W9-BZG-858

World Philosophers
and
Their Works

World Philosophers and Their Works

Volume III

Ockham, William of — Zhuangzi
Indexes

EDITOR
John K. Roth
Claremont McKenna College

MANAGING EDITOR
Christina J. Moose

PROJECT EDITOR
Rowena Wildin

SALEM PRESS, INC.
Pasadena, California   Hackensack, New Jersey

Managing Editor: Christina J. Moose   *Project Editor:* Rowena Wildin
Research Supervisor: Jeffry Jensen   *Research Assistant:* Jun Ohnuki
Acquisitions Editor: Mark Rehn   *Production Editor:* Cynthia Beres
Photograph Editor: Karrie Hyatt

Some of the essays in this work, which have been updated, originally appeared in the following Salem Press sets: *World Philosophy: Essay-Reviews of 225 Major Works, Great Lives from History: Ancient and Medieval Series, Great Lives from History: Renaissance to 1900 Series, Great Lives from History: Twentieth Century Series, Great Lives from History: British and Commonwealth Series, Great Lives from History: American Women Series, Critical Survey of Literary Theory.*

Library of Congress Cataloging-in-Publication Data

World philosophers and their works / editor, John K. Roth.
   p. cm.
   Includes bibliographical references and indexes.
   ISBN 0-89356-878-3 (set) — ISBN 0-89356-879-1 (v. 1) — ISBN 0-89356-880-5 (v. 2) — ISBN 0-89356-881-3 (v. 3)
   1. Philosophers — Biography — Encyclopedias.   I. Roth, John K.
B104.W67 2000
109—dc21   99-055143

First printing

Contents

Volume III

Contents

William of Ockham

Ockham held that intuition was the only form of knowledge and that God could be approached only through faith and revelation, not through the "proofs" of natural reason. Misconstrued, Ockham's nominalism—his rejection of the idea of abstract entities, or universals—had serious implications for the Church's teachings on the Eucharist.

Principal philosophical works: *Scriptum in librum primum sententiarum ordinatio*, 1317-1321 (commonly known as *Ordinatio*; partial translation, *Concerning the Distinction of Reason, the Problem of Universals, and the Nature of a Concept*, 1986); *Quodlibeta septem*, 1322-1327 (*Quodlibetal Questions*, 1991); *Summa logicae*, 1322 (*Ockham's Theory of Terms, Part I of the "Summa logicae,"* 1974, and *Ockham's Theory of Propositions: Part II of the "Summa logicae,"*1980); *Opus nonaginta dierum*, 1322 (*The Work of Ninety Days*, 1998); *Dialogus*, 1334-1346; *An princeps pro suo succursu*, 1338; *Octo quaestiones de potestate papae*, 1340-1342; *Breviloquium de principatu tyrannico*, 1341-1342 (*A Short Discourse on the Tyrannical Government Over Things Divine and Human*, 1992); *Consultatio de causa matrimoniali*, 1342; *De imperatorum et pontificum potestate*, 1347 (English translation, 1927; also known as *On the Power of Emperors and Popes*, 1998).

Born: c. 1285; Surrey, England
Died: 1347 or 1349; Munich, Bavaria (now in Germany)

Early Life

Nothing is known of William of Ockham's parents or childhood, except that he entered the Franciscan order before he was fourteen and received his early education at the Franciscan house at Southwark. In 1303, he was ordained a subdeacon by Archbishop Winchelsey and thereafter went to Oxford University, where he obtained the baccalaureate. He taught at Oxford, lecturing on Peter Lombard's *Sententiarum libri IV* (1148-1151; *The Books of Opinions of Peter Lombard*, 1970, 4 volumes; commonly known as *Sentences*), while at the same time writing the first version of his celebrated commentary on the four books of the *Sentences*, *Ordinatio*, and also works on logic. Around 1321, he left Oxford to return to the Franciscans in Southwark, where he taught philosophy, but there is no evidence for the story that he went to Paris University and there met Marsilius of Padua.

The period from 1314 to 1324 was perhaps the most productive of his entire life. In terms of originality and sheer intellectual brilliance, Ock-ham's was one of those minds that come early to fruition. In addition, he had a gift for rapid and prolific writing. This was the period when he revised (not for the last time) his commentaries on the *Sentences* of Lombard, wrote several commentaries on Aristotle, and completed *Ockham's Theory of Terms* and *Ockham's Theory of Propositions*. He also wrote most of *Quodlibetal Questions*, an undertaking of remarkable maturity, embodying a vast amount of reading and reflection within the Scholastic tradition. Yet despite his later, and posthumous, reputation as the philosopher who dissolved the Thomist-Aristotelian synthesis, Ockham, during his years in England, was essentially a mainstream thinker: original, controversial, but not necessarily dangerous. His ideas circulated widely among fellow teachers and students, and for a young man, he enjoyed a formidable reputation. Some of his statements were later questioned by opponents, and eventually accusations against his teaching reached the Papal Curia, but his excommunication in 1328 had nothing to do with his academic career in England. He raised issues of major intellectual concern to contemporaries, but he did not attack the Church or its teachings, nor did he rail against clerical wealth and corruption. A typical

English representative of his order, he did not (so far as is known) adopt the radical line of the Spiritual Franciscans with regard to the *vita apostolica* (apostolic life), and was uninfluenced (and was perhaps uninterested in) the Joachimite writings in favor with the Italian Fraticelli. He was involved neither in clerical politics nor in calls for reform, and he was certainly no self-proclaimed iconoclast.

Yet in 1323, Ockham was accused of error by John Lutterell, a former chancellor of Oxford University, who was eager to curry favor at the papal court, and Ockham was compelled to set off for Avignon, then the residence of the pope, in order to defend himself from the charges laid against him. Avignon was to be his home for the next four years, and although he may have suffered from some loss of freedom, he continued writing and revising his earlier works. Meanwhile, a commission appointed to examine his writings met during 1324-1325 and identified fifty-one propositions deserving of further scrutiny. Although it detected many errors, however, it found no evidence of heresy. In 1326, the commission began a second inquiry, perhaps as a direct result of papal prompting, and this time uncovered ten heretical propositions. The papers were then passed to the famous Inquisitor Jacques Fournier (the future Benedict XII), but apparently no further steps were taken prior to Ockham's flight from Avignon in 1328. It is not difficult to imagine, however, the frustration and uncertainty engendered during Ockham's stay in Avignon. As Ockham scholar David Knowles puts it:

> The brilliant young man had the mortifying experience of waiting upon the delays and debates of his judges, with his high hopes dashed, and in the demoralizing surroundings of a city of luxury and intrigue, where the atmosphere was rendered permanently electric by the irascible octogenarian autocrat Pope John XXII, an untiring generator of storm and lightning.

Life's Work

The year 1328 marked a virtual bifurcation in Ockham's career. Before that year, he had been an academic, a teacher of theology and logic. Thereafter, he became a committed and forceful po-

lemicist, the champion of the Spiritual Franciscans, the implacable opponent of Pope John XXII, whom he came to regard as a heretic, and a propagandist for the Holy Roman Emperor, Ludwig IV of Bavaria, the pope's bitter foe.

The event that provided the catalyst for the change in Ockham's life was the arrival in Avignon of Michael of Cesena, minister general of the Franciscans, who had been summoned there by the pope to answer charges relating to apostolic poverty. The Spiritual Franciscans had long held that neither Jesus nor his apostles had owned any personal belongings and that Saint Francis of Assisi had intended a similar evangelical poverty for his followers. Meanwhile, the success of the Franciscan movement had resulted in the order becoming the recipient of great wealth. This development the Spiritual Franciscans abhorred, just as they abhorred the all-too-visible wealth of the Church and the worldly and luxurious lifestyle of many clerics. Their radical idealism, therefore, constituted a profound challenge to the Church as an institution, and it was not a challenge that the Church could afford to disregard. The debate had gone on for years, but Nicholas III, deeply sympathetic to Franciscan idealism, had sought a compromise, by which the Church administered the property of the Franciscans on their behalf, thereby enabling them to maintain their founder's commitment to a life of apostolic poverty. This compromise had been further refined during the pontificate of Clement V.

John XXII, however, stirred up a hornet's nest of opposition when, in December, 1322, he issued the bull, or edict, *Ad conditorem canonum*, in which he handed back to the Franciscans the property that, since the time of Nicholas III, had been held in trust for them. In 1323, in a second bull, *Cum inter nonnullos*, John pronounced that it was heresy to teach the doctrine of Christ's absolute poverty and followed this up in November, 1324, with the bull *Quia quorundam*, in which he asserted his absolute authority to rule in such matters without reference to the pronouncements of his predecessors. Hitherto, Michael of Cesena had been a moderate, endeavoring to hold the middle ground within the Franciscan order and maintain a continuous dialogue with the Curia. John, however, was outraged by Franciscan intransigence, and he summoned Michael and a learned Franciscan canonist, Bonagratia of Bergamo, to answer for their flock.

Once in Avignon, and in considerable danger from John's anger, Michael of Cesena discovered that one of the most celebrated of Franciscan scholars was a fellow resident in the town, and he therefore commanded Ockham, as his subordinate, to review the various papal pronouncements on apostolic poverty from the point of view of a theologian. Hitherto, Ockham relates in a letter, he had deliberately avoided looking into these issues, fearful of what he might find, but ordered by his superior to examine the various bulls, he found in them statements that he later described as erroneous, foolish, ridiculous, fantastic, insane, defamatory, and worst of all, heretical. From this time forward, he was filled with horror at the thought that the pope himself had become a heretic and in consequence could no longer command the allegiance of the Church, views that came to be shared by Michael of Cesena and Bonagratia of Bergamo. On the night of May 28, 1328, the three men fled from Avignon, traveling down the Rhône to Aigues Mortes, where an imperial galley was waiting to transport them to Pisa. There they were well received by Ludwig and his entourage, which included the Italian author of the *Defensor pacis* (1320-1324; *The Defence of Peace*, 1535), Marsilius of Padua, who, like Ludwig himself, was a bitter foe of John XXII. Ludwig's quarrel with the pope went back to his election in 1314 by the German princes, which John had refused to recognize, but the disagreement had escalated when Ludwig had marched on Rome earlier in the year, had been crowned before the Roman people by a layman, Sciarra Colonna (the same who, a quarter of a century earlier, had assaulted Boniface VIII on behalf of the King of France), and had then formally announced the deposition of John XXII and his replacement by a Franciscan antipope, Nicholas V. At Pisa, the emperor was fresh from his triumphs in Rome. On entering Ludwig's presence, Ockham traditionally is said to have declared: "Defend me with your sword, and I shall support you with my pen." Regardless of whether this statement was uttered, Ockham lived for the next two decades under the emperor's protection in Munich.

From 1328 until his death, Ockham's writings were, in the broadest sense, political, personally attacking John XXII and his successor, Benedict XII, raising fundamental issues with regard to the governance of the Church, and vigorously upholding the rights of lay rulers. His very first polemic, *The Work of Ninety Days*, was a defense of Michael of Cesena, whose views had been condemned by John XXII in his bull *Quia vir reprobus* (November, 1329), and a refutation, sentence by sentence, of John's pronouncements on the question of evangelical poverty. The subject matter of this work is diverse, ranging from the nature of property and its usage to the authority of the pope. Throughout the work, it is clear that Ockham is acutely aware that a pope fallen into heresy must drag all Christendom down with him unless remedies are applied.

Far more ambitious is the *Dialogus* (dialogue), a work conceived in the form of a discussion between master and pupil, of which the first part was probably begun in 1333 and completed toward the end of 1334 (by which time John XXII had been succeeded by Benedict XII), followed by a second and, in 1346, by an unfinished third part. Heresy is the principal theme of the *Dialogus*. This is perhaps Ockham's most original political work, and it is marked by his characteristic concern for the precise meaning of words, for definitions, and for painstaking analysis.

It is not always clear where Ockham is taking his readers in the *Dialogus*. The direction becomes clearer in three later works of political philosophy. In the *Octo quaestiones de potestate papae* (1340-1342; eight questions on the power of the pope), which may have been written at the emperor's behest, he resuscitates the classic debate regarding the sources and extent of the authority of pope and emperor, and their relations with each other, issues that are also central to *A Short Discourse on the Tyrannical Government over Things Divine and Human* and the *De imperatorum et pontificum potestate*. Yet Ockham also addressed more immediate issues of his times. Thus, in the *An princeps pro suo succursu* (1338; on the right of kings), written on behalf of Edward III of England, he upholds the right of the English king to tax his clergy in times of national crisis. Similarly, in the *Consultatio de causa matrimoniali* (prior to February, 1342; advice on the right of the emperor to dispense from an impediment of consanguinity) and presumably on Ludwig's orders, Ockham takes up the problem of consanguinity, which seems to stand in the way of the marriage of Ludwig's son, Ludwig of Brandenburg, to Margaret, the heiress of the Tirol, arguing that in such a case the emperor possesses the authority to grant a dispensation. A further problem, however, was that Margaret was already married to someone else. To deal with this situation, Marsilius of Padua was called in, to argue in his *Defensor minor* (c. 1344; English translation, 1922), that in cases of a husband's impotence (as this one was said to be), the emperor had the authority to grant a divorce. In the light of Ludwig's poisonous relations with successive popes, there was not the slightest possibility of obtaining either a papal divorce or a papal dispensation with regard to consanguinity, and so the emperor turned to the two great luminaries of his court, Ockham and Marsilius, to legitimate a course of action on which he had set his heart. The "marriage" was celebrated on February 10, 1342.

That same year, Michael of Cesena died. He had long been stripped of his position as minister general, but he had remained the vicar of that minority of Franciscans who had broken permanently with Avignon. Thereafter, Ockham served as vicar until, in 1348, he sent the seal to Minister General William Farinier, perhaps in the course of negotiations for a reconciliation with the Church, from which Ockham had been excommunicated since 1328. It is uncertain whether it was Ockham himself or the Curia or perhaps Farinier who took the initiative. In any case, his position had become dangerously exposed since Emperor Ludwig's death in 1347 and the accession of Charles IV of Bohemia, a favorite with Avignon. Benedict XII had died in 1342, and his successor, Clement VI, a suave, Francophile diplomat, may well have been disposed to bring about the public reconciliation of a notorious heretic, who was also the most influential scholar of the age. Whether Ockham was reconciled prior to his death is a matter for speculation, but there has survived a form of submission drawn up by Clement, which was passed on to Farinier, presumably for transmission to Ockham. In it, there is no mention of those charges that had first brought him from England to Avignon a

quarter of a century earlier, but Ockham was required to disassociate himself entirely from the opinions of the late excommunicants, Michael of Cesena and the Emperor Ludwig; he was to deny utterly that the emperor possessed the authority to make or unmake popes; and he was to declare himself faithful to the official teachings of the Church.

Whether the document ever reached Ockham's hands, whether there was ever a formal reconciliation, or whether Ockham died before the arrangements could be completed will never be known. He died in 1349, probably in the course of the ravages of the Black Death, and tradition has it that he was buried in the Franciscan church in Munich, implying that he was no longer an excommunicant.

Influence
Ockham was the most powerful and perhaps the most original mind of the later Middle Ages. "No later reformer," writes scholar E. F. Jacob, thinking ahead to the age of Martin Luther, "is uninfluenced by his ideas," and David Knowles describes him as "one of the half-dozen British philosophers who have profoundly influenced the thought of western Europe." Yet those who study Ockham have found it difficult to categorize him, some regarding him as the apex of the medieval Scholastic achievement, others viewing him as the great skeptic whose dialectic helped to dissolve the Thomist-Aristotelian synthesis of the thirteenth century.

He is also a prime example of the "unfinished" thinker, whose tremendous intellectual activity as a young man virtually came to an end when he involved himself in the affairs of popes and emperors and the writing of propaganda. It is impossible now to conceive of what he might have written or in what direction he might have taken contemporary thought had he not abandoned teaching for polemics after 1328. Before judging him too harshly for the loss to philosophy, however, it is well to remember that to a man of Ockham's time, the issue of apostolic poverty and the terrible conviction that the head of the Church had lapsed into heresy were matters of such urgency as to outweigh entirely the claims of scholarship and the schools.

Gavin R. G. Hambly

William of Ockham: Selections

Type of philosophy: Epistemology, logic, philosophical theology

First transcribed: Early fourteenth century (*Ockham: Studies and Selections*, 1938; *Philosophical Writings: A Selection*, 1957, rev. ed. 1990)

Principal ideas advanced:

◇ All abstractive cognitions (knowledge derived from experience, made possible by reflection upon experience) depend on prior intuitive cognitions (sense experience of things).

◇ Our knowledge of the existing world is contingent on God's will, for he can affect our intuitive cognitions whatever the facts may be.

◇ Predication occurs only if the predicate term of a sentence refers to the object referred to by the subject term, and if the predicate term refers to the object not by naming it, but by referring to some feature of it.

◇ Universals are not single properties common to many things, but signs that have application to a number of things.

◇ An explanation involving fewer assumptions than an alternative explanation is preferable to the alternative; this is Ockham's razor.

William of Ockham is known for his "razor," for his logic, and for his nominalistic and empirical viewpoint. Living in the fourteenth century, he was the dominant figure in the movement away from Albertus Magnus, Thomas Aquinas, and John Duns Scotus, the great system builders of the thirteenth century. He was the inspirer of an empirically and nominalistically inclined movement that contended with the Thomistic, Albertist, Scotist, and Averroistic schools of the next several centuries. However, Ockham was not a skeptic. He undermined and rejected most of the metaphysics and a good deal of the natural theology of his contemporaries, but he was a theologian who accepted the traditional Christian dogmas on faith and who preferred to accept them on faith alone rather than to argue for them on dubious philosophic grounds.

Intuitive and Abstractive Cognition

His basic inclination toward empiricism is revealed in the distinction between intuitive and abstractive cognition. When we are looking at Socrates, he says, we can see that he is white. In this case, we are aware of the existence of Socrates, of the occurrence of the quality, and of the fact that this individual, Socrates, is white. That is, the senses enable us to know with certainty a contingent fact about the world. This is an instance of what Ockham calls *intuitive cognition*. However, we can think of Socrates when he is not present and of white when we are not seeing it, and we can think of Socrates as being white. In this case we are cognizing the same things, Socrates and white, and we are entertaining the same proposition, but we do not know that Socrates still exists or that the proposition is true. This is an instance of what Ockham calls *abstractive cognition*, abstractive not because the terms are abstract, but because we have abstracted from existence.

The terms of the intuitive cognition are sensed and are particular, while the terms of the abstractive cognition are not sensed and are common. In intuitive cognition, the cognition is caused in us by action of the object on our sensory and intellectual faculties, a process that culminates naturally, without any initiative on our part, in the knowledge that Socrates is white. No judgment, at least no explicit one, is involved here, for we simply see that Socrates is white. On the other hand, in abstractive cognition, the cognition is not caused by the object, for either the object is absent or, if present, it is not sufficiently close to produce a clear sensation. Under such circumstances, we scrutinize the data given by memory or sensation and, perhaps, go on deliberately to judge or refrain from judging that something is the case.

In abstractive cognition, an apparently simple idea, such as the concept "Socrates," must be understood as a complex of common terms, for neither Socrates nor any other individual is operating on us to produce the cognition of him. In such a cognition, we are entertaining such common terms as "intelligent," "snubnosed," "white," and "Athenian" that, when taken together, constitute a complex abstractive term limiting our attention to the one desired individual.

In contrast, in intuitive cognition, we apprehend Socrates in a different manner, for in this case the object itself is producing in us a noncomplex idea of itself. Indeed, we obtain the terms appearing in abstractive cognitions only by attending to and separating in thought the various features of the sensation. Thus, Ockham concludes, all abstractive cognitions depend on prior intuitive ones, and intuitive cognition must be the source of all our knowledge about the world. Furthermore, Ockham says that we intuit or sense nothing but individual things, and these are either sensible substances such as Socrates, or sensible properties such as the sensed whiteness of Socrates. Even relations are regarded as properties of groups of individuals.

Cause and the Senses

When we add to all these considerations Ockham's razor—"What can be explained by the assumption of fewer things is vainly explained by the assumption of more things"—his nominalistic and empiricistic views follow immediately, for now we have an epistemology that not only makes us start with the senses but also prevents us from going very far beyond them. The senses reveal to us a multitude of sensible individuals and provide us with a great deal of information about them and their temporal and spatial settings, but they do not reveal any necessary connections, causal or otherwise—and the razor prevents us from assuming any.

This epistemology obviously limits the scope of metaphysics but does not quite eliminate it, for the metaphysician can still tell us a little about God. Given the terms "being," "cause," and "first," all of which are derived from experience, and assuming that they are univocal terms, as Ockham does, we can form the complex idea of a being who is a First Cause. Furthermore, given intellectually self-evident principles such as "Every thing has a cause," we can demonstrate the existence of a First Cause that exists necessarily and that, as the most perfect existent, has intellect and will. However, we cannot prove that there is only one such God or that there might not have been a greater God, and we cannot demonstrate that he has the various features required by Christian dogma.

Contingency of Knowledge

The sort of world suggested by Ockham's epistemology is also required by his theology. Like Duns Scotus before him and French philosopher René Descartes after him, Ockham emphasizes God's will rather than his intellect. God can do

nothing that is contradictory, but this fact does not limit his will, for his ideas are not of his essence and are not exemplars between which he must choose. They are his creatures and the world is whatever he has cared to make it. Consequently, the world does not exist necessarily, and within this world nothing follows necessarily from anything else and nothing requires the existence of anything else. This radical contingency stems from God's complete power over the circumstances in which things shall or shall not come into existence. God ordinarily uses instruments to produce in us the experiences we have, but he could, if he wished, dispense with them and operate on us directly. For instance, Ockham says, it would require a miracle but God could make us see a star even where there actually is no star. That is, we could have exactly the same cognition that is normally caused in us by the star even if there were no star or any other physical cause. Because the seeing of the star is one distinct event and the star itself is another, it is not impossible that either should exist independently of the other.

The possibility of cognition without a corresponding fact reveals a limitation of intuitive cognition, for even though such a cognition makes us certain that something is the case, we could nevertheless be mistaken. Ockham skirts around the threat of skepticism by remarking that although an error of this sort can occur if God interferes with the natural order, miracles are rare. Consequently, the probability of error is insignificantly low. Yet, he acknowledges, it is still the case that our knowledge of the existing world is contingent upon God's will.

There is a remarkable agreement between Descartes and Ockham concerning the contingency of our knowledge. Because Descartes held a more extreme doctrine about the power of God, he took skepticism more seriously, but, of course, he believed he could escape by using reason. On the other hand, Ockham regarded the risk of empiricism as slight and claimed that it is better to exercise a little faith than to accept the grave risks of rationalism.

Terms

In his writings, Ockham, who was probably the best of medieval logicians, commences his discussion of logic by considering the nature of terms. First, he distinguishes between written, spoken, and conceptual terms. The latter are mental contents that function as private signs of things. Because these mental signs are not deliberately produced by us, but come about naturally through the operation of the object on us, they are called *natural* signs. Because spoken signs, on the other hand, are sounds that have been conventionally attached to particular mental signs, they are *conventional* signs. They denote the same object as the associated concept, thus enabling us to communicate what would otherwise be private. Written signs have a similar relation to spoken signs. Ordinarily, when Ockham speaks of terms he has in mind such terms as "man," "animal," "whiteness," and "white," which signify or denote things and which can function as the subject or predicate of a proposition. These terms, which he calls *categorematic* terms, are to be contrasted with *snycategorematic* terms such as "every," "insofar as," and "some," which do not denote anything when they stand by themselves. He also distinguishes between concrete terms such as "white" and abstract terms such as "whiteness," and between discrete terms such as "Socrates" and common terms such as "man."

A more important distinction is that between absolute terms and connotative terms. An *absolute* term is one that denotes directly, whereas a *connotative* term is one that denotes one thing only by connoting another. "Socrates," "man," and "whiteness" are absolute terms for they are used to point to, respectively, a specific individual, any one of a number of similar individuals, or to a property. A connotative term such as "white" is not used as a label, for there is no such thing as white. When it is used in a proposition such as "Socrates is white," it denotes the same object as does the subject term, but it does so by connoting a property of the object; namely, whiteness. The distinction can be formulated in another way. At least some absolute terms, such as "man," have real definitions in which each term, such as "rational" and "animal," can denote the same objects as the defined term. Connotative terms have only nominal definitions, for the definition will require a term in the oblique case that cannot denote the same object as does the defined term. Thus "white" may be defined as "that which has the property whiteness," but "white-

ness" does not denote the white thing. In certain definitions, connotative terms may occur, but these can always be defined in turn until we reach definitions that contain absolute terms only. That is, language is grounded in terms that denote only, and cognition is basically a matter of being aware of objects and features of objects by intuitive cognition.

This distinction also brings us back to Ockham's epistemology by indicating the way in which a proposition is related to the world. Because there are only particulars in the world, each term of a true proposition, such as "Socrates is white," can refer only to one or more individuals. Such a proposition does not assert that two different things are identical, nor that the subject and predicate are one and the same thing, nor that something inheres in or is part of the subject. In our example, "white" is not another name for Socrates, it is not the name of another individual, and it is not the name of the property *whiteness*; but it must denote something. It can only denote Socrates, but not, of course, as "Socrates" does. That is, it denotes him indirectly by connoting his whiteness. Predication occurs only if the predicate term denotes the very same object as the subject term, and the predicate term denotes the object not by naming it but by connoting some feature of it.

Universals

In the above discussion, we have mentioned abstract terms such as "whiteness" that are absolute and that denote properties rather than substances. Lest it seem that Ockham was a realist after all, we must turn to his discussion of universals. He denies emphatically that there are universals of either Platonic or Aristotelian varieties, for both doctrines require that something simple be common to many things. This state of affairs, he says, is impossible unless that simple something be plural, a condition that itself is impossible. Furthermore, he says, the problem should be turned around, for because the world is composed of particulars only, the problem is not the way in which some universal thing becomes particularized, but our reason for attributing universality to anything in the first place. The only thing to which we can attribute it is a sign and only by virtue of its function as a sign, for as a mere existent it is as particular as anything else. Thus a universal is a sign or concept that has application to a number of things.

The nature of this universal concept, or common term, can be understood better by considering what it is and how it is produced. First, as a result of intuitive cognition, there occurs in sensation, and then in memory, sensations or images that function as natural signs of the individual objects that cause them. Now, through the medium of these images the intellect notices the similarity of the objects so signified and notes that there could be still other entities similar to them. In noting these similarities, it produces naturally another entity that resembles the particulars in such a manner that it might very well be used as an exemplar for the construction of similar things. Ockham is not clear about the nature of this new entity, but he says that it is produced by ignoring the differences between the similar particulars. The new sign, or universal, is an indeterminate image that could represent any of the determinate particulars that fall under it. However, whatever it is, because it is a natural rather than a conventional sign, this resemblance has come into being as a sign that denotes indifferently any of the particulars it resembles. Ockham says this entity is a fiction only, for because it is not a particular sign produced in us by a particular object, it has no literal counterpart in the world. In Ockham's terms, if we say "Man is a universal," and insist that we are saying something is common to many things, then in this proposition, the concept "man" refers to itself (it has "simple *supposition*") and not to men (it does not have "personal *supposition*"), and the concept "universal" is of the second intention (it refers to a mental sign) rather than of the first intention (it does not refer to something other than a sign). That is, the universal "man" is only a concept that can be applied to many things; in the world there are only men.

It is to be noted that Ockham is not a nominalist of the Berkeleian-Humean sort, for his general ideas are not particulars standing for other particulars. Perhaps it would be more accurate to say that he holds to a kind of conceptualism. Later in his life, he applied his razor to his own doctrine to eliminate the fictitious entity we have just described, for he then argued that because the act

that produces the generalized picture must be able to generalize without the assistance of such a picture, such pictures must be superfluous. In the end, then, universals turn out to be acts of the intellect; the other features of his earlier doctrine are retained.

Finally, it is to be noted that though they have different grammatical functions, concrete substantives and their abstract counterparts (such as "man" and "manness") denote exactly the same things (men). Nonsubstantive qualitative terms such as "white" denote indifferently individuals such as Socrates and a piece of paper; and their abstract counterparts, such as "whiteness," denote indifferently similar features of individuals, such as a certain sensible feature of Socrates and a similar sensible feature of a piece of paper. In these ways, all common terms, whether they are concrete or abstract, denote particulars and particulars only.

Propositions and Arguments

Ockham discusses terms in great detail, and he goes on to discuss propositions and arguments. He was concerned primarily with formal syllogistic reasoning, but he did make a number of observations that impinge on the areas we know in symbolic logic as the propositional calculus and modal logic. Among other things, he discussed the truth conditions of conjunctive and disjunctive propositions, reduced "neither-nor" to "and" and "not," discussed valid arguments of the form "p and q, therefore p," "p, therefore p or q," and "p or q, not p, therefore q," pointed out the related fallacies, and stated Augustus De Morgan's laws explicitly.

At the end of his treatment of inference, he discussed some very general nonformal rules of inference. Assuming in appropriate cases that we are speaking about a valid argument, they are as follows:

(1) if the antecedent is true the conclusion cannot be false
(2) the premises may be true and the conclusion false
(3) the contradictory of the conclusion implies the contradictory of the premise or conjunction of premises
(4) whatever is implied by the conclusion is implied by the premises

(5) whatever implies the premises implies the conclusion

(6) whatever is consistent with the premises is consistent with the conclusion

(7) whatever is inconsistent with the conclusion is inconsistent with the premises

(8) a contingent proposition cannot follow from a necessary one

(9) a contingent proposition cannot imply a contradiction

(10) any proposition follows from a contradiction

(11) a necessary proposition follows from any proposition

He illustrated the last two with these examples: "You (a man) are a donkey, therefore you are God," and assuming God is necessarily triune, "You are white, therefore God is triune." Ockham concluded his discussion by saying that because these rules are not formal they should be used sparingly.

Leonard Miller

Additional Reading

Freppert, Lucan. *Basis of Morality According to William of Ockham*. Chicago, Ill.: Franciscan, 1998. Includes a biography, an autobiography, and letters. Focuses on Ockham's thoughts on ethics and moral philosophy.

Jacob, E. F. "Ockham as a Political Thinker." In *Essays in the Conciliar Epoch*. 2d ed. Manchester: Manchester University Press, 1953. A discussion of Ockham's impact on political philosophy.

Leff, Gordon. *The Dissolution of the Medieval Outlook: An Essay on Intellectual and Spiritual Change in the Fourteenth Century*. New York: Harper & Row, 1976. An excellent summary of Ockham's life and thought.

_____. *William of Ockham: The Metamorphosis of Scholastic Discourse*. Manchester: Manchester University Press, 1975. Leff's discusses the philosophy of Ockham.

McGrade, Arthur S. *The Political Thought of William of Ockham: Personal and Institutional Principles*. Cambridge, England: Cambridge University Press, 1974. An essential text for understanding the thought of Ockham.

Gavin R. G. Hambly,
updated by Howard Z. Fitzgerald

Origen

Origen is usually considered the greatest of the early Christian thinkers; he was the first not only to write extensive commentaries on most books of the Bible but also to study the main areas and problems within theology. He did so with such intelligence that often what he wrote determined the lines of all subsequent Christian thought.

Principal philosophical works: *Origenous tōn eis to kata ōannēn* , 218-238 (*The Commentary of Origen on Saint John's Gospel*, 1896); *Peri archōn*, 220-230 (also known as *De principiis; On First Principles*, 1936); *Peri euchēs*, 233 (*Treatise on Prayer*, 1954); *Eis marturion protrepticos*, 235 (*Exhortation to Martyrdom*, 1954); *Homilies on Jeremiah*, wr. 241-244, pb. 1995); *Kata Kelsou*, 248 (*Origen Against Celsus*, 1660).

Born: c. 185; Alexandria, Egypt
Died: c. 254; probably Tyre (now Sur, Lebanon)

Early Life

Origen was born at the end of the period that Edward Gibbon, the eighteenth century English historian, called the happiest and most prosperous the human race had known; he died during a time of civil war, plague, economic dislocation, and persecution of the Christian church. Alexandria, the city of his birth, was one of the great cities of the world; it used Greek as its first language and was the home of the largest library in the Mediterranean basin. There many of the best scholars of the Greek world taught and studied.

Origen was the oldest of nine children. His father, whom tradition names Leonides, was prosperous enough to provide him with a Greek literary education and concerned enough about his Christian formation to teach him the Bible. From childhood, Origen was a serious Christian and a learned Greek. The Old Testament from which he studied, the Septuagint, was a Jewish translation of the Hebrew Bible into Greek. It contained, in addition to translations of those Scriptures originally written in Hebrew, books originally written in Greek. Although the canon, or list of books considered properly to be in the Bible, was not completely set in Origen's day, for most purposes his New Testament is that still used by Christians. While young, Origen memo-

rized long passages of the Bible; thus as an adult he could associate passages from throughout the Bible on the basis of common words or themes. Like other Christians of his day, Origen accepted as authoritative a body of teaching held to come from the Apostles.

Origen imbibed from his father and the Christian community the dramatic and heroic idea that he, as an individual Christian, was a participant in the drama by which the world was being redeemed. Like many other Christians, he was uneasy about wealth and marriage and tended to see Jesus calling the Christian to poverty and celibacy (that is, to a heroic mode of existence). Although martyrdom was still relatively infrequent, it was exalted in the Christian community, and in many ways Origen saw himself throughout his life as a living martyr doing battle for the spread of Christ's kingdom. At an unknown date, thoroughly instructed in the faith, he was baptized. Around 202, when Origen was seventeen, his father was martyred and the family property was confiscated by the state. It may be argued that for the rest of his life Origen saw himself continuing his martyred father's work.

Life's Work

In the following years, Origen added to his knowledge of grammar and Greek literature a knowledge of Gnosticism, a form of dualism very common in the Greek world of his day, which condemned all things material, especially the appetites and passions of the human body, and celebrated the spiritual, especially the human soul and spirit. Salvation was seen to lie in the separation of the soul from matter, and before Origen's day, a form of Christian Gnosticism had developed. After his father's death, Origen was taken in by a Christian woman so that he could continue his studies, and he subsequently began to teach grammar. In this woman's house, Christian Gnosticism was practiced. Although Origen rejected much of what he heard there, he adopted the Gnostics' distinction between literal Christians, who understood only the literal sense of the Bible; psychic Christians, who went beyond this to consider the spiritual meaning of Scripture; and perfect Christians, who understood and followed the deepest meanings of the Bible. Origen also accepted a doctrine that was, after his death, to be condemned as heretical: He believed that ultimately all beings, and even Satan himself, would be reconciled with God.

One of the second century Gnostic documents discovered at Nag Hammadi in Upper Egypt in 1945 contains many teachings similar to those found in Origen's writings and represents a form of Gnosticism more acceptable to the Christian tradition in which Origen had been formed. In this work, as in Origen's, Christ was conceived of as very similar to God the Father, although subordinate to Him in being. It also, with Origen, conceived of human existence as a long process of education, in which evil and death prepare humans for union with God. Another writer, Marcion, whom Origen classified a Gnostic, provided a foil against which Origen developed the teaching that human suffering can be reconciled with God's power and goodness. Unlike Marcion, Origen held that difficult passages in the Scripture might be allegorized.

Sometime between 206 and 211, Origen added catechetical instruction (explanation of Christianity to those interested in conversion) to his duties as a grammar teacher. This period was again a time of persecution, and although he taught in secret, at one point Origen was discovered and almost killed; some of his students were martyred.

After the persecution, he gave up his work as a teacher of grammar, sold his books of Greek literature, became the chief Christian teacher in Alexandria, and gave himself totally to Bible study. He began to follow what became a lifelong practice of strictly imitating the hardest sayings of Jesus, fasting regularly, sleeping very little (the Bible had said to "pray without ceasing"), and possessing only one cloak; he also castrated himself.

In the years between 211 and 215, Origen learned much of the Platonic tradition, and that had a deep influence on him, especially the Platonists' insistence on both divine providence and human freedom and—against the Gnostics—on the fundamental, if limited, good of the created order. Sometime before 217, Origen traveled briefly to Rome, where he was exposed to growing controversies over the definition of the relation of Jesus Christ to God the Father. Also sometime between 215 and 222, Origen met a Hebrew-speaking convert to Christianity who had been

Origen. *(Archive Photos)*

trained as a rabbi, with whom he began to study Hebrew and Jewish biblical interpretation. He also met an Alexandrian, Ambrose, who became his lifelong patron. The first problem facing Origen as a biblical scholar was the establishment of a reliable biblical text; his response was to write first *Tetrapla* (third century) and ultimately, after he had settled in Palestine, *Hexapla* (231-c. 245), each of which contained various Greek translations in parallel columns next to a transliterated Hebrew Old Testament. In this task, he revealed lifelong characteristics—painstaking interests in textual criticism and historical problems. In his mind, these were completely compatible with his interest in mystical interpretation of the Bible. Origen's growing reputation is evident from an incident that occurred about 222, when he was summoned to Arabia by the Roman governor for the discussion of an unknown subject.

Most of his early writings, from between 222 and 230, have been lost, but one of his most important, *On First Principles*, survives. Heavily influenced by Platonism, it espoused the idea, later to be condemned, that the human soul before entering the body has existed eternally. Students were now flocking to Origen's lectures; of these he accepted only the most promising. Ambrose provided a staff of stenographers, who took down Origen's lectures in shorthand as he gave them, and of copyists, who then prepared a more finished text.

Probably in 230, after unspecified conflict with Bishop Demetrius of Alexandria, Origen moved, at first briefly, to Caesarea, in Palestine. Having returned to Alexandria, he again left in 231, summoned by the dowager empress, Julia Mamaea, to Antioch to teach her more about Christianity. After a brief return to Alexandria, he left for Greece, traveling via Caesarea, where he was ordained a priest. In 233, a final break with Bishop Demetrius took place, and Origen moved to Caesarea. Finally, works that he had long been developing, such as a commentary on the Gospel of John and *Treatise on Prayer*, the first thorough Christian examination of prayer as contemplation of God, were finished.

Even more productive were the years from 238 to 244, when he regularly preached and was consulted in matters of doctrine. Again, although most of his work has been lost, some has sur-

vived, including more than two hundred sermons. Following an estrangement from his bishop, Theoctistus, Origen departed for Athens, where he continued his writing. In 246 or 247, he returned to Caesarea, where he set to work on commentaries on the Gospels of Luke and Matthew and on *Origen Against Celsus*, a defense of Christianity. During roughly the last eight years of his life, he found himself in the midst of both theological controversy and serious persecution of the Christians by the emperor Decius. By 251, Origen, who had been imprisoned and tortured, was a broken man. The circumstances of his death are uncertain.

Influence

Origen was more important than any other early Christian thinker in assimilating the Jewish and Greek traditions into Christianity. The former he accomplished through his lifelong contact with rabbinic scholars and the latter through his lifelong devotion to the Platonic tradition. His conscious intent was always to be faithful to Christianity whenever there was a direct conflict between it and what he had inherited from the earlier traditions. Nevertheless, he also intended to be open to truth wherever it might be found. That Christians usually think of themselves as the heirs to both the Jewish and the Greek traditions is more his work than that of any other. He was the first Christian to discuss at length central problems such as the nature of free will and of God's relation to the world. As the first to do so, Origen did not always arrive at conclusions deemed correct by later standards. Thus, in spite of his genius, he has often been the subject of some suspicion in later Christian tradition. Yet arguably, he had as much influence in setting the terms of later Christian theology as any writer.

Origen subjected himself to great ascetic discipline, usually surrounded by his community of scribes and students, and his mode of life may be justly described as protomonastic; indeed, it was only about forty years after his death that the monastic movement began. Finally, with his great confidence in the ability of the disciplined intellect to rise above the world of sense to the vision of God, Origen stands near the source of the Christian contemplative tradition.

Glenn W. Olsen

On First Principles

Type of philosophy: Metaphysics, philosophical theology

First transcribed: Peri archōn, 220-230 (also known as *De principiis*; English translation, 1936)

Principal ideas advanced:

◇ God is incorporeal, the light, the truth, the good; he knows, and is known, as an intellectual being.

◇ The Trinity is eternal; although the Intellectual Principle (*nous*) and the Son are eternally generated by God the Father, they are eternal with him.

◇ The conception of the Holy Spirit is Christianity's unique contribution to religious doctrine.

◇ Every creature within the rational structure of the universe has its position in relation to God as a result of what it merits because of its free action.

◇ Scripture has a threefold meaning: the obvious sense, the essential meaning, and the spiritual meaning.

Origen is the first major figure in the Christian era who wrote—in Greek—with full philosophical training and with a full sympathy toward philosophical method. Saint Augustine is sometimes given this credit, but Origen preceded him, and Augustine owes much to Origen. In any inquiry into the sources of later philosophy and theology, Origen must be given wide attention. The infusion of Greek philosophical skill into theology gave Christian thought its unusual theoretical side and allowed it to develop close relationships with pagan philosophical interests.

Therefore, Origen's *On First Principles* subjected him to charges of heresy. His strong philosophical interests and training most likely led to a doctrine that did not conform to established ideas on every point. However, because the original Greek text of the work has, for the most part, been lost, these charges are difficult to establish. The elaborated Latin translation, *De Principiis*, by Rufinus contains indications that Origen's work was considerably altered in its rendering, and modern scholarship tends to find Origen not so extreme on some points as has sometimes been charged. Origen and Plotinus had the same

philosophical teacher, Ammonius Saccas, who is sometimes said to be the founder of Neoplatonism.

Origen begins by establishing the words and teachings of Christ as a central norm, and his fame as a biblical interpreter is widespread. To develop theological issues along the lines of philosophy, some interpretive scheme had to be devised to make biblical thought and expression amenable to philosophical treatment. Like many a sophisticated follower of religion, Origen was caught between the rough and untechnical nature of biblical expression and the abstract nature of technical and systematic analysis. In response, Origen attempted first of all to establish what can be taken as agreed apostolic teaching, because the church of his time provided for him no single unequivocal set of agreed doctrines.

Origen's *Kata Kelsou* (248; *Origen Against Celsus*, 1990) is sometimes thought to be more immediately relevant to philosophy, since Origen wrote it during the time of Philip the Arabian to refute the attack against Christianity by the Greek philosopher Celsus. Actually, it is less philosophical in the systematic sense than *On First Principles*, since it is in the latter work that Origen develops his principal doctrines. *Origen Against Celsus* is rather contrived and often shows philosophical reason at its worst, compiling lists of apparently rational arguments in order to overwhelm an opponent's point. It is true that *On First Principles* is much more inextricably involved with the details of Christian doctrine, but this fact should bother none but the antimetaphysical readers.

God

The opening chapter of the first of the four books is titled "On God." Such a starting point must spring from systematic interests, for the Bible contains little direct discussion of the divine nature, and none in technical form. Later philosophy agreed with Origen in beginning immediately with a discussion of the divine attributes, until the modern period began to swing the emphasis away from metaphysics. Origen then discusses the second and third persons of the Trinity and gives an account of the origin of sin or defection. After this he considers humans as rational creatures and the doctrine of last things, or eschatology. He ends the book by discussing the nature and function of angels, which to contemporary readers will seem the most artificial use of rational argument. In short, what Origen provides is a vast scheme, beginning with God and including all natural creatures in an account of the beginning and end of the world.

Origen is most concerned to prove God to be incorporeal and to deny any possible physical attributes. His love for the immaterial undoubtedly reflects his Platonic training, and Origen also stresses light symbolism in referring to God, another favorite Platonic sign. Like Saint Augustine, Origen uses "God" as a symbol and norm for truth, but he goes on to place God beyond final human comprehension. Like the "Good" of Plato, God is too bright for direct human vision. God's incorporeality, it turns out, has its primary example in the human intellect, which Origen takes to be equally incorporeal in its operation. God is not seen as a corporeal body is seen; he is known, and he knows, as an intellectual being.

The Trinity

When Origen turns to Christology, it is clear that his conception of divinity in its highest sense is personal, which is not true in Neoplatonism. The personal relationship of the three members of the Trinity is immediately apparent, and Origen establishes the coeternality of the Father and Son, despite the fact that the Son is said to have been "generated." Any Platonic, and especially Neoplatonic, framework can accept eternal generation as an intelligible concept, so that Origen's philosophical background helps to set the theological orthodoxy. Just as *nous*, the intelligible world (or principle), in Plotinus is the source of the natural order, containing the seeds and forms of all things, so the primary function of the Son, as Origen sees it, is to be the second person, the divine creative agent for the natural world. The world is not eternal and the three members of the Trinity are coequal and personal in nature. This view radically distinguishes Origen and Plotinus from a basic Neoplatonism, despite the many similarities.

The Son is the truth and life of all things that exist, and Origen goes on to argue that there should be a resurrection of the type that the Son

in fact undergoes in order to destroy the bond of death placed on humans. However, the Son is the Word (Logos), the intelligible structure of all things, and as such is not subject to sight but can be revealed only to the understanding. The incorporeality of the Son, and God, is again an overriding concern. Origen also takes the classical position in upholding the necessity of creation. God's omnipotence demands a world to govern and so he has no choice but to create a world through the agency of the second person of the Trinity, his Word.

Origen finds the sources for his doctrine of the Son, the divine intellectual and creative agency, in pagan philosophical views. He considers not the doctrine of the Son but that of the Holy Spirit to be the unique theological idea in Christianity. No pagan before, Origen believes, had conceived of the Holy Spirit; but such teaching is, he feels, in the Bible, both in the Old and the New Testaments. The Holy Bible is the divine agent, and Origen asserts that all rational beings, Christian or not, partake of reason. As a measure of the importance Origen gives to the Holy Spirit, he believes that a sin committed against the Son can be forgiven but that a sin against the Holy Spirit cannot.

Freedom of the Will

When Origen turns to discuss what a rational nature is, his famous doctrine of the freedom of the will becomes evident. Every rational creature is capable of earning praise or censure: Therefore, if people are censured for sins, it is not because they were incapable of different action. However, among rational creatures Origen lists angels and spiritual powers of wickedness along with humans. Angels and the powers of wickedness are also fully free to determine their course. Angels are free to fall, and they remain angels only as a reward for contrived choice of the good.

Every creature within the rational structure has its position because of the merit, or demerit, it has earned. The situation of every creature is the result of its own work and movement. Origen is adamant about keeping the responsibility for the fall of the angels, or human sin, away from God. No malignant powers were formed by God in creation, although such irrational forces now exist. They have come into being and now plague the world. Through a fall, they were converted into wicked beings and that fall resulted from their own choices. Such a power was formerly holy and happy, and from that state of happiness, it fell from the time that iniquity was found in it.

Our world is rationally governed, and it contained only good beings at its creation; but those beings were free to choose their own actions; they included powers and angels far stronger than humans. Once such divine powers fell, because their chosen iniquity was discovered, then rational humans came to have superior forces—both of good and evil—at play upon them. Humans are still free to determine their choices, but not in the easy way that existed before the transformation of some good powers into evil. Spotless purity exists in the essential being of none save the Father, Son, and Holy Spirit; it is an accidental quality in every created thing and thus can easily be lost. Yet it lies within humans, in their own actions, to possess either happiness or holiness.

When Origen comes to discuss the end of the world and the ultimate transformation and restoration of all things, he acknowledges immediately that such questions are not subject to strict definition but must take the form of speculative discussion. The Trinity can be set forth in propositional form: However, any account of the end of the world can only be conjecture, despite its obvious basis in Scripture. How things will be after such a day is known with certainty only to God.

There is no rational creature that is not capable of both good and evil. Because not even the devil was incapable of good, what people become is the result of their own decisions and not of any inevitable force. However, the righteousness of humans is only accidental, and it is easy for them to throw it away. Yet God has so constructed the world that no rational creature is compelled by force, against the liberty of its own will, to any course other than that to which the motives of its own mind lead it.

Origen has sketched his position, one that concedes a great deal of the directive powers of each rational individual, but he ends by admitting that his view is only a possible one. Let each reader, he says, determine for himself or herself whether any of the views he argues can be adopted or not. Origen trusts reason a great deal, and he makes

every question of theology a matter for rational discussion, but he does not believe his conclusions to be unavoidable or inevitable.

Scripture

Perhaps Origen's greatest ability is shown by how he treats Scripture's place in theological argument, a particularly interesting problem in view of his obvious attachment to philosophy and to rational argument on all points. The authority of Scripture as a norm must first be agreed to, Origen says, and in that sense, argument is prior to Scripture's authority. Thus, he first set down the *reasons* that lead us to regard Scripture as divine writings. The wide conversions to Christianity, he argues, attest to the special significance of its Scriptures. Origen argues for the deity of Christ, and thus for the divine inspiration of the Scripture that prophesied him, so that the authority of Scripture in theology really rests on the prior acceptance of the divinity of Christ. Scripture is not obviously authoritative for Origen, but it becomes so for those who are convinced of Jesus' divine authority, and one can be convinced through a process of reasoning.

Scripture hides the splendor of its doctrines in common and unattractive phraseology, and the inability to see through this is one of the most frequent reasons for rejecting scriptural passages as valid points in an argument. Thus the central problem is to state the manner in which Scripture is to be read and understood as its validity is not immediately obvious. Origen introduces his distinction of the "spiritual meaning" as opposed to the interpretation according to the "mere letter." Origen finds certain mystical economies in the Scriptures, but to see these, the words must be properly interpreted. Each individual, Origen insists, ought to receive the threefold meaning of Scripture: first, the obvious sense; second, the "soul," or essential meaning of the words; and third, the hidden wisdom or mystery of God contained in a "spiritual" meaning.

There are, then, esoteric and exoteric meanings in Scripture, and one cannot easily tell which of the three meanings will best fit a passage. Some people are better interpreters of Scripture than others and can divine the esoteric meanings of certain important passages, but the exoteric meaning is easily available, even to simple folk.

This being so, not all Scriptural accounts need to be factual. That is not their purpose. Interwoven in the historical accounts are reports of events that did not occur, some that could not have happened, and some that could have happened but did not. The biblical documents are not a pure history of events but were intended to convey meaning and truth on a threefold level, according to the scheme Origen has sketched. They reveal facts about the divine intention that no mere record of events could convey.

Many biblical accounts cannot be believed literally—for example, God walking in paradise in the evening—and when this is so, one knows that a deeper meaning must be sought beneath the literal phrase. Therefore, the biblical documents are, in themselves, no simple authoritative norm in theological debate, for their normative value depends on the prior working out, and acceptance of, a rational framework for interpreting the literature. Were the Bible to be taken literally, Origen argues, it would be incredibly irrational. Yet the passages that are true in their historical meaning are much more numerous than those that are interspersed with a purely spiritual signification. The reader must be careful to ascertain how far the literal meaning is true and how far it is impossible. Certainly this places the ultimate norm in the rational judgment of the individual interpreter.

Thus Origen sets Scripture into a rational framework, making it possible to use it in support of rational theological discussion. A modern reader may at first miss the philosophical importance of Origen's analysis in *On First Principles*. It is more the way in which Origen treats his material than the material itself that is philosophical. Furthermore, if Origen's approach to scriptural authority is basically rational, his philosophical interests can be seen even more clearly in his stress on the freedom of the will. For this is not basically a religious problem but one that a philosophical instinct might regard as important to theological doctrine. Classical philosophy had not laid great stress on the question of freedom; the contemporary importance of the problem of humanity's freedom stems from the movement of philosophical minds, such as Origen's, into a religious context that stresses the relation between a creating, ordaining God and all rational beings. Origen's philosophical background makes him sense that rational independence for humanity depends upon establishing some form of freedom of the will as the basis of independence from God's action. Such independence also solves the theological problem of God's responsibility for sin, which the religious doctrine stresses; and the result is to give to the question of freedom of the will a place of new importance for all succeeding philosophy.

Frederick Sontag

Additional Reading

Crouzel, Henri. *Origen*. Trans. A. S. Worrall. San Francisco: Harper & Row, 1989. A comprehensive treatment of Origen's life and writings, with sections devoted to Origen's work on exegesis, spirituality, and theology. Includes an index of biblical references.

Daniélou, Jean. *A History of Early Christian Doctrine Before the Council of Nicaea*. Vol. 2 in *Gospel Message and Hellenistic Culture*. Translated by John Austin Baker. London: Westminster Press, 1973. Contains fine sections on Origen's catechetical teaching, biblical interpretation, Christology, anthropology, demonology, and understanding of Christian Gnosticism. Daniélou is very precise on the meaning and practice of allegory for Origen.

Küng, Hans. *Great Christian Thinkers*. New York: Continuum, 1994. The chapter on Origen offers a general overview of his life and major ideas. Presents his synthesis of Greek philosophy and Christian spirituality as the first model of a "scientific theology."

Trigg, Joseph W. *Origen*. New York: Routledge, 1998. An accessible introduction to Origen's life and work. Includes translations of a representative selection of his writings and an index of scriptural citations.

Glenn W. Olsen, updated by William Nelles

José Ortega y Gasset

Ortega's books, journalism, and lectures commanded attention throughout Europe. His renown helped to bring Spain out of a long period of cultural isolation, and his thought contributed greatly to his country's intellectual reawakening.

Principal philosophical works: *Meditaciones del Quijote*, 1914 (*Meditations on Quixote*, 1961); *Españainvertebrada*, 1922 (*Invertebrate Spain*, 1937); *El tema de nuestro tiempo*, 1923 (*The Modern Theme*, 1931); *La deshumanización del arte*, 1925 (*The Dehumanization of Art*, 1948); *La rebelión de las masas*, 1929 (*The Revolt of the Masses*, 1932); *Misión de la universidad*, 1930 (*The Mission of the University*, 1944); *Estudios sobre el amor*, 1939 (*On Love*, 1957); *Del imperio romano*, 1941 (*Concord and Liberty*, 1946); *Historia como sistema*, 1941 (*Toward a Philosophy of History*, 1941); *¿Qué es filosofía?*, 1958 (*What Is Philosophy?*, 1960); *La idea de principio en Leibniz y la evolución de la teoría deductiva*, 1958 (*The Idea of Principle in Leibniz and the Evolution of Deductive Theory*, 1971).

Born: May 9, 1883; Madrid, Spain
Died: October 18, 1955; Madrid, Spain

Early Life

José Ortega y Gasset was born in Madrid, Spain, on May 9, 1883. His father, José Ortega y Munilla, was a novelist and had formerly been editor of *El Imparcial*, a leading Madrid newspaper founded by his grandfather. The young Ortega was first taught by private tutors. Subsequently, like so many European intellectuals before him, he was schooled by Jesuits, at the College of Miraflores del Pala in Málaga. He later studied at the University of Madrid and at the universities of Leipzig, Berlin, and Marburg in Germany. In 1904, he received a doctorate in philosophy and literature from the University of Madrid, and in the years that followed, he deeply imbibed neo-Kantian philosophy. Ortega was named professor of metaphysics at the University of Madrid in 1910-1911. His association with that institution was to continue until 1936, when he went into self-imposed exile during the Spanish Civil War.

The same year that he received his chair, he founded *Faro* (beacon), a philosophical review. Shortly thereafter, he founded a second journal, *Europa*. These were the first of many periodicals he was to found during his long journalistic ca-

reer. By roughly the age of thirty, Ortega was well launched upon his multifaceted career as philosopher, journalist, author, educator, and statesman. Having spent the years 1905-1907 at German universities, he had become conversant with northern European ideas. He believed that Spanish thought would tend to be superficial as long as Spain remained cut off from the cultural roots of Europe. In his own journals and in the newspapers, he tirelessly argued for a reintegration. By the time Spain's intellectual reawakening came to pass, Ortega was famous throughout the Spanish-speaking world.

Life's Work

For several years, Ortega had been writing on Spanish problems in his own reviews and in *El Imparcial*, but it was a speech he made in 1914 that catapulted him to national prominence. The speech, entitled "Old and New Politics" and delivered at the Teatro de la Comedia, denounced the monarchy. Shortly thereafter, the League for Political Education was founded, and Ortega participated in the establishment of its monthly organ, *España*.

Also in 1914, Ortega published *Meditations on Quixote*, which contained the germs of his philosophy. The work contrasts the depth and pro-

José Ortega y Gasset. *(UPI/Corbis-Bettmann)*

fundity of German culture with the perceived superficiality of Spanish and Mediterranean culture. At the same time, the German writer Thomas Mann was exploring in fiction the different frames of mind in northern and southern Europe. In 1917, Ortega conducted a lecture tour in Argentina. Upon his return to Spain, he became one of the founders of the liberal newspaper *El Sol*. The paper was intended to counter the conservatism of *El Imparcial*, which his father had once edited.

The 1920's were a period of great literary productivity for Ortega. The title *Invertebrate Spain* is a metaphor for the nation's lack of an intellectual elite that could lead it out of its morass. Many essays that Ortega originally wrote for *El Sol* appear in this book and in *The Modern Theme*. The latter explores the different concepts of relativity that have influenced the author and states his philosophy more systematically than do his first two books. Also in 1923, Ortega founded yet another magazine, *La Revista de Occidente*, a literary monthly that soon came to be held in very high regard. It was in this journal that many European writers first appeared in Spanish.

By the end of the decade, Ortega and his fellow philosopher Miguel de Unamuno y Jugo were recognized as the foremost intellectuals in Spain. In 1928, Ortega again traveled in South America, where he was even more popular than Unamuno. His reception was tremendously enthusiastic, but he soon returned to Spain to participate in the revolution that would lead in 1931 to the exile of King Alfonso XIII. In the same year, principally because of his work in the Association for Service to the Republic, he was elected deputy for Leon.

Ortega's political career was short-lived. In 1929, he had published *The Revolt of the Masses*, destined to become a best-seller in its English translation. This book, like the earlier *Invertebrate Spain*, had predicted that the hegemony of mass humanity would have dire consequences. When the republican movement rapidly proceeded far to the left of mere liberalism, Ortega broke with it. He also did not support the loyalists when civil war finally came. He fled to France instead.

His stated longings for the leadership of an intellectual aristocracy misled the theoreticians of the Falange, the Spanish Fascist organization. They believed that his sympathies were being altered in their favor, while he still desired a rule of enlightened liberalism. After the forces of Francisco Franco triumphed, Ortega was offered a position as Spain's official philosopher. The regime also offered to publish a deluxe edition of his works, provided that he would delete certain essays and certain passages from others. He declined and remained abroad. He moved to Argentina, where earlier he had been well received and, in 1941, became professor of philosophy at the University of San Marcos, in Lima, Peru. This was a difficult period for Ortega. All of his political impulses were liberal, but he feared the results of an undifferentiated egalitarianism. Thus, he was condemned by the right and left alike. He did not return to his native country until 1945.

During his exile of almost a decade, Ortega also lived in the Netherlands and Portugal. Upon his return to Spain, he chose not to reclaim his chair at the University of Madrid, although technically he still held the rank of professor there. Instead, he and Julián Marías founded a private institution of higher learning, the Instituto de Humanidades in Madrid.

Also in 1948, his influential treatise on modern art, *La deshumanización del arte* (1925), was translated into English under the title *The Dehumanization of Art*. His interests continued to be wide-ranging. Toward the middle of his career, he had offered his theories on higher education in *The Mission of the University*. During the last fifteen years of his life, he also addressed the daunting subjects of love in *On Love* and history in *Toward a Philosophy of History*.

Ortega was an intensely private man. Beyond his writings, he revealed little of himself to his readers. He was described physically by observers as a small, well-proportioned man, with dark olive features and bright, arresting eyes. During his last years, he lectured throughout Europe. He died in the city of his birth on October 18, 1955.

Influence

Ortega is acknowledged to be a beautiful stylist. Some critics have found his individual books disappointing and have implied that his style is superior to his thought. However, Marías, who edited several volumes of his posthumous works, asserts that, despite surface indications, Ortega's philosophy is highly systematic. He saw no transcendent purpose in life, and because life consists only of the present, he argued that one should approach life as one approaches a game. Ortega's insistence that people must remain totally free, so that they can create their own lives, has caused his name to be linked with existential philosophy. He held life to be the relationship between the individual and the environment—that is, each person is the ego plus its circumstances. He be-

lieved, therefore, that Aristotelian reason must be sometimes subordinated to the intuition and spontaneous insight that comes from life experiences. His adjective for this kind of biological reason is translated as "vital" or "living." Commentators have identified various influences upon Ortega's thought, foremost among them the differing relativities of scientist Albert Einstein and German writer Oswald Spengler.

Ortega's extensive use of the essay form meant that he often could not rigorously pursue ideas to their ultimate conclusions in the manner of a dissertation. Yet his breadth of interests and mastery of language have earned for him a readership much larger than most serious philosophers can attract.

Patrick Adcock

What Is Philosophy?

Type of philosophy: Existentialism, metaphysics
First published: ¿Qué es filosofía?, 1958 (English translation, 1960)
Principal ideas advanced:
◇ Philosophy aims to understand the universe (all that is) as a totality and as a system, by discovering how each thing fits into the whole.
◇ Philosophy must begin with self-evident or indubitable truth, which becomes its basic datum.
◇ That basic datum is one's life (and the lives of all others) and is composed of oneself and the world, which mutually interact in an indissoluble bond.
◇ Living, rather than being, is the fundamental category of philosophy.
◇ The three attributes of life are self-knowledge, freedom, and time.

What Is Philosophy? contains a series of lectures that José Ortega y Gasset gave in Buenos Aires, Argentina, in 1928 and then in Madrid, Spain, in 1929. The lectures were not a traditional academic course in philosophy introducing the perennial problems in the field but a course that analyzed the very activity of philosophizing.

Ortega explains that in the last half of the nineteenth century and the beginning of the twentieth, the prestige of philosophy suffered under the "imperialism of physics." Physics owed its success to its uniting within itself the rigor of mathematical deduction, the confirmability of its findings through observation, and the opportunity of making the world more comfortable through technology. Philosophy could boast of nothing comparable. However, by the end of the first quarter of the twentieth century, philosophy rebounded. One reason for this was the demotion of physics as the paradigm of knowledge. A second reason was a dissatisfaction with the individual sciences, which provide only those parts of reality that come within the province of their methods, unlike philosophy, which offers a total view, being rooted in a vital need to know, or to attain a synoptic vision of, the whole.

The Whole as a System

Philosophy has as its object each thing that exists as an integral part of the whole; it seeks to locate everything in the total scheme of things. Therefore, the object of philosophical knowledge is the whole as a system. The method of philosophical inquiry consists of the principles of *autonomy*, which stipulates that every truth in the philosophical system must be demonstrable entirely within the system itself, and of *pantonomy*, which stipulates that the philosopher should seek to grasp the whole by showing what every particular thing is and how it fits into the total scheme of things. What is known to be true must be directly intuited or immediately present in a manner appropriate to itself; therefore, knowledge of sensory objects requires that they be present to the senses and knowledge of concepts requires that they be present to the mind. Philosophy must determine what things have an absolutely certain existence because they are directly intuited. They constitute the basic "data of the universe."

The physical world with its contents does not qualify as such a datum because, as René Descartes showed, it may be doubted; hence, realism must be rejected. What does qualify as a datum is thought; as Descartes proved, even when doubting one is thinking. Thought, then, "is the only thing in the Universe whose existence cannot be denied, because to deny is to think." Moreover,

thought is unique inasmuch as that at the moment it occurs, it fully manifests itself as it really is; nothing of itself is hidden. All that one knows exists for certain is one's mind and its ideas; one cannot know that anything outside one's mind exists for certain. This is the philosophical doctrine of Idealism.

Idealism

Idealism understands that the external world and its contents are nothing other than ideas in one's mind; their existence somehow depends on one's perception of them. Therefore, if one simply closes one's eyes, the whole visible world instantly vanishes. However, where is the world? One cannot say it is outside one's mind because one cannot escape one's mind to see whether the world is really out there independently of one's thought. Hence, the world must in some sense be contained within one's mind. However, in saying this, one supposes that the part of one's mind containing external objects such as chairs and tables takes on their physical properties—so one is reduced to the absurdity of supposing that one's thought is round or square, has a certain color, and occupies space. If the idealist rejoins by saying that it is not the world itself that is inside the mind, but just an image of it, then one is left again with the untenable position that the world is completely outside the mind and therefore unknowable to it.

Ortega escaped the idealist's dilemma by suggesting that the world is neither literally inside nor wholly outside one's mind but is inseparably linked with one's thinking of it—just as right is linked with left or concave with convex. Thus, to think at all is to think of the world, and to think of the world is simply to think: "The external world does not exist except in my thinking of it, but the external world is not my thought." The world and oneself are necessarily coordinate, which implies that just as there is no world without a mind to perceive it, so there could be no mind without a world to think about. Thought and its object are mutually dependent.

In light of this, Ortega amends the fundamental insight of idealism. The basic datum of philosophy is "the joint existence of a self, a subjectivity, and of its world." The world and oneself, which are indissolubly linked, indubitably exist.

Moreover, this world that is coordinate with one-self is the one that a person not only thinks about but also responds to emotionally, succeeds in changing, and moves about and has one's being in—none of which one could do if one did not coexist with the world. However, the term "coex-istence" does not adequately describe this rela-tionship because it connotes separate beings con-tiguous with each other. The relationship between the world and oneself is much more intimate and dynamic. It is a mutual interaction. The world depends on the person who perceives it, acts on it, endures it, and loves or hates it; yet the world confronts and resists one. The relation-ship between the world and oneself, their coexis-tence, is more a mutual functioning, one toward another. This complex interaction of oneself and the world is nothing other than one's life. This means that the fundamental datum of philoso-phy—"the primordial reality"—is nothing other than one's life. Thus, the fundamental task of philosophy is to define human life, not merely biologically because biology, like philosophy, pre-supposes this very life to be defined. Philosophy itself is a form of life, a vital activity that seeks to understand that life.

Life as Fundamental Being

As the basic datum of philosophy, or that which can be intuited with absolute certainty, life is the fundamental being for Ortega. His conception of being is quite unlike the traditional concep-tions—the ancient conception of being as a "thing" or the modern conception of it as "inner-most subjectivity." For Ortega, being as living is an intimacy that one has with both the self and things. Unlike the old idea of being as something independent and self-sufficient, Ortega under-stands it is as mutual need: A person, to be, needs the world, and the world, to be, needs the person. "One's living" replaces "being" or "existence" as the fundamental term of philosophy; all else is encompassed by one's life. Ortega's position su-persedes, by absorbing and going beyond, ideal-ism and realism. In affirming life as the basic reality, Ortega equally affirms the reality of both the conscious self (subject) and the world (object) in which the self finds itself. Life is more primor-dial than either thought or the world. Thinking is but an activity of one's living self that would

cease if one were dead. Moreover, the world is the world one finds oneself in as a living being. There is nothing that can possibly contradict the reality of one's life because everything else can be doubted and presupposes that life.

Self-Knowledge, Freedom, and Time

More than what is described by biology, life is what one is, what one does, and what happens to one. Its first attribute (category) is *self-knowledge*, or self-discovery. What is known or discovered is not just the self but also the world that is insepa-rably linked with it; one is aware of living in the world, of acting within it, and of responding to things in it. Thus, one knows that one is an active agent who is productively occupied with things in the world—"life is preoccupation"; the world is the sphere of one's activity. One preoccupies oneself with things—making and acting—for the purpose of improving one's existence. In think-ing, for example, one is preoccupied with things insofar as one thinks them and produces truths (philosophy). Those things that preoccupy one exist (in their primary sense) insofar as they exist for one's purposes; they do not subsist or exist otherwise. However, when they cease to preoc-cupy, they obtrude themselves in one's mind as self-subsistent things or as existing apart from one (in their secondary sense). However, even their self-subsistence is one's concept or abstrac-tion, and abstracting is uniquely a human activ-ity or occupation. Hence, things subsist in them-selves by virtue of one's abstract preoccupation with them and so still exist for one. Through abstraction, one no longer occupies oneself di-rectly with things or immediately experiences them as part of one's life; one pushes them, and the life they represent, away from one, so to speak, and thereby transcend one's own life. In this process can be found the theoretical (philo-sophical) attitude wherein one supposes things as existing not for oneself but for themselves.

One does not choose this world or one's life and time within it; in this respect one's life is predetermined. However—and this is the second attribute of life—one does not see oneself as be-ing predetermined but as having some *freedom* to choose; daily one is confronted with choices one must make with respect to what one might do or become. Life, then, is a mixture of free will and determinism, of "fate in freedom, and freedom in fate." Before one acts, though, one needs to decide for what purpose one should act: "Life consists in deciding what we are going to be." Because one must decide and act purposively, one always has one's eye on and anticipates the future where preferences will be met: "Our life is in its very essence futurism." Life, then, is essentially paradoxical because who one is depends on what one will become, on what is not yet—living is wholly a living into the future. Hence, *time* is the third attribute of life; in considering what one ought to be, one must think of the future: "Life is what comes next, what has not yet come to pass."

What Is Philosophy? represents Ortega's mature thought. It adapts the ideas of several German philosophers, particularly Max Scheler, Martin Heidegger, Wilhelm Dilthey, Edmund Husserl, and Nicolai Hartmann. The book is significant in numerous ways. It formulated a novel ontology of human life in which being or existence is defined as the "radical reality" of "my life"; it fused traditionally distinct or opposed movements, such as vitalism with rationalism, idealism with realism, and existentialism with phenomenology; it again placed the ancient field of metaphysics at the center of philosophy; it offered the concept of "vital" or "historical" reason; and it cast philosophical ideas in highly poetic and dramatic terms. *What Is Philosophy?* is of interest as a work of literature no less than as a text of philosophy; furthermore, it is an important document in the cultural history of Spain in the twentieth century.

Richard A. Spurgeon Hall

Additional Reading

Graham, John T. *Theory of History in Ortega y Gasset: "The Dawn of Historical Reason."* Columbia: University of Missouri Press, 1997. This is a clear look at Ortega's theory of history.

Gray, Rockwell. *The Imperative of Modernity: An Intellectual Biography of José Ortega y Gasset.* Berkeley: University of California Press, 1989. An extensive intellectual biography of José Ortega y Gasset that shows the development of his thought in all his major works. It places him in the history of international modernism at the turn of the century and considers his reaction to Spain's cultural isolation.

Mora, José Ferrater. *Ortega y Gasset: An Outline of His Philosophy.* London: Bowes & Bowes, 1956. A concise and compact introduction to Ortega's main philosophical doctrines that is especially suited to general readers. Its special virtue is that it is written by a philosopher and therefore contains the trenchant insights of a fellow practitioner.

Oimette, Victor. *José Ortega y Gasset.* Boston: G. K. Hall, 1982. A study of the development of Ortega's thought against the social and political background of Spain in the first half of the twentieth century. It makes a good introduction to Ortega's philosophy.

Raley, Harold C. *José Ortega y Gasset: Philosopher of European Unity.* University: The University of Alabama Press, 1971. An insightful study of Ortega's political, historical, and cultural thought as it relates to Europe itself and Spain's place in European history and culture.

Silver, Philip W. *Ortega as Phenomenologist: The Genesis of 'Meditations on Quixote.'* New York: Columbia University Press, 1978. Focuses on a specific facet of Ortega's thought that had been neglected—namely, his existential phenomenology—and describes his relationship to German philosophers, particularly Edmund Husserl.

Tuttle, Howard N. *The Crowd Is Untruth: The Existential Critique of Mass Society in the Thought of Kierkegaard, Nietzsche, Heidegger, and Ortega y Gasset.* New York: Peter Lang, 1996. An examination of the thought of Ortega and others.

Patrick Adcock,
updated by Richard A. Spurgeon Hall

Parmenides

By exploring the logical implications of statements that use apparently simple terms such as "one" or "is," Parmenides established metaphysics as an area of philosophical inquiry.

Principal philosophical works: *Peri physeōs*, fifth century B.C.E. (only fragments exist, including "Aletheia" and "Doxa"; *The Fragments of Parmenides*, 1869, including "The Way of Truth" and "The Way of Opinion"; commonly known as *On Nature*).

Born: c. 515 B.C.E.; Elea (now Velia, Italy)
Died: Perhaps after 436 B.C.E.; possibly Elea (now Velia, Italy)

Early Life

In the mid-sixth century B.C.E., as the Persian Empire advanced through Asia Minor toward the Aegean Sea, some of the Greek city-states that were threatened accommodated themselves to the invaders, while others attempted to maintain their independence. In the case of one Ionian city, Phocaea, many of the inhabitants left Asia Minor entirely. They migrated to southern Italy, founding Elea around 540. Parmenides' father, Pyres, may have been one of the emigrants, or, like his son, he may have been born in Elea. At any rate, Parmenides' family background was in Ionia.

It is therefore entirely natural that Parmenides would eventually compose verse in the standard Ionic dialect that had earlier been used for Homeric epics. Philosophical influences on the young Parmenides must be more conjectural, but at least some interest in the Ionian philosophers of the sixth century, such as Thales of Miletus and Anaximander, seems entirely reasonable for someone growing up in a Phocaean settlement.

The ancient traditions about Parmenides, on the other hand, connect him with the poet and philosopher Xenophanes. Born circa 570 B.C.E., Xenophanes was from Colophon in Asia Minor, and like the Phocaeans, he fled before the Persians to the western Greek world. Some contact between him and Parmenides is therefore quite likely. It is not so clear, though, that one should regard Parmenides as in any real sense Xenophanes' student. A better case can be made for a close association of Parmenides with the otherwise obscure Ameinias, to whom, after his death, Parmenides built a shrine, according to Diogenes Laërtius. Ameinias was a Pythagorean, and therefore, the sixth century B.C.E. philosopher and mystic Pythagoras should be added to the list of early influences on Parmenides.

The date that Diogenes gives for Parmenides' birth is around 540 B.C.E. Plato's dialogue *Parmenidēs* (middle period, 388-368 B.C.E.; *Parmenides*, 1793), on the other hand, is inconsistent with this date. Most of the dialogue is clearly invented by Plato because it includes details of argumentation that Plato himself developed in the fourth century B.C.E. The conversation between Parmenides, Socrates, and others, therefore, can scarcely have taken place as described by Plato; still, the overall setting of the dialogue, which implies that the title character was born around 515 B.C.E., may be chronologically accurate. Possibly, the date given by Diogenes arose from a reference in one of his sources to the founding of Elea around 540 B.C.E. as a crucial event in Parmenides' background.

Life's Work

Pondering the implications of earlier philosophy, which saw a single unifying principle—such as water, the infinite, or number—behind the various phenomena of the world, Parmenides strove to uncover a paradox residing in any such analysis. He wrote one treatise, in poetic form, in which he set forth his views. This three-part poem, of which only fragments exist, is generally referred to as *Peri physeōs*, although it is not certain that Parmenides so entitled it. Of this poem, commonly known as *On Nature*, about 150 lines are preserved in Greek, along with another six lines in a Latin translation.

Parmenides' central concern, or at least that for which he is best known, lies in the implications of the Greek word *esti*, meaning "is." According to Parmenides, of the two predications "is" and "is not," only "is" makes sense. Merely to say "is not" gives some stamp of evidence to whatever one says "is not" and therefore involves self-contradiction. With "is not" thus rejected, all reality must somehow be single and unified, all-encompassing and unchanging. Such a view would seem to be essentially ineffable, but toward the middle of Parmenides' fragment 8, which gives the core of his argument, *what-is* is compared to a well-rounded ball, perfectly poised in the middle, with nothing outside itself.

Despite this thoroughgoing monism, the opening of Parmenides' poem (fragment 1) refers to two paths of inquiry—one of *aletheia* (truth) and one of *doxa* (opinion). The argument about the primacy of "is" over "is not" follows the path of *aletheia*, while the latter part of fragment 8 follows the path of *doxa*. (These sections are generally known as the "Aletheia," or "The Way of Truth," and the "Doxa," or "The Way of Opinion.") Ancient authors did not, on the whole, find the "Doxa" interesting. It was therefore not as often quoted in antiquity, and only about forty-five lines of it are preserved. As a result, many modern treatments of Parmenides concentrate on the better-preserved "Aletheia." Such an approach may also find a precedent in Plato's dialogue *Parmenides*. Other scholars, though, acknowledge "Doxa" as having been an integral part of the poem, and this approach is entirely supported by some of the ancient references to Parmenides. Aristotle, for example, refers in *Metaphysica* (second Athenian period, 335-323 B.C.E.; *Metaphysics*, 1801) to Parmenides as having been constrained by phenomena to acknowledge change and multiplicity in the sensible world.

Aristotle's line of interpretation is probably correct. Despite the paucity of direct information about the "Doxa," several crucial ideas in ancient science are consistently associated with Parmenides, either as originating with him or as being promulgated by him. For example, the simile that concludes the "Aletheia"—that what-is resembles a well-rounded ball—may have a more prosaic but still grander cosmic application to Earth as a sphere, poised in space. Fragment 14 refers to the Moon's shining, not of its own accord but by reflected light. Aëtius and Diogenes Laërtius ascribe to Parmenides the observation that the evening and morning star are the same body (Venus) as it travels through space. Strabo (who flourished during the first century B.C.E.), quoting an earlier source, refers to Parmenides as having divided Earth into five zones. Such astronomical and geographic interests, along with various references to his treatment of biology, anatomy, and psychology, suggest that Parmenides had a mind more concerned with the investigation of physical phenomena than his austerely logical treatment of "is" and "is not" would suggest.

Nevertheless, Plato's contrary focus on Parmenides as primarily a metaphysician provides the earliest biographical and descriptive vignette of Parmenides. Plato's account places Parmenides in Athens in 450 B.C.E., at the time of a quadrennial festival to the goddess Athena. According to Plato, the Eleatic visitor to Athens was then about sixty-five years old, already white-haired but still of a forceful and commanding appearance and quite capable, as Plato reveals in the rest of the dialogue, of engaging in a complicated philosophical discussion.

Unfortunately, there is nothing very specific in Plato's physical description of Parmenides. One might hope that the picture would be filled out by the bust from the first century C.E. found during excavations at Elea in 1966. The bust matches an inscription, "Parmenides the son of Pyres the natural philosopher," found in 1962; also, the inscription somehow connects Parmenides with Apollo as a patron of physicians. The existence of this statue obviously testifies to the regard in which Parmenides was held in Elea several centuries after his death. It is unlikely, however, that it actually portrays the visage of Parmenides because it seems to be modeled on the bust of a later figure, the Epicurean Metrodorus, who was chosen to represent the typical philosopher.

In his account of Parmenides' visit to Athens, Plato includes the detail that Zeno of Elea, who accompanied Parmenides on that occasion, had once been his lover. Athenaeus objects to this point as a superfluous addition that contributes nothing to Plato's narrative. Whatever the case may be, Zeno and the slightly later Melissus are often grouped with Parmenides as the founders of an Eleatic school of philosophy. In particular, the intellectual connection between Parmenides and Zeno may be especially close. Both were from Elea (Melissus was from the Aegean island Samos), and according to Plato, Zeno's paradoxes, purporting to show the impossibility of motion, were designed to support Parmenides' doctrine concerning the unified nature of reality.

The determination of direct influences of Parmenides beyond the Eleatic school is more tenuous. Theophrastus, however, connects two other fifth century figures with him: the philosopher-poet Empedocles and the founder of atomism, Leucippus. Also, although he is from a later generation, it is generally agreed that Plato himself owed much to Parmenides.

Of Parmenides' life after his possible visit to Athens in 450 B.C.E., nothing definite is known. Theophrastus's implication that Leucippus studied with him at Elea should possibly be dated after 450. Also, Eusebius of Caesarea implies that Parmenides was still living in 436 B.C.E.; this information leads scholars to believe Plato's chronology over that given by Diogenes Laërtius. According to Plutarch, Parmenides was a lawgiver as well as a philosopher, and subsequent generations at Elea swore to abide by his laws.

Influence

Some critics see fundamental flaws in Parmenides' reasoning. According to the modern scholar Jonathan Barnes, for example, it is perfectly acceptable to say that it is necessarily the case that what does not exist does not exist, but Parmenides erred in holding that what does not exist necessarily does not exist. Even if this objection is valid, Parmenides' lasting influence on subsequent thought is undeniable. Often, his arguments are presented without quibble in modern treatments of the history of philosophy, as having uncovered difficulties with which any process of thinking must cope.

It is also important to keep in mind the poetic medium that Parmenides used. His sixth century predecessors, such as Anaximander and Anaximenes, had used prose for their philosophical treatises. Parmenides, however, chose verse, perhaps to give some sense of the majesty and dignity of the philosopher's quest. The ineffable quality that Parmenides claims for ultimate reality may also find an appropriate expression in poetry. Above all, the use of verse puts Parmenides in a rich verbal tradition, stretching back to the earliest extant Greek poetry, that of Homer and Hesiod, and to even earlier oral poetry. The most obvious parallels are with Homer's *Iliad* (c. 800 B.C.E.; English translation, 1616) and his *Odyssey* (c. 800 B.C.E.; English translation, 1616). For example, the cattle of the Sun are described in the *Odyssey* as neither coming into being nor perishing, and this idea is also central to Parmenides' concept of what is. A close verbal parallel to Homer's description of the paths of night and day in the *Odyssey* is also found in Parmenides. More generally, one may note that Odysseus, after his manifold adventures in the outer reaches of the world, eventually returns home to Ithaca and to his wife, Penelope, exactly as Parmenides would both partake of and yet, somehow, eschew the realm of pure thought for the mundane world of *doxa*.

Parmenides thus emerges as a prime mediator between ancient Greek and later philosophy. While casting his thought in terms of the poetic imagery, metaphors, and formulas used by Homer and Hesiod, he still insisted emphatically on the paramount importance of reason that his contemporaries and successors, such as Zeno, Leucippus, and Plato, framed anew.

Edwin D. Floyd

The Way of Truth *and* The Way of Opinion

Type of philosophy: Metaphysics
First transcribed: Peri physeōs, fifth century B.C.E. (only fragments exist, including "Aletheia" and "Doxa"; *The Fragments of Parmenides*, 1869, including "The Way of Truth" and "The Way of Opinion"; commonly known as *On Nature*)

Principal ideas advanced:
◇ Reality is a solid, homogeneous sphere.
◇ All appearances of change and motion are illusory.
◇ Whatever exists could not have come from nothing; it must then have come from what exists—but if the existent can come only from the existent, there is no beginning to what exists: Reality is eternal and indestructible.
◇ Because the material of the universe consists of its sensible qualities and because to change would involve the nonexistence of qualities (which are eternal and indestructible), change is impossible.

Parmenides, it seems, began his philosophical career as a Pythagorean, but when still a young man, he attained the insight that reality consists of a solid homogeneous sphere, the appearances of diversity and change being altogether illusory. He set out this extraordinary doctrine in a poem in hexameter verse, consisting of a proem; "Aletheia" ("The Way of Truth"), a section expounding and defending the theory of the sphere; and "Doxa" ("The Way of Opinion"), a section in which he dealt with scientific theories (probably Pythagorean). The proem and "The Way of Truth" have been preserved substantially intact, but only a few fragments of "The Way of Opinion" remain.

The Goddess
The proem is an elaborate allegorical description of Parmenides' journey into heaven. In a chariot drawn by "immortal mares," he is conducted upward by the daughters of the Sun, who bring him to the "gates of the ways of Night and Day," the keys to which "severely chastising Justice" holds. At the entreaties of the maidens, Justice opens the portals, revealing "the goddess" who addresses Parmenides:

O youth, who come to our mansion in the company of immortal charioteers, welcome! It was no evil fate but right and justice that set you to travel on this way, far indeed from the path trodden by men. Meet it is that you should inquire into all things, the unshaking heart of well-rounded truth as well as the opinions of mortals in which is no true confi-

dence at all. Yet none the less you shall learn all things, even how seeming things—all passing through each—must really be.

The goddess warns Parmenides against relying on the senses for knowledge of reality: "Keep your thought away from this way of inquiry, and by no means let much-tried custom force you this way, to ply the unseeing eye and the ringing ear and the tongue" (considered to be the organ of taste, not of speech). "Rather, judge by reason the much-disputed proof which I expound." The much-disputed proof is strictly a priori, depending altogether on the law of identity:

Well then, I shall tell you—and do you attend and listen to my word—what are the only ways of inquiry there are to think of. The first, that IT IS, and that it is impossible for it not to be, in the way of conviction, for it follows truth. The other, that IT IS NOT, and that it must needs not be,—that, I tell you, is a path that none can learn of at all. For you could not perceive what is not—that is impossible—nor even think of it; for it is the same thing that can be thought and that can be.

The goddess's expressions are puzzling because it does not follow the rules of language (Greek or English) to say simply, "It is." We want to know what the "it" stands for; and if "it" is (for example) a radish, the expression "A radish is" still makes no sense. A radish is *what*? Nevertheless, the sense of the passage is unmistakable: If there is something real (and there is), then whatever characteristics it has, it has just those characteristics, and none other. *A* is *A*. It is impossible to think of *A* not being *A*, for to *say* that *A* is not *A* would be in effect to say that the thing having the characteristic *C* does *not* have the characteristic *C*; and this would amount to saying something and immediately retracting it, so that altogether nothing would be said. It is in this sense that "it is the same thing that can be thought and that can be." The goddess did not mean, of course, that there must be mermaids in the ocean because we can think of them. She meant that reality and thought must both be noncontradictory.

All this is perhaps innocent enough, but the goddess is going to use the principle thus laid down as a weapon to destroy belief in the reality of the world revealed by the senses. The first step is to draw the corollary "For this shall never be proved, that what-is-not is," for "it is not possible for what is nothing to be." The thought is that the word "nothing" means "that which is not"; consequently any sentence having the word "nothing" as its subject, and "is" as its verb, must be contradictory, "not to be thought of."

Having established this, it is easy for the goddess to prove that "what-is is uncreated and indestructible." She asks, "For what birth of it will you seek out? In what way and from what source its increase? I forbid you to say or to think that it came from what-is-not; for how what-is-not could *be* is neither speakable nor thinkable." The argument implied is a simple dilemma: If there is an origin of what-is, that origin must be either what-is or what-is-not. However, it cannot be what-is-not, for if so, the contradictory sentence "What-is-not is the origin of what-is" would be true, which is absurd. Also of course to say that the origin of what-is is what-is, while in a sense true, is so only trivially. Therefore what-is is uncreated.

The goddess advances another argument to prove the same conclusion: "And, if it came from nothing, what need could have made it arise later rather than sooner?" This is really an argument from an assumed causal principle; even if the objection be waived that "what-is-not" is unthinkable, mere nothingness or negation could not, by definition, afford any reason or cause why something, if it were to originate out of it, should suddenly appear at one time rather than another. However, without such a reason, nothing could appear at *any* time; hence, if there ever were a time at which there was just nothing at all, then there never could be anything at any other time. This argument was attractive to many subsequent philosophers, including Saint Thomas Aquinas and Thomas Hobbes. A similar argument (not given) would show that annihilation is also impossible. "Thus is generation extinguished and destruction not to be heard of."

The conclusions reached are those that were agreed to by all Greek philosophers before and after Parmenides: Nothing comes from nothing, and nothing disappears into nothing. However, the goddess makes additional conclusions:

Nor is it divisible, since it is all alike, and there is no more of it in one place than in another, to hinder it from holding together, nor less of it, but it is completely filled with what-is. Wherefore it is wholly continuous; for what-is is in contact with what-is. It is immovable in the bonds of mighty chains, not starting, not stopping, since generation and destruction have been banished afar, driven back by true conviction. Wherefore all these things are but names which mortals have given, believing them to be true—generation and destruction, being and not being, change of place and alteration of bright color.

These astounding conclusions are drawn as corollaries, without further argument. Motion was supposed to be impossible because if anything were to move, it would have to move into empty space; but because empty space would be "what-is-not," there cannot *be* any empty space. As for "alteration of bright color" or other qualitative change, this could not take place either, for if an apple, previously green, were to become red, this would entail the disappearance of the greenness into nothing, and the appearance of redness from nothing, both equally impossible because they are contradictory. The goddess has another surprise for Parmenides.

It abides the same, remaining in the same place, by itself; thus it stays, rooted to the spot. For mighty Necessity keeps it in the bonds of a limit which shuts it in round about. For this reason it is not right that what-is should be without an end. For it is not wanting; if it were, there would be need of everything. . . . Since, then, it has an outermost boundary, it is limited from every side, like the mass of a well-rounded sphere, extending equally from the center in every direction.

This emphatic assertion of a spatial limit to what-is is perhaps the hardest of all to absorb because one immediately is led to ask, in Parmenidean fashion, What is outside it? If more of what-is, then there is no limit after all; but if what is outside what-is is what-is-not, then it cannot exist as a limit. Indeed Parmenides' follower Melissus of Samos ventured to correct the master on this point; he asserted that what-is is spatially infinite. Parmenides' thought seems to have been that infinity (being *without* end) entails incompleteness and hence could not be predicated on what-is, which is perfect; indeed it was characteristic of Greek thought to prefer the tidy to the vast. However, this at most extenuates Parmenides without acquitting him of manifest inconsistency.

"Here shall I close my trustworthy reasoning and thinking for you about the truth," says the goddess. "Henceforward learn the beliefs of mortals, giving ear to the deceptive order of my words." After this unpromising beginning comes an account of the nature of things, more in keeping with the general tenor of early Greek thought. For instance, Parmenides states that the Moon shines by light "borrowed" from the Sun. However, the fragments of this part of the poem are too few to reconstruct the system with certainty. The purpose of including cosmological information seems to have been to forestall derisive criticism of Parmenides as ignorant of the science of his day: "I am telling you everything about this plausible cosmology, so that you may not be surpassed in insight by any mortal."

The Philosopher's Reasoning
No serious thinker in the fifth century B.C.E. could dismiss Parmenides' conclusions merely on the ground that they were incompatible with observed fact, because philosophy, which was still a new enterprise, consisted in an investigation of the world by *reason*. If in general the senses provided the data for the inquiry, no philosopher considered himself bound to conclude that things are in all respects as they appear to be. If the senses declared things to be a certain way, but reason indicated that they were otherwise, it was not by any means unheard of to dismiss the observations as deceptive. In throwing out *all* observation, Parmenides only carried to an extreme a preexisting practice.

Parmenides, the founder of formal logic, simply deduced the logical conclusion of the assumptions agreed on by his predecessors. These assumptions were as follow: (1) the stuff (whether water, the Boundless, mist, or fire) of which all things are made is of one kind only (monism); (2) this stuff, as such, is eternal, being neither created

nor destroyed, neither augmented nor diminished (conservation of stuff); (3) the qualities of things and the things qualified are not distinguished (phenomenalism). Thus heat and brightness were not thought of as properties of a fire-substance; heat and brightness literally *constituted* fire; (4) change is a real phenomenon (reality of change).

Once these assumptions are made explicit, Parmenides' philosophy becomes in a certain way obvious. If the stuff of things is ungenerated and indestructible, and if that stuff consists of its sensible qualities, then it is out of the question for it to change. For to say that it changes is precisely to say that it has a property at one time and lacks it at another, a conclusion that contradicts assumptions two and three. Thus what-is must be at least "frozen." However, there cannot be any diversity in it, if the premise of monism is taken seriously.

Parmenides' argument against motion on the ground that motion requires empty space, and empty space would be what is not and therefore nonexistent, is an obvious sophism. Oddly, though, his successors Empedocles and Anaxagoras deferred to it and denied the possibility of a vacuum. They attempted to make reason agree with observation by giving up the postulate of monism in favor of six kinds of stuff (Empedocles) or as many stuffs as there are perceived differences (Anaxagoras); and they tried to account for motion in a plenum as displacement, illustrated by a fish swimming in a jar "full" of water. Failing to see that the argument that empty space is nothing is independent of Parmenides' main contentions, and that change is inconsistent with the postulates of conservation and phenomenalism, they exposed themselves to the Parmenidean rebuttal of Melissus, who pointed out that "If there were a many, these would have to be of the same kind as I say that the One is. For if there is earth and water, and air and iron, and gold and fire, and if one thing is living and another dead, and if things are black and white and all that men say they really are,—if that is so, and if we see and hear aright, each one of these must be such as we first decided, and they cannot be changed or altered, but each must be just as it is."

In fact, if Parmenides' conclusions are to be escaped without abandoning either conservation or logic, it is necessary (besides clearing up the quibble about "empty" and "nothing") to distinguish between a thing and its properties (to abandon phenomenalism) and to distinguish, within properties, between qualities and relations. F. H. Bradley's *Appearance and Reality* (1893) demonstrated that if the reality of relations is denied (if relations are conceived as qualities or predicates of the things related), then a Parmenidean view of reality is inescapable. Of the ancients, Democritus, Plato, and Aristotle were the only philosophers who displayed some grasp of Parmenides' essential points and tried to come to grips with them. It is doubtful whether any of them was altogether successful.

Problems in Parmenides' System

It should not be thought, however, that Parmenides' philosophy is free of internal problems. Besides the difficulty of the "outermost boundary," the most obvious one is that it is not sufficient to reject sense-experience (or anything else) as illusion unless one can at least show the *possibility* of explaining, consistently with one's general position, how the illusion occurs. However, such a possibility seems to be ruled out in Parmenides' system. For if the assumption is made that in reality there exists nothing but a homogeneous rigid sphere, it seems that there cannot be any illusions at all because in order for there to be an illusion there must be—*really* be—a mind that is deceived, and a mind is by its very nature something that is changing or at least implies change (it thinks now one thought, now another).

There is the further paradox that Parmenides in effect reduced one of his premises to absurdity. As a matter of strict logic, all that Parmenides proved was that the four assumptions listed above are incompatible; the argument of itself did not show that the postulate of change was the one to be rejected. Parmenides evidently chose to deny it because of his (logically independent) argument for the impossibility of void (and perhaps also on religious grounds). Because there is no inconsistency in assuming at once monism, conservation, and change (as the atomists were to show), Parmenides' reasoning would have been invalid without the premise of phenomenalism. Yet this premise seems incompatible with his conclusion that what-is is not at all what we perceive. Perhaps, however, Parmenides interpreted the third premise as implying only that what-is must have (or be) *some* kind of quality capable of entering into *some* kind of consciousness—the property in question might have been just awareness itself. The fact that Melissus argued explicitly that the One could not "suffer pain" suggests that he thought it could "suffer" *something*, in other words, be somehow conscious. This lends some slight support to the conjecture that Parmenides' sphere, though undeniably a body, was also endowed with nondiscursive consciousness, whatever that might be. If so, then there is warrant for thinking of Parmenides as the father of idealism.

Wallace I. Matson, updated by John K. Roth

Additional Reading

Barnes, Jonathan. *The Presocratic Philosophers.* London: Routledge & Kegan Paul, 1982. Contains three chapters mainly on Parmenides, along with numerous other references. Barnes puts Parmenides' ideas into a modern philosophical framework. Includes a good bibliography.

Burnet, John. *Early Greek Philosophy.* London: Adam and Charles Black, 1930. A classic work on pre-Socratic philosophy, first published in 1892. Contains a clear, readable chapter on Parmenides and a chapter on Leucippus that suggests that Parmenides' reference to what-is as a self-contained sphere may have given rise to atomism.

Cornford, F. M. *Plato and Parmenides.* London: Kegan Paul, 1939. A general account of Parmenides' poem and Plato's dialogue *Parmenides*. Contains text, introduction, and running commentary.

Curd, Patricia. *The Legacy of Parmenides.* Princeton, N.J.: Princeton University Press, 1998. Curd offers a new interpretation of Parmenides that finds an important place for the "Doxa" and that makes his work more continuous with the rest of pre-Socratic philosophy. One of her principal claims is that while the thesis that there is only one thing may fairly be attributed to Melissus of Samos, a later figure who was inspired by Parmenides, it should not be ascribed to Parmenides himself. Contains an extensive bibliography.

Furth, Montgomery. "Elements of Eleatic Ontology." In *The Pre-Socratics: A Collection of Critical Essays*, edited by Alexander P. D. Mourelatos. 1974. Reprint. Princeton, N. J.: Princeton University Press, 1993. Furth offers an imaginative reconstruction of Parmenides' central argument in dialogue form. The anthology is the standard collection on the pre-Socratics.

McKirahan, Richard D., Jr. *Philosophy Before Socrates*. Indianapolis, Ind.: Hackett, 1994. Contains translations of key pre-Socratic fragments, which are then explored by McKirahan in a remarkably clear and accessible way. Includes a discussion of Parmenides and the other Eleatic philosophers. This is perhaps the best place for a new student of pre-Socratic philosophy to begin.

Mourelatos, Alexander P. D. *The Route of Parmenides*. New Haven, Conn.: Yale University Press, 1970. The main thrust of this work is Parmenides' philosophical program. It pays particular attention to the way in which material in the "Doxa" parallels statements in the "Aletheia," often through a more or less explicit appeal to paradox. Contains Greek text of fragments of Parmenides without translation.

Owen, G. E. L. "Eleatic Questions." In *Logic, Science, and Dialectic*. Ithaca, N.Y.: Cornell University Press, 1986. Owen's article has been enormously influential in shaping the standard reading of Parmenides. In it, he describes "Aletheia" as the philosophically important part of the poem and states that the ultimate conclusion of Parmenides' argument is that only one thing really exists.

Taran, Leonardo. *Parmenides*. Princeton, N.J.: Princeton University Press, 1965. Contains Greek text, translation, commentary, and critical essays. Taran argues that the subject of "Aletheia" is Being and that Parmenides regards the sensible world as an illusion.

Edwin D. Floyd, updated by Randall M. Jensen

Blaise Pascal

Pascal was a man of genius in many areas who made important contributions to mathematics and physics and invented an early form of the calculator. His major contribution, however, is the record of his religious and philosophical struggle to reconcile human experience, God, and the quest for happiness and meaning.

Principal philosophical works: *Lettres provinciales*, 1656-1657 (*The Provincial Letters*, 1657); *Pensées*, 1679 (*Monsieur Pascal's Thoughts, Meditations, and Prayers*, 1688; best known as *Pensées*).

Born: June 19, 1623; Clermont-Ferrand, France
Died: August 19, 1662; Paris, France

Early Life

Blaise Pascal was the third child of Étienne Pascal, a government financial bureaucrat, and Antoinette (née Begon), who died when Pascal was about three. After his mother's death, Pascal and his family moved to Paris. Pascal's father decided to educate his children himself, rather than making use of either tutors or schools. Étienne Pascal was associated with the intellectual circles of Paris and thereby exposed Pascal to the best scientific and mathematical thought of his time.

While still a teenager, the precocious Pascal attracted the attention of the court and, in 1640, published his first mathematical treatise. In 1642, he began developing a mechanical calculator to help in his father's work. He continued improving the device for the next ten years and in 1652 sent a version of it to Queen Christina of Sweden. In 1646, Pascal and his two older sisters first came under the influence of Jansenism, a strict, pietistic movement within the Catholic Church that stressed a life of devotion, practical charity, and asceticism. Pascal experienced what is usually called his "first conversion," feeling the need for religious renewal but not wanting to give up his scientific and mathematical endeavors. His scientific work at this time included experiments with vacuums, an important area of exploration in seventeenth century physics.

Life's Work

By his mid-twenties, Pascal had assumed a pattern of life that he would continue until his death. In 1647, he entered into the first of the public religious controversies that would preoccupy him on and off for the rest of his life. He also continued his scientific work on the vacuum, exchanging information with the great philosopher René Descartes and publishing his own findings. In 1648, he wrote a mathematical essay on conic sections. Throughout this period, Pascal was afflicted with serious illness, as he would be for the remainder of his life.

Pascal's sister Jacqueline continued to be influenced by Jansenism, and during this time, she expressed her desire to enter the Jansenist religious community at Port Royal. Both Pascal and his father objected, but after her father's death in 1651, Jacqueline entered the convent the following year. Pascal began a brief phase in which he indulged himself in the pleasures and pursuits of French society, finding the experience empty but also finding no other direction for his life at this time.

Pascal experienced a growing disillusionment with the skeptical worldliness of society life and greatly desired something more meaningful. During the middle of the night of November 23, 1654, he had an intense, mystical religious experience that lasted about two hours and changed the direction of his life. During this experience, Pascal felt powerfully and unmistakably the truth of God's existence and the blessing of his love and

Blaise Pascal. *(Library of Congress)*

its, and in January of 1656, Pascal wrote the first of a series of anonymous letters now entitled *The Provincial Letters*. These letters, eighteen in all, came out until May, 1657, and are masterpieces of satire, wit, analytic logic, and French prose style. Especially in the early letters, the fictitious writer adopts a pose of objective, naïve curiosity about the controversy between the Jesuits and Jansenists, which he is purportedly trying to explain to his fellow provincial back home. In reality, the letters are an impassioned defense of the principles and principals of the Jansenist movement and a stinging attack on the Jesuits. The letters were enormously popular, and the local authorities went to great lengths to try to suppress them and discover their author. Pascal's letters have been admired ever since as masterpieces of French prose.

Pascal was not satisfied, however, merely to defend a particular movement within the Catholic Church. He desired to write a great defense of Christianity as a whole at a time when religious faith was increasingly under attack by skepticism and rationalism. Prompted in part by what he took to be the miraculous cure of his young niece, Pascal began in 1657 to take notes for this work, which he once said would take ten years of steady effort to complete. As it turned out, Pascal never completed the work or even a draft of it. Instead, he produced approximately one thousand notes, some only a few words, others pages long and substantially revised. The majority of these notes were written in 1657 and 1658, after which time he fell into the extremely painful and debilitating illness that would largely incapacitate him until his death. They were first published in abbreviated form as *Pensées* in 1670 and have become one of the classic documents of Western culture.

Although Pascal never wrote his great apology for the Christian faith, he did organize many of his notes into groups, from which scholars have speculated as to his ultimate intentions. As enlightening as these speculations sometimes are, the timelessness of *Pensées* comes not from the tantalizing promise of some irrefutable defense

forgiveness. Pascal had been provided with the kind of experiential certainty for which his scientific mind yearned and, consequently, saw everything thereafter in spiritual terms. In reaction to this experience, Pascal went to Port Royal, the center of Jansenism, for a two-week retreat in early 1655 to begin the reformation of his life that he now sought. He was particularly concerned with overcoming the willful pride that had marked his life since his spectacular intellectual accomplishments as a boy and the selfishness that showed itself in his resistance to his sister Jacqueline's entrance into the community at Port Royal.

Jansenism was to dominate his life for the next few years. In 1653, Pope Innocent X had condemned the writings of Cornelius Jansen, Bishop of Ypres, upon which the Jansenist movement in the Catholic Church was based. The great enemies of the Jansenists were the rationalistic Jesu-

of religious faith but from Pascal's compelling, often painful insights into the human condition and from the process of watching one of history's great minds struggle with eternal questions of faith, spirit, and transcendence.

Many of Pascal's most powerful entries poignantly explore the tragedy and folly of the human condition if there were no God. He depicts humankind as lost in an alien and inhospitable world, given over to the empty baubles and distractions of society. Pascal portrays the world as a psychologically frightening place. Men and women are caught between the infinitely large and the infinitely small. They are torn by a divided nature that is neither angel nor beast, to use one of his images, but is capable of acting like either. Human beings yearn for something sure and permanent but find only illusion and transience. Pascal finds the solution for the human dilemma in the grace of God as manifested in Jesus Christ. Only by knowing who created them, Pascal argues, can humans know who they are and how they can be happy. He does not, however, offer this solution as an effortless one. Part of Pascal's enduring appeal is his very modern awareness of the difficulty of religious faith in a scientific and skeptical world.

Pascal was seriously ill much of the last four years of his life, but that did not prevent him from making at least sporadic efforts on a variety of projects. In 1658, he made further mathematical discoveries on the cycloid and publicly challenged the mathematicians of Europe to a contest in solving problems in this area. He was drawn briefly into the Jansenist controversy once again but then withdrew from it altogether. His concern for the poor led him to invent and launch a public transportation system in Paris in March of 1662. Additionally, when health permitted, he worked on his defense of Christianity that became *Pensées*. After much suffering patiently borne, Pascal died on August 19, 1662, at the age of thirty-nine.

Influence

Pascal is one of those handful of individuals in history whose wide range of accomplishments shows evidence of a fundamental genius that expressed itself wherever it was applied. Proof of his greatness is given by the number of different

fields of intellectual effort that claim him. He is considered a mathematician of the first rank, an important physicist at the early stages of that science, an inventor, a literary master of French prose, and, most important, a philosopher and religious thinker who has written brilliantly about fundamental questions of the human condition.

Standing at the beginning of the modern age, Pascal felt keenly the call of reason and science but realized the price to be paid if one were to lose a sense of the spiritual and transcendent. He felt caught between two contrary forces: the rationalism of rising seventeenth century science and the skepticism about all human efforts, reason included, as epitomized by his French predecessor, Michel de Montaigne. He sought an approach to life that avoided the arrogance and materialism of the former and the cynicism and moral passivity of the latter. In this sense, Pascal's situation anticipates the modern one. How does one find meaning, values, and faith in a rationalistic, skeptical world where most traditional guidelines are called into question? For more than three hundred years, men and women have found insight and inspiration in Pascal's answers.

Daniel Taylor

Pensées

Type of philosophy: Metaphysics, philsophical theology, philosophy of religion

First published: Pensées, 1679 (*Monsieur Pascal's Thoughts, Meditations, and Prayers,* 1688; best known as *Pensées*)

Principal ideas advanced:

◇ There are two essential religious truths: There is a God, and there is a corruption of nature that makes people unworthy of God.

◇ Reason is of little use in showing either the existence or the nature of God, but it does reveal humanity's finiteness and separation from God.

◇ It is a reasonable wager to stake everything on God's existence, for God either exists or does not exist. If God is, then the person who believes in God wins everything; if God is not, the person who believes in God suffers only a finite loss.

◇ In knowing that one is miserable, one achieves greatness.

◇ Because one's will is subject to one's passions, it is important that one obey custom simply because it is custom, and obey the law in order to avoid sedition and rebellion.

Blaise Pascal's reflections on religion make up a large body of notes, written between 1654 and his death in 1662, intended to develop a work called "Apologie de la religion catholique." Composed at different times after a moving mystical experience, the contents of *Pensées* appeared in print posthumously. These reflections reveal Pascal as belonging to the group of fervently Christian writers who reject the usual claims of natural theology in order the more sharply to separate faith from reason.

Jansenist Influence

Pascal's thought expresses the influence of the Jansenists, a seventeenth century Catholic order indebted to the theological views of John Calvin, one of the Protestant reformers. A group in conflict with the Jesuits, the Jansenists lived at Port Royal, near Paris, where they taught several central beliefs: the total sinfulness of humanity, salvation through God's predestination, grace as sole means to salvation, and the need of the faithful to hold to a Christian belief that can never be proved by reason.

Though never an official member of the Jansenist community, Pascal visited them frequently (his sister belonged) and wrote in their defense in a bitter controversy with the Jesuits. Pascal was a brilliant mathematician as well as a religious writer, aware of the significant mathematical developments of his day. Living an austerely self-disciplined life, he gave away his wealth in an effort to exclude all pleasure and vanity from his practices.

The Existence of God

Pensées expresses numerous reflections concerning a few central themes. The Christian religion as known by Pascal teaches two essential truths: "that there is a God, to whom men may attain, and that there is a corruption of nature which renders them unworthy of him." Pascal insists that if people deny either of these truths, they must fall into atheism, end up with the philosophers' god so popular among deistic thinkers of his time, or find themselves reduced to a complete pessimism. The Christian God worshiped by Pascal does not require a philosopher's proof of existence, and he writes, "It is a wonderful thing that no canonical author has ever made use of nature in order to prove God." Pascal argues that humanity's miserable state does not justify total pessimism for the reason that the God worshiped by Christians, as by Abraham, Isaac, and Jacob, is one of love and consolation.

Pascal claims that God becomes available to people only through the mediation of Jesus Christ. Although Pascal makes clear that a person is a "thinking reed," one's thinking capacity can nevertheless function religiously only to make clear one's absolute finiteness, one's total separation from God's actual infinity. In writing about faith, Pascal stresses the utter uselessness of reason for religious purposes. "Faith is a gift of God," he insists. "Believe not that we said it is a gift of reason." Yet reason is never to be disparaged, since it performs its own important functions and provides the key to whatever dignity humanity may achieve.

The Wager Argument

Nevertheless, Pascal sometimes does come close to a kind of reasoning about God—as in his famous wager argument for belief in God's existence (although this argument was intended primarily for skeptics who deny the importance of religious belief). In another place Pascal treats the relation of humanity's miserable condition to its finitude in such a way that he gives something resembling an argument for the necessity of God's existence. This latter argument rests on the awareness that the "I" of Pascal is really a thought. Had Pascal's mother died before his birth, the "I" of Pascal would never have existed. The conclusion is that Pascal is clearly not a necessary being. Pascal sees also that he is neither eternal nor infinite. He asserts that "I see plainly that there is in nature one being who is necessary, eternal, and infinite." This approximation to one of the classical demonstrations of God's existence indicates that Pascal was more concerned to argue that proofs cannot induce one to accept the Christian faith than to claim that proofs are unqualifiedly impossible of formulation. Such proofs, even if possible, turn out to be religiously useless and unimportant.

Pascal contends that people know *that* there is a God without knowing *what* God is. (In this claim he is inconsistent; he also asserts in one place that people can never *know* God's existence.) He insists that people also can know there is an infinite while remaining ignorant of its nature. Numbers cannot be brought to an end. This means simply that people can never mention a number that is the last one. Therefore, number must be infinite. Similarly, aware of the infinite's existence and unable to know its nature, people fail to know God's nature and existence because God lacks extension and limits. People have absolutely no correspondence with the God that Christians worship in faith. The Christians who refuse to give reasons for their faith are essentially right, according to Pascal. They present their God as a "foolishness" to a world that often complains because the Christians cannot prove this God's existence. Some critics reasonably criticize Christians for holding beliefs that are beyond proof. Pascal attempts to reply to these critics by arguing that it is reasonable to believe. This he does primarily by producing his famous wager argument.

The stakes are clear, in Pascal's view. "God is, or He is not." The agnostic can argue that because reason is unable to decide the issue, one need make no choice either way. Pascal insists that this will not do—that people must wager. They must choose. "It is not optional; you are committed to it." Pascal claims that people own two things as stakes in such a wager: their reason and their will (blessedness). They have two things to lose: the true and the good. Human nature involves also two things to avoid: error and misery. Now, according to Pascal, since reason is unable to make the decision, the issue must turn on humanity's blessedness. How is this to be decided? The answer is that if people wager on God's existence, they stand to win everything, losing nothing. Thus, to wager for God's existence means the possibility of either finite loss (if God does not exist) or infinite gain (if God does

exist). Humanity's wager stakes a possibility of finite loss against one of infinite gain; namely, happiness. People can therefore make only one wager: that God does exist.

What Pascal set out to prove was not that God exists but that people *ought to believe* in God's existence. Once made, however, the wager does not necessarily bring one to the Christian God, as Pascal was clearly aware. Yet the wager is a fruitful beginning. Doubters who make the wager can still use the possible way of "seeing through the game" associated with the reading and study of Scripture. They can also seek to control their passions. In this present life, the person who wagers will be better off for having made the wager. Such a person will be driven to associate with others who have already been cured of their malady. Like them, the person must act as if he or she believed. According to Pascal, no harm can come to such a person, for he or she will be "faithful, honest, humble, grateful, benevolent, a sincere and true friend."

Reason and the Will

To read Pascal as if he sought to debase the functions of human reason would be to read him wrongly. Because reason is incapable of knowing what God is does not alter the fact that humanity's greatness is tied to reason. Pascal insists that thought is not derived from body. Thought is its own kind of entity. Reason alone permits people to know the misery that marks their condition, but this very knowledge accounts for their dignity: "To be miserable is to know one's self to be so, but to know one's self to be miserable is to be great." Only humanity can possess this kind of knowledge, which is denied to the other elements in nature. What makes Christianity the solely adequate religion, in Pascal's view, is that Christianity teaches the otherwise peculiar doctrine that human misery and greatness are inseparable. People need to come to terms with their miserable condition, though they cannot fundamentally alter it. This gives both people and religion something important to accomplish. The central religious problem is to learn to control the human will rather than to pile up theological knowledge by reasoning. To cure pride, lust, and ego-centered aggressiveness remains the fundamental task of the Christian religion.

Concern about human willfulness occurs in numerous passages in *Pensées*. Unlike the reasoning powers, the will operates according to the human perspective. People find themselves in bondage to their passions. For this reason, custom is a most important necessity of any possible social existence. Against Michel de Montaigne, Pascal argued that people should obey custom simply because it is custom and not because it is reasonable. People should also obey law as law in order to avoid sedition and rebellion. Pascal insists that classical philosophers such as Plato and Aristotle wrote about politics with many reservations. "If they wrote of politics, it was as if to regulate a hospital for madmen." Pascal could not believe that such people thought reasoning about politics the most serious business of life.

Though he understood the limited possibilities of reasoning, Pascal never degraded reason. Reasoning allows people to encircle the universe in certain ways, but "instinct" and "the heart" are essential allies. "How few demonstrated things there are!" Pascal laments in one place. People are as much automata as minds. No one should ridicule custom in view of this fact. Agreeing with a philosopher such as David Hume, Pascal says it is custom that permits people to believe that tomorrow will dawn and that people must die. Custom influences people to act, while reason directs only the mind. Habit, including religious practice, remains a routine needed in every day and age. "We have to acquire an easier credence—that of habit—which without violence, art, or argument, makes us believe things and inclines all our powers to this belief, so that our mind falls into it naturally." Pascal claims that life would be easier for people if reason were unnecessary, but because nature has not so arranged matters, people need to supplement intuited first principles with limited demonstrations.

Knowledge vs. Judgment

Pascal makes a distinction between knowledge and judgment. For example, geometry is a matter of the mind, while subtlety is a function of intuition. People must judge things either literally or spiritually. Honoring reason, people should accept its limits, knowing what it can and cannot accomplish. Although there is criticism of the

Pyrrhonists (skeptics) for some of their beliefs, Pascal shows that he was favorably disposed to a partial skepticism concerning the powers of reason. People can at most achieve a "learned ignorance." Different from the natural ignorance of all people at birth, a learned ignorance is gained by a few "lofty souls who, having traversed all human knowledge, find that they know nothing. . . . This is a self-aware ignorance." Between these two kinds of ignorance dwell the great numbers of the intelligent who "disturb the world and judge wrongly of everything." Genuine philosophers are those who learn how to laugh at philosophy.

The imagination and human sickness are two important elements that shape people's constant susceptibility to deception. The wisest person can hope only to modify, never to eradicate, these two sources of illusion. People tend naturally toward wrong judgment. They find it difficult, if not impossible, to escape the binding conditions of their own vanity. Their actions are motivated by self-love. What makes the Christian view of Incarnation important is the radical cure it suggests for humanity's pridefulness. People must hate religion as long as it teaches what it must: that the misery of humanity is objective and absolutely ineradicable except by God's grace. This side of Pascal's thought shows a relation to the long tradition in Western thought concerned with the numerous psychological and cultural obstacles in the way of genuine discovery of self-knowledge. These obstacles are, for Pascal, as much connected with the human will as they are with the mind. It is as if people want, in some deep and buried way, to judge things wrongly.

Atheism and Deism

Pascal mentions atheism and deism as the greatest competitors of a genuine Christian faith. He understands how atheism may be a mark of a strong intellect, though only up to a point. Atheists have blind spots when they come, say, to the notion of immortality. Pascal asks why atheists should deny dogmatically the possibility that a person might rise from the dead. He wants to know which is the more remarkable: that a living being should appear at all, or that a once-living being should be reborn. By custom, the atheist accepts the fact that there are living beings and then seems astounded by the religious notion of rebirth. Here the atheist puzzles Pascal. On the other hand, the deist seeks to know God without revelation, meaning without the mediation of Jesus Christ. The deist thus misunderstands Christianity, ending with the philosopher's God of proofs and first principles rather than with the God of redemption. Pascal clearly aligns himself with those who assert that the Christian faith cannot fully be translated into philosophical terms.

Original Sin

Affirmation of the original sin of all people is a necessity for Pascal. The evidence for this affirmation is that all people are born disposed to seek their own interests, a disposition that runs counter to the necessary conditions of order. Wars and revolutions arise from people's pursuit of self-interest even when their reason tells them that they should attend to the needs of a commonwealth. People should usually seek the general as opposed to the particular interests of a community, but most often they do not. Facts like these Pascal takes as indicative of some basic flaw in human willing. The glory of the Christian religion stems from its insistence on people's inherent sinfulness. "No religion but ours has taught that man is born in sin," Pascal writes; "no sect of philosophers has affirmed it, therefore none has spoken the truth." This dark doctrine, so stressed by Pascal and borrowed from Calvinism, helped to bring him into disrepute among the Jesuits, who thought he emphasized it disproportionately. Yet he was quite aware of the nonrational nature of this doctrine and made no effort to prove it.

Legacy of Faith

What makes Pascal's *Pensées* an enduring work is the classical manner in which one aspect of the Christian tradition in theology receives forceful and passionate presentation. Its confessional and personal nature also makes it a work that can help individuals who, like Pascal, find themselves caught up in a struggle to make sense of Christian faith once they have abandoned belief that natural proofs of God's existence are possible. One-sided in emphasis, Pascal's work tries to show that Christian faith is reasonable on its own

terms even though not susceptible of rational proofs divorced from reasons of the heart. No matter how extremely emphasized, Pascal's views about the depravity of the will help to counterbalance the more optimistic humanistic conceptions of human perfectibility.

Through *Pensées* runs a sense of the fragility of human life—a constant reminder of something most people know when they think about it but which they often wish to forget. A sense of the contingency of life, of uncertainty about its duration, pervades Pascal's writings. A mystical sense that there is more to finite existence than meets the finite eye drives Pascal to fall back on intuition and feeling when reason proves unable to establish the kinds of certainty many religious persons hope to find.

Pascal's portrait of human misery involves a kind of metaphysical sickness. Reasoning people are caught between the finite and an infinite whose nature they can never hope to fathom. They own a will to self-deception, marked by an endless pursuit of means by which to divert attention from this very fact. On the other hand, a critic may well say that Pascal is too much a puritanical thinker—unwilling or unable to point out the genuinely redeeming features of natural processes. The Pascalian picture of humanity illustrates the more somber side of Puritan thought and feeling. "Imagine a number of men in chains, and all condemned to death, of whom every day some are butchered in sight of the others, those remaining seeing their own fate in that of their fellows, regarding each other with grief and despair while awaiting their turn; this is a picture of the condition of man."

Obviously, some of Pascal's thoughts reflect events of his own life. He shunned pleasure and picked up the radically austere notions of the Jansenists. Nevertheless, his version of Christian faith remains a recurring theme in the long, unresolved competition between those who argue for a natural theology and those others who insist that revelation is not to be explained in philosophical terms. Pascal's *Pensées* is the expression of a man who seemed to need this specific version of Christian faith to find life itself a meaningful affair.

Whitaker T. Deininger,
updated by John K. Roth

Additional Reading

Adamson, Donald. *Blaise Pascal: Mathematician, Physicist, and Thinker About God*. New York: St. Martin's Press, 1995. Explores how Pascal dealt with the insights and conflicts produced by his mathematical, scientific, and religious experiences.

Coleman, Francis X. J. *Neither Angel Nor Beast: The Life and Work of Blaise Pascal*. New York: Routledge & Kegan Paul, 1986. An insightful overview of Pascal's life and work, good at placing Pascal in the context of seventeenth century thought.

Davidson, Hugh M. *Blaise Pascal*. Boston: Twayne, 1983. This good first introduction to Pascal discusses his major philosophical and religious works.

_____. *Pascal and the Arts of the Mind*. New York: Cambridge University Press, 1993. Discusses Pascal's views on the nature and variety of human experience.

Jordan, Jeff, ed. *Gambling on God: Essays on Pascal's Wager*. Lanham, Md.: Rowman & Littlefield, 1994. Pascal scholars explain and evaluate the most controversial features of Pascal's philosophy of religion.

Kolakowski, Lezek. *God Owes Us Nothing: A Brief Remark on Pascal's Religion and on the Spirit of Jansenism*. Chicago: University of Chicago Press, 1995. An important philosopher of religion reflects on the main points of Pascal's views about faith and the relationship between God and humankind.

Krailsheimer, Alban. *Pascal*. Oxford, England: Oxford University Press, 1980. A short but serious overview of Pascal's thought, including his mathematical and scientific accomplishments.

Marvin, Richard O'Connell. *Blaise Pascal: Reasons of the Heart*. Grand Rapids, Mich.: W. B. Eerdmans, 1997. A worthwhile discussion of Pascal's efforts to reconcile the demands of human rationality and the yearnings of feeling and hope, especially as the latter are expressed religiously.

Morris, Thomas V. *Making Sense of It All: Pascal and the Meaning of Life*. Grand Rapids, Mich.: W. B. Eerdmans, 1992. A clear and sensitive interpretation of Pascal's struggle to identify what the meaning of human life may be.

Nelson, Robert J. *Pascal: Adversary and Advocate*. Cambridge, Mass.: Harvard University Press, 1981. Takes a psychological approach to Pascal's biography and work and offers extensive critical study of his individual works.

Rogers, Ben. *Pascal*. New York: Routledge, 1999. An excellent biographical introduction to the thoughts of the philosopher, clearly presented and requiring no special background. Bibliography.

Wetsel, David. *Pascal and Disbelief: Catechesis and Conversion in the "Pensees."* Washington, D.C.: Catholic University of America Press, 1994. A helpful discussion of Pascal's approach to an affirmative religious faith, which Pascal develops and defends in a context of skepticism.

Daniel Taylor, updated by John K. Roth

Charles Sanders Peirce

Largely unrecognized by contemporaries, except for his contribution to pragmatism, Peirce developed a system of philosophy that attempted to reconcile the nineteenth century's faith in empirical science with its love of the metaphysical absolute. His difficult and often confusing ideas anticipated problems central to twentieth century philosophy.

Principal philosophical works: "Questions Concerning Certain Faculties Claimed for Man," 1868; "Some Consequences of Four Incapacities," 1868; "On a New List of Categories," 1868; "Grounds of Validity of the Laws of Logic: Further Consequences of Four Incapacities," 1869; "Fraser's *The Works of George Berkeley*," 1870; "The Fixation of Belief," 1877; "How to Make Our Ideas Clear," 1878; "The Doctrine of Chances," 1878; "The Probability of Induction," 1878; "The Order of Nature," 1878; "Deduction, Induction, and Hypothesis," 1878; "A Guess at the Riddle," 1887-1888; "The Architecture of Theories," 1891; "The Doctrine of Necessity Examined," 1892; "The Law of Mind," 1892; "Man's Glassy Essence," 1892; "Evolutionary Love," 1892; *Reasoning and the Logic of Things*, 1898; *Pragmatism*, 1903; "What Pragmatism Is," 1905; "Issues of Pragmaticism," 1905; "Prolegomena to an Apology for Pragmaticism," 1906; "A Neglected Argument for the Reality of God," 1908; *Collected Papers of Charles Sanders Peirce*, 1931-1958 (8 volumes); *The Writings of Charles S. Peirce: A Chronological Edition*, 1982- (multiple volumes); *The Essential Peirce*, 1992-1994 (2 volumes).

Born: September 10, 1839; Cambridge, Massachusetts

Died: April 19, 1914; near Milford, Pennsylvania

Early Life

Charles Sanders Peirce, born on September 10, 1839, in Cambridge, Massachusetts, was the son of Benjamin Peirce, one of America's foremost mathematicians. During his childhood, Peirce's mother, Sarah Hunt (Mills) Peirce, took second place to his dynamic father, who personally supervised the boy's education and provided a role model that inspired his son but also proved impossible to emulate. Convinced of his son's genius, Benjamin Peirce encouraged his precocious development. Charles began the study of chemistry at the age of eight, started an intense scrutiny of logic at twelve, and faced rigorous training in mathematics throughout his childhood. In his mathematical training, he was seldom given general principles or theorems but rather was expected to work them out on his own.

At sixteen, Peirce entered Harvard, where his father was professor of mathematics. Contrary to expectations, Peirce proved a less-than-brilliant student, and he was graduated, in 1859, seventy-first out of a class of ninety-one. Although Peirce was probably too young and certainly too much the nonconformist to fit into the rigid educational system of nineteenth century Harvard, his inauspicious beginning in institutional academics was prophetic. Though he would continue his education, receiving an M.A. from Harvard in 1862 and a Sc.B. in chemistry the following year, his future did not lead to a distinguished career in academics or, indeed, in any conventional pursuit. His lot in life, in spite of so much promise, was frustration and apparent failure.

Peirce's difficulty in adjusting to the ordinary world was related to his unusual and often trying personality. Always his father's favorite, Peirce became convinced of his own genius and impatient with those who failed to recognize the obvious. Shielded and overindulged as a child, Peirce never developed the social skills required for practical affairs or the self-discipline necessary to make his own grandiose vision a reality. Such problems were exaggerated by his passion for

World Philosophers and Their Works

perfection and his abstract turn of mind. Peirce found real happiness only in the rarefied world of his own philosophical speculation.

As a youth, Peirce both attracted and repelled. Always prone to the dramatic gesture and, when he was inclined, a brilliant conversationalist, he could be an entertaining companion, but he could also use his rapier wit as a weapon. Of medium height, dark, swarthy, and fastidious in matters of dress, the handsome young Peirce reveled in his reputation as a lady's man and spent much energy in seeking the "good life." He actually paid an expert to train his palate so that he could become a connoisseur of fine wines. In 1862, Peirce married Harriet Melusina Fay, three years his senior and infinitely more mature and self-possessed. A feminist and intellectual in her own right, "Zina" worshiped her captive "genius" and labored for years to keep him out of serious trouble while restraining his extravagance. Yet she could also be jealous and posses-sive, and, though Peirce would experience some stability under Zina's influence, the marriage was doomed.

Life's Work

Upon his graduation from Harvard, Peirce went to work for the U.S. Coast and Geodetic Survey, a position acquired through his father's influence. Benjamin Peirce served as a consulting geometer for the organization and became its superintendent in 1867. Charles Peirce remained with the survey in various capacities until 1891, when he was asked to resign. This bureaucratic career, while terminated in less-than-desirable circumstances, was not without accomplishments. His deep commitment to the experimental method helped put the survey on a firm scientific basis, and Peirce became internationally known for his work on gravity research. He also continued an association with Harvard, once again through his father's influence, holding temporary lectureships in logic in 1865-1866 and 1869-1870 and from 1872 to 1875 serving as assistant at the Harvard Observatory. His observatory work on the measurement of light provided data for *Photometric Researches* (1878). Peirce hoped for a permanent appointment at Harvard, but his lack of a doctoral degree, his erratic lifestyle, and a personal quarrel with Harvard president Charles W. Eliot made the dream impossible.

More than his actual work, the atmosphere and personal contacts at Harvard helped mold Peirce's philosophical outlook. Never idle, Peirce spent his spare time studying the work of German philosopher Immanuel Kant, the ideas of the medieval Scholastics, and various theories in logic and mathematics. The most useful forum for his developing ideas was the so-called Metaphysical Club. In the meetings of this unusual group, which included William James, Oliver Wendell Holmes, Jr., Francis E. Abbot, and Chauncey Wright, Peirce had the opportunity to test his theories before a critical audience. It was there that he used the term "pragmatism" to describe the relationship be-

Charles Sanders Peirce. *(Preston Tuttle Collection, Institute for Studies in Pragmaticism, Texas Tech University)*

tween a conception and its effects, which allows one to understand the actual meaning of the original conception by knowing its effects. Although Peirce intended his idea as a theory of meaning, James, more than twenty years later, would popularize the term and expand it far beyond the original intention. In fact, objecting to his friend's interpretation, Peirce, in 1905, coined the term "pragmaticism" to distinguish his thought from James's version.

In his Harvard years, Peirce began to write articles for *The Journal of Speculative Philosophy* and other scholarly publications, as well as more popular magazines such as *Popular Science Monthly*. Such articles, along with numerous book reviews, provided his major public outlet for the remainder of his life. Ignored by much of the philosophical community, these writings contained important contributions to logic, mathematics, and metaphysics.

Peirce finally got his chance to teach when he was hired as a part-time lecturer at The Johns Hopkins University in 1879. Apparently an effective teacher, he produced some of his best work in logic and scientific methodology at Johns Hopkins. Yet his erratic behavior, coupled with his divorce from his first wife and remarriage to a twenty-six-year-old French woman, the mysterious Juliette Pourtalai, made it difficult for the authorities to accept him, no matter how brilliant, as part of the faculty. In 1884, Peirce was dismissed from his position because of unsuitable activities of a moral nature, probably connected with his divorce and remarriage.

Peirce's second marriage began a phase of his life that would be philosophically productive but personally frustrating, ending in self-imposed exile. In 1887, his academic career hopelessly in shambles and his labors for the survey drawing to a conclusion, Peirce moved to Milford, Pennsylvania, a resort area on the Delaware River. With a small inheritance, he was able to purchase land and begin construction of an elaborately planned home he called "Arisbe." Though Peirce was able to live in his retreat for the remainder of his life, the mansion was never really completed. Typically, Peirce had overextended himself. When he lost his government salary in 1891 and suffered severe losses in the depression of 1893, he began a long slide into poverty. His closest

and always tolerant friend, William James, tried to help as much as possible, arranging for a series of lectures in Boston in 1898 and finally convincing Harvard to allow the notorious philosopher to give a series of lectures at the university in 1903. No effort, however, even by the United States' most famous philosopher, would make Peirce acceptable to established society in the nineteenth century. Finally, James began collecting donations for a Peirce fund from interested and unnamed friends. From 1907 until his death in 1914, Peirce was largely supported by this fund, which amounted to about thirteen hundred dollars a year. Peirce, who had often been jealous of James and attacked his version of pragmatism with undisguised contempt, paid his friend a typical compliment by adopting Santiago (Saint James) as part of his name in 1909.

Even in his last years, which were marred by illness, Peirce was productive. He continued to work in isolation, leaving behind a massive collection of papers. Ironically, Harvard, the institution that had so often rejected him, recognized his worth and purchased the manuscripts from his widow. Between 1931 and 1958, the eight volumes of the *Collected Papers of Charles Sanders Peirce* were published by Harvard. This collection began what amounted to a revolution in American academic philosophy, making the ideas of Peirce a touchstone for twentieth century philosophical inquiry.

Unfortunately, the exact nature of Peirce's contribution to understanding is by no means clear. Numerous scholars have spent their careers examining his writings, never reaching a consensus. The confusion is rooted in the nature of Peirce's work. Not satisfied with a contribution in a single area of inquiry, Peirce envisioned a vast architectonic system ending in a complete explanation of all human knowledge. In short, Peirce strove to be a modern Aristotle. While admirable, this goal ran up against a central dilemma in human thought, providing a source of tension within Peirce's system as well as within the world in which he lived.

Science, in the last years of the nineteenth century, revealed a limited vision of reality, of what could be known. The world, according to this view, consisted of matter and could be fully explained through the scientific method. Many thinkers, unable to accept this so-called positivistic version of reality, countered with an explanation based on the mind itself as the source of everything. Best represented in the Idealism of Georg Wilhelm Friedrich Hegel, this view spawned many variations. Peirce could not fully accept either position. Positivism seemed to deny the possibility of metaphysics or a universe with meaning intelligible to people. Idealism seemed hopelessly subjective, denying the possibility of actually knowing the physical universe.

Peirce set out to reconcile the irreconcilable by carefully examining immediate experience. Characteristically, this examination would be grounded on clear and precise thinking such as his famous "pragmatic maxim." He also rejected nominalism and accepted the position of the medieval scholastic John Duns Scotus on the reality of universals. Peirce insisted that cognition itself is reality, and everything that is real is knowable. The structure of experience is revealed in what he called "phaneroscopy." This term is typical of Peirce's obsession with the invention of new words to explain concepts, which is one of the reasons his ideas are so difficult. Phaneroscopy is roughly analogous to the modern concept of phenomenology. From his phenomenological basis, Peirce deduced three categories or qualities of experience: Firstness, Secondness, and Thirdness. This division of experience allowed him to move from an essentially psychological analysis to logic itself through what he called the "semiotic," or the doctrine of signs. By signs, Peirce essentially meant those things in the mind that stand for the real things of the world. A word, for example, would be a sign but only one kind of sign. Peirce's analysis of signs and their relationships was a vast and complicated explanation of how human beings think and provides the logical basis for his whole system.

Most modern philosophers would agree that this difficult and obscure argument constitutes Peirce's most important contribution to philosophy, particularly logic. Its obscurity, however, has led to many different interpretations. Phenomenologists, for example, find considerable comfort in his explanation of experience, while the logical positivists, who seldom agree with phenomenologists, also see their ideas reflected in Peirce's theory of signs. In fact, most philosophical systems in the twentieth century find some part of Peirce's ideas important in either a positive or a negative way.

Peirce's logic, however, was only the foundation of a broad system that included a complete theory of knowledge as well as cosmological speculations. This system, while not as widely accepted as his semiotic, includes a number of important concepts. For example, Peirce develops what he calls "tychism," or the doctrine of chance, which explains irregularities within nature. This idea should be balanced with "synechism," which is the doctrine that continuity is a basic feature of the world. Here again, Peirce reconciles the irreconcilable, and the result provides a reasonable picture of the actual condition of scientific inquiry. Synechism represents scientific law, which Peirce calls habit, without which one could not understand the operation of the natural world. Tychism, however, explains how change is possible and prevents a deterministic version of reality, which is the logical result of scientific law. Science then, while based on research that, if pursued to infinity, will result in "truth," must in the practical world be based on probability. Even in logic itself, one cannot be sure that all statements are correct. While not denying absolute truth, this concept, which Peirce called "fallibilism," provides a healthy corrective to those who are convinced that they have found the ultimate answer to reality.

Influence

Few can profess to understand all of Peirce's philosophy, and his work will probably never appeal to the average person unschooled in the mysteries of philosophical discourse. Yet his attack on the central dilemma of modern thought, created by the advance of science and its clash with human values, is the necessary starting point for many twentieth century philosophers and, through their work, has a profound influence on the way the world is viewed. It may be true that Peirce ultimately failed in his attempt to reconcile the "hard" world of science with cherished human values represented by the "soft" world of Idealism, but unlike his tragic personal life, his philosophy was certainly a glorious failure. Moreover, Peirce remained a true optimist who believed in the inevitability of human progress through reason. His system of thought, while far from perfect, did provide a view of reality that would make such progress possible. His first rule of reason demanded that the road to new knowledge always be left open. The greatest sin against reasoning, he believed, consisted in adopting a set of beliefs that would erect a barrier in the path of the search for truth.

David Warren Bowen

Collected Papers of Charles Sanders Peirce

Type of philosophy: Epistemology, logic, pragmatism

First published: 1931-1958 (8 volumes)

Principal ideas advanced:

◇ A belief is a habit of action; different beliefs give rise to different modes of action.

◇ One's idea of anything is one's idea of its sensible effects; objects are distinguished according to the difference they make practically.

◇ True ideas are those to which responsible investigators, were they to push their inquiries far enough, would finally give assent; reality is what true ideas represent.

◇ Of the four methods of fixing belief—the methods of tenacity, of authority, of a priori judgments, and of science—the scientific is preferable as providing critical tests of procedures.

◇ By the conceptions of Firstness, Secondness, and Thirdness, a metaphysics of cosmic evolution can be developed; Firstness is the individual quality of a thing, Secondness is the relatedness of a thing to something other than itself, and Thirdness is the tendency to mediate or contribute to law.

◇ There is chance in the universe (tychism); the universe begins in a chaos of unpersonalized feeling and develops habits or patterns of action (synechism); finally, as laws develop, the universe moves toward a condition of perfect rationality and symmetry (agapasm).

In the late 1800's, Charles Sanders Peirce—in conversation with William James, Chauncey Wright, Nicholas St. John Green, and Oliver Wendell

Holmes at informal meetings of the Metaphysical Club in Cambridge, Massachusetts—developed and clearly expressed the central ideas that became the core of pragmatism. In the United States, pragmatism largely replaced idealism, gained numerous adherents, and influenced many American philosophers. The thoughts of American pragmatists can be seen in linguistic empiricism, developed by Vienna positivists, who grounded philosophical claims in experience, and the British philosophers who emphasized the study of ordinary language in the multiplicity of its uses.

However, Peirce was more than the creator of pragmatism; he was a scientist, mathematician, logician, and teacher, although his career as a professor was limited. He lectured at Harvard and The Johns Hopkins University. Peirce's failure to find, or to be offered, a university position suitable for one of his talents was a consequence of his independent and undisciplined nature. The result of his being free from academic restrictions was perhaps both fortunate and unfortunate. As an outsider, his creative powers had no formal limits; his intellect was brilliant, and he knew where to stop in his inventions and speculations. However, because he was an outsider, he had neither the security nor the incentive to fashion his essays into any coherent whole. Although he attempted, in later life, to write a great, single work in which his views on logic, nature, science, humanity, and philosophy would be developed in some mutually illuminating and supporting fashion, his poverty and isolation—together with his iconoclastic stubbornness—combined to frustrate his great ambition.

The *Collected Papers of Charles Sanders Peirce* is an eight-volume collection of Peirce's works, arranged thematically. The first six volumes were edited by Charles Hartshorne and Paul Weiss and the last two by Arthur Burks. Although critics and editors of Peirce's essays are not in complete agreement on what constitute the philospher's major works, most recognize certain essays as characteristic of Peirce at his best. These essays include "The Fixation of Belief," "How to Make Our Ideas Clear," "The Architecture of Theories," and "The Doctrine of Necessity Examined." Because these essays contain some of the most famous and revealing statements of Peirce's basic opinions, an examination of them will serve as an introduction to other significant essays.

Peirce's thought, varied and original as it was, falls naturally into four categories: the pragmatic, the epistemological, the logical, and the metaphysical. The poles are the pragmatic ideas of meaning and truth (ideas that condition the epistemological conceptions) and, at the other extreme of his thinking, the metaphysical ideas. The effort to relate these poles to each other rewards the student of Peirce with a synoptic idea of Peirce's philosophy that illuminates the otherwise confusing variety of essays to be found in the *Collected Papers of Charles Sanders Peirce*.

Doubt and Belief

In the essay "How to Make Our Ideas Clear," which first appeared in *Popular Science Monthly* in 1878, Peirce set out to interpret the vague conception of clarity to be found in French philosopher René Descartes's writings on method. The first step was to clear up the conception of belief. Peirce began by speaking of doubt as a kind of irritation arising from indecisiveness in regard to action; when one does not know what to do, one is uneasy, and this uneasiness will not abate until one settles upon some mode of action. Belief is "a rule for action," and as it is acted upon repeatedly, each time appeasing the irritation of doubt, it becomes a habit of action. Thus, Peirce concluded, "The essence of belief is the establishment of a habit, and different beliefs are distinguished by the different modes of action to which they give rise."

In a previous essay, "The Fixation of Belief," which appeared in *Popular Science Monthly* in 1877, Peirce had written of doubt as a state of dissatisfaction from which people try to free themselves and of belief as a satisfactory state. The struggle to remove the irritation of doubt and to attain belief, a rule of action, was described as "inquiry," and the settlement of opinion was set forth as the sole object of inquiry.

It was Peirce's conviction that logic, as the art of reasoning, was needed to make progress in philosophy possible; he anticipated logical positivism in urging that only "a severe course of logic" could clear up "that bad logical quality to which the epithet *metaphysical* is commonly applied."

Therefore, the first step in learning how to make one's ideas clear is to come to the realization that belief is a habit of action, the consequence of a process of inquiry undertaken to appease the irritation of indecisiveness. Because the entire purpose of thought, as Peirce conceived it, is to produce habits of action, it follows that the meaning of a thought is the collection of habits involved. If the question involves the meaning of a "thing," its meaning is clear once one knows what difference the thing would make if one were to become actively, or practically, involved with it. Peirce's conclusion was that "there is no distinction of meaning so fine as to consist in anything but a possible difference of practice."

As an example, he referred to the doctrine of transubstantiation and to the Catholic belief that the elements of the Communion, though possessing all the sense properties of wine and wafers, are literally blood and flesh. To Peirce, such an idea could not possibly be clear, for no distinction in practice could be made between wine and wafers, on the one hand, and what *appeared* to be ine and wafers, on the other. He argued that no conception of wine was possible except as the object of the reference, "this, that, or the other, is wine," or as the object of a description by means of which certain properties are attributed to wine. However, the properties are conceivable only in terms of the sensible effects of wine; "Our idea of anything *is* our idea of its sensible effects." Consequently, "to talk of something as having all the sensible characters of wine, yet being in reality blood, is senseless jargon." The rule for attaining clearness of thought, Peirce's famous pragmatic maxim, appears in "How to Make Our Ideas Clear" as follows: "Consider what effects, which might conceivably have practical bearings, we conceive the object of our conception to have. Then, our conception of these effects is the whole of our conception of the object."

Peirce's discussion of his maxim, revolving about examples, makes it clear that the rule for the clarification of thought was not designed to support a simple phenomenalism. Although Peirce used sentences such as "Our idea of anything *is* our idea of its sensible effects," he did not use the expression "sensible effects" to mean merely sensations. By conceiving, through the use of the senses, the effects of the action of a thing, one comes to understand the thing; one's habit of reaction, forced upon one by the action of the thing, is a conception of it, one's belief regarding it. The object is not *identifiable* with its effects, but the object can be conceived as "that which" one conceives only in terms of its effects.

Pragmatism and Pragmaticism

Peirce's pragmatic rule should be distinguished from philosopher William James's version of the same principle. James stressed an idea's becoming true; he used the misleading expression "practical cash-value" to refer to the pragmatic meaning of a word, and he sometimes emphasized the *satisfactoriness* of an idea, as constituting its truth, in such a way that no clear line was drawn between sentimental satisfaction and the satisfaction of a scientific investigator.

Peirce, on the other hand, in developing the ideas of truth and reality made careful use of the contrary-to-fact conditional in order to avoid any loose or emotional interpretation of the pragmatic method. He wrote, in "How to Make Our Ideas Clear," that scientific processes of investigation "if only pushed far enough, will give one certain solution to every question to which they can be applied." Again, in clarifying the idea of reality, Peirce came to the conclusion that "The opinion which is fated to be ultimately agreed to by all who investigate, is what we mean by the truth, and the object represented in this opinion is the real." In other words, those opinions to which systematic, responsible investigators *would* finally give assent, *were* the matter thoroughly investigated, are true opinions. It was Peirce's dissatisfaction with the tender-minded versions of the pragmatic method that led him finally to give up the name "pragmatism," which he invented, and to use in its place the term "pragmaticism."

The Scientific Method

Peirce's preference for the scientific method of inquiry is nowhere more clearly expressed and affirmed than in his early essay "The Fixation of Belief." Regarding the object of reasoning to be the discovery of new facts by a consideration of facts already known and having argued that a belief is a habit of action that appeases the irrita-

tion of doubt or indecisiveness, he went on to examine four methods of fixing belief: the method of tenacity, which is the method of stubbornly holding to a belief while resisting all criticism; the method of authority, which consists of punishing all dissenters; the a priori method, which depends on the inclination to believe, whatever the facts of the matter; and, finally, the method of science, which rests on the following assumption:

> There are real things, whose characters are entirely independent of our opinions about them; those realities affect our senses according to regular laws, and, though our sensations be as different as our relations to the objects, yet, by taking advantage of the laws of perception, we can ascertain by reasoning how things really are, and any man, if he have sufficient experience and reason enough about it, will be led to the one true conclusion.

Peirce strongly endorsed the scientific method of inquiry. He argued that no other method provided a way of determining the rightness or wrongness of the method of inquiry itself; the test of a procedure undertaken as scientific is an application of the method itself. In support of the realistic hypothesis on which the method of science is based, Peirce argued that the practice of the method in no way cast doubt on the truth of the hypothesis; furthermore, everyone who approves of one method of fixing belief in preference to others tacitly admits that there are realities the method can uncover. The scientific method is widely used, and it is only ignorance that limits its use. His final argument was that the method of science has been so successful that belief in the hypothesis on which it rests has been strengthened proportionately.

These passages should be of particular interest to those who suppose that Peirce, as the founder of pragmatism, was absolutely neutral in regard to commitments ordinarily regarded as metaphysical. He did not claim to know the truth of the realistic hypothesis, but it did seem to him eminently sensible, accounting for the manner in which nature forces experience upon people and making uniformity of opinion possible.

Firstness, Secondness, Thirdness

In the essay "The Architecture of Theories," published in *The Monist* in 1891, Peirce introduced the critical conceptions of Firstness, Secondness, and Thirdness, which he described as "principles of Logic," and by reference to which he developed his metaphysics of cosmic evolution. He defined the terms as follows: "First is the conception of being or existing independent of anything else. Second is the conception of being relative to, the conception of reaction with, something else. Third is the conception of mediation, whereby a first and second are brought into relation."

Arguing that philosophical theories should be built architectonically, Peirce offered the conceptions of Firstness, Secondness, and Thirdness as providing the logical principles of construction. Any adequate theory, he maintained, would order the findings of the various sciences by the use of the principles of Firstness, Secondness, and Thirdness. Thus, in psychology, "Feeling is First, Sense of reaction Second, General conception Third, or mediation." Significantly, as a general feature of reality, "Chance is First, Law is Second, the tendency to take habits is Third," and, Peirce maintained, "Mind is First, Matter is Second, Evolution is Third."

Peirce sketched the metaphysics that would be built by the use of these general conceptions. He wrote that his would be a "Cosmogonic Philosophy." It would describe a universe that, beginning with irregular and unpersonalized feeling, would, by chance ("sporting here and there in pure arbitrariness"), give rise to generalizing tendencies that, continuing, would become "habits" and laws. The universe, such a philosophy would claim, is evolving toward a condition of perfect rationality and symmetry.

Peirce elaborates on the ideas introduced in "The Architecture of Theories" in four papers collected in *The Essential Peirce* (1992-1994, 2 volumes), edited by N. Houser and C. Kloesel. They are "The Doctrine of Necessity Examined," "The Law of Mind," "Man's Glassy Essence," and "Evolutionary Love."

"Tychism" and "Synechism"

In "The Doctrine of Necessity Examined," Peirce argued for the presence of chance in the universe. However, Peirce's conception of chance was not the usual conception of the entirely uncaused and irregular, acting without cause or reason. He wrote of chance as "the form of a spontaneity which is to some degree regular," and he was careful to point out that he was not using the conception of chance as a principle of explanation but as an element in the description of a universe in which there is the tendency to form habits and to produce regularities. The doctrine of absolute chance was named "tychism," and the doctrine of continuity was named "synechism." The essay "The Law of Mind" develops the latter doctrine.

In "The Law of Mind," Peirce argued that there is but one law of mind, that ideas spread, affect other ideas, and lose intensity but gain generality and "become welded with other ideas." In the course of the article, Peirce developed the notion of an "idea" as an event in an individual consciousness. He argued that consciousness must take time and be in time, and that, consequently, "we are immediately conscious through an infinitesimal interval of time." Ideas are continuous, Peirce claimed, and there must be a "continuity of intrinsic qualities of feeling" so that particular feelings are present out of a continuum of other possibilities. Ideas affect one another, but to understand this, one must distinguish three elements within an idea: First, the intrinsic quality of the idea as a feeling, its *quale*; Second, the energy with the idea that affects other ideas (its capacity to relate); and Third, the tendency of an idea to become generalized (its tendency to be productive of law). Habits are established by induction; general ideas are followed by the kind of reaction that followed the particular sensations that gave rise to the general idea. Mental phenomena come to be governed by law in the sense that some living idea, "a conscious continuum of feeling," pervades the phenomena and affects other ideas. Peirce concluded "The Law of Mind" with the striking claim that matter is not dead, but it is mind "hidebound with habits."

Matter and Consciousness

In the essay "Man's Glassy Essence," Peirce argued that mind and matter are different aspects of a single feeling process; if something is considered in terms of its relations and reactions, it is regarded as matter, but if it is understood as feeling, it appears as consciousness. (This is a more sophisticated philosophy than James's radical empiricism, which resembles Peirce's hypothesis in some respects.) A person is a particular kind of general idea.

If it seems intolerable to suppose that matter is, in some sense, feeling or idea, one must at least consider that for Peirce an idea must be considered not only in its Firstness, but in its Secondness and Thirdness as well. In other words, an idea or feeling, for Peirce, is not *simply* a feeling as such; that is, a feeling is more than its quality, its Firstness. A feeling is also that which has the tendency to relate to other feelings with which it comes in spatial and temporal contact, and it works with other feelings toward a regularity of development that can be known as law. Peirce differs from a physical realist who maintains that matter is in no way feeling or mind. His philosophy is much more acceptable to one concerned with the multiplicity of physical phenomena than an idealism that regards ideas as static individuals existing only in their Firstness (merely as feelings).

"Agapasm"

In "Evolutionary Love," Peirce maintained that his synechism calls for a principle of evolution that will account for creative growth. How is it that out of chaos so irregular that it seems inappropriate to say that anything exists, a universe of habit and law can emerge? Chance relations develop, the relations become habits, the habits become laws; "tychism" emphasizes the presence of chance, "synechism" emphasizes the development of relations through the continuity of ideas, and "agapasm" (Peirce's term) emphasizes the evolutionary tendency in the universe. The logical (ordering) principles of Firstness, Secondness, and Thirdness make intelligible not only the idea (with its *quale*, its relatedness, and its tendency to contribute to the development of law), but also the person (who is a general idea), matter (which is mind hidebound with habits), and the character of the universe. The logical principles become metaphysical.

Peirce is important in contemporary thought primarily because of his pragmatic, logical, and epistemological views. There is a great deal of material in the *Collected Papers of Charles Sanders Peirce* that remains to be explored, and those who would picture Peirce as the forerunner of linguistic and empirical philosophy can find much to support their claims in his essays. His metaphysics is generally regarded as interesting though pragmatically insignificant. When interest in metaphysics revives, and there is no methodological reason why it cannot revive and be respectable, the metaphysics of Peirce, his theory of cosmic evolution or agapasm, will certainly be reconsidered.

Ian P. McGreal

Additional Reading

Almeder, Robert F. *The Philosophy of Charles S. Peirce: A Critical Introduction.* Totowa, N.J.: Rowman & Littlefield, 1980. An analysis of Peirce's philosophy, stressing his epistemological realism, which contains a perceptive and detailed discussion of his theory of knowledge.

Brent, Joseph. *Charles Sanders Peirce: A Life.* Bloomington: Indiana University Press, 1993. A study emphasizing how Peirce's dandy-like, almost demonic personality undermined his professional achievements but influenced the evolution of his ideas.

Conkin, Paul K. *Puritans and Pragmatists: Eight Eminent American Thinkers.* Bloomington: Indiana University Press, 1968. One of the finest overviews of American intellectual history. Places Peirce within the context of the development of American thought between Jonathan Edwards and George Santayana.

Corrington, Robert S. *An Introduction to C. S. Peirce: Philosopher, Semiotician, and Ecstatic Naturalist.* Lanham, Md.: Rowman & Littlefield, 1993. Begins with a brief biography contrasting personal failure with intellectual genius. Explores pragmatism, semiotics (particularly Firstness, Secondness, and Thirdness), and the evolution of Darwin's ideas and Peirce's metaphysical categories.

Goudge, Thomas A. *The Thought of C. S. Peirce.* Toronto: University of Toronto Press, 1950. One of the most perceptive studies of Peirce's thought. Sees Peirce's philosophy as resting on a conflict within his personality that produced tendencies toward both naturalism and Transcendentalism.

Hookway, Christopher. *The Arguments of the Philosophers: Peirce*. London: Routledge & Kegan Paul, 1985. The first section examines Peirce's pursuit of truth through analyses of logic, realism, naturalism, ethics and aesthetics, phenomenology, and a theory of signs. The second section looks at knowledge and reality through key ideas on perception, mathematical reasoning, induction and abduction, pragmatism, and evolutionary cosmology and objective idealism. For more advanced students.

Ketner, Kenneth Laine, ed. *Peirce and Contemporary Thought: Philosophical Inquiries*. New York: Fordham University Press, 1995. An interpretive guide by renowned scholars on Peirce's views of logic, science, and metaphysics.

Parker, Kelly A. *The Continuity of Peirce's Thought*. Nashville, Tenn.: Vanderbilt University Press, 1998. An analysis of four major areas: refining Immanuel Kant's architectonic and developing a blueprint for Peirce's classification of the sciences; revising Georg Cantor's theory of transfinite sets and refining mathematical categories; using the continuity principle to bridge the gap between metaphysics and mathematics; and examining cosmology.

Potter, Vincent G. *Charles S. Peirce: On Norms and Ideals*. Amherst: University of Massachusetts Press, 1967. An analysis of Peirce's attempt to establish aesthetics, ethics, and logic as the three normative sciences. The author places particular emphasis on the role of "habit" in the universe.

_____. *Peirce's Philosophical Perspectives*. New York: Fordham University Press, 1996. Highlights the British influence on the evolution of Peirce's philosophy. Examines three key issues in Peirce's ontology and theory of knowledge—realism, notion of substance, and foundationalism—and shows how continuity is a key mathematical notion.

Raposa, Michael. *Peirce's Philosophy of Religion*. Bloomington: Indiana University Press, 1989. An analysis of Peirce's conception of religious experience and belief in God. Explains that "theosemiotic" involves ways the self becomes attuned to the traces of God (the divine sign maker) in the world.

Rosenthal, Sandra B. *Charles Peirce's Pragmatic Pluralism*. Albany: State University of New York Press, 1994. An analysis of pluralism as the core of Peirce's philosophy. Interrogates "habit" in Peirce's mathematical essays, examines his proofs for realism, and connects metaphysics with a Kuhnian-Peircean interpretation of science.

David Warren Bowen, updated by Sue Hum

Alvin Plantinga

Plantinga's most famous contributions were to the philosophy of religion, although he also significantly influenced metaphysics, epistemology, and even philosophy of language.

Principal philosophical works: *Faith and Philosophy: Philosophical Studies in Religion and Ethics*, 1964; *God and Other Minds: A Study of the Rational Justification of Belief in God*, 1967; *The Nature of Necessity*, 1974; *God, Freedom, and Evil*, 1974; *Does God Have a Nature?*, 1980; *The Twin Pillars of Christian Scholarship*, 1990; *When Faith and Reason Clash: Evolution and the Bible*, 1991; *The Nature of Necessity*, 1992; *Warrant: The Current Debate*, 1993; *Warrant and Proper Function*, 1993; *Warranted Christian Belief*, 1999.

Born: November 15, 1932; Ann Arbor, Michigan

Early Life

Born while his father was pursuing a graduate degree in philosophy, Alvin Plantinga was heir to a long tradition of Dutch Calvinism. He attended Jamestown College (North Dakota), Calvin College, Harvard, and Calvin College (again) as an undergraduate, where he majored in philosophy and psychology and was particularly influenced by William Harry Jellema. In January, 1954, he entered the University of Michigan, where he took classes with William Alston, William K. Frankena, and Richard Cartwright. He then went to Yale, taking courses from Brand Blanshard, Paul Weiss, and Frederick Fitch and completing his doctorate in philosophy. He also taught at Wayne State University, Calvin College, and the University of Notre Dame, where he became the John A. O'Brien Professor of Philosophy.

Life's Work

Best known for his philosophy of religion, Plantinga addresses the problem of how an omnipotent, omniscient God and evil could coexist. He uses the notion of possible worlds and possible persons as well as logical reasoning to argue for the existence of God.

Plantinga is enthusiastic about the philosophical usefulness of the notion of a possible world. Two standard ways of explaining this notion appeal to maximal propositions and maximal facts.

A proposition is what is expressed by the standard use of a declarative sentence, namely an assertion of something. Thus what is expressed by "Two is twice one" is one proposition and what is expressed by "No U.S. president has been a Martian" is another proposition. Similarly, "two's being twice one" is one fact and "no U.S. president's having been a Martian" is another fact.

One proposition P entails another proposition Q if it is not logically possible that Q be false if P is true. Otherwise stated, P entails Q if and only if "P is true and Q is false" is self-contradictory. It is logically impossible that "Charles has always weighed less than two hundred pounds" be true and "Charles has always weighed less than three hundred pounds" be false. Thus the former proposition entails the latter.

Some propositions entail certain propositions and not others. "Two is twice one" entails "Two is not less than one" but it does not entail "The population of Ireland is not less than one." "No U.S. president has been a Martian" entails "No U.S. president has been a Martian male" but it does not entail that "No U.S. president has been male." However, if P is a *maximal* proposition, then for every proposition Q, either P entails Q or else P entails not-Q. A true maximal proposition thus contains an incredible amount of information. In fact, if P is a true maximal proposition, it is also *the* true maximal proposition; there can be only one. Each maximal proposition describes a different possible world; self-contradictory propositions do not count as maximal propositions. A maximal proposition describes a total way that things might be. Further, if *P* is a maximal proposition, then it is what logicians call a *logically contingent* proposition; it is logically possible or non-self-contradictory that *P* be false. Thus each maximal proposition describes exactly one possible world, and to say "Maximal proposition *P* is true" is the same as to say "The possible world that maximal proposition *P* describes exists."

One fact can include another; the fact of "Tom's being tired and Tess's being reflective" includes the fact of "Tom's being tired." One fact can preclude another; the fact of "Tom's being tired" precludes "Tom's not existing." A run-of-the-mill fact includes some facts and precludes others. A *maximal* fact *F* has this feature: For any fact *F**, *F* either includes *F** or *F* precludes *F**. If *F* is a maximal fact, then *F* either includes or precludes each of the following: "Maude's being a millionaire," "Hoover Dam's being in Colorado," "Berkeley's notebook on notions being discovered by the tallest woman in Rome," and "the starting quarterback of the Minnesota Vikings in 2001 being female." A maximal fact is a possible world. There are *possible* facts, which are facts that might obtain but do not. For example, "there being unicorns," "there being flying pigs," "there being money-bearing trees" and the like might have obtained. Because they do not obtain—because there are no unicorns, flying pigs, or trees whose fruit is cash—they are merely possible facts. Every maximal fact—every possible world—is a possible fact. All maximal facts are merely possible save for one, namely the maximal fact that is actual, the actual world. Thus, according to Plantinga, a possible world is described by each maximal proposition; every maximal fact is a possible world. The true maximal proposition describes the actual world; the actual world is the maximal fact that obtains.

A necessarily true proposition is one that is true in all possible worlds. "Two is twice one" is true in all possible worlds, and Plantinga holds that "God exists" and "There are propositions that are necessarily true, or true in all possible worlds." A necessarily false proposition or self-contradiction is true in no possible world and false in all possible worlds. "One is twice two,"

for example, is false in all possible worlds. Logically contingent propositions—propositions that are neither necessary truths nor necessary falsehoods—are true in some possible worlds and false in other possible worlds. "There are unicorns," "All U.S. presidents have been women," "Many caves are occupied by bats," and "In some cultures, weddings are arranged by the parents of the bride and groom" are true in some possible worlds and false in others.

There are also, in Plantinga's view, possible caves, possible plants, possible wombats, and possible persons. A crucial point to remember is if *X* is actual then *X* is possible (nothing impossible can be actual) but if *X* is possible then *X* may or may not be actual. If it is actual that a particular armadillo weighs exactly seven pounds for all of its adult life, then it is obviously possible that it have this weight for all of its adult life. However, just because it is possible that an armadillo weigh exactly seven pounds for all of its adult life it does not follow that one actually does have that weight for all of its adult life. To talk of *merely* possible caves, plants, wombats, and persons is to talk of ways things might have been but are not regarding caves, plants, wombats, and persons. If certain descriptions that might have been true had actually been true, then there would be caves, plants, wombats, and persons that there are not. A merely possible person is a description such that, had God made the description true, God would have made a person.

The notion of merely possible persons versus that of actual persons plays an important role in Plantinga's discussion of whether the existence of evil provides reason to think that there is no God. Some philosophers have held that "There is evil" and "God, who is omnipotent, omniscient, and morally perfect, exists" are logically incompatible claims; if one is true, the other is false. Plantinga argues that this cannot be correct. He uses the following consistency strategy: If a set of three propositions *A*, *B*, and *C* form a logically consistent set, then any pair selected from that triad of propositions will be logically consistent. Thus, if we begin with *A*: "Australia is not New Zealand," *B*: "Puppies are cute," and *C*: "Baseballs are not typically made of cabbage," and note that (1) none of *A*-*C* taken singly is self-contradictory, and (2) *A*-*C* taken collectively is logically consistent, then it follows that (3) any pair of propositions taken from *A-C* will be logically consistent. This is independent of the truth of *A-C*: It does not matter if all are true, all are false; or some are true and some are false, as long as (1) and (2) are the case, then (3) follows.

Consider, then, Plantinga suggests, these examples: *A*: "God exists," *B*: "God has a morally sufficient reason for allowing any evil that God does allow," and *C*: "There is evil." It is not too hard to see that *A-C* satisfy (1) and (2). None of *A-C* seems, by itself, self-contradictory. The group *A-C* seems to be not self-contradictory. However, if *A-C* satisfy (1) and (2), it follows that they satisfy (3). Any pair of propositions taken from *A-C* are logically compatible. "God exists" and "There is evil" are included in *A-C*. So "God exists" and "There is evil" are logically compatible.

This line of reasoning leads to a further objection of the following sort. It is logically possible that there have been persons that there are not. It is possible that Abe, who has one brother, had seven. It is possible that there not have been the persons that there are; Abe and his brother might never have existed. The core of the objection concerns a possibility that will hold if God exists. The condition is this: If God is omnipotent, omniscient, and morally perfect and creates the world, then God will create only persons who are morally perfect.

The reasoning behind this condition is as follows: Plantinga holds that in order for people to be moral agents, they must be free agents. People are free relative to an action at a given time if, under the conditions that actually prevail at that time, they can perform that action or can refrain from performing it. Neither performing it nor refraining is determined by the past. Suppose this is so, and consider some merely possible person—some description such that, if God makes the description true of something, God has made a person. Let this description include the element "actually makes morally relevant choices, makes them freely, and always makes them rightly." Let any possible person in whose description this element occurs be a possible moral saint. If every actual person is a moral saint, then there will be no moral evil. God can bring it about that every actual person is a moral saint by creating a possible world that contains persons all of whose descriptions contain the element "actually makes morally relevant choices, makes them freely, and always makes them rightly." If God makes only persons who correspond to descriptions of possible moral saints, no one will ever choose wrongly. Further, God will not have made them choose rightly; God will know that the recipes for possible persons are such that if the persons they are recipes for are created, those persons will freely always choose rightly. Therefore, these persons will be free agents in accord with Plantinga's requirement.

The result of this line of reasoning is simply that if God exists, God will create only persons who freely always choose rightly. People do not always freely chose rightly, so God does not exist. Alternatively, if God exists, God will make actual only a possible world with persons all of whom are moral saints. The actual world does not contain persons any of whom, let alone all of whom, are moral saints, therefore, God does not exist.

The objection is cast in possible-worlds terms, and so is Plantinga's reply. Consider a different element in the description of a possible person: "actually makes morally relevant choices, makes them freely, and sometimes makes them rightly" or, more simply, "freely makes some wrong morally relevant choices." Suppose, as logically possible, that every person who was actually created would do this. The crucial point that the objector has missed is this: What can consistently go into a description is a matter of logic alone. However, what some actual person would do is not a matter of logic alone. Therefore, the description that would be true of an actually created person partly depends on what that person would do if he or she were created. It might well be that one thing the person would do is sometimes freely choose wrongly. This might well be true of absolutely every actual person God created. After all, it seems to be true of every actual person as things stand. Suppose it is true of absolutely every actual person God created—suppose whatever description of a person God made true by making the corresponding person will in fact have the result of there being a person who sometimes freely acts wrongly. Then, we might say (following Plantinga), possible persons suffer from *transworld depravity*.

Plantinga's reply to the objection, then, is if it is logically possible that possible persons suffer from transworld depravity, then it is logically possible that God will not create only persons who are moral saints. It is logically possible there are not any possible moral saints to make actual. It is logically possible that possible persons suffer from transworld depravity. Hence, it is logically possible that God will not create only persons who are moral saints. However, if it is logically possible that God will not create only moral saints, then "God exists" does not after all entail "God creates only moral saints," and therefore, the fact that the world is not populated only by morally perfect people is not evidence that there is no God.

Plantinga also presents what he takes to be a modestly successful version of the traditional ontological argument, which is intended to show that it is logically impossible that God *not* exist and hence logically necessary that God *does* exist. The argument, in Plantinga's formulation, can be put succinctly as follows: Let a being who is omnipotent, omniscient, and morally perfect in some possible world W be maximally excellent—in W. Now consider a being who, for any possible world W^*, is maximally excellent—in W^*. Let this feature of having maximal excellence in every possible world be maximal greatness. The argument now takes advantage of this feature of propositions about all possible worlds, namely that they are, if possibly true, then necessarily true. Suppose P is a proposition about all possible worlds. Then either P is a necessary truth or a necessary falsehood. Suppose further that P is possibly true. Then P is not a necessary falsehood, and because it is either a necessary falsehood or a necessary truth, it is a necessary truth.

"God has maximal greatness" is a proposition about all possible worlds. Hence it is either a necessary truth or a necessary falsehood. However, it is not a self-contradiction; it is not a necessary falsehood. Therefore, it is a necessary truth, and it is true that God has maximal greatness, which entails that God exists in all possible worlds. Because God exists in all possible worlds, and the actual world is of course a possible world (if it were not possible, it would not be actual), God exists in the actual world. Further, no matter what world had been actual, God would have existed in it as well. So not only does God exist, but it is logically impossible that God not exist.

The problem with this argument is that it is not at all obvious that any of these three statements is self-contradictory:
(1) God has maximal greatness;
(2) God has maximal excellence in our world but lacks maximal greatness; or
(3) God has maximal excellence in every world in which God exists (in every world description that includes the claim that God exists, God is described as maximally excellent).
However, if either (2) or (3) is true, then (1) is false (and hence necessarily false). Plantinga's ontological argument does not show, but rather assumes, that it is (1), not (2) or (3), that is true. Hence it does not prove that it is logically necessary that God exists or that God exists.

Plantinga is aware of this (he pointed it out when he presented the argument) and claimed a more modest success, namely that it is perfectly rational to believe that the premises of his version of the ontological argument are true, and (because the argument is plainly valid) also perfectly rational to believe that God exists.

Influence

Plantinga published significant work on the philosophy of religion as well as metaphysics and knowledge theory (epistemology). He also offered theories in the philosophy of language and modal logic. One of his common themes, nature of knowledge, was examined at length in his trilogy *Warrant: The Current Debate*, *Warrant and Proper Function*, and *Warranted Christian Belief*. Plantinga's work in these areas has greatly influenced contemporary discussion on possible worlds, the problem of evil, the ontological argument, the notion of logical necessity, and the matter of when one is warranted in accepting something as true.

Keith E. Yandell

Warrant and Proper Function

Type of philosophy: Epistemology, philosophy of religion

First published: 1993

Principal ideas advanced:

◇ There is a correct account of knowledge.

◇ This account does not require that one have accessible evidence for what one knows (internalism is false).

◇ This account does require that our cognitive faculties operate properly in a congenial environment (externalism is true).

◇ An account of knowledge should be such that if it is true, one is warranted in accepting it.

◇ Only a monotheistic version of externalism has this feature.

Alvin Plantinga's *Warrant and Proper Function* offers a detailed version of a very widely accepted (and strongly disputed) analysis of knowledge. In this analysis, knowledge, for a person, is not to have evidence of his or her beliefs but rather for these beliefs to have been formed properly, for these beliefs to be the result of a reliable process of belief formation operating in a congenial environment under circumstances in which its operation is aimed at truth (rather than, for example, survival or convenience).

This book is the second of three books that form a trilogy in the theory of knowledge. The other two are *Warrant: The Current Debate* (1993) and *Warranted Christian Belief* (1999). *Warrant* examines in detail the debate concerning the nature of knowledge, asking what exactly it means for a person to know something. Plantinga attempts to analyze the claim "Jane knows that so-and-so is true if and only if . . . ," where the blank is filled in with a statement of the conditions that must be satisfied. The analysis is intended to be general so that regardless whether what Jane knows is that her shoes are white, that ten is greater than nine, that God exists, that it is wrong to torture for pleasure, or that quantum mechanics has replaced classical Newtonian mechanics, the analysis will fit perfectly. The analysis is intended to cover every actual and every possible case of knowing. *Warrant* examines various analyses of knowledge and rejects them in favor of Plantinga's analysis. *Warranted Christian Belief* discusses the relevance of the analysis offered in *Warrant and Proper Function* to questions of religious, particularly Christian, belief.

Internalism vs. Externalism

Warrant was written to show that *internalist* theories of knowledge are mistaken, and that while *externalist* theories of knowledge are the right sort of analyses, only Plantinga's externalist analysis has a certain very desireable feature and is not subject to refuting counter-examples. *Warrant and Proper Function* presents an in-depth examination of the theories set out in the first book, and an understanding of these theories is necessary to place the second work in its context.

The internalist versus externalist dispute occurs among philosophers who agree on at least two things. (1) A person can know something only if that something is true. It is what might be called propositional knowledge, or knowledge of what is expressed by true statements, that is under analysis, not knowledge by acquaintance or awareness of either external objects such as trees or internal items such as pains. Thus, these philosophers must agree that "Jane knows that *P*" entails "*P* is true." (2) For a person to know something, the individual must believe it. Knowledge must include true belief, but true belief is not enough for knowledge. If Jane believes that the most expensive tea in the world costs twenty thousand dollars an ounce and believes this because she read about a twenty-thousand-dollar car while she was drinking a cup of tea, even if the most expensive tea in the world does happen to cost twenty thousand dollars an ounce, Jane has just luckily stumbled onto a true belief; she does not know it to be true. So the question becomes, "What, besides her having a true belief, must be true of Jane if she is to know something?"

An *internalist* theory of knowledge insists that knowers have something available to them that constitutes evidence for what they know. There must be something that the knowers are conscious of or at least can be conscious of that provides evidential support for what is believed. If Jane knows that she is in pain, she must be aware of an internal negative feeling or state and know that this state is a pain; if Jane knows that there is a tree outside her window, she must be having a sensory experience in which it seems to her that she sees a tree. If she believes that two plus two is four, then she must have a familiar, though hard to accurately describe, sort of cognitive experience in which the content of "two and two is four" is understood in such a way as to make its truth plain. Absence of evidence, whether experiential, propositional, or another appropriate sort, is sufficient for absence of knowledge.

Plantinga argues in *Warrant* and *Warrant and Proper Function* that the varieties of internalism are inadequate, either that one can satisfy the conditions that they specify and fail to have knowledge or that one can have knowledge while failing to meet the conditions that they specify (or, even worse, that both these things are true), and that this is so for *all* varieties of internalism now available. Further, he takes this not to be an accidental result of the various forms of internalism that happen to be on offer. He takes it that the *sorts* of debilitating weaknesses that available internalisms have plague the entire species of internalist accounts.

Varieties of externalism other than the one he favors, Plantinga contends, suffer from two sorts of defects. First, they too are subject to counterexamples: Either one can satisfy their externalist conditions and not know or one can know without satisfying their externalist conditions. Second, they have this inelegant feature: It is not the case that if they are true, then one is warranted in believing them. The meaning and force of this suggestion will be examined shortly.

Plantinga's Externalism

According to Plantinga, for Jane to know that some proposition is true—that her hair is properly brushed or that seventeen is a prime number or whatever—is for her to have the belief that this proposition is true when it is and under conditions in which her faculties that produced the belief in question are functioning properly in a congenial environment where those faculties operate in accord with a design plan that orients them toward truth seeking and where the design plan is good (such that if our faculties follow it, the plan will typically yield true beliefs). Plantinga contends that reference to a design plan is crucial in offering any defensible version of externalism. He also argues, by critically considering various accounts that lack this feature, that the design plan must be more than simply metaphorical or used for convenience.

His view is that if our cognitive faculties simply developed in a naturalistic or creatorless evolutionary environment, there would be no reason to think that their functioning properly relative to survival would also involve their functioning reliably relative to truth (and in particular, there would be no reason to think that they do so relative to beliefs about matters not related to survival such as evolutionary theory and the nature of knowledge). He contends that if we are to have an externalist account of knowledge such that we can know the account of knowledge to be the correct one, we need an externalist account in which our cognitive faculties are objectively likely to yield true beliefs. This, he contends, will be the case only for a monotheistic externalist account in which God has made people in a way that they are knowers, an account in which God has established a design plan for people's cognitive faculties and an environment in which these faculties congenially operate so that their results (people's actual beliefs) are likely to be true beliefs and hence (given their manner of production) to constitute knowledge.

Keith E. Yandell

Additional Reading

Alston, William. *Perceiving God*. Ithaca, N.Y.: Cornell University Press, 1991. Offers a discussion of a wide variety of perspectives in the theory of knowledge by way of embracing the view that a theistic practice of belief formation can reasonably be believed to be reliable.

Dancy, Jonathan, and Ernest Sosa, eds. *Blackwell Companions to Philosophy: A Companion to Epistemology*. Oxford: Blackwell, 1992. A series of discussions of a wide variety of perspectives, theories, ideas, and arguments in theory of knowledge, including internalism and externalism.

Kvanvig, Jonathan L., ed. *Warrant in Contemporary Epistemology: Essays in Honor of Plantinga's Theory of Knowledge*. Lanham, Md: Rowman & Littlefield, 1996. This collection of essays examines Plantinga's views on warrant and proper function and his theory of knowledge. Includes bibliography and index.

Sosa, Ernest. *Collected Essays in Epistemology*. Cambridge, England: Cambridge University Press, 1991. Defends an account of knowledge in which one is justified within an environment and relative to a community of believers.

Tomberlin, James, and Peter van Inwagen, eds. *Alvin Plantinga*. Dordrecht: D. Reidel, 1985. Collection of essays on various aspects of Plantinga's work, including the work that provided the background for the trilogy on warrant.

Keith E. Yandell

Plato

Plato used the dialogue structure in order to pose fundamental questions about knowledge, reality, society, and human nature—questions that are still alive today. He developed his own positive philosophy, Platonism, one of the most influential thought systems in the Western tradition.

Principal philosophical works: Early period works (399-390 B.C.E.) are *Prōtagoras* (*Protagoras*, 1804); *Iōn* (*Ion*, 1804); *Gorgias* (English translation, 1804); *Lachēs* (*Laches*, 1804); *Charmidēs* (*Charmides*, 1804); *Euthyphrōn* (*Euthyphro*, 1804); *Lysis* (English translation, 1804); *Hippias Elattōn* (*Hippias Minor*, 1761); *Hippias Meizōn* (*Hippias Major*, 1759); *Apologia Sōkratous* (*Apology*, 1675); and *Kritōn* (*Crito*, 1804). Middle period works (388-368 B.C.E.) are *Cratylos* (*Cratylus*, 1793); *Symposion* (*Symposium*, 1701); *Politeia* (*Republic*, 1701); *Phaedros* (*Phaedrus*, 1792); *Menōn* (*Meno*, 1769); *Euthydēmos* (*Euthydemus*, 1804); *Menexenos* (*Menexenus*, 1804); *Phaedōn* (*Phaedo*, 1675); *Parmenidēs* (*Parmenides*, 1793); and *Theaetētos* (*Theaetetus*, 1804). Later period works (365-361 B.C.E.) are *Sophistēs* (*Sophist*, 1804) and *Politikos* (*Statesman*, 1804). Last period works (360-347 B.C.E.) are *Nomoi* (*Laws*, 1804); *Philēbos* (*Philebus*, 1779); *Timaeos* (*Timaeus*, 1793); and *Critias* (English translation, 1793).

Born: c. 427 B.C.E.; Athens, Greece
Died: 347 B.C.E.; Athens, Greece

Early Life

There is an ancient story (very likely a true one) that Plato was originally named Aristocles, but he acquired the nickname Plato ("broad" or "wide" in Greek) because of his broad shoulders. Both of Plato's parents were from distinguished aristocratic families, and Plato, because of family connections and expectations as well as personal interest, looked forward to a life of political leadership.

Plato was born in the wake of Athens's Golden Age, the period that had witnessed the emergence of Athens as the strongest Greek power (particularly through its leadership in repelling the invasions of Greece by the Persians); the birth of classical Athenian architecture, drama, and arts; and a florescence of Athenian cultural, intellectual, and political life. By the time of Plato's youth, however, the military and cultural flower that had bloomed in Athens had already begun to fade. A few years before Plato's birth, Athens and Sparta—Athens's rival for Greek supremacy—

had engaged their forces and those of their allies in the Peloponnesian War.

This long, painful, and costly war of Greek against Greek lasted until Plato was twenty-three. Thus, he grew up witnessing the decline of Athens as the Greek military and cultural center. During these formative years, he observed numerous instances of cruelty, betrayal, and deceit as some unscrupulous Greeks attempted to make the best of things for themselves at the expense of other people (supposedly their friends) and in clear violation of values that Plato thought sacred.

It was also at an early age, probably in adolescence, that Plato began to hear Socrates, who engaged a variety of people in Athens in philosophical discussion of important questions. It could fairly be said that Plato fell under the spell, or at least the influence, of Socrates.

When, as a consequence of losing the Peloponnesian War to Sparta, an oligarchy was set up in Athens in place of the former democracy, Plato had the opportunity to join those in power, but he refused. Those in power, who later became known as the Thirty Tyrants, soon proved to be ruthless rulers; they even attempted to implicate Socrates in their treachery, although Socrates had no part in it.

A democratic government was soon restored, but it was under this democracy that Socrates was brought to trial, condemned to death, and executed. Socrates' execution was the last straw for Plato. He never lost his belief in the importance of political action, but he had become convinced that such action must be informed by a philosophical vision of the highest truth. He continued to hold back from political life, devoting himself instead to developing the kind of training and instruction that every wise person—and political people especially, since they act on a great social stage—must pursue. Plato maintained that people would not be able to eliminate evil and social injustice from their communities until rulers became philosophers (lovers of wisdom)—or until philosophers became rulers.

Life's Work

In his twenties and thirties, Plato traveled widely, becoming aware of intellectual traditions and social and political conditions in various Mediterranean regions. During these years, he also began work on his earliest and most Socratic dialogues.

When he was about forty years old, Plato founded the Academy, a complex of higher education and a center of communal living located approximately one mile from Athens proper. Plato's Academy was highly successful. One famous pupil who studied directly under the master was Aristotle, who remained a student at the Academy for twenty years before establishing an independent philosophical position. The Academy continued to exist for more than nine hundred years; it was finally forced to close in 529 C.E. by the Roman emperor Justinian I on the grounds that it was pagan and thus offensive to the Christianity he wished to promote.

In 367 B.C.E., Plato went to Sicily, where he had been invited to serve as tutor to Dionysius II of Syracuse. The

project offered Plato the opportunity to groom a philosopher-king such as he envisioned in his *Republic*, but this ambition soon proved to be unrealizable.

One of the main tasks Plato set for himself was to keep alive the memory of Socrates by recording and perpetuating the kind of impact that Socrates had on those with whom he conversed. Virtually all Plato's written work takes the form of dialogues in which Socrates is a major character. Reading these dialogues, readers can observe the effects that Socrates had on various interlocutors and, perhaps more important, are themselves brought into the inquiry and discussion. One of the explicit aims of a Platonic dialogue is to involve readers in philosophical questioning concerning the points and ideas under discussion. In reading essays and treatises, readers too often assume the passive role of listening to the voice

Plato. *(Library of Congress)*

of the author; dialogues encourage readers to become active participants (at least in their own minds, which, as Plato would probably agree, is precisely where active participation is required).

The written dialogue is an effective mode of writing for a philosophy with the aims of Plato, but it sometimes leaves one uncertain as to Plato's own views. It is generally agreed among scholars that the earlier works—such as *Apology*, *Euthyphro*, and *Gorgias*, written between 399 and 390 B.C.E.—express primarily the thought and spirit of Socrates, while works from the middle to the last periods—such as *Meno*, *Symposium*, *Republic*, and *Theaetetus* (388-366 B.C.E.) and *Philebus* and *Laws* (360-347 B.C.E.)—gradually give way to the views of Plato himself.

The dialogues of Plato are among the finest literary productions by any philosopher who has ever lived, yet there is evidence that Plato himself, maintaining the superiority of the spoken word over the written word and of person-to-person instruction over "book learning," regarded the written dialogues as far less important than the lectures and discussions that took place in the Academy. There is, however, very little known about those spoken discussions, and the best evidence available for Plato's views is surely in his many dialogues.

The fundamental thesis of Plato's work is the claim that there are "forms" or "ideas" that exist outside the material realm, are the objects of knowledge (or intellectual cognition), and, unlike material objects, do not come into existence, change, or pass out of existence. These forms, rather than material things, actually constitute reality. This is Plato's well-known theory of forms (or theory of ideas).

The theory attempts to take two points of view into consideration and to define their proper relationship. The two points of view give the questioner access to a changing world (of sensible or material things) and an unchanging world (of intellectual objects). From the first perspective, human beings know that they live in a changing world in which things come into existence, change, and pass out of existence. If one tries to pin something down and determine whether various predicates apply to it (whether it is big, red, hot, or good, for example), one finds that the object can be viewed from a variety of standpoints. From some of these standpoints, the predicate applies, and from others, it does not. Socrates, for example, is big compared with an insect but not big compared with a building. This train of thought leads one, however, to the other point of view. An insect, Socrates (that is, his body), and a building belong to the changing physical world, in which the application of predicates is problematic or changing. In the nonphysical, or intellectual, world, however, there must be some fixed points of reference that make possible the application of predicates. These latter fixed points do not change. Whether one compares Socrates with the insect or with the building, when one judges which is bigger, one is always looking for the same thing. Bigness or largeness itself, Plato thought, must always exist, unchanging, and it must itself be big. It is this abstract or intellectual element with which a person must be familiar if the person is to be in a position to decide whether various objects in this changing material world are big.

The forms, or objects of intellect, are quite different from (and superior to) physical objects, or objects of sense. Plato thought of knowledge as occurring only between the intellect (or reason) and its objects, the forms. The bodily senses give human beings only belief, he said, not true knowledge.

Plato considered human beings to be composed of a rational aspect and an irrational aspect. The intellect or reason, that which communes with the forms, is rational. The body, which communes with the physical world, is irrational. Plato looked down on the body, considering it merely the seat of physical appetites. Additionally, there is a third, intermediate aspect of people: passions, which may follow intellect (and thus be rational) or follow the bodily appetites (and thus be irrational).

In each person, one aspect will dominate. Reason is best, but not everyone can achieve the state in which one's life is under the direction of reason. Thus, communities should be organized in such a way that those who are rational (and not led by physical appetites) will be in command. The philosopher-king is one who both attains philosophical insight into the world of the forms and holds power in the day-to-day changing world.

Influence

Plato defended the role of reason in human life, in opposition to many ancient Greek teachers called Sophists. The Sophists traveled from city to city and claimed to be able to teach young men how to be successful in life. They offered such services for a fee. Although the Sophists were never a unified school and did not profess a common creed, certain beliefs are characteristic of them as a group and almost diametrically opposed to the views of Plato. The Sophists mainly taught the art of speaking, so that a person could speak well in public assemblies, in a court of law, and as a leader. Plato thought, however, that such speakers were probably more likely to appeal to feelings and emotion than to reason. Such speakers may hold forth and sound impressive, but they tend not to be acquainted with the objects of the intellect, the ground of true knowledge. Plato argued that such speakers may, for example, be persuasive in getting a person who is ill to take medicine, but it is only a real doctor who can prescribe the right remedy. Plato also compared the Sophist to a makeup artist, who makes only superficial changes in people's looks; the true philosopher, on the other hand, is compared to a gymnastic trainer, who is genuinely able to bring health and soundness to people's bodies.

In Plato's view, however, the stakes are really much higher, for both Sophists and philosophers actually affect people's souls or inner selves, not their bodies, and Plato followed Socrates in thinking of the cultivation of the soul as much more important than the cultivation of the body. Moreover, Plato went beyond the views of other Greek philosophers and beyond the cultural norms of ancient Athens by affirming that women and men had the same potential for philosophical wisdom and community leadership. Many writers in the twentieth century have referred to Plato as the first feminist, although it is also true that the vast majority of ancient, medieval, and modern philosophical Platonists did not follow him in this particular. The Sophists, in any case, were false teachers and false leaders, in Plato's view. True leaders must have wisdom, and the acquisition of such wisdom, he believed, could only come about in a cooperative community of inquirers who were free to follow argument, not carried away by speech making.

Throughout the history of more than two millennia of Western philosophy, Plato has been one of the most influential thinkers. One twentieth century philosopher, Alfred North Whitehead, said that philosophy since Plato's time has consisted mainly of a series of footnotes to Plato. There have been numerous revivals of Plato's thought in Western philosophy. Platonists, Neoplatonists, and others have made their appearance, but Plato's influence is probably better gauged in terms of the importance of the questions he has raised and the problem areas he has defined, rather than in terms of the numbers of his adherents or disciples. From both dramatic and philosophical points of view, Plato's dialogues are so well constructed that in modern times, they serve well as a student's first encounter with the philosophical practice of inquiry and argument.

Stephen Satris

Protagoras

Type of philosophy: Epistemology, ethics, metaphysics
First transcribed: Prōtagoras, early period, 399-390 B.C.E. (English translation, 1804)
Principal ideas advanced:

◇ In a discussion with the Sophist Protagoras, Socrates raises some doubts concerning the claim that goodness can be taught; everyone is supposed to be qualified to speak about goodness, and good people have difficulty teaching goodness to their children.

◇ He then wonders whether the virtues—justice, wisdom, temperance, and courage—are identical; Protagoras claims that they are not, but Socrates maneuvers Protagoras into admitting that wisdom, temperance, and justice are identical because they are all opposite to folly.

◇ When Protagoras then insists that although three of the virtues discussed are identical, courage is different because it may be a reflection of passion, Socrates persuades him that no person is courageous who faces danger in passion and ignorance; only the wise are brave: Courage is wisdom.

◇ It is ironic, Socrates points out, that having begun by arguing that virtue cannot be taught, he ends by identifying virtue with wisdom or knowledge, which can be taught.

Plato's *Protagoras* is a brilliant dialogue and a splendid piece of argumentation. It incorporates a picture of the Sophist and a glimpse of the cultured aristocrats of the Periclean Age, facts that cannot fail to interest anyone who has a desire to know more about the life of classical Greece.

Protagoras, along with three middle period (388-368 B.C.E.) dialogues, *Politeia* (*Republic*, 1701), *Phaedōn* (*Phaedo*, 1675), and *Symposion* (*Symposium*, 1701), represents the high point of Plato's literary activity. Some experts believe the dialogue is surpassed in literary quality only by *Symposium*. Philosophical development and dramatic development parallel each other precisely in the dialogue, exemplifying the high level Plato achieved in the very special literary form he used to articulate his philosophy. The philosophical argument is presented clearly and distinctly, and the characters in the dialogue are drawn with great finesse. The reader comes to know not only the Protagorean position but also the man Protagoras.

The comic relief provided by Socrates' ridiculous analysis of Simonides' poem—a satire on the kind of literary criticism that must have been current in Periclean Athens—is a fine diversion, separating the preliminary discussion between Socrates and Protagoras from the final demonstration of the unity of the virtues. Another fine touch is the description of the Sophist Protagoras marching back and forth in Callias's house, followed by his coterie, who are careful always to execute the necessary close-order drill at the turns so that the flow of wisdom need not be interrupted. Then there is the irony of Socrates in saying how moved he is by Protagoras's long speeches, even though he cannot follow them—an emotion that Socrates' subsequent arguments clearly reveal he did not experience. Finally, there is Socrates' reduction of Protagoras to impotent fury at the end of the argument, so that when Socrates asks why he will no longer answer the questions, Protagoras explodes, "Finish the argument yourself!" Such a scene aptly describes a situation all philosophers would like to find themselves in vis-à-vis their opponents.

Socrates and Hippocrates

As the dialogue begins, Socrates explains to a companion how Hippocrates early one morning brought him the news that Protagoras was in Athens. Hippocrates hoped to be introduced to Protagoras by Socrates so that he might become one of Protagoras's pupils. Socrates was surprised at the request, and because it was still too early to go to Protagoras, the two friends spent the time in conversation until they could make the call. The dialogue goes back in time to that conversation.

Socrates asks Hippocrates why he wants to study with Protagoras. If he were to study with a physician, he would become a physician, or if with a statuary, he would become a statuary. However, what is Protagoras? The answer is that he is a Sophist. However, what does one learn from a Sophist? Does Hippocrates wish to become a Sophist? Hippocrates replies that he does not wish to become a Sophist, but he thinks he can learn from Protagoras how to be a good public speaker. Such a reply does not satisfy Socrates because Hippocrates will learn from Protagoras not merely how to say something but also what to say. The Sophist, Socrates points out, offers "food for the soul." The trouble is that one cannot first try a sample before buying food for the soul. The best advice in such a case is that one should exercise considerable care before letting another person "tend his soul." The two friends then go to call on Protagoras.

The Sophists' Teachings

Socrates and Hippocrates go to the home of Callias, where Protagoras is staying, and a servant grudgingly ushers them into Protagoras's presence. This occasion offers Plato an opportunity to give the reader an amusing description of the Sophist. Protagoras is pictured as pompous and as eager for the attention his fawning disciples are paying him. He is marching back and forth, passing judgment on important matters, followed by a group of admirers who cluster around him in a way not unlike modern-day reporters gathering around a celebrity.

Protagoras's pomposity contrasts noticeably with the straightforward manner of Socrates, who, when he comes up to the Sophist, introduces Hippocrates and, on his behalf, asks Protagoras what Hippocrates will learn if he studies with Protagoras. Protagoras frankly acknowledges that he is a Sophist, stating that he is the first to admit openly his profession. However, Socrates is not to be put off without an answer to his question, so he asks Protagoras to state specifically what he teaches his students. Protagoras then replies that his students become better each day as a result of his instruction. Socrates asks if this means that Protagoras teaches good citizenship, that is, how to be a good person in the context of the Greek city-state, and Protagoras replies that Socrates has understood him correctly.

Socrates then raises some doubts about whether this kind of goodness can be taught. He remarks that the Athenians, who are not all fools, recognize that particular people should be listened to as experts on such matters as shipbuilding or medicine, but they regard all people as equally well qualified to speak on matters of goodness. Furthermore, people who are renowned for their personal goodness (for example, Pericles) feel that they cannot offer instruction even to their own children in this subject. Therefore, it seems that at least some persons are not willing to admit that what Protagoras professes to teach really can be taught. Can Protagoras reply to this?

Protagoras replies by launching into a long speech. He recites the fable of Prometheus and Epimetheus. Epimetheus, under Prometheus's supervision, was given the job of distributing the various qualities to the animal kingdom—swiftness to animals who were sought as prey, fur to animals who lived in cold climates, and so on—but he distributed all the qualities without leaving any for people. Prometheus then stole fire and knowledge of the industrial arts from heaven to make up for people's deficiencies. However, in spite of their knowledge, people were forced to live in cities for their mutual protection. This was impossible unless people were made ethically sensitive, so Zeus commanded Hermes to distribute conscience and moral sense equally among all people. This myth describes the situation that exists, Protagoras says. All people are ethically sensitive, and all people must learn the principles of morality. All adults, quite properly, regard themselves as responsible for the moral education of the young, but some are better teachers than others in this area of moral instruction. Protagoras happens to be better than most people as a teacher.

The Virtues

Socrates professes to have been impressed by the splendid speech Protagoras has made, yet, characteristically, he has "a little question," which he is sure Protagoras can easily answer. Are the virtues—justice, wisdom, temperance, and courage—identical? Protagoras answers confidently that they are not, although they have certain likenesses and they are all parts of virtue, which itself is a unity. Socrates then presses to find out whether they are homogeneous parts of an aggregate (as a pail of water is a unity consisting of many uniform drops) or are heterogeneous parts that together make a unity (as eyes, nose, and mouth are parts of a face). Protagoras replies that they are heterogeneous elements that together make a unity.

Socrates now moves to the attack. He gets Protagoras to agree to the logical principle that a thing can have only one contrary opposite. He also gets the admission from Protagoras that *folly* is the opposite of both *wisdom* and *temperance*. This forces an alternative on Protagoras: Either he must admit that wisdom is identical with temperance or he must abandon the logical principle. Protagoras reluctantly admits the identity of wisdom and temperance, and he tacitly concedes that justice and holiness, too, are identical. Socrates then pushes for the final admission, that justice and temperance are identical. However, because Protagoras senses that the argument is beginning to turn against him at this point, he tries to divert the argument. He launches into a long-winded discourse about the relativity of goods: What is good food for animals is not always good food for humans; oil may be good for massaging the body but not good if taken as food.

However, Socrates will have none of this. He pleads that he has a bad memory and therefore cannot remember long answers—he can only handle short ones. He knows Protagoras can speak either at length or with brevity, but he protests that he himself cannot manage long speeches. Will not Protagoras please confine himself to short answers? Protagoras, however, recognizing that he is losing the argument, refuses to let Socrates determine the rules for the debate. The discussion almost collapses at this point; Socrates remembers that he has an appointment elsewhere that he must keep, and he begins taking his leave.

The listeners plead with the two disputants to continue. Plato uses this occasion to give the reader a brief glimpse of the other two Sophists who are present, Hippias and Prodicus, by having them offer suggestions about how the discussion may be resumed. Prodicus urges them to "argue" but not to "wrangle" so that they will win "esteem" and not merely "praise." This type of discussion will give the hearers "gratification" rather than "pleasure," the latter reaction being concerned only with the body, while gratification is "of the mind when receiving wisdom and knowledge." Prodicus's linguistic pedantry, akin to that of some modern linguistic philosophers, emerges clearly in one paragraph to delight the reader. Hippias, too, is the butt of Plato's wit. He is made to say that all those present are really "kinsmen," by nature if not by law, and should conduct themselves as such. He is an advocate of the brotherhood of humanity, lofty in speech but with very little thought to fill out his speech.

Socrates finally rescues the situation by suggesting that he and Protagoras reverse their roles; Protagoras will ask the questions and Socrates will answer. Later on, when Protagoras has asked all the questions he desires, Socrates will resume his customary role as questioner. Protagoras agrees, even though he does so half-heartedly, and thus the dialogue can continue.

Protagoras is not the master of cross-examination that Socrates is, however, and he soon loses the initiative. Protagoras begins questioning Socrates about a poem written by Simonides, pointing out an apparent contradiction in the poem. Socrates has a good deal of fun making long speeches that present a ridiculous literary analysis of the poem (and that show, incidentally, that he need not take a back seat to Protagoras in the matter of windiness). He appeals to Prodicus, the pseudoexpert on usage, to justify out and out equivocations; he cites the Spartans, who conceal their concern for knowledge under a counterfeit

cultivation of physical prowess, as the most truly philosophical of all the Greeks. Nothing is too wild for him as he dissolves the contradiction with an exegesis of the poem that is undoubtedly a satire on the excesses of silly literary criticism in the Athens of the day. His serious point is well taken, however, for he reminds Protagoras that one ought to judge a poem in the light of its total effect, instead of rejecting it because of one relatively minor flaw.

Socrates now gets back to the main argument. He asks Protagoras again whether the virtues are identical, and this time Protagoras admits that all are alike, with one exception—courage is different from the rest. Protagoras insists that people may be courageous either because they have knowledge or because they are in a passion. However, it turns out that people do not really regard the person in a passion as courageous but as foolhardy. What distinguishes brave people from foolhardy people who do the same deed is, of course, that the brave people know the possible consequences of what they are doing. Thus, it turns out that courage really is identical with wisdom.

Socrates does not arrive at this conclusion directly, however. After Protagoras states that people may act bravely either out of knowledge or out of passion, Socrates shifts his attention to another problem. He raises the question whether whatever is good is also pleasant. Neither he nor Protagoras accepts the hedonistic version of this doctrine, but for the sake of the argument both agree to develop its consequences. As the reader might expect, it turns out that wisdom and courage are the same. The argument is as follows: Ordinary people believe that one always acts so as to increase the ratio of pleasure over pain for himself. However, sometimes people say that they are "overcome by pleasure," and hence do not do the good that they should. However, if people always seek their own pleasure, and if whatever is good is also pleasant, this can only mean that they have chosen a lesser pleasure rather than a greater pleasure (or a lesser ratio of pleasure over pain instead of a greater ratio of pleasure over pain). If one adds that no one ever knowingly does evil unless the individual is "overcome by pleasure," then the inference is clear that when people do not do good, they have acted out of ignorance of what good is. They have chosen short-range pleasure instead of long-range pleasure. This choice results only from their having failed to estimate the consequences of their act properly. Proper estimation of the consequences, however, is a matter of knowledge. So the conclusion that must be drawn is that the wise person is the good person—knowledge being identical with goodness (justice).

A Reversal of Positions

At the end of the argument, Protagoras and Socrates part on surprisingly good terms, considering how near they came to conversational disaster earlier. Protagoras comments favorably on Socrates' skill in argument and predicts that he will become eminent in philosophy. Socrates courteously excuses himself and leaves. However, just before these closing compliments, Socrates points out the paradoxical reversal of positions that has taken place in the course of the dialogue. Protagoras had taken the position at the beginning that virtue can be taught and said that he himself had adopted the teaching of it as his profession. At the end of the dialogue, however, Protagoras had been maintaining that virtue was not knowledge, and thus, by implication, he was denying that virtue can be taught. Socrates, on the other hand, had begun by raising doubts that virtue can be taught; he ended by identifying virtue with knowledge, thus implying that it can be taught.

The reversal is not so strange as it seems at first glance, however. Protagoras had implicitly identified virtue with skill at getting along in public affairs. Such skill cannot, of course, be taught. One must acquire it by doing it, by practicing. Socrates denies only that virtue can be taught when "virtue" is defined as a skill. If, on the contrary, virtue is not a skill, but is a form of knowledge, then of course it can be taught. Socrates has not shifted his position in any fundamental sense. At the end of the dialogue, he still holds to his conviction that a skill cannot be taught. What he has done is to argue that virtue is knowledge, and, once this shift to the proper definition of virtue is made, he obviously must hold that virtue can be taught.

Robert E. Larsen

Gorgias

Type of philosophy: Epistemology, ethics
First transcribed: Gorgias, early period, 399-390 B.C.E. (English translation, 1804)
Principal ideas advanced:

◇ Socrates and Gorgias discuss the uses of rhetoric, and Socrates initiates the discussion by describing rhetoric as the art of persuasion.

◇ However, Socrates argues, if rhetoricians have no knowledge of what they proclaim, it is a case of the ignorant attempting to teach the ignorant; furthermore, if they discourse on justice, they must have knowledge of justice, and if they have knowledge of justice, they are just—consequently, they could not tolerate the unjust, which would be talking without having knowledge of what one was talking about.

◇ Because all people desire to act for the sake of some good, no one can act as one wills if one acts in ignorance of the good; if one acts wrongly, one acts in ignorance of the evil that one does.

◇ Consequently, punishment should aim at rehabilitation, and it is better to be punished for one's misdeeds than to escape punishment.

◇ From all this, Socrates argues, it follows that rhetoric should be used to make people aware of injustice and of the cure for injustice.

◇ Callicles argues that natural justice is the rule of the stronger, but Socrates suggests that the wise are the strong; Callicles then argues that the wise person seeks pleasure for the self, but Socrates shows that pleasure and pain are not identical with the good and the bad.

Plato's *Gorgias* is an interesting if somewhat rambling dialogue in which several issues typical of Socratic inquiry are discussed. Because Socrates himself was concerned with discussion as a means of arriving at the truth, he naturally examined the claims of others to have a "vocal" way to it. The Sophists were the itinerant teachers of ancient Greece, teaching their pupils to debate with others any side of an issue and to win the argument. Rhetoric was their art; by persuasion, they argued, one could control the state and gain wealth. Gorgias, one of the better-known Sophists, engages Socrates in discussion over the merits and meaning of rhetoric. The position he presents is not so arbitrary as some of the claims made by other Sophists, but it is nevertheless subjected to a scathing analysis by Socrates. Callicles, a rather ill-mannered member of the group, also joins in the debate. The larger question with which they are concerned is "What is the purpose of rhetoric, and, more generally, any kind of discussion?" Also discussed are justice, the role of punishment, and pleasure and pain as good and evil.

Rhetoric and Persuasion

Socrates is concerned in the opening of the discussion with finding out exactly what rhetoric is as an art. It is concerned with persuasive discourse and aims at giving those who practice it power over others. The recipients of this art (persuasion) are those present in the law courts and assemblies of the land, and the subject matter is the just and the unjust. Supposedly, in teaching an art, the Sophists know their subject and inform others. Socrates next discusses learning and believing, which are intimately connected with teaching and studying. When one has learned, then one has knowledge; one cannot be mistaken. If one only believes, then one can be mistaken, for there is false as well as true belief. Both Socrates and Gorgias agree that one can persuade others without regard to belief or knowledge—rhetoric apparently has to do with persuading people to believe. However, although it is not brought up here, the Socratic method of dialectical discussion, rather than rhetoric, is the persuasion that leads to knowledge.

Gorgias holds that the rhetorician has a powerful tool by which people may gain much; they may sway anyone and accomplish anything. Rhetoricians should be just, however, and should not use their power for evil consequences, although having taught it to others, they are not responsible for their misuse of it. (This point is of dramatic interest because at his trial Socrates was held responsible for the activities of his pupil, Alcibiades.)

Socrates rejects the view that one can teach anything of which one is ignorant. If rhetoricians persuade only those who are ignorant (those who know need no persuading) and they, themselves, do not know—hence, are ignorant—then is this not a case of the ignorant attempting to teach the ignorant? Gorgias has already stated that rhetoricians discourse on justice, injustice, good, and evil, but if they are ignorant of these, then the same paradox holds. Gorgias has also stated that rhetoricians should not make bad use of their art, but he admits the possibility of their doing so. Also, under Socrates' questioning, he concedes that if rhetoricians have knowledge of the just, then they are just; but if they are just, then they cannot be unjust. Practicing their art badly would be unjust. It appears to be inconsistent that rhetoricians could make bad use of their art unless one admits that they do not know their art. For it is a Socratic principle that one who knows, knows what to do and what not to do, whereas the ignorant know neither.

Socrates then questions whether it is proper to call rhetoric an art. He proceeds in the following manner. Both the body and soul may be considered under two headings: the body under gymnastic and medicine, the soul under legislative (wherein the art of politics is found) and justice. When these divisions function properly, individuals are sound in body and soul, and their highest good is approached; but there are sham divisions that bear a resemblance to the real ones but do not work for the best interests of individuals. They are, for the body, attiring, or dressing up, and cookery and, for the soul, sophistry and rhetoric. They are based on experience (belief or opinion) rather than on reason and make a pretense to knowledge.

When an objection is raised that those who can sway others (the rhetoricians) control the state and have real power, Socrates replies in a manner typical of him by distinguishing between the way people act and the way they ought to act. He argues that without knowledge, people cannot do as they will. People do things not for themselves but for some sake or purpose. In so doing, people do what they will. For Socrates, ultimately all that people will is done for the sake of the good. The good is a complicated concept in Plato's philosophy. Although his explanation is not meant to be complete, it means, at least, that in willing, one acts so that the health and harmony of the body and soul are maintained. Now, if to do good is to do that which one wills, then one cannot will to do evil. This is another instance of the Socratic maxim that no person does wrong knowingly. However, it is held that the person who can kill with impunity is in an enviable position. Socrates replies to this claim by an analysis of punishment and injustice.

Punishment

Socrates holds that those who act because they know what they will are the happy people, for they are masters of themselves. Unjust people in ignorance know not what they will, so that seeking what they mistakenly believe is good (no person does wrong knowingly), they are wretched in their failure to be at one with themselves. Punishment is not primarily retributive but aims at the rehabilitation of unjust people to prevent them from doing that which is bad; hence, punishment aims at their eventual happiness, for the wicked when punished are less miserable than when they go unpunished. In this view, the individuals who do injustice are worse or more evil than those who suffer injustice, and certainly not to be envied. When properly administered, punishment is the medicine of the soul. If rhetoric has a use, it is to allow people to become aware of their own injustice and seek a proper cure for it; if they are not unjust, then they had no use for rhetoric.

It is here that Callicles enters the discussion. He accuses Socrates of intentionally turning the whole of life upside down and of telling those who listen to his prattling that they are doing exactly the opposite of that which they ought to do. Philosophy may be amusing when practiced by the young, who in so doing are looked upon as precocious by their elders, but in an adult it is unseemly, especially for one such as Socrates, who ought to be out earning a living instead of annoying his betters. The life that Callicles asserts is the normal one is that in which the stronger rule their inferiors by force, the better rule the worse, and the noble have more than the lowly. When this state occurs, natural justice prevails.

However, Socrates takes Callicles quite literally (and thus paves the way for a discussion with him, because to make his position precise, he has to modify his initial statement). Socrates points out that although the many are the superior or stronger, they hold that to do injustice is more disgraceful than to suffer it. Callicles modi-

fies his point and claims that the stronger are the more excellent, not the mob; and they are also the wiser. Socrates counters that because those who practice an art are wiser with regard to it than those who do not, trained shoemakers or cobblers ought to receive more benefits than those inferior to them in these arts. In addition, Socrates points out that the wiser may also take less than those who do not know; for example, a wise dietitian may eat less food than the ignorant person. Knowledge does not always prescribe more but what is proper, and that may be more, less, or the same depending on what is needed. Again, Plato writes of the Socratic principle that wisdom is knowing what to do and what not to do.

Pleasure and Good

Callicles rejects this argument and brings up yet another, although related, position. Wise people know how to satisfy themselves, to realize their wants; the happy life is to strive for the satisfaction of pleasure. Socrates counters that intemperate people who are never satisfied are like a leaky vessel that cannot be filled because it empties at a faster rate than it fills. Such people are the slaves of their wants; they cannot be satisfied and hence cannot be happy; it is the one who wants not who is happy. For Callicles, one who wants not is dead; it is the continual gratification of desires that leads to the full life. Socrates retorts that such an all-embracing statement permits one to draw odd conclusions. The man with a constant itch who spends his life in scratching must then be a happy man.

The point is that unless people distinguish kinds of pleasures and pains and pursue some while avoiding others, there is not much to be gained from the sort of view that Callicles offers. Furthermore, the view under examination appears to equate pleasure with good and pain with evil, whereas Socrates holds them distinct. He proceeds as follows: It will be granted that opposites cannot exist together at the same time and in the same place. Good and evil are opposites, yet it can be shown that pleasure and pain can be present in the same individual at the same time. In order to satisfy thirst, which is painful, an individual may drink water that tastes pleasant and, according to Socrates, experience pain and pleasure at the same time in the same place. If pleasure and pain were identifiable with good and evil, then the bad person would be as good or as bad as the good person, because they have about the same amount of pleasures and pains. Lastly, with regard to this idea, when people slake their thirst, both the pain and the pleasure go respectively, but when people purge evil from their souls and the good is with them, the good remains.

Callicles is now willing, as Socrates suggested earlier, to differentiate between pleasures, calling some good and others bad. However, this takes the discussion back to the view that it is not pleasure alone that determines how people act, but rather that people must know what to choose and what not to choose as pleasures before they may pursue them; knowledge is the key to action. This fact takes Socrates back to his earlier discussion concerning true arts, flattery, and sham. Rhetoric, as discussed by its proponents, appeals only, and indiscriminately, to the pleasure of the individual and not to the good; hence it can be classified as a sham. It is the harmony and order of the soul or the body that must be aimed for, not the gratification of passions. Harmony of the soul and body is the criterion by which one must judge their fitness; when present in the body it is called "health," when in the soul, "law." From these spring the virtues of temperance and justice; the person who would practice the art of rhetoric should aim at bringing harmony to the citizenry. When people are sick, either physically or mentally, they seek the services of a doctor. When prescribing a cure, the physician may forbid the satisfaction of certain wants in order to improve the patient's health.

Rhetoricians who aim at getting what they want and abusing their society are much like the tyrant discussed in Plato's *Politeia* (middle period, 388-368 B.C.E.; *Republic*, 1701). Intent on satisfying his every desire, a slave to his passions, not knowing how to control himself, the tyrant can get the best of no one, for he knows not what is best for himself. He who would lead others must first know how to lead himself. The art of rhetoric is no art at all. The art of ruling, on the other hand, is perhaps the most difficult and serious art of all; it calls for people who have had experience and who have demonstrated their ability, so that when entrusted with the rule of society it will be

the good or benefit of the ruled that will be their primary objective. The benefit of an individual does not reside in a misdirected search for satisfaction but in that harmony of body and soul wherein lies health and law.

Theodore Waldman

Euthyphro

Type of philosophy: Ethics, philosophy of religion
First transcribed: Euthyphrōn, early period, 399-390 B.C.E. (English translation, 1804)
Principal ideas advanced:

◇ Socrates has been charged by Meletus with corrupting the youth of Athens and with inventing new gods, and he seeks to learn from Euthyphro, who is prosecuting his own father for murder, the distinction between piety and impiety.

◇ Euthyphro suggests that piety is prosecuting the unjust, those who have committed such crimes as murder or sacrilege; impiety is failure to prosecute such persons.

◇ However, Socrates points out that this is an example, not a definition; and thus Euthyphro suggests that piety is whatever is pleasing to the gods, and impiety is whatever is displeasing to them.

◇ However, Socrates rejects Euthyphro's definition on the ground that the gods do not agree in attitude concerning the acts of humans, nor is it satisfactory to say that the pious is what all the gods love, for the pertinent question concerns the nature of piety in virtue of which the gods love it.

◇ If, as Euthyphro then claims, piety is paying careful attention to the gods, by means of prayer and worship, for the benefit of humanity, then piety seems to be loved by the gods even though it is of no benefit to the gods; but this runs counter to the previous claim that piety is good not simply because the gods love it.

Euthyphro deals with some of the events culminating in Socrates' trial and death, portraying Socrates just before his trial. *Euthyphro* forms a sequence with the dialogues *Apologia Sōkratous* (early period, 399-390 B.C.E.; *Apology*, 1675), dealing with the trial; *Kritōn* (early period, 399-390 B.C.E.; *Crito*, 1804), dealing with Socrates' incarceration after his conviction; and *Phaedōn* (middle period, 388-368 B.C.E.; *Phaedo*, 1675), dealing with the execution of Socrates by the drinking of the poison hemlock.

Piety and Impiety

Euthyphro is one of the best examples of the Socratic method. Socrates is portrayed as seeking wisdom about the meaning of the terms "piety" and "impiety" so that he can defend himself against the charge of being impious. Euthyphro, presumably, knows what these terms mean. Socrates tries to learn from him by asking questions and by asking him to define the terms. Each answer given by Euthyphro is scrutinized by Socrates and found to be faulty. Euthyphro complains that Socrates will not let his statements "stand still." Instead, by his persistent questioning, he makes the statements "move away," until Euthyphro no longer knows what to say. Euthyphro finally quits the discussion, refusing to recognize his own ignorance concerning the matter in question and refusing to see how dangerous it is for him, or for anyone else, to act on the basis of such complete ignorance.

The discussion begins when Socrates and Euthyphro meet at the Porch of the King Archon, where cases dealing with crimes affecting the state religion are judged. Euthyphro expresses surprise at encountering Socrates in such a place. The latter explains that he is there because he has been charged with corrupting the youth of Athens and with inventing new gods while not believing in the old, official ones. In contrast, Euthyphro has come to court to charge his own father with murder. Socrates suggests that Euthyphro must be very wise if he knows that he is right in prosecuting his own father. Such wisdom about what is right and wrong can be of great assistance to Socrates in his own case, so he requests details from Euthyphro.

The charge that Euthyphro is bringing against his own father is based on a very strange story. A drunken laborer, who worked on the family farm, killed one of the slaves. Euthyphro's father caught the murderer, tied him up, and threw him into a ditch. The father then sent a messenger to Athens to find out what to do. While waiting for an answer, he completely neglected the bound murderer, who died from cold and hunger before the messenger returned. Euthyphro's family insisted that the father did not actually kill the laborer, and even if he had, the laborer was a murderer anyway, so he probably deserved death. Also, they maintained, Euthyphro should not get involved, because it is impious for a son to charge his own father with murder. Euthyphro, on the other hand, insisted that he was doing the right thing.

Socrates is so impressed by Euthyphro's assurance that what he is doing is right and pious, that he asks Euthyphro to instruct him so that he will be able to go to his own trial and explain to his accusers and his judges what is right and wrong. Because piety and impiety must have the same characteristics in all actions that are pious or impious, Socrates asks Euthyphro to explain the distinction between piety and impiety.

The first definition that Euthyphro offers is that piety consists of doing what he is doing; namely, prosecuting an unjust person who has committed a serious crime, even if such a person is a parent. Impiety, on the other hand, consists of not prosecuting such an individual. To justify what he is doing, Euthyphro also points out that the Greek god Zeus bound up his own father, Cronos, for committing the crime of devouring some of his children, and that Cronos also punished his father for wrongdoing.

Socrates points out that Euthyphro's statement does not actually constitute a definition of piety but is only an illustration of one pious action. Such a statement does not really help in ascertaining if other actions are pious or impious. What is needed, instead of an example, is a statement of the essential characteristic of piety that makes all pious actions pious. Such a statement would allow one to classify all actions because it would provide a general standard by which to judge which actions are pious and which are not. As Plato points out over and over again in his dialogues, one does not actually know a general concept like piety, justice, or courage if one can only cite examples of pious, just, or courageous activity. One cannot even be sure that these are examples of what one thinks, unless one also knows the meaning of the concepts; hence, general knowledge is crucial for identifying and comprehending the particular examples with which one is acquainted.

Pleasing the Gods

Euthyphro sees that he has not given a satisfactory definition of the term "piety" by citing the example of his case against his father. Therefore, he offers Socrates a more general statement about piety, saying that "what is pleasing to the gods is pious, and what is not pleasing to them is impious." Socrates congratulates him for giving him the kind of answer he wanted. All that remains, he states, is to find out if this definition is the true one. The truth will be ascertained by asking questions about the definition given.

Because Euthyphro accepts all the Greek mythological tales about quarrels and disagreements among the gods, Socrates asks him whether the gods disagree about matters of fact or matters of value. The latter, says Euthyphro. Then, Socrates argues, they are disagreeing about what pleases or displeases them. The same action is pleasing to some gods and displeasing to others, and hence, according to Euthyphro's second definition of "piety," that which is pleasing to the gods, the same action can be both pious and impious.

Euthyphro insists that this contradictory conclusion does not follow because the gods all agree on certain matters, such as that if one person unjustly kills another, that individual is to be punished. The gods may all agree, Socrates admits, about certain universal laws regarding punishment, but a disagreement still exists among both people and gods as to which cases fall under these laws. They disagree in their evaluations of various acts, some saying the acts are just, some that they are unjust. Even if Euthyphro is sure in his own case that the gods agree that his father's action was unjust, and that Euthyphro's action is just, it is still evident that Euthyphro's second definition of "piety" is inadequate. In view of the fact that the gods disagree about some of the actions that are pleasing or displeasing to them, an action cannot be pious simply because it pleases some gods because the same action would have to be classed as "impious" if it displeased other gods.

Another definition is presented to overcome the problem of divine disagreements. Something is pious if *all* the gods love it, and it is impious if they *all* hate it. In cases in which there is disagreement among the gods, the item in question is to be classed as neither pious nor impious.

Socrates immediately begins examining this new definition by raising the most serious point that is brought up in the dialogue. He asks Euthyphro whether the gods love piety because it is pious, or whether it is pious because the gods love it. The question at issue is whether the basic characteristic that determines piety is the fact that the gods love it, or whether piety has in itself some characteristic that accounts for the fact that the gods love it.

Euthyphro holds that the gods love piety because it is pious. Socrates then shows him that he has not offered a definition, but only an effect of piety in pointing out that the gods love it. Because, according to Euthyphro, piety has certain characteristics that make it what it is, and because those characteristics are what makes the gods love it, then he still has not given an adequate definition of "piety." He still has not revealed what the essential characteristics are that make it what it is.

Then Socrates asks Euthyphro once more to tell him what Euthyphro claims to know—namely, what piety and impiety are. By this point in the discussion, Euthyphro is bewildered; he complains that whatever he says in answer to Socrates' persistent questioning just gets up and moves away. His words and his ideas do not seem able to stay fixed and permanent. Socrates then offers to help by suggesting another way of approaching the problem.

Piety and Justice

He asks Euthyphro whether whatever is pious must also be just. When Euthyphro gives an affirmative answer, Socrates inquires whether piety is the same as justice, or whether piety is only part of what constitutes justice. The latter, he is told. In turn, Socrates demands to know what part of justice piety is. If he could find out, he tells Euthyphro, then he could go to his own trial and show his accusers that they should not prosecute him for impiety because he would then know what piety is and would act accordingly.

In answering the question, Euthyphro offers another definition of piety and states that righteousness and piety are that part of justice dealing with the careful attention that should be paid to the gods. The remaining portion of justice deals with the careful attention that ought to be paid to people. Socrates requests a clarification of the meaning of the phrase "careful attention." A clarification is needed, he points out, because in most cases where careful attention is paid to some object, such as a horse or a person, the object is benefited or improved by the attention. Is this also true of the gods? Are they benefited or improved by piety? No. Therefore, it must be a different kind of attention that is involved.

To make his point clear, Euthyphro says that the kind of attention he has in mind is that which slaves pay their masters. Then, Socrates points out, piety is a type of service to the gods. Every service aims at accomplishing something. A doctor's service produces health; a shipwright's service produces a ship. However, what does piety, which now seems to be a service, produce? Generally speaking, Euthyphro answers, the principal result achieved through piety, by means of words and actions in prayer and sacrifice that are acceptable to the gods, is the preservation of the state and of private families. The results of impiety are the undermining and destruction of everything.

In terms of this latest answer, Socrates again asks what piety and impiety are. Euthyphro now seems to be offering the view that piety is a science of prayer and sacrifice, a science that deals with asking of the gods and giving to them. Euthyphro insists this is exactly what he means, so Socrates proceeds to explore this latest definition of piety. To ask rightly of the gods is to ask of them what people need from them, and to give rightly to the gods is to give to them what they need from people. When Euthyphro agrees to this view, Socrates points out that piety is the art of carrying on business between the gods and people. However, it is a strange kind of business, since one side, humanity's, appears to receive all of the benefits. People are obviously benefited by what the gods give them. However, what do people give in return? Also, are the gods benefited by it?

Euthyphro answers that what people give in return are honor and praise, which are gifts acceptable to the gods. Then, Socrates argues, piety is acceptable to the gods, but it does not benefit them nor is it loved by them. Euthyphro disagrees and insists that nothing is more loved by the gods than piety. So, Socrates asserts, piety means that which is loved by gods. Euthyphro agrees wholeheartedly.

Socrates then goes on to show Euthyphro that he has simply been talking around in a circle, and it is his own fault that his words will not stay put. They had agreed earlier in the discussion that the gods love piety because it is pious, and it is not pious because the gods love it. The fact that the gods love it is an effect of its nature and not its essential characteristic. Hence, there must be something that constitutes the fundamental characteristic of piety, that makes it what it is and causes the gods to love it. Either this conclusion is wrong, or Euthyphro has yet to answer the question, "What is piety?" Then Socrates begins all over again by asking that question.

Socrates points out once more that Euthyphro must know the answer in order to pursue his case against his father. Surely, he would not risk doing the wrong thing and offending the gods. Euthyphro wearily protests that he has no more time for the discussion, and he must rush off about his business. Socrates protests that he is left without the help he needs for his trial so that he can report that he knows what piety is and hence will not commit any impieties in the future. At this point the dialogue ends.

Euthyphro is one of the several superb short early dialogues that portray Socrates exposing the ignorance of supposedly wise people. When pressed, they are shown not to know what they are talking about. They cannot define basic concepts they deal with, such as "piety," "justice," and "courage," yet they are sure that what they are doing is pious, or just, or courageous. They are unwilling to undertake the difficult task of seeking to discover the meanings and natures of these terms. Their actions, based on their ignorance, can be disastrous, as is illustrated by both Euthyphro's charges against his father and the impending trial of Socrates.

Richard H. Popkin

Apology

Type of philosophy: Ethics
First transcribed: Apologia Sōkratous, early period, 399-390 B.C.E. (English translation, 1675)
Principal ideas advanced:

◇ The oracle at Delphi has declared Socrates to be the wisest of all people, and Socrates suggests that if he is superior to other people in wisdom, it is only because he is aware of his own ignorance.

◇ Defending himself against the charge of impiety and corrupting the young, Socrates argues that the pretenders to wisdom, whom he has exposed by his critical questioning, must have spread rumors about him in order to discredit him.

◇ Socrates maintains that it would have been foolish for him to corrupt the very persons with whom he associated, for everyone knows that corrupt and evil persons harm even those who have once befriended them.

◇ If to point out the weaknesses in a state is to do the state a service, Socrates argues, then he had better be rewarded for performing the function of gadfly to the state.

◇ Having been condemned to death, Socrates declares that death is not to be feared, for either it is annihilation or it is a change to a better world where one might converse with noble souls.

The word "apology," the title of this famous dialogue, means "a defense," not a request for forgiveness. In meeting the accusation that he had corrupted the youth of Athens, Socrates did not for a moment assume an apologetic air, but with courageous faith in the worth of philosophy set forth the principles by which he governed his life.

The dialogue—the creation of Plato, who knew Socrates and had grown to love him both as a teacher and as a man—assumes the worth of Socrates' life and the rightness of his acts, especially of those acts of criticism that aroused the enmity of Socrates' accusers. *Apology* is one of three dialogues describing the final days of perhaps the greatest hero in the history of philosophy, one who took philosophy seriously enough

to die for it. Here Plato reports the trial and condemnation of Socrates. *Kritōn* (early period, 399-390 B.C.E.; *Crito*, 1804) reports his reasons for refusing to escape from prison, and *Phaedōn* (middle period, 388-368 B.C.E.; *Phaedo*, 1675) his last conversations and death. To read the dialogues in that order is to gain some understanding of the significance of Socrates' identification of wisdom with virtue, and some conception of the nobility of his character.

The Charges

As *Apology* opens, the prosecution, for which Meletus is the spokesperson, has already stated its case. Meletus was probably merely the spokesperson for the chief instigator of the trial, Anytus, respected leader of the restored democracy; the third accuser, Lycon, is barely mentioned in the dialogue. Meletus speaks only a few words, and the other accusers none, but Socrates repeats the charges made against him. He begins by pointing out that almost everything they have said is false, especially their warning to the court implying that Socrates is a persuasive speaker, unless they mean by that one who speaks truth. His words will be unpremeditated but spoken with confidence in the justice of his cause; it is to truth that the jury should attend, just as it is the speaker's duty to state only the truth. There are actually two sets of charges against him, Socrates says: the present ones of impiety and corruption of the young and some ancient ones his audience heard as children and that should now be refuted.

The latter were made by accusers largely unknown, except for Greek dramatist Aristophanes in his burlesque of Socrates in the comedy *Nephelai* (423 B.C.E.; *The Clouds*, 1708), which was written in fun rather than ill will. These accusations were that Socrates had theories about and conducted investigations into the heavens and things below the earth (that is, pursued physical sciences), and that he could make weaker arguments appear to overcome the stronger and taught others to do the same (that is, he was a Sophist). Such accusations are dangerous, Socrates argues, because uncritical listeners assume that such inquirers must be atheists. However, the accusations are false, for Socrates has no knowledge of physics, not from disdain but from lack of interest. Socrates asks whether anyone present ever heard him discussing these matters. As to the charge that he has taught others professionally for fees, this, too, is false. Socrates professes (ironically) to admire Sophists such as Gorgias, Prodicus, and Hippias, who are able to convince youths to forsake their usual company—which is free—and come to them for training in social skills—for large fees. Still, people will wonder how Socrates got this reputation if the accusations are false, so he will explain.

Perhaps he does have some degree of human wisdom, though that of the Sophists is undoubtedly superhuman. The tale he will tell now concerning the kind of wisdom he does have may seem exaggerated, but judgment should be reserved until the end. Chaerephon, an old friend known to all, asked the oracle at Delphi if anyone were wiser than Socrates, and the answer was no. Such an answer puzzled Socrates—surely the god was speaking in riddles, for he could not be lying. So Socrates set out to see whether he could disprove the oracle by finding a wiser person. He examined a politician with a great reputation for—and the conceit of—wisdom. Not only was the man not wise, but he resented Socrates' attempt to show him that he was not. Socrates came away realizing that at least he was himself wiser in awareness of his own ignorance. Others who heard the politician's examination resented the inquiry, too, but Socrates felt it a religious duty to determine the oracle's meaning. Having queried other politicians with the same effect, he went next to the poets and found that they could not even expound their own works. Not wisdom, then, but instinct or inspiration must be the source of poetry. Proceeding to the skilled craftspeople, Socrates discovered here a kind of technical knowledge he did not possess, but these men prided themselves so on their special competence that they mistakenly thought themselves expert on everything else. Naturally, Socrates' exposé of the ignorance of others made him unpopular with them, even though it was really to their good.

When bystanders heard him examine pretenders to wisdom, it was assumed that he had the knowledge, lack of which he uncovered in those questioned, even though this was not true. However, the real meaning of the oracle and the upshot of Socrates' search was that God alone is really wise, and human wisdom is of relatively little value. The oracle used Socrates' name merely to make a point: "The wisest of you men is he who has realized, like Socrates, that in respect of wisdom he is really worthless." Thus in exposing ignorance, Socrates continues, he obeys a divine command.

Socrates tells the court that young men of leisure, having heard him questioning their elders to the latter's discomfort, have tried to imitate his techniques and have aroused further hostility that has redounded to Socrates' discredit. When victims irritated at exposure are asked what Socrates has done or taught to mislead the young, however, they have no specific evidence and so "they fall back on the stock charges against any philosopher: that he teaches his pupils about things in the heavens and below the earth, and to disbelieve in gods, and to make the weaker argument defeat the stronger." It is thus because he has revealed the truth about them in plain language that the earlier calumniators have spread these rumors about Socrates, which are the underlying causes of the present attack by Meletus, Anytus, and Lycon.

The Real Complaint

It must be remembered that the prosecution could not afford to present its real complaint against Socrates. The pretext of "corruption of the young" concerned his supposed influence, discouraging unquestioning loyalty to the democracy, on former associates (Alcibiades, Critias, Charmides, and others) who had opposed the state. The charge of "irreligion" was probably related to the mutilation, in 415 B.C.E., of all the Athenian statues of Hermes on the night before Alcibiades led the military expedition to Sicily, for which Alcibiades was blamed, probably falsely. However, these matters were excluded from the jurisdiction of the present court by the Act of Oblivion that Anytus had sponsored. According to this act, offenses occurring under the old democracy had received general amnesty. During the year of Socrates' trial, 399 B.C.E., Anytus defended another person against charges of irreligion, so it is unlikely that he actually held such a grievance against Socrates. It is likely that Anytus regarded Socrates' influence as dangerous to the restored democracy and, consequently, as something that needed to be destroyed. Hence the trumped-up charges, the use of Meletus as mouthpiece, and the prosecution's unwillingness and inability to explain or substantiate the accusations made in public.

Consequently, on trial, Socrates exercises his argumentative abilities with humor and irony to show how ridiculous the prosecution's case is. He turns specifically to the charges of Meletus, stating them as follows: "Socrates is guilty of corrupting the minds of the young, and of believing in deities of his own invention instead of the gods recognized by the State." This passage has been interpreted as meaning that Socrates did not worship the official gods rather than that he did not believe in them, and that he practiced unfamiliar rites.

The Defense

Socrates now takes the line that Meletus must be joking about a serious matter in which he really has no interest. Who, he queries, exercises the best influence on the young? By a series of questions he leads Meletus to say that it is the whole Athenian citizenry—except Socrates. However, this is very odd; in fact, it is exactly opposite to the case of training horses, in which the many are incompetent and only a few expert trainers improve the animals.

Furthermore, because Meletus must admit that evil people harm their associates, he must also admit that Socrates would be unbelievably stupid not to know that by corrupting his young acquaintances, he would only be brewing trouble for himself. Thus, either Socrates has not been a bad influence, or if he has, he must have been one unintentionally. If the latter, however, what Socrates deserves according to the usual procedure is that he be given private admonition rather than punishment. However, far from instructing Socrates, Meletus has avoided his company until now.

How, specifically, has Socrates corrupted the young, especially in regard to teaching belief in new deities? Does he believe in gods different from those of the state or in none at all? Meletus takes the latter alternative. Socrates suggests that Meletus has deliberately and flippantly contradicted himself in order to test Socrates' logical prowess. It is charged both that Socrates believes in no gods and that he believes in new deities, that he is an atheist and yet believes in "supernatural activities" (this refers to Socrates' famous divine "sign," or inner voice). Now one cannot believe in activities without an actor, and if Socrates believes in supernatural activities, he must believe in supernatural beings. Thus, either Meletus was trying Socrates' wit or he was desperate for a genuine charge against him.

At this point, Socrates acknowledges that his destruction will be caused by the general hostility aroused by his conduct, not by these flimsy accusations, but that he has no regret for his behavior. Good people must not busily calculate the chances of life and death but must concern themselves with acting rightly. It would be most inconsistent if, after loyal military service through several engagements, Socrates were to fail through fear of death an assignment given by God himself to the philosophic life. To fear death implies knowledge of what occurs afterward, another form of the pretense to know what one does not; but to disobey a superior, human or divine, is a known evil.

Were it suggested that Socrates be acquitted on condition that he desist from his philosophical questionings, he would reply that, much as he appreciates the offer, he must still pursue his duty to God, asking Athenians, "Are you not ashamed that you give your attention to acquiring as much money as possible, and similarly with reputation and honour, and give no attention or thought to truth and understanding and the perfection of your soul?" Actually, Socrates conceives his divine service as the greatest benefit ever to fall on Athens, since he urges people to put the welfare of their souls above all else. If the Athenians kill him, they will inflict more harm on themselves; Socrates believes that divine law prevents injury by an evil to a good person. Of course they can banish or kill his body, but such acts do no harm to the soul, except of course to the soul of the evildoer.

Here Socrates introduces the famous "gadfly" metaphor. Comical as it sounds, he says, "God has appointed me to this city, as though it were a large thoroughbred horse that because of its great size is inclined to be lazy and needs the stimulation of some stinging fly" ("gadfly," in one translation).

It seems to me that God has attached me to this city to perform the office of such a fly; and all day long I never cease to settle here, there, and everywhere, rousing, persuading, reproving every one of you. You will not easily find another like me, gentlemen, and if you take my advice you will spare my life. I suspect, however, that before long you will awake from your drowsing, and in your annoyance you will take Anytus's advice and finish me off with a single slap; and then you will go on sleeping till the end of your days, unless God in his care for you sends someone to take my place.

Although such a description of his mission might be misinterpreted as conceited, careful study of its context and of other Socratic dialogues will convince the reader that it is only the frank self-appraisal of a prophet. As Socrates adds, proof of the sincerity of what he has said and done lies in the obvious fact of his poverty; he has neglected his private affairs in order to fulfill his duty.

Should someone ask why Socrates has not addressed himself to the state at large with his advice, the answer is that he has been forbidden to do so by the divine voice to which Meletus's charge made implicit reference and that comes to him occasionally to warn against a course of action. In regard to a political career, its warning was evidently provident, for otherwise Socrates would have been dead long ago—no person, he says, can conscientiously oppose a government by the masses and champion justice and live long. He would not act wrongly in obedience to any authority, as is evidenced by the few occasions of his public office. When a member of the council under the old democracy, he alone opposed the unconstitutional trial of ten military commanders *en bloc*, thus risking denunciation and arrest. Later, under the oligarchy, he disobeyed an unjust order to participate in the arrest of Leon of Salamis and probably would have been executed had not the government fallen.

Toward the end of his defense, Socrates repeats that he has never taught professionally nor privately but has allowed rich and poor to exchange questions and answers with him and, consequently, cannot be held responsible for the good or bad career of any individual. If some of those who have listened to his discourse have been corrupted by him, Socrates challenges them to bear witness now. That no one comes is ample evidence that Meletus lies. This constitutes Socrates' defense; he will not appeal, as is usual with defendants, to the sympathy of the jury by exhibiting his children and friends. To do so would be unfitting for one of Socrates' reputation. Besides, the defendant's business is to convince the jury by facts and argument rather than by sentiment, and the jury is to decide justly, not hand out verdicts as favors. Were he to ask them to perjure themselves as jurors, this in itself would convict him of guilt. Thus Socrates ends his speech and places himself in his judges' and God's hands.

The Verdict and Punishment

When the verdict is brought in, it is guilty, though obtained by a small margin, about 280 to 220. Meletus proposes the death penalty (although scholars believe Socrates' accusers did not wish to kill him but only to silence or banish him because according to the prevalent practices several alternatives of escape were open to the philosopher). It is customary for the convicted defendant to propose an alternate penalty and for the jury to choose which one would be enacted. However, Socrates will not admit guilt. Because he has not cared for money, a comfortable home, high rank, or secret societies—all the things having popular appeal—and has instead devoted himself to his mission to Athens, Socrates says it would therefore be appropriate that he be maintained at state expense as a public benefactor. Certainly he deserves this treatment more than do Olympic horse racers!

Of course Socrates does not expect this suggestion to be taken seriously in spite of its justice. What of other possibilities? He rejects that of imprisonment, which is a known evil compared to death, which is of uncertain value. As to banishment, it is clear that he would find no more welcome in other societies than he has in Athens, for his conduct and its results would be the same. Again, he cannot give up philosophy and "mind his own business," for "to let no day pass without discussing goodness and all the other subjects about which you hear me talking and examining both myself and others is really the very best thing that a man can do, and . . . life without this sort of examination is not worth living." As to a fine, it is not likely that what he could afford would be acceptable. At this point Plato, Crito, Critobulus, and Apollodorus offer to pay a fine thirty times that which Socrates suggests, an offer he transmits to the court.

However, the jury decides on the death penalty, and Socrates makes his final remarks. He reminds that part of the jury voting for death that nature would soon have brought about what they wished, but as it is, they will incur blame for having killed a wise man, whether he is one or not. His condemnation has resulted not from paucity of argument but from his bearing: He has not been brazen or servile, nor has he catered to their pleasure. The real difficulty is not to elude death but to outrun vice. Socrates, the old man, has been caught by the former, but they have been captured by the latter; his condemnation is by the court, but they are convicted of their wickedness by Truth. Hoping to stop his mouth by death, they will find that criticism of their actions will increase—the only escape for them is to become good people.

To those voting for acquittal, he notes that in nothing he has done this day has the inner voice opposed him, whereas in the past it sometimes stopped him in the middle of a sentence. This is clear evidence that the outcome is good and that even death is no evil. Death must be either total annihilation, in which case it is an unbroken rest or else a change to another world; and if it is true as reported that one can there converse with the great men of time past, how rewarding! To meet Homer, Hesiod, or the great heroes of the old days, especially those similarly condemned to death unjustly, would be worth dying for again and again. To talk and argue with them would be happiness beyond description, and presumably one is not killed there for asking questions.

Socrates concludes by encouraging the friendly jurors with the belief that "nothing can harm a good man either in life or after death, and his fortunes are not a matter of indifference to the gods." He has no ill will for those who condemned him, although they are guilty of intent to harm him. As a final favor, Socrates asks that his hearers treat his sons as he has treated the Athenians: If they put anything before goodness or are self-deceived about their virtues, he asks that the jurors take their "revenge by plaguing them as I plagued you."

So ends Plato's story of the legal but unjust trial of one regarded as philosophy's first martyr. The authenticity of his report has been questioned, but scholars have pointed out that many people present at the trial, including hostile critics, would have read Plato's account and detected any substantial deviation from the facts. It therefore may be regarded as an essentially accurate record of the serenity, wit, courage, and steadfastness of a philosopher whose justness gave him composure in the face of those who cheated him of life.

Marvin Easterling

Crito

Type of philosophy: Ethics
First transcribed: Kritōn, early period, 399-390 B.C.E. (English translation, 1804)
Principal ideas advanced:

◇ Although Socrates has been unjustly accused of corrupting the young and has been sentenced to death, he refuses to escape because to escape would be to break an implicit agreement with the state to abide by its laws and judgments.

◇ He argues that the important thing is not to live, but to live honorably.

◇ It is never right to defend oneself against injury by an act of retaliation.

◇ To remain in a state, after having been reared and educated under its laws, is, in effect, to agree to abide by its laws.

◇ If Socrates were to escape a punishment legally decided on by the state, he could no longer conduct himself as a philosopher devoted to justice and the love of wisdom.

Crito is a relatively short dialogue that should be read in conjunction with and between *Apologia Sōkratous* (early period, 399-390 B.C.E.; *Apology*, 1675) and *Phaedōn* (middle period, 388-368 B.C.E.; *Phaedo*, 1675). *Apology* gives an account of Socrates' trial and condemnation; *Phaedo* describes his last conversations and death; *Crito* recounts a friend's urgent plea for Socrates to avail himself of the ample opportunity to escape and the latter's justification on moral grounds for remaining in prison voluntarily, although the execution will occur two days later. The dialogue is probably meant to explain Socrates' personal reasons for taking this course of inaction, rather than to prescribe a universally applicable norm for the individual unjustly condemned by the state, and some writers have suggested that Plato himself would probably have chosen to escape rather than to accept the sentence. Yet profound political, social, and moral issues are raised to which there are no easy solutions; their complications are such that readers may find their own judgments falling on either side of an exceedingly fine line.

A Discussion of Escape

When the dialogue opens, Socrates has been in prison a month, for no death sentences could be carried out in Athens during the annual voyage of the state vessel to Delos, in commemoration of the legendary deliverance of the city from the Minotaur by Theseus. However, the ship is reportedly about to return, and Crito, having arrived at the prison before dawn, is waiting for Socrates to awake, in order to break the news and try to convince him to escape while there is yet time. It is typical of Socrates that he slumbers peacefully while Crito is wakeful and desperate, and that in the ensuing discussion it is Socrates who is the more rational and objective, though it is his own life that is at stake.

Crito's reasons for urging Socrates to escape, though perhaps on a less lofty plane than the latter's rebuttal, are not specious but are rather quite practical and persuasive. It is the weight of these, plus that of the circumstances under which Socrates was condemned, which gives the dialogue its moral significance. Crito begins by pointing out that if Socrates dies, an irreplaceable friend will have been lost, and besides, Crito will gain a reputation for loving money more than his friends, since many people will think he could have saved Socrates had he only been willing to put up the necessary cash; they will not believe that Socrates stayed in prison voluntarily.

Socrates answers that people of reason will believe only the truth; why should one regard majority opinion? Crito then points out that popular opinion is not to be taken lightly, which fact is confirmed by Socrates' present circumstances. However, the philosopher replies that common people, unfortunately, are of limited capacity to do evil—because otherwise they could likewise do great good. This segment of the dialogue reveals the Socratic identification of wisdom and virtue, and his belief that no real evil can happen to a good person even if one's body is destroyed.

Crito acquiesces in this point but continues by assuring Socrates that he need not be concerned about any consequences to his friends if he chooses to escape (which apparently would have been quite easy under the circumstances, if not actually desired or intended by those who brought Socrates to trial). They are prepared to risk a large fine, loss of property, or other punishment. There is plenty of money available to buy off informers, and Crito knows people who will take Socrates out of the country for a moderate fee. Not only Crito's money, but also that of Simmias and Cebes—foreigners who would not be so liable to punishment—is at Socrates' disposal. At his trial, Socrates had rejected banishment to a foreign society, but Crito assures him of comfort and protection among friends in Thessaly.

Furthermore, he continues, Socrates will do a wrong in voluntarily neglecting to save his life; he will be inflicting on himself the penalty his enemies wished. What of his young sons? Will he not be failing them by leaving their education unfinished and deserting them to the lot of orphans? Crito finishes his argument by expressing once more his concern for the reputation both Socrates and his friends will incur if he refuses escape, a reputation for cowardice and lack of initiative resulting from first, Socrates' unnecessary appearance in court (it was customary for Athenians whose conviction was probable to leave the country before trial); second, the manner in which the defense was made (Socrates had refused all compromise and had deliberately taken a position that might, and did, result in conviction); and third, the present situation, which will suggest sheer bungling and lack of spirit. In short, the suffering of Socrates' death will be augmented by disgrace.

Right and Wrong

To all this Socrates makes a reply remarkable for its calm, detached, and rational tenor. Much as he appreciates Crito's concern, he points out that his choice to face death is not a sudden impulse; his practice has always been to follow the course reason shows to be best. The question, then, is whether the opinions he has previously adopted are still true or whether their truth has been altered by the turn of events. One must not be frightened into a change of outlook, he reassures Crito, by imprisonment, loss of goods, or execution. With characteristic but kindly irony Socrates asks Crito to consider the matter with him, for since Crito is in no danger of death he is more likely to be impartial and objective.

Is it not true, he asks, that only some opinions are tenable and not all, that those to be respected are the good ones, and that these belong to the wise? Is it not the case that the opinions of the few qualified experts, rather than those of the masses, are to be regarded, as is illustrated in the case of athletic training? If this is true in general, then it follows that in the present case Socrates and Crito should be concerned only with what the expert in right and wrong will think, not with what the majority will say. The fact that the latter have the powers of life and death in their hands is really irrelevant to the argument.

In the considerations that follow, it is clear that Socrates is not at all interested in discussing the possibility or the means of escape, but rather its rightness or wrongness. His premises are that "the really important thing is not to live, but to live well. . . . And . . . to live well means the same thing as to live honourably or rightly." Crito's concern about expense, reputation, and the upbringing of Socrates' children are those of the common people, whose attitudes and acts are unrelated to reason. Socrates says:

> Our real duty . . . is to consider one question only. . . . Shall we be acting rightly in paying money and showing gratitude to these people who are going to rescue me, and in escaping . . . or shall we really be acting wrongly in doing all this? If it becomes clear that such conduct is wrong, I cannot help thinking that the question whether we are sure to die, or to suffer any other ill effect . . . if we stand our ground and take no action, ought not to weigh with us at all in comparison with the risk of doing what is wrong.

Wrongdoing, Socrates holds, is reprehensible not merely on most but on all occasions; there are no exceptions. Although most people think it natural and right to return wrongs done them, Socrates disagrees: "It is never right to do a wrong or return a wrong or defend one's self against injury by retaliation." If this is so, and it is agreed that one should always fulfill morally right agreements, then it follows, Socrates concludes, that it would be wrong for him to leave without an official discharge by the state, for he would be doing the state an injury by breaking an implicit agreement with it. He explains what he means by personifying the Athenian Laws and Constitution and imagining the dialogue that might occur between them and himself were he to favor escape.

They would first point out to him that such an act would subvert the Laws and the state; the latter cannot subsist if its legal decisions are to be set aside for the benefit of individuals. However, suppose that Socrates should retort that the proposed escape was in reprisal for the wrong done him by the state? The answer of the Laws to this would be that not only was there no provision made for such evasion and insubordination, but Socrates is under agreement to abide by the state's judgments. He has no legitimate complaint against them, the Laws continue, but rather positive obligations to abide by them. The Laws, by sanctioning the marriage of his parents, in a sense gave him life itself; they also provided a proper education for him. He is thus their child and servant, and as such does not have rights equal to theirs, any more than a son has the right to rebel against his father. Indeed, "compared with your mother and father and all the rest of your ancestors your country is something far more precious, more venerable, more sacred, and held in greater honour both among gods and among all reasonable men." Whatever it orders one must do, unless he can justly persuade it otherwise (and of course, during the trial Socrates failed to persuade the jury, though he was confident he might have done so if given more time).

Now, in spite of all the blessings vouchsafed to Athenian citizens, the Laws continue, any young man upon reaching maturity may evaluate the political order and the administration of justice, and if he disapproves, he is free to leave the state with all his possessions. If, on the other hand, he surveys the political and judicial arrangement and voluntarily stays, his act is equivalent to an agreement to abide by the state's commands—or rather its proposals, because they are not blunt dictates and the citizen has the choice of either obeying or persuading the state to change its decision. If Socrates should run away now, he would be more blameworthy than any other Athenian: His implicit agreement to abide by the law has been more explicit than that of any other citizen because he above all has remained at home, never crossing the border except while on military duty. Although he admired Sparta and Crete because of their good governments and respect for law, he has never emigrated to those city-states. And again, during the trial when the defendant was given the customary opportunity to propose an alternative penalty, Socrates did not choose banishment. His covenant with the state was thus made freely, consciously, and under no stress in relation to time—after all, he has spent seventy years in Athens.

Furthermore, the Laws ask, what will Socrates gain by escaping? The risk of banishment or loss of property would be inflicted on his friends. If he entered well-ordered states, he would be regarded as a lawbreaker by their citizens and would confirm the jury's opinion of him. However, if he chose to go to states with little or no respect for law and order, would that kind of life be worthwhile? He could not continue to converse as usual about goodness in persons and governments, for it would be hypocrisy to do so. He would not want to rear his children in such an environment, and if they remained in Athens, they would be more likely to receive good care with Socrates dead than with him alive illegally and in exile. Surely his friends, if true to their profession, would care for them.

In conclusion, the Laws advise Socrates, "Do not think more of your children or of your life or of anything else than you think of what is right; so that when you enter the next world you may have all this to plead in your defence before the authorities there." To disobey by escaping will not really better either his friends or Socrates in this world or the next. "As it is, you will leave this place, when you do, as the victim of a wrong done not by us, the Laws, but by your fellow-men." However, if he retaliates and returns evil for evil, breaking his agreement and wronging himself, his friends, his country, and the Laws themselves, he will incur the wrath of the Laws both here and in the next life.

Socrates thus concludes the speeches he has put in the mouth of the Laws and asks Crito whether he has anything to say in opposition to these arguments, which seem so persuasive that Socrates professes to be scarcely able to hear any others. Because Crito offers no refutation, the matter is decided: Socrates will obey the law even though it means his death.

Reasons for Socrates' Decision

Few readers will leave *Crito* without making a personal judgment on Socrates' decision and his justification for it. The difficulty of making an adequate one is complicated by several factors: Socrates' trial, as far as is known, was legal. In addition, the real reasons for which Socrates was prosecuted concerned matters for which general amnesty had been extended by the Act of Oblivion, and so the court could not have jurisdiction over these; hence the failure of Anytus and Meletus, Socrates' accusers, to explain their charges. However, though the ostensible charges were thus specious, and though Socrates showed them to be ridiculous, the jury had voted in proper order to convict him, and so the letter of the law had been fulfilled. The very fact that this case clearly showed that an innocent and supremely good man could be condemned unjustly under the law and hence that the law needed revision was cited as an excellent reason for escape, but Socrates argued that such reform should be demanded at a time other than that at which his own fate was affected in order that reform would not be motivated by mere favoritism.

However—as Socrates makes the Laws say in the dialogue—it is not the laws but the people administering them who wronged him. Socrates argued that respect for law in general is more valuable than one person's life lost by maladministration.

This again is a delicate point. Had the miscarriage of justice occurred merely through ignorance—though of course Socrates regarded vice as a kind of ignorance—it would have been easier to accept the sacrifice. However, the reader finds it difficult to avoid feeling that the court is more intent on ridding Athens of Socrates than it is on reaching a just verdict. It is true that Socrates argued that were he to evade the death penalty, people would think him insincere in his former teaching about integrity and obedience to the law—but Crito might well have turned one of his own statements against him by replying that it is only what reasonable and wise people think that really matters. Nevertheless, the example set by escape might have been harmful to people of less comprehension.

Socrates perceived the value of consistency and stability in the state and its dispensation of justice. A state does not consist merely of the persons administering and living in it at any give time; to function best, a state must have a continuity transcending the irregularities of individual fortunes. Presumably this was Socrates' intent in valuing the state above parents and ancestors, though modern Western readers may feel that Socrates revered the state too much. However, whether or not readers agree with Socrates' decision, they can hardly fail to admire the philosopher's devotion to principle, nor deny that the nobility of such a death enhances life for the living.

Marvin Easterling

Symposium

Type of philosophy: Metaphysics
First transcribed: Symposion, middle period, 388-368 B.C.E. (English translation, 1701)
Principal ideas advanced:

◇ During a banquet, a number of speeches praising the god Love are delivered; the first speech, by Phaedrus, makes the claim that love between virtuous men and youths is of the highest type, the chief motive to a noble life.

◇ Pausanias distinguishes between common love, which is of the body, and heavenly love, which is the love of virtue and philosophy.

◇ The physician Eryximachus argues that love is the principle of harmony that reconciles the hostile elements in the body.

◇ Aristophanes, satirizing physiological theories of love, maintains that the human body was originally round, having four arms, four feet, a head with two faces—and so forth—and that Zeus, to punish people for rebellion, split them in two. Ever since that time, the halves have sought each other avidly; the desire to be reunited is love.

◇ Agathon praises Love as the most beautiful and youngest of the gods, possessed of all the virtues.

◇ Socrates explains how from a love of the beauty of physical objects one can pass to the apprehension of the nature of Beauty itself, the ideal, and thereby share Love's divinity.

Symposium is perhaps Plato's masterpiece as a work of art, though other dialogues are of greater philosophical import. Its great range, from discussions of physical love to an almost mystical vision of eternal, absolute beauty, makes it both art and philosophy. The range of subject and level of discussion are reflected in the original Greek and in some translations by differences in the language and style of individual speakers, and the contrasts thus afforded contribute to the dramatic excellence of the work. The dramatic effect is also enhanced by the order and structure of the dialogue, which is an account by Apollodorous of a banquet described to him by Aristodemus. At the banquet, a number of speeches are made, leading to a final speech by Plato's beloved teacher and paragon of philosophy, Socrates.

Many Views of Love

The dramatic poet Agathon has just won the prize for his first tragedy and is celebrating at home with his guests. Because of the aftereffects of yesterday's drinking, it is agreed that the entertainment will consist chiefly of conversation. Eryximachus recalls Phaedrus's frequent observation that while other gods and heroes have had ample praises and honors, Love has been singularly neglected, so he proposes that each man deliver a speech praising this god. All agree to this proposal, Socrates remarking that he claims understanding of nothing other than this subject. Readers familiar with Socrates will see in this statement a hint that the symposium on Love will remain on no ordinary level, for Socrates, above all his contemporaries, is able to transcend the sensual.

Because the topic originated with Phaedrus, Plato's friend, he is invited to speak first. Phaedrus's speech is a rather commonplace encomium setting the stage for later speeches. He describes Love as the oldest of the gods, full of power and the author of the greatest blessings. Phaedrus conceives love of the highest type to be that between virtuous men and youths and believes that the desire for honor and the fear of dishonor and shame are the chief motives for leading a noble life. The love between men is above all else the source of this motive, for the lover and the beloved hate nothing more than disgrace in each other's eyes; hence, they are courageous and self-sacrificing, even to the point of death. A nation or army made up of such lovers would be almost invincible. Thus, Love not only serves as the chief source of virtue but also, as seen in the stories of Alcestis and Achilles, gives happiness after death.

Pausanias thinks the foregoing is indiscriminate. Love is not one but twofold; one part is noble and one part is not. There is an elder, heavenly Aphrodite, daughter of Uranus and having no mother, and also a younger, common Aphrodite, daughter of Zeus and Dione. Therefore, there are two Loves, the offspring of each. The common Love, whose mother was of both male and female parentage, desires either women or youths and is merely of the body, without regard for good or evil, the noble or the base, and being of the body in its craving, is also like the body in temporality. The heavenly Love, however, whose mother was born from the male alone, seeks the male as the more valiant and intelligent. Lovers of this sort seek out youths of promising virtue and intellect with the intent of educating and developing them. Lovers of the body have brought only disgrace on Love, and some societies disapprove of attachments between men and youths; the question of their propriety is not simple, depending on whether the attitudes and manners involved are honorable or not.

Pausanias thinks that when love of youths and the practice of philosophy and virtue coalesce, this love is noble and mutually profitable.

The next speech affords a transition to a higher plane when the physician Eryximachus declares his discovery from medicine that love is indeed twofold, but not just in humanity; this duality is a universal principle. His position, reminiscent of the teachings of Heraclitus and Empedocles, is illustrated by the fact that in the body there are hostile loves and desires both healthy and diseased; medicine is the art of satisfying the one type, eliminating or converting the other. Hostile elements in the body must be reconciled if there is to be health, just as a proper arrangement of high and low notes is needed to produce musical harmony, and an orderly combination of short and long beats to produce rhythm. Hot and cold, moist and dry must be blended by harmonius love in order to secure the well-being of men, animals, and plants; whereas if wanton love causes an excessive degree of one element, injury follows. Even divination or communion between humanity and the gods is concerned with enhancing the good and curing the evil love. The former originates happiness and harmony with gods and humanity.

Eryximachus's speech is serious and apparently intended to be scientific, but it is followed by that of the great comic dramatist Aristophanes, who satirizes current physiological theories. In order to explain the power of love properly, Aristophanes first gives the background of human nature: Originally there were three sexes—male, female, and the male-female. The body was round, having four arms, four feet, two sexual organs, and one head with two faces. This race became so powerful it attacked the gods in heaven. Zeus, in order to punish people without destroying them—because the gods would not wish to forgo the sacrifices and worship people provided—reduced their power and doubled their number by splitting them in two. The two halves, however, sought each other avidly, and when reunited would not separate long enough to tend to the usual affairs of life; hence, they began to perish.

While in the original division, the face had been turned around to the sectioned side, the sexual organs had not; now Zeus contrived to move them around so that when the two halves of the man-woman came together, conception and reproduction would occur, or if two halves of males or females embraced, sexual gratification would prepare them to return to their daily tasks. Consequently, sections of the double nature lust after members of the opposite sex, but halves of the other two sexes seek their own kind. Males who seek the male, therefore, are not shameless but rather desirous of the manly and best, as is evinced by the number of statesmen so inclined. The association is not merely sexual, however; it stems from a most fundamental desire for fusion into one being. Perfect satisfaction and happiness would lie in reunion with the original other halves of one's nature, but failing this, the next best is to find congenial loves. Thus Love leads one back to one's own nature in this life and the next, and hence it deserves highest praise. So ends Aristophanes' speech, in the main highly fantastic but with a germ of truth in its description of the desire for unity.

Agathon's turn is next. As might be expected of a dramatic poet, his remarks are rhetorically brilliant rather than philosophically cogent. He argues that Love is the most beautiful of the gods because he is the youngest, and the youngest because he is swift enough to outrun old age. Love is tender and soft because he goes about and dwells in the softest places, the hearts and souls of gods and people. He is just, neither suffering nor exerting force—all people serve him of their own wills. He is temperate, because temperance rules pleasure and no pleasure is greater than that of love. That he is courageous is evident in that Ares yielded to Aphrodite. He must be wise, for he is a poet and at his touch teaches everyone to become a poet. He is the creator of all animals, inspirer of all arts, peacemaker among the gods. His is the love of beauty rather than of deformity, and as the author of love of the beautiful he has originated every heavenly and earthly good. Agathon's praise ends in a grand flourish of words that win the acclaim of all present and that Socrates uses as occasion for pretended dismay as Agathon's successor.

Socrates Looks at Love

Plato exploits Agathon's florid but somewhat vacuous panegyric as a stage setting for the more substantial and more enduring lustrous speech of Socrates. He did not realize, Socrates says, that the intent was to praise Love by giving him every good quality without regard for the facts. Socrates knows only how to speak the truth, and he will proceed only if that is what the other wishes to hear. Upon reassurances, Socrates begins by asking questions, as is his wont, to which the answers given by Agathon lead up to the desired conclusions. By this dialectical method, he shows that because love is love *of* or desire *for* something, love cannot presently possess the object of its affection. Even when one is said to desire that which he has, what is really meant is that one desires its continued or future possession. Now it was stated that love is one of the beautiful rather than of the deformed; if so, it follows that love cannot itself be beautiful. Because there is a basic identity between the good and the beautiful, it follows also that love wants, rather than has, the good.

Socrates now proceeds to an account of Love allegedly taught him by a woman of wisdom, Diotima of Mantineia. Love is neither fair (handsome or beautiful) nor good, but this does not imply that he is ugly or evil. Just as there is a mean between wisdom and ignorance—right opinion, which is not wisdom because it cannot give adequate reason for its belief, and which is not ignorance because it is true—so there is a mean between beauty and ugliness, good and evil. Furthermore, Love is not a god, for the gods are admittedly happy, beautiful, and in possession of all goods. Love is neither mortal nor immortal, but an intermediate spirit who interprets between gods and people by forwarding prayers and sacrifices to the gods and commands and answers to people. The understanding of this function of Love is spiritual wisdom, whereas knowledge of skills and arts is of a much lower order.

As to Love's ancestry, Diotima told this tale: On Aphrodite's birthday, the gods held a feast at which Poros (Plenty), son of Metis (Discretion), became tipsy on nectar and lay down to sleep. Penia (Poverty), having come to the door to beg as usual, saw an opportunity to better herself and lay down by Poros; thus Love was conceived. Both because Aphrodite is beautiful and Love was born on her birthday, he is now her devotee.

However, in accordance with his mixed parentage are his character and fortune; because of his mother, he is poor, rough, squalid, without a roof over his head, but like his father he is scheming, bold, aggressive, clever, strong, a great enchanter. Neither mortal nor immortal, he flourishes at one moment, perishes the next. His intermediate nature also makes him a philosopher; gods and wise men already possess wisdom, and the ignorant are self-satisfied—this is the evil of ignorance—but Love as a mean between the ignorant and the wise is a lover of wisdom, since "wisdom is a most beautiful thing, and Love is of the beautiful." Socrates' and his companions' previous error in attributing qualities such as beauty and wisdom to Love lay in confusion between love and the beloved.

"Of what use is love to man?" Socrates asked Diotima. Her reply was that this amounted to asking what people desire in loving the beautiful; it turns out that what they really desire is possession of the good, which is what people mean by "happiness." However, one cannot ask again why one desires happiness because happiness is an ultimate end. All people seek happiness rather than something like the other half of themselves; love, then, is really "of the everlasting possession of the good." A further question concerned the manner of the pursuit of love's object. All people, Diotima continued, desire to procreate the beautiful, whether in body or in soul. Love is not, therefore, of the beautiful alone but of "generation" in beauty (creativity). This is true because only through generation or reproduction can that which is mortal gain a kind of immortality. Not only people but also other animals love and desire immortality, and because all physical things undergo constant change and succession, the only means of attaining permanence is by generating offspring to take the parents' places. This is why procreation is desired so passionately and offspring are given such anxious care, even to the point that parents sacrifice their lives if necessary. The desire for immortality accounts also for the otherwise senseless ambition that drives so many people. In fact, Diotima said, this desire motivates all things that people do, even the practice of great virtues that people hope will keep them in memory.

Thus, some procreation is not of the body; some men are "pregnant" in body only, but some are creative in soul: They write poems or paint pictures, they conceive wisdom and virtue, best of all wisdom about the organization of states and families. Such creations of statesmen, lawmakers, and artists are preferable to human children, being more beautiful and more immortal, and the friendships out of which they are born are actually closer than those that bring forth children in the flesh.

Although this account of love transcends the earlier ones, it is still only regarding what Diotima described as the "lesser mysteries of love." Yet if practiced in the right way, these point to the higher. Diotima's description of beauty is recalled by Socrates in a passage that is considered to be among Plato's most significant because its description of the dialectical ascent to vision of absolute beauty applies to knowledge of the other ideas or forms as well.

The proper procedure in the apprehension of beauty is to begin in youth to appreciate physical or external beauty of one object, letting this inspire fair thoughts. From this, one should grow into the realization that the beauties of all physical things are related and thus transcend narrow devotion to one. The next level is the insight that beauty of mind is preferable to that of outward appearance; at this stage, the lover is moved to nurture the character and intellect of promising youths. Then he is prepared to ascend to the next (each step is progressively more abstract)—that in which the beauty of institutions and laws becomes evident. The beauty of the sciences is even higher, and he who perceives this will then proceed to a vision of a unique science, that of beauty per se. The final reward and the goal of this laborious ascent is apprehension of the nature (which Plato in other contexts calls the form or idea) of beauty:

A nature which in the first place is everlasting, not growing and decaying, or waxing and waning; secondly, not fair in one point of view and foul in another, or at one time or in one relation or at one place fair, at another . . . foul, as if fair to some and foul to others, or in the likeness of . . . any . . . part of the bodily frame, or in any form of speech or knowledge, or existing in any other being, as, for example, in an animal, or in heaven, or in earth, or in any other place but beauty absolute, separate, simple, and everlasting, which without diminution and without increase, or any change, is imparted to the ever-growing and perishing beauties of all other things. He who from these ascending under the influence of true love, begins to perceive that beauty, is not far from the end. And the true order of going . . . to the things of love, is to begin from the beauties of earth and mount upwards for the sake of that other beauty, using these as steps only, and from one going on to two, and from two to all fair forms, and from fair forms to fair practices, and from fair practices to fair notions, until from fair notions he arrives at the notion of absolute beauty, and at last knows what the essence of beauty is. This . . . is that life above all others which man should live, in the contemplation of beauty absolute.

Socrates maintains that anyone living a life of communion with the ultimately real beauty—as Diotima has described it—will share Love's divinity and reality and goodness, becoming a friend of the gods and achieving immortality as far as is possible for man. There is no better aid to this end than that of Love, and this is why and how Love ought to be praised.

In Praise of Socrates

As Socrates thus ends his speech, a sudden change of tone is introduced by the entrance of the drunken Alcibiades, who adequately reinforces the Socratic teaching by recalling ways in which the master practices it. Willing to participate only if the others will drink, Alcibiades empties a half-gallon wine vessel and has it filled for Socrates, calling attention to the fact, however, that Socrates can drink any amount without becoming drunk. When asked to speak, Alcibiades admits that he is in no condition to vie with others in praise of Love, and he chooses to praise Socrates instead.

Socrates, he begins, looks like a satyr; indeed, he is like the busts of Silenus that open up to reveal images of gods inside them. He is like the satyr Marsyas, too, the marvelous flute player whose melodies charm all hearers, except that

Socrates pipes with words even more powerful than those of Pericles. He is the only man who is able to shame Alcibiades for neglecting his own soul to attend public affairs, and only the love of popularity tears him away from Socrates' spell. In spite of the latter's rough exterior and pretension of ignorance, he is full of temperance and true beauty, despising the popular versions of beauty, wealth, and honor. While still a youth, Alcibiades became enamored of Socrates because of the master's shining virtues and sought to become his beloved. But this association, had it been consummated—as it was not—would have been motivated solely by Alcibiades' desire to render service to a master admired for his wisdom and goodness and ability to impart these, for Socrates was certainly unattractive physically. However, Alcibiades recounts how his advances became more and more overt with absolutely no effect on Socrates, which made the handsome youth realize fully how genuine was the philosopher's self-control. This was only one of many occasions in which the almost superhuman virtues of Socrates were exhibited, Alcibiades continues. While at war, Socrates was able to go without food and rest with incomparable stamina; he marched better barefoot on the ice than did other soldiers whose feet were shod. Once, while engrossed in a difficult problem, Socrates stood in one spot from one dawn to the next, to the amazement of fellow soldiers who slept out in the open to keep watch on his endurance. However, Socrates was not just a dreamer; he rescued Alcibiades in battle and should have had the prize for valor that was awarded to the latter. Although he seems a satyr in appearance, also like the statues with gods inside are Socrates' words, ridiculous at first but, when examined, found to have unparalleled significance, to be "of the most divine, abounding in fair images of virtue, and of the widest comprehension, or rather extending to the whole duty of a good and honourable man."

Shortly after Alcibiades' lauding of Socrates, the banquet breaks up; some men leave, some drink themselves to sleep. When Aristodemus awakes at dawn, there is Socrates still holding forth in argument to an audience of only Agathon and Aristophanes. When they doze off, Socrates arises and departs.

So ends a dialogue remarkable for its picture of Socrates' outward appearance, moral character, and ability to take—or leave—the earthly point of departure for the realm of reason and intellect. Especially valuable for the student of Plato is its account of the dialectical approach to the vision of forms. Careful examination of the long quoted passage will reveal also that many other essential features of the theory of forms are suggested there—the forms are simple, unique, immaterial, immutable, eternal, ultimately real natures that give particular objects their being. The form of absolute beauty described here is obviously—on both internal and external evidence—that which Plato elsewhere calls the good. The reader might well compare the account in *Symposium* with those in other dialogues, especially with the Myth of the Cave in *Politeia* (middle period, 388-368 B.C.E.; *Republic*, 1701). However, *Symposium* glows with beauties of its own, mixing philosophical discourse on love and lovely discourse on philosophy.

Marvin Easterling

Republic

Type of philosophy: Ethics, metaphysics, political philosophy

First transcribed: Politeia, middle period, 388-368 B.C.E. (English translation, 1701)

Principal ideas advanced:

◇ The question arises, "What is justice?," and after some unacceptable answers, Thrasymachus suggests that justice is whatever is to the interest of the stronger party (because the stronger party makes the laws and enforces them); but Socrates argues that rulers sometimes err and that, in any case, the art of government, like other arts, is directed to the interests of those to be affected, the people themselves.

◇ Socrates claims that just people, provided they have knowledge, can rule both themselves and others, and that the concern of just people is not for themselves alone.

◇ To clarify the idea of justice and to prove its worth, Socrates leads a discussion concerning justice in the state; he constructs the idea of an ideal state, one that exhibits justice.

◇ Any state needs guardians (rulers), auxiliaries (soldiers), and workers; each class does its proper business without interfering with the others; analogously, the just person is one in whom the three elements of an individual's nature—the rational, the spirited, and the appetitive—are harmonized.

◇ The ideal republic is one in which the classes are carefully built up by controlled breeding, education, and selection; society is communized in order to eliminate quarrels about personal property.

◇ The guardians of the state should be educated as philosophers, having been prepared by training in music and gymnastics.

The *Republic* of Plato, perhaps the greatest single treatise written on political philosophy, has strongly influenced Western thought concerning questions of justice, rule, obedience, and the good life. The work is undoubtedly the best general introduction to Plato's philosophy. It contains not only his ideas on the state and human nature but also his theory of forms, his theory of knowledge, and his views of the role of music and poetry in society. Plato presents a penetrating analysis of each of the important philosophical questions. Socrates and his illustrious student Plato force the reader, by their dialectical technique of question and answer, of definition and exception, to take an active part in the philosophical enterprise.

The work is divided into ten books, or chapters, written as a dialogue with Socrates as the main character. One cannot fail to catch the magnificence of Plato's literary and philosophical style, for all the available translations contain passages of great force and beauty.

Justice

The opening book of the *Republic* is concerned with the question, "What is justice?" Invited by Polemarchus to the home of his father, Cephalus, Socrates and others (among them Glaucon, Adeimantus, and Thrasymachus) begin, in an easy fashion, the search for an answer. First Cephalus and then his son Polemarchus defend the idea that justice is the restoration of what one has received from another. Socrates asks if this definition would apply in a situation in which weapons borrowed from a friend were demanded by him when quite obviously he was no longer of sound mind. It is a homely example of the type that Socrates loved to give; and as usual, when examined, it raises important considerations. Justice, among other things, involves not only property but also conditions, such as a sound mind, which cannot be merely assumed.

The next definition is that justice is doing good to friends and harm to enemies. However, knowledge is needed in order to be able to judge who one's friends and enemies are. The definition is then modified: Do good to the just and harm to the unjust. Socrates brings up an objection that is a central feature of many of his discussions of the good life. He argues that doing harm to the unjust makes them worse than they are. He holds that it can never be just to make people worse than they are by doing harm to them.

The most serious discussion of this book, which sets the tone for the remainder of the *Republic*, occurs next. Thrasymachus, who had been sitting by listening to the argument with ill-concealed distaste, impetuously breaks in and takes it up. He presents a position that has since been stated many times: Because the stronger party makes the laws, justice is that which is to the advantage or interest of the stronger party. Socrates attacks this definition: He points out that people do not always know what their interest is or wherein it lies. When the stronger party errs in judgment, then what? Thrasymachus replies that rulers are not rulers when they err. Note that in admitting this, Thrasymachus has already moved away from his original position and toward that of Socrates, which is that might alone does not make right; might together with some kind of knowledge capable of preventing errors makes right. Socrates presses his advantage further. Whenever we consider an art and its practice, be it medicine, piloting a ship, or ruling, it is practiced not for the sake of the art or its practitioner but for those who are to receive its benefits, be they patients, passengers, or the ruled.

Thrasymachus angrily declares that anyone but a philosopher could see that society "honors" the powerful person over the powerless. Corrupt people with impunity dissolve contracts and pay no taxes. People may privately proclaim the virtues of justice, but publicly, the opposite prevails, and people are admired and respected for daring to practice that which is ordinarily frowned on. In fact, Thrasymachus claims, the tyrant is the happiest person. Socrates points out that Thrasymachus has challenged the whole conduct of living.

Socrates repeats the point that an art is practiced for the benefit of those for whom its services are intended and not for the benefit of the practitioner. Any payment received for practicing an art is independent of the aim of the art. In ruling, the benefit is for the ruled, not the ruler. No one rules willingly; people accept the responsibility only because they fear to be ruled by a worse person. Thrasymachus replies that ideal justice is a virtue that a person of intelligence cannot afford, whereas what is called "injustice" is in reality only good prudence. Under questioning, Thrasymachus admits that the just person does not try to get the better of other just people, but rather of unjust people who are the individual's opposites. "Get the better of" appears to mean "take advantage of" in the widest possible sense. Even to instruct someone is somehow to take advantage of him. In a vein much like the one taken above, Socrates argues that in every form of knowledge and ignorance (every art or its lack), the person who knows tries to benefit those who do not know, not those who know. When the ignorant are in control, not knowing the art, they do not know in what way to practice it or on whom. Hence, they try to get the better of all—be they wise or ignorant.

For Socrates, knowing one's art and for whom it is intended is a sign of virtue. "Virtue" appears to mean "the proper function of anything"; what the proper function of a thing is, however, demands appropriate study and knowledge. Those who are just try to get the better of only those who are unjust and of no others, whereas the unjust try to get the better of all. The latter, then, are the ignorant and the ineffectual; the former, the intelligent, and hence the wise and the good. The soul's virtue is found in proper rule of the individual. Just people with knowledge can rule themselves and others, whereas unjust men, factitious, disrupted, and not knowing what to do and what not to do, can rule neither themselves nor others.

The first book ends as Socrates reminds his disputants that they have been getting ahead of themselves; it is a bit foolish to talk about justice (a virtue) when they have not yet defined it.

The State

In book 2, Glaucon and Adeimantus press Socrates to prove that the just life is worth living, and Glaucon illustrates his wish by means of the legend of the ring of Gyges. Gyges, so the story goes, gained possession of a ring that when turned made its wearer invisible. With this advantage, he was able to practice evil with impunity. Socrates is to consider an individual with the advantage of Gyges and contrast him with a person who is his opposite. It is his task to show that the life of the just person, no matter what indignities are suffered, is worth living and that it is preferable to that of Gyges. He is to show that virtue is its own reward no matter what the consequences.

Socrates, with misgivings, takes on the task. He suggests, inasmuch as they are searching for something not easily found, justice, that they turn to a subject that will most readily exhibit it. The state is analogous to the individual, and justice, once found in the state, will apply also to its counterpart, the individual.

He begins his quest by a kind of pseudohistorical analysis of the state. People are not self-sufficient and thus cannot supply themselves with all the necessities of life. However, by pooling their resources, and by having people do what they are best suited to do, they will provide food, shelter, and clothing for themselves. The city that these people create then engages in exporting and importing, sets up markets, and steadily advances from its simple beginnings. From simple needs, the people pass increasingly to luxurious wants. Because the necessities of life are no longer sufficient, the people turn to warfare to accumulate booty. Armies are needed and a new professional is born: the soldier, with appropriate characteristics. The soldiers must be as watchdogs, gentle to their friends and fierce to their enemies. (Note that in discussing the characteristics of the soldiers, a spirited group that forms only a part of the state, and analogously, a

spirited part of the individual, Socrates suggests a feature formerly given as a possible definition of justice.) The soldier must know his friends, the citizenry, and his enemies, the barbarians, and be good to the one and harm the other. This may be an aspect of justice, but it is not the complete definition. The state also needs rulers, or guardians, who are to be carefully selected and trained.

Plato holds music and gymnastics to be a significant part of the guardian training. He concludes book 2 and takes up much of book 3 with arguments for censorship of the tales of Hesiod and Homer, especially any wherein the gods, who ought to be examples of noble, virtuous beings, are presented as deceitful, lustful, brutal, and petty. He believed that Greek society was in decline, that moral behavior was no longer understood or practiced by the Athenians, and that, to a large measure, the degrading tales of the gods were responsible. He no doubt mistook a symptom for a cause. The moral decline of a people involves many things of which trashy literature is only a sign; the desire for such things cannot be cured by censorship. He thought that the young imitate in their behavior the activities they perceive in the imitative arts. If they read stories in which the "heroes" are immoral, if they see plays in which the protagonists are effeminate and slavish, then they will tend to act similarly. Plato argues that the guardians may know of such people, but to act as they do will bring about bad habits. Furthermore, to imitate means to do or be more than one thing—that is, to be both that which one imitates and also one's own self—and in this society it is enough to do or be one thing and that well.

In order to convince the inhabitants of this state that people are fit for one and only one job—to be either guardians (rulers), auxiliaries (soldiers), or workers—the rulers will institute a "noble lie." This lie or myth will be to the effect that people are molded by the gods to be one of the three types noted. Plato likens these classes to gold, silver, and bronze and holds that the people are to look on themselves as having these "metals" in their makeup from birth. There will be some "mobility" between classes if ability is discovered, but generally they will remain static.

In book 4, Socrates holds that the city should be neither too wealthy nor too poor, neither too large nor too small, neither too populous nor too scarcely populated. It should be a place where men and women have equal opportunity and where each person does the task for which he or she is best suited. Such a city will be wise and brave, temperate and just. These are the cardinal virtues, and therefore, we are well on our way toward finding in the city those virtues we had hoped to see in the individual.

In the city, wisdom is found in the rule of the guardian; in the individual, in the rule of intelligence. To function properly, we saw, is to be virtuous. This, to Plato, is the essence of wisdom, especially since acting virtuously takes knowledge. Courage is a way of preserving the values of the city through education. Knowing what to fear and what not to fear, a knowledge gained through law, characterizes courage. Temperance is a kind of order; the naturally better part of the soul controls the worst part, as in the city the naturally superior part governs the inferior. Thus, the intelligence of the few controls the passions of the many, as people's intelligence governs their appetites through their will. Justice, lastly, is found in the truth that each one must practice the one thing for which one's nature is best suited. To do one's "business" and not to meddle with others, to have and to do that which is one's own—that is justice. Although within the class of artisans there may be some mixing of tasks—the carpenter may perform some other craft—there cannot be mixing of the classes of gold, silver, or bronze.

The Three Waves

In book 5, Plato discusses the "three waves" that are needed if the ideal state is to be possible. The rulers are to be selected from those who show the proper aptitude, women as well as men. This is the first wave. The second wave is that communal life must be shared by the ruling class. Marriage and children will be held in common. All within a certain age group are to be designated "parents," a younger group, "children" and "brothers and sisters," and so on. Plato argues that family loyalty is an asset that, when practiced on a public scale, will retain its value, whereas the deficits of private family life, such as the factiousness between families, will be eliminated. "Mine" and "not mine" will apply to the

same things. The ruler will arrange communal marriages by lot; unknown to the betrothed, however, the lottery will be fraudulently arranged for reasons of eugenics. Another myth or lie is told for the state's benefit. The third wave, and most difficult to bring about, is that philosophers must be kings, or kings, philosophers. If this can occur, then political power and intellectual wisdom will be combined so that justice may prevail.

In books 6 and 7, Plato presents three analogies to illustrate parts of the three waves. Plato believed that those features that objects of a certain kind have in common, for example, the features common to varied art objects, all beautiful, are all related to a single perfect ideal, or form, which he called "the feature itself," in this case "beauty itself." This is an intellectual reality properly "seen" by the rational element of the soul, just as the many instances are perceived by sight or by means of the other senses. The good itself, the highest of all forms, is the proper object of the philosopher's quest.

In his first analogy, Plato likens the good to the sun. Just as the sun provides light so that people can see physical objects, the good provides "light" so that the soul may perceive intellectual forms.

Plato's second analogy also emphasizes the distinction between the senses and the rational element of the soul as sources of knowing. Imagine a line whose length has been divided into two unequal parts; furthermore, these parts are then divided in the same proportion as the first division. If the line is labeled AE, the first point of division C and the other two points of the subdivisions B and D, then the proportions shown in the diagram hold. Hence $BC = CD$.

$$\frac{CE}{AC} = \frac{DE}{CD} = \frac{BC}{AB}$$

Now what do these segments represent? The first segment of the original line with its two segments Plato styles "the world of opinion," and he calls the first of its segments "conjecture" (AB) and the second "belief" (BC). We gain information regarding this world through our senses. We pass from creatures who let the world come to us with little or no thought, only conjecture—a world of shadows and reflections—to persons who have beliefs as to what the shadows represent—a world of physical objects such as trees, hammers, and houses.

The second segment of the original line is titled "the world of knowledge," and its sections "understanding" and "thinking" respectively; this is the world of forms mentioned in the analogy of the sun. Plato considers mathematics the mental activity most characteristic of *understanding* by the use of images. In geometry, there is, among other things, an attempt to define precisely the various mathematical figures (circle, triangle, square, and so forth). Unlike the world of physical objects, which is mutable, these definitions, which state the formal properties of these objects, are unchanging. In *thinking*, one finds the highest form of mental activity: dialectical thought, or thinking by the use of ideas. From contemplating the unchanging forms or ideas of physical things, the mind progresses to the reality of perfect beauty, justice, and goodness. The process of education in the perceptual world moves from bare opinion through belief, a practical rather than a theoretical understanding of the truths of the world of things seen, to understanding and thinking, wherein the eternal truths of the world of things thought are known.

Plato's third analogy is that of the cave. Imagine prisoners chained in a cave in a way that all they can see is a wall in front of them. On the wall, shadows appear cast from a parapet behind them where a fire burns and where bearers carry all sorts of objects. This is, of course, analogous to the world of shadows (sense experience) represented by the segment *AB* of the divided line. Miraculously, a prisoner frees himself and sees the cause of the images and the light that casts them; he is in the world of belief. Noticing an opening that leads out of the cave, he crawls into the sunlight, the world of forms, and is so dazzled that he is blinded. However, gradually he adjusts to the light, sees the true reality, the realm of ideas, and is tempted to remain there forever. However, he is compelled by a sense of obligation to return to the cave and to instruct the chained. They disbelieve, for all they know is the world of gloom and shadows, and they would jeer him, or worse, tear him to pieces; but he persists and rededicates his life to their instruc-

tion. Thus the philosopher, having the world of forms for his contemplation, must return to be king, to rule by a sense of duty, if there is to be justice.

Plato outlines an educational program for the philosopher-king that continues from the music and gymnastics taught the guardians. For ten years, he studies arithmetic, geometry, solid geometry, and astronomy. He is in the realm of understanding, and the point of his mathematical training is to prepare him for study of and grasp of ideal forms. For five years, he studies dialectical thought so that the ultimate principle of reason, the form of good, shall be known to him. Then, at the age of thirty-five, he begins his period of practical application of these principles, and after fifteen years, he ascends the throne at fifty.

The Decline of the State

In book 8, Plato discusses the decline of the state, which is paralleled by the decline of the individuals who make it up; the state is analogous to the individual. From the rational state, one moves to the spirited one (the guardians), the chief virtue of which is honor. When the spirited element is again dominated by appetites, then wealth is sought and the oligarchy born. From wealth, one goes to the government of the many who, overthrowing the few, proclaim the virtues of the group. Appealing to the mob, the demogogue takes over, and the full decline of the ideal state and its members has occurred.

There is a weird similarity; from love of reason to insatiable lust, the state and the individual have degenerated. There is the rule of one in both cases, but people have gone from one who knows what to do and what not to do to one who knows nothing and whose every impulse is one's master. People of intelligence use their reason to direct their will and thus to control their appetites, but tyrants control nothing. Tyrants are controlled by their appetites. People who are slave to their appetites are masters of nothing; those who are masters of nothing are the most miserable of people. They are always in pain. Thus book 9 closes, with the passage from true pleasure to pain, from the just person to the unjust. Socrates has shown Glaucon and Adeimantus what the happy life, the just life, is.

Book 10 contains the famous Myth of Er and touches somewhat on what Plato means by "idea" or "form" and on the danger of art in the state. To each class of particulars that have something in common, Plato holds there is a form or idea in which these particulars participate and that gives them their common quality. The quality is a reflection of the idea, so a bed painted by an artist has as its model a physical bed that has in common with other beds the idea of "bedness" itself. There can be but one idea-form of beds, for if there were another, the two forms would have a third in which they would participate, and so on, ad infinitum. Plato's criticism of art as imitation was based on the claim that art is three steps removed from reality (because works of art are copies of the aspects of things and things are themselves copies of the ideas).

The *Republic* closes with an argument for the immortality of the soul. The soul's only illness is injustice; yet injustice is not fatal. By loving justice—by harmonizing reason, spirit, and appetite—people can keep their souls healthy, and the soul will prosper forever.

Theodore Waldman, updated by John K. Roth

Phaedrus

Type of philosophy: Metaphysics
First transcribed: Phaedros, middle period, 388-368 B.C.E. (English translation, 1792)
Principal ideas advanced:

◇ Lysias is reported by Phaedrus as having argued that it is better to be loved by one who does not love than by one who does, for the lover is moved by passion and can do harm.

◇ Socrates at first agrees that love is irrational and therefore harmful, but on reflection, he maintains that madness is sometimes divine and that love is a kind of divine madness.

◇ The soul is like a winged charioteer driving a team of horses; the charioteer, if inspired by love of the ideal, is reason or intelligence in control of the good horse (will) and the bad horse (passion).

◇ Souls that have seen the most of Being, having known the eternal forms or ideas of all things,

pass into the bodies of philosophers, or lovers of wisdom; souls that are disciplined and full of wisdom return to their heavenly home.

◇ Good rhetoric depends on having true knowledge; the Sophists are mistaken in claiming that the appearance of knowledge is all that is necessary.

Phaedrus was probably composed around 370 B.C.E., but the dramatic date of the dialogue is about 410 B.C.E., about ten years before the trial and death of Socrates. *Phaedrus* is a direct dialogue; that is, Plato does not use in this dialogue a narrator who retells a conversation of Socrates. The scene, a walk outside the walls of Athens to a shady spot along the banks of the river Ilissus, is an unusual setting for Socrates. There are only two characters, Socrates and Phaedrus; Phaedrus also participates in two earlier dialogues, *Prōtagoras* (early period, 399-390 B.C.E.; *Protagoras*, 1804) and *Symposion* (middle period, 388-368 B.C.E.; *Symposium*, 1701).

There are several possible answers to the question, "What is *Phaedrus* about?" Love, rhetoric, and philosophy are all possible answers because all three subjects are significantly involved in the dialogue. Love is the subject of all three of the set speeches included in *Phaedrus*; this does not, however, necessarily make love the subject of the dialogue. Rhetoric is examined and criticized, and proposals are made for a reformed rhetoric capable of serving philosophy. Perhaps the most significant feature of this dialogue is Plato's continuation of his effort to justify philosophy as the most worthy life of the soul against the opposing claims of the Sophists. The dialogue also presents a special method of philosophy, dialectic, which involves collection and division.

Love

Phaedrus opens with a meeting between Socrates and Phaedrus. Phaedrus has spent the morning listening to a speech of Lysias on the subject of love. Socrates accompanies Phaedrus to a shady spot along the river Ilissus where Phaedrus reads a copy of Lysias's speech.

Scholars disagree on the genuineness of this long speech attributed in the dialogue to Lysias. Whether this speech was actually written by Lysias, or whether it is a clever caricature by Plato, it illustrates the reasons for Plato's criticism of the rhetoric of the Sophists. The speech argues on the basis of self-interest the advantage of yielding to someone who does not love rather than to someone who does love. The basic reason offered for yielding to someone who does not love rather than to a genuine lover is that a lover is prevented by his passion from making careful calculations and is therefore likely to injure his beloved.

When Socrates criticizes this speech of Lysias as repetitious and inferior to what he has heard from others on the same subject, Phaedrus challenges Socrates to construct a better speech. Socrates reluctantly agrees. Because Socrates insists that successful deliberation must follow definition, he begins his speech with a definition of love as irrational desire directed toward physical beauty, analogous to gluttony, which is irrational desire directed toward food. From this definition, which is the basis for Lysias's speech but is not the definition Socrates develops in his second speech, Socrates concludes that the lover is more likely than the nonlover to harm the beloved. After this first speech, Socrates declares his remarks to be, along with Lysias's speech, foolish, irreverent, and blasphemous. Socrates then proposes to atone for his offence in treating love as evil by delivering a second speech.

Socrates begins his second speech by denying the assumption of the first two speeches that all madness is evil. He asserts that madness is divine rather than evil when it inspires prophets to foretell the future, when it heals the sick by ritual purification, and when it stimulates the poet to the frenzy of composition. Socrates then declares that he will prove love to be a fourth type of divine madness. The first step in this proof is the argument for the immortality of the soul. This argument, which rests on the nature of the soul as the self-moving principle of motion, recurs in book 10 of *Nomoi* (last period, 360-347 B.C.E.; *Laws*, 1804); but is not present in considerations of immortality in two other middle period (388-368 B.C.E.) dialogues, *Phaedōn* (*Phaedo*, 1675) and *Politeia* (*Republic*, 1701).

The Soul

Although the immortality of the soul is demonstrated by argument, the nature of the soul is described indirectly by one of the most famous of Plato's myths. The soul is compared to a winged charioteer driving a team of winged horses. All the horses and charioteers corresponding to the souls of the gods are good, but the pair of horses corresponding to the human soul has one good horse and one evil horse. The souls travel through the heavens, but human souls lose their wings, fall to earth, and join bodies to form living beings. The three parts of the human soul are the same as those mentioned in the *Republic*: the winged charioteer corresponds to reason, the good horse to will or spirit, and the bad horse to the passions.

No human souls are able to follow the chariots of the gods to the place where true Being dwells, where the souls of the gods see with the eye of reason such forms or ideas as justice, temperance, and knowledge. In no human soul are the horses so completely under the control of the charioteer that the fullest vision of true Being can be achieved. However, some souls rise higher and thus come closer and see more than the others before falling back and losing their wings. The type of life assigned to a human soul at birth depends on how close the soul has come to the full vision of Being. Souls that have seen the most enter into the bodies of philosophers. Then, in descending order, souls that have seen less of Being enter into the following types of persons: a law-abiding ruler, a statesman, an athlete or physician, a prophet, a poet, a farmer, and finally the two lowest types, a Sophist and a tyrant.

After each period of a thousand years, a soul enters another human form until it finally regains its wings. Between the end of one life and the beginning of the next is a period of reward or punishment as earned in the previous life. It is possible for a human soul after the first life to be born in an animal, and for a human soul that has been born in an animal to be again born in a person. However, all souls born into human beings must have had some vision of Being because only this vision of the forms can explain how human souls can pass to universal concepts of reason from the particular impressions of the senses. For most souls, it takes ten thousand years to regain wings and return to their heavenly home. A philosopher, however, who chooses the philosophic life three times regains wings in only three thousand years.

The love of beauty is called by Socrates the fourth and highest type of divine madness because one who pursues the beautiful things of this world is reminded of the vision of the form beauty and thus of the other proper objects of contemplation, justice, temperance, and the other forms. Through love, the soul begins to regain its wings. The struggle in the soul of the lover against the purely physical carnal desires is represented in the myth by the difficult struggle of the charioteer to subdue the behavior of the bad horse. The highest form of love results from the complete subjection of physical desires by both the lover and the beloved. The happiest lovers are those who achieve the philosophical life by the victory of the higher elements in their souls over the lower. Socrates concludes his second speech with a prayer to the god of Love by which he atones for the blasphemous attack on love of his earlier speeches.

Rhetoric

Phaedrus praises this speech of Socrates and then agrees with Socrates that there is nothing bad in writing a speech but only in writing a bad speech. Socrates then proposes to examine the nature of good and bad writing. According to Socrates, the first requirement of a good speech is knowledge. Phaedrus replies with the claim of the defenders of rhetoric that what is believed to be knowledge by the audience is required rather than genuine knowledge. Socrates points out that rhetoric as the skill of persuasion depends on misrepresenting things. In order to mislead successfully, the rhetorician must himself have knowledge. Socrates then turns again to Lysias's speech, which reveals Lysias's lack of knowledge and his inability to organize a speech properly. On the other hand, Socrates finds in his own two speeches an illustration of the philosophical method, dialectic. The method of dialectic, which also looms large in *Sophistēs* (later period, 365-361 B.C.E.; *Sophist*, 1804), *Politikos* (later period, 365-361 B.C.E.; *Statesman*, 1804), and *Philēbos* (last period, 360-347 B.C.E.; *Philebus*, 1779), involves collection and division. Collection of similars under a single form and the division of generic forms into more specific forms (the form of living thing into the form of plant and the form of animal) are essential to the definition that must begin successful discussion.

Socrates reviews for Phaedrus the claims of the teachers of rhetoric and urges that allowances be made for their mistaken claims, since their ignorance of dialectic prevents them from properly defining rhetoric. As a positive example, Pericles' superiority in rhetoric is explained by his study of the philosopher Anaxagoras.

The claim of the teachers of rhetoric that knowledge of the truth is not necessary because probability or likeness to truth is enough for success is again rejected. A successful orator must have knowledge of his subject, knowledge about his audience, and the ability to use the method of dialectic. Even then, competence will be achieved only by those who practice diligently. Wise people who become successful orators will not direct their skill toward other people but toward speaking what is pleasing to the gods. Speaking the truth rather than manipulating the audience is the goal of wise people. Writing on paper is inferior to writing in the soul of the learner because a written composition can easily fall into the hands of those who are unable to understand it. The dialogue ends appropriately with Socrates' prayer to the gods, a prayer that the inward life may not be hampered by outward possessions.

John Linnell

Meno

Type of philosophy: Epistemology, metaphysics
First transcribed: Menōn, middle period, 388-368 B.C.E. (English translation, 1769)
Principal ideas advanced:

◇ Meno asks Socrates how to acquire virtue, and Socrates questions him in order to discover the nature of virtue; but Meno either uses the term in his definitions, gives examples, or offers circular definitions.

◇ The question arises as to how anyone can inquire about that which one does not know, for it would seem that one must know what one is inquiring about.

◇ Socrates suggests that people's souls are immortal, and that in the course of their travels between reincarnations, the souls acquire knowledge of all things; acquiring knowledge in this life, then, is an act of recollection.

◇ Virtue can be taught if virtue is knowledge, but as there appear to be no teachers of virtue, virtue must be a gift of the gods.

Plato's *Meno* does not have the high dramatic quality characteristic of some of the other middle period (388-368 B.C.E.) dialogues, including *Symposion* (*Symposium*, 1701) and *Phaedōn* (*Phaedo*, 1675). In addition, the philosophical problem discussed in the dialogue (whether virtue can be taught) receives better handling in other dialogues; Plato's best account of this question is found in *Prōtagoras* (early period, 399-390 B.C.E.; *Protagoras*, 1804). Nevertheless, *Meno* is a well-known and important dialogue, for it is the *locus classicus* of one of Plato's most important philosophical doctrines—the doctrine of recollection.

Defining Virtue

The dialogue opens with Meno asking Socrates how one acquires virtue. Socrates replies that this question cannot be settled without first reaching agreement on a prior one, namely, what the nature of virtue is. As usual, Socrates professes not to know what virtue is, and, furthermore, he says that he has never met anyone else who knows. Meno naïvely remarks that Gorgias knew, to which Socrates replies that he has "forgotten" what Gorgias said. Meno then agrees to act on Gorgias's behalf and to inform Socrates of what Gorgias held virtue to be. This, of course, sets up a view that Socrates can examine and refute by his usual method of question and answer.

Meno's first attempt at defining virtue turns out to be inadequate. Instead of offering a definition of virtue, he identifies what a man's virtue is and what a woman's virtue is, then says that each person has his or her own peculiar virtue. Virtue is relative to the person and the condition in which the person is situated. The idea that a thing's "virtue" is its *function*, mentioned here, is made explicit in *Politeia* (middle period, 388-368 B.C.E.; *Republic*, 1701). Meno's proposed definition fails because it does not define the term "virtue." He offers several other definitions, which can be summarized as the "virtue of *X* is *Y*." He does not recognize that all of these presuppose some common meaning for the word "virtue" itself. Socrates, by citing a number of analogous

cases, finally gets Meno to see what is involved and to offer a second definition.

Meno's second proposal is that virtue is the "power of governing mankind." This second definition does not have the same inadequacy as the first, but it still will not do, for the obvious reason that not all people govern others. Virtue must be possible for everyone, but if virtue is the power of governing, then it can be achieved only by the governors and must remain beyond the reach of the governed.

At this point, Meno slips into enumerating specific virtues, a mistake made by many of the people Socrates interrogates in the Platonic dialogues. Socrates then illustrates the kind of definition he is after by giving Meno an example of a proper definition for "figure" (in the geometrical sense).

For a third time, Meno makes an attempt to define "virtue," this time by saying that "virtue is the desire for honorable things and the power of attaining them." By cross-examining Meno, Socrates draws out the implications of his statement, showing it to be a circular definition. It amounts to saying that virtue is the power of achieving good with justice. That this is circular, in a sense, follows from Meno's admission that justice is one of the virtues. What it comes to, then, is this: Meno is saying that virtue *generally* is the power of achieving good in a *specifically* virtuous manner. This will not do, for "a specifically virtuous manner" is meaningless as long as "virtue generally" remains undefined.

At this point, Meno confesses his confusion, but he tries to lay the blame on Socrates; it is characteristic of Socrates, he says, to confuse those who talk with him—Socrates is like the torpedo fish who paralyzes all with whom he comes into contact. Socrates accepts the comparison provided he can add a qualification concerning a respect in which he differs from the torpedo fish. The torpedo fish itself is not paralyzed when it comes into contact with another fish; Socrates, by contrast, is just as ignorant as those with whom he argues. However, if this is so, Meno observes, there seems to be no point in trying to learn anything at all. He raises the stock puzzle of the Sophists: "How can one inquire about what one does not know; and if one already knows it, why should he inquire about it?"

The Theory of Recollection

In reply to this puzzle, Socrates puts forth the theory of recollection. He says that he heard from "certain wise men and women who spoke of things divine" that people's souls are immortal and undergo an endless cycle of deaths and rebirths. In the course of these endless rebirths, people's souls come to know all things, both in this world and in the other world. Knowing, therefore, is not a matter of acquiring something new but rather a matter of recollecting something known but forgotten. Meno is fascinated by this idea and asks if Socrates can prove it. Socrates does not offer a direct proof of the theory, but he does offer what is supposedly an illustration of it by getting Meno's slave boy, who has been given no training in mathematics, to construct a proof in geometry merely by answering certain questions Socrates puts to him.

The proof itself is fairly simple but not at all obvious. The problem is to determine how long the side of a square must be if its area is to be twice the area of a given square. Socrates diagrams a square and arbitrarily sets the side equal to two units. The area of the original square is, of course, four square units. Using the diagram, Socrates next shows the boy what the diagonal is. Then he asks the boy how many units long the sides of a square twice the area of the original square will be; that is, a figure that has an area of eight square units. At first the boy says that the side of the required figure will be four units long, but under questioning, and by referring to the diagram, he sees that this answer would yield a square whose area is sixteen square units rather than eight. He then guesses that the side of the required square should be three units long, but again he recognizes that this is not the answer because it yields a figure with an area of nine square units. Finally, he sees that by constructing a square on the diagonal of the original figure he will have the required solution, a square whose area is twice the area of the original one. Socrates, without telling the boy the answer, has elicited it merely by asking questions.

Socrates points out to Meno that the boy could not have learned the solution subsequent to his birth because he has never been given any instruction in geometry, nor did Socrates himself tell the boy the solution. Therefore, the boy must have known the solution all along, and Socrates' questions served merely as an occasion for the boy's recalling what he knew but had forgotten. The point of the example is to refute the claim of the Sophists that nothing can be learned. In spite of the apparent self-evidence of their paradox, the fact is that ignorant people can come to know something as a result of intellectual inquiry. It is better to engage in inquiry, even if it merely reveals that a proposed solution is inadequate, than it is to imagine that there is no value at all in intellectual inquiry.

Teaching Virtue

The discussion is shortly brought back to the original topic, whether virtue can be taught. Meno wants Socrates' own view of the matter. However, Socrates replies that he cannot deal directly with this question. He must, he says, first lay down a *hypothesis* because he and Meno have not yet defined "virtue." Considerable discussion has centered around what Socrates says here about hypotheses. He gives, as an example of a hypothesis, another illustration taken from geometry. He says that a geometrician, if asked whether a certain triangle can be inscribed within a given circle, may answer that he must first lay down a hypothesis. One scholar suggests that Socrates means that some geometrical problems are not susceptible to a general solution—only when some restriction is laid down is a solution possible. However, it is not necessary to pause here in an effort to determine all the niceties of the proper interpretation of the passage. The development of the dialogue can be seen without having to establish Plato's meaning in all its technical detail. The point is this: Socrates is willing to discuss the question whether virtue can be taught if Meno will grant the restriction that virtue is knowledge. This must be granted as an initial assumption (hypothesis) before the discussion can proceed. Meno agrees to the restriction.

Once it is granted that virtue is knowledge, the conclusion that it can be taught follows easily; indeed, the conclusion seems trivial. However, it raises another question that is not trivial; namely, who are the teachers of virtue? Meno suspects that there must be some such teachers, but Socrates again professes ignorance; he has found none. However, perhaps, Socrates suggests, Anytus, who is listening to the conversation, can tell Socrates and Meno who the teachers of virtue are.

Anytus has no uncertainties; of course there are teachers of virtue, but they are not to be found among the Sophists (such as, for example, Gorgias). Any Athenian gentleman is a fine teacher of virtue. (It adds to the irony of this part of the dialogue to know that Anytus was the leader of the group of Athenian "gentlemen" who prevailed on Meletus to bring the charges that led to the conviction and execution of Socrates.) However, Socrates wants to know who taught these Athenian gentlemen who teach virtue. Obviously, Anytus responds, a previous generation of Athenian gentlemen taught them. Plato does not pursue this matter; it is clear enough to any reader that this answer leads to a troublesome regress. However, on other grounds, Socrates is not satisfied with this general answer. He grants that there have always been good people to be found in Athens. However, if one takes time to look at the particular histories of some of these good Athenians and their sons, he finds many cases where the father has taken care to have his sons instructed in such things as horsemanship or wrestling, and the instruction has been successful. Yet in the matter of virtue, either the sons have received no instruction or else the instruction has not achieved its purpose, for the sons have turned out to be considerably less virtuous than the fathers. Themistocles and Pericles are good examples.

Anytus's argument has been shown to be inadequate, and he recognizes the fact, but instead of pursuing the question in the proper spirit, he loses his temper and issues a pointed warning to Socrates to watch his step in criticizing the Athenian aristocracy in this way. Socrates, in good-humored fashion, returns to Meno.

It seems, Socrates points out, that the outcome of the investigation into whether virtue can be taught is finally negative, in spite of the previous restriction. For if there are no teachers of virtue and no scholars of virtue, then the apparent conclusion is that virtue must not be capable of being taught. Perhaps, however, another possibility should be examined. Perhaps true opinion is just as good a guide for action as is knowledge. Perhaps people can become virtuous by holding true opinions. The only drawback to this theory is

that true opinions are like the statues of Daedalus—they are very valuable, but unless they are tied down they walk away. True opinions must be tied down by recollection of the truth; that is, true opinion must become knowledge. People can get along by holding true opinions that they get from great statesmen and poets, but true opinion must be converted into knowledge in order to become completely adequate. Virtue, then, is not something that is taught nor something that people have "by nature" (as the Sophists held). It is, finally, a gift from the gods. This is the explicit conclusion of the dialogue. However, Plato obviously expects the reader to amend this conclusion on his own. Plato expects the reader to recognize that knowledge and virtue are identical, and that it is really knowledge that is the gift of the gods.

The Soul

There is no doubt that Plato held a doctrine of recollection. References to it are to be found throughout Plato's writings, and it lies at the center of his theory of knowledge. The debate concerns just what the theory of recollection amounted to for Plato. Specifically, did Plato's belief in the doctrine of recollection include a belief in the preexistence of the soul? Scholars have given both affirmative and negative answers to this question. Regardless of how one settles this question, however, the crucial point for Plato's theory of knowledge is that he held that knowledge is in some sense innate.

The evidence cited by those who say that Plato really did believe in the preexistence of the soul includes the following points: First, Socrates calls the doctrine a "glorious truth" in *Meno*; second, the Platonic view that the ideas are separate from the things of sense and that the soul knows the ideas implies that the separation of the ideas and the preexistence of the soul stand or fall together; and third, the first argument for the immortality of the soul that is given in *Phaedo* assumes the truth of the doctrine of the preexistence of the soul. Each of these claims must be countered if one is to conclude that Plato did not hold to the preexistence of the soul.

With reference to the first claim, that Socrates calls the doctrine a "glorious truth," one may make the following observations. Plato here adopts his standard technique for introducing a myth in presenting the doctrine in *Meno*; that is to say, he does not put the doctrine into the mouth of Socrates directly. Instead, he has Socrates say that he heard this from certain poets and wise people. This is the device Plato repeatedly uses when he wishes to state a myth that expresses an important truth but that is not to be taken literally. Indeed, the emphasis in reading the words "glorious truth" seems to fall on "glorious" rather than on "truth," suggesting that the doctrine cannot readily be expressed in literal terms.

The second assertion that the separation of the ideas and the preexistence of the soul go together is too strong. Certainly no one can deny that Plato asserted the separation of the ideas and that he believed the soul was the element in a person who knows the ideas. However, Plato might very well hold these views without also holding that the soul existed before its incarnation in the body.

The third claim, that the first argument for immortality in *Phaedo* assumes the preexistence of the soul, neglects the fact that the first two arguments of *Phaedo* are questioned in that dialogue, and that the conclusion of *Phaedo* is finally made to rest on the claim that the soul is *essentially* alive; at the approach of its essential opposite, death, the soul either retires or is annihilated. Furthermore, the conclusion of *Phaedo* is that the belief in immortality is reasonable, not certain. Plato argues that the belief in immortality is consistent with other commonsense beliefs. The conclusion of *Phaedo* rests on *agreed* premises; Plato never claims that they are incontrovertibly *true*, as anyone who takes seriously the account of Socratic method given in *Phaedo* should immediately recognize.

If the foregoing arguments are sound, the most plausible conclusion is that it is impossible to determine whether Plato held that the theory of the preexistence of the soul was a necessary part of the doctrine of recollection. However, if this is the case, the question arises: Why, then, does he mention the preexistence of the soul? Given that preexistence is part of the myth and that this means that an important truth is being expressed—though not necessarily in literal language—the proper interpretation comes readily to mind. Plato means to say by his doctrine of recollection that knowledge is not learned but is in some sense innate. Undoubtedly Plato, who wrote his philosophy before Aristotle had made logic into an independent discipline, was not so sophisticated in logical matters as were philosophers who followed him. It would be highly unreasonable, therefore, to expect him to have recognized the significance of the relation of logical implication. A modern philosopher might say of the slave boy's demonstration that he recognized, under appropriate questioning, the logical implications of the geometrical situation Socrates diagramed, and that the ability to recognize such implications is innate. Such a view represents the spirit of the rationalist tradition in philosophy as it was given expression by such important thinkers as René Descartes and Baruch Spinoza. Plato's myth, it seems, is his expression of the rationalist's insight, an insight that had to wait for greater logical sophistication before it could be expressed properly. Plato had the insight, but he lacked the appropriate apparatus for expressing it in terms that present-day philosophers easily recognize.

Regardless of how one interprets the theory of recollection as it is presented in *Meno*, there can be no disagreement that *Meno* is an important element in the Platonic corpus. The subject of the dialogue, the relation between virtue and knowledge, is central to Plato's ethical views; the use of illustrations from geometry to clarify knowing reflects Plato's underlying mathematical bias; and the theory of recollection itself is closely tied to the central Platonic doctrine, the theory of ideas. *Meno* is a first-rate introduction to the thought of one of the truly great thinkers in the history of Western civilization.

Robert E. Larsen, updated by John K. Roth

Phaedo

Type of philosophy: Metaphysics
First transcribed: Phaedōn, middle period, 388-368 B.C.E. (English translation, 1675)
Principal ideas advanced:

◇ The philosopher is always pursuing death, for the body hinders the soul's search for knowledge, and death brings about a separation of body and soul.

◇ The philosopher attempts to acquire knowledge of the ideas—those eternal forms that are copied by individual things—but to gain such knowledge, the philosopher must practice a kind of death, freeing the soul so that it can discover ideas.

◇ Surely the soul survives the death of the body, for opposites are generated out of opposites, and life is the opposite of death.

◇ Furthermore, people possess certain ideas (such as the idea of equality) that could not have been acquired in this life; hence, people must have existed, as souls, prior to being born; people recollect the ideas encountered before birth.

Phaedo is Plato's literary and philosophical monument to the death, and to the life, of his master, Socrates. An excellent way to begin the study of philosophy is with this account of the end of the first member in the great trio in Greek thought, as written by the second. It describes the philosophic way of life as Socrates and, consequently, Plato saw it, explaining how the philosopher, so unlike other people in many ways, differs also in being unafraid of death. Its account of the soul's immortality ranges from the fanciful myth about the various destinies of good and evil souls to what is perhaps Socrates'—and certainly Plato's—most fundamental theory, the doctrine of forms. Although *Phaedo* must be complemented by the other Platonic dialogues in order to round out the picture of Socrates as a man and as a philosopher, it suggests powerfully the influence he and Plato jointly exercised in the history of Western thought.

The work consists of one dialogue within another: At the request of a friend, Phaedo recounts the conversation between Socrates and his companions and the final events of the day Socrates' unjust death sentence is executed. The inner dialogue occurs chiefly between the master and two of the several followers present, Simmias and Cebes. Quite naturally the talk turns to the true philosopher's attitude toward death.

Socrates' View of Death

Because Socrates appears willing to die and to justify this willingness, the question is raised: Is

suicide legitimate? Socrates' answer is that because we belong to the gods, the occasion of our death is in their hands, not ours. However, Cebes objects that if life is divinely directed, its continuance is desirable and voluntary escape from it would be folly. Socrates explains, however, that he expects to enjoy the company of other good and wise gods and people after death.

However, a stronger defense of his position is requested. Socrates surprises his listeners by asserting that the philosopher is always pursuing death, and that it would therefore be most inconsistent, now that death is at hand, to shun it. Simmias laughingly agrees that most people think the philosophic life is and deserves to be a kind of death, but he desires clarification. Socrates explains that the philosopher seeks and enjoys the pleasures of the body—those of food, drink, sex, and adornment—only to the extent that they are necessary to life and beyond this despises them. The bodily senses, desires, and feelings hinder the soul's search for knowledge of true existence. Thought is clearest, then, when the influence of the body is felt least or when there is the greatest possible separation between body and soul ("soul" in this context includes "mind"). However, what is such separation, when completed, but death itself? Hence the philosopher—whose object is truth beheld with the clear eye of the soul, not with the befuddled vision of the physical organ—is constantly practicing a kind of death.

In elaborating this position, Socrates introduces the famous doctrine of forms, variously described as "essences," "absolutes," and "ideas." For each class of objects and qualities (or at least for many classes), there is an absolute form or essence that is the true nature and reality shared by particular members of the class. For example, there are absolute justice, beauty, goodness, greatness, health, and strength. A beautiful object, say, is beautiful not in itself but by participation to some degree in the very essence of beauty. Each absolute is pure or self-identical, unique, eternal, and perfect in its kind—because ultimately it *is* the kind in reality and not simply by definition for the sake of classification. A healthy person, for instance, typically becomes more or less healthy, and eventually loses health altogether in death, but health is what it is without relation to time. Particular things, Plato explains elsewhere, are real only on a secondary level because they are changeable and perishable; they exist only by virtue of the ideal patterns they so variously but never perfectly copy.

Socrates asks how such forms are known. Certainly not, strictly speaking, by the senses; with the eye we see only this or that imperfectly beautiful thing or observe persons merely more or less just, whereas beauty, justice, and the other absolutes are adequately apprehended only by an arduous and purely intellectual process: "He attains to the purest knowledge of them who goes to each with the mind alone, not introducing or intruding in the act of thought, sight or any other sense together with reason, but with the very light of the mind in her own clearness searches into the very truth of each." However, if forms are known by mind alone, wisdom concerning true being can mature only after death, when the mind is wholly freed.

The Soul

It has not yet been established that the soul survives; Cebes expresses the common fear that upon bodily death, the soul simply disperses into nothing. Socrates therefore offers a number of considerations supporting his confidence in immortality. One translator of the dialogue suggests that Plato does not attempt a logical proof of this belief, but even in the translation phrases such as "sufficient proof" and "logical necessity" occur. It is true, however, that the arguments used vary greatly in plausibility for a modern reader.

It is observable, Socrates holds, that all things that are "generated" or that come into and pass out of being are generated from their opposites. Particular (rather than absolute) opposites give way to each other: That which becomes weaker must have been stronger, the worse comes from the better, and so on. Thus one finds all through nature both opposite states and the processes of coming into them; otherwise, if all things passed into conditions from which there was no return, the universe would become utterly static. Imagine, for example, a world in which waking was followed only by sleeping, or in which the processes of composition were never varied by those of division. Granted this point, Socrates argues that since life and death and living and

dying are opposites, and it is certain that the living die, according to this universal law of nature the living must return from the dead, and therefore the dead must exist somewhere prior to return.

Cebes suggests that the same implication follows from Socrates' familiar account of knowledge as recollection: knowledge of true being (that is, of the forms) turns out to be a recognition of what was known in a previous existence. Take, for example, people's comprehension of equality. If people see two similar objects, they may judge that they are equal or nearly so, but how do they recognize this relative equality? Such a judgment presupposes a concept of equality per se to serve as a standard for comparison. The concept of perfect equality cannot be derived from sensory observation because physical objects are never precisely equal. At the same time, however—and here Socrates tempers the extreme rationalism of the earlier account of knowledge of absolutes—people are reminded of absolute equality by the sight of imperfectly equal things; sensation is thus a necessary but not a sufficient condition of this recognition. However, because people have sensation at birth, knowledge of essences must be prior to the present life; it is recollection of what people had once known and had forgotten when the soul took on a body. It is clear then that preexistence of the soul and that of the absolutes are equally certain.

Nevertheless, say Simmias and Cebes, we still have insufficient proof that the soul continues to exist *after* physical death. However, Socrates reminds them that the latter argument, plus the one concerning opposites, does prove the point, for if the soul exists before birth (that is, in a state of "death" relative to bodily existence) and the living come from the dead, even as the dead come from the living, the soul thus exists both before and after the various bodies into which it is born. However, noticing that Simmias and Cebes still evince the natural human uneasiness about the soul's future, Socrates adds another and perhaps sounder argument.

It hinges on comparison of the nature of the soul as compared with that of the body, and it concludes that if they are materially different, there is no reason to assign them a common fate. In general the composite or compound is unstable, subject to change and hence to dissolution, whereas the uncompounded or simple must be indissoluble, as are the invisible, simple, self-existent, and unchanging forms. Comparison of body and soul shows that body is like all other compound and perishable physical objects, but soul resembles the absolutes in some ways and presumably will share their permanence. This dichotomy of soul and body appears in the knowing process. If the soul relies on sensation, it is dragged down to earth, as it were—to the unstable and the confused; but if it relies on its own reason, it approaches the pure and eternal. Communion with the immutable breeds similarity: "The soul is in the very likeness of the divine, and immortal, and intellectual, and uniform, and indissoluble, and unchangeable."

This conclusion leads Socrates to descriptions of the soul's fate after death that approach and finally cross the border between philosophy and fiction, but which, like many of Plato's myths, allegorically state significant hypotheses and profound insights. The soul's future, he says, will depend on its degree of purity in the present. Those impure souls enthralled by love of sensual pleasures and by evil passions are so weighed down by the corporeal that they may be reincarnated in animals similarly miserable in nature, such as in asses or wolves. The moderately virtuous soul might be given the body of an admirable social animal such as the ant or the bee or perhaps even another human body. However, only those souls purified of all bodily taint through philosophy may enter immediately into the blissful company of the gods and escape further reincarnation.

Philosophy is thus not merely an academic discipline or a profession; in the Platonic view it is a way of life and even the soul's salvation. Socrates describes the soul as previously shackled to the body, hoodwinked by the senses, enslaved by its own desires. Worst of all, the soul is deceived about true reality by opinions influenced by pleasure and pain—it mistakes violence of emotion for evidence of truth. Philosophy offers release from this deception and teaches the soul to rely on its own intellectual resources. Thus, "she will calm passion, and follow reason, and dwell in the contemplation of her, beholding the true and divine."

Objections Raised and Countered

After the almost poetic heights Socrates reaches in this account, he displays the equanimity of the truly philosophical inquirer when Simmias and Cebes still have serious doubts that he encourages them to broach. Simmias's objection presupposes the Pythagorean concept of the soul as a sort of harmony or attunement of the elements of the body, obtaining when these are in proper tension or proportion. By analogy to his previous arguments, Socrates would have to argue that the harmony of a lyre—which harmony is also invisible, perfect, and divine—could survive the destruction of the instrument. However, the absurdity of this suggests the absurdity of the belief that the soul exists when the body is destroyed. Cebes adds that while the soul may survive several deaths and reincarnations, it is possible that it finally wears out as does a body that has survived several coats.

These objections seem so cogent to the audience, just now persuaded by Socrates' train of thought, that a despair of the success of any argument whatever sets in. However, Socrates warns his friends of the dangers of misology; just as one may become a misanthropist by overconfidence in people, followed by disillusionment, so may one learn to distrust all argument by accepting conclusions hastily and without sufficient attention to logic, only to discover their falsity later. However, instead of adopting a cynically skeptical position that no arguments are valid, no truths about reality discoverable, one should think that the difficulty is one's lack of ability, which can be improved by further effort. It is fallacious to attribute the invalidity of one's own thinking to reason itself, and folly thus to forfeit the very possibility of learning the truth.

Socrates then proceeds to answer Simmias's objection by showing that it is inconsistent with previous and present admissions. Harmony or attunement is not prior to the elements organized or tuned, but the soul has been shown to exist prior to the body. Simmias cannot hold, therefore, both that knowledge is recollection and that the soul is harmony. Furthermore, harmony occurs in degrees; an instrument may be more or less in tune. However, people do not think that souls are more or less souls either in themselves or relative to others. Again, if the soul were a harmony, it could contain no vice, which is inharmonious, and consequently all souls would be equally good, which of course is absurd. Finally, if soul were a harmony of bodily elements, it would be dependent on them, but as a matter of fact, the soul, especially the wise one, acts as a governor of the body and hence is sometimes out of harmony with it.

To meet Cebes's objection that the soul may eventually deteriorate and vanish, Socrates appeals once more to the doctrine of forms to elaborate a theory of causation relevant to the problem. In his youth, he remembers, he studied physicalistic and mechanistic theories of causal explanation of human life and behavior. However, the detail (and presumably the mutual inconsistencies) of these frustrated and confused him. A gleam of hope appeared in the Anaxagorean view that mind (as universal rather than human) orders and causes all things, which philosophy Socrates thought would show that everything was ordered for the best. If one wished to discover the ultimate causes for the shape of the earth, the positions and movements of the heavenly bodies, one need only refer to the highest good that these arrangements serve. However, to his disappointment Socrates found Anaxagoras falling back on the familiar physical causes.

These offer partial but inadequate explanation of his own present behavior, Socrates continues. Of course he is engaging in his present activities in prison by means of bones, muscles, and their functions, but these are not the true causes of his behavior, which are that the Athenians have condemned him to die and he has thought it right to refuse escape and accept the penalty. Mechanistic philosophers ignore the distinction between conditions and causes (or between what Aristotle was later to call efficient and final causes); "of the obligatory and containing power of the good they think nothing." However, since Socrates claims that he has been unable to discover what the nature of the best is, he offers a substitute causal theory.

Although his procedure of adopting it may appear too rationalistic, further qualifications reveal much affinity to later scientific thought. His method is to select the theory judged most sound and then to accept or reject particular propositions by reference to it. However, the original hypothesis is not wholly arbitrary; it can be justified either by derivation from an established theory or (to judge from Socrates' practice) by examining its consequences for any inconsistencies. With this explanation, Socrates accounts for his present assumption of the theory of forms.

An implication of the theory is that participation in the forms accounts for the characteristics of objects; Socrates insists that for him this is the only intelligible *cause* assignable. Indeed, it applies to the very processes of becoming: There is "no other way in which anything comes into existence except by participation in its own proper essence." Two chief characteristics of forms are uniqueness and simplicity: They cannot admit their opposites. Furthermore, some particulars are so constituted that it is impossible they should admit forms opposite to those especially characteristic of their own natures; for example, the number two, having the form "even," cannot remain two and admit the form "odd." When one realizes that what renders body alive is soul and nothing else, it appears that soul has an essential relation to life and hence cannot admit its opposite, death, any more than fire can admit cold. Hence, again the soul has been proved to be immortal, this time to the satisfaction of all those present.

It follows, then, that the soul deserves the greatest care in the present life, preparatory to the next. Socrates proceeds to give an imaginative description of the details of life after death and the various regions good and evil souls will occupy. The orthodox Christian reader will find here a number of counterparts anticipating the traditions of heaven, hell, and even purgatory. Socrates adds, however, that "A man of sense ought not to say, nor will I be very confident, that the description which I have given of the soul and her mansions is exactly true. However, I do say that, inasmuch as the soul is shown to be immortal, he may venture to think, not improperly or unworthily, that something of the kind is true." The chief point is again that "there is no release or salvation from evil except the attainment of the highest virtue and wisdom."

Socrates' Death
That Socrates has by his own virtue and wisdom escaped the evil of fear of death is now abundantly evident. When the discussion is finished

and he has bidden his family good-bye, only Socrates among the entire assembly keeps his composure as the final preparations are made. Admonishing his friends to restrain their sorrow, Socrates quaffs the cup of poison as cheerfully as if it were wine.

Whether or not the reasoning associated with his attitude seems entirely valid, and some of it judged formally certainly is not, there is much in the Socratic teaching that is enduringly sound and recurrently fruitful. Some doctrines, such as that of the forms, may be rejected as metaphysics while renewed as logic or epistemology. However, theory aside, none can gainsay the value of Socrates' visionary courage, or fail to wish it perpetual in the human race. For an adequate intimation of the master's immortality, however, one must return to its original description by his most eminent disciple.

Marvin Easterling

Parmenides

Type of philosophy: Metaphysics
First transcribed: Parmenidēs, middle period, 388-368 B.C.E. (English translation, 1793)
Principal ideas advanced:

◊ Zeno has argued that if Being is many, it must be both like and unlike, which is impossible; but Zeno forgets that, although the universals likeness and unlikeness are not identical, particular things can be alike in some respect and unlike in some other respect.

◊ Socrates claims that there are absolute ideas (forms) of the just, the beautiful, the good, and the true; but perhaps there are no ideas of vile materials such as mud, hair, and dirt.

◊ Parmenides has various criticisms of the theory of ideas: If an idea is one and yet exists in many things, it is separated from itself; and if ideas cover things with only parts of themselves, anything partaking of smallness would be smaller than absolute smallness.

◊ Furthermore, Parmenides argues, the theory of ideas leads to an infinite regress of ideas, and if the ideas are absolute, they cannot be known by people.

◊ Parmenides then demonstrates his sophistical skill by arguing that if the one is, the one is not; and if the one is not, nothing is.

Parmenides is fascinating as a penetrating criticism of the theory of ideas, or forms, in its undeveloped state, as propounded by the youthful Socrates. According to the report given by Antiphon—a report of the conversation between Parmenides and Socrates, with some assistance from Zeno and Aristoteles—Socrates met Parmenides when the latter was about sixty-five years old and famous for his poem *Peri physeōs* (fifth century B.C.E.; *The Fragments of Parmenides,* 1869; commonly known as *On Nature*), in which he argued, with great ingenuity, that "All is one." It may very well be that this conversation occurred as reported, but what is more likely is that Plato, having heard that at one time young Socrates met the aging Parmenides, used this bit of historical information as a dramatic center about which to build a summary of Parmenidean criticism of his theory of ideas, taking some of the edge off the criticism by portraying Socrates as clever but immature in his thinking. Consequently, *Parmenides* serves as evidence that Plato was never entirely satisfied with the theory of ideas. Like all great philosophers, he kept coming back to his central thesis, subjecting it to critical scrutiny and modifying it in accordance with the discoveries of its weaknesses.

The presentation of the dialogue is somewhat complicated. Cephalus repeats an account originally given by Antiphon of the meeting between Parmenides and Socrates. The actual conversation presumably occurred several years earlier.

Socrates had gone with others to hear the writings of Zeno, who was visiting Athens with Parmenides. After hearing Zeno read from some of his writings, Socrates summed up Zeno's thesis as stating that "if being is many, it must be both like and unlike, and . . . this is impossible." The youthful Socrates then pointed out that this was simply a roundabout way of supporting Parmenides' doctrine that all is one, for to claim that Being is *not many* and to state that it *is one* is to make one and the same claim.

Zeno agreed with Socrates, but he defended himself by saying that his argument was designed to show the inconsistency in upholding the doctrine that Being is not one, but many.

Socrates then professed not to see the extraordinariness of saying that things could be both like and unlike. It would be paradoxical, he agreed, to say in regard to the *idea* of likeness that it could somehow partake of unlikeness; after all, the likeness that things might share could not in itself, as an absolute nature, be unlikeness. However, things—as distinguished from absolute ideas, or natures—could very well be alike in some respect or to some degree and unlike in some other respect or degree. To say that things are one simply because it is possible to speak of them as partaking of the idea oneness, while at the same time they might, in some other respect, partake of the idea of the many, is only to utter a truism. The impression left by Socrates' argument was that the view held by Parmenides and Zeno might very well be trivial, nothing but a truism.

Absolute Ideas

Apparently both Parmenides and Zeno were upset and impressed by Socrates' criticism, but the venerable Parmenides had no intention of allowing Socrates to escape scrutiny of his own views. He began to probe Socrates' distinction between *ideas* in themselves (or kinds of things) and *things* of certain kinds (partaking of ideas). He drew from Socrates the admission that Socrates believed in ideas (such as the idea of likeness), which can be considered as distinct from that which partakes of the ideas. Socrates emphatically asserted that there are absolute ideas of the just, the beautiful, the good, and such matters, but he was not certain that there are ideas of man, fire, and water—and he was certain that there are no absolute ideas of such vile materials as hair, mud, and dirt. Nevertheless, Socrates did admit that he sometimes thought that there is an idea of everything—that even the most vile things partake of absolute ideas—but that he was afraid that this extreme view would turn out to be nonsensical. Parmenides replied, in a somewhat condescending manner, that Socrates' reluctance to extend his view was caused by Socrates' youth, that the time would come when he would "not despise even the meanest things."

Then, by using the language of things to talk about ideas, Parmenides attempted to show the difficulties of claiming that many things can partake of a single absolute nature or idea. If the whole idea is one and exists as one in many things, then it is separated from itself (resulting in a condition, Parmenides suggested implicitly, which would not be possible). Socrates responded by saying that the idea is like the day—"one and the same in many places at once." However, Parmenides then took advantage of this spatial metaphor to argue that just as a sail spread over many people covers each with only a part of itself, so an idea spread over many things would cover each with only a part—not the whole of itself. However, if ideas cover things with only parts of themselves, then things partaking of equality, for example, would in fact be partaking of less than equality (a part of equality); and things partaking of smallness would be partaking of part of smallness, and because a part is smaller than the whole of which it is part, the part would be smaller than the absolutely small (which is absurd). Hence, Parmenides concluded, there are difficulties in Socrates' view, whether the idea covers things as a whole or only in part. Socrates conceded that he had no ready answer to this criticism.

Another objection was then advanced by Parmenides. If one compares greatness (the idea) to great things, it would seem that, according to Socrates' way of thought, there must be another idea by reference to which greatness and great things can be seen to be alike in partaking of this second greatness. However, there is no end to this mode of analysis, and one begins to wonder about the method.

Further criticism by Parmenides led to the rejection of the suggestion by Socrates that the ideas might be only thoughts (for if the ideas are *only* thoughts, the thoughts have no objects; but if, on the other hand, the thoughts are of ideas, there are ideas).

Socrates then proposed that ideas are patterns and that to say that something partakes of an idea (or nature) means only that it fits the pattern, is like the pattern in some respect. However, Parmenides then used a variant of one of his former arguments to maintain that this view would involve another infinite regress of ideas (for the pattern would be like the copy in respect of a certain idea, and that idea would be like the pattern in respect of a third idea, *ad infinitum*).

Another difficulty involved in the claim that there are absolute ideas, Parmenides told Socrates, is that if the ideas are absolute and not relative to us, they cannot be known by us, since all our knowledge is relative to us. Furthermore, he went on, God surely has absolute knowledge, but if so, he cannot know human beings by reference to the absolute ideas that he has (for the relative cannot be understood by the absolute). Yet to know them in any other way would be to know them in an inferior fashion. Thus, in Socrates' view, God is either ignorant in part or knows in some inferior fashion.

All Is One

Having with his adept criticism made Socrates uncomfortable, Parmenides then gave the young philosopher advice concerning his profession. He suggested that Socrates follow the practice of considering the consequences of any proposed hypothesis and also the consequences of the denial of the hypothesis. Socrates asked for an example, and after some urging Parmenides agreed to illustrate the method he endorsed by considering the hypothesis that one is (that Being is one) and then that one is not (that Being is not one).

To follow the logical analysis then offered by Parmenides, who supposed that he was somehow getting at the nature of reality, it is necessary to understand what might be meant by the claim that all is one—a claim sometimes put by the alternative expressions, "One is" and "Being is one." To say that all is one may be to say that whatever *is* must be one with whatever is—at least in respect of being. (My eraser and pencil are one in that they both *are*—they both exist.) If one tries to think of something that does not exist, then it is either something that is not part of the one that is (for example, a mermaid)—or else, if it is something like empty space, then it *is* empty space; it has being, and is one with anything else that has being. If one then refuses to talk about anything at all except in terms of its being or not being, it is of course evident that everything that *is* is one with everything (else) that is. However, one should not say "else," or even "everything," because to do so involves making a distinction in terms of something other than being.

Once this game is started, it is easy to take advantage of the multiplicity of uses of the word "is" and of the word "one" to defend the claim

that "One is" or that "Being is one, not many." Parmenides was so skillful at this game that his fame persists to this day, and he was persuasive enough to impress both Socrates and Plato, partly because they themselves sometimes played similar games under the same misconception: that they were learning about reality metaphysically.

To show Socrates how philosophy should be practiced, Parmenides sought the aid of young Aristoteles to give him the right answers to the questions put by Parmenides. Considering first the alternative that one is, he quickly established that if one is, it cannot be many; if it cannot be many, it can neither be a whole nor have parts (because in either case, it would be many). Because only something other than the one could limit the one, if the one is, it has no beginning, middle, or end; hence, it is unlimited, formless, existing nowhere, neither resting nor moving, and never in anything. The one could not be the same as or different from itself or anything other than itself; it could neither be equal to nor unequal to itself, nor to anything other; it could be neither the same age as, nor younger than, nor older than itself nor anything other. Finally, Parmenides concluded that no mode of being could be attributed to the one; consequently, the one is not. The assumption that the one is had yielded the conclusion that the one is not.

Parmenides then explored the proposition that the one is not, but only after having decided that if the one is, it partakes of being; and if it partakes of being, it must have being in every part and be infinitely multiple, thus not one. Further considerations only enforced the conclusion that if the one partakes of any mode of being, it must be multiple and not one. However, if the one is not, and if there is consideration of the hypothesis that the one is not, then the meaning of the expression "If one is not" is known. Furthermore, there is not only knowledge of the one who is not, but the one who is not must be something if it can be considered; however, on the other hand, being cannot be attributed to the one because it is not. As that which is not, the one must be different from the others which are; it must be like itself, which is not. Working out the implications of various interpretations of the ambiguous claim that the one is not, Parmenides finally came to the conclusion that if the one is not, nothing is, and he finished by saying: "Let this much be said; and further let us affirm what seems to be the truth, that, whether one is or is not, one and the others in relation to themselves and one another, all of them, in every way, are and are not, and appear to be and appear not to be."

It is worth one's while to attend to the logical play (undertaken in dead seriousness) in the latter part of *Parmenides*, if only to learn what happens when a philosopher mistakes logical facts for facts about the world; and the uselessness of such analysis makes the earlier discussion, concerning the Platonic ideas, seem all the more important by contrast. One receives the impression that Plato (and Socrates) enjoyed the game that logic makes possible, but at the same time they tended to regard Sophistical skills as unimportant, even improper, when contrasted with the practice of true philosophy.

The following passage—elementary in its logical development but sparkling enough to impress his uncritical listeners, the youthful Socrates and the guileless Aristoteles—serves as a final example of the sort of wordplay that occupied Parmenides and led to his famous thesis that "all is one."

> The one which is not, if it is to maintain itself, must have the being of not-being as the bond of not-being, just as being must have as a bond the not-being of not-being in order to perfect its own being; for the truest assertion of the being of being and of the not-being of not-being is when being partakes of the being of being and not of the being of not-being—that is, the perfection of being; and when not-being does not partake of the not-being of not-being but of the being of not-being—that is the perfection of not-being.

"Most true," commented the guileless Aristoteles.

Ian P. McGreal

Theaetetus

Type of philosophy: Epistemology
First transcribed: *Theaetētos*, middle period, 388-368 B.C.E. (English translation, 1804)

Principal ideas advanced:

◇ Theaetetus suggests that knowledge is perception, and Socrates identifies the theory as the Protagorean view that humanity is the measure of all things; but because the Protagorean theory applies only to sensation and because it is possible to see without knowing what one sees and to know without seeing, the theory is unsatisfactory.

◇ The Protagorean doctrine that the world of sense experience is a flux is unacceptable to Socrates because if everything were flux, knowledge would be impossible, for knowledge involves the unchanging by reference to which the changing is understood.

◇ To understand the raw data of sense one must refer to ideas, the forms or natures of sensible things; thus, one could not know by perception alone.

◇ The proposal that knowledge is true opinion does not provide a criterion for deciding definitely whether an opinion is true; nor is it satisfactory to say that knowledge is true opinion supported by reasons, for such an account is circular.

Theaetetus is one of the finest of Plato's middle-period dialogues. It may well have been written as a tribute to the historical Theaetetus shortly after Theaetetus's death from wounds suffered in battle. This conjecture rests on the fact that the speakers who introduce the main dialogue, but play no other role, refer to the return of the dying Theaetetus. This event serves as an occasion for them to read together a report of a conversation that took place a number of years previously between Socrates and Theaetetus. At the time, Socrates was awaiting his trial, so we are to assume that Socrates was seventy years old and that Theaetetus was a youth of about sixteen.

The dialogue proper opens with a conversation between Theodorus (Theaetetus's teacher) and Socrates in which Theodorus praises Theaetetus highly. Socrates is impressed, and he calls the boy over to converse with him to see if Theodorus's estimate is a fair one. Socrates tells Theaetetus of his occupation as an intellectual midwife and requests Theaetetus to let him use his art to see if Theaetetus will give birth to anything. The boy responds eagerly but respectfully, and the philosophical portion of the dialogue gets under way.

Knowledge as Perception

Socrates asks Theaetetus for a definition of knowledge, and Theaetetus replies that knowledge is perception. This possibility is then examined. Socrates, using his customary question-and-answer technique, proceeds to make the definition more precise. He begins by identifying the theory as that of Protagoras. With this identification, the theory is recognized as the familiar Protagorean view that humanity is the measure of all things. What the view comes to, Socrates states, is an identification of appearance with reality: "What *seems* or *appears* to me *is* to me." The world of knowledge is in some sense private to each knower. The theory is thus applied to sensation, which is interpreted as an interaction or resultant of two elements, a sense stimulus and the sensory response. The stimulus is given status as something objectively real. Nevertheless, because each knower's sense organs are private and the knowledge one obtains is conditioned by this private character, the result is a private world of knowledge.

Socrates wishes to clarify the theory still more, however. To do so, he points out that certain puzzles can arise if the theory is not fully understood. There are three "laws" that seem to be true, yet incompatible with experience:

(1) No object can become greater or smaller without having something added to or subtracted from it.
(2) No object to which nothing is either added or subtracted is made greater or smaller.
(3) Any object that now is, but previously was not, must have suffered becoming.

Against the background of these three apparently self-evident laws, it seems impossible that Socrates can now be taller than Theaetetus but yet within a year be shorter than Theaetetus, unless Socrates himself undergoes some change in height.

The resolution of the apparent conflict between the facts (Socrates' first being taller, then shorter, than Theaetetus) and the three laws rests on recognizing that the theory of sensation Socrates has attributed to Protagoras differs from the theory of sensation that is presupposed in gener-

ating the puzzles. The three laws, when taken in conjunction with the fact of Socrates' becoming shorter than Theaetetus, produce the puzzle only when largeness and smallness are interpreted as nonrelational properties; that is to say, only when they are interpreted as absolute qualities that are inherent in an object without making any reference to another object. In Plato's *Phaedōn* (middle period, 388-368 B.C.E.; *Phaedo*, 1675), there is a suggestion that size is an absolute rather than a relational property, that Socrates is short because of the presence of shortness (the idea) in Socrates. In such a view, the comparison of Socrates and Theaetetus would involve one in saying that initially tallness was present in Socrates, and then, a year later (without Socrates having undergone any change), shortness is present in Socrates. If sensation yields knowledge of the real, and Socrates becomes shorter than Theaetetus in virtue of shortness replacing tallness, one cannot say that Socrates really remains unchanged—yet Socrates does remain the same height. The contradiction lies in saying that Socrates changes and that Socrates does not change.

The account of sensation developed in this dialogue, however, is that the sensation of Socrates' height is the result of an interaction between the sense stimulus and the sense organ. This is a more sophisticated account that, it should be noted, is intended to deal with sense experience, not with knowledge of the ideas. The ideas cannot be known by sensation, so a part of the problem—*really* knowing the tallness in Socrates—is dispelled. What can be sensed is the world of becoming, and this, for Plato and Socrates, is a world of flux, not the world that truly can be known.

However, the sensation—that which can be "known" on the basis of the theory under consideration—is a product of the interaction of an element from the flux with the private sense organ of an individual knower. The externally real combines with a private sense organ to give rise to sensation. The real, as Protagoras understood it, may very well be a collection of apparently contradictory qualities, but the world of "knowledge" is private because it is conditioned by the privacy of the knower's sense organs. All sense knowledge is relative to a particular knower at a particular time. Thus, there is no contradiction in saying that Socrates is taller than Theaetetus, but later is shorter than Theaetetus. There is no stable, unchanging background to give rise to the (apparent) contradictions. The "laws" are thus revealed as resting on the conviction that there is an abiding, changeless structure to the world of sensation. Once this abiding character is rejected in favor of a flux, the "laws" lose their point. The external world is a flux, the knower himself is in flux, and sensation is a product of the two. If either changes, there is a different sensation.

Socrates' Criticisms and Defense

The theory is now fully stated, and Socrates moves on to the criticism of it. He first makes some rather trivial objections. He points out, in the first place, that the theory does not justify taking *humanity* as the measure of all things. With just as good reason, one might take a pig or a horse as the measure, if knowledge is merely an interaction between a flux and a private sense organ. The criticism is not developed seriously; nevertheless, there is a purpose in making it. It suggests, without explicitly stating, a crucial element in the discussion of knowing; namely, that a judging mind is involved wherever there is a genuine case of knowing. A judging mind is precisely what a pig or horse lacks; thus, it is ridiculous to say that a pig is the measure of all things. The other criticisms Socrates makes at this time also imply the same point, that a judging mind must be included in any theory of knowing.

Three additional criticisms are made here:

(1) The theory, because it rejects any common world shared by two knowers, provides no justification for Protagoras's life as a teacher. Protagoras cannot justify his role as a teacher who corrects his pupils unless he is in some sense the measure of his pupils' worlds.

(2) Sensations cannot be all there is to knowing because this would imply that one who cannot read would nevertheless *know* what is said on a page of writing when he merely *sees* it. Yet this clearly is not the case.

(3) The theory would require one to deny that people who close their eyes know what they have just seen.

Socrates next undertakes to defend Protagoras against these criticisms. He states that Protagoras would regard the criticisms as irrelevant because what should be refuted is either the claim that people's sensations are private or the claim that the object causing the sensation is private. Still speaking on behalf of Protagoras, Socrates adds that the earlier criticisms missed the point and spirit of Protagoras's position.

Protagoras could offer a justification of his teaching by pointing to the analogous case of a physician. The physician does not deny the reality of his patient's (distorted) world; instead, he changes the condition of the patient so that the patient's world is changed (thus losing its distortion). The wine really is bitter to a sick person, but the physician makes the patient well so that the same wine tastes sweet to the recovered individual. (In a sense, this is to say that the sick Socrates is not the same man as the well Socrates.) We can admit that the wine is both bitter and sweet without thereby destroying the right of the physician to perform his beneficial work.

This justification, however, rests on restricting our concern to what is *useful* rather than on raising the question of what is *true*. Questions of *truth* concern the external object of knowledge; questions of *utility* can be restricted to the state of the knower. Protagoras, as teacher, can justify modifying the state of the knower without rejecting his claim that the object is a part of a private world in which there is no difference between what *appears* and what *is*. The earlier criticism has not touched Protagoras's real claim; namely, that which *seems* or *appears* to be true for an individual knower *is* true for that knower.

Further Criticisms

After a digression, Socrates turns to a more serious criticism of the position of Protagoras, one that takes into account the justification Socrates has offered on behalf of Protagoras. Socrates is quite willing to admit that the Protagorean position is a fair account of what occurs in immediate sensation. The world of becoming, for Plato and Socrates, is a flux, and people's sensations are private. One cannot taste the apple another person is tasting, nor does one ever see a particular apple tree from quite the same perspective as that of one's companion. The "seeming" of the immediate data of sense is the "reality" of the immediate data of sense. However, the problem of knowledge is wider than the problem of data.

A theory of knowledge must account for other judgments besides those concerning the immediate data of sense, and it is this fact that finally undercuts the Protagorean theory. Once one recognizes that there is more to the problem of knowing than merely giving an account of the direct awareness of uninterpreted sense experience, the weakness of the Protagorean position becomes obvious. Socrates raises the question of justifying judgments that have a future reference; thus, he broadens the scope of the discussion to include a problem Protagoras's theory cannot explain. A physician and his patient, for example, may disagree today about whether the patient will have a fever tomorrow. It is clear that both cannot be judging truly, and obviously the physician's prediction is more reliable than is the patient's. Both are judging about a fact that is not at the moment a part of the immediate experience of either of them, and both cannot be right in their judgments; clearly one of them (the physician) is a better "measure" than is the other. When the consideration of knowing is thus broadened to include more than merely people's immediate experience, the Protagorean theory is seen to be inadequate.

Socrates next moves to a more critical examination of the doctrine that the world of sense experience is a flux. He examines the position of the followers of Heraclitus. Heraclitus had said that everything is in flux and that a person cannot step into the same river twice since "new waters are ever flowing." Some of his followers, however, had gone beyond this claim in saying that one cannot step into the same river even once. What these followers sensed, apparently, was that if everything is an absolute flux, then there is no point at all to mentioning "same." "Same" is a word that has meaning only in contrast with change, but if all is utter change, there is nothing that can be said to be "the same." This doctrine meshes well with the Protagorean doctrine; in fact, it is the Protagorean position stated in its most extreme form. Socrates therefore wishes to consider it.

The crucial point that the Heraclitean analysis omits is the recognition that there must be something that is exempt from the flux if there is to be any knowledge at all. If the world is nothing but a flux, in this extreme Heraclitean sense, then knowledge is impossible. Socrates rejects both the unrelieved flux of the extreme Heracliteans and its opposite number, the unchanging unity of the followers of Parmenides. Knowledge, in the strict sense, is of elements like the Parmenidean One, but the (almost) knowledge we have of the world of becoming is of a flux that moves within limits that are unchanging and fixed after the manner of the Parmenidean unity. The world of sense experience, for Plato, is a flux—as the Heracliteans recognized—but insofar as this world of sense experience can be known, it must be viewed against an unchanging set of limits having the character of the Parmenidean One. Knowledge of the world of sense experience, then, involves both the changing and the unchanging; neither is by itself sufficient to account for our knowledge. Absolute flux is radically unknowable.

Redefining Knowledge

From this criticism of the extreme Heraclitean position, Socrates moves on to a total rejection of the definition of knowledge that Theaetetus initially put forth; namely, that knowledge is perception. At the beginning of the examination of this theory, Socrates laid down two criteria for knowledge that now serve as a basis for the rejection of Theaetetus's first proposal. Socrates at that point stated—and Theaetetus had assented—that knowledge was of the real and infallible. The examination of the theory that knowledge is perception has issued in the recognition that sensation may very well yield something that is infallible, but it has also revealed that it is not of the real because the real is fixed and unchanging, not an ultimate flux. Yet Socrates goes even further in refuting Theaetetus's initial proposal. He introduces a consideration that had been hinted at earlier but was then left undeveloped; namely, that knowledge involves a mind that interprets the deliverances of sense.

Before anything even remotely resembling knowledge is achieved, the raw data of sense must be interpreted. One may taste an apple, but one cannot judge that it is sweet without evaluating the sense experience in the light of a standard that is not in itself part of the raw taste of the apple; one must know what sweetness is before one can determine that the apple tastes sweet.

This standard—which is the idea sweetness, the reader realizes, even though Plato avoids specific mention of the ideas in this dialogue—must be unchanging and real. It can be known, and it serves as the standard in terms of which the raw data of sense are interpreted. However, the sense organs by themselves cannot know the standard. On the contrary, it is the mind that knows the standard and judges that the sense experience is of such and such a character in the light of this standard.

Uninterpreted sense experience, therefore, cannot possibly be knowledge; even if it is interpreted, it still has as its object something that is less than real, and the interpretation presupposes a standard that is the genuine object of knowledge. When pursued far enough, the examination of sense experience leads to the Platonic position that knowledge must be restricted to the ideas; we cannot have genuine knowledge of the world of becoming. Plato reserves the discussion of the ideas in their own right for *Sophistēs* (later period, 365-361 B.C.E.; *Sophist*, 1804), but *Theaetetus* prepares the ground for this later direct analysis of knowing.

True and False Opinion

Theaetetus's first attempt to define knowledge has thus proved to be inadequate in the light of Socrates' examination of it. If the dialogue is to continue, Theaetetus must offer a new definition. This he does, proposing now that knowledge is true opinion. The examination of this possibility occupies Socrates and Theaetetus in the next portion of the dialogue. However, if there is any significance to the definition of knowledge as "true opinion," there must be something that is *false* opinion. It is to the elucidation of mistaken belief, or false opinion, then, that Socrates turns at this point.

Two well-known analogies occur in the account of false belief: the wax tablet analogy and the birdcage analogy. Socrates first suggests that belief may be analogous to fitting a new sense experience into an impression left in a wax tablet by a previous experience. When the new sense experience matches the impression in the wax, there is a case of true belief, but when the new experience is fitted into an impression that does not match, the result is mistaken belief.

The birdcage analogy takes into account some complications that the wax tablet analogy overlooks. The wax tablet analogy cannot account for mistaken belief about matters that do not have reference to sense experience. For example, a person might believe that seven plus five equals eleven, a mathematical belief that does not rest on sense experience. This situation is likened to a person who has a cage full of birds. At some time in the past, this individual got possession of the birds (learned the truths of mathematics) and put them into the cage. Later, he reaches into the cage to get possession of a particular bird. He may think he has grasped a parrot, even though he has a pigeon in his hand. Analogously, a person who once learned that seven plus five equals twelve may, when he tries to recall this truth, mistakenly believe that seven plus five equals eleven. He has in his possession, but not in his hand, the truth; thus, he describes incorrectly what he has in his hand.

These two accounts have a common feature. Both involve the interpretation of some conceptual object. It is the interpretation that brings in the difficulty, for whether one mistakenly judges that a stone is an apple (sense object) or whether one mistakenly judges that seven plus five equals eleven (mathematical object), one still is making an interpretation. Yet if the interpretation yields genuine knowledge, it must be infallible and of the real. A mistaken belief is clearly not infallible. If one knows and knows that one knows, one's initial judgment cannot be fallible. Neither the wax tablet analogy nor the birdcage analogy yields such certainty, however, and they therefore fail to do the job. Plato and Socrates want a psychological criterion for separating true from false beliefs. Neither the wax tablet nor the birdcage yields such a psychological criterion. Both accounts of mistaken belief are therefore inadequate, but the discussion is broken off at this point since further analysis would require Plato to introduce the ideas, something he wishes to postpone until the *Sophist*.

Theaetetus has one final proposal to make. He suggests that the difficulty encountered in the examination of false belief may be overcome by defining knowledge as true belief accompanied by a reason or correct explanation. This will indeed do the job, but it has one crucial flaw;

namely, it is a circular definition of knowledge. What the definition comes to is that knowledge is true opinion that is known to be true. An adequate definition, however, cannot use the term to be defined in the definition of the term. Theaetetus's final suggestion is inadequate, just as his earlier proposals have been.

A Negative Conclusion

The conclusion of the dialogue, then, is that knowledge is neither sensation nor true opinion—not even true opinion accompanied by an explanation. Theaetetus has labored, but he has not brought forth a legitimate intellectual offspring. Nevertheless, Socrates says, the discussion has been of value to Theaetetus, for he does not now think that he knows something that he does not know, and if he attempts to define knowledge again at a later time his present efforts will help him to avoid certain pitfalls.

The overt conclusion of the dialogue may be negative, but for one who reads Plato intelligently and enters into the dialogue as an attentive, though silent, participant, the positive conclusion is nevertheless obvious, even though it is not explicitly stated: Knowledge can only be of the forms or ideas. To give an adequate account of knowing one must introduce the ideas. This task Plato postpones until the *Sophist*, the dialogue that naturally follows *Theaetetus*.

One can hardly read *Theaetetus* without feeling that here is philosophy unsurpassed. Plato's problems, for the most part, retain their vitality, and his solutions retain their interest, even after more than two thousand years. When philosophical excellence of the very first order is given expression in literary and dramatic form of equally high quality, there is very little that can be said in criticism. Part of Plato's appeal undoubtedly results from the fact that he usually is occupied in rejecting inadequate positions, leaving his own positive doctrine to be worked out by the reader as the implicit alternative. It is certainly true that Plato made mistakes. Yet when his mistakes are all pointed out, and an allowance is made for his indirect manner of arguing for his own doctrine, the fact remains that the Platonic position is still in its essentials the same as that Plato himself held; the necessary corrections are minor. Platonism is a live alternative.

The student who wishes to see the inadequacies of a simple-headed empiricism that thinks it can do without a judging mind in accounting for knowledge can do no better than to study carefully Plato's Theaetetus.

Robert E. Larsen

Sophist

Type of philosophy: Epistemology, metaphysics
First transcribed: Sophistēs, later period, 365-361 B.C.E. (English translation, 1804)
Principal ideas advanced:

◇ Sophists claim that in teaching the art of rhetoric they teach all useful knowledge.

◇ Parmenides' claim—that the real is one being—is false, for the term "real" must refer to one idea and the term "one" to another.

◇ Those who claim that only the tangible is real are mistaken, for ideas are real; and life, soul, and intelligence are also real, yet none of these is tangible.

◇ The task of philosophers in their search for wisdom is to seek to discover which ideas combine and which do not.

◇ Sophists claim that people cannot speak of what is not, but they are mistaken, for to speak of what is not is simply to speak of that which exists as not having certain forms (ideas).

◇ Sophists are image makers who teach the art of deception through the use of language; they are not true philosophers.

Some scholars believe Plato intended to write a trilogy consisting of *Politikos* (later period, 365-361 B.C.E.; *Statesman*, 1804), the *Sophist*, and a third dialogue on the philosopher. Because the first two dialogues search for definitions that not only will delimit the statesman and the Sophist but also will show how, if at all, they differ from the philosopher, it seems likely that Plato planned a third dialogue in which he would define the philosopher and describe the appropriate search for knowledge. In the *Sophist*, Plato defines Sophists and describes the kind of activity that properly belongs to them. The dialogue *Theaetētos* (middle period, 388-368 B.C.E.; *Theaetetus*, 1804) is also intimately connected to this series, for in it Plato begins the quest for a proper definition of knowledge and for an answer to many of the problems that plagued him as he worked out his theory of ideas. The *Sophist* follows *Theaetetus* and carries on the search for an answer.

The Sophist Defined

In attempting to define "sophist," Plato makes use of the technique of classification by which he goes from the most general terms to the more specific. He makes use of a similar approach in the *Statesman* in order to distinguish the true ruler from apparent ones. In their pursuit of the nature of Sophists, Socrates and a stranger from Elea point out many facets of their character, especially with regard to what they profess to know, which indicate to them that although a correct definition ought to point to that, and that alone, which is essential to the nature of Sophists, they find that they profess to be master of many arts.

The Sophists' most pronounced trait is the ability to discourse persuasively; they claim that through the art of rhetoric, they can give one knowledge in all fields. It is denied by the stranger that one can have knowledge in all fields, a denial in accord with Plato's view expressed throughout his works and emphasized in *Politeia* (middle period, 388-368 B.C.E.; *Republic*, 1701) that one can know and do only one thing well. Therefore, Sophists, although they proclaim themselves experts in many areas, must have and present only the appearance or image of a subject rather than the reality. Sophistry, if it is an art (for how can the practitioners of sham be artists?), is the art of image making. The stranger then pursues an analysis of image making.

Reality and Appearance

Image making has two parts or kinds. First, one may copy an original; examples are the craftsperson who copies a natural object and the painter who makes a likeness of someone's face. Second, there are those who make semblances—what appear to be likenesses but are in some way out of proportion. The second type of image making raises certain questions. What is meant by this world of semblances? A semblance is apparently not real, and yet it cannot be said to be

unreal or nothing, for it is something. However, what kind of a something? Plato is again struggling with the Parmenidean problem of the existence of a world of appearances, which is neither of the world of forms or ideas nor of the world of not-being or nothing; rather, it seems to hover somewhere in between, to be a world of change, of becoming.

The Eleatic stranger had previously proclaimed himself, or had been proclaimed, a student of Zeno and of Parmenides, and he shows his indebtedness to them in his pursuit of these questions. The concern over the world of appearances brings up related problems over the judgments made about that world. For in dealing with that which is not real (that is, that which changes), one must use negative judgments, yet these judgments apparently refer to some object. Plato is emphasizing that when one uses a locution such as "is not," one seems to be denying the existence of something. However, of what? There is nothing that one can be talking about because apparently it, whatever it is, is not, and hence is not anything. This sort of puzzle sets off a discussion in the *Sophist* over certain aspects of epistemology and ontology that had troubled pre-Socratic philosophers and to which Plato addressed himself. The discussion concerns the three realms of not-being (nothing), becoming, and being, and what sort of knowledge and judgment is appropriate to each.

In discussing the worlds of reality and appearance, the stranger dismisses rather quickly that of not-being or the totally unreal. Generally speaking, the totally unreal cannot be the subject of discourse because one's statements cannot have *no* reference whatsoever; one cannot talk about nothing. In addition, the very attempt to do so is ambiguous and misleading. One seems to be talking about something, the totally unreal, and one uses pronouns as if they referred to a thing; and yet, as noted, one is not talking about anything. One contradicts oneself when attempting to talk about nothing because one must talk about something.

There is still a puzzle that must be solved: When one uses a statement that either tells one that something is or that something is not, then of either alternative one can say that it is true or it is false. In either case, one seems to be stating a sentence that conveys meaning. Hence, one cannot always be talking about the totally unreal or the meaningless when one utters negative or even false judgments. It remains to be seen if this problem can be treated successfully. The analysis given by Parmenides (who is the stranger's inspiration) that there is only that which is or is not cannot be adequate; false statements seem to refer to something "in between." Thus Plato parts company with Parmenides and holds that the realm of becoming, events in space and time that undergo change, has a status that cannot be ignored by the philosopher. Before this realm is examined, however, some attention must be given to what is meant by the "real." The Eleatic stranger begins by reviewing what some of the earlier philosophers have said about it.

The Eleatic stranger treats briefly those who had held that hot and cold are real, or that one is but the other is not, or that the real is a third thing. When he comes to Parmenides, he treats him in more detail. Parmenides had claimed that the real is one being. A question is raised in that Parmenides used two names, "one" and "real," to designate this entity: How can there be two names to designate one entity? Plato apparently believed that these two names designated two separate and distinct forms or ideas—the form of oneness and that of realness—hence Parmenides' analysis was not about one thing, but two. A more detailed analysis of this view is given. If the real is a whole made up of parts, then it cannot be unity or oneness itself; these imply a lack of parts, but obviously a whole made up of parts indicates a plurality of entities. In such a case, of course, one can speak quite properly of such a whole (made up of parts) as having unity, but one cannot say that there is only one being and no other. The real is not a whole, yet wholeness exists. The real, then, cannot be what is. That realness and wholeness must exist means that a plurality exists. Another possibility is, if wholeness does not exist, then the real will be a plurality of many parts with no totality. However, if so, it cannot then be that which is, nor can it ever become that which is.

Idealism vs. Materialism

The discovery of the unsatisfactory character of Parmenides' view of reality leads to a general discussion of idealism versus materialism as philosophical positions; Plato picturesquely calls this "the battle between the Gods and Giants," between those who dwell in the heavens—the realm of ideas—versus those who dwell on the earth—the realm of the tangible. The Giants, or materialists, claim that only the tangible is real, whereas the idealists, or Gods, point out that moral qualities can be present in some and absent in others; these are qualities that are not tangible yet must be admitted as real. The question as to what is real leads both camps to search for a mark or sign by which they may know the real. The materialists suggest, and the Eleatic stranger considers it tentatively, that only that which has the power to affect or to be affected by an agent is the real. The Eleatic stranger makes out the following objection to the materialists: The materialists demand a quality that they can sense before they proclaim something real; they admit, however, that they can be aware of the presence or absence of "justice" within themselves or others; but such awareness is not of a sensible quality but of an intellectual one, and its object, justice, is an idea.

In discussing the idealists, the Eleatic stranger first considers the view that proclaims that only that which is changeless can be an object of knowledge and truly real. However, can the changeless be an object of knowledge if to know is to act on in some sense? For if that which is an object of knowledge is acted on, then it is changed; but if it is changed, then it cannot be that which is changeless. Hence, either knowledge is not that which acts on something, or, if it is, then that which is changeless and, by definition, not capable of being acted on, cannot be known. It is here that the Eleatic stranger questions whether only that which is changeless is real. (He thus again breaks with the Parmenidean school.) He argues that life, soul, and intelligence—all of them "objects" that undergo change—belong to the domain of the real. The school of Heraclitus is next attacked—that school that had maintained that only change, flux, was real. If all is flux, there can be no intelligence in real things; for if nothing were the same from moment to moment, nothing could be known. Therefore the stranger from Elea concludes that reality must consist both of that which is changeless and of that which changes, if we are to have intelligence in the world.

Plato seems to wish to bridge the gap created by the Parmenideans and the followers of Heraclitus in their construction of what is real by pointing out that each group errs when it rejects that which the other regards as real. In this dialogue, the matter is not pursued further. Instead, a return to a previous discussion ensues that seems much like the one just concluded but is different. The discussion concerns "reality" rather than the "real," and it treats reality as a form among forms. It is in this sense that Plato holds reality to be changeless, and hence he does not contradict what he had just affirmed—that the real includes that which is changeless as well as that which changes. If reality included both change and changelessness, one would have three forms rather than one—but that is impossible.

The argument brings out an important point in Platonic metaphysics. Each time a combination of forms is considered, an impasse is reached when it is revealed that there is more than one form involved in the discussion. If the one is real (or exists), then oneness, unity, reality, and existence are all involved, for if reality were not present, we could not talk of the one as real.

Movement, Rest, and Reality

The Eleatic stranger then considers the questions raised in the discussion, questions concerning the possibility of the combination of forms and of negative judgments. The forms considered in this discussion are movement, rest, and reality (or existence). Some forms must be compatible with others in that some kind of combination must be possible between them if they are to be said to be real. Thus, unless movement combines with reality and unless rest does also, neither of them is real. Not all forms are compatible in this way, however, or else we would run into absurdities; for instance, movement cannot combine with rest, for if it did then we could say of movement that it is at rest, and of rest that it is in movement. The task of philosophers in their search for wisdom and truth is to investigate which forms combine and which do not; this task is to be accomplished by philosophic discourse—by dialectic. The Eleatic stranger reminds his cohorts in dis-

cussion that their task is to seek out the Sophist, who dwells in the realm of seeming or perhaps of not-being, rather than the philosopher. He suggests that after their present task is finished, they may come back to philosophers and their realm (thus giving credence to the view that Plato intended to write a dialogue on the philosopher). In the search for what is real, the purpose is to clarify the realm that the Sophist inhabits.

The stranger continues this discussion by bringing up two more forms: sameness and difference. He does so because in speaking of two or more forms, we are automatically involved with sameness and difference. For example, rest is the same as itself (partakes of sameness) and different from movement. Sameness and difference must be separate forms, for if movement and rest were equivalent to sameness then they would be equivalent to each other. That is, they would both partake of sameness and thus be the same; yet although they are the same with regard to themselves respectively, they are not with regard to each other. The same holds for difference.

Having pointed out that the five forms are separate and distinct, the Eleatic stranger then considers them with regard to judgments involving the locutions "is" and "is not." He points out an important feature of the verb form "is": It has at least two senses; namely, "exists" and "is identical to," or "is the same as." The statements considered are as follow: (1) motion is not (rest). Motion is (real or exists); (2) motion is not (the same). Motion is the same (as itself); (3) motion is not (the different). Motion is different (from difference).

The Eleatic stranger then concludes that of any form, we may say that it is not (any other form) and that it is (real or exists). It is here that the break with Parmenides is complete, for it can be shown that his statement, "'That which is' cannot 'not be'" is incorrect, because "That which is" *can* "not be" (be other than) all other existents; and thus we can have as a true statement the following: "'What is' can 'not be.'" Furthermore, we can also have as a true statement, "'What is not' can 'be.'" That which is not everything else is still itself (exists). Parmenides has thus been refuted in saying that "that which is" can in no sense "not be" and that "that which is not" can in no sense "be."

This argument can also be applied to Sophists, and they can be shown to be wrong when they state that we cannot speak of what is not; it has been shown that we can and do so speak, when, for example, we say that "is not" means "is not the same as." Can we reconcile the problem, however, when "is not" refers to "falsity"?

False Statements and Judgments

The Eleatic stranger presents an analysis of statements (essentially of descriptive statements) to clarify the problem of false judgments. Of every statement, it may be said that it must contain at least a name (an expression applied to that which performs the action) and a verb (an expression applied to the action). Every statement must also be about something. Lastly, every statement has a certain character; that is, we say of it that it is either true or false. The examples that the stranger considers are "Theaetetus sits" and "Theaetetus flies." The first is true for Theaetetus is in fact sitting. The second is false for it describes the subject Theaetetus as doing what he is not doing. Thus it states that things that are not, are (exist). It appears here that Plato in his analysis has presented us with an application of the views just worked out by the Eleatic stranger regarding the five forms and the possibilities of combination. Falsity occurs whenever the incorrect forms are used in describing the action of the subject (assuming that the correct subject is used). In this way, Plato feels that he has shown that false statements are meaningful.

Plato has so far dealt with the problem of false statements, and he has shown in what sense they are about something and in what sense they are meaningful. His analysis, although incomplete, points toward a fuller discussion that, as noted, was probably to be made in the dialogue on the philosopher. He tackled the problem, not as he felt the Sophists had done, with a shallow display of verbal paradoxes, but rather by a provocative analysis and a suggested solution in terms of his theory of forms or ideas. Descriptive statements are about something, often tangible, performed by something or someone—thus, they denote—but to an extent, they derive meaning from the relation they express between the action described and the form(s) of which they partake. With this attempt made, the Eleatic stranger returns to a final consideration of the Sophist.

He concludes that as a species of image maker, the Sophist belongs to those who deal in semblances. Their forte is in the construction of contradictions that, they freely admit, are intended to confuse and deceive. The mimicry they advocate is based not on knowledge but on opinion. Because it is an art that deals in a shadow-play of words, it is not a discourse that aims at wisdom. When Sophists encourage the use of their arguments to persuade the people and gain mastery over them, their profession is that of the demagogue and not of the statesman.

Theodore Waldman

Statesman

Type of philosophy: Ethics, metaphysics, political philosophy

First transcribed: Politikos, later period, 365-361 B.C.E. (English translation, 1804)

Principal ideas advanced:

◇ The problem confronting the Athenian stranger and Socrates is that of defining the ideal statesman.

◇ The statesman, or king, is a member of the class of those who direct action; he initiates directives and is distinguished from those who build lifeless things by the fact that his concern is with a living herd, the citizenry.

◇ The art of statesmanship is not a function of the kind of state to be governed; a good statesman can rule no matter what the form of government.

◇ Laws are necessary in a state, but the ruler is more important than the laws; in many cases, he must judge when the laws do not apply.

◇ The statesman is superior to other people who practice the various arts of ruling people in that he must decide which of the other arts is to be used for the benefit of the state; in that sense, statesmanship is the art of all arts.

In Plato's political works, he is mainly concerned with an analysis of the nature of the individual and of the state that is an appropriate reflection of the individual. Plato looked on the state as analogous to the individual, and he believed that the type of individual found in the state determined the sort of state it would be. In *Politeia* (middle period, 388-368 B.C.E.; *Republic*, 1701), he searches for justice in the state to discover the nature of justice in the person; and after he describes the ideal state and its ruler, he traces the state's decline by pointing to the concomitant decline in the soul of the individual. In *Nomoi* (last period, 360-347 B.C.E.; *Laws*, 1804), he concentrates on the second-best state, a government of laws, not people, and works out the constitution applicable to it. In the *Statesman*, written most likely between the *Republic* and the *Laws*, Plato attacks the problem of defining the king who would rule in the best state, distinguishing him from sham rulers.

The Art of Ruling

Plato looked on ruling as an art, and as with other arts, it has subject matter that only an expert can master. People who are ill turn willingly to a physician expertly trained in the art of medicine to cure them; people who are in need of transportation between lands separated by an open sea turn to a pilot expertly trained in the art of seamanship to guide them across perilous seas; yet in the most important problem they face—conducting themselves as citizens in the state that involves their very happiness—they seem content to trust their fortunes to people untrained in statesmanship, who know nothing of the art of governing. It is as if they turned to the first person they met for medical help or trusted anyone at all to sail them across dangerous waters. Plato believed that intelligent human beings would willingly turn to the expert for advice. He believed that if he could spell out the art of ruling and the training necessary to be an expert in it, intelligent people would willingly turn to true statesmen to rule them.

The Athenian stranger points out that we are to seek a definition of the statesman as a kind of expert, and, hence, a division of forms of knowledge will be necessary, for to be an expert takes knowledge, and knowledge of statecraft should be separated from that which is other than statecraft. In addition, we must also separate knowledge into that which is applied and that which is pure. The stranger points out that the ruler's art is closer to mental than to manual labor, and thus the distinction is needed, for the former is theoretical or pure rather than practical or applied.

Definitions

In his search for a proper definition, the Athenian stranger makes use of the logical technique of defining his terms by proceeding from the most general to the more particular, thus specifying what the statesman is as accurately as he can. He begins by examining appropriate subdivisions of the division of theoretical knowledge: the art of counting (which has nothing to do with applied work), and that of master builder, charged with directing action. The king is found in this class, which can itself be divided into those who give initial directives (the kind) and those who pass on to others commands that are given to them (the king's ministers).

As one who issues commands, the king aims at the production of something. That which is productive may itself be divided into the lifeless and the living. The king, who is a member of the directive class, may be distinguished at this juncture from the master builder, for whereas the builder produces lifeless things, the king is concerned with ordering living creatures, in flocks rather than singly. These, it must be remembered, are flocks of tame rather than wild creatures, of people rather than animals. The art that we are looking for, then, is that of shepherding humankind; it is the art of government, and the expert, the man of knowledge concerning this art, is the statesman or king, who is herder to a human, tame flock. It is a peculiar herd in that its members challenge the herder, and various members claim that they themselves are the true herders of humankind. Thus, it is not easy to get people to accept willingly the expert in governing as properly ruling over them; they do not recognize the art for what it is. Farmers, doctors, merchants, teachers, others, all put in their claims; some point out that even the statesman is fed by them.

Plato turns to one of his famous myths to aid us in our quest. This myth relates the reversal of the movements of heaven and earth and the changes that this brought about. Before the reversal, every herd of living creatures was watched over by a heavenly daemon. The herds were all under the great god Cronus, and they lived an idyllic existence. The reversal changed all this; when Zeus took over, the daemons left the human flocks and, unattended, they were prey to wild beasts. People were forced to learn to protect themselves; they had no crafts and were at the mercy of nature. With mastery of crafts came protection from and the control of nature; because the gods had abandoned the flocks, human herders had to take over. The Athenian stranger points out that the mistake they were making in defining the statesman was that they confused him with the divine herder, did not define his manner of rule, and forgot that nurture was to be subsumed under the flock in discussing the herder's function. The herder is concerned with people in flocks and it is to this fact that we must turn in our search for a definition.

In "tending men," sometimes rule has to be enforced and at other times it is willingly accepted. It is important that this distinction be made, for on it depends the distinction between a tyrant and a king. The true statesman has his "tending" freely accepted. If the state is to function properly, the rulers must be accepted willingly by the subjects; in any form of government, the ruled must obey the laws or face sanctions provided in the law.

In order to understand what kingly duties entail, the Athenian stranger continues, we must first distinguish those activities that are not part of statesmanship from statesmanship. First of all are those practical activities that contribute to the basic needs of the community and without which the community could not survive. (Nevertheless, it is not the kingly art to produce these things.) Under this category, we find such workers as those who preserve what has been produced; those who produce the support of things (the carpenters, for example); those who defend us from cold as well as from enemies—such people as builders and weavers; those who provide diversion for us, the poets and musicians; those who produce the basic materials to be used in other crafts, the skinners, the lumbermen, and so on; and those who provide food and nourishment for the community. We also find in the community other groups such as slaves or merchants, civil servants and priests; but the statesman is not to be confused with any members of any of these

groups, for none has independent authority and none is a ruler. Nor must we confuse the statesman with those who pretend to teach one how to rule, those who boast of their ability to argue any side of an issue, the Sophists who walk the land.

The Athenian stranger proceeds to discuss various types of states to see if the statesman fits one more than another. There are three major types, each with two subtypes. In monarchy there is rule by one, and this may be exemplified by a tyrant or a hereditary ruler in a constitutional monarchy. The next type is that in which a few wield power; this may be seen in an aristocracy or if wealth is the criterion for rule, an oligarchy. Lastly, there is the rule of many, called a democracy. The many may control either by force or by consent. Given that these are the forms of government, can we thus discover the art of rule?

For Plato, the art of statesmanship is not a function of the type of state. If a statesman is capable of ruling, then, whatever the constitutional form of government under which he rules, he is to be regarded as a ruler. Plato goes on to say that this is so whether there are subjects who are rich or poor, willing or unwilling, and regardless of whether there is a code of laws.

The Role of Laws

At this juncture, Socrates questions whether a good governor can govern without laws. This perhaps marks the midpoint between the *Republic* and *Statesman*, works concerned, respectively, with the best government and its ruler, and the *Laws*, a work that discusses the second-best government, a government in which the laws are prior in importance to the character of the ruler. The Athenian stranger answers that the art of kingship includes the art of lawmaking, but that the political ideal is not full authority for laws but rather for a person who understands the art and has the ability to practice it. If a law is an unqualified rule of human behavior, then it cannot with perfect accuracy prescribe what is right and good for each member of the community at any one time—this takes a king. Laws are necessary, however, because the legislator cannot give every individual his or her due with absolute accuracy; general codes of conduct must be spelled out for the bulk of the citizenry. In any particular case, if the statesman can legislate better than the laws, he should be permitted to do so, no matter what. Here Plato includes the possibility of forcing the citizen to accept this kind of ad hoc ruling.

A state in which the ruler is superior to the laws is the best state, but when that is not possible, it is best to adhere to a government of laws. The Athenian stranger points out how the laws grow through the experience of legislators in dealing with human affairs. The knowledge that is gained is that of a science. As such, it has the force of a scientific truth of the kind that Plato considers infallible. As rules of behavior, the laws must be obeyed, and no one is to act in contravention to them. The only better situation is that in which a king, having achieved the art of statesmanship, applies the knowledge that he has gained to a particular situation. The Athenian stranger hints at the work to be done in the *Laws* when he points out that imitative constitutions must keep strictly to the laws and never transgress written enactments or established national customs, if they mean to reproduce as far as they can that one real constitution that is government by a real statesman using real statecraft. The various types of government occur when the ideal constitution is copied in various ways; thus, when copied by the wealthy, the rule is called "aristocracy," and when aristocrats disobey the laws, that rule is called "oligarchy." When someone governs in imitation of the truly wise ruler, he is called "king"; however, calling him this contributes to confusion because a king who imitates the true statesman rules by right opinion without knowing the grounds for the art of statesmanship. When such a person rules not by right opinion but by passions, he is called "tyrant." Although people doubt that any statesman could be superior to the laws without being corrupt, such a statesman is the only one who could govern the commonwealth worthy of the name of best state.

Previously those functions in the state that were important to the very existence of the community were distinguished from kingly duties. However, what of those functions that resemble statesmanship, and what of those individuals who practice them? That is, what of generals, judges, rhetoricians, and the like, all of whom function something like a ruler, and all of whom have been suggested at one time or another for the office of ruler? Each of these people, in practicing his art, uses some form of action on other people; it may be by force (military action), or by persuasion (oratory or rhetoric), or through interpretation and judgment of the law (legal decisions). The Athenian stranger holds that the art that decides which of the foregoing forms of action is to be practiced is superior to the particular art employed. It is the statesman who decides whether to use persuasion or force against a group of people or to take no action at all. He can use oratory that is an adjunct of statesmanship but is not statesmanship itself; thus, the statesman is superior to the rhetorician. Similarly, he can decide whether the generals are to fight or whether friendly settlement is possible; thus, he is superior to the generals. The duty of the judge is to make honest judgments in accordance with the laws made by the statesman; thus, the judge is subservient to the statesman. As an art, statesmanship is concerned with which of these other arts is to be used on the right occasion in the great enterprise of statecraft. It is the art of arts as the good is the form of forms. The statesman must develop the best in the conflicting natures of his subjects—he is a royal weaver.

Theodore Waldman, updated by John K. Roth

Laws

Type of philosophy: Ethics, metaphysics, political philosophy

First transcribed: Nomoi, last period, 360-347 B.C.E. (English translation, 1804)

Principal ideas advanced:

◇ Laws are initiated when communities seek to fix custom, but societies fail when ignorance triumphs over wisdom, when intemperance defeats temperance, or when freedom is lost or becomes license.

◇ The best form of government is a combination of democracy and monarchy, for such a state combines freedom and wisdom.

◇ Legislation should be designed to ensure freedom, harmony, and understanding; the effort should be made to imitate the good and the gods.

◇ Where the laws are above the ruler, the state has the possibility of salvation; the best ruler is one who can enforce the laws by persuasion and command.

◇ The laws should provide for censorship of the improper kinds of music, dancing, poetry, eulogies, and drama; they should discourage all love but the love of soul, and they should provide for the rehabilitation of criminals.

◇ The gods must exist because the soul, that which can move itself, is essentially dependent on the divine.

Plato's three great political treatises, *Politeia* (middle period, 388-368 B.C.E.; *Republic*, 1701), *Politikos* (later period, 365-361 B.C.E.; *Statesman*, 1804), and the *Laws*, are undoubtedly unsurpassed in their influence on political thought. The first two represent Plato's attempt to argue for and describe the political body and the ruler that would be the best or ideal, and there is a serious question as to whether he believed these ideals to be possible. Some hold that the *Republic* represents Plato's attempt to sketch the form or idea of the state—stateness itself, as it were—along with the art of ruling itself. The *Statesman* further examines the art of ruling. The *Laws* sketches a state that is second best, one in which Plato no longer considers the rule of a philosopher-king, either because he no longer thought it possible or because it represented an unrealizable ideal. His concern, rather, is with the rule of law.

Western democracies generally hold that a government of laws is superior to one of people because of the arbitrary rule that may occur when tyrants are in power. People, however, must interpret the laws, for laws do not speak for themselves. Thus, in his presentation of the ideal state, Plato described the training and qualifications of rulers who would combine wisdom and morality with experience, so that given any problem of governing, they would arrive at the correct solution. Why should this type of rule have been considered better than the rule of laws? A law, broadly speaking, is a command issued in *general* terms by a ruler, or by those empowered to rule, for the regulation of the conduct of the members of society. When it is held that someone has broken the law, the person's act must be fit-

ted under the general law, as interpreted by properly constituted authorities. A wise person, moral in character, who, through training (education) and discipline, has attained knowledge of the good and who has spent many years in the practical application of that knowledge in governmental positions is best suited to sit in judgment of particular cases and come to decisions. For Plato, proper rule by laws demanded the ideal ruler.

Education

In the *Laws*, an Athenian stranger, thought by some scholars to represent Plato himself rather than Socrates, dominates the conversation. In the opening books, a discussion, reminiscent of many in earlier dialogues, ensues of the virtues, their importance to the good life, and the role of education in training citizens to rule themselves and to obey their rulers. The Athenian stranger inquires of Megillus whether he thinks that the program in Sparta to train the young to be courageous is adequate. Although much stress is put on endurance and resistance to pain, there is little, if any, preparation for resisting improper pleasures, especially flattery. Furthermore, in their educational scheme the Spartans have confused temperance with prohibition, by banishing revelry in all forms. Conviviality may be a benefit to the state when properly managed. In fact, the notion of "proper management" is the key to the temperance, and gaining knowledge of it a major feature of a correct education.

People are pulled from within by pleasure and pain, and the way in which they are pulled results in virtue or vice. The way in which people are pulled can be determined by their use of reason in directing their will to control their passionate nature or their enslavement to the demands of their desires. It is the role of education to prepare people to use their reason, so that their acts will be virtuous and not vicious. If children are observed carefully, and their instincts toward virtue are molded into suitable habits so that they learn to do that which they ought to do—by loving what ought to be loved and hating what ought to be hated—then education will be properly administered in the city. As in the *Republic*, Plato advocates as part of the program of education the correct use of music, and, again, he stresses imitation of the good as the standard by which it should be judged.

Legislation

In book 3 of the *Laws*, the Athenian stranger turns to an analysis of legislation, one that occupies him for much of the remainder of the dialogue, and he begins by considering the origin of governments. Recounting the legend of the destruction of civilization by the Deluge, he describes the rise of society again on a simple, pastoral level. People lived by custom, remembered from the "old days," and practiced the virtues that they inherited from their parents. Legislation began when the various communities discovered the differences in their customs and vied with one another to be the best. By arbitration, it was decided which were best, and the communities were united into city-states, from which federations were formed. Yet Sparta and two of its neighbors had broken their federation in recent times because they lacked the wisdom to remain united. Unless legislators endeavor to plant wisdom in states and banish ignorance, not only federations but also the state itself will be ruined. The stranger points out many examples of states that have come to ruin because of excesses rather than improper management.

Persia, he claims, fell because of the servitude of the people. When the most important principle of rule, that of the wise over the ignorant, is practiced as it ought, there exists a rule of law over willing subjects. When there is rule by compulsion, as in Persia, then the government will fall. On the other hand, too much freedom can also lead to the destruction of a state. The stranger refers to the fall of Athens as a case in point. Interestingly enough, in the light of his criticisms of certain poetical practices, he traces the downfall to excesses in music. He claims that at first the music was listened to in an orderly fashion and in silence, but the poets themselves introduced noisy innovations that led to noisy confusion. In addition, freedom was replaced by license, and equality proclaimed in all things, so that the view expressed by "It's all a matter of taste" replaced norms in morality as well as etiquette. The democracy that had consisted of educated persons in the role of judges degenerated to a situation in which anyone was qualified. When

freedom becomes excessive, when taste takes over, then reverence is lost and authority ignored; both the rulers and the laws are disobeyed.

In discussing a state that is well governed, Plato, in the *Laws*, indicates that he has modified the position on democracy he put forth in the *Republic*, in which he stated that it was next to tyranny as the worst of states. It is true that there he presented a picture of mob rule in which license and no moral laws prevailed. That conclusion was the main feature of a democracy when discussed in the *Republic*. In the *Laws*, he holds that when democracy is combined with monarchy, it is possible to join features that make for a well-governed state: friendship and wisdom with freedom. The Athenian stranger holds that legislation should aim to accomplish three things: ensure the freedom of the city, promote harmony so that the city is at one with itself, and foster understanding. Cleinias, who is to found a colony for Crete, asks the Athenian stranger to develop his views on legislation further so that he may profit by them.

Speaking rather generally, the Athenian stranger claims that it is preferable for a legislator to make laws in a state ruled by a young tyrant (king) with a good memory, one who is quick at learning, courageous, noble, and temperate. Because people tend to imitate their ruler, such a ruler is more likely to be obeyed and the laws of his kingdom are more likely to be the best. Besides, because he is more likely to honor the laws, he should rule, for where the law is subject and has no authority, there the state is on its way to ruin. Thus Plato, in the *Laws*, subscribes to the second-best view, for he goes on to say that where the law is above the ruler, there the state has the possibility of salvation. He stresses, as he did in the *Republic*, that the gods should be imitated, and he urges that legislators not give two rules for one point of law.

The Athenian stranger develops this point further by advising legislators to define clearly the terms of their laws so that there will be no ambiguity. This will be the true sense of moderation. When the laws are made, legislators should use both persuasion and command in framing them. The persuasive efforts will create good will on the part of the citizens who will be required to obey the laws.

It is important to realize the kinds of laws Plato is talking about. Legislators are described as framing laws to fit what ordinarily is called a constitution. (Plato is not always clear about this point, but the text supports such a view.) Both Niccolò Machiavelli, in his *Discorsi sopra la prima deca di Tito Livio* (1531; *Discourses on the First Ten Books of Titus Livius*, 1636), and Jean-Jacques Rousseau, in *Du contrat social: Ou, Principes du droit politique* (1762; *A Treatise on the Social Contract: Or, The Principles of Politic Law*, 1764), are indebted to Plato as they argue for a constitution written by a stranger (as does Plato), sanctioned by the gods, and consented to by the people.

A Virtuous State

In the fifth book, the Athenian stranger gives practical advice for the securing of a virtuous state. Next to the gods, people should honor their souls and then their bodies. They should live moderately, avoiding excesses, with regard to both their mental and physical activities. Those in society who are guilty of wrongdoing, if they appear curable, should be treated gently and with forgiveness. If, however, some citizens in the state are beyond cure or are incurably evil, they must be purged. Plato, again stressing the view that evil is a kind of disease of which punishment is the cure, argues for rehabilitation over vengeance; but when rehabilitation appears fruitless, then the state should put away those who are of no good to themselves or others. Oddly enough, from Plato's viewpoint, because no person ever does wrong knowingly, an incurable person would appear to be one who no longer can learn anything.

The state that the Athenian stranger plans would be small in size and population. The property would be divided among the citizens as fairly and justly as possible, and great effort would be made to keep the population constant. In the best state, the stranger proclaims, property would be held in common (as in the *Republic*), but if it must be held privately, then the owners should be taught that they owe their possessions to the state and that basically the property belongs to the whole citizenry. The city-state should be neither too wealthy nor too poor, for the excesses of both are dangerous to civic welfare. The laws should protect the city from these extremes by limiting wealth so that no one through property shall gain undue power.

Education and Custom

In the ensuing books, Plato continues to stress education, and he points out that a crucial function of it is to help transmit and enforce the customs (favorable) that have been developed in society. Laws are only a skeleton of the rules that govern a state. Between the "spaces," custom binds and knits the country, providing a ground for proper management of oneself. Custom can bring about reverence for the law by instilling in the young a respect for it. It is well to frown upon changes in the law, to make it difficult for changes to occur, for stability in the law is reflected in a satisfied people. Only the good is to be stressed. Plato was so concerned about the disquieting effect that "wrong" music can have on the populace that he advocated laws to control music, dancing, poetry, and eulogies. He advocated censorship of plays and other literary works for the youth. The Athenian stranger knows that the young will imitate the characters they watch on the stage and read about; only if these are presented with a high regard for morality can the imitation be safe. As in the *Republic*, Plato advocates that mathematics be taught, especially arithmetic, plane and solid geometry, and astronomy.

Because men and women are to be together in their education, some precautions must be taken to prevent promiscuity. In book 8, the Athenian stranger discusses love, pointing out that there are three types that become confused and that must be carefully distinguished by the laws. The three types are love of body, which leads to wantonness; love of soul, which enables one to search for virtues and for a kindred soul with whom to live chastely; and a mixture of the two. It is the second that is to be favored by the state; the others are to be forbidden. However, how will it be possible to enforce a law in support of the love of soul? Just as incest is not practiced because the customs and mores are such that it is held to be the most vile of crimes, so a similar attitude can be established regarding other vile unions. By combining the fear of impiety with a love for moderation, sexual temperance will be looked upon as a victory over base pleasures, and sufficient incentive will be provided to encourage obedience to the law. In addition, hard work will get rid of excess passion.

Crime and Punishment

Although the Athenian stranger finds it hard to believe that there will be crimes in his proposed state, he recognizes the need for criminal law. It is here that Plato once more declares punishment to be a form of rehabilitation, designed to cure or improve the criminal. It is interesting that Plato considers the robbing of temples to be a capital offense, punishable by death if committed by one who has been educated and trained. In *A Treatise on the Social Contract*, Rousseau reveals Plato's influence when he urges a similar punishment for this kind of crime.

Because Plato accepts the Socratic view that no person does wrong knowingly and that punishment should be a cure, he feels obligated to discuss the sources of crime. He finds it in three major aspects of people's makeup. The passions, as the lowest element of the soul, may drive people to act without reason's guidance. However, to act without reason's guidance is tantamount to slavery, and people who are slave to their passions may perform all sorts of crimes. Related to this is the fact that people who seek pleasures find that by persuasion and deceit they are led to pursue them, often to their ruin. Lastly, ignorance itself is a cause of crime. Socrates had found that he was proclaimed the wisest person in Athens because he knew that he did not know anything, whereas his fellow citizens were ignorant of their ignorance and fooled themselves into thinking that they knew. It is the conceit of wisdom that leads the ignorant person astray, causing the individual to commit crimes. The degree of the conceit is matched by the seriousness of the crime.

The Athenian stranger proclaims that laws are necessary for humankind because without rules to guide them, people would be no better than savage beasts. This position influenced Rousseau, who held that society would make a person of virtue out of a creature who, acting from instinct rather than reason, was little better than a savage beast. No person is able to know what is best for all of human society. A philosopher-king is hardly possible; thus, law and order must be chosen so that good people may be led to a good life, and those who refuse to be instructed, curbed.

Religion

In the final book (book 10) of the *Laws*, the Athenian stranger argues that as long as the gods are held in esteem, crimes of impiety will not be committed frequently. To the question of what can be done with those who do not believe in the existence of the gods, the stranger proposes to prove their existence. He does so with a proof that shows that the soul is prior to the body, and that because the spiritual nature of the soul is the same as that of the gods, they too must exist. The proof rests on the soul as a source of motion. Briefly, this proof may be demonstrated as follows: Some things are in motion; others are at rest. Motion itself is of several types: spinning on an axis, locomotion, combination, separation, composition, growth, decay, destruction, self-motion and motion by others, and change of itself and by others. Change of itself and by others is actually the first in terms of superiority, with self-motion and motion by others second. The "self-moving" principle is identified with life. Not only is the soul defined, in essence, as that which can move itself, but also it is the source of motion in all things. The body is essentially inert and has no moving power of its own; rather, it has motion produced within it. As the source of motion, the soul is prior in time to that which is moved by it. The body, which is moved by the soul, must be later than it in time. Not only is the soul the author of movement in and of the body, but of all bodies, including heavenly ones (planets, for example). Soul or spirit must exist prior to and concurrent with the heavenly bodies to have put and kept them in motion. Therefore the gods, who are spirits with spiritual qualities unencumbered by bodies, must exist.

Theodore Waldman

Philebus

Type of philosophy: Ethics, metaphysics
First transcribed: Philēbos, last period, 360-347 B.C.E.
  (English translation, 1779)

Principal ideas advanced:

◇ Philebus maintains that pleasure is the good, while Socrates contends that wisdom is better than pleasure.

◇ To decide the issue, Socrates considers whether a life of pleasure without wisdom or knowledge would be worthwhile; he decides that if pleasure is not known, or realized, it has no value.

◇ However, a life of wisdom that is in no way pleasant is also without value.

◇ Wisdom contributes more than pleasure does to the good, for by wisdom order and harmony are achieved, and they are the essential features of the good.

◇ In the final ordering of goods, as a result of the discussion, measure is ranked first; second is that which is ordered by measure, the symmetrical and the beautiful; third is mind or wisdom, which possesses more of beauty, symmetry, and truth than does pleasure; fourth is the class of arts, sciences, and true opinions; and fifth is the class of pure pleasures, those accompanying the practice of the pure arts and sciences.

Philebus asks whether pleasure or wisdom is the good. Philebus is represented as maintaining that pleasure is the good, while Socrates contends that wisdom, right opinion, and right reasoning are better than pleasure. It is agreed at the outset of the discussion that if a third state of being turns out to be better than either pleasure or wisdom, then neither Philebus nor Socrates will be considered the victor in the argument; but if either pleasure or wisdom turns out to be more akin to the good than the other, the victor will be the one who has defended the state allied with the better and happier life. Protarchus agrees to defend Philebus's position, and the discussion begins.

Socrates begins his criticism of Philebus's view by asking Protarchus to identify the quality common to pleasures of various sorts that Philebus designates by the word "good." Protarchus objects to the question, arguing that pleasures, insofar as they are pleasures, do not differ from one another. However, after Socrates points out that it would be ridiculous to say that the various sciences, because they are all sci-ences, do not differ from one another, Protarchus agrees to say that there are many different kinds of pleasures, just as there are many different kinds of sciences.

The dialogue here takes a fascinating, although technical, turn. Pleasures are one, but also they are many. This fact suggests the problem of the one and the many, a problem that has nothing to do with concrete things, for an individual person, for example, can easily be one person with many parts; it has, rather, to do with the question as to how a person (the universal) is one, a unity, while the class of people is many, a plurality. The problem is to explain how the one (the universal) can be distributed among the many without losing its unity. Socrates explains that his favorite way of learning is to begin with one idea, a unity, and to proceed to infinity by means of finite steps. A musician, for example, understands that sound is one but also knows that there are many sounds and realizes how these various sounds can be combined. Also, Socrates adds, if inquiry begins with the infinite, then one should proceed to the unity not directly but only by means of a definite number. Thus, beginning with the infinite number of sounds possible to humanity, some god or "divine man," perhaps the Egyptian Thoth, selected a definite number of sounds, and finally unified them by the art of grammar. In the present discussion, the problem is to determine, in the case of the unities pleasure and wisdom, the definite number of species or kinds of each, before passing on to the infinity of particular pleasures and instances of wisdom. Philebus interrupts to beg Socrates either to divide pleasure and wisdom, in the manner described, or to find between them some other way of settling the issue.

Pleasure or Wisdom Alone

Socrates suggests that perhaps neither pleasure nor wisdom is the good, and, if so, there is no need to divide either of them into species. To settle the question as to whether either of them is the good, the proper method would be to consider, first of all, a life of pleasure without wisdom, and then a life of wisdom without pleasure; for if either is the good, it is self-sufficient and does not depend on the other. Philebus and Protarchus assent to this suggestion.

Protarchus at first is convinced that he would like nothing better than a life spent in the enjoyment of the greatest pleasures. However, Socrates points out that if he had neither mind nor memory nor knowledge, he would have neither the intelligence nor the knowledge to know or to discover that he possessed pleasure or that he had possessed pleasure in the past; furthermore, he could not anticipate pleasure. Consequently, without knowledge, life would be reduced to the kind of existence an oyster has. Viewing the alternative in this way, Protarchus loses his enthusiasm for a life of pleasure.

Socrates then considers a life of wisdom without pleasure. It, too, appears unsatisfactory. It does seem to be the case that a life of both pleasure and wisdom, a third alternative, would be superior to a life of nothing but pleasure or nothing but wisdom.

Division into Finite and Infinite

The next pertinent question, then, is the question as to whether pleasure or wisdom is the element that makes the mixed life good. Socrates claims that wisdom, or mind, is the cause of the good; if he can establish his point, Philebus's claim that pleasure is the good will not take even third place. There is the possibility, briefly mentioned by Socrates, that the divine mind is the good; by the time the argument is over, pleasure has fallen to fifth place, and, even then, only as "pure" pleasure.

To lay the foundation of his argument in support of mind over pleasure, Socrates introduces a principle of division according to the distinction between the finite and the infinite. The finite and the infinite form two classes, the compound of them is a third class, and the cause of the compound is the fourth.

Socrates then shows that the infinite is many and that comparatives (such as the hotter and the colder) have no definite quantity because there is no end to the possibilities of degree. The comparative, then—whatever admits of more or less—belongs in the class of the infinite. In Socrates' terms, "the infinite . . . is their unity." Whatever has definite quantity and is measurable is, then, finite.

When the finite and infinite are combined, a third class appears: the class of the harmonious

and proportionate (because the finite is the class of the measurable and is therefore able to introduce number, or order, into the infinite). Health, music, moderate temperature, the seasons, beauty, strength, and "ten thousand other things" belong to the third class.

Protarchus is reminded that the fourth class is the cause of the union of the finite and the infinite. It is then decided that pleasure and pain belong to the class of the infinite, the unlimited. Wisdom (knowledge, mind), however, as that which orders the universe and the elements of the universe and provides human beings with souls and minds, must belong to the fourth class: the cause of the union of the finite and infinite in a state of harmony.

Pleasure and Pain

Socrates then explains that pain is the consequence of the dissolution of harmony in the body; the restoration of harmony is a pleasure. The pleasure of the soul is produced by expectation, a hope of pleasure. However, it is possible for a person to be in a condition of rest between periods of dissolution and restoration, and it may be that such a condition, possible to those who live a life of wisdom, is "the most divine of all lives."

The pleasures of memory are mentioned, and Protarchus is reminded that not all bodily affections reach the soul, for sometimes people are not conscious; to be conscious is to achieve union of body and soul. Memory is the preservation of consciousness, and recollection is the soul's power of recovering some feeling once experienced.

Because desire is the "endeavour of every animal . . . to the reverse of his bodily state"—as when a person who is hungry (empty) desires to be full—desire must be of the soul, or mind, which apprehends the replenishment when it occurs (remembering the state of being empty). Most people are in an intermediate state, as, for example, those who, experiencing pain, take some pleasure in remembering past pleasures.

A distinction is then made between true pleasures and false pleasures. Those persons who beguile themselves with false fancies and opinions derive pleasure from the false; consequently, their pleasures are false. Socrates also shows how the quality and quantity of pleasures can be misjudged when they are compared with different amounts of pain; pleasures compared with pains appear to be greater than they actually are: Such pleasures are also false. The greatest of bodily changes are felt as pleasure or pain, and they appear to be greater when the body is in an unhealthy state than when it is healthy. Furthermore, the pleasures of the intemperate are more intense than those enjoyed by the wise and temperate.

Socrates then carefully outlines the class of mixed feelings, combinations of pleasure and pain that are only of the body, or only of the soul, or common to both. The pleasure of scratching an itch, for example, is a mixed feeling of the body only; and there are certain kinds of anger, belonging to the soul, which are compounds of pleasure and pain.

Because neither false nor mixed pleasures could possibly rank very high in the scale of values, Socrates goes on to consider true and pure pleasures. If he can show that even these pleasures are inferior to wisdom or mind, he will win his case. Having previously rejected the notion that pleasure is merely the absence of pain, Socrates classifies the true pleasures as those given by beauty of color and form, by smooth and clear sounds, by sweet smells, and by knowledge when there is no hunger (pain) for knowledge. These pleasures are true and pure because they are unmixed with pain. Because the excessive pleasures have no measure, they are infinite; the moderate pleasures are finite. A small amount of pure pleasure is truer and more valuable than a large amount of impure, or mixed, pleasure.

Socrates then refers to the philosophical opinion that pleasure is a "generation"; that is, it is relative to some absolute essence that has true being. Because pleasure is not an end, or absolute, but is feeling provoked in a generative process toward an end and is thus allied with the instrumental, it cannot be truly good. The contrary view—that pleasure is good—would lead to the denial of the value of courage, temperance, understanding, and the other virtues; and it would further entail the absurd position that a person possessing pleasure is a person possessing virtue or excellence because only pleasure is good.

Knowledge

Turning to a consideration of knowledge, Socrates first distinguishes between productive knowledge (aiming at products) and educational knowledge. Arithmetic, measurement, and weighing are the pure elements of the productive arts; the rest is conjecture. Socrates claims that music, medicine, husbandry, piloting, and generalship involve more of the impure element of conjecture than does the art of the builder. Even the exact art of building, considered in its pure aspect, the arithmetical, is not always pure. One must distinguish between rough-and-ready practical calculation, where things are counted, and the pure arithmetic of the person who is concerned only with number.

Of the arts, the purest is dialectic, the science of being and reality; the knowledge at which dialectic aims is the highest kind of knowledge, the knowledge of the changeless and essential. The words "mind" and "wisdom" are most truly and exactly used to refer to the contemplation of true being.

The Ordering of the Goods

In summarizing, Socrates reminds his listeners, Philebus and Protarchus, that neither pleasure nor wisdom in isolation is a perfect good because neither would be acceptable without the other. The good, then, is a feature of the mixed life. At first it seems as if the greatest good could be achieved by mixing true pleasures with pure knowledge, but because life without knowledge of practical matters, to supplement knowledge of the essential, would not be worthwhile, all kinds of knowledge were admitted into the compound of the good. However, only the true pleasures are admitted, for wisdom knows the trouble that the impure can cause. Truth, too, is added. However, without measure to regulate the order of the parts of the good, no good would be possible. The mixture conceived by Socrates is regarded as the ideal because of the beauty, symmetry, and truth that order it.

The rival claims of pleasure and wisdom can now be judged by consideration of the beauty, symmetry (measure), and truth of each. On all three counts, wisdom wins; it surely has more of beauty, symmetry, and truth than does pleasure. The conclusion is now possible—the final ordering of the goods. Measure is first, because without measure nothing is worthwhile. Second is that which has been ordered by measure, the symmetrical and the beautiful. Mind and wisdom, as that which possesses the three essentials, is third. Then come the arts and sciences and true opinions that are the mind's activities and products. In fifth position are the pure pleasures of the soul, the pleasures accompanying the practice of the pure arts and sciences.

Although wisdom turns out to be only third in the list of goods, Socrates wins the argument, for pleasure—and only pure pleasure at that—is fifth. Furthermore, measure and the symmetrical, the first two on the list, characterize the mind and are the mind's objectives. Insofar as pleasure is allowed at all, it is only as the pure pleasure of wisdom.

Ian P. McGreal

Timaeus

Type of philosophy: Metaphysics
First transcribed: Timaeos, last period, 360-347 B.C.E. (English translation, 1793)
Principal ideas advanced:

◇ Whatever is apprehended by intelligence and reason always exists and has no becoming.

◇ The world (the universe) must have been created, for it is a sensible and not an intelligible thing; the world is a living creature endowed with soul and intelligence.

◇ The soul of the world is prior in existence and excellence to the body of the world; the soul's function is to know the rational and to rule the body.

◇ The universal nature that receives all things without changing its own nature is "that which is"; it is eternal, formless space.

◇ The three natures that make up reality are the ideas (the eternal forms of things), the sensible copies of ideas (existing objects), and space.

In most of the Socratic dialogues, Socrates is either the central figure or one of the central figures. For all of his assumed deference, Socrates knew himself to be the superior of his contempo-

raries in the art of philosophical elucidation and debate, and Plato honored him by making him the consistently victorious examiner of the pretenders to wisdom. However, *Timaeus* is one of the dialogues in which Socrates assumes a minor role; his personality is off to the side, glowing as usual, but only by grace of earlier dialogues in which he figures as an intellectual hero. *Timaeus* is not so much a dialogue—although there is some conversation—as it is a solo display of Pythagorean ideas about the origin and character of the universe by Timaeus, an enthusiastic Pythagorean astronomer.

Timaeus is interesting as an exhibition of the lengths to which imagination can go in the attempt to understand this mysterious universe. It is a characteristically curious mixture of immature science and mature invention—and it has almost no relevance to modern scientific and philosophical problems. Nevertheless, as part of the portrait of Greek thought, as a facet in the complex entity that was Plato's realm of ideas, and as the one dialogue that—thanks to a translation by Cicero—was influential in the Middle Ages, *Timaeus* continues to hold a place in the significant literature of philosophy.

As the dialogue begins, Socrates reminds Timaeus of a conversation on the previous day concerning the various kinds of citizens required in an ideal state. The main points of *Politeia* (middle period, 388-368 B.C.E.; *Republic,* 1701) are reviewed: The citizens will be husbandmen or artisans or defenders of the state. The defenders will be warriors or political leaders, "guardians" of the state. The guardians are to be passionately dedicated to their tasks and philosophical by temperament and training. Gymnastics and music will play important parts in their education. There will be no private wives or children, but all will work together and live together in a communal way. An effort will be made, by contrived lots, to mate the good with the good, the bad with the bad; and only the good children, morally and intellectually superior, are to be educated.

A Portrait of the Ideal State
Socrates, having reviewed the principal points, then invites Timaeus, Critias, and Hermocrates, as persons with practical experience in the art of

politics, to tell something of their adventures so that the portrait of the ideal state can begin to take on living character.

Critias begins by telling a story about ancient Athens, a tale told to him by his great-grandfather, Dropides, who heard it from Solon, the lawgiver. Solon told of hearing from a priest of Sais that Athens was a thousand years older than Sais, which had been founded eight thousand years before the time of Solon. Both Sais and Athens were founded by Athene, the goddess, so that, both in the division of classes and in laws, the two were alike. Athens became the leader of the Hellenes against the threatening forces from the great island of Atlantis, a powerful empire larger than Libya and Asia combined. Athens defeated Atlantis, but soon afterward both empires were utterly destroyed and hidden by earthquakes and floods. Critias suggests that Socrates regard the citizens of the imaginary city (as outlined in the *Republic*) as being, not imaginary, but the citizens of the actual city of ancient Athens. The justification for this would be that the ancient city and the imagined one agree in their general features.

Socrates is charmed by the idea, and it is agreed that Timaeus will give an account commencing with the generation of the world and ending with the creation of humanity. Critias is then to continue the account in order to complete the process of making actual the state that has so far figured in their conversation as an imaginary one.

The remainder of the dialogue is devoted to Timaeus's account. The dialogue *Critias* (last period, 360-347 B.C.E.; English translation, 1793) continues the conversation by giving Critias his turn in the historical-philosophical account of humanity's origin and progress.

After invoking the gods Timaeus asks the fascinating, complex question: "What is that which always is and has no becoming; and what is that which is always becoming and never is?" The answer is thoroughly Platonic (although it is also consistently Pythagorean): "That which is apprehended by intelligence and reason is always in the same state; but that which is conceived by opinion with the help of sensation and without reason, is always in a process of becoming and perishing and never really is." This answer—that idea (whatever is apprehended by intelligence) is

constant, while what is sensed is inconstant and consequently unreal—is Platonic in its giving priority to idea and in its identification of reality with whatever is constant and prior.

The World

The next important question to be settled is whether the world did or did not have a beginning. The answer by now is obvious: If whatever can be sensed is not eternal, but comes into being or is destroyed, and if the world is sensible, then it must have come into being. However, whatever comes into being must have a cause. Furthermore, because the world is fair and the maker of it must have been the best of causes, the pattern to which the artificer referred in making the copy that is the world must have been the pattern of the unchangeable—the ideas (although the word is not used here).

Timaeus continues by stating that the world must have been patterned after a perfect, intelligent animal (an idea), for the Deity could not have been satisfied with the imperfect, the unintelligent, or the inanimate. The world, then, became a living creature "endowed with soul and intelligence by the providence of God." In order to make the world visible, God had to use fire; in order to make it tangible, he had to use earth. Then, in order to supply two means by which a union of elements could be achieved and a world of solidity created, God introduced the elements of water and air. Because the world had to have a shape that would comprehend all others, God made the world (the living animal) in the form of a globe. The world is one, for it is a copy of the eternal form, which is one. It has no hands or feet, but revolves in a circle.

The soul of the world was made by God to be prior in existence and excellence to the body. The soul's function is to rule the body. To compose the soul, God made an essence in between the indivisible and the divisible. He then mixed this intermediate essence with the indivisible (the same) and the divisible (the other), and then divided the compound into parts, each of which contained each of the three essences. The division was very complicated, but orderly. The material was then made into strips, and an outer and an inner circle were formed that joined to form X's. The one circle became the circle of the same and was, consequently, undivided; the other, the circle of the other, was divided into seven circles (the seven planets) having different orbits.

The soul and the corporeal universe were joined together. Because the soul partakes of the essences of the same, the other, and the intermediate, it alone knows the characters of the sensible world and attains to perfect knowledge of the rational.

God wanted the world to be everlasting, but eternity is not possible for a corporeal being. Hence, he created time as the image of eternity. Stars were placed in the seven orbits to make time possible. God then made a great fire, the sun, to light up the heavens so that animals (people) might learn arithmetic by observing the stars in their courses.

The created animal was then made to have four species corresponding to the four kinds of ideas involved in the original: heavenly bodies (creatures of fire), birds (creatures of the air), creatures of the water, and creatures of the earth. Knowledge of the gods comes by tradition from those who were the children of the gods. From Earth and Heaven were born Oceanus and Tethys, whose children were Phorcys, Cronus, and Rhea, and from Cronus and Rhea were generated Zeus and Herè.

God then used a dilution of the essence of the universe soul to prepare the souls of living things. Souls that lived properly were destined to return to their native stars, but others would be forced to reside in women or brute animals. Human beings had their bodies fashioned by those gods who were the children of the father of the gods, and the bodies were made of the four elements welded together with tiny invisible pegs. Motions within the body or on it from external motions were carried to the soul, and the motions came to be called "sensations." Only when the soul is able to free itself from the influence of bodily motions can it begin to revolve as it should, acquiring knowledge.

The courses of the soul are contained in the head, which is a spherical body emulating the spherical body of the universe. All the other appendages of the human being are instrumental to the soul's functioning within the head. Light is a gentle fire that merges in the eye with the fire within the body, finally affecting the soul in an act of perception. The causes of sight must be distinguished from the purpose of sight. Sight exists to make knowledge possible: By observing heavenly bodies, people acquire knowledge of time, then of numbers and of philosophy. People learn by analogy, identifying the courses of heavenly bodies with the courses of individual souls.

The Four Elements

Having given an account of the genesis and development of the soul and of mind in terms of the soul's activity, Timaeus considers the consequences of the presence of the four elements (earth, water, air, fire) in the universe.

In addition to the changeless, eternal pattern of things and the copies of the pattern, there is the "receptacle" and "nurse" of all generation. Because the elements can pass into each other—water, for example, changing into a vapor, or air—no element is primary; in fact, one should not refer to fire, or water, or any element as "that" that is; but one should say of that which is that it is of "such" a nature, for example, fire. The universal nature, which receives all things without changing its own nature, is alone truly designated as "that" which is; it is formless; it is eternal space. Thus, there are three kinds of natures: the uncreated, indestructible kind of being (the eternal ideas); the sensible copies of the eternal (the objects of opinion and sense); and space, the "home of all created things." These are called, respectively, being, generation, and space.

Originally the four elements were tossed about in space, and they were neither fair nor good, but God, by the use of form and number, brought order and goodness. The elements were made up of triangles, for they are solids, and all solids are made up of planes that are, in turn, composed of triangles. Triangles are either isosceles or scalene (with unequal sides); of these, the most beautiful is that which is such that its double is an equilateral triangle. To achieve the most beauty, the isosceles, which has but a single form, and that one of the scalene forms that is such that, doubled, an equilateral triangle is formed, must have been used by God in the creation of the elements.

Timaeus retracts his earlier statement that the elements can all pass into one another. Earth can never become anything but earth. The other three, however, can pass into one another. Because earth is the most immovable of the four elements, it must be composed of cubical forms. Water is harder to move than either fire or air; hence, it must be composed of icosahedron forms ("made up of 120 triangular elements, forming twelve solid angles, each of them included in five plane equilateral triangles, having altogether twenty bases, each of which is an equilateral triangle"). Fire is made up of the smallest and most acute bodies, pyramids, while air is composed of octahedron solids. It can now be understood why earth cannot become something other than earth: Its solids cannot assume the forms necessary to the other elements.

After a discussion of the kinds of fire (flaming fire, light, and glow), the kinds of water (liquid and fusile, the latter divisible into gold, adamant, and copper; and the former into such various liquids as wine, oil, honey, and the like), and the kinds of earth (rock, stones, chemicals), Timaeus considers the effects of the elements on bodies and souls. Fire is sharp and cutting in its heat because it is made up of sharp pointed solids (pyramids: tetrahedra). Other sensations are accounted for by reference to contraction, compression, expansion, and so forth, caused by the impingement of various bodies on the sensing body. Pain is the result of a sudden change that disturbs the particles of the body; pleasure is the effect of the body's return to its natural condition.

The sensations resulting from the stimulation of the sense organs are explained as affectations caused by contractions and dilations, or by moistening or drying up, or by smothering or roughening of parts caused by the entrance of the particles of exterior objects. Sounds are blows that are transmitted to the soul, and hearing is a vibration that begins in the head and ends in the liver. Colors are flames coming from things that join with the streams of light within the body. With great care, Timaeus explains how various colors are formed by the combinations of fires.

Body and Soul

Returning to the account of humanity's origin, Timaeus argues that a person's immortal soul comes from God, but one has another, mortal soul given by the gods who fashioned one's body. One's mortal soul is subject to various destructive passions, among which are the love of pleasure and rashness and fear. The immortal soul is in the head, but the mortal soul is in the breast and thorax and is so divided that the part that has courage and passion is nearer the head, so that it might be better subject to reason.

The heart was designed by the gods to be a guard in the service of reason, sending the fire of passion to all parts of the body; and the lungs were designed to enclose the heart, thus cushioning its exertions and cooling it. The liver, solid and smooth like a mirror, was intended to distort the images of things of unworthy nature, giving them the distressing color of bile, while it also suffuses the images of worthy things with its natural sweetness. The spleen was made to keep the liver clean in order that it might function properly as the seat of divination. All parts of the body—the bowels, the bones, the marrow of the bones (which unites the soul with the body), the joints and flesh—were fashioned in such a manner as to encourage a person to be a creature of reason, not appetite. Fire travels through the body, giving the red color to blood and performing such necessary tasks as the digestion of food by cutting the food with the pyramidal solids that are the material of fire. Eventually, however, as the body grows older, the triangles are blunted, and digestion becomes more difficult. Disease and death are the results of the loosening or dissolving of the bonds by which the marrow holds the body and soul together. When death results the soul, "obtaining a natural release, flies away with joy."

The diseases of the mind are of two kinds: madness and ignorance. If anyone is bad, he or she is so involuntarily as the result of an indisposition of the body, and indisposition is simply the lack of that fair and good proportion that means health and sanity. To achieve a proper harmony of body and soul, exercise is necessary: gymnastic for the body, music and philosophy for the soul. Human beings need the food and motion that will encourage the growth and harmony of body and soul, and the motions most worth studying and emulating are the motions of the universe as revealed in the revolutions of the heavenly bodies. Intellect is supposed to be superior to desire, and thus one must give particular attention to the exercise of that divine part of his soul.

Cowardly men change into women in the second generation; simple, light-minded men give rise to the race of birds; and those without philosophy, who allow the breast to rule the head, become beasts. Those who become foolish are made to crawl on the ground, devoid of feet, while the senseless and ignorant become animals of the sea.

The generation of animals is the result of desire resulting from the respiration of the seed of life rising in the marrow. When the desire of man and woman is satisfied, unseen animals pass from the man to the woman, and they mature in her.

Timaeus concludes his account by summarizing in the following manner: "The world has received animals, mortal and immortal, and is fulfilled with them, and has become a visible animal containing the visible—the sensible God who is the image of the intellectual, the greatest, best, fairest, most perfect—the one only-begotten heaven."

Thus, by giving the center of the stage to a Pythagorean, Plato sketched out a conception of the origin of the universe. Perhaps he found the analysis of things in terms of triangles a reasonable, even probable, anatomy of nature; perhaps he was intrigued, but not convinced. In any case, Plato gave full allegiance to the theory of forms, or eternal essences, and he never wavered in his endorsement of the rational mode of life. Despite the bizarre character of the philosophy contained in *Timaeus*, the Greek love of wisdom makes itself felt and gives to the whole an enduring charm.

Ian P. McGreal, updated by John K. Roth

Additional Reading

Brumbaugh, Robert S. *Plato for the Modern Age.* New York: Crowell-Collier, 1962. A good introduction to Plato's thought and the Greek world in which he developed it.

Copleston, Frederick. *A History of Philosophy: Greece and Rome.* Garden City, N.Y.: Doubleday, 1969. Copleston devotes several clear chapters to a discussion of the full range of Plato's view.

Cropsey, Joseph. *Plato's World: Man's Place in the Cosmos.* Chicago: University of Chicago Press, 1995. Discusses Plato's views on human nature with attention to his political theories.

Gonzalez, Francisco, ed. *The Third Way: New Directions in Platonic Studies.* Lanham, Md.: Rowman & Littlefield, 1995. A helpful sampling of late twentieth century research on Plato, his continuing significance, and trends of interpretation in Platonic studies.

Irwin, Terrence. *Plato's Ethics.* New York: Oxford University Press, 1995. A thorough study of Plato's moral philosophy, including its political implications.

Jones, W. T. *The Classical Mind.* Vol. 1 in *A History of Western Philosophy.* 2d ed. New York: Harcourt, Brace & World, 1969. A reliable introduction to the main themes and issues on which Plato focused.

Kahn, Charles H. *Plato and the Socratic Dialogue: The Philosophical Use of a Literary Form.* New York: Cambridge University Press, 1996. A study of Plato's use of the dialogue form as a means for exploring and developing key philosophical positions and dispositions.

Kraut, Richard, ed. *The Cambridge Companion to Plato.* Cambridge, England: Cambridge University Press, 1992. Eminent Plato scholars analyze and assess key Platonic dialogues and issues in Plato's thought.

Moravcsik, J. M. E. *Plato and Platonism: Plato's Conception of Appearance and Reality in Ontology, Epistemology, and Ethics and Its Modern Echoes.* Cambridge, Mass.: Blackwell, 1992. A scholarly study of Plato's key distinction between appearance and reality and the continuing impact of that distinction.

Pappas, Nikolas, ed. *Routledge Philosophy Guidebook to Plato and the "Republic."* New York: Routledge, 1995. Helpful articles that clarify key Platonic concepts and theories.

Rutherford, R. B. *The Art of Plato: Ten Essays in Platonic Interpretation.* Cambridge: Harvard University Press, 1995. Well-informed essays on key elements of Plato's theories.

Tuana, Nancy, ed. *Feminist Interpretations of Plato.* University Park: Pennsylvania State University, 1994. Scholarly essays evaluate Plato's understanding of gender issues and appraise his philosophy from the perspectives of feminist theory.

Williams, Bernard A. O. *Plato.* New York: Routledge, 1999. An excellent biographical introduction to the thoughts of the philosopher, clearly presented. Bibliography.

Stephen Satris, updated by John K. Roth

Plotinus

As the founder of Neoplatonism, Plotinus exerted a profound influence on Western philosophical and religious thought, from his own day to the present.

Principal philosophical works: *Enneas*, c. 256-270 (*The Enneads*, 1918); *Plotinos: Complete Works*, 1918 (4 volumes); *Collected Writings of Plotinus*, 1994.

Born: 205; possibly Lycopolis, Upper Egypt
Died: 270; Campania, (now in Italy)

Early Life

Plotinus was born in 205, but almost nothing is known about his origins or his early life. His nationality, race, and family are unknown, and information about his birthplace comes from a fourth century source that may not be reliable. Plotinus told his disciples little about himself; he would not even divulge the date of his birth. Only one thing can be said with certainty: Plotinus's education and intellectual background were entirely Greek. This fact can be deduced from his writings; Plotinus shows little knowledge of Egyptian religion and misinterprets Egyptian hieroglyphic symbolism. Porphyry, Plotinus's pupil and biographer, reports that Plotinus had a complete knowledge of geometry, arithmetic, mechanics, optics, and music, and he must have acquired some of this knowledge during the early years of his education.

Porphyry reports that in 232, when Plotinus was twenty-seven, he felt a strong desire to study philosophy. He consulted the best teachers in Alexandria, but they all disappointed him. Then a friend recommended a teacher named Ammonius Saccas. Plotinus went to hear him and immediately declared, "This is the man I was looking for." Little is known, however, of Ammonius's philosophy; he was self-taught, wrote nothing, and made his followers promise not to divulge his teachings.

Beginning in late 232 or early 233, Plotinus studied with Ammonius for eleven years. Plotinus's long stay in Alexandria may be the only reason for the common belief that he was originally from Egypt. Plotinus wanted to learn more of the philosophy of the Persians and the Indians, and he joined the army of Emperor Gordianus III, which was marching against the Persians.

It is not known in what capacity Plotinus served; he may have been a scientific adviser, or he may have occupied a lower position. The expedition, however, did not achieve its objective. Gordianus was assassinated in Mesopotamia, and Plotinus escaped with difficulty to Antioch. He made no attempt to return to Ammonius (nor did he ever return to the East). Instead, in 245, at the age of forty, he traveled to Rome, where he was to remain for twenty-five years, until shortly before his death. The stage was set for him to emerge as the last great pagan philosopher.

Life's Work

For the next ten years, Plotinus established himself in Rome. He accepted private students and based his teaching on that of Ammonius. During this time, he wrote nothing, but by the time Porphyry joined him in 264, Plotinus no longer considered himself bound by the restrictions on publication that Ammonius had imposed (other pupils of Ammonius, such as Origen and Erennius, had already published). Plotinus had therefore written twenty-one treatises by 264, although none of them had circulated widely. Porphyry urged him to write more, and twenty-four treatises followed during the six years that Porphyry was his pupil.

Only one story survives about Plotinus's life in Rome before Porphyry's arrival. A philosopher named Olympias, from Alexandria, who was also a former pupil of Ammonius, attempted to "bring a star-stroke upon him [Plotinus] by magic." Plotinus, who apparently believed in the power of magic, felt the effects of this attack, but Olympias found his attempt recoiling on himself. He ceased his attack and confessed that "the soul of Plotinus had such great power as to be able to throw back attacks on him on to those who were seeking to do him harm."

During the time that Porphyry was his pupil, Plotinus lived comfortably in what must have been a large house, owned by a wealthy widow named Gemina. He earned a reputation for kindness and gentleness and was always generous in offering help to others. Many people entrusted their sons and daughters to his care, "considering that he would be a holy and god-like guardian." Although Plotinus was an otherworldly philoso-

pher, he also believed in the importance of the social virtues, that the practice of them contributed to the soul's ultimate liberation. He was therefore practical, wise, and diplomatic in daily affairs, taking good care of the worldly interests of the young people in his charge. For example, they would be encouraged to give up property only if they decided to become philosophers, and even this was a decision that they would have to make for themselves. The same was true of Plotinus's attitude toward the physical body and its desires. Although he believed in self-discipline, he acknowledged that legitimate physical needs must be looked after, and he never advocated the kind of asceticism that was found in some other ancient philosophical schools.

Plotinus often acted as arbitrator in disputes, without ever incurring an enemy. The only opposition he appears ever to have aroused (apart from that of Olympias) was when some Greek philosophers accused him of stealing some of his philosophy from Numenius, a charge that modern scholars have not accepted. Plotinus was also a good judge of character, and his advice was sound. When Porphyry, for example, confessed that he was contemplating suicide, Plotinus told him that the desire was caused by physiological reasons, not by rational thought, and advised him to take a vacation. Porphyry accepted his advice.

Plotinus had a number of aristocratic friends, and members of the senate attended his lectures. One of them, Rogatianus, relinquished his property and became an ascetic after being exposed to Plotinus's teaching. The Emperor Gallienus, sole emperor from 260 to 268, and his wife, Salonia, venerated Plotinus. Plotinus once asked them to found a "city of philosophers" in Campania, to be called Platonopolis, which would serve as a monastic retreat for him and his followers. The scheme failed, however, as a result of opposition in the Roman senate. Gallienus's assassination in 268 must have been a blow to Plotinus because Gallienus's successors showed no interest in Greek philosophy.

Plotinus. *(Giraudon/Art Resource)*

Plotinus's lectures were more like conversations; discussion was always encouraged. One of his pupils once complained that he would prefer to hear Plotinus expound a set treatise and was exhausted by Porphyry's continuous questions. Plotinus replied, "But if when Porphyry asks questions we do not solve his difficulties we shall not be able to say anything at all to put into the treatise." Plotinus was a thoroughly engaging teacher; when he was speaking, "his intellect visibly lit up his face: there was always a charm about his appearance . . . kindliness shone out from him."

Plotinus would never revise his written work; he complained that writing gave him eyestrain. He was careless in the formation of the letters, and he showed no interest in spelling. Porphyry comments that Plotinus would compose everything in his mind. When he came to write, the thoughts were already fully formed, and he wrote "as continuously as if he was copying from a book." Even if someone engaged him in conversation, he would continue writing and not lose his train of thought. This ability to focus on the inner life enabled him to achieve a high level of mystical experience. He attained complete mystic union four times during Porphyry's stay with him, and in a treatise written before Porphyry's arrival, Plotinus says that he had experienced it often.

In his final years, he suffered from a painful illness that may have been leprosy. Although he stopped teaching and withdrew from his friends and pupils, who feared contagion, he continued to write. Nine treatises appeared in his last two years, bringing the total to fifty-four, which were collected and edited by Porphyry, at Plotinus's request. Finally, Plotinus went away to the estate of his deceased friend Zethus in Campania, where he died alone, except for the presence of his doctor, Eustochius. His last words, according to Eustochius, were "Try to bring back the god in you to the divine in the All!"

Influence

Plotinus was the last great philosopher of antiquity and the only one to rank with Plato and Aristotle. His philosophy has exerted an enormous influence on the thought of his own period and on that of later times. Although he probably thought of himself as no more than an interpreter of Plato, Plotinus became the founder of Neoplatonism. His thought lived on in his pupils Porphyry and Amelius, and all Neoplatonic philosophers regarded him as a respected, although not a supreme, authority.

Plotinus's system was a comprehensive and original one. He brought to the best of Greek philosophy a dimension of mystical thought that in its force, immediacy, and beauty has rarely, if ever, been equaled in the West. *The Enneads* are not merely an ethical or metaphysical system; they are a guide to the soul's liberation, culminating in the experience and contemplation of the One. This experience is seen as the goal of the philosopher's quest, and that of all humanity.

Plotinus, and Neoplatonism in general, were also major influences on the development of Christian theology. Saint Augustine knew *The Enneads* and quotes Plotinus by name five times. The fourth century Cappadocian Fathers, especially Gregory of Nyssa, also came under his spell. His thought emerged again in the Renaissance in the work of Marsilio Ficino (who translated Plotinus into Latin) and Giovanni Pico della Mirandola. In modern thought, Plotinus's influence can be traced in the work of German Idealist philosopher Friedrich Schelling, French philosopher Henri Bergson, and English Romantic poets such as William Blake and William Butler Yeats, whose interest in Plotinus was prompted by the translations made by the English Platonist Thomas Taylor in the late eighteenth and early nineteenth centuries.

Bryan Aubrey

The Enneads

Type of philosophy: Metaphysics, philosophical theology
First transcribed: Enneas, c. 256-270 (English translation, 1918)
Principal ideas advanced:
◇ Reality is one, and the source of all being is the One, the divine unity.
◇ From the One emanates the divine mind (*nous*), the intellectual principle.

◇ The divine mind, in turn, spends the creative force of the One in giving rise to the divine soul.

◇ The One, *nous*, and the soul make up the divine Trinity.

◇ While lost in the contemplation of the One, the soul desires to return to its source of being, but in turning away from the One, it creates a lower (and hence, less perfect) order of souls and material objects by forming matter according to the ideas of the intellectual principle.

Only in recent years has the full importance of Plotinus been widely recognized. Previously, Neoplatonism, of which Plotinus is the greatest representative, and Platonism had not been clearly distinguished. Lacking the original writings to compare, scholars in the Middle Ages blended the two forms of thought together without a clear notion of their distinctive qualities. Historical research and the availability of the sources themselves have produced a growing awareness of the distinctiveness of Plotinus's thought and of his unique contributions in *The Enneads*. Its intimate connection with the Platonic tradition is readily admitted by Plotinus himself, but such closeness in origin need not mean similarity, as Plato's famous student Aristotle made clear.

In a strict sense, *The Enneads* are unsystematic. Neither Porphyry's ordering of the scattered writings nor scholarly reconstruction of possible temporal sequence can make the writings form any strictly logical order. Plotinus discussed with his students a few very central philosophical problems, each of which he returned to many times, and *The Enneads* represent in content but not in form the consistency of this continual development of certain central themes.

The Soul

Plotinus's metaphysical interest in the problems of the one and the many is well known, but his central interest in ethics and his fully developed aesthetic theory, which is one of the first to be elaborated, are not always so widely recognized. Most important of all, however, are Plotinus's explorations into philosophical psychology. The soul is central in all Plotinian thought, and he was the first major writer to put the analysis of the soul at the center of philosophical investigation.

The soul in Plato's world held an important place, and Plato devoted considerable time to describing it in *Politeia* (middle period, 388-368 B.C.E.; *Republic*, 1701) and *Phaedros* (middle period, 388-368 B.C.E.; *Phaedrus*, 1792). Yet somehow "soul" was never reconciled with "form" as a metaphysical principle. Plotinus began where Plato left off, making soul central, and the analysis of it is more direct and extended than Plato's mythical framework could allow. Despite the importance of Plato both as to the problems Plotinus treated and as to style, what many are surprised to find upon reading Plotinus is the large amount of Aristotelianism present, as well as a wide variety of other views. In some sense, Plotinus began with Platonic problems, but his scope takes in almost all previous philosophy.

Just as Plato had a strong interest in sense perception, so also Plotinus was led by the problems of sense perception to consider the soul as of first importance. Soul is intimately related to the body and clearly is combined with it. After considering most known theories of the soul, Plotinus went on to make the soul more perfect than the body in virtue of the soul's greater unity. Soul centralizes perception and is not subject to physical division as the body is.

The Intellectual Principle

In Plotinus's philosophy, sensation is only the beginning of knowledge. Above that stands the soul's grasp of intelligible forms. Sensation is dependent upon the soul's close association with a physical body, but because the soul in virtue of its greater unity stands higher in the order of being than the body, its grasp of intelligible form indicates that something in turn stands above it in the ontological order. This is the intellectual principle, the locus of the intelligible forms of all things and of the principle of thought itself. This principle, which is superior to the soul, is often called the divine mind because it exemplifies the union of universal thought with all the intelligible forms of thought. This is a level of unity that exceeds that possessed by the soul, just as the soul surpasses that of the physical world.

Physical body, as it looks away from soul's

guidance, tends to become sheer disorganized matter; on the other hand, as the body is subject to the soul's direction, it exemplifies harmony and order to the highest degree possible for it. As the soul's attention is absorbed by physical matter, it tends to forget itself and to be overcome with sensual desires; it goes out of itself seeking a multitude of things. However, when the soul considers the intellectual principle above it, then it tends to be drawn away from physical concerns and to regain its original and essential integrity, absorbed in contemplation.

The intellectual principle when considered in relation to soul appears as the rational structure of the world order, but in itself it is sheer intellection, involved with no motion or change and retaining no distinction except that between thought and object. All, then, has been hierarchically arranged in the Plotinian metaphysical scheme, beginning with the soul and ascending and descending according to the degree of unity. As far removed from the multiplicity of the physical world as the intellectual principle is, it still embodies the necessity of at least a distinction between thought and its object, as well as the distinctions between the various intellectual forms themselves.

Because unity has operated all along the way to delineate the various structures, Plotinus found himself driven to seek unity itself, beyond even the division between thought and its object. Such a first principle Plotinus called the One (sometimes the Good), and it stands at the pinnacle of the hierarchy as unity itself, from which all of the lower gradations of unity are in turn derived. These three central principles, One, intellectual principle, and soul (body is not given equal status), are nowhere simply defined, but they are refined through constant reference throughout the writings.

Evil

Evil was both a moral and a metaphysical problem for Plotinus. The deficiencies that the individual finds in this world are precisely what drove him to seek an order of existence higher than this world. Contrary to much popular opinion, Plotinus did not despise this world. Rather, he regarded the world as the fullest expression of beauty above. The natural world holds all the perfection that its lower order allows, and as such, it is the very embodiment and evidence of that from which it descends, its higher origin. Yet this is not necessarily a temporal origin because Plotinus never questioned the fact that the world is eternal. It is "origin" in the sense of the dependence of the lower orders upon the higher for the power of their existence.

Metaphysically speaking, evil was difficult for Plotinus. Because all must be accounted for by means of one principle that is without defect, the problem is to show how what is essentially perfect can eventually become bad. Plotinus did this through the image of gradually diminishing light and through increasing multiplicity. What is in itself One and perfect (the divine unity) as it goes out from itself to create lower orders, becomes in the process increasingly multiple and less perfect, until its final outreach is sheer matter (the negative of being), its moral equivalent, evil.

However, the process that leads down from the One to the creation of matter and evil also leads upward. The soul, by looking to itself and discovering its essentially higher nature through its essential difference from its body, grasps the basic distinction that can lead it away from matter toward matter's perfect and unitary source. Seeing the gradations of unity represented in the various levels, the soul may rise by intelligence to the intelligible world and then beyond it, at least momentarily, to the One beyond intellectual distinctions.

The One

The description of the One itself, of course, was an even more difficult problem for Plotinus than accounting for matter and evil. No explanation of evil is ultimately possible in a world that is eternal and whose structure is necessary. However, the description of the One is of necessity baffling, and both Plotinus and his interpreters have been painfully aware of this fact. The One as the first principle of all transcends all multiplicity and therefore all distinctions, whereas an intellectual grasp depends on the presence of at least a minimum of distinction.

Therefore, the One may be approached and may be grasped, but neither directly nor intellectually. Here the "negative method" comes to its fullest classical use. We may deny qualities inappropriately attributed to the One more easily than we can say what its characteristics are. Indirectly, from the process of denial and of paring away, we come to some grasp of the One, but this is not a discursive understanding. Such an apprehension does not induce conversation, and Plotinus said that if we are tempted to speak about the One, to give it a set of positive characteristics, then silence is more appropriate.

This difficulty leads to what is often called Plotinus's "mysticism." If the term is used carefully, it is quite accurate as applied to the Plotinian view. Plotinus was not needlessly vague, and surely he did not belittle the powers of reason. Everything discerned is grasped through reason's light. Yet above reason's highest level stands a more ultimate realm, the source of intelligence and all below it, a realm not itself subject to the distinctions that reason requires for its operation. Not that the One is empty; the One is the source of all below it, containing the power of all but without itself being any single thing.

Raising the Soul

The ethical aims of Plotinus were high. After he had devised this hierarchical scheme of the nature of things, each level determined by the multiplicity of its distance from the One, the goal then becomes to raise the soul in its considerations to the highest possible level. To do this, however, in some sense means that knowers must become the very level they contemplate. The soul ceases to be like the indefinite multiplicity below and actually becomes what it finds above it. Thus the soul tends not only to become good as it turns from matter and evil; it becomes godlike. Thus, the soul recovers the "essential humanity."

Beauty has a part in this conversion from the lower to the higher, and Plotinus here admitted his dependence on Plato's analysis of the use of beauty in *Phaedrus*. The apprehension of beauty draws the soul upward, reminding it of its true self and of the higher levels open to it. Beauty represents purity, and the truly happy and virtuous life is not a thing of mixture; it is an unchanging state. By its nature, beauty is present where a diversity has become a unity, which is why the pleasure derived from such beauty is itself essentially an unchanging state.

The whole process is not an easy one. It requires training and discipline. People must learn to cut away and to detach themselves from multiple concerns. Not that these concerns are in themselves bad or that beauty is not found in the multiplicity of the natural order, but the soul has become aware of something higher, something perfect that is possible to attain. Trained properly, the soul requires no guide for the last steps. The soul that wants the vision of beauty must first make itself beautiful through discipline and order. Action and effort are preparation for achieving a level beyond act. The Good, which is Plotinus's other name for the One, is self-sufficient, and through virtuous effort, people reach a level of essential rest.

Despite the absolute determinism of the natural structure as a whole that is eternal and without alternative, Plotinus still allowed for an area of freedom in human affairs. Some causation is due to environmental factors, but some causes originate from the soul, and this is the area of self-determination. Plotinus defined a free act as essentially one that springs from the individual's own nature, neither reflecting outside forces nor representing accidental features. It is the soul's clear vision of its own essential nature. Here the soul is guided by the reason principle above it, so that fate (freedom's opposite) prevails when action is contrary to reason. Thus Plotinus stands within the tradition: freedom means self-determination guided by rational apprehension of the structure of things.

In the intellectual principle above the soul, no spatial distinction can be found, no division, no incompleteness. It is a living intellection as one act within a unity, whereas the soul's intellection is a more multiple and temporal affair. In keeping with the classical idea of perfection, any widespread activity would represent defeat. The various ontological levels are thus characterized by a decreasing activity as well as by an increasing unity the nearer people move toward the One. Not that all activity is missing, but it here becomes fully realized activity.

The Natural Order

The inequality within the natural world and the inequality of the various ontological orders all are necessary. They are, in fact, the best expression possible to the One. Gradations and completeness of every possible kind from highest to lowest, from best to worst, are the fullest expression possible for the One as the first principle of all things. Its fullness requires expression, and the widest possible variety actually expresses its perfection best. In this way, Plotinus justified the presence of evil in a world that is essentially of good origin. Individual objects or events may be bad, but viewed as a part of the total panorama, their place can be seen to be within a necessarily good order.

Following Plato's suggestion in *Timaeos* (last period, 360-347 B.C.E.; *Timaeus*, 1793), Plotinus developed the view that the natural order is like an organism. As unity "fissures out," it reaches out to the furthermost extent of things and yet embraces all in one system; but with all its differentiation, it is still one organized living thing. Not everything can be equal; there must be levels from the highest to the lowest, but the overall scheme is that of the natural order as a living, self-sustaining organism.

In considering love, Plotinus made it clear that, once one has discovered the basic ontological levels and gained control over oneself through discipline, there is no reason why the beauties of the natural order may not be enjoyed. Viewed properly as the descendants of yet higher orders, natural beauties may be instructive and are not to be shunned. The usual picture of Plotinus as an ascetic and as rejecting the everyday world is not accurate. One must study and discipline oneself for metaphysical insight, but although the levels above the soul are to be preferred, the natural world and human life are to be enjoyed fully as representing the best possible expression of those higher principles.

"Matter" is perhaps Plotinus's most pressing problem in his effort to see the natural order as good and as being the best expression of the One. Matter seems to be opaque, the very opposite of the light that represents the One. However, Plotinus argued that, although matter is responsible for much evil and distortion, it is necessary to the One's essentially good production because it furnishes a base for the imprinting of forms. Without matter, the world would be insubstantial. Thus, despite its difficult properties, matter is necessary. As necessary to the order, it is in that sense good. This is not so much to explain matter as being in itself good as it is to account for it as necessary to the whole and as being good only in that indirect sense.

Time

In accounting for time, Plotinus foreshadows Saint Augustine's famous discussion of time in the *Confessiones* (397-400; *Confessions*, 1620). The intellectual principle is not temporal, although time lies, so to speak, self-concentrated there. Soul, on the other hand, must by nature move and produce, and thus soul's activity is the essential origin for time. This is not the soul perceived as a cosmic principle produced immediately by the intellectual principle, this is soul as it turns away from its origin to produce physical structures below it. In the process of producing the other orders below it, soul clothes itself with time. If soul withdrew and turned itself entirely toward its primal unity, time would once again disappear.

Augustine's dependence on Plotinus for his doctrine of time is one major illustration of the now recognized importance of Plotinus for all medieval philosophy and theology. Because Plato's own writings were unavailable, Plotinus was accepted as the representative of Platonism, with no distinction drawn between Platonism and Neoplatonism. Augustine's debt to Plotinus is heavy, as Augustine acknowledges. Through Plotinus, the Neoplatonic strain became extremely influential, particularly because it formed such a natural background for the rapidly developing Christian doctrine. For instance, Plotinus's ontology is based on a trinitarian concept, although the doctrine developed by Christian theologians differs from it in detail.

Philosophers Baruch Spinoza and Georg Wilhelm Friedrich Hegel are also much in Plotinus's debt; in this sense, much modern thought is Plotinus's heir. Wherever soul is stressed as a prime object of philosophical analysis, there is a strong kinship to Plotinus. Wherever reason is powerful but is ultimately to be transcended, there rational mysticism begins and has links to Plotinus. Whenever people are urged to seek their authentic existence and to turn back from multiple pursuits, the philosophical psychology and the metaphysics of Plotinus are not far away.

Upward Vision and Beauty

Contrary to some popular opinion, Plato actually stressed the practical application of philosophy, together with the constant necessity to blend practical skill with philosophical insight. Plato had his moments as a visionary, but Plotinus is far more visionary. Plato described his realm of forms in their perfection, but Plotinus's almost lyrical praise for the purity and repose of his intellectual principle is unrestrained and unqualified. Toward this vision all thought bends, and it is not modified as it is for Plato by the necessity for return to the practical world. Plotinus knew that that vision cannot be sustained, but the return to the sense world is simply a necessity; it is never a goal.

Ethically, then, Plotinus had a single direction: upward and beyond this world's structure. However, it would be false to say that this goal involves a disparagement of the natural world. Plotinus did not disdain ordinary affairs. He loved nature, but only for what it could tell him about the source of all things and for the guidance it could provide for transcending it.

This is why the apprehension of beauty is such a stirring phenomenon for a Plotinian. Such experience is a taste of the realm beyond being that the soul seeks. The sense of beauty is a natural guide in detecting and in separating the higher from the lower orders within nature. Such a sensitivity to hierarchy is absolutely essential because it is by establishing orders and levels that the mind is able to orient itself and to discern realms even beyond the natural order.

Thus the lover is very close to the philosopher, and philosophy's classical definition (the love of wisdom) fits Plotinus almost perfectly. Plato's *Phaedrus* is important here. Plotinus, like his revered predecessor, found in the phenomenon of love a philosophical key. Philosophers are stirred by love and moved by beauty; both of these experiences teach them to discern the higher from the lower in nature's sphere. Evil is not a question at this point. The natural tendency under the influence of beauty is away from evil's home (matter) and toward beauty's source, the intellectual sphere.

Plato described a world of forms different from the ordinary world, but Plotinus carried this transcendental tendency much further. In the as-cent that the apprehension of beauty has launched, we soon discover that each level has laws of its own, until we come finally to the One itself, where even the law of identity does not hold. Above this, the intellectual principle has been found to be free of all distinctions, whereas division and partition are the essential elements of every lower order. To learn to read Plotinus is to stretch the mind's natural habits and to learn to think and visualize in new ways. Contrast is the proper method: Bodies are exclusively many; the supreme is exclusively one.

Climb to the One

In some genuine sense, Plotinus was an evolutionist. That is, because his theory was based on levels, each of which is different in kind from the others, his primary task was to explain how the levels are related; that is, how each lower order came from a higher principle. Plotinus's theory differs from modern evolutionary theory in that this succession is not a temporal affair. The world and all its orders were, for Plotinus, eternal. However, each order is derived constantly from its superior, so that if each ontological realm exhibits basically different properties, then an evolutionary theory is required to show how something generated by one level can become unlike its origin in kind.

This continual attempt to trace the evolutionary cycle, now upward, now downward, is the substance of much of *The Enneads*. Beginning with the soul, Plotinus tried to explain how it could generate something different and inferior to it—physical body. Then the movement of the discourse turns upward to account for the soul's generation by the intellectual principle. Finally, we reach the One, the logical terminus that the delineation of the various realms below requires.

What the modern reader gains from Plotinus is a feeling for the necessary dialectical movement between qualitatively different realms. This constant passage from the One to the intellectual principle and then to the soul takes place all the while a multitude of traditional ethical and epistemological questions are being discussed. Yet, underneath this constant recovering of old ground, the picture of the Plotinian world gradually emerges. The reader begins to see how, within such a framework as Plotinus has constructed, Plotinus could hope to deal with practical questions successfully.

In a basic sense, the Plotinian view is a contemplative one, although it is incorrect to infer from this any aversion to everyday life. In addition to his contemplative quality, Plotinus was speculative. He did not claim to know his doctrines with finality, but he attempted an answer to all of philosophy's most fundamental and comprehensive problems. The scope is breathtaking: To grasp what Plotinus saw is still an exhilarating experience that gives life and energy to the philosophical quest.

Frederick Sontag, updated by John K. Roth

Additional Reading

Armstrong, A. H., ed. *The Cambridge History of Later Greek and Early Medieval Philosophy*. Cambridge, England: Cambridge University Press, 1970. A good introduction to Plotinus that provides a concise but rich exposition of his thought.

Copleston, Frederick. *A History of Philosophy: Greece and Rome*. Garden City, N.Y.: Doubleday, 1962. Copleston offers a brief but helpful chapter on Plotinus and the context in which his philosophy and theology emerged.

Gerson, Lloyd P., ed. *The Cambridge Companion to Plotinus*. Cambridge, England: Cambridge University Press, 1996. Plotinus scholars present diverse essays on multiple features of his thought and the development of Neoplatonic philosophy.

_____. *Plotinus*. New York: Routledge, 1994. A good introductory survey of Plotinus's life, times, and thought.

Hadot, Pierre. *Plotinus, or, the Simplicity of Vision*. Translated by Michael Chase. Chicago: University of Chicago Press, 1993. Explores how Plotinus arrives at and develops his distinctive view about the unity of all existence.

Jones, W. T. *A History of Western Philosophy: The Medieval Mind*. New York: Harcourt, Brace, 1969. A brief but lucid introduction to Plotinus.

O'Meara, Dominic J. *Plotinus: An Introduction to the "Enneads."* New York: Oxford University Press, 1993. A scholarly analysis of the best-known work produced by Plotinus.

Rist, J. M. *Plotinus: The Road to Reality*. Cambridge, England: Cambridge University Press, 1967. A scholarly work that includes detailed study of Plotinus's view about God, free will, and faith.

Wallis, R. T. *Neoplatonism*. New York: Charles Scribner's Sons, 1972. Shows how Plotinus developed his outlook from sources in Plato, Aristotle, and the Stoics and then goes on to show how Plotinus influenced his own philosophical successors.

Bryan Aubrey, updated by John K. Roth

Karl Raimund Popper

Popper became well known in the 1930's for his rigorous analysis of the logic of scientific research. During World War II, he wrote two influential works on the philosophy of politics and history.

Principal philosophical works: *Logik der Forschung*, 1935 (*The Logic of Scientific Discovery*, 1959); *The Poverty of Historicism*, 1944-1945 (serial), 1957 (book); *The Open Society and Its Enemies*, 1945 (2 volumes); "New Foundations for Logic," 1947; "Logic Without Assumptions," 1947; *Conjectures and Refutations*, 1962; *Objective Knowledge*, 1972; *The Philosophy of Karl Popper*, 1974; "The Rationality of Scientific Revolutions," 1975; *Unended Quest*, 1976; *The Self and Its Brain*, 1977 (with J. C. Eccles); *Die Beiden Grundprobleme der Erkenntnistheorie*, 1979; *Quantum Theory and the Schism in Physics*, 1982 (part 2 of *Postscript to "The Logic of Scientific Discovery"*); *The Open Universe*, 1982 (part 3 of *Postscript to "The Logic of Scientific Discovery"*); *Realism and the Aim of Science*, 1983 (part 1 of *Postscript to "The Logic of Scientific Discovery"*); "A Proof of the Impossibility of Inductive Probability," 1983 (with D. Miller); "Why Probabilistic Support Is Not Inductive," 1987; *A World of Propensities*, 1990; *In Search of a Better World*, 1992; *Knowledge and the Body-Mind Problem*, 1994; *The Myth of the Framework*, 1994.

Born: July 28, 1902; Vienna, Austria
Died: September 17, 1994; Croydon, England

Early Life
Karl Raimund Popper was the only son of a prominent Viennese lawyer. His mother and father were born Jewish but converted to Lutheranism and baptized their children in that faith, believing this action would help the family become assimilated into the Christian society of Austria. In 1918, Popper dropped out of secondary school and began to audit courses at the University of Vienna. From 1922 to 1924, he apprenticed himself to a cabinetmaker to learn how to work with his hands. He next spent a year volunteering at a clinic for neglected children run by Freudian psychologist Alfred Adler; he dismissed psychoanalytic theories as unscientific.

For a few months in the spring of 1919, Popper considered himself a Communist but became disillusioned when he observed his friends changing positions as new directives arrived from Moscow. When his comrades defended a disastrous protest demonstration in which students were killed by police, Popper was appalled by their

argument that the importance of their goal justified using any means to attain it. Popper's intensive study of Karl Marx's writings soon turned him into an anti-Marxist.

After formal matriculation at the University of Vienna in 1922, Popper earned a primary-school teaching certificate in 1924, completing work on his Ph.D. in 1928 and qualifying to teach mathematics and physics in secondary schools in 1929. In 1930, he obtained a position as a secondary-school science teacher and married Josephine Anna Henniger, a fellow student of education at the University of Vienna; they had no children.

Life's Work
Popper's doctoral dissertation on dogmatic and critical ways of thinking brought him to the attention of the Vienna Circle, a group of philosophers and scientists who were developing the theories of logical positivism. Despite his disagreement with many of their ideas—his nickname in the circle was "the Official Opposition"—Popper was a valued contributor to the discussion group. When he had difficulty getting his first book accepted, the circle published *The*

Logic of Scientific Discovery in a series they sponsored although they cut the manuscript to about half its original length.

The publication of *The Logic of Scientific Discovery* earned Popper an international reputation as an original contributor to the philosophy of science. Even though the book was not translated into English until 1959, Popper received many invitations to lecture at British universities. Popper defined his positions through debate, contrasting his own ideas with prevailing views of the course of scientific research. He also discussed the problem of distinguishing true science from nonscience. Popper rejected the traditional view, accepted by logical positivists, that accumulated experience led to scientific hypotheses, which in turn were verified by further factual observation. Instead, he contended that hypotheses developed first and were then tested by experiments designed to see if predictions based on the theories were falsified by experience. In support of his argument, he cited physicist Albert Einstein's theory of relativity, which made testable predictions about astronomy and physics. If any of the predictions proved false, the theory would be discredited; if, however, they proved true, the theory advanced scientific knowledge. What distinguished science from nonscience was that theories of science were empirically falsifiable, providing a rational basis for acceptance or rejection. In contrast, the theories of psychoanalysis were not scientific because they could not be formulated in a way that permitted a falsification test; however, they might contain useful and valuable insights. For Popper, absolute certainty was not attainable. Experience taught by correcting errors. No matter how many times a prediction derived from a theory proved true, the next prediction might reveal a flaw in the hypothesis that required correction. Popper, unlike the logical positivists, did not dismiss metaphysical speculations as nonsense statements. Noting the way cosmological myths of the ancient world led to the earliest development of testable scientific theories about astronomy, Popper argued that metaphysical ideas might lead to verifiable hypotheses and thus contribute to the advancement of science.

Popper's successful 1935 and 1936 lecture tours in Great Britain brought him to the attention of organizations devoted to rescuing scientists and scholars liable to persecution as liberals or Jews. Despite his baptism as a Protestant, both Popper and his wife were considered Jewish by the Nazis. Popper welcomed an offer in 1937, arranged by his British friends, of a lectureship in philosophy at Canterbury University College, Christchurch, New Zealand. He remained there throughout World War II. Despite his heavy teaching load as the only lecturer in philosophy—and the frowns of university authorities who considered his research and writing merely time stolen from his paid work as lecturer—Popper composed two major works on history and politics that established his reputation in those fields.

Popper called *The Poverty of Historicism* and *The Open Society and Its Enemies* his war work. By historicism, Popper meant the belief that there

Karl Raimund Popper. *(Hulton Getty/Liaison Agency)*

were laws of historical development that determined the future in the same way that astronomical laws determined the motion of the planets. This implied that the task of the social scientist was to discover such "laws" or "trends" and use them to make predictions about the social and political development of the world; if astronomers could predict eclipses, social scientists should be able to predict political revolutions. Popper rejected historicism, contending it was based on a view of natural science and its methodology that misunderstood the nature of science and the provisional character of scientific laws. More important, he considered it socially dangerous because it encouraged believers to think they could use their knowledge to control the course of history. Popper asserted that whether expressed from a right-wing point of view in Hegelian dialectic or from the left in Marxism, historicism inevitably led to totalitarianism and authoritarianism, resulting in government control of the individual and misguided attempts at large-scale social planning.

The Open Society and Its Enemies began as an attempt by Popper to clarify, through an analysis of specific thinkers, a part of historicism that puzzled his New Zealand friends. As his work grew in size, Popper turned it into a book that helped explain how totalitarianism had become intellectually respectable. In accordance with his belief that knowledge advanced through the correction of errors, Popper focused on a critical analysis of the thinkers who made the strongest case for restriction of human freedom. With the exception of Georg Wilhelm Friedrich Hegel, whose defense of Prussian absolutism repulsed him, Popper treated the philosophers he covered with considerable respect.

Volume 1 of *The Open Society and Its Enemies*, "The Spell of Plato," describes Greek philosopher Plato as a powerful thinker, responding to the political crises of Athens with great originality and creativity. The Greek idea of historical development treated change as degeneration—the golden age of the past deteriorated into the iron present. Plato observed that, as the closed world of traditional Athens gave way to a more liberal and open society, the rule of aristocratic oligarchs was replaced by a popular assembly led by demagogues, resulting in a loss of social privilege

by Plato's class and political chaos in the life of the city. Plato's solution to the problem of degeneration and decay was to break out of the process by arresting all political change. The way to escape political degeneration was to establish a utopian state so perfect that it need not participate in historical development.

Plato believed the fundamental problem of politics was determining who should rule the state. His solution was that it should be governed by the "best" people. Popper objected to the authoritarian implications that whoever was "best" was entitled to rule and that opposition to such rulers was wrong. All totalitarian governments made this claim. Although he acknowledged the necessity of political constraints, Popper was pessimistic about governmental power, wanting to limit the activity of the state to a minimum. For Popper, the real problem was how to organize political institutions so that citizens could rid themselves of bad or incompetent governments without violence.

Volume 2, "The High Tide of Prophecy: Hegel, Marx, and the Aftermath," briefly, but scathingly, rejected Hegel as a paid apologist for the kingdom of Prussia. Hegel used historicist ideas to defend the status quo, asserting that whatever existed was right because it was the result of reason working through history. Popper noted that both left and right totalitarians followed Hegel's historicist scheme—the left replacing Hegel's war of nations with the war of classes, the right replacing it with the war of races.

The nearly two hundred pages on Karl Marx are highly respectful of Marx as a person, while subjecting Marxist ideas to a withering analysis of their shortcomings. Popper noted that Marx's writings contained an implicit ethical theory that supported his denunciation of the exploitative capitalist system of his day. Popper considered Marx's belief that the state would ultimately wither away an indication that he really favored an open society. Popper credited Marx with a sincere though misguided attempt to create a science of society. However, Marx misunderstood the nature of science and, instead of the testable predictions on which true science depends, created dogmatic prophecies of what the future would hold. When Marx's prediction that capitalism would cause increasing misery for the general population did not come true, Marxists did not change their theory but rather looked for special circumstances to explain away the anomaly. Marx's followers believed his prophecies absolutely; they knew what the future would inevitably hold and defended any means used to achieve that end, however horrible the immediate results. Just as Plato's historicism justified the right of the "best" people to control the state, Marx's historicism justified the dictatorial dominance of society by a Marxist elite.

Popper preferred a policy of democratic liberalism. He rejected pure laissez-faire theories calling for totally free markets. Popper believed government was needed, both to protect free markets and to prevent the oppression of citizens. Popper insisted that "there is no freedom if it is not secured by the state; and conversely, only a state which is controlled by free citizens can offer them any reasonable security at all." Popper did not believe that voting and majority rule by themselves defined democracy; the majority might welcome tyranny, as the Austrians had done when they acclaimed Nazi Adolf Hitler's annexation of their country. What characterized a truly open society was a structure of government that provided peaceful means whereby citizens could remove a corrupt or oppressive regime.

Influence

The Open Society and Its Enemies was published shortly before Popper returned to England in January, 1946, to take up a position as reader in logic and scientific method at the London School of Economics. Promoted to professor in 1949, he continued there until his retirement in 1969. Popper's highly readable style and vigorous defense of freedom attracted a wide public. The book brought Popper both fame and controversy. He was invited to lecture at many colleges and universities, to participate in public forums, and to give radio talks for the British Broadcasting Corporation. His ideas antagonized leftists, who could not accept Popper's denunciation of Marxism, and classical scholars, who resented his negative view of Plato. Their attacks ensured that Popper's name and views would become widely known.

Although Popper was hailed by many scientists and philosophers as the most influential philosopher of science of the twentieth century, his views on the scientific method also came under attack. Believing that a critical and rational evaluation of ideas was the way to advance knowledge, Popper took his critics very seriously. Two collections of his major papers, *Conjectures and Refutations* and *Objective Knowledge*, show the development of his ideas as he argued with his critics. From 1955 to 1957, as Popper worked on the English translation of *The Logic of Scientific Discovery*, he began to prepare an addendum answering his critics, which grew so greatly in length that his three-volume *Postscript to "The Logic of Scientific Discovery"* was not published until 1982-1983.

Popper received numerous awards and honors. The University of Vienna offered him a professorship, which he declined. In 1965, he was knighted by Queen Elizabeth II. During the 1950's and 1960's, as his reputation as a philosopher of both physical and social science grew, he was invited to lecture at Harvard and other major universities in the United States, Britain, Australia, and the continent of Europe. Both *The Logic of Scientific Discovery* and *The Open Society and Its Enemies* have become recognized as classics. His major works remain in print, and his admirers created a Web site where a vigorous ongoing discussion testifies to the continuing relevance of Popper's ideas.

Milton Berman

The Logic of Scientific Discovery

Type of philosophy: Epistemology, philosophy of science
First published: Logik der Forschung, 1935 (English translation, 1959)
Principal ideas advanced:
◇ The method of testing in the empirical sciences is characterized not by inductive inference but by deducing empirically testable claims from proposed theories.
◇ Falsification, not verification, is crucial in science.
◇ Scientific propositions are to be distinguished from nonscientific in that only the former are empirically falsifiable.

◇ The asymmetry between verification and falsification makes it possible for a falsification criterion to succeed where the verification principle failed.

◇ A scientist proposing a theory must state the conditions under which it will be appropriate to reject it.

Karl Raimund Popper's *The Logic of Scientific Discovery*, one of the most important books ever written on the philosophy of science, begins with the problem of induction. An inference is inductive, Popper explains, if it moves from a singular statement (roughly, a statement whose subject term refers to some particular concrete thing) to one or more universal statements (roughly, statements whose subject terms refer to all the members of a class of things). In science, such inferences occur when one passes from descriptions of particular experimental results to hypotheses or theories alleged to be justified by these results. "All observed swans have been white" sums up a set of particular statements that report observations of concrete particular items. "All swans are white" expresses a universal statement one might inductively infer from that summary.

The Problem of Induction

Notoriously, Popper notes, such inferences are not deductively valid, and the problem of induction is the question of whether such inferences are ever rationally legitimate, and if so, under what conditions. One widely held view, Popper notes, is that the universal statements that express natural laws, or laws of science, or well-confirmed scientific theories, or the like, are known by experience; that is, singular statements are statements known by experience from which the natural-law-expressing universal statements may somehow legitimately be derived. Hence, in this view, the problem of induction has some proper solution.

This alleged solution, Popper continues, is often expressed in terms of a principle of induction—a proposition known to be true that can be placed in inferences from singular to universal scientific statements and whose presence in such inference renders the inference rationally compelling. Some philosophers have held that, without some principle of induction, science would

be without a decision procedure and could no longer distinguish solid theory from superstition.

This alleged principle of induction, Popper notes, cannot be a logical truth or a statement true by virtue of its very form or structure because no such proposition would legitimately lead one from "All observed *A*'s are *B*" to "All *A*'s are *B*," or from singular to universal statements in any other case. It must rather be synthetic or not contradictory to deny. How, though, Popper asks—consciously restating an argument offered by Scottish philosopher David Hume—should one rationally justify one's acceptance of this principle? The principle must be not a singular but a universal statement. One cannot certify its truth by logic alone. If, then, one tries to justify it from experience, one will again face the very sort of derivation of universal from singular statements the principle itself was meant to sanction, and so on ad infinitum if one appeals to a higher-order inductive principle. Perhaps, an inductive principle is accepted by "the whole of science"; however, Popper asks, cannot "the whole of science" err? It will not do to say that singular statements, while they do not *entail* universal conclusions, nevertheless render such conclusions probable, for then one would need some principle of probability, and while perhaps this would differ in content from a principle of induction, its justification would present similar difficulties.

Popper completely rejects the familiar inductivist view that, while not rendering universal statements certain or providing conclusive justification for them, true singular statements can provide good reason for universal statements or render them (at least to some degree) probable. Popper argues that, if some degree *N* of probability is to be assigned to statements based on inductive inference, then some sort of principle of induction must be somehow justified. How this is to be done remains utterly problematic, even if one weakens the alleged relationship between singular premise and universal conclusion ("providing some degree of reliability" replacing "inductively justifies") or the alleged status of the conclusion ("probable" replacing "true"). Other attempts to shore up induction, Popper feels, are equally unsuccessful.

Popper also rejects the views that induction needs no justification and that universal statements are merely, albeit perhaps infinite, conjuncts of singular statements. In this respect, Popper's view agrees with a remark by philosopher Bertrand Russell to the effect that there are two kinds of reasoning: deductive and bad.

Rejection of inductive reasoning, Popper holds, involves much gain and no loss. Obviously, however, if he rejects inductive inferences and hence inductive confirmation of theories, Popper must replace this account of scientific method by some other. It is this positive, constructive task that is the central topic of *The Logic of Scientific Discovery*.

Testing Theories

The basic task of the scientist, Popper contends, is to put forward, and then test, theories. Part of this task, of course, is the invention of theories, a matter Popper holds "neither to call for logical analysis nor to be susceptible of it." Study of the conditions, activities, and stages included in the invention of theories, he holds, is a matter for psychology, not philosophy. Philosophy, the *logic* of knowledge as opposed to the *psychology* of knowledge, is concerned with the testing part of the scientist's task.

This testing procedure, Popper says, begins by deducing consequences from the theory being tested; the theory, in effect, becomes a premise from which conclusions are deductively derived. This done, Popper continues, four lines of testing may be distinguished. First, the conclusions may be compared among themselves; this provides something of a test as to the internal consistency of the theory. Second, the conclusions may be examined to see if the theory has any empirical consequences, and so is scientific as opposed to tautological. Third, the conclusions may be compared with those of other theories to see whether the theory, if it survived empirical tests, is such that its acceptance would mean scientific advance. Fourth, the empirical conclusions or predictions, if any, are applied to experimental results to see if what the theory tells us will occur really does occur.

It is this fourth line of testing that is central for Popper. It is the new empirical consequences of a theory—empirical conclusions that follow from it but not from hitherto-accepted theories—that gain the assessor's attention. These predictions

are compared with the results of relevant experiments, old or new; if the predictions of what would happen under certain circumstances are not correct descriptions of what happened under those conditions, the theory, Popper notes, is falsified. (The form of deductive inference involved here is the simple and standard *modus tollens*: if p entails q, and q is false, then p is false.) If the predictions are correct, then the theory is (so far) verified. A theory that after numerous tests is not falsified is corroborated, although this is fundamentally a matter of not having been falsified. This doctrine of testing procedure raises various questions. What Popper emphasizes most, however, is that the procedure outlined above contains no inductive procedures whatever and yet does not leave the scientist, or the philosopher of science, without a rational decision procedure when faced with a choice between incompatible theories.

Science and Nonscience

Popper's "criterion of demarcation" requires that a genuinely scientific hypothesis must be (in principle) empirically falsifiable. Popper regards distinguishing the nonscientific (including what is logical, mathematical, or metaphysical) from the scientific—a task he designates "the problem of demarcation"—as an epistemological problem, perhaps the most basic one. He holds that appeal to inductive reasoning provides no solution to this problem and that his own testing-through-attempting-to-falsify account of scientific decision procedure solves it.

In contrast to traditional (for example, Humean) empiricism, which recognized as scientific only concepts analyzable in terms of sensory phenomena, Popper holds that statements, not concepts, are the basic elements of scientific theories. In contrast to later empiricism, which at least to some degree replaced analysis of concepts by analysis of statements but recognized as scientific only statements derivable from (or reducible to) elementary perceptual claims, Popper holds that any statement that entails a proposition that describes a possible experimental or observational result is scientific, whether or not it is itself entailed by some set of elementary perceptual claims. ("Scientific" here does not mean "part of science" and certainly not "true," but "within the scope of scientific interest." One might say that mathematical claims are those that, whether true or false, fall within the domain of mathematics in that they are decidable by its procedures; then one is using the word "mathematical" in a sense analogous to that in which "scientific" is used above.)

Popper's criterion of demarcation, he admits, rests, if not securely then at least squarely, on a convention. He distinguishes science from nonscience, he tells us, not on the basis of some discernible intrinsic difference between scientific and nonscientific propositions, but on the basis, in effect, of a decision that the science/nonscience distinction be made along the line of demarcation. This decision, he admits, is not beyond rational dispute; however, he adds that any such dispute can be only among those who share his purposes, and whether one does that or not, he holds, *is* beyond rational dispute. Thus if Popper succeeds in marking off what is of scientific interest from what is not, he feels he will have been triumphant. The logical positivists, he contends, shared his purpose but, by appealing to the verification principle (which, roughly, asserts that a sentence has truth value only if it is either a tautology or is empirically confirmable or disconfirmable) as their principle of demarcation, failed to provide a basis for distinguishing science from metaphysics. The core of their failure, Popper suggests, is found in their acceptance of induction as a confirmation method. By contrast, and without claiming anything about whether metaphysical propositions have truth value, Popper holds that his own criterion does mark out the desired distinction. If one has some other end in mind, there is neither reason nor need to suppose his criterion will serve that end.

Popper, then, views science as an empirical theoretical system—a system of synthetic or nontautological statements that represents not only a possible but also the actual world of experience. That a system does represent the world is guaranteed only by its having been exposed to unsuccessful falsification attempts. This, Popper notes, falls short of the ideal of philosophers who require that meaningful statements be conclusively verifiable or in principle determined as true. It replaces this ideal by another: that a scientific statement be capable of being refuted by experience. Lest this seem to trivialize natural laws,

Popper points out that the more ways there are of refuting a proposition, or the more ways there are of its going wrong, then the more information the proposition contains. Information content waxes proportionate to falsifiability potential.

Falsification Criterion

The falsification strategy, Popper notes, is made possible by an asymmetry between verification and falsification; that a proposition cannot be verified or established does not entail that it cannot be falsified or refuted, and that a proposition can be falsified does not entail that it can be verified. Further, although even if one limits oneself to propositions with empirical content, no set of singular statements will entail a universal statement, but a universal statement will entail singular statements. The failure of the verification principle, Popper asserts, is no reason to expect the falsification criterion to suffer a similar fate.

A complication, if not a problem, arises, however, from the fact that rarely if ever does a theory all by itself entail any predictions; it does so only together with auxiliary hypotheses. Schematically, one has not that T (theory) entails P (prediction), but that T and H (auxiliary hypothesis) entails P. If, then, one deduces P from T and H, and discovers that under the relevant controlled experimental conditions, P turns out to be false, various alternatives remain open. One could reject the rule of inference by which P was derived, claim that the experiment was not properly conducted, or deny that one's perception of the result was correct, although these alternatives may often seem radical. Or one could reject T, or else H. If one rejects H, one can retain T without recourse to any of the other alternatives noted. If one always rejects the auxiliary hypothesis, no theories will ever be falsified. To put it mildly, this would be inconvenient for Popper's perspective.

Popper is fully aware of the problem. To meet it, he specifies that when a member of a scientific community proffers a theory, the person must specify the conditions under which the theory itself (and not some other proposition, be it auxiliary hypothesis or whatever) is to be abandoned. In such fashion, as it were, those who play the game of science must be prepared to say when they will admit defeat.

Popper maintains that his view provides for the objectivity of scientific theories, which, he contends, lies in their being intersubjectively testable. If science is to have an empirical basis, he states, the propositions composing this basis must themselves be objective and hence intersubjectively testable. Therefore, they must entail predictions and so on ad infinitum so that science can contain no ultimate statements. The infinite regress thus produced, he argues, is not vicious. True, every claim can be tested, and testing must stop somewhere so that some claim is accepted that is not tested—some claims will be accepted as correct observational reports without their having run a falsification gauntlet. However, this, Popper reminds us, violates no tenet of his philosophy of science, and in principle, one can test any proposition one wishes.

The net effect of this is that scientific knowledge is possible without its being required to rest on allegedly indubitable propositions. Popper explicitly rejects the view that science is made up of propositions about which scientists are rightly epistemically certain—about which it is logically impossible to be wrong—and his methodology in philosophy of science rules out science's having, or needing, indubitable foundations. In this important respect, as in others, he differs from classical empiricism.

Keith E. Yandell, updated by John K. Roth

Additional Reading

Burke, T. E. *The Philosophy of Popper*. Manchester, England: Manchester University Press, 1983. Argues that, despite Popper's disclaimer, intellectual and moral relativism are inherent in his philosophy of science.

Levinson, Paul, ed. *In Pursuit of Truth: Essays on the Philosophy of Karl Popper on the Occasion of His Eightieth Birthday*. Atlantic Highlands, N.J.: Humanities Press, 1982. Laudatory articles that provide a good introduction to Popper's ideas and their impact on the philosophy of science. The last four essays focus on Popper himself.

Magee, Bryan. *Philosophy and the Real World: An Introduction to Karl Popper*. La Salle, Ill.: Open Court, 1985. First published as *Popper* in 1973, this brief but comprehensive exposition of

Popper's ideas remains the best introduction to Popper's thought for the general reader.

O'Hear, Anthony. *Karl Popper*. London: Routledge & Kegan Paul, 1980. A negative evaluation of Popper's philosophy of science, arguing against his rejection of certainty and denying Popper's contention that the principle of falsification is an adequate criterion for distinguishing what is true science from nonscience.

_____, ed. *Karl Popper: Philosophy and Problems*. Royal Institute of Philosophy series. Cambridge, England: Cambridge University Press, 1995. This collection of essays examines Popper's philosophy. Includes bibliography and index.

Raphael, Frederic. *Popper*. New York: Routledge, 1999. An excellent biographical introduction to the thoughts of the philosopher, clearly presented and requiring no special background. Bibliography.

Schilpp, Paul Arthur, ed. *The Philosophy of Karl Popper*. 2 vols. La Salle, Ill: Open Court, 1974. Contains thirty-three critical essays, mostly by noted philosophers; Popper's extensive "Replies to My Critics"; his intellectual autobiography (revised and separately published as *Unended Quest* in 1976); and a substantial bibliography.

Shearmur, Jeremy. *The Political Thought of Karl Popper*. London: Routledge, 1996. This book examines Popper's contributions to political science. Includes bibliography and index.

Stokes, Geoff. *Popper: Philosophy, Politics, and Scientific Method*. Key Contemporary Thinkers series. New York: Blackwell, 1998. This volume, one in a series on contemporary philosophers, focuses on Popper's contributions to social science methodology. Includes bibliography and index.

Williams, Douglas. *Truth, Hope, and Power: The Thought of Karl Popper*. Toronto: University of Toronto Press, 1989. Interprets Popper's social and political thought as a powerful defense of individualism and liberal democracy against the best known justifications of collectivism and utopianism in the Western philosophical tradition.

Milton Berman

H. H. Price

Price expressed perhaps the most complex version of sense-data theory, articulated a sophisticated theory of concepts and a detailed account of belief, and discussed various key topics in the philosophy of religion, including the notion of an afterlife.

Principal philosophical works: *Perception*, 1932; *Hume's Theory of the External World*, 1940; *Thinking and Experience*, 1953; *Belief: The Gifford Lectures Delivered at the University of Aberdeen in 1960*, 1969; *Essays in the Philosophy of Religion*, 1972; *Philosophical Interaction with Parapsychology*, 1995.

Born: May 17, 1899; Neath, Glamorgan, Wales
Died: November 26, 1984; place unknown

Early Life

Born at the end of the nineteenth century in Wales, Henry Habberley Price was educated at Winchester College and New College, Oxford. He was a shy and somewhat reclusive person; in later life he neither belonged to a school of philosophy nor sought to found one. He served as fellow of Magdalen College, Oxford, from 1922 to 1924. Price was appointed fellow and lecturer of Trinity College in 1924 and remained there until 1935. He became Wykeham Professor of Logic at New College in 1935, a position from which he retired in 1959. Like Henry Sidgwick, William James, and C. D. Broad, Price was interested in psychical research, publishing articles in journals devoted to this topic and serving as president of the Society for Psychical Research, London, and a charter member of the Parapsychological Association as well as a member of the professional philosophical associations the Aristotelian Society and the Mind Association. Price was visiting professor at Princeton University in 1948 and the University of California, Los Angeles, in 1962, and Gifford Lecturer at Aberdeen University in 1959-1960; his book *Belief* contains the substance of these distinguished lectures.

Life's Work

Price stated that his book *Perception* "is concerned in the main with only two points, the nature of perceptual consciousness and the relation of sense-data to the ordinary 'macroscopic objects' of daily life, such as tables and rocks." Price rejected the view that sense-data (sensory images private to the person who has them) are caused by material objects in such a way that perceiving is a matter of inferring back to their physical causes.

Philosopher John Locke held that physical objects cause private perceptions that later philosophers, including Bertrand Russell and G. E. Moore, came to call "sense-data." In Locke's view, in perception, we are directly aware of sense-data (Locke's term is "impressions of sensation"), which, in cases of veridical or reliable perception, partially resemble the physical objects that cause them. Specifically, color qualities and taste qualities, accessible to only one sense, are not present in physical objects, nor do they resemble any features of such objects. In contrast, shape and size qualities do resemble features of such objects. Perception, in this view, involves knowing there are mind-independently existing objects by inferring their existence from the private impressions with which we are noninferentially aware. George Berkeley and other philosophers were dubious about the reliability of any such inference and proposed instead that our sensory awareness is simply constituted by sense-data. John Stuart Mill proposed that physical objects are simply made up of (actual and possible) sense-data. Talk of physical objects, insofar as it refers to anything at all, refers to actual and possible sensory experiences.

Price rejected Locke's causal theory of the origin of sense-data and Mill's phenomenalism (so called because in this view physical objects are reducible to, or composed of, private sensory phenomena). Nonetheless, he held that it is sense-data that provide the immediate objects of perceptual awareness, the things that we are noninferentially aware of when we have sensory experiences. Price developed and defended this view in *Perception*, a view that is nothing if not detailed and complex.

The simplest way of denying Locke's and Mill's very different views would be to deny that there are sense-data. The idea of sense-data as items that come between the subject and the ultimate object of perception was rejected by Price. However, he held that there are sense-data that belong to material objects, and much of *Perception* is devoted to explaining what "belongs to" means. To perceive is to have sense-data that one takes to belong to mind-independent physical objects. Price's concept, unlike Locke's, does not require an inference to objects and, unlike Mill's, does not see objects as mere collections of sense-data.

The "belonging to" relation is analyzed so as to involve the notion of a family of sense-data; sense-data can fit together in the sense that together they form a single solid thing—a complete, three-dimensional figure. Price writes concerning such things as a table or a rock that it is:

> neither the family [of sense-data] alone or the physical object [a mind-independent occupant of a spatial location] alone, but something that consists of both; we mean a certain family [of sense-data] together with the physical object [the space occupier] coincident with it.

Perception struggles mightily with the task of saying how various sense-data (including visual, tactual, and auditory) form families that occupy a specious (momentary) present and can endure, and how they combine with space occupiers to form objects. In the preface to the second edition of *Perception*, Price seems to regard the view he developed more as a manifestation of a sort of perspective held by many at the time than something to be unreservedly accepted at a later date, though this is compatible with continuing to ac-

cept parts of his earlier view. He grants that talk of physical objects is logically prior to that of sense-data in that one must use concepts of physical objects in order to explain what sense-data are. He also grants that in typical veridical or reliable sensory experience we are not aware of any sense-data at all but only of material objects. These are strong concessions to the criticism of a theory of the sort Price had held.

In 1940, Price's *Hume's Theory of the External World* was published. It remains a classic account of its topic that has never been surpassed. In his next major philosophical work, *Thinking and Experience*, Price argued that to have a concept is to possess a representational capacity, not (as a popular competing theory had it) simply to be able to use a symbol correctly. He argues against any view in which having a concept was analyzed without remainder in terms of actual and potential behavior. He summarizes his view by saying:

> I have been recommending a *dispositional* version of Conceptualism [the view that universals are not mind-independent abstract objects, but rather are some sort of mental objects or activities], instead of the traditional introspective version *inspective* or introspective Conceptualism, which holds that concepts or abstract ideas present themselves to the mind as one sort of occurrent mental contents among others. It is true that we may still speak, if we please, of "having an abstract idea occurrently" as distinct from "having it dispositionally." However, having it occurrently does not consist in directing a kind of mental gaze at it. It is not any sort of intuitive apprehension or direct awareness. The nearest we get to anything of the kind is the inspection of generic images.

Price's *Essays in the Philosophy of Religion* contains his 1971 Sarum Lectures delivered at the University of Oxford. They include discussions of the sort of fear of God that is said to be the beginning of religion, petitionary prayer, motives for disbelief in an afterlife that he argues are just as powerful as desires that inspire belief in an afterlife, and an especially interesting discussion of two conceptions of afterlife. One is a conception of the afterlife in which its participants are conceived as embodied, and the other is a conception of the afterlife in which its participants are thought of as disembodied minds having dream-like perceptual states that are capable of being influenced by the telepathic powers of other minds, thus making communication possible even in the absence of a common physical environment. He argued that upon careful examination, the two conceptions are much closer than one might think possible. An unusual feature of these essays is their frequent reference to psychical research and its proposed findings, concerning some of which Price held a cautiously favorable view.

Belief contains the Gifford Lectures for 1959-1960. Price noted that belief is a mental state or act of which one can be introspectively aware. According to this view, which Price calls the mental occurrence theory of belief, the philosophical task concerning belief is the description and analysis of this occurrence. One endeavors to describe the necessary and sufficient conditions for its being true of someone that they are in the mental state that is belief. Traditionally, this has been the dominant account of belief.

In other views, beliefs are dispositions rather than occurrences. To say that someone believes that mice are smaller than rabbits is to say that the individual would tend to answer affirmatively to the question "Are mice smaller than rabbits?," to place rabbits in cages when asked to put the larger animals in a room filled with mice and rabbits in cages, and so on. This Price called the dispositional theory of belief. Those who hold the occurrence theory typically allow that belief has a dispositional component. One can believe that snails move slowly even when none of one's mental contents represents snails moving slowly, and what makes it true that, in the absence of any such representation, one still believes that snails move slowly is the sort of thing that the dispositional theory takes to entirely constitute belief. However, the occurrence theorist insists that it is belief as occurrence that is primary in properly describing the nature of belief. The dispositional analysis, as Price conceived it, simply leaves out belief as occurrence.

Price's purpose is to describe and defend a version of the occurrence theory. In so doing, he discusses various related topics: René Descartes versus David Hume on whether belief can be voluntary, the issue of whether beliefs can ever be self-verifying, John Locke and John Henry Newman on degrees of assent, whether there is an ethics of belief, belief *in* versus belief *that*, belief that a whole worldview is true, and belief and faith. He also argued that the epistemology of belief and the metaphysics of mind and body are interrelated issues.

Influence

Price's theory of perception is probably the most thorough version of a view that Price himself came to see as problematic. His theories of thought and belief went against the reductive views of his day, but they were argued in clear detail and are, at least in part, still defensible. The same is true of his discussions in the philosophy of religion, particularly those concerning the conceptual possibility of life after death.

Keith E. Yandell

Perception

Type of philosophy: Epistemology
First published: 1932
Principal ideas advanced:

◇ Sense-data are the given elements in our sense experience, the colors, odors, noises, and pressures of things as they are met in consciousness; such sense-data are particulars, not universals.

◇ Material objects are spatially complete, three-dimensional objects; but sense-data are spatially incomplete and private, and they are free from the causal relations that characterize material objects.

◇ Sense-data that fit together to form solids are said to be constructible, and solids perceptually constructed within a mediate range of vision in which perfect stereoscopy is possible are said to be constructed from perfectly constructible sense-data.

◇ The material object, known by reference to constructible sense-data, has causal properties that could not belong to any family of sense-data; consequently, phenomenalism is false.

In *Perception*, H. H. Price undertakes an examination of existing theories of perception, rejecting what is bad, retaining what is good, and adding original reflections to construct a new, more adequate theory avoiding the difficulties of the old. Price phrases the problem of perception in two separate questions:

(1) What is perceptual consciousness and how is it related to sensing?

(2) What is the relation of "belonging to" when we say a sense-datum "belongs to" a thing?

Consciousness contains givens—color expanses, pressures, noises, smells. These givens are *sense-data*, and the act of apprehending them intuitively is *sensing*. There are other data of consciousness, such as of introspection or memory. Sense-data differ from these solely in that they lead us to conceive of and believe in the existence of material things (whether or not such things *actually* do exist). By accepting sense-data as given, we do not commit ourselves to believing (1) that they persist when not being sensed (but only that they exist when sensed), (2) that the same sense-datum may be a datum of more than one mind, (3) that sense-data have some particular status in the universe, or (4) that they originate in any particular way.

Naïve Realism

Price examines and rejects naïve realism and its offshoots, the selective theory and the causal theory. He makes some use of the theory of phenomenalism and gathers the apparatus with which to exclude it only after stating most of his own theory. He never loses sight of his two basic questions, and all his very thorough and detailed arguments and rebuttals keep constant contact with them.

Naïve realism asserts that (1) perceptual consciousness is knowing that there exists an object to which a sense-datum presently sensed belongs and (2) for a visual or tactual sense-datum to belong to an object is for that sense-datum to be part of the surface of a three-dimensional object. Those who oppose the naïve realist usually regard hallucinations and perceptual illusions as ample refutation, but they commonly assume in their premises the theory they profess to upset. Price argues that the argument that actually disposes of naïve realism is simply that the many surfaces as seen, if they were really surfaces, simply would not fit together to construct the sort of three-dimensional solid in which the naïve realist believes. From the controversy, we can rescue the facts that the *totum datum* (the sum of all the data of all the senses at a particular time) has main parts, the somatic sense-data and the environmental, and that in certain respects these vary concomitantly. They are always copresent and covariant; that is, the *totum datum* is *somato-centric*. Similarly, from the remains of the effort to establish an improved form of realism that he names the selective theory, Price draws the lessons that we must account for abnormal and illusory sense-data as well as normal ones, that to various persons the same material things may be present to the sense in various ways, and that provision must be made for obtainable as well as actual sense-data.

The causal theory of perception states, as answers to Price's initial questions, that "belonging to" means "being caused by" a material thing, and that perceptual consciousness is fundamentally an *inference* from effect to cause. Although Price expects to refute the theory readily, he notes that it seems to be the official foundation for the natural sciences. The only plausible version of the causal theory is, if every event has a cause and if sense-data are events, something other than sense-data must exist: the *causes* of sense-data. However, we can know nothing of the character of the causes and cannot prove them to be material. The fact is that from the first, we are "on the lookout" for sets of sense-data of the sort that we already expect to adumbrate solids. We already have a notion of the material thing before being capable of formulating ideas of causality. This notion seems not only innate but a priori, a necessary condition of certain kinds of experience. This must be a whole complex notion of thinghood, including the factor of causality.

Price then progresses toward his own theory. Sense-data are not universals but particulars; not redness, but instances of red. They are not facts, but the bases for judging facts. Visual and tactual sense-data are the primary ones for establishing the existence of material things. A visual sense-datum can be called a colored expanse, but to call it a colored surface assumes too much. Sense-data are not substances; when suitable bodily and external conditions are present, they are created out of nothing and, when these conditions disappear, vanish into nothing. They have a finite, usually very small, duration. They take up no space and do not have causal characteristics, such as inertia or impenetrability. They are not so much like mechanical processes as *vital* processes. They are generated in neither the brain nor the mind alone, but in the substantial compound of the two, having certain characteristics that neither would have by itself.

Perceptual Consciousness

The primary form of perceptual consciousness of our sense-data is perceptual acceptance. As a sense-datum arises, a state of taking for granted the material thing to which the sense-datum belongs also arises. The question whether to believe simply does not occur with the first sense-datum, though it may be introduced later. Other than the datum itself, perceptual acceptance has no content. Although I take for granted that the front surface of what I see has a back, I leave it until later to determine the nature of the unseen part. Moreover, the first sense-datum does not completely specify the details of the accessible side, but rather it simply limits the possibilities to some extent. Further observation adds greater detail. I therefore do not take my first datum as identical with the front surface of the object, but simply take it that a thing now exists that has a certain general character.

Unlike the transitory sense-datum, a material thing persists through a period before and after the sense-datum. It is spatially complete in three dimensions, whereas a sense-datum is spatially incomplete. It is public and accessible to many minds, whereas a sense-datum, being somatocentric, is private. "Belonging to" it are sense-data of many, usually all, of the different senses. Finally, it has causal relations, whereas the relation between a sense-datum and the awareness of that sense-datum is not causal.

Price accounts for error, illusion, and even mere peculiarities of interpretation by referring to the difference in nature between sensing and perceptual consciousness. Sensing is undoubted and perfectly intuitive reception of the given. Perceptual consciousness is a mode of *taking as existing* a material thing, although that thing is not *necessarily* present; it *seems* intuitive only because it is instantaneous, not discursive, and is yet the raw material of judgment, not the product. However, the claim of any ostensibly sensed object to exist and have a certain character may be tested and corrected.

The further development of perceptual consciousness is perceptual assurance. Through additional perceptual acts, our primary acceptance is led to a settled conviction of the existence and nature of the material thing that first gave rise to sense-data. With succeeding acts of perception, the mode of reception is not mere acceptance, as it was with the first. Conditioned by the first sensing, it is now a progressive confirmation of the thinghood of what is sensed, a continual further specification of previously unspecified detail and addition of other parts not at first sensed. For we take the initial sense-datum as confirmable by other obtainable sense-data, which will fit together in a unified, enduring something that is spatially complete and has causal characteristics. As further acts of perception provide such confirmations, the existence of the thing and the specifications of its nature become settled rational beliefs. (Those cases with some confirmation but in which the way to adequate confirmation is blocked may be said to bring perceptual confidence, our ordinary state regarding most things.)

How Sense-Data Interrelate

Price carries out a subtle and complex analysis of the relation of sense-data to one another. From the separate sense-data of sense-fields, as both change, we gain our beliefs in the existence of individual things. The theory that sense-data that resemble one another compose a class, and that the thing is simply the class of resembling data, is inadequate because many of the data of an individual thing do not resemble one another in any sensible way. A better theory is that of gradual transition, which accounts not only for the changing of sense-data with motion of the observer but also for distorted data (as in perspective viewing) as well as for changing qualities (while, it is assumed, the thing itself does not change). According to this view, the whole group of changing data gathered as we move about a thing to get further specification of it "belong to" the particular thing. However, shapes, sense-data apprehended as spatial, must be related not only geometrically but also *locally*. We need an account of the manner in which sense-data "fit together" to form a solid. Price calls data that thus fit together *constructible*.

Price cites certain empirical facts. Although optical theory has not recognized it, vision has two types of stereoscopy, *perfect* and *imperfect*. The familiar sort associated with perspective seeing is the imperfect; it allows us to construct solid objects from its data but incompletely. Immediately before the eyes there is a range of depth in which the usual perspective effects are reversed—the parallel edges of a matchbox when held against the nose seem closer together at the nearer rather than farther end. Between this nearest range and the outer one, there is a range of perfect stereoscopy, in which the visual sense-data of any object small enough to lie within it *actually do coincide*, approximately, with the surfaces of the particular thing. In this range, things are seen without distortion. The rectangular sides of the matchbox are seen as rectangular, not trapezoidal, even though the three sides seen at once are facing in quite different directions.

These facts allow Price to conclude that the thing seen within the range of perfect stereoscopy is seen virtually as it is. The solid perceptually constructed in this range is constructed from *perfectly constructible sense-data*. He calls it a *nuclear solid*. Around it, we can arrange all constructible sense-data in order from the least deviation to the greatest. The variations in perspective order will form a *perspectival distortion series*, and those varying concomitantly with that series from greatest to least specification will form a *differentiation series*. The members limiting these series at the position of the nuclear solid are their *nuclear members*. The nuclear solid provides the ground for uniting both continua, and indeed the continua of all sense-data both of spatial and nonspatial senses. The nuclear members with respect to a single sense are standard forms—the nuclear visual sense-datum, for example, gives the *standard figure* and *standard color*. The nuclear solid constructed from the perspectival distortion series, amended by the best presentation (that with most specific detail) of the differentiation series, gives us the *standard solid*. The collection of all sense-data unified by a standard solid is a *family of sense-data*.

To establish the validity of the construction of material things from sense-data, Price cites three propositions that seem obviously true, although he cannot imagine a way to prove them.

(1) Some sense-fields are not momentary but have a finite duration.

(2) Some two sense-fields must be continuous rather than discrete in time and quality.

(3) Successive sense-fields sometimes overlap in time—have a part of their durations in common.

These are the logical requirements of three-dimensional construction. If they actually occur, then, given two sense-fields, one containing a pair of sense-data *AB* and the other containing a pair *BC*, each pair sensibly adjoining and also arranged in a spatial relation *R* (such as "to the right of"), we can know that *A* and *C* are also related by relation *R*. This *method of progressive adjunction* is our validation of the "beyond"—the existence of unseen surfaces.

It is easily seen that the nonnuclear data do not exist in space. The tabletop that is narrower at the far end exists in sense only, as a member of the family of sense-data of the table, not as a constituent of the standard solid of the table. The nuclear sense-data are not parts or surfaces of the standard solid but may be said to *coincide* with it. Position in physical space is not a characteristic of a single sense-datum but rather a *collective* characteristic of a whole group of sense-data constituting a standard solid.

A family of sense-data perhaps should not be said to *exist* in time and undergo change but to *prolong* itself through time and differ through time. The point of view of the observer, and its motion, are definable in terms of the space of standard solids. Obtainable sense-data are definable in terms of changes of the observer's point of view.

Causality

So far, it might seem that the theory of perception Price has offered is an elaborated phenomenalism, identifying a material thing with the family of sense-data. He shows, however, that this is not his theory. A material thing *physically*, as well as sensibly, occupies a space. By this we mean that it manifests in that space certain *causal* characteristics, most notably that of impenetrability.

When a chestnut drops on a stone and bounces away, it is a causal characteristic of the stone, not a sense-characteristic, that has acted on the chestnut. An obtainable sense-datum, on the other hand, is not an existent particular, but a fact of the form "If any observer were at such and such a point of view, such and such a sense-datum would exist." Because an individual observer can occupy only one point of view at a time, he or she can realize only one of the alternatively obtainable sense-data at a time.

The family of sense-data thus has a peculiar mode of existence, as a collection of actual sense-data, plus an infinite number of obtainable sense-data existing as contemporary alternatives, centering on a standard solid. This is not the kind of entity to which causal characteristics may belong. Further, in many instances, a family of sense-data is manifested in only one part of a region when a causal characteristic is being manifested in many parts of that region. Again, causes continue to be manifested during times when no sense-data are obtained. There is no necessary concomitance of caused events with sense-data, though there is concomitance among sense-data themselves. Accordingly, the causative physical occupant and the family of sense-data are not identical, and phenomenalism is false.

Collective Delimitation Theory

Now we see that for a sense-datum s to belong to a certain material thing M, first s must be a member of a family of sense-data prolonging itself through time and centering in a standard solid having a certain place in the system of standard solids; and second, the place must be physically occupied—causal characteristics must be manifested there. This is Price's theory, the collective delimitation theory. It stresses that the primary relation of "belonging to" is between an entire family and a material thing, the relation of a single sense-datum to the thing being derivative; moreover, that the family is related to the material thing by coinciding with the physically occupative portion of the thing.

Probably we get our first hint of the relation of causation to sense-data by observing other people's changed behavior in the face of certain evident changes in their environment. More important is the influence of the fact of our having

several senses. By reflection on the data of one, we discern how the data of another sense originate. Concomitant changes in our tactual sense-data, for example, with the introduction of objects of the visual field to the skin, are a source of knowledge. The *complete thing* is the physically occupative thing with causal properties plus the family of sense-data. A changing complete thing is not the cause of changes in our sense-data, for the data are part of the thing. However, a change in the thing *as physical occupant* of space may entail changes in the sense-data that depend upon the presence of both it and its observer. The laws of sense-data are of a different order from ordinary causal laws. We can define a given type of physical occupant only by reference to the kind of family of sense-data it is coincident with and to all those foreign ones whose mode of prolongation it influences. However, of the intrinsic qualities of physical occupants, we have no knowledge at all.

Beyond Phenomenalism

Price's *Perception* perhaps represents our farthest point of advance in its area. Whether his position is adopted, his close study of the problems and his careful solutions have much that is useful. For the introspective part of his procedure, Price asks of us only the accordance with our own experience. In addition, he seems to begin with the perhaps intuitive preconceptions that have made us suspicious of some of the stranger theories of perception and to exhibit and justify these conceptions. Finally, Price's convincing exposition of the differences between the separately certifiable orders, sense-data, and the manifestations of causality seems, by correcting the "emptiness" of phenomenalism, to be a considerable contribution.

John T. Goldthwait

Additional Reading

Davis, Stephen T., ed. *Death and Afterlife*. New York: St. Martin's Press, 1989. Discussions of the afterlife, from secular and a variety of religious perspectives with some references to H. H. Price; not every religious tradition teaches personal survival.

_____. "Survival of Death." In *A Companion to the Philosophy of Religion*, edited by Philip L.

Quinn and Charles Taliaferro. Oxford: Blackwell, 1997. Discussion of the notion of a person surviving the death of her body, with reference to Price's classic article, "Survival and the Idea of 'Another World.'"

Flew, Antony, and Alasdair McIntyre, eds. *New Essays in Philosophical Theology*. London: SCM Press, 1955. Essays by D. M. Mackinnon and Antony Flew regarding survival.

Lewis, H. D. *Persons and Life After Death*. New York: Barnes & Noble, 1978. Essays on the title topics by Lewis, with contributions from and discussions with Anthony Quinton, Bernard Williams, Antony Flew, and Sydney Shoemaker with numerous references to Price; Lewis favors the claim that persons survive the death of their bodies, and the others are critics of this claim.

Yandell, Keith. *The Philosophy of Religion*. London: Routledge, 1999. Contains discussions of views of persons and the afterlife as held in various religious traditions.

Keith E. Yandell

Hilary Putnam

Putnam is probably best known for his development and defense of Turing machine functionalism, for his concept of semantic externalism and the Twin Earth thought exercise, and for internal realism.

Principal philosophical works: *Philosophy of Logic*, 1971; *Mathematics, Matter and Method*, 1975; *Mind, Language, and Reality*, 1975; *Meaning and the Moral Sciences*, 1978; *Reason, Truth, and History*, 1981; *Realism and Reason*, 1983; *The Many Faces of Realism*, 1987; *Representation and Reality*, 1988; *Realism with a Human Face*, 1990; *Renewing Philosophy*, 1992; *Words and Life*, 1994; *Pragmatism: An Open Question*, 1995.

Born: July 31, 1926; Chicago, Illinois

Early Life
On July 31, 1926, Hilary W. Putnam was born in Chicago to Samuel and Riva Putnam. Samuel was a writer and a journalist and a member of the Communist Party during the Depression. Putnam's parents lived in France until 1934 and then in Philadelphia, where Putnam was graduated from the University of Pennsylvania in 1948. He studied at Harvard for a year before eventually earning his Ph.D. from the University of California, Los Angeles, in 1951.

At the age of twenty-two, Putnam married Erna Diesendruck on November 1, 1948. They divorced in 1962, and he married Ruth Anna Hall on August 11 of that year. He became the father of four children, two daughters and two sons.

Life's Work
Putnam began teaching philosophy as an instructor at Northwestern University in 1952. That year was followed by a stint at Princeton, where he advanced to assistant and later associate professor. He then taught, as a full professor, at the Massachusetts Institute of Technology from 1961 to 1965. Beginning in 1965, he taught philosophy at Harvard under various titles, including Walter Beverly Pearson Professor of Modern Mathematics and Mathematical Logic and Cogan University Professor. He served the Eastern Division of the American Philosophical Association as vice

president for 1975-1976 and as president for 1976-1977.

According to an article that appeared in the news magazine *U.S. News and World Report*, Putnam supported the draft resistance during the Vietnam War and later, having become more radicalized, assumed the position of Harvard faculty sponsor of Students for a Democratic Society (SDS) and joined a Maoist group, the Progressive Labor Party. According to Putnam, this Marxist period in his life may have been a retracing of his father's footsteps.

Putnam's topics include a vast array of philosophical issues, from the theoretical foundations of quantum physics to the epistemology of ethics, but as indicated by the title of his Ph.D. dissertation, *The Meaning of the Concept of Probability in Application to Finite Sequences*, his early work focused primarily on logic and the philosophy of mathematics. A notable contribution in these fields is his work with Martin Davies and Julia Robinson. Davies and Putnam teamed to write "Reductions of Hilbert's Tenth Problem," and Putnam, Davies, and Robinson wrote "The Decision Problem for Exponential Diophantine Equations."

In the late 1950's, Putnam proposed a program in the philosophy of mind that is now widely known as functionalism. Functionalism, according to Putnam, is the view that mental states, rather than being identified as some physical state, are defined by their inputs and outputs, or causes and effects. Putnam stated that the mind may be viewed as a "probabilistic automaton" of which, in some state, the transition to other states and the display of certain behaviors can be probabilistically predicted based on a given input, or set of inputs. The Turing machine, often used by Putnam to explain and defend functionalism, is a special type of probabilistic automaton with transition probabilities 1,0. That is, the strictly binary probabilities of the Turing machine are, more than probabilistic, deterministic.

Putnam's argument rests largely on the thesis that states such as pain are not physical-chemical states of the brain, but *functional* states of the entire organism. Given some typical state of the organism, pain is the state caused by a certain input, such as a pinch or a pinprick, that in turn causes other states, such as worry or apprehension, and behaviors (output) such as exclaiming, "Ouch!" What he intended to show, through functionalism, was that organisms composed of physically possible but different material could as easily exhibit mentality as do humans. From this we learn that what we really want to know about the mind is its functional organization, not the nature of its either mysterious or strictly physical substance.

About the time that Putnam became more politically radical, his philosophical views moved away from positivism and became less concerned with logic and the philosophy of mathematics. The focus of his work shifted to human experience and how human experience is affected by fields such as logic, philosophy of mathematics, epistemology, and other areas of philosophy.

Putnam often changed his mind. Early in his career, he was a strong proponent of the positivist movement, which he later abandoned and even criticized. In addition, although he defended and developed the theory of functionalism, he came to argue that functionalism fails because the intentional cannot be reduced to the computational or physical. However, Putnam basically held one position (though often revised) beginning in the late 1950's: The main concepts of that position are "semantic externalism" and "internal realism."

Semantic externalism, or the notion that "'meanings' just ain't in the head" was first introduced, using the Twin Earth thought experiment, in Putnam's 1975 essay, "The Meaning of 'Meaning.'" Twin Earth is exactly like Earth in every way except one—the word "water," though indicating the substance filling ponds, running through pipes, and drunk from glasses, does not refer to H_2O, but XYZ. In spite of its distinct chemical makeup, XYZ is utterly indistinguishable from water to the layperson, and it is only with the aid of modern science that Earth and Twin Earth inhabitants are aware of the difference between the two substances.

Putnam proposed semantic externalism as a response to the popular and pervasive notion according to which knowledge of meanings is private. A feature common to all theories of meaning, from those of Greek philosopher Aristotle to

Hilary Putnam. *(Courtesy of Hilary Putnam)*

those of Scottish philosopher David Hume, is that an individual in isolation can grasp any concept and that the individual's grasp of the concept completely determines the extension of that concept. The difference between the extension of "water" on Earth and the extension of "water" on Twin Earth is intended to show that extension of terms is at least partially dependent on factors *external* to any individual's mind.

An increasingly staunch critic of metaphysical realism, Putnam strove to show that the collapse of such realism does not require us to fall into relativism or postmodern skepticism. He introduced his concept of *internal realism* in a presidential address to the American Philosophical Association in 1976. Essentially, internal realism, or realism with a little "r," as Putnam termed it, takes both the commonsense view of things and the scientific view of things at face value without "helping itself to a notion of the 'thing in itself.'" In his 1987 essay "Is There Still Anything to Say About Reality and Truth?," Putnam said that "internal realism . . . is just the insistence that realism is not incompatible with conceptual relativity." That is, internal realism is not in conflict with the idea that we can, and perhaps should, use different theories about the world in different circumstances. To illustrate this idea, Putnam recalled that the typical person views a table as "solid," or as mostly solid matter, even though physics has shown that the table is, *in fact*, mostly empty space.

Other consistent themes in Putnam's work, particularly his later work, are his attack on the fact-value dichotomy and his praise of American pragmatism. Both themes are found throughout the papers in *Reason, Truth, and History* and *Words and Life*. In these works, he suggests that it is a mistaken view to claim that ethics and aesthetics do not deal in facts because they are ultimately value-based and to think that metaphysics is any less ultimately grounded in values.

These themes might both be considered a part of Putnam's push to bring philosophy back to the people, another central theme in his later work. As the Gifford Lecturer at the University of St. Andrews during the Martinmas term of 1990, Putnam presented a series of lectures to this end that were later published as *Renewing Philosophy*. Philosophy was taken from the people, in his

view, through its own mistaken views of its purpose and value. These views, which Putnam sometimes attributes to particular philosophers and other times simply to the discipline as a whole, grant either too much or too little importance to philosophy:

> For philosophy to see itself simply as thinking about a collection of riddles seems too small an ambition, but for philosophy to have the ambition of saving the world seems too extreme. Something in between has got to be right.

Influence

Putnam's influence on philosophy is difficult to measure because his writings span a wide breadth and contain evolving views. Nevertheless, some conclusions can be made with a fair amount of certainty.

Putnam, like many other scholars, benefited from the mass intellectual exodus of Europe resulting from Nazi occupation prior to and during World War II. A student of both Rudolf Carnap and Hans Reichenbach, Putnam frequently acknowledged Reichenbach's influence on his work. Among the connections to his teacher is the substantial contribution to the theoretical foundations of quantum physics.

In his works, Putnam drew extensively on the influence of both philosophers Immanuel Kant and Ludwig Wittgenstein and expressed a desire to think of some of his own views as Kantian. In addition, he wrote that though Kant was wrong about quite a bit, the solution lies not in asking new or different questions but in correctly answering the questions that Kant aptly raised.

There is no denying the strong influence of pragmatism on Putnam's work, his later work in particular. Putnam made no secret of his affinity to that school of thought and indeed seemed to view himself somewhat as a contemporary pragmatist. In the preface to *Words and Life*, he suggested that he should have called internal realism *pragmatic* realism. Also, in the preface to *Realism with a Human Face*, he allied his views with "the generous and open-minded attitude that William James called 'pragmatism'" as opposed to the "science worship" of the positivists.

Putnam's early work is likely to have a long-lasting impact on logic and the philosophy of mathematics. Likewise, his work on functionalism, though ultimately rejected by Putnam himself, was quite influential in the philosophy of mind. Though it is yet unclear whether Putnam's later work will accomplish his goal of renewing philosophy, it is likely that it will have significant implications for the field and that, if nothing else, Putnam's thought will play a part in rejuvenating the pragmatist movement in philosophy.

James C. Griffith

Realism with a Human Face

Type of philosophy: Metaphysics, epistemology
First published: 1990
Principal ideas advanced:
◇ "Conceptual relativity" is the idea that every true utterance contains a conventional and factual aspect.
◇ "Internal realism" is superior to metaphysical realism and relativism.
◇ The dichotomy between facts and values is untenable; metaphysical and epistemological claims are ultimately based on values.
◇ The American pragmatist tradition is important and viable.

Hilary Putnam argues that, historically, philosophical realism has pledged to save the world—to reveal the world to us so that we can better understand it. Modern philosophical realism seems to say that a better understanding of the world out there is not possible. Therefore, while "realism" relieves us of our "incorrect" commonsense view of the world, it replaces it with a scientific view that appears no more grounded in fact or truth. In a way, Putnam's "internal realism" is the hero of our commonsense view.

Like the earlier *Reason, Truth, and History* (1981) and the later *Words and Life* (1994), *Realism with a Human Face* focuses on Putnam's concept of internal realism as an alternative to metaphysical realism and relativism. Putnam seeks to de-

velop the idea and defend it against what he perceives as misunderstandings of the notion as it was presented in *Reason, Truth, and History* (published just five years after he introduced the idea in his address to the American Philosophical Association). The majority of the essays in this work were written in the early 1980's, some in response to criticisms of internal realism.

Something that goes hand in hand with internal realism and that Putnam feels provides a more human way of seeing the world, is the rejection of the fact-value dichotomy. He insists that basically, metaphysics and epistemology are no less based on values than are ethics and aesthetics.

Putnam suggests that none of the ideas for which he argues in this book are new. "All of these ideas," he writes in the preface, "are ideas that have been long associated with the American pragmatist tradition." After realizing that so many of his ideas are closely aligned with this tradition, Putnam sought to better understand the tradition in its entirety, "from [Charles Sanders] Peirce right up to [W. V. O.] Quine and [Nelson] Goodman." He includes his studies of American pragmatism to indicate the direction of his later interests and to further the understanding of this tradition in its many forms.

The book is broken into three parts, each with the purpose of emphasizing a particular area of Putnam's thought. It is important to understand that all three areas are intertwined to some degree throughout the book, though here they are treated separately. For example, although part 3 is dedicated to studying American pragmatism, as Putnam admits, all the ideas in the book are associated with that tradition.

Conceptual relativity, which Putnam stresses as extremely important in the preface, is not the focus of one of the three parts or even an essay but is instead woven throughout the book. Putnam anticipates his readers asking why they should give up metaphysical realism and provides a twofold answer. First, all the views that attempt to hold on to at least some part of metaphysical realism fail to adequately represent quantum mechanics, which he views as the most fundamental physical theory. More important, these views fail to do justice to the "pervasive phenomenon" he calls conceptual relativity. Essentially, conceptual relativity is the idea that for every *true* thing we say, there is a way in which it is a matter of convention and a way in which it is fact. However, Putnam argues that it is a mistake to conclude from this that the truth can in some way be separated into "conventional" and "factual" parts. These two aspects of the truth simply apply in different ways or at different times. Though this explanation, along with his concept of internal realism, may seem to place Putnam's ideas very close to those of philosopher Richard Rorty, Putnam distinguishes between their views. For example, Putnam insists that he does not share Rorty's skepticism about the existence of a substantial notion of truth. That is, Putnam does not think that truth is "whatever works."

Internal Realism

Part 1 is devoted to the development and defense of *internal realism*, and the first essay, "Realism with a Human Face," explains why the alternatives, metaphysical realism and relativism, are not acceptable and what distinguishes each from internal realism. To illustrate one of the points of the essay, Putnam relates a problem and controversy in quantum physics. He raises the point that quantum mechanics, at some base level, depends on classical physics to describe the device making measurements in quantum mechanics. (Quantum mechanics "replaced" classical physics because it provided a better, or "more accurate," picture of the world.) No real understanding of physics is necessary to see Putnam's point about conceptual relativity. He is simply highlighting the fact that the view being exercised, quantum physics, is in need of some other view, classical physics, to describe itself. Which theory provides the true picture of the way the world is?

The metaphysical realist believes that we can answer questions about the truth if we can just reach some objective viewpoint, a God's-eye view, from which we can observe that truth. The point is that because it is sometimes necessary, as in the case of quantum mechanics, to use one view to explain the other, it must be perfectly acceptable to sometimes hold one view and sometimes, the other—that there is no *one* truth that always applies under all conditions. However, because we are talking about views of

"truth" or "what the world is *really* like," metaphysical realists cannot accept this. For the metaphysical realist, there *is* only one truth in terms of "the way the world is." Thus Putnam believes that metaphysical realism is untenable.

In contrast, relativists relinquish all ties to realism, and Putnam also views this as a mistake. He suggests, quoting philosopher Stanley Cavell, that although philosophical problems are unsolvable, "there are better and worse ways of thinking about them," and we should not discard all epistemological principles simply because the quest for objective truth failed. Five such principles are

(1) Ordinarily, there is a fact of the matter as to whether or not statements are warranted.
(2) Such warrant is independent of the opinions of one's peers.
(3) As historical products, our standards for this "warranted assertibility" evolve in time.
(4) These always reflect our interests and values.
(5) All of our norms and standards, including these, are revisable.

Despite the tension some see in these principles, Putnam feels that they should be held jointly. The fourth principle is based on his claim that these norms and standards are informed by our picture of intellectual flourishing and that this picture is part of, and only makes sense as part of, our picture of human flourishing. (Putnam returns to this notion of flourishing when rejecting the fact-value dichotomy.) In short, he argues that we can justify our image of the world, but it "cannot be justified by anything but its success as judged by the interests and values which evolve and got modified at the same time and in interaction with our evolving image of the world itself." Therefore, we cannot have the God's-eye view sought by metaphysical realists, but we can avoid the skepticism of relativists with principles such as warranted assertibility.

In "A Defense of Internal Realism," Putnam begins the defense as another attack on metaphysical realism. He identifies the metaphysical realist's position and describes how that position is untenable. Metaphysics, he claims, is an impossible project. He argues that anyone who can show us how we *can* do metaphysics will have to do something truly revolutionary. A metaphysical system must not only contain more than what is indispensable to metaphysics—reference and justification—but also explain how we can have access to "metaphysical reality." The main point of the essay is that some sentences are true from the perspective of one theory yet false from another perspective. It is true, for example, in some theory that points exist in space and time, while in another theory, they are simply limits. Once again, this involves employing different pictures of the world at different times, so there can be no *one* truth. Despite this, Putnam thinks that the notion of truth as a property independent of an individual mind is something we need to retain. What we need to remember, however, is that truth can only be fixed, or evaluated, from within a particular language, theory, or picture of the world.

The Fact-Value Dichotomy

Although part 1 is officially dedicated to defending internal realism, both in this essay and while arguing that relativism and positivism are two sides of the same coin in "Why Is a Philosopher?," Putnam previews his attack on the fact-value dichotomy in part 2. For Putnam, the distinction between facts and values is an illusion. One method of attack, which he refers to repeatedly in this work, is the "companions in the guilt" argument. This argument is a response to the claim that ethical and aesthetic judgments are merely subjective and thus have no objective truth-value. The goal is to show that *if* such judgments are merely subjective, then the same is true of metaphysical and epistemological judgments. The argument accepts all the charges brought against ethics and aesthetics (disagreement exists across cultures about what is valuable, controversy cannot be settled "intersubjectively," and no reductive account exists of what value is) and then brings the same charges against metaphysics and epistemology.

The "facts" of these latter fields, Putnam charges, are just working assumptions, or standards, based on values identical to those of ethics and aesthetics. The values of ethics and aesthetics are a part of our picture of human flourishing. The values of metaphysics and epistemology are based on our picture of intellectual flourishing,

which is itself a part of our picture of human flourishing. Because we cannot provide scientific explanation for reference, warrant, or truth, no such explanation should be demanded of ethical or aesthetic values.

Pragmatism

Though the book deals with pragmatic concerns and ideas throughout, part 3 is dedicated to the American pragmatist tradition. Rather than introducing much new material, this section appears to serve as a tribute to Putnam's heroes. In the introduction to the volume, editor James Conant discusses Putnam's work in relation to his philosophical heroes, and this final section is perhaps best read in the context of Conant's introductory comments. This portion of the book includes discussion of pragmatist heroes such as William James, John Dewey, and Charles Sanders Peirce and allusions to other, nonpragmatist philosophers. References to Immanuel Kant and Ludwig Wittgenstein are peppered throughout several of the essays in this section, with particular attention paid to Kant's project in "The Way the World Is." The philosophy of Donald Davidson is given a supporting role in multiple essays, most notably in "Meaning Holism" and in "The Way the World Is," in which it is linked with the philosophies of Nelson Goodman and W. V. O. Quine, and all are linked with the American pragmatist tradition. Though the final essay is devoted to Goodman's *Fact, Fiction, and Forecast* (1954), Quine appears to be the star of the third section of the book. He is heralded as "The Greatest Logical Positivist." "The Way the World Is" provides a concise, favorable summary of Quine's *Word and Object* (1960), and Putnam builds "Meaning Holism" around Quine's philosophy. Conant suggests that shifts in Putnam's thought can be closely mapped to his abandonment of old heroes and adoption of new heroes. If this is true, then we can assume that Putnam was serious about his intention to forward the understanding of the American pragmatist tradition.

By the end of the twentieth century, the influence of the American pragmatist tradition had increased, and the accomplishments of these philosophers were receiving greater consideration. However, several philosophers besides Putnam implicitly paid tribute to the pragmatists in the latter part of the twentieth century, and it would be difficult to attribute this revival in pragmatist thinking to Putnam alone.

James C. Griffith

Additional Reading

Boolos, George, ed. *Meaning and Method: Essays in Honor of Hilary Putnam.* Cambridge, England: Cambridge University Press, 1990. Boolos presents a series of papers by several of Hilary Putnam's colleagues and former students. The papers cover a wide variety of philosophical subjects, reflecting Putnam's own interests and his pervasive influence on contemporary thought.

Clark, Peter, and Bob Hale, eds. *Reading Putnam.* Cambridge, Mass.: Blackwell, 1994. Papers from nine philosophers presented at an international conference on Putnam's philosophy at the University of St. Andrews in 1990 are collected in this volume. They represent a broad range of issues to which Putnam has contributed significantly. Two essays in particular, Simon Blackburn's "Enchanting Views" and Michael Dummet's "Wittgenstein on Necessity: Some Reflections," focus on Putnam's internal realism. Blackburn tells us what internal realism *is not*.

Goldberg, Sanford, and Andrew Pessin, eds. *The Twin Earth Chronicles: Twenty Years of Reflection on Hilary Putnam's "The Meaning of 'Meaning.'"* Armonk, N.Y.: M. E. Sharpe, 1996. This is a good initiation to one of Putnam's major ideas, "semantic externalism." This collection begins with an introduction, followed by "The Meaning of 'Meaning,'" Putnam's article challenging traditional views of the philosophies of language and mind. The remainder of the work is dedicated to arguably the best of many responses the article generated.

Harman, Gilbert. "Metaphysical Realism and Moral Relativism: Reflections on Hilary Putnam's *Reason, Truth, and History.*" *The Journal of Philosophy* 79, no. 10 (October, 1982): 568-575. This is a useful critique of internal realism, based on a defense of the fact-value distinction. This is one of two papers that generated Putnam's own "A Defense of Internal Realism" in *Realism with a Human Face.* The other, also in this issue, along with Putnam's brief responding comments, is Hartry Field's "Realism and Relativism" on pages 553-567.

James C. Griffith

Pythagoras

Pythagoras set an inspiring example with his energetic search for knowledge of universal order. His specific discoveries and accomplishments in philosophy, mathematics, astronomy, and music theory make him an important figure in Western intellectual history.

Principal philosophical work: No extant fragments. Primary source: Aristotle

Born: c. 580 B.C.E.; Samos, Ionia, Greece
Died: c. 500 B.C.E.; Metapontum, Lucania (now Metaponto, Italy)

Early Life

Pythagoras, son of Mnesarchus, was born about 580 B.C.E. His birthplace was the island of Samos in the Mediterranean Sea. Aside from these details, information about his early life—most of it from the third and fourth centuries B.C.E., up to one hundred years after he died—is extremely sketchy. Sources roughly contemporary with him tend to contradict one another, possibly because those who had been his students developed in many different directions after his death.

Aristotle's *Metaphysica* (second Athenian period, 335-323 B.C.E.; *Metaphysics*, 1801), one source of information about Pythagorean philosophy, never refers to Pythagoras himself but always to "the Pythagoreans." Furthermore, it is known that many ideas attributed to Pythagoras have been filtered through Platonism. Nevertheless, certain doctrines and biographical events can be traced with reasonable certainty to Pythagoras himself. His teachers in Greece are said to have included Creophilus and Pherecydes of Syros; the latter (who is identified as history's first prose writer) probably encouraged Pythagoras's belief in the transmigration of souls, which became a major tenet of Pythagorean philosophy. A less certain but more detailed tradition has him also studying under Thales of Miletus, who built a philosophy on rational, positive integers. In fact, these integers were to prove a stumbling block to Pythagoras but would lead to his discovery of irrational numbers such as the square root of two.

Following his studies in Greece, Pythagoras traveled extensively in Egypt, Babylonia, and other Mediterranean lands, learning the rules of thumb that, collectively, passed for geometry at that time. He was to raise geometry to the level of a true science through his pioneering work on geometric proofs and the axioms, or postulates, from which these are derived.

A bust now housed at Rome's Capitoline Museum (the sculptor is not known) portrays the philosopher as having close-cropped, wavy Greek hair and beard, his features expressing the relentlessly inquiring Ionian mind—a mind that insisted on knowing for metaphysical reasons the *exact* ratio of the side of a square to its diagonal. Pythagoras's eyes suggest an inward focus even as they gaze intently at the viewer. The furrowed forehead conveys solemnity and powerful concentration, yet deeply etched lines around the mouth, and the hint of a crinkle about the eyes, reveal that this great man was fully capable of laughter.

Life's Work

When Pythagoras returned to Samos from his studies abroad, he found his native land in the grip of the tyrant Polycrates, who had come to power about 538 B.C.E. In the meantime, the Greek mainland had been partially overrun by the Persians. Probably because of these developments, in 529 B.C.E. Pythagoras migrated to Croton, a Dorian colony in southern Italy, and entered into what became the historically important period of his life.

At Croton he founded a school of philosophy that in some ways resembled a monastic order.

Its members were pledged to a pure and devout life, close friendship, and political harmony. In the immediately preceding years, southern Italy had been nearly destroyed by the strife of political factions. Modern historians speculate that Pythagoras thought that political power would give his organization an opportunity to lead others to salvation through the disciplines of nonviolence, vegetarianism, personal alignment with the mathematical laws that govern the universe, and the practice of ethics in order to earn a superior reincarnation. Pythagoras believed in metempsychosis, the transmigration of souls from one body to another, possibly from humans to animals. Indeed, Pythagoras claimed that he could remember four previous human lifetimes in detail.

His adherents he divided into two hierarchical groups. The first was the *akousmatikoi*, or listeners, who were enjoined to remain silent, listen to and absorb Pythagoras's spoken precepts, and practice the special way of life taught by him. The second group was the *mathematikoi*, students of theoretical subjects, or simply "those who know," who pursued the subjects of arithmetic, the theory of music, astronomy, and cosmology. (Though *mathematikoi* later came to mean "scientists" or "mathematicians," originally it meant those who had attained advanced knowledge in a broader sense.) The *mathematikoi*, after a long period of training, could ask questions and express opinions of their own.

Despite the later divergences among his students—fostered perhaps by his having divided them into two classes— Pythagoras himself drew a close connection between his metaphysical and scientific teachings. In his time, hardly anyone conceived of a split between science and religion or metaphysics. Nevertheless, some modern historians deny any real relation between the scientific doctrines of the Pythagorean society and its spiritualism and personal disciplines. In the twentieth century, Pythagoras's findings in astronomy, mathematics, and music theory are much more widely appreciated than the metaphysical philosophy

that, to him, was the logical outcome of those findings.

Pythagoras developed a philosophy of number to account for the essence of all things. This concept rested on three basic observations: the mathematical relationships of musical harmonies, the fact that any triangle whose sides are in a ratio of 3:4:5 is always a right triangle, and the fixed numerical relations among the movement of stars and planets. It was the consistency of ratios among musical harmonies and geometrical shapes in different sizes and materials that impressed Pythagoras.

His first perception (which some historians consider his greatest) was that musical intervals depend on arithmetical ratios among lengths of string on the lyre (the most widely played instrument of Pythagoras's time), provided that these strings are at the same tension. For example, a ratio of 2:1 produces an octave; that is, a string twice as long as another string, at the same ten-

Pythagoras. *(Smithsonian Institution)*

sion, produces the same note an octave below the shorter string. Similarly, 3:2 produces a fifth and 4:3 produces a fourth. Using these ratios, one could assign numbers to the four fixed strings of the lyre: 6, 8, 9, and 12. Moreover, if these ratios are transferred to another instrument—such as the flute, also highly popular in that era—the same harmonies will result. Hippasus of Metapontum, a *mathematikos* living a generation after Pythagoras, extended this music theory through experiments to produce the same harmonies with empty and partly filled glass containers and metal disks of varying thicknesses.

Pythagoras himself determined that the most important musical intervals can be expressed in ratios among the numbers 1, 2, 3, and 4, and he concluded that the number 10—the sum of these first four integers—comprehends the entire nature of number. Tradition has it that the later Pythagoreans, rather than swear by the gods as most other people did, swore by the "Tetrachtys of the Decad" (the sum of 1, 2, 3, and 4). The Pythagoreans also sought the special character of each number. The tetrachtys was called a "triangular number" because its components can readily be arranged as a triangle.

By extension, the number 1 is reason because it never changes; 2 is opinion; and 4 is justice (a concept surviving in the term "a square deal"). Odd numbers are masculine and even numbers are feminine; therefore, 5, the first number representing the sum of an odd and an even number (1, "unity," not being considered for this purpose), symbolizes marriage. Seven is *parthenos*, or virgin, because among the first ten integers it has neither factors nor products. Other surviving Pythagorean concepts include unlucky 13 and "the seventh son of a seventh son."

To some people in the twentieth century, these number concepts seem merely superstitious. Nevertheless, Pythagoras and his followers did important work in several branches of mathematics and exerted a lasting influence on the field. The best-known example is the Pythagorean Theorem, the statement that the square of the hypotenuse of a right triangle is equal to the sum of the squares of the other two sides. Special applications of the theorem were known in Mesopotamia as early as the eighteenth century B.C.E., but Pythagoras sought to generalize it for a char-

acteristically Greek reason: This theorem measures the ratio of the side of a square to its diagonal, and he was determined to know the *precise* ratio. It cannot be expressed as a whole number, however, so Pythagoras found a common denominator by showing a relationship among the *squares* of the sides of a right triangle. The Pythagorean theorem is set forth in book 1 of Euclid's *Stoicheia* (c. 300 B.C.E.; *The Elements of Geometrie of the Most Auncient Philosopher Euclide of Megara*, 1570, commonly known as *Elements* or *Elements of Geometry*), Euclid being one of several later Greek thinkers whom Pythagoras strongly influenced and who transmitted his ideas in much-modified form to posterity.

Pythagoras also is said to have discovered the theory of proportion and the arithmetic, geometric, and harmonic means. The terms of certain arithmetic and harmonic means yield the three musical intervals. In addition, the ancient historian Proclus credited Pythagoras with discovering the construction of the five regular geometrical solids, though modern scholars think it more likely that he discovered three—the pyramid, the tetrahedron, and the dodecahedron—and that Theaetetus (after whom a Platonic dialogue is named) later discovered the construction of the remaining two, the octahedron and the icosahedron.

The field of astronomy, too, is indebted to Pythagoras. He was among the first to contend that the earth and the universe are spherical. He understood that the sun, the moon, and the planets rotate on their own axes and also orbit a central point outside themselves, though he believed that this central point was the earth. Later Pythagoreans deposed the earth as the center of the universe and substituted a "central fire," which, however, they did not identify as the sun—this they saw as another planet. Nearest the central fire was the "counter-earth," which always accompanied the earth in its orbit. The Pythagoreans assumed that the earth's rotation and its revolution around the central fire took the same amount of time—twenty-four hours. According to Aristotle, the idea of a counter-earth—besides bringing the number of revolving bodies up to the mystical number of ten—helped to explain lunar eclipses, which were thought to be caused by the counter-earth's interposition between sun and moon. Two thousand years later, Nicolaus Copernicus saw the Pythagorean system as anticipating his own; he had in mind both the Pythagoreans's concept of the day-and-night cycle and their explanation of eclipses.

Like Copernicus in his time, Pythagoras and his followers in their time were highly controversial. For many years, the Pythagoreans did exert a strong political and philosophical influence throughout southern Italy. The closing years of the sixth century B.C.E., however, saw the rise of democratic sentiments, and a reaction set in against the Pythagoreans, whom the democrats regarded as elitist.

Indeed, this political reaction led either to Pythagoras's exile or to his death—there are two traditions surrounding it. The first account, which is the more probable story, is that a democrat named Cylon led a revolt against the power of the Pythagorean brotherhood and forced Pythagoras to retire to Metapontum, where he died peacefully about the end of the sixth century B.C.E. According to the other tradition, Pythagoras perished when his adversaries set fire to his school in Croton in 504 B.C.E. The story is that, of his vast library of scrolls, only one was brought out of the fire; it contained his most esoteric secrets, which were passed on to succeeding generations of Pythagoreans.

Pythagoras's followers continued to be powerful throughout Magna Graecia until at least the middle of the fifth century B.C.E., when another reaction set in against them and their meeting-houses were sacked and burned. The survivors scattered in exile and did not return to Italy until the end of the fifth century. During the ensuing decades, the leading Pythagorean was Philolaus, who wrote the first systematic exposition of Pythagorean philosophy. Philolaus's influence can be traced to Plato through their mutual friend Archytas, who ruled Taras (Tarentum) in Italy for many years. The Platonic dialogue *Timaeos* (last period works, 360-347 B.C.E.; *Timaeus*, 1793), named for its main character, a young Pythagorean astronomer, describes Pythagorean ideas in detail.

Influence

"Of all men," said Heraclitus, "Pythagoras, the son of Mnesarchus, was the most assiduous in-

quirer." Pythagoras is said to have been the first person to call himself a philosopher, or lover of wisdom. He believed that the universe is a logical, symmetrical whole, which can be understood in simple terms. For Pythagoras and his students, there was no gap between the scientific or mathematical ideal and the aesthetic. The beauty of his concepts and of the universe they described lies in their simplicity and consistency.

Quite aside from any of Pythagoras's specific intellectual accomplishments, his belief in universal order, and the energy he displayed in seeking it out, provided a galvanizing example for others. Although the details of his personal life are sketchy, his ideals left their mark on later poets, artists, scientists, and philosophers from Plato and Aristotle through the Renaissance and down to the twentieth century. Indirectly, through Pythagoras's disciple Philolaus, his ideas were transmitted to Plato and Aristotle, and, through these better-known thinkers, to a much larger audience.

Pythagoras's systematic exposition of mathematical principles alone would have been enough to make him an important figure in Western intellectual history; however, the spiritual beliefs he espoused make him also one of the great religious teachers of ancient Greek times. Even those ideas that are seen as intellectually disreputable have inspired generations of poets and artists. For example, the Pythagorean concept of the harmony of the spheres, suggested by the analogy between musical ratios and those of planetary orbits, became a central metaphor of Renaissance literature.

Thomas Rankin

Pythagoras: Philosophy

Type of philosophy: Metaphysics, philosophy of mathematics
First transcribed: No extant fragments. Primary source: Aristotle
Principal ideas advanced:
◇ The principles of numbers are the principles of the cosmos and all things: All things are numbers.

◇ Ten is the essence of number, the perfect number.

◇ There are ten basic principles of being and ten heavenly bodies; the movement of the heavenly bodies gives rise to the music of the spheres.

◇ Fire is the center of the universe; the earth is a star.

◇ By number the unlimited was limited; the world soul breathes the air of the unlimited.

◇ All living things are akin.

◇ The virtues can be understood mathematically: justice is four.

◇ The soul is immortal and is reincarnated; one should aim at the purification of the soul through emulating the divine order and harmony.

Although there are no extant fragments of the writings of Pythagoras, his views were influential in the ancient world and have been referred to by a number of philosophical writers, among them Plato, Aristotle, Porphyry, and Diogenes Laërtius. As one might expect, the accounts are not entirely consistent, and it is often difficult to determine precisely or even approximately what view Pythagoras held on a question under discussion, but there is a body of beliefs that critics generally attribute to Pythagoras or to his followers. The followers are generally assumed either to have inherited the master's views or to have been inspired by his philosophy and practice to develop their ideas along lines that have a distinctive inherited character.

Pythagoras (like many ancient Greek philosophers) did not distinguish his metaphysical convictions from his beliefs about the physical world: His ontology (theory of being), cosmology (theory of cosmic origin and development), epistemology (theory of knowledge), theology, and ethics appear to be grounded in certain abstract mathematical ideas and beliefs and to be interrelated.

Number as a Basis

According to Aristotle, the Pythagoreans believed that all things are numbers in the sense that the principles of numbers are the principles of all things. "There is but one number, the mathematical," is a view attributed to Pythagoras by Aris-

totle, together with the related propositions that all objects of sense are numbers and that numbers are prior, both in power and existence, as well as logically, to physical objects. Accordingly, the Pythagoreans differed from the Milesian philosophers, who found in water, fire, or earth the fundamental substance and cause of things; for the Pythagoreans, the primary cause and substance of all things is number. Not only physical things but also justice and the other virtues, as well as the soul and reason, are in principle and composition numbers. The early writers attributed this philosophical tendency of Pythagoras and his followers—the tendency to take number as primary, creative essence and substance—to the Pythagoreans' having noticed similarities between numbers and objects of sense (although it is not clear what sorts of relationships counted as similarities). Thus, Aristotle writes, "They see many qualities of numbers in bodies perceived by sense" and "in numbers, . . . they thought they saw many likenesses to things that are and that are coming to be."

No doubt part of the belief in the creative power of numbers stemmed from the discovery of the numerical ratios involved in musical harmony. If numbers can so order sound as to achieve harmony, then it is credible that numbers so order the unlimited as to achieve a harmonious universe and that numbers so order the things within the universe as to endow them with distinctive numerical natures and to make physical harmony possible. Thus, since the Pythagoreans regarded ten as "the very nature of number" (Aetius) and as perfect (Aristotle), they declared that the number of heavenly bodies must be ten (although they had observed only nine and thereby presumed the tenth to be an unobservable body between the earth and the sun, a "counter-earth").

One is tempted to suppose that the Pythagoreans regarded number as the nature of things because they discovered constant and harmonizing arithmetical ratios in nature; it is as if they fastened on the abstract relationships that contemporary physics attempts to fix by mathematical equations. According to Aristotle, however, number for the Pythagoreans was not only the "first principle" of all things—the formal aspect or essence—but also "as it were the matter in things and in their conditions and states." Hence, number was not only form but also matter; the numbers themselves were quantities or magnitudes, not simply the formal aspects of that which has quantity. Pythagoras (or the Pythagoreans) believed that the odd and the even are the elements of numbers; the even is unlimited and is identified with the infinite; the odd is limited. Unity (the number 1) is the product of the odd and even, and all number arises from this original unity.

According to Aristotle, some Pythagoreans—proceeding from a dedication to ten as the perfect number—maintained that there are ten fundamental principles of all being, each principle consisting of a pair of opposites: the limited and the unlimited, the odd and the even, the one and the many, the right and the left, the male and the female, the resting and the moving, the straight and the crooked, the light and the dark, the good and the bad, the square and the oblong. Here again, Aristotle surmises, the principles appear to have been ranged "under the category of matter, for they say that being is compounded and formed from them, and that they inhere in it."

The Origin of the Universe

The Pythagorean account of the origin of the universe as an ordered system consistently accords to numbers the power of generation and the essential determination of the direction and quality of world order. According to Aristotle in *Physica* (second Athenian period, 335-323 B.C.E.; *Physics*, 1812), the Pythagoreans argued that void entered into heaven, which breathed it in from the Unlimited. Somehow "void defines the nature of things," and first of all defined numbers. Void is described as "a kind of separating and distinguishing factor between terms in a series." (It is not clear from Aristotle's account—and perhaps it was not clear to Aristotle—whether the Pythagoreans believed that number was somehow in void and then drawn out of void by a movement, like breathing, stemming from a resolution of tension between the limited and the unlimited, or that void somehow actually gave rise to number. In any case, the universe results from the forming power of number, according to the Pythagoreans.)

Aristotle remarks that although the common belief is that the earth is at the center of the universe, the Pythagoreans (who were dedicated astronomers) believed that a central fire is the center and that the earth creates day and night by circling about this fire. Fire as the center of space, matter, and nature also was regarded as the authoritative guard of all being, "the guard of Zeus."

Aristotle also comments on the Pythagorean view that there is a music of the spheres, a harmony of sound produced by the movement of the heavenly bodies in accord with the intervals determined by numbers. The belief in this heavenly music followed from their assumptions about the effect of the determination of all things by numbers (just as the belief in the tenth planet, the "counter-earth," was required by their belief in ten as the perfect number). The Pythagoreans accounted for the fact that human beings are not aware of the heavenly sounds by pointing out that because this sound is part of the nature of things and has been with us from birth, it is part of our lives, a constant background, and hence not noticeable.

Even the virtues can be understood mathematically, the Pythagoreans believed, according to the sources. Aristotle remarks in the *Ethica Nicomachea* (second Athenian period work, 335-323 B.C.E.; *Nicomachean Ethics*, 1797) that the Pythagoreans regarded the good as the limited and the evil as unlimited. (The idea of moral virtue as involving constraint within limits and even as exhibiting a kind of harmony was characteristic of the Greeks, including Plato and Aristotle.) Aristotle also mentions that the Pythagoreans defined the just as that which is reciprocal. Aristotle declares that Pythagoras was mistaken in attempting to discuss goodness by reference to numbers. Such a reference is inappropriate, Aristotle asserts; after all, he insists, "justice is not a square number."

Hippolytus's View

Hippolytus speaks of the Pythagoreans as combining astronomy, geometry, and music in their study of nature. He reports that Pythagoras claimed that God is a monad, and he mentions the Pythagorean belief that the universe is melodic and that the stars move rhythmically and hence melodiously. For the Pythagoreans, Hippolytus continues, number is the first principle, and this first principle is a male monad in substance, "begetting as a father all other numbers." The dyad is female, the triad male; that is, even is female; odd is male. All numbers are fours, and four generates ten, the perfect number. (If one adds the numbers 1, 2, 3, and 4, the total is 10.) The four parts of the decad—number, monad, power, and cube—by combining, account for all growth.

Hippolytus also calls attention to the Pythagorean belief in the immortality of the soul and in the soul's moving from one body to another. (He mentions the Pythagorean prohibition against the eating of beans because "at the beginning and composition of all things when the earth was still a whole, the bean arose.")

Others on Pythagoras

The Neoplatonic philosopher Proclus alludes to the Pythagorean discovery that the square of the hypotenuse of a right-angle triangle is equal to the sum of the squares of the other two sides. (The Pythagorean practice of arranging units or "dots" in squares may have contributed to some of their mathematical discoveries as well as to their metaphysical conviction that all things are numbers. As the Greek philosopher Speusippus points out, for the Pythagoreans 1 is the point, 2 is the line, 3 is the triangle, and 4 is the pyramid. The *tetraktys*, a triangle with a four dot base, then a line of three, then two, then one dot—making ten in all—was a key figure.)

Religious Beliefs and Practices

The Pythagoreans were subject to a number of rules of considerable moral and religious importance but hardly of philosophical significance (such as "Stir not the fire with iron," "Speak not of Pythagorean matters without light," and "Let not a swallow nest under your roof"). These rules, together with others—such as the prohibitions against the eating of flesh and beans and against the sacrifice of animals—stem from certain beliefs involved in the religion of the Pythagoreans as influenced by Orphism (the cult of Orpheus). The strictures against the eating of flesh and the sacrifice of animals, for example, are required by the belief in the transmigration of souls.

The moral emphasis in religious beliefs and practices of the Pythagoreans was on the purification of the soul. Porphyry writes of their beliefs that the soul is immortal and changes into other kinds of living things, that events recur in cycles, and that all living things be regarded as kin. Herodotus also speaks of the cyclical theory and applies it specifically to the transmigration of souls: From a human body, the soul enters the body of an animal born at the time of death of the human organism; the soul then makes the rounds of land and sea creatures; finally, after three thousand years, it enters a human body again. Diogenes Laërtius tells a tale in which Pythagoras calls upon someone to stop whipping a puppy because Pythagoras had recognized in the yelping of the dog the voice of a departed friend.

Through philosophy, the use of reason, music, religious observances, and the inculcation and development of a spirit of universal sympathy, the Pythagoreans sought the purification of the soul. (Because of the fundamental metaphysical belief in the ultimate reality and power of numbers, these various routes to purification were unified; the reliance on music, for example, was due at least in part to the discovery of the arithmetical proportions exhibited in musical harmony.) The soul, then, was to be educated, trained, ordered, and harmonized. Through the restraint of desire, the soul was to find its proper limits and balance; it could thereupon fit into the universal scheme of things, the universe itself exhibiting the beauty of harmony resulting from its essence in sacred numbers. As Aristotle wrote, for the Pythagoreans "the whole heavens were harmony and number."

Although the Pythagoreans apparently meant literally to claim that all things are numbers and that harmony is achieved through the proper arithmetical relationships, their philosophy probably could not have elicited the kind of dedication it did had not the emphasis on numbers been made "mystically"—that is, in such a way as to transform a mathematical metaphysics into a Greek ethics. Number as first principle was regarded as indefinable (according to Hippolytus); hence, it lent itself to symbolic extension as the possibility of order in life and to moral application in the form of injunctions calling for the attainment of inner harmony and the recognition of a universal harmony that provides an ideal, a ten. Although the discovery of the theorem that bears the master's name was a magnificent intellectual accomplishment, the moral use of metaphysics by the Pythagoreans contributed to the distinctive Greek emphasis on the use of reason, the recognition of opposites, the attainment of the mean, the setting of proper limits, and the harmonizing of the self and the world.

Ian P. McGreal

Additional Reading

Bamford, Christopher, ed. *Homage to Pythagoras: Rediscovering Sacred Science*. Hudson, N.Y.: Lindisfarne Press, 1994. This collection of essays touches on Pythagoras's ideas as they affect architecture and religion, among other topics. Includes bibliography.

Boudouris, K. I., ed. *Pythagorean Philosophy*. Athens: International Center for Greek Philosophy and Culture, 1992. This volume examines Pythagoras and the Pythagorean school. Includes bibliography.

Burkert, Walter. *Lore and Science in Ancient Pythagoreanism*. Translated by Edwin L. Minar, Jr. Cambridge, Mass.: Harvard University Press, 1972. This study, translated from the German, attempts to disentangle Pythagoreanism from Platonism and to describe the various aspects of Pythagoreanism, from music theory to what is called shamanistic religion. Includes extensive bibliography.

Godwin, Joscelyn, ed. *The Harmony of the Spheres: A Sourcebook of the Pythagorean Tradition in Music*. Rochester, Vt.: Inner Traditions International, 1993. This volume examines the effect that the philosophy and aesthetics of Pythagoras, particularly the concept of the harmony of the spheres, had on music. Includes bibliography and indexes.

Guthrie, W. K. C. *The Earlier Presocratics and the Pythagoreans*. Vol. 1 in *A History of Greek Philosophy*. Cambridge, England: Cambridge University Press, 1962. Contains an excellent, nearly two-hundred-page chapter on Pythagoras and a half dozen Pythagoreans.

Kingsley, Peter. *Ancient Philosophy, Mystery, and Magic: Empedocles and Pythagorean Tradition*. Oxford: Clarendon Press, 1995. This book illuminates Pythagorean philosophy by showing how it influenced Empedocles. It demonstrates the Pythagorean origin of Plato's myths. It examines connections between ancient magic, science, and religion, tracing a line of transmission from Empedocles and the Pythagoreans into the world of Islam.

Kirk, Geoffrey S., John E. Raven, and M. Schofield. *The Presocratic Philosophers*. 2d ed. Cambridge, England: Cambridge University Press, 1983. One chapter contains a scholarly account of Pythagorean philosophy; includes Greek text of testimony (no fragments).

Mourelatos, Alexander P. D. *The Pre-Socratics: A Collection of Critical Essays*. Princeton, N.J.: Princeton University Press, 1993. This volume includes two essays on Pythagoreanism. F. M. Cornford argues that the early Pythagorean school exhibited two radically opposed systems of thought, the mystical and the scientific, which have been mistakenly conflated. Charles H. Kahn addresses the question of how much of the Pythagorean doctrine can be traced back to some earlier period of the school and specifically to Pythagoras.

Thomas Rankin, updated by Priscilla K. Sakezles

W. V. O. Quine

Variously called the father of post-World War II American philosophy and the greatest philosopher of the second half of the twentieth century, Quine created a new framework or paradigm of philosophy, one that describes the way knowledge is actually obtained.

Principal philosophical works: *A System of Logistics*, 1934; "Truth by Convention," 1936; "New Foundations for Mathematical Logic," 1937; *Mathematical Logic*, 1940; *Elementary Logic*, 1941; "Steps Towards a Constructive Nominalism," 1947 (with N. Goodman); "On What There Is," 1948; *Methods of Logic*, 1950; "Two Dogmas of Empiricism," 1951; *From a Logical Point of View*, 1953; "Carnap on Logical Truth," 1960; *Word and Object*, 1960; *The Ways of Paradox and Other Essays*, 1966; *Ontological Relativity and Other Essays*, 1969; *The Web of Belief*, 1970 (with J. S. Ullian); *The Roots of Reference*, 1974; *Theories and Things*, 1981; *The Time of My Life: An Autobiography*, 1985; *Philosophy of Logic*, 1986; *Quiddities*, 1987; *Pursuit of Truth*, 1992; *From Stimulus to Science*, 1995.

Born: June 25, 1908; Akron, Ohio

Early Life

Willard Van Orman Quine was born into a self-made, upper-middle-class family, the younger of two sons. In his autobiography *The Time of My Life*, Quine wrote that his passions for foreign travel and intellectual discovery began when he was a boy. For him, the thrill of discovery in theoretical science and the discoveries and knowledge gained from foreign travel were both appealing. As a youth, Quine undertook a number of small ventures to earn money and to exploit his interests in travel and journalism. He sold postage stamps, created maps of Akron, and sold advertising for his own publication.

Quine's interest in philosophy predated his high school education. He said it was sparked by Edgar Allan Poe's essay "Eureka." His interests in philosophy and science were driven by his desire to understand how the universe works. Toward the end of high school, Quine developed an interest in the origins of words and how they are used in ordinary language. He would later investigate the role of language in a variety of philosophical disciplines.

As a student at Oberlin College in Ohio, Quine majored in mathematics and graduated with

honors. He wrote his thesis on mathematical philosophy, especially as it was developed and practiced by the English thinker Bertrand Russell. A poker companion introduced Quine to Russell's work in college. Russell derived the world from experience by logical construction. No one at Oberlin was familiar with the revolutionary developments in logic as developed by Gottlob Frege, Russell, and others. Quine's professors at Oberlin, however, encouraged him to explore the works of these thinkers on his own.

Life's Work

Quine chose to do his graduate work at Harvard University because of the strong reputation of its philosophy department, which excelled in logic. Alfred North Whitehead, the coauthor with Russell of *Principia Mathematica* (1910-1913), was then a Harvard professor. Whitehead eventually became Quine's dissertation adviser. Under the guidance of Whitehead, Quine completed his doctoral studies and dissertation in two years. Quine analyzed and advanced Russell's systems in his doctoral dissertation, "The Logic of Sequences: A Generalization of *Principia Mathematica*."

Russell had a profound influence on Quine's intellectual development. Quine used Russell's ideas to advance the power and scope of mathematical logic. As a graduate student and then as a postgraduate student, Quine also began to explore the branch of metaphysics called ontology, which is concerned with questions of what there is and with the relationship of nature and being.

Another major influence on Quine was the philosopher Rudolf Carnap, whom he described as his greatest teacher. For Carnap, the proper role of philosophy is the analysis, criticism, and refinement of the methods and concepts of science. Philosophers, he argued, should study the meanings of words and how words are put together to form clauses, phrases, and sentences. The study of the rules of language, or syntax, is key to Carnap's philosophy. Syntax is the basis not only for logic and mathematics but also for the entire logic of science and philosophy. A consequence of Carnap's perspective is that metaphysical commitment and logical rules are language-dependent.

Quine would eventually break with Carnap and offer an alternative to Carnap's system of how beliefs are justified. Quine opposed efforts to base logical and factual distinctions on linguistic considerations alone. For Quine, the goal of the philosopher is to escape from intuition and the shackles of linguistic convention. According to Quine, science, not philosophy, determines how a correct view of the real world is determined.

While a postdoctoral fellow at Harvard, Quine traveled to Europe and met many of the leading philosophers of the day, especially those associated with mathematical logic and linguistic and analytic philosophy as practiced in the then-leading intellectual capital cities of Europe such as Vienna, Prague, and Warsaw. Analytic and linguistic philosophers contend that the proper role of philosophy is to clarify language and thereby resolve disputes that originate in linguistic confusions. The goal of such activities was to make philosophical assertions clear and unambiguous. As a result of the lessons he learned in Europe, Quine expanded his own philosophical perspective and honed his technical skills, especially in the area of logic. Using what he learned, he conducted a number of philosophical investigations in the field of mathematical logic. Quine sought to develop what he described as an elegant set of

axioms from which ordinary mathematics could be developed.

Quine returned to Harvard in the fall of 1933 and was appointed a junior fellow in the prestigious Society of Fellows at Harvard. In 1938, he became a philosophy instructor at Harvard. During World War II, he worked as a Navy cryptographer deciphering messages intercepted from German submarines.

For Quine, the two major goals of philosophy should be to develop a theory to explain the world and to account for how the meager evidence we have of the world leads to our knowledge of reality. Quine rejected the idea that a "first" philosophy existed, one from which everything we know can be derived. In Quine's view, philosophy is the theory of scientific truth. According to him, there is only one reality. That one reality is the one the science of physics constructs. As he said repeatedly, the philosophy of science is philosophy enough. By attacking the notion that thought alone is sufficient to derive the basis of all human knowledge or prove the existence of a first philosophy, Quine was attacking a tradition dating back to the Greek philosophers Aristotle and Plato.

Quine also denied there is any such thing as a distinctive philosophical subject matter or method. For him, philosophy, like science, is concerned with matters of fact. According to Quine, the only evidence we have for our theory of what exists is sensory evidence. In Quine's view, philosophy had the potential to make logical and empirical what we know about the world. Philosophy, in other words, had the potential to be on a par with the exact sciences. From Quine's behaviorist perspective, we acquire our conception of reality as children by learning to speak. Children learn to speak by learning to identify things by their proper names and in a manner that all who speak the language can understand. In this manner, we acquire our understanding of the world. Our knowledge of the world is then ultimately grounded in logic, observation, and experimental verification and an exploration of its consequences.

Quine retired in 1978 but remained an emeritus professor of philosophy and mathematics at Harvard. His unusually productive career as a philosopher spanned more than six decades. As of 1999, his books had been translated and reprinted in more than fifty editions in at least seventeen languages. He lectured on six continents and visited approximately 113 countries. Perhaps most important of all, through his articles, books, lectures, and textbooks on mathematical logic he taught several generations of philosophers and their students how to do logic and appreciate its power. His textbooks *Elementary Logic* and *Methods of Logic* taught undergraduate and graduate students how to grasp a complete proof procedure and how to use logical notation. He taught students how to appreciate the precision and rigor of symbolic logic systems. Quine authored a number of journal articles that are now considered classics, including "New Foundations for Mathematical Logic," "On What There Is," and "Ontological Relativity," as well as such books as his most famous work, *Word and Object*. Quine is the author of one of the landmarks of twentieth century philosophy, "Two Dogmas of Empiricism," the paper that marked Quine's public break with Carnap.

Over his long career and in his many publications, the core of Quine's philosophical investigations remained the same. He attempted to find the answers to the fundamental questions of epistemology: How do human beings acquire their theory of the world and why does it work so well? What are the limitations and validity of our methods? How do we know what there is in the world? In his answers to these questions, Quine joined American pragmatists such as Charles S. Peirce and William James, who argued that the function of thought is to guide action. Quine belongs to the tradition of philosophers of science that includes thinkers such as Aristotle, Thomas Hobbes, and Baruch Spinoza, among others. In addition, he attempted to find a foundation for mathematics anchored by logic and set theory. Quine sought to simplify and refine the work undertaken by Russell.

Influence

Quine is often heralded as one of the titans of twentieth century philosophers, a peer group that includes the analytical philosopher Ludwig Wittgenstein and Russell. The philosopher A. J. Ayer went so far as to describe Quine as perhaps the greatest philosopher of his time. For his numerous contributions to philosophy, Quine received such prestigious awards as the Kyoto and Schock Prizes. The grantors of these prizes said Quine's body of work had a profound and powerful influence on twentieth century philosophy, especially in the areas of mathematical logic, epistemology, the philosophy of language, and the philosophy of science. Among his most influential contributions to logic and the theory of knowledge were his "New Foundations for Mathematical Logic" and *Word and Object*. Despite the fact that his work resulted in many fundamental advances in computer theory, Quine himself was not interested in computers. Rather, he was interested in theory, not in how his ideas were applied.

Quine was one of the first philosophers to promote the power of mathematical logic in America. He pioneered the development of mathematical logic from its infancy in Alfred White Northhead and Bertrand Russell's *Principia Mathematica*. Quine changed the legacy of analytical philosophy or logical positivism in the United States. Many of the central ideas and themes of philosophy in the United States during the second half of the twentieth century may be traced to him. His philosophy helped move philosophers away from Wittgenstein, another of the century's major philosophers.

Quine's reputation is that of an innovator and the creator of new approaches to logical theory and the philosophy of logic. As a logician, Quine refined and reformed the logical system of Russell. He did so by infusing it with generous dosages of American pragmatism and the power of the philosophies of the European philosophers. Quine used mathematical logic and the methods of science to prompt philosophers to rethink their approaches to long-standing philosophical disputes and controversies.

Quine is a revolutionary in that he successfully challenged and overthrew the ideas of philosophical movements such as analytical and linguistic philosophy as developed during the first half of the twentieth century. His ideas and insights forced philosophers in the analytical tradition to reassess the fundamental concepts and purpose of epistemology. To some historians, Quine represents a supreme achievement of twentieth century rational philosophy. Rational philosophy is empirically, linguistically, and logically oriented. He developed fresh philosophical techniques, novel devices, and new theories, and revised old ones. Quine developed a new kind of philosophy to describe the way knowledge is actually obtained. "Naturalized epistemology," as this approach is called, describes how contemporary science arrives at the beliefs held by the scientific community. Quine's work influenced the development of such philosophers as Donald Davidson and Daniel Dennett. His papers on the simplification of truth functions helped advance computer engineering.

Fred Buchstein

Word and Object

Type of philosophy: Epistemology, logic, philosophy of language
First published: 1960
Principal ideas advanced:
◇ Translation from one language into another is indeterminate. Two schemes of translation, incompatible with each other, might be equally adequate and acceptable.
◇ Two kinds of entities exist: physical objects and sets of objects.
◇ Entities are posited to exist if they are empirically attested to or have theoretical utility.
◇ First-order predicate logic with identity is a canonical notation.
◇ A canonical notation—that is, a logically perspicuous language—makes clear the ontological commitments of a theory.

Word and Object is W. V. O. Quine's magnum opus, the most complete expression of his views in a single place. It was written when he was at the height of his philosophical powers, roughly between 1955 and 1959, and continues the themes of his earlier articles in *From a Logical Point of View* (1953), of which the two most famous are "On What There Is," which discusses criteria for ontological commitment, and "Two Dogmas of Empiricism." The first dogma is that there is a clear distinction between analytic sentences (which are true by virtue of their meaning) and synthetic truths (which are made true by facts). The second dogma is that each meaningful sentence is reducible to an equivalent sentence, all the terms of which refer to immediate experience.

As these two articles make clear, Quine is equally interested in the problems of ontology and language, problems that he thinks are intertwined. Quine elaborated and refined the views of *Word and Object* in *Ontological Relativity and Other Essays* (1969). In the title essay of the latter book, which constitutes the first of the John Dewey lectures given at Columbia University in 1968, Quine admits his debt to Dewey. In *Word and Object* and other essays, he expresses his debt to Charles S. Peirce and his commitment to a kind of pragmatism. By his own admission, then, Quine is in the mainstream of traditional American philosophy.

Words and Language

Word and Object consists of three projects: One concerns words, one concerns objects, and one concerns the conjunction of words and objects. The first project is an attempt to give empirical foundations to language, to explain the human use of language in terms of human behavior and the perceptual environment. Quine restricts the theoretical terms of the explanation to these two because, he claims, they are the only available resources for the evidence upon which human beings learn language; thus Quine is very much concerned with reconstructing how a person—typically, but not invariably, a child—might come to learn a language. The second project concerns the classic problem of metaphysics: What kinds of objects are there? What really exists? Quine's short answer to these questions is that there are two kinds of objects that really exist: physical objects and sets or classes of objects. These first two projects come together in his discussion of the kind of language that is appropriate for expressing what there is. According to Quine, it is science that says what there is, and the language for science, what he calls "a canonical notation," is first-order predicate calculus with identity.

Quine's most famous or infamous thesis about language is what he calls the "indeterminacy of translation." The thesis is this: Two systems of translating one language into another can be devised such that each system is compatible with all the speech dispositions of those who know the language, yet the two systems are not equivalent. Quine develops his thesis in the course of describing the situation with which a linguist would be confronted when first coming upon a culture wholly alien to his or her own. How can the linguist correlate sentences of his or her own language with sentences of the native speaker? That is, how can the linguist come to translate between his or her own language and that of the native? This is the problem of radical translation.

Radical Translation

Suppose a rabbit hops by and the native says, "Gavagai." The linguist might plausibly guess that the utterance means, "There's a rabbit," or "Look at that rabbit." Of course the linguist might be wrong; in order to determine that, the linguist has to test his or her guess or hypothesis by interrogating the native in some way. However, how can one do this? One way is to say "Gavagai" the next time a rabbit appears and observe the reaction of the native. The linguist wants to see whether the native will assent to or dissent from the utterance. Assuming that a linguist can ask a native whether a given sentence is appropriate, Quine defines "affirmative stimulus meaning" as the class of stimulations that would prompt assent, "negative stimulus meaning" as the class that would prompt dissent, and "stimulus meaning" as the ordered pair of the two. Further, two utterances are stimulus-synonymous just in case they have the same stimulus meaning; that is, when they would produce assent or dissent in the same situations. Although the notion of stimulus meaning is well defined, the linguist is still faced with a cluster of problems, to which Quine is attentive. Which utterances of the native are to count as assent and which as dissent? Given that "evok" and "yok" are the utterances expressing each, which is which? Another problem is that a native will not always be willing or able to respond to the query. His or her glimpse of the object may not have been long enough to allow a response. Therefore, in addition to the assents and dissents there will be some lack of response. The native will sometimes make mistakes; perhaps he or she was looking in the

wrong direction or attending to the wrong object. Alternatively, the native might lie. Because of all of these possibilities for skewed results, stimulus synonymy is not what is ordinarily meant by "synonymy."

This partial catalog of the linguist's problem is not meant to imply that the linguist's task is impossible. The point is rather to indicate what difficulties one faces in learning a wholly alien language, what resources are available to learn it, and the strategy the linguist will employ in matching utterances with behavior. Given enough data, time, and imagination, the linguist will surely succeed in writing a manual of translation.

Quine helps us understand how the linguist will proceed with his or her job of translation beyond those utterances whose use is most closely tied to observation by explaining how the linguist might move from translating observation sentences like "Gavagai" to truth-functional sentences. The linguist comes to translate a linguistic element as expressing negation when and only when adding it to a short sentence causes a native speaker to dissent from a sentence previously assented to; the linguist comes to translate a linguistic element as conjunction when and only when it produces compounds from short component sentences that the native is disposed to assent to when and only when he or she is also disposed to assent to the components separately. The qualification "short" is added to guard against the native's becoming confused by a sentence of extreme length. Also, it applies only to the language-learning situation; once the terms are learned, there is no restriction on the length of the sentences to which the terms are applied.

After the observation sentences, the truth-functional ones, and some other related sorts are translated, how does the linguist proceed? Roughly, he or she divides the sentences he or she hears into those segments that are often repeated; these are counted as the words of the language. The linguist's task is then to correlate these words with words of his or her own language in such a way that the correlation conforms to the translation of the earlier sentences. Quine calls these correlations "analytical hypotheses." A further constraint on analytical hypotheses is that stimulus-analytic ones, those sentences that receive unanimous assent among the natives, should, if possible, be correlated with sentences that are stimulus-analytic for members of the linguist's own speech community; *mutatis mutandis* for stimulus-contradictory sentences. The parenthetical "if possible" is an escape clause. It is not always possible, without sacrificing the simplicity of the analytical hypothesis, to match a stimulus-analytic sentence of the natives with one of the linguist's community. It may be necessary, in the interests of simplicity, to translate a stimulus-analytic sentence of the natives as "All rabbits are people reincarnate." Such translations, however, are a last resort. By the principle of charity, one should always avoid attributing absurd or bizarre beliefs to foreigners.

There is another problem, or rather another result, of the thought experiment involving radical translation. The most fundamental relation between language and the world, the relation of reference, is infected by a kind of indeterminacy, which Quine calls "the inscrutability of reference." Suppose that one linguist has determined that "Gavagai," whatever its other uses, translates "rabbit" when it is used as a term. It remains a possibility that a second linguist, acting on the very same evidence as the first, will determine that "Gavagai" translates "rabbit stage" and a third that it translates "undetached rabbit part." Each of these preferred translations is consonant with all the empirical evidence, yet the references of "rabbit," "rabbit stage," and "undetached rabbit part" are different. In other words, there is no one correct answer to the question, "What does 'Gavagai' refer to?" Reference is inscrutable.

The situation of radical translation implies that the translator has a language and attempts to correlate the sentences of his or her own language with the sentences of a foreign language. In this regard, the problem of radical translation is different from the situation that infants are in when they begin to acquire language. However, there is an important respect in which infants are in the very same situation: They have the very same resources available to them as the linguist does. Like the linguist, infants must learn their language on the basis of perceptual stimulation and human behavior and must construct and test hypotheses about what an utterance means just

as the linguist, but self-consciousness is not essential to the learning process.

The babbling of human beings during the end of their first year of life becomes transmuted into an incipient language by selective, positive reinforcement. Among the randomly produced verbal sounds of the infant will be "mama" and "papa," which for the infant have no significance. They acquire significance when its mother and father reward the infant for producing those vocal sounds. Like a chicken learning to pull a lever for a pellet of food, a child first acquires language. The comparison of a child with a chicken is neither facetious nor unfair. Quine's model for the first steps of language acquisition is a stimulus-response model, and he approvingly refers to the work of his Harvard colleague B. F. Skinner in this regard. In an oblique response to the criticisms of Noam Chomsky, who trenchantly criticized Skinner's work, Quine concedes that, in addition to the stimulus-response mechanism, such innate forces as the natural tendency for an infant to smack its lips in anticipation of nursing and thereby to utter "mama" and a "basic predilection for conformity" play some role in a total causal account of infant language acquisition.

Among the most important things that the infant needs to learn are the distinctions among various types of terms. Quine distinguishes between singular terms, such as "Cicero" and "the orator who denounced Catiline," and general terms, such as "orator" and "apple." General terms, unlike singular terms, divide their reference among a number of objects. Definite and indefinite articles—"the" and "a(n)" respectively—and the plural ending are devices for the use of general terms in English. A person does not know how to use a general term in English if he or she does not know how to use such expressions as "an apple," "the apple," and "apples." Mass terms, such as "gold" and "water," are a kind of middle case, a kind of grammatical hermaphrodite. Syntactically, they are like singular terms in resisting indefinite articles and plural endings; semantically, they are like singular terms in not dividing their reference. However, they are like general terms in not naming one thing. The double role of mass terms extends to predication. In the subject position they are like singular terms ("Water is wet"); in the predicate position, they are like general terms ("That puddle is water").

Physical Objects and Abstract Objects

Quine's second project is to answer the question, "What is there?" His answer that there are physical objects (that is, four-dimensional spatiotemporal entities) and abstract objects (sets or classes of objects) is perhaps less interesting than his answer to several related questions, such as "What isn't there?" or, to put the question more perspicuously, "Why does Quine refuse to countenance various sorts of purported entities?" On the ground of economy, Quine does not accept sense data; they are not needed for science. Physical objects cannot be eliminated from science, and they do all the work that sense data do. Sense data are not needed even to account for reports of illusions and uncertainty. Quine accounts for them with the phrase "seems that" prefixed to a sentential clause about physical objects, and he then paraphrases them away in the same way he paraphrases away propositional attitudes toward sentences. Sense data are excess baggage.

Quine's rejection of sense data brings his standards for adjudicating conflicting claims for thinghood into high relief. Something has a claim to being an entity if it is empirically attested to or is theoretically useful. Competing claims to thinghood have to be weighed against both considerations. Sense data have empirical support but no theoretical use. Physical objects have at least some empirical support and a great deal of theoretical utility. Even if physical objects are not completely observable, or not "all there," positing the unobservable parts involves more conceptual continuity than inventing an abstract entity. Theoretical utility also recommends classes or objects for thinghood. Classes account for numbers and numbers for mathematics. Hence, there are classes.

There are no properties or attributes because, in contrast with classes, they do not have clear identity. Classes are identical just in case they have the same members. There is nothing similar to be said for properties. The same set of objects might have two different properties; all and only creatures with hearts are creatures with kidneys, but the property of having a heart is different from the property of having a kidney.

Also, there are no facts. Like properties, facts do not have well-defined identity conditions. There is no answer to the question, "Is the pulling of the trigger the same entity as the killing of the man?" Facts are objectionable on other grounds. "Fact" is a stylistic crutch; it helps support the word "that" in some grammatical constructions, such as "The fact that he left is no excuse," and the phrase "that fact" is a kind of standard abbreviation for a previously expressed assertion. As such, however, facts can be eliminated or altogether avoided by simple paraphrase.

Another question is, "Are objects given?" Quine says, "No." They are posits. To call something a "posit" is not, for Quine, to be derogatory. Although some posits are bad—theoretically unjustified—some posits are really real; we posit entities of certain sorts in order to explain phenomena. For Quine, our beliefs are replete with posits. If a posit fails to explain a phenomenon or if another posit explains better, then its justification fails. However, the best explanatory posits are justified and have the status of being real. In short, for Quine, two sorts of objects have this status: physical objects for natural sciences, and sets or classes for mathematics.

Conjunction of Words and Objects

Quine's third project is to explain how a person's ontological commitments can be clearly expressed in language. His explanation is that what is required is a canonical notation that is clear, precise, and unambiguous. Such a notation is the first-order predicate calculus with identity. A canonical notation has two purposes. The first is that it allows for simplification of theory. It allows a person to iterate a few constructions a large number of times to the same effect as the use of a larger number of constructions a small number of times. The use of a larger number of constructions may allow for psychologically simpler constructions but not a theoretically simpler one, and that is what is demanded. The second purpose of a canonical notation is clarity. There are no ambiguities and no hedged entities in a canonical notation. Everything that is meant is up front.

Quine's notion of philosophical explication is an important one in itself and important historically in contrast with some traditional notions of analysis. A philosophical explication does not purport to uncover or bring to light the hidden or implicit ideas of the people who use the problematic notion, and it does not purport to be synonymous with the problematic notion. In one stroke, Quine cuts the Gordian knot of G. E. Moore's paradox of analysis. Philosophical explication is informative because it replaces the problematic notion with unproblematic notions that serve the same purpose. The notions of the explication may well be unfamiliar to and difficult for the ordinary user, but that is irrelevant. Familiarity should not be confused with intelligibility. Philosophical explication requires philosophically acceptable notions, not familiar ones.

This view of philosophical explication introduces a certain latitude into the standard of correctness. A correct explication may not be a unique one; several nonequivalent explications may be equally acceptable, no one of which is more or less correct than the others, so long as each explication meets scientific standards and serves the original purpose. For example, it is indifferent whether one accepts Gottlob Frege's, John von Neumann's, Ernst Zermelo's, Richard Dedekind's, or someone else's definition of number, so long as the chosen one does the job. In short, explication is elimination: Out goes the bad air of familiar but unacceptable notions; in comes the good air of intelligibility. Quine thinks that his view of philosophical explication is in line with Ludwig Wittgenstein's doctrine that the goal of philosophy is to dissolve a problem by showing that, contrary to appearances, there really was no problem.

A. P. Martinich, updated by John K. Roth

Additional Reading

Arrington, Robert L., and Hans-Johann Glock. *Wittgenstein and Quine*. London: Routledge, 1996. The essays in this book address the similarities and differences between these philosophers, whom the authors rank as two of the leading philosophers of the twentieth century.

Borradori, Giovanna. *The American Philosopher*. Translated by Rosanna Croatto. Chicago: University of Chicago Press, 1994. Conversations with Quine and other leading philosophers are recorded in an easy-to-read, question-and-answer format. The interview with Quine reveals how he views his own philosophical development and place in the history of philosophy.

Brown, Stuart, Diane Collinson, and Robert Wilkinson, eds. *One Hundred Twentieth-Century Philosophers*. London: Routledge, 1998. Quine's essential ideas and influence are briefly summarized.

Clarke, D. S. *Philosophy's Second Revolution: Early and Recent Analytic Philosophy*. Chicago: Open Court, 1997. The author presents a readable and useful account of the origins and evolution of analytic philosophy, especially the role of Quine in the revolution. He argues that Quine's method of philosophical analysis marks a radical departure in contemporary philosophy.

Davidson, D., and J. Hintikka. *Words and Objections: Essays on the Work of W. V. Quine*. Dordrecht, Holland: D. Reidel, 1975. The essays are a response to the arguments presented by Quine in his classic *Word and Object*. Quine's responses to the remarks by the essayists are also included.

Gibson, Roger F., Jr. *Enlightened Empiricism: An Examination of W. V. Quine's Theory of Knowledge*. Tampa: University Presses of Florida, 1988. The premise of this book is that philosophers have not understood Quine as well as they might. Gibson's goal is to correct the situation.

Hacker, P. M .S. *Wittgenstein's Place in Twentieth-Century Analytic Philosophy*. Oxford, England: Blackwell, 1997. This text provides an account of Quine's place in analytic philosophy and compares his ideas with those of Ludwig Wittgenstein. The author documents the role of Quine's ideas in the decline of Wittgenstein's influence in analytical philosophy.

Hahn, Lewis Edwin, and Paul Arthur Schilpp, eds. *The Philosophy of W. V. Quine*. Peru, Ill.: Open Court, 1998. This handy guide includes an intellectual autobiography, a series of essays on Quine's work and achievements, and a bibliography.

Leonardi, Paolo, and Marco Santambrogio. *On Quine: New Essays*. Cambridge, England: Cambridge University Press, 1995. This collection of essays pays homage to Quine. It is also devoted to making Quine's work better understood in Europe.

Romanos, George D. *Quine and Analytic Philosophy*. Cambridge, Mass.: MIT Press, 1980. The author explores the relevance of Quine's methods to various philosophical problems. The book grew out of the author's doctoral dissertation. What makes this work especially useful is that Quine reviewed the author's work as it was being written.

White, Morton G. *Toward Reunion in Philosophy*. Cambridge, Mass.: Harvard University Press, 1956. This work focuses on solving philosophical problems in the "spirit" of Quine. It also places Quine's work in the context of philosophers who are his contemporaries.

Fred Buchstein

Sarvepalli Radhakrishnan

As the preeminent modern interpreter of Indian philosophy to the West and as a lifelong exponent of the "perennial philosophy," Radhakrishnan bridged the gap between two cultures and fostered the growth of universal spiritual values.

Principal philosophical works: *The Reign of Religion in Contemporary Philosophy*, 1920; *Indian Philosophy*, 1922, 1927; *The Hindu View of Life*, 1927; *Kalki: Or, The Future of Civilization*, 1929; *An Idealist View of Life*, 1932; *East and West in Religion*, 1933; *Freedom and Culture*, 1936; *India and China: Lectures Delivered in China in May 1944*, 1944; *Is This Peace?*, 1945; *Eastern Religions and Western Thought*, 1939; *Religion and Society*, 1947; *East and West: Some Reflections*, 1955; *Recovery of Faith*, 1955; *Fellowship of the Spirit*, 1961; *Religion in a Changing World*, 1967; *The Present Crisis of Faith*, 1970; *Our Heritage*, 1973.

Born: September 5, 1888; Tiruttani, India
Died: April 17, 1975; Madras, India

Early Life

Sarvepalli Radhakrishnan was born to orthodox Hindu Brahman parents in a small town fifty miles northwest of Madras. He was raised in a Hindu atmosphere, but because it was necessary for him to learn English if he was to attain secular success, his parents sent him to a Lutheran mission school when he was eight years old. He remained there for five years before going to Voorhees College in Velore, where he married a distant cousin, Sivakamu. She was to bear five daughters and a son.

Continuing his studies at Madras Christian College, he became very familiar with both Hinduism and Christianity. Radhakrishnan was distressed by his Christian teachers' criticisms of Hinduism, and he determined to study closely the religion into which he had been born. After choosing for his thesis the topic of ethics in the Vedanta, he was awarded an M.A. in philosophy in 1909. He was then appointed to the post of lecturer for the Provincial Education Service, and two years later, in 1909, he became assistant professor of philosophy at Madras Presidency College. He became a full professor in 1916.

Life's Work

In 1918, Radhakrishnan was named professor of philosophy at the University of Mysore. In the following three years he wrote his first books, a study of the Indian poet Rabindranath Tagore, and *The Reign of Religion in Contemporary Philosophy*, a book that made him well known in academic philosophical circles. As a result, he was invited to become the King George V Professor of Philosophy at Calcutta University, a position he was to occupy for nearly twenty years. The appointment marked the beginning of the most fruitful period of his intellectual life and quickly led to international recognition.

It was at Calcutta that he wrote his monumental two-volume *Indian Philosophy*. Not only did this work give a huge stimulus to the study of philosophy in Indian universities; it was the first work on Indian philosophy that could be appreciated by scholars trained in Western traditions, because Radhakrishnan had the unique gift of being able to discuss Indian thought in the light of Western philosophy. A decade later, Radhakrishnan explained that his principal purpose in writing *Indian Philosophy* was to show that Indian thought was not strange and antiquated but had a contribution to make to the spiritual awakening of the world.

In 1926, at a time when little was known in the West about Indian philosophy, Radhakrishnan was invited to deliver the annual Upton Lectures at Manchester College, Oxford University. He gave four lectures, speaking without the assistance of any notes, presenting Hinduism not as a set of fixed dogmas and rituals but as a tolerant faith with a wide vision and moral values that were relevant for contemporary life. These lectures were published as *The Hindu View of Life*, a small volume that has had lasting importance as an interpretation of Hinduism to Western readers.

In August of 1927, Radhakrishnan visited the United States and delivered the Haskell Lectures in comparative religion at the University of Chicago; he also lectured at Harvard University. *Kalki: Or, The Future of Civilization*, a critique of the ills of a technological society and an outline of how they might be overcome, was based on the Harvard lectures.

In autumn, 1929, Radhakrishnan returned to Oxford to take up the Upton Chair of Comparative Religion at Manchester College, Oxford, and he also gave the Hibbert Lectures at the Universities of Manchester and London, which cogently analyzed the idealist tradition of East and West. Radhakrishnan's international reputation as a philosopher of the first rank was now firmly established. In June, 1931, he was knighted by King George V, and on his return to India later that year, he became vice chancellor of Andhra University at Waltair.

In addition to his administrative duties at Andhra, Radhakrishnan continued to publish widely. The Hibbert Lectures appeared in 1932 as *An Idealist View of Life*, which was widely regarded by Western and Eastern scholars as a significant, original contribution to religious and philosophical thought. Radhakrishnan himself regarded it as his major work. *East and West in Religion*, which sought to establish that Eastern and Western traditions had throughout history borrowed from each other, followed in 1933, and *Freedom and Culture* in 1936. In that year Radhakrishnan was again invited to England, where he

Sarvepalli Radhakrishnan, left, pays an official visit to Yugoslavia in 1965. *(Library of Congress)*

became Spalding Professor of Eastern Religions and Ethics at Oxford University. He resigned from the position of vice chancellor at Andhra but continued as the George V Professor of Philosophy at Calcutta. It was agreed that each year he would spend six months in England and six months in India.

At Oxford his teaching duties were light and he was thus able to spend much time in writing and research. One of the fruits of this labor was *Eastern Religions and Western Thought*, in which he endeavored to create a synthesis of Eastern and Western religious and philosophical thought. His goal was to lay the groundwork for an inclusive philosophy that would carry greater spiritual force and profundity than existed in either tradition when considered in isolation.

In 1939, Radhakrishnan became the first Indian to be elected to the British Academy. He returned to India in July, and when World War II broke out in September, he applied for leave of absence from Oxford. That same year, he accepted the vice chancellorship of Benares Hindu University, the largest university in India. He served in this position throughout World War II, interrupted only by a trip to China in 1944, when at the invitation of the Chinese government he delivered twelve lectures on Indian and Chinese philosophies and religions in Chungking (Chongqing). These were published as *India and China* in the same year.

Radhakrishnan had long shown an interest in international affairs. From 1931 to 1936 he had been a member of the Committee of Intellectual Cooperation of the League of Nations, and in 1946 he was appointed leader of the Indian delegation to the United Nations Educational, Scientific, and Cultural Organization (UNESCO) at its conference in Paris. He became chairman of UNESCO'S executive board in 1948.

He continued to write books at a steady rate, including *Is This Peace?* and *Religion and Society*. The latter, which discussed the meaning of religion and its application to modern problems of war and peace, family, and marriage, was based on the Kamala lectures he had given at the University of Calcutta in 1932.

In 1948 Radhakrishnan resigned as vice chancellor of Benares University in order to accept a position as chairman of the Indian Universities

Commission, which had been established by the newly independent government of India. In the same year, Radhakrishnan published a translation of and commentary on a major work in the Hindu canon, the Bhagavad Gita, which he dedicated to the recently assassinated Mohandas K. (Mahatma) Gandhi. The ten thousand copies of the first printing of this book were sold out within twelve months, and it has long continued to be a popular and authoritative work. Its success is due to the fact that Radhakrishnan wrote not only for scholars but also for the general reader with an interest in spiritual matters. He believed that great works such as the Bhagavad Gita must be understood anew by each generation, in a way that provides insight into the problems of the time. To this end, he alluded in his explanatory notes and commentary to parallels between the Bhagavad Gita and other religious texts, and with modern philosophical literature. He continued with this method in his translation of the Buddhist work the Dhammapada, which was published in 1950.

In July, 1949, Radhakrishnan's involvement in public life deepened when he was appointed India's ambassador to the Soviet Union, although he still retained his professorship at Oxford, where he spent eight weeks of each year. He remained in Moscow until 1952, when he was elected vice president of India for five years by both houses of Parliament. Radhakrishnan's principal function as vice president was to preside over the Rajya Sabha, the upper chamber of the national legislature. During his years in this capacity, he won admiration from all political sides for his sense of fairness, his impartiality, and his ability to act as a conciliator.

In addition to fulfilling his public duties, Radhakrishnan continued his scholarly work. His translation of the Upanishads, *The Principal Upanishads*, was published in 1953, and in 1954 he gave the Sir Edward Betty memorial lectures at McGill University in Canada, which were published as *East and West: Some Reflections* in 1955. *Recovery of Faith* attempted to show how modern human beings could renew their religious faith by transcending dogma and sectarian differences. Another translation of a Hindu scripture, *The Brahma Sutra*, appeared in 1960, followed in 1961 by *Fellowship of the Spirit*.

In 1962, Radhakrishnan was elected president of India, a position he held until 1967. British philosopher and mathematician Bertrand Russell declared that Radhakrishnan's appointment as president was an honor to philosophy, and there were frequent allusions by commentators to Plato's ideal of the philosopher-king.

After retiring from public life, Radhakrishnan continued to write, publishing *Religion in a Changing World*, *The Present Crisis of Faith*, and *Our Heritage*. In 1975, shortly before his death, he became the first non-Christian to receive the Templeton Prize for Religion.

Influence

Radhakrishnan's universalist philosophy has its roots in the work of two nineteenth century Indian religious figures: Ramakrishna and Swami Vivekananda, both of whom had a strong awareness of religions other than Hinduism. Ramakrishna believed that all religious teachings represented different paths to the same goal, and this was the basis of the movement founded in 1897 by his follower Vivekananda, whom Radhakrishnan acknowledged as a formative influence on his own work.

In scope and philosophical depth, Radhakrishnan vastly extended the work of these earlier figures. He interpreted and developed the whole range of Indian philosophical thought to make it relevant for the times in which he lived. At a time when there was much ignorance and prejudice against non-Christian religions in the West, Radhakrishnan's work in comparative philosophy and his dedication to drawing out the unity between East and West laid the foundation for a great leap in intercultural understanding. His work ensured that Indian philosophy received its rightful place in world culture as a venerable tradition with much to offer to the modern world. His promotion of a universal religion that would meet the needs of a scientific and technological civilization that had lost its moral and spiritual compass has had a lasting impact. It revealed Radhakrishnan as at once a philosopher and a practical man of affairs with a deep concern for the well-being of humanity.

In spite of these major contributions to human thought, Radhakrishnan has not been immune to criticism. Some have disputed whether he was a philosopher in his own right. According to this view, Radhakrishnan was merely a historian or chronicler of Hindu thought, not an original thinker. His Western critics also argue that he grasped Christianity only from an outsider's point of view and frequently misinterpreted and distorted it in his eagerness to establish parallels with Indian thought. Critics in India claim the opposite, that he distorted the Indian texts in order to please the West.

Radhakrishnan's response to such criticism was to say that all great philosophers restate and interpret the thought of their masters and make no claim to originality. He would also reiterate the "perennial philosophy," the belief that all religious traditions point to the same underlying reality. Scholars of Radhakrishnan also point out that whatever Radhakrishnan may have said about his own work, in his writings he sometimes questioned ancient authorities, reserving the right to develop his thought on independent lines in pursuit of his goal of a vital philosophy that had power to heal a fragmented, secular, war-torn world.

Bryan Aubrey

An Idealist View of Life

Type of philosophy: Ethics, Indian philosophy, metaphysics
First published: 1932
Principal ideas advanced:

◇ The ideal world, which alone is real, lies beyond the phenomenal world of appearance yet dominates it; the center of the universe is the transcendent, the Absolute, Brahma.

◇ Intuition is the way to an integral apprehension of ultimate reality; it is a knowledge by identity that transcends the distinction between subject and object.

◇ Scientific certainty is not the only kind of certainty available to people, but in considering the mystical revelation as a source of certainty, one must distinguish between the content of the experience and the interpretation of it, for interpretation is historically conditioned and liable to error.

◇ The scientific view of the inorganic world and of life and mind is more compatible with idealism than with naturalism.

An Idealist View of Life has a marked mystical foundation in the theory of knowledge. In this regard, it may be said to express the main Hindu tradition in philosophy. This is one reason for its importance. The other is the author's familiarity with Western philosophy and science. Though his general standpoint guides him, there is no turning away from crucial problems.

Radhakrishnan's Idealism
Sarvepalli Radhakrishnan recognizes that the term "idealism" needs definition. It is clear that he is not a subjective idealist of the mode of the early George Berkeley. Nor does he much concern himself with Hegelian rationalistic Idealism. Rather, his emphasis is on the relation of value to reality. The truly real is replete with value. The alignment is with the Upanishads in India and the outlook of the Platonists, especially that of Plotinus, the father of the Western tradition of mysticism.

The book reflects the meeting of the East and the West. The broad sweep of Radhakrishnan's thought brings together Hindu classic thinkers with the Greek philosophers Plato and Aristotle, and with the Anglo-American idealists Francis Herbert Bradley and Josiah Royce. Less attention is paid to Western naturalism and realism. That is both the strength and the weakness of the book. It stands out as an excellent example of its perspective, and it has both scope and verve.

Radhakrishnan's general argument is that the ideal world, which alone is real, lies beyond the phenomenal one of appearance yet is tied in with it and dominates it. Spirit is working in matter that matter may serve spirit. In a sense, matter is an abstraction and not a concrete reality, such as spirit. That is why materialism can be absorbed and transcended. It is doubtful whether Western materialists would accept this thesis, but it goes quite logically with the author's outlook. For him, the center of the universe is the transcendent, the Absolute, Brahma, that which has *aseity*, being. However, despite this assurance—rather, because of it—he is sympathetic with other points of view because they have their partial truth.

Religion and Mysticism
The first of the eight lectures concerns itself with the modern challenge to the religious outlook on the universe as a result of scientific and social thought. Here the author confronts psychology specialists Sigmund Freud, John B. Watson, and Émile Durkheim. The second lecture notes contemporary movements such as humanism, naturalism, and logical positivism. These are tied in with science. In all this, the author is frank and well informed. He is not trying to defend specific orthodoxies. Like the Buddhist, he has no tradition of particular doctrines in geology and biology. Science is to be accepted but has its limits.

It is in the third lecture that Radhakrishnan states the basic claims of the religious consciousness, especially at the mystical level. He introduces *intuition* as a way of knowledge alternative to that of sense perception or discursive conception. He puts forward the claim for an integral apprehension of ultimate reality. It is a knowledge by identity that transcends the distinction between subject and object. Here, of course, is where dispute arises. Those who do not have the mystical vision are likely to deny its significance.

In the fourth lecture, Radhakrishnan develops the idea that scientific certainty is not the only kind of certainty available to us. A query may, of course, be raised as to the scientific claim that is usually more modestly put as an affair of working hypotheses. However, the author is ready to admit that, in the mystical revelation, we must distinguish between the kernel of it and the interpretation given, which is historically conditioned. Thus Hindu, Muslim, and Christian mystics have different accounts of the meanings of their experiences.

The fifth lecture takes up the nonconceptual, intuitive, imaginative, and affective ingredients of morality, art, and religion. The element of creativity is noted with reports from mathematicians, scientists, and poets. Just how do new ideas arise? What part does the subconscious play? It is generally agreed that there must be preparation. It takes a trained mathematician to have relevant ideas and to solve mathematical problems. There is extensive literature on this question and Radhakrishnan is familiar with it. He is at home in aesthetics and art and quotes freely from Benedetto Croce, Alighieri Dante, John Keats,

William Shakespeare, and Robert Browning. The stress, it is to be noted, is on creativity. The suggestion is that this is something higher in nature than perception and conceptual reasoning. Does it link up with his third kind of knowledge?

The sixth and seventh lectures are devoted to a brief formulation of the scientific view of the inorganic world, of life, and of mind. It was written in an era in which Sir Arthur Stanley Eddington and Sir James Hopwood Jeans were the avowed spokespersons of science. A semi-idealistic, semi-agnostic note was in the air. Relativity and quantum mechanics were transforming science away from Newtonian mechanics. Scientists were finding the world a subtler and more complex sort of thing than had been supposed earlier. The question at issue was whether naturalism could do justice to this development or whether it implied idealism. If these are the alternatives, there is no question as to which side Radhakrishnan adopts. He sees the development as favoring idealism. And it is well to have this alignment so beautifully carried out.

In the eighth, and last, lecture, the turn comes for metaphysics and its basis in an integral intuition of ultimate reality. Radhakrishnan presents an excellent example of transcendental metaphysics, something to which the logical positivist is so opposed with his insistence that sensory verification is essential for the meaningfulness of empirical statements. It is clear that much depends upon the certainty and value of the mystical experience. It is upon this foundation that Radhakrishnan builds. Nothing could be more desirable than such a confrontation.

Religion vs. Science
According to Radhakrishnan, even a person who remains skeptical of the mystical insight will be impressed by the idealism to which it leads. Though political leader Jawaharlal Nehru is more of an agnostic, one can note in him something of the same elevation of spirit.

The essential thing, Radhakrishnan argues, is to know what the problem is. Freud's queries help to bring this home. Is religion an illusion? That there have been illusory ingredients is undeniable. Popular religion has been too anthropomorphic and has laid too much stress on special providences. On the other hand, Newtonian ra-

tionalism led to deism and the absentee God. Of what use is an absentee God? Surely, that is not the sort of God the religious consciousness requires.

The influential feature of science has been its attack on parochialism and narrow ideas. Watson's behaviorism, for instance, has forced us to think more clearly about mind. These challenges must be met. For instance, the French school of sociology represented by Durkheim stresses the pressure of society but does not do justice to personality and self-consciousness. Again, the study of comparative religions should have the effect of enlarging our horizon. The so-called higher criticism of the Scriptures ought to have the same effect. Such a critical attitude is fairly common among thoughtful Hindus and Buddhists, and it is doubtful that the traditional proofs for theism are convincing. Radhakrishnan stresses an internal religious approach. It would appear that he regards the materialistic atmosphere of technology as the greatest enemy. It is not the mastery of nature as such that is at fault but the industrial and utilitarian climate.

The result of this frank approach is the contention that nothing can be true by faith if it is not true by reason. However, then reason must not be taken as limited to deduction from fixed premises. Radhakrishnan believes in a source of insight of a higher order.

Religion in the Modern World
However, what are the substitutes for religion offered these days? One is an atheistic naturalism. It appears that Radhakrishnan has in mind philosopher Bertrand Russell's early protest against a supposedly alien nature composed of blind atoms ruled by mechanical laws. This would be, in effect, a malign nature that might well be defied. Such an outlook would represent a mixture of naturalism, stoicism, and paganism. The stoicism reflects human beings' innate dignity.

Humanism is an old tradition that goes back to the Greeks, with their doctrine of inner harmony, and to the Romans, with their sense of decorum. There are elements of it in Chinese thought and in Immanuel Kant's work. Such humanism tends to be religion secularized and separated from a larger reality. It lacks *élan*. It sets up boundaries.

It is these boundaries that religion oversteps. On the other hand, it cannot be denied that humanism is humanitarian and stresses social reform.

Pragmatism is more an American development that emphasizes will and practice. It is a protest against the separation of knowledge and active planning. Modernism, on the other hand, is a halfway house. It seeks to revise religious tradition. It is confronted by the revival of authoritarianism. This regards itself as an escape from anarchy. However, loyalty to tradition should not involve bondage to it. There is often a secret skepticism in authoritarianism. All these movements seem to Radhakrishnan to lack something of the spiritual. There is a lack of profundity. What is needed is a synoptic vision.

Radhakrishnan's positive position holds that religious experience is factual in its own right. Philosophy of religion explores this domain and differs from dogmatic theology. Religion is not a form of knowledge but is more akin to feeling. It is inward and personal. It is the response of the whole person in an integral way to reality. It expresses an incurable discontent with the finite and seeks the transcendent.

The Hindu Tradition

At this point in Radhakrishnan's thinking, the Hindu tradition comes to the front, though it is soon connected with the mystical note in the West. The Vedic seers stressed the eternal and sought to raise themselves to this plane. In this respect, the early thinkers Plato, Saint Augustine, and Dante are examples of the same direction. Can this massive evidence be illusory? However, it involves a higher kind of knowledge or insight. That is the problem for philosophy of religion. The justification of this claim is taken up in the conclusion. This constitutes the debate with scientific empiricism and naturalism.

One must be very careful here, Radhakrishnan warns. There is danger in a purely negative approach. It is difficult to translate the mystical experience. Its note is timelessness and unity. When one uses language to bring out the contrast, this ultimate reality is called the Absolute. The term "God" is of the nature of a symbol. With the experience, says Radhakrishnan, goes a sense of harmony and unity. Self-mastery is involved. From this flows idealism and denial of what is selfish. The danger in this concentration is, perhaps, disregard of social ties. This should be guarded against.

According to Radhakrishnan, if all knowledge were of the scientific type (as some empiricists hold), then the challenge to the religious outlook on the world could hardly be met. Hence comes the importance of the question of intuitive knowledge, something that cannot be expressed in propositions, yet is justifiable. It is well to recall that sense qualities are confused and that logic and mathematics are essentially analytic and do not give us factual information.

In Hindu thought and in the works of Plotinus and philospher Henri Bergson, Radhakrishnan notes, emphasis is placed on direct intuition, which seems to be the extension of a sort of perception beyond the senses. Bergson sets limits to the intellect. He thinks it useful rather than true. Georg Wilhelm Friedrich Hegel criticizes immediacy and tends to ignore the importance of feeling and will. Yet he is opposed to the abstractions of the understanding. However, is not the unity of nature coordinate with the unity of the self? Kant emphasized the "I think" at the phenomenal level and believed in a noumenal world beyond. Faith and spiritual experience make their demands. It is well to look at the creative spirit in humanity, according to Radhakrishnan.

Radhakirshnan also notes that scientific discovery is more like intuition than people ordinarily realize. French mathematician Jules-Henri Poincaré's account of mathematical imagination is a case in point. There is something creative about it. We prove deductively but invent by intuition. There is here a kind of integrative passivity. English chemist Michael Faraday, who made many breakthroughs in electricity, is another case of unpredictable invention. The whole self is involved. When philosophers devote themselves to abstruse analysis, this creative factor may escape them.

The Arts

If we turn from science to poetry and the plastic arts, says Radhakrishnan, intuition stands out even more clearly. The poet feels himself to be inspired. This should not be taken too literally, yet it has meaning. There is emotional value and this has significance. It would seem that Italian philosopher Croce connects intuition and expression too closely. There must be room for communication. It is well to recall the testimony of Greek philosopher Plato and Scottish essayist and historian Thomas Carlyle. Emotional intensity goes with a sense of deep insight. Too much modern literature tends to be trivial and to avoid the agonies of spirit.

Creativity is a path to discovery and is to be connected with knowledge. It involves understanding of life and brings us into accord with it. In William Shakespeare's *Romeo and Juliet* (pr. c. 1595-1596), the heroine Juliet dies, but only after making us realize the greatness of love. If we turn to ethics, Radhakrishnan maintains, we find something similar. The moral hero, or saint, tends to be somewhat antinomian. He does not keep to conventions. It is because of this that moral heroes can make fools of themselves in the eyes of the world.

Science and Psychology

Modern science, notes Radhakrishnan, stresses abstraction and statistics. For Eddington and Jeans, matter tends to be reduced to thought. In terms of relativity and quantum mechanics, it is a term for a cluster of events possessing habits and potencies. The traditional idea of substance is in abeyance. There is a touch here of the Hindu notions of *samsāra*. All is becoming. There is another respect in which science suggests idealism. What we know is the effect things produce in us; all is experience and possible experience. This is the idealistic note.

If we turn to life, we find it to be of the nature of a dynamic equilibrium. The theory of evolution developed from Georges de Buffon and Jean-Baptiste-Pierre-Antoine de Monet de Lamarck to Charles Darwin and is still subject to improvement. Natural selection is a sifting process. Herbert Spencer made it too quickly into a philosophy.

Mind is under study in comparative psychology. The nature of nervous integration is under study. Russian physiologist Ivan Petrovich Pavlov and American psychologist John B. Watson were pioneers, but we now have gestalt principles opposed to purely mechanical notions.

Radhakrishnan then turns to human personality. Atomistic psychology is obsolete. The person is a unity and more than the sum of his parts. He is an organized whole. We must give up the notion of a changeless soul. The self is a growth constantly interacting with its environment.

The Concept of "Subject"

Radhakrishnan then deals with the term "subject." American psychologist William James and English psychologist James Ward differed in their views on this topic. James thought of the subjects as the passing thought. This concept seems inadequate; there must be something more enduring. The subject, by its very nature, cannot be an object. Why not hold it to be one with the simple, universal spirit? Here we are beyond the lower order of existence and are confronted by such problems as those of freedom and karma. Eastern and Western thought have long pondered these problems. It seems to Radhakrishnan that mere predestination is unethical. Freedom is not a matter of caprice nor is karma mere necessity. Suppose we take freedom to be a term for self-determination. It is the whole self that is involved in choice. The will is the active side of the self. It is not something in itself. Karma means, literally, action or deed. It is the principle of causal continuity. Thus, it is not opposed to creative freedom, unless one takes causality to demand mere identity or repetition. There is a good side to the idea of karma that is not always recognized. It involves sympathy. People may be more unfortunate than wicked. There is tragedy in the world.

Although there is a demand for a future life and personal immortality, people hardly know what they want. There are those who hold that immortality is a prize to be won. This is called conditional immortality. However, the idea seems to favor the more fortunate and to be semiaristocratic in motivation. It is certain that the modern mind cannot accept the idea of endless punishment that is not justified by improvement as a goal. Surely, no being is wholly evil. The Hindu idea of rebirth has its biological difficulties, but these are not insurmountable. There would need to be some kind of selectivity.

The Ultimate Reality

All this leads up to the speculative climax of Radhakrishnan's argument. How are we to envisage ultimate reality? Radhakrishnan summarizes the results of his survey of the world. The world is an ordered whole; everything is an organization with its mode of connection. There is a development in the direction of greater union with surroundings. Nature is a domain of becoming without fixity. Yet these changes are not meaningless. Evolution goes with progress on the whole. Lastly, the highest kind of experiences and personalities seem to indicate a goal of being.

These principles are opposed to traditional naturalism. It did not have a sufficient place for time. Radhakrishnan aligns himself in some measure with holism and Lloyd Morgan's emergent evolution. However, it would seem, he is most in sympathy with Alfred North Whitehead's Platonism, with its primordial God and Consequent God. God is the home of universals, of possibilities, and of ideal harmony.

The Eastern note in Radhakrishnan's conclusion is interesting. The Absolute is also absolute freedom in activity. All else is dependent, created reality, *maya*. One can speak symbolically of three sides of God's nature. In Hindu tradition, these are Brahma, Vishnu, and Siva. These must not be set apart.

It is clear that Radhakrishnan regards absolute idealism as representing the basis for a fusion of the Vedanta perspective in India and Western thought. It is debatable whether he has done justice to trends toward realism and analysis. However, he would be the last to hold that human thought has finished its task. Probably the most intriguing element in his thought is his belief that mystical apprehension is a genuine form of knowledge, though it is evocative and does not lend itself to description. Here, he would hold, we are capable—a few of us at least—of contact with the absolute and the eternal.

Roy Wood Sellars

Additional Reading

Agarwal, Sudarshan, ed. *Dr. Sarvepalli Radhakrishnan: A Commemorative Volume, 1888-1988*. New Delhi: Prentice-Hall of India, 1988. Records and honors Radhakrishnan's contribution to the functioning of parliamentary democracy in his capacity as first chairman of the Rajya Sabha, the second chamber of the Indian parliament.

Ahluwalia, B. K., ed. *Facets of Radhakrishnan*. New Delhi: Newman Group, 1978. Twenty-two essays that illuminate all aspects of Radhakrishnan's work as philosopher, diplomat, humanitarian, scholar, and patriot. Many of the essays are by prominent people who had known Radhakrishnan personally.

Arapura, J. G. *Radhakrishnan and Integral Experience*. Bombay: Asia Publishing House, 1966. A critical study of Radhakrishnan's methodology, epistemology, and "perennial philosophy."

Banerji, Anjan Kumer, ed. *Sarvepalli Radhakrishnan: A Centenary Tribute*. Varanasi: Benaras Hindu University, 1991. Contains the texts of some rare lectures and letters as well as reminiscences of those who knew Radhakrishnan. Covers his work as statesman, philosopher, and scholar.

Gopal, Sarvepalli. *Radhakrishnan: A Biography*. London: Unwin Hyman, 1989. A comprehensive biography. Although it is written by Radhakrishnan's son, it is an objective account of Radhakrishnan's life: well-documented, readable, and balanced in its conclusions. Contains thirty-one photographs.

Harris, Ishwar. *Radhakrishnan: The Profile of a Universalist*. Calcutta, India: Minerva Associates, 1982. A study of Radhakrishnan's religious thought that emphasizes his universalism. Covers the tradition of universalism in Indian thought, the evolution of Radhakrishnan's views, the influence on him of Christianity and other faiths, and of Vivekananda and Tagore, and a comparison of his thought to that of Western theologians Paul Tillich and Frithjof Schuon.

Minor, Robert N. *Radhakrishnan: A Religious Biography*. Albany: State University of New York Press, 1987. Much of this is based on interviews with Radhakrishnan's family, friends, students and acquaintances. It seeks to place his thought in the context of his experience, to analyze the method by which he formulated his philosophical outlook and to highlight his own definitions of his major concerns.

Murty, K. Satchidanda, and Ashok Vohra. *Radhakrishnan: His Life and Ideas*. Delhi, India: Ajanta Publications, 1989. The authors describe themselves as "critical admirers" of Radhakrishnan, and this is a compact, balanced introduction to all aspects of his life and work. Not as detailed as Gopal, above.

Parthasarathi, G., and D. P. Chattopadhyaya, eds. *Radhakrishnan: Centenary Volume*. Delhi, India: Oxford University Press, 1989. Contains twenty-nine articles by Eastern and Western scholars on Radhakrishnan's philosophical thought and his achievements as a statesman.

Rodrigues, Clarissa. *The Social and Political Thought of Dr. S. Radhakrishnan: An Evaluation*. New Delhi: Sterling Publishers, 1992. An in-depth examination of Radhakrishnan's social and political views.

Bryan Aubrey

Ayn Rand

Rand first achieved success as a writer of fiction with strong political and ethical content. She later expanded on the ethical and political theme of Objectivism, along with her idea that self-interest is morally good and altruism is corrupting to the human spirit and ultimately self-defeating.

Principal philosophical works: *We the Living*, 1936; *Anthem*, 1938, rev. ed. 1946; *The Fountainhead*, 1943; *Atlas Shrugged*, 1957; *For the New Intellectual*, 1961; *The Virtue of Selfishness*, 1964; *Capitalism: The Unknown Ideal*, 1966; *Introduction to Objectivist Epistemology*, 1967; *The Romantic Manifesto*, 1969; *The New Left: The Anti-Industrial Revolution*, 1971; *Philosophy: Who Needs It?*, 1982; *The Early Ayn Rand: A Selection from Her Unpublished Fiction*, 1984.

Born: February 2, 1905; St. Petersburg, Russia
Died: March 6, 1982; New York, New York

Early Life

Ayn Rand, born in St. Petersburg, Russia, on February 2, 1905, as Alisa (Alice) Rosenbaum, was raised in a middle-class family. She showed an early love of storytelling and decided at the age of nine to become a writer. In school, she showed academic promise, particularly in mathematics. The Revolution of 1917 devastated her family because of the social upheavals brought by the revolution and fighting, and because her father's pharmacy was confiscated by the Soviets. The family moved to the Crimea to regroup financially and to escape the harshness of life that the revolution had brought to St. Petersburg. The family later returned to Petrograd (the new name given to St. Petersburg by the Soviets), where Rosenbaum was to attend university.

At the University of Petrograd, Rosenbaum concentrated her studies on history, with secondary focuses on philosophy and literature. She was repelled by the dominance of communist ideas and strong-arm tactics, which had the effect of suppressing free inquiry and discussion. As a youth, she objected to the communists' political program; as an adult, she would become more fully aware of the destructive effects that the revolution had had on Russian society.

Having studied American history and politics at the university, and having long been an admirer of Western plays, music, and films, she came to value American individualism, its vigor, and its optimism, seeing it as the opposite of Russian collectivism, decay, and gloom. Believing that she would not be free under the Soviet system to write the kinds of books she wanted to write, she resolved to leave Russia and go to the United States.

Rosenbaum graduated from the University of Petrograd in 1924. She then enrolled at the State Institute for Cinema Arts to study screenwriting. In 1925, she finally received permission from the Soviet authorities to leave the country to visit relatives in the United States. Officially, her visit was to be brief; however, she had decided not to return to the Soviet Union.

After several stops in Western European cities, Rosenbaum arrived in New York City in February, 1926. She adopted the name Ayn Rand. From New York, she traveled to Chicago, Illinois, where she spent the next six months living with relatives, learning English, and developing ideas for stories and screenplays. She had decided to become a screenwriter, and, having received an extension to her visa, she left for Hollywood, California.

On Rand's second day in Hollywood, an event occurred that was worthy of her dramatic fiction

Ayn Rand. *(Library of Congress)*

and had several major effects on her future. She was spotted by Cecil B. deMille, one of Hollywood's leading directors, while she was standing at the gate of his studio. She had recognized him as he was passing by in his car, and he had noticed her staring at him. He stopped to ask why she was staring, and Rand explained that she had recently arrived from Russia, that she had long been passionate about Hollywood films, and that she dreamed of being a screenwriter. DeMille was then working on *The King of Kings* (1961); he gave her a ride to the set and signed her on as an extra. During her second week at deMille's studio, Rand met Frank O'Connor, a young actor also working as an extra. Rand and O'Connor were married in 1929, and they remained married for fifty years, until his death in 1979.

Rand also worked for deMille as a reader of scripts, struggling financially while working on her own writing. She held a variety of nonwriting jobs until, in 1932, she was able to sell her first screenplay, *Red Pawn*, to Universal Studios. In 1934, her first stage play, *Night of January 16th*, was produced in Hollywood under the title *Woman on Trial*; it later appeared on Broadway.

Life's Work

Rand's life was often as colorful as those of the heroes in her best-selling novels *The Fountainhead* and *Atlas Shrugged*. Rand first made her name as a novelist, publishing *We the Living* in 1936, *The Fountainhead* in 1943, and her magnum opus *Atlas Shrugged* in 1957. These philosophical novels embodied themes she would then develop in nonfiction form in a series of essays and books written in the 1960's and 1970's.

Rand worked for years on her first significant novel, *We the Living*, and finished it in 1933. Various publishers rejected it over the course of several years, until in 1936 it was published by Macmillan in the United States and Cassell in England. Rand described *We the Living* as the most autobiographical of her novels, its theme being the brutality of life under communist rule in Russia. *We the Living* did not receive a positive reaction from American reviewers and intellectuals. It was published in the 1930's, sometimes called the "Red Decade," during which American intellectuals were often pro-Communist and respectful and admiring of the Soviet experiment.

Rand's next major project was *The Fountainhead*, on which she had begun to work in 1935. Whereas the theme of *We the Living* was political, the theme of *The Fountainhead* was ethical, focusing on individualist themes of independence and integrity. The novel's hero, architect Howard Roark, is Rand's first embodiment of her ideal man, one who lives a principled and heroic life.

As with *We the Living*, Rand had difficulties getting *The Fountainhead* published. It was rejected by twelve publishers before being accepted by Bobbs-Merrill. Like *We the Living*, it was not well received by reviewers and intellectuals, but it nevertheless became a best-seller, primarily through word-of-mouth recommendations. *The Fountainhead* made Rand famous as an exponent of individualist ideas, and its continued sales brought her financial security. Warner Bros. produced a film version of the novel in 1949, starring Gary Cooper and Patricia Neal, for which Rand wrote the screenplay.

In 1946, Rand began work on her most ambitious novel, *Atlas Shrugged*. At the time, she was working part-time as a screenwriter for producer Hal Wallis. In 1951, she and her husband moved to New York City, where she began to work full-time on *Atlas Shrugged*. Published by Random House in 1957, it is her most complete expression of her literary and philosophical vision. Dramatized with a strong element of mystery, in the form of the question "Who is John Galt?," it concerns characters who try to stop the motor of the world. The plot and characters embody the political and ethical themes first developed in *We the Living* and *The Fountainhead*, integrating them into a comprehensive philosophy including metaphysics, epistemology, economics, and the psychology of love and sex.

Atlas Shrugged was an immediate best-seller and Rand's last work of fiction. Her novels had expressed philosophical themes, although Rand considered herself primarily a novelist and only secondarily a philosopher. The creation of plots and characters and the dramatization of achievements and conflicts were her central purposes in writing fiction, rather than presenting an abstract and didactic set of philosophical theses.

The Fountainhead and *Atlas Shrugged*, however, attracted to Rand many readers who were strongly interested in the philosophical ideas the novels embodied; many readers wished to pursue these ideas further. Among the earliest of these followers who later became prominent were psychologist Nathaniel Branden, philosopher Leonard Peikoff, and economist Alan Greenspan, later chairman of the Federal Reserve Board. Her interactions with these and several other key individuals were partly responsible for her turning from fiction to nonfiction writing to develop her philosophy more systematically.

From 1962 until 1976, Rand wrote and lectured on her philosophy, now officially named Objectivism. Her essays during this period appeared primarily in a series of periodicals: *The Objectivist*, published from 1962 to 1965; the larger periodical *The Objectivist*, published from 1966 to 1971; and *The Ayn Rand Letter*, published from 1971 to 1976. The essays written for these periodicals form the core material for a series of nine nonfiction books published during Rand's lifetime. Those books develop Rand's philosophy in all its major categories and apply it to cultural issues. Perhaps the most significant of the books are *The Virtue of Selfishness*, which develops her ethical theory; *Capitalism: The Unknown Ideal*, devoted to political and economic theory; *Introduction to Objectivist Epistemology*, a systematic presentation of her theory of concepts; and *The Romantic Manifesto*, a theory of aesthetics.

During the 1960's, Rand's most significant professional relationship was with Nathaniel Branden. Branden, author of *The Psychology of Self-Esteem: A New Concept of Man's Psychological Nature* (1969) and now well known as a leader in the self-esteem movement in psychology, wrote many essays on philosophical and psychological topics that were published in Rand's books and periodicals. He was the founder and head of the Nathaniel Branden Institute (NBI), the leading Objectivist institution of the 1960's. Based in New York City, the NBI published, with Rand's sanction, numerous Objectivist periodicals and pamphlets. It also presented many series of lectures live in New York, then distributed taped recordings around the United States and the rest of the world. The rapid growth of the NBI and the Objectivist movement came to a halt in 1968, when, for both professional and personal reasons, Rand and Branden parted ways.

Rand continued to write and lecture consistently until she stopped publishing *The Ayn Rand Letter* in 1976. Thereafter, she wrote and lectured less as her husband's and her own health declined. Rand died on March 6, 1982, in her New York City apartment.

Influence

The impact of Rand's ideas has been enormous. All the books she published during her lifetime remained in print for decades, selling more than twenty million copies, and they continued to sell hundreds of thousands of copies each year until the end of the twentieth century. A survey jointly conducted by the Library of Congress and the Book-of-the-Month Club early in the 1990's, asking readers to name the book that had most influenced their lives, resulted in *Atlas Shrugged* being named second only to the Bible. Excerpts from Rand's works are regularly reprinted in college textbooks and anthologies, and several volumes containing her early writings, journals, and letters have been published posthumously.

Those inspired by her ideas have published books in many academic fields and founded several institutes. Noteworthy among these is the Cato Institute, the leading libertarian think tank in the world. Rand, along with Nobel Prize winners Friedrich Hayek and Milton Friedman, was hugely instrumental in attracting generations of individuals to the libertarian movement. Also noteworthy are the Ayn Rand Institute, founded in 1985 by philosopher Leonard Peikoff and based in California, and the Institute for Objectivist Studies, founded in 1990 by philosopher David Kelley and based in New York.

Stephen R. C. Hicks

The Virtue of Selfishness

Type of philosophy: Ethics, social philosophy
First published: 1964
Principal ideas advanced:
◊ Self-interest is morally good.
◊ Happiness is the goal of life, and self-responsibility is the means to that goal.
◊ Self-interest is the basis for free enterprise economics and liberal politics.
◊ The seven cardinal virtues of self-interest are rationality, productiveness, integrity, independence, honesty, justice, and pride.
◊ Selflessness and sacrifice for others are not moral values.
◊ There are no fundamental conflicts of interest.

The provocative title of Ayn Rand's *The Virtue of Selfishness* matches an equally provocative thesis about ethics. Traditional ethics has always been suspicious of self-interest, praising acts that are selfless in intent and calling amoral or immoral acts that are motivated by self-interest. A self-interested person, in the traditional view, will not consider the interests of others and thus will slight or harm those interests in the pursuit of his or her own. Rand's view is that the exact opposite is true: Self-interest, properly understood, is the standard of morality, and selflessness is the deepest immorality.

A New Theory of Self-Interest
According to Rand's philosophy of Objectivism, self-interest, rightly understood, is to see oneself as an end in oneself. That is to say that one's own life and happiness are one's highest values, and that one does not exist as a servant or slave to the interests of others. Nor do others exist as servants or slaves to one's own interests. Each person's own life and happiness are that person's ultimate ends. Self-interest, rightly understood, also entails self-responsibility: One's life is one's own, as is the responsibility for sustaining and enhancing it. It is up to each person to determine what values his or her life requires, along with how best to achieve those values, and to act to achieve those values.

Rand's ethic of self-interest is integral to her advocacy of classical liberalism. Classical liberalism, more often called libertarianism in the twentieth century, is the view that individuals should be free to pursue their own interests. This implies, politically, that governments should be limited to protecting each individual's freedom to do so. In other words, the moral legitimacy of self-interest implies that individuals have rights to their lives, their liberties, their property, and the pursuit of their own happiness, and that the purpose of government is to protect those rights. Leaving individuals free to pursue their own interests implies in turn that only a capitalist or free market economic system is moral: Free individuals will use their time, money, and other property as they see fit, and they will interact and trade voluntarily with others to mutual advantage.

Rationality
Fundamentally, the means by which people live their lives is by reason. The capacity for reason is what enables humans to survive and flourish.

People are not born knowing what is good for them; that is learned. Nor are they born knowing how to achieve what is good for them; that too is learned. It is by reason that one learns what is food and what is poison, what animals are useful or dangerous, how to make tools, what forms of social organization are fruitful, and so on.

Thus, Rand advocates rational self-interest: One's interests are not whatever one happens to feel like; rather, it is by reason that one identifies what serves one's interests and what does not. By the use of reason, one takes into account all the factors one can identify, projects the consequences of potential courses of action, and adopts principled policies of action. The principled policies a person should adopt are called virtues. A virtue is an acquired character trait; it results from identifying a policy as good and committing to acting consistently in terms of that policy.

Virtues

One such virtue is rationality. Having identified the use of reason as fundamentally good, Rand asserts that being committed to act in accordance with reason is the virtue of rationality. Another virtue is productiveness: Given that the values one needs to survive must be produced, being committed to producing those values embodies the virtue of productiveness. Another is honesty: Given that facts are facts and that one's life depends on knowing and acting in accordance with facts, being committed to awareness of facts entails the virtue of honesty.

Independence and integrity are also core virtues for Rand's account of self-interest. Given that one must think and act by one's own efforts, being committed to the policy of independent action is a virtue. In addition, given that one must both identify what serves one's interests and act to achieve those interests, a policy of being committed to acting on the basis of one's beliefs is the virtue of integrity. The opposite policy of believing one thing and doing another is the vice of hypocrisy; hypocrisy is a policy of self-destruction, in Rand's view.

Justice is another core self-interested virtue. In Rand's account, justice means a policy of judging people, including oneself, according to their value and acting accordingly. The opposite policy of giving to people more or less than they deserve is injustice. The final virtue on Rand's list of core virtues is pride, the policy of "moral ambitiousness," in Rand's words. This means a policy of being committed to making oneself be the best one can be, of shaping one's character to the highest level possible. According to her, pride is a virtue rather than a sin.

The moral person, then, according to Rand, is someone who acts and is committed to acting in his or her self-interest. It is by living the morality of self-interest that one survives, flourishes, and achieves happiness. This account of self-interest is a minority position, though it has always attracted many followers. The contrasting view typically pits self-interest against morality, holding that one is moral only to the extent that one sacrifices one's self-interest for the sake of others, or, more moderately, to the extent that one acts primarily with regard for the interests of others. For example, standard versions of selflessness hold that one is moral to the extent that one sets aside one's own interests to serve God, or the weak and the poor, or society as a whole. In these accounts, the interests of God, the poor, or society as a whole are held to be of greater moral significance than one's own interests; accordingly, one's interests should be sacrificed when necessary. These ethics of selflessness thus believe that one should see oneself fundamentally as a servant, as existing to serve the interests of others, not one's own interests.

Conflicts of Interest

The core difference between Rand's self-interest view and the selfless view can be seen in the reason why most advocates of selflessness think self-interest is dangerous: conflicts of interest. According to traditional ethics, conflicts of interest are fundamental to the human condition, and basic ethical principles exist to advise in these conflicts and to state whose interests should be sacrificed to resolve these conflicts. If there is, for example, a fundamental conflict between what God wants and what humans naturally want, then religious ethics will make fundamental the principle that human wants should be sacrificed for God's. If there is a fundamental conflict between what society needs and what individuals want, then some versions of secular ethics will make fundamental the principle that the individual's wants should be sacrificed for society's.

Taking conflicts of interest to be fundamental almost always stems from one of two premises: that human nature is fundamentally destructive or that economic resources are scarce. If human nature is fundamentally destructive, then humans are naturally in conflict with one another. Many ethical philosophies start from this premise, such as Plato's myth of Gyges, Jewish and Christian accounts of original sin, and Sigmund Freud's account of the id. If what individuals naturally want to do to one another is rape, steal, and kill, then these individual desires need to be sacrificed in a functioning society. A basic principle of ethics then will urge individuals to suppress their natural desires so that society can exist. In other words, self-interest is the enemy.

Scarcity of economic resources, with not enough to satisfy everyone's wants or needs, puts human beings in fundamental conflict with one another: For one individual's want or need to be satisfied, another's must be sacrificed. Many ethical philosophies begin with this premise. For example, English economist and philosopher Thomas Malthus's theory that population growth will outstrip growth in the food supply falls into this category, and Karl Marx invigorated socialism with his theory that brutal competition for scarce resources leads to the exploitation of some by others. Philosopher Garret Hardin's famous use of the lifeboat analogy asks people to imagine that society is like a lifeboat and that there are more people than its resources can support. To resolve the destructive competition caused by inadequate resources, a basic principle of ethics will urge individuals to sacrifice their interests in obtaining more (or even some) so that others may obtain more (or some) and society can exist peacefully. In other words, in a situation of scarcity, self-interest is the enemy and must be sacrificed to serve the interests of others.

Rejecting Premises
Rand rejects both the scarce resources and destructive human nature premises. Human beings are not born in sin or with destructive desires, nor do they necessarily acquire them in the course of growing to maturity. Instead, one is born tabula rasa ("blank slate"), and through one's choices and actions, one acquires character traits and habits. As Rand phrases it, "Man is a being of self-made soul." Chronic desires to steal, rape, or kill others are the result of mistaken development and the acquisition of bad habits, just as are chronic laziness and the habit of eating too much junk food. Just as one is not born lazy but can, by individual choices, develop into a person of vigor or sloth, one is not born antisocial but can—again by individual choices—develop into a person of cooperativeness or conflict.

Nor are resources scarce in any fundamental way, according to Rand. By the use of reason, humans can discover new resources and how to use existing resources more efficiently, including recycling where appropriate and making productive processes more efficient. Humans have, for example, continually discovered and developed new energy resources, including animal energy, wood, coal, oil, and nuclear and solar power. In this perspective, there is no end in sight to this process. At any given moment, the available resources are fixed in quantity, but over time, the stock of resources is constantly expanding.

Because humans are rational, they can produce an ever-expanding number of goods, so human interests do not fundamentally conflict with one another. Rand holds that the exact opposite is true: Because humans can and should be productive, human interests are deeply in harmony. For example, one person's choice to produce more corn is in harmony with another person's choice to produce more peas, because by being productive and trading with each other they both become better off. It is in each person's interest that the other be successful, because that will expand the total amount of resources—in this example, food—available.

Conflicts of interest do exist within a narrower scope of focus. In the immediate present, available resources are more fixed, and competition for those resources results. That competition produces winners and losers. Economic competition, however, is a broader form of cooperation, a way to allocate resources socially without resorting to physical force and violence. Through competition, resources are allocated efficiently and peacefully, and in the long run more resources are produced. Thus, a competitive economic system serves the self-interests of all its members.

Rand argues that her ethic of self-interest is the basis for personal happiness and free and prosperous societies. Her novels and books of nonfiction have sold tens of millions of copies, thus having a wide influence. Her work on ethics, particularly her advocacy of self-interest as morally good, is perhaps the most controversial part of her philosophy. That her views have an established place in the canon is indicated by the facts that excerpts from her works are regularly reprinted in college textbooks and that several academic and policy institutes have arisen to articulate and advance her philosophy of Objectivism.

Stephen R. C. Hicks

Additional Reading

Binswanger, Harry. *The Biological Basis of Teleological Concepts*. Los Angeles: Ayn Rand Institute Press, 1990. Written by a philosopher, this is a scholarly work focused on the connection between biology and the concepts at the roots of ethics.

Branden, Nathaniel, and Barbara Branden. *Who Is Ayn Rand?* New York: Random House, 1962. This book contains three essays on Objectivism's moral philosophy, its connection to psychological theory, and a literary study of Rand's methods in her fiction. It contains an additional biographical essay, tracing Rand's life from birth to her mid-fifties.

Hessen, Robert. *In Defense of the Corporation*. Stanford, Calif.: Hoover Institution Press, 1979. Hessen, an economic historian, argues and defends from an Objectivist perspective the moral and legal status of the corporate form of business organization.

Kelley, David. *The Evidence of the Senses*. Baton Rouge: Louisiana State University Press, 1986. Written by a philosopher, this is a scholarly work in epistemology, focusing on the foundational role the senses play in human knowledge.

Mayhew, Robert. *Ayn Rand's Marginalia*. New Milford, Conn.: Second Renaissance Books, 1995. This volume contains Rand's critical comments on more than twenty thinkers, including Friedrich Hayek, C. S. Lewis, and Immanuel Kant. Edited by a philosopher, the volume contains facsimiles of the original texts, with Rand's comments on facing pages.

Peikoff, Leonard. *Objectivism: The Philosophy of Ayn Rand*. New York: Dutton, 1991. This is the first comprehensive overview of all aspects of Objectivist philosophy, written by the philosopher who was closest to Rand during her lifetime.

_____. *The Ominous Parallels: The End of Freedom in America*. New York: Stein & Day, 1982. A scholarly work in the philosophy of history, arguing Objectivism's theses about the role of philosophical ideas in history and applying them to explaining the rise of National Socialism (Nazism).

Rasmussen, Douglas, and Douglas Den Uyl, eds. *The Philosophic Thought of Ayn Rand*. Urbana: University of Illinois Press, 1984. A collection of scholarly essays by philosophers, defending and criticizing various aspects of Objectivism's metaphysics, epistemology, ethics, and politics.

Reisman, George. *Capitalism: A Treatise on Economics*. Ottawa, Ill.: Jameson Books, 1996. A scholarly work by an economist, developing capitalist economic theory and connecting it to Objectivist philosophy.

Sciabarra, Chris Matthew. *Ayn Rand, the Russian Radical*. University Park: Pennsylvania State University Press, 1995. A work in history of philosophy, this book attempts to trace the influence on Rand's thinking of dialectical approaches to philosophy prevalent in nineteenth century Europe and Russia. Also provides an introduction to and overview of the major branches of Objectivist philosophy.

Stephen R. C. Hicks

John Rawls

A creative and original thinker, Rawls sought to present the basic political structure of democracy as a set of principles of justice obtained from a hypothetical social contract, a system of cooperation among equal citizens having a common allegiance.

Principal philosophical works: *A Theory of Justice*, 1971; *Political Liberalism*, 1993; *Collected Papers*, 1999.

Born: February 21, 1921; Baltimore, Maryland

Early Life

In 1921, John Bordley Rawls was born to William Lee Rawls and Anna Abel Stemp Rawls. Rawls was educated at the Kent School, Princeton University, and Cornell University. He served in the United States Army from 1943 until 1946. He married Margaret Warfield Fox in 1949, and they had two sons and two daughters. He was an instructor at Princeton from 1950 until 1952, a Fulbright fellow at Oxford University from 1952 until 1953, and then an assistant and later an associate professor at Cornell from 1953 until 1959. He was a visiting professor at Harvard University from 1959 until 1960, a professor at the Massachusetts Institute of Technology from 1960 until 1962, and the James Bryant Conant University Professor of Moral Philosophy at Harvard University from 1962 until his retirement sometime after 1993.

Life's Work

Rawls's primary and most significant work is *A Theory of Justice*, published in 1971. In this highly controversial volume, Rawls presents a liberal, egalitarian, and moral conception of society and aims to explain and justify the basic structure of a constitutional democracy.

The principal themes of Rawlsian justice have created an enormous literature among many diverse academic disciplines—among them philosophy, political science, economics, and sociology—having in common an interest in liberty, equality, and social justice. Critics of Rawls believe that his foundations are flawed and that his position signals the death of the era of liberalism and the demise of the Enlightenment tradition. After *A Theory of Justice* appeared, there was an academic shift caused by the critiques of libertarian Robert Nozick and communitarian Michael Sandel.

While acknowledging his indebtedness to the ethics of German philosopher Immanuel Kant, Rawls presents his social contract as a public conception of justice. He argues that free persons who are equally situated and ignorant of their historical circumstances would agree to certain principles to secure their equal status and independence and to pursue their conceptions of the good.

In *A Theory of Justice*, Rawls develops an imagined agreement meant to express terms of fair cooperation among free and equal citizens in a modern constitutional democracy. Rawls's aim is "to provide the most appropriate moral basis for a democratic society." Rawls views persons as free, equal, rational, and endowed with a moral capacity for a sense of justice. Because of differences in knowledge and circumstances, free persons will develop different conceptions of the good. Toward this end, they make conflicting claims on scarce resources. These scarce resources, along with the benefits and burdens resulting from social cooperation, must be divided using some principles of justice. Rawls contends that the appropriate way to decide such principles for a democratic society is by use of conjecture as to what principles free persons would agree to, among themselves, if they were given the opportunity. To ensure that this agreement is fair, they must bring to this task their own awareness of justice as well as historical circumstances, desires, and conceptions of the good. A key concept in Rawls's theory is the "veil of ignorance." When deciding the principles to which they would agree, people are assumed to be behind such a veil. They know general social, economic, psychological, and physical theories of all kinds, and they are aware that there are certain all-purpose means that are essential to achieving their good. These "primary social goods" are rights and liberties, powers and opportunities, income and wealth, and the basis of self-respect. People in Rawls's principles-deciding task, however, do not know which social, economic, racial, or other class they will belong to after the principles of justice have been established.

These restrictions render Rawls's parties strictly equal, enabling him to carry to the limit the intuitive idea of the democratic social contract tradition: that justice is what could, or would, be agreed to among free persons from a position of equality. Rawls views his strong equality condition and other moral conditions as reasonable restrictions on arguments for principles of justice for the basic structure of society. These conditions define the "original position," the perspective from which rational agents are to agree. Rawls argues that the parties, after being presented with a list of all known conceptions of justice, would unanimously agree to justice as fairness, comprising two principles: (1) Each person has an equal right to a fully adequate scheme of equal basic liberties, compatible with a similar scheme of liberties for all; and (2) social and economic inequalities must be attached to offices and positions that are open to all, under conditions of equality of opportunity, and must benefit the least advantaged members of society (the "difference principle"). Included in one's conception of the good are the religious and philosophical convictions and ethical ways of life that give one's existence meaning.

The principles of justice are prioritized. The principles chosen from the original position apply to political, social, and economic institutions and the rules that govern them, not to individu-

als. The principles are concerned with the distribution of "primary goods," or things that every rational human is presumed to want, whatever that person's goals, aspirations, and desires. There are two kinds of primary goods: social (income and wealth, opportunities and powers, rights and liberties) and natural (health, intelligence, vigor, imagination, and natural talents affected by social institutions but not directly distributed by them).

According to Rawls's two principles of justice, the basic liberties of citizens are political liberty (the right to vote and to be eligible for public office), the freedom of speech and assembly, liberty of conscience and freedom of thought, freedom of the person and the right to hold personal property, and freedom from arbitrary arrest and seizure. Rawls does not discuss limitations on these liberties that might be enacted to ensure "equal liberty for all."

Rawls's second principle contains a solution called "democratic equality," that is, equality of fair opportunity supplemented by the principle of efficiency with the difference principle. All in society should benefit, the least well off as well as the advantaged. If entrepreneurs accumulate too much wealth, creating great disparity with the working class, the government is justified in taxing them at a greater rate to pay for benefits for the working class that would reduce the disparity. Such an application of the difference principle greatly constrains the inequalities in the distribution of primary goods that can exist in society. The two principles of justice are meant to express fair terms of cooperation by which equal moral persons would be willing to cooperate with all members of society throughout their whole lives. When the principles are applied, citizens will act with full autonomy.

Many read *A Theory of Justice* as claiming a methodology for achieving the most rational principles of justice. In subsequent writings, Rawls explained that his more modest aspiration was to set out principles for liberal democracies that would best capture the fundamental idea of "a fair system of cooperation between free and equal persons." He believes that appropriate principles of justice are ones that are sustained by an overlapping consensus of comprehensive views. Principles of justice can be argued to be valid or desirable or appropriate without reliance on any particular comprehensive view. In a well-ordered society, a plurality of reasonable comprehensive views will support the basic political structures and ideas of justice. One aspect of justice in a liberal democracy will be a principle of common reason, a unifying force among members of society.

Recognizing that certain obscurities existed in *A Theory of Justice*, Rawls wrote *Political Liberalism* to clarify problematic aspects of the former work. While continuing to emphasize the importance of the original position, he denies that the original position is designed to set up a choice situation that can be resolved solely through rational decision theory. The work is based substantially on a series of articles that Rawls had already published, albeit in a somewhat different form. Now claiming that his theory is a specifically political theory of justice and not a comprehensive critical moral theory, Rawls regards comprehensive and general moral theories as overlapping on the independently justified political conception of justice.

The first part of the book is a reworking of Rawls's three Dewey Lectures presented in 1980; in fact, Rawls refers to the main divisions of his book as lectures rather than chapters. The second part of the book consists of three more lectures that weave together various parts of published and unpublished materials on "public reason." The final part of the book consists of previously published articles, presented as originally published. The one fully new part of the book is an introductory essay.

The most significant feature of his new theory is that Rawls takes the public political culture of a contemporary democratic society from four "model conceptions" or "fundamental ideas": the idea of the person or citizen, the idea of social cooperation for reciprocal benefit, the idea of the well-ordered society and its basic institutional structure, and the idea of a linking or mediating conception that sets out the standards for discussion and for decision making that citizens could follow in reaching a rational and reasonable decision on the governing principles of political justice. *Political Liberalism* strengthens and enriches Rawls's account of how basic liberties and rights are justified and limited.

Influence

Rawls's theories had a significant impact on American lawyers and judges, having been cited in at least thirty-nine state and federal court opinions as of March, 1994. Rawls's theories have been included in nearly every American law school course in jurisprudence or legal philosophy dealing with rights, and they have set the agenda of political thinkers and academicians. Finally, Rawls has given philosophers and political scientists perspective and structure through which to accept or criticize his theories. Rawls has caused a reconsideration of the institutions of a constitutional democracy. By breaking with tradition, he caused a rethinking of the concept of justice as fairness and the protection of basic liberties. The philosophical liberal tradition shifted to considerations of communitarianism, emphasizing the group rather than the individual.

Marcia J. Weiss

A Theory of Justice

Type of philosophy: Ethics, political philosophy
First published: 1971
Principal ideas advanced:

◇ The principles of justice are whatever would be agreed to by rational, self-interested, and unenvious persons who knew they were to enter a society structured according to their agreement but did not know what positions they would have or what their natural endowments and particular interests would be.

◇ Justice is fairness.

◇ The first principle of justice is equal and maximum feasible liberty for all.

◇ The second principle of justice is that power and wealth are to be distributed equally except where inequalities would work for the advantage of all and where all would have equal opportunity to attain the higher positions.

Possibly the most ambitious and influential work in social philosophy of the later twentieth century, *A Theory of Justice* attempts to show what the principles of social justice are and why they can be satisfied only in a liberal society that partially redistributes income and wealth for the benefit of its least advantaged members. John Rawls revives the social contract tradition of philosophers John Locke, Jean-Jacques Rousseau, and Immanuel Kant, in opposition to utilitarianism.

Justice as a Virtue

Justice, the author declares, is the first and indispensable virtue of social institutions, as truth is of theories. Even the welfare of society as a whole cannot morally override the inviolability that each person has, founded on justice. This is why utilitarianism, which examines only the sum of welfare and permits the sacrifice of the few for the good of the many, is not a tenable moral theory.

In this book, Rawls is concerned with social justice only, not with the justice that individuals may display in private dealings. Society is a cooperative venture for mutual advantage: If people cooperate in the production of goods, there will be more goods than if every person produces things only for his or her own consumption. People, however, do not merely cooperate in the production of social goods; they also compete for them, and everyone prefers more rather than less. These facts give rise to the problem of distributive justice: On what principles should goods and the benefits of social cooperation be distributed?

There is scope for the operation of justice whenever many individuals coexist in a territory and are similar enough so that no one is able to dominate the rest. Social goods must be moderately scarce, so that there will be conflicting claims that cannot all be satisfied.

Rawls makes a distinction between the *concept* of justice, on which all agree, and different *conceptions* of justice. The concept, he says, is that "institutions are just when no arbitrary distinctions are made between persons in the assigning of basic rights and duties and when the rules determine a proper balance between competing claims to the advantages of social life." Different conceptions are generated when people differ in their interpretations of which distinctions are arbitrary and what balances are proper.

The social justice of which Rawls writes involves the basic structure of society: the way in which major social institutions, chiefly governmental, distribute fundamental rights and duties and divide up the product of social cooperation. This is the distributive aspect of the basic structure of society, not a complete social idea. Rawls claims that his conception of distributive social justice tallies with the traditional Aristotelian notion that justice consists of giving everyone his or her due, because notions of what people are entitled to ordinarily are derived from social institutions.

Rawls's basic idea is that the correct principles of justice are what free and rational people, concerned with furthering their own interests, would agree to accept as defining the fundamental terms of their association, if their agreement were made under conditions that were fair to all parties. This is "justice as fairness." The conditions of fairness obtain when no party to the agreement is in a position of any advantage over other participants in furthering his or her own interests. Such a fair position, which Rawls calls "the original position," demands that all participants be equal. This corresponds to the "state of nature" in traditional contract theory. Rawls requires in addition that contracting parties not know what their places will be in the society that they are to enter, nor to what class they will belong, nor what their social status will be, nor even their fortunes in the distribution of natural assets and abilities such as intelligence, strength, and particular psychological traits. This is the "veil of ignorance," drawn to prevent the parties from pressing their particular selfish interests. It would not be "fair" if the parties could be influenced in their deliberations by the morally irrelevant contingencies of natural chance (to which natural endowments are due) or social circumstances. Rawls assumes, however, that all parties know the "laws" of psychology and sociology and the general facts about social life. They are also to be mutually disinterested—that is, they take no interest in the interests of other people. They are rational in the sense that they take the most effective means to whatever they put before themselves as their ends. Rawls assumes, finally, that they are not motivated by envy; that is, they will not forgo goods for themselves merely to prevent others from enjoying them. Although the parties are not allowed knowledge of what their particular conceptions of the good will be, they are ensured motivation by a "thin theory of the good": They all want to pursue rational plans of life, in which rights, liberty and opportunity, income and wealth, and the bases of self-respect are primary goods, for it is rational to desire these things, and good is the object of rational desire. Principles of justice, then, are to regulate the distribution of these primary goods.

The Original Position

No actual person is ever ignorant in the ways specified, nor are actual persons equally rational, disinterested, and free of envy. The restrictions of the original position, however, are not arbitrary or fantastic but serve to rule out of discussion factors that are irrelevant to justice. The conception of justice that results must be one that validates people's strongest intuitions—for example, that religious and racial discrimination are unjust. People must aim for "reflective equilibrium" in which their intuitions about justice are harmonized with their principles. This may require adjustment in either or both. The conditions of the original position are those that people do in fact accept, Rawls avers—or that people could be "persuaded" to accept.

Certain formal constraints are embodied in the concept of right: Principles should be general, universal in application, public, capable of ordering conflicting claims, and final. These conditions are satisfied by the notion of deliberation in the original position: Because the individuals cannot identify themselves, they cannot tailor principles to their own advantage; nor would there by any point in their trying to strike bargains with one another. Rawls assumes, furthermore, that because everyone is equally rational and similarly situated, each is convinced by the same arguments. Anyone—any actual person—can enter the original position at any time by arguing in accordance with its restrictions.

Two Principles of Justice

The parties in the original position would agree, Rawls claims, in choosing two principles of justice. The first is that everyone is to have equal rights to the most extensive basic liberty (political, intellectual, and religious) consistent with equal liberty for others. The second is that social and economic inequalities are to be arranged so that they are (1) to everyone's advantage (this is called the difference principle) and (2) attached to positions open to all. The first principle is prior to the second—that is, it must be fully satisfied before the second comes into play; no trade-offs of liberty for economic or social advantage are to be permitted.

The general conception of justice behind this is that all social values should be equally distributed unless an unequal distribution turns out to be to everyone's advantage—for example, by providing incentive for greater production to be shared by all. Rawls defines injustice as "inequalities that are not to the benefit of all."

It is supposed to follow deductively from the specifications of the original position that the parties will vote unanimously for the two principles. The argument is this: The voters not only do not know what their position will be in the society they are forming, but they also do not have any basis on which to calculate the likelihoods of alternatives. Moreover, Rawls claims, a person in the original position will care little for what he or she might gain above the minimum that will be given to everyone. Also, the situation is one of grave risk: If the principles of justice allow unacceptable positions to exist in the society, every voter runs some risk—the magnitude of which cannot be guessed—of ending up in it. Under these conditions, the theory of rational choice is said to dictate a "maximin solution": Choose principles such that the worst possible outcome for the chooser will be better than the worst possible outcome under alternative principles. In other words, voters will choose as if their enemy is to assign them their social place.

The maximin strategy would lead to choice of equal distribution of all social goods were it not for the fact that some inequalities may be such as to bring about the production of more social goods to be distributed, so that by permitting these inequalities it will be possible for everyone, including the worst off, to have a larger amount of goods than if the distribution were equal. Because the choosers want more rather than less, and in addition are not envious, there is no reason why they should not adopt such an idea, called the difference principle: Inequalities are to be permitted when everyone, including the worst off, benefits from them. This principle, being chosen under fair conditions of equality, is just.

Liberty

The social good of liberty is to be distributed equally. People in the original position must adopt a principle of equal religious liberty if they are to adopt any principle at all. As for toleration, the principle is that limitations on liberty must be for the sake of preventing even greater violations of it and must be supported by arguments capable of convincing any rational person. Applying this principle to the question of tolerating the intolerant, Rawls holds that it cannot be unjust for the tolerant to suppress the intolerant in self-defense, but when the intolerant do not constitute a real threat, they must be tolerated. Paternalism—governmental protection of citizens against their own weakness and irrationality—is acceptable, because rational persons in the original position would foresee that they might become irrational and need such help.

Only in the distribution of wealth, income, and authority are inequalities to be allowed. Here, too, equality is the "benchmark"—equal distribution would not be unjust, only inefficient. Rawls recognizes that people are born with unequal natural endowments, both physical and mental, and that social and familial conditions may accentuate them. These inequalities, however, are "arbitrary from the moral point of view"—no one deserves his or her natural endowments, and even a sober and industrious disposition is dependent on the accidents of nature and nurture. The "system of natural liberty," which rewards people in proportion to what they have the talent and industry to produce, thus permits distribution to be improperly influenced by the "natural lottery." The difference principle represents an agreement to consider the total pool of natural talents as a common asset in which everyone shares. Although the natural lottery is neither just nor unjust, societies that base distribution of goods on it are unjust: There must be redress for the undeserved inequalities of birth and natural endowment. It is unjust that people should get more because they are born with more.

Under the difference principle, those who are less favored by nature have no ground for complaint of inequalities, because they benefit from the existence of inequalities. The more favored should realize that their well-being depends on cooperation, which must be obtained on reason-

able terms that the difference principle specifies. Thus, the difference principle promotes fraternity, making society more like a family.

The only sense in which people can be said to deserve anything is this: If, in accordance with the difference principle, it has been announced that those who produce more will get more, then the higher producers deserve their differential, and it would be unjust to withhold it from them.

Social Institutions

The background institutions for distributive justice may be either democratic capitalist or socialist, but they must include a public school system, equality of economic opportunity, a social minimum, and social security. Rawls recommends a governmental organization including four branches. Allocation will keep prices competitive and will prevent too much economic concentration by adjusting taxes and subsidies. The stabilization branch will guarantee full employment. The transfer branch will correct competitive pricing (which by itself ignores need) to ensure that total income is allocated according to need. The distribution branch, through taxes and adjustments in the rights of property, will correct the distribution of wealth. A proportional expenditure tax (the total amount of tax paid rises as expenditures rise, and taxes paid increase by the same percentage of expenditure no matter the level of expenditure) is preferable to a graduated income tax.

Rawls claims that his theory is in the spirit of German philosopher Immanuel Kant, who held that moral principles are the objects of rational choice by free and equal rational beings. The original position is devised in accordance with this conception. One acts autonomously when action is the expression of freedom and rationality. In the original position, it is impossible to choose heteronomous principles. Moreover, the Rawlsian principles of justice are categorical imperatives: They do not assume that anyone has any particular aims. Justice as fairness, however, improves on Kant by showing how, in choosing principles of justice, people are fully expressing their natures as rational and free individuals—their noumenal selves. In justice as fairness, moreover, the basis of equality is being a moral person, which means having the capacity to have a conception of one's own good and a sense of justice. Moral persons are all persons who would be capable (contingencies aside) of taking part in the initial agreement.

To give people really fair opportunities, the family ought to be abolished, but this reform, Rawls allows, is not urgent.

The most important social good, Rawls avers, is self-respect, which he defines as "a person's sense of his own value, his secure conviction that his conception of his good, his plan of life, is worth carrying out," together with confidence in the ability to carry it out. Justice as fairness furthers the equal distribution of the bases of self-respect.

Although the assumption that persons in the original position are not motivated by envy is contrary to present facts about real persons, Rawls holds that in the just society there will be little occasion for, or incitement to, envy. It is not right to claim, as conservative writers do, that the modern tendency toward equality is based on envy. In any case, the two Rawlsian principles of justice cannot be so based, for by hypothesis they are chosen by envy-free people.

Wallace I. Matson

Additional Reading

Alejandro, Roberto. *The Limits of Rawlsian Justice.* Baltimore: The Johns Hopkins University Press, 1998. A new critique of Rawls's theories.

Barry, Brian. *The Liberal Theory of Justice: A Critical Examination of the Principal Doctrines in "A Theory of Justice" by John Rawls.* Oxford: Clarendon Press, 1973. An early book-length critique of Rawls.

Baynes, Barry. *The Normative Grounds of Social Criticism: Kant, Rawls, and Habermas.* Albany: State University of New York Press, 1992. An attempt to clarify social criticism, including Rawlsian refinements of Kantian arguments. Extensive bibliography.

Boucher, David, and Paul Kelly, eds. *The Social Contract from Hobbes to Rawls.* London: Routledge, 1994. An overview of the social contract and its critics. Also contains bibliographical references and an index.

Daniels, Norman, ed. *Reading Rawls: Critical Studies on Rawls' "A Theory of Justice."* Stanford, Calif.: Stanford University Press, 1989. A collection of major critical reactions to *A Theory of Justice.* Contains a Rawls bibliography covering the years 1971 to 1974.

Griffin, Stephen M., and Lawrence B. Solum, eds. Symposium on John Rawls's *Political Liberalism. Chicago Kent Law Review* 69, no. 3 (1994). Contains nine articles by professors of philosophy on the later work of Rawls, with comparisons with the earlier work. A good resource for conflicting views and criticism.

Martin, Rex. *Rawls and Rights.* Lawrence: University Press of Kansas, 1985. Focuses on the basic rights central to Rawls's theories.

Murphy, Cornelius F., Jr. *Descent into Subjectivity: Studies of Rawls, Dworkin, and Unger in the Context of Modern Thought.* Wakefield, N.H.: Longwood Academic, 1990. Outlines the antecedents of the social contract tradition (Jean-Jacques Rousseau and Immanuel Kant) and places the philosophers under discussion in context, relating them to the earlier philosophical tradition. Written from a legal perspective. Deals with governmental institutions.

Pogge, Thomas W. *Realizing Rawls.* Ithaca, N.Y.: Cornell University Press, 1989. A defense and constructive critique of Rawlsian theories of justice.

Schaefer, David Lewis. *Justice or Tyranny? A Critique of John Rawls' "A Theory of Justice."* Port Washington, N.Y.: Kennikat Press, 1979. A critical assessment of Rawls's work.

Wolff, Robert Paul. *Understanding Rawls: A Reconstruction and Critique of "A Theory of Justice."* Princeton, N.J.: Princeton University Press, 1977. A critical assessment of Rawls's work.

Marcia J. Weiss

Thomas Reid

Famous for his criticism of "the way of ideas" and its attendant skepticism, Reid defended "common sense" and human freedom.

Principal philosophical works: *An Inquiry into the Human Mind on the Principles of Common Sense*, 1764; *Essays on the Intellectual Powers of Man*, 1785; *Essays on the Active Powers of Man*, 1788 (also published as *Essays on the Active Powers of the Human Mind*).

Born: April 26, 1710; Strachan, Kincardineshire, Scotland
Died: October 7, 1796; Glasgow, Scotland

Early Life

Thomas Reid was born into distinguished families. His father and ancestors for several generations had been clergymen in the Church of Scotland. On his mother's side, the Gregory family included the inventor of the reflecting telescope, two mathematics professors in Scotland, and a professor of astronomy at Oxford University. Reid's own career alternated between the vocations of pastor and professor.

Reid was home schooled until he entered Marischal College, Aberdeen, at the age of twelve. By the time he graduated four years later, he had embraced George Berkeley's immaterialist philosophy. Reid trained for five years for the Christian ministry, then took the position of librarian at Marischal College between 1733 and 1737, which allowed him to continue his study of John Locke's philosophy and Isaac Newton's physics.

In 1737, Reid became the pastor at New Machar, a rural parish just outside Aberdeen. Because the congregation had little input into his appointment, Reid's ministry had a troublesome start. He married his sixteen-year-old cousin, Elizabeth, four years later. She helped smooth the situation in New Machar, and the congregation grew to love their pastor and his wife during their ten years of service together. The Reids had nine children, but eight died in infancy and

young adulthood. Only a daughter, Martha Carmichael, survived.

Reid was forty-one years old when he accepted the invitation in 1751 to become a regent professor at King's College, Aberdeen. A regent

Thomas Reid. *(Archive Photos)*

professor taught a group of college students all their courses for three years, then presented them for graduation. Reid taught the sciences and mathematics for two years. Only in the third year would he teach ethics and philosophy, the subjects on which he published. In 1758, he helped organize the Aberdeen Philosophical Society, affectionately called the Wise Club by the small group of professors and ministers who gathered twice a month at a local pub. Reid's first book, *An Inquiry into the Human Mind on the Principles of Common Sense*, grew from his presentations and discussions in that group.

Life's Work

Reid was fascinated by the great Scottish philosopher David Hume's *A Treatise of Human Nature* (1739-1740). He pored over it as a young pastor and later reviewed the book intensely with his friends in the Aberdeen Philosophical Society.

Hume claimed in *A Treatise of Human Nature* that people have only two sorts of knowledge and that both are grounded in perceptions of ideas. One either notices necessary relations between ideas (as when noting that "dolphins are mammals") or knows that things contingently exist because one perceives ideas of them (as when seeing that "there swims Flipper the dolphin"). The young Reid accepted this view. He was genuinely shocked at the skeptical conclusions that Hume carefully deduced from these apparently simple claims. Hume argued that if people perceive only ideas, then they cannot know any reality that is different and beyond those ideas. Ideas are fleeting and entirely separate from one another, not at all like the enduring objects that people believe to exist and to interact one with another. Consequently, from the experience of ideas, people can give no reason to believe that bodies and minds exist, that God exists, or that anything (or anyone) actually causes any event to occur.

Reid accepted the challenge of explaining how people can know such realities through experience. In *An Inquiry into the Human Mind on the Principles of Common Sense*, he questioned Hume's key assumption (which Reid variously termed "the ideal theory" or "the way of ideas") that people perceive ideas. Reid thought this assumption was the root of skepticism in the work

of all modern philosophers (whom he judged to be René Descartes, John Locke, and their followers down to his contemporary, David Hume). People mistakenly accept the ideal theory, Reid said, because they confuse sensation and perception. They mistakenly believe that they perceive their sensations. Reid, therefore, kept these processes separate. Sensations are fleeting and separate episodes in consciousness; they just happen to people. Perceptions, on the other hand, involve acts that people do; usually, perceptions are about things that exist continuously outside consciousness. For example, when people type by touch, their sensations are slight momentary pains. They perceive, however, an enduring three-dimensional keyboard at their fingertips. Reid's point is that people do not perceive the sensations (unless, as when thinking about this example, they concentrate on those brief pains), but they perceive something outside consciousness, the keyboard. They conceive the keyboard and then have perceptual beliefs about the keyboard existing, being on the desk, having a light key touch, and so on. In other words, the object of perception is not ideas, but an enduring, causally engaged reality outside the perceiver.

Hume had declared that conceptions are copied from prior sensations (for example, one can think of cerulean blue because one has had sensations of the blue sky). Reid's new position was that conceptions usually are nothing like sensations. The conception of an enduring three-dimensional keyboard is nothing like a momentary pain, but upon feeling the latter, the mind thinks of the former. If (as Reid said) there is no similarity between sensations and objects of perception, why, when people have sensations, do they think of a particular object of perception? That is just how the human mind works, Reid argued. Many conceptions and perceptual beliefs are basic and unexplainable. It is a law of human nature that certain sensations are the occasion of certain conceptions and perceptual beliefs, just as it is a law of nature that physical objects attract one another gravitationally. As observers, people can discover these laws, but they cannot explain why the laws work as they do.

Reid's reputation as a philosopher spread. He accepted the prestigious Chair of Moral Philosophy at the University of Glasgow in 1764 so that he could concentrate on his study of the human mind and agency. He nevertheless lectured busily and did not publish his research for sixteen years. Aware of his diminishing strength in old age, Reid entered semiretirement in 1780. A colleague taught Reid's assigned classes, giving Reid the opportunity to revise his lectures for two final publications: *Essays on the Intellectual Powers of Man* and *Essays on the Active Powers of Man*.

Reid is most famous for his doctrine of common sense. It has been widely misunderstood as an easily refuted view—somewhere in the intellectual neighborhood of "anything that most people believe must be true," or "people should keep their unexamined prejudices regardless of overwhelming counterevidence." Reid, however, meant nothing of the sort. He carefully defined his terms in *Essays on the Intellectual Powers of Man*. By "common," he meant what people must be like if one is to talk and interact with them; "sense" meant judgment—in both its meanings, as a belief and as a power to form beliefs. By "common sense," Reid meant the beliefs people must have so that others can live with them and, consequently, the faculties that they need to form such beliefs.

Reid argued that beliefs arise from a network of evidence-giving faculties such as self-consciousness, sense perception, memory, trust of other people's testimony, something like "seeing" basic logical patterns, reasoning (following arguments), and noticing the presence of causal agents. When these faculties function properly, they provide true basic beliefs such as these: A person has existed for (at least) as long as he or she remembers existing; other people have experiences; physical objects that people perceive really do exist; 2 + 2 = 4; and if "A" and "A then B," then "B." Other philosophers wanted proofs that physical objects, other minds, and causes exist. Reid responded that there could be no proofs, because people know nowhere else to start. These are basic beliefs from which other beliefs are proved. As a thought experiment, consider the following: A person asks someone to prove that other people have minds. To whom is this argument made? From what shared beliefs can the argument begin?

Faculties of common sense sometimes mal-

function—as when a person is poked in the eye, the memory is clouded by drugs, or reasoning is distorted by a powerful desire to dominate a debate. Can people be absolutely certain that their faculties are functioning properly at any given moment? That is, can people know that they know? Reid answered negatively—people's knowing is fallible. That is no reason, however, to distrust people's faculties, because people have no other way to know when they are malfunctioning. People spot a faulty memory by using their faculties: by other remembering, by trusting another person's testimony, or by reasoning from present evidence.

Reid criticized especially Descartes's project in *Meditationes de prima philosophia* (1641; *Meditations on First Philosophy*, 1680). Descartes had begun by doubting the faculties of sense experience. He later argued that God exists and guarantees that human senses are trustworthy after all (when used as carefully as God intended). Reid objected that if one or several faculties are totally doubted for any reason, then all knowing faculties must be doubted (for that same reason)—including people's ability to reason about God's existence. Descartes had dug a pit of skepticism out of which no one could climb.

This objection to Descartes's method is crucial for understanding Reid's own position concerning God and knowledge. One cannot prove God's existence before trusting one's knowing faculties. Reid did think, however, that theists have a reason ultimately to trust people's knowing faculties, namely, that these were designed by a loving Creator for the task of obtaining true beliefs. Nontheists do not have this reason, and they well may have other beliefs (for example, that human faculties were an unintended result of physical processes) that undermine trust in these faculties' truth-getting function.

Reid gave a powerful defense of human free will in *Essays on the Active Powers of Man*. When people act freely, they determine what they choose, and choice governs what they do. (Not all actions are free, of course; something might determine choice, or people might not act as they choose.) People are morally responsible for these free actions because no other persons or events totally determine those actions.

People are creatures embedded in the causal

patterns of the universe, leading to the question of whether freedom of choice is possible. One might question whether every act of choosing has some cause, which might be some prior event beyond one's choosing or control. Reid agreed that free choices have a cause, but that cause is the human agent, not some prior event. This is compatible with radical human freedom.

In later life, Reid became deaf, but he still enjoyed his favorite activities: one-on-one conversations, walking several miles each day, gardening, and working out mathematical proofs as a hobby. Reid's wife, Elizabeth, died in 1792, and Reid died four years later after a brief violent illness.

Influence

Reid imaginatively appraised seventeenth and eighteenth century philosophy. From Irish philosopher Berkeley, he rescued the insight that people have a notion of mind even though they do not experience minds; thus, they must be able to form conceptions of something other than of sensations. The innateness of these concept-forming abilities is a fertile reworking of Descartes's theory of innate ideas. To explain the relationship between sensation and perception, Reid borrowed Berkeley's theory signs. Reid said sensations are signs that signify conceptions and beliefs about objects of perception. Locke's realism and trust in experience also found their echo in Reid's optimistic account of knowledge.

Philosophers in the United States early in the nineteenth century were looking for an adequate response to the skepticism and atheism implicit in modern philosophy. Many of them believed Reid supplied that answer. Charles Sanders Peirce, the founder of pragmatism, continued to develop Reid's theory of signs. By the twentieth century, however, skepticism and atheism were preferred views among intellectuals. Reid's reputation suffered as a thinker who had struggled futilely against the drift of modern thought. His theory of knowledge went out of fashion as, once again, many philosophers claimed to find certainty in the evidence of immediate consciousness or sense experience.

By the late twentieth century, the intellectual drift was going another way. Many believed that modern thought was a grand mistake, and they heralded the coming of a "postmodern" age. Moderns, they said, longed for certainty in knowledge, mistakenly believed they had found it, and then used their opinions to dominate and rule out all others. The postmodern thinkers instead endorsed human fallibility and preached tolerance. Reid had anticipated these critiques of modern philosophy, yet where postmodern thought itself led toward moral skepticism and a distrust of theism, Reid would not have followed. It is not surprising that a number of distinguished American philosophers, including Roderick Chisholm, Keith Lehrer, Nicholas Wolterstorff, William P. Alston, and Alvin Plantinga, became proponents of Reid's alternative way of avoiding the skepticism and hubris of modern philosophy.

Robert B. Kruschwitz

Essays on the Intellectual Powers of Man *and* Essays on the Active Powers of Man

Type of philosophy: Epistemology, ethics
First published: Essays on the Intellectual Powers of Man, 1785; Essays on the Active Powers of Man, 1788 (also published as *Essays on the Active Powers of the Human Mind*).
Principal ideas advanced:

◇ There is no intermediate between the mental act and the object of knowledge; perception is the direct experience of things present to the senses.

◇ All the intellectual powers involve both apprehension of some content and judgment.

◇ People have immediate experience of spatial extension and of temporal duration, and this intuitive knowledge supplies first principles.

◇ Through perception and memory, people acquire probable knowledge; through conception and abstraction, they acquire knowledge of necessary truths.

◇ God has supplied people with consciences that provide intuitive knowledge of the right and the wrong; in following one's own moral sense, one need not fear a conflict of interest and duty.

At the age of seventy-one, Thomas Reid resigned from his University of Glasgow professorship to prepare for publication his celebrated classroom lectures on mental and moral philosophy. The intellectual world already knew the general thrust of the new Scottish Realism through his *Inquiry into the Human Mind on the Principles of Common Sense* (1764); however, the full articulation and defense of the system awaited the appearance of his two books of essays, works so lucid and so plausible that they became almost at once the basis of the orthodox philosophy of the English-speaking world. Reid's philosophy is everything that a "public philosophy" should be. Although it lacks the graceful style of certain eighteenth century philosophers, it has a masculine strength and a directness that still arouses admiration.

Intellectual Powers

Essays on the Intellectual Powers of Man contains eight essays of rather unequal length, each (except the Introduction) concerning one of humankind's intellectual powers or faculties. It is characteristic of Reid's philosophy that, like those of Joseph Butler and Francis Hutcheson, it makes no effort to reduce the different activities to a common denominator. Sense perception, memory, conception (imagination), abstraction, judgment, reason, and taste are so many distinct and irreducible activities, although they may also occur in combination. Reid begins each essay by identifying the power in question and explaining its typical features. There follows a historical account telling how other philosophers have dealt with the subject. Often, in addition, one of the British empiricists is selected for quotation and detailed refutation—not the least profitable part of the work.

Reid was a conscientious empiricist, pledged to carry out the program of English philosopher Francis Bacon for the mental and moral sciences. By observation and investigation, he hoped to arrive at fundamental laws comparable to those that English physicist Isaac Newton had found in natural philosophy. His method is basically introspective: One can learn to attend to one's own mental activities, describe them, and relate them to one another. In this manner, people can map out the "human constitution." Description, however, is all that humanity can attain, because humankind is not given to know the causes of things. In fact, with Reid, as with most of his contemporaries, the underlying assumption (as basic to them as evolution was to the late nineteenth century) was that by a perfect wisdom, all the parts of the world are adjusted to one another.

In addition to his appeals to introspection, Reid makes frequent appeal to common speech to support what he takes to be the witness of humanity's constitution. An example is this: Is beauty properly said to be an emotion in the mind of the perceiver, or a property of the object viewed? Language witnesses the latter. Are heat, hardness, and the like perceived as ideas in the mind or as qualities in bodies? People's speech testifies that they are perceived as qualities.

Reid's attitude toward the history of philosophy (which he regarded as the history of error) is central to his own "common sense" point of view. He shared the optimism of the eighteenth century, which held that the truth is always near at hand and that the first step toward enlightening humankind is to clear away ignorance, prejudice, and artificiality. In Reid's view, all the complications in mental philosophy stem from the very old error of thinking of the mind after the analogy of body. People observe that, in the physical world, there is no action at a distance, and they suppose that similarly the mind can act and be acted on only by what is immediately present to it. The ancient philosophers taught that bodies give off films that, passing through the sense organs, leave impressions on the mind. The moderns, following French philosopher René Descartes, refined their doctrine and retained the old "phantasms" under the new name of "ideas." According to Reid, the progress of philosophy is ensured if the "ideal hypothesis" (which remains to plague the writings of Cartesians and Lockeans alike) is relegated to the rubbish heap along with other scholastic notions.

Perception and the Senses

In Reid's theory of knowledge, there is no intermediate between the mental act and the object of knowledge. Perception is the direct experience of things present to the senses, memory is the experience of things past, consciousness is experience of the mind's own activity, and sensation and emotion are pure states of consciousness. It is characteristic of all these powers that they include, first, a notion or apprehension of some content, and second, a judgment or belief about existence. Reid is full of scorn for Scottish philosopher David Hume's suggestion that belief is simply a degree of the vivacity of an object.

Reid makes use of the distinction between primary and secondary qualities of things, even though he does not hold to the existence of ideas. Perception is a complex act that includes sensation but is not reducible to it. Thus, says Reid, when one touches a table, one has a sensation that, however, one does not ordinarily attend to; the mind passes over it to attend to the quality of the thing—that is to say, such characteristics as hardness or smoothness. There is, according to Reid, a natural symbolism here that people cannot understand: The Creator has attached the perception of the quality to the particular sensation, and this is a mystery—just as it is a mystery that certain vibrations in the brain are regularly attached to certain sensations. The case is otherwise with secondary qualities. When people smell an odor, Reid says, the sensation is likely to be mistaken for the physical object, although introspection reveals that when people smell, say, a rose, all that is really attested is the existence of some external cause of the characteristic sensation: People learn to connect the odor with the object of their other senses. This is partly true of vision as well; however, the purely mental experiences of color are inseparably blended with spatial properties.

Perception and memory, besides the notion of and belief in the object toward which they are directed, carry with them other truth. As Reid says, one knows that one exists as knower, and that some external cause exists adequate to give rise to one's perceptions and memories. Through perception, one comes to know the reality of space, and through memory, one knows the reality of time—these are presupposed by extension and by duration, of which people have immediate experience. These are examples of what Reid calls intuitive truths. They serve as first principles for people's knowledge of the world and humankind. Other truths follow from them by reasoning or demonstration, but the first principles (requisite to every science) must be known immediately.

The principles so far mentioned all have to do with existence. By means of conception and abstraction, it is possible for the mind to invent objects of a different order. These could be called "ideas" without offense—Platonic, rather than Cartesian, ideas. They are objects of the mind and do not represent anything beyond themselves. They do not, as Greek philosopher Plato supposed, exist apart from the mind but are pure essences completely discerned by the mind. Among these theoretical objects, axioms of a different sort are discovered. People call them intuitive also, but they differ from those axioms dealing with contingent truths in that they are seen to be necessary.

Two Kinds of Knowledge

The two kinds of principles previously mentioned yield two kinds of knowledge: Necessary truths (for example, mathematics) yield demonstrative knowledge, and contingent truths (astronomy) yield probable knowledge. Reid is dissatisfied with Hume's suggestion that probable knowledge is less certain than demonstrative knowledge and accuses that philosopher of using the word "probability" in a strange fashion. One's knowledge, for instance, that the capital of France is Paris is no less certain than a demonstration in geometry.

Discussing demonstrative knowledge, Reid takes issue with English philosopher John Locke's contention that moral judgments are of this sort because the terms of moral judgments are not real essences but nominal ones. According to Reid, moral judgments are judgments about contingent matters, and they flow not from definitions but from intuitions. They depend on moral axioms, more or less clearly discerned by all civilized peoples, and they are properly discussed under the actual rather than the intellectual powers of the mind.

Problems of taste, however, which very much interested philosophers of the eighteenth century, are dealt with under intellectual powers. Reid is interested in the power of the mind to combine images in meaningful patterns—he is dissatisfied with the purely mechanistic account of thinking expounded under the name of associationism. Here, in the broadest sense, is the basis for art:

purposiveness. People not only invent meaningful combinations but also recognize them and rejoice in them in the handiwork of other people and in nature.

Reid follows the usual division of aesthetic objects into those of curiosity, grandeur, and beauty. The perception of any of these is a complex act involving both an emotion and a notion and judgment respecting the object. There is an analogy between this and his analysis of sense perception: as sensation is to physical quality, so emotion is to aesthetic quality. Curiosity (like smell, for example) is almost entirely subjective. Not so with grandeur and beauty: People are aware of a property in the thing. It may be that the property is "occult"—in which case people's judgment of beauty is like their perception of color, and they do not understand what it is in the object that gives rise to their pleasant emotion. Sometimes, however, the property is perfectly intelligible, in which case judgment of beauty is analogous to perception of primary qualities.

Reid's philosophy radiates confidence and good will. He is not nervous about his position, and although he indulges in ridicule (he justifies it as one of the ways in which common sense asserts itself), it is never cruel or malicious as is so much eighteenth century wit. Reid does have a genuine enemy: skepticism. He thanks Hume for carrying the "spirit of modern philosophy" (Reid's own expression) out to its logical conclusion: If one hypothesizes "ideas," skepticism is inevitable. Skepticism, in Reid's eyes, is merely defeatism of the sort that prevailed in natural philosophy until the miasmas of peripateticism were cleared away by such men as Galileo and Newton. Happily, a return to common sense makes possible new experimental gains in mental and moral philosophy.

Reid's Moral Philosophy

Essays on the Active Powers of Man carries the investigation from mental philosophy into the field of moral philosophy. This work is only half as long as *Essays on the Intellectual Powers of Man*; hence, it can be inferred that it was not Reid's major field of interest, but not that he considered the active life less important than the speculative one. On the contrary, he glows with enthusiasm

for those remarkable endowments that set humankind above the other animals and give humans the means of remaking the world in the interests of human happiness. The intellectual powers are only instruments in the service of humankind's active powers.

Moral philosophy, almost until the present, included the psychology of motives as well as the principles of normative action. In Reid's philosophy, these can scarcely be disjoined. The clue to his system may be found in Alexander Pope's *An Essay on Man* (1733-1734) as well as in Joseph Butler's *Fifteen Sermons Preached at the Rolls Chapel* (1726). It lies in the belief that humanity's constitution has been fashioned by a wise and benevolent Creator who always orders the part with a view to the perfection of the whole. There are many motives in humankind and, though they often seem to be at odds, careful examination reveals a hierarchy among them. Every motive is good at the right time and place, and there are superior principles that determine when and where the inferior are intended to function. Thus, a purely descriptive account of human nature contains by implication a moral code. In practice, however, people have a readier guide. One of the higher principles with which people are endowed is conscience, which gives them an intuitive sense of right and wrong. Because it is bestowed on them by the Creator, the architect of their being, it can be trusted to lead them toward their proper end.

By the same token, interest and duty are seen to be complementary. It is part of the office of reason to judge between desires and to steer the course that promises to be good for humanity on the whole. The person who follows reason is said to be prudent, and insofar as that person is successful, he or she achieves a happy life. Such intelligence, however, never extends very far, and for humankind as a whole, it is not an adequate guide. In addition to calculating their interest, people should study duty, disclosed to them through the moral sense. Here they are not merely provided with moral truth, from which they may infer their obligation; the deliverances of conscience are also attended with strong feelings of approval and disapproval, which add greatly to its effectiveness as a guide. Although there can be no opposition between these two principles, the rule should be to follow duty rather than interest, on the reasonable presumption that under a wise and benevolent Administration it is impossible that doing what is right should ever result in anything but happiness.

In somewhat the same way, egoistic and altruistic motives are proved not to be in conflict. People's animal impulses, whether appetites or desires, by themselves are neither selfish nor unselfish, neither bad nor good. It is only with reference to larger considerations that they become one or the other. Rightly ordered, they promote both the happiness of the person and that of fellow humans. Reason would, if it were perfect, so regulate them. Because of the limits of humankind's reasoning power, however, God has taken the precaution of undergirding his intention and, to secure people's social well-being, has implanted in them certain affections that are above the particular desires but beneath reason and conscience. Benevolence, the first of these, is the source of such affections as filial love, gratitude, compassion, friendship, and public spirit. There is also malevolent affection, however, which manifests itself in emulation and resentment. (Reid is not sure that they should be called "malevolent.") In themselves, they are not evil, being the basis for such honest attitudes as the desire to excel and the disposition to resist and retaliate injury. If they are not brought under the government of reason or conscience, they become evil, but this is also true of people's benevolent affections.

Moral Liberty

The question of moral liberty inevitably finds a place in Reid's discussion. The problem, as he sees it, is not whether a person has the power to act, but only whether he or she has the power to will. Seventeenth century English philosopher Thomas Hobbes, who defined the question in the former manner, equated liberty with freedom from external impediment; at the same time, he held that all human actions are causally determined. For Reid, it is this last contention that needs to be examined. The matter is complex. Reid holds it to be a self-evident truth that every event in the material world, including the motion of a person's body, must have an efficient cause, but that the nature of the causal nexus is mysteri-

ous. Presumably, the divine Spirit is the source of the motions in nature at large. The question is whether the human spirit has received a somewhat analogous power. Reid holds that it has; otherwise, all human notions of duty and responsibility, and of praise and blame, would be without foundation. As he looks for the source of this freedom in the human constitution, it seems to him to lie on the side of reason as opposed to passions. The latter are impressions on the mind that have their origin in matter, but the former seems to be independent of these motives and free to direct its attention from one object to another, to weigh their respective merits, to select a goal, and to plan a course of action. Insofar as reason is externally motivated, the things that influence it are final (not efficient) causes, together with such considerations as truth and duty.

Although Reid regards the active powers as a natural endowment, he does not suppose that they occur full blown in any person. Conscience is a good example. It does not make itself felt at all in infants or in imbeciles, and even in the adult, it is extremely subject to education, both for weal and for woe. In this respect, moral competence is like other natural endowments, like the ability to dance or sing, or to reason logically. The unpleasant fact is that the great part of humankind in every age is sunk in gross ignorance and fettered to stupid and unprofitable customs. Even as the intellectual powers have a natural affinity for truth, however, so the active powers incline humanity toward virtue and well-being. This is manifest in the institutions of all civilized people and in the law of nature and of nations widely recognized as the foundation of political rights and duties.

Reid distinguishes between moral judgment and the theory of morals. Just as a person may have a good ear that has been improved by practice in the art of music and still be ignorant of the anatomy of hearing and the theory of sound, so one may have exact and comprehensive knowledge of what is right and wrong in human conduct and yet be ignorant of the structure of moral powers. Moral theory is important as a part of the philosophy of the human mind, but not as a part of morals.

Common Sense

It is usual to think of Reid as the apostle of "common sense." The term occurs frequently in his writings, not always with the same meaning. In some places, it means "good sense"—that degree of reason that makes a person capable of managing his or her own affairs and answerable in his or her conduct toward others. In other places, it refers to the opinions of the person in the street. In the technical sense that came to characterize the system of Reid and of the Scottish school, it stands for that part of people's mental constitution by which they know the truth of the principles or axioms that underlie all experience and all inference and are the indispensable foundations of science and morality.

> We ascribe to reason two offices, or two degrees. The first is to judge of things self-evident; the second to draw conclusions that are not self-evident from those that are. The first of these is the province, and the sole province, of common sense; and, therefore, it coincides with reason in its whole extent, and is only another name for one branch or one degree of reason.

The most obvious difference between the two kinds of reason mentioned here is that, whereas the second is "learned by practice and rules," the first is "purely natural, and therefore common to the learned and the unlearned, to the trained and the untrained." Whatever the difficulties of formulating its deliverances, there is, native to the human mind, a capacity to grasp the essential truths concerning human existence.

Common sense, so understood, underlies the realism of Scottish philosophy. In his analysis of experience, Reid avoided sensationism and nominalism only because, at each critical juncture, he refused to wear the blinders of technical reason. He professed to repudiate metaphysics, and he agreed with his age that humans ought to content themselves with observed laws and phenomena. He was little disposed, however, to measure heaven with a span.

> A man who is possessed of the genuine spirit of philosophy will think it impiety to contaminate the divine workmanship, by mixing it with those fictions of human fancy, called theories and hypotheses, which will always bear the signature of human folly, no less than the other does of divine wisdom.

John Linnell

Additional Reading

Beanblossom, Ronald E., and Keith Lehrer, eds. *Thomas Reid's Inquiry and Essays*. Indianapolis, Ind.: Hackett, 1983. This inexpensive paperback contains generous selections from Reid's published writings.

Dalgarno, Melvin, and Eric Matthews, eds. *The Philosophy of Thomas Reid*. Boston: Kluwer Academic, 1989. The essays in this anthology are representative of the current interest in Reid's philosophy.

Diamond, Peter J. *Common Sense and Improvement: Thomas Reid as Social Theorist*. New York: Peter Lang, 1998. A keen study of Reid's thoughts on social theory.

Fraser, Alexander C. *Thomas Reid*. Bristol: Thoemmes Press, 1993. An informative and thorough biography of Thomas Reid.

Gallie, Roger D. *Thomas Reid: Ethics, Aesthetics, and the Anatomy of the Self*. Boston: Klumer Academic, 1998. An important evaluation of Reid's moral philosophy and his aesthetics aimed at the advanced undergraduate to graduate level.

Lehrer, Keith. *Thomas Reid*. New York: Routledge, 1989. An excellent introduction to Reid's thought.

Rowe, William L. *Thomas Reid on Freedom and Morality*. Ithaca, N.Y.: Cornell University Press, 1991. In this fine study of Reid's *Essays on the Active Powers of Man*, Rowe develops a defense of Reid's theory of human freedom.

Robert B. Kruschwitz

Nicholas Rescher

Rescher not only contributed significantly to logic, philosophy of science, and the history of philosophy but also developed a system of pragmatic idealism that placed him squarely in the mainstream of the history of American philosophy.

Principal philosophical works: *Distributive Justice: A Constructive Critique of the Utilitarian Theory of Distribution*, 1966; *The Philosophy of Leibniz*, 1967; *The Coherence Theory of Truth*, 1973; *A Theory of Possibility: A Constructivistic and Conceptualistic Account of Possible Individuals and Possible Worlds*, 1975; *Methodological Pragmatism: A Systems-Theoretic Approach to the Theory of Knowledge*, 1977; *Scientific Progress: A Philosophical Essay on the Economics of Research in Natural Science*, 1978; *Cognitive Systematization: A Systems-Theoretic Approach to a Coherentist Theory of Knowledge*, 1979; *The Logic of Inconsistency: A Study in Non-standard Possible-World Semantics and Ontology*, 1979; *Induction: An Essay on the Justification of Inductive Reasoning*, 1980; *The Limits of Science*, 1984; *The Strife of Systems: An Essay on the Grounds and Implications of Philosophical Diversity*, 1985; *Ethical Idealism: An Inquiry into the Nature and Function of Ideals*, 1987; *Rationality: A Philosophical Inquiry into the Nature and the Rationale of Reason*, 1988; *Pluralism: Against the Demand for Consensus*, 1993; *A System of Pragmatic Idealism*, 1992-1994 (3 volumes); *Objectivity: The Obligations of Impersonal Reason*, 1997; *Communicative Pragmatism and Other Philosophical Essays on Language*, 1998.

Born: July 15, 1928; Hagen, Westphalia, Germany

Early Life
In 1938, Nicholas Rescher and his mother emigrated to the United States from Germany to join his father, who had arrived in New York a year earlier. The elder Rescher had made the decision to leave Germany when his law practice began to lose clients after 1933, partly because of his antipathy to Nazism. Rescher quickly became Americanized, a process abetted by the Beechurst community where he lived and the school on Long Island Sound he attended. However, during his adolescence he had an acute awareness of the cultural difference between the Old and the New Worlds and of his being something of a cultural amphibian who belonged to both. He consequently retreated from the life of society to the life of the mind and cultivated the habits of introspection and reflection.

In 1942, the economic conditions spawned by World War II forced his father to sell his business at a considerable loss. That same year, the Reschers moved to Armonk, Westchester County. During high school, Rescher discovered his aptitude and interest in mathematics, particularly algebra. He was naturalized as an American citizen in 1944. In 1945, he read Will Durant's *Story of Philosophy* (1926), which awakened his interest in philosophy. He went on to read the works of thinkers such as René Descartes, David Hume, and Arthur Schopenhauer. He was particularly interested in logic, where philosophy and mathematics intersected.

In 1946, he entered Queens College in New York, majoring in philosophy and mathematics. He continued to study classical languages and to read extensively in world literature, believing that the culture transmitted by the academy was integral and that inquiry in any one field fed inquiries in others. He eventually chose philosophy over mathematics because, although proficient in mathematics, he felt he lacked that facility in the field that made for true distinction. Philosophy appealed to him because of the importance and challenge of its questions and the beauty and rigor of logic. Furthermore, this field gave him ample scope to indulge his generalist bent and enabled him to integrate his interests in the sciences and humanities. Among his teachers at Queens were Carl G. Hempel, Donald Davidson, and Arnold Isenberg.

Rescher began graduate studies in philosophy at Princeton University in 1949. There he studied logic under Alonzo Church; the philosophies of F. H. Bradley, Alfred North Whitehead, and Bertrand Russell under Walter T. Stace, whose interest in mysticism and deep commitment to philosophy impressed him; and epistemology with Paul Ushenko, whose book on logic he had read in high school.

During his first year of graduate studies, Rescher—stimulated by Russell's *A Critical Exposition of the Philosophy of Leibniz* (1900) and philosopher Louis Couturat's *La Logique de Leibniz* (1901; Leibniz's logic)—wrote an essay on Gottfried Wilhelm von Leibniz's cosmology, which dealt specifically with Leibniz's application of science to philosophy. He was intrigued by Leibniz's multifaceted thought and his method of using logic and mathematical symbols to solve philosophical problems, a method that would become Rescher's own. His interest lay not so much in Leibniz's doctrines as in his method. Rescher felt an affinity with this philosopher because he confronted a period of upheaval in philosophy represented by the advent of Cartesianism. Rescher's *The Coherence Theory of Truth* was in part inspired by Leibniz. His interest in Leibniz took a practical turn when he became a member of the council of the International Leibniz Society and of the editorial board of *Studia Leibnitiana*, its official journal, and helped organize the American Leibniz Society. From 1951 to 1953, Church enlisted Rescher as a reviewer for *The Journal of Symbolic Logic*. In the same period, Rescher collaborated with Paul Oppenheim on an essay that analyzed logically the concept of the gestalt; this represented his entry into the philosophy of science. He received a doctorate in 1952.

Life's Work

From 1952 to 1954, Rescher served in the U.S. Marine Corps, where he was employed in amphibious reconnaissance and in the administra-

tion of correspondence courses at the Marine Corps Institute. He attributed his later indefatigableness in writing philosophy to a need to compensate for the time wasted during these two years. However, his military service did give him invaluable practical experience of the "real world" and contributed to his later reflections on the issues of life as well as thought. Between 1954 and 1956, he went to work in the Mathematics Division of the Corporation for Research and Development (the Rand Corporation), a military think tank in Santa Monica, California. His projects were to determine how much damage the U.S. economy could sustain in an aerial bombardment yet remain militarily viable and to assess the human and economic impact of a Soviet nuclear attack on the United States. His work at Rand helped him lay the theoretical foundations for the Delphi method of expert prediction.

Religion played only a marginal role in Rescher's boyhood and youth. However, he became increasingly receptive to it because his experiences as a refugee and as a soldier during the Korean War made him realize the radical contingency and vulnerability of human existence. Following his mother's example, he attended the Friends Meeting in Santa Monica. He was impressed by the warmth of the Quakers, by their idea of a still, small voice calling one to higher things, and by the utter simplicity and silence of their way of worship. He particularly liked the Friends' lack of any creed that might give a philosophical skeptic pause and their peaceful resolution of conflict (the need for which was brought home to him during his stints at Rand and in the Marines). His increased commitment to Christianity was the highlight of his California years and a factor in his decision to leave Rand. At the think tank, Rescher learned the value of collaboration in research and the usefulness of empirical inquiries in the social sciences as the basis for social philosophy. It also gave him the opportunity to develop an intimate knowledge of the practical issues of public policy.

From 1957 to 1961, Rescher taught philosophy at Lehigh University in Bethlehem, Pennsylvania. There his interest in the pre-Socratic philosophers was reawakened, and he pioneered work in the joint fields of the history and the philosophy of science. The cousin of Rescher's father, Osker Rescher, a distinguished but eccentric scholar of Asian languages who had converted to Islam and lived in Istanbul, sparked Rescher's interest in Arabic. Rescher promptly learned the language and used it to read Arabic philosophers, especially logicians such as Al-Farabi. Among the fruits of his research was the restoration of the text of a polemical tract by Alexander of Aphrodisias, a commentator on Aristotle. The original Greek text had been lost, and the work survived only in an Arabic translation. In 1961, he joined the philosophy department at the University of Pittsburgh.

A signal event in Rescher's life was his formal reception in 1981 into the Roman Catholic Church. From 1966, he had begun to worship regularly in the Church, being particularly drawn by the drama of its liturgy. His Christian commitment was motivated more by feeling than by thought. On the whole, he felt a greater intellectual and personal kinship with believers, among whom he felt at home, than with nonbelievers. Religion put things in perspective for Rescher and accommodated his insight that life has more questions than answers. His theology was liberal and pluralistic. His membership in the Catholic Church reinforced his belief that adherence to tradition and the observance of traditional rituals and ceremonies were essential to a civilized life.

Rescher was a polymath who, in more than fifty books and two hundred articles, contributed—sometimes significantly—to virtually every field of philosophy. Of his many contributions to the history of philosophy, his *The Philosophy of Leibniz* stands out. He also wrote works in the fledgling field of medical ethics, logic, epistemology, the philosophy of science, metaphysics, and social philosophy. Rescher began with abstract and theoretical issues in mathematics and logic, moved to the philosophy of the natural sciences (biology, cosmology) and the social sciences (economics), and then addressed issues in philosophical anthropology (human culture).

Like Leibniz, Rescher was more than a cloistered scholar; he was engaged in the practical affairs of founding and editing journals and administering academic societies and organizations. He helped found the *American Philosophical*

Quarterly (1964), founded the *History of Philosophy Quarterly* (1984) and the *Public Affairs Quarterly* (1987), and organized *The Journal of Philosophical Logic* (1971). He served as secretary of the Logic, Methodology, and Philosophy of Science branch of the International Union of History and Philosophy of Science (1969-1975) and as the administrative director of the Philosophy of Science Center at Pittsburgh. He was named to the board of directors of the International Federation of Philosophical Societies and elected president of the Eastern Division of the American Philosophical Association (1989-1990). His manifold accomplishments earned him a number of awards, including the Doctorate of Humane Letters from Loyola University and the Humanities Research Prize from the Alexander von Humboldt Foundation.

Influence

Rescher's mission in philosophy was to tackle the perennial questions that were jettisoned by positivism using contemporary and rigorous methods of logical analysis along with the resources of the past. Rescher's own continuity with the history of philosophy is evident in his rehabilitation of the historical movements of idealism and pragmatism and his implementation of the methodology of Leibniz. A persistent theme in Rescher's philosophy is human limitations and the imperfection (and imperfectability) of human knowledge. However, he does not succumb to skepticism, nihilism, or relativism, all of which he roundly rejects. He argues on pragmatic grounds that there is an objective reality that is intelligible, the truth of which can be obtained by human reason; and though perfect knowledge is impossible, adequate knowledge for the realization of human ends is not.

Perhaps Rescher's crowning achievement is his trilogy, *A System of Pragmatic Idealism*, a synthesis and systematization of his multifaceted thought. In this work, he presents a system of pragmatic idealism. This system is idealistic insofar as it affirms the mind's active role in the construction of reality; however, it also acknowledges that people's interests and needs, arising adventitiously from their environment, constrain and restrain their subjectivity. It is pragmatic insofar as it values what works well for all human beings as opposed to what works well for one individual or a select group; hence, this pragmatism is *objective*, not *subjective*. Undergirding this trilogy is the idea of the dynamic and evolutionary character of human thought, derived from George Wilhelm Friedrich Hegel and Charles Sanders Peirce.

Rescher is a quintessentially American philosopher inasmuch as he—like Peirce, C. I. Lewis, and W. V. O. Quine—fused analytic technique with historical concerns and rehabilitated the specifically American philosophy of pragmatism. Moreover, Rescher is intellectually kin to Josiah Royce, a classic American philosopher who was also a pragmatic idealist. Rescher's philosophical reputation rests on the following achievements: first, the revival of idealism within the analytic tradition; second, a theory of induction and scientific method based on the coherence theory of truth; third, the reconception of pragmatism; fourth, the development of a logic that accommodates inconsistency and the rediscovery of the medieval Arabic logicians' theory of temporal modality; fifth, a theory of progress in the sciences; and sixth, a critique of utilitarian ethics. With respect to his enormous output and the wide range of his achievements, he has few rivals in the history of philosophy. His philosophical system is a monument of twentieth century philosophy.

Richard A. Spurgeon Hall

Objectivity

The Obligations of Impersonal Reason

Type of philosophy: Epistemology, metaphysics, ethics, axiology, ontology
First published: 1997
Principal ideas advanced:

◇ Objectivity is grounded in human reason and seeks to transcend the limitations imposed by personal interests and inclinations and establish uniform standards of rationality valid for all persons.

◇ The reality of objectivity is disclosed by the fact that some means are more effective and expeditious than others in realizing ends (especially cognitive ones).

◇ Objectivity is a necessary postulate of human communication that presupposes the existence of an objective order, the truths of which can be communicated.

◇ Objectivity is a necessary postulate of experience and knowledge of the world; faith in objectivity is vindicated pragmatically by its fruitfulness in advancing scientific knowledge.

◇ Moral laws and principles are objective because morality is a functional institution that involves achieving practically worthwhile ends; moral objectivity is rooted in the inherent rationality of morality.

◇ Certain values, having to do with what is truly in one's best interest, are objective insofar as they may conflict with and stand in judgment over one's personal desires.

Nicholas Rescher's *Objectivity: The Obligations of Impersonal Reason* is his critique of the subversion of objectivity and rationality by three intellectual trends that gathered steam in the last quarter of the twentieth century. The first of these trends was cultural relativism, a dogma of the social sciences that maintained that because codes of value emerge from and depend on particular cultures, there is no way to judge their relative superiority and, therefore, they are all equally valid. The second trend was a liberal egalitarianism that denied that any set of values (particularly Western values) is superior to another and urged tolerance of them all. The third trend was postmodernism, which contended that there are no objective, transcendent, and absolute values in the world such as truth, goodness, and beauty, and that the normative distinctions between truth and fiction, or sense and nonsense, are wholly subjective.

Rescher's aim in this volume is to defend the claim of objectivity against its various cultured despisers. He argues that a relativistic indifference to truth and rightness is inherently self-destructive and self-contradictory. To abandon objective standards of truth in fields such as physics, history, and ethics is in effect to abandon those fields altogether. The source of objectivity, Rescher claims, is found in human rationality itself. Thus, to relinquish objectivity is nothing less than to relinquish reason. He conceives of rationality in terms of pragmatism (the view that the meaning and truth of a statement is the sum of its logical and physical consequences) and the coherence theory of truth (the view that the truth of a statement is determined by its consistency with other statements in a system of logically consistent statements). The prestige of objectivity suffered a decline among some thinkers in the last quarter of the twentieth century because either its link to rationality was not understood or, if it was, rationality itself was disparaged for some reason.

Objectivity requires putting aside one's prejudices and personal preferences in choosing one's beliefs, values, and actions and instead following the dictates of impartial reason—in other words, consulting one's head rather than one's heart. Reason is universal: What is rational for one person to believe, value, or do must be so for anyone else in the same situation. Reason does not accommodate itself to the idiosyncratic needs, dispositions, or needs of any individual. Though it does not ignore differences in people's situations or contexts, rationality (objectivity) stipulates that people in similar contexts ought to believe, evaluate, and act in uniform ways.

Misunderstanding Objectivity

Various academic groups have attacked objectivity for different reasons. Some anthropologists have claimed that different cultures have different kinds of rationality, none of which is universal and transcendent. Some historians and sociologists have despaired of ever attaining objectivity in their respective fields. Personalists have believed that objectivity conflicts with our humanity. Feminist epistemologists and Marxists have thought that objectivity, even if attainable, would be undesirable. Postmodernists have regarded all claims to objective truth as specious and nothing more than subjective opinions. Social activists have deemed objectivity illegitimate because it is incompatible with personal commitment. However, Rescher contends that all these attacks are based on misunderstandings of the nature of objectivity.

One such misunderstanding is that one must enter into a consensus or agreement with others concerning truth to meet objectivity's requirement that personal idiosyncrasies be ignored. However, this is not so. Consensus does not guarantee the truth at which objectivity aims; only in an ideal world would consensus be a decisive indicator of truth. However, in some disciplines—science, for example—consensus is epistemically significant; and in the realm of general principles, with which philosophy deals, its pursuit may be fruitful.

A second misunderstanding is that objectivity requires one to ignore the fact that knowledge and truth necessarily emerge from a specific culture or a particular kind of collective experience. Thus, cognitive relativism, which denies that there is a body of objectively true knowledge against which all claims to knowledge must be judged, rejects objectivity. It does so on the basis of an egalitarianism according to which there are different criteria of truth, each criterion being determined by the particular social group from which it emerges, with none being more valid than any other. However, its claim that there are equivalent "alternative standards of rationality" is incoherent; there is only a single, decisive standard of rationality. However, a uniform rational standard does not mean that rationality may not be exercised in diverse contexts or within different domains of experience; it does not demand a uniformity in human experience. Indeed, the exercise of reason is bound to particular social and cultural contexts. Cognitive relativists fail to realize that human activities, particularly scientific inquiry, are purposive, and certain procedures are more effective in realizing those purposes than others. Hence, the effectiveness of the means used to achieve one's ends provides a criterion of the objective adequacy of those means to their ends.

A third misunderstanding of objectivity is that it reduces all human experience and knowledge to that which can be quantified and measured. However, Rescher states that objectivity does not presuppose quantification, and quantification by itself does not guarantee objectivity. Furthermore, measurement is something more than quantification; only occasionally do quantities actually measure anything. Measurement is a sufficient but not necessary condition for objectivity.

To the objection that the quest for cognitive objectivity does not guarantee certain success in human endeavors, Rescher replies pragmatically that the best hope people have of achieving their goals is through rational means, which presuppose an objective basis. Being rational in pursuit of ends makes more sense than not.

Objective Reality

Rescher demonstrates that objectivity is a necessary presupposition of language and science: It is a postulate that makes these activities possible. Thus, ordinary language is committed to the existence of objective standards of truth. The existence of an intercommunicative community fosters objectivity. People's beliefs about the world are always provisional; the correctness of their beliefs depends upon their rightly discovering the important properties of things. However, discovery of these properties depends on human intercommunication over time. Thus, human thought and knowledge revolve around the possibility of communal inquiry into and interpersonal communication about an objective order of things. Without the assumption of that objective reality, human intercommunication about a shared world would cease to work. The existence of objective knowledge rests on the existence of an objective reality that serves as a functional or "regulative" presupposition of it. Ontological objectivity is not discovered but postulated. If people's purely subjective opinions wholly determined reality, then communication and the advance of knowledge would be impracticable.

Physical objects, which help make up the real world, cannot be perfectly known. This means that the world people know is only a limited part of the world that exists. This limited knowledge of the world suggests that there is a vaster reality out there independent of people's minds (the thesis of metaphysical realism). This objective reality is not discovered through experience but is presupposed by people's experience and empirical inquiries. Its presupposition (postulation) is justified not by evidence but by its enabling people to learn and know. Objective reality, then, is a functional postulate of experience and knowledge, it is ultimately justified pragmatically by being an essential part of a useful and necessary cognitive enterprise (the sciences).

Objectivity and Values

Rescher next turns to the objectivity in value theory, particularly ethics. Morality, by definition, claims to be objectively true, and therefore to reduce it to subjectivity is to abandon it. Morality is an inherently functional institution insofar as it serves a purpose. Moral reasoning and disputes are possible only because morality is functional. Because morality involves the goods in life that people should pursue, there can be rational thought about the nature of these goods and how best to acquire them. Though the moral codes operative in various cultures differ, the moral principles underlying all these codes display a functional uniformity. Despite the diversity among moral codes, the moral code of a particular society should be normative for its citizens. Morality formulates moral rules and duties that are objective and universal, which means that all human beings must abide by them and that they are rational and true. Moral rules and obligations get their objective force from neither the social benefits that will accrue from abiding by them (utilitarianism) nor from a mutual promise to obey them (the social contract), but solely from their inherent rationality. Because moral principles are part of rational principles, which are absolutely true and universal, moral principles share these characteristics. Obeying moral rules and meeting obligations benefits everyone; thus, the polity of a just society will seek to harmonize morality with the self-interest of individuals.

The issue of whether values in general (moral and nonmoral) are objective boils down to the issue of whether rational thought about them is possible. Philosophers who are disciples of Scottish philosopher David Hume claim that values are purely subjective, being nothing but expressions of personal desire—of people's wants and preferences. However, humans have interests that may conflict with their desires and determine their validity. As soon as people start seriously to evaluate what is really in their best interest, independently of whether they desire it, they commit themselves to a rational activity. That people can rationally weigh their values means that they are not merely subjective but have a rational and, therefore, objective element.

Rationality and Texts

Rescher finally considers objectivity as it applies to the interpretation and meaning of texts. He claims, against deconstructionists, that texts do have an objective meaning that is rationally discoverable. Deconstruction, a relativist theory about the meaning of texts, holds that no one interpretation of a text is correct or true to the exclusion of other interpretations and, therefore, that all interpretations are equally valid. The meaning of a text is purely subjective and relative to its reader's viewpoint. However, notes Rescher, deconstructionists woefully misunderstand and underestimate the critical role played by a text's broadest context in its interpretation. Indeed, it is the consistency of the interpretation of a text with its context—how well its presumed meaning fits in with the larger meaning of its background—that helps determine whether that interpretation is the right one and provides the basis for its rationality and objectivity. In communication, people's purposes help establish whether their interpretations are appropriate or not.

It is perhaps a psychological necessity that each person has a private domain where subjectivity is the rule and one's imagination is given free play, where one can freely indulge one's prejudices, biases, idiosyncrasies, whims, and personal peculiarities. However, this necessity, if it is a fact, is objective and is disclosed to one by rational inquiry. There is, then, no limit to the scope of rational objectivity because it determines even the fact and propriety of a subjective domain.

Objectivity is significant because it defends the values of objectivity and rationality using pragmatism and the coherence theory of truth. More specifically, it demonstrates how pragmatism, which originated as a theory of scientific explanation, can be fruitfully used to combat subjectivism, skepticism, nihilism, relativism, and other manifestations of the cult of irrationality. It also shows the continuing relevance of pragmatism, which is arguably the United States' most distinc-

tive contribution to the history of philosophy, and demonstrates the relevance of the coherence theory of truth to domains outside its traditional ones of philosophy and the sciences.

Richard A. Spurgeon Hall

Additional Reading

Almeder, Robert, ed. *Praxis and Reason: Studies in the Philosophy of Nicholas Rescher*. Washington, D.C.: University Press of America, 1982. This volume, which is intended for specialists, considers specifically Nicholas Rescher's pragmatism and theory of truth.

Marsonet, Michele. *The Primacy of Practical Reason: An Essay on Nicholas Rescher's Philosophy*. Washington, D.C.: University Press of America, 1995. This is perhaps the best introduction for the general reader because it deals synoptically with Rescher's philosophy. It puts the philosopher's thought in historical perspective as well as locates its place in contemporary philosophical thought.

Pragmatic Idealism: Critical Essays on Nicholas Rescher's System of Pragmatic Idealism. Atlanta, Ga.: Rodopi, 1998. This book, addressed to specialists in the field, is a discussion of different perspectives of Rescher's distinctive philosophical system.

Rescher, Nicholas. *Instructive Journey: An Essay in Autobiography*. Lanham, Md.: University Press of America, 1997. This informative work introduces the man as well as the philosopher and is particularly valuable in showing how Rescher's distinctive ideas emerged from his life's experience.

Sosa, Ernest, ed. *The Philosophy of Nicholas Rescher: Discussion and Replies*. Boston: Kluwer Academic, 1979. This book records the discussion of Rescher by Ernest Sosa and L. Jonathan Cohen together with Rescher's responses to their critique. It is most suitable for advanced readers who already have some background in Rescher's thought.

Richard A. Spurgeon Hall

Richard Rorty

Rorty revitalized the pragmatism and naturalism of William James and John Dewey by incorporating elements of linguistically oriented analytic philosophy, critiquing the quests for certainty and for the foundations of knowledge and championing creative individualism, political liberalism, and a consciousness of existential uncertainty.

Principal philosophical works: "Mind-Body Identity, Privacy, and Categories," 1965; *The Linguistic Turn: Recent Essays in Philosophical Method*, 1967, 2d ed. 1992; *Philosophy and the Mirror of Nature*, 1979; *Consequences of Pragmatism: Essays, 1972-1980*, 1982; "Contemporary Philosophy of Mind," 1982; "Diskussion/Discussion: A Reply to Six Critics," 1984; "Thugs and Theorists: A Reply to Bernstein," 1987; *Contingency, Irony, and Solidarity*, 1989; *Objectivity, Relativism, and Truth: Philosophical Papers*, 1989; *Essays on Heidegger and Others: Philosophical Papers*, 1991; "Feminism, Ideology, and Deconstruction: A Pragmatist View," 1993; "Putnam and the Relativist Menace," 1993; "Does Academic Freedom Have Philosophical Presuppositions?" 1994; "'Who Are We?' Moral Universalism and Economic Triage," 1996; *Achieving Our Country: Leftist Thought in Twentieth Century America*, 1998.

Born: October 4, 1931; New York, New York

Early Life

Born in New York City, Richard McKay Rorty recalls a childhood of politics and culture. His parents were active antimilitarists and temporarily members of the Communist Party. They broke with the Party in 1932 when they realized the extent to which it was run from Moscow. "Because my father had once been thrown in jail for reporting on a strike, I associated the police with goon squads who, in those days, were regularly hired to beat up strikers." As a teenager, Rorty knew personally many of the so-called New York intellectuals who were political leftists and staunchly anti-Stalinist.

At the age of fourteen, after skipping several grades in school and with literary aspirations, Rorty enrolled as an undergraduate at the University of Chicago. At the age of seventeen, he decided to become a philosopher, and he began studying pragmatism, the history of philosophy, and newly developing analytical philosophy. As a graduate student at Yale, he wrote his doctoral dissertation on Aristotle and Alfred North Whitehead. Rorty's first, most conventional, writings

appeared in the early 1960's. Articles on the mind-body problem, Whitehead, metaphilosophy, and pragmatism evidenced Rorty's broad interests and his appreciation of many competing schools of philosophy.

Life's Work

With the development of modern formal logic at the turn of the century, logic and linguistic analysis became increasingly central to Anglo-American philosophy. Rorty's anthology *The Linguistic Turn: Recent Essays in Philosophical Method* collected pieces written during the previous fifty years that exhibited "the reasons which originally led philosophers in England and America to adopt linguistic methods, the problems they faced in defending their conception of philosophical inquiry, alternative solutions to these problems, and the situation in which linguistic philosophers now find themselves." Thirty years later, Rorty described his anthology as trying and failing "to explain what was so important about linguistic method in philosophy." The linguistic method is one of many approaches that Rorty came to reject; however, the rejection is combined with an appreciation that it was "genuine philo-

Richard Rorty. *(Princeton University Library)*

Darwinian pragmatism and naturalism of American philosophers William James and John Dewey to reflect the claims and concerns of analytic philosophy. Second, he venerates the fecundity, artistic self-creation, playfulness, and irony that he finds in writers such as Jacques Derrida, Vladimir Nabokov, and Marcel Proust. Third, Rorty defends a version of liberalism strongly influenced by the socialist tradition. The final theme is also found in existentialism (philosophers such as Friedrich Nietzsche and Jean-Paul Sartre): God is dead, the good is contingent and precarious, and people should be wary of the temptation to recreate God, to find something bigger and better to idolize (such as science, a political party, tradition, language, or one's true self).

Philosophy and the Mirror of Nature, a complex book with many themes, catapulted Rorty to international prominence. The most discussed part was Rorty's attack on analytic philosophy as insufficiently historical and presumptuous in its search for a philosophical method that distinguished legitimate from illegitimate knowledge claims. The attack drew attention because Rorty, then a professor at Princeton, was writing from within a stronghold of analytic philosophy. Rorty rejected the hope of analytical philosophy to make philosophy more like a science and to develop logical and linguistic methods to authorize legitimate inferences and justifiable concepts. Rorty maintained that insufficient awareness of history made analytical philosophers imagine themselves pursuing a timeless quest; they tended to forget their subject's recent and idiosyncratic origins with German philosopher Immanuel Kant.

By noting his debt to James and especially to Dewey, Rorty highlights many features of his philosophy: (1) a philosophical appreciation of naturalist Charles Darwin's demonstration that humans are on a continuum with nonhuman animals, (2) the denial of metaphysical and moral realism, (3) fallibilism and the anti-Cartesian point that doubt needs as much justification as

sophical progress" to focus on language rather than the more nebulous concepts of consciousness and experience, as previous philosophers had done.

In the late 1960's, Rorty's marriage to Amelie Oksenberg Rorty began to come apart, and he went through a personal and professional crisis that he later termed a year of clinical depression. Although he was unable to write during this period, he examined John Dewey's work and found in it a way of connecting philosophy to the optimism and sense of possibility found in the works of such writers as Ralph Waldo Emerson and Walt Whitman, and in American culture in general. In 1972, he met and married Mary Varney.

Four themes run through Rorty's mature writings. First, Rorty modifies and extends the post-belief, (4) the recognition that cognition and reasoning evolve and are collective, (5) an account of morality that avoids both absolutism and skepticism, (6) the refusal to draw sharp fact/value or science/nonscience lines, and (7) the embrace of democracy and left liberalism. Significant differences also exist between Rorty's philosophy and that of his predecessors. For example, Rorty views humans as created through socialization and denies that there is any such thing as human nature, whereas Dewey's philosophy of education rests on a rich conception of human nature.

Consequences of Pragmatism, which collects Rorty's essays from the 1970's, clarifies his identification with both Dewey's and philosopher Ludwig Wittgenstein's opposition to philosophical theories. Donald Davidson, a sophisticated philosopher of language, emerges as a key figure in helping Rorty work out the technical details of his neopragmatism. Reaching beyond the Anglo-American tradition, Rorty finds and highlights commonalities with Martin Heidegger and Jacques Derrida. He criticizes what he sees as the excessively narrow, overly technical professionalism of most academic philosophy. Reflecting his keen reservations about academic philosophy and his broadening cultural interests, Rorty left Princeton in 1982 to become a professor of the humanities at the University of Virginia.

Analytical philosophers are the intended audience for *Philosophy and the Mirror of Nature*; Rorty's later writings, including *Contingency, Irony, and Solidarity*, are those of a public intellectual addressing the educated public. The word "contingency" in the title sounds existential themes; "irony" echoes the romantic rebel; and "solidarity" signals social concerns. Like Nietzsche and Sartre, Rorty envisions life without God or what Rorty takes as God's shadows, namely, moral absolutes, perfect objectivity, atemporal truth independent of human reality, or "something other and bigger." People are walk-ons who must improvise and cope as best they can. Rorty champions an ironic stance that recognizes people's metaphysical rootlessness and worries that the language and socialization with which people are at home may be faulty—faulty not in God's eyes, but faulty by people's own considered judgment, developed in conversation with others.

Rorty recognizes that many people will feel homeless and adrift (nihilistic) if they accept his philosophy of radical contingency. For example, Russian writer Fyodor Dostoevski said, "If God does not exist, everything is permitted." Rorty turns to American poet Whitman and to Dewey for a liberal philosophy of hope, decency, and community that acknowledges human contingency. Upon leaving home, a young adult may feel lost or may feel liberated; Rorty would have people delight in the freedom and the possibilities of liberation.

Contingency, Irony, and Solidarity contains an imaginative response to traditional concerns about the appropriate relationship between the individual and the state (or community). Rorty stresses a classical liberal dichotomy (as exemplified in the thought of John Stuart Mill) between the public and the private spheres; the need for experimental, piecemeal improvements ("meliorism"); and the importance of irony. For Rorty, imagination, irony, and creativity, if restricted to private life, are all to the good, but the public sphere requires rules and regulations. By locating the individual's search for perfection in the private sphere, Rorty is explicitly at odds with Greek philosopher Aristotle as well as most political philosophers, who tend to give primacy to the public sphere.

Rorty maintains that novels, films, and television have long since taken over from philosophy the social role of educating the young. By the 1980's, Rorty wrote as often on literary topics, particularly the novels of Vladimir Nabokov, George Orwell, and Marcel Proust, as on philosophy; these essays foreshadow Rorty's becoming a professor of comparative literature at Stanford University in 1998.

Achieving Our Country: Leftist Thought in Twentieth Century America is unique among Rorty's works in being partially autobiographical and being primarily devoted to American social movements and politics. Strongly identifying with the pursuit of social justice, Rorty concerns himself primarily with the relative silence and ineffectiveness of liberals and "the Left" during the 1980's and 1990's as the distribution of income and benefits became increasingly skewed toward the affluent. He calls for a revitalization of political liberalism by focusing on concrete problems: the large percentage of the American population that have no health care insurance, the extraordinary influence of money in politics, and the decline in working-class politics and union membership.

Rorty champions a position at odds both with the Right (conservatives) and with many on the Left (liberals and socialists). Describing himself as a patriot in the tradition of Whitman and Dewey, Rorty attacks the Right as the party of the status quo, dedicated to maintaining and expanding enormous inequality. The Right is unwilling to sufficiently acknowledge a legacy of slavery, discrimination, American Indian genocide, and social inequality. Rorty also faults the Left, which, since the Vietnam War in the early 1970's, has been so absorbed with what is and has been wrong with the United States that it insufficiently acknowledges an often laudable past (for example, labor organizer and socialist Eugene Debs and civil rights activist Martin Luther King, Jr.) and the potential for a better future. From Rorty's perspective, too many of society's effective agents are on the Right, furthering the interests of the affluent, and too many on the Left are content to be disheartened, knowing spectators. The greedy, Rorty maintains, reshape the world to their ends while the opposition spins out grand, gothic theories along the lines of philosopher Michel Foucault about how awful things are. The progressive social movements of the last third of the twentieth century—feminism, gay rights, multiculturalism, and environmentalism—are praised for their goals but challenged by Rorty for their insularity.

Rorty criticizes Leftists who continue to study Karl Marx. Contrary to Marxism, he says, revolutions merely exchange one set of rulers for another, there are no iron laws of history, and the working class is not an agent of change with privileged insight. Rorty perceives that Marxism, like God, is dead. He longs for a time when Marx's evolutionary theories feel as Victorian and quaint as those of English philosopher Herbert Spencer do.

The four themes mentioned above in Rorty's work—philosophical pragmatism, romantic individualism, political liberalism, and existentialism—are sometimes at odds. For example, atheism can only hinder liberal politics in a nation of believers. Additionally, it is easy to slide from irony and a concern with artistic self-creation into political quietism. Still another tension is between the solidarity required by Dewey's community of inquirers and the autonomy demanded by the individualist.

Rorty's rhetorical style is enticing, potent, and sometimes frustrating. He combines engaging narratives, insightful summaries, pithy asides, and plainspoken metaphors with words in German, Latin, and ancient Greek; allusions to an astounding number of writers; and subtle distinctions. Deflationary and debunking tones overshadow the lyric and grand. Given to learned hyperbole, Rorty can irritate specialists by oversimplifying complex issues and reading selectively. His interpretations of the philosophers he heralds (such as Dewey or Derrida) are inevitably controversial. Rorty might respond that Socratic gadflies are useful irritants, and without such irritants it may be impossible to break through what Dewey called the crust of convention.

Rorty at times has appeared to be a postmodernist who denigrates philosophy as nothing more than a misguided collection of failed foundational projects and who favors the end of philosophy. He counters this misreading by identifying with the pragmatist and progressive traditions. To end philosophy of one sort, even the prevailing sort, is not to end philosophy. For Rorty, the nonfoundationalist elements within the philosophical tradition provide a rich set of tools and perspectives not found elsewhere.

Influence

Although Rorty was one of the most prominent philosophers in the world at the end of the twentieth century, his influence was marked by controversy. There are few Rortyans but numerous critics of Rortyism. Most critics rise to the defense of programs that he has attacked (such as conceptual analysis, neopositivism, realism, and poststructuralism).

The most common criticism of Rorty is that he is a relativist. Critics argue that without absolutes and eternal standards, anything might be believed. In response to this charge of relativism, Rorty stresses that although he rejects putative absolutes, he does not accept the sophomoric and self-refuting view that any belief is just as good as any other. He describes himself as an ethnocentrist who affirms the Western idea of rationality and thinks there are often immeasurably better reasons (by usual standards) for accepting a sentence rather than its negation. What Rorty denies is that there are moralities, standards for rationality, or foundations for knowledge that are independent of a culture and a way of life. Rorty is too erudite, stylish, and prolific to ignore, and his compelling skepticism, irony, liberal politics, and debunking style are a recipe for continued prominence and controversy.

Drew Christie

Philosophy and the Mirror of Nature

Type of philosophy: Epistemology
First published: 1979
Principal ideas advanced:

◇ People's vocabularies, languages, and theories are fallible tools for coping with human problems, not accurate representations of a human-independent truth or reality.

◇ It is unfortunate that the philosophical tradition has been dominated by foundational projects that attempt to provide general grounds for sharply distinguishing legitimate from illegitimate knowledge claims.

◇ Contemporary analytic philosophy, which uses logic and the analysis of language, often continues to pursue untenable, traditional foundational projects.

◇ Philosophical questions are not timeless questions that occur to any reflective person; rather, they are problems with a history that are embedded in a culture.

◇ Philosophers have been too slow to assimilate Charles Darwin's discovery that people are continuous with the nonhuman animals, a discovery with profound philosophical implications.

◇ There are no eternal essences or fundamental categories. Differences among the natural sciences, the human sciences, and the humanities are differences in degree, not differences of kind.

◇ There is no God. People are on their own and should celebrate their capacity for novelty, creation, and human betterment.

◇ Philosophy, reconceived as edification, has the important role of cultural critique and of promoting dialogue among the disciplines.

Richard Rorty describes himself as carrying on the tradition that he finds in his twentieth century philosophical heroes—John Dewey, Ludwig Wittgenstein, and Martin Heidegger—a tradition of debunking attempts to make philosophy scientific. Although the pretensions of intellectuals have often been mocked, Rorty's work stands out as a sophisticated, internal critique by one trained in analytical philosophy. *Philosophy and the Mirror of Nature* is the most detailed development of Rorty's critical side; his positive views are most fully expressed in *Contingency, Irony, and Solidarity* (1989).

One broad strand in Rorty's thought, instrumentalism, extends the pragmatist's thesis that good theories are tools that work and the post-Darwinian thesis that humans are one among many evolved species that are coping as best they can. A second broad strand in Rorty's thought continues what is called the disenchantment of the world that began with the Enlightenment and recalls German philosopher Friedrich Nietzsche's provocative statement, "God is dead." Rorty believes that people are on their own, without an intrinsic nature, and should celebrate their capacity for self-creation.

Responding to Logical Positivism

The most explicit influences on *Philosophy and the Mirror of Nature* are important responses to logical positivism that appeared in the 1950's and 1960's. The logical positivists, as influential as any philosophical movement in the first half of the twentieth century, regarded mathematics and the physical sciences as paradigms of knowledge. By contrast, art, morality, religion, and metaphysics were seen by the positivists as purely subjective. From their perspective, the social sciences and humanities were legitimate only insofar are they emulated the physical sciences. Logical positivism was widely criticized after World War II, and attacks by Wittgenstein, W. V. O. Quine, Wilfrid Sellars, and Thomas S. Kuhn on elements of positivism are key components in Rorty's philosophy.

Wittgenstein, who as a young philosopher was an important influence on the development of positivism, abandoned the movement in his later work, *Philosophical Investigations* (1953; bilingual German and English edition). Rejecting broad philosophical theories altogether, Wittgenstein came to see different practices and cultures as employing distinct "language games" that cannot be hierarchically ranked and are sometimes impossible to compare.

Since the work of eighteenth century German philosopher Immanuel Kant, philosophers have distinguished between analytical statements, which are true in virtue of the meaning of words (e.g., bachelors are unmarried), and all other statements, which they refer to as synthetic. The distinction is considered important by some philosophers because they view a prime task of philosophy as the analysis of meaning. Rorty follows Quine in rejecting the analytic/synthetic distinction. Quine, in his famous essay "Two Dogmas of Empiricism" (1951), gave three broad reasons for this rejection: the distinction cannot be defined without appeal to equally problematic terms such as "meaning," many statements are hard to classify, and no statement is immune to rejection based on new empirical evidence.

In "Empiricism and the Philosophy of Mind" (1956; published in book form in 1997), Sellars maintains that awareness in a linguistic affair and knowledge of sense impressions cannot provide an independent foundation for empirical knowledge because such knowledge presupposes extensive general knowledge. Rorty takes Sellars's critique to undermine the empiricist program of founding knowledge on unconceptualized, immediate experience.

Kuhn, a historian of science, challenged the positivist's image of strict scientific method in *The Structure of Scientific Revolutions* (1962). According to Kuhn's alternative picture, scientists either apply a prevailing theory or, during revolutionary periods, they engage in vigorous, nonrational debate concerning which theory ("paradigm") to accept. By offering extensive historical detail, Kuhn shows that the selection of scientific theories is not accomplished by the mechanical application of a scientific method.

Rorty contends that the picture that holds traditional philosophy captive is that of the mind as "a great mirror, containing various representations—some accurate, some not—and capable of being studied by pure, nonempirical methods." Rorty describes traditional philosophy as the attempt to use these special philosophical methods to inspect, polish, and repair the mirror to obtain more accurate representation. Positivism, with its goal of banishing metaphysics and making philosophy scientific, is the most prominent recent attempt to make philosophy foundational. Additional targets of Rorty's skepticism and debunking include "conceptual analysis," "phenomenological analysis," "explication of meanings," analysis of the "logic of language," and Kant's attempts to find the necessary presuppositions of any possible experience.

Historicism and the Nature of Science

Rorty emphasizes that philosophical problems are not eternal but are products of historical development. This perspective, known as "historicism," often weakens the grip of an idea by showing its context-specific, contingent evolution. To show that much of philosophy might be what he calls "optional" (best ignored), Rorty notes that the academic discipline now called philosophy did not achieve its current identity as a discipline distinct from science and religion until the mid-nineteenth century. Two key events preceded the creation of academic philosophy as a separate discipline. First, the development of science in the seventeenth century replaced metaphysics (speculation about the heavens and the Earth) with physics. Second, Kant discovered a plausible way to make philosophy foundational by allegedly revealing the necessary presuppositions and structure of knowledge.

The sometimes rocky relationship between science and religion has been a pivotal cultural question since the rise of modern science in the seventeenth century. For philosophers, the cluster of issues associated with science and religion has focused on the nature of justification for scientific and for moral propositions. Kant set the parameters for contemporary discussion by making a sharp distinction between the empirical (scientific) and moral realms, each with distinct forms of philosophical justification. The positivists followed Kant in making a sharp distinction but denied that moral statements were capable of justification. Rorty, like Dewey, refuses to draw sharp lines between facts and values or between science and nonscience, though he acknowledges that science and morality differ in subject matter. Furthermore, scientists are usually more likely to agree among themselves than are moralists. For Rorty, however, neither scientific nor moral statements reveal the true nature of things or correspond to an independent reality. Both scientific and moral statements are part of evolving human practices that are fallible ways of meeting human needs and goals. For Rorty, science and morality are no more capable (or in need of) a philosophical justification than are the rules of etiquette or the current conventions of artistic performance.

The Mind-Body Problem

The first of the three parts of *Philosophy and the Mirror of Nature* explores the mind-body problem because it is the "mind" that inspects the mirror of nature. Rorty recounts the history of philosophy to highlight the seventeenth century creation of the mind-body problem and the subsequent transformation of the problem that gave ontological prominence to a physical/mental dichotomy. Rorty is a materialist who believes that everything is physical and that as science progresses, descriptions using mental attributes will be replaced by physical descriptions. It is a physical world, and what people want to learn about pains will come from scientists studying the brains of people in pain. Consciousness, according to Rorty, is a natural phenomenon that is too often wrongly revered as a divine spark separating humans from beasts. Rorty stresses that humankind is merely one more species coping with reality as best it can. He is vigilant concerning ethereal interpretations of natural phenomena.

The Epistemology of Language

The central and most controversial part of *Philosophy and the Mirror of Nature* is part 2, "Mirroring." Rorty focuses on the epistemology (theory of knowledge) and the philosophy of language. The principal targets of his critique are philosophers, such as the positivists, who follow Kant in

thinking that philosophers can and should provide a foundation for knowledge. One foundational project is to show how knowledge of the external world is possible. Another is to provide timeless criteria for distinguishing good from bad theories, or legitimate from illegitimate approaches to inquiry. The most prevalent form of contemporary foundationalism is the view that science alone discovers truth, and further, that truth can be acquired only by appropriate application of the scientific method.

Philosophers have attempted to provide a foundation for knowledge by either grounding knowledge in perception (John Locke and the empiricist tradition) or determining the broad structure of knowledge (Kant and the rationalist tradition). According to Rorty, both of these strategies were decisively undermined in the twentieth century. He relies on Sellars's critique of empirical foundationalism in "Empiricism and the Philosophy of Mind" and on Quine's critique of the analytic/synthetic distinction that was first introduced by Kant.

For at least a century, a significant number of scientists and thinkers have maintained that physics is the paradigm of empirical knowledge; that all other sciences are reducible, at least in principle, to physics; and that the humanities and social sciences should strive to become more scientific (more like physics). A movement for the "unity of science" was a prominent part of positivism in the 1920's and 1930's. Rorty counters that theories do not mirror reality; rather, they are tools. Physics is just one among many vocabularies and languages, though one that is exceptionally fruitful in terms of prediction and control. Rorty also stresses that successful reductions (thermodynamics to molecular motion) are rare and that there is no reason to think that they will or should become the norm. Finally, it is misguided and harmful to hope to achieve the degree of consensus in all branches of inquiry that currently prevails in some parts of the physical sciences. It is harmful because it misdirects inquiry toward what is likely to be an unattainable and futile ideal. Disagreement in the humanities and the social sciences is a sign of health, not failure. Faced with the questions of what to value and what relations and institutions to create, humanity will always disagree and struggle. Rorty sees no hope of finding the one right answer, just as there is no hope of finding the one right way to interpret a novel. Hope lies in finding many better answers.

Hermeneutics and Edification
In the third and final part of *Philosophy and the Mirror of Nature*, Rorty endorses a picture of philosophy as hermeneutics and edification. The word "hermeneutics" is taken from Hans-Georg Gadamer's *Wahrheit und Methode: Grundzüge einer philsophischen Hermeneutik* (1960; *Truth and Method*; 1975). Rorty uses Gadamer's insight that interpreting a novel language or way of talking requires a fruitful back-and-forth exchange between learning specific words and learning the overall point. By edification, he means the numerous changes that occur within people as they discuss unfamiliar ideas, read broadly, explore novel cultures, and experience the arts. Rorty's edification is liberal education, provided that such education is not limited to the young. Philosophy's contribution to the benefits of a liberal education are those of a tradition with some of the most imaginative ways of seeing things and some of the most intriguing (if unanswerable) questions. Rorty believes that philosophy, stripped of arrogant foundational projects, richly deserves a place among the humanities. Philosophers are well trained to build bridges among patterns of thought. Rorty warns against the inevitable new attempts to create a super theory that can judge among the claims made by different language games.

Rorty's Legacy
Philosophy and the Mirror of Nature, which has been widely translated, established Rorty as an international scholar. His critique of analytic philosophy was much praised and widely adopted. Rorty became a central figure in discussions of postmodernism, literary analysis, legal theory, and the nature of the social sciences and of the humanities. Many have seen Rorty's philosophy as a cure for "physics envy" (the dream of making every area of culture scientific). Others fear that Rorty's philosophy supports shoddy thinking and a lack of concern for rigor. His broad popularity, especially among nonphilosophers, strengthens the firestorm of protest against Rorty

among analytic philosophers, who often feel misunderstood and betrayed.

Drew Christie

Additional Reading
Festenstein, Mathew. *Pragmatism and Political Theory*. Chicago: University of Chicago Press, 1997. Rorty's philosophy is greatly clarified by Festenstein's excellent explication of and comparisons among Rorty, John Dewey, Hilary Putnam, and Jürgen Habermas. Dewey is shown to have a much more developed (thus, more controversial) account of human nature than Rorty. Various strands in Rorty's thought are neatly disentangled.

Hall, David L. *Richard Rorty: Prophet and Poet of the New Pragmatism*. SUNY Series in Philosophy. Albany: State University of New York Press, 1994. The best of the secondary literature in terms of placing Rorty's work in historical and cultural context. Hall examines Rorty's narratives (short histories) and discusses their similarity to allegories. His discussion of alternative narratives (e.g., what Max Weber might write) is particularly valuable. Writing with flair, Hall captures the letter and the spirit of Rorty's work.

Kolenda, Konstantin. *Rorty's Humanistic Pragmatism: Philosophy Democratized*. Tampa: University of South Florida Press, 1990. A sympathetic, accessible exposition of Rorty's writings.

Malachowski, Alan R., Jo Burrows, and Richard Rorty. *Reading Rorty: Critical Responses to Philosophy and the Mirror of Nature (and Beyond)*. Oxford, England: Basil Blackwell, 1990. A valuable if sometimes exhausting collection of sophisticated critical essays by specialists.

Murphy, John P., and Richard Rorty. *Pragmatism: From Peirce to Davidson*. Boulder, Colo.: Westview Press, 1990. Written as part of a curriculum project. Murphy develops discussions of the readings for a one-semester undergraduate course on pragmatism. As noted in the introduction by Rorty, Murphy emphasizes antirepresentationalist, anti-Cartesian themes. The book shows Rorty as he sees himself within the history of American pragmatism.

Saatkamp, Herman J., Jr., ed. *Rorty and Pragmatism: The Philosopher Responds to His Critics.*

Nashville, Tenn.: Vanderbilt University Press, 1995. A wonderful dialogue between Rorty and his pragmatist critics (including his first philosophy teacher), this book also includes two illuminating essays by Rorty.

Sellars, Wilfrid, Richard Rorty, and Robert Brandom. *Empiricism and the Philosophy of Mind.* Cambridge, Mass.: Harvard University Press, 1997. Rorty's introduction and Brandom's study guide help readers through this long essay by Sellars that was a dominant influence on Rorty. Sellars criticizes what he calls the Myth of the Given, namely, the empiricist view that one has immediate, incorrigible access to what is sensed.

Drew Christie

Franz Rosenzweig

Rosenzweig, a German-Jewish philosopher, is best known for his work on Georg Wilhelm Friedrich Hegel's political philosophy and on his own philosophy of religion, which developed as he examined his identity as a Jew. The chief characteristics of Rosenzweig's works are the questions that he provokes and the originality and wealth of his insights.

Principal philosophical works: *Das älteste Systemprogramm des deutschen Idealismus: Ein handscriftlicher Fund*, 1917; *Zeit Ists: Gedanken über das judische Bildungsproblem des Augenblicks, an Hermann Cohen*, 1918 ("It Is Time," 1955); *Hegel und der Staat*, 1920; *Der Stern der Erlösung*, 1921 (*The Star of Redemption*, 1970); *Das Büchlein vom gesunden und kraken Menschenverstand*, 1921 (*Understanding the Sick and the Healthy: A View of World, Man and God*, 1953; also as *God, Man, and the World: Lectures and Essays*, 1998); "Das neue Denken: Einige nachträgliche Bemerkungen zum *Stern der Erlösung*," 1925 (*Franz Rosenzweig's "The New Thinking,"* 1998); *Kleinere Schriften*, 1937 (includes "Urzelle," "Atheistiche Theologie," and "Das neue Denken").

Born: December 25, 1886; Kassel, Germany
Died: December 10, 1929; Frankfurt am Main, Germany

Early Life

Though raised in a Jewish community, Franz Rosenzweig was educated in the classical German school system. The ongoing significance of these factors for students of his life is that they provide possibilities for ways to think about and live through the realities of religious and ethnic differences. As a German Jew, he was unavoidably confronted with fierce pressures, social and economic, to assimilate to the dominant Christian and secular community. His assimilated father was a successful businessperson, and his more devout mother maintained a more or less typical bourgeois household, with the exception that the Rosenzweigs continued to observe Jewish festivals and maintain social links to the Jewish community. Despite pressures to assimilate, Rosenzweig did learn a great deal from his uncle Adam Rosenzweig about classical Jewish sources, such as the Torah, Commentaries, Talmud, Kabbala, the Hebrew language, and Jewish ritual life. As a German citizen and an engaged member of the greater German community, he was exposed to and trained in classical German literature, art (including painting and architecture), philosophy, music (violin), and Greek and Latin literature.

As a young man, Rosenzweig actively pursued the study of medicine, history, art, and philosophy. In 1905, he began studying medicine at the Universities of Göttingen, Munich, and Freiburg, to the point of sitting for his preliminary medical examinations. However, Rosenzweig became disillusioned with the technical aspects of medicine and turned ever more frequently to reading works of Johann Wolfgang van Goethe and Friedrich Nietzsche and to cultivating his interest in German culture, history, literature, and philosophy. In passionate exchanges with fellow students; his cousins, Hans and Rudolf Ehrenberg; and especially his friend Eugen Rosenstock, all of whom had converted to Christianity, he changed course in 1907 and began studying history and philosophy at the Universities of Berlin and Freiburg. In a diary notation, Rosenzweig wrote:

Why does one philosophize? For the same reason that one makes music, literature or art. Here too, in the last analysis, all that matters is the discovery of one's own personality.

Under the tutelage of the noted historian Friedrich Meinecke, he studied Georg Wilhelm Friedrich Hegel's political philosophy and received his Ph.D. in 1912 for work that became a section of *Hegel und der Staat* (Hegel and the state).

Life's Work

Rosenzweig's first exposure to academic philosophy was a close reading of Immanuel Kant's *Kritik der reinen Vernunft* (1781; *The Critique of Pure Reason*, 1838) under Jonas Cohn at Freiburg University. On his own, he continued to read Goethe, Plato, Moses Mendelssohn, G. E. Lessing, and Nietzsche, as well as Christian, Roman, and Zionist authors such as Jacob Klatzkin and Ahad Ha-Am (pseudonym of Asher Ginsberg). As he matured intellectually, he became ever more occupied with questions about the dynamic relations of Judaism, Christianity, and secularity in contemporary Germany.

In 1908, he began studying history with Meinecke at Freiburg University, who with Wilhelm Dilthey and Ernst Troeltsch is counted as one of the founders of a new kind of historicizing built on the history of spirit and ideas. Rosenzweig applied this fusion of balancing the elements of intellectual personality and historical research, which he learned with Meinecke, when he began his study of Hegel's philosophy with Heinrich Rickert in the winter semester of 1910. As a philosophy student, he spent considerable time going through original manuscripts in order to form his biographical sketch of Hegel's formulation of a globalizing, political-spiritual philosophy. Together with other impassioned students, Rosenzweig formed the Freiburger Circle. Within this group, he developed his philosophy of history. It was influenced by the anti-Semitism directed at him by other students in the circle. His principal antagonists were the history student Siegfried A. Kaeler and Viktor von Weizsacker, who was to later become Rosenzweig's doctor. The developments within this circle fed Rosenzweig's skepticism about the German academic environment and most likely influenced his decision to direct the Lehrhaus instead of pursuing a traditional university career. Both Rosenzweig, the critical political liberal, and Kaehler, the faithful political conservative, were promoted to the Ph.D. by Meinecke. Rosenzweig left the circle,

but Kaehler later dedicated the publication of his dissertation work in 1927 to that same circle, leaving out Rosenzweig's name.

In 1913, Rosenzweig moved to study jurisprudence at the University of Leipzig and to be close to his cousin Rosenstock, with whom he struggled through a mutual dissatisfaction with contemporary academic philosophy and its political conservatism. After an intellectual and spiritual crisis, Rosenzweig decided to become a Christian but only "qua Jew." However, on October 11, 1913, after a Yom Kippur (Day of Atonement) service at an Orthodox synagogue in Berlin, he came to the realization that he must "remain a Jew."

In 1914, two important events took place: a creation and a discovery. First, Rosenzweig wrote the essay "Atheistische Theologie" (atheistic theology), which he described as a "programmatic affirmation of the idea of revelation." Second, in going through some Hegel manuscripts, he discovered an essay on ethics in Hegel's handwriting but which, he argued, based on a comparison of philosophical styles, could only be Friedrich Wilhelm Joseph Schelling's work copied by Hegel in 1796. These two events influenced the two paths upon which Rosenzweig then found himself.

He made use of the latter material in an essay entitled *Das älteste Systemprogramm des deutschen Idealismus* (the oldest program of a system for German Idealism), which was published by the Heidelberg Academy of Sciences. The outline of the Schelling fragment that he had found was a plan for a comprehensive system of philosophy that would combine ethics and physics and allow an individual to think of the physical world in conjunction with moral freedom. Moreover, such a system would be dedicated to "absolute freedom" and would include ethics, physics, politics, myth, and religion. At the peak of the system would be philosophy presented as an aesthetic act. This vision was important for Rosenzweig's own development as a creative philosopher because this outline, which he adapted for his own work, entailed an aesthetic act that joins the rational realm with the sensuous realm. The masses, moved only by sensual images, must then become rational and the philosophers, concerned only with rationality, must become sensuous or mythmakers in a unified vision of enlightenment of the masses and a practical engagement of the philosophers.

After the outbreak of World War I, Rosenzweig spent time both physically and intellectually in the trenches of Europe, patriotically fighting for Germany and also forming his own ideas. At first, he enlisted in the Red Cross as a nurse, then joined the regular army in 1915 and continued to work on *Hegel und der Staat*. After training in artillery and ballistics, he was sent as part of an antiaircraft unit to the Balkans, where he remained until the end of the war. In a secluded and relatively safe bunker, he began reading the works of writers and philosophers such as Saint Augustine, Martin Buber, Franz Kafka, Martin Luther, and Hermann Cohen, all the while corresponding formally and informally on German and Jewish cultural and political matters with family, friends, and intellectual colleagues. Rosenzweig also formulated a plan to reform Jewish religious instruction in Germany, organizing his thoughts in what would eventually become the treatise "It Is Time." Finally, in addition to reading deeply in the Bible and other Jewish sources, he sketched the basic outline for *The Star of Redemption* on a series of postcards that he sent home to his family.

The Star of Redemption is Rosenzweig's most original and major contribution to the field of philosophy in particular and intellectual life in general. As part of the overall fabric of Rosenzweig's life, it should be noted that he wrote the entire text in an inspired six-month period, finishing it after the end of the war and in the context of Germany's humiliating defeat. This political situation was highly determinative for the remainder of Rosenzweig's brief but highly productive life. Under that cataclysmic historical impetus, Rosenzweig's chief focus was to contribute to a renewal of Jewish life in the diaspora.

In 1920, Rosenzweig was appointed director of the Frankfurter Volkshochschule (community learning center) for the Jewish community. He renamed it the Freies Jüdisches Lehrhaus (free Jewish learning house). Under his directorship, a renaissance of Jewish community began. It was based on education involving the study of Hebrew, classical Jewish texts such as the Torah, and non-Jewish philosophical, literary, and historical

texts and movements. In this new institution, the students had to assume active roles in the learning process by being personally challenged by the texts and each other. This method of hermeneutics was also made popular as a way of interpreting seminal texts, but in a different institutional setting, by Rosenzweig's more famous contemporary Martin Heidegger. Where Heidegger used this method to examine classical philosophical texts in an original way, Rosenzweig's choice for such a method arose out of his own commitment to renewing a traditional Jewish study that bound students, teachers, and texts together in interpretive practices.

Influence

Diagnosed with amyotrophic lateral sclerosis (Lou Gehrig's disease) in 1921, Rosenzweig spent the last eight years of his life working to effect changes that he envisioned. That vision is reflected in five major areas of Rosenzweig's writing, which was roughly divided between his two major philosophical texts and his essays and translations. His two major works, *Hegel und der Staat* and *The Star of Redemption*, deal with German Idealism and his coming to terms with the human immersion in and production of history. The latter work displays his systematic philosophical standpoint, which would dictate certain directions in Jewish philosophy for the rest of the twentieth century. In his own lifetime, his work on *The Star of Redemption* caused him to recognize the need to verify the philosophy or standpoint of his own life and thus led to his later works, including his translations into German of the poetry of Judah ha-Levi, the translation into German of the Bible with Martin Buber, and many letters and short essays.

Through his writing and charismatic teaching, Rosenzweig deeply impressed the Jewish intellectual community of Weimar Germany in the critical years leading up to the Nazi assumption of power. His enduring influence can be traced in the works of other notable Jewish scholars in the twentieth century, among them Erich Fromm, Walter Benjamin, Emmanuel Lévinas, Emil L. Fackenheim, Jacques Derrida, Stephan Moses, Norbert Samuelson, Robert Gibbs, and Yudit Greenberg. He also deeply influenced such Christian scholars as Catholic theologian Bernard

Casper, Protestant theologian Rheinhold Mayer, and the American Protestant scholar Paul Van Buren. Finally, there are several institutes of Jewish learning that have been established throughout the United States and Europe based upon the Lehrhaus institute that Rosenzweig directed.

Despite the near-total destruction of the European Jews by the Nazis, his own relatively early death, and the difficulty and inaccessibility of his major philosophical works, Rosenzweig's seminal philosophical works are increasingly read and discussed, especially by Jewish and Christian philosophers and theologians.

Julius J. Simon

The Star of Redemption

Type of philosophy: Jewish philosophy, metaphysics, philosophy of religion
First published: Der Stern der Erlösung, 1921 (English translation, 1970)
Principal ideas advanced:
◇ The history of philosophy, especially as it is exemplified in Hegelian Idealism, does not adequately account for the existential relations of humans with each other, the world, and God.
◇ A hermeneutical method is presented for how to think, believe, and act in the world; it is based upon a broad and in-depth analysis of the nature of metaphysics, physics, psychology, aesthetics, and ethical relations.
◇ That hermeneutical method combines elements of a powerful speech-act logic in conjunction with midrashic and dialogical tools drawn from the Jewish tradition of study and community.
◇ The idea of revelation is presented as a fixed orienting event to counteract the relativity of the philosophical currents of modernity.

Franz Rosenzweig's text presents a challenging critique of a traditional rationality that has dominated Western thought systems, and therefore political and social life, from its Greek inception with the Ionian pre-Socratics to its culmination in the pervasive European versions of Georg Wilhelm Friedrich Hegel's philosophical system. Rosenzweig sees this system of rationality breaking up under the spur of revised Kantian versions of the philosophical-ethical standpoints exemplified by Arthur Schopenhauer, Søren Kierkegaard, and especially Friedrich Nietzsche. His inclusion of such philosophers signifies that Rosenzweig intends to pursue an ethical line throughout the text. This intention is emphasized by his choice to end his first introduction with references to Friedrich Wilhelm Joseph Schelling's *Die Weltalter* (1861; *Ages of the World,* 1942), which provides for a temporally significant revelation; the neo-Kantian Hermann Cohen's *Logik der reinen Erkenntnis* (1914; logic of pure cognition), whose mathematics Rosenzweig uses; and an approving utilization of Immanuel Kant's rational-ethical metaphysics.

Rosenzweig's emphasis on the ethical was instrumental in his attack on the educational thought structures that led to totalitarian political and social systems dominating European, but especially German, universities at the end of the nineteenth and beginning of the twentieth century. From Rosenzweig's perspective, these educational structures validate a universal and dialectical historical process that could only result in the kind of oppositional violence and human destruction of World War I, which Rosenzweig witnessed and in which he fought. Besides attacking conservative political tendencies, Rosenzweig criticizes the Marxist alternative of a dialectical-material progressive political system. None of this, however, is clearly evident in the opening pages of the first section of his text. Rather, in the beginning, Rosenzweig takes his reader on what initially appears to be a Faustian journey to know and experience all, via a descent into the depths of the struggle for knowledge. This descent requires profound encounters with our presuppositions that we know something about the world, the human, and God.

From Negation to Affirmation
One overarching motif of this text is Rosenzweig's philosophical orientation, which moves the reader from thinking about death on the first page to a proposal for acting in life on the last. It begins with the thought of death and uses that point of departure as a starting point for a claim

to comprehensive, absolute knowledge that leads to an existential affirmation of the irreducibility of individual existence. Such a movement of negation from death to life is influenced by his choice to include Kierkegaardian anguish tempered by Nietzschean joy in people's radically finite lives. In fact, following Schopenhauer and Nietzsche, Rosenzweig argues that one does not "give up" one's life for the sake of philosophical, religious, or ethical immortality. On the contrary, Rosenzweig's work represents a critical response to the absolute epistemological and ontological claims of idealist: dialectical philosophy in favor of a philosophical stance that ethically affirms the differences of particular, individual humans.

The Star of Redemption is divided into three formally parallel parts within which there are numerous ways to read and reread the text, ranging from an innovative philosophy of religion to a postmodern critique of idealist philosophy to a critical social philosophy that includes religious communities as viable life-affirming paths. Throughout, Rosenzweig develops a powerful speech-act philosophy that he uses to construct dynamic links between the various readings.

Each of the three parts is divided into three books, and each part has its own introduction and an epilogue that serves as a bridge to the next part. Each unit formally presents a different type of religion and a corresponding kind of language, as well as a corresponding aesthetic theory. Although architectonic in formal construction, the content itself is fluid and dynamic, and the configuration of the Star of David as the symbol of the text can, with benefit, be compared to the star of a Koch curve of contemporary chaos theory. The final "bridge" at the end of the text signifies the passage from textual work to a hoped-for verification of the life of ethical human relations beyond the text. Through the three movements of the three major parts, the reader is led to the final pages of the text for an affirmation of life and an invitation to engage the human other via a face-to-face encounter sealed with a kiss of promise, commitment, and love.

The Three Elements

Rosenzweig organizes part 1 along the lines of a hypothetical construct that corresponds to three unordered points of his projected star. The three points correspond to three elements of reality that encompass three logical constructs, each capable of being understood on its own terms. Moreover, the three elements correspond to the three branches of the rational sciences of Kant's critical philosophy, namely, physics, logic, and ethics. Rosenzweig claims that any thinking at all begins with the negation of all other as an affirmation of the unity of the thinking subject. Following Nietzsche, such a unity also entails existential factors such as the irreducibility of embodied existence to an abstract conceptual structure.

Rosenzweig goes on to consider each of the elements as a hypothetical construct based on a phenomenological principle of the fusion of thinking and existing. Adapting Hermann Cohen's calculus of infinitesimal asymptotes to a three-variable symbolic logic to represent the constitution of these constructs, Rosenzweig gives us the process formulas of $A = A$ (freedom becoming nature) for thinking the inner dynamic of the element God, $B = A$ (particularity becoming logos) for thinking the inner dynamic of the element World, and $B = B$ (free will becoming character) for thinking the inner dynamic of the element Human. What we are left with are the isolated forms of Antiquity: the mythic, secluded God; the plastic, generative world; and the defiant, tragic self.

Each of these formulas is based on a sentential logic that corresponds to a propositional form roughly capable of the generative capacities of Chomskian deep-structure forms or even the rigid logical structures of an ideal language proposed by Ludwig Wittgenstein in his "Logisch-philosophische Abhandlung" (1921; best known by the bilingual German and English edition title of *Tractatus Logico-Philosophicus*, 1922, 1961). Rosenzweig's difference is that he weds his phenomenological analysis of speech-forms with negations of the historical occurrences of negative theology with respect to God (negating Maimonides' thought structure); negative cosmology with respect to thinking the World (negating René Descartes's thought structure); and negative psychology with respect to thinking the Human (negating Kant's thought structure).

In other words, Rosenzweig's argument is that there are philosophical figures who have created thought structures that play into how these developments of the hypothetical constructs come about in the first place, and if one begins with the assumption of the unavoidability of one's constitution as a finite human being whose thinking proceeds as a negative limit function of that very finitude, a negation of these constructs as definitive is the first step one takes in one's own original thinking of those elements. Hence, following Rosenzweig's linguistic logic, one will inevitably arrive at the kinds of conclusions about the humanly constructed character of a secluded God, a plastic World, and a tragic Human toward which Rosenzweig guides the reader.

Through a series of inversions in thinking the elements proposed in part 1, one moves into a different order out of the empirical and epistemological chaos that holds in reflecting on such elements. On Rosenzweig's analysis, humans impose such an order a posteriori on the elements themselves in their dynamic relations of language and responsibility. Using an interpretation (a midrash) of the Song of Songs as his model, Rosenzweig claims that human-embodied response to the proximity and love demands of the other directs attention outward from secluded and tragic introversion. This revelatory event, which Rosenzweig associates with the theological categories of creation, revelation, and redemption, is also the key moment of ethical determination. The lover, as other, spontaneously but intentionally calls to his or her beloved in love and the lover answers freely in responsibility forming a relational bond that eventually serves as the sound basis for redemptive community life.

Philosophical Theology

The language of part 1 involves what people can know and that people can know that they do not know something. This is opposed to Hegelian philosophical claims that people can know absolutely all and includes an analysis of ancient myths and religions via mathematical-symbolic logic. The language of part 2, on the other hand, is based on a philosophical theology, the dialogical and ethical origins of monotheistic myths and religions, and is presented as the grammar of spoken language and the revelatory relations of love.

In the final part of *The Star of Redemption*, Rosenzweig elaborates sociohistorical issues and the communities in which the temporality of lived histories and life relationships of actual communities are set in vital relations. Because Rosenzweig examines historical realities as kinds of idealized social types in order to carry on the initial Cohenian-Kantian-Schellingian asymptotic logic of ideal relations, his social theory reflects his desire to fuse the givenness of chaotic brute sensuality with a humanly ordered cosmos.

The form of communication with which Rosenzweig ends part 2 and begins part 3 is prayer. However, this is a peculiar kind of prayer that is more a cry of hope than of petition or penitence as a result of the very love relationship formed in part 2. The final hope is to redeem the world in such a way that the partisanship of religious particularity no longer holds sway. Furthermore, where the philosopher-scientist is the chief spokesperson of part 1 and the theologian-poet of part 2, the human-prophet is the spokesperson of part 3. This is so because Rosenzweig is committed to a Messianic vision of the world, where the end of days would be a time when from out of the blazing fire of the family love of Judaism, the redeeming rays of Christian love of neighbor would extend to and enlighten, and thereby bring to passionate life the darkened pagan world. Although this means that there would no longer be any pagans in such an enlightened world, because his is a Messianic vision, it also means that there would be no Christians or Jews. Rather, the very human face of each radically individual other would characterize the lived social world of relational responsibility.

As a framing device, *The Star of Redemption* itself, both as symbol and as text, gives us an aesthetic-philosophical picture of reality. As such a textual picture, the reader experiences a literary thought-world guided by the transformative/performative event of reading itself. Approached from the perspective of any one of the series of tri-form structures that Rosenzweig presents in the text—philosophical, theological, communal; thinking, speech, ritual activity; temporal dimensions of past, present, future; or mathematical signs, grammatical signs, social signs—a rich mosaic of textual texture takes shape. Moreover, although created out of his Jewish particularity,

Rosenzweig's stated aim was to enable his book to be understood philosophically, so he intentionally wrote in a way that allowed the text to be transparent to any reader who would open its pages: Jew, Christian, Muslim, Buddhist, Hindu, pagan, or atheist.

Julius J. Simon

Additional Reading

Cohen, Richard A. *Elevations: The Height of the Good in Rosenzweig and Levinas*. Chicago: University of Chicago Press, 1994. In this collection of essays, Cohen recognizes in Franz Rosenzweig a voice calling for the revitalization of traditional Jewish thought and ethical practice.

Fackenheim, Emil L. *To Mend the World: Foundations of Future Jewish Thought*. New York: Schocken Books, 1982. One of the best contemporary empirical applications of Rosenzweig's ideas to a problematic world issue, namely, the Holocaust.

Fackenheim, Emil L., and Raphael Jospe, eds. *Jewish Philosophy and the Academy*. Madison, N.J.: Fairleigh Dickinson University Press, 1996. This work was published in conjunction with the International Center for University Teaching of Jewish Civilization. It looks at Jewish philosophy, particularly that of Rosenzweig and Emmanuel Lévinas. Contains bibliographical references.

Gibbs, Robert. *Correlations in Rosenzweig and Levinas*. Princeton, N.J.: Princeton University Press, 1995. Gibbs pairs Rosenzweig with Emmanuel Lévinas, one of the most influential French-Jewish philosophers of the twentieth century, to make his case that Rosenzweig is a postmodern philosopher because of his rejection of the primacy of reason and his acceptance of the particularities of tradition, time, and place.

Glatzer, Nahum N. *Franz Rosenzweig: His Life and Thought*. New York: Schocken Press, 1976. 2d ed. Glatzer draws from his own personal relationship with Rosenzweig when they studied and taught together in the Lehrhaus. Glatzer comments on chronologically ordered selections from Rosenzweig's collected letters and papers, which cover the philosopher's views on a broad and diverse range of intellectual, religious, social, political, and aesthetic issues.

Greenberg, Yudit Kornberg. *Better than Wine: Love, Poetry, and Prayer in the Thought of Franz Rosenzweig*. American Academy of Religion Reflection and Theory in The Study of Religion series. Atlanta, Ga.: Scholars Press, 1996. This volume examines Rosenzweig's work in Jewish philosophy. Contains bibliographical references and index.

Mendes-Flohr, Paul, ed. *The Philosophy of Franz Rosenzweig*. Hanover, Md.: University Press of New England, 1988. Topics in this collection of essays range from exploring the affinities of Rosenzweig's work with Jewish Kabbala to examining his place in the German philosophical tradition. There are also recollections of his significance by Glatzer, a former colleague, and Ernst Simon, a former disciple.

Mosès, Stephane. *System and Revelation: Philosophy of Franz Rosenzweig*. Translated by Catherine Tihanyi. Detroit, Mich.: Wayne State University Press, 1992. The most extensive point-by-point elaboration of Rosenzweig's *The Star of Redemption*. Mosès's work includes a very thorough bibliography.

Samuelson, Norbert M. *An Introduction to Modern Jewish Philosophy*. Albany: State University of New York Press, 1989. One of the founders of the Academy of Jewish Philosophy, Samuelson provides a rigorous summary and explanation of each of the major sections of Rosenzweig's *The Star of Redemption* as well as a detailed list of paragraph topics. He also includes helpful diagrams and lists of Rosenzweig's symbols, signs, and Jewish liturgical expressions.

Vogel, Manfred H. *Rosenzweig on Profane/Secular History*. South Florida Studies in the History of Judaism series. Atlanta, Ga.: Scholars Press, 1996. This volume, part of a series on the history of Judaism, examines Rosenzweig's view on history and on the history of philosophy. Includes bibliographical references and index.

Julius J. Simon

Jean-Jacques Rousseau

Rousseau helped transform the Western world from a rigidly stratified, frequently despotic civilization into a predominantly democratic civilization dedicated to assuring the dignity and fulfillment of the individual.

Principal philosophical works: *Dissertation sur la musique moderne*, 1743; *Discours sur les sciences et les arts*, 1750 (*The Discourse Which Carried the Praemium at the Academy of Dijon*, 1751; better known as *A Discourse on the Arts and Sciences*, 1913); *Discours sur l'inégalité*, 1754 (*A Discourse on Inequality*, 1756); *Lettre à d'Alembert sur les spectacles*, 1758 (*A Letter to M. d'Alembert Concerning the Effects of Theatrical Entertainments*, 1759); *Du contrat social: Ou, Principes du droit politique*, 1762 (*A Treatise on the Social Contract: Or, The Principles of Politic Law*, 1764); *Émile: Ou, De l'éducation*, 1762 (*Emilius and Sophia: Or, A New System of Education*, 1762-1763); *The Works*, 1763-1773 (10 volumes); *Le Sentiment des citoyens*, 1764; *The Miscellaneous Works*, 1767 (5 volumes); *Quatre Lettres à M. le président de Malesherbes contenant le vrai tableau de mon caractère et les vrais motifs de toute ma conduite*, 1779; *Les Dialogues: Ou, Rousseau juge de Jean-Jacques*, 1780, 1782; *Œuvres complètes de Jean-Jacques Rousseau*, 1959-1969 (4 volumes); *Essai sur l'origine des langues*, 1781 (*On the Origin of Languages*, 1967); *Les Rêveries du promeneur solitaire*, 1782 (*The Reveries of the Solitary Walker*, 1783); *Les Confessions de J.-J. Rousseau*, 1782, 1789 (*The Confessions of J.-J. Rousseau*, 1783-1790); *Political Writings*, 1915, 1954; *Religious Writings*, 1970.

Born: June 28, 1712; Geneva (now in Switzerland)
Died: July 2, 1778; Ermenonville, France

Early Life

Jean-Jacques Rousseau was born of middle-class parents in the fiercely independent Protestant municipality of Geneva. His mother, the former Suzanne Bernard, died within days of his birth, and he was reared until age ten by his watchmaker father, Isaac Rousseau, with whom the precocious boy shared a passion for romantic novels, a passion that helped shape Jean-Jacques's emotional and highly imaginative nature. Young Rousseau and the irresponsible Isaac often neglected sleep as they devoured their beloved romances, an escapist reading regimen that Rousseau supplemented with more substantial works by such writers as Plutarch and Michel Eyquem de Montaigne.

This earliest phase of Rousseau's life came to an abrupt end when his father was forced to flee from Geneva to escape imprisonment for wounding a former military officer during a quarrel in the autumn of 1722. Left in the care of a maternal uncle, Rousseau was soon placed, along with his cousin Abraham Bernard, in the home of the Lambercier family, a Protestant minister and his sister, in the village of Bossey, a few miles outside Geneva.

The essentially carefree two years spent with the Lamberciers were followed by a short period of distasteful employment with the district registrar, and a longer apprenticeship to an engraver. Petty thefts and other breaches of discipline earned for Rousseau, now in his teens, a series of beatings that in no way altered his recalcitrant behavior but instead augmented his hatred of authority. After nearly three years of these confrontations, in March of 1728, he abandoned his apprenticeship and, with it, his native city.

Rousseau was introduced to twenty-nine-year-old Madame de Warens, eventually to be one of the great loves of his life, who sent the destitute and still-directionless teenager to Turin's monastery of the Spirito Santo, where, within a few days of his arrival, he found it expedient to embrace the Catholic faith. Released into the streets of Turin with little money, Rousseau held several jobs but eventually returned, probably by mid-1729, to Madame de Warens.

Rousseau's duties as record keeper to Madame de Warens were light enough to allow him ample time for wide reading, but his genius still had not manifested itself, and after his patron left on a journey to Paris, the aimless youth took the opportunity to add to his ample store of life adventures. At Lausanne, he attempted, despite insufficient knowledge of music, to conduct an orchestral work of his own composition; the performance was a fiasco.

Succeeding months saw Madame de Warens establish herself as Rousseau's mistress and Rousseau busy himself with the study and teaching of music. Over the next several years, Rousseau also undertook the intensive study of most other branches of human knowledge in an eminently successful effort to overcome the handicap of his earlier haphazard education.

Life's Work

By 1740, Rousseau had begun serious attempts to write, but he remained essentially unknown. His first minor recognition came in 1742, during his second visit to Paris, when he suggested a new method of musical notation to the Academy of Science. Although the method was judged inadequate, Rousseau's presentation earned him the respect of and eventual introduction to several figures of importance in the French intelligentsia, most notably philosopher Denis Diderot. In 1743, at the salon of Madame Dupin, Rousseau widened his circle of influential acquaintances, and eventually he became Madame Dupin's secretary.

While traveling to Vincennes to visit Diderot, who had been imprisoned in 1749, Rousseau happened across an essay competition that would ensure his lasting fame. Had the advancement of science and art, the Academy of Dijon wished to know, improved the moral state of mankind? Rousseau argued in the negative, and his essay, *A Discourse on the Arts and Sciences*, was awarded first prize on July 10, 1750. Rousseau's central contention, that modern advances in the arts and sciences had produced an abandonment of primitive sincerity and simple virtue, inspired a plethora of attacks and defenses and helped prepare the way for the Romantic reaction against Enlightenment rationalism.

Rousseau's next success was the composition of an operetta, *Le Devin du village* (1752; *Cunning-Man*, 1766), which gained for him some financial security and was honored with a command performance before the French court on October 18, 1752. By refusing an audience with the king and then entangling himself in a dispute over the relative merits of French and Italian music, however, Rousseau almost immediately lost the regal favor he had just gained.

Jean-Jacques Rousseau. *(Library of Congress)*

Following this unpleasant interlude, Rousseau achieved another of his great intellectual triumphs with the publication of *A Discourse on Inequality*, again written in response to a topic proposed by the Academy of Dijon. An analysis of the beginnings of human inequality, this work continues Rousseau's theme of the relative superiority of primitive man to civilized man. Distinguishing the irremediable inequality produced by natural circumstance from the imposed inequality encouraged by artificial social convention, Rousseau attacked many of the assumptions underlying the political and social order of mid-eighteenth century Europe.

With the publication of *Julie: Ou, La Nouvelle Héloïse* (1761; *Eloise: Or, A Series of Original Letters*, 1761; also known as *Julie: Or, The New Eloise*, 1968; better known as *The New Héloïse*), Rousseau's career took a new turn. An epistolary novel of sentimental love, *The New Héloïse* focuses on the passionate relationship of the aristocratic Julie d'Étange and her tutor Saint-Preux, a relationship doomed by the disapproval of Julie's intolerant father. The novel's emotional intensity, its portrayal of the corrupting influence of the city, and its association of sublime sentiment with the beauty and grandeur of nature engendered tremendous popularity and established a model for emulation by Romantic writers of the ensuing one hundred years.

More in keeping with his previous publications, *A Treatise on the Social Contract: Or, The Principles of Politic Law* is Rousseau's fullest statement on the proper relationship between a nation's government and its people. *A Treatise on the Social Contract* admits that, in practice, any of the range of governmental structures, from pure democracy through aristocracy to monarchy, may be the most appropriate for a particular state, but he insists that the source of sovereignty is always the people and that the people may not legitimately relinquish sovereignty to despots who would subvert the general will. If a government acts contrary to the will of the people, the people have a right to replace it.

His next work, *Emilius and Sophia: Or, a New System of Education*, contains his most influential statements on education and religion. The book insists that the developing child be allowed adequate physical activity and that the pace of the child's education be determined by the gradual emergence of the child's own capacities and interests. A slow and deliberate individualized education is infinitely preferable to an education that rushes the child toward an identity that subverts his natural inclinations. Furthermore, the purpose of education should not simply be the acquisition of knowledge but the formation of the whole human being, whenever possible through life experiences rather than through heavy reliance on books.

From the beginning of his career as a writer and thinker, Rousseau had been the center of controversy. With his publications of the early 1760's banned in some areas of Europe and burned in others, he found himself again becoming an exile. He left Paris in June of 1762 to avoid imminent arrest and spent the next eight years living for varying periods in Switzerland, England, and France, sometimes driven by actual persecution and sometimes by a growing paranoia. Much of his literary effort during this period went into the composition of the posthumously published *The Confessions of J.-J. Rousseau*, among the most intimately detailed and influential of all autobiographies. A remarkable experiment in self-revelation, his confessions helped to establish the vital relationship between childhood experience and the development of the adult psyche. The work also inspired countless self-analytic memoirs emphasizing their various authors' growth toward a unique individuality, despite Rousseau's belief that he would find no imitators.

By 1770, Rousseau was able to return to Paris, where he supported himself largely as a music copyist and wrote two further experiments in self-revelation, the defensive *Les Dialogues: Ou, Rousseau juge de Jean-Jacques* (the dialogues, or Rousseau as judge of Jean-Jacques) and the more serene *The Reveries of the Solitary Walker*, both published posthumously. On July 2, 1778, Rousseau died at Ermenonville, just outside the French capital. In 1794, his remains were transferred to the Pantheon in Paris in honor of the influence of his ideas on the French Revolution.

Influence

Rousseau is one of those rare individuals whose life and career epitomize the transition from one historical epoch to another. He was a man perpetually at odds with the world around him, a world dominated by ancient privilege and entrenched power. Through the eloquence of his words, he helped to transform that world. Whatever he might have thought of the various revolutions that swept away the old social order, those revolutions would not have occurred so readily without his ideas to justify them. Nor would the constitutions of the new nations that replaced the old have been framed exactly as they were if he had not written on government and popular sovereignty. His hatred of despotism and of a conformity enforced by authoritarian rule shaped a world in which equality and individuality, if not universally to be encountered, were at least more frequently possible than they once had been. Furthermore, his emphasis on allowing individuals to develop according to their own nature rather than according to some externally imposed standard had a profound effect on how modern societies educate their children.

Robert H. O'Connor

A Treatise on the Social Contract

Or, The Principles of Politic Law

Type of philosophy: Ethics, political philosophy
First published: Du contrat social: Ou, Principes du droit politique, 1762 (English translation, 1764)
Principal ideas advanced:
◇ Whatever rights and responsibilities the rulers and citizens have in a state are derived from some agreement; no social right is derived from nature.
◇ In a state of nature, people live to preserve themselves; to make cooperation possible and to assure common security, states are instituted by social contracts.
◇ According to the contract, when people place themselves under the control of a sovereign, they are placing themselves under the control of themselves and their fellow citizens, for a sovereign exists in order to safeguard the citizens.
◇ The sovereign is limited to the making of general laws; he or she cannot pass judgment upon individuals.
◇ As a result of the joining of wills by the social contract, a general will, distinguishable from a collection of individual wills, comes into being.
◇ The ideal government is a small, elected group; the ideal state is small enough to allow the citizens to know one another.

Jean-Jacques Rousseau is perhaps best known for *A Treatise on the Social Contract,* one of the great classics in political philosophy. Rousseau was concerned with the relationship between the state and the individual. He recognized that the state has tremendous power over individuals, that it can command them, coerce them, and determine the sort of life they are to live, and also that individuals make many demands on society, even if they do not have the power to back them up. However, he insisted, the relations between the state and the individual cannot be simply those of naked power, threats, coercion, arbitrary decrees, and fearful or cunning submission, for people do speak of justified authority, the legitimate exercise of force, the rights of citizens, and the duties of rulers. The big question, then, is this: What is the source of the rights and responsibilities of both the citizen and the ruler?

In *A Treatise on the Social Contract,* Rousseau repudiates those who argue that the stronger have the right to rule the weaker, insisting that strength as such amounts to coercion. If a robber brandishing a pistol stops me and demands my purse, I am forced to hand it over, but his strength does not justify his act and my weakness does not make my reluctance blameworthy. Nor does this right of society over the individual flow from nature. True, the simplest social group, the family, does rest upon the natural requirement that the parents care for the child—survival is the first law of nature—but because the family often holds together much longer than is needed to satisfy this requirement, it is evident that the rights and obligations that continue to exist within the family organization are not supported or required by nature. Rather, these obligations and rights depend upon tacit agreements between parents and children that certain relationships shall be maintained and respected within the group, agreements tacitly admitted when the son chooses to stay within the family and the father welcomes his continued presence. Agreements of this sort mark the transition from the amoral state of power and submission to power to the moral state of acknowledged rights and responsibilities. What is true of the family is also true of that larger society, the state, for whatever rights and responsibilities the rulers and citizens possess could only have evolved as the result of some agreement. Rousseau insists, like Thomas Hobbes, John Locke, and many other philosophers, that society is based upon some implicit contract.

A Social Contract

This social contract delivers us from a prior state of nature. Before people lived in societies, they were motivated primarily by the basic urge to preserve themselves, an urge that manifested itself in physical appetites and desires and released itself instinctively through actions designed to satisfy these. People were not governed by reason or by moral considerations, for there were no rights or moral relationships to be respected. Rousseau does not claim that presocietal people were vicious or that they had no gregarious instincts, but he does claim that each person's life was dominated by the amoral, unreflective pursuit of the individual's own welfare. As a result of this marked individualism and the rude circumstances of nature, life was uncertain and precarious, cooperation impossible, and aggression common. Such a state could be transcended only by instituting, by common consent, some sort of body politic within which cooperation would be possible and security guaranteed.

According to Rousseau, the society instituted by the contract brings about a marked transformation in humanity, for rational behavior replaces instinct, a sense of responsibility replaces physical motivation, and law replaces appetite. Latent capacities and faculties finally flower, and out of "a stupid and dull-witted animal," there emerges "an intelligent being and a man." In these respects, Rousseau differs from Locke and political leader Thomas Jefferson, who maintained that before the contract, humanity was already rational and moral and possessed rights. The contract does not change people or affect their rights; it only safeguards what they already have. However, for Rousseau a person's debt to

society is far greater because rights, morality, and an individual's very status are consequences of being a member of a body politic. Rousseau also differs from Hobbes, not about the nonexistence of morality in a state of nature, but about human nature. For Hobbes, people are so egoistic that they can only be restrained, not transformed. For Hobbes, Locke, and Jefferson, people are essentially individualistic, whereas for Rousseau, they are essentially social creatures. This view leads to two different conceptions of the function of political society. In the former, social institutions have only the negative function of securing what people already have by controlling excessive individualism, whereas in the latter, social institutions have the positive function of enabling people to fulfill their natures. In the former, political institutions are a necessary evil, but for Rousseau, they are a blessing.

In the contract that establishes the state, people agree with one another to place both themselves and their possessions under the complete control of the resultant body politic and to give to it the power and responsibility of safeguarding them and of providing the framework within which they can jointly pursue their common welfare.

The Terms of the Contract

It may sound as if Rousseau were advocating a rather extreme despotism, but this is not so. First, according to the terms of the contract, civil power and responsibility are not turned over to a king or to some small group of persons, but are kept in the hands of the contractors themselves, who thus become jointly sovereign. Consequently, when people contract to place themselves under the control of the sovereign, their action means only that they, like every other person, place themselves under the control of themselves and their fellow citizens.

Second, while the state has control over the individual, the scope of its control is limited to matters pertaining to the preservation and welfare of all. If it transgresses these limits, the contract is void and the citizen is released. Thus, for instance, although new citizens hand all their possessions over to the state, the state immediately hands them back and, by giving them title to these possessions, institutes property rights as distinguished from mere possession. According to the contract, the state retains control only in the sense that it has the right to appropriate the individual's property if the public interest should require that it do so. Similarly, the state can command the individual only to the extent that control is needed for the public welfare. At all other times and in all other respects, it guarantees the individual freedom from the encroachment of the government and of other individuals. In this way, the contract brings human rights into being and specifies their scope.

Again, the individual is safeguarded insofar as the function of the sovereign group is restricted to the making of laws and insofar as the object of the law is always general. The sovereign power can pass laws attaching rewards or punishments to types of action and privileges to certain offices, but it cannot pass judgment upon individuals. The latter is the function of the executive or administrative branch, not that of the legislative. Rousseau maintains emphatically that the legislative and administrative functions shall not be discharged by the same group.

The General Will

The transformation wrought in the individual and the nature of the sovereign act are both expressed in what is perhaps the most basic of Rousseau's concepts, that of the "general will." Even though people are initially motivated by self-interest, the awareness that a contract is desirable forces them to think about others and their interests. Once the contract is made and the mechanism of democratic assemblies put into practice, individuals will be forced to consider those other interests more seriously than ever before. This consideration may result solely from prudence in the first place, but the deliberate joining of lots, the debating, the compromises to accommodate others, and the conscious recognition that they have common ideals cannot fail to encourage a genuine concern for the welfare of all. People become social creatures with social consciences, and what would otherwise have been a mere collection of individuals with individual goals and individual wills becomes a collective person with a single general will and a single goal. There comes into being a *res publica*, a republic, a body politic with many members.

Rousseau stressed that people are not really citizens as long as they accept society from prudence alone, that they become real citizens only when they develop a genuine concern for the welfare of all. There is an emphasis here that is not found in the English and American social contract writers. Of course, Rousseau does not write that people's interest in themselves will disappear; he claims, rather, that a new dimension has been added. Insofar as people are still self-centered, they must be subjects, but insofar as they are socially conscious persons, they can assume their responsibilities as sovereigns.

Rousseau insists that the general will must be distinguished from the many individual wills. If the citizens jointly form a body politic, the general will is the will of that body, a will that comes into being when they jointly concentrate their attention on the needs of that body. This will exercises itself through democratic assemblies of all the citizens and lets its intentions be known through the decisions of such assemblies. An assembly expresses the will of the whole people and not that of a part, but it requires only the voice of the majority *if* the views of the minority have been fairly heard and fairly considered. The general will cannot be ill-intentioned; it is concerned with the good of all, and it cannot be mistaken unless it is ill-informed. Simple, unsophisticated people are quite capable of exercising sovereign power provided that they are socially conscious and well-informed and that they act after full discussion and are not subject to pressure groups. Because sovereignty is the expression of the general will, and the general will is the expression of the will of all, sovereignty cannot be alienated by anyone or delegated to anyone—king or elected representative.

Although he sometimes spoke in a rather idealistic manner, Rousseau could also be hardheaded. He was quite aware that the conditions just mentioned are not always fulfilled. Pressure groups do exist; citizens become so indifferent or so preoccupied with their own concerns that they fail to discharge their civic responsibilities, and administrators seek to control those they are supposed to serve. In these and other ways, sovereignty can be destroyed. No human institution, he writes, will last forever. In addition, it is not likely that simple people can themselves establish the proper kind of state. Some well-intentioned and exceedingly gifted lawgiver is needed to provide a constitution, help establish traditions, and guide the fledgling state with a hidden but firm hand until the people have developed the ability, stability, and desire to carry on for themselves.

A Small State

Through the expression of their general will, then, the people exercise the sovereignty that they have and must retain in their own hands, but they do not administer the resultant laws. To do so, they establish an executive branch that functions as their agent. The form and structure of the administration will depend upon the size of the state, and other things being equal, the number of rulers tolerable for efficiency will vary inversely with the number of citizens. This is so because a larger state will require the tighter administrative control that can be achieved only if the executive power is restricted to a small number of administrators. On the other hand, a very small state might get along by allowing all the citizens to take part in the administration. Having in mind a moderately sized city-state, such as his native Geneva, Rousseau suggests that the ideal government would be a small elected group. He says that the function of the executive is restricted to the support and administration of the law and to the preservation of civil and political liberty and that the sovereign assembly is restricted to legislating, but he does not specify these functions in detail nor does he discuss the relationship between them. Furthermore, he does not discuss a judiciary, but this is presumably included in the administrative complex.

He is clear, though, in his insistence that the administrator be the servant of the assembly. To ensure that this be so, the people enter into no contract with their administrator and, unlike the Hobbesian contractors, transfer no rights. They extend to him nothing more than a revocable commission, thereby retaining control without being bound. When the sovereign assembly meets, as it does very frequently, all commissions granted by it at previous meetings become void until they are renewed.

Rousseau favors a moderately sized state something like the communes of Switzerland, wherein every citizen can come to know all the others, for in the large state relations between citizens become impersonal, and their interests, problems, and fortunes become diversified. If there are many provinces, customs will not be uniform and one body of law will not be sufficient. The number and levels of subordinate government will multiply, and as the cost increases, liberty will decrease. Chains of command become attenuated to such an extent that administration at the bottom levels becomes indifferent, weak, or corrupt, and supervision from the top becomes difficult. The control of the government by the people becomes impossible, as does the democratic legislative process. Indeed, a very large state cannot avoid being a dictatorship both legislatively and administratively, and that is the best form of government for it. If a state is to be a democratic state, it must be small, as small as it can be without inviting encroachment by its neighbors.

It is interesting to speculate what Rousseau would say of modern democracies, which have millions of citizens and embrace hundreds of thousands of square miles. Would he find that contemporary means of communication obviate some of the difficulties he had in mind and that security usually requires a considerably larger state than was necessary in his day? Quite possibly, he would admire many of the ingenious ways by which people have delegated both legislative and administrative powers and controlled these powers, but he might argue sadly that people are bedeviled by many of the difficulties inherent in size. Gone forever is the small autonomous political group with its intimacies, its personal concern, its shared interests and problems, and its joint endeavors.

Rousseau's views have influenced many thinkers and political movements, partly because of the central problem with which he was concerned and partly because of the vigor and clarity with which he wrote. However, unresolved tensions in his thought have permitted partisan readers to place rather different interpretations upon him. His emphasis on equality, liberty, and the supremacy of the citizen made him a favorite author among the leaders of the French Revolution, and these emphases plus those on democracy and the control of the administrators have always made him attractive to those who have supported a republican form of government. However, his claim that people realize their full nature only by participating in the life of a society has impressed those who believe that the state should play more than a negative regulatory role. This claim, along with his assertion that the individual is under the complete control of the sovereign power and his sometimes near reification of the general will have seemed to others to foreshadow the engulfing national spirit of German philosopher Georg Wilhelm Friedrich Hegel and his followers and to be congenial to tyrannical forms of nationalism. The truth, of course, is that each of the foregoing views requires that interpreters select passages and, in some cases, stretch them considerably, whereas in fact, Rousseau presents a rich array of ideas that are not worked out completely or consistently. These fresh ideas are what make *A Treatise on the Social Contract* one of the great classics of political philosophy.

Leonard Miller, updated by John K. Roth

Additional Reading

Copleston, Frederick. *A History of Philosophy: Modern Philosophy*. Garden City, N.Y.: Doubleday, 1964. Copleston places Jean-Jacques Rousseau against the backdrop of the Enlightenment, suggesting both his affinities and his points of disagreement with his philosophical contemporaries.

Cranston, Maurice William. *The Solitary Self: Jean-Jacques Rousseau in Exile and Adversity*. Chicago: University of Chicago Press, 1997. Explores Rousseau's views on individual experience with special reference to solitude, exile, and adversity.

Crocker, Lester G. *Jean-Jacques Rousseau: The Quest (1712-1758)*. New York: Macmillan, 1968. A biography that places heavy emphasis on Rousseau's eccentric psychological development.

Cullen, Daniel E. *Freedom in Rousseau's Political Philosophy*. Dekalb: Northern Illinois University Press, 1993. An assessment of Rousseau's philosophy of freedom and its impact on his broader moral and political views.

Dent, N. J. H. *Rousseau: An Introduction to His Psychological, Social, and Political Theory*. New York: Basil Blackwell, 1988. A helpful analysis of Rousseau's views about education, rights, community, and other social and political issues.

Grant, Ruth H. *Hypocrisy and Integrity: Machiavelli, Rousseau, and the Ethics of Politics*. Chicago: University of Chicago Press, 1997. An instructive comparative analysis of two important figures in political philosophy.

Grimsley, Ronald. *The Philosophy of Rousseau*. Oxford: Oxford University Press, 1973. A reliable survey of Rousseau's ideas with an emphasis on his social thought.

Havens, George R. *Jean-Jacques Rousseau*. Boston: Twayne, 1978. A concise introductory account of Rousseau's life and career with analyses of his major works.

Hulliung, Mark. *The Autocritique of Enlightenment: Rousseau and the Philosophes*. Cambridge, Mass.: Harvard University Press, 1994. Shows how Rousseau both reflected and departed from main currents in Enlightenment philosophy.

Morgenstern, Mira. *Rousseau and the Politics of Ambiguity: Self, Culture, and Society*. University Park: Pennsylvania State University Press, 1996. Analyzes Rousseau's political theory and its historical context, showing how Rousseau's thought introduced notes of ambiguity that remain in contemporary political life.

Wokler, Robert. *Rousseau*. New York: Oxford University Press, 1995. A concise and lucid introduction to Rousseau's life and thought.

Robert H. O'Connor, updated by John K. Roth

Josiah Royce

Royce was the last major philosopher of the twentieth century to integrate theological or religious topics with idealistic philosophy and to present his system to the general reader in terms of community and loyalty. He advanced philosophic idealism and played a significant role in Harvard University's intellectual development.

Principal philosophical works: *The Religious Aspect of Philosophy*, 1885; *California from the Conquest in 1846 to the Second Vigilance Committee in San Francisco (1856): A Study of the American Character*, 1886; *The Feud of Oakfield Creek: A Novel of California Life*, 1887; *The Spirit of Modern Philosophy: An Essay in the Form of Lectures*, 1892; *The Conception of God*, 1897; *Studies of Good and Evil*, 1898; *The World and the Individual*, 1899-1901 (2 volumes); *The Philosophy of Loyalty*, 1908; *Race Questions, Provincialism, and Other American Problems*, 1908; *William James and Other Essays on the Philosophy of Life*, 1911; *The Sources of Religious Insight*, 1912; *The Problem of Christianity*, 1913; *War and Insurance*, 1914; *The Hope of the Great Community*, 1916; *Lectures on Modern Idealism*, 1919; *Fugitive Essays*, 1920; *The Basic Writings of Josiah Royce*, 1969; *The Letters of Josiah Royce*, 1970.

Born: November 20, 1855; Grass Valley, California
Died: September 14, 1916; Cambridge, Massachusetts

Early Life

Josiah Royce was born November 20, 1855, in Grass Valley, California. His parents, Josiah Royce, Sr., and Sarah Bayliss Royce, had come to California during the gold rush of 1849. They were pious, evangelical Christians. Because Royce's father was never successful in any of his various business activities and, as a salesperson, was often absent from the home, his mother played a major role in shaping young Josiah's world. He was a sickly boy, short, freckled, with wild red hair; his mother did not allow him to play with the other children in the community. According to later autobiographical remarks, Royce was fascinated by the problem of time: He considered his hometown old, yet people referred to Grass Valley as a "new community." Meanwhile, in 1866, Royce entered Lincoln Grammar School in San Francisco, the family having moved there for better economic opportunities and educational possibilities for "Jossie." After a year at San Francisco Boy's High School, which in 1869 had a distinct militaristic manner

that Royce hated, he entered the preparatory class at the University of California in Oakland. Within five years, Royce received his bachelor of arts degree in classics. As a result of his achievement, local patrons of the university sponsored him for a year's study in Germany.

Accordingly, from 1875 to 1876, Royce studied at Heidelberg, Leipzig, and Göttingen. His area of study was philosophy. His early concerns about time, the individual, and the community now found expression in his study overseas and at The Johns Hopkins University. Enrolling in 1876, Royce completed his Ph.D. degree at Johns Hopkins within two years. Jobs teaching philosophy were scarce, and—very unwillingly—Royce returned to the University of California, where he taught English rhetoric and literature for the next four years. He did not, however, give up his study of philosophy.

In 1880, Royce married Katharine Head; the couple produced three sons. Royce kept his public role and private life separate, although the latter often indirectly revealed itself in his letters. Royce had met William James while at Johns Hopkins and regularly corresponded with him. In 1883, Royce joined the Harvard faculty as a temporary replacement for James, who was on

Josiah Royce. *(Library of Congress)*

academic leave. Royce could now be a full-time philosopher.

Life's Work

Having published fifteen articles by the time of his temporary appointment, Royce worked very hard, teaching and writing, to gain a permanent place on the Harvard faculty. Within six years, he would achieve tenure and have a nervous break-down. *The Religious Aspect of Philosophy* was based on his lectures, and most of his later books would derive from lectures. Exceptions were *California from the Conquest in 1846 to the Second Vigilance Committee in San Francisco (1856): A Study of American Character*, a state history, and *The Feud of Oakfield Creek: A Novel of California Life*, a novel; both books were early reflections of Royce's lifelong interest in community and indi-vidual behavior.

After spending most of the year 1888 traveling to Australia as a cure for his nervous condition, Royce returned to Harvard with a fuller grasp of his ideas as well as the energy to express them. After publishing *The Spirit of Modern Philosophy: An Essay in the Form of Lec-tures*, he was appointed professor of the history of philosophy at Harvard. He continued to write on an extraordinary range of topics, but his basic focus was on religious values and philosophy; *The Conception of God* and *Studies of Good and Evil* were typical expressions of that focus. During the years 1894 through 1898, Royce was chairman of the De-partment of Philosophy, and he signifi-cantly shaped the courses and the fac-ulty at Harvard.

Royce published his Gifford Lectures as *The World and the Individual*. In the last sixteen years of his life, his scholar-ship was truly remarkable. His writ-ing continued to be both broad and technical: *The Philosophy of Loyalty* and *Race Questions, Provincialism, and Other American Problems* were the results of his efforts to have philosophy inform both the scholar and the general public.

Although his scholarly achievements were many, in his personal life Royce suffered many setbacks. His marriage was a strain. His wife was often caustic and hypercriti-cal, and his children disappointed him in various ways. Christopher, his oldest son, who suffered from mental illness most of his adult life, was committed to Danvers State Hospital in 1908 and died two years later. A month before the death of Royce's son, his closest and dearest friend, Wil-liam James, died. Despite these tragic events, Royce continued to work, publishing *William James and Other Essays on the Philosophy of Life*. Within a year, he had completed *The Sources of Religious Insight*. Despite a major stroke, Royce struggled back to health and continued his philo-sophic work with a significant book, *The Problem of Christianity*.

World War I was a philosophical crisis for Royce. After much thought, he became a strong advocate for U.S. intervention. Worn out by personal worries and poor health, Royce died on September 14, 1916, in Cambridge, Massachusetts.

Influence

Royce left no school of thought or prominent disciples. His philosophy of metaphysical idealism fell out of fashion as pragmatism, logical positivism, and existentialism gained currency in the academic world and the larger society. His use of the German idealism of Immanuel Kant and Georg Wilhelm Friedrich Hegel also limited Royce's appeal.

In his varied writings, Royce stressed the primacy of the individual while holding fast to his emphasis on community. Royce recognized the damage done to individuals and to society by the alienation in American life. Also significant in his thought was the distinction between the world of appreciation or value and the world of factual description. The world of appreciation gives meaning, shape, and value to the human condition.

Finally, Royce was not a naïve thinker. He recognized evil in the world in various manifestations. His philosophy of the Absolute recognized three kinds of evil: metaphysical evil, anything short of the Absolute that is not perfect; natural evil, anything that offends humanity's ethical sense or that humanity cannot accept because of the limits of human intelligence (the problem of Job); and human evil, sin or voluntary inattention. Royce was a philosopher whose ideas have application to the modern world. Like Peirce and James, Royce during his lifetime and in his writing contributed to the golden age of American philosophy.

Donald K. Pickens

The World and the Individual

Type of philosophy: Metaphysics
First published: 1899-1901 (2 volumes)
Principal ideas advanced:
◇ Being can be understood as an absolute system of ideas that embody the fulfillment of purposes.
◇ All knowledge is of matters of experience.

◇ The individual self must be defined in ethical terms by reference to a life plan.
◇ As a free individual, each person contributes to the world and to God's will.
◇ Although no perfection is found in the temporal world, the Eternal Order is perfect.
◇ People are finite, but union with the infinite God is realized.

Josiah Royce proved to be the most durable American proponent of the metaphysical position, absolute idealism. *The World and the Individual* is composed of two series of Gifford Lectures delivered before the University of Aberdeen in 1899 and 1900, the first entitled "The Four Historical Conceptions of Being," and the second, "Nature, Man, and the Moral Order." In these lectures, Royce developed, with some significant changes, earlier ideas that he had presented in such works as *The Religious Aspect of Philosophy* (1885) and *Studies of Good and Evil* (1898). A summary of Royce's philosophical position appears in the last lecture of the second volume:

> The one lesson of our entire course has thus been the lesson of the unity of finite and of infinite, of temporal dependence and of eternal significance, of the World and all its Individuals, of the One and the Many, of God and Man. Not only in spite, then, of our finite bondage, but because of what it means and implies, we are full of the presence and the freedom of God.

This is a truly revealing statement considered not only as a condensation of Royce's central claim but also as an indication of the characteristic mode of argument that gives Royce's philosophy its individual content and flavor, distinguishing it from other versions of idealism. Royce maintains that from human finitude, God's infinite presence and freedom follow. Royce supposed that the finite, the limited, is conceivable only by comparison with an actual infinite. It is as if he had argued that humanity, in virtue of its limitations, suggests the actual unlimited, the Absolute—otherwise, there would be no sense in saying that humanity is "limited," that it does not come up to the mark. Royce's words are reminiscent of French philosopher René Descartes's argument that knowledge of humanity's imperfection leads to knowledge of the actuality of God's perfection and, hence, of God's existence.

Royce's argument claims that from imperfection, knowledge of perfection follows. Hence, from knowledge of purpose, knowledge of fulfillment follows; from knowledge of error or of its possibility, knowledge of the actuality of truth follows; from knowledge of the partial, knowledge of the Absolute; from knowledge of the individual, knowledge of the community—and from knowledge of the unfulfilled and finite individual and community, knowledge of the fulfilled, infinite, "Individual of Individuals," or God, follows.

Error and Infinity

In "The Possibility of Error," a chapter in *The Religious Aspect of Philosophy*, Royce argued that the possibility of error implies the actuality of "an infinite unity of conscious thought to which is present all possible thought." Royce suggested that an error is a thought that aims at being a complete thought in regard to its chosen object, and it is only by comparing the incomplete or inadequate thought with a complete or adequate thought that the incomplete thought can be known to be erroneous. Furthermore, not only could the error not be *known* to be erroneous were there not a complete thought present to a thinker who could compare the complete thought with the erroneous thought, but the error could not even be an error were there not such an actual complete thought and actual, knowing thinker. An idea could not be incomplete by reference or comparison to *nothing* or by reference to something other than a thought; for an error to be an error, an actual, adequate thought (and thinker) must exist. Since "there must be possible an infinite mass of error," there must be an *actual*, infinite, all-knowing thought.

A pragmatist such as William James or Charles Sanders Peirce would say that a belief can be understood to be erroneous if what one would receive in the way of experience, were one to act appropriately, would run counter to one's expectations. However, the mere possibility of a more satisfactory and adequate experience was not enough for Royce. Unless there were actually a complete idea, no belief could possibly be erroneous, for no belief could fail to measure up to a complete idea unless there actually was such a complete idea.

Internal and External Meanings

In the preface to *The World and the Individual*, Royce writes: "As to the most essential argument regarding the true relations between our finite ideas and the ultimate nature of things, I have never varied, in spirit, from the view maintained in . . . 'The Possibility of Error.'" He refers to a number of books in which the argument was used, then states that "In the present lectures, this argument assumes a decidedly new form." The new version of the argument is presented in "The Internal and the External Meaning of Ideas," chapter 7 of the first volume of *The World and the Individual*. The argument concludes with the fourth (and final) conception of Being considered by Royce: "What is, or what is real, is as such the complete embodiment, in individual form and in final fulfillment, of the internal meaning of finite ideas." The three conceptions of Being that Royce examined and rejected before settling on this final idea were those of realism, mysticism, and critical rationalism. The fourth conception of Being, for all of the novelty of its presentation, is fundamentally that with which readers of Royce's earlier works are familiar; and the argument in its support is, strictly speaking, not a new argument distinguishable from the one to be found in "The Possibility of Error" and *The Conception of God* (1897), but—as Royce himself wrote—the argument in "a decidedly new form."

To understand the argument in its new form a distinction must be drawn, in Royce's terms, between the "internal and external meaning" of ideas. According to Royce, an idea "is as much an instance of will as it is a knowing process"; that is, an idea is a partial fulfillment of the purposive act of desiring to have an adequate conception of something. By the "internal meaning" of an idea, Royce meant the "conscious embodiment" of the purpose in the idea. If one tries to get a clear idea about someone, then to the extent that one's thoughts are directed by that interest and come to have something of the content they would have were one entirely clear in one's conception, then to that extent one's idea has internal meaning. Unless to some extent one fulfills the purpose of one's thought by thinking accurately, one cannot be said to have an object of thought: In thinking about someone, one has to think accurately enough, at least, to identify that person as the object of one's conception. Internal meaning, then, is a function of, and consequence of, human will and purpose.

However, ideas refer beyond themselves to something external, not part of their content. Royce asks, "How is it possible that an idea, which is an idea essentially and primarily because of the inner purpose that it consciously fulfills by its presence, also possesses a meaning that in any sense appears to go beyond this internal purpose?" The answer is that the external meaning of an idea is the "completely embodied internal meaning of the idea." In other words, a finite thought fulfills itself to some extent by managing to be *about* something; but what one aims at is a more complete and adequate idea, a fuller conception, one that fulfills one's purpose in thinking. Yet unless there is such an adequate idea, such an external meaning, then the incomplete thought, the unfulfilled idea, the partial conception, aims at nothing. If it has no objective, it cannot fail; and if it cannot fail, it cannot be incomplete or partial. Hence, the possibility of unfulfilled internal meanings implies the actuality of external meanings, and the totality of external meanings is God. God is the "Other," the fulfillment of purpose, which alone can be the object of thought. An idea is true to the extent that it "corresponds, even in its vagueness, to its own final and completely individual expression."

Royce built his conception of God in such a manner that God, or that Being that is the absolute fulfillment of all individual wills, "sees the one plan fulfilled through all the manifold lives, the single consciousness winning its purpose by virtue of all the ideas, of all the individual selves, and of all the lives."

Another insight that serves to illuminate Royce's philosophy and his method is the realization that for Royce, "the world is real only as the object of true ideas." To be the "object" of an idea is to be that at which the idea aims, its objective; and the objective of the idea (of the thinker) is a completely adequate thought, one that fulfills the original purpose in thinking. Hence, if "the world is real only as the object of true ideas," the world is real only as an absolutely adequate

thought, itself an expression of will. The consequence is that God alone is real—but, then, insofar as any individual or any thought fulfills the purpose that has being because of the finite individuals and wills, then just to that extent the finite individual or thought is real, part of Being. Thus, unity is achieved despite the variety and finitude of things. The individual contributes to the Being who fulfills the purposes of the individuals.

A Theory of Knowledge

With the final conception of Being, the first volume of *The World and the Individual* comes to a close. In the second volume, Royce worked out the implications of his conception to present an idealistic theory of knowledge, a philosophy of nature, a doctrine about self, a discussion of the human individual, a portrait of the world as "a Moral Order," a study of the problem of evil, and some conclusions concerning the bearing of these matters on natural religion.

Royce's idealistic theory of knowledge is a reaffirmation of his central predisposition to accept as real only that which fulfills the purpose of an individual will. Realists talk about "hard" facts, he writes, but analysis shows that "hard" facts are understandable as facts that enable us "even now to accomplish our will better than we could if we did not acknowledge these facts." A fact is "*that which I ought to recognize* as determining or limiting what I am here consciously to do or to attempt." A distinction is drawn between the ethical Ought, definable by reference to a more rational purpose than one's own, and a theoretical Ought, definable by reference to a world of recognized facts that embodies and fulfills purposes. To know, to apprehend a fact, is to come to have the thought that the present thought would be were its purpose (its internal meaning) fulfilled by further considerations (the external meaning). To know is to think what you *ought* to think relative to the purpose of your thought. Facts are *objective* in that they are "*other than*" the present, incomplete thoughts; one's grounds for acknowledging facts are *subjective* in that they are related to one's purposes, the intentions of one's wills; however, the objective and subjective are synthesized by "the essential *Teleological* constitution of the realm of facts"—a teleological constitution that is understood once reality or Being is recognized as absolutely ordered and fulfilling will.

Royce argues that to those who see reality in a fragmentary fashion, facts appear to be disconnected; but there is, he claims, a linkage of facts that illuminates the particular character of each fact. Analogously, through temporal failures and efforts, the reality of eternal fulfillment is won.

To Royce, it appears that people's wills are such that they cannot be satisfied by the mere addition of content, additional facts; for the full expression of will, other wills are necessary. Finally, fulfillment comes only from a system of wills that is such that Being is a unity, a one out of many, a will (the Individual of Individuals) that is the infinite, eternal embodiment of individual wills that, by their temporal efforts, have contributed to the reality of the whole.

According to Royce, the idea that nature is hopelessly divided between matter and mind is itself the product of a scientific enterprise motivated by social concerns. The fulfillment of that social concern is best served by recognizing the unsatisfactory character of a conception that maintains a diversity in nature, an irreconcilable tension between matter and mind. The conception of the natural world "as directly bound up with the experiences of actually conscious beings" is more in accord with the fourth conception of Being that the first series of lectures was designed to advance. The idea of a nonconscious, nonliving, nonwilling reality is unacceptable, for to *be*, to be *real*, is to be the conscious fulfillment of purpose. Thus, if nature is real, nature is the conscious fulfillment of purpose.

The Self and Moral Order

The idea of the human self is constructed not by reference to any "Soul-Substance" but by reference to an "Intent always to remain another than my fellows despite my divinely planned unity with them." There is no ultimate conflict between individual selves and the Divine Will, "for the Divine Will gets expressed in the existence of me the individual only in so far as this Divine Will . . . includes within itself my own will, as one of its own purposes."

To justify the claim that reality exhibits a moral order, Royce insists that every evil deed must sometime be "atoned for" or "overruled" by some individual self; in this manner, perfection of the whole is realized. The evil of this world is in its incompleteness, its partial fulfillment of purposes—but because the incomplete and the unfulfilled make sense only by reference to an actual Absolute, by being incomplete they make Being possible as an ordered whole.

Royce regarded God, or Absolute Being, as a person, that is, as "a conscious being, whose life, temporally viewed, seeks its completion through deeds." God is the totality of all conscious efforts, but viewed eternally, God is an infinite whole that includes temporal process. People are also persons, but not absolute; reality finally consists in God's reality.

Because the self possesses individuality, a uniqueness of purpose, it can be satisfied only by what is Other, by what fulfills that purpose, namely, God. However, God is eternal. Consequently, the immortality of self is assured.

One can come to understand, provided one views Royce's arguments with sympathetic tolerance, how if the self is realized only in God, there is a sense in which the self (the individual) and God are one—although viewed from the varying perspectives of time and purpose, they are distinct. However, if the self and God are one, then, in the respect in which they are one, they are alike: God's eternity, then, is humanity's, and this is humanity's immortality. Although the individual self, in being distinguished from other selves by its peculiar purposive striving, is only partial, in contributing to the reality of the Absolute and in becoming unified with the Absolute, it is itself absolute. The part is equal to the whole, even though, considered otherwise than by reference to the final unity, the part is distinguishable from the whole.

The World and the Individual is eloquent witness to Royce's moral sincerity and intellectual acumen. Fantastic as the idealistic image is to realists who presuppose an unconcerned and unconscious material world, it has a certain intellectual charm and moral persuasiveness to one who is willing to sympathize with the interest that leads Royce to deny that anything could be *real*, could be worthy of the honorific name "being," that did not show itself to be a conscious effort to go beyond the limits of fragmentary knowledge and experience to a recognition of and identity with the whole of such effort. If such a proposition as "All Being is the fulfillment of purpose" is taken not as a description of the facts of the matter in regard to the kind of world the physicist studies, but as a suggestion that all human effort be directed to the ideal cooperation of all seekers after truth and goodness, *The World and the Individual* comes to be recognizable as a revolutionary manifesto directed to the human spirit—something quite different from the naïve speculative expression of an idealistic philosopher remote from the world of hard facts.

Ian P. McGreal, updated by John K. Roth

Additional Reading

Clendenning, John. *The Life and Thought of Josiah Royce.* Madison: University of Wisconsin Press, 1985. Taking a chronological approach, Clendenning argues that there is a close relationship between the particulars of Josiah Royce's life and his metaphysical thought.

Hine, Robert V. *Josiah Royce: From Grass Valley to Harvard.* Norman: University of Oklahoma Press, 1992. This worthwhile historical study of Royce and his times stresses the importance of Royce's California upbringing.

Kegley, Jacquelyn Ann K. *Genuine Individuals and Genuine Communities: A Roycean Public Philosophy.* Nashville: Vanderbilt University Press, 1997. Uses Royce's outlook to develop a social philosophy that emphasizes the interdependence of individuality and community.

Kuklick, Bruce. *Josiah Royce: An Intellectual Biography.* Indianapolis: Bobbs-Merrill, 1972. Relating Royce to the issues of his time, Kuklick provides a reliable study of Royce's ideas and their place in the history of American philosophy.

McDermott, John J., ed. *The Basic Writings of Josiah Royce.* Chicago: University of Chicago Press, 1969. McDermott's introductions show how Royce set a "herculean task" for himself, namely, to provide a complete philosophical account of the nature of experience.

Oppenheim, Frank M. *Royce's Mature Ethics.* Notre Dame: University of Notre Dame Press, 1993. This detailed study by an important Royce scholar shows how Royce's moral philosophy developed and why it emphasized communal relationships so strongly.

_____. *Royce's Mature Philosophy of Religion.* Notre Dame: University of Notre Dame Press, 1987. A thoughtful appraisal of Royce's developing understanding of God and religious experience as key ingredients in his metaphysical idealism.

Roth, John K., ed. *The Philosophy of Josiah Royce.* Indianapolis: Hackett, 1982. Roth suggests that Royce's lasting contributions are to be found more in his analysis of finite human experience than in his metaphysical conclusions.

Smith, John E. *The Spirit of American Philosophy.* Rev. ed. Notre Dame: University of Notre Dame Press, 1983. This classic study attempts to locate a common American spirit among five varied thinkers by interpreting the philosophies of Charles Sanders Peirce, William James, John Dewey, and Alfred North Whitehead as well as the thought of Royce.

Smith, John E., and William Klubach. *Josiah Royce: Selected Writings.* New York: Paulist Press, 1988. This book's introductory material and selections emphasize Royce's contributions to religious thought and understanding.

Trotter, Griffin. *The Loyal Physician: Roycean Ethics and the Practice of Medicine.* Nashville: Vanderbilt University Press, 1997. Shows how Royce's ethics and their emphasis on loyalty have important implications for the practice of medicine.

Donald K. Pickens, updated by John K. Roth

Richard L. Rubenstein

One of the first Jewish thinkers to explore deeply the ethical and religious implications of the Holocaust, Rubenstein not only questioned the credibility of claims about God's presence in history but also addressed overpopulation, modernization, bureaucracy, and the persistent threat of genocide in the modern world.

Principal philosophical works: *After Auschwitz: Radical Theology and Contemporary Judaism*, 1966 (revised and enlarged as *After Auschwitz: History, Theology, and Contemporary Judaism*, 1992); *The Religious Imagination: A Study in Psychoanalysis and Jewish Theology*, 1968; *Morality and Eros*, 1970; *My Brother Paul*, 1972; *Power Struggle*, 1974; *The Cunning of History: Mass Death and the American Future*, 1975; *The Age of Triage: Fear and Hope in an Overcrowded World*, 1983; *Approaches to Auschwitz: The Holocaust and Its Legacy*, 1987 (with John K. Roth).

Born: January 8, 1924; New York, New York

Early Life

A 1940 graduate of Townsend Harris High School in New York City, Richard Lowell Rubenstein did not experience the Holocaust firsthand. While Nazi Germany's "final solution of the Jewish question" destroyed European Jewry, he was a student at Hebrew Union College in Cincinnati, Ohio, where he studied from 1942 to 1945, and then at the University of Cincinnati, where he took his bachelor of arts degree in 1946. Nevertheless, the Holocaust marked Rubenstein's life profoundly. That disaster was a governing influence on his substantial body of philosophical writings about religion, theology, politics, and ethics.

Raised in an assimilated Jewish home, Rubenstein received strong parental encouragement to develop intellectually—so much so that his avid reading and disinterest in sports led to grammar school teasing that dubbed him "The Professor." His family, however, was less than enthusiastic about Rubenstein's eventual decision to become a rabbi, which led to his ordination when he graduated from the Jewish Theological Seminary of America in 1952. For the next four years, Rubenstein served Jewish congregations in Brockton and Natick, Massachusetts, but his academic interests proved stronger than his commitment to these rabbinical positions. Graduate study at Harvard University, where Christian theologian and philosopher Paul Tillich influenced him considerably, led to his master's degree in theology in 1955 and to his Ph.D. in 1960. Rubenstein served as chaplain to Jewish students at Harvard from 1956 to 1958 and then as director of the B'nai B'rith Hillel Foundation and chaplain to Jewish students at the University of Pittsburgh and Carnegie Mellon University from 1958 to 1970. During these years in Pittsburgh, Pennsylvania, Rubenstein emerged as a Jewish writer whose thought would be even more significant than it was controversial—and Rubenstein's thought definitely turned out to be controversial.

Life's Work

In 1961 in the Netherlands, Rubenstein planned to begin a research trip to West Germany on Sunday, August 13. That same day, the East Germans created a major Cold War crisis by hastily building a wall between East and West Berlin. Postponing his trip for two days, Rubenstein arrived in Bonn, the West German capital, and accepted an invitation from his hosts, the Bundespressamt (Press and Information Office) of the Federal Republic, to fly to Berlin to see the unfolding crisis. In an atmosphere charged with fear that nuclear war might erupt, Rubenstein took the opportunity to interview Heinrich Grüber, a prominent German Christian leader who had resisted the Nazis under Adolf Hitler, rescued Jews, and suffered imprisonment in a Sachsenhausen concentration camp. Earlier in 1961, Grüber had been the only German to testify for the prosecution at the Jerusalem trial of Adolf Eichmann, a leading Nazi perpetrator of the Holocaust.

With American tanks rumbling through the streets of Dahlem, the West Berlin suburb where Grüber lived, Rubenstein interviewed him in the late afternoon of August 17. When their conversation turned to the Holocaust, this meeting became a turning point in Rubenstein's personal and intellectual life. Grüber affirmed a biblical faith in the God-who-acts-in-history. More than that, he held that the Jews were God's chosen people; therefore, he believed, nothing could happen to them apart from God's will. When Rubenstein asked Grüber whether God had intended for Hitler to destroy the European Jews, Grüber's response was yes—however difficult it might be to understand the reason, he told Rubenstein, the Holocaust was part of God's plan.

Rubenstein was impressed that Grüber took so seriously the belief that God acts in history, a central tenet of Judaism and Christianity. To Grüber, that belief meant specifically that God was ultimately responsible for the Holocaust. Although Grüber's testimony struck him as abhorrent, Rubenstein appreciated the consistency of Grüber's theology, and the American Jewish thinker came away convinced that he must persistently confront the issue of God and the Holocaust. The eventual result was Rubenstein's first and immensely important book, *After Auschwitz: Radical Theology and Contemporary Judaism*, which appeared in 1966. A second edition of *After Auschwitz*, so extensively enlarged and revised as to be virtually a new book, was published in 1992 with a different subtitle: *History, Theology, and Contemporary Judaism*.

After Auschwitz was among the first books to probe systematically the significance of Auschwitz for post-Holocaust religious life. Its second edition advanced its unsettling explorations. Rubenstein's analysis sparked ongoing debate because it challenged a belief that many people have long held dear. After Auschwitz, Rubenstein contended, belief in a redeeming God—one who is active in history and who will bring a fulfilling end to the upheavals in the human condition—is no longer credible.

In the late 1960's, the stir caused by *After Auschwitz* linked Rubenstein to a group of young American Protestant thinkers—Thomas Altizer, William Hamilton, and Paul van Buren among them—who were called "death of God" theologians. The popular media, including *Time* magazine, picked up the story, and the movement ignited public discussion for some time. Although the spotlight eventually moved on, these thinkers' contributions—especially Rubenstein's—did not fade. Their outlooks posed questions and their testimonies raised issues too fundamental to disappear. Yet neither the labeling nor the clustering of these thinkers was entirely apt. None was atheistic in any simple sense of the word. Nor were their perspectives, methods, and moods

Richard L. Rubenstein. *(Courtesy of University of Bridgeport)*

identical. What they loosely shared was the feeling that talk about God did not—indeed could not—mean what it apparently had meant in the past. In that respect, the term "radical theology" described their work better than the more sensationalistic phrase "death of God." Creating breaks with the past and intensifying discontinuities within traditions, they ventured to talk about experiences that were widely shared even though most people lacked the words or the encouragement to say so in public. Unlike his Protestant brothers, however, Rubenstein put the Holocaust at the center of his contributions to radical theology in the 1960's. *After Auschwitz* provoked real soul searching about that historic catastrophe.

With controversy about *After Auschwitz* and the "death of God" movement still swirling, Rubenstein kept writing. Between 1968 and 1974, he published four important works. An award-winning study, *The Religious Imagination: A Study in Psychoanalysis and Jewish Theology*, drew on Sigmund Freud's thought to interpret religion. It was followed by *Morality and Eros; My Brother Paul*, a work that discussed the differences and similarities Rubenstein saw between Saint Paul's outlook and his own; and *Power Struggle*, in which Rubenstein offered instructive insights about his life and scholarly work. None of these works, however, would be as widely noted as *After Auschwitz* or a brief but pointed book called *The Cunning of History: Mass Death and the American Future*, which appeared in 1975.

The Cunning of History defended several disturbing propositions. First, far from being an aberration or a sign of the decline of "progress," the Holocaust, Rubenstein argued, was an extreme expression of the mainstream of Western civilization. In no way did Rubenstein condone the Holocaust, but he held that key developments in modern society—overpopulation, technology, "problem-solving" calculation, and bureaucracy as well as nationalism and "scientific" racism— could make state-sponsored population riddance a "rational" policy. Rubenstein contended that Nazi Germany enacted such policies against the European Jews. In doing so, moreover, the Nazis revealed the functional inadequacy of morality and religion to prevent such destruction. As a result, Rubenstein affirmed, it no longer makes sense to say that human beings possess rights by

nature. Human beings have rights as members of political communities or they do not have rights at all.

At first, *The Cunning of History* received limited attention, but one of its readers was novelist William Styron. He reviewed the work favorably in *The New York Review of Books* and then discussed it approvingly in *Sophie's World* (1979), his best-selling Holocaust novel. By that time, a new paperback edition of *The Cunning of History*, introduced by Styron, had appeared, and the book's prominence in Holocaust studies was assured.

Rubenstein relocated to Florida State University in 1970, where he became the Robert O. Lawton Distinguished Professor of Religion in 1977 and taught until 1995. It was also in the late 1970's that Rubenstein became interested in the work of the Reverend Sun Myung Moon's Unification Church. This interest led to Rubenstein's presidency of two institutions affiliated with the Unification Church: The Washington Institute for Values in Public Policy, a public policy research institute in Washington, D.C., which he led from 1981 to 1992, and the University of Bridgeport (Connecticut), where Rubenstein became president in 1995. Rubenstein's links with Unification Church projects encouraged his interest in international relations and, in particular, Asian culture, economics, politics, and religion.

Rubenstein's *The Age of Triage: Fear and Hope in an Overcrowded World* reflected his growing concern about international issues. Elaborating the ideas of surplus populations and population riddance introduced in *The Cunning of History*, Rubenstein linked modernization and mass death in a study that encompassed such *apparently* diverse events as the enclosure movement in England during the Enlightenment, the nineteenth century famine years in Ireland, and a variety of twentieth century events—a nonexhaustive list includes the Armenian genocide at the hands of Turks, the slaughter of Soviet citizens under Joseph Stalin, and the devastation of Cambodia, as well as the destruction of the European Jews.

A surplus population, Rubenstein explained, is "one that for any reason can find no viable role in the society in which it is domiciled." Rubenstein recognized that population redundancy exists partly because of sheer numbers but even more because the dominant intentions that energize modern society tend to be governed by the belief that money is the measure of all that is real. More than any other, he claimed, that belief drives the modernization process, which has been under way and intensifying over the last five centuries. One effect of this process is that the intrinsic worth of people diminishes. Their worth is evaluated functionally instead. Hence, Rubenstein contended, if persons are identified as nonuseful—they can be so regarded in any number of ways, depending on how those in power define their terms—a community may find it "sensible" to eliminate the surplus. In modern times, that action has been facilitated, indeed instigated and promoted, by governmental power. As Rubenstein understood it, then, triage entails state-sponsored programs of population elimination: through eviction, compulsory resettlement, expulsion, warfare, and outright extermination, roughly in that order. This winnowing process, more or less extreme in its violence, enables a society to drive out what it does not want and to keep what it desires for itself.

Influence

Rubenstein's wide-ranging scholarship also includes *Approaches to Auschwitz: The Holocaust and Its Legacy*—coauthored with John K. Roth in 1987 and one of the first studies of the Holocaust jointly written by a Jew and a Christian—as well as additional books and many articles about the global connections between religion, ethics, and politics. These writings typically analyze how violence is provoked—and might also be checked—by religious commitments and institutions. They provide further evidence that Rubenstein's influence derived from his unflinching and unrelenting attention to the "dark side" of human existence: violence, genocide, the Holocaust. In his writings, he also affirmed that humankind's persistent ways of destruction and death may be limited, if not checked completely, by the best religious, ethical, and political commitments that human beings can muster. If Rubenstein's incisive writings are more sobering than optimistic, his readers recognize that humankind cannot afford to ignore his thoughts.

John K. Roth

After Auschwitz

History, Theology, and Contemporary Judaism

Type of philosophy: Philosophy of religion, ethics
First published: After Auschwitz: Radical Theology and Contemporary Judaism, 1966 (revised and enlarged as *After Auschwitz: History, Theology, and Contemporary Judaism*, 1992)
Principal ideas advanced:

◇ The Holocaust calls into question the most fundamental beliefs of Jews and Christians.

◇ After Auschwitz, belief in a redeeming God—one who is active in history and who will bring the upheavals of human existence to a fulfilling end—is no longer credible.

◇ As far as the post-Holocaust credibility of belief in a redeeming God is concerned, we live in the time of the "death of God."

◇ A post-Holocaust view that envisions God mystically as the Holy Nothingness offers a credible alternative to belief in the God of history.

◇ Theology's basic relevance is anthropological—what it tells us about humankind.

Calling their regime the Third Reich, Adolf Hitler and his Nazi Party ruled Germany from 1933 to 1945. The Holocaust, Nazi Germany's planned total destruction of the European Jews and the actual murder of nearly six million of them, took place during those years. More than a million Jews were gassed at Auschwitz. The catastrophe that befell his people, the Jews, during the Holocaust led Richard L. Rubenstein to write *After Auschwitz*. The first edition, published in 1966, assured Rubenstein's significance in Jewish theology. Revised and expanded in 1992, this book remains required reading for anyone interested in post-Holocaust philosophy and religion.

Significantly, the Holocaust did not occur until the mid-twentieth century, but conditions necessary, though not sufficient, to produce it were forming centuries before. *After Auschwitz* helps to show how Christian anti-Judaism and its demonization of Jews were decisive antecedents of the Holocaust. It also discusses the importance of the post-Holocaust emergence of the state of Israel, but the book is best known for its emphasis on a collision between faith in the God of history—some Christian beliefs about such a God have produced Christian anti-Judaism—and the disastrous reality of the Holocaust.

The 1992 version of *After Auschwitz* is more a new book than a second edition of an old one. Nine of the original version's fifteen chapters were eliminated; those that remain were substantially rewritten. Ten new chapters, which had been published elsewhere, were added to the revised edition, which is the source for all of the quotations in this article.

A Meeting with a Swami

In the 1992 edition of *After Auschwitz*, Rubenstein describes a meeting with Swami Muktananda of Ganeshpuri, a deeply religious man. "You mustn't believe in your own religion," the Swami advised him, "I don't believe in mine. Religions are like the fences that hold young saplings erect. Without the fence the sapling could fall over. When it takes firm root and becomes a tree, the fence is no longer needed. However, most people never lose their need for the fence."

Rubenstein found the Swami's advice helpful because he received it at a time when he was feeling very pessimistic about humanity, a mood that included what he acknowledged as an intolerance toward people in his own Jewish tradition who apparently declined to face difficulties about the relationship between a God of history and the Holocaust. Rubenstein heard the Swami saying something that spoke to him in ways that are reflected in the opening paragraph of *After Auschwitz*'s second edition. The first version, Rubenstein explained, contained a "spirit of opposition and revolt, which was an almost inevitable consequence of my initial, essentially uncharted attempt to come to terms theologically with the greatest single trauma in all of Jewish history." Governing the second edition, he went on to say, was a "spirit of synthesis and reconciliation." Rubenstein stated that he had kept his fundamental insights but had done so in the second edition "with a greater degree of empathy for those who have reaffirmed traditional Jewish faith in the face of the Holocaust." Rubenstein discerned that Swami Muktananda had urged him not to give up his fundamental insights but

to use them to look deeper and to see beyond their limited meanings.

The "Death of God" Movement

Even before receiving the Swami's advice, Rubenstein showed that he had already been practicing some aspects of it in the first edition of *After Auschwitz*. This book challenged some of the most fundamental beliefs held by Jews and Christians. Specifically, Rubenstein argued, the Holocaust calls into question the existence of a redeeming God, one who is active in history and who will bring the upheavals of human existence to a fulfilling end. In the late 1960's, *After Auschwitz* provoked considerable controversy. One result was that Rubenstein found himself linked with three American Protestant thinkers—Thomas Altizer, William Hamilton, and Paul van Buren—and all four were identified as key players in what came to be known as the "death of God" movement.

At the time, the three American Protestants hailed the "death of God" with considerable enthusiasm. Optimistic about the human prospect, they celebrated the liberation that men and women could experience when they moved beyond an outmoded theological past to see that the whole world was no longer in God's hands but solely in those of the people. Rubenstein's outlook differed in important ways. He was not alone among those thinkers in denying that he was an atheist who literally believed "God is dead," but Rubenstein made clearer than most his view that "the ultimate relevance of theology is anthropological," a perspective reflected in his long-standing use of psychoanalytic insights when he has spoken about religion. What Rubenstein meant was that whenever people speak about God, they are talking about what they believe about God, which is not the same as talking about God directly. Therefore, it can make sense to say, as Rubenstein did in *After Auschwitz*, that "we live in the time of the death of God," but as Rubenstein explained further, we cannot say whether "the death of God" is more than an event within human culture.

Rubenstein's emphasis on the anthropological dimensions of theological discourse did not mean that he was indifferent about the nature of ultimate reality. One place, for example, where he parted company with the Christian "death of God" theologians involved his impression that they "'willed' the death of the theistic God" with very little regret. In contrast, Rubenstein found himself unwillingly forced to conclude that the idea of a God of history lacked credibility after Auschwitz and felt saddened by that outcome. He recognized that history had shattered—at least for him—a system of religious meaning that had sustained people, especially Jews and Christians, for millennia. The destruction of such meaning was no cause for celebration. To the contrary, it suggested to Rubenstein the melancholy prospect that human existence is ultimately absurd and meaningless.

Another View of God

That conclusion, however, was not to be Rubenstein's last word on the subject. Seeking an alternative that could work for him and for others who might share his outlook about the God of history, Rubenstein went on to write movingly and positively about his vision of "God after the Death of God," as the final chapter of the revised version of *After Auschwitz* is titled. Instead of "faith in the radically transcendent Creator God of biblical religion, who bestows a covenant on Israel for His own utterly inscrutable reasons," Rubenstein affirmed that "an understanding of God which gives priority to the indwelling immanence of the Divine may be more credible in our era."

Drawing on both Eastern and Western mystical traditions, including strands from his Jewish heritage, Rubenstein amplified the idea of divine immanence by speaking of God as the Holy Nothingness. Submitting that "omnipotent Nothingness is Lord of all creation," he used that concept to refer to "the ground, content, and final destiny of all things," adding that "God as the 'Nothing' . . . is not a thing" but "no-thing." Beyond distinctions between the masculine and the feminine or human understandings of good and evil, Rubenstein's Holy Nothingness is not the "absence of being, but a superfluity of being . . . a *plenum* so rich that all existence derives therefrom." The best metaphor for this concept, he suggested, is that "God is the ocean and we the waves. Each wave has its moment when it is identifiable as a somewhat separate entity. Nevertheless, no wave is entirely distinct from the ocean, which is its substantial ground."

This perspective's advantages, Rubenstein argued, include "a judgment on the overly individualistic conception of the self which has predominated in the Western world." Emphasizing the interdependence of all things, Rubenstein insisted that "the world of the death of the biblical God need not be a place of gloom or despair. One need not live forever for life to be worth living. Creation, however impermanent, is full of promise." Granted, if omnipotent Nothingness is Lord of all creation, we can ask but never really answer the question "Why is there something rather than nothing?" Far from reducing the horror of "ethnic cleansing" and the Holocaust, that outcome may make human life more tragic than ever. However, it does remove the theological "problem of evil" that intrudes when such devastations are interpreted as part of a world created and sustained by a powerful biblical God of history whose providential purposes are supposedly governed by goodness, justice, and love.

However, the concerns that drove Rubenstein to reject the traditional God of history were never directed by unsatisfactory attempts to solve a dilemma whose dissonance had been reduced to the abstract question, "If there is radical evil in the world, how can God be omnipotent and completely good?" His issue was far more concrete, particular, and historical. After Auschwitz, how could sense be made of a Jewish tradition of covenant and election, a perspective in which Jews interpreted themselves to be specially chosen by God, bound to God in a covenant that entailed God's blessing for faithfulness and God's judgment against infidelity? Common to that tradition's self-understanding was the belief that "radical communal misfortune," as Rubenstein called it, was a sign either that God found the Chosen People wanting and dispensed punishment accordingly, or that God called on the innocent to suffer sacrificially for the guilty, or that an indispensable prelude for the messianic climax of Jewish history was under way, or some combination of such outlooks. In any case, the Holocaust, an event in which Nazi Germany was hell-bent on destroying Jewish life root and branch, made Rubenstein collide head-on with the biblical tradition of covenant and election, which seemed to him to lead consistently to a positive answer to the question: "Did God use Adolf Hitler and the Nazis as his agents to inflict terrible sufferings and death upon six million Jews, including more than one million children?" Such an answer Rubenstein could not accept. He wrote *After Auschwitz* instead.

A Distinctive Journey

Rubenstein had to decide whether to affirm the logical implication that he found belief in the God of history to entail, namely, that God was ultimately responsible for Auschwitz. Finding that affirmation obscene, he looked elsewhere to make sense of his Jewish identity. Rubenstein's developing religious perspective led him to reject a providential God and to emphasize instead a sense of the sacred in which "creation and destruction are part of an indivisible process. Each wave in the ocean of God's Nothingness has its moment, but it must inevitably give way to other waves." Nevertheless, Rubenstein affirmed, we have considerable freedom to direct the journey we take during our limited time on earth. That journey can be joyful and good.

After Auschwitz was a crucial departure point for Rubenstein's distinctive journey. Decades later he returned to that work and saw that "no person writing about the religious significance of contemporary history can rest content with what he or she has written at a particular moment in time. As history is an ongoing process, so too is theological writing concerning history." As the second edition of *After Auschwitz* made clear, however, Rubenstein consistently followed his conviction that theology's basic relevance is anthropological—what it tells us about humankind. Thus, the accent of his work fell increasingly on history, politics, economics, and sociology—always with reference to religious thought and practice but with emphasis on the conditions that produce human conflict and the safeguards that must be shored up to limit that conflict's destructiveness.

Important though they are, none of Rubenstein's other books is likely to eclipse the significance of *After Auschwitz*. Particularly in the United States, its sustained impact has rightly been considerable in Jewish circles and on many Christian audiences as well. Rubenstein's reflections were among the first to probe the signifi-

cance of Auschwitz for post-Holocaust religious life. Few, if any, have better stood the test of time.

John K. Roth

Additional Reading

Braiterman, Zachary. *God After Auschwitz: Tradition and Change in Post-Holocaust Jewish Theology*. Princeton: Princeton University Press, 1998. Braiterman thoughtfully interprets and assesses Richard L. Rubenstein's contributions to debate about God's relation to history and to the Holocaust in particular.

Cohn-Sherbok, Dan. *Holocaust Theology*. London: Lamp Press, 1989. Surveying various theological responses to the Holocaust, this book contains a good introductory chapter about Rubenstein's thought written by a well-qualified interpreter of his work.

Cooper, John Charles. *The Roots of Radical Theology*. Philadelphia: Westminster, 1967. Provides early perspective on the "death of God" movement as it emerged in the 1960's.

Haynes, Stephen R., and John K. Roth, eds. *The Death of God Movement and the Holocaust: Radical Theology Encounters the Shoah*. Westport, Conn.: Greenwood Press, 1999. Rubenstein joins other scholars, including Thomas Altizer, William Hamilton, and Paul van Buren, to discuss retrospectively the Holocaust's impact on the "death of God" movement in theology.

Jacobs, Steven L., ed. *The Holocaust Now: Contemporary Christian and Jewish Thought*. East Rockaway, N.Y.: Cummings and Hathaway, 1996. This work features significant essays on post-Holocaust theology that frequently address Rubenstein's concerns and theories.

Katz, Stephen T. *Post-Holocaust Dialogues: Critical Studies in Modern Jewish Thought*. New York: New York University Press, 1983. In this noteworthy study, an important Jewish philosopher and Holocaust scholar includes a critical discussion of Rubenstein's work and its implications.

Kliever, Lonnie D. *The Shattered Spectrum: A Survey of Contemporary Theology*. Atlanta, Ga.: John Knox Press, 1981. Provides useful insights about Rubenstein's role in the upheaval and development of post-Holocaust religious thought.

Murchland, Bernard, ed. *The Meaning of the Death of God: Protestant, Jewish and Catholic Scholars*

Explore Atheistic Theology. New York: Random House, 1967. Important scholars comment on the "death of God" movement, including Rubenstein's relation to it.

Roth, John K., ed. *Ethics after the Holocaust: Perspectives, Critiques, and Responses*. St. Paul, Minn.: Paragon House, 1999. In a dialogue format, Leonard Grob, Peter J. Haas, David Hirsch, David Patterson, Didier Pollefeyt, and John K. Roth discuss post-Holocaust ethics in ways that often draw on Rubenstein's thought.

Rubenstein, Betty Rogers, and Michael Berenbaum, eds. *What Kind of God? Essays in Honor of Richard L. Rubenstein*. Lanham, Md.: University Press of America, 1995. This valuable book contains extensive biographical and bibliographical information about Rubenstein as well as significant essays about his work by important Holocaust scholars, philosophers, and theologians.

Sontag, Frederick, and John K. Roth. *The American Religious Experience*. New York: Harper & Row, 1972. Rubenstein's work is discussed in a chapter on "The Death of God in American Theology."

John K. Roth

Jalāl al-Dīn Rūmī

Rūmī's poetry and prose teachings guided Sufis on Islamic teachings by revealing the way to God in the context of the Qur'an and the life of the Prophet Muhammad. He showed the way of loving God as a personal transfiguration of radical and profound proportions for individuals who reach spiritual perfection.

Principal philosophical works: *Fīhī mā fīhi*, early thirteenth century (*Discourses of Rumi*, 1961); *Dīvan-e Shams-e Tabrīz*, 1244-1273 (*Selected Poems from the Dīvani Shamsi Tabrīz*, 1898; better known as *The Sufi Path of Love: The Spiritual Teachings of Rumi*, 1983); *Ma'navī-ye Ma'navī*, 1259-1273 (*The Mathnavī of Jalālu'ddīn Rūmī*, 1925-1940); *Majāles-e Sab'a*, 1315-1319 (*Seven Sessions*, 1983); *Maktubāt*, 1335 (*Letters*, 1983); *Mystical Poems of Rūmī*, 1968; *The Essential Rumi*, 1995.

Born: September 30, 1207; Balkh (now in Afghanistan)
Died: December 17, 1273; Konya, Asia Minor (now Turkey)

Early Life

Jalal al-Din Rūmī's father, Baha' Walad, was a Sufi preacher, author, and lawyer in Balkh, present-day Afghanistan, where Rūmī was born in 1207. He influenced many, including Rūmī himself, in placing spiritual values ahead of legal and practical ones of other Muslims, and he irritated learned men with his criticisms of Greek philosophy. Rūmī's father fled his home city when it was threatened by invading Mongols in 1219. He took the family first on a pilgrimage to Mecca, and then he moved them to Konya, located in modern Turkey, where he soon acquired prominence and influence. Rūmī began his studies in Konya, mastered the Turkish, Persian, Arabic, and Greek languages, and then went to study at Damascus, proceeding from basic knowledge to theology and philosophy. He married Gevher Hatun in Karaman and his son, Sultan Veled, was born in 1226 in Konya. In 1231, when Rūmī was twenty-four, his father died, and Rūmī assumed his father's place as a preacher and legal scholar.

Life's Work

Rūmī's explicit education in Sufi beliefs was guided by one of his father's disciples, Burhan al-Dīn Tirmidhi, from 1232 to Tirmidhi's death in 1240. After his death, Rūmī continued to preach and discourse on spiritual law. Then there appeared in 1244 the most important person in Rūmī's adult life, the mysterious Shams al-Dīn of Tabrīz. This man's friendship turned Rūmī from a life of prudent teacher of law into an enthusiastic mystic devoted to ecstatic worship of God, expressed in strong Persian poetry of sensuous and intoxicated love. Shams was Rūmī's closest friend and companion for about two years, and then Shams disappeared forever from Rūmī's life and from history. The pain of this loss was a significant cause for Rūmī to compose poetry for the rest of his life. Thus did the poems of *The Sufi Path of Love: The Spiritual Teachings of Rumi* arise from human love and its loss, but their significance was heightened by Rūmī's use of that love as a form to worship God. After Shams's disappearance, Rūmī ceased to perform as a public preacher; instead, he gave the rest of his life to the training of Sufi worshipers.

The Sufi Path of Love is a collection of more than three thousand of Rūmī's *ghazals*, or love poems. Other than those that are in *The Mathnavī of Jalālu'ddīn Rūmī*, the poems of *The Sufi Path of Love* are all of Rūmī's poetry produced over a span of nearly thirty years. Most of them are dedicated to Shams, but a few other persons are mentioned in some. They are inspired by Shams, but transcend him for celebrations and praises of God. Love for a person is but a step along the path toward love of God, which is consciousness of universal unity.

The Mathnavī of Jalālu'ddīn Rūmī is a set of six books of poems in couplet style; there are some twenty-five thousand verses in all. It was written at the request of one of Rūmī's disciples beginning in 1259 so that his didactic teachings might be passed down to posterity in poems that could be memorized. The last book was left unfinished at Rūmī's death. Rūmī composed orally, and his disciples transcribed his verses for recitation. The follower of Rūmī is instructed to exhibit good works in contrast to the enemies of God, who display only sensual desires. A good work involves praising God, as in the recitation of these poems, made by one who cannot turn good things into bad ones, like God, but merely hold up a mirror to show forth the bad and ugly forms of the world. Although *The Mathnavī of Jalālu'ddīn Rūmī* shows more didactic intent than *The Sufi Path of Love*, it is nevertheless only as systematic as the religious framework from which it draws its inspiration and texts for moral edification. The work ought to be read as a companion text to *The Sufi Path of Love*.

The verses of *The Mathnavī of Jalālu'ddīn Rūmī* also differ from those of *The Sufi Path of Love* in that they are largely anecdotal and narrative in contrast to the more lyrical and figurative poetry inspired by Shams. The anecdotes were Rūmī's versions of folklore and commentaries on passages of the Qur'an. There is a moral to each anecdote and it is intended to develop Islamic beliefs with special emphasis on spiritual or mystical insights stressed by Sufis. Unlike the poems of *The Sufi Path of Love*, however, those of *The Mathnavī of Jalālu'ddīn Rūmī* provide more commentary on mystical experience and less on its apprehension or embodiment. After Rūmī's death, scholars and mystics began to compose commentaries on his poetry, including *The Mathnavī of Jalālu'ddīn Rūmī*, which is itself a commentary on the distinctions between laws and love. In this work, Rūmī says that the law can, like a lamp, show the way to the path of love, but once a person is on the path itself, he or she will be taken directly to the goal of truth at the end. Rūmī's way in *The Mathnavī of Jalālu'ddīn Rūmī* is the path; the goal is grasped in the truth of *The Sufi Path of Love*.

Rūmī explains that knowledge that lacks unity with God is merely form without substance, an empty vessel or a branch without fruit. Some of the verses of *The Mathnavī of Jalālu'ddīn Rūmī* satirize those scholars who lack the substance of God's love; they are like birds who cannot fly all the way across the ocean of existence. Those poor in knowledge of substance are like schoolboys who study only books, whereas those who are rich in substance are nourished by a spiritual fountain. The fourth book of *The Mathnavī of Jalālu'ddīn Rūmī* develops this simile in a story of the universal intellect bubbling up inside the spirit; it cannot be blocked by any exterior object of the world. If one looks at the forms of experience, one sees a competition of contraries, of good and evil, but in the reality of God's absolute love there is no good or evil. The verses of *The Mathnavī of Jalālu'ddīn Rūmī* explain this by comparison with the poison of a serpent, which is evil to humans but good to the serpent. It is quaintly explained that one person's candy is another's poison, until the vision of God dissolves such disparities.

Discourses of Rumi is a prose work with a paradoxical and teasing title that literally means, "It has in it what it has in it." This work, composed at the end of Rūmī's life, is a transcription of his various talks to disciples. It employs anecdotes and similes to communicate Rūmī's wisdom. For example, it says that one who sees the light of a candle may know only the bodies of experience, whereas those who are consumed by the fire that gives that light know the spirit of God. Frequently this work is marked by satire, as when Rūmī says that Muhammad may have been poorly educated but anyone who can write on the moon is rich in something. Rūmī mocks the sophisticated wise people who pursue what they call knowledge. He says there must be ignorance, or one could never find God. This praise of ignorance is a playful way of putting down the proud and encouraging the humble. The quality and tone of this work constitute a tribute to Rūmī's gentle humanity, tolerance, and sense of humor.

Two other works are also prose, *Seven Sessions* and *Letters*. The first is a collection of sermons and the second Rūmī's 145 letters written to people who lived in his city of Konya on behalf of Rūmī's friends. The sermons of *Seven Sessions* include simple comparisons that drive home Rūmī's teachings. For example, he says that many serpents in the sea may have the form of fish, but the substance of a snake is still that of a snake. In one of the sermons, Rūmī develops at length his mocking point about Muhammad's reputed illiteracy, a theme favored in *Discourses of Rumi*. There are unlettered people who write without a pen those things that others can write with the pen: The orphaned Muhammad learned impossible truths without benefit of formal knowledge or penmanship. Muhammad learned directly from God, the tutor who teaches all things. The sermons do, of course, contribute to knowledge of his philosophy, but the date of their composition is the subject of scholarly dispute. The sermons may have been delivered before Rūmī met Shams and so demonstrate that Rūmī's beliefs were well established early in his life and that Shams's significance was to inspire the poetry that expressed those beliefs.

Rumi's *Letters* is a collection of letters more personal than public; they do not contain much discussion of Rūmī's beliefs and philosophy. Nevertheless, Rūmī teaches even in the letters, as in the first letter, when he describes the true believer as a bird of the day, who loves the light of the sun, and the false believer as the bird of night, who loves merely darkness. He incorporates teaching in his messages, as when he tells a correspondent in the eighth letter that his good news is a preview of God's best news. The fifty-eighth letter contrasts the good fortune of this world with the good fortune of the next; in this life of games is a model for reflection, a correspondence, for the more serious game of the spirit.

Influence

After Rūmī's death in Konya on December 17, 1273, his disciple Husameddin Celebi assumed Rūmī's place as beloved master. When Celebi died in 1284, Rūmī's son Sultan Veled became the master and contributed to the organization of the major mystical sect of Islam that came to be known as the Mevlevi Sufi. These followers knew Rūmī as Mevlana, or Mawlana ("our master"), and they took their name from him. Rūmī's influence over art and literature, as well as philosophy, is largest in those parts of the world where Islam is strong. His intent was to bring people to

God, overcome divisions, and unite contraries, and his works have encouraged universal toleration. The Mevlevi dervishes celebrate the night of his death as the Night of Union. They recite his poetry in their symbolic rituals and imitate his cosmic order in their whirling dances. They conclude their ritual with a prayer to Rūmī as their master. For some Muslims, Rūmī's work has become the standard interpretation of the Qur'an.

Richard D. McGhee

The Sufi Path of Love

The Spiritual Teachings of Rumi

Type of philosophy: Aesthetics, ethics, Islamic philosophy, philosophical theology
First transcribed: Dīvan-e Shams-e Tabrīz, 1244-1273 (*Selected Poems from the Dīvani Shamsi Tabrīz*, 1898; better known as *The Sufi Path of Love: The Spiritual Teachings of Rumi*, 1983)
Principal ideas advanced:

◇ Justice is the will of God bringing all things to their proper place in the cosmic scheme.
◇ Intellect must be used to overcome the ego, which interferes with divine justice.
◇ Reason and faith embolden one for Holy War, the *jihad*, against evil.
◇ When the ego is obliterated by union with God, shadows dissolve into the light of the First Cause.
◇ The Sufi is the person who has purified himself from desire for anything except the love of God.

Rūmī was a scholar and teacher of Islam, learned in the Qur'an and sayings of the Prophet Muhammad. He developed his special messages from insights into human experience of conflict and struggle, love and hate. Through the experience of love, he realized that wisdom can come directly from God, without dependence on formal education and training, which are only guides to wisdom itself. What Islam needed was the Sufi emphasis on mystical revelation to the individual prepared to surrender absolutely to the love of God. This is what Rūmī brought from his background for his contemporaries and posterity.

The Sufi Path of Love: The Spiritual Teachings of Rumi is a large collection of poems, totaling forty thousand lines, making it by far the longest of Rūmī's works. These lines are composed in three kinds of poems: *ghazals*, or Persian love poems; *tarji'ats*, made up of two or more *ghazals*; and quatrains known as *ruba'iyyats*. The poems were composed over a period of nearly three decades, dating from the arrival of Shams in 1244 to Rūmī's death in 1273. Although the poems are inspired by Shams and many persons are mentioned in them, they are taken by Sufi followers as representations of states of spirituality on the Sufi path of love.

The Divine Lover

Early in *The Sufi Path of Love*, there is an array of holy images, described in ecstatic visions, celebrated as versions of the image of God. The loving poet-speaker is taken up by this image and transformed by its possession. The image is perceived as a form of God but felt as the love of the divine creator, fully available to the poet's loving imagination.

This divine lover can be wrathful, however, like any jealous lover. The human soul is cautioned never to forget how angry and severe God can be if one forgets that his true self, his spirit, belongs to God. The human lover must not pollute himself by loving things of the world before and beyond love of God. To do otherwise would be to wallow in excrement. Rūmī pleads with the lover to leave the pleasures of excrement and find the joys of the spirit in God. In metaphysical imagery, the poems say the human form needs to keep itself empty of earthly things to make room for the divine feast, especially for the intoxicating wine of God's love.

As soon as the lover catches a glimpse of the divine image, the lover will be consumed with desire that annihilates all other interests in life. This may be experienced as pain, because the human suffers separation from God and absolute reality. A direct and full view of the divine lover is denied; there is a screen, sometimes seen as tresses of hair, concealing his view. The human lover can hold onto the tresses and prevent falling away. This vision bestows intellect on the

human lover, a knowledge of God that brings suffering as well as comfort. Through the beloved human, such as Shams of Tabrīz, may this divine love be discovered. When Shams disappears, great suffering remains, and the human lover must battle despair. Memory of the beloved threatens madness when separation has divided the lovers.

It is clear that Shams brought something special to Rūmī, who found in Shams a mirror of God. In their relationship, Rūmī contemplated all the attributes of God and praised the path of love as the way to God. Shams is not the only person in whom Rūmī found God's attributes, but it was in Shams that he found most, even perfection. One of the paradoxes of divine truth is that those human beings in whom God shows himself may not themselves recognize that God is in them. The lover wonders what it takes for human beings to see God regularly: intellectual or spiritual strength. Do the angels or Jesus or Moses see God in his highest sphere? It is clear that God's beauty would burn the lover into cinders if God is viewed directly; therefore, a mirror must be used.

Divine Justice

The glimpse of the beloved is a sign of the way to return to God, who has put everything in its proper place. Thus to find God is actually to return to God after fulfilling a role in the history of the world. This is Rūmī's concept of justice, which operates as the will of God bringing all things to their proper place in the cosmic scheme. Each kind of creature or thing will find its just place and function in eternity, because each has come from that place in the beginning. Although in the world there are struggles and conflicts between opposites, in divine justice, like objects will attract only like subjects at the appropriate level and distance from the divine origin.

For the human soul, intellect must be used to overcome the ego, which interferes with divine justice. Help may be found from the prophets and saints, such as Moses, Jesus, and the Prophet Muhammad, who possess the highest form of intellectual power. Eventually, however, each individual must develop his or her own intellect to reach the place destined by God. There is no doubt that intellect is a primary attribute created for humans by God, but when God is achieved in the divine bliss of vision, intellect is annihilated in the absolute divinity. Angels are embodiments of the highest form of intellectual power, as Gabriel was to the Prophet. However, the angel Gabriel was not able to go all the way to God, and therefore the human lover cannot count on intellect to be there in the final union with the divine. It is love that annihilates the separation between humans and God, and therefore love transcends intellect in Rūmī's philosophy, however significant and necessary intellect may be for human progress. It seems that intellect is too closely attached to ego to get to God; love must dissolve both intellect and ego.

There are several *ghazals*, such as number 182, that caution people to leave intellect behind in the ascent to love, the *mi'raj*. At this level, intellect is like the smell of dung on the wind. The intellectual effort is slow in progress; love flies to the seventh sphere while intellect labors like a camel across the desert. Ascent is the way of love from the physical world (which ends in the ninth sphere), through the spiritual, and ultimately to God himself.

Love As the Way to God

The poems of *The Sufi Path of Love* express great discipline of mind and heart, following such Islamic practices as fasting and prayer, but they go deeper into the essence, or mystery, of the divine experience. They make their way to God through invocation of his name and attributes. This is crucial to remembering the source from which all things come. If it is not done correctly, however, as through meditation or with the guidance of a spiritual master (a *shaykh*), it may not succeed on account of an interfering pride of ego. Such discipline and guidance presume great faith in the human lover, and the faith is substantiated by intellect. There is no division between reason and faith in Rūmī's writings. The person emboldened by these qualities will be ready to enter into a Holy War, the *jihad*, against evil. There is no distinction between the inner spiritual battle within a person and the external objective battle against evil in society and the world. Poem number 312 includes even prayer and wakefulness, fighting off sleep, as acts of *jihad*.

No matter what kind of love is experienced, true or false, it is in the end love only for God.

Those unable to love God truly in this life will find God after death and then it is too late to unite with him. The true believer does not make this mistake, loving God as the only beloved. As in Western Platonism, the belief of Rūmī is that things of the world are but shadows of God the ideal and absolute. Love of the beauty of nature is purely derivative as an illusion that misleads, as described in verses 336-338. At best, a person may find in human love the practice that can prepare him or her for love of God, which is a gift of his grace, although the human's way can be strengthened with the guidance of a master *shaykh*, God's messenger, as in *ghazals* 374 and 695. Eleven poems later, the purified lover is celebrated as deserving the reward of resurrection through death in the Garden of Eden.

Joy and happiness are rewards of true love and they are signs that the love is true. The spirit of the lover is taken up in God's spirit and made intoxicated as with music, dancing, and drinking wine in *ghazal* 81. Many poems celebrate this intoxication of union with God, as number 391, which calls for a minstrel to play a tune of drunken revelry. The person of intellect is sober, the person of love is lost in the annihilating power of God. Then, in number 419, the beloved is felt through his kiss, which cracks and chaps the lips of the human lover, set on fire by God, who lopped off the head of reason in poem number 33. These experiences seem to the rational and sober person to be signs of madness, and for Rūmī there is a deep kinship between love of God and insanity.

Ironically, poetry is without value to Rūmī, unless the poems convey his love of God. Poetry can inspire love of God through the energy of imagination, but this imagination must be burned into annihilation by divine reality. Like all other forms of experience, poetry is empty unless it has the meaning of devotion to God. The philosophical idealism of Rūmī is manifested in this theme of divine essence permeating all forms to give them meaning. Many of the poems express this point as a matter of duality, between the light of God as the First Cause and the shadows of experience as secondary (in *ghazal* 41). When God's light is recognized in the annihilation of love, it is felt as the only thing that exists (poem 1400). All shadows disappear and all other things dissolve in its absoluteness, which is beyond both existence and nothingness (*ghazal* 1019). When the self, or ego, is obliterated by union with God, shadows dissolve into the pure light of the First Cause. Drunk on God, men find true essence in death and nothingness (poem 2102), leaving existence for women (poem 1601), who are dominated by ego and forms.

The Sufi is a poor person, because nothing belongs to the Sufi. All is annihilated in devotion to God, the only richness that counts (*ghazal* 260). The Sufi is literally the person who wears wool, practicing self-denial, and so the Sufi is also the person who has purified the self, eliminating desire for anything except the love of God. This lover of God breaks through the veil of ego, rips it away, and beholds the face of the beloved as the hidden treasure of absolute reality in poem number 3003. This experience can be had several times in a lifetime, and so an individual may experience death and resurrection several times on the path to God, as expressed in *ghazal* 582. When a person declares "there is no God but God," as a declaration of faith, this person is expressing the Sufi principle of contraries between annihilation, or negation, and affirmation, or realization, of God: Each person must experience both of the contraries, passing through nothingness before reaching the absolute (as in poem number 734), in which it is manifested that ultimately all things are lovers, because all reality is infused with God's love, from the fruit that drops from a tree to the hook that sticks in the mouth of a fish (*ghazal* 2327). When the lover finds God, then the lover may truly say he or she exists.

These poems have had profound influences throughout the Islamic world. They have called forth commentaries by generations of scholars, and they have inspired the ceremonies and rituals of Sufi practitioners, especially by the Mevlevi sect of dervishes organized and developed by Rūmī's own son but still vital to this day. In addition, translations of his poetry into English by A. J. Arberry and others have made his art an increasingly popular subject for pleasure and study.

Richard D. McGhee

Additional Reading

Arasteh, R. *Rumi the Persian: Rebirth in Creativity and Love.* Lahore, Pakistan: Sh. Muhammad Ashraf, 1965. An appreciation of the mystical values that can come from devoted readings of Rūmī's poetry.

Chelkowski, P. J. *The Scholar and the Saint.* New York: New York University Press, 1975. This book contains several useful essays on Rūmī and the importance of his work, such as his place in the culture of Turkey, the philosophical concepts to be found in his poetry, the style of his compositions, and the art of his narratives.

Iqbal, A. *The Life and Work of Muhammad Jalal-ud-Din Rumi,* 3d. rev. ed. Lahore, Pakistan: Institute of Islamic Culture, 1974. An appreciation and survey of the poet's life, with respect for Rūmī's influence throughout the Islamic world.

Keshavarz, Fatemeh. *Reading Mystical Lyric: The Case of Jala al-Din Rumi.* Studies in Comparative Religion series. Columbia: University of South Carolina Press, 1998. This work looks at Rūmī's poetry and its religious content. Includes bibliographical references and index.

Nasr, Seyyed Hossein. *Jalāl al-Dīn Rūmī: Supreme Persian Poet and Sage.* Tehran: Shura-ye 'Ali-ye Farhang o Honar, 1974. A good account of the impact made by Shams on Rūmī, including the use of the friendship as a symbol, or exteriorization, of love for God.

_____. *Sufi Essays.* Albany: State University of New York Press, 1972. This book contains eleven essays on various aspects of Sufism in religious thought, Persian literature, and philosophical orientations. Rūmī receives generous credit for contributions to all these areas. Particularly useful is the fourth essay, "The Sufi Master as Exemplified in Persian Sufi Literature."

Renard, John. *All the King's Falcons: Rumi on Prophets and Revelation.* Albany: State University of New York Press, 1994. This book looks at prophets and religion in the works of Rūmī. Contains bibliographical references and index.

Schimmel, Annemarie. *The Triumphal Sun: A Study of the Works of Jaalaaloddin Rumi.* Albany: State University of New York Press, 1993. This book examines the work of the Persian philospher Rūmī. Includes bibliographical references and indexes.

Richard D. McGhee

Bertrand Russell

Russell's original work in the areas of logic, mathematics, and the theory of knowledge was complemented by several important volumes of philosophical popularization, and in his later years, Russell emerged as a major figure in the peace movement.

Principal philosophical works: *German Social Democracy*, 1896; *An Essay on the Foundations of Geometry*, 1897; *A Critical Exposition of the Philosophy of Leibniz*, 1900; *The Principles of Mathematics*, 1903; *Principia Mathematica*, 1910-1913 (with Alfred North Whitehead, 3 volumes); *The Problems of Philosophy*, 1912; *Theory of Knowledge*, 1913; *Our Knowledge of the External World: As a Field for Scientific Method in Philosophy*, 1914; *Principles of Social Reconstruction*, 1916; *An Introduction to Mathematical Philosophy*, 1919; *The Practice and Theory of Bolshevism*, 1920; *The Analysis of Mind*, 1921; *The ABC of Relativity*, 1925; *On Education*, 1926; *The Analysis of Matter*, 1927; *Marriage and Morals*, 1929; *The Conquest of Happiness*, 1930; *The Scientific Outlook*, 1931; *Education and the Modern World*, 1932; *Freedom and Organization*, 1934; *An Inquiry into Meaning and Truth*, 1940; *A History of Western Philosophy*, 1945; *Human Knowledge: Its Scope and Limits*, 1948; *Logic and Knowledge: Essays, 1901-1950*, 1956; *Portraits from Memory*, 1956; *My Philosophical Development*, 1959; *The Autobiography of Bertrand Russell*, 1967-1969 (3 volumes); *Essays in Analysis*, 1974.

Born: May 18, 1872; Trelleck, Monmouthshire, Wales

Died: February 2, 1970; near Penrhyndeudraeth, Wales

Early Life

Bertrand Arthur William Russell was born on May 18, 1872, in Trelleck, Monmouthshire, Wales. His mother, née Kate Stanley, was the daughter of the second Baron Stanley of Alderley and a leader in the fight for votes for women; his father, Lord Amberley, was the eldest son of the first Earl Russell and a freethinker who lost his seat in Parliament because of his advocacy of birth control. Both parents were considered extremely eccentric, and both died before Russell reached the age of four. Russell and his older brother were brought up by their rigidly conventional paternal grandmother, and they spent a rather solemn childhood being educated at home by a succession of governesses and tutors.

At the age of eighteen, Russell entered Trinity College, Cambridge, where it did not take him long to make a positive impression. He was taken under the wing of the philosopher Alfred North Whitehead, with whom he would later collaborate on *Principia Mathematica*, and was much influenced by fellow student G. E. Moore, who helped him develop his early ideas on the independent existence of what is perceived by the senses. In 1894, Russell married Alys Pearsall Smith, an American Quaker five years older than he was, and in 1895, he was elected a Fellow of Trinity College for his dissertation "An Essay on the Foundations of Geometry." In the following year, he and his wife spent three months in the United States, thus beginning a lifelong interest in and involvement with American affairs.

In the late 1890's, Russell achieved wide recognition as a professional philosopher of promise, as he subjected the dominant idealist thought of the period to an increasingly rigorous critique. His personal life revolved around the strains of a deteriorating marriage, which in 1902 reached a crisis when Russell told his wife that he no longer loved her. Although they continued to live together until 1911, the pressures of conflict at home and a demanding professional career made this the most difficult period of Russell's life. It was also, however, a very productive time for him, highlighted by the publication of perhaps his greatest single work: *The Principles of Mathematics*, which took the groundbreaking step of removing metaphysical notions from the concept of numbers and arguing that logic alone could serve as the basis for a true science of mathematics. After the publication of this volume, even those who took issue with Russell's views had to acknowledge his status as a major contributor to contemporary philosophical and mathematical thinking.

Russell's striking personal appearance became part of the folklore of Cambridge. His tall, thin frame and sharply chiseled, almost hawkish facial lines were seldom observed at rest, as his penchant for vigorous intellectual disputation was matched by a passion for strenuous walking. Russell kept his distinctive looks to the end of his life, with the only significant change being a whitening of his full head of hair, which added a mature dignity to his craggy features. The heavy media coverage of his public appearances on behalf of the peace movement in the 1960's reflected the charismatic appeal of his majestically leonine figure, which seemed to many observers to possess an almost biblical air of wisdom and authority.

Life's Work
The decade preceding the outbreak of World War II found Russell achieving success as a professional philosopher and undertaking what would be the first in a tempestuous string of love affairs and marriages. His collaboration with Whitehead on the three volumes of *Principia Mathematica* developed the ideas touched upon in *The Principles of Mathematics* into a coherent and influential formal system, and he was fruitfully stimulated by his pupil Ludwig Wittgenstein, who helped him clarify his thoughts about the proper conduct of philosophical analysis. Russell's growing interest in the theory of knowledge resulted in his *The Problems of Philosophy*, the first in what would be a series of books concerned with such perennial philosophical issues as

the nature of reality and the operations of the mind. In 1911, he began an intense love affair with Lady Ottoline Morrell, which lasted until 1916 and put an end to his first marriage.

Russell was deeply affected by the horrors of World War I and found himself compelled to become active in the pacifist movement. His *Principles of Social Reconstruction* signaled a deepening involvement with questions of human relations, and his antiwar efforts led to his being fined in 1916, imprisoned for six months in 1918, and as a result deprived of his lectureship at Trinity College. In 1916, he met Dora Black, a fellow free-thinker who became his second wife in 1921. As a couple, they had two children and briefly ran an experimental school at Beacon Hill. A visit to

Bertrand Russell. *(The Nobel Foundation)*

postrevolutionary Russia produced *The Practice and Theory of Bolshevism*, in which he recorded his disillusionment with the gap between the Soviet Union's promise and its performance, and he became somewhat notorious for his advocacy of free love—a doctrine that he practiced in a string of extramarital affairs—in the book *Marriage and Morals*.

Russell continued to do serious work in philosophy during the interwar period, although his refusal to accept Trinity College's offer of reinstatement meant that he had to spend more time writing financially profitable books and journalistic articles. Thus, popularly oriented titles such as *The Conquest of Happiness* and *Education and the Modern World* were interspersed with the more technical philosophical works such as *An Inquiry into Meaning and Truth*, and Russell also became a popular lecturer on topics such as divorce, sexual relations, and pacificism. His personal life continued to be turbulent, as he divorced his second wife in 1935 and married his third, Patricia Spence, in 1936; they had a son the following year.

In 1938, Russell and his new family moved to the United States, where he held several university posts and made a number of extensive lecture tours. He was in continual difficulty as right-wing pressure groups attacked his liberal views, and in 1943, he even had to go to court to collect his salary from the outraged head of a charitable foundation. The main positive result of his American sojourn was *A History of Western Philosophy*, a popular success whose royalties would comfortably support him for the remainder of his life. The Russells returned to England in 1944, and he decided to accept a five-year lectureship at Trinity College and endeavor to settle down into a less hectic pattern of existence.

The award of the Order of Merit in 1949 and the Nobel Prize in Literature in 1950 indicated that Russell's achievements now commanded general respect. This did not, however, seem to have a stabilizing effect upon his domestic life: He divorced his third wife in 1949 and married his fourth, Edith Finch, in 1952. Disappointed by the indifference of his academic colleagues to his last serious philosophical work, *Human Knowledge: Its Scope and Limits*, Russell devoted more and more time to antiwar activities. He helped to found the Campaign for Nuclear Disarmament in 1958, organized its militant wing, the Committee of 100, in 1960, and was jailed for seven days for participating in a Whitehall sit-in in 1961.

Although Russell's physical powers began to weaken, he remained an effective propagandist for the pacifist movement and in the late 1960's was a prominent member of the international opposition to the U.S. presence in Vietnam. His final days were spent resting quietly at his home in northern Wales, where he died on February 2, 1970.

Influence

Russell brought keen intellectual perception to every task that fired his imagination. As a philosopher, he was instrumental in the development of modern analytical techniques; as a mathematician, he helped to anchor speculative hypotheses on the firm ground of formal logic; and as a political activist, he cut through the verbiage of politicians with a clarion call to abandon nuclear weapons before they produced a global holocaust. Although the content of his ideas has in some cases been rejected by subsequent commentators, there is an almost universal acknowledgment of his methodological contributions to his areas of academic specialization.

Yet Russell was not merely a man with a great mind. His charismatic public persona and his ability to write for a general readership extended his influence into regions usually closed to the professional academic, and the range of his published work is extraordinarily impressive. His volatile emotional life also reflected the immense energy and appetite for new experiences that, in combination with his outstanding intellectual prowess, made Russell one of the seminal figures of his time.

Paul Stuewe

Our Knowledge of the External World

As a Field for Scientific Method in Philosophy

Type of philosophy: Epistemology, metaphysics
First published: 1914

Principal ideas advanced:

◇ The method of logical analysis makes the resolution of philosophical problems possible by defining the limits of scientific philosophy so as to exclude speculative metaphysics.

◇ We can account for our knowledge of the external world by realizing, through logical analysis, that the world as we know it is a construction from the data given in sense experience; an individual's "private world" is the class of all data within his or her perspective, and a perceived object is the class of all aspects to be found in all the perspectives that include the object.

◇ The conception of permanent things can be constructed by reference to appearances if points are defined by reference to an enclosure-series of spaces, and if time is defined by reference to classes of events simultaneous with each other.

◇ Zeno's paradoxes of motion can be resolved by use of the mathematical theory of continuity.

The significance of *Our Knowledge of the External World* is that it proposed a new method for philosophizing. Although the method suggested was not strictly novel (it had been previously used by such mathematical logicians as George Boole, Giuseppe Peano, and Gottlob Frege), it was modified by Bertrand Russell and transferred from mathematical to philosophical subject matter. Russell called it the "logical-analytic" method or the method of "logical atomism." Since the publication of these lectures, the method has been taken over and radically modified and broadened by a large school of philosophers who call themselves "analysts" and who constitute an important group in the modern philosophical world.

The analytic method, as Russell formulated it, is less ambitious than that of classical philosophy in that it does not claim to determine the nature of reality or the universe as a whole. What it does is both less speculative and less sweeping, but more scientific. It uses the techniques of modern logic and modern mathematics and employs such concepts as *class*, *relation*, and *order* for the purpose of clarifying and solving some of the perennial problems of philosophy that have not yet yielded to satisfactory solution. There are many such problems, but Russell here considers those concerned with the nature of the external world, with how the world of physics is related to the world of ordinary sense experience, and with what is meant by space, time, continuity, infinity, and causation. The book consists of illustrations of the application of the logical-analytic method to these problems for the purpose of showing its fruitfulness. Russell insists that his results are to be taken as tentative and incomplete, but he believes that if any modification in his method is found necessary, this will be discovered by the use of the very method that he is advocating.

The Faults of Traditional Logic

The philosophies of two typical representatives of the classical school—F. H. Bradley and Henri Bergson—are first examined in order to show the errors that these men made. Bradley found the world of everyday life to be full of contradictions, and he concluded that it must be a world of appearance only, not of reality. His error lay in his attempt to determine the character of the world by pure reasoning rather than by going to experience and examining what he found. Bergson believed that reality is characterized fundamentally by growth and change; he then concluded that logic, mathematics, and physics are too static to represent such a world and that a special method called "intuition" must be employed. His mistake was twofold: First, he supposed that because life is marked by change and evolution, the universe as a whole must be so described; he failed to realize that philosophy is general and does not draw conclusions on the basis of any of the special sciences. Second, his emphasis on life suggests that he believed philosophy to be concerned with problems of human destiny. However, such is not the case; philosophy is concerned with knowledge for its own sake, not with making people happier.

One reason why the logical-analytic method was not more widely employed earlier, according to Russell, is that it was new and only gradually replaced some of the earlier and erroneous conceptions of logic. Traditional (syllogistic) logic had been quite generally abandoned as inadequate. The inductive logic of Francis Bacon and John Stuart Mill had been shown to be unsatisfactory because it cannot really show why people believe in such uniformities as that the sun will rise every morning. Belief in universal causation cannot be a priori because it is very complicated when formulated precisely; nor can it be a postulate, for then it would be incapable of justifying any inference; nor can it be proved inductively without assuming the very principle that one is trying to prove. Russell claims that Georg Wilhelm Friedrich Hegel made the mistake of confusing logic with metaphysics, and that only mathematical logic provides the tool by which one may hope to solve philosophical problems.

The Logical-Analytical Method

Mathematical logic is both a branch of mathematics and a logic that is specially applicable to mathematics. Its main feature is its formal character, its independence of all specific subject matter. Looked at formally, it can be said to be concerned with propositions. The main types of propositions are *atomic* propositions, such as "Socrates is a man"; *molecular* propositions, which are atomic propositions unless connected by *and*, *if*, or *unless*; and *general* propositions, such as "All men are mortal." In addition, there must be *some* knowledge of general truths that is not derived from empirical evidence. For example, if we are to *know* that all men are mortal, we must also know that the men we have examined are all the men there are. This we can never derive from experience because empirical evidence gives us only particular truths. Thus, there are certain general truths that, if they are known, must be either self-evident or inferred from other general truths.

It is obvious that one of the oldest problems of philosophy is the problem concerning knowledge of the external world. In applying the logical-analytical method to this problem, Russell finds that what we have to begin with (something that is always vague, complex, and inexact) is knowledge of two kinds: First, our acquaintance with the particular objects of everyday life—furniture, houses, people, and so on; and second, our knowledge of the laws of logic. These may be called "hard" data because doubt in such cases, while it *could* occur, normally would not, and if it did, would probably be considered pathological. Most of us would be willing to add to these data

certain facts of memory, some introspective facts, spatial and temporal relations, and facts of comparison, such as the likeness or unlikeness of two shades of color.

However, Russell argues that certain very common beliefs probably should be excluded from our data. One is the belief that objects persist when we are not perceiving them. Another is the belief in the existence of other minds and of things outside our experience that are revealed by history and geography. These should be called "soft" data because they can be doubted and are actually derived from our belief in hard data. The problem, then, is to determine whether the existence of anything other than our own hard data can be inferred from these data.

In formulating the question by asking whether we can know of the existence of anything independent of ourselves, Russell finds that the terms "independent" and "ourselves" are too vague to determine whatever solution we happen to be seeking. What we *can* show, however, is that the appearances of an object—its color, shape, and size—change as we move toward it or away from it, or around it. Russell calls these appearances "sense-data," and he then defines a "private world" as an object seen from a certain perspective. If we move around an object we shall discover that the sense-data change and that correlated with these changes are the bodily sensations associated with our movements. Then, if we assume the existence of other minds, we can correlate their private worlds and perspectives with ours and define an object as the *class* of all of its perspectives. This is much safer than inferring a *thing* that exhibits itself in these perspectives. The *perspectives* are certainly real and constitute hard data; the thing is an inference and may be mistaken. A class is merely a logical construction, and we have thus substituted a logical construction for an inferred entity. This explanation fits the facts, has no empirical evidence against it, and is free from logical contradictions. Russell thus regarded himself as having solved the problem of how we know an external world.

Sense-Data and Physics

Another philosophical problem that yields to Rusell when his logical-analytic method is applied to it is that of the relation between the world of physics and the world of sense-data. According to physics, the world consists of material bodies, located in space and time and having a high degree of rigidity and permanence. Although the bodies themselves may change, they are made up of particles that are themselves unchanging and indestructible. On the other hand, the world of sense-data for any one of us comes and goes; even such permanent things as mountains become data for us only when we see them; they are not known with certainty to exist at other moments. The problem of "getting these worlds together" involves the attempt to construct things, a single space and a single time out of the fleeting data of experience.

Permanent things can be constructed if we can find some way of connecting what we commonly call "appearances of the same thing." Although some sort of continuity among appearances is necessary, it is not sufficient to define a thing. What is needed in addition is that the appearances of a *single* thing obey certain physical laws that the appearances of *different* things do not.

In much the same way, the dimensionless points (no one has ever seen a perfect point) of physics must be constructed out of the surfaces and volumes of our sensory experience. Using the fact that spaces can be observed to enclose other spaces (like Chinese boxes), Russell constructs "enclosure-series," which can be called "point-producers" because points can be defined by means of them. Russell does not, however, define a point as the lower limit of an enclosure-series, for there may be no such limit. Instead he defines it as the series itself; thus, a point is a logical entity constructed out of the immediate data of experience.

Time and Continuity

It can now be seen how Russell derives the concept of durationless instants of time. Events of our experience are not instantaneous; they occupy a finite time. Furthermore, different events may overlap in time because one event may begin before the other, but there may be a common time during which they both occur. If we restrict ourselves to the time that is common to more and more overlapping events, we get durations that are shorter and shorter. Then we can define an instant of time as the class of all events that are simultaneous with one another. To state accurately when an event happens, we need only to specify the class of events that defines the instant of its happening.

Russell recalls that since the days of Zeno, philosophers have wondered about the problem of permanence and change, and especially about the apparent paradox of motion. Some motions, such as that of the second hand on a watch, seem to be continuous because we can actually *see* the movement; other motions, such as that of the hour hand, seem to be discontinuous because we can observe only a broken series of positions. Russell's solution to this apparent contradiction in the nature of motion lies in the mathematical theory of continuity.

Continuity is regarded as, first, a property of a series of elements, of terms arranged in an order, such as numbers arranged in order of magnitude. Second, a continuous series must in every case be "compact," which means that no two terms are consecutive and that between any two terms there is always another. If space is thought of as being made up of a continuous series of points, and time as a similar series of instants, then motion will consist of a correlation between a series of different points in space and a series of different instants in time. However, Russell cautions that we must not say that a body moves from one point in space to the next, for if the series is truly compact, there is no next point in space, no next instant in time. This takes care of the difficulty we experience in thinking of a continuous motion as consisting of a very rapid series of jumps from one position to another.

Bergson argued that motion is simple, indivisible, and not validly analyzable into a series of states. In replying to him, Russell argues that on grounds of physiology, psychology, and logic there is no incompatibility between the mathematical theory of continuity and the evidence of the senses. From physiology, we learn that sensations do not cease instantaneously but gradually die away. Thus when we see a rapid motion, we do not perceive it as a series of jerks because each sensation blends into its successor. From psychology, we learn that there are actually cases of sense-data that form compact series. If a blindfolded person is holding a weight and to this a small additional weight is added, he may not observe the added weight if it is small enough. If still another weight is added, he may still not notice it. However, if both weights had been added at once, he might have detected the difference. This proves that weights form a continuous series. Finally, on grounds of logic, Bergson must be mistaken. For if analysis always falsifies, there could never be two facts concerning the same thing, and this would make motion, which depends on the distinction between earlier and later, impossible.

Zeno's Paradoxes

After a discussion of German philosopher Immanuel Kant's conception of infinity, Russell turns to an analysis of Zeno of Elea's famous paradoxes. Zeno had four arguments designed to show the impossibility of motion—all based on his theory of the infinite divisibility of space and time. His first argument was designed to prove that a runner cannot get to the end of a race course, for if space is infinitely divisible, he will have to cover an infinite number of points in a finite time, and this is impossible. According to Russell, Zeno's error came from thinking that the points must be covered "one by one." This would, apparently, require an infinitely long time, for the series has infinitely many elements. However, the series actually has a limit of 1, and this specifies the instant when the runner will complete the race.

Zeno's second argument attempts to show that Achilles can never overtake the tortoise if he gives it a head start, for by the time Achilles reaches the point where the tortoise was at any given time, the tortoise will always be slightly ahead. Achilles must then make up this distance, but again the tortoise will be slightly in advance. Achilles gets always closer to the tortoise but never is able to pass him. Russell claims that Zeno's error here is the same as in the previous case—an infinity of instants does not necessitate an infinitely long time.

Zeno's third argument begins with the claim that whatever occupies a space equal to itself must be at rest. An arrow in flight always occupies a space equal to itself; hence, it cannot move. Here Zeno supposes that the arrow could not move through an instant because this would require that an instant have parts, and this cannot

be. However, Russell points out that the mathematical theory of infinity has shown that, because there are no consecutive points or instants, an instant *can* have parts. When this is realized, Zeno's difficulty disappears.

Zeno's last argument attempts to prove that "half the time may be equal to double the time." This is illustrated by a column of soldiers passing another column at rest and a third column marching in the opposite direction. In the first case, the soldiers pass only half as many soldiers as in the second case, yet these actions both take place during the same time. The error again disappears for Russell with the recognition that there is no "fastest" motion that requires that slow motion have intervals for rest interspersed.

Infinite and Finite Numbers

According to Russell's analysis, infinite numbers differ from finite numbers in two ways: First, infinite numbers are *reflexive*, while finite numbers are not, and second, finite numbers are *inductive*, while infinite numbers are not. A number is reflexive when it is not increased by adding 1 to it. Therefore, the number of members in the class 0, 1, 2, 3 . . . n is the same as the number in the class 1, 2, 3, 4 . . . n plus 1. Even more surprising, the number of even numbers is equal to the total number of numbers (even and odd). It is therefore possible in the case of infinite numbers for a part of a class to equal the whole class.

Infinite numbers are also noninductive. Inductive numbers possess a certain property that can be called "hereditary." This is like the property of being named "Jones," which, if it applies to a man in many Western societies, also applies to all of his male descendants. Every property that belongs to 0 and is hereditary belongs to all of the natural numbers, and the natural numbers can be defined as those that are inductive. To all such numbers, proof by mathematical induction applies.

Philosophers have tried to define numbers, but without much success. Russell refers to the mathematician Frege, who recognized that numbers are neither physical nor mental but logical—that is, numbers are properties of general terms or general descriptions and thus are applicable to classes, not to things. The author asks: "When do two classes have the same number of members?" and answers "When a one-to-one correlation can be set up between them." This applies both to finite classes, which can be counted, and to infinite classes, which cannot. As an example, Russell refers to monogamous countries where the number of husbands is the same as the number of wives, though we may not know how many of both there are because the relation of marriage is a correlating relation. The number of a class can then be defined as the class of all classes that are similar to it—that is, which have a one-to-one correlation with it. Note that number is not a *property* of a class but is a *class of classes*. This is a valid conception even if classes are considered to be fictions, for there is a method for translating statements in which classes occur to statements in which they do not.

Causation and Free Will

Russell's final application of the logical-analytic method is to the problem of causation and free will. Causation is a complicated relation that must be described by a carefully worded formula: "Whenever things occur in certain relations to each other (among which their time-relations must be included), then a thing having a fixed relation to these things will occur at a date fixed relatively to their dates." The evidence for causation in the past is the observation of repeated uniformities, together with knowledge of the fact that where there appears to be an exception to such uniformities, we can always find wider ones that will include both the successes and failures. The only guarantee we could have that such a causal law would continue to hold in the future would be some sort of a priori principle. The law of causality is therefore an *ideal* law, possibly true, but not known to be true.

Determinism can be demonstrated, Russell believes, only if we can show that human actions are theoretically predictable from a sufficient number of antecedents. This we cannot do, he claims. In the great majority of cases, volitions probably have causes, but the only evidence for this is the fact of repeated instances. Furthermore, because causes do not *compel* their effects, the will is free in the sense that our volitions are the results of our desires, and we are not forced to will something that we would rather not will.

A. Cornelius Benjamin

An Inquiry into Meaning and Truth

Type of philosophy: Epistemology
First published: 1940
Principal ideas advanced:

◇ Empirical knowledge has its basis in percepts (sense experiences); from basic propositions about percepts, empirical knowledge is constructed.

◇ Although basic propositions are not indubitably true, as propositions of the utmost particularity, referring to percepts, they are the most dependable propositions of empirical inquiry.

◇ Empirical knowledge requires provision for general statements, for stating logical relationships, and for modes of inference.

◇ Propositions are both objective and subjective; they are objective in that they indicate factually, and they are subjective in that they express the state of mind of the speaker (belief, denial, or doubt).

◇ Sentences are true if what they indicate is the case; to know a sentence to be true one must perceive its verifier (the event the sentence indicates).

According to Bertrand Russell, the phrase "theory of knowledge" has two meanings. One kind of theory, the lesser, accepts whatever knowledge science presents and seeks to account for it. Russell's concern is with the wider kind, which embraces all problems of establishing the nature and validity of all knowledge. Confining his attention in this work to empirical knowledge, he undertakes to discover two things: (1) What is meant by "empirical evidence for the truth of a proposition"? (2) What can be inferred from the fact that there sometimes is such evidence?

Russell brings to the problem of a theory of empirical knowledge the full force of its counterpart, logical knowledge, to whose modern development he is a foremost contributor. He attacks the problems of his general task by translating their elements into formal logical symbols so as to achieve a precision lacking in the language in which the problems are usually couched. Yet the book does not consider problems of logic as such, except when they are relevant to epistemology.

Language

To talk about epistemological matters, Russell sets up a modern linguistic apparatus. He conceives a hierarchy of languages, at whose base is the object-language, or primary language. Terms in the object-language include subjects and predicates. While ordinary language may provide a beginning, every subject of the object-language should be transformed into a unique proper *name*, making use of coordinates in the visual field and of measures of time for discriminating the object named. The name will apply to a complex; and sometimes names must be given to complex wholes without knowing what their constituents are. People learn the names of things ostensively, and only of those things they actually perceive while hearing or coining their names. The names are employed as subjects in propositions of the simplest sort, called *atomic* propositions. Their predicates may be designated *relations*. Letting R stand for the relation "above," the proposition "$A R B$" consists of the relation R and the names A and B, and asserts that A is above B. This is a dyadic relation. Predicates may take any number of terms. The predicate of a single name is a monadic relation: "$f(A)$" states that a characteristic f is an attribute of A.

The secondary language consists of statements about the primary language (and must include the primary language within it). Therefore all words for logical conceptions, such as "is true," "is false," "or," "if," belong to the secondary language. All logical truths, because they depend for their truth on rules of syntax, are at least on this level, if not higher. An important group of propositions of the secondary language are those stating *propositional attitudes*, such as "A believes proposition p."

Propositions

The distinctive feature of empirical rather than logical truth is, of course, its basis in percepts, the sense images by which perception is possible. Russell adapts A. J. Ayer's phrase "basic propositions" to designate those propositions arising as immediately as possible from percepts. A basic proposition "is a proposition which arises on occasion of a perception, which is the evidence for its truth, and it has a form such that no two propositions having this form can be mutually

inconsistent if derived from different percepts." Examples in ordinary language are "I am hot," "That is red." Many basic propositions may arise describing a single percept, for people perceive a sensory whole combining the entire fields of vision, touch, and so on; and within this field people identify smaller wholes of sensory complexes—the individual objects of the world. Basic propositions need not be atomic propositions. An important group includes some propositions stating propositional attitudes—"I believe proposition p"—and thus basic propositions may occur in the secondary language as well as in the primary.

Unlike most prior writers, Russell does not affirm that basic propositions are indubitably true. He is quite willing to doubt them, particularly those involving the memory of percepts. However, what distinguishes basic propositions from others is their immediacy, whereas other propositions rest to some degree on inference. The evidence for a basic proposition is the momentary percept that causes it, and nothing can ever make a percept more or less certain than it is at the moment of its occurrence. It is from basic propositions that Russell proceeds to erect the structure of empirical knowledge. Because basic propositions are based on the least questionable objects of experience, they are the most dependable propositions in empirical inquiry. Thus, empirical knowledge is founded on propositions of the utmost particularity. Russell criticizes other writers for failing to screen out all traces of inference in the propositions they have regarded as basic.

Empirical Knowledge

A pure empiricism, depending only upon percepts for validation, would be self-refuting. It must contain some general proposition, which cannot be a basic proposition, about the dependence of knowledge upon experience; and the consequence is that such a proposition could not itself be known. Empirical knowledge requires certain additional elements besides basic propositions. These include provisions for making general statements and for stating logical relationships. Empirical knowledge, in other words, needs some epistemological premises as well as factual premises. Modes of inference are also required. These modes include the usual logical operations of deduction. More important in empirical knowledge, however, are nonlogical patterns of inference, namely, reasoning by analogy and by induction. For example, Russell throughout assumes that things perceived *cause* perceptions, and that perceptions *cause* propositions. His notion of cause is that it is a convenient device for collecting together propositions of certain percepts; it is something that one can arrive at inductively from appropriate combinations of percepts. Without some such organizing scheme for relating percepts, one would have nothing resembling empirical science. Yet neither causality nor induction is perceived, nor are they validated by logical syntax.

An innovation, no doubt startling to logicians, that Russell finds necessary to epistemology is to supply substantial meaning rather than merely formal meaning to logical terms. He finds these in psychological fact. "Or" rises from a hesitation, a conflict between two motor impulses when the organism is suspended between two courses of action. "Not" expresses a state of mind in which an impulse to action exists but is inhibited. "True" has its psychological ground in an expectation that is fulfilled; "false" in the surprise when an expectation is defeated. Such interpretations as these become possible when one accepts into epistemology not only logic but psychology and physical science, as one must in order to account for empirical rather than purely logical knowledge.

A Theory of Significance

Russell is now able to develop a theory of significance. Regarded epistemologically, a proposition has two sides, objective and subjective. The objective side is what it *indicates* factually. The subjective side is what it *expresses* about the state of mind of its originator; this is called its *significance*. What it expresses may be belief, denial, or doubt. These distinctions, not needed in logic, solve many puzzles of epistemology. The points concerning significance are independent of truth or falsity of the proposition; truth and falsity come into the relation of the proposition to what it indicates. A proposition does not necessarily consist of words; it is psychological, of the stuff of belief, not language. However, words may always be found to state the belief that, as a proposition, may underlie the many possible ways of saying it, in one or in various languages. Russell provides a sample language to show that the psychological conditions of significance can be translated into precise syntactical rules.

Logical sentence patterns can start from particular propositions recording percepts and extend one's thought over material that one has not experienced, and in this way one can expand one's body of statement. If one knows "Socrates is mortal," one can think "Something is mortal," or "Everything is mortal," and so on. Then further inquiry so as to have new percepts may test whether the new statements should be added to belief. Simple statements of immediate percepts may be expressed with constants—particular names—and predicates. However, any statement covering a percept one has not actually had must contain a variable term in place of a constant, for one can neither give nor learn a name (in Russell's sense) for an object one has not perceived. An epistemological language will need names, whereas a logical language does not deal with particulars and has no use for names. By the use of variables rather than names, it is possible to have propositions transcending one's experience. This is in fact what happens whenever one receives information from another person.

Thus far Russell has investigated meaning. In effect, he has constructed an epistemological language so that one can know what kinds of sentences are possible as statements of percepts and their relationships. It remains to examine the relationship between meaning and truth, between language and the world.

A Theory of Truth

Among the many possible theories of truth, Russell adheres firmly to a correspondence theory. Truth is defined by events, not percepts, although it becomes known by percepts. Truth is thus a broader concept than knowledge. The truth of a proposition is established by perception of its *verifier*. The sort of sentence that provides the model for truth is a spontaneous sentence that expresses what it indicates—that is, in which the subjective and the objective content coincide. Such a sentence is "I am hot!" Provided the sentence is stimulated by the immediate circumstances of the moment, there is no reason to doubt it. The verifier of a true sentence is what the sentence *indicates*; in other words, what makes that sentence true is that I was hot when I said it. Similarly, the verifier of a sentence about the future is the occurrence of what it indicates, and when that occurrence is perceived, the sentence is verified. A false sentence has no verifier, and it indicates nothing. Obviously, some verifiers may never be perceived, and there are some sentences whose truth or falsity is never known. Sentences are true if their verifiers occur, but when verifiers are not perceived, the sentences cannot be said to be known. The presence of an observer, Russell affirms, is no requisite of verifiers occurring.

The verifier of a basic proposition is a single occurrence at a moment of time. As to sentences containing variables, there is (usually) not just one but a collection of verifiers for them. The actual verification of such sentences depends on what is said. "All men are mortal" says "For any *x*, if *x* is a man, then *x* is mortal." This can never be verified by empirical knowledge because it would be impossible to examine all values of the variable—all men. "Some men live in Los Angeles" says "There is an *x* such that *x* is a man and *x* lives in Los Angeles." This can be verified by one of a very large number of verifiers, since any individual man living in Los Angeles can be the assigned value of the variable. In this fashion, propositions that are not basic, but that, rather, by the use of variables indicate occurrences beyond the speaker's experience, may be verified. One can give in advance a description of the occurrence that would make the proposition true, but one cannot name the occurrence. The relation between a sentence and its verifier is often much more remote than the explanation of simple cases would suggest.

Russell denies that either the verification or the verifier of a sentence constitutes its meaning. The verifier, as what the sentence indicates, relates to its truth; but one must know what the proposition means before one can know either its significance or its verifier; that is, before one can know either what it expresses or what it indicates. This knowledge is based ultimately on ostensive learning of object-words.

Known error arises in the experience of surprise upon a disappointed expectation. Its simplest case requires a combination of expectation, perception, and memory, in which either the expectation or perception must be negative, the others being positive. This combination accounts for perceptions that seem to be negative perceptions, such as in "There is no cheese in this cupboard." We examine every object in the cupboard having a size that might result in a percept of cheese, but in every such case, the expectation is disappointed.

The relation of empirical knowledge to experience is explained by Russell as follows: I must depend completely upon my own experience for all beliefs whose verbal expression has no variables; these include only basic propositions of immediate experience and memory. Though not indubitable, they are highly trustworthy. All my knowledge of what transcends *my* experience, including everything I learn from others, includes variables. When someone tells me, "A is red," using a proper name for something I have not experienced, if I believe him, what I believe is not "A is red" because I am not immediately acquainted with A, but "There is an *x* such that *x* is red." (Future experience giving me a percept of A together with a percept of the name "A" may later entitle me to believe "A is red.") Such a view of the nature of empirical knowledge would commit us either to depleting the body of knowledge to an intolerably small set of beliefs or else to relaxing our insistence that only the belief in true statements may be called knowledge. In order to admit the statements we believe on testimony, statements of things ever experienced anywhere by other human beings, and statements assumed in physical science, we should have to do the latter. In fact, upon examining the limitations of pure empiricism, Russell concludes there are no true empiricists.

Logical Difficulties

Certain principles of logic present difficulties in epistemological language when one attempts to apply nonsyntactic criteria of truth. They are the principles of extensionality and atomicity. Loosely, the principle of extensionality allows one to insert any atomic proposition in the place of a given atomic proposition in a sentence in the secondary language. However, this will obviously not do for sentences stating propositional attitudes. "A believes *p*" should not entitle one to say, by substitution, that *A* believes any or all propositions whatever. The principle of atomicity in effect requires one to reduce the complex parts of any proposition on a higher language level to their components on the atomic level, then be governed in assessing the truth of the whole by the relationships thus exhibited. Difficulties that these two principles raise in logic were attacked by Ludwig Wittgenstein and other philosophers by distinguishing between the assertion of a proposition and the mere consideration of a proposition. Russell affirmed, however, that the appropriate distinction to be made is between indication and significance.

The principle of extensionality will be found to apply to all occurrences of a proposition within a larger proposition when its indication is what is relevant, but not when only its significance is relevant, as is the case with sentences of propositional attitudes. Russell is less sure whether atomicity must be accepted or denied; upon considering the immediacy of perception and, in contrast, the elaborateness of inference involved in applying the principle of atomicity, he is inclined to believe that its application is irrelevant to the theoretical construction of empirical knowledge.

Another matter arising in logic is the challenge to the law of the excluded middle (which says that a proposition must be either true or false, not a third thing). It has been suggested that sentences as yet unverified should not be called either true of false. However, Russell clings to a realism, and a correspondence theory of truth, declaring that a sentence is true if its verifier occurs, even though its perception may not be part of anyone's experience. This outlook is extremely helpful in framing hypotheses, he says, and one should not attempt to do without it.

A continually recurring question in any investigation involving logical and nonlogical knowledge is whether anything about the structure of the world can be inferred from the structure of language. Because words are sensible objects, Russell believes that such inference is possible. While the investigation is confined to names and their objects, there is no reason to attempt such inference. However, on examining sentences, one discovers that those like "*A* is to the left of *B*"

cannot be explained without raising the question of universals. There is no escape from admitting relations as part of the nonlinguistic constitution. A universal is the meaning of a relation-word. "Above" and "before," just as truly as proper names, mean something in perception. Thus, in a logical language, there will be some distinctions of parts of speech that correspond to objective distinctions. Again, when one asks whether the word "similar" in recurring instances means the same thing or only similar things, there is no logical escape from granting that it means the same thing, thus establishing the universal "similar." Russell concludes, although with admitted hesitation, that there are universals and not merely general words. Knowledge must then be not of words alone but of the nonlinguistic world also. One who denies this fact must deny that one even knows when one is using a word; a complete agnosticism is not compatible with the maintenance of linguistic propositions. Hence, Russell believes that the study of syntax can assist us to considerable knowledge of the structure of the world.

With this work, given as the William James Lectures at Harvard University in 1940, Russell performed at least three worthy services for modern epistemology. By asserting that more than one thing can be known from one experience, that there is more than a single kind of knowledge, and that the mind can attain negative knowledge through perception, he assigned to the mind a fuller role in shaping its life than that accorded it by positivists and reductionistic philosophers. He pointed out the necessity for a metaphysic, if only a very simple one, and in doing so gave strength to the counterclaim against logical positivism that logical positivism is itself a metaphysic. Most important, his penetrating criticism showed the importance of the limitations upon empirical knowledge that its advocates, in their consciousness of the limitations of other kinds of knowledge, are prone to overlook.

John T. Goldthwait

Additional Reading

Dejnozka, Jan. *Bertrand Russell on Modality and Logical Relevance.* Avebury Series on Philosophy. Aldershot: Ashgate, 1999. This work presents a criticism and interpretation of modality and logical relevance in the work of Bertrand Russell. Includes index.

Grayling, A. C. *Russell*. Past Masters series. Oxford: Oxford University Press, 1996. This work, part of a series on great thinkers, covers the life and accomplishments of Russell. Includes an index.

Irvine, A. D., ed. *Bertrand Russell: Critical Assessments*. London: Routledge, 1999. This book critically examines the life and work of Russell, including his philosophy.

Landini, Gregory. *Russell's Hidden Substitutional Theory*. New York: Oxford University Press, 1998. This work takes a closer look at one of Russell's logical theories. Includes index.

Monk, Ray. *Bertrand Russell: The Spirit of Solitude*. London: J. Cape, 1996. This biography of Russell examines the philosopher's life and works. Includes bibliographical references and index.

_____. *Russell*. New York: Routledge, 1999. An excellent biographical introduction to the thoughts of the philosopher, clearly presented and requiring no special background. Bibliography.

Monk, Ray, and Anthony Palmer, eds. *Bertrand Russell and the Origins of Analytical Philosophy*. Bristol, England: Thoemmes Press, 1996. This collection of essays looks at Bertrand Russell and analytical philosophy. Includes bibliographical references.

Pampapathy Rao, A. *Understanding Principia and Tractatus: Russell and Wittgenstein Revisited*. San Francisco: International Scholars Publications, 1998. This work compares the philosophies and beliefs of Ludwig Wittgenstein and Russell.

Roberts, George W., ed. *Bertrand Russell Memorial Volume*. Atlantic Highlands, N.J.: Humanities Press, 1979. Essays from notable scholars focusing on the philosophical achievements of Russell.

Saintsbury, Richard Mark. *Russell*. London: Routledge & Kegan Paul, 1979. This text serves a twofold purpose as an analysis of Russell's ideas and as a critique of their adequacy.

Tait, Katharine. *My Father, Bertrand Russell*. New York: Harcourt Brace Jovanovich, 1975. Tait describes her father's flaws as a parent. This text offers a sensitive angle on the intellectual life of Russell and brings his social and educational theories under the critical lens of practice.

Vellacott, Jo. *Bertrand Russell and the Pacifists in the First World War*. New York: St. Martin's Press, 1981. This book documents the origins of the pacifist movement in Great Britain, focusing on its socialist and Quaker roots.

Paul Stuewe, updated by Howard Z. Fitzgerald

Gilbert Ryle

Ryle was a leader in what became known as "linguistic analysis." From 1947 to 1971, he edited *Mind*, the premier philosophical journal of Great Britain.

Principal philosophical works: *Philosophical Arguments*, 1945; *The Concept of Mind*, 1949; *Dilemmas*, 1954; *A Rational Animal*, 1962; *Plato's Progress*, 1966; *The Thinking of Thoughts*, 1968.

Born: August 19, 1900; Brighton, Sussex, England
Died: October 6, 1976; Whitby, North Yorkshire, England

Early Life

Gilbert Ryle, one of ten children of a physician whose interests were quite broad (ranging from astronomy to philosophy), read avidly in the philosophical works that were contained in his father's extensive library. As a boy, Ryle was educated locally, attending Brighton College. In 1919, he went to Queen's College, Oxford University, where he read Classic Honour Moderations and "Greats"—the first and second part of the undergraduate Literae Humaniores curriculum, comprising primarily classics, ancient and modern philosophy, and ancient history. While an undergraduate at Oxford, Ryle participated in the Jowett Society, a philosophical society; he was captain of the Queen's College Boat Club; and he earned First Class honors in examinations in both parts of the Literae Humaniores program. Ryle went on to study in what was then a new program—the school of Philosophy, Politics, and Economics. Again, his examinations yielded First Class honors. In 1924, Ryle became a lecturer at Christ Church, Oxford University.

During the time that Ryle was an undergraduate and a beginning lecturer, Oxford was in a state of change, though the change was gradual. The old guard—including neo-Hegelian idealists and historians of philosophy—was fading, but analytic Oxford philosophy, much of which Ryle himself was instrumental in establishing, was yet in the future. Oxford had lost some of its former glory, but the new British philosophy (emanating from Cambridge) and the new continental philosophy were only then coming into being. Ryle, like many at Oxford, had pursued study of historical figures in philosophy, especially Plato and Aristotle, but unlike many, he had also studied philosophers on the European continent, especially German, Austrian, and Italian writers. In addition, and also unlike many of the philosophers at Oxford, Ryle was interested in the new and revolutionary movements then beginning to get under way at Cambridge University.

At Oxford itself, there was a generation gap between the relatively older philosophers, who were too old to have fought in World War I, and the relatively younger philosophers, who were too young to have fought. While the more senior philosophers held weekly meetings called "The Philosophers' Teas" (to which junior philosophers were also invited, but at which they were always outranked), Ryle and a few junior philosophers organized weekly "Wee Teas," at which the discussions belonged to the newer generation, and the ideas that were expressed charted new directions for Oxford philosophy.

Life's Work

One early sign of change was Ryle's famous paper "Systematically Misleading Expressions," published in *Proceedings of the Aristotelian Society* (1931-1932), in which he argues that many statements, as they occur in ordinary language, are misleading indicators of the underlying logical structure of the facts that they represent. (Ryle makes it clear that ordinary people are not misled

Gilbert Ryle. *(Hulton Getty/Liaison Agency)*

thinking that statements that actually must be analyzed very differently from each other—like "Mr. Pickwick is a fiction" and "Charles Dickens is a writer"—are in fact similar. A statement such as "Mr. Pickwick is a fiction" is an example of what Ryle calls a "systematically misleading expression." In fact, the world simply does not contain people who are fictions along with people who are writers. In this case, however, and in a host of others, philosophers are often misled. As a result of being misled, they often assert the existence of entities and qualities that do not really exist. To take one more example from Ryle, alleged murderers are not really a subset of murderers. Although in these simple cases, people have little or no difficulty in avoiding being misled, in other cases, in which people speak of "the meaning of *x*," for example, they may think that the world contains meanings as well as *x*'s.

Even at this early stage of Ryle's philosophical development, certain characteristic Rylean moves can be discerned. One is the use of "Ockham's razor"—roughly, the principle that of two competing theories that perform equally well, the simpler one is better. (William of Ockham was a philosopher and theologian who studied and taught at Oxford in the early fourteenth century.) Ryle himself later spoke of his "Ockhamizing zeal" in his early writings. In this particular case, he uses Ockham's razor to cut away the idea that the world contains fictional people, or that there are entities such as word meanings. Again, in the ordinary sense in which it can be said that words mean something, or in which it can be said that language learners are learning the meanings of words, or that they are looking up the meanings in a dictionary, there is no problem. Problems can arise, however, when a philosopher asserts that there are meanings and that philosophy should investigate these entities. Similarly, there is no problem when one ordinary person tells another that Mr. Pickwick is fictional, but if philosophers think of fic-

by the statements, but that philosophers often are.) For example, the statement "Mr. Pickwick is a fiction," although bearing a superficial grammatical resemblance to statements such as "Charles Dickens is a writer" or "*Pickwick Papers* is a novel," is really not about Mr. Pickwick at all, because there is no Mr. Pickwick: He is a fictional character. Rather, such a statement is really about the writer Dickens or the novel *Pickwick Papers* (1836-1837). According to Ryle's position in this article, it is the task of philosophy to disclose the correct logical structure of statements. In fulfilling this task, however, some philosophers are misled by superficial grammatical features into

tional people as a certain kind of person—like tall ones or short ones—Ryle would want to apply Ockham's razor.

A second Rylean move is the use of what are called *reductio ad absurdum* (literally, "reduction to absurdity") arguments. Such arguments draw out conclusions from assumed premises such that the conclusion conflicts with well-grounded beliefs that people already hold, or it even conflicts with the given premises themselves. For example, if one assumes as a premise that (the fictional) Mr. Pickwick is indeed a certain kind of person, then, because every person was born in a certain year, it follows that Mr. Pickwick was born in a certain year. This conclusion conflicts with the original idea that Mr. Pickwick is a fictional character.

Behind these arguments is Ryle's attempt to articulate the particular task of philosophy. This is not one of investigating shadowy entities such as meanings, but of helping people to think more clearly. At least in the early 1930's, Ryle thought that this required penetrating to the real logical structure of the facts that language records.

When Ryle returned to Oxford in 1945, following his service in the Welsh Guards in World War II, he was chosen as the Waynflete Professor in Metaphysical Philosophy. The title was traditional, but it was in many ways ironic that Ryle assumed this title, because he was particularly interested in uncovering mistakes that lay at the base of much traditional metaphysics; moreover, he was interested not in producing a new metaphysical system that would avoid those mistakes but in showing that philosophy itself was a matter of making clear "the logical geography of concepts." In Ryle's view, philosophy was not a matter of metaphysical system building at all.

In 1949, Ryle published his most famous work, *The Concept of Mind*. In it, he coined two phrases that have become part of the general philosophical lexicon: "category mistake" and "the ghost in the machine." Philosophical mind-body dualism regards the body as something like a machine and the mind as something like a ghost that inhabits that machine. This dualism, however, is a myth, and the "ghostly" conception of the mind, says Ryle, is largely the result of treating mental concepts as some sort of unusual physical concepts. Mind-body dualism is largely the result of

applying ideas that fit one sort of thing to a different sort of thing, but to apply ideas in this way is to commit what Ryle calls a category mistake.

It was Ryle's general belief not only that philosophical problems are distinct from scientific ones but also that scientific facts (and metaphysical speculations) can make no contribution to philosophical investigation. Ryle was confident that everything a person needs to know to come to grips with philosophical problems is already a matter of common knowledge. The problem is that of reminding oneself of these facts and of resisting being misled.

In 1947, Ryle succeeded G. E. Moore as editor of *Mind*, the leading philosophy journal of Great Britain and one of the most prestigious philosophy journals in the world. In 1953, he was invited to give the Tarner Lectures at Trinity College, Cambridge. These lectures were published as *Dilemmas*. In them, Ryle turned his attention to several specific dilemmas, such as those concerning freedom and fatalism or the everyday world and the world of science, and he aimed to untangle thinking about such things. Again, what was needed was a proper understanding of concepts, to be achieved by careful attention to language and the world; there was no call for technical or scientific facts or for metaphysical speculations.

Influence

Ryle had an immense impact on the development of philosophy at Oxford University, and through Oxford, on the development of philosophy in the English-speaking world. Ryle had great influence in opening up Oxford University to philosophical developments elsewhere, especially in Vienna and Cambridge. This was important for a number of reasons. Prior to Ryle, Oxford was philosophically insular, but in the early part of the twentieth century, philosophically revolutionary events were taking place in Vienna and Cambridge. Ryle was largely responsible for bringing Oxford into the revolution. He also was instrumental in establishment of the bachelor of philosophy degree at Oxford, involving a formal program of advanced philosophical study that attracted students from around the world. In addition, Ryle was one of a number of Oxford philosophers (such as J. L. Austin and those who practiced "ordinary language" philosophy) to whom the rest of the world looked for philosophical guidance and authority. Moreover, as editor of *Mind*, the premier philosophy journal in Great Britain and one that is highly respected around the world, Ryle had an enormous impact on the direction of philosophy in the twentieth century.

A foe of sects, denominations, and limited schools of thought, which he referred to as "isms," Ryle was a force for philosophical ecumenism rather than exclusivity. He was a firm believer in (and practitioner of) the use of ordinary (rather than technical or pseudo-scientific) language in philosophy. This was not because he believed that ordinary language held some authoritative position from which it could determine the solutions to philosophical problems but because he believed that philosophy required that people understand concepts and that the concepts that give people the most trouble are those of ordinary language—for example, the concept of mind. Generally, the concepts of specialists are carefully constructed and cause little or no trouble (and if they do cause problems, they do so mainly for specialists).

Ryle thought of philosophy as a serious and academic discipline, but, without being a popularizer, he wrote in such a way as to be understood by ordinary people who were not academic philosophers. Ryle detested the use of showy technicalities and obscure writing. The point of philosophy was to examine the "logical geography of our conceptual system," and philosophy that is not clearly written is not likely to achieve that goal.

Stephen Satris

The Concept of Mind

Type of philosophy: Metaphysics, philosophy of mind, philosophy of language
First published: 1949
Principal ideas advanced:

◇ To suppose that the mind is a ghost mysteriously embodied in a machine is to commit the category mistake of confusing the logic of discourse about bodies and things with the logic of discourse about minds.

◇ To talk of a person's mind is to talk of his or her ability to perform certain kinds of tasks; words such as "know" and "believe" are disposition-words indicating that under certain circumstances certain kinds of performance are forthcoming.

◇ What are called mental processes are not processes; they are dispositions, or ways of acting, not themselves acts.

◇ Pronouns, such as "I," do not function as proper names but are index words; index words function in a variety of ways.

◇ One's knowledge of oneself comes from observing one's own behavior.

◇ To imagine is not to look at pictures in the theater of the mind; it is to perform any one of a number of various kinds of acts (such as telling a lie or playing at being an animal).

According to Gilbert Ryle, it is not the function of philosophy to furnish information about minds. Teachers, magistrates, historians, and plain people of all sorts already know the kinds of things that can be known about them, and knowing more is merely a matter of extending one's experience. Philosophers have access to no special facts; however, if they ply their trade properly, they can help "rectify the logical geography of the knowledge which we already possess."

As Ryle sees it, most people know how to make correct use of concepts that apply to mental situations but cannot state the "logical regulations governing their use." Consequently, they do not know how to correlate such concepts with one another or with concepts that refer to matters other than mental facts. The philosopher has the task of clearing up confusions and correcting mistakes that have their source in this kind of ineptness.

It is particularly incumbent on philosophers to do this because, in Ryle's opinion, most of the difficulties that occur in talking about these matters—for example, the mind-body problem, solipsism, and knowledge of "other minds"—have their origin in the errors of philosophers. In particular, modern European thinkers have great difficulty in throwing off the two-substance doctrine so forcibly stated by French philosopher René Descartes, according to which a person has immediate knowledge of his or her own mind by a kind of interior illumination, greatly superior to the kind of knowledge—never more than an inference—that the individual has of material things. According to this view, which Ryle calls "the official doctrine," minds dwell in bodies but share none of the characteristics of material things. He frequently stigmatizes it as "the dogma of the ghost in the machine."

The Logic and Meaning of Statements

In attacking this dogma, Ryle carries over into epistemology the battle that the logical positivists previously waged against metaphysics. The lines of his attack, if not the weapons, are familiar. The first line of attack has to do with the logic of statements: whether the expressions are related to one another in a coherent fashion. The second has to do with the meaning of the statements: under which conditions they can be verified or confirmed. For the purpose of carrying through the former of these attacks, Ryle sets up a series of "categories," deliberately reviving the Aristotelian term but relating the discovery of categories to linguistic analysis.

Ryle explains "the official doctrine" in terms of what he calls a "category mistake." To suppose that "the university" is an entity in the same sense that its component colleges, libraries, laboratories, and so forth are entities, would be to make a category mistake. Another would be to suppose that "team spirit" has the same kind of reality that batters, fielders, and umpires do. These extreme examples to one side, the danger is ever present, Ryle says, that people who know how to apply terms correctly in familiar situations will fall victim to the fallacy of mixing up terms of different orders when they try to think in abstract ways. In his opinion, most mistakes in thinking about "mind" are of this sort.

The Nature of Mind

The categories people use in describing the physical world are "thing," "stuff," "attribute," "state," "process," "change," "cause," and "effect." The error of philosophers, and of ordinary people when they try to theorize, consists of supposing that there are "things" called "minds" comparable to things called "bodies," except for having different attributes, and that there are mental "events," like physical ones, that have

causes and effects. Ryle designates attempts to talk about minds in these terms as "paramechanical." Mind is thought of as a ghost in the sense that it is regarded as immaterial, but it is believed to press levers, open windows, receive shocks, and exert reactions much as if it were material.

A special feature of "the official doctrine" that has impressed epistemologists is the teaching that mind knows itself in a peculiarly direct manner. Ryle supposes that this view reflects the strong influence upon seventeenth century European thought of the Protestant affirmation that people's minds are "illuminated" by divine truth, a mode of thought that was reinforced by a preoccupation with optical phenomena on the part of Galilean science. As a result, the paramechanical hypothesis of the mind's operation was supplemented by a paraoptical hypothesis of its self-knowledge.

Ryle, for his part, does not admit that there is any such *thing* as mind. It is, he says, a solecism to speak of the mind as knowing this or choosing that. The correct thing to say is that a *person* knows or chooses. Some actions of humans exhibit qualities of intellect and of character; Ryle says that the fact that a person knows or chooses can be classified as a "mental fact" about that person. He regards it as "an unfortunate linguistic fashion" that people then say that there are "mental acts" or "mental processes" comparable to "physical acts" and "physical processes."

Ryle's book is an attempt to show how it is that, though there is no such thing as a mind, people sometimes talk as if there were. The fault derives both from people's failure to distinguish different types of statements and from supposing that what is characteristic of words in one kind of sentence is also characteristic of words in other kinds of sentences.

Disposition-Words and Occurrence-Words

Take, for example, words such as "know," "believe," "aspire," "clever," and "humorous." These are, in Ryle's terminology, *disposition-words*. Statements in which they occur do not assert matters of fact; they discuss capacities, tendencies, propensities, and so forth. To say of a sleeping man that he knows French is not to affirm an additional fact about him comparable to saying that he has gray eyes and is wearing a blue suit. Dispositional statements correspond, rather, to the hypothetical propositions of modern logic: They are indicative sentences and may be true or false in the sense that they are verifiable under certain conditions. A man knows French *if*, when he is spoken to in French, he responds appropriately in French. No one criterion of performance, however, is sufficient. A mistake arises when it is supposed that every true or false statement is categorical and either asserts or denies that there exists some object or set of objects possessing a specified attribute.

Occurrence-words apply to people's higher-grade activities, referred to as "mental." If, as suggested above, "knows" designates a disposition, "heeds" would seem to designate an occurrence, as, for example, when a person is said to heed what he is doing. A doubling process misleadingly suggests itself in this instance, with the bodily activity (say, driving a car) going on more or less by itself and an intermittent mental process trying to parallel what is going on in the body. According to Ryle, however, there are not two processes, but one. Driving a car is an occurrence; paying heed is a state of readiness, or a disposition. To say that people heed what they are doing while driving is to make a semihypothetical, or a "mongrel categorical," statement. The heedful person drives differently, perhaps, in that he or she is alert to potholes and pedestrians, but the heeding is not itself an act in addition to the act of driving, and it presupposes no agent other than the one who is driving the car.

Causation and Laws of Nature

Ryle suggests that the wide currency of "the official doctrine" results in great part from the "bogy of mechanism." The successes of physical science since the days of Galileo have excited in many theorists the expectation that the world ultimately may be explicable in terms of the motions of bodies according to laws that can be mathematically demonstrated. In the interests of human freedom, moral and religious thinkers have countered this prospect by asserting the autonomy of mind. According to Ryle, however, the fear is baseless.

In the first place, "laws of nature" are not "fiats." Law-statements are "open" hypothetical sentences, ones in which the conditional phrase

contains a universal term such as "any" or "whenever." Such sentences do not, like categorical sentences, affirm the existence of anything. Causal connections, in other words, do not exist in the same sense as, say, the existence of bacteria and the disease they are alleged to cause. To assume that they do is "to fall back into the old habit of assuming that all sorts of sentences do the same sort of job, the job, namely, of ascribing a predicate to a mentioned object." Statements about physical laws do not "mention" anything. They are merely predictive of behavior.

In the second place, according to Ryle, the mechanistic account of nature is no threat to human freedom because many questions concerning human behavior cannot be answered in terms of physical law, and not all questions are physical questions. The same process, says Ryle, is often viewed in terms of two or more principles of explanation, neither of which can be reduced to the other, although one commonly presupposes the other. For example, if a child asks a chess player why he or she moves a certain piece (say, a knight) to a certain spot, the answer the child requires is a statement of the rules of the game, whereas if an experienced player asks the question, the answer required will be in terms of "tactical canons." Another example is the rules of grammar, which apply equally to all books written in a particular language irrespective of style or content. In the same manner, says Ryle, the laws of physics apply to everything—animate as well as inanimate—but they do not explain everything. Even for describing a game of billiards, mechanical principles, though necessary, are not sufficient. The purpose of the game, its rules, and its tactics are equally important. These "appraisal concepts" are not in conflict with the law-statements; rather, they presuppose them.

Ryle safeguards the meaning of purpose in human activity by distinguishing between questions about the *causes* of a person's acts and the *reasons* for it. Suppose the event to be explained is a man passing the salt to his neighbor at the table. The question about causes demands to be answered in factual or categorical sentences such as "He heard his neighbor ask for it" or "He saw his neighbor's eye wandering over the table." "Seeing" and "hearing" are events that may stand in the chain of causal explanations. The question about reasons does not admit of categorical answers. One might say, "He passed the salt out of politeness" or "He did it out of friendliness." These are reasons and not causes. They refer to motives or dispositional states, and they are expressed in lawlike or hypothetical propositions. That people constantly appeal to them in explaining human behavior testifies to the incompleteness of "causal" explanations. Moreover, according to Ryle, they express all that people actually intend when speaking of human acts as being free or voluntary.

The Pronoun "I"
Ryle finds that there is good sense in saying "I know that I am free." To infer, however, that the pronoun "I" must be the name of a distinct entity is to misunderstand the true function of pronouns. They do not function like proper names but instead are "index" words that point to different things at different times. Because of the complexity of human experience, the pronoun "I" (with "me" and "myself") is used in a variety of ways. Sometimes, a speaker uses "I" to refer to his or her body, as when a man says, "I was cut in the collision." He may even use "I" to refer to his mechanical auxiliaries, such as his car, as in the sentence, "I collided with the police car." These cases offer no particular difficulty. It is different, however, when one says, "I am warming myself before the fire." Here, "myself" could be replaced by "my body," but not "I." Even more complex are such statements as "I was ashamed of myself" and "I caught myself beginning to dream." Ryle's explanation is that the pronouns are "used in different senses in different sorts of contexts." Human behavior frequently involves what Ryle calls "higher order actions," ones in which the second agent is concerned with actions of a first agent, as in spying or applauding. A person's higher order acts may be directed upon his or her own lower order acts, as in self-criticism. This, according to Ryle, is what people ordinarily mean by "self-consciousness." There is nothing here to support the view that one looks into one's own mind and discovers its workings. What is known as "introspection" is in fact "retrospection." The attempt to glimpse oneself in the act of thinking is hopeless.

Ryle therefore rejects the much-touted claims of introspective psychology, founded on the paraoptical model of knowledge. He does not deny that people know their feelings immediately; however, he is careful to distinguish feelings, which are agitations, from moods and tendencies, which are dispositions. Of the latter, people have no immediate knowledge. Only as they eventuate in actions can people form any estimate of them. One's knowledge of oneself, therefore, comes from observing one's own *behavior* and is in principle no different from one's knowledge of other persons. Ryle recognizes many grades of self-knowledge: One may know that one is whistling "Tipperary" and not know that one is doing so to keep up one's courage, or one may be aware that one is trying to keep up one's courage without realizing that what makes one afraid is a guilty conscience. In no case, however, does one have "privileged access" to one's own mental states.

Ryle continues:

> No metaphysical Iron Curtain exists compelling us to be forever absolute strangers to one another, though ordinary circumstances, together with some deliberate management, serve to maintain a reasonable aloofness. Similarly, no metaphysical looking-glass exists compelling us to be forever completely disclosed and explained to ourselves, though from the everyday conduct of our sociable and unsociable lives we learn to be reasonably conversant with ourselves.

Ryle's treatment of sensation and observation is refreshing in that he candidly admits that his analysis is not satisfactory to him. He attributes his difficulty to contamination by sophisticated language. In ordinary language, the words "sensation" and "feel" signify perceptions, but in philosophical language, they refer to presumed bases for perceptual inference. Words like "hurt" and "itch" are not the names of moods, nor are they the names of certain kinds of perceptions, nor are they terms by which achievements are reported. Ryle confesses, "I do not know what more is to be said about the logical grammar of such words, save that there is much more to be said."

Imagination and Intellect

Ryle's discussion of imagination is perhaps the most provocative part of the book. The ordinary myth-view of imagination is that in the private box or theater of people's minds, they view private pictures. The logic of discourse involving the word "imagination," however, does not entail any such fanciful assumption. To imagine is to lie, to play at being an animal, to write a story, or to invent a machine. There is no need to suppose some internal, private operation to which the word "imagine" calls attention; in fact, the word does no such thing—it calls attention to publicly observable behavior.

In his discussion of "intellect," Ryle rejects, as by now one might expect, any analysis describing intellect as an organ, an internal lecturer, or a private thinker. As a result of producing various kinds of things—such as sums, books, or theories—people are said to have been engaged in intellectual processes. Confusing the grammar of intellect with the grammar of production, and working out an erroneous analogy, people tend to regard intellect as a hidden faculty of mind. Ryle's analyses discredit such a notion. He makes the interesting suggestion that such words as "judgment" and "deduction" belong to "the classification of the products of pondering and are misrendered when taken as denoting acts of which pondering consists." Such words, he argues, are "referees' nouns, not biographers' nouns"—that is, they are properly used to describe the products people have produced but are misleadingly used to talk about some hidden performances within the mind.

Links to Psychology

Ryle, in concluding his book, discusses the relation between his approach to the "concept of mind" and that which engages psychologists. It is his stated opinion that, with the collapse of the two-world view, psychology has ceased to have an identifiable aim and is more like medicine, a "fortuitous federation of inquiries and techniques." The wrong sort of promise, he feels, is being made when people are told that psychology will disclose causes of human actions that are hidden from such observers as economists, historians, anthropologists, and novelists. "We know quite well what caused the farmer to return from the market with his pigs unsold. He found the prices were lower than he had expected." The explanation of competent mental behavior does not require a psychologist; it is apparent to ordinary good sense. Where the psychologist can be of service is in explaining why people's competencies often fail. "The question why the farmer will not sell his pigs at certain prices is not a psychological but an economic question; but the question why he will not sell his pigs at any price to a customer with a certain look in his eye might be a psychological question."

Ryle recognizes a certain debt to behaviorism. Often confused by its practitioners with "a not very sophisticated mechanistic doctrine," it was originally a methodological program which insisted that the theories of psychologists "should be based upon repeatable and publicly checkable observations and experiments." This program, according to Ryle, has been of first importance in overthrowing the two-world myth, and it does not in any way entail mechanistic assumptions. According to Ryle, the rise of the biological sciences and the fact that the Newtonian system is no longer the sole paradigm of natural science make it unnecessary for scientists to consider a man as a machine. "He might, after all, be a sort of animal, namely, a higher mammal. There has yet to be ventured the hazardous leap to the hypothesis that perhaps he is a man."

Jean Faurot

Additional Reading

Addis, Laird, and Douglas Lewis. *Moore and Ryle: Two Ontologists.* The Hague: Martinus Nijhoff, 1965. A somewhat technical comparison of the thoughts of Ryle and G. E. Moore, a leading philosopher at Cambridge University.

Ayer, A. J. *Language, Truth and Logic.* London: Gollancz, 1936. 2d ed., with a new introduction, 1946. This influential book is a classic in logical positivism and did the most to take that particular strain of thought from Vienna to England. Although Ryle himself was not a logical positivist, he had suggested to Ayer that he go to Vienna and learn at first hand about the new philosophical developments there. This book, the result of that journey, serves as one more testament to the way in which Ryle—unlike many at Oxford—was open to philosophical input from abroad.

Flew, Anthony G. N., ed. *Logic and Language: First and Second Series*. Garden City, N.Y.: Doubleday and Company, 1965. Originally published by Blackwell in Oxford as two volumes in 1951 and 1953, the American volume comprises both collections (or series) of philosophical articles. Ryle has articles in both series, and Flew provides useful introductions to both series. Ryle is shown in action and in his historical context. The articles are all drawn from the years 1931 to 1953.

Lyons, William. *Gilbert Ryle: An Introduction to His Philosophy*. Atlantic Highlands, N.J.: Humanities Press, 1980. Lyons provides a biography of Ryle and a thorough and detailed account of his philosophical thought. This introductory book is accessible and reliable.

Quinton, A. M. "Contemporary British Philosophy." In *A Critical History of Philosophy*, edited by D. J. O'Connor. New York: Free Press, 1964. This essay contains a good exposition of (pre-1964) twentieth century British philosophy and Ryle's place in its development.

Rao, B. Narahari. *A Semiotic Reconstruction of Ryle's Critique of Cartesianism*. New York: W. de Gruyter, 1994. As its title suggests, this book presents Ryle's critique of Cartesianism and explains Ryle's definition of philosophy.

Urmson, J. O. *Philosophical Analysis: Its Development Between the Two World Wars*. New York: Oxford University Press, 1956. This book traces the development of British analytical philosophy from World War I to World War II. Although Ryle is rarely mentioned by name, this brief volume reviews the analytic philosophy with which Ryle is so closely associated.

Warnock, Geoffrey J. *English Philosophy Since 1900*. 2d ed. New York: Oxford University Press, 1969. The seventh chapter of this brief book specifically focuses on Ryle.

Wood, Oscar P., and George Pitcher, eds. *Ryle: A Collection of Critical Essays*. New York: Doubleday, 1970. This anthology contains an autobiographical article by Ryle, many articles that discuss specific points about Ryle's philosophy, and a bibliography of Ryle's writings from 1927 to 1968.

Stephen Satris

Samkara

Samkara was the greatest teacher and commentator of Advaita Vedanta Hinduism, a religious and philosophical tradition based on a nondualist, monistic reading of the Hindu sacred texts, the Upanishads. This perspective has been the dominant reading of these writings among Brahman teachers and a widely accepted perspective among Hindu philosophers.

Principal philosophical works: *Brahmasūtrabhāsya*, early eighth century (*The Vedānta Sūtras of Bādarā-yana with the Commentary of Samkara*, 1890-1904); *Upadesasāhasrī*, early eighth century (*A Thousand Teachings*, 1949); *Vivekachudamani*, early eighth century, authorship questionable (*The Crest Jewel of Wisdom*, 1890).

Born: 788; Kaladi (now in Kerala, India)
Died: 820; Himalayas

Early Life

According to tradition, Samkara (also known as Sankara, Shankara, Sankarācārya) left his mother at age eight to wander India as a Hindu ascetic, gained wisdom, came to be viewed as an incarnation of the god Shiva, and founded monasteries to preserve and spread his teachings. According to one story, he tricked his mother by pretending to be captured by a crocodile who would release him only if he adopted the life of a religious ascetic. According to another story, he left his mother at the age of eight, promising to return to do his duty by her burial needs. Some scholars doubt this story on the grounds at least that an enlightened ascetic would be free from all worldly concerns and thus not properly responsible for the burial rites of anyone, even a mother. There are stories of his winning disputes with competing philosophers. He wrote poetry and hymns to various gods.

Life's Work

The aphorisms of Badarayana are one source of authoritative teachings within the Hindu Vedantic tradition. Samkara's commentary on these sacred and esoteric sayings, *The Vedānta Sūtras of Bādarāyana with the Commentary of Samkara*, became a highly influential source of Vedantic teachings. The Bhagavad Gita ("the song of the blessed lord"), technically not an authoritative scripture but treated with great respect and in practical terms treated as having scriptural status, is perhaps the most loved of Hindu religious texts. The Upanishads, of which there are many, are Hindu scripture, as are the Vedas; the former are the more doctrinal of these documents. Samkara's commentaries on these works (the Bhagavad Gita and various of the Upanishads) are essential parts of his overall corpus, and they are also part of the authoritative texts of the Advaita Vedanta tradition. Although not regarded as the founder of Advaita Vedanta, which its adherents regard as having been taught by all of the Hindu scriptures, Samkara is thought of as having given this perspective its de facto definitive statement, and his work was central to a revival of Hinduism after a period of its waning in the light of Buddhist influence in India.

Badarayana's sutras are a series of aphorisms on which a major thinker of the Vedantic tradition must comment. Samkara's *The Vedānta Sūtras of Bādarāyana with the Commentary of Samkara* is a very influential commentary on this work, reading Badarayana's work as a presentation of Advaita Vedanta thought. Aphorisms are notoriously capable of diverse interpretations. The same work by Badarayana is interpreted very differently by other major Vedantic thinkers. Samkara's thought is best understood in comparison with the other major thinkers within the general Vedantic tradition to which Samkara belongs. Preeminent among these are Ramanuja, whose writings express Vsistadvaita (qualifiedly nondual) Vedanta, and Madhva, whose works advocate Dvaita (dualistic) Vedanta. Ramanuja and Madhva are much closer to one another in their views than either is to Samkara; they are both monotheists and Samkara is a monist.

The major religious difference between Samkara's view and the views of Ramanuja and Madhva, then, is that the latter are monotheists, believing in a personal deity, and Samkara is a monist, holding that Brahman or ultimate reality is apersonal. Badarayana's aphorisms, the Bhagavad Gita, and the Upanishads can be read monotheistically, and they can be read monistically. In particular, there are passages that, taken literally, teach that Brahman is a personal God and other passages that, taken literally, teach that Brahman is an apersonal reality. Because all these passages are taken to be scriptural and hence authoritative, none of them can be taken to be false. If both sorts of passages are properly read as literal, then one sort of passage must be false. Hence, the reasoning goes, one sort of passage must be taken literally and one sort of passage must not. The crucial question is which text merits a literal reading. Samkara reads the "Brahman is apersonal" passages literally and the "Brahman is a personal God" passages as nonliteral. Ramanuja and Madhva take exactly the reverse position. Interpreting the same authoritative text, Samkara and Ramanuja and Madhva come up with radically different religious perspectives. It is the monotheistic reading that had the greatest religious impact in India, and probably Samkara's monistic reading that had the greatest impact on Brahman philosophers.

The basic philosophical difference between Samkara and Ramanuja and Madhva is that Samkara distinguishes between the level of appearance and the level of reality. Understanding this distinction is basic to comprehending Samkara's philosophical perspective. The level of reality is constituted by Brahman and nothing else. Brahman here is conceived as *nirguna* ("not quality" or "qualityless"). Viewing Brahman in this manner makes it impossible to think of Brahman as creator of the world, as someone exercising any providential guidance, as a hearer of prayer, or as someone graciously forgiving the

sins of those who repent and ask for forgiveness. It also renders nonexistent the world that is apparently revealed to us by sensory experience and by commerce with other persons, as well as our awareness of our introspective state. Further, there is, in this account, no world for science to learn about or to which morality should relate. While Advaita Vedantins point out that in their view, this is so only from the level of reality, critics wonder what force the "only" has, because of course the level of reality is supposed to be the way things really are. So construed, if the view is even possibly true (a point hotly disputed between Samkara and his followers on the affirmative side, and Ramanuja and Madhva and their followers on the negative side), the idea is that Brahman is completely undifferentiated consciousness. It is not anyone's consciousness; it is not a consciousness of anything or possessed of any content. When Samkara characterizes it as bliss (Nirvana), his critics point out that *being blissful* is a quality and hence cannot characterize Brahman on Samkara's own terms.

The level of appearance is constituted, according to Samkara, by the way things appear to us when we have not been enlightened—that is the way at least almost everyone takes them to be. There appear to be, Samkara says, persons, physical objects, and God. He provides a vigorous defense of mind-body dualism that holds that humans are essentially enduring self-conscious beings that are nonessentially embodied. He argues, largely on the basis of its being altogether reasonable to take our sensory experience and the experience of our contact with others as reliable and unreasonable not to do so, for the existence of a plurality of minds and mind-independent physical objects. He contends as well for the truth of monotheism and accordingly practices worship. In all of this, he is in agreement with Ramanuja and Madhva, except, of course, for his claim that all of this is merely the level of appearance.

It is obvious to all sides that things cannot be both as the level-of-reality account says they are—only one undifferentiated consciousness exists—and as the level-of-appearance account says they are—a plurality of distinct individual minds, of distinct individual physical items, and a personal God. Samkara's reading of *sruti* (the

Vedas and Upanishads) leads him to claim that the level-of-reality account (as of course the term chosen to describe that account suggests) is the correct one. Ramanuja's and Madhva's readings of those same texts lead them to think that there is nothing at all that corresponds to the level-of-reality account, and that the level-of-appearance account is actually the correct view of what exists.

There is another factor that leads Samkara to claim that what his view calls the level of appearance is unreal and that qualityless Brahman is all there is. He appeals to enlightenment, or *moksha*, an experience in which one is said to learn that the level-of-reality account is the correct one, to come to see, with full cognitive clarity and transforming existential force, that this is so.

Ramanuja and Madhva also appeal to religious experience that is referred to by the same term but is radically different. In their view, the enlightenment experience is experience of God and God's grace, where God (Brahman) is conceived as personal. For them, there is nothing merely apparent about the divine being encountered in such experiences. Their claim regarding Samkara's *moksha* experience is that, for one thing, no experience could possibly confirm or provide evidence for the existence of a qualityless Brahman. An experience in which one learns something, is grasped by some truth, or is transformed by some insight is possible, but it is not a qualityless experience. Furthermore, one's having a qualityless experience and one's not having any experience at all are alternative descriptions for the same state of affairs (or absence thereof). In addition, they and their followers argue, Samkara's Advaita Vedanta claims that all those who are not enlightened, who have not come to see that the level-of-reality account is correct, are (in a technical but disastrous sense) ignorant. However, suppose that the level-of-reality account were true. Who, then, would be ignorant? To whom would one's own existence as a person, the reality of other persons, the existence of physical items, or the grace of God appear? Were the level-of-reality account true, then there could be no level of appearance.

Samkara's critics argue that his view is logically inconsistent or self-contradictory in at least two important and ineliminable ways. One is

that it is simply logically impossible that anything both exists and altogether lacks qualities; the notion of a qualityless existent is just as self-contradictory as the notion of the number two being odd or the number three being even. The other is that the idea behind Advaita Vedanta is that it provides the cure for people's deep religious disease of ignorance, yet if the cure were correct, it would be impossible that the disease existed. If there is a level of appearance, then it cannot be true that the level of reality is as Advaita Vedanta describes it; if there is the problem that Advaita Vedanta says there is, its solution to that problem cannot possibly be correct. Samkara's teachings are Advaita Vedanta's teachings to the degree that the fact that these are objections to Samkara's fundamental doctrines is sufficient for them to be objections to Advaita Vedanta's fundamental doctrines.

Influence

Due in part to the fact that Sarvepalli Radhakrishnan, philosopher and a president of India, was a devout follower of Samkara's Advaita Vedanta, almost all of the earlier presentations of Indian philosophy in Europe and the United States treated Advaita Vedanta as its basic content. This imbalance has been corrected by the publication of such works as Surendranath Dasgupta's *History of Indian Philosophy*. Nonetheless, much of the history of Indian philosophy after Samkara comes by way of response to his views, arguments, and interpretations.

Keith E. Yandell

The Crest Jewel of Wisdom

Type of philosophy: Ethics, Indian philosophy, metaphysics

First transcribed: Vivekachudamani, early eighth century, authorship questionable (English translation, 1890)

Principal ideas advanced:

◇ In this existence, all is illusion (*maya*).

◇ To achieve liberation, wise individuals will discriminate between the permanent and the transitory; they will be indifferent to the fruits of action; they will achieve tranquillity of mind, self-control, cessation of action by the mind, forbearance of suffering, faith, and deep concentration on Brahman; and they will yearn to be liberated from the bonds of ignorance and egoism.

⋄ Liberation from this existence can be achieved only through direct perception of the oneness of the individual self (*atman*) with the universal self (Brahman).

⋄ The self is none of the five sheaths of the human being.

⋄ To achieve Nirvana, disciples must overcome the feeling of "I," follow their guru's teachings, study the scriptures, and come to full awareness of the truth of the mystic formula: "This is Brahman; that thou art."

It would be incorrect to speak about the "philosophy" of Samkara, because he and other great Indian sages never claimed a philosophy of their own but were merely expounders of the great spiritual knowledge bequeathed them by a long lineage of predecessors. They differ according to the emphasis placed on the various aspects of that knowledge, and their greatness is measured by the degree to which they mastered it. By that measure, Samkara was perhaps the greatest of the historical Hindu sages, not including, however, Gautama the Buddha.

The Three Doctrines

In the East, the belief is common that there is a "soul-redeeming" *truth* that can make of its possessor a divine being, one liberated from the wheel of *samsara*, that is, from obligatory rebirth. The state of liberation, Nirvana, is the supreme aim, the *summum bonum* of all six Hindu schools of philosophy, as well as of the various Buddhist sects. The Western reader must, therefore, constantly keep in mind that there are three basic doctrines of Asian philosophy: (1) the doctrine of *rebirth*, or reincarnation, meaning the periodic appearance of the same human egos in new physical bodies; (2) the doctrine of *karma*, or moral retribution, the regulatory law under which rebirth takes place; and (3) the doctrine of *spiritual evolution* by which a relative perfection is attainable, in principle, by all beings—those of the lower kingdoms of nature included.

We can realize why no Hindu sage bothers to prove or defend these three doctrines, for they are never questioned even by an opponent. This will also explain the universal belief in India of the existence of advanced human beings who have acquired supernormal powers (*siddhis*) and who are no longer subject to the normal laws of birth and death. Having learned the hidden secrets of nature—mainly by following the Delphic injunction "Man, know thyself!"—they discovered that a thorough knowledge and understanding of their own egos enabled them to become masters not only of themselves (that is, of the actions of the outer body and the inner mind) but also of external nature to an extent that the Western reader would be inclined to call miraculous. Yet it is claimed by these sages that their supernormal powers are definitely not supernatural, but are exerted within the framework of nature's laws, which therefore, they are able to make use of, whenever the occasion calls for the exercise of their *siddhis*.

Such a sage was Samkara. Because many of his successors adopted the same name, Samkara, there is a great confusion as to when he lived as well as what he wrote. Many of the writings of the later Samkaras have been fathered upon their illustrious predecessor, not always to the benefit of the latter. Although some biographers place him as early as 510 B.C.E., most scholars are agreed that he was born much later, in about the eighth century C.E.

The Commentaries and Treatises

Samkara, by writing his commentary on the Brahma sutras of Badarayana, the *Brahmasūtrabhāsya* (early eighth century; *The Vedānta Sūtras of Bādarāyana with the Commentary of Samkara*, 1890-1904), in which he stressed nondualism, became an important leader in the Advaita system of the Vedanta school of Hindu philosophy. Samkara's writings consist of a number of important commentaries as well as original treatises of various lengths. Of his commentaries, the one on the Brahma sutras is of the greatest importance for his followers. Also important are those on some of the principal Upanishads as well as his commentary on the Bhagavad Gita.

Most of Samkara's original treatises seem to have been written for his disciples' use only.

Among these is a very short one consisting of precisely ten quatrains, and a somewhat longer one consisting of 101 quatrains. Of his two compendiums of Advaita philosophy, *Upadesasāhasrī* (early eighth century; *A Thousand Teachings*, 1949) consists of 116 numbered prose paragraphs and 649 couplets arranged in nineteen chapters. The other compendium, whose authorship is subject to question, is *The Crest Jewel of Wisdom*, which consists of 581 stanzas, most of which are couplets and quatrains with a few triplets interspersed.

The Vedanta viewpoint (*vedantadarsana*) was firmly established by Badarayana in the Brahma sutras. Badarayana is believed to be the same person as Krishna Dvaipayana, the compiler of the Vedas, to whom the Mahabharata is attributed. However, the Vedas were compiled in 3100 B.C.E. according to Brahman chronology, and this is, perhaps, too early a date for Badarayana's sutras.

Badarayana's Sutras

The Vedānta Sūtras of Bādarāyana with the Commentary of Samkara starts with an inquiry into Brahman, the world soul, then continues with a refutation of erroneous views, after which the means of reaching union with Brahman are discussed. Finally the fourth and last part is dedicated to the nature of liberation from the cycle of rebirth and discusses the kinds of liberated beings. The sutras (which are actually aphorisms) are extraordinarily terse, often consisting of only one or two words, and generally without any verbs. Commentators are needed to explain these riddles. However, as one would expect, commentators are wont to disagree among themselves, and so the Vedanta school split into three main systems, known as the Advaita, or nondual system; the Vsistadvaita, or qualifiedly nondual system; and the Dvaita, or dualistic system. Of these, the first system is that of Samkara and his commentary; the second is that of Ramanuja and his great commentary (*S'ribhasya*); the third system is that of Madhva, or Anandatirtha, and his *Sutrabhasya*.

Samkara teaches the unity of the human self with Brahman and that their apparent separation is an illusion (*maya*). Ramanuja, while admitting that the human self can unite with Brahman, claims that both are real. His system is theistic and anthropomorphic, based on religious devotion rather than on rules of logic, as is that of Samkara. Madhva, however, teaches that the duality of the human soul and Brahman persists, that both are real and independent of each other. His dualism is unqualified and opposes Samkara's monistic views as well as the views of Ramanuja.

There have been other commentators on the Brahma sutras. Perhaps the most recent is Baladeva (eighteenth century), whose extensive commentary, known as *Govinda Bhasya*, gives the Vaisnava viewpoint, because he was a follower of Sri Chaitanya. The *Govinda Bhasya* is therefore theistic, like the one by Ramanuja.

A Guide to Spiritual Wisdom

The Crest Jewel of Wisdom was written by Samkara to assist the would-be aspirant to spiritual wisdom in his efforts to free himself from incessant rebirths. There is a strong similarity between the teachings and methods of Samkara and the Buddha. Both aimed to teach humankind how to conquer pain and suffering, how to reach the acme of adulthood, and finally how to obtain the highest spiritual state possible while still living on earth. Both considered conditioned existence as *unreal* and stressed its illusory character (*maya*). Neither of the two had any use for personal gods (*devas*), knowing themselves superior to the latter. The Buddhists and Advaita Vedantists have been called atheists by their opponents, and Buddha as well as Samkara discarded rituals completely. There is no real difference between the path leading to Buddhahood and the path leading to the state of a *Jivanmukta*. All this makes it more difficult to explain the nearly complete silence of the Buddha on the subject of the self (*atman*) and the almost continuous reference to the *atman* by Samkara. Buddha's silence led many Buddhists as well as non-Buddhists to believe that Buddha denied the existence of the *atman* and, therefore, of a soul, which, of course, would contradict Buddha's statements upon a number of other subjects.

Samkara's writings are too metaphysical, even for the average Hindu, to be useful for any but advanced disciples in Hindu mysticism. This he frankly admits at the outset of most of his treatises. In the case of *The Crest Jewel of Wisdom*, he directs himself to a "wise man" (*vidvan*) who strives for liberation and has renounced his desire for the enjoyment of external objects. He advises the wise man to apply to a true and great spiritual teacher for guidance. After some further advice of a general nature, he states the qualifications necessary for success in this venture, apart from being learned and of strong intellect: *discrimination* between things permanent and transitory; *indifference* to enjoyment of the fruits of one's actions in this world and in the next; *yearning to be liberated* (*mumuksuta*), which is the desire to be liberated by knowing one's own real nature and the bonds made through ignorance, from egoism down to the body; and the six accomplishments: (1) *s'ama* (tranquillity), which is a state of mind devoted to its goal; (2) *dama* (self-control), which is the fixing in their own proper sphere of both the organs of perception and of action, after reverting them from their objects; (3) *uparati* (cessation), which is the spontaneous abstaining from action by the mind; (4) *titiksa* (forbearance), which is patient endurance of all suffering, without retaliation, free from anxiety and complaint; (5) *s'raddha* (faith), which is reflection and meditation on the truth of the words of the guru and of the sacred texts; and (6) *samadhana* (deep concentration), which is the constant fixing of the discriminating mind (*buddhi*) on the pure Brahman and not the indulging of the mind (*citta*).

The Guru

The necessary qualifications for the guru, the teacher whom the well-equipped aspirant to liberation or Nirvana must now seek, are even more severe. The guru, through whom freedom from bondage is to be attained, must be spiritually wise, conversant with sacred knowledge, sincere, and not suffering from desires; he must know the nature of Brahman; he must be one who is at rest in the eternal, like a fire that is tranquil when destitute of fuel, one who is a river of disinterested compassion, a friend of all living creatures.

Having found such a preceptor and having asked him for guidance, the disciple, when found worthy, is then instructed by the master, who praises him or her for the desire to rid the self of the bonds of ignorance (*avidya*). The disciple is told that liberation can be achieved only through the *direct perception* of the oneness of the individual self (*atman*) with the universal self (Brahman). Neither the Vedas nor the scriptures (*sastras*) nor the incantations (*mantras*) nor any medicine can help those who are bitten by the snake of ignorance.

It is necessary to know how to discriminate between spirit and non-spirit, between the self and not-self. In order to show the difference between spirit and non-spirit, the guru outlines the visible and invisible part of nature, beginning with the grossest of humans' constituent vehicles.

The *gross body* is produced from the five subtle elements, whose functions are responsible for the five senses. The guru warns of the danger of sense enjoyments and of desires pertaining to the body, and he describes the danger in no uncertain terms. The *internal organ* consists of *manas*, the mental faculties of postulating and doubting; the intellect, having the characteristic of certainty about things; the ego-conforming power, producing the conception "I"; and the mind, having the property of concentration. The *vital principle* manifests itself, according to its transformations, as one of the five "vital airs." The *subtle or astral body* is the vehicle of the five faculties, the five sense organs, the five vital airs, the five elements, ignorance, desire, and action. It is also known as the vehicle of characteristics, and is active in dreams. The *causal body* of the self is the unmanifested condition of the three universal qualities. Its state is that of dreamless sleep. The three universal qualities are purity, action, and darkness. When the purity is unalloyed there will be perception of the self.

The guru now defines in many ways the supreme spirit (*paramatman*), through the knowledge of which isolation (*kaivalya*) or freedom is obtained.

The Five Sheaths

A description follows of the five sheaths (*kosa*), another way of looking at the constituents of a human being. They are the *annamaya*-sheath, sustained by physical food—that is, the gross body; the *pranamaya*-sheath, the vehicle of the vital forces, through which the ego performs all the actions of the gross body; the *manomaya*-sheath, consisting of the organs of sensation and *manas*, the latter mental faculty being the cause of igno-rance and consequently the cause of the bondage of conditioned existence, although the same *manas* when pure becomes the cause of liberation; the *vijnanamaya*-sheath, consisting of intellect and the powers of perception, the doer of actions and the cause of the rounds of rebirth, the embodied ego that has no beginning in time and that is the guide of all actions; the *anandamaya*-sheath, the reflection of absolute bliss, yet not free from the quality of darkness.

The guru explains that these five sheaths are *not the Self*. The latter is self-illumined and re-mains after the subtraction of these sheaths. It is the witness of the three states, of the waking, dreaming, and deep-sleep state.

The Disciple Advances
The disciple is now given subtler teachings about the self and the supreme spirit. The mystic for-mula: "This is Brahman, that thou art (*tat tvam asi*)," paraphrasing the Chandogya-Upanishad, is repeated in a number of stanzas.

The subject of the mental impressions that are the seeds in the mind through which *karma* mani-fests subsequently to any act is now discussed by the guru, and the disciple is told how to exhaust them. At the same time, the disciple must over-come the feeling of "I," the power of egoism, and many stanzas are dedicated to the elaboration of this subject. Other subjects are interwoven in the discussion, such as that of *nirvikalpa samadhi*, a superior type of meditation.

The stanzas become more and more abstruse as the disciple advances in spiritual matters. The characteristics of *jivanmukta*, a person who is *lib-erated while living on earth*, are described, and also the consequences of this achievement, especially in relation to the three kinds of *karma*.

Finally comes the moment when the disciple, through the guru's teaching, through the evi-dence of the revealed scriptures, and through his or her own efforts, realizes the full truth and be-comes absorbed in the universal self. The disciple speaks and informs the master about his or her spiritual experiences, describing the absolute (*parabrahman*) and spiritual bliss. He or she is without attachment and without limbs, sexless, and indestructible. The disciple is neither the doer nor the enjoyer, for he or she is without

change and without action. The disciple, now the self-illumined *atman*, bows down before the guru through whose compassion and greatly esteemed favor the disciple has achieved the goal of his or her existence.

The guru, greatly pleased, explains the posi-tion of the knower of Brahman in the remaining stanzas. At the end, the disciple salutes the guru respectfully. Liberated from bondage, with the guru's permission, the disciple goes away.

Willem B. Roos

Additional Reading

Aleaz, K. P. *The Relevance of Relation in Samkara's Advaita Vedanta*. Delhi: Kant, 1996. This work looks at the concept of relation in Samakara's philosophy. Includes index.

Isaeva, N. V. *Shankara and Indian Philosophy*. SUNY Series in Religious Studies. Albany: State University of New York, 1993. This vol-ume looks at Samkara and Indian philosophy with an emphasis on religion. Includes index.

Pande, Govind Chandra. *Life and Thought of Sankaracarya*. Delhi: Motilal Banarsidass, 1994. This biography of Samkara traces his life and examines his work and beliefs. Includes in-dexes.

Potter, K. H., ed. *Advaita Vedanta Up to Samkara and His Pupils*. Vol. 3. *Encyclopedia of Indian Philosophies*. Delhi, India: Motilal Barnasidas, 1981. Summary of many works by Advaita Vedantins with an introduction by a leading interpreter of Indian philosophy.

Radhakrishnan, Sarvepalli. *Indian Philosophy*. 2 vols. London: Allen & Unwin, 1923. A his-tory of Indian philosophy from an unrelent-ingly Advaita Vedanta standpoint.

Ru, S. Suba. *The Vedanta-Sutras with the Commen-tary by Sri Madwacharya: A Complete Translation*. Madras: Minerva Press, 1904. The only transla-tion of Madhva's interpretation; extremely rare translation of the work of a great scholar.

Sankaranarayanan, S. *Sri Sankara: His LIfe, Phi-losophy, and Relevance to Man in Modern Times*. Madras, India: Adyar Library and Research Center, 1995. This volume published by the Theosophical Society looks at Samkara and at-tempts to relate his philosophy to modern times. Includes index.

Keith E. Yandell

George Santayana

Combining a deep sense of the enduring and ideal nature of classic Greek culture with a learned sense for the immediate and natural, Santayana produced a series of philosophical and literary works as well as personal commentaries on the life and cultures of his times. He has been deemed the "Mona Lisa" of philosophy.

Principal philosophical works: *The Sense of Beauty: Being the Outlines of Aesthetic Theory*, 1896; *Interpretations of Poetry and Religion*, 1900; *Reason in Common Sense*, 1905; *Reason in Society*, 1905; *Reason in Religion*, 1905; *Reason in Art*, 1905; *Reason in Science*, 1906; *The Life of Reason: Or, The Phases of Human Progress*, 1905-1906 (collective title for previous 5 works); *Three Philosophical Poets: Lucretius, Dante, and Goethe*, 1910; *Winds of Doctrine: Studies in Contemporary Opinion*, 1913; *Egotism in German Philosophy*, 1916; *Character and Opinion in the United States*, 1920; *Soliloquies in England and Later Soliloquies*, 1922; *Scepticism and Animal Faith*, 1923; *The Realm of Essence*, 1927; *The Realm of Matter*, 1930; *The Realm of Truth*, 1938; *The Realm of Spirit*, 1940; *The Realms of Being*, 1927-1940 (collective title for previous 4 works); *Persons and Places*, 1944; *The Middle Span*, 1945; *Dominations and Powers*, 1951; *My Host the World*, 1953.

Born: December 16, 1863; Madrid, Spain
Died: September 26, 1952; Rome, Italy

Early Life

George Santayana was born December 16, 1863, in Madrid, Spain. His mother, Spanish by birth, was first married to a member of the Sturgis family of Boston, an American merchant in the Philippines, where, until her husband's death in 1857, she lived and reared three children. Santayana's father was a friend of the Sturgis family, having served as a civil servant in the Philippines and authored a book on the natives of the Island of Mindanao. In 1862, the couple returned to Spain and were married in Madrid. Shortly thereafter, Santayana's mother returned to Boston with her older children while Santayana remained with his father in Spain. In 1872, he was brought by his father to Boston.

When Santayana arrived in Boston, he knew no English. Only Spanish was spoken in his home, but he soon picked up English outside the home and from his reading and was able to speak it without a marked accent. He attended Brimmer School, Boston Latin School and Harvard College, where he was graduated summa cum laude in 1886. In 1883, after his freshman year at Harvard, he returned to Spain to see his father. There, he considered a career in either the Spanish army or as a diplomat but decided instead to return to the United States and pursue a career as a writer. His attachment to Europe, however, remained strong.

At Harvard, Santayana had studied with philosphers Josiah Royce and William James. Having already published since 1880 in *The Boston Latin School Register*, he became a regular contributor of cartoons and literary pieces to the *Harvard Lampoon*. He helped found *The Harvard Monthly* and provided it with a continuous flow of poetry and articles.

In physical appearance, Santayana was a gentle-looking man of medium size. He had lively eyes, was bald, and for a while wore a handsome beard; later, he wore a mustache. He was fastidious about his clothes, often wearing black.

Life's Work

Santayana's first major philosophical work, *The Sense of Beauty: Being the Outline of Aesthetic Theory*, was published in 1896 when he was thirty-three. A book of sonnets and a series of pieces of literary criticism were also published that year. This was also the year that Santayana went to study with Henry Jackson at Trinity College, Cambridge. He undertook careful examination of the works of classical Greece, particularly those of Plato and Aristotle. This experience led to the production of one of Santayana's major philosophical works, the five-volume *The Life of Reason: Or, the Phases of Human Progress*. In it, Santayana attempted to present a summary history of the human imagination, a panorama of the whole life of reason and of human ideas as they are generated out of and controlled by humanity's animal life and nature. This was Santayana's first major effort at combining a skeptical naturalism and humanism with a Platonic idealism. A variety of pieces of literary philosophical criticism followed, and in 1914 his famous piece "The Genteel Tradition in American Philosophy" appeared.

In that year, Santayana received news of a legacy. He promptly retired from Harvard at the age of fifty, and in January, 1912, he left the United States for Europe, never to return. Santayana had been an extremely gifted teacher, and his sudden departure for Europe astonished his colleagues. Yet, although he was interested in his students, he disliked academic life and wished to devote himself to his writing. Also, his dual Spanish American heritage, although contributing extraordinary range and perspective to his thinking, awoke in him conflicts from which he was thankful to escape. He went to France, Spain, and England, and finally to Rome, Italy, where he lived for eleven years in the monastery of the Blue Sisters. From there, Santayana produced a number of penetrating pieces on the life and culture of his times, including *Winds of Doctrine* and *Egotism in German Philosophy*, a book much read by the Germans during the war, although it strongly demonstrated his loyalty to the Allied cause. In 1920, he wrote *Character and Opinion in the United States*. A major philosophical work appeared in 1923, *Scepticism and Animal Faith*, followed by his magnum opus, the four-volume *Realms of Being*. In 1935, he produced a novel reflective of his American experience entitled *The Last Puritan: A Memoir in the Form of a Novel*.

Santayana's *Persons and Places*, a kind of autobiographical travelogue, captures much of the spirit of Santayana's writing. It presents him as a traveler who, however appreciative or critical of the places and people encountered, is always a stranger, catching glimpses of people and places and recomposing these images as an artist would a painting. Santayana, in his work, too, conveys a constant sense of detachment, reflecting his reclusive spirit. Yet his works of speculative philosophy, with precision, depth, and coherence, elucidate complex ideas with what has been described as "luminous succinctness."

Santayana's life ended with characteristic ambiguity. Although he considered himself Catholic and lived among the nuns for eleven years, he did not officially return to the Roman Catholic Church and did not receive the Sacraments on his deathbed. He died in September, 1952, a few

George Santayana. *(Library of Congress)*

months before his eighty-ninth birthday. He was buried in Rome, on ground reserved for Spanish nationals.

Influence

To many Americans, Santayana was a great man of letters, a civilized hermit, and an isolated sage. His works were eloquent and penetrating but always a bit of a mystery. Santayana spent forty years in the United States and wrote eleven books as well as numerous other works. Yet he left the United States in 1912 never to return. As Santayana himself noted, however, his intentional detachment from the United States must be balanced by the fact that he was detached from every other place as well. He never did have a sense of home, yet he clearly believed that "it was as an American writer he was to be counted."

Like Transcendentalist Ralph Waldo Emerson, Santayana was essentially concerned with the conditions of life, with the bearing of events on people, and with the emergence of values and the possibilities for happiness. His account of the many sides of human experience—ethical, social, artistic, and religious—shows an interweaving of themes normally kept separate in modern philosophy and is expressed in prose that is polished to great beauty. Although his philosophy was much influenced by classical culture, it also contains much of the dynamic, fresh, naturalistic aspects of American culture. Santayana's profound belief in the life and power of the human mind and imagination and in the creativity and freedom of the human spirit produced a series of truly noteworthy works that expressed the American spirit at its best.

Jacquelyn Kegley

The Sense of Beauty

Being the Outlines of Aesthetic Theory

Type of philosophy: Aesthetics, ethics
First published: 1896
Principal ideas advanced:
◇ Our preferences are ultimately nonrational; things are good because they are preferred.

◇ Beauty is pleasure objectified; when a spectator regards pleasure as a quality of the object seen, the person calls the object "beautiful."
◇ Form pleases when in perception the excitation of the retinal field produces a semblance of motion while the mind synthesizes the elements perceived.
◇ The aesthetic component "expression" is the result of the emotional associations excited by contemplation of the aesthetic object.

George Santayana is one of the few philosophers whose writings have a beauty of style that can be appreciated independently of their philosophical worth. Literary ability should not be taken as a substitute for clarity in presenting ideas; but at his best, Santayana had the fortune of combining both well. In this early work, not only does he present a provocative account of aesthetics in what may be called a "naturalistic" vein, but in addition he gives an insight into the development of his later metaphysics and ontology.

The Sense of Beauty is divided into four parts. In the opening part, Santayana discusses the nature of beauty. He points out that the term "aesthetics" originally meant "perception" and that it was associated, by use, with a particular object of perception and its study, that which we call "the beautiful." This can be put in a different but related manner if we speak of a perceptual quality that we are to analyze; namely, beauty. Here one should remind oneself of words that make use of the "perception" meaning of "aesthetics"; for example, we use the term "kinaesthesis" to refer to a certain sense that our muscles have, and we speak of "anaesthesis" as the loss of our sensations.

Value

To return to the sort of perceptive activity with which this analysis is to be concerned, it should be pointed out that we are not examining the world of facts considered independently of any observer. Such a world is neutral as far as value is concerned, for it is not good (or evil) for any one. Herein we see a basis for Santayana's naturalism. The existence of worth or value depends upon the presence of somebody's consciousness; nature has purpose or growth only in that one values what nature exhibits. Nature is not itself aware of the changes. Because the consciousness that observes must also appreciate if it is to hold patterns of value, there is a nonrational as well as rational basis for our judgment of the world as one in which phenomena are loved or hated. Santayana lays bare his indebtedness to philosophers Baruch Spinoza and David Hume when he proclaims that our preferences regarding the events of the world are ultimately nonrational. Things are good because we prefer them; they are not preferred because they are good.

One should point out, however, that Santayana's view that values must be separated from facts rests upon a distinction that is false in fact. It is not meaningless to contend that we are creatures who have desires because objects in the world provoke our interests; in this sense, it is as much true that we desire things because they are good as that they are good because we desire them. Either philosophical view, the one that says that values are independent of consciousness and intrinsic to the world (the so-called absolutist position) or that which claims values wholly dependent on and relative to the attitudes of subjects, is incomplete and only part of the story.

Santayana goes on to discuss the difference between moral and aesthetic values. The analogy that he draws is between work and play, between duty and amusement. Morality prepares us for the serious aspects of life: death, disease, passion, and, only against the background of these, the possibility of salvation. To seek pleasure, to enjoy experience—these are but futile pursuits, trivial and potentially dangerous against the stark reality of existence. Actions are looked upon in terms of the consequences they will have in preparing us for our stern lives. There is no time to give oneself to the pleasure of an experience enjoyed for its own sake, which aims at nothing else. This attitude toward the world is akin to the biblical attitude toward work; one must labor by the sweat of one's brow because of humanity's first disobedience, which brought death and disease into the world. As the pressures upon a society lessen and it becomes more secure in its struggle with its environment, the seriousness of life lifts and individuals are more likely to take on a holiday air. Play and freedom go together and with them the love of immediate pleasures for their own sake, free from fear and independent of con-

sequences. In the distinction between duty and pleasure, work and play, and constraint and freedom is to be found the difference between moral and aesthetic values.

Beauty as Pleasure

In defining beauty, Santayana points out that as a pleasure it has certain peculiar characteristics that allow us to distinguish it from other pleasures. Most pleasures that we get from perceiving (in the wide sense of the term) can be distinguished from the object perceived. We usually go through certain actions before the pleasure is felt. In eating, drinking, inhaling, the activity is begun, then pleasure follows. There are certain pleasures that seem to occur in the process of perception itself; when this happens to us, we intuit the pleasure as a quality of the thing perceived. Santayana holds that the very mechanism or structure of the mind by which we perceive various qualities as one homogeneous object also objectifies this type of pleasure, so that it, too, is felt as an integral part of the object. This is the kind of pleasure that is considered to be intrinsic, enjoyable in itself, and, of course, of positive value in the sense that it belongs to the play, holiday, or free class rather than to the moral one. For Santayana, beauty is *positive, intrinsic, objectified pleasure*, or *pleasure regarded as the quality of a thing*.

Although some hold that in nature we can find such aesthetically pleasant objects, generally speaking it is to humans and their creations that we look for objects in which we can take some contemplative pleasure. Santayana has a problem, however, in considering beauty as he does; for if we identify those objects as works of art, we then have the problem of tragedy and of painful works of art. We shall later see how he meets this challenge.

Substance and Form

In "The Materials of Beauty," Santayana discusses the substance of beauty—sound, color, and fragrance—as well as other topics concerned with the appeal of our lower senses in relation to the total aesthetic experience. There are those who have argued that the experiences that we must have by *direct* contact with an object (because of the structure of certain parts of our sensorium) cannot be of the beautiful. The bouquet and taste of wine, the touch of brocade, of marble, or sandalwood, are pleasant yet do not seem to be beautiful. Santayana claims, however, that all contribute to the ultimate experience of beauty in that they teach us to appreciate the pleasant, to delight in things sensuous. Those who find the height of aesthetic experience in objects appealing to the eye and ear through their formal structure must recognize that form and meaning can be presented only in something sensible. To divorce content from a work of art is to present something utterly barren.

In the third part of his work, Santayana analyzes form as a main aspect of beauty. In the previous section, he noted that certain elements presented to the senses charm or please in themselves. We need look no further than the coolness of a summer breeze to explain the pleasure we feel in its company. However, we also encounter a pleasure that, although immediate and intrinsic, is yet puzzling and perhaps mysterious when we come upon it. These pleasures are presented to us as objects that have elements—none of which is particularly pleasing in itself—yet that, because of their arrangement, combination, or pattern, are pleasing. Aestheticians refer to this as the *form* of the object. To reduce an object to its elements destroys its distinctive, pleasing effect, although without those elements there could not be form.

Santayana turns to the psychology of perception to explain, hypothetically, the pleasure that one derives from form in its various manifestations as well as to indicate why some forms are either boring or incomplete as visual wholes. (He concentrates on visual form and specifically omits auditory form as too technical to analyze in this work, although he indicates that in principle it should be the same.) Briefly, he claims that the visual image is gathered as a series of sensitive points about the center of the retina. These points or spots each have their peculiar quality of sensation and are associated with the muscular tension and relaxation that occurs with the turning of one's eyes. As the associations are formed, they establish a field that is such that when certain elements (or perhaps a single element) are presented to the eye, the entire field is excited. The excitation produces a semblance of motion; there is a radiation about the points that tends to re-

create the associated image, so that the point leads the mind to the possible field. Various geometrical figures affect the eyes in ways that lead to a graceful and rhythmic completion by the mind (depending to a certain degree, if not entirely, on the figure given) that is pleasing. The muscular movement is not itself smooth, but rather a series of jerks; the visual effect, however, is one of movement full and graceful, combining actual and possible (or perhaps imaginary) rays. The form presented does not automatically produce a pleasing effect. Because of their gross or tiny size, some forms fail to excite the eye and its muscles significantly.

Symmetry is a good example of aesthetic form; where it is an aid to unification, where it helps us to organize, discriminate, and distinguish—in other words, to bring a semblance of harmonic order to a confused or chaotic jumble—the effect is pleasing. Form then may be viewed as the perception of unity in variety. Though a conscious and attentive effort, we are able to bring comprehension to what might otherwise not be understood. In this sense, it is an activity of mind as well as of perception. The elements may stimulate and excite, but it is the mind that synthesizes that has an insight into the order of the elements.

Santayana goes on to discuss various aspects of form that illustrate both its aesthetic value and its dangerous (from an aesthetic point of view) possibilities. There is unity in variety, as noted, but also there is multiplicity in uniformity. The starry skies present a picture of an infinite number of similar bodies. The field that is the sky is peppered by a multiplicity of objects that is overwhelming, yet they do not blend into one, for each retains its individuality. The heavens' beauty is increased by the very material composing it—the blackness of the heavens glittering with the light of the stars—so that form and substance are blended in perfect union.

It should be noted that multiplicity as an aesthetic component may lead to boredom and disinterest if not properly presented. The attention span of individuals and their ability to synthesize may be brief when the same elements are given repeatedly. Just as sheer variety becomes another name for confusion, so mulitiplicity is synonymous with dullness when presented for its own sake.

Aestheticians have long pondered the question, "Are all things beautiful?" Santayana addresses himself to this question, and it is not difficult, cued as we are by what has been presented of his system so far, to guess what his reply would be. Because the world independent of consciousness and will would be valueless and because what is good (or beautiful) depends on our desires, nothing in principle can be ruled out as a possible object of beauty. One makes a mistake, however, if one concludes from this possibility that everything is equally beautiful. As Santayana states:

> All things are not equally beautiful because the subjective bias that discriminates between them is the cause of their being beautiful at all. The principle of personal preference is the same as that of human taste; real and objective beauty, in contrast to a vagary of individuals, means only an affinity to a more prevalent and lasting susceptiblity, a response to a more general and fundamental demand. And the keener discrimination, by which the distance between beautiful and ugly things is increased, far from being a loss of aesthetic insight, is a development of that faculty by the exercise of which beauty comes into the world.

The most important aspect of form, and the one which best expresses Santayana's view, is that in a neutral universe, there are elements that are susceptible to the imaginative activity of our mind. By means of such activity, the world is constructed by reference to ideals into unities from elements that are diverse in themselves. In this activity lies the basis for the life of reason and contemplation and for the discovery of the world of phenomena that we know and the beauty that it has. Although a naturalist in his outlook on value, Santayana comes close to a variety of Kantian idealism in his consideration of the imaginative, synthesizing character of mind by which the world of objects and the beauty therein is constructed.

Expression

In the final section of *The Sense of Beauty*, the aesthetic component called "expression" is discussed. In the presence of beautiful objects, the mind is affected by and contributes to both the material and the formal aspects of the aesthetic object. There is an additional feature, however, which, given the object and the mind's activity, must be mentioned. There is present, both with the immediate perception of the object and after it is no longer perceived, an emotional overtone that colors the sensation and our memory of it. This aura is the result of associations that we have made and that affect our memory as well as our immediate perceptions; this quality we call "the expression of the object."

Form and substance constitute aesthetic value in the first term, whereas expression is value in the second term. The latter value is found in the associations, the moral values, the history, the accouterments—all of which may go with the presentation of a work of art. These, accompanying the work itself, are raised to the level of beauty, when in themselves they present a joy and sweetness that transcends the utilitarian or functional character that they ordinarily have.

The difficult question that was raised earlier as to the place of tragedy as an aesthetic object in a theory that emphasizes that pleasure is beauty when seen as the quality of a thing can now be answered. It is by expression that tragedy is beautiful. The events of playwright William Shakespeare's *Hamlet* can be imagined as reported in a newspaper; in this context, they would hardly constitute that which we would call "beautiful." Moral and pathetic, perhaps, if written well, but the utility of the journalistic presentation would doubtless preclude any feeling of pleasure. The horror, the pain, the sadness of life would come through; the world of moral value, of duty, of work, and, rather than that of beauty, of play, and of joy would be given to us. However, these events can, when placed in the context of the theater or treated under the brush of the painter or pen of the composer, take on a positive value and thus move, as it were, to a new plane. The moral, negative in itself, may then take on the character of a first-term value and become positive.

In this way, the evil in life is turned into a good; we see in the tragic lesson something to be learned, something that makes us better for it, something that points toward a possible and, we hope, realizable perfection. In the transference of the negative value into something good, we prepare the way for the events to be a source of pleasure. The tragic elements are there, but through their expressiveness they have been made by mind into a thing of beauty. It is in this way that Santayana analyzes the object of beauty into its material, formal, and expressive aspects and prepares the way for an analysis of the Life of Reason through which humanity raises the world that is given, a world of no value, into one in which, ultimately, good is supreme.

Theodore Waldman

The Life of Reason

Or, The Phases of Human Progress

Type of philosophy: Metaphysics, philosophy of history

First published: Reason in Common Sense, 1905; *Reason in Society*, 1905; *Reason in Religion*, 1905; *Reason in Art*, 1905; *Reason in Science*, 1906

Principal ideas advanced:

◇ The philosophy of history is an interpretation of humanity's past in the light of its ideal development.

◇ The life of reason, which gives meaning to history, is the unity given to existence by a mind in love with the good.

◇ By the use of reason, humans distinguish between spirit and nature and come to understand their own wants and how to satisfy them.

◇ Instinct, which originally showed itself only in animal impulses, takes on ideal dimensions and leads humanity into service for society and God.

◇ Finally, in art, which is the imposing of form on matter, but most of all in science, which puts the claims of reason to the test of fact, the life of reason reaches its ideal consummation.

In his autobiography, George Santayana says that *The Life of Reason* had its origin in a course he gave at Harvard University entitled "Philosophy of History." It drew heavily from Plato and Aristotle, but also from Francis Bacon, John Locke, Montesquieu, and Hippolyte-Adolphe Taine. Other

influences evident in the work are those of Arthur Schopenhauer, who was the subject of Santayana's doctoral dissertation, and his professor William James, whose biologically oriented psychology left a strong impression on Santayana.

For Santayana, the philosophy of history implies no providential plan of creation or redemption but is simply "retrospective politics"; that is to say, an interpretation of humanity's past in the light of its ideal development. It is the science of history that deals with events inferred from evidence and explained in terms of causal law. However, not content with a mere knowledge of what has happened, humans have a strong propensity toward trying to find meaning in events as if history were shaped to some human purpose. Admittedly, history is not; still, the exercise is profitable, for it is one of the ways in which we discover the goals we wish to pursue in the future. The failures and successes of our forebears, as their acts will appear when measured by our ideals, can help us appraise our standards and to enlighten us with respect to how far they can be attained. However, it can serve its function only if we remember that it is ideal history—an abstract from reality made to illustrate a chosen theme—rather than a description of actual tendencies observable in the world.

The Life of Reason

The theme that Santayana selects as giving meaning to history is the rise and development of reason. Unlike his idealistic counterparts, who think of nature as the product and embodiment of reason, he conceives reason as a latecomer on the evolutionary scene and very much dependent on what has gone before. This is not to say that there is no order in nature prior to the dawn of consciousness in humanity. Santayana's contention, on the contrary, is that reason, which is too often thought of in the abstract, schoolmasterly fashion, is in reality an extension of the order already achieved in organized matter. In its earliest phase, it is nothing more than instinct that has grown conscious of its purposes and representative of its conditions. For in the dark laboratories of nature, life has already solved the hardest problems, leaving to its strange child, reason, nothing to do at first but amuse itself with the images that drift through the mind while the body goes about its accustomed business. We can scarcely call it reason until, distinguishing these mental states from objects, reason gradually sees what the parent organism is about, what it runs from, what it pursues, and how it manages each new eventuality. Then it begins to play its role.

Although instinct is dependent on present cues, reason can summon thoughts from afar, suggest shortcuts, and balance likelihoods. Often its well-meant suggestions lead to destruction; however, its occasionally fruitful counsels tend to perpetuate themselves in habits and customs, as a shelter of branches, devised for one night's protection, remains standing and becomes a rudimentary home. It is in this way that reason, an adjunct of life, comes to have a "life" of its own. Reason, by this accounting, is the servant of will or interest. It is these that determine what is good. Santayana calls the Life of Reason the unity inherent in all existence.

Nature and Spirit

Santayana traces reason's career through five phases, devoting one book to each. *Reason in Common Sense* may be regarded as introducing the other books. It outlines the origins of the two realms, nature and spirit, whose fortunes are followed through the rest of the work. Out of an originally chaotic experience, humans learn to distinguish first the stable, predictable realm of nature. Regularity and order are present there; and things occurring repeatedly can be identified and their habits noted. However, in a great part of experience, images come and go in no discernible pattern and combine in innumerable ways. This remainder people come to designate as spirit: It is the seat of poetry and dreams, and later of philosophy and mathematics.

Human progress may be viewed as the gradual untangling of these two realms. The rich garment of sight and sound under which nature appears to our senses conceals its structure and beguiles us into supposing that trees and rivers have spirits and pursue purposes not unlike our own. It is practical experience—fishing and agriculture—that gradually teaches us otherwise, enabling us to strip off irrelevant qualities, and discern the mechanical process underneath. Not surprisingly, we are sometimes reluctant to leave behind the more congenial picture of poetry and myth. However, insofar as we become aware of our advantage, we learn to prefer things to ideas and to subordinate thinking to the arts of living.

Almost as difficult as discerning nature is the task of deciding what is good. Before consciousness awakened, instinct guided the body toward the satisfaction of genuine, if partial, needs. However, when ideas appeared, impulse was diverted, and moral perplexity began. False gods arose, which exist only in imagination, and these must be set aside in favor of ideas that live up to their promises. There is the further problem of subordinating the claims of competing goods under a common ideal. Reason must discover the truth and order of values. By understanding our wants and the limits of our existence, reason points us toward our highest fulfillment, that is, our happiness.

Viewed in these larger aspects, the rational life is sanity, maturity, and common sense. It justifies itself against romanticism, mysticism, and all otherworldliness that betoken a failure to distinguish between ideal and real, or a misguided flight from nature to the world of dreams.

The Social Expression of Reason

Reason in Society follows the course of humanity's ideal attachments from the passionate love of a person for one of the opposite sex to the fancies of a person of taste and finally to the devotions of a saint. The instincts that unite the sexes, bind parents and offspring, and draw the lonely from their isolation into tribes and cities, when illuminated with the flame of consciousness, take on ideal dimensions and give rise to love, loyalty, and faith. It is the mark of love to combine impulse and representation; and no one who has truly loved can be entirely deaf to the voice of reason or indifferent to the liberal life toward which it calls.

Santayana groups societies into three classes. The first, which he calls *natural* societies, includes not merely the family but also economic and political groups. In these, association is more instinctive than voluntary. However, they serve reason well when the regimen that they prescribe becomes the means of fashioning strong, reliant individuals who, without disloyalty to their origins, form *free* societies based on mutual attachments and common interests. Such persons, in possession of their own wills, may go further and create *ideal* societies, which is what we do when, forsaking the company of others, we make beauty or truth our companion.

In its social expressions, perhaps more than anywhere else, reason has to draw the fine line between crude fact and irresponsible fancy. Somewhere between the shrewd materialism of Sancho and the lofty madness of Don Quixote, there is a way of living that incorporates the ideal in the actual, whether in love or in politics. Therein lies the liberal or free life for humanity.

Religion and Reason

Reason in Religion develops the view that religion is a halfway station on the road from irresponsible fancy to verifiable truth. It is neither to be rejected out of hand as imbecile and superstitious, nor rationalized and allegorized until it agrees with science. In the story of human progress, it fulfills a civilizing function but under serious disabilities: For although it pursues the same goal as reason, it relies on imagination instead of logic and experiment. On the positive side, its occasional profound insights into moral reality have spurred humankind to needed reforms; but this gain is offset by its stubborn adherence to an anthropomorphic view of nature that closes the way to systematic advance.

A lifelong student of the religions of the West, Santayana illuminates his theme with detailed criticisms of the major traditions. The Hebrew religion gets high marks for its wholesome emphasis upon morals but is censured for its dogmatic and intolerant spirit. The Christian gospel, which dramatizes one's efforts to transcend human nature, is an important step toward the goal of freedom; but it needs to be blended with pagan ritual if people are not to lose sight of their moral dimensions. Such a paganized Christianity developed along Mediterranean shores; however, it remained strange to Christian converts in the northern forests. Gothic art, philosophy, and chivalry are, by contrast, a barbarized Christianity and have as their proper motif the native religion of the Teutons. This it was that, coming of age, threw off the world-denying gospel and emerged in its proper sublimation, first as Protestantism, then as Romanticism and Absolute Ego-

tism. Less mature, and further divorced from reality than Catholicism, Gothic Christianity lingers on in various idealisms—moral, political, philosophical—obscuring the path of reason.

Art and Reason

Reason in Art is broadly conceived to include every activity that "humanizes and rationalizes objects." For Santayana, with his classical bias, artistic activity consists in imposing form upon matter. Like religion, art is preoccupied with imagination; but its concern is more wholesome because, instead of mistaking fancies for facts, it fashions facts according to its ideal preferences. Thus, each genuinely artistic achievement is a step toward the goal of rational living.

Humanity's earliest constructions must have been clumsy and unprepossessing, not even rivaling the spontaneous products of nature. Compared, for example, with the prancing of a stallion, the movements of primitive people performing the first war or mating dances were probably crude and lacking in fluidity. However, when art frees the dance from the excitement of war or courtship and makes the intention its study, a new form of discipline and social control appears that purges the soul. Through art, we tame our own spirit and gladden it with sights and sounds.

The advance of civilization is not always friendly to free creation. Customs, acquiring almost the force of instincts, stifle invention; and products have a way of enslaving their producers. A society that views art as truancy from business condemns artists to vagrancy and robs their genius of its normal incentive. Such a society has entered a postrational phase because it has lost touch with humanity's genuine needs. Art is no mere pleasurable accessory to life. We are engaged in liberal and humane enterprise in the measure that, transcending our animal needs and vulgar ambition, we become the master of the conditions of our existence, visit on them our kind of perfection, and render their tragic aspects endurable by clothing them in intelligible and regular forms.

Science and Reason

Reason in Science brings the Life of Reason to its *logical* conclusion; for, as Santayana defines science, it is the consummation of the rational ideal in the light of which the other phases of human life have been interpreted and alongside which they have been judged. Insofar as the standard has been presupposed all along, this final volume is somewhat anticlimactic. What saves it from this lot is the feeling of contemporaneousness that goes with the word "science," together with the belief (characteristic of the period in which the work appeared) that humankind has *actually* entered the scientific era for which all previous history was but the prelude. Science, says Santayana, is practically a new thing: Only twice in history has it appeared—for three hundred years in Greece and for a comparable time in the modern West. Art and religion have had their day, and nothing more is to be expected from them. They bow before the new techniques of measurement and verification. The fruits of science, however, have scarcely begun to appear, and the morrow is sure to bring many surprises.

Santayana's purpose, however, was not primarily to trumpet the dawn of a new day. Optimism with respect to the future was never one of his characteristics. However, he was concerned to defend tough-minded naturalism against tender-minded idealism and against all kinds of compromise. His trumpet blast might be described as an effort to frighten off the enemies of science who, he thought, would yet have their way.

To this end, he stresses the sharp distinction between the realm of nature and the realm of spirit. There is a science corresponding to each of these, which, using classic terms, he designates respectively as *physics* and *dialectic*.

Physics and Dialectic

The ideal expression of physics is mechanics, because the laws governing the behavior of matter are there made perfectly intelligible. However, mechanics is exceptional, true only in the gross. The forms and repetitions of nature are never simple and never perfect. Nevertheless, all knowledge that deals with facts must adopt a mechanical principle of explanation. This is true, Santayana insists, even in the sciences that treat of humanity—notably history and psychology. There are no special "historical forces," such as idealists are wont to suppose: Historical causation breaks up into miscellaneous natural pro-

cesses and minute particular causes. Similarly, there are no "moral causes," such as biographers and literary psychologists presume: The part of psychology that is a science is physiological and belongs to human biology.

As physics comprehends all sciences of fact, dialectic includes all sciences of idea. Its perfect expression is mathematics, which makes possible the deductive elaboration of hypotheses in physics. However, another branch of dialectics elaborates the relationship between conflicting human purposes or ideals. Socrates, who pioneered in its development, first established rational ethics. Purely a normative science, it sheds great light on human undertakings and is presupposed in any study (such as the present one) that attempts to deal intelligently with problems of good and evil. However, it is limited to ideas and cannot take the place of observation and experiment in questions that have to do with existence.

Postrational Systems and Science

Questions of purpose are far more fateful than questions of fact because it is within the former's domain to decide whether the life of reason is to be pursued. Here Santayana considers at length the subject of postrational ethics and religion. The age of the Greeks passed. In mathematics, physics, and medicine, knowledge continued to progress; however, a sense of worldweariness descended on people's minds, causing them to turn their backs on worldly enterprise and seek consolation in pleasure or compensation in ecstasy or to deaden disappointment by asceticism and obedience. The humanism of Socrates gave place to Stoicism, Epicureanism, Skepticism, and to a revival of pagan cults, all founded on personal or metaphysical despair. In Christianity, a similar experience of disillusion forced the imagination to take wings and seek its hope beyond the clouds.

In Santayana's judgment these postrational systems are not to be condemned. They witness the fact that life is older and more persistent than reason and knows how to fall back on more primitive solutions to its problems when its bolder experiments fail. Even in retreat, they hold on to certain conquests of reason, which they fortify and furnish in rare fashion. Therefore, true sages can flourish and true civilizations can develop in retrogressive times, and super-naturalism can nourish a rational and humane wisdom.

This, however, is not to admit that the postra-tional systems are an advance over the rational even in the solution of humanity's spiritual enig-mas. When the same despair breeds arbitrary substitutes for physical science, it is time to sound the alarm. Santayana's final chapter, "The Validity of Science," is devoted to criticisms of science, particularly from theologians and tran-scendental philosophers. The former wish to combine scientific explanation with relics of myth, and thereby preserve a sanction over moral and political behavior. What the latter seek is less clear. Their attack consists in showing (what was never in doubt) that the findings of science are relative; such philosophers, appar-ently, aim at freeing their minds of intelligible notions so that they can swim in the void of the vegetative and digestive stage of consciousness.

Science is not beyond criticism. A healthy skepticism respecting the claims of reason is ever in order. It is an integral part of science to review its findings, and purge itself of arbitrariness and bad faith. For its whole aim is to free the mind from caprice by bringing it under the control of objective principles. Santayana quotes Heracli-tus's saying, "Men asleep live each in his own world, but when awake they live in the same world together." Religion and art are too much like dreaming; when people brings their dreams under the control of the real world, on the one hand, and the principle of contradiction, on the other, they pass from mere faith and aspiration to knowledge and expectation.

Jean Faurot

Additional Reading

Arnett, Willard E. *George Santayana*. New York: Twayne, 1968. This brief yet clear introduction concentrates on the basic themes in George Santayana's thought, especially his aesthetics and his view of spirituality. It also contains a short biography and a bibliography of his works.

_____. *Santayana and the Sense of Beauty*. Bloom-ington: Indiana University Press, 1955. The author probes Santayana's view of beauty and art, revealing a highly elaborated theory of aesthetics. The work also deals with the place of religion in Santayana's thought.

Cory, Daniel L. *Santayana: The Later Years: A Por-trait with Letter*. New York: George Braziller, 1963. Using letters and personal anecdotes, Cory gives a biographical and intellectual de-scription of the man who was his friend and colleague from 1928 until Santayana's death.

Kirby-Smith, H. T. *A Philosophical Novelist: George Santayana and the Last Puritan*. Carbondale: Southern Illinois University Press, 1997. This work looks at Santayana's philosophy in lit-erature. Includes index.

Lamont, Corliss, ed. *Dialogue on George Santayana*. New York: Horizon Press, 1959. This thin vol-ume is a transcript of a conversation about Santayana by friends and scholars, providing biographical detail along with philosophical insights. The editor was a close friend of San-tayana.

Levinson, Henry Samuel. *Santayana, Pragmatism, and the Spiritual Life*. Chapel Hill: University of North Carolina Press, 1992. This book situates Santayana as a pragmatist who differs from John Dewey and the mainline pragmatists in that he takes the religious life seriously. Levin-son criticizes some contemporary interpreta-tions of Santayana.

McCormick, John. *George Santayana: A Biography*. New York: Knopf, 1987. This biography traces Santayana from his birth in Madrid to his pro-fessorship of philosophy in the United States, and then back again to Europe. McCormick quotes extensively from Santayana's public works and his private letters.

Munson, Thomas N. *The Essential Wisdom of George Santayana*. New York: Columbia Uni-versity Press, 1962. This critical examination of Santayana's thought from a neo-Thomist point-of-view attempts to show that he failed at achieving true philosophy. The book is valu-able for its bibliography of articles by and about Santayana and its letters from Santayana to the author questioning the book's thesis.

Schlipp, Paul Arthur, ed. *The Philosophy of George Santayana*. Evanston, Ill.: Northwestern Uni-versity Press, 1940, 1951. This serious study surveys all aspects of Santayana's life and work, with a critical examination of his major themes by eighteen scholars. The volume also contains Santayana's reply to his critics as well as a bibliography of Santayana's writings.

Sprigge, Timothy L. S. *Santayana: An Examination of His Philosophy*. 1974. 2d ed. London: Routledge, 1995. This work clarifies the philosophical issues in Santayana's rich prose to provide an introduction to his thought. The author focuses on Santayana's treatment of skepticism, but also includes chapters on truth and ethics. It also includes the author's reflections on contemporary discussions of Santayana's work. It includes a bibliography of secondary sources on Santayana.

Tejera, V. *American Modern, the Path Not Taken: Aesthetics, Metaphysics, and Intellectual History in Classic American Philosophy*. Lanham, Md.: Rowman & Littlefield, 1996. This work examines several modern philosophers, including Santayana, Justus Buchler, C. H. Peirce, and John Dewey. Includes index.

Jacquelyn Kegley, updated by Patrick S. Roberts

Jean-Paul Sartre

A powerhouse of intellectual energy, French existentialist Sartre poured out novels, plays, screenplays, biographies, criticism, political essays, and philosophy. Journalist, teacher, and perennial activist, he served in the first rank of worldwide liberal causes.

Principal philosophical works: *L'Imagination*, 1936 (*Imagination: A Psychological Critique*, 1962); *Esquisse d'une théorie des émotions*, 1939 (*The Emotions: Outline of a Theory*, 1948); *L'Imaginaire: Psychologie phénoménologique de l'imagination*, 1940 (*The Psychology of Imagination*, 1948); *L'Être et le néant: Essai d'ontologie phénoménologique*, 1943 (*Being and Nothingness: An Essay of Phenomenological Ontology*, 1956); *L'Existentialisme est un Humanisme*, 1946 (*Existentialism*, 1947; also as *Existentialism and Humanism*, 1948); *Réflexions sur la question juive*, 1946 (*Anti-Semite and Jew*, 1948); *Baudelaire*, 1947 (English translation, 1950); *Qu'est-ce que la littérature?*, 1947 (*What Is Literature?*, 1949); *Situations I-X*, 1947-1975 (10 volumes; partial translation, 1965-1977); *Saint-Genet: Comédien et martyr*, 1952 (*Saint Genet: Actor and Martyr*, 1963); *Critique de la raison dialectique, précédé de question de méthode*, 1960 (*Search for a Method*, 1963); *Critique de la raison dialectique, I: Théorie des ensembles pratiques*, 1960 (*Critique of Dialectical Reason, I: Theory of Practical Ensembles*, 1976); *Les Mots*, 1963 (*The Words*, 1964); *L'Idiot de la famille: Gustave Flaubert, 1821-1857*, 1971-1972 (3 volumes; partial translation, *The Family Idiot: Gustave Flaubert, 1821-1857*, 1981, 1987); *Un Théâtre de situations*, 1973 (*Sartre on Theater*, 1976); *Les Carnets de la drôle de guerre*, 1983 (*The War Diaries of Jean-Paul Sartre: November, 1939-March, 1940*, 1984); *Le Scénario Freud*, 1984 (*The Freud Scenario*, 1985).

Born: June 21, 1905; Paris, France
Died: April 15, 1980; Paris, France

Early Life

Jean-Paul Sartre was the only child of Anne-Marie Schweitzer and Jean-Baptiste Sartre. Jean-Baptiste had been a promising naval officer, active in several engagements in China, where he contracted the enterocolitis that killed him in September, 1906. The young widow and her son, then fifteen months old, returned to her parents' home. Charles Schweitzer, Anne-Marie's father, an overbearing intellectual, undertook the education of the precocious boy, who was soon reading voraciously and writing imitations of adventure comic books. Anne-Marie kept her son in long, golden curls. When the curls were finally cut, he recognized himself as ugly, with one eye turned out and blinded by an early illness. This ugliness and his small adult stature (five feet, two inches) fueled his self-consciousness. Formal schooling was intermittent until he was enrolled in the Lycée Henri-Quatre in 1915. After a rocky start, he was academically successful and began making friends.

In 1917, Anne-Marie remarried and moved with her son and new husband to La Rochelle. The move was unhappy for Sartre, who returned to Paris in the fall of 1920 as a boarding student. Thus began a happy period of his life. He renewed and deepened his school friendships and in 1924 entered the rigorous École Normale Supérieure. He shared an interest in philosophy with several classmates and spent hours in reading and discussion, and in the fun of movies, music, jokes, and girl watching. Sartre loved the regimented life of all-male schools with their camaraderie and emphasis on intellectual achievement. He read widely, preferring the Greek philosopher Plato or the French philosopher René Descartes to his living professors. He also began to develop his own philosophical attitudes.

Probably his stubborn originality lay behind his failure at the *agrégation* in 1928. Because this competitive exam offered the sole entry into teaching in the national system of secondary schools and universities, failure made a would-be academic unemployable. Sartre began a year of concentrated preparation for a retake. Early that year, he met Simone de Beauvoir, a brilliant philosophy student also preparing for the *agrégation*. Although Sartre's romantic life was already crowded, de Beauvoir soon took the central position. They became partners, each the other's first reader and critic. They openly shared all experiences, and although both had other lovers, they never broke with each other. They took the *agrégation* in July, 1929; Sartre took first place, de Beauvoir second.

In November, 1929, Sartre was called up for military service. Trained as a meteorologist, he spent his spare time reading and writing. Both Sartre and de Beauvoir felt driven to put everything on paper, but neither had published when he was demobilized in February, 1931. Both accepted teaching jobs, and Sartre's unconventional style made him a favorite with students. He spent 1933-1934 in Berlin, studying the works of philosopher Martin Heidegger and the phenomenology of Edmund Husserl. Sartre finally gave up teaching for professional writing in 1945.

Life's Work

In the years before World War II, Sartre settled into a lifelong pattern of regular hours of work, often at café tables and while traveling. Very prolific, he was unconcerned with the fate of his manuscripts, losing some and leaving several works unfinished. In 1937-1939, he published philosophical essays on imagination, ego, and emotions. Simultaneously, he published the novel *La Nausée* (1938; *Nausea*, 1949) and a collection of short stories, *Le Mur* (1939; *The Wall and Other Stories*, 1948). These writings were well received, in spite or because of their pessimistic view of absurd human life. The writer Albert Camus, later a close friend, was an early, enthusiastic reviewer.

Sartre was called into active service as a meteorologist on September 2, 1939, the day after German troops invaded Poland. His military duties were minimal, and he spent most of his time writing letters, a journal, and the first draft of a novel, *L'Âge de raison* (1945; *The Age of Reason*, 1947), first of the planned tetralogy, *Les Chemins de la liberté* (1945-1949; *The Roads to Freedom*, 1947-1950). Equally important was his philosophical work *Being and Nothingness*, begun in the same period. In June, 1940, he was captured and sent to a German prison camp. Paradoxically, Sartre felt liberated as a prisoner. He enjoyed the solidarity of inmates against their jailers. He discussed theology and philosophy with the priests who served the camp and wrote his first play, *Bariona: Ou, Le Fils de tonnere* (1962; *Bariona: Or, The Son of Thunder*, 1970), a Christmas story published much later that camouflaged a call to resistance against for-

Jean-Paul Sartre. *(Library of Congress)*

eign invasion. When he escaped in March, 1941, he returned to occupied Paris and resumed teaching.

Sartre and de Beauvoir were active in the Resistance as writers and distributors of underground material, but Sartre also continued writing philosophical and literary texts. *Being and Nothingness* was completed in October, 1942. The second novel of his tetralogy, *Le Sursis* (1945; *The Reprieve*, 1947), was finished in November, 1943. In 1943, *Les Mouches* (*The Flies*, 1946), a play based on the Greek myth of Orestes' revenge on his mother Clytemnestra, appeared in Paris, using an ancient story to mask a call to violent resistance past the German censors. During rehearsals, Sartre met Camus. They became friends, and Sartre wrote for Camus's underground paper, *Combat*. In May of 1944, he presented a new play, *Huis-clos* (1944; *No Exit*, 1946). The direct audience contact of the theater was congenial. As he had in his novels, Sartre used the conventions of plot and character to present his philosophical concepts to a wider public.

During the war, Sartre and de Beauvoir collected a family of former lovers, students, and friends who ate or starved together, with de Beauvoir coordinating the scanty rations. A social network of avant-garde artists and writers met for all-night parties in defiance of wartime curfews. Sartre, an accomplished jazz pianist, played and sang. A heavy drinker and smoker, he always preferred café atmosphere to academic circles. Shortages of food and goods meant little to him. He did not collect property. He idealized the solidarity of students, prisoners, and Resistance fighters and, in the decades that followed, would yearn for and never quite recapture the euphoria of the war years. He remained on good terms with his mother and, after the death of his stepfather, shared an apartment with her from 1946 until 1961, when bomb threats made the arrangement dangerous for her. She died in January, 1969.

The end of the war coincided with Sartre's entry into full-time writing and celebrity. Between 1945 and 1965, he wrote eleven plays and film scripts, set in times and places as disparate as occupied France and medieval Germany. He promised a study on ethics to follow *Being and Nothingness*; it never came, but many considerations of good and evil were transposed into his biography of the outlaw genius Jean Genet, *Saint*

Genet: Actor and Martyr. He published a major biographical essay entitled *Baudelaire* in 1947, but his massive biography of Gustave Flaubert, *The Family Idiot: Gustave Flaubert, 1821-1857*, was never finished. His own autobiography, *The Words*, covers only the early years of his childhood. He published *La Mort dans l'âme* (1949; *Troubled Sleep*, 1950), the third volume of his tetralogy, but the projected fourth book never appeared. Even his *Critique of Dialectical Reason I: Theory of Practical Ensembles*, was never finished, although some themes were transposed into other works. The sheer press of demands from all sides, coupled with the ferment of his ideas, made completion of these works unlikely, but their open-ended state gave an illusion of freedom; he still had the option of working on them. A series of essays, gathered in collections entitled *Situations I-X*, dealt with specific issues, rather than philosophical generalizations. His emphasis was less on systematic consistency than on spontaneity of thought in relation to individual circumstances. His *What Is Literature?* examines aesthetics, especially in literature, and makes the case for the "engaged writer," who aims at action in the world and rejects "art for art's sake."

Sartre was the most prominent of a group loosely defined under the label "existentialist," and his writings of the 1940's and 1950's most clearly define the terms of that movement in French literature, criticism, and philosophy. Sartre detested all labels. He argued that each man is responsible for himself, that the external definitions of history or religion conceal the chaos to which actions give shape, and that choice of those actions defines human liberty. To a France bowed down by the shame of defeat, existentialism offered a fresh start with a clean slate.

Immediately after the war, Sartre worked to found a new journal, *Les Temps modernes*, whose diverse editorial board encouraged freewheeling discussion of political and literary subjects. By the time of the French student uprisings of May, 1968, Sartre spoke a frank Maoist line and loaned his name to the editorial boards of radical underground journals, helping to distribute them in defiance of the law.

Sartre died of long-standing vascular illness on April 15, 1980. He had been virtually blind since 1973, able to work only with the help of patient friends such as de Beauvoir, who would talk with him and record his words. He had remained active, going to demonstrations and speaking at rallies, but gradually decaying flesh triumphed over will. He had been idolized and hated by a diverse, worldwide audience.

Influence

A listing of Sartre's plays, articles, biographies, philosophical studies, causes he espoused, travels, talks, demonstrations, and volatile friendships is dizzying. He declined a Nobel Prize in Literature in 1964, the first person ever to do so, because he said he preferred not to be made an institution. The example of writers of the Resistance who risked their lives in their work defined his artistic position. In a sense, Sartre always believed himself to be such a Resistance writer. As he worked for liberal causes around the world, he was never deterred by fears of ridicule. His flirtation with the French Communist Party and the governments of Cuba, the Soviet Union, and China was long-standing. A frequent apologist for Marxist movements, he still opposed oppression within the Eastern Bloc, speaking out against the Soviet use of force in Hungary and Czechoslovakia.

Sartre's ideas influenced scholars, artists, and ordinary people. The novels and plays that brought his ideas directly before the public continue to be read and studied throughout the world. Situational ethics grew out of the existentialist milieu, as did the contemporary antihero, a figure whose anguish is measured by his individual reactions to life rather than eternal standards of good and evil. Although literary and critical fashion passed him by in the 1970's, some fifty thousand people followed his funeral procession through the streets of Paris.

Anne W. Sienkewicz

Being and Nothingness

An Essay of Phenomenological Ontology

Type of philosophy: Ethics, existentialism, metaphysics

First published: L'Être et le néant: Essai d'ontologie phénoménologique, 1943 (English translation, 1956)

Principal ideas advanced:

◇ Being is never exhausted by any of its phenomenal aspects; no particular perspective reveals the entire character of being.

◇ Being-in-itself (*en-soi*) is fixed, complete, wholly given, absolutely contingent, with no reason for its being; it is roughly equivalent to the inert world of objects and things.

◇ Being-for-itself (*pour-soi*) is incomplete, fluid, indeterminate; it corresponds to the being of human consciousness.

◇ Being-in-itself is prior to being-for-itself; the latter is dependent upon the former for its origin; being-for-itself is derived from being-in-itself by an act of nihilation, for being-for-itself is a nothingness in the heart of being.

◇ Freedom is the nature of humanity; in anxiety one becomes aware of one's freedom, knows oneself responsible for one's own being by commitment, seeks the impossible reunion with being-in-itself, and in despair knows oneself forever at odds with the "others," who by their glances can threaten one, turning one into a mere object.

The subtitle of *Being and Nothingness: An Essay on Phenomenological Ontology*, clearly states the central intention of the author. Jean-Paul Sartre is at one with Greek philosophers Parmenides and Plato in his contention that the chief problem of philosophy is the problem of being. Significant differences, however, emerge in a comparison of the ontological investigations of the ancient Greeks with those of Sartre. The adjective "phenomenological" in the subtitle indicates one of these significant differences.

Sartre's ontology is an ontology that follows in the wake of German Immanuel Kant's critical philosophy, Edmund Husserl's phenomenological reduction, and Martin Heidegger's ontology of *Dasein*. *Being and Nothingness* has all of the Kantian reservations about any philosophy that seeks to proceed beyond the limits of possible experience, draws heavily from the phenomenological investigations of Husserl, and exhibits basically the same form of analysis and description as was used in Heidegger's *Sein und Zeit* (1927; *Being and*

Time, 1962). Nevertheless, Kant, Husserl, and Heidegger intermittently throughout the work fall under some rather trenchant Sartrian criticism. Kant's chief mistake was his appeal to a "thing-in-itself" that somehow stands behind the phenomena. In Sartre's phenomenological ontology, nothing is concealed behind the phenomena or the appearances. The appearances embody full reality. They are indicative of themselves and refer to nothing but themselves. The Kantian dualism of phenomena and noumena, appearance and reality, is abolished, and being is made coextensive with phenomena. Husserl comes in for a similar criticism. His hypothesis of a transcendental ego is pronounced useless and disastrous. The fate of such a view, according to Sartre, is shipwreck on the "reef of solipsism." The faults of Heidegger are not as grievous as those of Kant and Husserl. As becomes apparent on every page of *Being and Nothingness*, Sartre's analysis is markedly informed by Heideggerian concepts. Yet Heidegger, argues the author, neglects the phenomenon of the lived body, has no explanation for the concrete relatedness of selves, and misinterprets the existential significance of death.

Being

Being, in Sartre's analysis, evinces a *transphenomenal* character. Although there is no *noumena* and no *thing-in-itself* that lies concealed behind the phenomenal appearances of being, being is never exhausted in any of its particular phenomenal aspects. Being, in the totality of its aspects and manifestations, never becomes wholly translucent to consciousness. Everything that has being "overflows" whatever particular categories, designations, and descriptions human knowledge may attach to it. Being evinces relationships and qualities that escape any specific determination. Although being is reduced to the whole of its phenomenal manifestations, it is in no way exhausted by any *particular* perspective that humanity has of the phenomena. All phenomena overflow themselves, suggesting other phenomena yet to be disclosed. This primordial being, transphenomenal in character, expresses a fundamental rupture into "being-in-itself" (*en-soi*) and "being-for-itself" (*pour-soi*).

Being-in-itself designates being in the mode of fullness or plenitude. It is massive, fixed, complete in itself, totally and wholly given. It is devoid of potency and becoming, roughly equivalent to the inert world of objects and things. It has no inside and no outside. It expresses neither a relationship with itself nor a relationship to anything outside itself. It is further characterized by an absolute contingency. There is no reason for its being. It is superfluous (*de trop*). "Uncreated, without reason for being, without connection with any other being, being-in-itself is superfluous for all eternity."

Being-for-itself is fluid and vacuous rather than fixed and full. It is characterized by incompleteness, potency, and lack of determinate structure. As being-in-itself is roughly equivalent to the inert and solidified world of objectivized reality, so being-for-itself generally corresponds to the being of human consciousness. These two modes of being, however, are not granted an equal ontological status. Being-in-itself is both logically and ontologically prior to being-for-itself. The latter is dependent upon the former for its origin. Being-for-itself is inconceivable without being-in-itself and is derived from it through an original nihilation (*néantisation*). Being-for-itself thus constitutes a nihilation of being-in-itself. Being-for-itself makes its appearance as a nothingness that "lies coiled in the heart of being—like a worm." The being of the for-itself is a "borrowed" being that emerges from the in-itself by virtue of its power of negation. The source of the power of nothingness remains inexplicable and mysterious. The for-itself simply finds itself *there*, separated and at a distance from the absolute fullness of the in-itself. The for-itself emerges as an irreducible and ultimate datum.

Nothingness

One of the fateful consequences of the primordial rupture of the for-itself from the in-itself is the introduction of nothingness. Sartre makes it clear that it is through human consciousness that nothingness comes into the world. In his discussion on nothingness, Sartre is intent on rejecting the Hegelian dialectical approach and substituting for it a phenomenological account. For Hegel, being and nothingness are dialectical concepts that take their rise from the same ontological level of mediated reality. Sartre maintains in his phenomenological approach that nothingness is dependent upon being in a way that being is not dependent upon nothingness. Nothingness is not an abstract idea complementary to being, nor can it be conceived outside being; it must be given at the heart of being. Nothingness demands a host, possessing the plenitude and full positivity of being, from which it borrows its power of nihilation. Thus, nothingness has only a borrowed or marginal being. Although Sartre never acknowledges his debt to early Christian philosopher Saint Augustine on this point, his analysis seems to draw heavily from Augustinian sources. Augustine had already described evil as a tendency toward nothingness, the movement presupposing perfect being as a host in which evil exists as a privation of the good. It would indeed seem that in its basic outlines, Sartre's analysis of nothingness is little more than a secularized Augustinianism. The introduction of nothingness raises the question of its relation to negative judgments.

As Heidegger had done before him, Sartre insists that nothingness is the origin and foundation of negative judgments, rather than vice versa. This foundation finds its clarification in the context of human expectations and projects. Sartre, as an example, tells of expecting to find a person (Pierre) in a café when in fact he is not present. His expectation of finding Pierre has caused the absence of Pierre to happen as a real event pertaining to the café. He discovers his absence as an objective fact. He looks for him and finds that he is not there, thus disclosing a synthetic relation between Pierre and the setting in which he has expected him to be. There obtains a *real* relation between Pierre and the café, as distinct from the relation of *not-being* that characterizes the order of thought in simple negative judgments. To make the negative judgment that Pierre is not in the café has purely abstract meaning. It is without real or efficacious foundation.

It is through humanity that nothingness comes into the world. The question then arises: What is it about human beings that occasions nothingness? The answer is freedom. The freedom that is here revealed should in no way be identified with a property or a quality that somehow attaches to humanity's original nature. Freedom *is* the "nature" of humankind. There is no difference between one's being and one's being-free. As becomes apparent later in *Being and Nothing-*

ness, Sartre's ontology of humanity is a philosophy of radical and total freedom. This consciousness of freedom is disclosed in anxiety. "It is in anxiety that man gets the consciousness of his freedom, or if you prefer, anxiety is the mode of being of freedom as consciousness of being; it is in anxiety that freedom is, in its being, in question of itself." An internal connection exists among nothingness, freedom, and anxiety. These are interrelated structural determinants of human existence.

Bad Faith

Nothingness, freedom, and anxiety provide the conditions that make possible the movement of "bad faith" (*mauvaise foi*). Bad faith is a form of self-deception that in making use of freedom denies it. Bad faith is akin to lying, yet not identical to it. In lying, one hides the truth from others. In bad faith, one hides the truth from oneself. In the former there is a duality of deceiver and deceived; in the latter there is a unity of a single consciousness. Bad faith does not come from the outside. Consciousness affects itself with it.

In describing the pattern of bad faith, Sartre develops the example of a woman who consents to go out with an amorous suitor. She is fully aware of his intentions and knows that sooner or later she will have to make a decision. An immediate decision is demanded when he caresses her hand. If she leaves her hand there, she encourages his advances; if she withdraws it, she may well preclude any further relationship with the suitor. She must decide, but she seeks means for postponing the decision. It is at this point that bad faith comes into play. She leaves her hand in his but does not notice that she is doing so. She becomes all intellect, divorces her soul from her body, and transforms her body into an object or thing—into the mode of "being-in-itself." Her hand becomes "a thing," neither consenting nor resisting. She objectivizes her body, and ultimately herself, as in-itself, and thus stages a flight or an escape from herself as for-itself. She loses her subjectivity, her freedom, and her responsibility for decision. She exists in bad faith.

Consciousness

The pursuit of being leads to an awareness of nothingness, nothingness to an awareness of freedom, freedom to bad faith, and bad faith to the being of consciousness that provides the condition for its possibility. People are thus led to an interrogation of the immediate structures of the for-itself as consciousness. The immediate consciousness in which the self experiences presence is what Sartre calls nonpositional consciousness. This consciousness characterizes the level of primitive awareness and is prior to the positional consciousness that is the reflective consciousness of the intentional action. Nonpositional consciousness is prereflective; therefore, Sartre describes it as a prereflective cogito (*cogito pre-reflexif*). This prereflective cogito quite clearly precedes the Cartesian cogito, which is a movement of reflection, and becomes the foundation for it.

Positional consciousness, on the other hand, is reflective in character, directed toward some intentional object. Sartre has taken over Husserl's doctrine of intentionality and has made it central to his description of the positional consciousness. Positional consciousness is always consciousness *of* something. It is directed outward into a *world*. However, the positional consciousness can also be directed reflexively upon itself. Consciousness can become conscious of itself as being conscious. It is in this way that the ego or the self is posited or derived. Both the world and the ego or self are posited by the projecting activity of the for-itself in its nonpositional freedom, and they become correlative phenomena inextricably bound up at their very source. Without the world there is no ego, and without the ego, there is no world. Both the world and the ego are hypostatized through reflection as unifying, ideal limits.

The For-Itself
One of the central structural elements of the for-itself is facticity. The for-itself apprehends itself as a lack or decompression of being. It is not its own foundation. It is a "hole" in the heart of being, infected with nothingness, abandoned to a world without justification. It discovers itself thrown into a situation, buffeted by brute contingencies, for the most part superfluous and "in the way." Facticity indicates the utter contingency and irrevocable situationality of the being of the for-itself. Without facticity, consciousness could choose its attachments to the world—it would be

absolute and unfettered freedom. However, the freedom that the for-itself experiences is always restricted by the situation in which it is abandoned. Nevertheless, the freedom of the for-itself is a *real* freedom, and even in its facticity, the for-itself perpetually relates itself to itself in freedom. One does not become a bourgeois or a French person until one *chooses* to become such. Freedom is always present, translating facticity into possibility. In the final analysis, the for-itself is totally responsible for its being.

Value and possibility provide two additional structures of the for-itself. Value is an expression of an impossible striving toward a coincidence of being. The for-itself perpetually strives to surpass itself toward reunion with the in-itself, thus achieving totality by healing the fundamental rupture in being. However, this totality is an impossible synthesis. As soon as the for-itself would become coincident with the in-itself, it would lose itself as for-itself. A final totality remains forever unattainable because it would combine the incompatible characteristics of the in-itself (positivity and plenitude) and the for-itself (negativity and lack). The impossible striving for reunion gives rise to the unhappy or alienated consciousness. The for-itself is "sick in its being" because it is haunted by a totality that it seeks to attain but never can without losing itself as for-itself. "The being of human reality is suffering because it emerges in being as perpetually haunted by a totality which it is without being able to be it, since it would not be able to attain the in-itself without losing itself as for-itself. Human reality therefore is by nature an unhappy consciousness, without the possibility of surpassing its unhappy state." Now possibility, as an immediate structure of the for-itself, provides further clarification of the meaning of the for-itself as lack. The possible is what the for-itself lacks in its drive for completeness and totality. It indicates the *not yet* of human reality, the openness of its constant striving.

Time
The structures of the for-itself are ontologically rooted in temporality, which provides their unifying ground. This temporality is understood in Sartre's phenomenological analysis as a synthesis of structured moments. The "elements" or direc-

tions of time (past, present, and future) do not constitute an infinite series of nows, or collected "givens," in which some are no longer and others are not yet. If time is understood as an infinite series of discrete nows, then the whole series is annihilated. The past nows are no longer real, the future nows are not yet real, and the present now is always slipping away, functioning only as a limit of an infinite division. In such a view, time evaporates and is dissolved into an infinite "dust of instants" that are ontologically anemic. A phenomenological analysis of the time of the immediate consciousness avoids this dissolution of temporality by describing the elements of time as "structured moments of an original synthesis."

Following Heidegger, Sartre speaks of time as an *ecstatic* unity in which the past is *still* existentially real, the future *already* existentially real, and in which past and future coalesce in the present. However, Sartre differs from Heidegger in refusing to ascribe ontological priority to the future. No ecstasis of time has any priority over any of the others; none can exist without the other two. If, indeed, one is to accent any ecstasis, Sartre maintains that it would be phenomenologically closer to the facts to accent the present rather than the future. The past remains an integral part of one's being. It is not something that one had or possessed at one time; it is something of which one is aware here and now. The past is always bound to one's present. One is always related to one's past, but one is at the same time separated from it insofar as one engages in a constant movement from the self as past to the self as future.

The past tends to become solidified and thus takes on the quality of an in-itself. It is defined as a for-itself that has become an in-itself. It takes on a character of completeness and fixity, but it still remains one's own, and as long as it remains a part of one's consciousness it can be recovered in an act of choice. The past provides the ontological foundation for facticity. In a very real sense, the past and facticity indicate one and the same thing. The past makes possible one's experience of abandonment and situationality.

In contrast to the past, which has become an in-itself, the present remains a full-embodied for-itself. Sartre defines the present as a "perpetual flight in the face of being." It exhibits a flight from the being that it was and a flight toward the being that it will be. Strictly speaking, the for-itself as present has its being outside itself—behind it and before it. It was its past and will be its future. The for-itself as present is not what it is (past) and is what it is not (future). The future is a mode of being that the for-itself must strive to be. As a mode of being, it designates an existential quality that one *is*, rather than an abstract property that one *has*. The future is a lack that is constitutive of one's subjectivity. As the past provides the foundation for facticity, so the future provides the foundation for possibility. The future constitutes the meaning of one's present for-itself as a project of possibilities. The future is not a series of chronologically ordered nows that are yet to come. Rather, it is a region of one's being, which circumscribes one's expanding possibilities and defines one as a for-itself who is always on the way.

Self and Other

The temporalized world of the for-itself is not an insulated world experienced in isolation. In the world of the for-itself, the "others" (*autrui*) have already made their appearance. Hence, the being of the for-itself is always a being-for-others as well. The discussion of the problem of the interrelation of personal selves occupies a lengthy and important part of *Being and Nothingness*. Sartre begins with an examination and criticism of the views of Hegel, Husserl, and Heidegger, and then proceeds to a positive formulation of his own. The "other" is already disclosed in the movements of the prereflective, nonpositional consciousness. Shame affords an example of a prereflective, disclosure of the "other," as well as a disclosure of oneself as standing before the other. Through shame one discovers simultaneously the "other" and an aspect of one's being. *One* is ashamed of *oneself* before the *"other."* The "other" reveals oneself to one. One needs the "other" in order to realize fully all the structures of one's being. It is thus that the structures of being-for-itself and being-for-others are inseparable.

In the phenomenon of "the look" (*le regard*) is another example of the prereflective disclosure of the self and the other. It is through the look that the "other" erupts into one's world, decentralizes and dissolves it, and then by reference to the other's own projects reconstitutes it and the freedom that one experiences. When one is "looked at," the stability of one's world and the freedom that one experiences as for-itself are threatened. The other is apprehended as someone who is about to steal one's world, suck one into the orbit of his or her concerns, and reduce one to the mode of being-in-itself—to an object or a thing. "Being-seen-by-the-other" involves becoming an object for the other. When the movement of the look is completed, one is no longer a free subject; one has fallen into the slavery of the other.

> Thus being-seen constitutes me as a being without defenses for a freedom which is not my freedom. It is in this sense that we can consider ourselves as slaves in so far as we appear to the other. However, this slavery is not the result of a life in the abstract form of consciousness. I am a slave to the degree that my being is dependent at the center of a freedom which is not mine and which is the very condition of my being.

It is in this way that the existence of the other determines one's original fall—a fall that can be most generally described as a fall from oneself as being-for-itself into the mode of being-in-itself. One's only defense is the objectivization of the other. Through *one's own* look, one can seek to shatter the world of the other and take away his or her subjective freedom. Indeed, one seeks to remove the other from one's world and put him or her out of play, but this can never succeed, because the existence of the other is a contingent and irreducible fact. One *encounters* the other; one does not *constitute* the other. The other remains, threatening to counterattack one's defenses with a look. This creates a constant cycle of mutual objectivization. One affirms one's freedom by rendering the other into an object. Then the other affirms freedom by rendering one into an object. Then one stages an existential counterattack, and the cycle repeats itself. The upshot is an irreconcilable conflict between the self and the other, with a consequent breakdown of all communication. Alienation remains in Sartre's doctrine of intersubjectivity. The reader who searches for a positive doctrine of community may search in vain. All forms of "being-*with*" find their common denominator in an alienating "being-*for*."

The Body

In the relation of the for-itself with the other, the body appears as a central phenomenon. The body is discussed in the context of three ontological dimensions: first, the body as I exist it, second, the body as utilized and known by the other, and third, the body as I exist it in reference to its being known by the other. The body as I exist it is not the objectivized body constituted by nerves, glands, muscles, and organs. Such an objectivized body is present for the physician when he gives me a medical examination, but I do not apprehend my body in this way. I apprehend my body in its lived concreteness as that phenomenon that indicates my possibilities in the world. The body as *concretely lived* signifies a level of being that is fundamentally different from the body as *objectively known*. The body as concretely lived reveals an original relation to the world of immediate and practical concerns. I carry out my practical concerns through instruments or utensils.

Sartre, in the development of his concept of the world, draws heavily from Heidegger and defines the world of immediate experience as an instrumental world. Instruments refer to one's body, insofar as the body apprehends and modifies the world through the use of instruments. One's body and the world are thus coextensive. One's body is spread out across the utensils that one uses. One's body is everywhere in the world. To have a body and to experience that there is a world are one and the same thing. However, not only does one exist in one's body, but one's body is also utilized and known by the other. This second ontological dimension indicates one's body as a body-for-the-other. One's body as known by the other, and so also the other's body as known by one, is always a body-in-a-situation. The body of the "other" is apprehended within the movements of a situation as a synthetic totality of life and action. The isolated appendages and gestures of another's body have no significance outside the context of a situation. A clenched fist in itself means nothing. Only when the clenched fist is apprehended as an integral part of a synthetic totality of life movements is the lived body of the "other" disclosed. A corpse is no longer in a situation, and hence can be known only in its modality of death as an anatomical-physiological entity.

The third ontological dimension indicates the reappraisal of one's body as a body that is known by and exists for the other. Thus alienation enters one's world. One's body becomes a tool or an object for the other. One's body flows to the other, who sucks it into the orbit of his or her projects and brings about the dissolution of one's world. This alienation is made manifest through affective structures such as shyness. Blushing, for example, expresses the consciousness of one's body not as one lives it for oneself, but as one lives it for the other. One cannot be embarrassed by one's own body as one exists in it. Only a body that exists for the other can become an occasion for embarrassment.

In the concrete relation of the for-itself with the other, two sets of contradictory attitudes make their appearance: the attitudes of love and masochism and the attitudes of hatred and sadism. In the love relationship, the beloved is for the lover not simply a thing that one desires to possess. The analogy of ownership breaks down in an explanation of love. Love expresses a special kind of appropriation. The lover wants to assimilate the love of the beloved without destroying the other's freedom. However, this relationship of love ultimately founders because it is impossible to maintain an absolute subjectivity or freedom without objectivizing another as the material for one's freedom. This accounts for the insecurity of love. The lover is perpetually in danger of being made to appear as an object. In masochism, the annihilation of subjectivity is deliberately directed inward. Masochists put themselves forward as an in-itself for the other. They set up conditions so that they can be assimilated by the other; thus, they deliberately transform themselves into an object. Hatred and sadism constitute the reverse attitude. Here there is an attempt to objectivize the other rather than the self. Sadists seek to "incarnate" the other by using their body as a tool. The other becomes an instrument in their hands; in this way, they appropriate the freedom of the other. However, this attempt results in failure because the other can always turn back on the sadists and make objects out of them. Thus, again, the futility of all attempts to establish harmonious relations with the other is demonstrated. This inability to achieve genuine communication leads to a despair in which nothing remains for the for-itself but to become involved in the circularity of objectivization in which it passes from one to the other of the two fundamental attitudes.

The Will and Psychoanalysis

Sartre concludes his phenomenological essay with a restatement and further elucidation of the nature and quality of human freedom, and a delineation of his program of existential psychoanalysis. Freedom is discussed in relation to the will, in relation to facticity, and finally in relation to responsibility. The will can never be the condition of freedom; it is simply a psychological manifestation of it. The will presupposes the foundation of an original freedom in order to be able to constitute itself as will. The will is derived or posited by reflective decision. It is a psychological manifestation that emerges within the complex of motives and ends already posited by the for-itself. Properly speaking, it is not the will that is free. Human existence is free. The will is simply a manifestation of humanity's primordial freedom. Freedom in relation to facticity gives rise to the situation. The situation is that ambiguous phenomenon in which it is impossible clearly to distinguish the contribution of freedom and the determinants of brute circumstance. This accounts for the paradox of freedom. There is freedom only in a situation, and there is a situation only through freedom.

Sartre delineates five structures of the situation in which freedom and facticity interpenetrate each other: one's place, one's past, one's environment, one's fellow humans, and one's death. Insofar as freedom always interpenetrates facticity, one becomes wholly responsible for oneself. One is responsible for everything except for the fact of one's responsibility. One is free, but one is not free to obliterate fully one's freedom. One is condemned to be free. This abandonment to freedom is an expression of one's facticity. Yet one must assume responsibility for the fact that one's facticity is incomprehensible and contingent. The result is that one's facticity or one's final abandonment consists simply in the fact that one is condemned to be wholly responsible for oneself. Although freedom and facticity interpenetrate, it remains incontestable that human freedom is given a privileged status in the Sartrian view.

The touchstone of existential psychoanalysis is a concentration on humanity's fundamental project (*projet fondamental*). This fundamental project is neither Heidegger's *Sein-zum-Tode*, nor is it psychoanalyst Sigmund Freud's libidinal cathexis. The method of existential psychoanalysis resembles that of the Freudians in that an effort is made to work back through secondary and superficial manifestations of personality to an ultimate and primary project, but the existentialist differs with Freud concerning the nature of this project. The Freudian localizes the project in a libidinal attachment that is determined by the past history of the self. The existential psychoanalyst broadens the framework of explanation to include the future projects of the self as well. The fundamental project is thus understood in the context of one's temporalized being, which includes the ecstatic unity of past, present, and future. The irreducible minimum of this fundamental project is the *desire to be*. Quite clearly, it is impossible to advance farther than being, but in having advanced thus far, one has undercut the simple empirical determinants of behavior. The goal of this desire to be is to attain the impermeability, solidity, and infinite density of the in-itself. The ideal toward which consciousness strives is to be the foundation of its own being. It strives to become an "in-itself-for-itself," an ideal that can properly be defined as God. One can thus most simply express the fundamental human project as the desire to be God. However, the idea of God is contradictory, for in striving after this ideal, the self can only lose itself as for-itself. Humanity's fundamental desire to give birth to God results in failure. One must therefore reconcile oneself to the fact that it is a useless passion.

Calvin O. Schrag, updated by John K. Roth

Additional Reading

Beauvoir, Simone de. *Adieux: A Farewell to Sartre.* Translated by Patrick O'Brian. New York: Pantheon 1984. A discerning look at Jean-Paul Sartre by his long-time companion.

Copleston, Frederick. *A History of Philosophy: Maine de Biran to Sartre.* New York: Doubleday, 1977. Copleston's clear exposition of Sartre's

existentialism and political philosophy situates Sartre in the French philosophical tradition.

Danto, Arthur C. *Sartre.* 2d ed. London: Fontana, 1991. A good introductory overview to Sartre's life and thought.

Dobson, Andrew. *Jean-Paul Sartre and the Politics of Reason: A Theory of History.* Cambridge, London: Cambridge University Press, 1993. An assessment of Sartre's perspectives on history and politics, emphasizing that human rationality is always situated in particular times and places.

Fournay, Jean-François, and Charles D. Minahen, eds. *Situating Sartre in Twentieth Century Thought and Culture.* New York: St. Martin's, 1997. Sartre scholars offer varied interpretations on the significance of Sartre's philosophical and literary works.

Fullbrook, Kate. *Simone de Beauvoir and Jean-Paul Sartre: The Remaking of a Twentieth Century Legend.* New York: Basic Books, 1994. A worthwhile study of the relationship between two important twentieth century philosophers who helped to establish existentialism as an important movement.

Hayman, Ronald. *Sartre: A Life.* New York: Simon & Schuster, 1987. A valuable scholarly study, this biography focuses on the progression of Sartre's ideas and his changing philosophical stance.

Howells, Christina, ed. *The Cambridge Companion to Sartre.* Cambridge, London: Cambridge University Press, 1992. Contains helpful articles on diverse aspects of Sartre's philosophical and literary works.

Jones, W. T. *A History of Western Philosophy: Kant to Wittgenstein and Sartre.* New York: Harcourt, Brace, 1969. A good introduction to Sartre and his place in twentieth century existential philosophy.

Kerner, George C. *Three Philosophical Moralists: Mill, Kant, and Sartre, an Introduction to Ethics.* New York: Oxford University Press, 1990. A comparative study of three of the most influential ethical thinkers in modern Western philosophy.

McBride, William L. *Sartre's Political Philosophy.* Bloomington: Indiana University Press, 1991. A thoughtful interpretation of the main points in Sartre's political theory and their implications for the future.

Wider, Kathleen Virginia. *The Bodily Nature of Consciousness: Sartre and Contemporary Philosophy of Mind*. Ithaca, N.Y.: Cornell University Press, 1997. Underscores the emphasis that

Sartre places on the embodied nature of human consciousness and relates Sartre's views to important contemporary theories about the mind-body relationship.

Anne W. Sienkewicz, updated by John K. Roth

Ferdinand de Saussure

Primarily through a book written by colleagues after his death, Saussure established the foundations of twentieth century linguistics. His focus on the systematic structure of language is the fundamental principle of structuralism in linguistics, anthropology, and literary criticism, and he provided the theoretical basis of semiology, the study of signs.

Principal philosophical works: *Mémoire sur le système primitif des voyelles dans les langues indo-européennes*, 1879; *Cours de linguistique générale*, 1916 (*Course in General Linguistics*, 1959).

Born: November 26, 1857; Geneva, Switzerland
Died: February 22, 1913; Vufflens, near Geneva, Switzerland

Early Life

When Ferdinand de Saussure was enrolled in chemistry and physics courses at the University of Geneva in 1875, he was following a tradition long established on his father's side of the family. Ferdinand's great-grandfather was Horace-Bénédict de Saussure, a famous scientist; his grandfather was professor of geology and mineralogy; and his father, Henri, had a doctorate in geology. Ferdinand, too, was to become a scientist, but it was the science of linguistics that captured his attention at an early age.

Adolf Pictet, a friend of the family, and Count Alexandre-Joseph de Pourtalès, Ferdinand's maternal grandfather, encouraged the young boy to study languages. By the age of twelve, Ferdinand had read chapters of Pictet's book on linguistic paleontology. He knew French, German, English, and Latin, and he began Greek at the age of thirteen. The year before entering the university, the young Saussure, on Pictet's advice, studied Sanskrit from a book by the German scholar Franz Bopp.

Saussure's career in physics and chemistry lasted for only two semesters. During that time, he continued his studies of Greek and Latin and joined the Linguistic Society of Paris. By autumn, 1876, he had transferred to the University of Leipzig in Germany. For the next four semesters,

Saussure attended courses in comparative grammar, history of the German language, Sanskrit, Greek, Old Persian, Celtic, Slavic languages, and Lithuanian. His teachers were the leading figures of the time in historical and comparative linguistics, including, among the younger generation, the "Neogrammarians," scholars of Indo-European languages who established the famous principle that sound changes in the historical development of languages operate without exception.

In the Leipzig environment of August Leskien, Hermann Osthoff, and Karl Brugmann, Saussure wrote extensively, publishing several papers through the Linguistic Society of Paris. At age twenty-one, in 1878, he produced the monograph that was to be the most famous work of his lifetime, *Mémoire sur le système primitif des voyelles dans les langues indo-européennes* (1879; memoir on the original system of the vowels in the Indo-European languages). When it appeared, he was in Berlin studying Sanskrit. Returning to Leipzig in 1880, he received his doctoral degree with honors.

Life's Work

Saussure's *Mémoire sur le système primitif des voyelles dans les langues indo-européennes* was a daring reconstruction of an aspect of proto-Indo-European languages that was met in Germany with little understanding and even with hostility. Yet the work was very well received in France; in the fall of 1880, Saussure moved to Paris. He attended courses in classical languages, lectures by the leading French linguist Michel Bréal, and meetings of the Linguistic Society of Paris. The next year, on October 30, 1881, with Bréal's strong support, he was unanimously named lecturer in Gothic and Old High German at the École des Hautes Études. His lifelong career as a teacher began a week later.

Saussure's courses dealt primarily with comparative grammar of the Germanic languages, but he was highly critical of the earlier nineteenth century German tradition in such studies. Comparison of individual words in different languages or over time within one language seemed to him haphazard, unfruitful, and unscientific. In his *Mémoire sur le système primitif des voyelles dans les langues indo-européennes*, he had used the notion of a language as a structured system in which all forms are interrelated, and this fundamental concept had led him to hypothesize forms in Indo-European languages that had disappeared in the languages for which there were historical records. It was a half century after the publication of the *Mémoire sur le système primitif des voyelles dans les langues indo-européennes* that evidence was discovered in Hittite proving him correct.

At the École des Hautes Études, Saussure's courses attracted substantial numbers of students, and, with Bréal, he set the foundation for comparative grammar in France. He taught Sanskrit, Latin, and Lithuanian as well, and some of his students and disciples became the most prominent French linguists of the early twentieth century. One of these, Antoine Meillet, was later to emphasize the intellectual excitement and commitment generated by Saussure in his classes. So engrossed was Saussure in his teaching during the Paris years that his publications became increasingly infrequent, but he was greatly admired, and when he left the École des Hautes Études for a position at the University of Geneva in the winter of 1891, his French colleagues nominated him for the Cross of the Legion of Honor.

At Geneva, too, students and colleagues were devoted to Saussure and committed to his teachings. Were it not for this dedication, there would be little more to say about Saussure. He married Marie Faesch; they had two sons. He ceased to publish entirely, rarely traveled, and attended only a few local scholarly meetings. From 1891 until 1899, he taught primarily comparative grammar and Sanskrit, adding a course on French verse in 1899; once in 1904, he taught a course on German legends.

Between 1906 and 1909, he conducted research on a topic that some scholars have called "esoteric"; others, more direct, labeled it "strange." Saussure believed that he had found "hidden texts" within Latin verse—deliberately concealed proper names, relevant to the meaning and repeated throughout the poems, whose spellings could be detected distributed among the words

Ferdinand de Saussure. *(Library of Congress)*

of the verse. He called these "anagrams," and he compiled more than a hundred notebooks of examples. He abandoned this work, without publishing a single paper on the topic, after receiving no response from a contemporary poet to whom he had written seeking confirmation of this poetic device.

The work on anagrams seems to have been an escape from Saussure's overriding preoccupation: probing the very foundations of the science of linguistics. Toward the end of his life, he confided to a former student that he had added nothing to his theory of language since the early 1890's, yet he struggled with the subject off and on for many years. At the University of Geneva, his teaching responsibilities for fifteen years in specific languages and comparative grammar precluded the incorporation of his general linguistic theory into his lectures. Then, in December, 1906, upon the retirement of another faculty member, Saussure was assigned to teach a course on general linguistics and the history and comparison of the Indo-European languages. He accepted the assignment reluctantly.

The course was offered three times, in alternate academic years. The first offering, in 1907, was actually only half a year, and Saussure focused almost entirely on the historical dimension. Five or six students were enrolled. In 1908-1909, there were eleven students, and, again, the emphasis was on the historical study of languages, although this time Saussure did begin with more general topics. For 1910-1911, Saussure spent the entire first semester on general linguistic theory. There were a dozen students in the course. Before he could teach the course again, Saussure fell ill in the summer of 1912. He died near Geneva on February 22, 1913, at the country home of his wife's family.

Two of Saussure's colleagues at the University of Geneva gathered the few lecture notes that Saussure had not destroyed and collected course notes from students who had attended his classes in general linguistics. Using the third offering of the course as a base, Charles Bally and Albert Sechehaye attempted "a reconstruction, a synthesis" of Saussure's thought on the science of linguistics. First published in 1916, Saussure's *Course in General Linguistics* initially received mixed reviews and relatively little attention.

In Europe, Saussure's views on linguistics, as represented in *Course in General Linguistics*, were discussed and adopted, often with alterations, only among members of the Copenhagen, Moscow, and Prague Linguistic Circles. It was not until the 1930's that *Course in General Linguistics* had any significant affect on linguistics in France. In the United States, little attention was paid to Saussure's work until the 1941 arrival in New York of Roman Jakobson, a founding member of the Linguistic Circles of both Moscow and Prague. In the development of the discipline of linguistics, Saussure has been more acknowledged in retrospect than followed directly.

Influence

In *Course in General Linguistics*, Saussure made a sharp distinction between what he termed synchronic linguistics and diachronic linguistics. The latter is the study of change in language; to a great extent, diachronic work had dominated the nineteenth century. Synchronic linguistics, however, concentrates on a static view of language, as it exists for speakers at a particular point in time, and this became the major focus of twentieth century linguistics, particularly in the United States. Saussure also maintained that the proper object of study in linguistics should be not the actual speech of individual members of a linguistic community (which he labeled *parole*) but rather the common code, the language (*langue*), that they share. This distinction became so widely recognized that Saussure's original French terms are still in international use.

Of all the concepts for which Saussure is now known, however, the most influential has been his view of a language as a system of signs, each of which is meaningful and important only in terms of its relationships to the other signs in the system. This system of relationships constitutes a structure, and it is this notion that is the foundation of twentieth century structuralism not only in linguistics but also in anthropology and literary criticism.

In his discussion of signs, Saussure proposed that linguistics was only one dimension of a broader science of the study of signs that he called "semiology." Referred to as semiotics in the United States, this field has been all but ignored by linguists, but for many nonlinguists, the name of Saussure is intricately intertwined with semiology. It is interesting, therefore, to note that semiology is mentioned in less than a dozen paragraphs in the entire *Course in General Linguistics*.

Course in General Linguistics has been the subject of numerous commentaries, and scholars have explored the origins of Saussure's ideas and compared the work with the notes from which it was constructed. This research shows that some of the concepts often credited to Saussure may have their origins with other nineteenth century scholars, and there has been a continuing debate about the "authenticity" of the work in representing Saussure's views. Regardless of these findings, the assessment of Saussure provided in a 1924 review of *Course in General Linguistics* by the great American linguist Leonard Bloomfield has been confirmed by the twentieth century: "He has given us the theoretical basis for a science" of language.

Julia S. Falk

Course in General Linguistics

Type of philosophy: Epistemology, philosophy of language
First published: Cours de linguistique générale 1916 (English translation, 1959)
Principal ideas advanced:
◊ Language is a universal phenomenon.
◊ To comprehend this universality, language must be understood as having two aspects.
◊ One aspect of language, called *parole*, is language as it is used by each of us everyday in our individual instances of speaking, listening, reading, or writing; this is the ever-changing and variable aspect of language.
◊ Language has a more permanent, more universal aspect called *langue*, which is the basic structure of a given language, such as English, that every fluent speaker learns with the acquisition of the language.
◊ A user of a language may or may not engage in acts of *parole* on a given day, but *langue* will always be carried with the user.
◊ Langue is composed of signs not sentences.

◊ Signs are sounds (*phons*) or combinations of sounds that make up the fundamental distinction between various signs; for example, the difference in first sounds between "cat" and "rat" distinguishes between the sign for a feline and for a rodent.
◊ Signs or signifiers refer to the signified; for example, the signifier "red" in English refers to a certain color.
◊ The relationship between signifier and signified is completely arbitrary; consequently, though "red" is the sign in English for a particular color, *rouge* is the sign in French for the same signified.
◊ Signs gain their meaning by negating other signs.

When Ferdinand de Saussure delivered a series of lectures on linguistics in Geneva in 1907-1911, he prompted an entirely new direction in philosophy, one that came to be known as the philosophy of language. Before Saussure's time, philosophers saw their task as trying to solve classical philosophic problems by carefully considering how certain words were used. For example, is it more exact to say "entrance" and "exit" or to say "entrance" and "not an entrance"? The philosophy of language does not concern itself with these issues, but rather aims to provide philosophically illuminating descriptions of certain general or universal features of language such as structure, reference, truth, meaning, and necessity.

Saussure considered himself a linguist rather than a philosopher, and his ideas about language as a sign system had been proposed by others such as philosopher Charles Sanders Peirce. At the turn of the century, philosophy was crossing new frontiers, spinning off new disciplines such as sociology and anthropology and new approaches such as that followed by the ordinary language school at Oxford University, which sought to solve perennial philosophic problems by appealing to linguistic theory. However, it remained for Saussure to lead twentieth century philosophers to seek answers in a new philosophy of language.

Because the *Course in General Linguistics* was not published by Saussure but compiled from lectures and notes after his death, there is some controversy about whether the 1916 French edition accurately reflects Saussure's intentions, and a revised edition was published in 1922. Although the editions differ on the details, certain concepts and lines of thought are clear in both versions. Saussure argues that a theory of language is part of a larger theory, not a theory of actions but a theory of signs, and therefore it is part of a theory of society or culture. Before discussing his theory of signs, Saussure presents two fundamental concepts: *langue* and *parole.*

Langue and Parole

Parole is our experience of language in everyday life. Whenever we attempt to communicate through speech or through writing, we are engaging in *parole. Parole* is as various as the number of people sharing a speech community and the number of attempts each of them makes to communicate. Nothing in the way of universal principles can be formed from *parole,* nor can any general idea be inferred from studying its multitudinous instances. All that can be asserted is that *parole* is infinitely diverse.

Underlying *parole* is *langue,* the general structure of a language, which Saussure defines as the sum of impressions deposited in the brain of each member of the speech community. Every speaker and listener can draw on this sum of impressions in the construction or reception of particular speech acts or instances of *parole.* In our daily lives, we give little conscious thought to *langue.* Instead we employ *parole,* the multitudinous varieties of *langue,* as a communication tool.

Langue underlies—and makes possible—every instance of *parole. Langue* is a universal structure that is innate in all functional human brains. It may have certain grand variations—such as French, Japanese, and English—but the tendency to overarching linguistic structure is common to each of these speech communities.

Signs

The fundamental structure of *langue* is not sentences but signs. Each sign, Saussure argues, has a twin aspect. Each sign signifies a concept and is also signified by an auditory unit, a sound pattern. In writing, the auditory unit is represented by visual symbols substituting for the sound pattern. However, the auditory unit is fundamental,

for there are some speech communities that have no written system. These two aspects, the sign and its signification by an auditory unit or pattern, are as inseparable as the two sides of a coin. Where there is no signifying, there is not a sign but only noise. Hence, if some one shouts "run" to a tree, that person is only "making noise." Conversely, where there is nothing being signified, there is no sound, only a shapeless intellectual blur. Consequently, if a non-French speaker overhears a conversation in French, he or she knows something is being signified but is powerless to make any connections.

Individual sounds, or *phons,* in the total pattern are used to distinguish one sign from another. Hence, the initial sound in the signs "cat" and "rat" differentiate the feline from the rodent. Sometimes the differentiation requires a full sound pattern, as in the phonic distinction between "cat" and "dog." Signs so distinguished may be called signifiers, for they signify an external reality or another sign, which may be called the signified. Saussure, in disagreement with his predecessors, argues that the relationship between the signifier and that which is signified is completely arbitrary. Hence, in English, we may signify a particular color by the sign "red." In French, the same color is signified by the sign *"rouge."* One sign has no particular advantage over another, nor does its use in any way alter the phenomenon signified. In a particular speech act, we may speak of a color as "red" when others choose to signify it with the sign "scarlet." The color will not change simply because the sign changed.

A Synchronic Theory of Language

Saussure borrows a metaphor from chess to develop his idea of the arbitrary relationship between signifier and concept signified. It matters not at all whether the chess piece is made of wood or ivory. The game may be played with either. What is not arbitrary, and therefore absolutely necessary to the construction of a linguistic theory, is the relationship between the signs. Such relationships resemble the "grammar" or rules of the chess game. These "grammatical structures" are what determine the value of a chess piece in a rule-governed universe.

Of course, the value of the piece varies with

the state of the game at a given moment, and we can describe that state without knowing any previous moves. It is this argument that Saussure uses against the long tradition of philology, which assumes that the basic understanding of a language is discovered in its developmental history. Saussure claims that this approach is unnecessary. A linguist can develop a *synchronic* theory of language; that is, the linguist may learn just as much or more by analyzing a language as it exists at any given moment, just as the current state of a chess game may be described. The linguist may disregard *diachronic*, or historical, issues. Saussure, of course, admits that there are fundamental differences between chess and language. The chess player may alter the conditions of the game at will, just as the *parole* may be manipulated by the individual, but *langue*, language's underlying structure, always eludes the individual and the social will.

Relations Among Signs

Just exactly what is this structure? Saussure proposes that the irreducible linguistic structure is the relationship of one sign to another or to a group of other signs. This relationship is found not in the similarity of one sign to another but in the differences between signs. This difference is what makes them independent signs, as in the difference between the initial sounds of "cat" and "rat." At the signifying level, sounds are differentiated if they distinguish one word from another; if they do not, we ignore the sounds. In Japanese, for example, no word is differentiated from another by whether it uses the sound "l" or "r." Consequently, Japanese ignore the distinction between these sounds: They simply do not *hear* the difference. From this, Saussure concludes that the auditory pattern is not simply "given" as a "sense-datum"; our language itself determines what we hear as a "distinct sound."

Further, Saussure postulates that the significance of a sign is that it occurs where other signs might have been used. Consider, for example, "She *danced* home," when other signs such as "walked" or "ran" might have been used instead of "danced." The sign "danced" signifies by virtue of its being chosen over other possible signs. For comparison, Saussure examines a statement such as "It is a short distance . . . walk," where

only "to" will fill the gap. In this instance, "to" does not signify; it is not a sign. Indeed, Saussure concludes, concepts are purely differential and are defined not by their positive content but negatively by their relationship to other parts of the system. This is the essential nature of *langue*. A concept is not simply there waiting to be named. If it were, Saussure argues, words in different languages would be exactly equivalent. They are not. However, in all languages, signs exist only in and through negating other signs.

Impact on Other Disciplines

Saussure's work had a profound and widespread impact on twentieth century thinking. Fellow linguists such as the Russian theorist Roman Jakobson translated Saussurean concepts to aesthetics where they influenced the so-called formalist critics of art and literature. Previously, paintings and works of literature were thought to refer to the world outside the artist and writer, or at least to the artist as a person. After Saussure, works of art were considered formal structures, like language, which referred mainly to patterns inherent in the art form itself.

Soon the theory of inherent structures spread to other disciplines, including psychology as practiced by the influential Jean Piaget in his study of the stages of childhood and human development and cultural anthropology in the works of Claude Lévi-Strauss. Roland Barthes, the influential French literary critic, looked to Saussure for instruction, as did the eminent psychoanalyst and philosopher, Jacques Lacan. Among philosophers, the entire continental structuralist school—led by Jean-François Lyotard, Michel Foucault, and Jacques Derrida—owe a deep debt to Saussure, as do the influential Anglo-American philosophers of language such as Noam Chomsky, who followed Saussure's lead in developing his widely debated concept of the "deep structures" of language. Ludwig Wittgenstein, along with the German philosopher Martin Heidegger, extended Saussure's ideas to a belief in language's universality as a "prison house" for individuals. To complete this illustrious company, Umberto Eco and other linguists have built modern semiotics, the science of signs, upon Saussurean foundations.

August W. Staub

Additional Reading

Culler, Jonathan. *Ferdinand de Saussure*. Rev. ed. Ithaca, N.Y.: Cornell University Press, 1986. This is a very readable account of Ferdinand de Saussure's theory and legacy in linguistics and semiotics, with suggestions for additional reading.

Furton, Edward J. *A Medieval Semiotic: Reference and Representation in John of St. Thomas' Theory of Signs*. New York: Peter Lang, 1995. A look at Saussure's theory of semiotics.

Gadet, Françoise. *Saussure and Contemporary Culture*. Translated by Gregory Elliott. London: Hutchinson Radius, 1989. Part 1 offers extended quotations from Saussure's *Course in General Linguistics* with exegesis, and part 2 deals with the editorial fortunes of the book and its reception and influence.

Harris, Roy. *Language, Saussure, and Wittgenstein: How to Play Games with Words*. New York: Routledge, 1988. Outlines several points of contact between the linguistic approach to language taken by Saussure and the philosophical approach taken by Wittgenstein. Argues that the analogy between language and rule-governed games is central for both views.

_____. *Reading Saussure: A Critical Commentary on the "Cours de linguistique générale."* London: Gerald Duckworth, 1987. A personal reading of Saussure with chapter-by-chapter commentary and summations of general issues by the author of a controversial translation; assumes basic background in linguistics and some familiarity with Saussure's place in intellectual history.

Harris, Roy, and Talbot J. Taylor. *Landmarks in Linguistic Thought: The Western Tradition from Socrates to Saussure*. New York: Routledge, 1989. The chapter on Saussure provides a brief introduction to his major ideas, aimed at students approaching his work for the first time.

Holdcroft, David. *Saussure: Signs, System, and Arbitrariness*. Cambridge, London: Cambridge University Press, 1991. Offers a revised ordering for Saussure's *Course in General Linguistics* and a detailed exposition of the work's central theses. Each chapter ends with a useful summary of its major points.

Koerner, E. F. K. *Ferdinand de Saussure, Origin and Development of His Linguistic Thought in Western Studies of Language: A Contribution to the History and Theory of Linguistics*. Braunschweig, West Germany: Vieweg, 1973. The most extensive biographical information available in English, with considerable coverage of possible sources of Saussure's thought. Includes a substantial bibliography.

Sampson, Geoffrey. "Saussure: Language as Social Fact." In *Schools of Linguistics*. Stanford, Calif.: Stanford University Press, 1980. Sampson provides a clear and engaging discussion of several of Saussure's most influential concepts, including the distinction between *langue* and *parole*. Other chapters treat a variety of twentieth century approaches to linguistics, most of which deal with issues raised by Saussure.

Thibault, Paul J. *Re-reading Saussure: The Dynamics of Signs in Social Life*. New York: Routledge, 1997. An examination of Saussure's work and its influence in the language of philosophy.

Julia S. Falk, updated by William Nelles

Arthur Schopenhauer

In the tradition of Immanuel Kant, Schopenhauer developed a pessimistic system of philosophy based upon the primacy of will.

Principal philosophical works: *Über die vierfache Wurzel des Satzes vom zureichenden Grunde*, 1813 (*On the Fourfold Root of the Principle of Sufficient Reason*, 1889); *Über das Sehen und die Farben*, 1816; *Die Welt als Wille und Vorstellung*, 1819 (*The World as Will and Idea*, 1883-1886, 3 volumes); *Über den Willen in der Natur*, 1836 (*On the Will in Nature*, 1888); *Die beiden Grundprobleme der Ethik*, 1841 (*The Basis of Morality*, 1903); *Parerga und Paralipomena*, 1851 (*Parerga and Paralipomena*, 1974); *Selected Essays of Schopenhauer*, 1951.

Born: February 22, 1788; Danzig (now Gdansk, Poland)

Died: September 21, 1860; Frankfurt am Main (now in Germany)

Early Life

Arthur Schopenhauer was born on February 22, 1788, in the Hanseatic city of Danzig, then under nominal control of Poland. His father, Heinrich, was an affluent merchant of Dutch aristocratic lineage, cosmopolitan in outlook and republican in politics. After Danzig lost its freedom to Prussia in 1793, he moved his family and business to Hamburg. Schopenhauer's mother, Johanna, also of Dutch descent, later became a successful Romantic novelist.

Because Heinrich Schopenhauer planned a mercantile career for his son, Arthur's education emphasized modern languages, which came easily to him. At age nine, he was sent to Le Havre to learn French, the first of six foreign languages he mastered. In return for agreeing to enter a merchant firm as an apprentice, his father rewarded him with an extended tour—lasting nearly a year and a half—of England, Scotland, France, Switzerland, Austria, and Germany, an experience that strengthened his own cosmopolitan perspective and further developed his facility with languages.

As an apprentice and later a clerk, Schopenhauer found the work tedious and boring, and

after the death of his father by drowning, presumed a suicide, in 1805, he altered his life's goals. With an inheritance adequate to assure independence and with encouragement from his mother, he entered grammar school at Gotha and then studied under tutors in Weimar, mastering Latin and Greek. At age twenty-one, he enrolled as a medical student in the University of Göttingen, changing to philosophy in his second year. His first influential teacher, G. E. Schulze, advised him to concentrate on Plato and Immanuel Kant, the two thinkers who would exert the strongest impact on his philosophy.

In 1811, Schopenhauer attended lectures at the University of Berlin by Johann Gottlieb Fichte and Friedrich Schleiermacher; scathing responses in his notes set the tone of his lifelong contempt for German academic philosophy. When revolution against Napoleonic rule flared in Berlin, Schopenhauer fled to the village of Rudolstadt, where he wrote his dissertation for a doctorate from the University of Jena. In *On the Fourfold Root of the Principle of Sufficient Reason*, he explores types of causation: physical, logical, mathematical, and moral.

After receiving his doctorate, Schopenhauer returned to Weimar to live in his mother's house, but the two could not agree. She found him moody, surly, and sarcastic; he found her vain and shallow. Disagreements and quarrels led her

Arthur Schopenhauer. *(Library of Congress)*

to dismiss him, and he left to establish his residence in Dresden in 1814, there to begin his major philosophical work. For the remaining twenty-four years of Johanna Schopenhauer's life, mother and son did not meet.

Life's Work
In Dresden, after completing a brief treatise on the nature of color, Schopenhauer was ready to begin serious preparation of his greatest philosophical work, *The World as Will and Idea*. Its three books, with an appendix on Kantian philosophy, include the conceptual ideas that Schopenhauer developed and elaborated throughout his career as an independent philosopher. Book 1 explains the world, everything that the mind perceives, as representation, a mental construct of the subject. Through perception, reasoning, and reflection and by placing external reality within the mental

categories of time, space, and causality, one understands how the world operates. Yet one never understands reality as it exists, for the subjective remains an essential element of all perception.

The fundamental reality that eludes understanding is, as book 2 makes plain, the will, that Kantian thing-in-itself. Understood in its broadest sense, will exists in everything—as a life force and much more. In plants, it drives growth, change, and reproduction. In animals, it includes all of these as well as sensation, instinct, and limited intelligence. Only in humans does the will become self-conscious, through reflection and analysis, though the will is by no means free in the usual sense. Every action is determined by motives—to Schopenhauer another name for causes—that predetermine one's choices. Thus, one may will to choose but not will to will. With its conscious and unconscious drives, will presses each person toward egoistic individualism; yet demands of the will, far from bringing peace, well-being, and gratification, lead only to additional struggle and exertion. As a consequence, unhappiness in life inevitably exceeds happiness.

As a respite from the imperious demands of the will, people find solace in the beauty that exists in nature and art, and the awakening of the aesthetic sense serves to tame the will by leading it toward disinterested contemplation. To enter a room and discover a table filled with food is to anticipate involvement, consumption, and interaction with others. To look at a painting of the same scene invites simply reflection and appreciation, removing any practical considerations from the will, thereby suspending its feverish activity.

Yet the solace afforded by beauty is only temporary. In book 4, Schopenhauer explores saintliness, which implies denial and permanent taming of the will. By recognizing that others experience the same unrelenting strife that the will creates in oneself, one can develop compassion. Through the power of reflection, one can recognize one's own motives and, through studying motives, become aware of those previously unknown and unacknowledged. Thus, while one cannot achieve freedom of choice, one may acquire a negative capability of rejecting and taming the will. Renunciation, denial of the will, represents for Schopenhauer the path to Nirvana. The best attainable life is that followed by the Hindu *sanyasas* and the ascetic saints of early Christendom.

After publishing his magnum opus, Schopenhauer left for a vacation in Italy, confident that his work would be recognized as a true account of the philosophy foreshadowed by German philosopher Immanuel Kant and accepted as a solution to all outstanding problems of philosophy. Instead, the work was ignored both by the reading public and by academic philosophers. From Dresden, he moved to Berlin, where he expected to become a university professor. Appointed to lecture on philosophy at the university, he selected a schedule that competed with lectures by Georg Wilhelm Friedrich Hegel, then at the height of his popularity, whose optimistic system was the antithesis of Schopenhauer's. Unable to attract students, Schopenhauer spent more than a decade in reading and desultory wandering, though with Berlin as his primary residence. In 1833, he settled in Frankfurt, where he remained for the final years of his life.

There his life assumed a measure of regularity and simplicity. His modest wants were easily met on his inherited income. Although he gave serious consideration to marriage more than once during his lifetime, he rejected the idea, choosing casual relationships instead. He lived in a boardinghouse, took regular walks for exercise, and dined in company at the Englische Hof Hotel. His day began with work in the morning, followed by a brief diversion through playing the flute. In the afternoons, he stopped by the public library for reading and study; an omnivorous reader, he was widely knowledgeable in the arts and sciences and, like his father, read the London *Times* almost every day of his adult life. He was short of stature, with a thick neck—characteristics, he thought, of genius. His portraits show penetrating blue eyes; a lined, intelligent face; a prominent, forceful nose; and, in old age, two curled locks of white hair on either side of a bald head.

Schopenhauer produced a series of minor works as further elaboration of his system, including *On the Will in Nature* and *The Basis of Morality*. After issuing a much-expanded second edition of his major work in 1844, he completed two volumes of essays and miscellaneous writings on a wide variety of subjects, *Parerga and Paralipomena*. With its graceful if sometimes barbed style and its combination of brilliant insights and freely indulged speculation, it expanded the philosopher's reading public.

During his final decade, Schopenhauer experienced the fame and adulation he had long anticipated. A third edition of *The World as Will and Idea* appeared in 1859, this time owing to popular demand. His work was widely discussed and became the subject of university lectures throughout Europe. He began to attract followers, some drawn more by his lucid, jargon-free prose than by his ideas, and on his birthdays, tributes poured in from admirers. Shortly before his death, he began to experience recurring chest pains; on the morning of September 21, 1860, he sat down to breakfast at his usual time. An hour later, his doctor, stopping by to check on him, found him still seated in the chair, dead.

Influence

A philosopher in the tradition of Kant, Schopenhauer modified Kantian terms and categories to accord primacy to will, regarding it as the inscrutable thing-in-itself. Far from an optimistic view, his alteration implies a largely blind force striving for individual advancement and doomed to frustration and defeat. Confronted with this pessimistic reality, the reflective person seeks to tame the will through asceticism. In the Upanishads, his favorite bedtime reading, Schopenhauer discovered that Eastern religious thinkers had anticipated important ideas of his system, and he himself helped popularize Hindu and Buddhist thought in Europe.

Schopenhauer's successors have generally accepted portions of his system while rejecting others, and his influence has been almost as varied as his system. Philosopher Friedrich Nietzsche followed him in granting primacy to the will but envisioned will as a constructive force for progress. Eduard von Hartmann attempted a synthesis of Schopenhauer and Hegel in his *Philosophie des Unbewussten* (1869; *Philosophy of the Uncon-*

scious, 1931). Scholars have discovered a profound debt to Schopenhauer in Hans Vaihinger's *Die Philosophie des Als-Ob* (1911; *The Philosophy of "As If,"* 1924); Ludwig Wittgenstein was influenced by Schopenhauer as well. Sigmund Freud acknowledged that, in large measure, his theory of the unconscious was anticipated by the philosopher.

Because Schopenhauer gives aesthetics a prominent and honorable place in his system, it is not surprising to discover that he has influenced artistic creation significantly. Composer Richard Wagner enthusiastically embraced Schopenhauer's speculations on music, in part because he accorded music first place among the arts. Writers such as Leo Tolstoy in Russia, Thomas Mann in Germany, Guy de Maupassant, Émile Zola, and Marcel Proust in France, and Thomas Hardy, Joseph Conrad, and W. Somerset Maugham in Great Britain are, in varying degrees, indebted to Schopenhauer for their worldviews and for their pessimistic depiction of human life and character. One should note, however, that the enthusiasm for blind will that forms the base of twentieth century fascism is a perversion of Schopenhauer's thought. Passages in Schopenhauer that reflect racism, anti-Semitism, and misogyny—attitudes undeniably present in his work—should be placed within the context of his overall pessimism concerning human nature.

Stanley Archer

The World as Will and Idea

Type of philosophy: Metaphysics
First published: Die Welt als Wille und Vorstellung, 1819 (English translation, 1883-1886, 3 volumes)
Principal ideas advanced:

◇ The world is my idea—this is a truth for every person, since the world as it is known depends for its character and existence upon the mind that knows it.

◇ By understanding, one forms the world of phenomena, and by reason, one achieves harmony in a world of suffering.

◇ The entire world of phenomena, including the human body, is objectified will.

◇ The will is a striving, yearning force that takes various forms according to its inclinations.

◇ By losing oneself in objects, by knowing them as they are in themselves, one comes to know the will as Idea, as eternal form.

In his preface to the first edition of *The World as Will and Idea*, Arthur Schopenhauer states that his chief sources are German philosopher Immanuel Kant, Greek philosopher Plato, and the Upanishads. He does indeed blend these three into his own philosophical system, but he gives the whole his own philosophical interpretation.

Idea

In the opening book, "The World as Idea," Schopenhauer presents his modified scheme of Kant's "Copernican revolution" in philosophy. Kant had held that the world of phenomena that we perceive is to be understood as a world that is made known to us through various features of our understanding. Events appear to us as in space and time; for Kant, these were ultimately to be understood as forms of intuition or perception that, as it were, gave to events their spatial and temporal characteristics. In his famous analogy, the forms of intuition are the spectacles through which we view the world in its spatial and temporal aspects. In addition, we know the world in terms of traditional categories among which cause is a primary one. For Kant, these categories are also of the understanding. Thus, the world of appearances is in the final analysis one in which undifferentiated "stuff" is formed in space and time and categorized by the understanding into the related events that science studies. However, to repeat, at bottom it is a mind-formed world. Schopenhauer accepted the Kantian view of the world, and rather brilliantly reduced the twelve categories in Kant's *Kritik der reinen Vernunft* (1781; *The Critique of Pure Reason*, 1838) to one, that of the principle of sufficient reason (causation). This principle, with its fourfold root in science, logic, morality, and metaphysics, formed the basis of Schopenhauer's analysis of the world of phenomena.

"The world is my idea" means, then, that the world of objects that I perceive depends for its existence as a perceived system of things upon the mind of consciousness that perceives it. Schopenhauer follows Kant in that he distinguishes mere sense impressions from perceptions (or ideas). Sense impressions are received by the mind from the external world; through the forms of space and time and the principle of sufficient reason, the understanding gives form to sensations, making them into ideas. Because it is the understanding that makes ideas what they are, perception is essentially intellectual. The subject or conscious mind becomes aware of object or body first through sense knowledge of its own body. Schopenhauer believed that the subject infers from sense effects immediately known to the self's body and to other bodies. It is in this way that the world of ideas is constructed.

The world of ideas may be considered in two ways. The understanding itself contains the potentiality to form a world of perceptions. However, it would remain dormant if the external world did not excite it. In this sense, then, there is an objective side to the possibility of knowing the world; the world must be capable of acting upon the subject to make perceptions possible. The subjective expression of the world, however, actually converts this possibility into a world of phenomena, for the law of causality springs from and is valid only for it. This means that the world of events as existing in space and time and causally related to one another is formed by the understanding. Additionally, the sensibility of animal bodies makes possible the body as an immediate object for the subject.

Although the understanding makes meaningful the world of objects (there would be but undifferentiated sensations otherwise), there is yet another aspect of mind that has an important role to play, and that is reason. Reason distinguishes humans from other animals in that by its use they are able to deal in abstract ideas or concepts and thus to plan, choose, and build—in general, to act prudently. If humans merely perceived the world of objects through their understanding, they would never be able to transcend and contemplate it. In the quiet life of contemplation, humans rise above the hustle and bustle of everyday activities; they can achieve stoical calm, peace, and inner harmony in a world of pain and suffering.

Will

In the second book, "The World as Will," Schopenhauer considers the reality behind the world of appearances, what had been for Kant unknowable, the thing-in-itself. It is traditional for philosophers to speculate upon the why of things, to try to understand what makes things what they are. For Schopenhauer, this question cannot be answered by searching within the world of phenomena, but only beyond that world. The key is to be found in the subject, who, as an individual, has knowledge of the external world rooted in the experience of the body—object to the self. Body is given to the individual in two ways. It is given first as an idea; an object among objects subject to the law of objects, that is, to the law of cause and effect. Second, it is given as an act of will; when the subject wills, the apparent result is a movement of the body. This aspect of Schopenhauer's philosophy can also be found in Kant. Kant had held that for morality to be possible, the will must be autonomous and not subject to the same laws as phenomena. Otherwise our actions would be causally explainable, and hence no more morally responsible than a rolling stone's action. As autonomous, the will is part of the noumenal world of things-in-themselves and is thus free. The result of willing, for Kant, was a physical movement subject to scientific laws, part of the world of phenomena. The cause of the movement was not itself part of the world of phenomena; hence, not a cause in the scientific sense, it was thus morally free.

The term "cause" has a curious history in philosophical works. There is a sense of cause that might be called the creative sense, that which brings an event into being and keeps it existing. In this sense, the word is often used to refer to something outside the world of events (usually a being such as God) regarded as responsible for the creation and continuity of that world. However, there is another sense of "cause" that, while not original with David Hume, has since his time been in more popular use among many philosophers: that is, cause as a constant conjunction of events within the world of phenomena; what there might be outside that world as a cause of it is held to be subject not to knowledge but perhaps to faith. It is a religious sense of cause. When Kant refers to the autonomous action of the will, he refers to an action that is not part of the world of events, yet one that has a consequence there—a bodily movement. The sequence of bodily movements is a sequence of events (or ideas) that is subject to causal analysis in the second sense mentioned above; but because the will is not part of the world of phenomena, its activities are free from scientific analysis, and thus responsible. It is this sense of the Kantian notion of will that Schopenhauer accepts.

Because an act of will is known as a movement of body, which is itself an idea, Schopenhauer regards the body as objectified will. He states also that the entire world of ideas, the realm of phenomena, is but a world of objectified will. For Schopenhauer, the world of noumena is nothing but a world of will, that which is "beyond" the world of events, yet is its very ground. We also have knowledge of the noumenal world; there is a unique relationship between the subject and the body in which the subject is aware of "noumenal" willing and the resulting physical movements. It is possible to look upon the entire world of events, including other subjects known only as ideas, as one's own world. However, Schopenhauer would not be satisfied with solipsism.

In holding that body is but objectified will, Schopenhauer argues that the various parts of the body—for example, teeth, throat, and bowels—are but expressions of will, in this case of hunger. For Schopenhauer, there is a force in all things that makes them what they are: the will. Recall, however, that phenomenally this force is not perceived; because all we know are events subject to the principle of sufficient reason, the will here is groundless. However, in self-consciousness, the will is not hidden but is known directly, and in this consciousness, we are also aware of our freedom. We are aware of an activity that cannot itself be part of the world of events that follows from that activity.

Although it has been customary in the history of philosophy for philosophers to raise questions concerning the purpose or end of existence, of creation, Schopenhauer claims that such questions are groundless. In effect they refer to the activity of the will; but the will has no purpose. It moves without cause, has no goal; it is desire itself, striving, yearning, wanting without rhyme or reason.

The Artist

The third book of Schopenhauer's work is also entitled "The World as Idea," but "idea" is now seen as a product of reason rather than as a perceptual event. It is here that Plato's concept of the idea or form is used by Schopenhauer, and his prime purpose is to develop his theory of art by means of it. He begins by pointing out that the will is objectified not only in the many particulars that we come to know as events in space and time, subject to change and, hence, explainable under the principle of sufficient reason; but it also manifests itself in universals, which are immutable and thus not susceptible to causal analysis. Schopenhauer holds that the will as universal presents us with a direct objectification, a Platonic form, whereas as a particular it is indirect.

How are individuals to know these direct objectifications? They may gain knowledge of them by transcending the world of events, of space and time and causality, and looking at things as they are in themselves. They do so by losing themselves in the object, by giving up their own subjectivity and becoming one with that which they perceive. In such a state, Schopenhauer holds, an individual becomes the pure will-less, painless, timeless subject of knowledge. The individual becomes a knower of ideas or forms and not of mere particulars; the object is now the *Idea*, the form, of the species. This seems to be something like the sort of knowledge that has been attributed to the mystic, and, no doubt, the influence of Eastern thought upon Schopenhauer can be seen here; but he likens the apprehension of forms to art. The artist repeats or reproduces Ideas grasped through pure contemplation; knowledge of the Ideas is the one source of art and its aim is the communication of this knowledge. With this in mind, we can see that Schopenhauer's definition of "art" fits closely with his views. It is the way of knowing things independently of the principle of sufficient reason. The person of genius is one who by intuition and imagination most completely frees himself from the world of events to grasp the eternal present within it.

Schopenhauer writes that the aesthetic mode of contemplation involves two features: the object known as a Platonic idea or form and the knowing person considered not as an individual in the ordinary sense, but as a pure, will-less subject of knowledge. When the knower gives up the fourfold principle of sufficient reason as a way of knowing things and assumes the aesthetic mode of contemplation, he or she derives a peculiar pleasure from that mode in varying degrees depending upon the aesthetic object.

Ordinarily it is difficult and, for most persons, impossible to escape from the world of desires and wants, the world that gives rise to our willing and that can never be satisfied. Our wants are without satiation; thus, suffering, frustration, and a sense of deficiency are ever-present. However, if by some external cause or inner disposition, we are raised above the cares of the daily world, our knowledge is freed from the directives of will and the temporal aspects of events, and we can achieve that transcendent state of peace, the painless state that separates the world of forms from that of suffering. This is the state of pure contemplation of which the great Greek philosophers spoke.

Artists who have attained this state and then represent it in their works allow others to escape the vicissitudes of life and to contemplate the world of forms free from the machinations of the will. These works of art are a means by which we can attain these artists' heights. Nature, too, in certain circumstances, can present objects in such a way that we transcend the world and enter into the realm of forms. However, the slightest wavering of attention on our part returns us to the world of phenomena; we leave contemplation for desire. Aesthetic enjoyment can also be obtained in the remembrance of things past. Schopenhauer points out that individuals, in contemplating their memories, finds them freed from the immediate tinges of suffering and pain that events often have. Generally speaking, aesthetic pleasure arises whenever we are able to rise above the wants of the moment and to contemplate things-in-themselves as no longer subject to the principle of sufficient reason; pleasure arises from the opposition to will; it is the delight that comes from perceptive knowledge.

When a contemplated object takes on the Idea of its species, we hold it to be a beauty. The nineteenth century aestheticians were concerned with the sublime also; Schopenhauer sees it in the ex-

altation that arises when one forcibly and consciously breaks away from the world of events and enters the world of forms. The object transfigured in this contemplative act yet carries an aura of its existence as an event created by will. As such it is hostile to the perceiver, yet in being "made" into a form, it is the object of pleasure and beauty. If the hostility crowds out the beauty, then the sublime leaves. When the sublime is present, we recognize our own insignificance alongside that which we perceive, yet, Schopenhauer feels, we also recognize the dependence of the object on us as one of our ideas. We are both humble and monumental in its presence.

Tragedy is the summit of poetical art; it presents the terrible side of life, the pain and evil, the want and suffering. We see in nature the all-consuming war of will with itself. When we learn of this inner struggle through tragedy, we are no longer deceived by the phenomena about us. The ego, which is so involved in the world of events, perishes with that world as we see it for what it is. The motives that keep the will striving are gone; they are replaced by knowledge of the world. This knowledge produces a quieting effect upon the will so that resignation takes place, not a surrender merely of the things of life but of the very will to live. (This is not to be confused with a "desire" to commit suicide, which is a definite act of will tormented by the world of events; rather, it is a renunciation of all desire as one becomes one with the eternal.)

Denial of the Will

The last book is also entitled, like the second, "The World as Will," but in the second aspect of will, Schopenhauer further examines the renunciation of the will to live. In this particular book, Schopenhauer emphasizes the Eastern religious and philosophical view of denial and renunciation. He also concentrates on the idea of life as tragic. It is interesting that Schopenhauer develops a theory of the act of generation as an assertion of the will to live. His discussion is reminiscent of Freud's account of the libido as a general drive manifesting itself throughout humankind and accounting for much, if not all, of human behavior. Freud is supposed to have been shown the passages in Schopenhauer that were similar to his. He claimed not to have read Schopenhauer, but he did acknowledge the similarity of the views.

Schopenhauer believed that in each phenomenal object, the will itself is present fully, in the sense that the object is the reification of the will. However, the will in its noumenal nature is most real. In inner consciousness, the individual is directly aware of the will. Individuals within the world of events, aware of pure will in themselves, desire everything for themselves. Schopenhauer believed that in this way, selfishness arises. Recall that indviduals have within themselves the entire world of phenomena as ideas as well as the world as will. Recall, too, that all other selves are known by individuals as their own ideas—thus individuals hope to have all, to control all. Thus, death ends all for individuals, although while they live they seek the world for themselves. In this eternal war with one another, people deserve the fate that the world as will has for them: a life of tragedy, of want, of pain and suffering. Ultimately, also, the will, in trying to express itself at the expense of others, punishes itself.

Only those who can rise above their principle of individuation, above the world of cause and effect, who can see the world as one of woe and suffering, can triumph over it. Once one has seen the world for what it is, there is no need to go on willing and striving. One renounces the world of ideas and of will; knowledge quiets the will. This freedom found outside the world of necessity is akin to grace, therein, believed Schopenhauer, lies one's salvation.

Theodore Waldman

Additional Reading

Atwell, John E. *Schopenhauer on the Character of the World: The Metaphysics of Will*. Berkeley: University of California Press, 1995. Atwell's extended analysis of *The World as Will and Representation* attempts, against the views of others, to establish that Arthur Schopenhauer has a metaphysics, though a severely limited one. In a closely reasoned text, Atwell delves into epistemology and ethics as well. A major feature is his discussion of the concepts of time, space, and causality. Like other explorations of will, this one gives primacy to intellect and thus unearths numerous inconsistencies.

_____. *Schopenhauer: The Human Character*. Philadelphia, Pa.: Temple University Press, 1990. In a topical, highly readable approach, Atwell explores Schopenhauer's ethics. Like other critics, he presses Schopenhauer's examples logically to the point that they break down and reveal contradictions. Major divisions concern the self, ethics, virtue, and salvation. Recognizing Schopenhauer's inclination toward hyperbole and paradox, Atwell offers a clear interpretation of the philosopher's concepts of virtue and ethical action.

Fox, Michael, ed. *Schopenhauer: His Philosophical Achievement*. Brighton, England: Harvester Press, 1980. A collection of essays by distinguished scholars. The book is divided into three sections: general articles, giving overviews of Schopenhauer; articles dealing with basic philosophical issues; and comparative studies that relate Schopenhauer's philosophy to others' and explore intellectual debts.

Gardiner, Patrick L. *Schopenhauer*. Bristol, United Kingdom: Thoemmes Press, 1997. A piercing analysis of Schopenhauer's life and philosophy.

Hamlyn, D. W. *Schopenhauer*. Boston: Routledge & Kegan Paul, 1980. A general survey of Schopenhauer's philosophy. Clarifies his terms, explains his epistemology, and offers extensive analysis of his philosophical debt to Kant.

Jacquette, Dale, ed. *Schopenhauer, Philosophy, and the Arts*. New York: Cambridge University Press, 1996. A penetrating look at Schopenhauer's philosophy and aesthetics.

Janaway, Christopher. *Schopenhauer*. Oxford: Oxford University Press, 1994. Janaway's concise though dense overview of Schopenhauer's life and philosophical system represents an excellent introduction. Synopses of the major works are skillfully supplemented by cogent references to lesser-known titles. Janaway exposes some limitations and contradictions in Schopenhauer's system, notably in his concepts of will, freedom, ethics, and pessimism.

Magee, Bryan. *The Philosophy of Schopenhauer*. New York: Oxford University Press, 1983. A scholarly introduction to Schopenhauer's philosophical system. Explores the effects of his early life on his system and places his ideas in their philosophical tradition. Numerous appendices trace his influence on others.

Safranski, Rüdiger. *Schopenhauer and the Wild Years of Philosophy*. Cambridge, Mass.: Harvard University Press, 1990. Essentially a biography, the book recounts the life and works of Schopenhauer. Safranski suggests that events in Schopenhauer's life contributed to his outlook and the formation of his pessimistic system. In addition, he places the philosophy within the aesthetic and intellectual currents of Schopenhauer's time.

Tanner, Michael. *Schopenhauer*. New York: Routledge, 1999. An excellent biographical introduction to the thoughts of the philosopher, clearly presented and requiring no special background. Bibliography.

Wallace, William. *Life of Arthur Schopenhauer*. London: Walter Scott, 1890. A comprehensive overview of Schopenhauer's life, philosophical system, and influence. Biographical information draws heavily upon previous studies in Germany and offers an illuminating account of his daily life.

Stanley Archer

Alfred Schutz

Drawing on Edmund Husserl's phenomenology and Max Weber's sociology, Schutz developed an account of meaning and action that addressed the actor's knowledge, intersubjectivity, and the nature of sociological analysis.

Principal philosophical works: *Der sinnhafte Aufbau der sozialen Welt*, 1932 (*The Phenomenology of the Social World*, 1967); *Collected Papers*, 1962-1996 (4 volumes; includes *The Problem of Social Reality*, *Studies in Social Theory*, *Studies in Phenomenological Philosophy*, *Volume 4*); *Reflections on the Problem of Relevance*, 1970; *The Structures of the Life-World*, 1973-1989 (with Thomas Luckmann, 2 volumes).

Born: April 13, 1899; Vienna, Austro-Hungarian Empire
Died: May 20, 1959; New York, New York

Early Life

In 1899, Alfred Schutz was born to a middle-class family in Vienna, Austria. Before Schutz's birth, his father died, and Schutz was raised by his mother and his stepfather, a bank executive.

Schutz graduated from high school during World War I. The Austro-Hungarian army was in short supply of officers, so the seventeen-year-old Schutz was immediately drafted into the army. After a short stint of training, the army commissioned Schutz as an officer and dispatched him to the Italian front.

On leave in late 1918, Schutz returned home, but the city to which he returned was not the one he remembered. Schutz found Vienna in a state of dramatic economic deterioration, with a large segment of its population suffering from starvation. Moreover, Schutz found that he himself had fundamentally changed during his military service. This experience probably shaped and informed Schutz's 1945 essay "The Homecomer," in which he employed phenomenology to explore the problems faced by soldiers returning home from World War II.

In the aftermath of World War I, Schutz studied law and social science at the University of Vienna, under the guidance of a handful of prominent teachers, including Hans Kelsen (law), Ludwig von Mises and Friedrich von Wieser (economics), and Othmar Spann (sociology). Through his studies, Schutz developed an interest in the work of the German sociologist Max Weber, in particular Weber's writings on the methodology of the social sciences. Intrigued by Weber's treatment of social action in terms of its subjective meaning for the actor, Schutz was nevertheless frustrated by what he felt to be ambiguities in Weber's position. In particular, Schutz was skeptical of Weber's treatment of "meaning" (*Sinn*) and "interpretive understanding" (*Verstehen*).

During the 1920's, as Schutz made the transition from student to scholar, he initially attempted to address Weber's conceptions of subjective understanding, experience, and action by adopting the perspective of Henri Bergson, a French philosopher popular among students and scholars in Schutz's Vienna. By 1928, however, Schutz had concluded that Bergson's perspective, though useful, was not wholly adequate to the task. Nonetheless, throughout his subsequent work, Schutz continued to draw on selected aspects of Bergson's work, including especially Bergson's distinction between "inner" time (*durée*), as subjectively experienced, and "outer" time, as measured by clocks.

A student and friend of Schutz, Felix Kaufmann, suggested that Schutz turn to phenomenology and, in particular, the writings of Edmund Husserl as a foundation for Schutz's ongoing effort to address issues raised by Weber about the interpretation of human action. Finally heeding Kaufmann's repeated suggestions, Schutz undertook the systematic study of Husserl's thought. Schutz distilled from Husserl a phenomenologically informed and sociologically relevant approach to the explanation of how subjective meanings produce an apparently objective social world. Schutz would spend the rest of his career developing Husserl's phenomenological conception of meaning as a method for addressing the ambiguities in Weber's sociological conception of action.

Life's Work

Schutz's first major publication, *The Phenomenology of the Social World*, addressed central issues in the philosophy of the social sciences, including the nature of the distinction between subjectivity and objectivity, the problem of interpreting social action in terms of its *subjective meaning*, and the fundamental question of whether—and to what extent—the social sciences can provide genuine understanding of human beings and their conduct. As such, this book formulated the themes and posed the problems that Schutz would work on his entire life.

In *The Phenomenology of the Social World*, Schutz explained action in terms of subjective experience, meaning, and the consciousness of time. Humans, Schutz argued, make sense of the social world, as well as of each other's conduct, in terms of *typifications*: Actors plan their own actions—and interpret the actions of others—based on typified conceptions of motivation and intention. In analyzing the relationship between action and motivation, Schutz developed the highly original distinction between "in-order-to-motives" and "because-motives."

The Phenomenology of the Social World was the only major study that Schutz published while living in Europe. In the mid-1930's, the Nazis' rise to power in Germany made intellectual life in Vienna uncertain. In 1938, while Schutz, a successful banker in addition to his career as a philosopher, was in Paris on a business trip, the Nazis invaded Austria. Though Schutz wanted to return to Vienna, where his family remained, friends discouraged him from doing so. Schutz obtained entry visas for his family, and he and his family lived in France for a year, during which time he worked tirelessly to help a number of his friends and associates escape Nazi-occupied Austria.

In 1939, Schutz and his family relocated to the United States, where a number of intellectuals from Germany and from various Nazi-occupied nations were in exile. Schutz took a position as part of the graduate faculty at the New School for Social Research in New York, a situation that afforded him regular contact with Aron Gurwitsch, Dorion Cairns, and his lifelong colleague Felix Kaufmann, each of whom had studied with Husserl.

After settling in the United States, Schutz began to develop and amplify the themes introduced in *The Phenomenology of the Social World*. The resulting writings—some thirty-two published titles, including his *Collected Papers*, published posthumously in four volumes—can be seen as an interrelated whole, across which Schutz sought to explicate a systematic (and accessible) treatment of the philosophy of the social sciences on the basis of phenomenology.

The major themes of Schutz's life work are concisely presented in his 1954 paper "Concept and Theory Formation in the Social Sciences." Schutz wrote this paper in response to the neopositivist approach to social science championed by Rudolf Carnap, Carl Hempel, and Ernest Nagel, among others. Proponents of the neopositivist perspective argued that first, the methodological procedures of science are unitary regardless of the domain of application; second, the goal of science is the explanation of individual phenomena by reference to general laws; and third, scientific statements must be testable by reference to publicly observable events. Taken together, these three claims amounted to a simple refusal to acknowledge the paramount significance of sense making as a *subjective* aspect of human action and social reality, as Schutz had argued in *The Phenomenology of the Social World*.

In his 1954 essay, Schutz presented a point-by-point response to the neopositivist account of social science. First, Schutz argued that the social sciences differ from the natural sciences in that the events and relationships that the social sciences analyze are "pre-interpreted"—or meaningful, in the first place, to the actors who are the subjects of social scientific inquiry. In contrast, in the world of nature, events and relationships do not "mean" anything to the molecules, atoms, or electrons that are, for example, the subject matter of physics. "The social world," Schutz argued, "is experienced from the onset as a meaningful one." As such, the social world requires interpretive understanding (*Verstehen*) of exactly the sort dismissed by the neopositivist as a nonscientific mode of understanding.

Second, Schutz addressed the idea that science should aim to explain individual phenomena by reference to general laws. Such a claim is based, Schutz argued, on an assumption that *rational* action is, or should be, the yardstick by which actual conduct is measured. However, humans act and make sense of action using concepts, categories, and constructs that they *presume* to be valid and socially shared "for all practical purposes" and "until demonstrated otherwise."

Actors in the social world interpret one another's behavior as meaningful action by imputing goals, motives, and intents to other actors on the basis of their public, observable behaviors. This is not the same, Schutz makes clear, as claiming that actors have immediate access to what other actors "really" experience; other actors' actual experiences are essentially inaccessible. Nevertheless, by employing socially shared, commonsense categories and constructs to interpret one another's behaviors, humans make *reasonable* sense of that behavior as meaningful action, in terms of usual motives, identities, or actions in typical situations.

These categories and constructs constitute a "stock of knowledge" that actors treat as *contingently* valid, or useful "for all practical purposes" and "until proven otherwise." Elsewhere, Schutz referred to this orientation as a "natural attitude" toward the social world, in which the actors treat their understanding of the world as practically adequate. From such a perspective, the actor simply believes that "as s/he sees things, so they are." The natural perspective does not, therefore, encompass a scientific or Descartian skepticism about the objectivity of perception, the adequacy of knowledge, or the utility of past experience. Thus, Schutz concludes, the employment of scientific rationality as the primary means of interpreting human action (as advocated by the

neopositivists) is inadequate to explain the conduct of actors who employ commonsense reasons to act and to interpret others' actions. Based as it is on unproven but shared assumptions about what is typical, commonsense reason *cannot* be "rational" in strictly scientific terms—nor is it taken to be so by the actors themselves.

Third, Schutz addresses the neopositivist idea that scientific statements must be testable. Schutz's response is simple but profound: Social science, like commonsense reason, unavoidably relies on constructs as a means of interpretive sense-making. That is, social scientists themselves employ typified models of human action. It follows that social scientists whose models ignore the role and influence of subjective constructs and interpretation in human action replace the real world of human conduct with a fictional, nonexisting representation of it, one that exists only as a (social scientific) construction.

When Schutz died in 1959, he was preparing a manuscript that he intended to be the final, comprehensive statement of his life's work. Thomas Luckmann, a former student of Schutz, completed this manuscript and saw it published as *The Structures of the Life-World*. Continuing to draw on Husserl's phenomenology, Schutz articulated his own conception of the "life-world" (*Lebenswelt*), the total sphere of experiences consisting of the objects, persons, and events encountered in practical action. The life-world, Schutz argued, is the "paramount reality" of life; and as such, the life-world is organized in terms of the "natural attitude" and its constituent features, as Schutz described in his previous writings.

Influence

Schutz's body of writings retain their significance as one route of development from Husserl's phenomenology. Existentialism, as developed by Maurice Merleau-Ponty and especially Jean-Paul Sartre, also drew primarily on Husserl. An alternative to existentialism, Schutz's sociological phenomenology offers novel analyses of human action, the problem of freedom, and what distinguishes human beings. Schutz's articulation of the social bases of intersubjectivity also has striking, potentially rich parallels in the philosophy of

Ludwig Wittgenstein, which argues against the privacy of language and "other minds."

Schutz was not the first thinker to attempt a synthesis of phenomenology and sociology, but his systematic, comprehensive effort to do so is original, nonetheless. Schutz's account of human action as meaningful, based on his analyses of the social foundations of subjectivity and intersubjectivity, remain among the most important and influential contributions in phenomenology and the philosophy of the social sciences.

Andrew L. Roth

The Phenomenology of the Social World

Type of philosophy: Epistemology, phenomenology, social philosophy
First published: Der sinnhafte Aufbau der sozialen Welt, 1932 (English translation, 1967)
Principal ideas advanced:
◇ The social world is interpreted by its members as meaningful and intelligible in terms of social categories and constructs.
◇ Therefore, scientific study of the social world must take into account the subjective interpretation of behavior as *meaningful* action.
◇ This point does not preclude scientific study of the social world, but it distinguishes such study from the natural sciences.
◇ A scientific explanation of action as meaningful must deal with the problem of *intersubjectivity*: How can two or more actors share common experiences of the world and how can they communicate about them?
◇ The achievement and maintenance of intersubjectivity is a *practical* "problem," which is routinely "solved" on the basis of shared assumptions about the nature of experience.
◇ In the absence of direct experience, social actors rely on *typified* conceptions of action, social identity, and context to make sense of the social world.

Originally published in 1932, *The Phenomenology of the Social World* has its deepest roots in the nineteenth century, when scholars (especially in Germany) made great advances in the study of history, economics, and social institutions. The modern conception of the social sciences arguably has its origins in the intellectual advances of this period. However, in conjunction with the development of the social sciences, questions arose about their status as *scientific* enterprises: Could human thought and activity be explained in terms of general laws? To what extent could the study of human thought and activity be free of value assumptions? Are the methods of the natural sciences appropriate for the social sciences? Timeless as these questions may seem, they held special prominence for the generation of philosophical and social scientific thinkers that came to intellectual maturity in the early decades of the twentieth century.

In orienting himself to these questions, Alfred Schutz drew on the phenomenology of Edmund Husserl and the methodological writings of sociologist Max Weber. Husserl sought to describe the relationship between objects of experience and the subjective structures through which humans become conscious of those objects; Weber championed an interpretive approach to the explanation of social action in terms of its subjective meaning. Schutz found shortcomings in both Husserl's and Weber's thought, but he also believed that a synthesis of the two thinkers' works—that is, a phenomenological study of the basic concepts of the social sciences—would address the questions about the *scientific* potential of the social sciences. Schutz's commitment to the *synthesis* of phenomenology and social science can be seen in the following pair of facts: He dedicated this book to Husserl, and he conceived of it as a "preface to interpretive sociology."

A Review of Weber
Schutz begins by introducing the sociological background of the problems that he intends to address. This involves a critical review of Weber's methodological writings. In *Wirtschaft und Gesellschaft* (1922; *The Theory of Social and Economic Organization*, 1947; also as *Max Weber on Law in Economy and Society*, 1954; *The Sociology of Religion*, 1963; and *Economy and Society: An Outline of Interpretive Sociology*, 1968), as well as elsewhere, Weber argued that the social sciences ought to be value-free (*wertfrei*) and that social

phenomena ought to be analyzed in terms of "ideal types," logically controlled and unambiguous concepts that, although removed from historical reality, nonetheless serve as a means of objectively interpreting the social world. From such a perspective, Weber argued, social action could be interpreted scientifically. Weber defined social action as behavior to which subjective meaning is attached.

Although Schutz agrees with Weber that social science must be interpretive, he believed that Weber failed to develop a clear account of the concepts essential to such an undertaking, including "understanding" (*Verstehen*), "subjective meaning" (*gemeinter Sinn*), and "action" (*Handeln*). Ambiguities in the explication of these foundational concepts weakened the enterprise of interpretive sociology, Schutz believed. For instance, although Weber made "subjective meaning" a key aspect of social action, Schutz argued that Weber did not adequately specify whether that term referred to the actor's own understanding or to the understanding of the sociological observer of the action. This ambiguity made the concept of "action" problematic. Consider the example of a person turning a doorknob: Is the relevant action "opening the door"? What if the person in question is a locksmith, who might be "checking the lock"? Or an actor who might be "rehearsing a scene"? In sum, Schutz objects to the idea, advanced by Weber, that there is a "course of behavior" to which "subjective meaning" is "attached." Such a formulation conveys the sense, Schutz argues, that "meaning" is somehow separate from "behavior," when in fact the two concepts are necessarily intertwined in actual human action. The problem for Schutz becomes a matter of determining more precise ways of specifying these concepts. To do so, he turns to Husserl and phenomenology.

Husserl

From Husserl, Schutz adapts the phenomenological conception of lived experience as lacking in *inherent* meaning or discrete identity. Instead, experience depends on acts of reflection, recognition, identification, and so forth. The meaning of experience is established in retrospect, through reflective interpretation. "It is misleading to say that experiences *have* meaning.

Meaning does not lie *in* the experience. Rather, those experiences are meaningful which are grasped reflectively." It follows that not all experiences are meaningful; meaningful lived experience is *constituted* as such in the individual's own "stream of consciousness" through active reflection. Likewise, Schutz proposes that humans are also capable of ascribing meaning *prospectively* to future experiences. If action is behavior directed toward the realization of a determinate future goal, it involves projection: The actor pictures the completed action as it is in progress, phase by phase.

Motives and Intersubjectivity

On this basis, Schutz proposes the highly original distinction between the "in-order-to-motive" (*Um-zu-Motiv*) of action and the "because-motive" (*Weil-Motiv*) of action. The in-order-to-motive refers to the future-oriented project of the action; in contrast, the because-motive refers to the past event that led to the action. For instance, in opening an umbrella as it begins to rain, an actor may be said to act on the bases of the perception of rain and knowledge about the effect of rain on clothing, as a because-motive, and the aim of "staying dry," as an in-order-to-motive.

Drawing on the interpretive resources gleaned from Weber and Husserl, Schutz proceeds to analyze "intersubjective understanding"—that is, socially shared knowledge—and the bases for it in human experience. Whereas Husserl had attempted to address intersubjectivity as a "transcendental problem" by seeking to demonstrate how we know that there *are* other minds, Schutz sidesteps this issue by arguing that, in everyday life, individuals assume the existence of others. Schutz argues that intersubjectivity is a *practical* problem: Given that individuals postulate—and, indeed, take for granted—the existence of other minds, how do they come to *know* and *share* one another's lived experiences? Schutz responds that in everyday life, the "problem" of intersubjectivity is recurrently "solved" through reliance on socially shared categories and constructs for interpreting behavior *as* meaningful action.

In interaction, individuals treat one another's behavior—including gestures, mannerisms, bodily comportment, and facial expressions—as *indicators* of subjectively meaningful processes. We know, Schutz might say, how to tell the difference between the blink of an eye that results from a speck of dust (behavior that is not subjectively meaningful) and the wink that is intended as an act of flirtation or affiliation (behavior that is subjectively meaningful). The treatment of physical behavior as an indicator of subjective states is premised on the assumption that individuals' experience of *time* is synchronized. In fact, in interaction, individuals' experience of time may become interlocked, as the successive behaviors of each individual, interpreted as meaningful acts, come to constitute a context for continued (meaningful) action.

In providing an account of intersubjectivity, Schutz is careful to maintain a distinction between experiences that are *irremediably* private and those that are *contingently* shared: Behavior can only be an indirect indication of others' subjective states, and consequently the maintenance of intersubjectivity has no other guarantee than individuals' continued reliance on a shared set of practices for making sense of one another's conduct. Precarious as this arrangement sounds, it is nonetheless stable in practice, Schutz contends.

The Social World
Given intersubjectivity, individuals experience the world as a *social* world. Schutz then proceeds to attempt to explain the "multiform structure" of the social world. The structuring of the social world is, he contends, integral to humans' ways of perceiving and understanding one another's subjective experiences. This claim holds both for *everyday* interpretation of the social world and for *scientific* interpretation of it. An underlying aim of Schutz's examination of the structure of the social world is to distinguish between the categories that ordinary actors (approaching the world from a "natural standpoint") use in making sense of the social world and the categories that social scientists (approaching the world from the perspective of their professional discipline) use in classifying the social world, including ordinary actors' efforts to make sense of it.

Schutz aligns with Weber in proposing that the social world is properly understood in terms of the concept of "social action." Drawing on Weber and Husserl, Schutz defines "social action" as

action whose in-order-to-motive contains some reference to another individual's stream of consciousness. Thus Schutz establishes the relevance of analyzing social *relationships*.

Social Relationships
Schutz distinguishes among three types of social relationships and their corresponding orientations: In a *thou-relationship*, one person in direct, face-to-face contact with another person orients to the other as a specific person; a *we-relationship* arises when two persons in a face-to-face situation orient to each other as in reciprocal *thou-relationships*; and, in contrast with the previous two types, a *they-relationship* refers to a situation in which the actor orients to others with whom there are no direct dealings and only general notions.

The import of the distinctions between the different types of social relationships and orientations hinges on the distinction between *directly* and *indirectly* experienced social reality. Schutz's analysis of this distinction yields a novel reinterpretation of Weber's conception of "ideal types." In instances of direct experience, an individual has available a number of interpretive resources that are not available to others who have only indirect access. Consider, for example, the differences between listening to a friend talk and reading a letter from the friend. In making sense of the friend's *spoken* words, a diverse array of interpretive resources are available on the basis of direct observation of that person—including, for example, the friend's tone of voice and accompanying gestures. Moreover, on the basis of this direct access, the listener can actively transform the situation, for example, by asking a question.

In contrast, in the absence of *direct* social relationship or observation, the interpreter must necessarily rely on relatively generalized, abstract means of interpretation. The indirect observer, Schutz writes, must resort to the employment of relatively anonymous "course-of-action types" and "personal types" to interpret social actions and relationships. In brief, indirect observation necessarily relies on the use of "ideal types" of the sort described by Weber. However, in contrast with Weber, who understood ideal types as unique to social scientific interpretation, Schutz argues that the use of ideal types is necessary to *any* interpretation based on indirect experience. In consequence, reliance on ideal types cannot be what distinguishes scientific observation from nonscientific observation.

Social Science

This analysis allows Schutz to provide an answer to the question: What is social science? Social science necessarily involves the interpretation of social action and the social world on the basis of ideal types; consequently, the knowledge of the social world thus generated can only be indirect. In this regard, social science is no different from other forms of indirect knowledge. However, social scientific knowledge differs from everyday forms of indirect knowledge in one crucial respect: No directly experienced social reality is *pregiven* to social science. Schutz writes, "In scientific judgment no presupposition nor any pregiven element can be accepted as simply 'at hand' without need of any further explanation. On the contrary, when I act as a scientist, I subject to a detailed step-by-step analysis everything taken from the world of everyday life." On this basis, Schutz concludes that the enterprise of social science is none other than an "objective context of meaning" constructed out of and referring to "subjective contexts of meaning."

Not surprisingly, given its focus on the methodology of the social sciences, the influence of *The Phenomenology of the Social World* has been most pronounced in sociology. The book made a profound impression on Harold Garfinkel, who (along with Aaron Cicourel) established the sociological field of ethnomethodology. Garfinkel saw in Schutz's work a significant resource for his own extension and critique of Talcott Parsons's then-dominant theory of social action. Similarly, Schutz's writings have a foundational status in the area of social constructionism. More generally, by insisting that sociology, including its theories and methods, is itself a social construction, Schutz's phenomenological approach to the social sciences stands as an important corrective to trends in sociology toward positivistic theorizing and research methods.

As a profound and thoroughgoing investigation of the fundamental concepts of social science—including "action," "meaning," "subjectiv-ity," and "objectivity"—Schutz's first book had an immediate and lasting effect on practitioners of the social sciences.

Andrew L. Roth

Additional Reading

Embree, Lester, ed. *Worldly Phenomenology: The Continuing Influence of Alfred Schutz on North American Social Science*. Washington, D.C.: University Press of America, 1988. A collection of essays that evaluate Alfred Schutz's continued influence on the practice of phenomenology and the social sciences.

Gorman, Robert A. *The Dual Vision: Alfred Schutz and the Myth of Phenomenological Social Science*. London: Routledge & Kegan Paul, 1977. A critical account of Schutz's work and especially the claim that phenomenology can provide an objective basis for the social sciences.

Grathoff, Richard, ed. *The Theory of Social Action: The Correspondence of Alfred Schutz and Talcott Parsons*. Bloomington: Indiana University Press, 1978. Reproduces the 1940-1941 correspondence between Schutz and sociologist Talcott Parsons, arguably the most influential American social theorist of the twentieth century. The letters document Schutz's attempt to convince Parsons of the need to base any sociological theory of action on phenomenological foundations, and Parsons's resistance to this approach; the exchanges offer fascinating insights into the minds of two of the century's most important social thinkers. Grathoff's introductory and concluding essays help to orient readers who are new to the writings of Schutz or Parsons.

Heritage, John. "The Phenomenological Input," In *Garfinkel and Ethnomethodology*. Oxford: Polity Press, 1984. Provides a clear, succinct overview of Schutz's phenomenology, as well as a more detailed account of Schutz's influence on Harold Garfinkel and the development of ethnomethodology, a phenomenologically informed field of sociology.

Schutz, Alfred. *Alfred Schutz: On Phenomenology and Social Relations*. Edited by Helmut R. Wagner. Chicago: University of Chicago Press, 1970. A systematic representation of the full scope of Schutz's writings, arranged and combined topically; includes a concise, accessible introduction to Schutz and his work by the editor, Helmut Wagner. Highly recommended.

Vaitkus, Steven. *How Is Society Possible? Intersubjectivity and the Fiduciary Attitude as Problems of the Social Group in Mead, Gurwitsch, and Schutz.* Dordrecht, The Netherlands: Kluwer Academic Publishers, 1991. Compares Schutz's account of knowledge and how it is socially shared with the explanations advanced by pragmatist George Herbert Mead and another phenomenologist, Aron Gurwitsch.

Wagner, Helmut R. *Alfred Schutz: An Intellectual Biography.* Chicago: University of Chicago Press, 1983. Perhaps the definitive source for information on Schutz and his writings. Wagner's treatment is clear and comprehensive.

Webb, Rodman B. *The Presence of the Past: John Dewey and Alfred Schutz on the Genesis and Organization of Experience.* Gainesville: University Presses of Florida, 1976. Compares the philosophic attitudes of John Dewey and Schutz, as well as their accounts of the fundamental concepts of "experience," "relevance," and "reality." Better suited for readers who already have some familiarity with Schutz and phenomenology.

Andrew L. Roth

John R. Searle

Searle elaborated on speech act theory and developed theories of intentionality and consciousness. His famous thought experiment, "the Chinese room argument," is arguably the most influential argument against artificial intelligence.

Principal philosophical works: *Speech Acts: An Essay in the Philosophy of Language*, 1969; *Expression and Meaning: Studies in the Theory of Speech Acts*, 1979; *Intentionality: An Essay in the Philosophy of Mind*, 1983; *Minds, Brains, and Science*, 1984; "Indeterminacy, Empiricism, and the First Person," 1987; *The Rediscovery of the Mind*, 1992; *The Construction of Social Reality*, 1995; *The Mystery of Consciousness*, 1997.

Born: July 31, 1932; Denver, Colorado

Early Life

John Rogers Searle was born to G. W. Searle, an electrical engineer, and Hester Beck Searle, a physician. He attended the University of Wisconsin from 1949 to 1952, then studied philosophy at Oxford University, where he was a Rhodes scholar. He received his B.A. from Oxford in 1955 and his M.A. and D.Phil. from Oxford in 1959. He taught as a lecturer in philosophy at Christ Church in Oxford from 1956 to 1959. In 1959, he was appointed to the philosophy department at the University of California, Berkeley, where he eventually became the Mills Professor of Philosophy. On December 24, 1959, he married Dagmar Carboch, an attorney, with whom he had two sons.

Life's Work

One of Searle's earliest and most important contributions was in the area of philosophy of language, especially speech act theory. While he was at Oxford, Searle studied under British philosopher J. L. Austin, who had developed speech act theory. Austin demonstrated that many utterances are significant not so much in terms of what they say, but rather in terms of what they do. In other words, some utterances do not simply state facts but instead are performances in and of themselves. Speech act theory distinguishes between what Austin referred to as con-stative and performative, or illocutionary, speech acts, or utterances. An utterance that only describes an event is called constative. An utterance is performative if it describes a certain action accomplished by its speaker and producing this expression amounts to accomplishing that action. For example, a sentence such as "I promise you I will pay you back" is performative, because by using it, one accomplishes the act of promising; not only does one say that one is promising, but one actually promises. Other examples of performative utterances are those of betting, commanding, greeting, requesting an action, acknowledging, and insulting.

Searle is credited with having elaborated and expanded speech act theory by examining the importance of rules in communication and by introducing the role of intentionality in constituting the meaning of speech acts. His first major book, *Speech Acts: An Essay in the Philosophy of Language,* took as its hypothesis the idea that speaking a language is engaging in a rule-governed form of behavior. One type of rule that is important to speech act theory is what Searle calls a constitutive rule. A rule is constitutive with respect to a certain form of activity if failure to observe the rule takes away from the activity its distinctive character; for example, the rules of chess are constitutive with respect to chess, because one ceases to play chess as soon as one disregards these rules. Searle believed that the rules establishing the performative value of utterances are constitutive with respect to the use of these utterances. For example, one cannot say "I promise I will pay you back" without actually taking on the obligation to accomplish what is promised. One may not keep the promise, but it is a constitutive rule that in promising, one makes a commitment. Searle refined his earlier analyses and extended speech act theory to new areas such as indirect and figurative discourse, metaphor, and fiction in *Expression and Meaning: Studies in the Theory of Speech Acts*.

While examining the role played by speakers' and receivers' intentions in creating the meaning of speech acts, Searle became interested in the philosophy of mind. He formulated a comprehensive theory of intentionality that he explains in *Intentionality: An Essay in the Philosophy of Mind*. This book, although it was published after *Speech Acts* and *Expression and Meaning*, provides the philosophical foundations for Searle's work in speech act theory. According to Searle, intentionality is the capacity of the mind to represent objects and states of affairs in the world other than itself. He uses "intentionality" as a technical term meaning that feature of representations by which they are about something or are directed at something. Intentionality has no special connection with intending. For example, intending to go to the store is just one kind of intentionality.

An important component of Searle's theory of intentionality is that of collective intentionality. Searle believes that humans have a capacity to share intentional states such as beliefs, desires, and intentions. The crucial element in collective intentionality is a sense of doing or wanting or believing something together; the individual intentionality of each person is derived from the collective intentionality that they share. For example, two men who are participating in a prize fight are engaging in collective intentionality, but a man who sneaks up behind another man in an alley and beats him is not engaging in collective intentionality.

Another important feature of intentionality is what Searle calls the "Background." Searle argues that the structure of human institutions is a structure of constitutive rules, but that no rule or meaning is self-interpreting; rather, a person needs a contextual understanding to arrive at the correct interpretation. The Background helps to provide this context and operates as the precondition for the intelligibility of representation and intentionality. The Background consists of two parts: the Deep Background and the Local Background. The Deep Background consists of neurophysiological functions, biological skills, and universally human capacities, such as eating, walking, and talking. The Local Background is made up of culturally bound skills and capacities, such as knowing the purposes of culturally specific objects and which behaviors are appropriate for certain culturally bound occasions.

Searle describes several ways that Background is important to intentions. First, Background enables linguistic interpretation to take place. Second, Background enables perceptual interpretation to take place. Third, Background structures consciousness. Fourth, Background facilitates certain kinds of readiness that help to structure the nature of human experiences. Finally, Background disposes people to certain kinds of behavior. Searle's work on intentionality and Background helps to form the basis of one of his most influential books, *The Construction of Social Reality*.

Searle became increasingly interested in the question "What is consciousness?" His theory of biological naturalism is an attempt to answer this question; it is described in detail in *The Rediscovery of the Mind* and *The Mystery of Consciousness*. Searle defines consciousness as a subjective state of sentience or awareness that begins when one wakes up in the morning and continues throughout the day until one goes to sleep at night, or falls into a coma or dies. He theorizes that mental phenomena such as thoughts, emotions, and desires are caused by neurophysiological processes in the brain and are themselves features of the brain. Above all, he says, consciousness is a biological phenomenon. Searle says consciousness should be thought of as part of ordinary biological history, along with digestion, growth, mitosis, and meiosis; however, it has some features that other biological phenomena do not. The most important of these, Searle says, is what he calls "subjectivity." This is the sense in which each person's consciousness is private to that person. Searle believes that consciousness is essentially a first-person, subjective phenomenon, and thus talk of conscious states cannot be reduced or eliminated in favor of third-person, objective talk about neural events. According to Searle, brain processes cause consciousness, but the consciousness they cause is not some extra substance or entity: It is just a higher level feature of the whole system. The two crucial relationships between the brain and consciousness are that lower level neuronal processes in the brain cause consciousness and that consciousness is simply a higher level feature of the system that is made up of the lower level neuronal elements. Searle acknowledges that although it appears that certain brain functions are sufficient for producing conscious states, limited knowledge of neurobiological matters prevents researchers from concluding that brain functions are necessary for producing consciousness.

Much of Searle's later career was concerned with arguing against artificial intelligence (AI), the basis of which is the claim that computers can think, or at least have the potential to do so. In "Minds, Brains, and Programs," published in *Behavioral and Brain Sciences* in 1980, he presented a thought experiment he called the Chinese room argument; it has become one of the best-known and most widely credited counters to artificial intelligence. In this argument, Searle targets what he calls "strong AI," in which the computer is not just a tool in the study of the mind but really is a mind, in the sense that computers given the right programs can be said literally to understand and to have other cognitive states.

In the Chinese room argument, he asks readers to imagine themselves to be monolingual English speakers locked in a room and given a large set of Chinese writing, a second set of Chinese script, and a set of rules in English for correlating the second group with the first group. The rules correlate one set of syntactic symbols with another set of syntactic symbols. A third group of Chinese symbols and more instructions in English enable readers to correlate elements of this third group with elements of the first two groups and instruct readers to give back certain sorts of Chinese symbols with certain sorts of shapes in response. Those who provide readers with the symbols have terms for each of the groups of symbols. They call the first set of Chinese writing a script, which is a data structure with natural language processing applications. The second set is called a story, the third set is called "questions," the set

of rules in English is called "the program," and the symbols readers would give back are called "answers to the questions." The readers engaged in the experiment know none of this, but they become so skilled at following the instructions that from the viewpoint of someone outside the room, their responses are indistinguishable from those of a Chinese speaker. In producing answers by manipulating uninterpreted formal symbols, they have behaved like a computer, but they still do not understand a word of Chinese.

According to Searle, the argument against strong AI is based on two truths: Brains cause minds, and syntax does not suffice for semantics. No matter how intelligently a computer behaves and no matter what programming makes it behave that way, because the symbols it processes are meaningless and lack semantics, it is not really intelligent and it is not really thinking. In *Minds, Brains, and Science*, Searle expanded his argument, providing this axiom: Syntax is not sufficient for semantics; programs are syntactic; minds are semantic; therefore, no program (or computer) is sufficient for the mind. His position against strong AI has become more forceful with time; in *The Mystery of Consciousness*, he argues that the Chinese room argument gives too much credit to computers. He says the argument wrongly took as unproblematic the assumption that computer programs are syntactic or symbolic in the first place, because there is nothing intrinsic in the physics of computers that makes their operations syntactic or symbolic. The ascription of syntax or symbolic operations to a computer program, therefore, is a matter of human interpretation.

Influence

Searle has made major contributions in the areas of philosophy of language and philosophy of mind, but his work also has been important in other scholarly fields. His contribution to speech act theory is important for communication and cultural studies because it counters the simplistic linear flow models of communication that see communication simply in terms of information transfer or exchanging ideas. Searle's contributions also have been influential in studies of social interaction because they provide an analytic tool for a variety of research traditions ranging from discourse analysis to ethnography of communication. His work in philosophy of mind, especially in terms of consciousness and artificial intelligence, has engendered great discussion in academic circles. Searle has been a prolific lecturer and researcher, acting as visiting professor at prestigious universities across the United States and around the world, in such cities as Venice, Florence, Frankfurt, Toronto, Oslo, Berlin, and Oxford. His works have been translated into twenty languages.

Karen Anding Fontenot

The Construction of Social Reality

Type of philosophy: Epistemology, philosophy of mind, social philosophy
First published: 1995
Principal ideas advanced:

◇ Two types of facts exist: institutional facts, which depend on human agreement for their existence, and brute facts, which require no human institutions for their existence. Money is an institutional fact; a mountain or river is a brute fact.

◇ Many species of animals, including humans, have a capacity for collective intentionality. This means that they share intentional states such as beliefs, desires, and intentions.

◇ Through collective intentionality, humans are able to impose certain functions on phenomena that cannot be achieved solely in virtue of physics and chemistry but require continued human cooperation in the specific forms of recognition, acceptance, and acknowledgment of a new status to which a function is assigned. This is the key element in the creation of institutional facts.

◇ Institutional facts require some form of language.

◇ The structure of human institutions is a structure of constitutive rules.

◇ The "Background" is a set of nonintentional or preintentional capacities that enable intentional states of function. It is the Background that enables people to relate to rule structures such as language, property, money, and mar-

riage in cases in which they do not know the rules and are not following them either consciously or unconsciously.

◇ There is no opposition between culture and biology; different cultures are different forms through which an underlying biological substructure can be manifested.

◇ The connecting terms between biology and culture are consciousness and intentionality.

John R. Searle first presented the ideas in *The Construction of Social Reality* as the Immanuel Kant Lectures at Stanford University in 1992. Subsequent versions were presented at various lectures and seminars in the United States and Europe. Searle wrote the book in part as a reaction against an increasingly relativistic view of reality that became popular with many philosophers and social scientists. Searle rejects the view that all of reality is created by humans. That view states that there are no brute facts, but only facts dependent on the human mind. His main purpose in writing this book was to answer the question, "How is a socially constructed reality possible?" Searle says there are things in the world that exist only because people believe them to exist, such as marriage, money, property, and governments; however, many facts regarding these things are objective in the sense that they are not a matter of human preferences, evaluations, or moral attitudes. How, then, do people come to believe them?

Consciousness and Intentionality

Searle begins by stating this fundamental ontology: People live in a world made up entirely of physical particles in fields of force, organized into systems such as planets, mountains, rivers, animals, and humans. Some of these systems are living, and some of these living systems have evolved, through natural selection, nervous systems capable of causing and sustaining consciousness. Consciousness is a physical, biological, and mental feature of humans and certain other animals that can create intentionality. Intentionality is the capacity of the mind to represent, to itself, objects and states of affairs in the world. Many species of animals, especially humans, have a capacity for collective intentionality. This means that they engage in cooperative behavior and, more important, that they share intentional states such as beliefs, desires, and intentions. Searle says that even most forms of human conflict require collective intentionality. Two prize-fighters, opposing litigants in a court battle, or two countries at war with each other are all engaging in cooperative collective behavior at a higher level, within which the antagonistic hostile behavior can take place.

One of Searle's most important and controversial points concerns his distinction between brute facts and institutional facts and the role played by constitutive rules. Brute facts exist independently of any human institutions; they would exist even if humans did not exist. Institutional facts can exist only within human institutions. Constitutive rules are rules that create the very possibility of certain activities. For example, the rules of chess create the very possibility of playing chess. The rules are constitutive of playing chess in the sense that playing chess is constituted in part by acting according to the rules. If one does not play according to at least a large subset of the rules, one is not playing chess. Institutional facts exist only within systems of constitutive rules. Money is an institutional fact because there are certain constitutive rules that govern its existence and use. The fact that the earth is ninety-three million miles from the Sun is a brute fact; it, and all other brute facts, require the institution of language to state the fact, but the distance would remain the same even if there were no humans.

Institutional Facts

Searle describes several important features of institutional facts. First, many social concepts are self-referential; that is, the attitude a person takes toward the phenomenon is partly constitutive of the phenomenon. If someone gives a huge cocktail party at which events become violent and there are many casualties, it is still a cocktail party. Part of an event being a cocktail party is that it is thought to be a cocktail party, just as part of being a war is being thought to be a war. Second, a very large number of institutional facts can be created by explicit performative, or declarative, utterances. Utterances such as "War is hereby declared" and "I now pronounce you husband and wife" create the very state of affairs

that they represent, and in each case the state of affairs is an institutional fact. Third, there can be no institutional facts without brute facts. For example, just about any substance can be money, but money has to exist in some physical form or another. Fourth, an institutional fact cannot exist in isolation but only in a set of systematic relations to other facts. For example, for anyone in a society to have money, that society must have a system of exchanging goods and services for money, and for a system of exchange to exist, the society must have a system of property and property ownership. Fifth, social objects are always constituted by social acts, and, in a sense, the object is simply the continuous possibility of the activity.

Searle describes the process of creation of an institutional fact in a clear and concise manner, using the example of money. First, collective intentionality assigns a new status to some phenomenon, where that status has an accompanying function that cannot be performed solely by virtue of the intrinsic physical feature of the phenomenon in question (there is nothing intrinsically valuable about the green and white pieces of paper that U.S. citizens use as money). This assignment creates an institutional fact. Second, the form of the assignment of the new status function can be represented by the formula "X counts as Y in C": This rectangular sheet of paper (brute fact X) counts as money (institutional fact Y) in the United States (context C). The "counts as" term is crucial: Because the function in question cannot be performed solely in virtue of the physical features of the X element, it requires agreement or acceptance that it be performed. Third, the process of the creation of institutional facts may proceed without the participants being conscious that it is happening according to this form. People may simply think, "This is money" or "This is valuable" without having to think, "We are collectively imposing a value on something that we do not regard as valuable because of its purely physical features." As long as people continue to recognize the X as having the Y function, the institutional fact is created and maintained. Fourth, where the imposition of status function according to the formula becomes a matter of general policy, the formula acquires a normative status and becomes a constitutive rule.

This is shown by the fact that the general rule creates the possibility of abuses that could not exist without the rule, such as counterfeit money. Searle states that the secret to understanding the continued existence of institutional facts is simply that the individuals directly involved and a sufficient number of members of the relevant community must continue to recognize and accept the existence of such facts. Because the status is constituted by its collective acceptance, and because the function, to be performed, requires the status, it is essential to the functioning that there be continued acceptance of the status. For example, at the moment that all or most of the members of a society refuse to acknowledge property rights, as in a revolution, property rights cease to exist in that society.

Language plays an essential role in the creation of institutional facts and thus social reality. Searle says that institutional facts are language dependent because the thoughts that are constitutive of institutional facts are language dependent. This is true for several reasons. First, some thoughts are of such complexity that it would be empirically impossible to think them without being in possession of symbols. Second, language is epistemically necessary. Language is necessary for its naming or labeling function in creating many institutional facts. Third, because institutional facts are inherently social, they must be communicated. If social systems are to function, then the newly created institutional facts must be communicable from one person to another, even when invisible to the naked eye. Fourth, because institutional facts persist through time independently of the duration of the urges and inclinations of the participants in the institution, there must be some way for people to leave a record of institutional facts for those who live in the society later.

Causation

Searle next attempts to answer the question of causation. If the structure of human institutions is a structure of constitutive rules, and the people who are participating in the institutions are not conscious of these rules, what causal role can these rules play in the actual behavior of those who are participating in the institutions? He rejects the idea that people follow rules uncon-

sciously and instead proposes an alternative explanation that he calls the Background. He defines Background as the set of nonintentional or preintentional capacities that enable intentional states of function. By capacities he means abilities, dispositions, tendencies, and causal structures, including neurophysiological causation. The Background enables linguistic and perceptual interpretation to take place, structures consciousness, and disposes people to certain kinds of behavior.

Although the major thrust of Searle's book is development of a general theory of the ontology of social facts and social institutions, he devotes the last three chapters to defending realism and the correspondence conception of truth. Searle believes in "external realism," the view that the world exists independently of human representations of it. Human beings have a variety of interconnected ways of representing features of the world to themselves, including perception, thought, language, beliefs, desires, and pictures. Because these representations are human creations, they are arbitrary. It is possible to have a number of different representations of the same reality. This idea is called "conceptual relativity." Some of these representations purport to represent how things are in reality. They are true if and only if they correspond to the facts in reality. This is the correspondence theory of truth. Actual human efforts to obtain or create true representations of reality are influenced by cultural, economic, and psychological factors. Complete objectivity is difficult, if not impossible, because actual investigations occur within certain cultural and historical contexts.

In this book, Searle builds on theories that he introduced in *Speech Acts: An Essay in the Philosophy of Language* (1969) and *Intentionality: An Essay in the Philosophy of Mind* (1983). One valuable contribution of *The Construction of Social Reality* is that it brings explicit unity to different aspects of Searle's works; however, by far the most important impact of Searle's book resulted from its denunciation of relativism. Many critics welcomed Searle's application of philosophical rigor to the issue of how reality is socially constructed. Even critics of the book, who felt that his hypothesis regarding the logical structure of institutional reality needed further exploration, welcomed his examination of social and cultural objects. Searle describes the philosophical and psychological basis for why and how people confuse physical and symbolic realities in a novel manner.

Karen Anding Fontenot

Additional Reading

Burkhardt, Armin, ed. *Speech Acts, Meaning, and Intentions: Critical Approaches to the Philosophy of John R. Searle*. Berlin: Walter de Gruyter, 1990. A detailed look at Searle's contributions to speech act theory, especially his work on illocutionary logic, intentionality, meaning, and metaphor. Although the book is primarily concerned with Searle's work on speech act theory, the final chapter discusses his work on philosophy of mind and critiques the Chinese room argument.

Lanigan, Richard. *Speech Act Phenomenology*. The Hague: Martinus Nijhoff, 1977. Provides an introduction to the philosophy of human communication that gives a good foundation for studying Searle. This is one of the most comprehensive and in-depth treatments of speech act theory available. It provides useful information but is most suitable for advanced undergraduates.

Lepore, Ernest, and Robert Van Gulick. *John Searle and His Critics*. Oxford, England: Basil Blackwell, 1990. The authors, both philosophy professors, analyze the importance and influence of Searle's work in the philosophy of language and the philosophy of mind. The book provides a thorough analysis of Searle's theories and impact. Each chapter concludes with a summary and a response from Searle himself.

Searle, John R., et al. *(On) Searle on Conversation*. Amsterdam: John Benjamins, 1992. Although Searle is listed as the major author, this book should be considered an excellent secondary source. It consists of eight articles by various scholars critiquing Searle's work on speech acts, with replies by Searle.

Van der Auwera, Johan. *Indirect Speech Acts Revisited*. Antwerp, Belgium: Universiteit Antwerpen, 1980. This is a short (75-page), well-written discussion of Searle's research on indirect speech acts. It is easy to read and understand, and it is useful in that it gives many conversational examples. A good resource for readers not very familiar with speech acts.

Vanderveken, Daniel. *Meaning and Speech Acts*. Cambridge, England: Cambridge University Press, 1990. This book gives a good overall explanation and description of speech act theory. The discussion of Searle's research on illocutionary acts is particularly valuable.

Karen Anding Fontenot

Wilfrid S. Sellars

Sellars is best known for his attack on the "myth of the given," his attempt to synthesize the "manifest" and the "scientific images," and his philosophy of mind.

Principal philosophical works: *Science, Perception, and Reality*, 1963; *Philosophical Perspectives*, 1967; *Science and Metaphysics: Variations on Kantian Themes*, 1968; *Essays in Philosophy and Its History*, 1974; *Naturalism and Ontology*, 1979; *Pure Pragmatics and Possible Worlds: The Early Essays of Wilfrid Sellars*, 1980; *The Metaphysics of Epistemology: Lectures*, 1989; *Empiricism and the Philosophy of Mind*, 1997.

Born: May 20, 1912; Ann Arbor, Michigan
Died: July 2, 1989; Pittsburgh, Pennsylvania

Early Life

Wilfrid Stalker Sellars was the elder of two children born to Roy Wood and Helen Stalker Sellars. His father was a critical realist philosopher who taught at the University of Michigan for many years. Sellars's early life in Ann Arbor was marked by a year spent in New England when he was nine years old, followed by a year in Paris where he attended the *Lycée Montaigne*. Back in Ann Arbor, Sellars attended the high school run by the University's School of Education, where he particularly enjoyed mathematics. After graduation in 1929, Sellars returned to Paris with his mother and sister. He entered the *Lycée Louis le Grand*, where philosophy was in the curriculum and Marxism was in the air. This was Sellars's first contact with philosophy, for he had not discussed philosophy before with his father. He thus began in philosophy as a French Marxist. When his father joined the family in the spring of 1930, father and son finally began the philosophical dialogue that lasted throughout their lives.

After six months studying in Munich, Sellars returned to the United States in 1931, beginning his undergraduate studies at the University of Michigan. He was soon caught up in traditional English-speaking strains of philosophy: the critical realism of his father, the analytical philosophy of Bertrand Russell and G. E. Moore, the work in logic of C. I. Lewis and C. H. Langford. His stud-

ies at the *lycée* enabled Sellars to test of enough courses that he graduated with his cohort in 1933 and moved on to graduate school at Buffalo, New York, where he studied Edmund Husserl and Immanuel Kant with Marvin Farber and wrote a master's thesis on the metaphysics of time in 1934.

Sellars won a Rhodes scholarship to study at Oxford University, where he read for the B.A. in philosophy, politics, and economics at Oriel College with W. G. Maclagan as his tutor and H. A. Prichard and H. H. Price, other significant influences. He took first class honors in 1936 and returned in the fall of that year for a D.Phil., attempting a dissertation on Kant under T. D. Weldon. Unable to bring that enterprise to completion, Sellars returned to the United States in the fall of 1937, undertaking graduate studies at Harvard and passing his prelims in the spring of 1938. He wedded his first wife, Mary, in 1938 as well. Sellars then took a position as assistant professor of philosophy at the University of Iowa, where he was primarily responsible for covering the history of philosophy. During this period, Sellars developed the outlines of the comprehensive view of the history of philosophy that informed his later writing. Sellars never did finish the dissertation at Harvard and was plagued for a number of years by an inability to get his thoughts down on paper. His Oxford M.A. became his last official degree. (Doctoral degrees from Oxford were still relatively uncommon at the time, and the Oxford M.A. was considered a terminal degree.)

World War II interrupted Sellars's academic career. He spent 1943-1946 in the U.S. Navy, first as an instructor in antisubmarine warfare and then in naval air intelligence. Upon release from the Navy, Sellars closeted himself to focus entirely on his writing and, after many drafts (seventeen by his own count), produced his first publishable paper, "Realism and the New Way of Words." This marked a watershed for Sellars, for he had finally discovered a writing process that enabled him to be a productive scholar.

Life's Work

In 1946, Sellars accepted a post as assistant professor at the University of Minnesota, where he rejoined Herbert Feigl, who had originally hired him at Iowa. Having now discovered his writing process, Sellars began publishing steadily. He also undertook several projects that made his name familiar to English-speaking philosophers everywhere: In 1950, Feigl and Sellars founded *Philosophical Studies*, the first journal expressly devoted to analytic philosophy. He and Feigl also published *Readings in Philosophical Analysis* (1949), which quickly became a classic collection of analytic philosophy. Sellars combined with John Hospers to produce *Readings in Ethical Theory* (1952), an equally significant collection for moral theory. Sellars was promoted to professor of philosophy in 1951 and chaired the department at Minnesota from 1952 to 1959, a time that also saw the flowering of the Minnesota Center for the Philosophy of Science.

Perhaps the most fundamental theme in Sellar's philosophy is his commitment to developing a naturalism that is nonetheless rich enough to accommodate without loss the domains of discourse distinctive of metaphysical and normative reflection. This requires combining rationalism's insights into the logical grammar of metaphysical and epistemological predicates with empiricism's rejection of the Platonism typical of rationalism. In his earliest publications, 1947-1954, Sellars recast classical philosophical problems of metaphysics and epistemology in an explicitly linguistic key and, playing off Rudolf Carnap's philosophical semantics, sought to approach these problems by developing a "pure pragmatics" that would analyze the relation of a richly structured language to the world in which it is used. In later years, Sellars sought increasingly to locate and clarify his methods and doctrines by responding to major figures from the history of philosophy, especially Kant.

Another constant theme in his work, coordinate with his naturalism, is scientific realism. Sellars was deeply involved in the Center for the Philosophy of Science while at Minnesota and developed a sophisticated understanding of the nature of scientific theory and its relation to observational evidence and to the broader conceptual framework within which science initially emerges. His belief that the theoretical language or languages of science are grounded in observation without being translatable or reducible to the language of observation became a key insight that served as a model for other nonreductive relationships between domains of discourse.

By 1956, the fundamental principles of Sellars's systematic philosophy were evident in print, with two major essays that dropped some idiosyncrasies of the earliest works and laid out the framework for much of his subsequent thought. In "Some Reflections on Language Games," Sellars developed his account of meaning as functional classification, which enables him to construct a nonreductive but thoroughly nominalistic treatment of meaning in tune with his naturalism. The insights thus garnered were applied in "Empiricism and the Philosophy of Mind," which was quickly recognized as a revolutionary step in philosophy. In this work, he introduced a groundbreaking critique of empiricist foundationalism—a particularly salient form of the myth of the given—and a broadly nonreductive but physicalistic philosophy of mind.

Sellars moved to Yale University as professor of philosophy in 1959. Another watershed for Sellars came shortly thereafter, in 1963: His first book, *Science, Perception, and Reality*, a collection of his most influential essays, was published, as well as his essay in ontology, "Abstract Entities," in which he worked out the details of his theory of meaning and nominalism and first developed the concept of dot-quotation that he subsequently employed to explain his theory. That same year, he also became university professor at the University of Pittsburgh.

Sellars's inaugural lecture at Pittsburgh, "Philosophy and the Scientific Image of Man," provided an overview of his philosophical mission and was reprinted in *Science, Perception, and Reality*. In that piece, he distinguished between the "manifest image," the conceptual framework that has been slowly refined by ages of intellectual labor and in which we are able to encounter ourselves reflectively, and the "scientific image," a conceptual framework that, by postulating imperceptible entities to explain the behavior of perceptible things and thereby revising the basic categorial scheme used by the manifest image, has come to constitute a significant challenge to the manifest image.

These two images, "each of which purports to be a complete picture of man-in-the-world," must somehow be fused into one vision. The scientific image, Sellars argues, must be granted ontological primacy: "In the dimension of describing and explaining the world, science is the measure of what is, that it is, and what is not, that it is not." However, personhood, agency, and the norms constitutive of such concepts do not appear within the scientific image. If we are self-reflective persons, the manifest image—the only point of view from which our personhood appears—must be adjoined to the scientific image. Sellars believes these two images can be unified once we realize that the norms constitutive of personhood are to be analyzed in terms of the most general common intentions of a community, and that the language of community and individual intentions can be joined onto the language of science without conflict.

During his years at Pittsburgh, Sellars elaborated the themes that he had set out by 1963, deepening the levels of analysis and enriching the interconnections among the various parts of his system. He wrote numerous pieces revisiting important figures in the history of philosophy, especially Kant, refining his attack on the given, elaborating his theory of meaning and intentionality, articulating his treatment of action, agency, and the mind-body problem, and treating fundamental issues of ontology. He was also a very productive supervisor of doctoral degree students and continued as editor of *Philosophical Studies* until 1975. Slowed by a stroke in 1984, he continued teaching until his death in 1989.

Sellars visited numerous universities during his career and gave a number of distinguished lecture series, including the John Locke Lectures at Oxford (1965-1966), the Matchette Foundation Lectures (1971), the John Dewey Lectures at the University of Chicago (1973-1974), the Paul Carus Lectures for the American Philosophical Association (1977-1978), and the Ernst Cassirer Lectures at Yale in 1979. Sellars served as president of the Eastern Division of the American Philosophical Association in 1970-1971.

Influence

Sellars revolutionized several aspects of philosophy, but he has not always been given full credit for everything he accomplished. For example, he has long been known for his attack on the given in "Empiricism and the Philosophy of Mind," but that essay also contains the first clearly functionalistic treatment of intentional states, well before Hilary Putnam's essays, which are usually credited with being the first to contain this treatment. Although he was among the fathers of functionalist philosophy of mind, Sellars did not fall prey to its excesses: He was never attracted to a narrow machine functionalism, and from the very beginning, he was aware that sensations need a very different treatment from intentional states. He sought on numerous occasions to argue that reconciling sensations with the physical sciences would prove such a challenge that physics would ultimately have to make a special accommodation for them, treating sensations as basic entities in their own right. Thus Sellars also anticipated the resurgence of interest in the 1990's in the "hard problem" of consciousness.

Sellars's essays, each of which went through a tortuous process of repeated revision, have a reputation for being very dense and difficult to understand, though those who attempt them seriously find them to be profound, subtle, and richly rewarding. He is a thoroughly systematic philosopher. As deep and complex as each essay might be, it reveals only a small piece of a much larger picture that must be pursued in numerous other difficult essays to be fully understood. He was, however, a brilliant lecturer and teacher who inspired many students who have gone on to introduce their own students to this penetrating thinker. While the complexity and extent of Sellars's philosophy have discouraged some, for many others, his philosophy has provided a sophisticated framework within which to work out further issues or against which to elaborate alternative positions.

Willem A. deVries

Science, Perception, and Reality

Type of philosophy: Epistemology, metaphysics, philosophy of language
First published: 1963
Principal ideas advanced:

◇ Naturalism is ontologically monistic (every existent is an element in the causal fabric of space-time) but linguistically pluralistic (there are many dimensions to our linguistic and conceptual activity, dimensions that we sometimes misunderstand as representing different realms of reality).

◇ The "manifest image," the conceptual framework in which humans become capable of reflecting on themselves, gives birth to the "scientific image," a framework in which newly conceived microentities are postulated to explain the behavior of sensible objects.

◇ The scientific image possesses ultimate ontological authority; however, certain aspects of the manifest image—namely, the action-oriented language of intentions and norms—cannot be duplicated in the scientific image and need to be preserved by being adjoined thereto.

◇ Platonism, or a belief in the independent existence of abstract entities, results from taking at face value sentences that are really disguised metalinguistic assertions about the formal features of linguistic expressions.

◇ Meaning statements do not express "relations" between expressions and special entities called "meanings"; they classify expressions functionally by exhibiting another expression (in the language of the speaker) that plays the same linguistic role.

◇ Traditional empiricist conceptions of concept acquisition and the structure of justification—the "entire framework of givenness"—are erroneous; instead, there exists a complex interplay of internalist and externalist factors that

is significantly coherentist without losing causal, sensory contact with the world.

◇ Psychological language is modeled on semantical language; concepts of the psychological and intentional are modeled on concepts of the semantical.

◇ Knowledge of the psychological neither is derived from nor is a form of direct "acquaintance" in which mental states are given in their intrinsic nature.

◇ Sensory states of organisms differ in kind from intentional states and cannot be given a functionalistic treatment; to preserve physicalism, the natural sciences must recognize the sensory among the fundamental ontological elements of the world.

This volume collects a number of significant essays that Wilfrid S. Sellars wrote between 1951 and 1962. These essays explore topics in metaphysics and epistemology and give a good picture of Sellars's philosophical system in these areas, but they do not exhaust the range or depth of his thought. Sellars is reacting in part against the logical empiricism that dominated the American philosophical scene at the time. There is a Kantian flavor to his response to empiricism, distinguishing between the (strictly speaking, phenomenal) realm of the conceptual, normative, and social and the realm of causal, physical reality. However, Sellars accommodates the insights of the rationalists and idealists without abandoning his naturalism by treating the conceptual and social as normatively constituted dimensions of human activity that supervene on the physical. The opening essay, "Philosophy and Scientific Image of Man" remains the best statement of Sellars's philosophical mission, and "Empiricism and the Philosophy of Mind" is still his most influential work.

Manifest and Scientific Images

Sellars's view of the philosophical enterprise is extremely liberal: namely, that it is the attempt to "understand how things in the broadest possible sense of the term hang together in the broadest possible sense of the term." Yet he pinpoints the principal challenge facing philosophy: Though we have come to understand the world by employing a conceptual framework called the "manifest image," itself a dynamic structure of concepts and categories that has been and continues to be revised in the light of experience, this framework engenders a rival, the "scientific image," enriched by the explicit postulation of unobservable microentities. The two images are not straightforwardly compatible. Each claims completeness-in-principle, but they disagree both about ontology (the basic entities in the world) and about ideology (the basic properties exemplified by basic entities). Sellars argues that the scientific image is, in matters of ontology, authoritative and will displace the manifest image in that regard. However, the ideology of science is confined to those aspects of the world relevant to causal explanation, whereas the ideology of the manifest image also includes normatively constituted, action-oriented or (in the Kantian sense) practical concepts. This other dimension can be joined to the scientific image in a synoptic vision.

The Intentional and Sensory

Sellars's underlying theme is unifying the scientific image of humans as complex structures of microphysical entities with our self-understanding as cognitive and moral agents. This requires developing a theory of the nature of the cognitive and the practical and their relation to the physical. Sellars does not deal significantly with the moral as such in *Science, Perception, and Reality*, leaving that topic for other works. His theory of the relation of the cognitive to the physical is sophisticated and left a lasting mark in philosophy. According to Sellars, a theory of cognition requires two parts: a theory of the intentional or conceptual, and a theory of the sensory. The *locus classicus* for Sellars's discussion of these issues is "Empiricism and the Philosophy of Mind," but the other essays in this volume augment these ideas.

An adequate theory of the intentional and its relation to the physical must overcome the errors of both rationalism and empiricism. The rationalists had sound insight into the logical, normative structure of the intentional realm but tended to understand the intentional in terms of relations to abstract entities. This Platonizing tendency is not consistent with a thoroughgoing naturalism. The empiricists tended to nominalism but assimilated the intentional to the sensory. Both accepted the "myth of the given"—the belief that there are certain states of a human, the natural properties of which fully determine its epistemic status without regard for its epistemic relations to other states. Most commonly, this myth has adopted the form that our own mental states are known to us directly, "by acquaintance."

In "Empiricism and the Philosophy of Mind," Sellars attacks this conception on several fronts. He argues that there are persistent, unresolved tensions in sense-datum theories of knowledge, that appearance theories mistake the grammar of "looks" statements, and that abstractionist theories of concept acquisition are circular. He further proposes an anti-Platonist theory of meaning *cum* theory of concept acquisition and claims that the cognitive has a normative dimension that renders it irreducible to natural fact.

Sellars proposes, positively, that a subject, S, knows observationally that p only if S is disposed spontaneously to report that p, S's disposition is a reliable symptom that p, and S knows that S's disposition is a reliable symptom that p—an analysis of perceptual knowledge that prefigures externalist themes that emerged elsewhere only a decade later yet retains a significant commitment to internalism.

A Theory of Knowledge

Sellars then proposes, via a "countermyth," a theory of our knowledge of the mental that is consonant with his theory of direct, perceptual knowledge. Sellars hypothesizes a community of proto-persons who possess a language for public objects with the basic logical operators and structures (especially the subjunctive conditional), including semantical discourse (for example, meaning-and truth-predicates) but lacking any psychological vocabulary. In Sellars's myth, the folk hero Jones proceeds to add psychological vocabulary to the language in order to explain certain complex kinds of human behavior. Jones uses two different models in extending his language. To explain how humans can exhibit intelligent action even when not accompanying their behavior with overt speech, Jones postulates "inner speech" that is modeled on overt language (in that it has structure and content) and is causally responsible for overt speech and for guiding action. Call this "thought." To explain how humans can sincerely engage in behavior appropriate to the observation of objects or conditions that do not obtain, Jones postulates internal sensory states modeled on the objects or conditions that typically cause them. These sensory states, or sense impressions, can occasionally occur in nonstandard ways, say, in a perceptual illusion.

Having adopted this fruitful new theory of behavior, Jones and his comrades become able to apply it directly—that is, noninferentially—to each other and, most particularly, to themselves. This enables them to make first-person reports of their inner mental lives without using any theoretical, inferential machinery. This countermyth undermines the Cartesian principles that we must know our own minds first and best, and that mental states must inhere in a nonphysical substance.

The essays other than "Philosophy and Scientific Image of Man" and "Empiricism and the Philosophy of Mind" all relate to some part of this general line of argument. "Being and Being Known" and "Truth and Correspondence" focus on the difference between the intentional order and the natural, causal order and on the importance of a *picturing* relation within the causal order between symbols and reality, a relation that must be distinguished from semantic signification or designation, which always remains within the intentional order. "Phenomenalism" develops Sellars's attack on phenomenalistic metaphysics and epistemologies. "The Language of Theories" details his analysis of theoretical constructs and outlines his scientific realism and the phenomenality of the manifest image. "Naming and Saying," an interpretation of Ludwig Wittgenstein's "Logisch-philosophische Abhandlung" (1921; best known by the bilingual German and English edition title of *Tractatus Logico-Philosophicus*, 1922, 1961), "Grammar and Existence: A Preface to Ontology," and "Particulars" all contribute to the defense of Sellars's nominalism. "Is There a Synthetic Apriori?" and "Some Reflections on Language Games" both elaborate Sellars's theory of meaning. His idea is that meaning is determined by an expression's functional role in a complex linguistic economy and that semantical statements such as "*Rot* (in German) means *red*" convey information about the similarity of role of the two expressions involved without explicitly *stating* that they are similar or *describing* the role they play. This idea is important both to his defense of nominalism and to his explication of the nature of intentional states.

Sellars's Impact

Science, Perception, and Reality left a significant mark on twentieth century Anglo-American and German philosophy. Sellars's distinction between the manifest image and the scientific image is widely known, and the phrases have acquired a life of their own in the literature. Sellars is widely credited with a major assault on the myth of the given in "Empiricism and the Philosophy of Mind," though there is disagreement about the exact nature of his argument. Sellars's assault, together with W. V. O. Quine's attack in "Two Dogmas of Empiricism" (1951), was principally responsible for foundationalist epistemology's falling into disfavor in the last half of the twentieth century.

Less universally acknowledged, but no less significant, is Sellars's tremendous influence on the philosophy of mind. He is properly given credit for developing a functionalist treatment of intentional states as a middle path between logical behaviorism and type-identity theories of mind. He also anticipated the criticisms of functionalist treatments of sensation that were raised against the generalization of functionalism. His own treatment of the sensory has found fewer adherents, however.

Other significant figures in late twentieth century philosophy, such as Robert Brandom and John McDowell, find inspiration in various Sellarsian doctrines, including his inferential theory of meaning and his insistence that semantical and epistemic concepts are normative and practical concepts are properly located in the "logical space of reasons."

Sellars is also responsible for several ideas developed by others into philosophical positions that he himself would not accept. For instance, Sellars originally developed the notion of a language of thought, or "Mentalese," to flesh out his claim that our concepts of the mental are a transposition of semantical concepts into a new key, but he would not accept the idea that Mentalese is an innate, unlearned language, as Jerry Fodor has argued. Sellars's comparison of psychological concepts to theoretical concepts led some, notably Richard Rorty, Paul M. Churchland, and Patricia Churchland, to claim that such folk psychology is not only a theory, but a bad theory—one that will, with the development of science, be eliminated in favor of a more directly neurophysiological theory.

Willem A. deVries

Additional Reading

Bernstein, Richard J. "Sellars' Vision of Man-in-the-Universe." *Review of Metaphysics* 20 (1965-1966): 113-143, 290-312. An extensive critical review of Wilfrid S. Sellars's book, still an excellent, lucid exposition of Sellars's thought.

Castañeda, H-N., ed. *Action, Knowledge, and Reality*. Indianapolis, Ind.: Bobbs- Merrill, 1975. A collection of articles examining aspects of Sellars's philosophy as well as his "Autobiographical Reflections" and "The Structure of Knowledge." Includes an extensive bibliography of Sellars's publications.

Delaney, C. F., Michael J. Loux, Gary Gutting, and W. David Solomon. *The Synoptic Vision: Essays on the Philosophy of Wilfrid Sellars*. Notre Dame, Ind.: University of Notre Dame Press, 1977. Notre Dame philosophy faculty examine aspects of Sellars's work. A highly readable complete general overview of the philosopher's system.

Pitt, Joseph C., ed. *The Philosophy of Wilfrid Sellars: Queries and Extensions*. Dordrecht, Holland: D. Reidel, 1978. Revised proceedings of a workshop on the philosophy of Sellars held at Virginia Polytechnic Institute and State University, Blacksburg, Virginia, in November, 1976. The essays focus principally on Sellars's philosophy of science and philosophy of language, but two deal with his views on practical inference and altruism.

_____. *Pictures, Images, and Conceptual Change: An Analysis of Wilfrid Sellars' Philosophy of Science*. Dordrecht, Holland: D. Reidel, 1981. A thorough treatment of Sellars's philosophy of science.

Rosenberg, Jay F. "Wilfrid Sellars' Philosophy of Mind." In *Philosophy of Mind*. Vol. 4 in *Contemporary Philosophy*, edited by Guttorm Floistad. The Hague: Martinus Nijhoff, 1983. A general exposition of Sellars's philosophy of mind by one of his leading expositors.

_____. "The Place of Color in the Scheme of Things: A Roadmap to Sellars' Carus Lectures." *The Monist* 65 (1982): 315-335. An intelligible study of Sellars's controversial treatment of sensory states.

Seibt, Johanna. *Properties as Processes: A Synoptic Study of Wilfrid Sellars's Nominalism*. Atascadero, Calif.: Ridgeview, 1990. An explication and defense of Sellars' nominalism.

Vinci, Thomas C. *Cartesian Truth*. New York: Oxford University Press, 1998. A look at how science and metaphysics are closly interwoven in the work of Descartes.

Willem A. deVries

Tsenay Serequeberhan

Employing intellectual tools fashioned by phenomenology, existentialism, and, especially, hermeneutics, Serequeberhan sought to articulate a postcolonial African philosophy rooted in the "lived experience" of African political liberation.

Principal philosophical works: "The Idea of Colonialism in Hegel's Philosophy of Right," 1989; *The Eritrean People's Liberation Front: A Case Study in the Rhetoric and Practice of African Liberation*, 1989; *The Hermeneutics of African Philosophy: Horizon and Discourse*, 1994; "Reflections on *In My Father's House*," 1996.

Born: May 18, 1952; Tehran, Iran

Early Life

Tsenay Serequeberhan has a dual parentage, natural and political. He is the son of his father, Serequeberhan Gebrezgi, and his mother, Assegedetch Aradom; however, Serequeberhan is also the child of Eritrea's protracted struggle for freedom and self-determination. Less than four months after his birth, Eritrea, on September 11, 1952, was federated with Ethiopia, largely as a result of the geopolitical interests of the United States. The union was not one of equals. The Ethiopian regime, under Emperor Haile Selassie, repeatedly violated the terms of the federal agreement. Finally, on November 14-15, 1962, Eritrea was annexed and made a province of Ethiopia.

Resistance to Ethiopian domination and movements for Eritrean liberation began even before the 1962 annexation. During the early and mid-1950's, students became increasingly militant, partly in conjunction with armed liberation movements such as the Eritrean Liberation Movement (ELM), established in 1958, and the Eritrean Liberation Front (ELF), formed in 1961. Secondary school students, including Serequeberhan, were often involved in protests and demonstrations. The ideological orientation of the activists became increasingly Marxist, especially after the demise of the ELM and the subsequent splintering of the ELF and its ultimate replacement by the Eritrean People's Liberation Front (EPLF) in the early 1970's.

However, Serequeberhan pursued a philosophical rather than directly political path. He left Eritrea to continue his education in the United States, a center of overseas Eritrean activism. He received a bachelor of arts degree in political science from the University of Massachusetts at Boston in 1979. His undergraduate specialization suggests the continuation of his early Eritrean political focus, as does his membership in the Eritrean Mass Association for Independence. However, events in Ethiopia during the late 1970's hinted at the difficulties of a strictly Marxist approach. The Haile Selassie regime had been overthrown in 1974 by the Provisional Military Advisory Committee, called the Derg. A period of chaos ensued, ending in February, 1977, with a coup led by Mengistu Haile Mariam. Mengistu, employing massive military aid from the Soviet Union, attacked and scattered the EPLF, which had been on the verge of success in Eritrea. A Soviet-backed Marxist regime in Ethiopia had decided that a Marxist-oriented liberation movement in Eritrea was no longer "progressive."

Life's Work

Serequeberhan's change in focus from political science to philosophy signaled the start of his search for intellectual foundations to assist in the support of African political liberation. Political developments in Eritrea, Ethiopia, and other African nations during the 1970's and early 1980's revealed the limitations of Marxism as a political philosophy. Marxism was European in its origins and Eurocentric in its outlook. It was abstract and "totalizing" in its social, economic, and political analyses, dogmatic in its philosophical presuppositions, and deeply involved in superpower rivalries and the Cold War. Despite its faults, for Serequeberhan and many other African political intellectuals Marxism remained of some use, especially in its emancipatory aspirations and its critical, dialectical approach. However, it was far more modern European than African and therefore more neocolonial than postcolonial.

Serequeberhan's first attempts to develop an African political philosophy consistent with indigenous liberation movements occurred within the context of African philosophy. When Serequeberhan began his graduate work in philosophy at Boston College in about 1980, African philosophy fell into two categories: ethnophilosophy and professional philosophy. Broadly speaking, ethnophilosophers were Christian missionaries and their African students who understood philosophy in terms of traditional African religion; professional philosophers were Marxists for whom philosophy was to be scientific. To the minds of Serequeberhan and some other young African philosophers, this debate was both anachronistic and irrelevant to contemporary African realities. It was repeating, to no useful purpose, the nineteenth century European argument between religion and science. Implicitly, the terms of the debate merely relegated Africa and Africans to philosophical nonexistence.

These critical considerations squarely pose Serequeberhan's problem: How—that is, in what terms—is Africa to have philosophical existence? The answer that he returns is deceptively simple (and therefore requires some extended discussion): Africa is to have philosophical existence in terms of existence. Which is to say that Africa is to have philosophical existence in terms of post-Nietzschean philosophies of experience, existence, and historicity. Also, Africa is to have philosophical existence through (reflection on) the practical process of liberation from colonial and neocolonial subjection. In other words, Africa will move from nonexistence (or dependent existence) to (autonomous or self-determining) existence by "making itself" in the process of "making history." This history—or more accurately, these *histories*—will be political, and the existence that

they provide will be both historical and philosophical. The comprehensive process, therefore, will be "historical African political philosophies."

In the early 1980's, Serequeberhan began the detailed studies required for the realization of this ambitious philosophical project. He drew primarily on historical/philosophical and contemporary/political sources. He worked with an eye toward demonstrating the partial utility of continental European thought for the predicament of neocolonial Africa. He was convinced that Africa must liberate itself, but he grasped the important truth that the twentieth century European thinkers Edmund Husserl, Martin Heidegger, and Hans-Georg Gadamer were, on balance, philosophical supporters of the African cause.

Husserl (phenomenology), Heidegger (existentialism), and Gadamer (hermeneutics) have, as far as Serequeberhan is concerned, one most fundamental lesson to teach. That lesson is that any philosophical doctrine or system is rooted in and limited by the "existential" (the historico-linguistic) situation of the philosopher. In terms first articulated by Friedrich Nietzsche, elaborated by Gadamer, and adopted by Serequeberhan, that existential situation is the philosopher's horizon. The horizon is determined by one's standpoint or viewpoint; it is literally "as far as one can see." No standpoint is nonsituational; therefore, every horizon is limited, no matter what the viewer, the theorist may claim.

Given this insight into the relation between philosophy and existence, Serequeberhan worked through two implications. First, European philosophy could not possibly live up to any claims to universal or absolute truth. Especially, Hegelian or Marxist claims to grasp the "meaning of history" and thus to end it (on European terms) are necessarily spurious. To the extent to which all schools of African philosophy implicitly operated within a European framework (and Serequeberhan became convinced that they did), these schools became an unconscious, ironic affirmation of European hegemony and neocolonialism. However, Africans could be free if they took post-Nietzschean philosophy seriously.

The second implication is the positive practical corollary of the first. Africans could not liberate or create themselves by merely studying post-Nietzschean European philosophy. Instead, they

1771

had to practice—act out—that philosophy. If liberation is active existence, then African liberation requires African action.

Given this necessity for action, for Serequeberhan, the word "source" acquired a different meaning, one that is both fuller and deeper that its use in European contexts. European sources are textual, and although African sources are becoming textual, they nevertheless remain closer to the underlying experiences. Because Africans are in the process of making history, African philosophers are simultaneously African activists. With this understanding, Serequeberhan investigated the "thoughtful activism" (or "activist thinking") of twentieth century philosopher-revolutionaries Amilcar Cabral and Frantz Fanon.

The practical revolutionary work and writings of Cabral (in Guinea-Bissau and Cape Verde) and Fanon (in Algeria) posed this question for Serequeberhan: What is specifically *African* liberation? In other words, in what ways do the past, present, and projected historical experiences of Africans differentiate them from other "social entities"—peoples, classes, genders, believers, and so forth—who have been suppressed and have desired the self-realization dependent upon freedom?

Gradually and creatively, Serequeberhan grasped the relationship of two ideas from Fanon and two from Cabral and began to weave them together into the outlines of a broad historical-political-philosophical process. Fanon contributed these ideas: First, Africans had been very thoroughly "colonized," especially to the extent to which middle-class Africans had been "assimilated" to European habits by formal education; second, this colonization of body, mind, and spirit had rendered the African a "thing" devoid of "internal" humanity. Although Fanon had died at an early age, Cabral had lived to see the liberation process develop further in his homeland; accordingly, his ideas were more hopeful and positive. Cabral understood that revolutionary intellectuals were committed to liberation but very abstract in their thinking. Sensitivity to particular practical circumstances was needed. First, the leaders needed to turn away from universalistic modern European thought-ways and to "return to the source," the ordinary, far less indoctrinated African. Second, sustained contact with

these Africans, especially those in the countryside, permitted the spiritual reconversion—in Cabral's term the "re-Africanization"—of the urban intellectual.

These four concepts—colonization, thingification, return to the source, and re-Africanization—outlined for Serequeberhan the specifically African liberation process. The articulation of this process and of its philosophical foundations in the "lived experience" of existential phenomenology and the "horizons" of hermeneutics is of course a matter of academic philosophy. Executing this broad and original synthesis occupied Serequeberhan throughout the remainder of the 1980's and the early 1990's. He earned his doctorate in philosophy from Boston College in 1988 with a dissertation entitled "The Possibility of African Freedom: A Philosophical Exploration." This dissertation served as the basis of Serequeberhan's influential work *The Hermeneutics of African Philosophy: Horizon and Discourse*. In the period between the dissertation and publication of that book, he edited the important collection *African Philosophy: The Essential Readings* (1991) and published or presented numerous philosophical papers.

Husband of Nuhad Jamal and father of sons Nesim-Netssere and Awate-Hayet, Serequeberhan would teach philosophy, African philosophy, and African studies at Boston College, the University of Massachusetts at Boston, Hampshire College, Simmons College, and Brown University. Throughout his career, writing as an African philosophically concerned with African autonomy, he would produce writings on African politics, particularly issues concerning Eritrea.

Following the setbacks of the late 1970's, Eritrea's EPLF had followed a course similar to and partially inspired by Cabral's Partido Africano da Independencia da Guine e Cabo Verde (PAIGC). EPLF's long-term "strategic retreat" during the 1980's had resulted in a PAIGC-like moderation of Marxist ideology and closeness to the common people. The result was strong, deep support for Eritrean independence. Military successes in 1988 and 1991 led to the collapse of Mengistu's Derg, the transformation of EPLF into the Provisional Government of Eritrea, and in a referendum held on April 23-25, 1993, a 99.8 percent vote for Eritrean independence. The liberation struggle, which effectively began in the year of Serequeberhan's birth, thus ended. Overseas Eritreans began to return home, to assist in addressing the problems of nationhood. In 1999, Serequeberhan began his association with the Research and Documentation Center of the People's Front for Democracy and Justice, Asmara, Eritrea.

Influence

In 1998, about five years after publication of *The Hermeneutics of African Philosophy* and about ten years after the research on which it was based, Serequeberhan published an article entitled "Africanity at the End of the Twentieth Century." In it, he argued that African identity or "Africanity" is a work in progress, of which formal political liberation is only a first step. African existence, in Eritrea and most other African nations, remains a struggle, in Serequeberhan's opinion, for that mass-participatory political and economic democracy necessary for complete humanity.

By the age of forty-seven, Serequeberhan had brilliantly exploited the political potential of European philosophy. He turned existential and hermeneutical philosophy away from universality and toward historicity and particularity. Serequeberhan demonstrated, through his study of leaders such as Cabral and Fanon and movements such as PAIGC and EPLF, that postcolonial African historicity is explicitly political.

Serequeberhan thus helped to open the way for the development of African political philosophy. This philosophy, as envisioned by Serequeberhan, is political because it issues forth from the continuing struggle against neocolonialism and creates a positive African identity that is not a mere negation of Europeanization. However, Serequeberhan cautioned against not only a universal but also a continent-wide political philosophy. Instructed by European classicists such as Gadamer and modern Africans such as Cabral, Serequeberhan had become well aware that many of the sources of African identity are particular and that identity is forged in emerging nationhood. His own "existential" return to Eritrea at the end of the twentieth century suggests a move toward developing Eritrean political philosophy.

John F. Wilson

The Hermeneutics of African Philosophy

Horizon and Discourse

Type of philosophy: African philosophy, epistemology, ethics, political philosophy
First published: 1994
Principal ideas advanced:

◇ The philosophical task at hand is to elaborate a radical hermeneutics of contemporary African philosophy.

◇ A hermeneutical approach reveals that the "horizon," or implicit framework, of the major schools of African philosophy is neocolonial.

◇ Because both "discourses" are neocolonial, neither the particularistic antiquarianism of "ethnophilosophy" nor the abstract universalism of "professional philosophy" provides an adequate ground for African liberation.

◇ For liberation to occur, the interrupted historicity of African experience must be reclaimed and resumed.

◇ That historicity is being reestablished through African liberation movements, which are often violent reactions to European colonial violence.

◇ These movements, to be successful, must "fuse" the "horizons" of Europeanized urban intellectuals and the deeper African "source," the common country folk.

◇ This fusion constitutes the hermeneutics of the "lived situation" of contemporary Africans and leads to the development of autonomous political communities.

A distinction, initially very sharp but progressively less distinct, must be drawn between the philosophical and the political contexts of *The Hermeneutics of African Philosophy*. Philosophically, the context is an academic struggle between approaches to "African philosophy." Specifically, an "ethnophilosophical" orientation, which researched and elaborated "traditional African wisdom," generated an opposition by "professional philosophy." Professional philosophers, working in the Marxist and neo-Marxist traditions, emphasized a "scientific"—quantitative, technical, and historico-materialistic—approach to reality.

1773

The political context is African decolonization. After the European powers withdrew, willingly or otherwise, the immediate euphoria of independence gave way to a growing awareness of Africa's subordinate status. A connection was soon made, especially by professional philosophers, between a continuing colonialism and the nonscientific, religious psychology attributed to Africans by ethnophilosophers. Conversely, the "scientific" philosophers saw their own views as progressive. However, as self-proclaimed Marxist regimes came to power across the continent and, at best, imposed Western notions of "development" on Africans, a third generation of African philosophers began to suspect that the "scientists" were themselves neocolonial. Tsenay Serequeberhan is a leading member of that third generation.

The structure of *The Hermeneutics of African Philosophy* is as follows. After a relatively short introduction and before a brief conclusion, the book is divided into four quite distinct chapters. The first chapter interprets the contemporary historical situation in Africa as neocolonial, the second conducts a lengthy critique of the schools of African philosophy, the third considers the situation of the colonized in Africa, especially in terms of violence and counterviolence, and the fourth discusses contemporary liberation movements, including the political thought associated with them, as the "lived historicity" of postcolonial Africa. Overall, the movement of the text is from neocolonial to postcolonial, from subordination to liberation, and from the "horizon" of the old discourse to that of the new.

Hermeneutics

Like any philosophical work, *The Hermeneutics of African Philosophy* is most fundamentally conceptual and definitional. The leading concept is that of "hermeneutics." Following philosophers Martin Heidegger and Hans-Georg Gadamer, Serequeberhan understands hermeneutics, or interpretation, as the most characteristic human activity. Those things that are distinctly human are not given to us directly. Instead, they must be understood within a (largely implicit or unspoken) context. In any given situation, that context is our "horizon." The "situatedness" of any and all horizons constitutes their "historicity." It fol-

lows that, for human beings, "to know" is to understand "hermeneutically" and "historically." Further, because all knowledge is given symbolically, usually linguistically, understanding occurs in and among human communities. Any other claims to knowledge—individual, transcendental, absolute, and so forth—are based on insufficient reflection concerning the conditions of knowing.

To understand hermeneutically the "discourse" of African philosophy, then, is to place it within its "horizon." This placement requires, according to Serequeberhan, the use of another hermeneutic concept, "misunderstanding." Despite its name, misunderstanding is helpful because it sets hermeneutics in motion and engages its interpretative powers. In the African situation, it is "liberation" and "freedom" that are misunderstood. Instead of being representations of reality, where "freedom" means genuine self-determination, these terms are "estranged." That is, they do not reflect the lived experience that gave rise to them originally. In contemporary African discourse, "independence" obscures what Serequeberhan bitingly calls the "lethargic inertness of neocolonialism."

This interpretation establishes the horizon of African philosophy as neocolonial. However, it is important first to identify the ground of Serequeberhan's interpretation. That ground is experiential; the experiences in question are, above all, those of ordinary Africans. They know that they are not free because the dimensions of freedom do not include being brutally oppressed, starved, and murdered. Serequeberhan pulls no punches here. He regards many, perhaps most African regimes as criminally incompetent—an incompetence resulting from their dependence on outside powers rather than their own people. Simply put, African rulers have not been required to govern well because they have been able to survive while barely governing at all.

"Ethnophilosophers" and "Scientists"

For Serequeberhan, African philosophy reflects this dependent, neocolonial political situation. Like African governing elites, African philosophers are dependent on external "sources." For the "particularistic antiquarianism" of the missionary ethnophilosophers, including Placide

Tempels, Alexis Kagame, and John Mbiti, that source is ultimately colonial Christianity. For the "abstract, scientific universalism" of, above all, Kwame Nkrumah and Paulin J. Hountondji, the source is neocolonial Marxism-Leninism.

Serequeberhan interprets and critiques these views at length, especially those of the authoritarian, developmentally oriented "scientists." The most extended and interesting criticism, however, is of Leopold Sedar Senghor, the Senegalese poet, philosopher, and statesman. Although Serequeberhan considers Senghor's views to be basically ethnophilosophical, he acknowledges that Senghor's "essentialist particularism" is not identical to the particularistic antiquarianism of the missionaries. In plainer language, the ethnophilosophers are discussing traditionally religious Africans; Senghor views Africans in terms that are contemporary, existential, humanistic, and communal. Certainly, Senghor does contend—although quite noncontentiously—that there is an essence to "Africanity." However, the issue, for Serequeberhan, is whether Senghor's construction of African identity/character is other than an implicit, unconscious acceptance of European racism. This racism, Serequeberhan charges, inclines Senghor to characterize Africans as intuitive rather than analytical, mystical not empirical, and so forth. For Serequeberhan, these characterizations confuse historical contingencies with essences and thus are neocolonial.

As mentioned, the tone of Senghor's writing is mild, tolerant, even gentle. It is in sharp contrast to both the tone and substance of Frantz Fanon's work, which Serequeberhan considers in discussing violence in the third major section of *The Hermeneutics of African Philosophy*. Because, as Serequeberhan points out, a discussion of violence is unusual in a philosophical work, Fanon's argument must be examined very carefully.

"Thingification"
The important hermeneutical concept of "historicity" is central here. The historicity, or the social-historical Being, of African peoples was violently interrupted by the European incursions. In other words, European violence and subsequent colonization violently interrupted the very temporal existence of Africans. In a colonized situation, Africans ceased to make, and thus to have, their own history. They became, to use Fanon's (and Aimé Césaire's) term, "thingified"—that is, mere biological organisms stripped of those history-making activities that make us human *beings*.

For "de-thingification" to occur and interrupted African history (or histories) to resume, colonial violence must be countered by decolonizing violence. Serequeberhan is understandably equivocal in arguing the case for counterviolence. The colonized do not choose violence; it is a condition of existence imposed upon them by the colonizer and by the very nature of the decolonizing "historical process" itself. The process of colonization and decolonization is violent. However, it appears that virtually all of European philosophy and European history is also violent. Then, does violence begin and end with "Europe"? Or, is all history, and therefore all peoples who would make history and thus possess historicity, similarly violent? In other words, contrary to many of the premises of hermeneutics, is there a universal (violent) "human nature," which is the condition (and price) for possessing "historical human Being"?

Serequeberhan does not explicitly raise these traditional, difficult questions of (Western) political philosophy. Situationally, African liberation necessarily requires violence; Senghor's "subordinate passivity" freezes Africans into an ahistorical, neocolonial existence.

Liberation
The question of liberation, discussed in the fourth and final major section, begins with consideration of the fundamental "fracture" in neocolonial African societies. That fracture is between Europeanized urban intellectuals and professionals and the rural peasant and nomad masses that have been subjected to but have not internalized European control.

Both of these groups have become historically disabled, but the condition of the Westernized African is considerably more impaired. The rural people have merely had their indigenous histories interrupted by colonialism. For the most part, they are frozen in time. However, the urban intellectuals have more or less willingly adopted an external, alien history as their own. They are thus further from indigenous "sources" than the "uneducated masses" are. Nevertheless, the educated urbanites have the advantage of extensive familiarity with the modern "outside" world to which all contemporary Africans must adjust.

The differing perspectives of rural and urban Africans might be understood as "ethnophilosophy" and "professional philosophy," respectively; and their conjunction as a "synthesis" of the perspectives. However, Serequeberhan resists this interpretation, and not only because he understands both perspectives as neocolonial. He presents a lengthy passage from the French philosopher Michel Foucault, in which Foucault argues that "liberation" properly understood requires the "practices of liberty" in political society. Overcoming the fracture between rural and urban, traditional and modern is a matter of political practice and not (merely) philosophical argumentation. In fact, the latter—because it must be done by urban intellectuals—would privilege professional philosophy and thus perpetuate elitism.

Given this fundamental understanding, Serequeberhan discusses African "repair," the healing of the fracture, in terms both practical and hermeneutical. The "horizons" of urban activists and rural peoples must be "fused." However, the fusion is primarily the acceptance by intellectuals of the viewpoint of the common people. This is not because that viewpoint is traditional and ethnophilosophical, but instead for two political reasons. The first is that ordinary Africans entertain no illusions that they are "liberated," given their "post"-colonial experiences. The second is even more fundamental. The rural "horizon" is relatively unobscured by colonialism. Rural people thus have a greater practical understanding of their interrupted political autonomy and historicity.

Amilcar Cabral's terms of "re-Africanization" and "return to the source," then, acquire a considerably deeper meaning, given Serequeberhan's hermeneutics. The source is not merely the common people and their Africanity, and the return is not merely an extended stay in the countryside. Instead, the common people and Africanity themselves have a source. It is, Serequeberhan believes, the deepest existential, historical ground—the ethical wholeness that accompanies political autonomy. In other words, fusion, while it occurs historically and provides historicity, is after all ethical and political.

Deconstruction and Reconstruction

The Hermeneutics of African Philosophy concludes with a brief but important discussion of the distinction between the "deconstructive" and "reconstructive" challenges facing African philosophers. Deconstructively, the last residues of colonialism must be eliminated. For Serequeberhan, this requires that both of the traditional types of African philosophy—ethnophilosophy and professional philosophy—be treated hermeneutically and revealed as neocolonial. The implication is clear, although scholars and practitioners of African philosophy have not yet fully realized its impact: *The Hermeneutics of African Philosophy* is a new kind of discourse in African philosophy.

However, deconstruction is considerably less important than reconstruction. The more fundamental intention of *The Hermeneutics of African Philosophy* is to liberate African philosophy. In this endeavor, it is the intellectual, literary equivalent of contemporary African political liberation movements (whether directed against European or African subjugators). However, African philosophy is not merely the analogue of African politics; liberated African philosophy is an outgrowth and consequence of a new "horizon," a genuinely postcolonial, liberated African politics.

Serequeberhan expresses his reconstructive purpose in terms of the "lived situatedness" and "lived present" that hermeneutics discloses. This may and, to realize its fuller impact, should be said more simply. The reconstruction of African philosophy literally brings philosophy to life. This does not mean that formal—and therefore antiquarian or foreign—philosophy is taught to ordinary Africans. On the contrary, professors and other bureaucratized intellectuals must understand practically the real concerns of everyday living—if, that is, horizons are to be fused.

The new, reconstructed type of African philosophy alluded to in *The Hermeneutics of African Philosophy*, then, is African practical philosophy. In practical philosophy, there is a meeting of the concerns of elites and the masses, rulers and ruled. Previously separated concerns move toward commonality. Practical philosophy is political philosophy and, because common, democratic political philosophy. The implication, and thus the potential impact, of *The Hermeneutics of*

African Philosophy is assistance in the development of African political communities.

John F. Wilson

Additional Reading

Cabral, Amilcar. *Unity and Struggle: Speeches and Writings*. Translated by Michael Wolfers. New York: Monthly Review Press, 1979. An extensive collection of Cabral's theoretical and practical writings, which have been a major influence on Tsenay Serequeberhan's thought. Includes an introduction by Basil Davidson and very useful biographical notes.

Connell, Dan. *Against All Odds: A Chronicle of the Eritrean Revolution*. Trenton, N.J.: Red Sea Press, 1993. An eye-witness account by an American journalist of the EPLF's long struggle for Eritrean independence. In addition to the reportage, Connell provides a solid account of EPLF's PAIGC-like evolution from rigid Marxism to pragmatism. Includes moving photographs of all aspects of the war situation.

Dallmayr, Fred. *Alternative Visions: Paths in the Global Village*. Lanham, Md.: Rowman & Littlefield, 1998. A discussion of the philosophical aspects of global multiculturalism. Serequeberhan's *The Hermeneutics of African Philosophy* is considered in the context of Cabral's "return to the source."

Fanon, Frantz. *Black Skin, White Masks*. Translated by Charles Lam Markmann. New York: Grove Press, 1967. First published in French in 1952. The work that represents Fanon's "psychological" influence on Serequeberhan, in terms of African identity. Chapter 5, "The Fact of Blackness," is especially important.

_____. *The Wretched of the Earth*. Translated by Constance Farrington. New York: Grove Press, 1966. First published in French in 1961. Fanon's seminal discussion of violence in situations of liberation from colonialism, deeply influential for Serequeberhan's treatment of these issues. Contains a preface by Jean-Paul Sartre.

Iyob, Ruth. *The Eritrean Struggle for Independence*. Cambridge, England: Cambridge University Press, 1995. A scholarly study of the entire sweep of Eritrean history from 1941 to 1993. Iyob's work is especially useful in sorting out and tracing the development of the many groups involved in liberation. Contains an extensive bibliography.

Okere, Theophilus. *African Philosophy: A Historico-Hermeneutical Investigation of the Conditions of its Possibility*. Lanham, Md.: University Press of America, 1983. May be read as the philosophical preface to Serequeberhan's much more political *The Hermeneutics of African Philosophy*. Okere's conclusion points in a practical direction.

Owomoyela, Oyekan. "Deconstruction and Capitulation: African Responses to European Misconstruction and Objectification." *Research in African Literatures* 27 (Summer, 1996): 151-154. A review article that emphasizes the deconstructive, philosophical rather than reconstructive, practical aspects of Serequeberhan's *The Hermeneutics of African Philosophy*.

Senghor, Leopold Sedar. *On African Socialism*. Translated by Mercer Cook. New York: Frederick A. Praeger, 1964. Senghor's work is characterized by one African philosopher as an endlessly discussed myth, and the philosopher was criticized by Serequeberhan for his "passivity." Nevertheless, Senghor's thought is a touchstone for consideration of Africanity.

Zegeye, Abebe, and Siegfried Pausewang, eds. *Ethiopia in Change: Peasantry, Nationalism, and Democracy*. London: British Academic Press, 1994. A collection of scholarly essays exploring the past and present relationships between Ethiopia and Eritrea. Chapter 5, discussing student movements during Serequeberhan's youth, is of special interest.

John F. Wilson

Sextus Empiricus

Promoting Pyrrhonian radical Skepticism, Sextus compiled arguments against dogmatic philosophers of Stoicism, Epicureanism, and Academic Skepticism, and in doing so he laid the foundation for modern philosophy.

Principal philosophical works: *Pyrrōneiōn Hypotypōseōn* , c. second century C.E. (also known as *Pyrrhoniarum hypotyposes*; *Outlines of Pyrrhonism*, 1591); *Pros Mathēmatikous*, c. second century C.E. (also known as *Adversus mathematicos*; *Against the Mathematicians*, 1591).

Born: c. 140-160 C.E.; Greece
Died: c. 220-230 C.E.; Greece or Alexandria, Egypt

Early Life

Little is known about Sextus Empiricus. He was an obscure Hellenistic writer but the only Greek Pyrrhonian Skeptic whose works survived and eventually made a great impact on Western intellectual history. He is said to be the last of the Alexandrian radical Pyrrhonist leaders.

Life's Work

Experts speculate that Sextus was a physician by profession. He refers to Asclepias as the founder of "our science" (medicine), and Diogenes Laërtius and Galen, personal physician to several Roman emperors in the first and second centuries C.E., mention that he belonged to the Empirical school of medicine. Sextus was also a philosophy teacher and a kind of therapist advocating mental tranquillity through suspension of judgment.

Sextus was not an original philosopher but an excellent and methodical expounder and compiler of Pyrrhonist arguments handed down to him by his teacher Herodotus and other Skeptics. Being a physician and, in the modern sense, a scientist perhaps gave him a natural talent for meticulous compilation and classification of arguments.

Sextus was part of a radical movement, the Alexandrian Pyrrhonists, which believed in returning to traditional Pyrrhonian principles and engaging in relentless struggle against certain dogmatic philosophical ideas. One of the major goals of the group was to construct arguments against any kind of dogmatism, particularly Stoicism, Epicureanism, and the Academic Skepticism prevalent in Plato's Academy. Sextus argued against Academic Skepticism and its famous teachers, Arcesilaus and Carneades. Pyrrhonian Skeptics considered the Academic Skeptics dogmatic philosophers for taking the position that nothing is knowable. Sextus argued that we are not allowed even this much knowledge; the best course is to suspend judgment.

Sextus was an ardent follower of Pyrrho of Elis, sometimes called the founder of Skepticism. It is said that Pyrrho, through strict observance of Skeptical practices, achieved an extraordinary tranquillity and indifference. Like Socrates, Pyrrho did not write down his thoughts and lectures. What is known about Pyrrho comes from surviving fragments written in poems by one of his devoted pupils, Timon of Philius, in the third century B.C.E. Sextus attempted to capture Pyrrho's basic teachings and compiled a massive collection of varied arguments against philosophers and professionals of all sorts, much as Plato did for Socrates.

Pyrrho and later Sextus did not establish a school of thought and were not interested in institutionalizing their philosophy, as Plato and Aristotle had been. Pyrrho's, and indeed Sextus's, philosophical method was to attack other philosophers and dogmatists. Pyrrho's basic Skeptical attitude, according to Sextus, was that objects in the world are indifferent and unfathomable, and we cannot determine them because our senses and judgments are indifferent—they are neither true nor false. We should suspend judgment on everything. If we do so, we will achieve tranquillity in life.

Skepticism began to change from Academic to Pyrrhonist with the teachings of Aenesidemus in Alexandria as early as the first century. Aenesidemus had been a student at the Academy and was disenchanted with its radical Skeptics. Sextus contends that Aenesidemus's policy of "determining nothing" resulted in happiness and Pyrrhonian tranquillity.

Pyrrhonism developed mainly among medical doctors in Alexandria, with Sextus as one of the movement's leaders. Two of Sextus's works survive in nearly complete form: *Outlines of Pyrrhonism* and *Against the Mathematicians*. In these books, Sextus describes Skepticism as the mental attitude that opposes the sources of certainty: appearances, objects of sense experience, and judgments people make about them. Through detailed and varied arguments, he shows that any dogmatic construction of knowledge only results in philosophical paradox and the illusion of knowledge. His books are rich sources of information about the ancient Greek philosophies.

The *Outlines of Pyrrhonism* is a methodical summary of Pyrrhonist Skeptical philosophy. It also compares the Skepticism of Pyrrho with that of the Academic Skeptics and attempts to show the weaknesses of the latter and the superiority of the former. The work is divided into three books. The first gives a general description of Pyrrhonist Skepticism and its terminology. The second and third present arguments against the basic premises of each of the divisions of philosophy: ethics, logic, and natural philosophy. Sextus's arguments in this work and *Against the Mathematicians* are targeted mainly against three schools of "dogmatist" philosophers—Epicureans, Stoics, and Academic Skeptics—who believed they have knowledge of *something*.

Against the Mathematicians is divided into two major parts, "Against Professors of Liberal Studies" and "Against Dogmatists," with eleven books in all. Sextus complies a detailed and meticulous taxonomy of arguments against many "dogmatist" philosophers, including the latter-day Aristoteleans and professionals and technicians such as medical doctors, military tacticians, musicians, astrologers, arithmeticians, geometricians, rhetoricians, and grammarians.

Like his Pyrrhonian predecessors, Sextus does not have an explicit set of beliefs or views of how the world is or ought to be. Instead, his objectives are to deconstruct the arguments of others within the system from which they have arisen. This is a more radical and controversial form of Skepticism than the Academics offered. At the end of *Outlines of Pyrrhonism*, Sextus claims that his arguments are mere pragmatic devices; they have no inherent value or superiority over any other arguments.

Sextus criticized Academic Skeptics as too dogmatic. Even the statement made by the Academics that nothing is knowable is itself a dogmatic claim of knowledge. This leads the Academic Skeptic into an irresolvable paradox—making an absolutist argument to support a relativist claim.

One of the most paradoxical claims, according to Sextus in his *Outlines of Pyrrhonism*, is the Academic Skeptics' claim about truth. According to the Academic Skeptics, to decide any dispute about truth, the accepted criterion must be spelled out. However, discovery of the criterion becomes "impracticable" because a criterion cannot be adopted without adopting a criterion for *that* criterion, creating a hopeless regression *ad infinitum*. Sextus claims that this kind of circular reasoning afflicts any claim of truth, be it mathematical, empirical, religious, aesthetic, or ethical. In opposition to dogmatists, he announces that humanity is *not* the measure of truth.

What is important to recognize about Sextus's version of Skepticism is that he does not state that there is or is not such a thing as truth. He merely suggests that we do not know. All we can do is to forgo making judgment one way or the other. He takes pains to explain this point and separates himself from the Academic Skeptics who claim they know with certainty that there is no truth. Sextus considered their view paradoxically dogmatic and against the spirit of Pyrrhonian Skepticism.

Sextus describes ten arguments, or "tropes," developed by Aenesidemus for suspending judgment. All deal with the paradoxical nature of ascertaining whether our sense experiences belong to real objects existing in the external world or to our perceptions alone. He distinguishes between what modern philosophers of mind such as Daniel Dennett call "qualia," the perceptions of sensory experiences, such as the redness of a tomato, and the external or physical attributions, such as light waves and chemical nature. Sextus claims that neither phenomenon is trustworthy. The same object may affect different people in different ways in different contexts.

Sextus believed that if Pyrrhonian Skepticism were adopted as a way of life, it would cure people of dogmatism, give them humility, and prepare them for a life of tranquillity. He says in *Outlines of Pyrrhonism* that Pyrrhonists like himself love humanity and want to save people from suffering and self-destruction caused by humankind's "rashness" and "self-deception," maladies of dogmatic living. People who need the Pyrrhonist cure, according to Sextus, are of two kinds: those who believe they have found the truth, such as Aristotelians and Epicureans, and those, such as Academic Skeptics, who believe they will never find it.

Sextus contends that various dogmatic schools of Hellenistic philosophy—the Stoic, Epicurean, and Academic—are all looking for "peace of mind" and that their theories of knowledge and truth are intended to lead to such "quietude." Dogmatists, however, never achieve peace because they worry about whether their theories are true. The Skeptics have no such worries because they suspend judgment about knowledge and truth. The suspension of judgment, according to Sextus, produces calm indifference. In turn, this state of mind produces the tranquillity that the dogmatist seeks in vain.

Influence

It has been said that modern philosophy began with the historical accident of rediscovery of Sextus's books in the fifteenth and sixteenth centuries. It changed Western intellectual development forever. However, Sextus's writings had minimal influence on his contemporaries, and he was almost completely unknown in the Middle Ages. Only a handful of scholars had read his works before the first publication of his books in 1562 in France.

The first serious attempt to use Sextus's books as major philosophical texts was made by Michel Eyquem de Montaigne, who established his own unique genre of skepticism inspired by Sextus.

Montaigne had much to do with the popularization of Sextus's works, which resulted in new translations in Italian, French, and English appearing in the sixteenth and seventeenth centuries. The new Pyrrhonism of Montaigne and his disciples, addressing the intellectual, scientific, and theological crises of their time, led to *nouveaux Pyrrhoniens* as the intellectual avant-garde of Europe. By the seventeenth century, Sextus had been metamorphosed into the "divine Sextus" and was regarded as the father of modern philosophy. The effect of his thoughts about the problem of the criterion of truth stimulated a quest for certainty that gave rise to the new rationalism of René Descartes and the "constructive skepticism" of Pierre Gassendi and Marin Mersenne.

The first detailed explication of Sextus's views was written in 1520 by Giovanni Pico della Mirandola, who used the philosopher's books to demolish rational philosophy. His argument, however, was not that one should hold a radical doubt in everything, but rather that one would turn to humanity's only guide in this "vale of tears," the Christian Revelation. Thus, Pico della Mirandola, using Sextus's arguments, established a kind of Christian Pyrrhonism that led to its later, more popular transformation propagated by Montaigne and his followers.

Theologians used Sextus's arguments to combat skepticism's corrosive influence on Christianity. Sextus's works provided material for varied interests in the Renaissance and Reformation eras. Thinkers such as Montaigne, Mersenne, Gassendi, and Francisco Sanches turned to Sextus for inspiration in dealing with various intellectual crises.

The rediscovery of Sextus stimulated great works for and against Skepticism. For example, Descartes in his meditations used skeptical devices to reach his certainty of *Cogito, ergo sum* ("I think, therefore I am"). On that foundation, he climbed back to the claims of the existence of the external world, God, and even Christianity. On the other hand, Scottish philosopher David Hume's ingenious radical skepticism attempted to abolish any and all foundations for religion, morality, and the notion of physical causation. George Berkeley's solipsism denied all external or physical existence in favor of an entirely mental world of existence. Sextus's influence is felt even in 1970's and 1980's postmodern philosophies such as Jacques Derrida's deconstructionism.

Sextus has been both admired and reviled. During his lifetime, he was accused of implicit dogmatism himself. In response, Sextus said that what he advocates has only the appearance of truth to him and that no one should take that as a dogmatic assertion of truth. However, there are still many unresolved problems and paradoxes in Sextus's varied arguments. For example, the claim that one has to suspend judgment about everything turns out to be circular, for the statement itself becomes subject to suspension of judgment. On close examination, Sextus's answers to this paradox are not satisfactory. Neither are rationalists' responses to Sextus's ingenious skeptical arguments, which will continue to capture people's intellectual imagination for the foreseeable future.

Chogollah Maroufi

Outlines of Pyrrhonism

Type of philosophy: Epistemology
First transcribed: Pyrrōneiōn Hypotypōseōn , c. second century C.E. (also known as *Pyrrhoniarum hypotyposes*; English translation, 1591)
Principal ideas advanced:
◇ Skeptical arguments are designed to cure dogmatists of the disease of supposing that knowledge is possible.
◇ The Skeptic relies on appearances and avoids the error of passing judgment.
◇ To suppose that it is possible to judge truth and falsity is to ignore the relativity of perception and judgment.

The writings of Sextus Empiricus are the only surviving texts that expound the view of the Pyrrhonian Skeptical movement of ancient times. The movement takes its name from Pyrrho of Elis

(c. 367-275 B.C.E.), who doubted that there is any way by which one can attain knowledge. He urged that judgment be suspended as to whether any particular assertion is true or false. He argued that to suspend judgment leads to a state of indifference toward the world and to a kind of inner tranquillity that enables one to live at peace in a troubled world.

The actual school of Pyrrhonian thought began much later, in the first century B.C.E. It developed out of the radical Skepticism that had been prevalent in Plato's Academy under Arcesilaus and Carneades. The Academic Skeptics developed a series of brilliant arguments to show that nothing can be known; they recommended that one live by probabilities. The Pyrrhonists regarded the Academics as too dogmatic, and the former maintained their doubts, even about the skeptical contention that nothing can be known. Starting with Aenesidemus, who had been a student at the Academy, the Pyrrhonian movement developed in Alexandria, primarily among medical doctors. Aenesidemus and his successors set forth a series of arguments against various dogmatic philosophies, including the Academic Skeptics. The arguments purported to show that every dogmatic attempt to gain knowledge leads to difficulties that cannot be resolved. Instead of seeking knowledge, one should suspend judgment, thus gaining peace of mind.

Sextus was one of the last leaders of the Pyrrhonian school. Besides the fact that he was a doctor and a teacher, practically nothing is known about him. His writings—probably copies of lectures—consist of compilations of the arguments that his predecessors had worked out on any and all subjects. The *Outlines of Pyrrhonism* is a summary of the Pyrrhonian position, whereas his other work, *Pros Mathēmatikous* (c. second century C.E., also known as *Adversus mathematicos*; *Against the Mathematicians*, is a much more detailed exposition of the arguments that the school had developed regarding each particular area in which other philosophers had claimed to have discovered true knowledge. Sextus's writings are veritable storehouses of skeptical arguments designed to confound all other philosophers. Although very repetitious, they contain both good and bad arguments.

In the last chapter of *Outlines of Pyrrhonism,*

Sextus explains the uneven character of his book in answering the question of why Skeptics sometimes propound arguments that lack persuasion. Skeptics, he writes, are lovers of humankind. They are seeking to cure an ailment called "self-conceit and rashness," from which the dogmatic philosophers suffer. Just as doctors employ remedies of different strengths depending on the condition of the patient, Skeptics employ arguments of different strengths depending on how "sick" the dogmatic philosophers are. If the therapy can succeed with a weak argument, good. If the case is severe, a strong argument is needed. Hence, the Pyrrhonists offered a variety of arguments, good and bad, weak and strong, because their avowed aim was to cure dogmatists of the disease of supposing that they knew something.

The *Outlines of Pyrrhonism* begins by dividing philosophers into three groups: the dogmatists, such as Aristotle and Epicurus, who say that they have discovered the truth; those such as Carneades, who say it cannot be found; and the Pyrrhonian Skeptics, who keep seeking for it. The aim of the Pyrrhonian arguments is to cure people from holding either of the first two views. Sextus guards against being accused of "secret dogmatism" by saying that the statements in his work are not to be taken as positive assertions of what is true, but only as expressions of what *appear* to him to be matters of fact.

The Nature of Skepticism

Sextus describes Skepticism as the ability or mental attitude that opposes appearances, the objects of sense experience, to judgments that can be made about them, so that suspense of judgment is achieved and one neither affirms nor denies anything. This state is followed by the state of "quietude," in which one is untroubled and tranquil. The various dogmatic schools of Hellenistic philosophy—the Stoic, the Epicurean, and the Academic—were all looking for peace of mind, and their theories of knowledge and of the real nature of the universe were intended to lead one to mental peace. The Skeptics contend that the dogmatists never achieve peace because they worry about never knowing whether their theories are true. However, Skeptics, who suspend judgment, achieve peace of mind because they escape such worry.

If Skeptics suspend judgment about everything, how do they live? Sextus answers by declaring that Skeptics accept the world of sense experience undogmatically. It seems to Skeptics that they see certain things, have certain feelings, and so on, but they do not know whether such is really the case. They suspend judgment about all that is not immediately evident to them. Then, without judging, they follow nature and custom, so that—for example—when they seem to be hungry, they eat. They have peace of mind because they do not judge, and they are guided in their lives by their experience, their feelings, and the laws and customs of their society.

The Ten Tropes and More

To achieve this tranquillity, one must first achieve suspension of judgment. Skeptical arguments are offered by Sextus to encourage such suspension. He first offers the ten tropes, or arguments, of Aenesidemus, which show why we should suspend judgment about whether sense objects really are as they appear to be. (Sextus prefaces these and all the other arguments he sets forth with the disclaimer that he is not asserting dogmatically the exact number, nature, or truth of the arguments, but only that it seems to him that they are a set of arguments.) The ten tropes all deal with difficulties in ascertaining when features of our sense experience belong to real objects existing independently of our perceptions.

(1) Sextus points out, different animals experience things differently according to the nature of their sense organs. We cannot tell which animal has the correct experience.

(2) Humans experience the same object differently, and we have no basis for deciding which person has the correct experience.

(3) The same object affects different senses in different ways. Honey is sweet to the tongue but sticky to the finger. We cannot tell which quality really belongs to the object.

(4) Our impressions of things vary according to our state of mind or our condition.

(5) Things appear different from different positions.

(6) We never perceive objects individually, but only together with other objects, so that we never know what they are like by themselves.

(7) Objects look different when decomposed or analyzed from how they appear when whole; we cannot judge which is their true nature.

(8) Everything that we perceive is seen relative to its position in space and time, so we do not know what it is like out of position.

(9) We regard things differently according to whether they occur frequently or rarely.

(10) Because different nations and cultures have different laws and customs, we cannot judge what things are really right or wrong.

These ten tropes should lead us to suspend judgment because they show that our sense impressions vary and are different, and we have no means for deciding which are correct ones.

Sextus follows with five additional tropes, or reasons for suspending judgment, attributed to Agrippa, a Skeptic of a century earlier. These are more general reasons for doubting dogmatic contentions.

(1) First of all, there is interminable controversy about everything, so we cannot tell who is right.

(2) Every judgment must be proved if it is to be accepted as true; however, the proof will require a further proof, and so on *ad infinitum*.

(3) Any judgment is relative to the judge and may not be true of the thing itself.

(4) The dogmatists must assume something in order to make judgments, but we cannot tell if these assumptions or hypotheses are true.

(5) The only way to escape from the infinite regress of proofs of proofs, or from starting with some unwarranted hypothesis, is to employ a circular argument in which something that is to be proved is used as part of the proof itself.

Further sets of tropes are offered, including Aenesidemus's arguments against any dogmatic theory of causation. Then the first book of *Outlines of Pyrrhonism* concludes with an explanation of Skeptical terminology (showing how the Skeptics can say what they do without making dogmatic assertions) and with a comparison of other Greek philosophies with Pyrrhonian Skepticism.

Knowledge

The second and third books of *Outlines of Pyrrhonism* show why Skeptics suspend judgment with regard to knowledge claims in various specific disciplines. The second book treats problems of logic and the theory of knowledge, while the third is a collection of arguments about theology, metaphysics, mathematics, physics, and ethics.

The second book presents the disturbing problem of whether Skeptics can deal with the arguments of the dogmatists without admitting that they, the Skeptics, know something, namely what the opponents are talking about. After contending that he deals only with what seems to be the dogmatists' view, Sextus turns to what he regards as crucial to any theory of true knowledge, the question of whether there is any criterion for judging what is true. Philosophers disagree as to whether there is such a criterion. To settle the dispute, a criterion is needed, but it is not known whether one exists. Further, any proposed criterion of knowledge would have to be judged by another criterion to tell if it were a true one, and that criterion by still another, and so on.

If the dogmatic philosophers insist that humanity is the judge or criterion of true knowledge, then a problem exists: whether all people or only some are judges of truth. If all, then another criterion is needed to settle disputes among people. If only some, then a criterion is needed to tell which people are proper judges and under what conditions. The Stoics, for example, claim that the wise person, the sage, is the judge. However, by what standards can one tell *who* is the sage and whether what the person says is true? Other philosophers say that the criteria are the faculties of sense and reason. However, under what conditions are they the criteria? By what standards shall we judge? Also, whose sense and reason are standards?

It is not even obvious that anything true exists. Therefore, if somebody asserts that truth exists, he will not be believed unless he offers proof. However, is the proof true? Further proof has to be offered. However, is *that* true? Unless some criterion of truth can be established, we cannot tell. However, how can we ever determine if the criterion is the true one?

Further, one can ask, what sort of truths are they—apparent or nonapparent? Because there is disagreement about everything (and Sextus appeals to the fact that there have been philosophers who disputed everything), it is not obvious that something is true. If truths are not apparent, some standard is needed for ascertaining what is true, but all the aforementioned difficulties arise when one attempts to apply a standard of truth.

Signs

Philosophers, especially the Stoics, maintain that they can gain true knowledge by means of signs or inferences that connect what is obvious or evident with that which is not. What is nonevident, Sextus says, falls into one of three categories: the *temporarily nonevident*, such as that which is on the other side of the wall one is facing; the *naturally nonevident*, those things that can never under any circumstances be perceived, such as the pores in the skin, but that can be inferred from what is evident; and finally, the *absolutely nonevident*, whatever can never be known at all, such as whether the number of stars is odd or even. There is a type of sign, called the suggestive sign, which connects what is obvious, our immediate experience, with what is temporarily nonevident. Smoke suggests that there is a fire. Skeptics, like anyone else, accept suggestive signs and act by them, because this is the natural way of relating present experience to possible future experience. However, suggestive signs do not provide true knowledge, only predictions or expectations about the future course of events.

Philosophers hope to gain true knowledge by means of another kind of sign, the indicative sign. This is defined as "an antecedent judgment in a valid hypothetical syllogism which serves to reveal the consequent." In a syllogism of the form "If A, then B; A, therefore B," A is an indicative sign if it, itself, is evident, if it reveals that B, which is naturally nonevident, is true, and if the syllogism is valid. Sextus offers many arguments against the existence of indicative signs, including the contention that one can determine if a hypothetical syllogism is valid only if one knows whether the consequent is true or false. The consequent in this case is a statement about what is naturally nonevident, which can be revealed only by an indicative sign. Hence, one is always involved in circular reasoning because it requires knowing what is naturally nonevident to tell if an indicative sign actually exists, and one can tell what is naturally nonevident only by means of indicative signs.

Demonstrative reasoning consists of using signs to reveal conclusions. Hence, similar doubts can be cast as to whether anything at all can be demonstrated or proved. Sextus offers many arguments to show that nothing can be proved, and then, to avoid establishing the negative conclusion, he offers evidence to show that something can be proved. Therefore, one has to suspend judgment on the question.

A very brief criticism is leveled against induction, pointing out that if a general conclusion is drawn from some particular instances, it may be disproved by other cases. If generalizations can properly be made only after a review of *all* particular cases, it is obviously impossible to survey all of the data, and hence, to generalize.

Religion, Metaphysics, and the Sciences

The third book of *Outlines of Pyrrhonism* rapidly surveys the various sciences from theology and metaphysics to mathematics, physics, and ethics, and indicates that in each of these areas the fundamental concepts are meaningless, that the basic principles are open to question, and that, as a result, one must suspend judgment about whether anything can be known in any of these areas.

Though Skeptics accept the customs of their society and hence its religious views, undogmatically, Sextus points out that the arguments for the existence of God and for atheism are inconclusive, and that the conceptions of God offered by various philosophers are conflicting and often inconsistent in themselves. Further, various problems, such as the problem of evil, cast doubt on the claim that a good, all-knowing deity exists.

With regard to metaphysics and physics, the basic notions such as "cause," "matter," and "body" contain difficulties. We cannot even be sure that anything causes anything else or that bodies exist. We seem to have no way of gaining indisputable knowledge in this area. Arguments such as those of Zeno of Elea, of the fifth century B.C.E., indicate that paradoxical conclusions can be drawn about the nature of bodies, motion, and so on. There are also paradoxes with regard to mathematics, such as the odd argument Sextus offers to show that six equals fifteen. The whole equals the sum of its parts, and the parts of six are five, four, three, two, and one. Therefore, six equals fifteen.

The disagreements among philosophers and mathematicians and the various paradoxical arguments, whether valid or not, that had been developed in ancient times suffice to raise doubts as to whether anything can be known about the world or about mathematics. Hence, we must again suspend judgment.

Ethics

When Sextus turns to ethical matters, he points out that philosophers disagree about what is good and bad. There is not even adequate evidence that anything really good or bad exists. The variety of beliefs and opinions about what is good and bad in the various known cultures leads one to suspend judgment about whether there are any objective moral values in the world. (Sextus even points out that some people and some societies condone incest and cannibalism. Who can say that they are wrong?) Skeptics live undogmatically, not judging whether things are good or bad, but living according to the dictates of nature and society. Skeptics, like others, may suffer from physical pains, but they will avoid the additional mental suffering that results from judging that pains are bad or evil.

The writings of Sextus seem to have had little or no influence in their own time and to have been practically unknown during the Middle Ages. Their rediscovery in the Renaissance greatly influenced many modern thinkers from Michel Eyquem de Montaigne, onward, for Sextus's writings proved to be a treasure house of argumentation on all sorts of subjects. Philosophers such as Pierre Gassendi, George Berkeley, and David Hume, among others, used arguments from Sextus in setting forth their own theories. Pierre Bayle contended that modern philosophy began when arguments of Sextus were introduced on the philosophical scene. The arguments of the Skeptics continue to stimulate twentieth century minds caught between the power of faith and the faith in power.

Richard H. Popkin

Additional Reading

Barnes, Johnathan. *The Toils of Scepticism*. Cambridge, London: Cambridge University Press, 1990. This is a technical but clear and engaging exposition of Pyrrhonian Skepticism by one of the foremost Oxford philosophers. Includes bibliographical references.

Hookway, Christopher. *Scepticism*. London: Routledge, 1990. Chapters 1 and 2 give a general account of Pyrrhonian Skepticism through the view of Sextus Empiricus. The rest of this book contains a detailed account of the influence of skepticism in various areas of modern philosophy.

Popkin, Richard H. *The History of Scepticism: From Erasmus to Spinoza*. Los Angeles: University of California Press, 1979. This is an excellent, readable, and informed historical treatment of Sextus and Pyrrhonian influences on the foundation of modern Western philosophy. In chapter 2, Popkin presents a clear and accessible account of the revival of skepticism in Europe in the sixteenth century.

Schmitt, C. B. "The Rediscovery of Ancient Skepticism in Modern Times." In *The Skeptical Tradition*, edited by Myles Burnyeat. Berkeley: University of California Press, 1983. This article gives a thorough account of the accidental rediscovery of Sextus's two books and their effect on the modern philosophy of the West. Chapters 2-9 of this book are basically devoted to discussions of ancient and Pyrrhonian Skepticism, and chapters 10 to 17 are excellent expositions of modern skepticism as a byproduct of its ancient Hellenistic prototype.

Sharples, Robert W. *Stoics, Epicureans, and Sceptics: An Introduction to Hellenistic Philosophy*. London: Routledge, 1996. Accessible reading on history and the principles of Sextus's Pyrrhonism. The chapters on stoicism and Epicureanism are quite helpful in understanding Sextus's arguments, for they are directed partially against these Hellenistic philosophies.

Zeller, Eduard. *The Stoics, Epicureans, and Sceptics*. Translated from the German by Oswald J. Reichel. New York: Russell and Russell, 1962. Chapters 22 and 23 describe in a clear and detailed manner the Pyrrhonian and the Academic versions of ancient Skepticism.

Chogollah Maroufi

Third Earl of Shaftesbury

Anthony Ashley Cooper

Shaftesbury emphasized common sense as opposed to logical systems and introduced the theory of the moral sense as an influential element of ethical theory. Although he drew on numerous traditions in philosophy, his work demonstrates a debt to Plato in both form and substance.

Principal philosophical works: *An Inquiry Concerning Virtue*, 1699 (unauthorized edition; also published as *An Inquiry Concerning Virtue or Merit*); *A Letter Concerning Enthusiasm*, 1708; *Sensus Communis: An Essay on the Freedom of Wit and Humour*, 1709; *The Moralists: A Philosophical Rhapsody*, 1709; *Soliloquy: Or, Advice to an Author*, 1710; *Characteristics of Men, Manners, Opinions, Times*, 1711; *The Life, Unpublished Letters, and Philosophical Regimen of Anthony, Earl of Shaftesbury*, 1900; *Second Characteristics: Or, The Language of Forms*, 1914; *The Shaftesbury Collection*, 1995.

Born: February 26, 1671; Dorset, England
Died: February 15, 1713; Naples, Italy

Early Life

Anthony Ashley Cooper, third earl of Shaftesbury, was born into a prominent noble family. At the time of his birth, his grandfather, the first earl of Shaftesbury, towered in the forefront of English politics as a champion of liberty and an advocate of Parliamentary power. He was to become an important founder of the Whig Party and a contributor to the development of the two-party system. Because of his son's ill health and frailty, he became his grandson's guardian and oversaw the boy's early education, until the age of eleven. The first earl's political activity placed him in opposition to King Charles II, and to escape a charge of treason, he was forced to flee to Holland, where he died in 1683. Afterward, Anthony's father, the second earl, who suffered from an incurable malady that left him an invalid, assumed responsibility for his son.

Anthony's early education followed the principles of his grandfather's secretary, philosopher John Locke, who selected a young woman named Elizabeth Birch as his tutor. Known for her ability in Latin and Greek, she enabled her pupil to master these languages by the age of eleven. Evidence suggests that, even from an early age, classical literature and philosophy were congenial to the young earl's temperament. Following the death of Anthony's grandfather, Anthony's father sent him to a preparatory school, Winchester College, where schoolmates taunted him about his grandfather's Whig politics. Before completing his studies, he left Winchester to take a three-year grand tour of Europe, accompanied by a tutor and his lifelong friend, Sir John Cropley. They traveled to France, Italy, Bohemia, Austria, and Germany before returning to England in 1689. Following his return to England, he devoted an additional five years to his studies.

Life's Work

In 1695, he was elected to the House of Commons, in which he served three years. In Parliament, he remained a loyal Whig, voting for measures that would extend the liberty of the king's subjects, but his brief career was not distinguished, largely because of his shy and reticent nature. In 1698, hoping to improve his frail health, he left for Rotterdam, Holland, where Locke had earlier lived. In the liberal atmosphere of Rotterdam, Anthony conversed with learned men, both Dutch and English, and continued his study of the classics. The extensive library of his friend, merchant Benjamin Furly, enabled him to continue his studies.

In November, 1699, upon the death of his father, he inherited his title and was placed in charge of large estates. He spent two years in the House of Lords, but the polluted London air aggravated his chronic asthma, so he retired from public life and left London in 1702. He devoted himself primarily to learning, art, managing his properties, and corresponding and conversing with friends. It is often noted that he retired from public life to devote himself to other pursuits because of his frail health, but it is equally noteworthy that his retirement coincided with the accession of Queen Anne and the return to power of the Tory Party that he opposed. His voluminous correspondence indicates that he spent much effort guiding promising young men in their studies and careers and taking care of his interests in England.

His retirement from public life did not offer him much comfort, because after 1704, he was in chronically bad health. The exact cause remains unknown, but his letters refer to asthma, colds, and recurring fevers; it seems likely that he suffered from tuberculosis. During 1703 and 1704, he again lived for a year in Holland, but afterward he resided in England until 1711. There, he lived in numerous places—at his country estate Wimborne St. Giles in Dorsetshire; at Chelsea and Reigate, where he owned houses; and at the houses of friends. His frequent relocations were often motivated by efforts to improve his health.

In 1709, Shaftesbury married Jane Ewer, the daughter of Thomas Ewer, a country gentleman of Hertfordshire. Their union produced one son, also named Anthony Ashley Cooper, who was to become the fourth earl. In 1711, accompanied by Lady Shaftesbury and their servants, he left England for Europe to seek a more favorable climate. He settled in Naples, but after fifteen months, he died there in 1713. Near the end of his life, too enervated to write, he had others copy his letters from dictation.

Shaftesbury's early publications were for the most part anonymous. In 1698, he wrote a preface to an edition of sermons by Benjamin Whichcote, a moderate clergyman associated with the Cambridge Platonists. In his preface, Shaftesbury observes that true virtue is not motivated by hope of future rewards or fear of punishments, a viewpoint indicative of the ethical cast of thought that formed a major theme of his writings.

His first important philosophical work, *An Inquiry Concerning Virtue*, appeared anonymously

Anthony Ashley Cooper, third earl of Shaftesbury. *(Library of Congress)*

in an unauthorized edition in 1699. In it, he outlines his moral sense theory for the first time. A revised version appeared in the first edition of *Characteristics of Men, Manners, Opinions, Times*.

In 1708, he published his *A Letter Concerning Enthusiasm*, also anonymously. The work was prompted by events of the early 1700's. A splinter group of French Huguenots, known as Camisards, had adopted religious observances that included speaking in tongues and specific prophecies. Camisards who had settled in England predicted the imminent destruction of London by fire and set a specific date when one of their number would arise from the grave, a prophecy sufficiently specific to be easily discredited. Numerous Englishmen, unaccustomed to religious zeal so extreme, argued that the Camisards should be suppressed for their "enthusiasm." In his pamphlet, Shaftesbury suggests that the proper antidote for excessive zeal is satire though raillery and ridicule. His solution, though moderate by comparison, opened him to the animosity of those who thought that nothing associated with religion should be ridiculed. He developed his position on satire further in *Sensus Communis: An Essay on the Freedom of Wit and Humour*, arguing the propriety of wit and raillery in the marketplace of ideas.

The Moralists: A Philosophical Rhapsody outlines Shaftesbury's optimism and religious views. It attempts to explain the ways of God to humankind, depicting the Creator as one who created not the best world imaginable but the best possible. Written in dialogue form, *The Moralists* is perhaps Shaftesbury's most ambitious work. The year after *The Moralists* appeared in print, he published *Soliloquy: Or, Advice to an Author*, outlining his essentially neoclassic literary principles and accounting for the formation of taste. In this work, he makes the Platonic assertion that truth and beauty are one.

In 1711, these works, along with miscellaneous reflections, were gathered into his major work, *Characteristics of Men, Manners, Opinions, Times*. Shaftesbury spent his final months in Naples revising and expanding this work for its 1713 edition and writing other works largely concerned with aesthetics. He left numerous letters, fragments, and miscellaneous writings that were later published, but his influence was based essentially on the works included in *Characteristics of Men, Manners, Opinions, Times*.

In philosophy, Shaftesbury limited himself to ethics, aesthetics, and religion; thus, he cannot be considered a systematic thinker. In fact, he disapproved of systems, considering them too restrictive; as an admirer of Socrates, he believed truth should be sought through dialectic and discourse. His writings, often published anonymously, reflect unusual diversity of genre: letters, dialogues, minor treatises, essays, and, as in *The Moralists*, for example, a blending of genres.

In religion, Shaftesbury, like other intellectuals of his time, distinguished between personal observances and publicly expressed philosophical views. He outwardly conformed to the Church of England, considering support of the national church essential to the good order of society, yet his religious writings are essentially deistic in that he advocates a general, rational, and somewhat impersonal religion. Unlike earlier deists of the seventeenth century, however, he did not argue for innate ideas. His concept of deity was of an impersonal, wise, benevolent Creator who ruled the world through general laws. Despite his opposition to the Camisards, Shaftesbury was inclined toward tolerance of religious diversity, including non-Christian religions. An advocate of general religious principles that are shared by numerous faiths, he distrusted accounts of miracles and abhorred what he termed *enthusiasm*, or excessive zeal. He believed that the nature of the Creator might be inferred from the order found in nature and the universe, and he advocated an optimistic view holding that the existing universe represented the best possible one. Although he was an exponent of progress, he considered the classical tradition a better foundation for progress than the Hebraic.

In ethics, he began as an opponent of English philosopher Thomas Hobbes, who had advanced a purely egoistic, self-centered ethics, based on determinism. Shaftesbury argued for a more compassionate ethics based on what he termed the moral sense, a concept that he introduced to philosophy. His views are based on assumptions about human psychology heavily influenced by classicism and represent an effort to establish ethics on a nonreligious basis.

Unlike other creatures, human beings are capable of reason and reflection. These powers enable them to discern the order and beauty that exist in the universe. This quality, in turn, leads to a social sense, an appreciation of the order of human society that improves and enriches human life. The moral sense focuses on what upholds and advances this order of society and the universe, whereas evil consists of disrupting the order. A virtuous life consists of a balance between self-interest and the social affections. Although Shaftesbury realized that humankind often falls prey to destructive tendencies brought about by what he terms unnatural affections, human beings are in his view basically good and find beauty in improvement. Where pain and suffering are concerned, Shaftesbury, believing them inevitable, commends Stoic acceptance.

Shaftesbury's aesthetics was such that he may be more an art critic than a philosopher. Although he held a broad interest in classical art and antiquities, his writings center on painting and literature. As a literary critic, he is firmly neoclassical, upholding the principles of classical Greek and Roman literature as he understands them. In art, he admires balance, proportion, and idealized nature. The painters he recommends include Raphael for his natural, balanced rendition of human emotion, and Claude Lorraine and Nicholas Poussin for their mythological and classical landscapes that idealize the natural setting. Convinced that ordered art improves one's morals, he scorned art that he labeled "gothick"—strained, violent, excessive, or unbalanced.

Influence

Paradoxically, despite Shaftesbury's emphasis on classicism in philosophy and art, he is generally regarded as a pre-Romantic thinker, and important themes of his work sustain such a view. His view of the natural goodness of humanity, his emphasis on liberty, his optimism about the potential for improvement of humankind and society, his inclination to see people as part of a larger world system infused with spirituality, his general acceptance of the idea of progress, and his distrust of systems and science all represent ideas and positions advocated by Romantics of various stripes. His ideas were readily available to early Romantics, for *Characteristics of Men, Manners, Opinions, Times* went through nine editions be-

tween 1711 and 1790 and was translated into French and German.

Shaftesbury absorbed the dominant intellectual currents of the Enlightenment and transmuted them into his own optimistic system. His work achieved popularity in part because of his graceful, genteel, somewhat precious style. On the whole, his influence was widespread but not deep. His cosmic optimism is reflected in Alexander Pope's *An Essay on Man* (1733-1734) and selected essays in Joseph Addison's *The Spectator* (1711-1712, 1714; with Richard Steele). Philosopher Francis Hutcheson attempted to derive a systematic ethics derived from Shaftesbury's concept of a moral sense. Hutcheson attempted to demonstrate how individuals develop a social sense as a kind of logical response to observations involving pleasure and pain. Other philosophers who reflect Shaftesbury's influence include Bishop Joseph Butler, Adam Smith, and David Hume, though they sometimes discredit rather than accept his positions. In both France and Germany, Shaftesbury was cited by numerous philosophers and thinkers, though his optimism was easily reduced to absurdity through a slight distortion. The belief that the world was the best possible creation might be extended to the idea that evil and suffering are good, an idea that Shaftesbury did not propose. This idea was attacked by Voltaire in *Candide: Ou, L'Optimisme* (1759; *Candide: Or, All for the Best*, 1759) and Samuel Johnson in *Rasselas, Prince of Abyssinia: A Tale by S. Johnson* (1759).

Stanley Archer

Characteristics of Men, Manners, Opinions, Times

Type of philosophy: Aesthetics, ethics
First published: 1711
Principal ideas advanced:

◇ Metaphysics has little to offer humanity either in regard to a proof of the nature of the self or concerning one's morality; in such matters, it is better to count on common sense.

◇ True philosophy is the search for what is just in society and beautiful in nature.

◇ Nature is orderly, and virtue for humankind consists of following nature and enthusiastically seeking out the true, the good, and the beautiful.

◇ Conscience and aesthetic judgment are alike in being faculties for the discovery of the beauty of nature, the reflection of an order given to nature by God.

◇ People must exercise their reason by discussing opinions and by examining themselves.

Anthony Ashley Cooper, third earl of Shaftesbury, was a grandson of the famous Whig statesman of the same name. When his own career in politics was cut short by ill health, he turned his liberal and humanitarian efforts into literary channels, bringing to the task, besides a Puritan sense of moral responsibility, an aesthetic sensibility disciplined by the study of Greek and Roman models. His assorted essays, published under the title of *Characteristics of Men, Manners, Opinions, Times,* develop the ideal of humankind working out the purposes of God through moral and spiritual striving. He opposed the dehumanizing tendencies of the Cartesian and Newtonian philosophies, much in the same way that Socrates had opposed the naturalism of an earlier day. Like the famous Athenian, Shaftesbury taught his age that humankind should know itself.

Influences from Locke and Descartes
Philosopher John Locke, who was for many years secretary to the elder Shaftesbury, was tutor to the author of the *Characteristics of Men, Manners, Opinions, Times* and may be credited with imparting to him a liberality of spirit and a general trust in reason. Shaftesbury, however, rejected Locke's theory of ideas and the whole philosophical enterprise that, beginning with French philosopher René Descartes, pursued the ideal of certitude based on self-evident truths.

Far from putting a stop to skepticism, said Shaftesbury, the attempt initiated by Descartes to demonstrate the rationality of nature and morality played directly into the hands of sophists and triflers. Descartes's statement of existence, *Cogito, ergo sum* ("I think, therefore I am"), merely stated a verbal identity. It left untouched the real problems, "what constitutes the I" and "whether the I of this instant be the same with that of any in-

stant preceding or to come." One has nothing but memory, Shaftesbury said, to warrant one's belief in one's own identity, and if one wishes to play the metaphysical game, the question about the "successional I" must remain undecided:

> I take my being upon trust. Let others philosophise as they are able: I shall admire their strength when, upon this topic, they have refuted what able metaphysicians object and Pyrrhonists plead in their own behalf.

Shaftesbury noted that persons of breeding habitually respond to the pedantry of scholars with irony or "wit." Appealing to this, Shaftesbury constructed a metaphysical theory of morals that showed, after the fashion of the Stoics and of Baruch Spinoza, that, if one accepts the theory of ideas, humanity's well-being consists of learning to entertain only those thoughts that will not disappoint. This excursus into "dry philosophy" and the "rigid manner" of metaphysical disputes was, however, only half serious. It was useful, he said, to be able to argue in this way with "moonblind wits . . . who renounce daylight and extinguish in a manner the bright visible outward world, by allowing us to know nothing beside what we can prove by strict and formal demonstration." Also, in any case, "it is in a manner necessary for one who would usefully philosophise, to have a knowledge in this part of philosophy sufficient to satisfy him that there is no knowledge or wisdom to be learnt from it."

Views on the Nature of Philosophy
Because it had become engrossed in introspection, Shaftesbury said, philosophy had fallen into ill repute among men of judgment. The philosopher was now what was formerly intended by the word "idiot"—a person who can attend to nothing except his or her own ideas. Persons concerned with bringing honest reason to bear on the affairs of life stood "to gain little by philosophy or deep speculations of any kind." In a passage often appealed to during the eighteenth century, Shaftesbury said, "In the main, 'tis best to stick to common sense and go no farther. Men's first thoughts in this matter [morals] are generally better than their second: their natural notions better than those refined by study or consultation with casuists." He added,

Some moral and philosophical truths there are withal so evident in themselves that 'twould be easier to imagine half mankind to have run mad, and joined precisely in one and the same species of folly, than to admit anything as truth which should be advanced against such natural knowledge, fundamental reason, and common sense.

Shaftesbury, however, was unwilling to give up the word "philosophy." A person does not become a philosopher by writing and talking philosophy, he said. In reality, a philosopher is one who reasons concerning humankind's main interests, and there are good and bad philosophers, separated as to whether they reason skillfully or unskillfully. In Shaftesbury's hands, therefore, the bald contrast between philosophy and common sense was not a philistine repudiation of the life of reason but an attempt to vindicate a venerable tradition against the pretensions of "the new learning."

Although he was committed to the political ideals of the rising bourgeoisie, Shaftesbury was alarmed at what appeared to be its want of sound moral foundations. For the greater glory of God, the followers of religious leaders Martin Luther and John Calvin repudiated nature, and for the greater glory of humankind, the followers of philosophers Francis Bacon and Descartes repudiated the past. To remedy these defects, Shaftesbury turned to the Greek philosophers Plato and Aristotle and to the living tradition of Renaissance Platonism. The aim of philosophy is "to learn what is just in society and beautiful in Nature and the order of the world," and this with a view to enabling humanity to realize the highest ideal of being.

The Order of Nature

The starting point of Shaftesbury's moral philosophy was the conception of nature as an orderly whole. The daylight philosopher, in contrast to those who fumble among ideas in the cellars of their own minds, recognizes with Plato that nature is a system in which each part is ordered with a view to the perfection of the whole. Shaftesbury was no less impressed than were his contemporaries by the regular motion of the heavens. Even more remarkable, in his opin-

ion, was the microscopic life revealed by the new biology. The latter, in particular, suggested that the world is a self-sustaining whole composed of subordinate wholes, each having a life and nature of its own but so adjusted that while it pursues its private end, it also functions in the interest of the systems that comprehend it.

From this point of view, all excellence consists of following nature. Shaftesbury said that he was a realist, holding that virtue or excellence is "really something in itself and in the nature of things; not arbitrary or factitious; not constituted from without, or dependent on custom, fancy, or will; not even on the supreme will itself, which can no way govern it; but being necessarily good, is governed by it and ever uniform with it." Animal breeders know what is natural and what is unnatural behavior in a dog or in a horse; they know a good animal from a mediocre one, and they know what constitutes the excellence of the former. So it is with people. By a native endowment, each individual knows what is just, fair, and honest in people's character and conduct.

The human soul, as Shaftesbury represents it, is like every other living form in that it has a natural constitution. Within the systems of nature and society, each human being is a system in which passions, inclinations, appetites, and affections have their place. Some of these are purely local, such as the appetite for food; others are more comprehensive, such as pride, embracing the individual's general interest; others, such as parental love and friendship, bind the individual to society. Each is good in its proper place, and people are endowed with reason to regulate them.

Reason, Morality, and Beauty

According to Shaftesbury, reason or reflection is that faculty by which people review their mind and actions and pass judgment on them, either approving or disapproving. It manifests itself in two quite different ways, which may be designated "prudence" and "conscience." By the former, people judge what is to their advantage; by the latter, they judge what is proper and right. Shaftesbury denies that prudence gives adequate direction for an individual's life; for this purpose, people have been given conscience. It follows, according to Shaftesbury, that the goal of life lies not in happiness, whether in this world or in that to come, but in the perfection of the soul itself and its harmony with the total order of things.

In opposition to the religious doctrine of human depravity, Shaftesbury maintains that all people are endowed with a sufficient sense of right and wrong to enable them to achieve virtuous lives, and that the only obstacles are passion and vice. He describes appetite or passion as the elder brother of reason, striving to take advantage of reason, but when reason grows strong enough to assert itself, appetite, "like an arrant coward . . . presently grows civil, and affords the younger as fair play afterwards as he can desire." Vicious habits and customs present a more difficult problem. One source of these, according to Shaftesbury, is "corrupt religion and superstition," which teaches people to regard as praiseworthy practices that are "most unnatural and inhuman." Another is idleness, such as befell the "superior" classes in his day. Without a proper goal in life, people fall, he says, into a "relaxed and dissolute state" in which passions break out.

As Shaftesbury pictures it, conscience or moral insight is all of a piece with aesthetic judgment. There is a "natural beauty of figures," for example, that causes a mere infant to be pleased with the proportions of a ball or a cube or a dye. If, in more intricate cases, where color, texture, motion, sound, and the like are involved, there is room for dispute as to which is the finer fabric, the lovelier face, or the more harmonious voice, it remains as a fundamental assumption "that there is a beauty of each kind." "All own the standard, rule, and measure; but in applying it to things disorder arises, ignorance prevails, interest and passion breed disturbance." Nor is it otherwise, Shaftesbury continues, in matters of conduct. That there is a "fitness and decency in actions" can never be denied as long as people preserve the distinction between "that which interests and engages men as good" and "that which they admire and praise as honest."

Ultimately, for Shaftesbury, the beautiful and the good are the same. When speaking of a building, a picture, or the human body, people might call the object beautiful. When speaking of action, life, or a physical operation, people might instead use the word "good." There are, according to Shaftesbury, three degrees of beauty. The first is the beauty of "dead forms"—of pictures and statues—that exhibit harmony and proportion but have "no forming power, no action or intelligence." The second, which possesses all that the former lacks, is a double beauty: It is the beauty of "forming forms"—of artists and craftsmen. There is a third order of beauty, that which forms the "forming forms." Principally, this is the beauty of nature itself, or of the mind that informs it. This parent-beauty, because it fashions people's minds, "contains in itself all the beauties fashioned by those minds, and is consequently the principle, source, and fountain of all beauty," even including "architecture, music, and all which is of human invention."

The admiration that people owe to this highest beauty is, for Shaftesbury, the foundation of true religion. He raised no opposition against Christianity, except to question whether it was conducive to true worship and piety to dwell on the evil of creation, as contemporary divines were wont to do. He thought of himself as a deist, but he denied that the world is like a machine that the Maker, having completed, could leave to its own operation. He rejected the usual "proofs" of God based on the necessity for a first cause; he appealed instead to the immanence of a continuing Providence that orders all things well.

Thus, Shaftesbury held morality to be the foundation for belief in God, rather than the contrary. Carried further, true religion, or the apprehension of the divine creativity in nature, raises people's eyes to a higher vocation for themselves than they otherwise would know. As the offspring of divinity, people are themselves divine and are called on to be themselves creators—not merely in the sense of imposing form on matter, but in the sense of forming their own nature and that of other rational creatures. In this way, people participate in the highest beauty:

> He only is the wise and able man who, with a slight regard to [bodies and outward forms] applies himself to cultivate another soil, builds in a different matter from that of stone or marble; and having righter models in his eye, becomes in truth the architect of his own life and fortune, by laying within himself the lasting and sure foundation of order, peace and concord.

Such wisdom comes only to those who exercise their reason in an extraordinary degree. Mere knowledge of the world does not suffice, nor do ordinary deliverances of conscience. A person must find ways of examining opinions that seem true to themselves and their generation to pass from ignorance into knowledge. Shaftesbury recommended "soliloquy" as the best way for a person to rectify opinions, especially for those addicted to being "talkers or haranguers" in public. "'Tis the hardest thing in the world," he said, "to be a good thinker without being a strong self-examiner." For the same reasons, Shaftesbury wished for more honest discussion "in the way of dialogue, and patience of debate and reasoning, of which we have scarce a resemblance left in any of our conversations at this season of the world." Philosophy, or wisdom, as he conceived it, is not the sort of thing that can be transmitted as information. It is a discipline of the mind, a step beyond good breeding.

Nature, Evil, and Optimism

Shaftesbury's reaffirmation of design in the world raised in an acute form the problem of evil. His answer was similar to that given by the Stoics and by Saint Augustine. Suffering and loss are bound to appear evil to people because of their limited perspective. When better instructed, people find cause for admiration in the arrangement by which individuals sacrifice their lives for the species, and even in the relentless forces of earthquake and fire. Monstrous and abnormal births, he said, do not mitigate against the design of nature, because they result not from any natural failure but from the natural conflict of forces.

'Tis good which is predominant," says one of the characters in his dialogue, "and every corruptible and mortal nature by its mortality and corruption yields only to some better, and all in common to the best and highest nature which is incorruptible and immortal.

The optimism of Shaftesbury was far from being forced. As opposed to materialists, such as philosopher Thomas Hobbes, he found in the conception of nature as a system grounds for rejecting the doctrine of egotism and the war of each against all. He contended that besides the self-regarding passions, people also have passions that impel them to act for the interest of others. Both kinds are necessary in the economy of things. Private affections are necessary, not only because they assist the survival of the individual but also because they contribute to the public good. Similarly, social affections, such as parental love and friendship, further the interests and fill out the happiness of the individual. Shaftesbury argued that the purely selfish person does not, in fact, serve his or her own interest. On the other hand, it is possible for a person to be too much affected with the needs of others for even the public good. Thus, the happy life coincides with the life of virtue, in which reason is allowed to prevail over impulse.

The foundations of art, like those of morals, must, according to Shaftesbury, be laid in natural harmonies and proportions that the styles and humors of a particular age cannot brush aside with impunity. True beauty, he said, is not that which appeals to the senses, but that wherein the rational mind may come to rest. Its enjoyment is a disinterested contemplation, totally different from the pleasures that have their seat in desire; hence, the artist should not aim to represent objects that people find enjoyable but instead to create new unities analogous to those that make up the fabric of nature. True beauty lies deep. Many things that seem shocking and offensive at first are later known and acknowledged as the highest beauties.

The influence of Shaftesbury's thought was far-reaching. The French Encyclopedists and the early German Romantics were in his debt no less deeply than the moral philosophers of England and Scotland. The fact that in the Age of Reason "philosophy" freed itself from the knottier problems of metaphysics and epistemology and engaged the attention of poets and economists, as well as statesmen and propagandists, was in the main his doing.

Jean Faurot

Additional Reading

Bernstein, John Andrew. *Shaftesbury, Rousseau, and Kant: An Introduction to the Conflict Between Aesthetic and Moral Values in Modern Thought.* London: Associated University Press, 1980. Bernstein explores Shaftesbury as a precursor to modern ethics and aesthetics. Whereas

Shaftesbury assumed a kind of Platonic unity and harmony between the two, later thinkers have seen them as divided and even opposing. The chapter on Shaftesbury demonstrates how his view of both is at base psychological and is dependent on his generally deistic religious outlook.

Brett, R. L. *The Third Earl of Shaftesbury: A Study in Eighteenth-Century Literary Theory*. London: Hutchinson's University Library, 1951. Brett places Shaftesbury within the Augustan literary context of his time. A major thesis is that Shaftesbury attempted to keep philosophy attuned to the arts, in opposition to empiricism, which tended toward science. Brett stresses the Christian element in Shaftesbury's thought and credits him with providing general guidelines for literary theory of the Augustan Age. He somewhat exaggerates the philosopher's influence on contemporaries and on the Romantics.

Grean, Stanley. *Shaftesbury's Philosophy of Religion and Ethics: A Study in Enthusiasm*. Athens: Ohio University Press, 1967. In the two major parts of his book, Grean places Shaftesbury's philosophy within its historical contexts. Part 1 explores views on the nature of philosophy and religion, with extensive probing of Shaftesbury's views on enthusiasm. The book's second part explores ethics, its relation to religion, and the meaning of beauty. Grean strongly defends the internal logic and consistency of Shaftesbury's ideas.

Klein, Lawrence E. *Shaftesbury and the Culture of Politeness: Moral Discourse and Cultural Politics in Early Eighteenth-Century England*. Cambridge, England: Cambridge University Press, 1994. Analyzes Shaftesbury's Whig political views as they appear in his life and writings. Klein argues that his politics are influenced by his concept of politeness. He draws heavily on *An Inquiry Concerning Virtue* and Shaftesbury's personal notebooks, applying modern discourse analysis to illuminate Shaftesbury's methods of writing and clarify his social intent. The book's second part explores Shaftesbury's ideas that institutions such as the church and monarchy must be further limited in society for liberty and culture to advance.

Shaftesbury, Anthony Ashley Cooper, Earl of. *The Life, Unpublished Letters, and Philosophical Regimen of Anthony, Earl of Shaftesbury*. Edited by Benjamin Rand. London: Thoemmes Press, 1995. A look at Shaftesbury's ideas through an examination of his life and letters.

Voitle, Robert. *The Third Earl of Shaftesbury, 1671-1713*. Baton Rouge: Louisiana State University Press, 1984. Voitle's book, the most reliable biography available, provides a careful examination of Shaftesbury's writings. Thoroughly researched, the book draws heavily on unpublished and previously suppressed writings to interpret Shaftesbury's life and works. An examination of revised and unrevised versions of the writings enables Voitle to trace the development of Shaftesbury's thought, revealing differences between the earlier and later writings.

Stanley Archer

Henry Sidgwick

A proponent of higher education for women and an advocate of research into paranormal phenomena, Sidgwick attempted in philosophy to reconcile an intuitive approach to morality with that of utilitarianism. His reasoned defense of the resulting ethical method produced one of the most significant works on ethics in English, the capstone of nineteenth century British moral philosophy.

Principal philosphical works: The Ethics of Conformity and Subscription, 1870; The Methods of Ethics, 1874; The Principles of Political Economy, 1883; The Scope and Method of Economic Science, 1885; Outlines of the History of Ethics for English Readers, 1886; The Elements of Politics, 1891; Practical Ethics: A Collection of Addresses and Essays, 1898; Lectures on the Ethics of T. H. Green, H. Spencer, and J. Martineau, 1902; Philosophy, Its Scope and Relations, 1902; The Development of European Polity, 1903; Miscellaneous Essays and Addresses, 1904; Lectures on the Philosophy of Kant and Other Philosophical Lectures and Essays, 1905.

Born: May 31, 1838; Skipton, Yorkshire, England
Died: August 28, 1900; Cambridge, Cambridge-
    shire, England

Early Life

Henry Sidgwick was born on May 31, 1838, the son of William and Mary (Crofts) Sidgwick, both from northern England. His father, an Anglican clergyman and headmaster of the Skipton, Yorkshire, grammar school, died in 1841. Henry's early life was characterized by frequent moves, which apparently brought on a kind of stammer that never left him. In 1852, Henry was sent to Rugby School, and the rest of the family, his mother and three other surviving children, settled in Rugby the following year.

Sidgwick was strongly influenced in his early life by one of his Rugby masters, Edward White Benson, a cousin nine years older than he. Benson soon joined the Sidgwick household; he would later marry Sidgwick's sister, Mary, and would be the Archbishop of Canterbury from 1883 until the year of his death. The precocious Henry came to idolize his cousin and followed his advice by enrolling at Trinity College, Cambridge, after his graduation from Rugby in 1855. Cambridge was to be his home for the rest of his life.

Sidgwick's early university experience brought a host of academic awards, and as an undergraduate he was elected to the Apostles Society. The Apostles were dedicated to the pursuit of truth, wherever it might be found, and Sidgwick found himself taken by the spirit of honest inquiry into religion, society, and philosophy. He would devote his life to the great philosophical questions, seeking always for honesty and truth to triumph over rhetoric. Indeed, Sidgwick's writing is characterized by a kind of zealous balance, the author being at pains to give each aspect of an argument or counterargument its due.

Some readers of Sidgwick have taken this balancing effort as a fault and have yearned for the simple dogmatic statement which Sidgwick was loath to make. He was not a system builder in philosophy; his was the task of honest elucidation and tentative judgment.

In curious contrast to the stodgy feel of his major works, Sidgwick the man was a witty conversationalist (using his stammer at times as a dramatic device) and a lover of poetry. Small in stature, his large, silken beard flapping in the breeze as he ran along the street of Cambridge to his lectures, he was vigorous, sturdy, and good-humored. The academic life suited him perfectly.

Life's Work

In 1859, Sidgwick's sister married Edward Benson. That same year, Sidgwick was elected a fellow of Trinity and appointed to an assistant tutorship in classics, thus beginning his career as a teacher and writer. It was a time of ferment in the intellectual world; that same year, *On the Origin of Species by Means of Natural Selection*, by Charles Darwin, first saw publication, as did *On Liberty*, by John Stuart Mill. Mill became a major influence on Sidgwick, though the two often took differing philosophical positions. Through his contact with the Apostles, Sidgwick became convinced that the truth of Christianity was an open question. The influence of Benson's Anglican orthodoxy had begun to wane.

Henry Sidgwick. *(Library of Congress)*

Sidgwick did not lightly dismiss the Christian story, yet even an intense study of the ancient Semitic texts left him unsatisfied. He realized that he was dealing with philosophical issues: If the miracle stories from the Scriptures were true, then reports of miracles from all ages must be considered, but then the accuracy of science itself (which admits of no supernatural interventions in its descriptions of the regularities of the world) is called into question. It appeared to Sidgwick that the probability of a real miracle was much less than the likelihood that witnesses were erroneous, untruthful, or credulous. "I still hunger and thirst after orthodoxy," he wrote, "but I am, I trust, firm not to barter my intellectual birthright for a mess of mystical pottage." Yet Sidgwick, never given to fanaticism, produced no anti-Christian propaganda. He recognized the value of the faith for others, but honesty compelled him to a skeptical view of Christianity. He would wrestle with the idea of theism for the rest of his life.

Sidgwick's honesty became a *cause célèbre* in 1869, when he resigned his fellowship at Cambridge rather than continue to subscribe to the Thirty-nine Articles of the Church of England, which was required by law for the post. Though by 1869, affirmation of the Anglican doctrines was an empty formality in academic circles, it is characteristic of Sidgwick that he took the matter seriously. It is further a recognition of his abilities as an instructor that, far from being relieved of his duties, Sidgwick was appointed to a special post at Cambridge that did not require doctrinal subscription and was reappointed as a fellow when such tests were abolished in 1871. In 1872, he was passed over for the Knightsbridge Professorship of Moral Philosophy but was elected to the post in 1883 after the death of the incumbent. Sidgwick continued teaching at Cambridge, in one post or another, until his death, with only occasional lectures elsewhere.

Sidgwick began his academic duties as a lecturer in the classics, but his interests soon encompassed moral and political philosophy, economics, and epistemology.

His most enduring contribution came in *The Methods of Ethics*, first published in 1874, which ran to seven editions (the last, published after his death, came in 1907).

The Methods of Ethics does not seek to build a theoretical system of ethics but rather to discover if some coherence can be brought to the moral judgments actually made by men and women and if two apparently conflicting sources of moral imperatives can be reconciled. One source, intuitionism, was exemplified by the "common sense" philosophy of Thomas Reid, who made conscience the self-evident supreme authority in moral choices, and William Whewell, who allowed for a progressive intuition of moral concepts. Ethics must be based on principles derived by reason (the so-called moral faculty) and not on some calculation of the consequences of an action. This, the second source, is utilitarianism (or "universal hedonism"), which calls those actions right that produce the greatest happiness for the greatest number. Its varied exemplars included William Paley, who disavowed some inherent moral sense, Jeremy Bentham, associated with political reform movements and a secular approach to ethics, and John Stuart Mill, who deprecated intuitionism as merely the consecration of deep-seated prejudices.

Sidgwick agreed with the intuitionists that the common moral judgments of humankind could be ordered only by some self-evident first principle, but he attempted to demonstrate that this first principle was none other than the utilitarian dictum. Thus, moral choices are actually made on the basis of the self-evident principle of maximizing the good. Yet there were really two kinds of utilitarianism: universal hedonism (or rational benevolence), which strived to maximize the universal, or societal, good, and egoism (or prudence), which strived for maximizing the agent's good. When these two forms of utilitarianism are in conflict (when, for example, an agent must choose to save either himself or his fellows), can a rational choice be made between them? Is it possible to determine the cases in which egoism should take precedence over altruism?

For Sidgwick the answer was no. Without bringing in additional assumptions (for example, that God exists and will ultimately reward the altruistic choice), it is impossible to pronounce

egoism or altruism the more rational way. Sidgwick was left with a kind of fundamental dualism of the practical reason, needing some cosmic postulate in which to ground ethical choice. Yet God's existence is far from self-evident, and the mere desire that virtue be rewarded is not proof that it will be. Here *The Methods of Ethics* concludes, leaving for others the task of placing ethics in a larger context and so avoiding Sidgwick's dilemma.

Sidgwick's interest in psychic phenomena paralleled his quest for some evidence that might justify belief in another realm of existence and so provide the "cosmic postulate" for practical ethics. He had become interested in the paranormal when he was twenty-one; in 1882, in response to a sustained fascination with the subject, Sidgwick became the first president of the newly formed Society for Psychical Research. Though he would often observe purported mind readers or those with "second sight," Sidgwick's greatest contribution was in validating the very existence of such an organization. As he put it, "My highest ambition in psychical research is to produce evidence which will drive my opponents to doubt my honesty or veracity."

Sidgwick married Eleanor Mildred Balfour, the sister of Arthur James Balfour, in 1876; as a couple, they became deeply involved in probing supposed psychic events. Eleanor was perhaps the more credulous; she was convinced that telepathy was a reality, while her husband was never quite certain.

Sidgwick was certain that speculative philosophy did not excuse him from practical responsibilities. He had long been interested in the education of women and, after reading *The Subjection of Women* (1869) by Mill, laid plans for giving university lectures to women. Victorian thought generally assumed women were by nature unable to reach higher learning, but Sidgwick eventually saw the opening of Newnham Hall for Women, as part of Cambridge, in the year of his marriage. In 1892, Eleanor Sidgwick became president of the college. Childless, the Sidgwicks lived there the rest of their lives.

Sidgwick was a prolific writer. An essay for the *Encyclopædia Britannica* in 1878 was issued in 1886 as *Outlines of the History of Ethics*. In 1883, he published *The Principles of Political Economy*; *The*

Elements of Politics followed in 1891. His life was terminated by cancer on August 28, 1900. He had requested that these words should accompany the simple burial service: "Let us commend to the love of God with silent prayer the soul of a sinful man who partly tried to do his duty."

Influence

Sidgwick believed he had failed to develop a coherent ethics without reliance on some cosmic postulate that would guarantee a reward for the selfless. Others would attempt to place ethics within the context of evolutionary thought, and still others would ground ethics on metaphysics (idealism, for example). Nevertheless, Sidgwick's masterwork, *The Methods of Ethics*, was a hallmark in Victorian philosophy not for its originality but for its clarity and exquisitely precise exploration of reason in ethical decision making. Sidgwick concluded that reason alone could not resolve the conflict facing beings who had an ego life and at the same time a life in community. He had shown in his history of ethics that the Greek idea of the Good involved both pleasure and virtue (or duty); now the two had become separated, with reason powerless to mediate between individual pleasure and one's duty to society.

Sidgwick has been characterized as the last of the classical utilitarians. In his work, he prepared the way for new approaches to ethics by marshaling the data of common sense and articulating how far the principle of universal hedonism could be taken. He embodied in his life, as well as in his writing, the qualities of caution, good sense, an irenic spirit, balance, and the conviction of the supreme importance of moral choices.

Dan Barnett

The Methods of Ethics

Type of philosophy: Ethics
First published: 1874
Principal ideas advanced:

◇ Modern people use three different methods of ethics, three ways of resolving moral problems: egoism, intuitionism, and utilitarianism.

◇ Egoistic hedonism, the theory that one ought

to seek one's own pleasure, is one of the natural methods of ethics; its primary disadvantage is the difficulty of measuring and evaluating pleasures.

◇ The ethics of right and duty employs an a priori method, utilizing intuition, or direct cognition, as a way of discovering duties; but it is difficult to find moral principles that do not need qualification and that do not admit exceptions.

◇ Certain moral principles are manifestly true: the principle of impartiality, the principle of prudence, and the principle of benevolence.

◇ Utilitarianism is true to the principles of impartiality and benevolence; but it is difficult to reconcile egoism and utilitarianism.

Henry Sidgwick held that ethics focuses on the reasons people use in deciding between two courses of action and that the study of ethics is the attempt to bring these reasons together in a coherent system. Modern Western people use three different "methods" of ethics; that is, three different ways of answering the question, "Why should I do such and such?" They may reason with a view to self-interest; they may ask what their duty is; they may try to estimate the effect of the action in question on the general well-being. Sidgwick held that ordinary people do not find it necessary to choose between these methods: On some occasions they use one, and on other occasions another.

Professed moralists, however, have condemned this slackness and have insisted that all ethical reasoning should proceed from one principle and employ one method. Some have maintained that ethics is the reasoned pursuit of happiness, whether one's own or that of all humankind. Others have denied this and maintained that human reason knows immediately what acts are right and what are wrong. In Sidgwick's view, neither of these approaches could be carried through consistently without unduly constraining the moral intention of ordinary people. He accepted the ideal of unity and consistency that governs all theoretical inquiry; but he was wary of Procrustean solutions, and thought it better to leave certain questions unresolved than to do violence to important aspects of moral experience. Thus, instead of championing only one method, he sought to find a higher unity in which the distinctive contribution of each of "the methods of ethics" is preserved.

A work with such a thesis might have turned out to be a tiresome piece of eclecticism. Actually, it is a masterpiece in philosophical analysis. The strength of Sidgwick's work lies in the sympathetic treatment that he accorded each method, the care he expended in defining and testing claims, and the hopeful and tentative manner in which he developed rival positions.

Sidgwick broke with the practice, which had prevailed in English philosophy before his time, of treating moral philosophy as an adjunct of metaphysics, or of divinity, or of psychology. Whether moral law has its foundation in the will of God or in the evolution of society, whether human will is an efficient cause, whether humans are naturally selfish or social are questions that do not enter into ethical inquiry. Ethics is a search for "valid ultimate reasons for acting or abstaining." Problems concerning God, nature, and self belong not to ethics but to general philosophy. "The introduction of these notions into Ethics is liable to bring with it a fundamental confusion between 'what is' and 'what ought to be,' destructive of all clearness in ethical reasoning."

Limiting his field, therefore, to what could be called "the phenomenology of morals," Sidgwick brought under review three methods of ethical reasoning and their corresponding principles. He called them, for brevity, egoism, intuitionism, and utilitarianism. British ethical opinion, when his book first appeared, could fairly well be summed up in these three positions.

Egotistical Hedonism

The first method discussed by Sidgwick is egoistical hedonism. Sidgwick aimed to separate ethical questions from psychological ones; however, historically, ethical hedonism has always been closely connected with psychological hedonism and has been thought to draw support from it. For example, Jeremy Bentham maintained that "the constantly proper end of action on the part of any individual" is his own happiness. This is an ethical proposition. However, Bentham also said that "on the occasion of every act he exercises, every human being is inevitably led to pursue that line of conduct which, according to his

view of the case, taken by him at the moment, will be in the highest degree contributory to his own greatest happiness." This is a psychological proposition. Sidgwick said that, if the psychological statement be construed strictly, the ethical statement is meaningless: There is no point in maintaining that one "ought" to pursue the line of conduct that will bring one the greatest happiness if one is incapable of following any other line. However, even if the psychological law is taken in a weak and approximate sense, "there is no necessary connection between the psychological proposition that pleasure or absence of pain to myself is always the actual ultimate end of my action, and the ethical proposition that my own greatest happiness or pleasure is for me the *right* ultimate end."

Ethical hedonism does, however, deserve consideration as a method of ethics apart from the alleged psychological law. When people make "cool self-love" the ordering principle of their lives, they are, according to Sidgwick, using one of the "natural methods" by which people judge between right and wrong conduct. The philosophical egoist who defines the good in terms of pleasure is doing no more than stating this view in clear and meaningful terms.

One problem implicit in the popular conception of estimating satisfactions—for example, the relative value of poker and poetry—is to find a common coin by which they can be measured. Pleasure, conceived of as "the kind of feeling that we seek to retain in consciousness," serves as that coin. To give the theory further applicability, pain may be regarded as commensurable with pleasure, along a scale on either side of a "hedonistic zero."

Sidgwick submitted these notions to searching criticism, the most damaging of which, in his estimation, was the impracticality of methodical and trustworthy evaluation of the pleasures involved in two different courses of action. He did confess, however, that "in spite of all the difficulties that I have urged, I continue to make comparisons between pleasures and pains with practical reliance on their results." He concluded that for the systematic direction of conduct, other principles were highly desirable. He thought that this would be recognized by those who are concerned only with their own happiness.

Intuitionism

Common morality, however, although it allows a place for reasonable self-love, does not admit that people have the right to live for themselves alone. This leads to the second "method" of ethics, which Sidgwick called intuitionism. From this point of view, right conduct has very little to do with desires and selfish enjoyment; what matters is duty and virtue.

Sidgwick held that the notions of "right" and "ought," which are fundamental to the intuitionist point of view are "too elementary to admit of any formal definition." They cannot be derived from the idea of the good, if this is understood to consist of happiness. If, on the other hand, it is understood to consist of excellence, this is merely another way of referring to what ought to be. The judgment that a certain course of action is right presents itself as a direct cognition. It may be accompanied by feelings, such as sympathy or benevolence, but it is itself a dictate of reason. Unlike egoistic hedonism, which reasons a posteriori in its effort to estimate future good, the ethics of right and duty employs an a priori method, reasoning from self-evident truth. Sidgwick called it, therefore, the method of intuition.

Sidgwick maintained, however, that it is one thing to recognize the *prima facie* claims of moral insight—that they are simple and categorical—and something else to grant that their claims are veridical. The point he wished to make is that people would not have the notions of morally right and wrong (as distinct from instrumentally right and wrong and logically right and wrong) except for some kind of direct moral insight.

The systematic moralist soon discovers that not all moral intuitions are trustworthy. There are, said Sidgwick, three levels on which the claims of obligation present themselves to the conscience. First, there is the kind of judgment ordinarily referred to as the voice of conscience, which functions after the analogy of sense perception and testifies to the rightness or wrongness of single acts or motives. However, the slightest experience with others is enough to convince people that conscience, in the sense of an intuitive perception, is not infallible. Virtuous people differ in their judgment of a course of action. In their effort to persuade one another, they appeal from the particular instance to gen-

eral rules that seem to be self-evident. This is the second level of intuitive moral reasoning. It is made up of rules such as these: that we govern our passions, obey laws, honor parents, and keep promises.

To the unreflective mind, these rules seem unexceptionable. Nevertheless, a serious attempt to give them precise meaning and application discloses at once their ambiguity. For example, it is said to be intuitively certain that promisers are bound to perform what both they and the promisees understood to be undertaken. On examination, however, all sorts of qualifications come into view, which are just as obviously reasonable as the original principle. The promisee may cancel the promise; and there are circumstances in which it seems that promises should be annulled if the promisee is dead or otherwise inaccessible. Again, a promise may conflict with another obligation, or a promise may have been made in consequence of fraud or concealment. Sidgwick explored these and other possibilities in detail, and concluded "that a clear consensus can only be claimed for the principle that a promise, express or tacit, is binding, if a number of conditions are fulfilled," and that "if any of these conditions fails, the consensus seems to become evanescent, and the common moral perceptions of thoughtful persons fall into obscurity and disagreement."

Recognizing the weakness of common moral axioms, philosophers, ancient and modern, have sought to raise the principle of intuition to the level of an axiomatic science by formulating abstract principles of morality so clearly that they cannot conceivably be doubted or denied. For example, "we ought to give all people their own," and "it is right that the lower parts of our nature should be governed by the higher." These alleged axioms are self-evident, but only because they are tautologies. Sidgwick called them "sham axioms." They are worth even less than popular moral rules.

It might seem, from this analysis, that the entire attempt to base ethical reasoning upon intuition was a mistake and should be abandoned, but this was not Sidgwick's contention. "It would be disheartening," he said, "to have to regard as altogether illusory the strong instinct of common sense that points to the existence of such principles, and the deliberate convictions of the long line of moralists who have enunciated them." If the "variety of human natures and circumstances" is so vast that rules are not helpful in determining particular duties, there are, nevertheless, "certain absolute practical principles, the truth of which, when they are explicitly stated, is manifest."

The first such principle is that of justice or impartiality. It states that "if a kind of conduct that is right for me is not right for someone else, it must be on the ground of some difference between the two cases other than the fact that I and he are different persons." Sidgwick saw this as an application of the principle of the similarity of individuals that go to make up a logical whole or genus.

The second principle is that of prudence. It states "that Hereafter *as such* is to be regarded neither less nor more than Now." In other words, one ought to have a care for the good of one's life as a whole and not sacrifice a distant good for a nearer one. Sidgwick said that this was an application of the principle of the similarity of the parts of a mathematical or quantitative whole.

The third principle is that of benevolence, and follows from the other two. If we combine the principle of justice (equal respect for the right of every man) with the principle of the good on the whole, we arrive at "the notion of Universal Good by comparison and integration of the goods of all individual human—or sentient—existences." "I obtain the self-evident principle that the good of any one individual is of no more importance, from the point of view of the universe, than the good of any other. . . . And it is evident to me that as a rational being I am bound to aim at good generally."

In Sidgwick's opinion, these formal principles of intuition are an indispensable part of systematic ethics, providing the rational necessity on which the whole structure is based. Egoistic hedonism would have no kind of rational foundation apart from the axiom of prudence here expressed, nor would universal hedonism, or utilitarianism, without the other two axioms, those of justice and benevolence.

The axioms of intuition do not offer practical guidance by themselves. They must be given content and direction in terms of the good—not merely in terms of the formal concept of the good

as "excellence" but also in terms of the material concept of the good as "happiness," that is, "desirable consciousness." We have seen the validity of this concept in connection with egoism. All that remains is to accept it as the ultimate criterion or standard that ought to govern our actions toward others.

Utilitarianism

Sidgwick's discussion of utilitarianism, the third of his three "methods," is brief. It need not be extensive because its main principles have already been stated—that the good is pleasure was shown under egoism and that the right action has regard to the happiness of the whole was shown under intuitionism. Sidgwick does not try to base our duty to humankind at large on "feelings of benevolence," or "natural sympathy." It rests on a moral cognition. Sidgwick declared that utilitarianism requires people to sacrifice not only their private happiness but also that of persons whose interests natural sympathy makes far dearer to them than their own well-being. Its demands are sterner and more rigid than traditional notions of duty and virtue.

The fact that he found the rationale of utilitarianism implicit in the axioms of intuitionism was, for Sidgwick, a great step toward bringing the diverse methods of ethics into a higher synthesis. That egoism finds its rule of prudence among them was also encouraging. However, one fundamental breach remained to be healed: how to reconcile egoism with utilitarian duty.

Theologians have resolved the problem by the doctrine of immortality and eternal rewards, but Sidgwick refused that solution in the interests of preserving the autonomy of ethics. He did not deny the desirability of such an arrangement, but he saw no rational evidence for it. "It only expresses the vital need that our Practical Reason feels of proving or postulating this connection of virtue and self-interest, if it is to be made consistent with itself. For the negation of this connection must force us to admit an ultimate and fundamental contradiction in our apparent intuitions of what is Reasonable in conduct."

That would be tantamount to admitting that rational ethics is an illusion. It would not mean abandoning morality, "but it would seem to be necessary to abandon the idea of rationalizing it completely." This, in turn, would have the practical consequence that in a conflict between duty and self-interest, the conflict would be decided by "the preponderance of one or other of two groups of non-rational impulses."

Sidgwick's conclusion has about it the inconclusiveness of many a Socratic dialogue. He suggested that we may be faced with the alternative of accepting moral propositions "on no other grounds than that we have a strong disposition to accept them," or of "opening the door to universal scepticism."

Jean Faurot, updated by John K. Roth

Additional Reading

Blanshard, Brand. *Four Reasonable Men*. Middletown, Conn.: Wesleyan University Press, 1984. Blanshard includes Sidgwick in this book, which reveals Blanshard's admiration for Sidgwick's thought.

Broad, C. D. *Five Types of Ethical Theory*. Patterson, N.J.: Littlefield, Adams, 1959. A detailed and thorough critical work on *The Methods of Ethics*, which is Henry Sidgwick's most important contribution to moral philosophy.

Copleston, Frederick. *A History of Philosophy: Modern Philosophy*. Garden City, N.Y.: Doubleday, 1967. In a chapter on "Empiricists, Agnostics, Positivists," Copleston provided a brief but helpful account of Sidgwick's contributions to ethical theory.

Havard, William C. *Henry Sidgwick and Later Utilitarian Political Philosophy*. Gainesville: University of Florida Press, 1959. This historical study defines Sidgwick's place in the British utilitarian tradition.

James, David Gwilym. *Henry Sidgwick: Science and Faith in Victorian England*. New York: Oxford University Press, 1970. Situates Sidgwick and his philosophy in the British context of his time.

The Monist. LVIII, no. 3 (July, 1974). This issue of the journal is devoted to Sidgwick's philosophy. Contains several excellent historical and critical articles.

Schneewind, J. B. *Sidgwick's Ethics and Victorian Moral Philosophy*. New York: Clarendon Press, 1977. A well-crafted and thoughtful study of Sidgwick's ethical theory in the context of his historical period.

Schultz, Bart, ed. *Essays on Sidgwick*. New York: Cambridge University Press, 1992. Careful studies by able scholars trace the development, insights, and implications of Sidgwick's moral philosophy and his interpretations of utilitarianism in particular.

Dan Barnett, updated by John K. Roth

Peter Singer

Blending classical and preference utilitarianism, Singer has applied his theory to animal welfare, environmental ethics, famine relief, euthanasia, abortion, civil disobedience, and aid to refugees.

Principal philosophical works: *Democracy and Disobedience*, 1973; *Animal Liberation: A New Ethics for Our Treatment of Animals*, 1975, 1990; *Practical Ethics*, 1979, 1993; *Marx*, 1980; *Animal Factories*, 1980 (with Jim Mason); *The Expanding Circle: Ethics and Sociobiology*, 1981; *Hegel*, 1983; *The Reproduction Revolution: New Ways of Making Babies*, 1984 (with Deane Wells); *Should the Baby Live? The Problem of Handicapped Infants*, 1985 (with Helga Kuhse); *How Are We to Live? Ethics in an Age of Self-Interest*, 1993; *Rethinking Life and Death: The Collapse of Our Traditional Ethics*, 1994.

Born: July 6, 1946; Melbourne, Australia

Early Life

Three of Peter Albert David Singer's grandparents died in Nazi concentration camps. His parents, Cora and Ernst Singer, emigrated from Vienna in 1938 to escape persecution of Jews after the political union of Austria and Germany. Arriving in Australia, Ernst Singer established a tea and coffee import business, and Cora Singer, after overcoming restrictions then placed on overseas practitioners, resumed her work as a medical doctor.

The Singers were not religious believers. They were determined to integrate Peter and his sister Joan into Australian culture. They spoke to their children in English only and enrolled them in prestigious Protestant schools. Peter's childhood was comfortable and unremarkable. He participated in Boy Scouts, rooted for the local football team, enjoyed annual skiing holidays with his family, and earned high marks at school. He continued his education at Melbourne University, where he studied law, history, and philosophy.

While at Melbourne University, Singer met a fellow student, Renata Diamond, whom he married in 1968. He enrolled as a graduate student in moral and political philosophy at Oxford University in 1970. There, the Singers met a group of students who abstained from eating meat for ethical reasons. Their association and discussions with these vegetarians changed their lives. They became vegetarians themselves and began to see the general relationship between human and nonhuman animals in a different light.

Life's Work

In 1973, Singer published *Democracy and Disobedience*. In that book, he argues that in a model democratic society, there are important reasons for obeying the law that do not exist in other forms of government. The first is that such a society is a fair compromise between competing and otherwise irresolvable claims to power by majority and minority interests. The second is that participating in a decision-making procedure results in an obligation to act as if one consented to be bound by the conclusions of that procedure. Singer argues, however, that the modern forms of Western democracy are not fair compromises between competing groups; thus, for groups and individuals with less than an equal say in decision making, the argument based on fair compromise does not apply, and the argument from participation, while still applicable to those who vote, is weakened by the absence of adequate reason, for many dissenters, to vote. With this work, Singer expressed his unwavering conviction that moral and political philosophy should be relevant to issues of current concern.

Two other publications established Singer as an influential applied ethicist. In "Famine, Affluence, and Morality" (1972), he argues that the affluent of the world have strong moral obligations to prevent absolute poverty in the world when this can be done without sacrificing anything of comparable moral significance. Written in the clear, unadorned style that was to become Singer's trademark, this article demonstrates how a simple, easily acceptable principle of morality could have radical implications for the way people live. Many charitable organizations, particularly those involved with famine relief, embraced Singer as their ideological mentor.

In *Animal Liberation*, Singer addresses the question of how people ought to treat other animals. He tries to expose the indefensible prejudices that underlie people's attitudes and behavior. Singer argues that using animals for scientific experimentation, wearing furs and leather goods, and eating commercially produced meats are based on speciesism, discrimination grounded on the morally irrelevant characteristic of membership in a particular species. Drawing parallels between speciesism and racism, Singer argues that morality requires that humans treat animals as independent sentient beings and not as mere means to human ends. He claims that animals possess interests based on their capacities for suffering and enjoyment and that such interests must be given equal consideration to the like interests of humans. Preferences for humans can be based only on their possession of interests that animals lack; however, such preferences cannot justify cruelly disregarding the important interests of animals to satisfy trivial human interests.

Animal Liberation was criticized strongly by some scientists, medical experimenters, and factory farmers. Nevertheless, the book sold more than 400,000 copies, was translated into eight languages, and became the chief sourcebook for the international animal liberation movement. With this book, Singer proved that moral philosophy, written and pitched in a certain way, could fuel striking changes in social practices.

Singer expanded his application of philosophy to current moral issues with *Practical Ethics*. His aim was to demonstrate how a broadly utilitarian theory successfully treats such problems as moral equality, animal rights, abortion, euthanasia, obli-gations of the affluent to the impoverished, and the justification of means to ends.

Singer's views in *Animal Liberation*, although hotly contested in the philosophical and scientific communities, did not attract violent reaction. Most of those who rejected Singer's conclusions nevertheless saw him as a well-intentioned, albeit misguided, person. His views on bioethics, however, drew forceful opposition.

Two of Singer's bioethical conclusions repelled many. First, he argued that the intrinsic wrongness of killing a fetus and the intrinsic wrongness of killing a newborn infant are not markedly different. Restrictions on morally permissible infanticide can be grounded only in the negative effects of infanticide on others, such as the parents of the potential victim, not on the inherent value of the infant. Because he rejected appeals based on potential, Singer evaluated only the actual capacities of entities at the time of consideration. Fetuses and newborns do not have conscious desires to continue living, nor are they capable of making choices. Accordingly, the lives of fetuses and newborns are of no greater inherent value than the lives of animals at similar levels of rationality, self-consciousness, awareness, and capacity to feel. In this vein, Singer supported destructive experimentation on early human *in vitro* embryos because they are nonsentient beings who cannot suffer, and thus have no interests.

Second, Singer rejected the traditional medical distinction between passive and active euthanasia. Singer found no morally relevant difference between deliberately allowing a patient to die and helping a patient to die. Although the former is accepted medical practice in clearly defined circumstances, the latter is prohibited. Singer argued, on the contrary, that it is sometimes better to take active steps to end a patient's life, especially if doing so prevents the unnecessary suffering that often accompanies passive euthanasia. Thus, active euthanasia is either morally equivalent or superior to passive euthanasia when comparable cases are examined. Furthermore, Singer argued that it is often morally permissible to perform nonvoluntary euthanasia, in cases in which a person has never had or has irretrievably lost the capacity to choose to live or die. Nonvoluntary euthanasia decisions pertain to severely deformed infants, older humans who have been severely mentally retarded since birth, and subjects who once were able to choose between life and death but have irretrievably lost the capacity.

Beginning in the late 1980's, opposition to Singer's views on euthanasia became especially harsh in Germany and Austria. A professor at the University of Duisburg who offered a course in which *Practical Ethics* was the principal text abandoned the course after organized, repeated disruption by protesters. The protesters objected to the use of the book because in it, Singer advocates active euthanasia when the parents of severely disabled newborn infants, together with their physicians, decide that their infants should die rather than live. Because of other organized protests, conferences and symposia on philosophy and medicine in Bochum, Vienna, Kirchberg, Marburg, and Dortmund were cancelled or moved, or organizers withdrew invitations to Singer or those sympathetic to his views. The popular press in Germany published attacks on Singer by the leader of a militant organization of disabled people. Overlooking the fact that Singer's view was designed to reduce the power of the state in crucial life and death decisions, these attacks drew parallels between Singer's views and euthanasia as carried out in the Third Reich.

At the University of Saarbrücken, Singer was greeted by shouts and whistles from a minority of the audience determined to prevent him from speaking. His talk and a discussion with members of the audience eventually took place. He was not so fortunate at the University of Zurich. Even though his lecture was on the rights of animals, Singer was shouted down by a sizable minority of the audience who opposed his views on euthanasia.

As a political activist, Singer has lobbied governments and interest groups and participated in numerous demonstrations and protests that publicize wrongful practices. To demonstrate the plight of battery hens, he sat in oversized cages on city squares, led peaceful marches, and held vigils in front of factory farms and fur shops. He and fellow animal liberationists were arrested for trespassing when they tried to take photos of cruelly confined pigs owned by the prime minister of Australia.

In 1993, Paola Cavalieri and Singer edited *The Great Ape Project*. The book is a collection of essays by scientists and philosophers who argue that chimpanzees, gorillas, and orangutans are entitled to basic moral and legal protection. Beginning with a "Declaration on Great Apes," modeled after the United Nations Declaration of Human Rights, *The Great Ape Project* sought to ensure the right to life, the protection of individual liberty, and the prohibition of torture to nonhuman great apes. The book triggered the formation of an international organization founded to work for the removal of the great apes from the category of property and for their inclusion within the category of persons.

Singer, a founding member of the Victorian branch of a political party known as the Australian Greens, headed the list of the party's Senate candidates in the 1996 federal election. He received about 3 percent of the vote, less than half of what he required to win election. In addition, Singer taught at Oxford University, New York University, the University of Colorado at Boulder, the University of California at Irvine, and La Trobe University. Beginning in 1977, he was professor of philosophy at Monash University in Melbourne and, after 1983, was director or deputy director of the Monash University Centre for Human Bioethics. In 1999, he accepted an appointment at Princeton University as DeCamp Professor of Bioethics. In addition to writing a number of books, he edited or coedited numerous anthologies, the most influential of which is *A Companion to Ethics* (1991).

Influence

Socrates and Plato assumed that the point of philosophy is determining how people ought to live. As academic philosophy, especially in the Anglo-American world, took a scientific and linguistic turn in the twentieth century, professors retreated from the practical into highly abstract theory. Too often withdrawing into technical jargon and evading the real problems of everyday life, academic philosophy became a highly stylized form of communication among specialists. Singer's work was important in changing that trend. He addressed the most pressing social problems in an accessible way. He not only advanced ongoing debates about abortion, euthanasia, and the environment but also pointed out the relevance of less popular topics such as famine relief and animal liberation. Through his writings and political activism, Singer helped put academic philosophers back on the job of asking what really matters in life.

Raymond Angelo Belliotti

Practical Ethics

Type of philosophy: Ethics
First published: 1979
Principal ideas advanced:

◇ People must give equal weight in their moral deliberations to the like interests of all those affected by their actions.

◇ Utilitarianism is the minimal moral position reached by universalizing moral decision making.

◇ To give greater weight to the interests of members of one's own species when there is a clash between their interests and the interests of those of other species is speciesism.

◇ A person is a rational, self-conscious creature whose self-consciousness involves seeing himself or herself with a future and having desires related to that future, including the desire to continue living.

◇ There are utilitarian and nonutilitarian reasons for holding that the killing of a person is more seriously wrong than the killing of a nonperson.

◇ The affluent have an obligation to help those in absolute poverty that is just as strong as their obligation to rescue a drowning child from a pond when they can help without sacrificing anything of comparable moral significance.

Peter Singer was already one of the most influential applied ethicists before the publication of *Practical Ethics*. He made his mark through his work on civil disobedience, famine relief, and animal liberation. In *Practical Ethics*, Singer expands on some of his earlier arguments and extends his analyses to other contemporary moral problems. The book is written in a clear, un-

adorned style that makes its arguments accessible to nonspecialists without sacrificing philosophical subtlety.

Singer's overall aim is to show how a broadly utilitarian theory successfully treats such problems as moral equality, animal rights, abortion, euthanasia, obligations of the affluent to the impoverished, and the justification of means to ends.

The Nature of Ethics
Singer begins with a chapter on the nature of ethics. He counters common misconceptions, pointing out that ethics is not a set of prohibitions primarily concerned with sex, it is not merely a theoretical model that cannot be applied in everyday life, it is not dependent on a religious context, and it is not relative. Instead, Singer understands the point of ethical judgments to be the guiding of human practices. Moreover, the objectivity in ethics involves the kinds of reasons and justifications that are offered within the moral enterprise. Ethical reasons are universal: They go beyond one's own likes and dislikes and rise to the standpoint of the impartial spectator or ideal observer, which elevates them from the merely relative or subjective.

The moral point of view requires that one's own interests cannot, simply because they are one's interests, count more than the interests of anyone else; thus, one must give equal weight to the interests of all. Singer insists that the universal aspect of ethics therefore provides a persuasive, although not necessarily conclusive, reason for taking a broadly utilitarian position. In fact, utilitarianism, the view that an action is morally sound if and only if no other action available will foreseeably produce better overall consequences to those affected, is the minimal moral position reached by universalizing moral decision making. To go beyond utilitarianism, says Singer, people must be provided additional good reasons.

The moral point of view thus requires the principle of equal consideration of interests: One must give equal weight in moral deliberations to the like interests of all those affected by one's actions. An interest is an interest, whoever's interest it may be. The principle of equal consideration does not depend on a belief in factual equality, the belief that all people or all interest-bearers are actually equal in relevant physical and mental respects. Instead, it depends on the conviction that the most important interests, such as the interest in avoiding pain, in developing one's abilities, in satisfying basic needs, in enjoying personal relationships, and in being free to pursue projects, are not affected by factual inequalities.

The rest of the book works out the implications of the principle of equal consideration of interests from a utilitarian standpoint. In general, Singer argues that people's moral calculations and practices should change: People should accord more weight to the interests of animals than they currently do and less weight to members of their own species, such as fetuses, newborns, the severely retarded, and the senile, whose possession of interests is problematic. Consequently, some nonhuman lives, judged from the standpoint of richness of interests, are of higher quality than some human lives. In certain cases, abortion, euthanasia, and the killing of defective infants are justified, and some types of treatment of animals are morally prohibited. Singer adds that it is speciesism to give greater weight to the interests of members of one's own species when there is a clash between their interests and the interests of those of other species.

Applying Utilitarianism

Singer applies the principle of equal consideration from a combination of classical and preference utilitarian theories. Classical utilitarianism is formulated around maximizing pleasure and minimizing pain, whereas preference utilitarianism is formulated around maximizing the fulfillment of desires and preferences. In his discussion of racial, sexual, and species equality, Singer emphasizes a version of classical utilitarianism. In his discussion of killing people and animals, he highlights preference utilitarianism in the case of persons, while referring to classical utilitarianism in the case of nonpersons. A person, for Singer, is a rational, self-conscious creature whose self-consciousness involves seeing oneself with a future and having desires related to that future, including the desire to continue living.

Practical Ethics contains an extensive discussion of the wrongness of killing. Preference utilitarianism provides a direct reason for not killing persons: Killing frustrates the person's future-related desire to continue living. Classical utilitarianism provides only an argument from side effects, at least when the killing is instantaneous and painless, which is merely an indirect reason for not killing. The argument is that painlessly killing some people increases the unhappiness of surviving people who will worry that they might be killed in the future. Thus, there are two utilitarian reasons for holding that the killing of a person is more seriously wrong than the killing of a nonperson: The classical utilitarian concern with side effects and the preference utilitarian concern with the frustration of the victim's desires and plans for the future. Singer also entertains, although he does not explicitly endorse, two nonutilitarian reasons: the argument that the capacity to have desires about one's future is a necessary condition of a right to life, and respect for autonomy.

In the case of killing animals for food, clothing, medical experimentation, and sport, people must first determine whether the animals in question are persons. Singer offers chimpanzees, gorillas, monkeys, whales, dolphins, seals, bears, pigs, dogs, and cats as candidates for personhood. He rejects fish, reptiles, chickens, and other birds. If an animal is a person, then, at least, the strong preference utilitarian objection to killing holds. If it is not a person, then none of the utilitarian reasons against killing hold when the killing is painless and no other animals are adversely affected. Killing an animal that is not a person would still reduce the amount of pleasure in the world because it eliminates one sentient being, but this is a relatively weak reason not to kill. Singer, acknowledging this, departs from his earlier work on animal liberation by accepting a replaceability argument and admitting that "in some circumstances—when animals lead pleasant lives, are killed painlessly, their deaths do not cause suffering to other animals, and the killing of one animal makes possible its replacement by another who would not otherwise have lived— the killing of a nonself-conscious animal [a nonperson] may not be wrong."

Abortion and Euthanasia

Regarding abortion, Singer rejects the view that a fetus embodies moral significance because it is a potential person. He concludes that the life of a fetus or even a newborn has no greater value than the life of a nonhuman animal at a similar level of rationality, self-consciousness, awareness, and capacity to feel. The grounds for not killing persons therefore do not apply to fetuses or newborns. Restrictions on infanticide should issue only from the argument from side effects: the adverse effects of infanticide on others, particularly the parents of the victim. In cases of abortion where the people most affected, such as the prospective mother, want the abortion, the argument from side effects typically will not create moral prohibitions.

Singer also argues that voluntary euthanasia, the killing of a person with that person's consent, is often morally permissible. When a person suffering from a painful and incurable disease wishes to die, neither the usual utilitarian nor nonutilitarian objections to killing apply. Under certain circumstances, Singer also endorses nonvoluntary euthanasia: when those killed lack the capacity to understand the choice between their continued existence or nonexistence, when that capacity will not be recovered or gained, when the foreseeable quality of life of the subject will be extremely poor, and when the argument from side effects creates no moral prohibition.

Distribution of Wealth
Singer's most passionate arguments are directed at the reallocation of wealth from the developed nations to the poor of the undeveloped nations. He rejects the view that there is a morally relevant distinction between acts such as killing and omissions such as letting others die who require aid to survive. Singer argues that the relatively affluent have an obligation to help those in absolute poverty that is just as strong as their obligation to rescue a drowning child from a pond when they can help without sacrificing anything of comparable moral significance. He provides numerous facts and examples that highlight the consequences of people's typical neglect of the impoverished of the world. Singer suggests a minimum ethical standard: Those earning average or above average incomes in affluent societies, unless they have an unusually large number of dependents or other special needs, ought to give one tenth of their income to reducing absolute poverty.

Morality as a Means to Happiness
When addressing the issue of why people should act morally, Singer claims that the notion of ethics has become misleading to the extent that moral worth is attributed only to actions taken because they are right, without any ulterior motive. He suggests that to act morally probably will make people happy, because fulfillment can be gained from the outward-looking, impartial way of life instead of from a direct search for happiness. Happiness can be an internal reward for moral achievements. Although those who do not follow the process are not necessarily irrational, self-awareness and reflection on the nature and point of human existence may lead people toward concerns broader than narrow self-interest.

Practicability and a Revised Edition
Practical Ethics has been widely used in philosophy courses in North America, the United Kingdom, and Australia, and it has been translated into German, Italian, Spanish, and Swedish. The book solidified Singer's standing as the most influential contemporary utilitarian philosopher. Many organizations concerned with animal rights, famine relief, and euthanasia regard Singer as their ideological mentor.

Critics, however, charge that Singer fails to demonstrate why thinking ethically and impartially about everyone's interests requires people to add up these interests and weigh them overall in a utilitarian calculus. Nonutilitarian methods permit people to evaluate the interests of everyone impartially without weighing them overall. More fundamentally, Singer never persuasively explains why morality requires people to consider all interests equally without regard for whose interests they are. That in mind, *Practical Ethics* may tacitly adopt an inadequate concept of the value of personal relations. Universal benevolence and sympathy—treating all others as equal objects of concern, respect, and intimacy—are insufficient. A world of no friendship and of no neighborly or family affection is one that few would choose to inhabit even on the condition that it yielded slight gains in overall happiness. If people's natural desires toward partiality do not translate into behavioral partiality, they become deeply conflicted. Can people have deeply felt bonds of love but still remain impartial when meting out resources and service goods? Does Singer's 10 percent solution adequately lessen the conflict?

Moreover, Singer may not have adequately dealt with a fundamental objection to utilitarianism: that it can justify sacrificing the paramount interests of a few for the minor interests of many others. Singer claims that the principle of equal consideration of interests does not permit such a result, but his examples fail to establish that claim. Finally, Singer's refusal to be swayed by results that sometimes seem radically at odds with considered judgments calls into question what he takes to be the criteria of soundness for ethical theories. Appeals to self-evidence ring hollow to those not already committed to utilitarianism.

In 1993, a second edition of *Practical Ethics* was published. All the chapters of the first edition were revised. One new chapter applies the arguments on equality and poverty to the problem of international refugees. Another applies Singer's blend of classical and preference utilitarianism to environmental ethics. The appendix outlines Singer's experiences in Germany and Austria, where his views on euthanasia met widespread criticism, especially from those acutely sensitive to the horrifying human experiments of the Nazi regime and from the disabled. Many parts of the book are updated to take into account certain technical developments since the first edition, such as *in vitro* fertilization, embryo experimentation, assisted suicides, and the emergence of environmental activism.

Raymond Angelo Belliott

Additional Reading

Bambrough, Renford, ed. *Philosophy* 53 (October, 1978): 433-563. A special issue of *Philosophy* devoted entirely to the discussion of the relations between humans and animals. Seven philosophers critically examine Singer's positions on the moral treatment of animals.

Cottingham, John. "Ethics and Impartiality." *Philosophical Studies* 43 (January, 1983): 83-99. The author attacks the impartiality thesis endorsed by Singer and argues that people are morally justified in giving special weight to their own interests and those of family and friends. Cottingham claims that the impartial-

ity thesis is an inadequate foundation for Singer's ethical globalism.

Fox, Michael. "Animal Liberation: A Critique." *Ethics* 88 (January, 1978): 106-118. Fox argues that it makes no sense to ascribe rights to animals because rights exist only within the context of the moral community, and animals lack certain crucial capacities required for membership therein. Fox argues that Singer is wrong in thinking that animals' capacity to enjoy and suffer is an adequate basis for assigning moral rights to them.

Glock, Hans-Johann. "The Euthanasia Debate in Germany: What's the Fuss?" *Journal of Applied Philosophy* 11, no. 2 (1994): 213-224. Glock claims that Singer's position on euthanasia is immoral but that his expression of those views is protected by freedom of speech. The author argues that Singer's views do not pose the kind of threat to other legal and moral values that would license a suspension of freedom of expression. Although it is illegitimate to silence Singer, Glock concludes that it is legitimate to protest against Singer because Singer denies that some of the lives of the disabled are worth living, in disregard of their own preferences.

Jamieson, Dale, ed. *Singer and His Critics*. Malden, Mass.: Blackwell, 1999. An examination of Singer's philosophical thoughts and responses to those philosophies.

Lockwood, Michael. "Singer on Killing and the Preference for Life." *Inquiry* 22 (Summer, 1979): 157-170. Lockwood argues against Singer's formulation of preference utilitarianism and the greater value Singer places on human, as opposed to nonhuman, life. He concludes that it is counterintuitive to regard animal lives as wholly replaceable.

Narveson, Jan. "Animal Rights." *Canadian Journal of Philosophy* 7 (March, 1977): 161-178. Narveson denies that animals have strong moral rights such as the right not to be killed for food. He argues from a contractarian perspective and against Singer, that people have no moral obligations to animals but do have duties to weaker humans.

Oderberg, David, and Jacqueline Laing, eds. *Human Lives: Critical Essays on Consequentialist Bioethics*. New York: Macmillan, 1997. A collection of original papers by philosophers from Britain, the United States, and Australia. The aim of the book is to undermine the persuasiveness of consequentialist views, such as utilitarianism, in the field of bioethics. The book contains excellent criticisms of Singer's positions on euthanasia, abortion, environmental ethics, animal welfare, and speciesism.

Rowlands, Mark. *Animal Rights: A Philosophical Defence*. New York: St. Martin's Press, 1998. Rowlands examines the philosophical aspect of the animal rights movement in Singer's *Animal Liberation*.

Sterba, James. "Abortion, Distant Peoples, and Future Generations." *Journal of Philosophy* 77 (July, 1980): 424-439. Sterba argues that many of the arguments advanced by those, such as Singer, who favor a liberal view of abortion are inconsistent with a defense of the rights of distant peoples to basic economic assistance. On this account, the author claims that those, such as Singer, who favor a liberal view of abortion and the rights of distant people must moderate their support of at least one of those positions.

Raymond Angelo Belliott

Adam Smith

Smith was one of the major luminaries of the eighteenth century Scottish Enlightenment. His *The Wealth of Nations* became the bible of nineteenth century liberals, and twentieth century conservatives were similarly animated by his vision of the beneficent results of the free marketplace. Economists, whatever their personal ideologies, continue to pay homage to Smith for his contribution to the study of economic development.

Principal philosophical works: *The Theory of Moral Sentiments*, 1759; *An Inquiry into the Nature and Causes of the Wealth of Nations*, 1776 (commonly known as *The Wealth of Nations*); *Essays on Philosophical Subjects*, 1795.

Born: June 5, 1723 (baptized); Kirkcaldy, Fifeshire, Scotland
Died: July 17, 1790; Edinburgh, Scotland

Early Life

Adam Smith was born in Kirkcaldy, a fishing and mining town near Edinburgh. His exact date of birth is unknown, although records show that he was baptized on June 5, 1723. His father, also named Adam, had died before his son's birth. His mother, the former Margaret Douglas, was thus the most important influence in young Smith's life. After attending the local school, Smith entered the University of Glasgow in 1737. In 1740, he won the Snell Exhibition, receiving a scholarship for study at Balliol College, Oxford, and spent the next six years there reading widely in the classics, literature, and philosophy. From 1746 to 1748, Smith lived with his mother in Kirkcaldy, until a group of friends arranged for him to give a series of public lectures in Edinburgh. These lectures proved so successful that he was named to the chair of logic at the University of Glasgow in 1751. When the equivalent position for moral philosophy became available that same year, he was elected to the place. Smith proved to be not simply a popular and effective teacher; he became heavily involved in university administration, serving as quaestor for six years, then as dean of faculty and as vice rector.

At Glasgow, Smith lectured on a broad range of topics: rhetoric and belles lettres, natural theology, ethics, and jurisprudence (law, government, and economics). Although nothing is known about his lectures on natural theology (except for a former student's report that they dealt with "the proofs of the being and attributes of God, and those principles of the human mind upon which religion is founded"), student notes on his rhetoric and economic lectures have been published. Smith's lectures on ethics became the basis of his first book, *The Theory of Moral Sentiments*. The work was an immediate success, it was translated into French and German, and it went through nine editions during Smith's life. Influential politician Charles Townshend was so impressed that he engaged Smith to tutor his stepson, the young duke of Buccleuch. In early 1764, Smith gave up his Glasgow chair to accompany his charge on a Grand Tour of the Continent that lasted until late 1766. After his return, Smith worked briefly as an adviser to Townshend, who was then Chancellor of the Exchequer. Given a generous lifetime pension by Buccleuch, Smith then went back to Kirkcaldy to work on what would be his masterpiece. From 1773 to 1776, he was in London advising the government on economic matters, simultaneously continuing with his own writing. The publication of *An Inquiry into the Nature and Causes of the Wealth of Nations* (commonly known as *The Wealth of Nations*) on March 9, 1776, was a landmark in Western thought.

Adam Smith. *(Library of Congress)*

for imaginatively identifying with others: "This is the only looking-glass by which we can, in some measure, . . . scrutinize the propriety of our own conduct."

Smith regarded justice as the "main pillar" upon which society rested. He defined this justice in negative terms—as consisting of refraining from injuring another person or from taking or withholding from another what belonged to him. More important, Smith realized the impossibility of relying exclusively upon the spontaneous and natural operation of people's impulses toward their fellows' feelings for the attainment of justice. The force of what he termed sympathy was strongest among those sharing a common social bond—membership in the same family, church, town, guild, or other social group. The wider the distance, physical or social, that separated people, the weaker was the bond's influence: "All men, even those at the greatest distance," he wrote, "are no doubt entitled to our good wishes, and our good wishes we naturally give them. However, if, notwithstanding, they should be unfortunate, to give ourselves any anxiety upon that account seems to be no part of our duty." Accordingly, people formulate general rules to govern their actions and institute governments to enforce those rules by legal sanctions. Smith recognized that people were moved simultaneously by self-regard and by social passions. The key to his later book, *The Wealth of Nations*, was his belief in the primacy of the self-regarding motives within the economic sphere, given the impersonality and anonymity of the marketplace. People, he believed, are dependent upon the goodwill of their neighbors but cannot depend on their generosity alone to provide it. To ensure the proper feeling, they must show others that it is to their own benefit to help them: "It is not from the benevolence of the butcher, the brewer, or the baker, that we expect our dinner, but from their regard to their own interest."

Smith's larger purpose in *The Wealth of Nations* was to identify the reasons behind what is called economic development, or what he called the

Life's Work

Smith first made his reputation with *The Theory of Moral Sentiments*. The problem he set for himself in this book was to explain the forces responsible for the socialization of the individual to fit him for membership in a social group. Reflecting the optimistic deism of the Scottish Enlightenment, his starting point was that God had endowed human beings with inborn "moral sentiments" that bound them together. One such sentiment was the desire each person had for the praise and approval of others: "Nature, when she formed man for society, endowed him with an original desire to please, and an original aversion to offend his brethren. She taught him to feel pleasure in their favourable, and pain in their unfavourable regard." The second was people's capacity

"progress of opulence." One such cause was the "propensity to truck, barter, and exchange one thing for another," which Smith considered to be "one of those original principles in human nature, of which no further account can be given." The second was people's similarly natural ambition to gain the esteem of others by improving their economic status and thus their rank in society.

These impulses interacted to promote economic development through the mechanism of an increasingly extensive division of labor. Smith's major contribution to economic theory lay in his explanation of the ways in which the specialization of function, accompanying the division of labor, increased productivity by reducing the time wasted in shifting from one task to another, sharpening workers' skills, and facilitating the invention of improved machinery. Smith envisaged the size of the market as the major limitation upon the extent to which the division of labor could go. Thus, he saw the process progressing almost automatically toward always higher levels of well-being. The more productivity was increased, the larger the population that could be supported; the larger the population, the larger the market; the larger the market, the more extensive the division of labor. Smith's argument for international free trade rested upon the same ground. Each country specializing in the kinds of production in which it had a comparative advantage would increase the total wealth of all. A major target of the book was the mercantilist policies of Smith's time, which aimed at promoting national autarky, which Smith attacked for forcing "part of the industry of the country into a channel less advantageous than that in which it would run of its own accord."

Behind Smith's exaltation of the beneficent economic results of the pursuit of self-interest lay Sir Isaac Newton's vision of a universe governed by self-regulating laws. Under a regime of free exchange, each person unintentionally promotes the good of his nation's economy when he "endeavours as much as he can both to employ his capital in support of domestick industry, and so to direct that industry that its produce may be of the greatest value; every individual necessarily labours to render the annual revenue of the soci-

ety as great as he can." He also assumed a tendency toward a self-correcting equilibrium in the economy. Aggregate income and output were automatically in balance; free competition would assure that whenever prices, wages, or the return on capital rose above or fell below their "natural" rates, supply and demand would bring about the required adjustment. The corollary was that government regulation will always distort the most efficient utilization of resources by interfering with the "natural balance of industry."

The first edition of *The Wealth of Nations* sold out within six months of publication. Smith published a revised edition in 1778 and followed it with a substantially expanded third edition six years later. The work was translated into French, German, Danish, Dutch, Italian, and Spanish. In 1777, Smith was appointed commissioner of the customs in Edinburgh, where he would live for the rest of his life. The income from this position, combined with his pension from the Duke of Buccleuch, made Smith a comparatively wealthy man. He maintained close ties with his mother until her death in 1784, and he never married. Nevertheless, he was active in the social life of Edinburgh's intellectual and scientific community. Among the honors he received was election in 1787 to the rectorship of the University of Glasgow. Although notorious for his absentmindedness, Smith maintained his broad intellectual interests. He revised and added to *The Theory of Moral Sentiments*. His *Essays on Philosophical Subjects*, published posthumously in 1795, included a lengthy piece on the history of astronomy that has earned for him recognition as a pioneer in the history and philosophy of science. He continued to write, but he destroyed the bulk of his manuscripts shortly before his death at the age of sixty-seven on July 17, 1790.

Influence

The Wealth of Nations became the bible of those who favor laissez-faire—that is, no interference by the government with the individual's pursuit of self-interest in the marketplace. Nevertheless, Smith was not the uncritical admirer of private enterprise that many later admirers thought him to be. He was deeply suspicious of the tendency of businesspeople to seek special privileges from the government and to combine to extort monopoly profits. When monopoly could not be avoided, he preferred government to private control. Nor was he dogmatic in his support for laissez-faire. He upheld the responsibility of the state to provide public services that would benefit society as a whole, but only when they were "of such a nature, that the profit could never repay the expence to any individual, or small number of individuals, and which it therefore cannot be expected that any individual or small number of individuals should erect or maintain." He explicitly endorsed publicly supported compulsory elementary education to offset the stultifying effects of the division of labor. He similarly qualified his support for international free trade by allowing for protectionist measures when they were required for national defense, a priority "of much more importance than opulence."

Even though his position was distorted by later exponents of laissez-faire, Smith's prescriptive recommendations would have a major impact on governmental policies not simply in Great Britain but throughout the Western world as well. Writing in 1857, the historian H. T. Buckle concluded that "looking at its ultimate results, [*The Wealth of Nations*] is probably the most important book that has ever been written, and is certainly the most valuable contribution ever made by a single man toward establishing the principles on which government should be based." A later reaction against laissez-faire spurred the resultant downgrading of Smith, but many twentieth century free marketeers found a continued source of inspiration in his writings.

Smith's intellectual influence transcended the economic implications of his work. Smith was a pioneer in the application of the historical approach to the analysis of economic phenomena. His arguments rested not only upon his astute observations of contemporary society but also upon a vast accumulation of data drawn from his wide reading in history. Even more important, his work was the first comprehensive and systematic exploration of how a capitalist market economy worked. His emphasis upon the central role of the division of labor would be followed by later students—including those, such as Karl Marx, who found more to damn than to praise.

John Braeman

The Theory of Moral Sentiments

Type of philosophy: Ethics
First published: 1759
Principal ideas advanced:

◇ The origin of moral sentiments is sympathy, placing oneself imaginatively in the situation of another in order to realize the passions that affected the person.

◇ One approves the passions of another and regards them as suitable if, imagining oneself in like circumstances, one believes that one would have similar feelings.

◇ The amiable virtues of condescension and indulgence stem from sympathy; the respectable virtues of self-denial and self-command arise in those who are the objects of sympathy.

◇ The unsocial passions, hatred and resentment, are disagreeable; the social passions such as generosity, kindness, and compassion are agreeable; and the selfish passions are mixed, neither as disagreeable as the unsocial passions nor as agreeable as the social.

◇ The propriety of an action is the fitness of its motivating feeling to the cause of that feeling; the merit or demerit of an action rests upon the character of the consequences of the action.

◇ Conscience is the faculty of judgment of the person within the breast, the inward person who knows the actual motivations of his or her actions.

Adam Smith was a professor of moral philosophy in the University of Glasgow. He is perhaps better known for his work in economic theory, *An Inquiry into the Nature and Causes of the Wealth of Nations* (commonly known as *The Wealth of Nations*; 1776), than for *The Theory of Moral Sentiments*, his other major work. Smith was a contemporary and friend of Scottish philosopher David Hume. Accepting Hume's moral doctrines on the whole, Smith offered the theory of moral sentiments as a treatment of an area Hume left only vaguely outlined. Smith considered the science of ethics to have as its business the description of the moral rules with a justness and nicety that would both ascertain and correct one's ideas of proper conduct.

Smith was close on the heels of the "moral sense" philosophers, the third earl of Shaftesbury (Anthony Ashley Cooper) and Francis Hutcheson. Unlike them, however, he did not ascribe moral perception to an inner sense such as the exterior senses, a sense capable of recognizing moral quality in a manner analogous to the way the eye perceives color and shape. Smith asserted that philosophers should give greater attention to the causes of the passions along with the due heed paid to their consequences.

Sympathy

Smith regarded the origin of the moral feelings to be in the process of sympathy with the passions. This process consists of placing the self in imagination in the place of another, of conceiving the self as undergoing the same events and, consequently, having the same feelings as the other person. One does not have *the other person's* feelings, which is simply impossible; but imagination copies one's own feelings upon earlier occasions and supplies them anew to one's mind. Thus, a sympathetic feeling could be one of compassion for the misery of an unfortunate person or the joy of one delivered from danger. Because one is not actually, but only imaginatively, in the situation of the other, one can never have feelings in such great strength as the other. Furthermore, some passions do not arouse fellow feeling but rather act as stimuli to some opposing feeling. Sometimes when one perceives a person's anger, one is aroused against the individual rather than against those toward whom the person's anger is aimed; or one may experience fear of the person rather than anger. A sympathetic response is aroused more by the knowledge of the situation in which the other's feeling first arises than it is by the perception of the other's feeling. This is shown when one occasionally sympathizes with the dead, who actually have no feelings at all. The exercise of sympathy brings pleasure both to those who give and to those who receive it. The pleasure of receiving sympathy in the disagreeable passions is more intense than in the agreeable and may serve as a measure of relief.

The basis of one's approval of the feelings of other people is whether perfect concord exists between one's own sympathies and theirs, when one is aware of the other's situation. One determines in this way that their passions are suitable and proper to their objects. Just as to have the same opinion as another is to approve of the person's having it, so with the feelings; one approves the other's feeling if, in like circumstances, one would have the same feeling. Even in cases in which one does not actually have sympathetic feeling with another, experience leads one to learn the nature and the amount of feeling appropriate to the other's circumstances, and thus to approve of his feelings.

People's natures are so constituted that they can be at variance with their fellows in their feelings, yet tolerate or even enjoy one another's company, as long as the matters that arouse them are items of indifference to people's particular lives. However, when an event touches one directly, one hopes for the greatest possible concord of the spectator's feeling with one's own, and one is likely to select one's company only from those who feel similarly. Yet recognizing that no other can feel precisely what one feels, because the person cannot imagine all the conditions that stir the feeling in one, people restrain and moderate their own feeling to a degree. Thus, one's desire for their approval and the satisfaction one can expect from it act as a curb on the extremes of our feelings, and the society of those who have fellow feeling with one aids in restoring and preserving the tranquillity of one's mind.

Virtues and Passions

Two classes of virtues follow from these tendencies. The *amiable* virtues of "candid condescension and indulgent humanity" stem from the sympathy of the spectator, and the *respectable* virtues of self-denial and self-command come from the moderation of passion in the person involved. "To feel much for others and little for ourselves . . . to restrain our selfish, and to indulge our benevolent affections, constitutes the perfection of human nature; and can alone produce among mankind that harmony of sentiments and passions in which consists their whole grace and propriety." The *propriety* or the impropriety of an affection is in its "suitableness or unsuitableness, in the proportion or disproportion which the affection seems to bear to the cause or object which excites it." Certain qualities are favorable but not necessarily admired; those that excite not only approbation but also wonder and surprise are the admirable qualities. This is true of one's actions. Many, perhaps most, actions exhibiting propriety do not require virtue; but those that arouse people's admiration at their uncommon delicacy of feeling or strength of self-command are signs of the admirable degree of the amiable or respectable virtue.

Passions originating with the body, such as hunger or pain, are objects more of disgust than of sympathy, since the onlooker can enter into them only to a very low degree. However, those that originate in the imagination, such as the loss of one's fortune or the frustration of an ambition, can readily take on the configuration of the imagination of the person affected. A tragic drama may fitly turn on such an event, but not even on so great a physical loss as the loss of a leg.

The passions fall into a set of classifications. The *unsocial* passions are hatred and resentment, with their variations. They arouse in the spectator rival feelings, which must work against each other, for the spectator has as much tendency to sympathize with the person hated as with the person showing hatred. These passions are disagreeable both to the spectator and the person feeling them. They tend to drive people apart and destroy society. The *social* passions, such as generosity, humanity, kindness, compassion, friendship, and all the benevolent affections, are felt with enjoyment; they bring people together and cement society. People enter into a feeling of satisfaction both with the person who shows them and with the person who is their object. Finally, the *selfish* passions take a middle place between the others. They are grief and joy when arising over the particular good or bad fortune of the person by whom they are felt. These become neither as disagreeable as the unsocial passions, for there is no rival to arouse a contrary sympathy, nor as agreeable as the social passions, for there is no additional beneficiary in whose satisfaction one would share.

The qualities of merit and demerit are the qualities of deserving reward or punishment, distinct species of approbation and disapprobation. Whereas the propriety of an action is the fitness of its motivating feeling to the cause of that feeling, the merit or demerit of the action rests upon the beneficial or hurtful effects that the action tends to produce. An action appears to deserve reward if it is the proper object of gratitude. Similarly, an action appears to deserve punishment if it is the proper object of a fitting resentment. These passions of gratitude and resentment, like every other, "seem proper and are approved of, when the heart of every impartial spectator entirely sympathizes with them, when every indifferent bystander entirely enters into, and goes along with them."

The "Impartial Spectator"

In one passage, Smith refers to the impartial spectator as "every human heart," but again he modifies this to "every body who knows of it." While he thus apparently sets up a standard of popular approbation, he seems to regard its basis—"the impartial spectator"—as an abstraction from instances of the human heart rather than as a census by count. Thus it is possible to have moral judgments in a case in which no feelings, or the "wrong" feelings, have been stirred; it is possible to judge of the demerit of an injury to a person who is unaware of injury; and it is possible to alleviate the apparent demerit of an act that is accidental rather than springing from an improper resentment. Judgments of merit are based on direct sympathy with the agent, through which one approves or disapproves the affection giving rise to the action, and upon a sympathy, indirect but no less strong, with the recipient affected. Smith's view makes retaliation a natural impulse and incorporates it, in due degree, into the body of proper actions.

However, the standard of the impartial spectator undergoes a further transformation. "I divide myself, as it were, into two persons; . . . I, the examiner and judge, represent a different character from that other I, the person whose conduct is examined into and judged of. The first is the spectator . . . The second is the agent, the person whom I properly call myself." The first of these persons Smith refers to again and again as "the man within the breast." Thus imagination and sympathy become the account of conscience or the voice within.

People naturally desire not only to be approved of by society but also to be what ought to be approved of, to be worthy of approbation. Therefore, the "man within the breast" has a powerful voice in determining one's actions, so much so that in many cases inward approval may completely replace that of others. The inward person knows one's inmost secrets of motivation and is not contented to approve merely external appearances of rightly motivated actions.

The general rules of morality are formed inductively upon instances of what one's moral faculties approve or disapprove. These rules, together with good habits of action, serve as guides to one's conduct when one's involvement is great and one's passions violent, conditions in which the "ideal man" within is deceived or haste prevents his being consulted. One's sense of duty is one's regard for these general rules. Some actions, such as marks of gratitude, are of course better when they are prompted by an immediate feeling than when done solely from a sense of duty. The commandments of justice are the most exact duties; they admit of only such exceptions as may also be derived from the same just principles and with the same precision. Justice is an ordinary virtue, largely negative because on most occasions it only avoids harm rather than doing positive good. Nevertheless, it is the foundation of society, for where people are ready to do each other harm without restraint there can be no society. On the other hand, benevolence, which is free and never required, is the ornament of society and often an admirable virtue.

Nature has made all people concerned first of all for the preservation and health of their own bodies. People soon learn to transfer their diligence in these regards toward obtaining social desires, such as the respect of their equals and credit and rank in society. The care of such objects as these, upon which one's happiness depends, is the virtue called prudence. It is perfectly respectable, yet neither endearing nor ennobling. Insofar as one's actions may injure or benefit others, the character of the individual may affect the happiness of others. The concern for others prompts the virtues of justice and benevolence. The only motive that can justify one's hurting or interfering with the happiness of one's neighbor is proper resentment for injustice attempted or actually committed; and the punishment should be more aimed at making the person aware of the hurt inflicted and at drawing the person's disapproval toward the motive of it than at inflicting

harm. While prudence, justice, and benevolence may often summon the approval of people, their passions may yet mislead them. Therefore, still another virtue is needed, that of self-command. Its best form shows greatness and steadiness of the exertions over self-love, with the strong sense of propriety needed to make and maintain that exertion. The degree of self-estimation, neither too high nor too low, which the impartial spectator would approve, is the same as that which will secure for the individual the most happiness.

The Nature of Virtue

Smith sharpens the outlines of his doctrine by adding, in the final part of his book, an examination of various systems of moral philosophy. He divides his subject according to two questions: First, wherein does virtue consist? Second, by what power or faculty of the mind is this character of virtue recommended to us? These represent the traditional questions, metaphysical and epistemological respectively, around which the philosophy of morals has centered in Western thought. Smith recognizes three possible answers to the first question: First, virtue consists either in propriety, the "proper government and direction of all our affections," which considered singly may tend either toward good or toward evil; or second, virtue consists in prudence, the pursuit of one's own happiness; or third, it consists in benevolence, the promotion of the happiness of others.

Smith places the ethical systems of Greek philosophers such as Plato, Aristotle, and the Stoics within the group making the first answer. He claims that Plato's system is consistent with his own description of propriety. Aristotle differs in having virtue consist of habits of action rather than sentiments and judgments. The Stoics, he insists at some length, mistake entirely the kind of a system nature made for people, for they reduce to nothing the importance of what one has the most power over, one's immediate circumstances; and they would deaden the sentiments that are the very basis of moral judgments. Smith adds to the group the systems of Samuel Clarke, William Wollaston, and the third earl of Shaftesbury, remarking that they fail to supply what he has provided, the element of sympathy on which morality is based.

Smith finds Greek philosopher Epicurus giving the second answer, that virtue is in prudence. Epicurus, however, was too eager to rest everything on a single principle, bodily pleasure and pain; he failed to notice the powerful satisfaction that people take in the approval of others.

Philosophers proposing the third answer, regarding the principle of benevolence as the primary virtue, included Ralph Cudworth, Thomas More, and John Smith of Cambridge, but especially Francis Hutcheson, "the soberest and most judicious." Smith commends these philosophies of benevolence as nurturing the most agreeable and noblest affections, but he objects that Hutcheson and the others fail to provide an adequate account of the real worth of the lesser virtues, such as prudence. Their works in that respect are not true to human nature. Bernard Mandeville, who urges that all society and all virtue are founded on self-love, also did people an injustice, for he presents any passion that is ever vicious as always vicious, and to the utmost degree.

For Smith, the problem of the knowledge of moral worth is the problem of approbation. To him, the three possibilities seem to be self-love, reason, and sentiment. Against Thomas Hobbes, Samuel Pufendorf, and Mandeville, he argues that society cannot have been founded simply as a means of furthering private interest because sympathy is not a selfish principle; rather, a sympathetic feeling arises entirely on account of the other individual. Cudworth and other opponents of Hobbes advanced reason as the source of moral knowledge. Smith agrees that reason gathers the moral rules inductively but argues that people must have some source, some "first perceptions," from which the reason gathers its instances. Smith commends Hutcheson for first seeing to what extent moral distinctions arise in reason and to what extent they are founded on immediate sense and feeling. However, on grounds of the nature of experience, he opposes Hutcheson's claim to have discovered an inner moral sense. The inner sense, said to have as its sole purpose the judging of the rightness of actions, could not function as claimed because right actions do not always have the same appearance or form. Further, sentiments, whether proper or improper, feel inwardly the same. If the inner sense is devoted to identifying proper approba-

tions, a species of moral feeling, it is superfluous, for one does not require particular inner senses to account for other species of feelings that are unrelated to the moral. Still further, the inner moral sense is never detected operating apart from allied feelings such as sympathy or antipathy, and there is therefore no evidence of its existence such as its single operation would afford.

Finally, Smith affirms that the ancient sort of moralists, who delineated characters in general, in accordance with recognizable virtues, were much superior to later writers, such as the casuists, who attempted to lay down particular rules covering human conduct in advance of the fact. For conduct will always be various, and systems of human law will never be equal to natural justice, made known to people by their sympathies.

The moral system of Adam Smith stands at an interesting place in the development of ethics. It was not a brilliant constructive performance in itself, being here and there imprecise, and advancing very few grounds for the claims made. It did, however, serve to ameliorate some of the more extreme views of its time by helping to emphasize the complexity and subtlety of human experience and conduct. Although it was among the last of the works to found morality upon a plan of virtues, it was among the early efforts to provide a sound psychological basis for choices of conduct. Although it provides clear glimpses of the narrowing influence of Smith's own temperament and of the culture and times in which he lived, the work also presents acute and instructive interpretations of human motives. Despite its copious didactic passages, the work shows a hearty desire not to let one's wishes for the moral elevation of humanity get in the way of one's seeing the facts of a person's actual moral life.

John T. Goldthwait

The Wealth of Nations

Type of philosophy: Ethics, social philosophy
First published: An Inquiry into the Nature and Causes of the Wealth of Nations, 1776 (commonly known as *The Wealth of Nations*)

Principal ideas advanced:

◇ Capitalism is an economic system in which the means of production are privately owned.

◇ Economic order and political order should remain separate entities.

◇ Business organizations create goods for a market guided by the forces of supply and demand.

◇ Financial systems must encourage loans to maintain and expand production.

◇ Privately owned enterprise is the most productive economic action.

◇ The marketplace is fluid and cannot be controlled by any individual or group.

◇ Efficiency leads to profits and inefficiency to losses.

◇ Competition promotes the best interests of society, and a free market system is ruled by competition.

The Wealth of Nations was a critique of the existing organization of state controls referred to by social philosopher Adam Smith as mercantilism. Although rudimentary forms of capitalism existed as far back as ancient times, modern capitalism began to unfold in the late Middle Ages with the development of a merchant class. Continued exploration during the next few centuries and the formation of joint-stock companies allowed the development of mercantilism, a state-dominated commercial system that primarily endeavored to use commerce to strengthen state power. Factors such the Protestant Reformation, which supported a more positive view of wealth, the rise of scientific reasoning, and corresponding population increases influenced the desire for new economic systems. Drawing on Enlightenment thought—individual human beings came to replace God at the center of things—humans, with their rational minds, could improve themselves and society through systematic and rational action.

In the late seventeenth century, philosopher John Locke proposed that the state had a responsibility for maintaining people's rights—one right, in particular, the right to own property. Smith's economic theories met the desire for economic change that would benefit the individual. However, mercantilism, which stimulated economic nationalism and encouraged government intervention in every aspect of trade, was the major economic system in the still primarily agricultural economy of late eighteenth century Britain.

The publication of *The Wealth of Nations*, the first comprehensive system of political economy, in 1776 marks the birth of economics as a separate discipline. The central theme is the growth of national wealth, which Smith, the moral and social philosopher, saw as the nation's annual production of goods and services among the three classes: laborers, landlords, and manufacturers. Smith theorized that the liberty to trade unhindered by government intervention would result in increased abundance and wealth for all involved. Deeply opposed to mercantilist practices, which encouraged government intervention in every aspect of trade, Smith's policy of free-trade economic liberalism, otherwise known as laissez-faire ("Let it be, let it go") led to extraordinary economic growth, particularly in Britain and the United States.

Economic Systems and the State

In his immensely popular and wide-ranging *The Wealth of Nations*, Smith provides an elaborate analysis of how economic systems function and develop over time, outlining the four main revolutionary economic stages that motivate society: the original "rude" state of hunters, a second stage of nomadic agronomy, a third period of feudal "farming," and a fourth and final stage of business interdependence. During the hunter stage, a legal system remains unnecessary because "there is scarce any property . . . so there is seldom any established magistrate or any regular administration of justice." However, as society becomes more complex and people begin to enclose flocks of animals, an legal system becomes paramount. Although Smith frowned on government controls, he clearly recognized the need for law enforcement for "the defence of the rich against the poor, or of those who have some property against those who have none at all." Feudalism, the next stage in economic evolution, Smith describes primarily as a transition period leading from a guild-determined to a market-driven economy. The final phase, commercial capitalism, Smith referred to as a self-correcting system of "perfect liberty."

The crux of the Scottish Enlightenment philosopher's argument was that economics and politics should remain separate and independent. A proponent of efficiency, Smith argued that state intervention not only reduces freedom to trade but also is economically inefficient. His major thesis strongly maintains that the state should refrain from interfering with the economic life of a nation and limit itself to "legitimate areas of government"—protecting and defending property, enforcing contracts and maintaining certain public works. Free of government intervention, the market would maintain sole responsibility for production (land, labor, and capital) and distribution (channels through which goods move from the producer to the market) among different groups and people, and would flourish as a result. In addition, Smith viewed the labor involved in government jobs are "unproductive" because the work did not generate wealth.

Society would be better served if merchants and business people could be free to seek their own interests. When this freedom was granted, Smith proposed, the economy would be guided "as if by an invisible hand . . . without knowing it, without intending it, [to] advance the interest of the society." Smith viewed merchants and business people primarily as selfish, their motives suspect. People who participate in the same type of trade, he wrote, never socialize together or conspire against each other or constantly attempt to raise prices. With the marketplace as the center of a capitalist system, Smith explained, the market itself would determine prices, what products would be produced, who would produce them, and even to whom to distribute the resultant profits.

This free-market commercial type of system, historians and economist argue, far outweighed the benefits of mercantilism because capitalism's circular and diffuse nature assured that no one individual or group could ever control the marketplace. Rewards in the form of fortune and profit would naturally come to those who worked hard and, most important, efficiently; but punishment in the form of financial losses, or ruin, would be the consequence for inefficient work methods.

Further, Smith criticized the supporters of mercantilism who advocated state intervention in international trade. Using the Law of Comparative Advantage, Smith asserted that nations should export goods that they were most efficient at producing and import only goods that they were less efficient in producing. If there were no international barriers to the exchange of goods, a market guided by the forces of supply and demand increased the wealth of nations, while government intervention and restrictions only decreased the nation's wealth.

Competition and Society

In addition, competition promoted the best interests of society. Monopolies, private or state-controlled were evil, Smith believed. The natural trend of economic development is upward, and a framework of an "obvious and simple system of liberty," or perfect competition, is vital to this movement. Competition in the marketplace, he stated, would automatically result in the availability of goods that consumers desired. More firms producing the same product would result in increased efficiency and ultimately lower costs to the consumer: in other words, spur economic growth.

Economic growth depended upon the accumulation of capital, distinguished by Smith from land and labor, the two other major factors of production. His primary concern focused on a system of "natural liberty" that would result in "maximizing general welfare." He emphasized that it was not nature but human effort that produced commodities and strongly suggested that people possessed a desire to advance socially: "a desire that comes with us from the womb, and never leaves us until we go into the grave." To advance upward, people needed to accumulate capital by saving and investing for the future. This innate desire at "self-betterment," Smith viewed as a direct outcome of people's natural competitive nature.

Taking the idea of innate competition one step further, Smith argued that this constant internalized competitive struggle not only forced the prices of commodities down to their "natural" level but also regulated the distribution of income among workers in the form of wages, in the form of rents to landlords, and to manufacturers in profits. In addition, he pointed out that the impetus behind this acquisitive drive would guarantee the steady increase of national wealth.

However, Smith did not foresee the tendency of individual businesses to increase dramatically in size. Industrial plants grew ever larger to gain the advantage of lower unit costs from mass production. Businesses expanded from small shops to large corporations employing thousands of workers, and corporations ultimately merged together forming enormous trusts, which in fact threatened a competitive economy.

Smith's Considerable Influence

The Wealth of Nations has to be considered one of the most influential studies of Western civilization. It provides a comprehensive view of political and social evolution. Indeed, economists and historians maintain that Smith's theory of a laissez-faire or free-market economy transformed society. Certainly Smith, often called the founder of modern economics, played a major role in the development of the Industrial Revolution first in Britain, France, and Germany and later in the United States. As a result of a free-market economy, large corporations and industrial cities developed. Such business innovations as the ability of the public to purchase stocks and bonds enabled corporations to accumulate wealth. Under the watchful eyes of stockholders anxious for profitable returns on investments, more qualified managers and workers were hired. Naturally, attacks on capitalism ensued, particularly the writings of Karl Marx and Friedrich Engels, which ultimately acted as the foundation of socialism and communism.

M. Casey Diana

Additional Reading

Brown, Maurice. *Adam Smith's Economics: Its Place in the Development of Economic Thought*. London: Routledge, 1992. Scholarly but approachable work sets forth the economic and historical contexts of Smith's theories.

Campbell, R. Hutchinson, and Andrew S. Skinner. *Adam Smith*. New York: St. Martin's Press, 1985. This volume not only provides biographical information on the philosopher but also furnishes facts on eighteenth century Scotland and Smith's well-known circle of acquaintances, which included such luminaries as Benjamin Franklin.

Fay, Charles R. *Adam Smith and the Scotland of His Day*. Cambridge, London: Cambridge University Press, 1956. A loosely linked collection of essays that places Smith in the larger context of his time and place.

_____. *The World of Adam Smith*. New York: A.M. Kelley, 1965. Classic work on the philosopher. This book presents an historical, economical, and philosophical overview of Scotland and England in the eighteenth century, providing insight into the development of Smith's philosophy. It particularly illustrates the reasoning behind his disdain for mercantilism.

Glahe, Fred R., ed. *Adam Smith and the Wealth of Nations: 1776-1996*. Bicentennial Essays. Boulder: Colorado Associated Press, 1978. A collection of appreciations by twentieth century champions of the free market.

Heilbroner, Robert. *The Nature and Logic of Capitalism*. New York: W. W. Norton, 1985. Well-recognized authority on Smith dissects the philosopher's works, in particular *The Wealth of Nations*, to indisputably establish Smith as a predominant figure in the rise of capitalism and a free-market economy.

Hollander, Samuel. *The Economics of Adam Smith*. Toronto: University of Toronto Press, 1973. The best survey of Smith's economic ideas.

Lindgren, J. Ralph. The *Social Philosophy of Adam Smith*. The Hague: Martinus Nijhoff, 1973. Undertakes to survey the full breadth of Smith's philosophy, including moral judgment, psychology, religion, and science.

Muller, Jerry Z. *Adam Smith in His Time and Ours: Designing the Decent Society*. New York: Free Press, 1993. Broad, relatively nontechnical view of Smith's analysis and philosophy, defending his relevance for modern society.

Pack, Spencer J. *Capitalism as a Moral System: Adam Smith's Critique of the Free Market Economy*. Brookfield, Vt.: Edward Elgar, 1991. Draws out Smith's criticisms of laissez-faire and of capitalism.

Raphael, D. D. *Adam Smith*. Oxford: Oxford University Press, 1985. A brief intellectual biography written for the general reader.

Rashid, Salim. *The Myth of Adam Smith*. Lyme, N.H.: Edward Elgar, 1998. The author argues that Smith's economic analysis is greatly overrated and finds inaccuracies in factual data and inconsistencies and fallacies in Smith's analysis.

Skinner, Andrew S. *A System of Social Science: Papers Relating to Adam Smith*. Oxford: Clarendon Press, 1979. A collection of essays dealing with different aspects of Smith's thought by a leading authority on the subject.

Tawney, Richard H. *Religion and the Rise of Capitalism*. New Brunswick, N.J.: Transaction Publications, 1998. Reprint of Harcourt Brace's popular 1926 edition. The author dramatically illustrates the social conditions of eighteenth century Britain and the role Christianity played as the religion of capitalism.

Wood, John Cunningham, ed. *Adam Smith: Critical Assessments*. 4 vols. London: Croom Helm, 1983. Presents 150 articles and excerpts, many of which extend beyond Smith's economic analysis.

Young, Jeffrey T. *Economics as A Moral Science: The Political Economy of Adam Smith*. Lyme, N.H.: Edward Elgar, 1997. Stresses the moral and ethical dimensions of Smith's economic ideas.

Paul B. Trescott and M. Casey Diana

Herbert Spencer

Best known as the leading Social Darwinist of the nineteenth century, Spencer was a broad-ranging thinker who epitomized the scientific mentality of his age. He coined the phrase "survival of the fittest" and attempted to build a comprehensive philosophical synthesis based on evolution.

Principal philosophical works: *The Proper Sphere of Government*, 1843; *Social Statics: Or, The Conditions Essential to Human Happiness Specified, and the First of Them Developed*, 1851; *The Principles of Psychology*, 1855; *Essays: Scientific, Political, and Speculative*, 1858-1874 (3 volumes); *Education: Intellectual, Moral, and Physical*, 1860; *The Synthetic Philosophy*, 1862-1896 (includes *First Principles*, 1862; *The Principles of Biology*, 1864-1867, 2 volumes; *The Principles of Psychology*, 1855; *The Principles of Sociology*, 1876-1896, 3 volumes; *The Principles of Ethics*, 1892-1893, 2 volumes); *The Study of Sociology*, 1872; *The Man Versus the State*, 1884; *The Nature and Reality of Religion*, 1885; *Facts and Comments*, 1902; *An Autobiography*, 1904.

Born: April 27, 1820; Derby, Derbyshire, England
Died: December 8, 1903; Brighton, Sussex, England

Early Life

Herbert Spencer was born on April 27, 1820, in Derby, Derbyshire, England. An only child, he was educated until the age of ten by his father, a private tutor. His unorthodox father, a Dissenter, and the lack of peers molded the young Spencer into an intellectual introvert. He was reared amid discussions of the great political and philosophical issues of the day, and his father's associates consisted primarily of Quakers and Unitarians. Spencer received further education, mostly in mathematics and mechanics, from his uncle, Thomas Spencer, who headed a school near Bath. The enormous learning that he later demonstrated was acquired principally through his own efforts.

Declining an offer from his uncle to send him to Cambridge, in 1837 Spencer took a job as a civil engineer with the London and Birmingham railway company. He worked for a number of different railways, traveled widely, introduced several technical innovations, and advanced in his career. He had, however, developed a deep interest in politics, and in 1841, he left his engineering career and returned to Derby to live on his savings while writing political commentary.

Initially, Spencer dabbled in radical politics rather unselectively, but some of his early pieces in the *Nonconformist* reveal that his narrow view of the role of the state had already developed. In 1843, he moved to London, where he believed he could advance his literary career He did very poorly, selling only a few items, most of them on phrenology. Soon, his funds depleted, he returned to engineering work. He quickly became disillusioned with the world of business, and he left it in 1846, exposing railway fraud in an essay in the *Edinburgh Review*.

At the age of twenty-six, Spencer had largely failed in engineering, politics, and journalism. He was both lonely and alone in his increasingly deep meditations. His dedication to philosophical inquiry and his serious reading precluded a social life, and he never married. His dark brown hair was beginning to recede, and in later life, he was partially bald, a feature he sought to counter by wearing his hair long on the sides, with bushy sideburns. His face was calm, but pale, and in general his slight figure suggested frailness and delicacy. He was an excellent conversationalist but somewhat abrupt and quite fixed in his opinions.

Life's Work

In 1848, Spencer's career took a turn for the better when his schoolmaster uncle assisted him in securing a position in London as subeditor of *The Economist*. With this position, Spencer had not only a modest level of financial security but also the spare time to work on the great philosophical project he had been contemplating. At *The Economist* Spencer found like-minded individualists, and his laissez-faire attitude hardened into the rigidness for which he would become famous.

The serious writing effort on which Spencer had been working for some time was completed in the summer of 1850 and published the following year under the title *Social Statics*. With his job and his book, Spencer enjoyed a wider social life, but he continued his father's traditions of nonconformity and enjoyed being something of an eccentric who flaunted convention. In 1853, the death of his uncle, who had aided him so greatly,

brought him a legacy, which was small but sufficient for him to leave *The Economist* and live independently as an author. That same year, however, he suffered the first of a series of physical and nervous ailments that plagued him for the rest of his life. He traveled widely in search of better health, argued with his friends, remained lonely and unhappy, and became a confirmed hypochondriac.

Spencer continued, however, to write prolifically. In 1855, he published *The Principles of Psychology*, and in 1860 he announced his plan to produce a multivolume work with the general title *The Synthetic Philosophy*. He suffered a serious nervous breakdown and treated himself with opium, but the work was finally completed in 1896. He financed his work by selling subscriptions, with the subscribers receiving installments of about ninety pages every three months. Some interest in the work was expressed in Great Britain, but it was support from the United States that actually gave Spencer the financial wherewithal to complete his work. An inheritance from his father, along with the proceeds from the sale of his books, allowed him to live comfortably for the rest of his life. He died on December 8, 1903, and the remains of his cremation are at Highgate Cemetery.

At the basis of Spencer's philosophy lay two fundamentals: first, the tremendous importance given to science that was characteristic of his age; second, the sanctity of political and economic laissez-faire that he acquired from his Dissenter and radical background. In fact, Spencer combined these two to make laissez-faire a natural law. He was not, however, the only one to do this. Both science and the idea of laissez-faire were dominant in the mid-nineteenth century, as was the idea of pro-

Herbert Spencer. *(Library of Congress)*

gress, also very important to him. Spencer, however, was the foremost spokesperson of these ideas, and he set them forth in his volumes in a way that convinced his contemporaries.

Spencer was, moreover, the only one of his time to attempt a synthesis of all thought, based on science and especially evolution, including philosophies of education, biology, psychology, sociology, and ethics, as well as politics. Such a comprehensive system was possible only to the nineteenth century mind, which embraced science in such an enthusiastic and general fashion. Most of Spencer's proofs rested on mere analogies, usually biological, and by the time of his death such generalizations were outdated in a world that had become highly technical and specialized. Having been the most popular thinker of his time, especially in the United States, Spencer fell from favor as rapidly as he had risen, and by the early years of the twentieth century he was largely forgotten, dismissed by philosophers as not being sufficiently philosophical and by scientists as being too much the generalist. Spencerian thought, however, remains well worth studying, not only for what it suggests about the nineteenth century mind but also for what it reveals about the origins of the modern social sciences.

Spencer is always linked, and rightly so, to Darwinian evolution, but it is not merely as a disciple of Charles Darwin that he is important. The evolutionary perspective was current before Darwin produced his famous *On the Origin of Species* in 1859. Geological evidence supported evolution, and Spencer was aware of these investigations and had been moved to that view by his own observations during excavations for railways. Moreover, his own writings on competition in business influenced Darwin, and while Darwin's work revolutionized Spencer's thinking, as it did that of so many others, it was Spencer who coined the term "survival of the fittest." Spencer, it should be noted, never became a complete Darwinist; for example, he continued to hold to the pre-Darwinian notion of the inheritability of acquired characteristics. It was Spencer, though, who was the most energetic in applying the principles of evolution and natural selection to society, and in doing so he became the archetypal Social Darwinist.

The great work, *The Synthetic Philosophy*, that Spencer announced in 1860 took more than thirty years to complete and is divided into several separately titled parts. *First Principles* appeared in 1862 and is both metaphysical with its insistence on the existence of an ultimate unknowable, which could be appreciated but never understood, and scientific with its assertion that evolution is the motor of all development, change, and progress. *The Principles of Biology*, a two-volume work published in 1864 and 1867, was both a survey of developmental physiology and an assertion of the iron law of evolution in the movement from lower to higher forms. Spencer followed his evolutionary theme in *The Principles of Psychology* by insisting that consciousness, too, had gone through successive stages.

Spencer's most influential thesis was *The Principles of Sociology*, which appeared in three volumes from 1876 to 1896. In this work, he set forth his view that a society is like an organism. In making this analogy, Spencer introduced the study of structure and function into the field of sociology and proved the value of comparative analysis. He also stated in the strongest terms his extreme individualism and negative view of government. From such attitudes has come the tradition that Spencer was rather brutal and pessimistic. In fact, he viewed progress as a natural process, but progress involved the elimination of the weak and unfit. The last portion of the great synthesis was *The Principles of Ethics*, in which he took lessons from nature to create a moral code. In the preface to the last volume of *The Principles of Ethics*, he included a note indicating that evolution had not been the absolute principle, at least in ethics, that he had hoped. In addition to these works, he completed an autobiography in 1889 (published in 1904), and in 1902, a year before his death, he was nominated for the Nobel Prize in Literature.

Influence

Enormously popular in his day, by the middle of the twentieth century, Spencer was entirely neglected by serious scholars, except to be mentioned as the classic proponent of Social Darwinism, an honor that served only to strengthen his negative image. Nevertheless, Spencer made important contributions in the study of society, particularly in the areas of social evolution and the problem of the individual versus the state. If nothing else, his version of natural selection, which he expressed in the phrase "survival of the fittest," has secured for him a permanent historical significance.

Roy Talbert, Jr.

First Principles

Type of philosophy: Epistemology, philosophy of science, social philosophy

First published: 1862

Principal ideas advanced:

◇ The business of philosophy is to formulate the laws concerning phenomena common to all the branches of scientific knowledge.

◇ From the principle of the persistence of force can be derived the other principles of natural philosophy, among them the principles of the uniformity of law, the transformation of forces, and the line of least resistance.

◇ The principle of evolution and dissolution is the dynamic and unifying principle of nature; evolution is an integration of matter and a dissipation of motion, during which matter passes from homogeneity to heterogeneity; dissolution occurs when resistance overcomes equilibrium and a system loses its force without adding to its organization.

◇ Society is a kind of superorganism that exemplifies the same principles of differentiation.

◇ Reality is unknowable; we know only appearances.

Herbert Spencer intended _First Principles_ to be an introduction to his comprehensive study of the world, entitled _The Synthetic Philosophy_ (1862-1896). However, he made it an independent work, complete in itself, that not merely announced the principles of evolutionary naturalism but illustrated them amply with examples from all fields of knowledge. For good measure, he also raised the issue of science and religion and proposed an amicable solution.

Spencer shared the classical positivist conviction that knowledge consists solely of empirical generalizations or laws. Particular sciences, he held, have the task of formulating the laws that govern special classes of data; however, inasmuch as there are phenomena common to all branches of knowledge, a special science is needed to gather them up into laws. This, he claimed, was the business of philosophy. In his view, that business was now completed. The synthetic philosophy included not only general laws but also one law from which all other laws, both general and specific, could be deduced a priori. He therefore offered a new definition of philosophy: It is "completely unified knowledge."

Evolution and Dissolution

Two highly general principles of natural philosophy were already well-established in Spencer's day, namely, the continuity of motion and the indestructibility of matter. Work in the field of thermodynamics had more recently shown that matter and motion are, in fact, different forms of energy, making it possible to combine these principles into one, which Spencer called the principle of the persistence of force. Here, in his opinion, was a fundamental truth from which all other principles could be deduced. The first principle that Spencer inferred from it was that of the persistence of relations of force, more commonly known as the uniformity of law. The second was that of the transformation of forces, namely, that every loss of motion is attended by an accretion of matter, and vice versa. The third was that motions follow the line of least resistance.

None of these principles, however, sufficed to explain the origin and structure of the ordered world of our experience. What Spencer needed was a unifying principle that applies equally to the burning candle, the quaking earth, and the growing organism. All these events he saw as instances of one vast "transformation." The problem was to find the dynamic principle that governs this metamorphosis as a whole and in all its details. The answer he found in the principle of evolution and dissolution.

Spencer regarded it as his special contribution to philosophy that he was able to show deductively what others (notably the embryologist K. E. von Baer) had concluded experimentally and on a limited scale: that change is always from a state of homogeneity to a state of heterogeneity. According to Spencer, it is self-evident that homogeneity is a condition of unstable equilibrium. At least this is true of finite masses—though if centers of force were diffused uniformly through infinite space, it might possibly be otherwise; however, Spencer held such a state of affairs to be inconceivable. It follows that, because of the inequality of exposure of its different parts, every finite instance of the homogeneous must inevitably lapse into heterogeneity.

Primarily, according to Spencer, evolution was a passing from the less to the more coherent form of energy, for example, the formation of the solar system out of a gaseous nebula. However, because the same instability is found in each part of the universe as is found in the whole, the differentiation process will be recapitulated within each new aggregate, giving rise to a secondary evolution, for example, the stratification of the surface of the earth. Primary evolution is a process of integration, the passage from a less to a more coherent form with the dissipation of motion and the concentration of matter. Secondary evolution adds to this a process of differentiation, in the course of which the mass changes from a homogeneous to a heterogeneous state.

However, not all heterogeneity is constructive, for example, a tumorous growth. Thus, Spencer had to qualify his law of change: Evolution is change from the indefinite to the definite, from the confused to the ordered. Finally, the same process that has hitherto been stated in terms of matter might equally well be stated in terms of motion: Evolution is a concentration of molecular motion with a dissipation of heat. In sum:

> Evolution is an integration of matter and concomitant dissipation of motion; during which the matter passes from an indefinite, incoherent homogeneity to a definite, coherent heterogeneity; and during which the retained motion undergoes a parallel transformation.

It was clear to Spencer, however, that evolution cannot go on forever. The redistribution of matter and motion must eventually reach a limit beyond which a simplification takes place: lesser movements are integrated into greater ones, as when the secondary gyrations of a spinning top subside into the main motion. Spencer called this tendency "equilibration." In a harmonious environment, suitably integrated motions continue indefinitely without undergoing noticeable change. Nevertheless, a change is taking place. Resistance, ever so minor, must in time produce its effect upon the system, wearing it down, causing it to dissipate its force without adding to its organization. Even the solar system, which is nearly a perfectly equilibrated system, is losing its energy and must continue to do so until in the distant future it no longer radiates light or heat.

Evolution, therefore, according to Spencer, is only one aspect of the process; it is paralleled by its opposite, dissolution, about which, however, he had little to say because he found it lacking in the interesting features that attend evolution. Still, it is not to be ignored, nor is it a stranger to us. The death of any living organism is "that final equilibration which precedes dissolution, is the bringing to a close of all those conspicuous integrated motions that arose during evolution." The process of organic decay is dissolution. Particular systems decay while more general systems are still in the state of integration, and Spencer was far from being of the opinion that the evolution of the planetary system has reached its height.

This bare skeleton of Spencer's argument remains unconvincing without the illustrations that he used. To show that the principle of coherence governs even such matters as the evolution of human speech, he pointed out that the primitive Pawnee Indians used a three-syllable word, *ashakish*, to designate the animal that the civilized English called by the one-syllable word "dog." The history of the English language offers illustrations of the same tendency toward coherence and integration: witness the passage from the Anglo-Saxon *sunu* through the semi-Saxon *sune* to the English *son*; or, again, from *cuman* to *cumme* to *come*. Other examples are taken from politics, industry, art, religion—not to mention the physical sciences. A characteristic one is the following, which shows the change toward heterogeneity in manufactures:

> Beginning with a barbarous tribe, almost if not quite homogeneous in the functions of its members, the progress has been, and still is, toward an economic aggregation of the whole

human race; growing ever more heterogeneous in respect of the separate functions assumed by separate nations, the separate functions assumed by the local sections of each nation, the separate functions assumed by the many kinds of makers and traders in each town, and the separate functions assumed by the workers united in producing each community.

Biological and Social Evolution

It was in connection with his argument that homogeneous masses are always unstable that Spencer gave his most explicit account of biological evolution. Given a homogeneous mass of protoplasm, the surface will be subject to different forces from those of the interior, and consequently the two will be modified in different ways. Moreover, one part of the surface is exposed differently from another, so that the ventral features will differ from the dorsal. Again, two virtually identical blobs of protoplasm that chance to arise in different environments—for example, moist and dry—will be modified in different ways. Spencer's theories in these matters had already been published before Darwin's *On the Origin of Species* (1859) appeared, and he saw no reason to change them afterward. In his view, the real cause of differentiation between species lay in the environmental influences. He thought it probable that modifications in the parent are transmitted through heredity to their offspring. However, in any case, it *must* sometimes happen

> that some division of a species, falling into circumstances which give it rather more complex experiences, and demand actions that are more involved, will have certain of its organs further differentiated in proportionately small degrees. . . . Hence, there will from time to time arise an increased heterogeneity both of the Earth's flora and fauna, and of individual races included in them.

No doubt Darwin's principle of natural selection facilitates the differentiation, he explained in a footnote, but the varieties can be accounted for without it; and without the changes caused by the environment, natural selection would accomplish little.

Spencer's theory of social evolution paralleled his account of biological origins. In his view, society is a kind of superorganism, which exemplifies the same principles of differentiation as those that appear on the inorganic and the organic planes. His was a system of strict determinism that explained social dynamics in terms of universal laws and denied any role to human purpose or endeavor. His guiding principle was the formula that motion follows lines of least resistance. Thus, migrations and wars result from the reaction of societies to climate, geography, and the like. Likewise, internal movements, such as the division of labor and the development of public thoroughfares, arise from the effort to fulfill human desires in the most economical manner. To the objection that this was only a metaphorical way of viewing social change, Spencer replied that it was not: People are, he said, literally impelled in certain directions, and social processes are in fact physical ones.

Psychology provides further instances. What we think of as mental processes are, from a more fundamental point of view, material ones. Spencer cited as an example the processes of thought engaged in by a botanist who is classifying plants. Each plant examined yields a complex impression; and when two plants yield similar impressions, this "set of molecular modifications" is intensified, "generating an internal idea corresponding to these similar external objects." It is a special case of the general principle called by Spencer "segregation," which states that like units of motion will produce like units of motion in the same or similar aggregates, and unlike will produce unlike.

The Unknowable

Such is the tenor of Spencer's system. Philosophy in the traditional sense hardly concerned him. His objective, like that of French philosopher René Descartes, was to put all knowledge on a deductive basis, and his *First Principles*, like Descartes's *Meditationes de prima philosophia* (1641; *Meditations on First Philosophy*, 1680), merely laid the foundation for the superstructure that was to follow. Unlike Descartes, however, Spencer pleaded ignorance of the underlying nature of things. Following philosophers David Hume and Immanuel Kant, he professed that what we know are only appearances, ideas, or impressions in the mind. Reality is unknowable.

Spencer had no intention of wasting his energies on the transcendental problems that concerned Kant and the German speculative philosophers. However, he did devote the first hundred pages of his book to "The Unknowable." In this section, he dealt, very much in the manner of T. H. Huxley, with the limits of human understanding, especially with the claims of revealed religion and of scientific metaphysics. He found it conveniently admitted by Canon H. L. Mansel of the Church of England that the object of religious devotion cannot be thought. In Mansel's opinion, this belief was due to the relativity of human knowledge, whereas God is, by definition, absolute. Of course, said Spencer, it is not merely the object of religion that is unknowable. The reality that science describes is also unknowable, if one tries to think of it absolutely. Kant's paralogisms and antinomies make it clear that such concepts as space, time, motion, consciousness, and personality have meaning only in the limited world of experience and tell us nothing about reality.

Nevertheless, said Spencer, the notion of the Absolute is not entirely negative: There is something that defines and limits the knowable; we have a vague, indefinite notion of a being more and other than what we know. Perhaps our closest approach to it is by analogy to the feeling of "power" that we experience in our own muscles. The true function of religion is to witness nature from its mysterious side, as the true function of science is to discover its knowable side. Here, as elsewhere, Spencer discerned a process of differentiation. The conflict within culture between science and religion is due to "the imperfect separation of their spheres and functions. . . . A permanent peace will be reached when science becomes fully convinced that all its explanations are proximate and relative, while religion becomes fully convinced that the mystery it contemplates is ultimate and absolute."

However, according to Spencer, writing and talking about the problem will not do any good. Cultural changes are not furthered by discussion alone. As presently constituted, people are not ready morally or socially to do without theology: They still need to believe that the Absolute is a person like themselves in order to strengthen their resolve to act rightly. By the time science and religion have differentiated themselves completely, people will presumably have evolved morally to the point that they do good spontaneously.

Jean Faurot

Additional Reading

Duncan, David. *The Life and Letters of Herbert Spencer*. London: Methuen, 1908. Useful because of the primary sources included.

Elliot, Hugh. *Herbert Spencer*. London: Constable, 1917. Interesting because of the early date and because it clearly shows that Herbert Spencer's decline had already begun.

Gray, Tim. *The Political Philosophy of Herbert Spencer: Individualism and Organicism*. Brookfield, Vt.: Avebury, 1996. A clear introduction to Spencer's political beliefs and thoughts.

Hofstadter, Richard. *Social Darwinism in American Thought*. Rev. ed. Boston: Beacon Press, 1955. An excellent examination of Spencer's considerable influence in the United States.

Kennedy, James G. *Herbert Spencer*. Boston: Twayne, 1978. A brief but useful and available survey of Spencer's life and thought.

MacRae, Donald G., ed. *The Man Versus the State*. Baltimore, Md.: Penguin Books, 1969. An excellent essay assessing Spencer's importance regarding individualism vis-à-vis big government; introduces eight pieces by Spencer.

Paxton, Nancy L. *George Eliot and Herbert Spencer: Feminism, Evolutionism, and the Reconstruction of Gender*. Princeton, N.J.: Princeton University Press, 1991. Analyzes Spencer's views and his influence on Eliot's views on the place of gender in the Victorian debates about nature, religion, and evolutionary theory.

Taylor, Michael W. *Man Versus the State: Herbert Spencer and Late Victorian Individualism*. New York: Oxford University Press, 1992. A study of Spencer's political philosophy and of his influence on the ideas of the British Individualist group of political theorists in the late nineteenth century.

Turner, Jonathan H. *Herbert Spencer: A Renewed Appreciation*. Beverly Hills, Calif.: Sage, 1985. A sympathetic view, citing Spencer's contributions to modern sociological methodology and theory.

Weinstein, David. *Equal Freedom and Utility: Herbert Spencer's Liberal Utilitarianism*. New York: Cambridge University Press, 1998. A very readable analysis of Spencer's political philosophy.

Wiltshire, David. *The Social and Political Thought of Herbert Spencer*. Oxford: Oxford University Press, 1978. A good biographical overview that concentrates on political theory.

Roy Talbert, Jr., updated by William Nelles

Baruch Spinoza

Spinoza attemped to show the nature and existence of God using geometrical models. He contributed much to the emergence of political and religious tolerance and helped lay the groundwork for future developments in philosophy and letters.

Principal philosophical works: *Renati des Cartes principia philosophiae*, 1663 (*Principles of Descartes' Philosophy*, 1905); *Tractatus theologico-politicus*, 1670 (*A Theologico-Political Treatise*, 1862); *Opera posthuma*, 1677; *Ethica*, 1677 (*Ethics*, 1870); *Tractatus politicus*, 1677 (*A Political Treatise*, 1883); *De intellectus emendatione*, 1677; *Epistolae doctorum quorundam virorum ad B.D.S. et auctoris responsiones*, 1677 (*Letters to Friend and Foe*, 1966); *Compendium grammatices linguae hebraeae*, 1677 (*Hebrew Grammar*, 1962); *Tractatus de deo et homine eiusque felicitate*, 1862 (*A Short Treatise on God, Man, and His Well-Being*, 1963).

Born: November 24, 1632; Amsterdam, United Provinces (now The Netherlands)
Died: February 21, 1677; The Hague, United Provinces (now The Netherlands)

Early Life

Baruch Spinoza (also known by the Latin name Benedictus Spinoza and the Portuguese name Bento de Espinosa) was born November 24, 1632, in Amsterdam. His parents, Michael and Hanna Deborah, were Spanish-Portuguese Jews who had emigrated to Holland to escape religious persecution. This persecution was relatively recent in origin. Jews living in Spain during the late Middle Ages had experienced a period of tolerance under the Moors, who were Islamic. The return of Christian rule utterly reversed this trend. Subject to all manner of plunder and murder during the Spanish Inquisition, many Jews decided to convert to Christianity. A large number of these converts, however, continued to practice Judaism in private. That led to a new round of persecution and finally to the expulsion of Jews from Spain in 1492. Some converted Jews (or *marranos*, as they were called) sought refuge in Portugal. Over time, persecution arose there as well. Holland became a logical next step for Jews who desired the freedom to practice their religion and pursue fruitful commerce. Spinoza's parents are believed to have been *marranos* who had

sought refuge in Jodenburt, the Jewish quarter of Amsterdam. There they could practice Judaism openly, enjoying the fruits of religious tolerance unmatched in all Christendom. They were also free to pursue a broad range of commercial opportunities.

This relatively self-contained community first nurtured Spinoza, providing him with material comforts and an extensive education in Jewish religion and philosophy. Ultimately, however, Spinoza was cast out. How and why that came about is pivotal to an understanding of Spinoza's early life as well as to his subsequent career.

Spinoza's father was in the import-export business and is believed to have been highly successful. Spinoza helped in the family business but at some point became far more interested in his studies than he was in commerce. He wished, moreover, to broaden his studies beyond the usual fare, exploring the less orthodox canons within Jewish thought and acquainting himself with non-Jewish sources of learning. This, in itself, was not unusual. Many members of the Jewish community had opened themselves to the world around them. As a result, Spinoza's father was agreeable, arranging for Spinoza to study Latin outside the Jodenburt in the home of Francis Van den Ende, a freethinker and something of a political radical. The study of Latin enabled Spinoza to explore the rationalist philosophy of

Baruch Spinoza. *(Library of Congress)*

first by attempting to bribe Spinoza with a generous monetary allowance in return for his outward compliance with orthodox beliefs. Spinoza refused this offer. Shortly thereafter, he was tried and found guilty of what amounted to a charge of heresy. In 1656, Spinoza was excommunicated.

Why Spinoza's accusers acted is not as self-evident as it might seem. The Jewish community in Amsterdam permitted a fair amount of diversity, and Spinoza was outwardly quiet about his dissenting opinions in theological matters. He was not, so far as is known, a gadfly in the image of the Greek philosopher Socrates. These circumstances have led some scholars to explain Spinoza's excommunication as a response by Jewish leaders to their fear of renewed persecution by Christians flowing either from Spinoza's apparent atheism or from his association with Dutch political radicals. The fact that Spinoza had already begun to divorce himself from the Jewish community (he was no longer living in the Jodenburt at the time of his excommunication) supports such an interpretation. Another theory is that Spinoza was thought dangerous because of his opposition to wealth and privilege within the Jewish community. Whatever the motivation, Spinoza was excommunicated at the age of twenty-four. Shortly afterward, he was forced by Dutch authorities to leave Amsterdam's city boundaries—this, too, at the urging of the Jewish leaders.

René Descartes. Though Descartes did not openly disparage traditional religion, his philosophy was an attempt to understand the world through reason rather than faith. Spinoza also launched into what was, for a Jew, even more controversial, a study of the New Testament.

The result of these unorthodox studies was that Spinoza moved irretrievably beyond the dominant beliefs of the community into which he had been born, rejecting its commercialism as well as the exclusiveness of the Jewish faith. Indeed, it appeared to some that he was rejecting religion altogether. As Spinoza's beliefs became known, the leaders of the Jodenburt responded

Life's Work

Though Spinoza's excommunication was of great symbolic importance, it did little to change the way he actually conducted his life. Spinoza left behind his Hebrew name, Baruch, substituting for it the Latin equivalent, Benedictus (both mean "blessed"). Yet he did not become a Christian. Nor did he marry. He lived quietly, first in Rhijnsburg, later in Voorburg, accumulating only as much money as he needed to pay his bills. A good neighbor and well loved by friends, he devoted the rest of his life to his studies.

What income Spinoza did have may have come from his knowledge of optics and skills as a lens grinder. Although this has become part of the Spinoza legend, there is no evidence that he actually earned a living in this way. It has, therefore, been hypothesized that, in order to sustain himself, Spinoza accepted moderate amounts of money from friends, though here, too, the evidence allows for little more than an educated guess. What is known is that Spinoza repeatedly rejected large gifts from wealthy friends and also that he refused a professor's chair at the University of Heidelberg.

Two reasons have been advanced for this behavior: Spinoza's humble tastes and, most important, his devotion to writing what he thought was true, regardless of who might be offended. Such candor required thoroughgoing independence. This is not to say that Spinoza led an entirely isolated existence. He exchanged ideas with numerous intellectuals, religious reformers, and political activists until the end of his life. The outcome of this combination of lively discourse and independence of thought was a body of work that drew immediate attention from avid supporters as well as critics and that has stood the test of time.

Spinoza's earliest work of note was his *Principles of Descartes' Philosophy*. Though the work is little more than an exegesis, it demonstrates Spinoza's profound grasp of the system he spent much time criticizing. The appeal of Descartes for Spinoza lies in Descartes's stated goal of explaining the world through the use of reason alone, thus taking a giant step beyond medieval Scholasticism, which, at best, gave reason status nearly equal to that of revelation. Spinoza's central criticism of Descartes was that he continued to take much on faith.

In 1670, Spinoza's *A Theologico-Political Treatise* was published anonymously. In this work, Spinoza broke new ground, writing perhaps the most eloquent defense ever of religious freedom. The treatise includes a critical essay on the Bible

that points out its rather haphazard assembly of very different works from different eras into a single text. It also distinguishes the role of reason, which is to discern truth, from that of religion, which is to foster piety. Although these points may seem innocent enough to modern readers, the treatise was greeted with a chorus of criticism from a variety of clerics, many of whom branded its author an atheist, and the Catholic Church, which banned it. Spinoza's circle of friends and supporters, on the other hand, deeply appreciated his achievement.

The rancor with which *A Theologico-Political Treatise* was received may well have persuaded Spinoza that it would be neither wise nor prudent to publish again during his lifetime. Although prudence in this matter is easily understood, it is likely that wisdom also played a role in Spinoza's decision. Throughout his life, Spinoza demonstrated a high regard for the atmosphere of tolerance in the United Provinces, which permitted the Jewish people to worship and he himself to think freely. To publish controversial works openly might risk the habits of tolerance that were just then taking root. His other major works remained unpublished until after his death in 1677 and even then remained anonymous (actually, authorship was designated by the use of Spinoza's initials). These include his unfinished *A Political Treatise*, which, beginning from Hobbesian premises about human nature, ends up with a very un-Hobbesian defense of democratic principles, and *Ethics*, Spinoza's most substantial and most famous work.

In *Ethics*, Spinoza borrows the language of Descartes (including such notions as "substance," what might be called matter, and "extension," what might be called form) to finish the interpretation of the world as it is known through reason. Although God plays a central role in Spinoza's worldview, it is not the role to which one is accustomed by traditional religion. Instead, God is depersonalized and indifferent. For many readers, this translated into atheism; for others, it is a form of pantheism. Whatever one's interpretation, the distinctiveness of *Ethics* lies in the direct connection of this metaphysical framework with a theory of how human beings should seek to do what is right and achieve happiness in the absence of divine commandments. Ethical conduct and happiness flow from the proper combination of emotion (or passions) and reason, neither being completely dominant over the other.

Ethics is clearly not designed to be edifying or stylish. It is argued through what Spinoza thought to be the philosophical equivalent of geometric proofs. Yet, for many of those who were not offended by Spinoza's view of God, the book conveyed breathtaking beauty and insight, giving off a special aura that is a mixture of intellectual, literary, and spiritual elements.

In addition to his formal writing, Spinoza left behind a large body of correspondence that is indispensable to an understanding of his life and thought. These letters not only provide a running commentary on Spinoza's philosophical works but also indicate the considerable interest his ideas inspired and the affection in which he was held by many friends. These friends mourned deeply when Spinoza died suddenly and, it is believed, peacefully, on February 21, 1677, at the age of forty-four.

Influence

During his lifetime, Spinoza established an underground reputation as one of the greatest philosophers of his day. Even philosophers such as Gottfried Wilhelm Leibniz, who openly disparaged, him could not ignore the forcefulness of his thought. In addition to his purely intellectual achievements, Spinoza served as an inspirational figure for the circle of freethinkers with whom he was in contact. For them, Spinoza's devotion to truth, defense of tolerance, and humility made him a rallying point in their attempts to bring about further progress. At the same time, however, in the eyes of many observers, Spinoza's name was synonymous with atheism, which was widely held to be nothing less than diabolical.

Over time, the viewpoint of Spinoza's supporters has easily outdistanced that of his critics. It is true that the predominance of analytic philosophy in Anglo-American universities tended to devalue the broad synthetic enterprise in which Spinoza was engaged, and there is an archaic quality to Spinoza's terminology. Nevertheless, Spinoza's stature as one of the three great rationalist philosophers (along with Descartes and Leibniz) and his influence on later philosophers such as Georg Wilhelm Friedrich Hegel,

who themselves became seminal thinkers, is well established.

Yet Spinoza's influence goes beyond the discipline of philosophy. Literary figures such as Gotthold Ephraim Lessing and Johann Wolfgang von Goethe were profoundly influenced by the beauty, if not the logic, of Spinoza's worldview. Psychologists continue to debate Spinoza's treatment of emotion and its relation to knowledge. Libertarians still celebrate his quest for religious freedom and free expression. Intellectual historians look to Spinoza in their search for a bridge between Asian and Western values or for the roots of modern democracy. There are others who read Spinoza's work or study his life simply for insight into their own lives. In short, Spinoza remains an inspirational figure for many people. Paradoxical as it may seem, there is something deeply spiritual about this man who was excommunicated by Jews for heresy and repeatedly condemned by Christians as an atheist.

Ira Smolensky

Ethics

Type of philosophy: Ethics, metaphysics
First published: Ethica, 1677 (English translation, 1870)
Principal ideas advanced:

◇ Whatever is the cause of itself exists necessarily.

◇ Only substance is self-caused, free, and infinite; and God is the only substance.

◇ God exists necessarily and is possessed of infinite attributes.

◇ However, only two of God's infinite attributes are known to us: thought and extension.

◇ Because thought and extension are features of the same substance, whatever happens to body happens also to mind as another phase of the same event.

◇ A false idea is an idea improperly related to God; by achieving adequate ideas, we become adequate causes of the body's modifications. This is human freedom, freedom from the human bondage to the passions.

◇ The highest virtue of the mind is to know God.

The figure of Baruch Spinoza has often attracted as much attention as his work, and he stands, along with the Greek philospher Socrates, as one of the few genuine heroes in a field not much given to hero worship. A Jew, ostracized by his own people and excluded from his homeland, he insisted on following his own ideas despite their heretical tendencies. Spinoza's *Ethics* remained unpublished in his lifetime but would become the work upon which his great reputation and reservoir of influence was based. Georg Wilhelm Friedrich Hegel and many of the later Romantics acknowledge Spinoza as the modern thinker whose thought suggests the direction for their later developments.

Although Spinoza is sometimes called a philosophers' philosopher because of the abstract and technical nature of *Ethics*, few philosophers' general views are more widely known among the nonphilosophical public. Although his views are often oversimplified, they are circulated extensively. Despite his central theological orientation, Spinoza's appeal is, moreover, wide-ranging. Many people who find traditional religious beliefs unacceptable discover in Spinoza a rational and a naturalistic form of religion. His views on God, humanity, and the emotions also have popular influence.

A Geometrical Approach

A great deal of argument has been generated by the style or form in which Spinoza chose to write *Ethics*. The continental rationalists (René Descartes, Gottfried Wilhelm Leibniz, and Spinoza) were all much impressed by the exciting developments in mathematics, and all of them reflect something of the geometric temper in their writings. Spinoza elected to write *Ethics* as a geometrical system—with definitions, axioms, and propositions. Some argue that this form is essential to Spinoza's doctrines; others feel that *Ethics* can just as easily be read in essay style. All seem agreed that the work does not really have the full deductive rigor of geometry; yet the form indicates Spinoza's desire to be clear and simple in his expression, to be straightforward in his assertions, and to connect the various parts of his thought systematically. All this he achieves with the barest minimum of explanation and with little external reference.

Fortunately, a full understanding of Spinoza's attitude toward this geometrical method of philosophizing is not necessary to appraise its success or to grasp the central features of his thought. The geometrical method represents an attempted revolution in philosophical thought. Spinoza agreed with other modern revolutionaries of his era in stressing methodology and the need for a thorough reexamination of traditional philosophical and theological methods. His break with the Scholastic method is complete. Spinoza firmly believed that the human intellect can be carefully examined and improved and thereby made able to produce a more rigorous and more complete understanding of things—all this through its own strengthened power.

Properly corrected, reason is self-sufficient, its own guide and its own judge. This is, for Spinoza, as true in ethical affairs as in speculative matters. He does not belong in the class of dogmaticians; there is no indication that he believed his own views to be either complete or final. What is evident is his trust in the human intellect to work out an acceptable and a comprehensive schema. Spinoza depended heavily on previous theological views, but his modern temperament transformed them by placing them in a new humanistic perspective.

The five parts of *Ethics* take up in order God, the nature and origin of the mind, then the emotions, and finally the twin questions of human bondage and human freedom.

God, or Substance

In beginning with a consideration of the divine nature, then developing all other theories in this light, Spinoza was influenced by medieval theology. Theory of knowledge and attention to human powers of knowing received a more prominent place with Spinoza, but systematically speaking, a theory of the divine nature was still first. Spinoza called his first principle sometimes God, sometimes substance. Aristotle had defined "substance" as that capable of independent existence. Spinoza interpreted this with absolute rigor and asserted that only God, a substance of infinite attributes, could fulfill this definition exactly.

Ethics opens with the traditional distinction between that which requires no external cause to account for its existence (cause of itself) and that which owes its existence (causally) to another being. That which is the cause of itself exists necessarily and needs nothing other than itself to be conceived. This Spinoza calls substance. On the other hand, what is finite is what is capable of being limited by another thing of its own kind, whereas substance is absolutely infinite, in that it possesses infinite attributes.

Spinoza defines an "attribute" as that which the mind sees as constituting the essence of substance. A "mode" is some modification of substance. "Freedom" means to exist from the necessity of one's own nature alone (only substance as cause of itself fulfills this requirement) and to be set in action by oneself alone. Only substance, or God, is perfectly free, dependent on nothing else for its existence or action; it is absolutely infinite and thus one of a kind.

From here Spinoza turns to a classical definition of knowledge: One can say one knows something only when one understands it through its causes. He then begins his proof that there could be only one substance that would be absolutely infinite and thus be its own cause. These "proofs" are simply a modern version of the traditional arguments for God's existence, although in the *Ethics*, they take a novel form. The burden of Spinoza's point is that either nothing exists or else a substance absolutely infinite exists. Something does exist, and the presence of such an absolutely infinite substance precludes the existence of more than one such, and it includes everything else as part of itself.

Because God, or substance, consists of infinite attributes, each one of which expresses eternal and infinite essence, God necessarily exists and excludes the existence of anything else not a part of it. Spinoza goes on to argue that such a substance cannot be divided, nor can the existence of a second such substance even be conceived. From this Spinoza turns to the statement of perhaps his most famous doctrine: Whatever is, is in God, and nothing can either be or be conceived without God. Popularly this belief is called "pantheism," but such a doctrine (that the world taken as a whole is God) is too simple to express Spinoza's view. It is not enough to say that the natural order as a whole is God, for what really is true is that Spinoza takes all of the usual transcendental

qualities of a traditional God and, combining them with the natural order, calls the sum of these God, or substance absolutely infinite.

Spinoza's doctrine of the infinite attributes of God is easy proof against a simple label of pantheism. In addition to God's infinity in each kind (in thought and extension), Spinoza posits an infinity of attributes as belonging to God, only two of which (thought and extension) are known directly in the natural world. Thus God, as Spinoza conceives him, is infinitely larger than the natural order, because the world with which people are familiar actually represents only a very small part of his vast nature. This is a speculative doctrine, as intriguing as it is baffling.

Divine Nature

Because everything must be conceived through, and has its existence in, God, the knowledge of any natural event requires a reference to the divine nature. Spinoza begins *Ethics* with a discussion of God's nature because the understanding of everything else, including ethical life, depends on this. Nothing can be understood in isolation, and all adequate understanding involves locating the particular events and their immediate causes within the larger scheme of a substance absolutely infinite. God in traditional theology was used to explain the natural world as a whole; now every phenomenon is to be seen as a part of him and is to be explained on a part-whole analogy. What it is true to say about the divine nature, then, is also in some sense true of every part of the natural world.

Nothing remains unrealized in such a divine nature. Infinite numbers of things in infinite ways will all become real in the course of time, and time is without beginning or end. Rejecting medieval theories of creation, Spinoza returned to a more classical view of the world as eternal. The natural order is equal in duration with God. One side of his nature is timeless, but the side that includes the natural order is temporal. Time applies to God, but only to one aspect. There are no alternatives to any natural fact because infinite possibilities will all be realized eventually. God's existence is necessary and so is his production of the natural order as a part of his nature.

Although this production of the natural order is necessary and its pattern without alternative, nothing outside God's own nature compels him to act, and in that sense, God's activity is free. Yet God is absolutely the only genuinely free agent; in nature there is nothing contingent, but everything is determined necessarily in whole or in part by factors and causes outside its own nature. "Will" had been stressed as a causal agent by philosopher John Duns Scotus; again Spinoza reverts to a more classical doctrine and denies that will can be a free cause. Will, he says, is nothing other than reason's tendency to recognize and to accept a true idea. Things could have been produced, by God or by humanity, in no other manner and in no other order than they are and were.

God and the Natural World

In the appendix to book 1, which contains the discussion of God's nature as it includes the world as a part, Spinoza goes on to elaborate his refutation of teleology. Christian doctrine necessarily depicts God as acting to achieve certain ends, or otherwise the drama of sin, atonement, and salvation would be difficult to present. God acts to accomplish his purpose, according to the orthodox conception. All of this Spinoza denied. According to *Ethics*, thought is only one of God's infinite attributes, so that although he is a personal being in some sense, he is so only in part. Will has been denied and thought is not dominant; such a being cannot be said to act purposefully to attain an end unachievable without his conscious action. What happens in nature is simply the necessary outpouring of the divine, absolutely infinite substance, to which there is no alternative conceivable. Although Spinoza's first principle is different, he is very close to the traditional Neoplatonic theories of the necessary (although good) emanation of the world from God.

In book 2, Spinoza begins to trace the nature and the origin of the mind, one of the infinite things that necessarily follow from the nature of God. Although the mind is only one attribute among an infinite number, Spinoza readily admits that it concerns people most and is vitally important for ethical conduct. First, he must distinguish between an idea (a concept of the mind) and an adequate idea (one that has all the internal signs of a true idea). Such a distinction is extremely important because from it will come the whole of the later ethical theory.

For more traditional thought, God alone was considered perfect and all the natural order somehow less perfect (as is implied by a doctrine of Original Sin). Spinoza takes a radical position and actually equates reality with perfection. Nothing in nature has an alternative or can be different from what it is, and all things are a part of God and follow necessarily from his nature. God could not be complete without the whole natural order. Thus, it is logical that each part of God (each aspect of the natural order) should be just as perfect as it is real.

Then Spinoza turns to another radical idea: God is extended, or material things are a part of his nature. Christian views had had to make God responsible for the creation of the physical world, but none had made God himself material even in part. Within Spinoza's view, the material world is no longer somehow less than perfect, and so it can be made a part of God without lessening his perfection.

Thought and Extension

Every material thing has an idea paralleling it, although ideas affect only other ideas and physical things affect only things physical. The attribute of extension is reflected fully in the attribute of thought, although the two are only parallel and do not intersect each other. Substance thinking and substance extended are one and the same substance, now comprehended under this attribute, now under that. Nothing can happen in the body that is not perceived by the mind, and the essence of humanity consists of certain modifications of the attributes of God. People perceive all things through God, although some perceptions may be confused.

How is such confusion as does arise to be corrected? All ideas, insofar as they are related to God, are true. Thus, correct understanding means to take the idea and to place it in its proper locus within the divine nature, rather than to treat it as an independent phenomenon. No idea in itself is false; it is simply improperly related to other ideas if it is confused. For instance, people are sometimes deceived in thinking themselves to be free, but this simply reflects their ignorance of the total causal chain within the divine nature of which their actions are a part. When actions are viewed in isolation, such confusion is possible, although no idea in itself is false.

It is the nature of reason to perceive things under a certain form of eternity and to consider them as necessary. Temporal viewpoints and a belief in contingency simply reflect an unimproved reason, unable to assume its natural viewpoint. For the human mind is actually able to possess an adequate knowledge of the eternal and infinite essence of God. In many previous theological views, the human mind was thought incapable of comprehending God. For Spinoza, the human mind is to be seen as a part of the divine intellect, and as such it has within its own nature the possibility for grasping the whole of the divine mind, although to do so requires a great deal of effort.

Emotions and Ethics

When Spinoza begins to discuss the emotions in book 3, he begins to enter the ethical part of the work proper. However, Spinoza's approach is not standard; he claims that no one before has determined both the nature and the strength of the emotions or has treated the vices and follies in a geometrical method. The emotions (hatred, anger, envy) follow from the same necessity as do all other things in nature. The Greek philosopher Aristotle and others thought that conduct was not amenable to scientific knowledge, but Spinoza's natural necessity, plus the connection of every event with the divine nature, subjects the emotions to the same laws as those that govern all natural phenomena.

Spinoza says that we act when we are the adequate cause of anything; we suffer when we are the cause only partially. An emotion is a modification of the body's power to act. The emotion is an action and the body's power is increased when we are the adequate cause of the modification; the emotion is passive and the body's power of acting is decreased when we are only partially the cause. Our mind acts when it has adequate ideas; it suffers necessarily when it has inadequate ideas.

The law of existence, Spinoza tells us, is that everything should do its utmost to persevere in its own mode of being. This striving is the very essence of every living thing. We feel "joy" when we are able to pass to a higher state of being; we feel "sorrow" when through passivity and suffer-

ing we pass to a lower state. Joy, sorrow, and desire are the primary emotions. Love attaches to the things that give us joy (an active and a higher existence); hatred attaches to what gives us sorrow (a passive and a lowered existence). Naturally we endeavor to support those things that cause joy, and just as naturally we tend to destroy whatever we imagine causes us sorrow. Love can overcome hatred and thus increase our joy, and Spinoza recommends that we attempt to return love for hate for that reason. On the other hand, Spinoza feels that the traditional Christian virtue of humility produces impotence and sorrow and therefore is to be avoided.

Spinoza is often thought of as an unrestrained optimist concerning the powers of human reason, but his treatment of human bondage in book 4 should correct any such impression. In one of the longest books in *Ethics*, Spinoza outlines in detail the inevitable causes that bind people to the blindness of their emotions and work against any attempted liberation. Good and evil are defined here as, respectively, what is useful to people and what hinders them from possessing something good. Appetite is what causes people to do anything, and virtue and power are defined as being the same thing. This is a classical definition of a naturalistic ethical theory.

If people's only virtue is whatever power they possess naturally, and if good means only what is useful to them, what on earth could bind people? Spinoza says that there is no individual thing in nature not surpassed in strength and power by some other thing, which means that people's power is always threatened and their current well-being always subject to loss. Other things are stronger than people are and continually challenge their powers, which places them in bondage to the passive emotions (sorrow) that necessarily accompany any such threat. The force that people have at their disposal is limited and is infinitely surpassed by the power of external causes. People suffer insofar as they find themselves to be merely a part of nature surpassed in power and thus threatened by the other parts.

An emotion can be restrained or removed only by an opposed and stronger emotion. Thus our ability to withstand the pressures around us, to prevent sorrow, depends upon our natural power to oppose the emotions surrounding us with an equal vigor. Such a task never ceases and any victory is constantly in danger of being reversed in a weak or lax moment. Yet the highest virtue of the mind is said to be to know God. Why? Simply because such knowledge renders our ideas more adequate; as our ideas become more adequate, our power of action is increased. People disagree as far as their ideas are disturbed by emotions; when guided by reason, they tend to understand and thus to agree.

Freedom

In book 5, Spinoza turns finally to an appraisal of the powers of the intellect that make it free, because freedom comes only through the possibility of increased understanding. The primary fact on which he bases his hope for human freedom is that an emotion that is a passion and thus destructive of our power ceases to be a passion as soon as we form a clear idea of it. Thus, we cannot prevent the constant challenge to our power to continue our existence, but we can come to understand all the causes that play upon us. To the extent to which we understand the causes impinging on us, just to that extent, we can successfully oppose any threat to our freedom or our power.

There is nothing of which we cannot, theoretically speaking, form an adequate idea, including of course God himself. The way toward increasing freedom is open and is identical with an increased understanding. Such striving toward an increase of our understanding has for its object all or part of God. This is the highest effort of the mind and its highest virtue, since it is the source of the individual's increased power of existence. Such understanding is rarely achieved and is exceedingly difficult, but its unobstructed possibility is a challenge to humanity and is the source of such freedom as people may have.

Frederick Sontag

Additional Reading

Browne, Lewis. *Blessed Spinoza: A Biography of the Philosopher*. New York: Macmillan, 1932. A lively, well-written account of Baruch Spinoza's life by a professional biographer. A good introduction to Spinoza the man. Should be augmented by more current research.

Chappell, Vere, ed. *Baruch de Spinoza*. New York: Garland, 1992. A very short biography of Spinoza accompanied by a series of essays explaining and discussing his ideas.

Deleuze, Gilles. *Spinoza: Practical Philosophy*. San Francisco: City Lights Books, 1988. A difficult book about a difficult man. It has the graces of being small, of offering a biography of Spinoza, and of discussing his work succinctly.

Della Rocca, Michael. *Representation and the Mind-Body Problem in Spinoza*. New York: Oxford University Press, 1996. Are the mind and body identical? What are the requirements for having a thought about an object? To this author, those are important questions, and he believes Spinoza had ideas about them and that the ideas of Spinoza are often misunderstood.

Garrett, Don, ed. *The Cambridge Companion to Spinoza*. Cambridge, England: Cambridge University Press, 1996. Baruch Spinoza, who later called himself Benedictus, was a mass of conflicting ideas. In the introduction, Garrett tries to place Spinoza's work in the tradition of philosophy, and in the opening essay, W. N. A. Klever offers us a biography of Spinoza and a discussion of his works in general. What follows is a series of essays examining specific parts of Spinoza's thought.

Gullan-Whur, Margaret. *Within Reason: A Life of Spinoza*. London: Jonathan Cape, 1998. A feminist account of Spinoza's life that contrasts his acceptance of the male domination of society with his egalitarian republican ideals. Contains a bibliography and an index.

Hampshire, Stuart. *Spinoza*. London: Faber & Faber, 1956. A highly accessible introduction to Spinoza's philosophical system. Places Spinoza's thoughts in a clear historical context and discusses the relationship between Spinoza's metaphysics and other aspects of his philosophy.

Harris, Errol F. *Spinoza's Philosophy: An Outline*. Atlantic Highlands, N.J.: Humanities Press, 1992. A book for beginners, discussing Spinoza's life and style, his principal works, and the means of understanding his methods and his writings.

Hunter, Graeme, ed. *Spinoza: The Enduring Questions*. Toronto: University of Toronto Press, 1994. A series of essays that attempt to settle Spinoza's place in the history of philosophy.

Scruton, Roger. *Spinoza*. New York: Routledge, 1999. An excellent biographical introduction to the thoughts of the philosopher, clearly presented and requiring no special background. Bibliography.

Woolhouse, R. S. *Descartes, Spinoza, Leibniz*. London: Routledge, 1993. The three seventeenth century philosophers are examined in relation one to another. René Descartes is recognized as the father of the modern shape of philosophy (not of all of its twists and turns), and Spinoza and Gottfried Wilhelm Leibniz are examined as to their agreements and disagreements with Descartes.

Dwight Jensen

Leo Strauss

A renowned political philosopher, Strauss searched the texts of both the ancients and the moderns to construct his vision of a viable politics that included the rule of the wise.

Principal philosophical works: *Die Religionskritik Spinozas als grundlage seiner Bibelwisssenschaft*, 1930 (*Spinoza's Critique of Religion*, 1965); *The Political Philosophy of Hobbes: Its Basis and Its Genesis*, 1936; *On Tyranny: An Interpretation of Xenophon's Hiero*, 1948, rev. ed. 1963; *Persecution and the Art of Writing*, 1952; *Natural Right and History*, 1953; *Thoughts on Machiavelli*, 1959; *What Is Political Philosophy?*, 1959; *The City and Man*, 1964; *The Argument and the Action of Plato's Laws*, 1975.

Born: September 20, 1899; Kirchhain, Hessen, Germany

Died: October 18, 1973; Annapolis, Maryland

Early Life

Leo Strauss was born into an orthodox Jewish family in Kirchhain, Hessen, Germany, on September 20, 1899. He received a classical education in a *Gymnasium* (secondary school) and served in the German army. By the age of seventeen, he was a firm believer in Zionism, the belief that a Jewish homeland should be established in Palestine. His later writings included discussions of Jewish history, philosophy, and culture. He studied philosophy and natural science at the universities of Marburg, Frankfurt, Berlin, and Hamburg, and he earned his Ph.D. from the University of Hamburg in 1921.

Strauss studied with Edmund Husserl, the founder of phenomenology, an extremely influential philosophy built on the premise that there could be a science of phenomena. Husserl argued that the philosopher could develop a system describing phenomena, a system that would be as rigorous as the natural sciences. Strauss's other important teacher, Martin Heidegger, one of Husserl's students, rejected phenomenology to concentrate on a study of being, the human awareness of existing in time (temporality), and how this awareness influences the human personality and its consciousness of death. These two thinkers stimulated Strauss to develop a philosophy treating politics as phenomena that could be accurately described while acknowledging that politics is subject to temporality; that is, historical processes change the significance of politics over time.

In 1932, Strauss won a Rockefeller grant to study in Paris, where he concentrated on medieval Jewish and Islamic philosophy. After 1933, when Nazi leader Adolf Hitler took power in Germany, it became impossible for Strauss to return to Germany, and in 1937, he migrated to the United States, taking a position as a research fellow at Columbia University in 1937. The next year, he became a research fellow at the New School for Social Research. In 1949, he began teaching political philosophy at the University of Chicago, where he embarked on the works of his mature career.

Life's Work

Following Husserl, Strauss emphasized the idea of the *whole*, a term he would employ in several of his books. To acquire knowledge, the thinker has to have a sense of the whole—that any particular idea is related to a body of ideas and that those ideas make sense only because of their connection to a whole. By the same token, the thinker could have an awareness of the whole only by examining particular ideas. Sometimes called the hermeneutical circle (a circle because interpretation or hermeneutics constantly shifts from part to whole and from whole to part), this concept became valuable to Strauss as he tried to show that good government is not a historical phenomenon but instead a set of ideas developed by the ancient Greeks and others, a set of ideas that could be obscured by historical developments but could be recovered by a persistent thinker and commentator on the classic texts of political philosophy.

In his early career, Strauss focused on theology, exploring the thinking of Thomas Hobbes and Baruch Spinoza, two philosophers from earlier centuries who attacked traditional religion and many of the traditional explanations for the foundations of political states. Like these philosophers, Strauss explored the meanings of reason and revelation because he saw the conflict between religion and philosophy as the core of Western civilization that contributed to its dynamism.

Allan Bloom, a professor at the University of Chicago and a disciple of Strauss, divided Strauss's career into three phases. In the first, Strauss produced two major books, *Spinoza's Critique of Religion* and *The Political Philosophy of Hobbes*. He began to explore what later became his mature program of study: how to interpret the fundamental tension between the need to set up a civilized state and the philosopher's often corrosive explorations of truths that could undermine belief in the civilized state.

Strauss contended that the state rested on "noble fictions" about its founding: that it arose out of a gift of the gods or otherwise had a divine sanction. In fact, the state often resorted to violence and other forms of compulsion to establish and to maintain its existence. No state, Strauss believed, could survive without employing coercive means. Thinkers who come into conflict with the state or who openly expose the state's suspect substructure can expect to be punished. Noting how philosophers such as Socrates and Spinoza had been persecuted and even put to death because of their unorthodox ideas, Strauss sought a method of commentary on these thinkers and on others that emphasized the need for both exoteric (explicit) and esoteric (implicit) teaching to safeguard both the philosopher, whose wisdom could guide the state, and the state, which could profit from such wisdom only indirectly and gradually.

In his second phase, Strauss began to elaborate what he meant by exoteric and esoteric philosophy. Examining the texts of great philosophers, he found passages that seemed deliberately obscure, as if certain philosophers had put up obstacles to an easy grasp of their ideas. Writers such as John Locke, Strauss reasoned, were perfectly capable of writing plainly, so there must be a reason for their abstruse passages. Strauss suggested that Locke wrote on different levels for different audiences. Ideas that were not controversial or that could be readily absorbed and accepted were stated directly; however, ideas that might jeopardize the philosopher's authority or the authority of the state were couched in much more subtle and even elusive language and were meant only for thinkers who could approach the philosopher's own sophistication. In this sense, philosophy's meanings are hidden; they are there, in the text, but they have to be dug out and analyzed by a persistent commentator.

As Bloom argued, Strauss began, in this second phase, to adopt the two-tier method he analyzed in philosophers—using an accessible style for unobjectionable ideas and an evasive style for his more challenging arguments. Regardless of historical period, Strauss found philosophers engaging in the same maneuvers of both courting and eluding their readers. As his titles from this phase suggest, Strauss (under the shadow of Hitler) was acutely conscious of writing in a world full of danger for philosophers. These titles include *Persecution and the Art of Writing*, *Natural Right and History*, and *On Tyranny*.

In his third phase, Strauss began to expand his own use of the exoteric/esoteric method. Reviewers were often baffled by his books because they did not obey the rules of conventional scholarship, which demanded that scholars be explicit about their ideas. On the contrary, Strauss seemed to be concealed in his commentaries on the great philosophers, daring the enterprising, resolute reader to understand him just as Strauss believed the philosophers he wrote about challenged him. Even Straussians such as Bloom, however, confess that they find certain of Strauss's books from this period difficult to comprehend, especially titles such as *Thoughts on Machiavelli*, *The City and Man*, and *The Argument and Action of Plato's Laws*.

A consistent theme in all of Strauss's work is his attack on the modern social sciences. He decried the dominant methods of academic sociologists and political scientists who tried to describe society and politics in value-neutral terms. Their moral relativism and refusal to make judgments appalled Strauss, who saw this intellectual stance as a dereliction of the thinker's responsibility. There exists a wisdom of the ages on which social scientists should draw and which they should use to assess the contemporary world. To the argument that different societies have different standards and should not be assessed in absolutist terms, Strauss replied that societies might differ as to the nature of the *summum bonum* (Aristotle's term for the supreme good) but that did not mean that there is no such thing. Thinkers should always argue for what they see as the truth, even if there is a dispute about what that truth is.

Influence

Strauss's influence on his colleagues and students grew steadily during nearly twenty years of teaching at the University of Chicago. After he retired in 1968, he taught briefly in California at Claremont Men's College (later renamed Claremont McKenna), then spent his remaining years as a scholar in residence at St. John's College in Annapolis, Maryland—a fitting destination because of the school's emphasis on the "great books" curriculum and its rigorous education in the classics of philosophy, more rigorous even than that provided at the University of Chicago. When he died, he was the recipient of lavish tributes, many of them printed in *National Review*, a conservative weekly magazine.

As Shadia Drury observes in her study of Strauss, his reputation grew considerably after his death. Reviewers often mistook the aims of his books, and in his own lifetime he was regarded primarily as a historian of ideas, not as a philosopher. He seemed to subordinate himself to the texts he expounded, and he preferred to call his writing teaching. Although Strauss did not make any claims to being an original philosopher, Drury (not a Strauss disciple) and many others treat him as an innovative, unconventional figure whom contemporary philosophy is just beginning to understand and to assimilate.

Drury and others would argue that Strauss's indirect presentation of ideas was deliberate and was in itself a demonstration of his belief that philosophers cannot enunciate their most inflammatory and unorthodox ideas openly. On the contrary, philosophy must proceed obliquely—in a sense, politically. Political philosophy is not just about politics; it is itself a part of politics and must proceed in a political fashion. The concrete result is that philosophers must be acutely aware of their audience, of how much their audience can absorb, and of how to advise the state and its leaders without undermining their authority.

Although the nature and significance of Strauss's ideas have been subject to many different interpretations, it is uncontestable that he is regarded as the inspiration for several generations of conservatives. Many of them, like Bloom, began as Strauss's students. Others have become political advisers to conservative administrations, following Strauss's view that philosophers can become indispensable advisers to rulers, if not rulers themselves.

Plato's idea of the philosopher-king and Niccolò Machiavelli's idea of the philosopher as adviser to the prince inform much of Strauss's view of philosophy and philosophy's role in the modern political state. He was "conservative" in the sense that he believed that his fundamental ideas derived from the teachings of the Greeks and the Hebrews and that modern philosophy's role is to rediscover the truths of the ancients.

Strauss believed there are universal ideas, and he had a vision of politics that transcends individual cultures. He did not deny cultural differences or that history shapes the thinker's understanding of universals, but the fact that interpretations may clash and societies may implement universals in contradictory fashions does not destroy the idea of universals. It is in this sense that he was conservative. Conservatives have taken him as a mentor because he believed in a tradition that must be recovered and maintained against what has been called historicism, the doctrine that ideas grow out of and are changed by history, and that no idea can be said to be permanent. Historicism claims that all ideas are the product of their time and place. As a conservative and antihistoricist, Strauss became the leading light for conservatives and others who wish to examine and perhaps even to slow down the momentum of political change.

Carl Rollyson

Natural Right and History

Type of philosophy: Ethics, political philosophy
First published: 1953
Principal ideas advanced:

◊ The Greeks and other ancient writers discovered in nature the right of people to establish and to govern the state.

◊ The natural right to rule has been challenged by modern thinkers who believe that the only sanction for authority derives from historical process or the development of different cultures over time.

◊ The error in historicism's location of the right to rule in historical process is the conceit that historicism can replace natural right; historicism itself is a temporary development in the history of thought.

◊ Modern thought must recover a sense of the "unchanging framework which persists in all changes of human knowledge of both facts and principles."

Leo Strauss wrote his classic text in an age dominated by historicism, the notion that ideas and values are a result of historical processes, a concept that itself emphasizes change and development. In political philosophy and in the social sciences, historicism means that each culture should be judged in its own terms and not measured against a universal standard. It would be wrong, for example, to condemn one society for not behaving by the standards of another. The point is to understand the evolution of each society's codes of behavior. This attitude is often called relativism because it recognizes no absolute truths that apply to all groups.

Strauss strenuously objected to what might be called a permissive approach to the study of the state. States might differ in their interpretation of standards and values, he realized, but that did not mean that a permanent canon of precepts did not exist. On the contrary, the ancients had discovered and promulgated an unchanging, universal framework that modern thinkers had nearly obliterated but that could be recovered by reconsidering and commenting on the classics of political philosophy.

The Concept of Natural Right

Chapter 1, "Natural Right and the Historical Approach," develops Strauss's idea of what philosophy itself means, and more specifically, how philosophy turned toward a study of politics. If theology is the study of God, then philosophy is the study of nature. There can be no philosophy without this distinction, Strauss argues, and no way for humanity to exercise its ability to reason. He observes that in the Bible, nature as a concept does not exist: There is only God's word. All authority stems from the divine, which means that humanity derives its knowledge from revelation. In the Bible, it is not humanity's task to discover the world but instead to receive it as a gift from God.

When the Greeks discovered nature, they simultaneously discovered philosophy, which began an inquiry into the interpretation of nature. Putting a premium on knowledge meant that the concept of natural right became associated with wise people and the right of wise people to rule. Their authority, in other words, was based on their closeness to nature and on their ability to read it, so to speak. The concept of natural right became associated with the wise, who enunciated first principles and universal standards derived from their close inspection of nature.

Beginning in the seventeenth century, the doctrine of natural right began to be replaced by the doctrine of natural law, which enlarged the concept of nature as an authority to which all people might appeal. Knowledge and political power no longer were matters of the rule of a small select group of the wise. In the age of revolution, beginning in the eighteenth century, the belief in universal standards was demolished. History, not nature, became the standard of judgment. Because societies differed over the course of time, there could be no uniformity of values, only an "indefinite variety of notions of right or justice." In other words, Strauss concludes, "there cannot be natural right if there are no immutable principles of justice, but history shows us that all principles of justice are mutable."

The trouble with historicism (the concept that all values must be treated historically) is that it is also a product of history and hence also impermanent; it cannot be used, therefore, as a means of knowledge. Instead, thinkers must return to the approach of the ancients, the "humanizing quest for the eternal order." Strauss realizes there will be much debate over what that eternal order means, but without such a quest, humanity loses its "pure source of human inspiration and aspiration."

Facts and Values

In Chapter 2, "Natural Right and the Distinction Between Facts and Values," Strauss demonstrates that Western philosophy from Plato to Georg Wilhelm Friedrich Hegel believed that it could address fundamental political problems that were "susceptible to a final solution." Whatever their differences, in other words, philosophers agreed to pursue the constant dialogue of philosophy that began with Socrates, a dialogue that addressed the fundamental issue of how humankind ought to live. It is from this vantage point of Western philosophy that Strauss attacks the modern idea of value-free sociology and political science. Strauss insists that scholars in both disciplines cannot simply study a society; they must evaluate it according to standards of truth that they take to be constant: "The sociologist cannot be obliged to abide by the legal fiction which a given group never dared to regard as legal fiction; he is forced to make a distinction between how a given group actually conceives of the authority by which it is ruled and the character of the authority in question." In other words, the sociologist cannot simply take a group's rationale ("legal fiction") for its authority at face value; the very nature of that authority has to be questioned, and such an inquiry cannot be conducted without a set of standards that transcend those of any particular group, a set of standards derived from concepts of natural right, not from a study of changing history.

Natural Right

Chapter 3, "The Origin of the Idea of Natural Right," fully develops the distinction between the Bible as revelation and philosophy as the study of nature. Philosophers seek to know what is good by the study of nature, not the conventions established by different societies; thus, the "discovery of nature is identical with the actualization of a human possibility," Strauss maintains. Nature becomes a way of recovering first principles that otherwise can be suppressed by authoritarian societies; nature is an appealing source because it is the "ancestor of all ancestors."

In chapter 4, "Classic Natural Right," Strauss surveys the development of philosophy from Socrates to the American constitution, contrasting it in chapter 5 with "Modern Natural Right," founded on an identification with history. Whereas the concept of a natural right grounded in a perception of nature expanded human possibility and helped humanity understand its place in the whole of creation, the concept of history makes humanity "oblivious of the whole or of eternity." Strauss concedes that the concept of history "fulfils the function of enhancing the status of man and of his world," but only at the expense of obliterating a more fundamental knowledge of the universe.

Thinkers such as seventeenth century English philosopher Thomas Hobbes sought to separate humans from nature, making the quest for knowledge a value in itself rather than an extension of humanity's desire to reconnect itself with nature. Knowledge, valued for itself, becomes merely a product of human history, and humanity loses a sense of a universal context in which it can measure its claims to knowledge. Niccolò Machiavelli had earlier initiated political philosophy as a study of what the prince (or politicians) actually does rather than continuing the ancient tradition of asking what the prince (or the rulers of the state) ought to do. His revolt against the classical tradition, his realism, devalues the idea of both political virtue and the contemplative life. The result is a lowering of standards and expectations. Just as Hobbes claimed that the goal of knowledge was more knowledge (not an understanding of nature), Machiavelli claimed that the proper actions of the prince consisted of achieving the political virtue of patriotism, a loyalty to the state, but with no overriding grasp of the state's origins in nature. Compared with the ancient Greeks, then, modern political philosophy represents a decline—even a degradation of what human beings can achieve, Strauss implies. Natural right or law, then, becomes merely a deduction from the way people actually live, not from how they ought to live. The quest for moral virtue and intellectual excellence has been depreciated.

Rousseau and Burke

Chapter 6, "The Crisis of Modern Natural Right," concludes Strauss's survey of the ancient and modern worlds of political philosophy with a juxtaposition of Jean-Jacques Rousseau and Edmund Burke. Rousseau reinterpreted both the ancient and modern views of nature. He contended that in a state of nature, humanity lacked virtually everything that might be called human nature. Nature was the primitive state. Human nature had evolved out of humanity's separation from the state of nature and the creation of a human state. What was human, in other words, was not a gift of nature but precisely the opposite of nature. Rousseau therefore justified the finding of human standards in history: "man's humanity is the product of the historical process," as Strauss puts it.

Rousseau then faced a predicament: How could it be proved that the results of historical process were deliberate? Was not much of history the product of accident? How could true principles be derived from the haphazard workings of history? Strauss finds no satisfactory answer to these questions and implies that in a historicist context, the rationale for finding first principles that are tied to historical developments is suspect.

Burke saw no way out of Rousseau's dilemma, except to return to the study of the ancients. He wished to conserve the sense of rights deriving from nature while also arguing for prudence in the exercise of those rights. History, for Burke, could be a guide not to universal values but to the way in which those values were observed and enforced by society. For him, the arguments for the French Revolution were too speculative, too theoretical, and too legalistic. The people had rights, to be sure, but to exercise those rights in every case meant chaos and intolerable destruction. The American Revolution, on the other hand, which derived from the same principles as the French, nevertheless seemed to him justifiable in terms of its practical and judicious aims.

For Strauss, it seems to be the tension between nature and history in Burke's thought that is most appealing. He does not resolve the debate between natural right and history so much as he finds a way to concede the value of history without substituting it for the claims of classic natural right.

That Strauss should end his book with Burke suggests that he did not believe that modern political philosophy had advanced much beyond Burke. It must continue to recover and conserve the wisdom of the ancients while responding, flexibly, to the demands of history.

Mixed Reception

Like many of Strauss's books, *Natural Right and History* received mixed and often puzzled reviews. Philosophers took issue with his contrast between reason and revelation, arguing that the terms need not be as mutually exclusive as he supposed. Others praised his antihistoricist method and his effort to recover the ancient conceptions of natural right. Still others initiated discussions of political philosophy that imitated Strauss's method of commenting on the thought of philosophers while presenting his own views indirectly, in brief asides. In his lifetime, however, Strauss was generally considered not a philosopher in his own right but rather a historian of ideas.

Since Strauss's death in 1973, an impressive number of scholars have treated him as presenting a coherent political philosophy. He is regarded as one of the founders of modern conservatism, influencing not only political philosophers but also policymakers and governmental leaders. Strauss's students and colleagues have perpetuated his methods, so much so that the term "Straussian" is commonly used to describe thinkers trained by him or influenced by his body of work. Indeed, like the ancient philosophers whom he praised for seeking knowledge that is eternal and universal, and for inspiring other thinkers to aspire after this permanent legacy of learning, Strauss and his work have become a focus for new generations of scholars who seek to confirm his recovery of ancient wisdom.

Carl Rollyson

Additional Reading

Bloom, Allan. "Leo Strauss: September 20, 1899-October 18, 1973." *Political Theory* 2 (November, 1974): 372-392. An often cited intellectual biography by one of Strauss's students and colleagues at the University of Chicago.

Coser, Louis A. *Refugee Scholars in America: Their Impact and Their Experiences.* New Haven, Conn.: Yale University Press, 1984. Singles out Strauss as the only refugee scholar who gained a devoted following of students and colleagues who perpetuated the influence of his work. Coser also casts important light on Strauss's efforts to come to terms with postwar America.

Deutsch, Kenneth L., and Walter Nicgorski, eds. *Leo Strauss: Political Philosopher and Jewish Thinker.* Lanham, Md.: Rowman & Littlefield, 1994. Includes an excellent introduction to Strauss's life and work, along with essays on his major books and his influence on other thinkers.

Devigne, Robert. *Recasting Conservatism: Oakeshott, Strauss, and the Response to Postmodernism.* New Haven, Conn.: Yale University Press, 1994. Chapters on British and American conservatism and on new conservative theory. Devigne shows how in Britain and in the United States, Oakeshott and Strauss reshaped the meaning of conservatism according to their interpretation of principles derived from classical philosophy.

Drury, Shadia. *Leo Strauss and the American Right.* New York: St. Martin's Press, 1997. A valuable source on Strauss's contributions to political science.

_____. *The Political Ideas of Leo Strauss.* New York: St. Martin's Press, 1988. Contains an excellent biographical/critical introduction and chapters on Strauss as teacher and philosopher; on his theology; on his interpretation of Socrates, Machiavelli, Hobbes, Plato, and Nietzsche; and on modernity. Concludes with a critique of Strauss's ideas. Notes, annotated bibliography, and index.

Emberly, Peter, and Barry Cooper, eds. *Faith and Political Philosophy: The Correspondence Between Leo Strauss and Eric Vogelin, 1934.* University Park: Pennsylvania State University Press, 1993. In addition to the correspondence between the philosophers, which explores Strauss's views on reason and revelation, the volume includes essays by Strauss and Vogelin, along with commentaries by other scholars on the Strauss/Vogelin dialogue.

Gadamer, Hans-Georg. *Truth and Method.* New York: Seabury Press, 1975. Contains an explanation and criticism of Strauss's antihistoricism.

Jaffa, Harry V. *American Conservatism and the American Founding.* Durham, N.C.: Carolina Academic Press, 1984. Chapters 8-10 are especially helpful in situating Strauss within the history of American conservatism.

Lampert, Laurence. *Leo Strauss and Nietzsche.* Chicago: University of Chicago Press, 1996. A very readable account of Strauss's ideas and his interpretation of Nietzsche. A bibliography and index are included.

National Review 25 (December 7, 1973): 1347-1357. This issue, entitled "The Achievement of Leo Strauss," includes tributes to Strauss's work and to his influence. One of the more accessible introductions to Strauss's impact on American conservatives.

Rosen, Stanley. *Hermeneutics as Politics.* New York: Oxford University Press, 1987. A useful explanation of how Strauss uses hermeneutics (interpretation) in his studies of political philosophy.

Scott, Warren. *The Emergence of Dialectical Theory: Philosophy and Political Inquiry.* Chicago: University of Chicago Press, 1984. Examines Strauss's criticism of value-free social science and his handling of classical political philosophy, which Scott finds disappointing.

Carl Rollyson

Peter Strawson

Strawson developed a relatively informal logic in comparison to W. V. O. Quine's unrelentingly formal approach, offered a chastened and influential account of Immanuel Kant's metaphysics and epistemology, and presented an account of the general conceptual scheme as an exercise in descriptive metaphysics.

Principal philosophical works: *Introduction to Logical Theory*, 1952; *Individuals: An Essay in Descriptive Metaphysics*, 1959; *The Bounds of Sense: An Essay on Kant's "Critique of Pure Reason,"* 1966; *Philosophical Logic*, 1967; *Logico-Linguistic Papers*, 1971; *Freedom and Resentment, and Other Essays*, 1974; *Subject and Predicate in Logic and Grammar*, 1974; *Skepticism and Naturalism: Some Varieties*, 1985; *Analysis and Metaphysics: An Introduction to Philosophy*, 1992; *Entity and Identity: And Other Essays*, 1997.

Born: November 23, 1919; London, England

Early Life

Peter Frederick Strawson was born in the London borough of Ealing to schoolteacher parents, the second child among three brothers and a younger sister. His parents met when they were graduate students in English literature at Goldsmith's College. He was brought up in Finchley, near London, and attended Finchley County School. After a year there, his parents transferred him to Christ's College, a male-only school with high academic standards. There his specialist subjects were French, Latin, history, and English. He particularly enjoyed English prose, poetry, and grammar. He earned an open scholarship in English to St. John's College, Oxford.

In 1937, at the age of seventeen, Strawson entered Oxford and switched his field of study to philosophy, specifically to the program in philosophy, politics, and economics. Influenced by Jean-Jacques Rousseau's *Du contract social: Ou, Principes du droit politique* (1762; *A Treatise on the Social Contract: Or, The Principles of Politic Law*, 1764) and the semipopular philosophical writings of C. E. M. Joad, he found himself skillful both at constructing arguments and at critiquing the arguments of others. At the same time, although a lover of poetry, he found his own poetic skills not of the same caliber as his philosophical

talents. He was unexcited by economics and the history of politics, finding philosophy more congenial. He therefore focused his studies on logic, the philosophy of language, metaphysics, epistemology, and the philosophy of Immanuel Kant. His principal tutor was J. D. Mabbott, known for his work in political philosophy and ethics and a fine small book on David Hume's philosophy. However, the major philosophical influence among his teachers was the well-known philosopher of language H. P. Grice. Upon graduation in 1940, Strawson was inducted into the Royal Artillery, where he took courses in radar technology and became the commander of a radar station in Sussex. He was commissioned in 1942 in the Royal Electrical and Mechanical Engineers. He reached the rank of captain, was posted to Italy and Austria, and served as a defending officer at various courts-martial. In 1945, he married Grace Hall Martin. He was demobilized in 1946.

Life's Work

Leaving the armed forces in 1946, Strawson became assistant lecturer of philosophy at the College of North Wales, lecturer at University College (1947-1948), and fellow and praelector in philosophy at University College, Oxford (1948-1968, promoted to reader in 1966). He was appointed to the Chair of Wayneflete Professor of Metaphysics and Fellow of Magdalen College, in which position he served from 1968 through 1987. He was visiting professor at Duke University (1955-1956), Princeton University (1960-1961), and the University of Colorado-Boulder (fall, 1991). Among his many honors, he was created Knight Bachelor in 1977.

Perhaps Strawson's interest in English prose, poetry, and grammar led naturally to his interest in logic and the philosophy of language and influenced him to prefer a more informal approach to these topics than some other philosophers have taken. Strawson took this approach in rejecting one of philosopher Bertrand Russell's analyses. Russell held that sentences such as "The present king of France is bald" should be thought of as expressing two propositions, namely (1) that there is a present king of France and (2) that this person is bald. In an approximation of the formal talk of *Principia Mathematica* (1910-1913), which Russell wrote with Alfred North Whitehead, this becomes, "There is an x such that x is the present king of France and x is bald." Thus the original sentence is seen as expressing not one proposition but two, and the resulting conjunction is true only if both its parts, or conjuncts, are true ("P and Q" is true if and only if P is true and Q is true). In Russell's view, "The present king of France is bald" is false because "There is a present king of France" is false.

Strawson found that this idea violated both common sense and good sense. His view is that "The present king of France is bald" expresses neither a truth nor a falsehood. The reason for this, he holds, is that judgments to the effect that something has or lacks a property presuppose the existence of the thing said to have or lack the property. Because there is no such being as the present king of France, there is no truth about the baldness or otherwise of such a thing. A follower of Russell will find this inadequate; Strawson's proposal will entail that the logician is unable to represent sentences (or the propositions they seem to express) such as "The Canadian unicorn is silver" and "Santa Claus takes a yearly world tour." Plainly such sentences can be represented in logical expressions and appear in arguments (only truths and falsehoods can appear in standardly represented arguments). They can be seen to entail and be entailed by other sentences (or the propositions these sentences express).

We can, without trying to adjudicate this dispute here, note one argument relevant to it. Assuming that Strawson's account is right, suppose I offer to sell you my beautiful horse for a thousand dollars, you hand over the money, and I leave, telling you my horse is in the stable all saddled and waiting for you to ride it. Suppose, further, I have never had a horse. When you confront me about the matter, I tell you that, because I had no horse, my telling you "My horse is beautiful and is worth a thousand dollars" cannot be false. It could be false only if there had been such a horse. Because lying to you includes telling you something false, I cannot have lied to you. You cannot say that (1) "My horse is beautiful and is worth a thousand dollars" entails (2) "I have a horse," because given that "I have no horse," the statement "My horse is beautiful and is worth a thousand dollars" is neither true nor false, and only things that are true or false have any entailments. (It follows that "P presupposes Q" cannot mean "not-Q entails not-Q.") A Strawsonian response will assert that I have misled you to suppose that the presupposition of "My horse is beautiful and is worth a thousand dollars" had truth value when it lacked it.

Strawson's most famous books are *Introduction to Logical Theory, Individuals: An Essay in Descriptive Metaphysics*, and *The Bounds of Sense: An Essay on Kant's "Critique of Pure Reason."* In the first book, he argued that induction needs no justification and offers his views of the connections between logic and natural language.

In *Individuals*, Strawson examines the idea that there is a conceptual scheme that all human beings share. The task of descriptive metaphysics is to map this scheme, identifying its basic concepts and their interrelationships. A revisionary metaphysic would proffer and contend for changes in this scheme. In accord with the overall linguistic orientation in British philosophy in the years in which he worked, Strawson takes the primary object of metaphysics to be not the world *per se* but people's thoughts about it. Those thoughts, he holds, occur within the context of a general conceptual system in which the notion of a spatio-temporal basic particular to which both mental and physical properties may be ascribed is central.

In *The Bounds of Sense*, Strawson offers a somewhat chastened version of Kantianism. Kant embraced what he termed transcendental idealism. This theory held that perception provides people with objects as experienced and that empirical knowledge is not knowledge of how things are but how they appear. Strawson finds Kant's arguments for transcendental idealism wanting. He finds Kant's view in the *Kritik der reinen Vernunft* (1781; *The Critique of Pure Reason*, 1873) much more defensible without transcendental idealism than with it.

What Strawson wishes to retain from Kant is essentially the idea that if a series of experiences are to be the experiences of a single experiencing subject, they must also be the experiences of an objectively ordered world. An essential element in such objectivity is the possibility of distinguishing between how things merely appear and how they actually are. According to Kant, subjectivity requires objectivity; being a subject of experience and viewing the world as distinct from and independent of oneself inherently go together.

Strawson agrees with Kant's claims and finds in them the basis for a refutation of skepticism. According to Strawson, skeptical philosophers, who doubt or deny the existence of any external world perceived through the senses, must use in the formulation of their doubts the concepts of enduring objects and individual perceivers. However, these concepts themselves, Strawson argues, are such that skeptics can hold them only if they believe there is a genuine distinction between experiencing subject and experienced objective world. It remains controversial whether, in their Kantian or Strawsonian form, arguments of this sort—transcendental arguments—succeed. For example, skeptics could respond that the fact that there seems to be an objective world is sufficient for one to have the concepts needed for the formulation of skepticism, and that is all skeptics need. However, there can seem to be an objective world in the absence of there actually being one.

In *Skepticism and Naturalism: Some Varieties*, Strawson pursued a line of thought suggested in different ways by David Hume and Ludwig Wittgenstein: We cannot in fact doubt that there is an external world that we experience; we are not psychologically up to this feat. This correlates with the thesis that skepticism about induction is inappropriate because inductive rules define a practice we engage in (a form of life that has its own internal rules that cannot be questioned and rejected without abandoning the practice they define). Similarly, our practice of formulating perceptual beliefs based on sensory experiences is a practice that has its internal rules, and we cannot escape the practice.

Philosophers have questioned, however, whether—even granting the psychological claim that we cannot actually protractedly accept an explicit skepticism—this shows skepticism to be false. It is logically possible that continuing to trust induction or perception has no rational justification, and neither the fact that even heroic efforts to continually believe this nor the fact that there are practices that assume such trust is rationally appropriate shows that this logical possibility is not also the fact of the matter. Thus philosophers who are not themselves skeptics have doubted that Strawson's adaptations of Hume and Wittgenstein refute the skeptical position regarding either induction or perception.

Influence

Strawson's work, done in the context of the linguistic philosophy dominant in Oxford during the years he wrote and taught, did much to return an interest in metaphysics to respectable status in Anglo-American philosophy. His work on informal logic, the philosophy of language, Kant's philosophy, and descriptive metaphysics was widely discussed in seminars, articles, and books.

Keith E. Yandell

Individuals

An Essay in Descriptive Metaphysics

Type of philosophy: Epistemology, metaphysics
First published: 1959
Principal ideas advanced:

◊ A descriptive metaphysic maps "our" conceptual system, which is shared by everyone.

◊ Revisionists such as George Berkeley and Thomas Hobbes see our conceptual system as faulty and attempts to gain consistency and coherence by excising some part of the system and working with the remainder or adding new material.

◇ In our conceptual system, particular things exist and are identifiable by reference to their places in a spatiotemporal framework.

◇ The concept of a person is primitive and cannot be analyzed into a mind plus a body or a collection of mental and physical states.

The intent of Peter Strawson's *Individuals: An Essay in Descriptive Metaphysics*, in accord with the linguistic philosophy that characterized the philosophy being conducted at Oxford when Strawson wrote his book, was to give an accurate description of the fundamental features of "our" conceptual system, not (as in most of traditional metaphysics) of the world itself. The intended system is "ours" in that it is shared by everyone, learned or unlearned, Greek or barbarian, wise or unwise, living ten thousand years ago or now.

The justification for taking the scheme to be "ours" in this wide sense, Strawson contends, is that everyone who is able to think and experience at least begins with this system of concepts. Of course, even philosophers who agree that there is such a conceptual system, possession of which is fundamental to thought and experience, may differ in the way in which they describe this scheme. For example, Greek philosopher Aristotle and German philosopher Immanuel Kant, both of whom influenced Strawson, offer a theory of categories or basic concepts whose logical interconnections define a cognitive system. However, while there are significant points of agreement among them, there are also differences. Any effort to offer a description of our conceptual system will have to include a defense of the claim that our system is as described. All such endeavors are subject to the question of why one should think that our concepts are properly mapped by the offered account. Even with such a defense, a descriptive metaphysic will face competitors.

Other Philosophers' Views
Aristotle was a descriptive metaphysician, an articulator of the assumptions of common sense. Kant, Strawson suggests, is also fundamentally a descriptive metaphysician with (unfortunate) revisionary tendencies. George Berkeley and Gottfried Wilhelm Leibniz, as idealists, are revisionists. Thomas Hobbes, as a reductive materialist (assuming he is one), is equally revisionist. Revisionists see our conceptual system as in some way fundamentally faulty, perhaps by way of some basic inconsistency or through holding together diverse elements that cannot be combined into a coherent whole. A revisionist then proposes a way of gaining consistency and coherence by excising some part of our conceptual system and then either adding new material or making do with what is left. There are both speculative revisionary metaphysicians (those who add) and reductive revisionary metaphysicians (those who make do)

Aristotle took himself to be investigating the fundamental characteristics of being—of things as they are independent of human thought. Proper thought reflects, corresponds to, represents the structure and content *of the world*, as well as of the structure of our thought concerning it. Kant took himself to be investigating the logically necessary conditions of our thought and experience, with the crucial addition that the results tell us the ways in which we must think of things, not the way the things thought about mind-independently are. Strawson, in contrast to Aristotle, takes the task of metaphysics to be the correct description *of our shared conceptual system* and, in contrast to Kant, does not hold that our conceptual scheme is closed off from what exists distinct from and independent of our thinking.

The Concept of a Person
Our conceptual system, Strawson says, is one in which particular things exist and are identifiable (and reidentifiable) by reference to their places in a single spatiotemporal framework. These particulars are conceived of as relatively enduring, publicly observable physical bodies. Among these are persons, bodies so conceived that it is their nature to be describable by mental and physical predicates. The concept of a person, Strawson contends, is primitive or unanalyzable either into a mind plus a body or a collection of mental and/or physical states. This approach to persons echoes Aristotle and rejects both French philosopher René Descartes's (and Greek philosopher Plato's) view that persons are centers of

self-consciousness that may or may not be embodied and David Hume's theory that a person at a given time is simply a bundle of states and over time is a series of such bundles. Both of these accounts—Descartes's and Hume's—are, in Strawson's view, revisionist and hence objectionable. Descartes presumably would deny that his account is revisionist; he seems (not implausibly) to think that his mind-body dualism, in which self-conscious things and spatially extended things are viewed as belonging to different kinds, to be as commonsensical as anything can be.

Berkeley also (perhaps rather less plausibly) also took his idealism (the view that there are self-conscious minds but that what talk of bodies refers to is, in the end, really only sensory experiences that these minds have) to be but common sense. He thought that philosophers (in particular, Aristotle) have perverted common sense and that his idealism merely returned thought to its original commonsense purity. Even Hume, in his *Philosophical Essays Concerning Human Understanding* (1748; best known as *An Enquiry Concerning Human Understanding*, 1758) takes his account of our experiences as composed, not of awareness of Strawsonian enduring things, but of fleeting impressions and ideas, and speaks as one who is merely describing what is evident to every observant participant in thought and perception. The salient point, then, is that in claiming merely to be describing "our" conceptual scheme, Strawson arguably is unintentionally engaging in what he designates as revisionary thought. Whether or not this is so is controversial.

To say that a kind of individual is primitive in our conceptual scheme is to deny that there is any other sort of individual that we need refer to in order to identify or refer to it. A sort of individual is nonbasic if, in order to refer to it, we must refer to particulars or individuals and predicate terms represent and indicate characteristics of individuals. Predicate terms can be negated; if having a quality is a feature of an individual, so would lacking that quality be a feature of an individual. However, subject terms cannot be negated; this claim links Strawson's idea that sentences of the form "The *A* is *Q*" are neither true

nor false if there is no individual that *A* designates. Strawson had earlier claimed that a sentence of the form "The *A* is *Q*" does not entail a corresponding sentence of the form "There is an . . . " because (he argued) there can be entailments only between things that have truth value (are either true or false), and the former sentence lacks truth value if there is nothing that is indicated by *A*.

Strawson rejects the idea that belief in a publicly accessible and mind-independently existing world requires justification by appeal to something whose existence is more securely known. He writes, "It is difficult to see how such beliefs could be argued for except by showing their consonance with the conceptual scheme [with] which we operate, by showing how they reflect the structure of that scheme."

The idea is that there is nothing more basic to appeal to than the discerned presuppositions of our common conceptual scheme. With this, presumably, goes the dialectical point that denying such presuppositions is self-defeating in some way, perhaps in that one (allegedly at least) could not make one's objection were it well founded.

Keith E. Yandell

Additional Reading

Ayer, A. J. *The Concept of a Person.* London: Macmillan, 1964. Contains A. J. Ayer's discussion of Peter Strawson's view of what a person is.

Hahn, Lewis Edward, ed. *The Philosophy of P. F. Strawson.* Library of Living Philosophers series. La Salle, Ill.: Open Court, 1998. An intellectual biography of the subject. Contains some twenty essays on his philosophy and a reply to each by the subject himself.

Sen, P. B., and R. R. Verma, eds. *The Philosophy of P. F. Strawson.* New Delhi, India: Indian Council of Philosophical Research, 1995. A collection of papers on Strawson's work with his replies.

Van Straaten, V., ed. *Philosophical Subjects.* Oxford: Clarendon Press, 1980. A collection of papers that touch on Strawson's work. Contains some difficult material.

Keith E. Yandell

D. T. Suzuki

Through his teaching, lectures, writings, and translations, Suzuki is credited with bringing Buddhism to the Western world. Emphasizing the unity of spiritual thought and synthesizing Eastern and Western religions, he defined the nature of Buddhism in Western philosophy and widened the influence of Zen Buddhism internationally.

Principal philosophical works: *Outlines of Mahayana Budddhism*, 1907; *A Brief History of Early Chinese Philosophy*, 1914; *Essays in Zen Buddhism*, 1927 (first series); *Studies in the Lankavatara Sutra, One of the Most Important Texts of Mahayana Buddhism*, 1930; *Essays in Zen Buddhism*, 1933 (second series); *Essays in Zen Buddhism*, 1934 (third series); *An Introduction to Zen Buddhism*, 1934; *The Training of the Zen Buddhist Monk*, 1934; *Manual of Zen Buddhism*, 1935; *Buddhist Philosophy and Its Effects on the Life and Thought of the Japanese People*, 1936; *Japanese Buddhism*, 1938; *The Essence of Buddhism*, 1946; *The Zen Doctrine of No-Mind: The Significance of the Sutra of Hui-neng*, 1949; *Living by Zen*, 1949; *A Miscellany on the Shin Teaching of Buddhism*, 1949; *Studies in Zen*, 1955; *Zen Buddhism: Selected Writings*, 1956; *Mysticism: Christian and Buddhist*, 1957; *Zen Buddhism and Psychoanalysis*, 1960; *The Field of Zen: Contributions to The Middle Way, the Journal of the Buddhist Society*, 1969; *Shin Buddhism*, 1970; *What Is Zen? Two Unpublished Essays and a Reprint of the First Edition of "The Essence of Buddhism,"* 1971; *Sengai, the Zen Master*, 1971; *Collected Writings on Shin Buddhism*, 1973; *Buddha of Infinite Light*, 1997.

Born: October 18, 1870; Kanazawa, Japan
Died: July 12, 1966; Kamakura, Japan

Early Life

Raised in a region of Japan and by a family steeped in Shin Buddhism, in 1875 Teitaro Suzuki (who later added the Buddhist name of Daisetz to become Daisetz Teitaro Suzuki) entered primary school shortly before the death of his physician father. In 1883, he entered middle school but was forced to temporarily abandon his formal studies in 1889 when he began teaching English first at Noto Peninsula and at Ishikawa in 1890 when his mother died.

In 1891, he entered Tokyo Senmon Gakko (Waseda University), and later he studied at Tokyo Imperial University. There he began his formal studies in Buddhism under the mentorship of Imagita Kosen Roshi, who died in 1892. Suzuki continued his Buddhist studies under Soyen Shaku and American publisher Paul Carus, who took Suzuki with him to La Salle, Illinois, in 1897, where Suzuki acted as translator for Shaku.

Suzuki translated works on Eastern religion for Open Court Publishing. Fluent in English, German, French, Chinese and Japanese, trained in religious philosophy, and skilled in oral and written communications, Suzuki was uniquely prepared to become an important spokesperson for Eastern thought in the twentieth century.

Life's Work

From the first publication of his essays on Zen Buddhism in 1927 until his death in 1966, Suzuki was known as one of the most knowledgeable exponents of Zen, although from the outset of his writing career, he clearly wanted to demonstrate the unity of all spiritual thought, including Mahayana, Shin, Tibetan, and Zen Buddhism, Daoism, Confucianism, and Western mystical Christianity. This desire to link modern religious faiths was first revealed in 1907, when he delivered a series of lectures in Maine that resulted in the publication of the first of his 125 books and articles in English, *Outlines of Mahayana Buddhism*. However, his name became closely associ-

D. T. Suzuki. *(Library of Congress)*

liance on empirical science can be equated with using standardized fishing nets that will catch only what fits into preestablished, inflexible systems of thought.

For both Western and Eastern audiences, Suzuki defined the notion of Buddhist Prajna intuition, a metaphysical state in which one can perceive things as they actually are rather than distorted in the mental layers of personal and cultural experience that yield unhealthy attachments for earthly matters. He taught the Buddhist principle that enlightenment is a final psychic fact that takes place when religious consciousness is expanded to extremity. This Buddha-conscious state clarifies thought and ends self-centered mental illusions created by subject-verb-object distinctions of duality or polarity.

Believing in the elements of "truth, progress, and life," which he championed despite the negative influences of the two world wars, Suzuki claimed progress began with one single significant intuitive moment that must follow a period of inner anguish. This moment is rekindled over and over in a person's life as the individual responds to life's demands in a state of moment-to-moment awareness of what is actually happening. Suzuki defined this day-to-day practice of "mindfulness" as "suchness" or "as-it-is-ness." Restating the ancient teachings of Buddhism, Suzuki wrote and spoke of affirming life primarily through the Great Compassion, or Oya-sama, for all living things.

Although none of these ideas was originated by Suzuki, he was the first to convey them to the Western world in understandable language, and he was the first Eastern spiritual leader to devote his life to successfully spreading these essentials of Buddhist thought to a largely non-Eastern audience. In this endeavor, Suzuki was aided by his studies in Western thought, notably his read-

ated with Japanese Zen because of the popularity of his three-part series, *Essays in Zen Buddhism*.

Suzuki's career was motivated by his determination to synthesize what he saw as single spiritual truths in the Buddhist state of satori. Satori, as described by Siddhārtha Gautama (known as the first Buddha), is one moment of heightened opening of consciousness, an awareness of the essential spirit of all religions and philosophies that comes to enlightened seekers. Suzuki believed that spiritual longing could be addressed beyond the limitations of logic and reason. He repeatedly wrote that spiritual matters cannot be dissected by the intellect, claiming Western re-ing of the works of the American philosopher and innovator in psychology, William James. Because of the breadth of his scholarship and his appreciation for varying approaches to spirituality, Suzuki was more than a spokesperson for his primary religion. By encompassing the long history of Buddhist thought and his synthesis of international religious schools, he was the one of the important interpreters of Buddhism in modern times and largely shaped how Buddhism would be received in the West.

Suzuki's long involvement in academic, religious, and cultural projects focused on three major tasks. First, he set out to introduce Mahayana Buddhism to the Western world using Zen teachings as a tool to open understanding. Second, he sought to unify and ally the various schools of Buddhism in Japan, ending the sectarian divisions in Buddhism. Third, he sought to uncover the essential aspects of religion as a whole, believing that both Buddhism and Christianity contained aspects of one central truth and that these religions were variations of one central faith deeply imbedded in the human soul.

Suzuki's expansive and inclusive studies in religious philosophy were lifelong and literally global. In 1908, he left the United States to tour Europe, where he was invited by the Society of Emanuel Swedenborg to translate one of works of the Swedish philosopher, scientist, and mystic into Japanese. In 1910, he was appointed professor at Gakushuin in Tokyo, where he taught until 1921 before returning to the United States to begin lecturing at a number of prominent universities. In 1911, Suzuki was married to Beatrice Erskine Lane, an American kindred spirit who supported Suzuki's work. With his wife, who died in 1939, Suzuki founded an animal shelter in Kita Kamakura, Japan, in 1929. In 1914, he took a class of students on a tour of China resulting in that year's *A Brief History of Early Chinese Philosophy*. In 1921, Suzuki began editing the magazine *Eastern Buddhist*. In 1934, he toured Korea, Manchuria, and China. In 1936, he attended the World Congress of Faiths in London, England, and lectured at Oxford, Cambridge, Durham, Edinburgh, and London universities. In 1946, he began editing the magazine *The Cultural East* (1946).

He received a number of awards and medals, including the Cultural Medal in Japan (1949), the Asahi Cultural Award (1955), and the Rabindranath Tagore Birth-Centenary Medal (1964). Suzuki gave a lecture on Buddhism before the emperor of Japan in 1947 and was elected to the Japanese Academy in 1949. He received an Honorary Doctorate of Law from the University of Hawaii in 1959. Suzuki was an important leader at the second East/West Philosopher's Conference in Honolulu in 1949, the third in 1959, and the fourth in 1964.

During the 1950's, Suzuki was part of the faculty at Columbia University in New York, where he published his signature book, *Mysticism: Christian and Buddhist*. In that work, he stated that the two religions are mirrors of each other, comparing the Christian doctrine of the Holy Ghost with the writings of Zen master Zhuangzi. In 1957, in Cuernavaca, Mexico, he joined forces with the influential American psychologist and writer, Erich Fromm, noted for his work on the individual versus society, to explore linkages between Zen and psychoanalysis. Their conversations resulted in the work *Zen Buddhism and Psychoanalysis*. Throughout the decade, he lectured in Paris, London, Zurich, Munich, Rome, Stuttgart, Vienna, Brussels, and Mexico City. He moved to Cambridge, Massachusetts, in 1957 to work with Shin'ichi Hisamatsu on a series of lectures at Harvard, the Massachusetts Institute of Technology (MIT), Wellesley, Brandeis, Radcliffe, and Amherst universities.

During celebrations of his ninetieth birthday in 1960, Suzuki spent four weeks in India, and in 1961, he wrote *Sengai*, a commentary on the artist's drawing for a traveling exhibit. In 1964, he met with Father Thomas Merton, the noted Catholic theologian and author of a series of books on Buddhism from the Christian perspective.

On July 13, 1966, one day after his death, Suzuki's ashes were placed behind the Tokei Temple. In recognition of his achievements, the senior grade of the third court rank was posthumously bestowed on him by the imperial household of Japan. A number of works were published posthumously, including *Sengai, the Zen Master*, which states that Zen masters should neither affirm nor negate but speak and act with the simple power of awareness. The *Collected Writings on Shin Buddhism* was published in 1973, and a series of transcriptions of Suzuki's lectures appeared in the 1980's in the *Eastern Buddhist*. In 1997, *Buddha of the Infinite Light* was published by the American Buddhist Academy, a revised edition of a talk by Suzuki explaining the philosophy of "Purer Land" Buddhism.

Influence

The 1927 publication of *Essays in Zen Buddhism* (first series) is considered a significant landmark in philosophical history, equated with the first European-language translations of Aristotle and Plato. Before Suzuki, Western writers influenced by Eastern thought such as Henry David Thoreau and Ralph Waldo Emerson could not distinguish between Buddhism, Hinduism, and other Eastern systems of thought largely because few publications were available in Western languages. The popularity of Suzuki's books elevated Western interest in Buddhism to a level equivalent to the interest shown in Daoism and Confucianism by nineteenth century Western writers. Suzuki's translations of both religious scriptures and verse made available many texts previously unknown outside their country of origin.

Suzuki, aided by twentieth century literary movements interested in Eastern poetics such as the Imagists and Beats as well as the post-World War II influx of Asian immigrants and return of soldiers who had been stationed in Asia, made Buddhism a prominent influence in postwar Western cultural thought. His significant participation in the growing milieu of multiculturalism also helped expand interest in Eastern art and culture as a whole. In the 1950's, he was acknowledged as one of the foremost leading living experts on Zen and was championed by writers such as Alan Watts, whose 1957 *The Way of Zen* spoke highly of Suzuki. Interest in Eastern philosophy in the 1960's and 1970's, particularly among the young, can be traced largely to Suzuki's presence, and his books remained in print and continued to have a wide readership long after his death.

Suzuki was not an inventor of systems or philosophy but rather a figure who gave universality to Zen and extended the audience for Buddhist thought. His doctrine of unifying the separate schools of Buddhism helped redefine the importance of Zen in Japan and created the

climate for unity later favored by Tibet's spiritual leader the Dalai Lama. Before Suzuki, Zen was a narrowly structured school of thought; after him, it became synonymous with enlightenment, awareness, and spiritual awakening.

Wesley Britton

Zen Buddhism

Selected Writings

Type of philosophy: Buddhism, Japanese philosophy, ethics
First published: 1956
Principal ideas advanced:

◇ Zen is a way of life, of seeing and knowing by looking into one's own nature.

◇ The truth comes through active meditation, and enlightenment is sudden and intuitive.

◇ Zen does not rely on the intellect, the scriptures, or the written word, but on a direct pointing at the soul, a seeing into one's own nature as making Buddhahood possible.

◇ Zen masters make the moment of enlightenment (satori) possible by referring directly to some natural and commonplace matter; the immediate recognition of the unity of being follows.

◇ The chief characteristics of satori are irrationality, intuitive insight, authoritativeness, affirmation, a sense of the beyond, an impersonal tone, a feeling of exaltation, and momentariness.

◇ The methods of Zen are paradox, going beyond the opposites, contradiction, affirmation, repetition, exclamation, silence, or direct action (such as a blow, or pointing).

Zen Buddhism shares with other philosophies and faiths that stress intuition and awareness the ironic condition of desiring to communicate what cannot be communicated. Like the theologies of the Middle Ages, it urges an understanding of true being by a kind of direct insight into one's own being, but it disdains any intellectual or formalistic methods of achieving that insight. The profession of conviction, then, is largely negative;

the emphasis, insofar as discourse is concerned, is not on what can be said but on that on which we must be silent. Zen masters are not lecturers; they are directors who turn the attention of disciples to some natural fact that, properly apprehended, reveals everything. Of those who have made the effort to explain Zen Buddhism, few have been more successful than the Japanese philosopher and professor, D. T. Suzuki, whose *Essays in Zen Buddhism* (1927, 1933, 1934), *The Zen Doctrine of No-Mind* (1949), and *Studies in Zen* (1955) provide the selections collected and edited by William Barrett under the title *Zen Buddhism*. This volume provides a good introduction to Suzuki's work and to Zen Buddhism; it deals with the meaning of Zen Buddhism, its historical background, its techniques, its philosophy, and its relation to Japanese culture.

The Origin of Zen

According to the legendary account of Zen, given by Suzuki, Zen originated in India, and the first to practice the Zen method was Sākyamuni, the Buddha. He is reputed to have held a bouquet of flowers before his disciples without saying a word. Only the venerable Mahakasyapa understood the "silent but eloquent teaching on the part of the Enlightened One." Consequently, Mahakasyapa inherited the spiritual treasure of Buddhism.

According to historical accounts, however, Zen Buddhism originated in China in 520 C.E. with the arrival of Bodhi-Dharma from India (the twenty-eighth in the line of patriarchs of Zen, according to the orthodox followers). The message brought by Bodhi-Dharma became the four-phrase summation of the Zen principles: "A special transmission outside the scriptures; No dependence upon words and letters; Direct pointing at the soul of man; Seeing into one's nature and the attainment of Buddhahood." These are not the words of Bodhi-Dharma, but of later disciples who formulated his teachings. The method of "direct pointing," of referring to some natural thing or event as the focal point of meditation, preparatory to an instantaneous enlightenment, continues to be the most characteristic method of Zen Buddhism.

Dharma came to be known as the *biguan* Brahman, or the "Wall-contemplating Brahman," be-

cause of his practice of contemplating a monastery wall—reputedly for nine years. One of the most familiar stories of his teaching has to do with the persistent seeker after truth, the monk Shen Guang, described in legend as having stood in the snow until he was buried to his knees and as having cut off his arm in order to show the sincerity of his desire to learn. Finally, gaining audience with Dharma, he said, "My soul is not yet pacified. Pray, master, pacify it." Dharma replied, "Bring your soul here, and I will have it pacified." Suzuki finishes the story: Guang hesitated for a moment but finally said, "I have sought it these many years and am still unable to get hold of it!" "There! It is pacified once for all." This was Dharma's sentence.

The Chinese founder of Zen, Suzuki reports, was Huineng (638-713), who was so deeply touched by a recitation of the Diamond Sutra (Vajracchedikasutra) that he made a monthlong journey to beg the patriarch Hongren to allow him to study under him. Hongren recognized Huineng's spiritual quality and transferred the patriarchal robes to him. (The account may not be accurate, having been composed by the followers of Huineng.)

It was Huineng who taught that Zen is the "seeing into one's own Nature." According to Suzuki, "This is the most significant phrase ever coined in the development of Zen Buddhism." Allied with this idea was the "abrupt doctrine" of the Southern School of Huineng. According to the Platform Sutra, "When the abrupt doctrine is understood there is no need of disciplining oneself in things external. Only let a man always have a right view within his own mind, no desires, no external objects will ever defile him. . . . The ignorant will grow wise if they abruptly get an understanding and open their hearts to the truth." In opposition to the view that enlightenment can be achieved by passive or quiet meditation, Huineng emphasized apprehending the nature of the self while the self is in the midst of action. Huineng began the Zen tradition of getting at the truth directly, intuitively, not intellectually. "When the monk Ming came to him and asked for instruction," Suzuki recounts, "[Huineng] said, 'Show me your original face before you were born.'" Suzuki comments: "Is not the statement quite to the point? No philosophic discourse, no elaborate reasoning, no mystic imagery, but a direct unequivocal dictum."

Seeing into the Nature of One's Being

Suzuki's essay "The Sense of Zen," the first chapter in *Zen Buddhism*, states at the outset that Zen is "the art of seeing into the nature of one's own being." He argues that Zen Buddhism contains the essence of Buddhism, although it differs from other forms of Buddhism because it does not stress rules, scriptures, authorities, and the intellectual approach to the truth. Zen Buddhism assents to the Buddha's Fourfold Noble Truth, which is built on the basic claim that life is suffering and that to escape suffering one must overcome desire and find truth. There is a struggle in the individual between the finite and the infinite, so that the nature of one's being, which provides a clue to the resolution of the conflict within the self, must be directly grasped. However, books are of no help nor is the intellect; the only way to Buddhahood is through a "direct pointing to the soul of man," as one of the four statements claims. "For this reason," Suzuki writes, "Zen never explains but indicates. . . . It always deals with facts, concrete and tangible." Suffering is the result of ignorance, and ignorance "is wrought of nothing else but the intellect and sensuous infatuation."

Direct teaching or pointing is sometimes a silent reference, as with the Buddha's flower. However, it may appear in the use of an apparently irrelevant, even ridiculous, or apparently senseless remark. To appreciate the method of direct pointing, Suzuki cautions, one must regard the attempt to learn as no mere pastime. For Zen Buddhists, Zen is an ethical discipline, an attempt to elevate one's spiritual powers to their ideal limits. The brief answers of the masters to their students' questions were never intended to be intellectual riddles or symbolic utterances. To talk by the use of metaphorical imagery would not be to point directly. Perhaps one can say that although some of the statements attributed to the masters appear to be symbolic in import, there may very well be more direct meanings that are the significant meanings of the statements. Suzuki gives some illustrations of the Zen practice of uttering a few words and demonstrating with action: "What is Zen?" The master: "Boiling

oil over a blazing fire." "What kind of man is he who does not keep company with any thing?" The master (Baso): "I will tell you when you have swallowed up in one draught all the waters in the West River."

There is perhaps no more difficult point to make than that such answers from the Zen masters are important not as charming and archaic riddles or irrelevancies but as "direct pointings" to the truth. The tendency of the Western mind is to go at these remarks intellectually, to make sense out of them. However, Suzuki argues with convincing sincerity that for the Zen Buddhist, such remarks are instruments of enlightenment that can be comprehended simply and naturally with the "opening of a third eye," the sudden enlightenment by which one sees into the nature of one's own being. The name for the moment of enlightenment or awakening is "satori," and the means to it is meditation of the proper sort. The term "Zen" comes from the Japanese word *zazen*, which means "to sit or meditate," and is equivalent to the Chinese *chan* and the Indian *Dhyana*. The distinctive feature of Zen is that meditation and action are one. Suzuki said, "Zen has its own way of practicing meditation. Zen has nothing to do with mere quietism or losing oneself in a trance."

Satori

To achieve satori, or enlightenment, involves "meditating on those utterances or actions that are directly poured out from the inner region undimmed by the intellect or the imagination." Again, Suzuki offers examples from the masters to suggest the direct method of Zen. Referring to his staff, Zen master Yeryo said, "When one knows what that staff is, one's life study of Zen comes to an end." Ye-sei said, "When you have a staff, I will give you one; when you have none, I will take it away from you."

Some suggestive remarks by Suzuki put the Zen method into a perspective accessible to Western minds. If one considers that the direct method is possible for the Zen masters because *any* point of meditation, properly caught in the fullness of its being, is infinitely illuminating, one can come to appreciate the pertinence of apparently irrelevant and abrupt remarks. If one's study of Zen ends with knowledge of the master's staff, it may be that it also ends, as Suzuki suggests, with knowledge of the flower in the crannied wall. The poet Alfred, Lord Tennyson's image may have much the same significance as the Zen master's image.

Referring to the Buddhist scriptures, Suzuki argues that "enlightenment and darkness are substantially one," that "the finite is the infinite, and *vice versa*," and that "the mistake consists in our splitting into two what is really and absolutely one." All of this is reminiscent of the philosophy of the metaphysical mystics; there is a close resemblance to the views of such men as Nicholas of Cusa and Giordano Bruno. Suddenly to appreciate the unity of all being and to recognize that unity in an illuminating moment of knowing one's own nature to be the nature of all being, and therefore the nature of whatever it is to which the master's abrupt remark calls attention, is surely not an act of intellect. For intellect to "work it out" would be to spoil the whole effect, as if one were to try to embrace the quality of a rug as a whole by tracing out its separate threads and their relationships to other threads. Satori, if it occurs, has to be a moment of "grasping," of knowing "all at once," and it is not at all surprising that the masters of Zen have come to rely on the abrupt remark as a sudden direct pointing.

In the essay, "Satori, or Enlightenment," Suzuki defines satori as "an intuitive looking into the nature of things in contradistinction to the analytical or logical understanding of it." It involves a new view, a new way of looking at the universe. The emphasis of the Zen masters, as with the patriarch Huineng, is not on direction or on instruction but on seeing into one's own nature in order to see the nature of all, to achieve Buddhahood, and to escape the cycle of birth and death.

Here again Suzuki emphasizes the masters' methods of bringing the seekers of enlightenment abruptly to satori. "A monk asked Joshu . . . to be instructed in Zen. Said the master, 'Have you had your breakfast or not?' 'Yes, master, I have,' answered the monk. 'If so, have your dishes washed,' was an immediate response, which, it is said, at once opened the monk's mind to the truth of Zen." Such remarks are like the strokes and blows, or the twisting of noses,

which the masters sometimes resorted to, as if suddenly to make the disciple aware of himself and of the obscuring tendencies of his old perspectives. By referring to commonplace matters in the context of a desire to know all, the masters somehow refer to all. By being apparently irrelevant, they show the relevance of everything.

The chief characteristics of satori, Suzuki writes, are *irrationality*, the nonlogical leap of the will; *intuitive insight*, or mystic knowledge; *authoritativeness*, the finality of personal perception; *affirmation*, the acceptance of all things; *a sense of the beyond*, the loss of the sense of self together with the sense of all; *an impersonal tone*, the absence of any feeling of love or "supersensuality"; *a feeling of exaltation*, the contentment of being unrestricted and independent; and *momentariness*, an abruptness of experience, a sudden realization of "a new angle of observation."

Zen Methods

In "Practical Methods of Zen Instruction," Suzuki discusses methods for arriving at the realization of the absolute oneness of things. A proper appreciation of these methods, even in outline, depends on unabridged explanations and examples, but the methods can be mentioned. Zen sometimes utilizes *paradox*, but by concrete images, not by abstract conceptions. Another method is to attempt to think the truth without using the ordinary logic of affirmation and denial; it is the method of *"going beyond the opposites."* The third method is the method of *contradiction*, the method of denying what has already been asserted or taken for granted. The method of *affirmation* is the method frequently referred to: stating almost blithely some commonplace matter of fact in answer to an abstruse and apparently unrelated question. *Repetition* serves to return the self to what it has already seen and not recognized. *Exclamation*, particularly when used as the only answer and when the sound is meaningless, is sometimes used; and even the method of *silence* has provoked satori. However, of all the methods, the *direct method* of illuminating action—even though the action be commonplace or almost violent, such as a blow on the cheek of a questioner—is most characteristic of Zen, perhaps because it is the action of everything to which Zen directs attention.

The *koan* exercise is the Zen method of teaching the uninitiated by referring them to answers made by Zen masters. The student is either enlightened or encouraged to "search and contrive" in order to understand the state of mind of the master whose koan he is considering. Suzuki devotes an interesting chapter to a discussion of the koan exercise, and he offers several examples.

Zen Principles

The basic principles of Zen, particularly as related to the teachings of Huineng, are examined anew in the essay, "The Zen Doctrine of No-Mind," in which the emphasis on the no-mind, the unconscious, brings out the essential concern with active, nondiscursive, intuitive insight. By avoiding the conscious effort to understand intellectually and by participating in ordinary action, one prepares oneself for the moment of enlightenment.

Zen differs from pragmatism, Suzuki maintains, in that pragmatism emphasizes the practical usefulness of concepts, while Zen emphasizes purposelessness or "being detached from teleological consciousness." Suzuki describes Zen as life; it is entirely consistent with the nonintellectualism of Zen that Zen has implications for action in every sphere of human life. However, Zen is concerned not so much with the quality or direction of action as with the perspective of the actor. The emphasis is on "knowing and seeing." Like existentialism, Zen recognizes the antinomy of the finite and the infinite and the possibilities that relation of apparent opposition opens up; but unlike existentialism, Zen does not involve any conception of an absolute opposition and, consequently, does not entail any "unbearable responsibility," or nausea in the face of the necessity for action. Once the division of finite and infinite, individual and other, is seen to be the consequence of intellectual analysis so that the idea of individuality is succeeded by the idea of oneness, there is no fear of plunging into the abyss.

In his discussion of Zen and Japanese culture, Suzuki shows how sumi-e painting (ink sketching on fragile paper, with no corrections possible), swordsmanship, and the tea ceremony are expressions of Zen principles.

Suzuki's essays on Zen Buddhism contribute immeasurably to an appreciation of Asian religion and philosophy. They also may shed light on the intuitive mysticism that runs through Western metaphysics despite its prevailing realistic and pragmatic directions and diminish the sense of opposition between realism and mysticism.

Ian P. McGreal, updated by John K. Roth

Additional Reading

Abe, Masao, ed. *A Zen Life: D. T. Suzuki Remembered*. New York: Weatherhill, 1986. This indispensable anthology contains a bibliography of D. T. Suzuki's complete works and biographical accounts published through the copyright date. Many insights into Suzuki's life and works appear in more than twenty articles by Japanese and Western writers with an emphasis on Suzuki's literature about Shin Buddhism.

Eastern Buddhist New Series, no. 2. (August, 1967). This memorial issue of the magazine Suzuki founded contains accounts of various phases of Suzuki's life by friends and fellow masters.

Fields, Rick. *How the Swans Came to the Lake: A Narrative History of Buddhism in America*. Boulder: Shambhala, 1981. This account of how Buddhism came to the West includes numerous lengthy passages on Suzuki and his family, particularly on his youth, motivations, training, and his early days in La Salle, Illinois, while he worked for Open Court Publishing. Fields also recounts anecdotes about Suzuki's lectures in New York City. Includes photographs of Suzuki and friends. This study is highly recommended as the best, most readily available full-length text on Suzuki.

Merton, Thomas. *Mystics and Zen Masters*. New York: Farrar, Strauss, & Goroux, 1961. Immersing himself in the study of Zen from the perspective of a Catholic Trappist monk, Father Merton relies heavily on Suzuki and refers to him frequently. In this work, Merton compares Suzuki with Greek philosophers and discusses Suzuki's comments on the training of Zen monks and monasticism.

_____. *Zen and the Birds of Appetite*. New York: New Directions, 1968. In this work, Trappist monk Merton devotes one chapter to Suzuki, discussing personal conversations between the two religious leaders, including twenty pages of letters.

Snelling, John. *The Buddhist Handbook: A Complete Guide to Buddhist Schools, Teaching, Practice, and History.* Rochester: Inner Traditions International, 1991. Throughout this comprehensive study of Buddhist history and practice, Snelling points to Suzuki's connections to and interpretations of a number of Buddhist schools of thought and Suzuki's influence on psychotherapy. Snelling praises Suzuki for making Buddhist scriptures available in the West and recounts anecdotes of Suzuki's public appearances.

Switzer, Irwin. *D. T. Suzuki: A Biography.* London: The Buddhist Society, 1985. This first account of Suzuki's life is short but authoritative. Contains a useful chronology and was compiled from a manuscript left by the author with Christmas Humphreys, president of the Buddhist Society and a personal friend of Suzuki. The text was augmented with material from Peter Fields's *How the Swans Came to the Lake.*

Wu, John C. H. *The Golden Age of Zen.* New York: Doubleday, 1996. Strongly influenced by Suzuki's writings and letters as well as a personal acquaintance with Suzuki, Wu discusses Suzuki's teachings on parallels between mystical Catholicism and Buddhism, summarizing and noting the key points in Suzuki's *Mysticism: Christianity and Buddhism.* Wu discusses Suzuki's opinions on Confucianism and Daoism. Includes anecdotes and reminiscences of Suzuki and reprints of letters between Wu and Suzuki.

Wesley Britton

Rabindranath Tagore

Nobel laureate Tagore, known for his lyric poetry, synthesized Eastern and Western spirituality in his numerous literary and philosophical works. He described a "religion of man," which emphasized the divinity of humanity and the humanity of God.

Principal philosophical works: *Sadhana*, 1913; *Jivansmriti*, 1912 (*My Reminiscences*, 1917); *Personality*, 1917; *Nationalism*, 1919; *Greater India*, 1921; *Glimpses of Bengal*, 1921; *Creative Unity*, 1922; *Talks in China*, 1925; *Lectures and Addresses*, 1928; *Letters to a Friend*, 1928; *The Religion of Man*, 1931; *Mahatmaji and the Depressed Humanity*, 1932; *The Religion of an Artist*, 1933; *Man*, 1937; *Chhelebela*, 1940 (*My Boyhood Days*, 1940); *Sabhyatar Samkat*, 1941 (*Crisis in Civilization*, 1941); *Towards Universal Man*, 1961; *A Tagore Reader*, 1961.

Born: May 7, 1861; Calcutta, India
Died: August 7, 1941; Calcutta, India

Early Life

Rabindranath Tagore was born on May 7, 1861, into a prosperous Bengali family in Calcutta, India. The fourteenth child and eighth son of Debendranath Tagore and Sarada Devi, he grew up surrounded by the artistic and intellectual pursuits of his elders. Agricultural landholdings in East Bengal supported the family's leisurely lifestyle, and their Calcutta mansion was a center for Bengalis who, like the Tagores, sought to integrate Western influences in literature, philosophy, arts, and sciences into their own culture. Young Tagore was a sensitive and interested child who, like his siblings, lived in awe of his father, a pillar of the Hindu reform group Brahmo Samaj. Cared for mainly by servants because of his mother's ill health, he lived a relatively confined existence, watching the life of crowded Calcutta from the windows and courtyards of his protected home.

From an early age, Tagore's literary talents were encouraged. Like the other Tagore children, he was thoroughly schooled in Bengali language and literature as a foundation for integrating culturally diverse influences, and, throughout his long career, Tagore composed most of his work in Bengali. In 1868, he was enrolled in the Oriental Seminary, where he quickly rebelled against formal education. Unhappy, transferring to different schools, Tagore nevertheless became appreciated as a budding poet during this time both in school and at home. In 1873, he was withdrawn from school to accompany his father on a tour of northern India and the Himalayas. This journey served as a rite of passage for the boy, who was deeply influenced by his father's presence and by the grandeur of nature. It also provided his first opportunity to roam in the open countryside.

Returning to Calcutta, Tagore boycotted school and, from 1873 on, was educated at home by tutors and his brothers. In 1874, he began to recite publicly his poetry, and his first long poem was published in the monthly journal *Bhārati*. For the next four years, he gave recitations and published stories, essays, and experiments in drama. In 1878, Tagore went to England to prepare for a career in law at University College, London, but he withdrew in 1880 and returned to India. Tagore's stay in England was not a happy one, but during those fourteen months, his intellectual horizons broadened as he read English literature with Henry Morley and became acquainted with European music and drama.

Life's Work

Returning to India, Tagore resumed his writing amid the intellectual family life in Calcutta, especially influenced by his talented elder brothers, Jyotirindranath (writer, translator, playwright, and musician) and the scholarly Satyendranath. Tagore's view of life at this time was melancholy; yet, with the metrical liberty of his poems in *Sandhya Sangit* (1882; evening songs), it became clear that he was already establishing new artistic and literary standards. Tagore then had a transcendental experience that abruptly changed his work. His gloomy introspection expanded in bliss and insight into the outer world, and Tagore once again perceived the innocent communion with nature that he had known as a child. This vision was reflected in *Prabhat Sangit* (1883; morning songs), and his new style was immediately popular. By his mid-twenties, Tagore had published devotional songs, poetry, drama, and literary criticism and was established as a lyric poet, primarily influenced by the early Vaishnava lyricists of Bengal and by the English Romantics. In 1883, he married Mrinalini Devi and continued to reflect his optimism in a burst of creativity that lasted for the next twenty years. During this period, he began to write nonsymbolic drama, and his verse *Kari O Komal* (1887; sharps and flats) is considered a high point in his early lyrical achievement.

In 1890, Tagore's father sent him to Shelaidaha, the family home in eastern Bengal, to oversee the family estates, and thus began the most productive period of Tagore's prolific career. His sympathetic observation of the daily activity of the Bengali peasant, as well as an intimacy with the seasons and moods of the rural countryside, sharpened Tagore's literary sensitivity and provided him with subject matter for his poems and essays during the 1890's. Tagore also wrote short stories—developing the genre in Bengali literature—and in 1891 started the monthly journal *Sadhana*, in which he published some of his work. In addition to literary output, Tagore began to lecture and write on his educational theories and the politics of Bengal, and he came more and more into public life. In 1898, he took his family to live in Shelaidaha, planning to

spare his children the schooling against which he rebelled by educating them himself. The family soon moved to Santiniketan at Bolpur, where Tagore founded his experimental school, which became a lifelong commitment. He continued to write ceaselessly during this time: stories, poems, essays, textbooks, and a history of India. In 1901, he became editor of *The Bengal Review* and also launched into a period as a novelist, reflecting the political situation of the time in his work. Tagore's *Gora* (1910; English translation, 1924) is considered by many to be the greatest Bengali novel.

The year 1902 saw the school in serious financial condition and also brought the death of

Rabindranath Tagore. *(The Nobel Foundation)*

Tagore's wife. Others close to him passed away—his daughter in 1903, his favorite pupil in 1904, and his father in 1905—and Tagore experienced a time of withdrawal. In 1905, he was pulled back into public life by the division of Bengal. Tagore served as a highly visible leader in the antipartition nationalist movement and composed patriotic prose and songs popular with the people. In 1907, however, concerned about growing violence in the movement and its lack of social reform, Tagore suddenly withdrew from politics and retired to Santiniketan, where he resumed a life of educational and literary activity and meditation. Tagore's intuitive belief in the spirituality of life and the inherent divinity of all things was reflected in his work during this time: educational addresses at his school, a series of symbolic dramas that criticized monarchy, and an outpouring of religious poetry expressing his extremely intimate realization of God. A collection of such poems was published as *Gitānjali* (1910; *Gitanjali* [*Song Offerings*], 1912). During his time in relative seclusion, Tagore the individual poet became, more and more, Tagore the universal person. When next he emerged, it would be to international acclaim.

Tagore became known outside India through the influence of the English painter William Rothstein, the organizer of the India Society in London. Rothstein arranged to publish a private edition of *Gitānjali* for India Society members, and, in 1912, Tagore's English translation appeared with an introduction by William Butler Yeats. Tagore and his poetry were introduced to influential critics and writers such as George Bernard Shaw, H. G. Wells, John Galsworthy, John Masefield, Ernest Rhys, and Ezra Pound. His reputation spread to Europe and to the United States, where, in 1912, his work appeared in the journal *Poetry* and a public edition of *Gitānjali* was published in 1913. In 1912, and again in 1913, Tagore lectured in the United States on religious and social themes, bringing the wisdom of the East to the West in his desire to move the world toward a true humanity. In November, 1913, he was awarded the Nobel Prize in Literature. In December, the University of Calcutta conferred upon him an honorary doctorate of letters, and he was knighted by the British government in 1915.

Underlying Tagore's success at this time was his apprehension about the future. Essentially a nonconformist and solitary soul, Tagore believed that he would have no peace from that time on; this, indeed, did prove to be true. Sudden international recognition brought Tagore intense public response, ranging from adulation to disenchantment, and he was an often misunderstood public figure for the rest of his life. At the height of his popularity, Tagore published *Balaka* (1916; *A Flight of Swans*, 1955, 1962), which enhanced his reputation as a mystical poet and is considered by many to be his greatest book of lyrics. He also toured Japan and the United States, giving a series of successful lectures later published as *Nationalism* and *Personality*.

Yet Tagore's reputation began to diminish almost as soon as it reached its peak. Some critics have proposed that the materialistic West was not able to appreciate the spiritual depth of the East, while others suggest that the poet and his publishers were themselves to blame for inept translation and unsystematic presentation. Forced to abandon his lecture tour in 1917 because of ill health, Tagore returned to India to a period of tragedy.

Although he was greatly disturbed by World War I and denounced it in his writings, Tagore was also unable to endorse wholeheartedly the activities of his own culture. In 1918, with the money received from his writing, lectures, and the Nobel Prize, Tagore founded an international university, Visva-Bharati, at Santiniketan. Yet in 1919, as he was forming the nucleus of the faculty, political turmoil in India caused Tagore to resign his knighthood in protest against the British massacre of Indians at Amritsar. As Tagore sought to unify humanity in a world that seemed at odds with his philosophy, he began to find himself less and less popular.

In 1920, Tagore undertook another international lecture tour to raise funds for the school, but the reception in England and the United States was particularly disappointing. During the last two decades of his life, despite increasing ill health, which often forced him to cancel lectures, and problems with public relations, Tagore traveled widely in support of his ideals of a universal humanity and world peace. He also continued to write until the end of his life, mainly poetry—

which critics perceive as uneven—and essays. In addition, Tagore began painting as a hobby in his later years and pursued it with increasing seriousness. In 1930, Tagore delivered the Hibbert Lectures at Oxford University, which were published in 1931 as the *Religion of Man*, and, in 1940, Oxford awarded him an honorary doctorate of letters. Because of frail health, Tagore received this honor at Santiniketan, which had become a permanent residence in his later years. On August 7, 1941, Tagore died at his family home in Calcutta.

Influence
Internationally known as a humanist who sought to reconcile such apparent opposites as humans and nature, materialism and spiritualism, and nationalism and internationalism, Tagore expressed a philosophy that was uniquely his own. His vision of the underlying wholeness of life was based on intuitive synthesis of classic Eastern religious texts and the works of early Indian poets and philosophers with Western thought and modern European literature. In the East, he is known as a great poet and thinker; in the West, he is best known as the author of *Gitānjali*, which is characteristic of his work and considered to be his masterpiece. Recognized as a prolific and accomplished writer in all genres, Tagore is internationally acclaimed as one of the world's greatest lyric poets as well as a great Eastern philosopher.

Tagore, a man of great courage and gentleness, of nobility and grace, is generally viewed as a symbol of the integration of East and West. Yet, many critics believe that the West has known him only superficially. They suggest that much of Tagore's best work remains accessible only in Bengali, and reading Tagore in translation—even his own translation—offers no real appreciation of his scope or the depth of his genius. Tagore's biographer, Kripalani, stated that "he lived as he wrote, not for pleasure or profit but out of joy, not as a brilliant egoist but as a dedicated spirit, conscious that his genius was a gift from the divine, to be used in the service of man." Although his writing is deeply rooted in Indian social history, Tagore's gift for expressing the unity of life and the grandeur of humanity gives it universal appeal.

Jean C. Fulton

The Religion of Man

Type of philosophy: Ethics, Indian philosophy, metaphysics, philosophy of religion
First published: 1931
Principal ideas advanced:
◇ The essence of religion is the divinity of humanity and the humanity of God.
◇ Humans realize the infinity of their true being through the arts of civilization: science, philosophy, religion, art, and music.
◇ The purpose of civilization is to hold up a mirror of the ideal, eternal person, to which all individuals aspire.
◇ The most important components of true religion are love, the renunciation of self, and service to others.

The Religion of Man was based on the Hibbert Lectures that Rabindranath Tagore delivered at Manchester College, Oxford, in May, 1930. The ideas he presented were the culmination of many years of Tagore's thought. Many of them can be found, for example, in earlier books such as *Personality* (1917) and *Creative Unity* (1922), as well as the later *The Religion of an Artist* (1933). *The Religion of Man* represents the final stage of Tagore's mature thought, the position he reached following his earlier attempt to forge a synthesis between the best elements of Hinduism and the new religion of Brahmanism (founded by Raja Rammohan Roy in 1828).

Realizing the Spirit of God
The main theme of *The Religion of Man* is the divinity of humanity and the humanity of God. Tagore pursues this theme through endless variations. Religion develops human consciousness and enables it to realize the eternal spirit, through science, philosophy, literature, and the arts. Tagore was a poet and artist rather than a systematic philosopher, and the ideal he proposes is to be attained not through philosophical reasoning but through direct experience of the union of the individual self and the eternal spirit.

In his chapter "The Vision," Tagore relates his own experience of this process, which crystallized when he was eighteen years old. He was watching the sun rise when he suddenly felt as if a mist had been lifted from his eyes, and a world of infinite joy, both within and without, was revealed to him. All trace of the commonplace had vanished, and he had a strong sense of the significance of all things, including humanity. All the apparently divergent waves of life were revealed as part of a boundless sea. This revelation of the "superpersonal" human world lasted for four days, after which in his perception the world relapsed into its former disguise as a collection of mere facts. However, he was left with the feeling that some being larger than himself was seeking expression through him, and this became the foundation of his life's work.

In the first two chapters, Tagore approaches the "religion of man" from the standpoint of science, arguing that the process of evolution finds its full meaning only in humanity. He accepts the truth of the Darwinian theory of natural selection but uses it to promote a theistic rather than atheistic view of life. According to Tagore, there is a shaping spirit of life that introduces more and more complex and interrelated forms of life in the evolutionary process, culminating in the creation of mind. Mind is the revelation of some truth or inner value that is not limited by space and time, and the vehicle of this revelation is humanity, through which the eternal comes to realize itself in history. This is accomplished by people's continual efforts to develop truth and active love. The latter is achieved when people realize themselves in others, making up a great societal and cosmic wholeness that frees all humans from their consciousness of separateness.

In chapter 3, Tagore explains his theory of "surplus," which lies at the heart of his religion of humanity. Throughout humanity's long history, people have always been aware that their lives somehow transcend their apparent smallness or limitations. Their inner compulsion is to break out of the restrictions that nature imposes on them, to develop a life that is not limited to the body. This is why people develop a vision, expressed in the religions of the world, of a being who exceeds them and yet is closely related to them; they know intuitively that they belong to a universal reality that they must manifest to the fullest extent that they are able. This universal reality, according to Tagore, is simply people's innate sense of their own fully developed consciousness.

Tagore develops this idea in the following chapter, in which he defines yoga as the union between the individual and the supreme divine reality, which is not an abstraction but is within people. Yoga is the realization of the "person" described in Vedic literature as *purushah*. The infinite is revealed not through creation but through humanity. This is the message delivered by all great religious founders and leaders. The danger for human beings is that they become lost in the objective, material world, forgetting that true freedom lies in the manifestation of inner truth, not the pursuit of externals or the formation of abstract systems of thought.

Tagore then extols the contribution of the Iranian prophet Zarathustra to the religion of humanity. According to Tagore, Zarathustra was the first man to preach a religion based on moral values rather than external rituals. He also was the first prophet to expound a monotheism that was accessible to all people, not just those belonging to a particular group.

Religion of the Heart
After discussing some personal experiences in the following chapter, including the vision described above and other moments when he felt the beauty of the natural world as a personality that flowed into and harmonized with his own deepest nature, Tagore explores in chapter 7 the difference between institutionalized religion and what he calls the "religion of the heart." He states that he grew out of the former when he discovered it to be sterile and artificial, and embraced the latter when he heard the simple emotional sincerity of the songs of the Baül sect of Bengal. Lacking all ceremonial aspects of religion, members of this sect simply declared their love for God through God's expression in humanity. Tagore then praises other poets of India who have celebrated their love for the universal, divine person revealed through individuals.

In this chapter, Tagore clearly distinguishes his own religion from a major aspect of the Vedantic philosophy, which at many other points it seems to resemble. The religion of humanity has no place for the experience of God as a negation, beyond all sense experience, known by the yogi when his or her consciousness becomes transcendental and still, free of any object. Tagore does not dispute the truth or the value of such experience, but for him, it does not come within the domain of religion. Humans are more perfect as humans than when their individual consciousness is dissolved into formlessness.

It is for this reason that Tagore emphasizes the value of personality, a term to which he attaches a special meaning. In its limited sense, "personality" refers to the individual's sense of the self as separate from the whole, but in the positive sense, the term refers to the aspect of people that, through their activities, feelings, and knowledge, gives them access to infinity. It is in the latter sense that personality is the true agent of religion because true religion is the pursuit of an ideal unity that is none other than people themselves in their most expanded, infinite state.

How people attain this sense of infinity is described in part in chapter 9, which examines the function of the arts. For Tagore, everyone is an artist because people are cocreators of their world. They do not passively record a preexisting, objective truth but rather create their truth by molding, through their feelings and their imagination, harmonious relationships between things. The conscious artist merely does this to a more intense degree. Sounding very much like his fellow poet William Blake, whose mystical-humanist philosophy resembles Tagore's in many ways, Tagore exalts the function of the creative imagination. It is the imaginative faculty that brings before humanity the sense of its true being and the full extent of it. For this reason, art is "the response of man's creative soul to the call of the Real."

Religious Unity

After an amplification of humanity's true nature in chapter 10, Tagore proceeds in chapter 11, "The Meeting," to put in a plea for a universal religion. In the past, humanity's consciousness of spiritual unity has been obscured by geographical separation, but because of modern communications, the time for this has passed. People's idea of God should no longer be limited by rites and theologies that are particular, not universal, and there should be an end to "race egotism" and race isolation. The way toward this goal is through the power of creative, spiritual love.

This leads Tagore to outline in the following chapter how the religion of humanity brings opposites together. Both the Indian tradition of contemplation and detachment and the Western ideal of service to humanity are necessary. Together they can create an ethic of love in action, which is the only way that perfect knowledge, conceived as wisdom, can be obtained. This realization of spiritual freedom requires the renunciation of the small, isolated self in order to reveal transcendental truth, beyond the world of appearances. As another way of putting it, it requires a confluence of two aspects of the human mind, the outer, which seeks satisfaction in external objects, and the inner, which seeks unity in truth.

Tagore's final chapter discusses the progress of the soul in terms of the four stages of life in Indian tradition. These four stages are *brahmacharya* (education and discipline), *garhasthya* (worldly work), *vanaprasthya* (retreat), and *pravrajya* (the awaiting of freedom with death). In Tagore's formulation, the four stages become, first, the early life of the individual; second, the forming of ties with the human community; third, the development to universal awareness of the supreme person; fourth, at death, the entry of the soul into infinity.

Four appendices include the text of a conversation between Tagore and Albert Einstein on the nature of reality and an address given by Tagore in the Chapel of Manchester College in May, 1930.

Acceptance by the West

The publication of *The Religion of Man* coincided with an increase in Tagore's prestige in the West, as demonstrated by his visit to the United States in late 1930, where he met leading poets, writers, and statespeople, including President Herbert Hoover. In 1931, the American Tagore Society was formed in New York.

At a time of disillusionment with conventional religion and steady growth in materialism, Tagore's visionary and optimistic philosophy pointed the way to the recovery of a faith in the limitless potential of humanity. Tagore's belief that the function of civilization was to keep alive the faith in the possibility of ideal perfection, that human culture should be understood as an unfolding discovery of a new level of humanity, beyond the individual self, fell with freshness on jaded Western ears. In addition, *The Religion of Man*, along with Tagore's other works and the works of Indian philosopher Sarvepalli Radhakrishnan from the same period, fostered an understanding of the philosophies of the East in a West that had too often in the past looked on other cultures with a disdainful eye.

Bryan Aubrey

Additional Reading

Banerjee, Hiranmay. *Rabindranath Tagore*. 2d ed. New Delhi: Government of India, 1976. One of a series about eminent leaders of India, this biographical narrative presents the depth and diversity of Rabindranath Tagore's character and his contributions to the heritage of India. It includes genealogical tables and a chronological list of his important works.

Cenkner, William. *The Hindu Personality in Education: Tagore, Gandhi, Aurobindo*. Columbia, Mo.: South Asia Books, 1976. Focuses on Tagore's role as the leading Asian educator of the first half of the twentieth century. Surveys his life, thought, and educational theories.

Chatterjee, Bhabatosh. *Rabindranath Tagore and Modern Sensibility*. Delhi: Oxford University Press, 1996. This book offers criticism and interpretation of Tagore's work.

Dutta, Krishna, and Andrew Robinson. *Rabindranath Tagore: The Myriad-Minded Man*. New York: St. Martin's Press, 1996. This work focuses on the many facets of Tagore.

Ghose, Sisirkumar. *Rabindranath Tagore*. New Delhi: Sahitya Adademi, 1986. This short, interesting survey focuses on Tagore's life and his poetry, drama, short stories, and novels. It also includes chapters on Tagore's thoughts about religion, beauty, art, and education.

Kripalani, Krishna. *Rabindranath Tagore*. 2d ed. Calcutta: Visva-Bharati, 1980. Written by a scholar well acquainted with the Tagore family, this interesting, 450-page work is considered the best English biography of Tagore. Includes twenty-three photographic illustrations as well as a detailed bibliography of Tagore's fiction, nonfiction, and musical compositions.

Lago, Mary M. *Rabindranath Tagore*. Boston: Twayne, 1976. This literary study concentrates on representative works by Tagore as a lyric poet and writer of short fiction. It suggests a perspective from which to view the national and international response to Tagore's distinguished career and includes a chronology and selected bibliography.

Mitra, Indrani. "I Will Make Bimala One with My Country: Gender and Nationalism in Tagore's *The Home and the World*." *Modern Fiction Studies* 41 (1995): 243-64. Outlines the historical context of Tagore's novel and analyzes its treatment of political action and women's oppression.

Mukherjee, Kedar Nath. *Political Philosophy of Rabindranath Tagore*. New Delhi: S. Chand, 1982. In this volume, Mukherjee presents an analysis of Tagore's political philosophy—in order to fill what he perceives as a gap in the literature on Tagore—and emphasizes the value of Tagore's philosophy in contemporary political situations, both in India and the world.

Singh, Ajai. *Rabindranath Tagore: His Imagery and Ideas*. Ghaziabad, India: Vimal Prakashan, 1984. This comprehensive consideration of Tagore's imagery relates Tagore's images to his thoughts on life, love, beauty, joy, and infinity. It also includes a selected bibliography.

Thompson, Edward. *Rabindranath Tagore: His Life and Work*. 2d ed. New York: Haskell House, 1974. A reprint of an earlier edition, this brief survey of Tagore's writing prior to 1921 includes commentary based on Thompson's own translations of Tagore's work.

_____. *Rabindranath Tagore: Poet and Dramatist*. London: Oxford University Press, 1926. This was among the first detailed literary studies of Tagore's work as poet and dramatist and is still considered one of the best.

Jean C. Fulton, updated by William Nelles

Saint Thomas Aquinas

By adapting pagan philosophy as a handmaiden to Christian doctrine, Thomas created both a magisterial systematization of medieval Catholic faith and a philosophical system with implications for ethics, law, psychology, semantics, and the nature of reason itself.

Principal philosophical works: *Scriptum super "Libros sententiarum,"* 1252-1256 (English translation, 1923); *Summa contra gentiles,* c. 1258-1264 (English translation, 1923); *Summa theologiae,* c. 1265-1273 (*Summa Theologica,* 1911-1921).

Born: 1224 or 1225; Roccasecca, north of Naples, Kingdom of Sicily (now Italy)

Died: March 7, 1274; Fossanova, Latium, Papal States (now Italy)

Early Life

Thomas Aquinas (Tommaso d'Aquino) was the youngest son of Count Landulf (Landolfo) of Aquino and his second wife, Donna Theodora of Naples, who was descended from Norman nobility. Landulf, along with his older sons, had been employed as a soldier by Emperor Frederick II to defend Sicily from the Papal States to the north. Thomas was born in the family castle near the old city of Aquino in 1224 or 1225 (the testimony from Thomas's first biographers is conflicting). When he was five, he was taken to the nearby Benedictine monastery of Monte Cassino; there he received his early religious instruction. Hostilities between Frederick II and the pope had calmed for the moment, and it is thought that Thomas's parents hoped that their son would one day become an abbot. The feudal system brought little prospect of family stability; perhaps Thomas's eventual clerical influence would provide for the future.

The emperor was excommunicated in 1239; in return, he threatened Monte Cassino; most of the monks there were sent into exile. That year, Thomas returned to his parents, who sent him to the *studium generale* (later to become the university) in Naples, a school that had been founded by the emperor in 1224 to compete with similar church institutions. Frederick welcomed the introduction of Islamic as well as Christian scholarship into his university. Thomas's studies included logic, grammar, natural philosophy, and metaphysics, and it was probably at Naples that he began his first serious study of the Greek philosopher Aristotle. Portions of Aristotle's works were being translated from the Greek, making their way into the Latin West often accompanied by interpretations of Arabic scholars, most notably the twelfth century Islamic philosopher Averroës.

It was an age of ferment: Intellectually, the new learning, especially Aristotle's teaching on the eternity of the world, threatened Christian doctrine. Politically and militarily, with the continued clash of secular and ecclesiastical powers, the old feudal order was coming to an end.

At Naples, Thomas was drawn to the Order of Friars Preachers, the Dominicans, founded in France in 1216 by Saint Dominic. The Dominicans taught obedience and poverty (and thus the begging of alms), as did the Franciscan Order (founded by Saint Francis of Assisi less than a decade earlier), but the Dominicans also put special emphasis on the life of study, preaching, and teaching. The order penetrated many of the universities of Western Europe, opening study houses devoted to theology and philosophy. Though reared to appreciate the Benedictine cycle of prayer, worship, sleep, and manual labor, Thomas found the new order better suited to his temperament.

Saint Thomas Aquinas. *(Library of Congress)*

An early biographer notes that in 1248, Thomas joined Albert in Cologne and a new *studium generale* there, where Thomas was often referred to as the "dumb ox." This sobriquet did not pertain to his intelligence but to his massive physique. Though Thomas was a bit taller than his peers, he was corpulent, slow of movement, quiet, and often withdrawn. Yet Albert saw deeper; Thomas's mentor remarked that the bellowing of this ox would be heard throughout the world.

Life's Work

Upon Albert's recommendation, Thomas returned to the University of Paris in 1252 to prepare for his degree in theology. Not yet thirty years of age, Thomas would have little more than two decades of life remaining. In that time, he was to produce an enduring systematization of the Catholic faith, numerous commentaries on the works of Aristotle, liturgical works, and polemical pieces.

Already he was discussing theological issues in public disputations and lecturing on the era's standard theological textbook, *Sententiarum libri IV* (1148-1151; books of sentences), by Peter Lombard. The "sentences," or opinions, were collected from church fathers and medieval theologians and arranged by doctrines. Book 1, for example, treated God; book 2, the Fall of Man. Theology students, "bachelors of the sentences," tried to harmonize the varying viewpoints and elucidate the fine points; nuance was everything. Thomas's own *Scriptum super "Libros sententiarum"* joined more than a thousand other commentaries on the sentences. The structure of Thomas's book was derived from the oral tradition of the public disputation. The master would employ his students in framing theological arguments, both pro and con, with debate sometimes lasting six or eight hours. The master then met in private with his students, analyzing the arguments and formulating a written version of the dispute. Many of Thomas's theological works are based on the form of the disputation and thus were not intended for lay audiences. In the multiplicity of distinctions and definitions, Thomas's

His decision to join the Dominicans in 1244 was not without controversy. His mother, now a widow, persuaded Thomas's older brothers to abduct and imprison him until he changed his mind. There is a story, perhaps based on fact, that when his brothers brought a prostitute into Thomas's cell to break his resolve, he picked up a burning stick from the fire and drove her from the room. Taken to Roccasecca, Thomas remained steadfast, and after about a year of detention, he was permitted by his family to join his Dominican brothers at the University of Paris in 1245. His novitiate was under the tutelage of the German Dominican theologian Saint Albertus Magnus.

writings exemplified a Scholastic style popular during the Middle Ages but stigmatized in later eras as hollow and pedantic.

In 1256, Thomas obtained his license to teach theology at the university. For three years thereafter, he continued to lecture, primarily on the Gospel of Matthew, and to participate in public disputations. During this time, he began work on a theological guidebook for Dominican missionaries as they engaged in disputes with Muslims, Jews, and heretical Christians in North Africa and Spain. This treatise, *Summa Contra Gentiles*, was completed after he returned to Italy to lecture at the papal court in 1261. In 1265, he left Orvieto and Pope Urban IV for a two-year stay in Rome. It was while he was in Rome, teaching Dominican students, that Thomas began his masterwork, *Summa Theologica*. He finished the first part, on God's existence and attributes, during his stay at the papal court of Clement IV in Viterbo, Italy, from 1267 to 1268. There Thomas was apparently associated with William of Moerbeke, a Flemish Dominican who was working on more accurate translations of Aristotle than those that had come to the West via the Arabic. In 1268 or 1269, Thomas was sent back to the University of Paris for his second tenure as a professor and found himself in the midst of a seething controversy.

Masters and students at the university had become fascinated not only with the speculative works of Aristotle but also with those of his Arab interpreter Averroës. Though at least nominally a Muslim, Averroës taught, contrary to Islam and certainly contrary to Christianity, that there was a fundamental duality between reason and faith. That is, philosophy might conclude that the world existed from eternity (as Aristotle did), while faith might speak of Creation. Both assertions, though contradictory, would be "true" in their own realm. Averroës also brought into question the nature of the soul and, using Aristotle's writings, concluded that it was doubtful that each individual had a separate, immortal soul, as the Church taught. In 1266, the Latin Averroist Siger of Brabant had begun to popularize Averroës's understanding of Aristotle and to attract disciples among the university's faculty. Thomas plunged into dispute with Siger, attempting to argue that Averroës had misinterpreted Aristotle

on matters of the soul and that though the eternity of the world might be a reasonable conclusion of science, such a conclusion was not absolute. Faith supplemented or fulfilled reason (not contradicting it) by teaching the Creation.

Nevertheless, Thomas was caught in the middle. When radical Averroism was officially condemned in 1270, Thomas's own reliance upon Aristotle's reasoning was also brought into question. Thomas was criticized by the followers of Saint Augustine's more mystical Neoplatonism, who claimed that human reason had been hopelessly compromised in the Fall. Although Thomas condemned the doctrine of double truth (believing, apparently mistakenly, that Siger and others were teaching it), he did maintain that natural reason can discover certain fundamental theological truths by studying the effects of God's working in the universe—thus the celebrated five proofs for God's existence. Reason, however, can take people only so far. Grace completes nature by revealing what cannot be learned from reason—for example, that God is triune. There are not two truths here: Because God is responsible for both reason and revelation, the two can never be contradictory. Thomas sought to separate Aristotle from his heterodox interpreters but, at the same time, was forced to defend his own use of the philosopher.

In the first three years after his return to the University of Paris, Thomas finished both the first and second sections of part 2 of *Summa Theologica*, dealing with happiness, virtue, sin, law, and grace and, in the second section, with specific moral questions. It is said that Thomas sometimes employed four secretaries at a time to take his dictation and that he would often dictate in his sleep. One story has Thomas sitting next to King Louis IX at a banquet. Completely forgetting himself, Thomas lifted his head from a trance, banged his hand on the table, and called for his secretary to dictate some prize answer to Christian heretics.

In 1272, Thomas returned to Naples to set up a Dominican study house at the university there. His attention was also given to completing part 3 of *Summa Theologica*, on the person and work of Christ. Yet on December 6, 1273, three months before his death, he put aside his writing, explaining that all he had written seemed as straw and that he could not continue. It is not known whether Thomas suffered a stroke or received a mystical vision or whether his faculties simply collapsed as a result of overwork. In 1274, he was summoned to attend a church council at Lyons. In poor health to begin with, he found himself unable to complete his journey after he struck his head on a tree or branch that had fallen in the road. He stopped at his niece's castle near Fossanova; a few weeks later, he was taken to the nearby Cistercian monastery, where he died on March 7, 1274.

Though Thomas never completed *Summa Theologica*, a supplement drawn from his earlier work was added to round out the presentation. In its two million words, *Summa Theologica* contains more than five hundred questions, twenty-six hundred articles, and ten thousand objections and replies. The prolific Thomas had produced more than one hundred other works as well.

Though in 1277 an official church body in Paris condemned some 219 theological propositions, including twelve held by Thomas, by 1319, inquiries had begun concerning Thomas's possible canonization. Thomas Aquinas was canonized a saint in 1323 (the Paris condemnation concerning his teachings was canceled in 1325), and in 1567, he was named Doctor of the Church, his works sanctioned as a repository of orthodoxy.

Influence

For the Roman Catholic Church, the thirteenth century was a time of synthesis. The writings of Aristotle and other ancients posed a new challenge to the Christian tradition, as did the influx of teachings from the Muslim world. It was the abiding passion of Thomas's life to integrate faith and reason, exploring systematically the teachings of the Church by taking natural reason as far as it might go and supplementing it with the reasonableness of revelation. To him, the Christian faith was both reasonable and rationally defensible.

Aristotle supplied many of the categories by which the nature and content of theology might be profitably organized. The philosopher maintained that the world was purposive, and Thomas adopted this idea of a final cause. Thomas also used Aristotle's conception of matter and form and act and potentiality in formulating his *Summa*

Theologica. Moreover, although Thomas disputed with the Augustinians, he also adapted Neoplatonism for his purposes, much as he did Aristotelianism. Creation was ordered in a kind of chain of being, with humans occupying a unique place, sharing earthly existence with other creatures but also possessing the capacity of receiving the vision of God after death and thus complete happiness. Critics have called *Summa Theologica* the capstone of passionless Scholasticism, the last gasp of medieval society in its effort to hold the world together by outmoded categories. Others have called Thomas an elitist who preferred order to freedom, citing his description of women as naturally inferior to men, his preference for monarchy, and his attitude toward Jews as examples of his outmoded beliefs. In response, twentieth century Thomists have attempted to demonstrate that certain historically conditioned positions should not invalidate Thomas's method or his insights and that Thomistic thought can be modified in favor of freedom, human rights, and democracy. Through Jacques Maritain in France and Mortimer Adler in the United States, generations of intellectuals have been introduced to Thomas's thought. Thomas's influence in theology has diminished since the Catholic Church ceased to promulgate Thomism after the Second Vatican Council ended in 1965; yet his contribution to philosophy as an interpreter of Aristotle continues to be widely recognized.

Dan Barnett

Summa Contra Gentiles

Type of philosophy: Metaphysics, philosophical theology
First transcribed: c. 1258-1264 (English translation, 1923)
Principal ideas advanced:
◇ The wise person is one who deals with the first beginning and the last end of the universe; truth is the final end, and the divine nature must first of all be considered if one is to understand first and last things.
◇ No truth of faith is contrary to principles known by reason.

◇ God understands not temporally but eternally; he understands all things at once by understanding their intelligible counterparts, but he knows individuals as well as universals.

◇ God's will is free, having no cause but his own wisdom; he does not of necessity love things other than himself.

◇ In God, there is active power but no potentiality; he is essentially infinite, and his knowledge and understanding are infinite.

◇ Because humans are rational creatures, their final happiness lies in the contemplation of God; however, this end cannot be achieved in this life.

Summa Contra Gentiles is less widely known and much less widely read than Saint Thomas Aquinas's later, longer *Summa theologiae* (c. 1265-1273; *Summa Theologica*, 1911-1921). *Summa Contra Gentiles* is simpler in its structure and in that sense more readable and less involved, but the *Summa Theologica* has become better known, perhaps because it is more widely used in church dogmatics. *Summa Contra Gentiles* is the more philosophical of the two works, as its author intended, and more likely to be of more interest to the non-Catholic reader. It is an earlier work, but Thomas's ideas did not change radically, and a comparison of the basic doctrines does not reveal any wide discrepancy.

Whereas *Summa Theologica* begins with an apologetic approach, explaining the relation of philosophy to theology and arguing for the existence of God, *Summa Contra Gentiles* begins immediately with God as he is in himself. As a work directed to the non-Christian, the reverse might have been expected. However, *Summa Contra Gentiles* is less doctrinal in style and does not base its arguments on a prior acceptance of Scripture as authoritative, as the *Summa Theologica* does. The earlier work is more directly metaphysical, defining the "wise person" as one who deals with the first beginning and the last end of the universe. Truth is conceived of as the final end of the whole universe, and the treatise begins directly with a consideration of the divine nature as that which must be delineated if one is to explain first and last things.

Thomas agrees with classical philosophy in holding that the chief aim of humanity is to achieve wisdom. In his case, however, this consists specifically of a knowledge of God. Because the Bible must be accepted as authoritative in order to be convincing, it cannot be used to prove any question about God's nature. With Jews, of course, a Christian may use the Old Testament as a basis for argument, and even heretics may recognize the New Testament as valid evidence; they simply do not agree with the orthodox interpretation. For those who are neither heretics nor Jews, all argument must be based solely on natural reason. The first thing to establish is what mode of proof is possible where God is concerned. Some things true of God are beyond the scope of human reason, as, for example, that God is three in one. Other things, such as the unity and existence of God, are demonstrable under the light of natural reason. Yet human reason cannot go on to grasp God's substance directly. Under the conditions of present natural life, the knowledge understanding can obtain commences with sense-data.

To discover anything true about God is exceedingly difficult, and not many have either the time or the natural capabilities for such arduous work. Some people devote themselves to business affairs and never study theology seriously. Furthermore, first of all, one must master philosophy, which means that a study of divine nature requires a lot of preparation. Thus, in one sense, it is a study better suited to old age, when some naturally disturbing influences have subsided. Theology is difficult, restricted, and demanding; therefore, faith was provided so that all people need not find out about God for themselves. It was necessary, Thomas argues, for the real truth about divine things to be presented to people with a fixed certainty by way of faith.

God and Faith

Reason and faith must agree, however, and Thomas begins by asserting that it is impossible for the truth of faith to be contrary to principles known by natural reason. No opinion or belief, Thomas is sure, is sent to humanity from God as an item of faith that is contrary to natural knowledge. For one thing, although for human beings knowledge begins with sense objects, these retain in themselves some trace of the imitation of God. Here is Saint Bonaventure's doctrine of the natural world seen as a sense world but also as one containing traces within itself of its supernatural origin as a creation of God. Thomas also affirms the use of the negative method, another traditional doctrine. People may have some sort of knowledge of the divine nature by knowing what it is *not*.

Proofs for God's existence appear in *Summa Contra Gentiles*, but they are in briefer form than in *Summa Theologica* and seem less fully developed. One might have expected this work, directed at pagans and not dependent upon Scripture for its arguments, to make more use of the "proofs." Instead, the proofs receive less stress, and Thomas moves directly into a discussion of the divine attributes. He discusses in sequence God's eternality, his freedom from potentiality, his lack of composition, and his incorporeality. All of these are rather directly stated as if they needed little expansion.

Summa Contra Gentiles appears to be the framework upon which *Summa Theologica* was finally built. The arguments need expanding, and more biblical material is included, but the structure is very much the same. In *Summa Contra Gentiles*, very few authors are quoted, and the argument is simply advanced in a straightforward way. Later, in *Summa Theologica*, Thomas attempted to blend a number of important views and to reach a more detailed conclusion. In the earlier work, however, he seems satisfied to provide the outline of the important questions and the basic structure of each argument. Little of great significance is changed in the later work, but the arguments receive a great many refinements, and the reasoning is made both subtler and more complex in order to deal with the multiplicity of views presented there.

God's Understanding and Nature

Aquinas considers God's understanding at length and describes its difference from humanity's. God does not understand temporally but eternally. He does not understand by knowing an object directly but by knowing its intelligible counterpart in his own understanding. God's understanding does contain a multitude of objects, but he understands all things at once and together. Propositional truth is also present in the divine understanding, and God also knows indi-

viduals, not merely universals. Nonexistent things are known by God, even though they never will become actual, and he knows individual events, contingent upon humanity's action, as they will happen. In order to do this, God must know the motions of the human will as well as his own will, and through these he understands evil as well as good.

Aquinas agrees to the traditional self-sufficiency of God's nature: God does not of *necessity* love things other than himself. Things outside God need him in a way that he does not depend on them. God's will is free, subject to no external conditions, and has no cause other than his own wisdom. His goodness is the reason he wills all things, and in that sense it is possible to assign a reason for the choice of God's will. Will, understanding, and goodness exist in God, but not passion, because that would indicate imperfection. There is love in God, but not such that he suffers from it or is subject to anything else because of it. God cannot, it is true, will evil, but such a limitation is no imperfection. God hates nothing, although his attributes are such that it is proper to describe him as "living."

In contrast to this extended and direct discussion of God's nature, philosophy considers humanity and the natural order as these things are in themselves. Philosophy makes no necessary reference to God, but the Christian faith considers natural beings, not in themselves, but inasmuch as they represent the majesty of God. Furthermore, Christians focus specifically on that in humans that is directly involved in their relation to God's will. The other human qualities are not as important in the Christian view. Philosophers take their stand on the immediate and natural causes of things; but Christians argue from God as First Cause, indicating what things are revealed and what people can learn about the divine nature. Philosophically, one begins with creatures and then may be led to a knowledge of God; faith studies creatures only in their relation to God and so studies God first and creatures after that.

God's Power

Turning then directly to God, Aquinas asserts that God's power and his action are not distinct. They are not two things, and this view actually results in a stronger doctrine of necessary predestination here than Thomas was to adopt in *Summa Theologica*. God does not create the natural world out of anything preexistent, and therefore he does not create merely by moving material. The act of creation means bringing a thing into being without any preexistent material, not even potentiality. Nor is creation a successive movement. Creation takes place in an instant. A thing is at once in the act of being created and is created. Such a drastic form of creation is an action proper to God alone, and he creates directly with no intermediaries. God's power extends to every possible thing, except to those that involve a contradiction.

In God there is an active power but no potentiality. Whatever would necessarily involve potentiality, those things are impossible to God. Nor could God make one and the same thing to be and not to be, because that would involve a contradiction. He cannot make a thing that lacks any of its essential constituents. His will cannot be changeable; he cannot cause what once was willed not to be fulfilled. On the other hand, God's knowledge or understanding is bounded by no limits in its view. This means that God is essentially infinite, although all other things are limited. The infinite reach of God's understanding means that his knowledge extends even to things that neither are, nor shall be, nor have been.

Creation of the Natural Order

God needs nothing and depends on nothing other than himself; every other being is in his or her neighbor's debt on God's account. In all these matters, God is not a debtor to any creature, but a debtor to the fulfillment of his own plan. There is no absolute necessity for the being of any creature. The creature begins to exist in time exactly when God from eternity arranged that it should begin to exist. God brought into being creation and time simultaneously. Thus, questions that concern a "before creation" are improperly asked. There is no account to be given of why he produced a creature *now*, and not before, but only why the creature has not always been. Having thus been always willed, a new thing that has not always been may be produced by God without any change in him. However, if time has not always been, one may mark a nonexistence of time prior to its being.

Multiplicity and variety characterize creation, to the end that the perfect likeness of God can be found in creatures and in each according to his or her measure. Taken all together, they are very good, because the order of the universe is the finest and noblest creation. Of course, in created intelligences, both potentiality and actuality are present in a way in which they are not in God. The potential intellect in humanity does not subsist apart from matter but is intimately dependent on the body's functions. In each person, it is individual, just as one's body is individual. There is no common potential intellect that is the same for all people. Despite the individuality of the human intellect and its close association with the passive intellect, particularly with the functioning of the body, the human soul does not perish with the body but is capable of independent existence. However, this does not mean that the human soul is of the same substance as God, because they differ quite markedly in basic nature. Neither is the human soul an eternally existing thing nor is it transmitted by generation; it is, rather, brought into being by a creative act of God himself.

Aquinas's description of the divine nature is metaphysical; his doctrine of the creation of the natural order can stand on its own logical ground. It fits into Christian doctrine, it is true, but Aquinas does not expect it logically to depend upon this, nor does he consciously derive his two doctrines from specifically or exclusively Christian materials.

The End of Humanity

Two objectives of the vast scheme remain: to consider the end of humanity and the created world in relation to God, and to consider finally what God can be said to have revealed. Using a quotation from the Psalms, Aquinas begins his discussion of the last end of humanity with the assertion that God will not abandon his creation once constituted. Every creature acts to attain some end, so that the natural world in this sense seems constantly directed toward the attainment of some goal. Furthermore, the goal desired is always some good; evil is a thing aside from the attention of an agent. In fact, the very cause of evil is something that in itself is good; and even when evil appears, it never cancels out completely the good upon which it is based.

Because the end of everything is always some good, the ordained end of all things is actually the source of all good: God. God is the end of all things in the sense that all rational creatures desire to be like God, to understand him. Happiness in any ultimate sense does not consist, for humanity, in bodily pleasures. Humans know, as rational creatures, that all final happiness lies in the contemplation of God. However, this happiness is not based on a general knowledge of God or upon the knowledge of God's existence that is to be had by demonstration. The problem is that people cannot in this life see God as he essentially is, which means that the final happiness of humanity cannot be attained in this life. Nor can any created substance of its own natural power arrive at a point where it can see God as he essentially is. To achieve its aim in life, a created intelligence needs an influx of divine light enabling its intellect to be lifted up to see God. Yet even in seeing God, no created intelligence could comprehend the divine substance or see all things that can be seen in God. Nevertheless, this is not an exclusive affair; every intelligence of every grade can, by being lifted up, partake of the vision of God.

Those who do see God will see him forever, and in that final happiness every desire of humanity will be fulfilled. Because God is the cause of the activity in all active agents, God is everywhere and in all things. The progress toward humanity's final goal, then, is within the scope of divine providence. The providence of God watches immediately over all individual things. This does not deny a freedom of the will because the action of divine providence is not direct but operates by means of secondary causes. However, the motion of the human will is caused by God and subject to his providence.

Christian Doctrines

From this point, Thomas moves on to consider specifically the utility of prayer, the question of fate, miracles (which God alone can work), and the purposes for the giving of a divine law for human conduct. The divine government of humanity here on this earth is like paternal govern-

ment because people's acts are punished or rewarded by God. Of course, not all punishments or rewards are equal. There is a distinction between venial and mortal sin, the latter being material in determining final reward or punishment. Because people cannot attain happiness for themselves, they need divine assistance, or grace. The presence in people of grace causes people to love God and produces faith. Such grace is given gratuitously. People can, it is true, easily do good from time to time, but they need the assistance of grace in order to persevere in good action. People may be delivered from sin but only by grace.

All these things people need to know if they are to understand their final goal and the possibility for achieving it. Yet the human mind cannot of itself arrive at the direct vision of the divine substance. God cannot, Thomas has established, abandon his creation; therefore, revelation is necessary in order to show humans the way. God himself is prevented by his nature from descending to humanity, but here is the heart of Christian doctrine. For the Son of God, as a coequal member of the Trinity, is at the same time God and capable of descending to humanity to make the necessary revelation to humanity's knowledge of its final end and the means thereto. Thomas began by addressing rational arguments to non-Christians, but the discourse is brought to the place where the Christian doctrine of revelation through Christ is considered to be necessary for the completion of creation's plan.

Thomas, having laid the rational groundwork for considering the nature of Jesus, examines various theories of Christology and their adequacy. Revelation through an agent of God himself is necessary to the fulfillment of this rational plan, and now everything depends upon describing Jesus's nature so that he is seen as fulfilling this role successfully. No one needs to be converted to Christianity by this means, but at least its rational basis can be examined. Thomas rejects Arian and Sabellian views as heretical, as orthodox Christians have done, and goes on to discuss each person of the Trinity and to work out a theory of their functions and relationships. Next, a theory of the Incarnation is developed. The human nature assumed by the Word (Christ) must be perfect in soul and body in every respect and from the instant of conception.

The need for sacraments and the doctrine of Original Sin are discussed. Because Thomas concludes with a discussion of the office of the minister and the resurrection of the body, one might almost forget that *Summa Contra Gentiles* was written for non-Christians. However, its non-Christian basis still remains: It aims to present Christian doctrine on the basis of arguments and materials that do not themselves depend for their validity on the prior acceptance of authority. Thomas had no intention of avoiding specifically Christian doctrines, but what he meant to do was to present them in the form of rational discourse, moving on from a theory of God and the nature of humanity to show the consistency of Christian doctrine with such a rationally developed view. Taking in as it does nearly every major metaphysical, theological, and ethical question, this work is truly a vast *summa* (summation), written to present Christian doctrine upon the basis of rationally structured argument.

Frederick Sontag

Summa Theologica

Type of philosophy: Metaphysics, philosophical theology

First transcribed: Summa theologiae, c. 1265-1273 (English translation, 1911-1921)

Principal ideas advanced:

◇ Humans require more than philosophy in their search for truth; certain truths are beyond human reason and are available only because of divine revelation; theology, which depends on revealed knowledge, supplements natural knowledge.

◇ The existence of God can be proved in five ways: by reference to motion (and the necessity of a First Mover), by reference to efficient causes (and the necessity of a First Cause), by reference to possibility and necessity, by reference to the gradations of perfection in the world, and by reference to the order and harmony of nature (which suggests an ordering being who gives purpose to the created world).

◇ God alone is the being whose nature is such that by reference to him, one can account for

the fact of motion, efficient cause, necessity, perfection, and order.

◇ God's principal attributes are simplicity (for he is noncorporeal and without genus), actuality, perfection, goodness, infinitude, immutability, unity, and immanence; but the created intellect can know God only by God's grace and only through apprehension not comprehension.

It is a difficult task to comment on Saint Thomas Aquinas's *Summa Theologica* briefly; it has meant and can mean many things to many people. Partly this is because of its length; it runs to many volumes. It is also because of the scope of the questions considered; they range from abstract and technical philosophy to minute points of Christian dogmatics. The situation is complicated because of Thomas's style. Such works were common in his day, and his is only one of many that were written in this general form. The work consists entirely of questions, each in the form of an article in which the views Thomas considers important are summarized and then answered. Objections to the topic question are listed, often including specific quotations, and then an equal number of replies are given, based on a middle section ("I answer that"), which usually contains Thomas's own position. However, this, in turn, is sometimes based on some crucial quotation from a philosopher or theologian.

Out of this complexity and quantity many have attempted to derive Thomistic "systems," and both the commentators and the group of modern Thomists form a complex question in themselves. Thomas was considered to be near heresy in his own day, and his views were unpopular in some quarters. From the position of being not an especially favored teacher in a very fruitful and exciting era, he has come to be regarded as perhaps the greatest figure in the Catholic philosophy and theology of the day. His stature is due as much to the dogmatization and expansion of his thought that took place (for example, by Cardinal Cajetan and John of Saint Thomas) as it is to the position Thomas had in his own day. Without this further development, his writing might have been important, but perhaps it would have been simply one among a number of significant medieval works. The Encyclical

Letter of Pope Leo XIII, "On the Restoration of Christian Philosophy," published in 1879, started the Thomistic revival. The modern developments in philosophy had gone against the Church of Rome, and Thomas was selected as the center for a revival and a concentration upon Christian philosophy. Since that time, Thomas has been widely studied, so much so that it is sometimes hard to distinguish Thomas's own work from that of those who followed him.

Part 1 contains 119 questions, including treatises on Creation, on the angels, on humanity, and on the divine government. The first part of part 2 consists of 114 questions, including treatises on habits and law, and in general, it covers ethical matters in contrast to the metaphysical and epistemological concentration that marked part 1. The second part of part 2 is made up of 189 questions, and part 3 contains ninety. These cover laws, the ethical virtues, and questions of doctrine and Christology. Taken as a whole, it is hard to imagine a more comprehensive study. Thomas's earlier study, _Summa contra gentiles_ (c. 1258-1264; English translation, 1923), literally, a "summation against the Gentiles," was intended as a technical work of apologetics for those who could not accept the premises of Christian theology. Many of the arguments in the later work were first presented in the earlier work. _Summa Theologica_, then, has as its unspoken premise the acceptance of certain basic Christian propositions, whereas _Summa Contra Gentiles_ attempts to argue without any such assumptions.

The influence of any single philosopher or theologian on Thomas's thought is difficult to establish, and probably too much has been made of Thomas's use of the Greek philosopher Aristotle. It is true that Aristotle is quoted in _Summa Theologica_ more than any other pagan author and that Thomas refers to him on occasion as "the philosopher." The availability of Aristotle's writings in fairly accurate translation in Thomas's day had a decided influence upon him and upon others of his era. The works of many other Greek philosophers such as Plato were still largely unknown, so Thomas quotes few philosophers outside the Christian tradition other than Aristotle. Particularly in psychology and epistemology, Thomas seems to have followed at least an Aristotelian tradition, if not Aristotle himself.

However, the authors Thomas quotes with favor cover a wide range, including frequent citations of the Neoplatonic pseudo-Dionysius and Saint Augustine. Moreover, in a theologically oriented _summa_, or summation, the Bible and church tradition must play a major role, so that to sort out and label any strain as dominant is extremely difficult in view of the peculiar nature of a _summa_. There are positions that can clearly be recognized as Thomas's own, but the real perplexity of understanding Thomas is to grasp the variety of sources blended in his works and to hold them all together for simultaneous consideration and questioning, as Thomas himself did.

Theology and Philosophy

The first question, consisting of ten articles, presents Thomas's definition of the nature and the extent of sacred doctrine or theology, and it opens by asking whether humanity requires anything more than philosophy. Thomas's contention that the Scriptures are inspired by God and are not a part of philosophy indicates the usefulness of knowledge other than philosophy. Scriptural knowledge is necessary for humanity's salvation, for Scripture offers the promise of salvation and pure philosophic knowledge does not. Philosophy is built up by human reason; however, certain truths necessary for humanity's salvation but that exceed human reason have been made known by God through divine revelation. Such knowledge is not agreed to be reason; it is by nature accepted only on faith.

Now the question arises: Can such revealed knowledge be considered as a science (a body of systematic knowledge) along with philosophy? Of course, such a sacred science treats of God primarily and does not give equal consideration to creatures. This means that it is actually a speculative undertaking and is only secondarily a practical concern. Yet it is the most noble science, because of the importance of the questions it considers, and in that sense all other forms of scientific knowledge are theology's handmaidens. Wisdom is knowledge of divine things, and in that sense theology has chief claim to the title of "wisdom." Its principles are immediately revealed by God, and within such a science, all things are treated under the aspect of God.

Naturally, there can be no argument on these terms with one who denies that at least some of theology's truths are obtained through divine revelation, for such a person would not admit the very premises of theology conceived of in this fashion. That is the sense in which this *summa* is a *summa* of theology intended for Christians. Because its arguments, at least in some instances, involve a claim to revealed knowledge, *Summa Theologica* may be unconvincing to the non-Christian. Thus, the reception of grace, sufficient to become a Christian, is necessary to understand the arguments. In the Christian conception, the reception of grace enables the receiver to accept the truth of revelation. However, Thomas's famous doctrine here is that such reception of grace does not destroy nature (natural knowledge) but perfects or completes it. Nothing is countermanded in philosophy's own domain; grace simply adds to it what of itself could not be known.

The Existence of God
As compared with other classical theologians, Thomas believed in a fairly straightforward approach to questions about God. However, Thomas did admit the necessity of the familiar "negative method" because where God is concerned, what he is *not* is clearer to us than what he is. The proposition "God exists" is not self-evident to us, although it may be in itself. The contradictory of the proposition "God is" can be conceived.

In this case, Thomas seems to oppose Saint Anselm's ontological argument, although the opposition is not quite as straightforward as it seems. Thomas denies that people can know God's essence directly, even though such vision would reveal that God's essence and existence are identical and thus support Anselm's contention. However, the ontological argument, he reasons, is built upon a kind of direct access to the divine that human reason does not have.

The existence of God, then, needs to be demonstrated from those of his effects that are known to us. Thomas readily admits that some will prefer to account for all natural phenomena by referring everything to one principle, which is nature itself. In opposition, he asserts that God's existence can be proved in five ways: first, the argument from motion; second, the argument from the nature of efficient cause; third, the argument

from possibility and necessity; fourth, the argument from the gradations of perfection to be found in things; and fifth, the argument from the order of the world. Without attempting individual analyses of these arguments, several things can be noted about them as a group. First, all are based on the principle that reason needs a final stopping point in any chain of explanation. Second, such a point of final rest cannot be itself within the series to be accounted for but must be outside it and different in kind. Third, in each case, it is a principle that is arrived at, not God himself, but these principles (for example, a first efficient cause) are shown to be essential parts of the nature of God. God's existence is agreed to by showing reason's need for one of his attributes in the attempt to explain natural phenomena.

Divine Nature and Its Attributes
It is probably true that Thomas's five proofs have been given a disproportionate amount of attention, for following them, Thomas goes into elaborate detail in a discussion of the divine nature and its primary attributes. Simplicity, goodness, infinity, and perfection are taken up, and then the other chief attributes are discussed before Thomas passes on to the analysis of the three persons of the Trinitarian conception of God. Taken together, these passages form one of the most elaborate and complete discussions of God's nature by a major theologian, and it is here that much of the disagreement about Thomas's philosophy centers, rather than in the more formal and brief five proofs.

In spite of Thomas's use of Aristotelian terms, he indicates his affinity with the Neoplatonic tradition by placing the consideration of "simplicity" first. This is the divine attribute most highly prized and most stressed by Neoplatonists, and Thomas concurs in their emphasis. God's simplicity is first protected by denying absolutely that he is a body in any sense because what is corporeal is by nature subject to division and contains potentiality, the opposite of God's required simplicity and full actuality. Nor is God within any genus, nor is he a subject as other individuals are. The First Cause rules all things without commingling with them.

God's primary perfection is his actuality because Thomas accepts the doctrine that a thing is perfect in proportion to its state of actuality. All created perfections preexist in God also because he is the source of all things. As such a source of the multitude of things in this world, things diverse and in themselves opposed to each other preexist in God as one, without injury to his simplicity. This is no simple kind of simplicity that Thomas ascribes to his God as a perfection. God is also called good, although goodness is defined primarily in terms of full actuality, as both perfection and simplicity were. Everything is good insofar as it has being, and because God is being in a supremely actual sense, he is supremely good. An object can be spoken of as evil only insofar as it lacks being. Because God lacks being in no way, there is absolutely no evil in his nature but only good.

When Thomas comes to infinity, he is up against a particularly difficult divine attribute. By his time, infinity had become a traditional perfection to be ascribed to God, but Aristotle had gone to great lengths to deny even the possibility of an actual infinite. Concerning this point, Thomas makes one of his most significant alterations in the Aristotelian concepts that he employs. Aristotle had considered the question of an actual infinite in the category of quantity. Thomas agrees with him: There can be no quantitative infinite and the idea is an imperfection. Form had meant primarily limitation for Aristotle, but here Thomas departs. The notion of form, he asserts, is not incompatible with infinity, although the forms of natural things are finite. In admitting the concept of the form of the infinite, Thomas departs from Aristotelian conceptions quite markedly and makes a place for a now traditional divine perfection. Nothing besides God, however, can be infinite.

Turning to the question of the immanence of God in the natural world, Thomas makes God present to all things as being the source of their being, power, and operation. However, as such, God is not in the world. For one thing, God is altogether immutable, whereas every natural thing changes. He must be, since he is pure act and only what contains potentiality moves to acquire something. It follows that in God, there is no succession, no time, but only simultaneous presence. God's unity further guarantees that only one such God could exist. Of course, a God

of such a nature may not be knowable to a particular intellect, on account of the excess of such an intelligible object over the finite intellect; but, as fully actual, God is in himself fully knowable. The blessed see the essence of God by grace; for others, it is more difficult. However, a proportion is possible between God and humans, and in this way, the created intellect can know God proportionally. This is not full knowledge, but it establishes the possibility for a knowledge relationship between God and humans.

The created intellect, however, cannot fully grasp the essence of God, unless God by grace unites himself to the created intellect, as an object made intelligible to it. It is necessary in the case of God only that, for a full grasp, the natural power of understanding should be aided by divine grace. Those who possess more charity will see God more perfectly and will be more beatified. This is Thomas's statement of the goal of the beatific vision. Even here God is only apprehended and never comprehended because only an infinite being could possess the infinite mode necessary for comprehension, and none is infinite except God. God alone can comprehend himself, yet for the mind to attain an understanding of God in some degree is still asserted to be a great beatitude. God cannot be seen in his essence by a mere human being unless the person is no longer alive. Thomas echoes Exodus 33:20: "Man shall not see Me, and live."

For Thomas, faith is a kind of knowledge because a more perfect knowledge of God himself is gained by grace than by natural reason. Such a concept of faith has had wide implications. That God is a Trinity, for instance, cannot be known except by faith, and in general, making faith a mode of knowledge has opened to Christianity the claim to a more perfect comprehension than non-Christians possess.

Names can be applied to God positively on Thomas's theory, but negative names simply signify his distance from creatures, and all names fall short of a full representation. Not all names are applied to God in a metaphorical sense, although some are (for example, God is a lion), but there are some names that are applied to God in a literal sense (for example, good, being). In reality, God is one, and yet he is necessarily multiple in idea, because the intellect represents him in a manifold manner, conceiving of many symbols to represent him. However, univocal predication is impossible, and sometimes terms are even used equivocally. Others are predicated of God in an analogous sense, according to a proportion existing between God and nature.

God's Knowledge

In the first thirteen questions, Thomas considers God as humans approach him. He then considers the world as it is viewed from the standpoint of the divine nature. Even the attributes of perfection that Thomas discussed, although they truly characterize God's nature, are not separate when viewed from the divine perspective. The question is how God understands both himself and the world, and the first thing that must be established is that there actually is knowledge in God. This might seem obvious, but the Neoplatonic tradition denies knowing to its highest principle as implying separation and need. Thomas admits a mode of knowing into the divine nature, but he denies that God knows as creatures do. God understands everything through himself alone, without dependence on external objects; his intellect and its object are altogether the same and no potentiality is present. God's knowledge is not discursive but simultaneous and fully actual eternally. This is true because of God's role as the creator of the natural world; God's knowledge is the cause of things being as they are. God knows even some things that never were, nor are, nor will be, but it is in his knowledge not that they be but that they be merely possible.

God knows future contingent things, the works of humanity being subject to free will. These things are not certain to humanity because of their dependence upon proximate, contingent causes, but they are certain to God alone, whose understanding is eternal and above time. There is a will as a part of God's nature, but it is moved by itself alone. The will of humans is sometimes moved by things external to them. God wills his own goodness necessarily, even as people will their own happiness necessarily. Yet his willing things apart from himself is not necessary. Supposing that he wills it, however, then he is unable not to will it because his will cannot change. Things other than God are thus "necessary by supposition." God knows necessarily whatever

he knows but does not will necessarily whatever he wills. The will of God is always reasonable in what it wills. Yet the will of God is entirely unchangeable, Thomas asserts, because the substance of God and his knowledge are entirely unchangeable. As to evil, God neither wills evil to be done, nor wills it not to be done, but he wills to permit evil to be done; this is good because it is the basis of humanity's freedom. However, all things are subject to divine providence, not only in general, but even in their own individual selves. It necessarily follows that everything that happens from the exercise of free will must be subject to divine providence. Both necessity and contingency fall under the foresight of God.

The Soul and Will

Thomas devotes considerable time to a consideration of the nature and function of angels. Part of his reason for doing so, of course, is undoubtedly their constant presence in the biblical record. Part of his interest comes from the necessity of having intermediary beings between God and humans. Having assigned to God a nature so different from humanity's nature, beings who stand somewhere in between are now easy to conceive. When Thomas comes to describe human nature, he follows much of the traditional Aristotelian psychology, which he finds more amenable to Christianity than certain Platonistic theories. Angels are not corporeal; humans are composed of a spiritual and a corporeal substance. The soul has no matter, but it is necessarily joined to matter as its instrument. The intellectual principle is the form of humanity and in that sense determines the body's form. Because Thomas claims that the intellect in each person is uniquely individual, he argues against some Arabian views of the universality of intellect. In addition to a twofold intellect (active and passive), humans have appetites and a will.

The will is not always moved by necessity, but in Thomas's view, it is subject to the intellect. When he turns to the question of free will, Thomas's problem is to allow sufficient causal power to human will without denying God's providence and foreknowledge. His solution to this problem is complicated, but essentially it involves God's moving humans not directly and by force but indirectly and without doing violence to human nature.

To obtain knowledge, the soul derives intelligible species from the sensible forms that come to it, and it neither has innate knowledge nor knows any forms existing independently from sensible things. The principle of knowledge is in the senses. The intellect can know the singular in material things directly and primarily. After that, intelligible species are derived by abstraction. Yet the intellectual soul cannot know itself directly but only through its operations. Nor in life can people's intellect know immaterial substances directly. That is a knowledge reserved for angels, but it means that humans cannot understand immaterial substances perfectly (through natural means). People know only material substances, and they cannot represent immaterial substances perfectly.

Human Nature

The human soul is not eternal; it was created. It is produced immediately by God, not by any lesser beings (as is suggested by Plato, for instance). Soul and body are produced simultaneously because they belong together as one organism. Humans were made in God's image, but this in no way implies that there must be equality between Creator and created. Some natures may be more like God than others, according to their disposition and the direction of their activities. All humans are directed to some end. Just as their end is worthy of blame or praise, their deeds are also worthy of blame or praise. There is, however, one last fixed end for all humans, and people must, of necessity, desire all that they desire for the sake of that last end. People's happiness ultimately is not found in wealth, fame, honor, or even power. Thomas never doubts that the desired end is to be happy, but he does deny that the end can consist of goods of the body. No created good can be humans' last end. Final and perfect happiness can consist in nothing else than the vision of the Divine Essence, although momentary happiness probably does depend on some physical thing.

It is possible for humans to see God, and therefore it is possible for people to attain ultimate happiness. Of course, there are varying degrees of happiness, and it is not present equally in all people. A certain participation in such happiness can be had in life, although true and perfect happiness cannot. Once attained, such happiness cannot be lost because its nature is eternal, but people cannot attain it by their own natural powers, although every person desires it.

Next Thomas considers the mechanics of human action, voluntary and involuntary movement, individual circumstances, the movement of the will, intention, and choice. His discussion forms an addition to his psychology and a more complete discussion of the ethical situation of humanity. Thomas acknowledges that some actions of people are evil, although they are good or evil according to circumstance. As far as the interior act of will is concerned, good and evil are essential differences in the act of will. The goodness of the will essentially depends on its being subject to reason and to natural law. The will can be evil when it abides by an erring reason. The goodness of the will depends upon its conformity to the divine will.

In his more detailed psychology, Thomas discusses the nature and origin of the soul's passions, joy, sadness, hope, fear, and love and hate. Pleasure, pain or sorrow, hope, despair, and fear all are analyzed in a way that anticipates Baruch Spinoza's discussion of the emotions. When Thomas comes to virtue, his opinion is largely based on Aristotle's. There are intellectual virtues and moral virtues, and to these he adds the theological virtues of faith, hope, and charity. Moral virtue is in a person by nature, although God infuses the theological virtues into people. For salvation, of course, there is need for a gift of the Holy Ghost.

Thomas continues with a discussion of sin, its kinds and causes. Such discussion has been extremely important both to church doctrine and in church practice. Not all sins are equal; therefore, sins must be handled in various ways. The carnal sins, for instance, are of less guilt but of more shame than spiritual sins. Mortal and venial sins are distinguished, but the will and the reason are always involved in the causes of sin. Original Sin as a concept is of course extremely important to Christian doctrine, and Thomas discusses this in detail.

The treatise on law is one of the better-known parts of *Summa Theologica*, for it is here that Thomas develops his theory of natural law. First, of course, there is the eternal law of which natural law is the first reflection and human (actual legal) law is a second reflection. The eternal law is one and is unchanging; natural law is something common to all nations and cannot be entirely blotted out from people's hearts. Human law is derived from this common natural law, but human law is framed to meet the majority of instances and must take into account many things, as to persons, as to matters, and as to times.

A brief survey such as this cannot do justice even to the variety of topics considered in *Summa Theologica*, nor can it give any detailed description of the complex material presented or of the views Thomas distills from it. The impression that *Summa Theologica* gives is that of an encyclopedia to be read and studied as a kind of source book for material on a desired issue. In fact, the only way for any reader to hope to understand Thomas and his *Summa Theologica* is to become engrossed and involved in it for himself or herself—undoubtedly what Thomas intended.

Frederick Sontag

Additional Reading

Bradley, Denis J. M. *Aquinas on the Twofold Human Good: Reason and Human Happiness in Aquinas's Moral Science*. Washington, D.C.: Catholic University of America Press, 1997. Bradley argues that Saint Thomas Aquinas was a theologian first and philosopher second. He contends that to avoid misinterpretation, Aquinas's writings should be approached from a theological, rather than a philosophical, approach.

Chesterton, G. K. *St. Thomas Aquinas*. New York: Sheed & Ward, 1933. A superb introduction to the life and thought of Thomas, "the Angelic Doctor." Aimed at non-Christian readers, or those with little experience in theology.

Copleston, F. C. *Aquinas*. Harmondsworth, England: Penguin Books, 1955. A scholarly yet accessible discussion of the philosophy of Thomas. Spends little time in dealing with Thomas himself but instead focuses on God and creation, body and soul, morality and society. The discussion of modern Thomism is dated. Copleston's analysis provides insight into Thomas's use of Aristotle (he notes that the ancients were concerned with *how* things came into being; Thomas was concerned with *why*).

Kenny, Anthony. *Aquinas*. New York: Hill & Wang, 1980. This volume in the Past Masters series covers Thomas's life in fewer than one hundred pages. Thomas's theories are explored, including his conception of Being (which Kenny believes is hopelessly flawed) and his notion of the nature of Mind (which Kenny praises for the questions Thomas asks). Latter chapters introduce the reader to medieval categories of thought, but Thomas the Christian is almost submerged.

McInerny, Ralph. *Ethica Thomastica: The Moral Philosophy of Thomas Aquinas*. 1982. Rev. ed. Washington, D.C.: Catholic University of America Press, 1997. This work is one of the finest introductions to Thomas's moral philosophy. Covers selected themes in Thomistic moral thinking, including moral goodness, judging good and evil moral actions, work of virtues, functions of conscience, and relation of ethics to religious belief.

_____. *St. Thomas Aquinas*. Boston: Twayne, 1977. An accessible study of Thomas's thought in chapters dealing with Aristotle, Boethius (whose philosophy was introduced to modern times through Thomas's writings), and Platonism. In a chapter on the tasks of theology, the author explains Thomas's distinction between believing and knowing. The book is filled with examples and includes a useful chronology of Thomas's life plus a short, annotated bibliography.

Sigmund, Paul E., ed. *St. Thomas Aquinas on Politics and Ethics*. New York: W. W. Norton, 1987. An introduction to Thomas, with eighty pages devoted to pertinent excerpts of Thomas's work, newly translated by the editor. Selections are generally quite short and range from Thomas's writings on government to selections from his treatise on God in *Summa Theologica*. Excerpts from background sources are also presented, with the remainder of the volume devoted to interpretations of Thomas.

Dan Barnett, updated by Lisa A. Wroble

Paul Tillich

Tillich believed orthodoxy to be intellectual Pharisaism, and he challenged many accepted tenets of Christianity. He rejected faith in a personal God, the historic fall into sin, the work of Christ, and the validity of prayer.

Principal philosophical works: *Die religiose Lage deer Gegenwart*, 1926 (*The Religious Situation*, 1932); *Die sozialistische Entscheidung*, 1933 (*The Socialist Decision*, 1977); *The Protestant Era*, 1948; *Systematic Theology*, 1951-1963 (3 volumes); *The Courage to Be*, 1952; *Love, Power, and Justice*, 1954; *Dynamics of Faith*, 1957; *Theology of Culture*, 1959; *Gesammelte Werke*, 1959-1975 (14 volumes); *Christianity and the Encounter of the World Religions*, 1963; *Main Works/Hauptwerke*, 1987-1993 (6 volumes).

Born: August 20, 1886; Starzeddel, Brandenburg, Germany
Died: October 22, 1965; Chicago, Illinois

Early Life

Paul Johannes Tillich was born August 20, 1886, in Starzeddel, in the province of Brandenburg in eastern Germany, an area that later became part of Poland. His father, a Lutheran pastor from eastern Germany, instilled in his son a love for philosophy. Much of Tillich's later attitude toward traditional authority, however, was a negative reaction to the stern conservativeness of his father. Tillich was deeply fond of his mother, the more influential of his parents. She was from the progressive western part of Germany and encouraged her son to explore new ideas. The family also included two daughters.

Tillich loved the country life, where, although his family was in the upper class, he went to a public school and made most of his close boyhood friends from among the poorer classes. His later leanings toward socialism were begun in these friendships. When his father was called to a new position in Berlin in 1900, the fourteen-year-old Tillich found that he was also strongly attracted to the excitement of Berlin. In addition, he found great relaxation and contemplative value at the shore of the Baltic Sea, where the family vacationed each year.

When Tillich was seventeen, his mother died of melanoma, a painful form of cancer. This trag-edy left him psychologically and spiritually destitute. The feeling of abandonment and betrayal, as if he had lost all direction, meaning, and stability, was to color his entire personal and professional life.

With his university work at Breslau, he earned a doctor of philosophy degree in 1910, going on to earn a licentiate of theology from Halle. He identified membership in a Christian student organization called the Wingolf Society as the most influential chapter in his life. This group of seventy men spent late nights in deep theological and philosophical debates, followed by smaller, quieter conversations continuing until nearly dawn. In August of 1912, he followed in his father's footsteps, receiving ordination in the Evangelical Lutheran Church.

When he was twenty-seven, Tillich married Grethi Wever, a woman much older than he. That same year, with the outbreak of war in Europe, he volunteered for service in the army as chaplain. During the next four years, he earned two Iron Crosses for valor, even though he suffered three nervous breakdowns during his service. While Tillich was in the army, his wife had an affair with one of his friends and gave birth to a child. A child born earlier to the Tillichs had died in infancy. After a two-year separation, the couple was divorced in 1921.

In the meantime, Tillich became involved in the decadence and excesses that marked German society in the postwar period. Some even suggested that he resign from any further work in theology. It was in that social setting that he met Hannah Werner, who was already engaged to be married. Despite her engagement, they maintained a heated romance for a time, then resumed it after she left her new husband to return to Berlin to be with Tillich. She brought with her an infant child, whom she placed in a nursing home. When the child died there, her husband divorced her, and she married Tillich in 1924. A daughter, Erdmuthe, was born to them in 1926, and nine years later, a son, René Stephan.

Life's Work

Tillich began his career as a teacher in 1919, when he accepted a position as instructor at the University of Berlin. Because of the nature of the position, he needed the financial support of others during this time.

His private life was very much in turmoil during those years. In addition to his divorce and remarriage, he suffered the death of his older sister. Yet he was able to establish himself as a competent teacher and remained at Berlin until 1924. His lectures began to receive a somewhat wider audience, and he was able to publish a number of articles.

From Berlin, Tillich left with his wife for Marburg for a position as associate professor of theology at the university there. During this time, his first real success came with the publication of his book *The Religious Situation*. Yet the Tillichs were unhappy in the smaller community of Marburg, and after three semesters, in 1925, they moved to the Dresden Institute of Technology, where he had a full professorship. Over the next four years, he continued to publish and gain recognition as a speaker. He also took a position as adjunct professor of systematic theology at the University of Leipzig. In 1929, Tillich accepted a full professorship at the University of Frankfurt. There, he lectured on religion, culture, the social situation, and philosophy.

The growing power of Adolf Hitler and his National Socialist Party (the Nazis) disturbed Tillich. He spoke and wrote with increasing strength against Nazi tactics. As a result, he lost his position at Frankfurt and was advised by friends and officials to go into exile. By the fall of 1933, he was being followed by members of the Gestapo.

His writings, however, had gained some international recognition. When efforts were made in New York City to bring to the United States those German intellectuals who were in trouble because of their resistance to Hitler, Union Theological Seminary in New York invited Tillich to join the faculty. Early in November, 1933, he arrived in New York and began an intensive study to learn the English language.

Tillich's early lectures at the seminary were interrupted by occasional outbursts of laughter

Paul Tillich. *(Archive Photos)*

among the students over the instructor's attempts to use the right words in the right order. He blushed easily and, for a while, had a difficult time dealing with the new environment; in Germany, it would have been unthinkable for students to laugh at the professor for any reason. Tillich's lectures introduced to the students some ideas that they had never heard presented in a classroom situation. His thinking very much reflected the influences of personal as well as social and political events. It was his contention that "truth is bound to the situation of the knower."

Tillich's view that God is unable to speak to humans meant that God must therefore reveal truth not only in the biblical records or in Jesus Christ alone, but also through other means, including the human predicament and human expressions such as art and literature.

Although for Tillich the Scriptures were the primary source for theological study, they certainly were not the only source. Church history, the Reformation, and the flow of culture were equally valid sources for his systematic theology. Tillich's study of theology thus began as an analysis of the human condition and the philosophical questions arising from it. This marked a keynote of his thinking. He maintained that any theological study originated in a philosophical question. Without philosophy, according to Tillich, theology had no questions, and therefore, nothing to study.

One of his statements, which led many to accuse him of being an atheist, was that God does not exist. His explanation was that God is existence itself, being itself, not some existing being who is simply higher than all other beings. He said that he did not know if there was a devil and that he was uncertain about his own salvation. In the United States, Tillich did not participate in the local church and its programs. In fact, he often saw enemies of the church, who worked for social change, as more useful than the church.

Tillich's grasp of social issues, political viewpoints (he was a Socialist but disavowed any political affiliation while in the United States), art, religion, and psychology, blended with his natural intelligence and almost actorlike quality of presentation, made him a favorite among the

Union faculty. Seminary president Henry Sloane Coffin said, "I don't understand what he says, but when I look at his face, I believe." In the twenty-two years he was in New York, Tillich also taught at Columbia University. In 1940, at age fifty-three, he became a citizen of the United States. In 1948, fifteen years after he left his native country, he made the first of several trips back to Germany.

Tillich moved to Harvard University Divinity School in 1955 and was soon named university professor, which freed him to study and teach in any discipline he chose. During this period, his growing reputation gained for him worldwide recognition. Some of his classes at the school were so popular that students would come an hour early simply to get a good seat in the lecture hall. A position as professor of theology at the Divinity School of the University of Chicago was offered to him, and Tillich moved to the Midwest in the fall of 1962. He also conducted seminars in the winter quarters of 1963 and 1964 at the University of California, Santa Barbara.

His health began to fail while he was in Chicago. Even so, in the spring of 1965, Tillich received two offers—a full professorship at Santa Barbara and an invitation to hold the chair of philosophy at the New School for Social Research in New York City. Tillich accepted the position in New York, to begin the following year, but on October 12, 1965, he suffered a heart attack. He died in Chicago ten days later, after asking his wife, Hannah, to forgive him for his unfaithfulness to her. His body was cremated, and after seven months in the East Hampton, New York, cemetery, his ashes were reinterred in a park named in his honor in New Harmony, Indiana.

Influence

Tillich wanted to be a philosopher and called himself a theologian. It was this combination that determined his approach to religion and won for him many devoted followers as well as many severe critics. It also was the means to widespread recognition. His influence extends around the world. Scores of books and articles by Tillich and hundreds more about him and his views have been published on nearly every continent.

John D. Wild

The Courage to Be

Type of philosophy: Existentialism, metaphysics, philosophy of religion
First published: 1952
Principal ideas advanced:

◇ Considered from the ethical point of view, courage in people is a sign of their caring for something enough to decide and to act despite opposition; considered in terms of its effect on their being (ontologically), courage is the self-affirmation of one's being.

◇ These points of view are united in the conception of courage as the self-affirmation of one's being in the presence of the threat of nonbeing; anxiety is the felt awareness of the threat of nonbeing, and courage is the resolute opposition to the threat in such a manner that being is affirmed.

◇ Three types of anxiety—ontic, moral, and spiritual (the anxiety of fate and death, of guilt and condemnation, of emptiness and meaninglessness)—are present in all cultural ages, but spiritual anxiety is predominant in the modern period.

◇ Existential anxiety cannot be removed; it can be faced only by those who have the courage to be.

◇ The courage to be involves the courage to participate, to be oneself, and to unite the two by absolute faith in the God above God, "being-itself."

The material in Paul Tillich's book, *The Courage to Be*, was first presented in the form of a series of lectures given at Yale University in 1950-1951, under the sponsorship of the Terry Foundation. The central task that the author has assumed in these lectures is that of a dialectical analysis and phenomenological description of courage as a structural category of the human condition.

Defining Courage

Courage, as understood by Tillich, is both an ethical reality and an ontological concept. As an ethical reality, courage indicates concrete action and decision that expresses a valuational content. As an ontological concept—that is, as illuminating a feature of being—courage indicates the universal and essential self-affirmation of one's being. Tillich argues that these two meanings of courage must be united if a proper interpretation of the phenomenon is to be achieved. In the final analysis, the ethical can be understood only through the ontological. Courage as an ethical reality is ultimately rooted in the structure of being itself.

These two meanings of courage have been given philosophic consideration throughout the whole history of Western thought. The author provides a brief historical sketch of the attempt to deal with the phenomenon of courage by tracing its development from the Greek philosopher Plato through the German philosopher Friedrich Nietzsche. There is first the tradition that begins with Plato and leads to medieval philosopher Saint Thomas Aquinas. In the thought of Plato and Aristotle, the heroic-aristocratic element in courage was given priority. Plato aligned courage with the spirited part of the soul, which lies between reason and desire, and then aligned both courage and spirit with the guardian class (*phýlakes*), which lies between the rulers and the producers. The class of guardians, as the armed aristocracy, thus gave the Platonic definition of courage an indelible heroic-aristocratic stamp. Aristotle preserved the aristocratic element by defining the courageous person as one who acts for the sake of what is noble. However, there was another current of thought developing during this period. This was the understanding of courage as rational-democratic rather than heroic-aristocratic. The life and death of Socrates, and later the Christian tradition, gave expression to this view. The position of Thomas is unique in that it marks the synthesis of a heroic-aristocratic ethic and society with a rational-democratic mode of thought.

With Stoicism a new emphasis emerges. Taking as the ideal sage the Athenian Socrates, the Stoics became the spokespeople for an emphatic rational-democratic definition of courage. Wisdom replaces heroic fortitude and the democratic-universal replaces the aristocratic ideal. The "courage to be" for the Stoics was a rational courage, indicating an affirmation of one's reasonable nature, or Logos, which countered the negativities of the nonessential or accidental. However, this courage to be, formulated independently of the Christian doctrine of forgiveness and salvation, was ultimately cast in terms of a cosmic resignation. The historical significance of the ethical thought of Spinoza, according to Tillich, is that it rendered explicit an ontology of courage. This ontology of courage was one that made the Stoic doctrine of self-affirmation central but that replaced the Stoic idea of resignation with a positive ethical humanism.

Nietzsche stands at the end of the era, and in a sense is its culmination. Nietzsche transforms Baruch Spinoza's "substance" into "life." Spinoza's doctrine of self-affirmation is restated in dynamic terms. Will becomes the central category. Life is understood as "will-to-power." Courage is thus defined as the power of life to affirm itself in spite of its negativities and ambiguities—in spite of the abyss of nonbeing. Nietzsche expressed it thus: "He who with eagle's talons *graspeth* the abyss: he hath courage."

Anxiety

Tillich, in formulating his ontology of courage, keeps the tradition from Plato to Nietzsche in mind. His definition of courage, as the universal self-affirmation of one's being in the presence of the threat of nonbeing, receives its final clarification only in the light of the historical background that he has sketched. In the author's definition of courage, the phenomenon of anxiety is disclosed as an unavoidable consideration. Courage and anxiety are interdependent concepts. Anxiety is the existential awareness of the threat of nonbeing. Courage is the resolute facing of this anxiety in such a way that nonbeing is ultimately embraced or taken up into being. Thus, the author is driven to formulate an ontology of anxiety. There is first a recognition of the interdependence of fear and anxiety.

Fear and anxiety are distinct but not separate. Fear has a determinable object—a pain, a rejection, a misfortune, the anticipation of death. Anxiety, on the other hand, has no object; paradoxically stated, its object is the negation of every object. Anxiety is the awareness that nonbeing is irremovably a part of one's being, which constitutes the definition of human finitude. Anxiety and fear are thus distinct. Yet they are mutually immanent within each other. Fear, when it is deepened, reveals anxiety; and anxiety strives toward fear. The fear of dying ultimately ceases to

be a fear of an object—a sickness or an accident—and becomes anxiety over the nonbeing envisioned "after death." Conversely, anxiety strives to become fear, because the finite self cannot endure the threatening disclosure of nonbeing for more than a moment. The mind seeks to transform anxiety into fear, so that it can have a particular object to deal with and overcome. However, the basic anxiety of nonbeing cannot, as such, be eliminated. It is a determinant of human existence itself. Tillich distinguishes three types of anxiety: *ontic anxiety*, or the anxiety of fate and death; *moral anxiety*, or the anxiety of guilt and condemnation; and *spiritual anxiety*, or the anxiety of emptiness and meaninglessness.

Fate threatens humans' ontic self-affirmation relatively; death threatens it absolutely. The anxiety of fate arises from an awareness of an ineradicable contingency that penetrates to the very depth of one's being. Existence exhibits no ultimate necessity. It manifests an irreducible element of irrationality. Behind fate stands death as the absolute threat to ontic self-affirmation. Death discloses the total ontic annihilation that is imminent in every moment of existence. For the most part, people attempt to transform this anxiety into fear, which has a definite object. They partly succeed but then realize that the threat can never be embodied in a particular object. It arises from the human situation as such. The question then is posed: Is there a courage to be, a courage to affirm oneself in spite of the threat against humanity's ontic self-affirmation?

Nonbeing threatens on another level. It threatens by producing moral anxiety—the anxiety of guilt, which threatens relatively, and the anxiety of condemnation, which threatens absolutely. The self seeks to affirm itself morally by actualizing its potentialities. However, in every moral action, nonbeing expresses itself in the inability of humans to actualize fully all of their potential. They remain estranged from their essential being. All of their actions are pervaded with a moral ambiguity. The awareness of this ambiguity is guilt. This guilt can drive people toward a feeling of complete self-rejection, in which they experience the absolute threat of condemnation. The question then arises whether people can find the courage to affirm themselves in spite of the threat against their moral self-affirmation.

Lastly, there is the anxiety of emptiness and meaninglessness, which reveals the threat to spiritual self-affirmation. Emptiness threatens this self-affirmation relatively, meaninglessness threatens it absolutely. Emptiness arises out of a situation in which the self fails to find satisfaction through a participation in the contents of its cultural life. The beliefs, attitudes, and activities of tradition lose their meaning and are transformed into matters of indifference. Everything is tried but nothing satisfies. Creativity vanishes and the self is threatened with boredom and tedium. The anxiety of emptiness culminates in the anxiety of meaninglessness. People find that they can no longer hold fast to the affirmations of their tradition or to those of their personal convictions. Truth itself is called into question. Spiritual life is threatened with total doubt. Again, the question arises: Is there a courage to be that affirms itself in spite of nonbeing—in this case, nonbeing expressed in the threat of doubt that undermines one's spiritual affirmation through the anxiety of emptiness and meaninglessness?

These three types of anxiety find a periodic exemplification in the history of Western civilization. Although the three types are interdependently present in all cultural ages, we find that ontic anxiety was predominant at the end of ancient civilization, moral anxiety at the end of the Middle Ages, and spiritual anxiety at the end of the modern period. The anxiety of fate and death was the central threat in the Stoic doctrine of courage; it received expression in the transition from Hellenic to Hellenistic civilization, which saw the crumbling of the independent city-states and the rise of universal empires, introducing a political power beyond control and calculation; and it is present on every page of Greek tragical literature. In the Middle Ages, the anxiety of guilt and condemnation was dominant, expressed in the theological symbol of the "wrath of God" and in the imagery of hell and purgatory. Ascetic practices, pilgrimages, devotion to relics, the institution of indulgences, heightened interest in the mass and penance—all bear witness to the moral threat of nonbeing as it manifests itself in guilt and condemnation. Modern civilization, born of the victory of humanism and the Enlightenment, found its chief threat in the threat to spiritual self-affirmation. Here the anxiety of

emptiness and meaninglessness becomes dominant. Democratic liberalism calls into question the security and supports of an absolute state; the rise of technology tends to transform selves into tools and thus displace people's spiritual center; skepticism replaces philosophical certitude. All cultural contents that previously gave people security no longer afford satisfaction and meaning. Modern people are threatened with the attack of emptiness and meaninglessness.

Tillich concludes his ontology of anxiety by distinguishing existential anxiety, in the three types discussed, from pathological or neurotic anxiety. Existential anxiety has an ontological character and is thus understood as a universal determinant of the human condition. Existential anxiety cannot be removed; it can only be courageously faced. Pathological anxiety, on the other hand, as the result of unresolved conflicts in the sociopsychological structure of personality, is the expression of universal anxiety under special conditions. It is the consequence of people's inability to face courageously their existential anxiety and thus take the nonbeing that threatens into themselves.

The neurotic self still affirms itself, but it does so on a limited scale. Such affirmation is the affirmation of a reduced self that seeks to avoid the nonbeing that is constitutive of its universal finite condition. However, in thus seeking to avoid nonbeing, the neurotic self retreats from the full affirmation of its being. Tillich defines neurosis as "the way of avoiding nonbeing by avoiding being." The neurotic personality always affirms something less than what it essentially is. Potentialities are sacrificed in order to make possible a narrow and intensified affirmation of what remains of the reduced self. The neurotic is unable to take creatively into the self the universal existential anxieties. In relation to the anxiety of fate and death, this produces an unrealistic security, comparable to the security of a prison. Because neurotics cannot distinguish what is to be realistically feared from those situations in which they are realistically safe, they withdraw into a castle of false security so as to insulate themselves from all threats of existence. In relation to the anxiety of guilt and condemnation, pathological anxiety expresses an unrealistic perfection. Neurotics set up moralistic self-defenses against all actions that would widen the horizons of their reduced and limited actualized state, which they consider to be absolutely perfect. In relation to the anxiety of emptiness and meaninglessness, which expresses itself in a radical existential doubt, pathological anxiety drives the self to an unrealistic certitude. Unable to face the doubt regarding the contents of cultural tradition and personal beliefs, neurotics construct a citadel of certainty, from which they fend off all threat of doubt on the basis of an absolutized authority. This absolutized authority may be either a personal revelation, a social or religious institution, or a fanatical leader of a movement. In any case, they refuse to accept doubt and reject all questions from the outside. They are unable courageously to accept the reality of meaninglessness as a universal phenomenon in existential reality.

The Courage to Be

The courage to be is the movement of self-affirmation in spite of the threat of anxiety as the existential awareness of nonbeing. This courage is conceptually clarified by Tillich through the use of the polar ontological principles of participation and individualization. The basic polar structure of being is the polarity of self and world. The first polar elements that emerge out of this foundational polar structure are the elements of participation and individualization. The relevance of these elements to Tillich's doctrine of courage is evident. Courage expresses itself as "the courage to be as a part," exemplifying the polar element of participation, and as "the courage to be as oneself," exemplifying the polar element of individualization. Finally, these two polar exemplifications of courage are transcended and united in "absolute faith." Absolute faith, grounded in transcendence, provides the final definition of the courage to be.

First, the author examines the manifestation of courage as the courage to be as a part. This is one side of people's self-affirmation. They affirm themselves as participants in the power of a group, a historical movement, or being as such. This side of courage counters the threat of losing participation in the world. The social forms that embody this manifestation of courage are varied. Tillich briefly discusses four of these forms: *collectivism*, *semi-collectivism*, *neocollectivism*, and *democratic conformism*.

All of these forms attempt to deal with the three types of anxiety—ontic, moral, and spiritual—by channeling their individual expressions into an anxiety about the group. Thus, it becomes possible to cope with these existential anxieties with a courage that affirms itself through collective or conformal participation. The individual anxiety concerning fate and death is transcended through a collective identification. There is a part of oneself, belonging to the group, that cannot be hurt or destroyed. It is as eternal as the group is eternal—an essential manifestation of the universal collective. So, also, a self-affirmation is made possible in spite of the threat of guilt and condemnation. Individual guilt is translated into a deviation or transgression of the norms of the collective, and the courage to be as a part accepts guilt and its consequences as public guilt. The anxiety of emptiness and meaninglessness is dealt with in the same way. The group becomes the bearer of universal meaning, and the individual derives his or her personal meaning through a participation in the group. The ever-present danger in the radical affirmation of the courage to be as a part is the absorption of the self into the collective, with the consequent loss of the unique, unrepeatable, and irreplaceable individual.

The courage to be *as oneself* expresses the other side of self-affirmation. This movement is made possible through the ontological polar element of individualization. The courage to be as oneself has found a concrete embodiment in *romanticism*, *naturalism*, and *existentialism*.

Romanticism elevated individuals beyond all cultural content and conferred upon them a radical autonomy. In some of its extreme expressions, as in Friedrich von Schlegel, the courage to be as oneself led to a complete rejection of participation.

Naturalism, whether of the "philosophy of life" variety or of the American pragmatic variety, follows basically the same path. Nietzsche, in his definition of nature as the will-to-power, granted priority to the individual will and made it the decisive element in the drive toward creativity. In Nietzsche, individual self-affirmation reaches a climactic point. American pragmatism, in spite of its roots in democratic conformism, shares much of the individualistic attitude characteristic of European naturalism. It finds its highest ethical principle in growth, sees the educational process as one that maximizes the individual talents of the child, and seeks its governing philosophical principle in personal creative self-affirmation.

It is in existentialism that the courage to be as oneself is most powerfully presented. Tillich distinguishes two basic expressions of existentialism: as an attitude and as a philosophical and artistic content. Existentialism as an attitude designates an attitude of concrete involvement as contrasted with an attitude of theoretical detachment. Existentialism as a content is at the same time a point of view, a protest, and an expression. However, in all of its varieties, existentialism is the chief protagonist for the reality of the individual and the importance of personal decision. It is concerned to salvage the individual from the objectivization of abstract thought, society, and technology alike. Existentialists struggle for the preservation of the self-affirmative person. They fight against dehumanization in all of its forms. The task of every individual, according to the existentialist, is to be oneself. Philosopher Martin Heidegger has profoundly expressed this existentialist courage to be as oneself in his concept of resolution (*Entschlossenheit*). Resolute individuals derive their directives for action from no external source. Nobody can provide for one's security against the threat of ontic annihilation, moral disintegration, or spiritual loss of meaning. They themselves must decide how to face their imminent death, how to face their moral ambiguity, and how to face the threat of meaninglessness that strikes at the root of their existence.

The danger in the courage to be as a part is a loss of the self in the collective. The opposite danger becomes apparent in the various forms of the courage to be as oneself—namely, a loss of the world as a polar structure of selfhood. The question then arises whether there can be a courage that unites both sides of self-affirmation by transcending them.

Courage understood as absolute faith exemplifies this union through transcendence. A courage that can take the three types of anxiety creatively into itself must be grounded in a power of being that transcends both the power of oneself and the power of one's world. The self-world correlation is still on this side of the threat of nonbeing;

hence, neither self-affirmation as oneself nor self-affirmation as a part can cope successfully with nonbeing. The courage to be, in its final movement, must be rooted in the power of being-itself, which transcends the self-world correlation. Insofar as religion is the state of being grasped by the power of being-itself, it can be said that courage always has either an explicit or implicit religious character. The courage to be finds its ultimate source in the power of being-itself and becomes manifest as absolute faith. As long as participation remains dominant, the relation to being-itself is mystical in character; as long as individualization remains dominant, the relationship is one of personal encounter; when both sides are accepted and transcended, the relation becomes one of absolute faith. The two sides are apprehended as contrasts, but not as contradictions that exclude each other.

This absolute faith is able to take the threefold structure of anxiety into itself. It conquers the anxiety of fate and death in its encounter with providence. Providence gives humans the courage of confidence to say "in spite of" to fate and death. Providence must not be construed in terms of God's activity but as a religious symbol for the courage of confidence that conquers fate and death. Guilt and condemnation are conquered through the experience of divine forgiveness that expresses itself in the courage to accept acceptance. The courage to be in relation to guilt is "the courage to accept oneself as accepted in spite of being unacceptable." In relation to the anxiety of emptiness and meaninglessness, the courage to be, based on absolute faith, is able to say "yes" to the undermining doubt and to affirm itself in spite of the threat. Any decisive answer to the question of meaninglessness must first accept the state of meaninglessness; this acceptance constitutes a movement of faith. "The act of accepting meaninglessness is in itself a meaningful act. It is an act of faith." Through their participation in the power of being-itself, humans are able to conquer emptiness and meaninglessness by taking them into themselves and affirming themselves "in spite of" these factors.

The content of absolute faith is the "God above God." Tillich rejects the God of theological theism, who remains bound to the subject-object structure of reality. A God who is understood as an object becomes an invincible tyrant who divests people of their subjectivity and freedom. This is the God whom Nietzsche pronounced dead and against whom the existentialists have justifiably revolted. Theism must be transcended if absolute faith is to become a reality. The "God above God" is the power of being-itself, which, as the source of absolute faith, is not bound to the subject-object structure of reality. Being-itself transcends both self and world and unites the polarities of individualization and participation. The courage to be, which is ultimately grounded in the encounter with the "God above God," thus unites and transcends the courage to be as oneself and the courage to be as a part. This courage avoids both the loss of oneself by participation and the loss of one's world by individualization.

Calvin O. Schrag

Additional Reading

Calâi, Grace. *Paul Tillich, First-Hand: A Memoir of the Harvard Years.* Introduction by Jerald C. Brauer. Chicago: Exploration Press, 1996. An interesting and readable biography of Tillich.

Crossman, Richard C. *Paul Tillich: A Comprehensive Bibliography and Keyword Index of Primary and Secondary Writings in English.* Matuchen, N.J.: Scarecrow Press, 1983. A source book for titles of all of Paul Tillich's writings in English and of articles, books, dissertations, theses, and reviews about Tillich.

_____. *Tillich.* Philadelphia: Presbyterian and Reformed Publishing, 1962. An interesting work that fiercely assails Tillich's work in two areas: his view of God and his view of Revelation.

Grigg, Richard. *Symbol and Empowerment: Paul Tillich's Post-Theistic System.* Macon, Ga.: Mercer University Press, 1985. This book examines the theological, philosophical, and psychological aspects of Tillich's system of thought.

Johnson, Wayne G. *Theological Method in Luther and Tillich.* Washington, D.C.: University Press of America, 1981. Defends Tillich's approach to theology by making comparisons at different points to the theology of Martin Luther.

Lyons, James R. *The Intellectual Legacy of Paul Tillich.* Detroit, Mich.: Wayne State University Press, 1969. Printed versions of lectures by three scholars as they evaluate Tillich as philosopher and theologian and as an observer of psychiatry. Includes brief biographical notes and a letter Tillich wrote to Thomas Mann in 1943.

Mahan, Wayne W. *Tillich's System.* San Antonio, Tex.: Trinity University Press, 1974. A good outline of Tillich's thought.

May, Rollo. *Paulus: Reminiscences of a Friendship.* New York: Harper & Row, 1973. Extremely personal glimpses of Tillich by the man recognized as his best friend during his thirty-two years in the United States.

Newport, John P. *Paul Tillich.* Waco, Tex.: Word Books, 1984. One of the best and most complete books on Tillich. Includes an excellent biographical section, plus chapters on Tillich's views and evaluations of those views.

Stone, Ronald H. *Paul Tillich's Radical Social Thought.* Atlanta: John Knox Press, 1980. Relates biographical information to Tillich's social philosophy. This work contains some biographical material not found in older volumes.

Towne, Edgar A. *Two Types of New Theism: Knowledge of God in the Thought of Paul Tillich and Charles Hartshorne.* New York: Peter Lang, 1997. A good examination of Tillich's thought process.

John D. Wild, updated by Patrick S. Roberts

Tzvetan Todorov

Todorov, a structuralist critic of literature and poetry, turned his talents toward analysis of human behavior during the Holocaust of World War II, examining the virtues that inspired heroic conduct and the forces that produced horrific evil in the concentration camps.

Principal philosophical works: *Littérature et signification*, 1967; *Grammaire du Décaméron*, 1969; *Introduction à la littérature fantastique*, 1970 (*The Fantastic: A Structural Approach to a Literary Genre*, 1973); *Poétique de la prose*, 1971 (*The Poetics of Prose*, 1977); *Dictionnaire encyclopédique des sciences du langage*, 1972 (with Oswald Ducrot; *Encyclopedic Dictionary of the Sciences of Language*, 1979); *Poétique*, 1973 (*An Introduction to Poetics*, 1981); *Théories du symbole*, 1977 (*Theories of the Symbol*, 1982); *Symbolisme et interprétation*, 1978 (*Symbolism and Interpretation*, 1982); *Les Genres du discours*, 1978 (*Genres in Discourse*, 1990); *Mikhaïl Bakhtine: Le Principe dialogique*, 1981 (*Mikhail Bakhtin: The Dialogical Principle*, 1984); *La Conquête de l'Amérique: La Question de l'autre*, 1982 (*The Conquest of America: The Question of the Other*, 1984); *Critique de la critique: Un Roman d'apprentissage*, 1984 (*Literature and Its Theorists: A Personal View of Twentieth-Century Criticism*, 1987); *Frêle bonheur: Essai sur Rousseau*, 1985; *La Notion de littérature et autres essais*, 1987 (slightly revised versions of eight essays from *Les Genres du discours* and two essays from *Poétique de la prose*); *Nous et les autres: La Réflexion française sur la diversité humaine*, 1989 (*On Human Diversity: Nationalism, Racism, and Exoticism in French Thought*, 1993); *Les Morales de l'histoire*, 1991 (*The Morals of History*, 1995); *Face à l'extrême*, 1991 (*Facing the Extreme: Moral Life in the Concentration Camps*, 1996); *Les Abus de la mémoire*, 1995; *La Vie commune: Essai d'anthropologie générale*, 1995.

Born: March 1, 1939; Sofia, Bulgaria

Early Life

Tzvetan Todorov was born on March 1, 1939, in Sofia, Bulgaria, to Todor Borov Todorov, a university professor, and the former Haritina Todorova, a librarian. After taking his M.A. in philology at the University of Sofia in 1963, he emigrated to France and enrolled at the University of Paris. Roland Barthes directed his doctoral thesis, which was published in 1967 as *Littérature et signification* (literature and meaning). Todorov took his *doctorat de troisième cycle* (equivalent to the Ph.D.) in 1966 and his *doctorat ès lettres* in 1970. He was appointed to his post as a director of research at the French Centre Nationale de la Recherche Scientifique in 1968. In 1970, he helped to found the journal *Poétique*, of which he remained one of the managing editors until 1979. With Gérard Genette, he edited the Collection Poétique, the series of books on literary theory published by Éditions de Seuil, until 1987.

Life's Work

Although his work is clear, systematic, and analytically rigorous, Todorov's theoretical stance shifted radically over the years from that of a "scientist" to that of a "humanist" and "moralist." He also moved from a consideration of only literature to a wider evaluation of social reality and morality. His early work, beginning with *Littérature et signification*, the published version of his 1967 doctoral thesis, to the late 1970's, most clearly aspired to being scientific. During that period, Todorov was the most representative of the French structuralist literary theoreticians. His reputation as a moral philosopher stemmed largely from his later works, including *Facing the Extreme: Moral Life in the Concentration Camps*.

Todorov frequently discussed the opposition between "poetics," the study of the general laws of literature, and what he variously called "description," "interpretation," "commentary," "criticism," and "exegesis"—the study, from various perspectives, of the individual literary work.

While Todorov recognized the value of these activities, he, like most of the French structuralists, was primarily a poetician rather than an exegete.

Todorov observed that one sense of "structuralism" is "the study of abstract structure." Poetics is by definition structuralist in this broad sense because the object of poetics is an abstract structure, the general laws of literature. Yet his work was also structuralist in a narrower sense. In *Literature and Its Theorists*, he said that Northrop Frye's *Anatomy of Criticism* (1957) is structuralist in that it combines two traits: an "internal approach to literature" and a "systematic attitude." In *The Fantastic*, however, he judged Frye's theory to be insufficiently "internal" and "systematic" because the categories that make up Frye's classificatory scheme were all "borrowed . . . from philosophy, psychology, or a social ethic." Because Frye did not indicate that he used these categories in special literary senses, "they lead us outside of literature." Thus, to take an "internal" approach to literature in Todorov's sense is to try to understand literature as constituted by its own categories and the relations between those categories.

What most clearly distinguishes Todorov's work from other internal, systematic theories of literature is its heavy reliance on structural linguistics and on semiotics as sources for the basic categories in terms of which it describes the systems of literature. Although French structuralist poeticians generally agree that their adoption of linguistic categories is authorized to some extent by the fact that language and literature are both sign-systems, they disagree among themselves about just how intimate the relationship between language and literature is. Todorov, however, hypothesized rigorous homologies between language and literature; in *The Poetics of Prose*, he quoted with provisional approval poet Paul Valéry's dictum: "Literature is, and can be nothing other than, a sort of extension and application of certain properties of language." In *Grammaire du Décaméron*, an examination of Giovanni Boccaccio's *Decameron: O, Prencipe Galetto* (1349-1351; *The Decameron*, 1620), he adopted the "methodological hypothesis" of a kind of deep-structural identity between language and literature: Underlying all sign-systems is a "universal grammar," which is also universal in the sense

that "it coincides with the structure of the universe itself."

Todorov devoted a great deal of attention to the theory of genre. In *The Fantastic*, his most extended discussion of genre, he considered a given genre as a system of interrelated features. According to Todorov, texts belonging to the historical genre of the "fantastic" have three basic features. The first is verbal: The "implicit reader," whose perception, unlike that of the actual reader, "is inscribed in the text with the same precision as the movements of the characters," must hesitate between the natural and supernatural explanations of a narrated event. The second feature is both syntactic and, because it results in the thematization of the fantastic hesitation, semantic: A central character may also (although not necessarily) experience the fantastic hesitation, thus helping to promote the first feature by providing a model within the story for the implicit reader's hesitation. The third feature "transcends" the three aspects of literature, being a requirement for a particular "mode" of reading: The fantastic text must "refuse an allegorical or 'poetic' interpretation" because both of these modes of reading interfere with the evocation of the fiction, and the first, defining feature of the fantastic is precisely the implicit reader's attitude toward the fiction.

Todorov generalized his notion of genre to include all forms of discourse established by social convention. "Scientific discourse," for example, displays certain relatively constant "generic" traits, including the exclusion of "reference to the first and second persons of the verb, as well as the use of other tenses than the present." This development is in part a consequence of Todorov's questioning the possibility of distinguishing between "literature" and "nonliterature" on the basis of purely structural, internal features.

By 1973, Todorov had decided that there probably is no structural trait or group of traits that is possessed by every instance of what is called literature and that is not possessed by any instance of nonliterature. If there is some greatest common denominator of what is called literature, it is not structural but "functional"; that is, literature may perhaps be distinguishable from other discourses not by what it is, but by what it does. The role of poetics has been primarily "transitional": Because it has focused on the most "opaque" discourses, it has sharpened its audience's awareness of discourse as such; all the "genres of discourse" should now be given the careful attention that has hitherto been accorded to literature.

Todorov's rejection of the idea of an essential opposition between literature and nonliterature seems to align him with poststructuralism. Yet Todorov never denied the value of structuralism; he only denied that by itself it can account for every important dimension of literature. Moreover, his ideas about the way language works put him into clear opposition to what Robert Scholes, in *Textual Power: Literary Theory and the Teaching of English* (1985), calls "hermetic interpretation," the current of poststructuralism that "sees texts as radically self-reflective and non-referential." For example, the grounding premise of Todorov's analysis of indirect verbal signification, *Symbolism and Interpretation*, that there is an essential difference between the way one arrives at the "direct," or "literal" sense of a given utterance and the way one arrives at its "indirect," or "symbolic" sense, is directly contrary to deconstructive thought about language, as Todorov recognizes.

In *Symbolism and Interpretation*, Todorov analyzed two different interpretive strategies in detail: "biblical exegesis," which is a form of what he calls "finalist" interpretation, interpretation that takes the content of the text to be interpreted as a given (the given content of biblical exegesis was Christian dogma) and that sees its primary task as showing how one may get from the text to the given truth; and "philological exegesis," which is a form of what he calls "operational" interpretation, interpretation that takes the ways of getting from a text to its meaning as a given and that sees its task as restricted to determining that meaning, without asking whether it is "true." What most strikingly distinguishes Todorov's work in this area, both from poststructuralism and from his own earlier structuralism, is his rejection of a purely "operational" interpretive strategy, one that renounces any consideration of questions of "truth."

Todorov saw that in rejecting operational "relativism," one risks lapsing into a finalist dogma-

tism; in *Literature and Its Theorists*, he explored the thought of twentieth century literary aestheticians in an attempt to find a way to "transcend" this "dichotomy." The form that Todorov finally suggested the critical "search for truth and values" should take is partly inspired by ideas advanced by Mikhail Bakhtin. Todorov called for a "dialogic criticism"—one that does not try to deny, either by rendering the critic's "voice as inaudible as possible" or by assuming a position of mastery with regard to the literary text, that it partakes of what Bakhtin saw as the essential "dialogism" of all discourse, its orientation toward the discourse of other subjects. Taking truth as "an ultimate horizon and a regulating idea" rather than as "given in advance," the critic should attempt to engage in a dialogue with the author of the text he or she is studying, granting the author as far as possible full status as a speaking subject and equal partner in the exchange.

In the 1980's and 1990's, Todorov turned his attention increasingly to questions of ethics and morality in such works as *On Human Diversity* (1989), *The Morals of History* (1991), *Les Abus de la mémoire* (1995; the abuses of memory), and *La Vie commune* (1995; the common life). One of his most influential of these later works is *Facing the Extreme: Moral Life in the Concentration Camps*, in which he examined the heroic virtues—strength, courage, and solidarity—that maintain humanity during the toughest times, despite the evils and morals laid bare by people's experiences in the Nazi and Soviet concentration camps during the Holocaust of World War II.

Influence

Todorov's greatest influence was in structuralism. A synthesizer and organizer, Todorov helped to define the program of structuralist poetics by providing it with its most coherent and comprehensive manifesto in his *An Introduction to Poetics*, and he helped to give structuralist poetics its most important forum, as a cofounder and coeditor of the journal *Poétique*. In addition, although he was not the first to attempt to formulate a grammar of narrative syntax, he did develop the structural parallel between narrative and the sentence in greater detail and with greater rigor than anyone before him.

Nevertheless, Todorov will also be remembered for his positive view of human moral behavior in the face of brutality such as that of the Holocaust. This turn toward what has been named Todorov's "critical humanism" characterizes an important late twentieth century return to the components of moral behavior, and how moral behavior is sustained and propagated, in a century marked by increasing violence.

Scott Vaszily

Facing the Extreme

Moral Life in the Concentration Camps

Type of philosophy: Ethics, philosophy of history, social philosophy

First published: Face à l'extrême, 1991 (English translation, 1996)

Principal ideas advanced:

◇ The major virtues that sustain humanity are strength, courage, and solidarity—the heroic virtues—and dignity, the life of the mind, and caring—the ordinary virtues.

◇ The major evils that are self-destructive to humanity arise from totalitarianism and hostility to freedom, social and individual fragmentation and depersonalization, indoctrination into hate, lust for power, and moral indifference.

◇ These virtues and evils are revealed most starkly by focusing on life inside the Nazi and Soviet concentration camps.

◇ Valuable lessons of both dire warnings of human evil and inspiring examples of human goodness are to be learned from the experiences of the Nazi and Soviet concentration camps.

◇ If these lessons are studied, remembered, and internalized, humanity will benefit greatly.

This important work of internationally renowned writer and literary theoretician Tzvetan Todorov synthesizes the major research and insights of scores of scholars and writers about human behavior in the concentration camps of the two major totalitarian states of the twentieth century, Nazi Germany and the Soviet Union. Such stud-

ies began to emerge immediately after the horrors of World War II and tended to emphasize the radical evils and dehumanization that were perpetrated in the camps. In the 1980's and 1990's, however, new works explored the countless examples of kindness practiced by the victims and the rescuers of Jews, exploring the possibility that helping behavior is part of "human nature"—a finding as significant as its negative counterparts of aggression, envy, fanaticism, sadism, and human corruptibility. Todorov acknowledges that this more positive theory about human nature began in the Enlightenment with figures such as Jean-Jacques Rousseau.

Todorov was inspired to write *Facing the Extreme* during a trip to Warsaw. In Poland, he heard awe-inspiring stories of the Jewish resistance against the Nazis in the Warsaw Ghetto in the spring of 1943 and of the futile heroics of the Polish uprising against the Nazis the very next year. Todorov set out to analyze those virtues that were revealed by these events and then proceeded to explore the unprecedented world of the concentration camps.

Virtues

Todorov was impressed that the Jews of the Warsaw Ghetto uprising knew that they would die and that their attempt would nevertheless make a statement about their ideals for future generations. What kind of virtues shaped their great efforts? Todorov distinguishes between what he calls "heroic virtues" and "ordinary virtues." The heroic virtues are the qualities of moral strength, courage, willpower, and solidarity.

For Todorov, the ordinary virtues are no less important, perhaps even more so, because courage and willpower can be put to evil purposes, as they were at the hands of the Nazis. The ordinary virtues that are most important are dignity, self-respect, the development of the life of the mind (sometimes characterized as critical thinking), and care for others. Todorov wisely remarks that the Warsaw Ghetto uprising was a sane, practical reaction to the Nazi aim to kill every Jew in Warsaw and the rest of Europe.

After his discussion of the Warsaw Ghetto uprising, Todorov turned to the extreme situations experienced by human beings in the concentration and death camps of Nazi Germany and Soviet Russia. This was the major focus of his work, for Todorov realized that moral life is best understood under the impact of extreme situations. His concern was heightened by the fact that he himself lived in communist Bulgaria until he was twenty-four years old and that the Bulgarian communists perpetrated the evils of dictatorship, indoctrination, and selective killing of existing and potential political opponents.

At the outset of his study of the camps, Todorov shares the now conventional wisdom that the Nazis and Soviets created a new form of social organization akin to the seventeenth century English political philosopher Thomas Hobbes's "state of nature," in which humans would be reduced to beasts and where life would be a struggle of all against all. Indeed, camp life gave rise to many instances of cannibalism, betrayal, corruption, and meanness—all produced by the desperate struggle to survive. What is remarkable for Todorov is that within this horrific system, many people were striking exceptions to this rule. For example, the Italian Jew Primo Levi, who was a prisoner in Auschwitz, was saved by an Italian Gentile who brought him extra food every day. The Polish writer Tadeusz Borowski, who was also in Auschwitz, created works that stood as a moral act of testimony to both good and evil. This was also characteristic of the great Russian writers who served time in the Gulag, the network of Soviet slave-labor camps. Acts of goodness in the camps were much more telling than those in the ordinary world.

Todorov then proceeds to give a brief survey of the ideas of heroism and saintliness in the Western world. Starting with the ancient Greeks, Achilles and Hector exemplified the qualities of bravery, self-sacrifice, and the struggle for excellence. Socrates represented the virtues of justice and the life of the mind. The chivalric hero of the Middle Ages gave way to the individualistic idealist of the eighteenth and nineteenth centuries. The twentieth century produced military and patriotic heroes as well as the absurd or comical heroes of the dramas of Samuel Beckett and films of Charlie Chaplin. Moreover, there were always heroes in the public spheres of politics and business and the private spheres of the intellect and of personal relationships. However, these people became heroes under largely normal circum-

stances. How must heroism and virtue be defined and redefined in the extreme context of concentration or slave-labor camps?

In the camps, there were courageous heroes who led the revolts in Auschwitz and Sobibor, and quiet heroes who smuggled food and saved children from the gas chambers. Still, Todorov makes a distinction between heroes who gave their lives for a cause and those who saved lives. At this point, Todorov felt it necessary to classify acts of what he called "ordinary" virtues. The first is dignity, which could mean self-respect or moderation, perhaps social recognition or personal autonomy. The struggle for dignity was of critical importance in the camps because the camps were the greatest systematic assault on human dignity ever conceived. The Nazis actually declared the Jews not worthy of the dignity of life itself. There were many instances of the struggle for dignity. Primo Levi, for example, was determined always to walk erect, keep himself as clean as possible, and shine his shoes because he realized that the camp was a machine intended to turn human beings into beasts.

The exercise of will is another virtue because it relates to the value of freedom and individual autonom. Prisoners exercised this value in different ways. Some committed suicide to have control over their own death; the Jewish crematorium workers wrote down their experiences and buried them in the hope that someday their existence and the story of the camp would be remembered; other prisoners refused to obey Nazi orders or sabotaged the Nazi war machine.

Todorov examines the moral ambiguities of the perpetrators. Todorov reminds the reader that many concentration camp functionaries were "good people"—hardworking, kind to animals, good husbands and fathers, conscientious and competent at their jobs—yet they were mass murderers. Todorov resolves this paradox by showing that dignity must work for a good end. Unfortunately, in their own minds the Nazis thought that they were doing good.

The virtues of solidarity and the life of the mind are also frought with ambiguity. Solidarity can be a helping virtue but can also create group selfishness to the exclusion of others. Many Nazis and Russian communists valued the classics, loved music and poetry, and prized scientific discovery. Once again, it is the aims and goals of culture and education that determine whether the life of the mind will have ethical and moral results. Todorov also raises the question of whether virtue has any gender-specific implications. He argues that women were stronger than men both physically and psychologically. Women bonded better and helped each other more than men did. For Todorov, women are the nurturers and the caring gender of the human species. He claims that present-day feminists can fall into the trap of imitating the traditionally masculine values of aggression, competition, and power. In Todorov's view, men are more conceptual, women more practical: These qualities of women must be practiced to complement those of men.

The experiences of the camps revealed to Todorov that the value of caring is the most important of all. When the individual reaches out to the community, he or she gives the life of the mind a humane goal. The value of caring makes people look upon others as individuals, not as abstract ideals. Caring means kindness, pure and simple. It knows no boundaries or ideologies. There were countless acts of life-saving kindnesses in the camps. The height of caring behavior was found in those few thousand "dissidents" who rescued Jews during the Holocaust.

The Evils

After this catalog of the virtues, Todorov proceeds to analyze the evils that resulted in the camps and the deaths of millions. For him, most of the German Nazis and Russian communists were ordinary people; only a small proportion were pathologically abnormal. Ordinary people were turned into mass murderers by totalitarianism; mass murder was defined as good and authorized by the state. The "ordinary vices" include fragmentation (splitting) of the private bourgeois self and the murderous public self, indoctrination and "depersonalization" of both the perpetrator and the victim, the value of technical competence over moral competence, the lust for absolute power and certainty and, not least, indifference.

Some controversial aspects of Todorov's analysis include his equating the nature of the Nazi and the Soviet camps, his omission of the impact of the family as a force in the development of morality, his perhaps excessively optimistic view of human nature, and his bifurcation of humanity into masculine and feminine characteristics. Todorov ends his work with some important observations on how justice—as opposed to revenge—is possible after the fall of Nazi and Soviet totalitarianism. Todorov understands the desire for revenge as a response to extreme humiliation and suffering but prefers that justice recognize degrees of guilt, between perpetrators and bystanders, for example, and that there be a permanent world court of justice for crimes against humanity.

According to Todorov, there are some crucial lessons to be learned from the experience of the dark side of the twentieth century. The facts of the camps must be studied and remembered, but so should their larger implications. Knowledge must be accompanied by "telling, judging, and understanding." Todorov evaluates some important works in this area. He believes that Primo Levi's *Survival in Auschwitz* (1961) is balanced and rational, while *Shoah*, the 1985 film of Claude Lanzmann, is colored by anger. His favorite work is *Into That Darkness* (1974) by Gitta Sereny, a study of how Franz Stangl, the commandant of Treblinka and Sobibor, was able to oversee mass murder and to justify and rationalize his deeds, thereby adding still another evil to his career.

Facing the Extreme had a great impact on the field of moral philosophy. It was reviewed favorably and cited for its thesis that human beings are capable of moral behavior under the worst of conditions, presenting some reassurance and comfort in the knowledge that moral behavior can continue in the worst of circumstances. Todorov's positive models of morality during some of the darkest times in the twentieth century—the groups, individuals, and regions that saved Jewish lives during the Holocaust, the helping behavior of many women who exhibited true virtue, the individuals who committed numerous acts of kindness within the camps—provide some hope for humanity. In this way justice, the highest goal of politics, can be furthered most. Todorov demonstrated convincingly that morality must be bestowed on other individuals and must be practiced and nurtured as well as taught.

Leon Stein

Additional Reading

Culler, Jonathan. *Structuralist Poetics*. Ithaca, N.Y.: Cornell University Press, 1973. A balanced overview of structuralist criticism. Covers many of Tzvetan Todorov's important ideas in passing, including his contributions to the structuralist concepts of character, genre, narration, plot, and theme.

Gorman, David. "Tzvetan Todorov: An Anglo-French Checklist to 1995." *Style* 31, no. 4 (Winter, 1997): 702-729. A comprehensive listing of all of Todorov's French publications through 1995 and of all of the English translations of them. Includes Todorov's many important translations of works from Slavic languages into English.

Jefferson, Ann. "Structuralism and Post-Structuralism." In *Modern Literary Theory: A Comparative Introduction*, edited by Ann Jefferson and David Robey. 2d ed. London: B. T. Batsford, 1986. Discusses Todorov's work in the context of an overview of structuralism and narratology. Focuses on Todorov's readings of Boccaccio's *Decameron* (which she finds unsuccessful) and of the stories of Henry James (which she finds much more successful).

Marchitello, Howard, ed. *Tzvetan Todorov and the Writing of History*. *South Central Review* 15, no. 3–4 (1998): 1–104. Includes an important new essay by Todorov, "The Morality of the Historian," and five essays by literary critics who use that essay to respond to the "critical humanism" of Todorov's writings of the 1980's and 1990's. The most valuable treatment available of his recent work.

Merquior, J. G. *From Prague to Paris: A Critique of Structuralist and Post-Structuralist Thought*. London: Verso, 1986. Devotes a few pages to approval of Todorov's shift toward humanism and away from "structuralitis" in the 1980's.

Scholes, Robert. *Structuralism in Literature: An Introduction*. New Haven, Conn.: Yale University Press, 1974. Relies on Todorov's theory of reading as the model for showing how structuralism works when applied to specific texts. Also discusses his theory of genres and his analysis of Boccaccio's *Decameron*.

Scott Vaszily, updated by William Nelles

Leo Tolstoy

Tolstoy, an accomplished novelist for the first half of his life, achieved worldwide renown as a pacifist, social activist, and moral philosopher in his later years. He worked alongside the peasants and wrote numerous works critical of war, injustice, and the church.

Principal philosophical works: *Ispoved'*, 1884 (*A Confession*, 1885); *V chom moya vera*, 1884 (*What I Believe*, 1885); *O zhizni*, 1888 (*Life*, 1888); *Kritika dogmaticheskogo bogosloviya*, 1891 (*A Critique of Dogmatic Theology*, 1904); *Soedinenie i perevod chetyrekh evangeliy*, 1892-1894 (*The Four Gospels Harmonized and Translated*, 1895-1896); *Tsarstvo Bozhie vnutri vas*, 1893 (*The Kingdom of God Is Within You*, 1894); *Chto takoye iskusstvo?*, 1898 (*What Is Art?*, 1898); *Tak chto zhe nam delat?*, 1902 (*What to Do?*, 1887); *The Diaries of Leo Tolstoy, 1847-1852*, 1917; *The Journal of Leo Tolstoy, 1895-1899*, 1917; *Tolstoi's Love Letters*, 1923; *The Private Diary of Leo Tolstoy, 1853-1857*, 1927; *"What Is Art?" and Essays on Art*, 1929; *L. N. Tolstoy o literature: Stati, pisma, dnevniki*, 1955; *Lev Tolstoy ob iskusstve i literature*, 1958; *Leo Tolstoy: Last Diaries*, 1960.

Born: September 9, 1828; Yasnaya Polyana, Russia
Died: November 20, 1910; Astapovo, Russia

Early Life

Leo Tolstoy traced his aristocratic origins back to the founding of the Russian state in the ninth century. His ancestors, at times faithful servants, at times opponents of the Crown, amassed fame as well as respectable wealth over the centuries. Thus Tolstoy, though orphaned at age eight, grew up in comfort under the care of relatives at the various Tolstoy residences. He subsequently shaped a vague memory of his mother, who died when he was two, into an idealized portrait of the perfect woman and featured such a paragon in many of his major works. His first published narrative, *Detstvo* (1852; *Childhood*, 1862), re-creates a boy's tender relationship with and painful loss of his mother.

A flamboyant lifestyle, filled with carousing and gambling, prevented Tolstoy from completing university study, but he revealed an early talent for writing and meticulously recorded daily details, from purest thoughts to debauched acts, in his diaries. He continued keeping such journals until old age, providing future literary historians with rich source material for every stage of his life. His elder siblings and relations, dismayed at the young count's irresolution and wantonness, sent him in 1851 to the Caucasus, where Russia was engaged in sporadic military operations with hostile natives.

Tolstoy's subsequent participation in the Crimean War put an end to the unstable years of his youth. Active service during the siege of Sevastopol motivated him to set down his impressions of the carnage in a series of sketches, "Sevastopol' v dekabre," "Sevastopol' v maye," and "Sevastopol' v avguste" (1854-1856; collected in translation as *Sebastopol*, 1887). His original and above all truthful accounts pleased a public that had grown tired of the prevailing vainglorious, deceitful war reports. So convincingly did Tolstoy chronicle the horror of battlefield life and communicate his disillusionment with war that czarist censors moved to alter his exposés. Tolstoy's later devotion to nonviolence stems from these experiences. His perceptions about the ineptitude of military commanders juxtaposed to the courage and common sense of foot soldiers resurface in his major work, *Voyna i mir* (1865-1869; *War and Peace*, 1886). Moreover, his dispute with the authorities over his forthright reporting set the stage for a lifelong confrontation with the imperial autocracy.

Life's Work

Tolstoy's long literary career followed several distinct directions. The labors of his younger years belong to the field of aesthetic literature, though he embarked on that course only after lengthy deliberation. When he returned to St. Petersburg in 1855 following military service, high society lionized the young hero and for a time drew him back into the swirl of its carefree amusements. His strong didactic bent and quarrelsome nature did not, however, endear him to the literary establishment. He soon antagonized writers on all sides of the social and political spectrum and in the end thought it best to develop his talents without the help of contemporaries. The deaths of two brothers and an execution witnessed in Paris in 1857 led him to approach life in a more serious vein. He opened and directed a school for peasant children on his estate, using pedagogical methods that he himself established, and entered into lively journalistic polemics with other educators over his scheme of placing moral teachings above the acquisition of knowledge. These and other controversial public exchanges brought renewed government interference that impelled Tolstoy to turn to less antagonistic activity. In 1862, he married Sophia Behrs, sixteen years his junior, became a country gentleman, and settled down to a life of writing.

The 1860's were almost wholly devoted to the composition of the epic *War and Peace*, which went through so many revisions and changes of focus, even as it was being serialized, that no clearly definitive version of the novel exists. Among the diverse issues embedded in the finished product are Tolstoy's own interpretation of the Napoleonic Wars, a richly drawn panorama of early nineteenth century Russian upper-class society

supplemented by many biographical details, a firm conviction that the values of close-knit family life are far superior to social rituals, and a wealth of sundry philosophical observations. *War and Peace* owes its immense success to the author's vast descriptive talents, which manage to neutralize his lifelong tendency to sermonize.

Reflections on the importance of stable domestic existence also dominate Tolstoy's second major work, *Anna Karenina* (1875-1877; English translation, 1886), in which he chronicles the fates of three aristocratic families and demonstrates that the title figure's insistence on personal happiness to the detriment of family duty engenders tragedy for all concerned. The novel also develops Tolstoy's pet notion that Russian peasant mores are morally superior to high society's ideals. Ideas about the meaning of death and the validity of suicide also represent an important strain

Leo Tolstoy. *(Library of Congress)*

in *Anna Karenina*, reflecting Tolstoy's own frequent contact with death, as he lost several children and other close relatives in the 1870's during the composition of the novel. The themes of these two major works are echoed in the many shorter pieces produced by the prolific Tolstoy during the same period.

The late 1870's represent a watershed for Tolstoy, a time when a prolonged spiritual crisis forced him to evaluate both his privileged life and his literary endeavors. A drastic reorientation evolved from this period of introspection. No longer able to justify his considerable wealth in the face of millions of illiterate, destitute peasants and laborers, Tolstoy resolved to make amends by placing his talent and means at the disposal of the poor. In consequence, he actively challenged what he perceived to be the hypocrisy of Russia's ruling institutions. Because the Russian Orthodox Church worked closely with the conservative czarist government to maintain the status quo, it too became a target of Tolstoy's dissatisfactions. After publication of the strongly anticlerical *Voskreseniye* (1899; *Resurrection*, 1899), Tolstoy found himself excommunicated, an action he dismissed lightly, having over the years developed a personal Christianity that became the basis of much of his nonfictional writing. His spiritual anxieties and search for an acceptable faith are chronicled in *A Confession*.

Both Tolstoy's literary style and his subject matter underwent extreme changes during this time. The works became shorter, using more succinct and simpler language, and became decidedly more opinionated. Fiction largely gave way to social and philosophical commentary, and even the remaining fictional pieces were intricately shaped to transmit Tolstoy's moral messages. Thus, *Smert' Ivana Il'icha* (1886; *The Death of Ivan Ilyich*, 1887) presents Tolstoy's view of the proper attitude toward death and dying, and the play *Vlast' t'my* (1887; *The Power of Darkness*, 1888) warns of the grim consequences engendered by evil thoughts and deeds. Tolstoy justified the political nature of this type of fiction by challenging the very morality of aesthetic detachment. Because even his polemical commentaries adhered to respectable literary standards, he never lost his readership. On the contrary, people of all persuasions debated his works with interest, even fascination.

Tolstoy's efforts to use his name and fortune in support of favorite causes gave rise to severe disharmony within the Tolstoy family. For years, the spouses battled over property and copyright privileges. These quarrels led Tolstoy to replace his earlier emphasis on family unity with issues of personal salvation and questions of ethics. He returned to the theme of family in one of his most controversial narratives, *Kreytserova sonata* (1889; *The Kreutzer Sonata*, 1890). In this work, he denies that marriage is a valid social institution by defining its main purpose as the gratification of lust, detrimental to women and destructive of personal integrity. The major character, Pozdnyshev, murders his wife in a bout of jealousy and proposes the abolition of all sexual acts, even at the expense of humanity's extinction.

Not all of Tolstoy's later views express such absolute negatives, but most of his mature output was disputational in nature. For example, his treatise *What Is Art?* sets forth his revised opinion on the nature and role of literature. He dismisses most art, including his own earlier writings, as immoral and undemocratic, suggesting instead that all art forms be morally instructive and executed in simple, guileless fashion accessible to the multitudes.

Throughout his long life, Tolstoy continued to espouse peaceful settlement of international conflicts. In time, his advocacy of nonviolent resistance made him into a prominent spokesperson against war and the death penalty. His regard for the impoverished masses and his many controversial stands brought him worldwide fame. The image of the revered, bearded, aged "repentant nobleman," holding court and expounding his position on national and global topics while dressed in homemade rural attire, drew diverse crowds from far and wide. His very renown prevented an angry czarist government from treating him harshly. To prevent the total dissolution of his domestic bonds, Tolstoy permitted the family to remain at the imposing country estate, but he himself withdrew to a humble corner of it to observe a rigorously modest lifestyle. At the age of eighty-two, he decided to cut even these ties and secretly left home to live henceforth entirely according to his convictions. Illness almost immediately forced him to abandon the train journey, and he died at the station master's house a week later, surrounded by dignitaries and reporters. He lies buried in a distant corner of his estate. His simple, unadorned grave and the mansion, converted into a Tolstoy museum after the Russian Revolution, are a favorite stop for countless visitors and tourists.

Influence

Tolstoy's impact as both artist and moralist continues undiminished. His fictional works, especially his earlier ones, retain a charm that is proof of his enormous descriptive powers. Yet even these works express personal preferences and values, which the author elucidates at every opportunity. Thus, it is, in the final analysis, Tolstoy the teacher, moralist, and public commentator who dominates. Through his doctrine of nonviolent resistance, which he based on the words of Jesus and through which he resisted many inequities of the state, he set examples for similar movements in India under Mohandas K. Gandhi and the United States under Martin Luther King, Jr. Although his pronouncements on behalf of the poor often assume an overly shrill tone, he backed these convictions with solid action. Not only did his income and efforts facilitate great humanitarian projects, from famine relief to resettlement of religious dissenters, but also he himself found no peace until he had adjusted his lifestyle to fit the humblest. His deliberations on death and ideas on how to cope with it cut through the stilted social conventions of his time to find universal appreciation and application in the twentieth century.

Closely linked to Tolstoy's thoughts about death and dying was his quest for a new religious attitude. By examining the doctrines and practices of the Russian Orthodox Church as well as other religions and finding them incompatible with Jesus' words, he pointed to alternative approaches, advocating a way of life based on the Gospels, not church dogma. In this, too, he anticipated certain twentieth century movements toward a personal fundamentalism.

Tolstoy also generated opposition. His dogmatic and frequently cantankerous method of conveying his beliefs alienated many potential adherents. In the manner of all prophets, he brooked no contradiction of his scheme of universal ethical improvement. Even so, his many achievements and contributions as major writer, social activist, and moral philosopher remain universally acknowledged.

Margot K. Frank

What Is Art?

Type of philosophy: Aesthetics, ethics
First published: Chto takoye iskusstvo?, 1898 (English translation, 1898)
Principal ideas advanced:
◇ Art is the intentional communication of feelings.
◇ Artists use colors, sounds, words, or other materials to create objects that will provoke in spectators the feeling the artists themselves had and which they intend to pass on to others.
◇ True art is not only sincere but infectious; the more widespread the appeal and effectiveness of the work as a means for the communication of feeling, the better the work is as art.
◇ The highest art is that which communicates the feeling of brotherhood and sisterhood and love for one's neighbor.

Leo Tolstoy, like the Greek philosopher Plato, believed art too important to be judged in terms of art alone. Because art is capable of making people better or worse, the social and ethical consequences of art must be considered in judgments about art. Tolstoy denied that a work of art can be great but corrupting, artistically good but morally evil.

A Definition

Tolstoy published *What Is Art?* when he was sixty-eight, nearly thirty years after the publication of his masterpiece *Voyna i mir* (1865-1869; *War and Peace*, 1886). The answer Tolstoy found to the question "What is art?" is very simple. Art is the intentional communication of feelings. According to Tolstoy, the creation of a work of art proceeds along the following lines. First, artists have an experience or feeling, such as fear, joy, grief, anger, hope. They then desire to share this feeling with others, to infect them with it, to make them fearful, joyous, grief-stricken, angry, or hopeful. In order to communicate their feelings to others, they create a work of art, a story, a song, a poem, a play, a painting. If they are successful, if they have created a genuine work of art, their creations will restore their original feeling, and more important, these works will give others the same kind of feeling. Art is essentially a means of communication; it is the most direct and immediate form of communication because the very feelings that led artists to create their works of art are experienced by their audience. Artists do not merely describe their feeling of joy or grief, nor do they merely reveal or show their feeling of anger or fear; the artists share their feelings with others by creating something that makes them feel joy, grief, anger, or fear.

It is not very surprising that Tolstoy rejected as pseudoart much of what is usually accepted as art. Art must originate with an experience or feeling of the artist. Much pseudoart comes from insincerity, or the attempt to create a work of art that does not grow from an actual experience or feeling. The aspiring artist, lacking any feeling that could be conveyed by a genuine work of art, tries to imitate the accepted artists. In an effort to achieve recognition, the artist who has nothing to communicate tries to give the public what they want by copying the popular fashions or by following the formulas learned in school. Tolstoy denies that anything created in answer to an external inducement rather than to an inner need can be genuine art.

Nevertheless, sincerity, however necessary, is not sufficient. Even if aspiring artists are sincere, they may fail in their efforts to create a work of art. The attempt to communicate the genuine feeling may be ineffective. Artists are judged not by their feelings but by their creations. Good intentions are not enough. In addition to feeling, a work of art requires adequate form. However, Tolstoy recognizes only one measure of adequate form, infectiousness. A work of art must infect the audience; it must compel the audience to feel what the artist felt. Adequate form requires individuality rather than imitative repetitiousness, brevity rather than bulkiness, clarity rather than obscurity, simplicity of expression rather than complexity of form. The adequate form of a genuine work of art is shown by the universality of its appeal. A genuine work of art does not need an interpreter. A genuine work of art is not restricted to the elite, to the happy few. A genuine work of art directly and immediately creates in others the feelings of the artist.

Art and Morality

Art, then, demands the adequate expression of genuine feeling. However, Tolstoy adds yet a third requirement, not a requirement that determines whether something is art, but a requirement that determines whether something is good art—morally good, worthy of support and encouragement. Tolstoy recognizes that art can be morally corrupting, that art which is good art judged by the sincerity of the artist's feeling and the successful communication of this feeling might still be undesirable. The feeling communicated is also important. If the feeling or the experience that the artist is communicating is evil or perverse or trivial or silly, it is possible for the work of art to be artistically good but morally bad. Tolstoy says that art demands sacrifices not only from the artist but also from others. Artists are members of society; their efforts must be supported in many ways by others. The question of what kind of art is worth the sacrifice demanded is a moral question; Tolstoy's answer to this question is clearly a moral answer. The feelings communicated by a work of art are not relevant when we are trying to decide whether it is a work of art, but they are relevant when we are trying to decide whether it is good, whether it is worthy of support and encouragement.

Tolstoy rejected orthodox Christianity; he was excommunicated by the Synod of the Russian Church in 1901 and after his death in 1910 was interred without Christian burial. Tolstoy attacked Church Christianity as a corruption of the original teachings of Jesus. The brotherhood of man, the golden rule, the turning of the other cheek, love for all people (including those who hate you) are the essential teachings Tolstoy sees in the New Testament but not in the Church. There is a very close connection between Tolstoy's views on art and on religion. Art is the handmaiden of religion. The feelings communicated by artists to others by their works of art will in the case of the best art be feelings that unite people, that increase their love for one another. The final judgment on a work of art must be a moral judgment as well as an aesthetic judgment. Tolstoy writes, "The estimation of the value of art (or rather, of the feelings it transmits) depends on men's perception of the meaning of life; depends on what they hold to be the good and evil of life."

True Art

The connection between art and religion, the service art is expected to give religion, and the consequences for art of Tolstoy's perception of the meaning of life are clearly stated in the closing paragraphs of *What Is Art?*

> The task for art to accomplish is to make that feeling of brotherhood and love of one's neighbor, now attained only by the best members of society, the customary feeling and instinct of all men. By evoking under imaginary conditions the feeling of brotherhood and love, religious art will train men to experience those same feelings under similar circumstances in actual life; it will lay in the souls of men the rails along which the actions of those whom art thus educates will naturally pass. And universal art, by uniting the most different people in one common feeling by destroying separation, will educate people to union and will show them, not by reason but by life itself, the joy of universal union reaching beyond the bounds set by life.

Tolstoy saw in the art of the Middle Ages an example of true art. In that period, religion provided a basis common to the artists and the mass of the people, so that the feelings experienced by the artist could be communicated to the mass of the people. This true art, shared by the whole community, ended when the people who rewarded and directed art lost their religious belief. The universality of the art of the Middle Ages was followed by a split between the art of the upper classes and the masses of the people. The development of an exclusive art, incomprehensible to most people, seriously weakened and almost destroyed art itself. The subject matter of art became impoverished; the only feelings acceptable for communication were pride, discontent, and sexual desire. The artist became a professional, living by his or her art, creating counter-

feits of art rather than genuine works of art. Critics, perverted but self-confident, took away from plain people the valuation of art.

Genuine art, Tolstoy argues, needs no critics. If the work succeeds in transmitting the feeling of the artist, there is nothing for the critic to do. If the work fails to transmit the feeling of the artist, there is nothing the critic can do. The final perverted and perverting consequence Tolstoy ascribes to the reduction of art to an amusement for the upper classes is the establishment of art schools. Tolstoy, a teacher as well as an artist, denies that a school can evoke feeling in a person or teach someone to manifest feeling in a way that will transmit this feeling to others. Art schools destroy the capacity to produce real art in those who have the misfortune to enter them; they do nothing more than train imitators of artists, professionals who produce on demand the counterfeits of art that amuse the perverted upper classes, provide the critics with an excuse for their activity, and debase the taste of the masses.

"Bad" Art

If there is any danger that admiration for the artistic achievements of the author of *War and Peace* will lead to uncritical acceptance of Tolstoy's theories about the nature and purpose of art, it is more than balanced by the danger that contempt for Tolstoy's critical judgments will lead to uncritical rejection of these theories. Criticism of Tolstoy's point of view as perverse and even stupid may be caused by Tolstoy's remarks on particular works of art rather than by his theories as to the nature and purpose of art. *War and Peace*, and in fact all his own work except the stories "Bog pravdu vidit, da ne skoro skazhet" (1872; "God Sees the Truth but Waits," 1906) and "Kavkazskii plennik" (1872; "A Prisoner of the Caucasus," 1887), fall, in Tolstoy's eyes, into the category of bad art. Examples of good art include the Psalms, the writings of the Jewish prophets, Homer's *Iliad* (c. 800 B.C.E.; English translation, 1616) and *Odyssey* (c. 800 B.C.E.; English translation, 1616), Miguel de Cervantes's *El ingenioso hidalgo don Quixote de la Mancha* (1605, 1615; *The History of the Valorous and Wittie Knight-Errant, Don Quixote of the Mancha*, 1612-1620; better known as *Don Quixote de la Mancha*), Charles Dickens's *Pickwick Papers* (1836-1837) and *A*

Christmas Carol (1843), Harriet Beecher Stowe's *Uncle Tom's Cabin: Or, Life Among the Lowly* (1852), and Millet's drawing *The Man with the Hoe*.

Tolstoy praises as true art Alexander Pushkin's short stories and poems but calls his *Boris Godunov* (wr. 1824-1825, pb. 1831; English translation, 1918) "a cold, brain-spun work" produced under the influence of false criticism. Sophocles, Euripides, Aeschylus, Aristophanes, Dante Alighieri, John Milton, William Shakespeare, Johann Wolfgang von Goethe, Raphael, Michelangelo, Johann Sebastian Bach, Ludwig van Beethoven, Richard Wagner—these are among the artists judged and found wanting by Tolstoy. Michelangelo's *Last Judgment* is called absurd; Beethoven's Piano Sonata in A major, Opus 101 (Hammerclavier) is bad art because it "artificially evoked obscure, almost unhealthy, excitement"; Beethoven's Ninth Symphony is bad art because it neither transmits the highest religious feeling nor unites all people in one common feeling; from Shakespeare's *Hamlet, Prince of Denmark* (pr. c. 1600-1601) Tolstoy received "that peculiar suffering which is caused by false imitations of works of art." Charles Baudelaire is criticized on two counts: the feelings transmitted are "evil and very base" and these feelings are expressed with "eccentricity and lack of clearness," in fact with "premeditated obscurity." Baudelaire is judged lacking in "naïveté, sincerity, and simplicity," but overflowing with "artificiality, forced originality, and self-assurance."

Tolstoy directs his most detailed and extensive criticism in *What Is Art?* against Wagner's operas. He describes a performance of *Siegfried*. Tolstoy calls this a "model work of counterfeit art so gross as to be even ridiculous." He was unable to sit through the entire performance and "escaped from the theatre with a feeling of repulsion." Tolstoy sees in *Siegfried* almost everything he detests in pseudoart. It would be incomprehensible to a peasant with unperverted taste; it is accepted because fashionable by the "cream of the cultured upper classes"; it requires a great deal of wasted labor; it provides the art critics with an excuse for their activity; and it perverts and destroys the capacity to be infected by genuine art.

It would be a mistake to judge Tolstoy's view on art by the examples he chooses. Tolstoy himself says that he does not attach great importance to his selection because he believes he is among those whose taste has been perverted by false training. Because the examples appear to be chosen to illustrate or explain Tolstoy's theory, they are less important than the theory itself.

Others have agreed that art is the language of emotions, that art expresses or communicates feelings. However, the distinctive feature of Tolstoy's theory is his claim that the actual experience is communicated by art. We do not merely recognize that the poem is an expression of grief; we do not merely recognize that the author was moved by an authentic feeling of grief. If the poem is a genuine work of art, we grieve. The connection between art and life cannot be made closer. Tolstoy, like Plato, denies the autonomy of art, the uniqueness of aesthetic experience.

John Linnell

Additional Reading

Bayley, John. *Leo Tolstoy*. Plymouth, United Kingdom: Northcote House, 1997. Criticism and interpretation of Tolstoy's work.

Benson, Ruth Crego. *Women in Tolstoy: The Ideal and the Erotic*. Urbana: University of Illinois Press, 1973. Concentrates on Leo Tolstoy's changing vision of the role and importance of family life. Suggests that Tolstoy struggled most of his life with a dichotomous view of women, regarding them in strictly black-and-white terms, as saints or sinners. Analyzes the female characters in the major and several minor works in terms of such a double view. An interesting and provocative piece of feminist criticism.

Bloom, Harold, ed. *Leo Tolstoy*. New York: Chelsea House, 1986. A collection of critical essays, encompassing the years 1920-1983. The views expressed give a very good sampling of the wide range of opinions about Tolstoy prevalent among Western critics. Many of these critics assign a prominent place in literary history to Tolstoy, comparing him to, among others, Homer and Johann Wolfgang von Goethe. Some of the articles deal with specific works; others define Tolstoy's contributions to nineteenth century European intellectual movements. Limited bibliography.

De Courcel, Martine. *Tolstoy: The Ultimate Reconciliation*. Translated by Peter Levi. New York: Charles Scribner's Sons, 1987. A detailed biography, annotated with selected bibliography, which relies heavily on the notebooks and diaries of Tolstoy and those of his wife, Sophia. Concentrates on Tolstoy's domestic life but has extensive references to his general public activity. Posits the unique notion that Tolstoy left home at the end of his life in order to return to aesthetic literature.

Orwin, Donna Tussing. *Tolstoy's Art and Thought, 1847-1880*. Princeton, N.J.: Princeton University Press, 1993. Reconstructs the personal, philosophical, and historical contexts of the first three decades of Tolstoy's creative life.

Pinch, Alan, and Michael Armstrong, eds. *Tolstoy on Education: Tolstoy's Educational Writings, 1861-62*. Rutherford, N.J.: Fairleigh Dickinson University Press, 1982. Pinch provides an introductory essay on the historical context of Tolstoy's writings on education, and Armstrong contributes a long essay outlining Tolstoy's theories on education and mental development.

Rowe, William W. *Leo Tolstoy*. Boston: Twayne, 1986. Concise introduction to Tolstoy's life and work, with special emphasis on the major novels and later didactic writings. Discusses, briefly, most of Tolstoy's major concerns. Excellent treatment of individual characters in the major novels. Selected bibliography.

Tolstaia, Sophia Andreevna. *The Diaries of Sophia Tolstoy*. Edited by O. A. Golinenko et al. Translated by Cathy Porter with an introduction by R. F. Christian. New York: Random House, 1985. Illustrated. This massive personal record of Tolstoy's wife, detailing their life together, spans the years 1862-1910. Sophia Tolstoy kept an almost daily account of her husband's opinions, doubts, and plans concerning his literary activity and social ventures as well as of his relationship with other writers and thinkers. The diaries often portray Tolstoy in an unfavorable light because the couple were temperamentally incompatible, and she chafed under his domination. She collaborated closely with Tolstoy for many decades, however, and her notes give a fascinating and intimate view of the Tolstoy family and of the extent to which this family served as background for many of the literary episodes.

Wilson, A. N. *Tolstoy*. New York: W. W. Norton, 1988. A long but immensely readable biography, breezy, insightful, and opinionated, by a prolific and highly regarded British novelist. Illustrated; includes a useful chronology of Tolstoy's life and times as well as notes, bibliography, and index.

Margot K. Frank, updated by William Nelles

Stephen Toulmin

A philosopher of remarkable breadth and interests, Toulmin believed that the idea of rationality has been too closely tied to issues of formal logic and therefore analyzed rationality afresh in numerous fields of theory and practice.

Principal philosophical works: *An Examination of the Place of Reason in Ethics*, 1950; *The Philosophy of Science: An Introduction*, 1953; *The Uses of Argument*, 1958; *Philosophy of Science: An Introduction*, 1953; *The Fabric of the Heavens*, 1961 (with June Goodfield); *Foresight and Understanding: An Enquiry into the Aims of Science*, 1961; *The Architecture of Matter*, 1962 (with June Goodfield); *Human Understanding*, 1972; *The Discovery of Time*, 1965 (with June Goodfield); *Wittgenstein's Vienna*, 1972 (with Allan Janik); *Knowing and Acting: An Invitation to Philosophy*, 1976; *The Return to Cosmology: Postmodern Science and the Theology of Nature*, 1982; *The Inner Life, the Outer Mind*, 1985; *The Place of Reason in Ethics*, 1986; *Cosmopolis: The Hidden Agenda of Modernity*, 1990.

Born: March 25, 1922; London, England

Early Life

Professionally, Stephen Edelston Toulmin began in physics at Cambridge University, working on radar from 1942 to 1945. He read philosophy in the last years of philosopher Ludwig Wittgenstein's tenure at Cambridge. For his doctoral degree, Toulmin wrote a dissertation that became a book, *An Examination of the Place of Reason in Ethics*. Although Wittgenstein was not Toulmin's dissertation adviser, he was Toulmin's intellectual mentor.

When Toulmin and Wittgenstein were interacting intellectually, Wittgenstein was in his famous "later period," in which he treated meaning and language as dependent on contextual factors rather than on objective pictorial representations, as he had in his early work "Logisch-philosophische Abhandlung" (1921; best known in its bilingual German and English edition, *Tractatus Logico-Philosophicus*, 1922, 1961). Wittgenstein was examining the relationship between forms of life and language games of distinctive communities and the enculturation of a particular mode of life within a language. However, Wittgenstein also held that ethics lay beyond the treatment of any "linguistic" or rational analysis or interpretation.

Toulmin both followed and diverged from Wittgenstein's position. Toulmin's doctoral dissertation advanced a Wittgensteinian analysis of ethical argumentation, arguing that "good" and "bad" reasoning (if not actually formal induction and deduction) are embedded in ethics as much as in science or law or any other realm of human activity.

Toulmin then moved to Oxford University as university lecturer in the philosophy of science, and he wrote in that field until 1960. Toulmin used the skeptical pragmaticism of Wittgenstein's later philosophy to challenge the reliance on formal logic so prevalent in the philosophy of science practiced in Vienna and in the United States. Toulmin generalized this challenge in *The Uses of Argument*, in which he emphasized the "field dependence" of reasoning and the need to view arguments of all kinds—whether in science, ethics, law, politics, or medicine—as arising out of the varied practical activities of these different enterprises.

Life's Work

While at Oxford, Toulmin published a much-admired, much-anthologized article entitled "Do Submicroscopic Entities Exist?" in the journal *Philosophy of Science*. A scientific realist holds that unobservable entities, such as electrons, exist in the way the chemical or physical theory claims they exist. Toulmin, taking an antirealist position, began by analyzing several different senses of the word "exist" and argued that while some submicroscopic entity may exist, it does not need to exist in the way the theory says it exists.

To prove his point, he created an analogy using the contour lines on a topographical map. For example, he said, although these lines represent the different elevations of a hill, we would not expect to see the lines on the actual hill. In any case, Toulmin argued, scientists need not and do not worry over these types of ontological problems, for scientific theories proceed very well even if these questions of existence are unresolved. For example, in 1905, Albert Einstein showed that the phenomenon of Brownian motion supported the idea that atoms and molecules really exist. However, by 1905 physicists were already showing, through the development of quantum theory by Niels Bohr, that the atomic theory was not the last word in physics, and some of the foundations of this very theory of atoms were being severely attacked. Paradoxically, then, one finds that the theory of atoms was being supported by Einstein's argument concerning Brownian motion at the same time quantum physicists were regarding the atom as hardly more than a useful fiction.

After his *Philosophy of Science: An Introduction*, Toulmin wrote *The Uses of Argument*, in which he applied Wittgenstein's "linguistic" approach to logic and epistemology. As a model of human understanding, Toulmin proffered "the common law," or the jurisprudence model, in which reasoning and argumentation are founded on empirical evidence and precedents. Although neither strictly deductive nor inductive, legal reasoning and courtroom argumentation proceed from "facts" and "principles" in order to present and gain acceptance of *the best possible argument*. For Toulmin, all human understanding should be viewed in this way, that is, using the best possible reasoning at a given time, often with truth (as opposed to justice) as its ultimate goal.

From the late 1950's to the mid-1970's, Toulmin's works explored the practical contexts of reasoning, relating issues of epistemology—even issues in natural science—to the historical evolution of concepts and practices as found in the work of the Oxford philosopher and historian R. G. Collingwood.

Toulmin greatly admired Collingwood, whom he described as a talented philosopher and a first-class writer of history. It was Collingwood who impressed on Toulmin the fundamental historicity of human thought as well as the basic danger of historical analysis. Collingwood argued that historically conceptual presuppositions underlie all instances of human understanding. However, Toulmin saw the dangers of historical analysis in Collingwood's own work, specifically the development of an unwarranted epistemological relativism that can emerge from such historical treatments. Nevertheless, Toulmin is indebted to

Stephen Toulmin. *(Irene Fertik)*

Collingwood for initiating his own strategic task: the quest for an historical view of human understanding that allows for conceptual change and that does not at the same time allow for intellectual anarchism (relativism). Toulmin fundamentally saw Collingwood's vision of philosophy as a study of the methods of argument that at any historical moment served as the ultimate "court of appeal" in the various intellectual disciplines.

After spending a year (1954 to 1955) in Australia, Toulmin visited the United States and moved there in 1965. At Brandeis University, he wrote *Wittgenstein's Vienna* with Allan Janik, in which they presented a radical thesis to the effect that Wittgenstein's early work, *Tractatus Logico-Philosophicus*, is not so much a treatise on language and ontology as it is a treatise on ethics. Also in 1972, Toulmin wrote *Human Understanding*, a treatise on conceptual change in natural science.

Human Understanding is characterized by Toulmin's moving into the borderland between epistemology and the sociology of knowledge by way of the history of science. Toulmin analyzed the historical development of the procedures and concepts that guide human understanding, particularly (but not exclusively) in the sciences. Influenced again by the later-period Wittgenstein, Toulmin focused on the actual *use* of concepts. However, this analysis was joined to an explicitly Darwinian analysis of the evolution of concepts. Toulmin used the term "intellectual ecology" to characterize his approach. He argued that in any given population of concepts (say, in chemistry or physics), certain concepts are better adapted to current demands or pressures or forces in the intellectual and social environment. These concepts will be used more often and thus perpetuate themselves. However, as the demands or population pressures of concepts in a given area change, the survival value of these concepts may decrease and that of others may increase. This transformation is *conceptual evolution* and is guided by "rationality," defined as the adaptation of the procedures and patterns of argument to the demands of the changing problem. Toulmin also extended his treatment of conceptual "growth" to include analyses of concept acquisition and judgments of value. Overall, *Human Understanding* is a major treatment of the subject that has formed the basis of evolutionary epistemology and is a major contribution to the nature of human understanding.

Beginning in 1973, Toulmin concentrated on the study of practical reasoning—for example, by relating clinical medicine and other activities to Aristotle's discussion of *phronesis* in book 6 of *Ethica Nicomachea* (second Athenian period, 335-323 B.C.E.; *Nicomachean Ethics*, 1797). For fifteen years, Toulmin worked on problems in clinical medical ethics, first in human experimentation and later in hospital work, at the University of Chicago Medical School. At the same time, Toulmin's position on the Committee on Social Thought at the University of Chicago led him to focus on the development of the humanities, as exemplified, above all, in the sixteenth century tradition from Desiderius Erasmus and Martin Luther to Michel Eyquem de Montaigne and William Shakespeare.

At this stage of his work, Toulmin contrasted the concrete particularity of the sixteenth century humanists and the abstract generality aimed at in natural philosophy, from the time of the scientist Galileo and French philosopher René Descartes. This work resulted in his reanalysis of modernity in *Cosmopolis: The Hidden Agenda of Modernity*. In this work, Toulmin interprets the rise of the exact sciences as one response to the political, social, and spiritual crisis of early modern Europe, as displayed in the theologically rationalized brutalities of the Thirty Years' War. Toulmin argues that the Westphalian settlement in Europe after 1648 was built on static ideals of order in nature and society and nourished by Newton's physical worldview. Only at the end of the twentieth century was this alliance of science and politics directly challenged, with chaos and complexity theory in the natural sciences and with the critique of the sovereign nation-state as the natural unit of political order.

After his formal retirement in 1992, Toulmin began to work at the University of Southern California, Los Angeles, in multiethnic and transnational studies and to make regular visits to Europe, notably Sweden, Austria, and Holland. His focus became the evolving institutions of science, politics, and "civil society"—often nongovernmental or supranational institutions of science—and the loss of centrality for nation-state governments.

Across a spectrum from theory to practice, Toulmin argued that the effective loci of action reside in dispersed "functional networks" rather than localized "point sources" of power. He argued that the basic concepts can be found less in the axiom system of a physical theory (as in the 1650's) than in the ecological categories of biological science. In clinical medicine, technology, and practical politics equally, Toulmin wanted to show that our fundamental ideas of logical structure and national sovereignty are often more misleading than trustworthy for the purpose of practical decision and argument. For Toulmin, nothing is entirely stable and immutable, yet nothing is in total flux either.

Toulmin was the 1997 Thomas Jefferson Lecturer of the National Endowment for the Humanities. In his lecture, he discussed the value of *dissent* in philosophy, politics, and religion. He focused on the theologian, chemist, and philosopher Joseph Priestly, who corresponded with Jefferson long before emigrating to the United States in 1794. Toulmin argues that dissenters form their own opinions by their own judgments and are ready for honest debate. By contrast, dogmatists condemn dissenters as *dissidents* and dismiss them as troublemakers. Toulmin concludes that dogmatism is an enemy of freedom in science, politics, and religion. Toulmin also argues that, rather than denounce people whose ideas we do not share, we need to listen to what they say and see what is at stake for these people in those ideas. The alternative is the philosophical distrust of language that Socrates knew as *misology*. Toulmin concedes that during a time of bitterly contested ideas, tolerance may not be an easy lesson to learn.

At the end of the twentieth century, Toulmin's philosophical work focused mainly on the methods of the human sciences, with particular attention to the practical uses of economics. Indeed, in a lecture entitled "The Humanity of the Human Sciences," which Toulmin delivered in 1998 to the symposium Science and Culture, sponsored by the Student Philosophy Association at California State University, Long Beach, Toulmin noted that one of the curious things about the history of the human sciences is that psychology, sociology, and economics modeled themselves for so long on physics rather than biology. Physics, it is claimed,

is a "hard" science, full of mathematical and logical rigor, strictly "factual" and free from "values." However, Toulmin also notes that the activities of human beings are much more like those of animals than like the movements of physical objects, such as the planets going around the sun.

Toulmin asked what was the source of "physics envy" in the human sciences. On examining the "theory" model on which the human sciences are fashioned, Toulmin found that the model does not fit the actual work of physics itself. Instead, Toulmin argued, it is preferable to think of the human sciences as concerned, exactly, with the *values* of human life, that is, with how things go well or badly in human affairs, in one way or another. As a result, Toulmin argues that development economics stays closer to the historical, social, and/or cultural facts of human life than do formal analyses of general theory. Development economics also stays closer to concrete particular practice rather than abstract general theory.

At the end of the century, Toulmin also became interested in demonstrating the "clinical" character of the human sciences (ethics included) and accounting for the relation between theory and practice in terms of a contrast between the concepts of rationality and reasonableness.

Influence
Toulmin blended a background of physics and philosophy in his diverse writings. A common thread uniting many of his works is his challenge of the reliance on formal logic in the philosophy of science. His work in evolutionary epistemology contributed largely to human understanding of the processes involved in the quest for knowledge. His writings on argumentation and the human sciences acted as the source for much further discussion and debate on these issues.

Paul C. L. Tang

An Examination of the Place of Reason in Ethics

Type of philosophy: Ethics
First published: 1950

Principal ideas advanced:
◊ Traditional approaches to problems of ethics—the objective, regarding goodness as a property; the subjective, relating goodness to a person's feelings or attitudes; and the imperative, focusing on the persuasive functions of language—are false and misleading.
◊ A study of the logic of moral reasoning shows that what is central in ethics are good reasons for action.
◊ A good reason is one that refers to the moral code of the community or to a principle that harmonizes interests and minimizes avoidable suffering.

The central problem of ethics, according to Stephen Toulmin, is that of finding a way to distinguish good moral arguments from weak ones, good reasons from poor ones, and deciding whether there comes a point in the course of moral argument when the giving of reasons becomes superfluous. The inquiry he undertakes in *An Examination of the Place of Reason in Ethics* centers on the question of what makes a particular set of facts that bear on a moral decision a "good reason" for acting in a particular way. The author contends that he has no interest in a circular argument to the effect that a "good reason" is one that supports the kind of act he would regard as a "good act"; his task is to clarify the nature of moral reasoning and the kind of logic that goes into it.

Toulmin's conclusion is that moral reasoning is a kind of inductive reasoning: One examines how various courses of action have worked out and determines to what degree those courses of action have reduced conflicts of interest and to what degree and in what respects certain ways of life lead to satisfaction and fulfillment and minimize or eliminate misery and frustration—and then one appeals to the results of empirical inquiry as providing good reasons for adopting certain principles (or following established ones) and for pursuing certain ways of life.

The discussion of the problem is divided into four major areas of inquiry: "The Traditional Approaches," "Logic and Life," "The Nature of Ethics," and "The Boundaries of Reason." The author begins with a discussion of the traditional approaches to ethics because the tradition has

had a considerable influence, and there is the possibility that some traditional theories have something helpful to say about moral reasoning.

Traditional Approaches to Ethics

The traditional approaches, despite differences in details, fall into three classes, according to Toulmin: The "objective" approach regards such terms as "good" and "right" as attributing some property to whatever is so designated; the "subjective" approach regards such words as reports of feelings; and the "imperative" approach claims that value terms are without meaningful content ("pseudo-concepts") but are used as persuasive devices.

The critique of the objective approach begins with a classification of properties (characteristics). Toulmin uses the term "simple qualities" to refer to such properties as redness, blueness, softness, hardness—properties perceived by the senses, characteristics we become aware of through seeing, smelling, hearing, touching, and tasting. "Complex qualities," such as that of a polygon's having 259 sides, are recognized only by undertaking a complex procedure of sense observation involving the use of criteria of identification. Finally, "scientific qualities" are those that cannot be directly perceived through the use of the senses but involve, in addition to sense observation, reference to scientific theory. Because philosophers generally have tended to regard goodness, if it is a property, as either a simple or a complex quality, Toulmin confines his attention to those two possibilities.

Terms used to refer to simple properties are taught ostensively, Toulmin argues; one uses the term while giving examples or by pointing to things having the qualities. However, he argues, one certainly cannot teach the use of the term "good" in this way; hence, it is unlikely that goodness is a simple property. When two persons disagree in their descriptions of simple qualities they both clearly indicate, their difference is a linguistic one: They talk about the same simple quality but use different words in doing so. However, those who use value terms, when it is clear they are talking about the same thing, do not regard a difference in the application of value terms as merely a linguistic difference. Again, it is unlikely that goodness is a simple quality.

Nor is goodness a complex quality, Toulmin argues. Ethical disagreements cannot be settled by agreeing on procedures of observation and translation rules. Hence, goodness is not a directly perceived quality at all. (Also, Toulmin argues, it does not help matters to insist that goodness is a "nonnatural" quality; such an expression is either meaningless or contradictory—like "nontauroid bull.")

The objective approach fails because it cannot provide a method for agreeing on the identification of values as properties. Toulmin suggests that the objective view appealed to many thinkers because they suppose that "It is red" and "It is good" are alike in attributing properties to things and that when people disagree about values, they are disagreeing about properties. However, Toulmin accounts for disagreements about values—about the rightness of an act, say—by pointing to differences in the reasons given for doing or not doing the act or differences of opinion as to whether the reasons are good reasons. Accordingly, Toulmin rejects the objective approach as not only unhelpful but also "a positive hindrance" to anyone interested in understanding moral reasoning.

The subjective approach is also unsatisfactory, Toulmin argues. In contending that what is fundamental in moral disagreement, once there is agreement as to the relevant facts, is a difference in feeling or attitude, the subjectivist denies that moral reasoning can finally have criteria of validity other than by appeals to attitudes. It is not enough to know, Toulmin insists, what one's attitudes are toward various matters; one wants to know what they *ought* to be; and of the reasons that are given in support of moral judgments, one wants to know which are *good* reasons (not simply which of the reasons happens to appeal to one at the time).

Toulmin's conclusion is that such terms as "good" and "right" refer neither to objective properties nor to subjective relations; he contends that it is a mistake to ask, "Are values objective or subjective?" as if they had to be one or the other. The key terms of moral reasoning are to be understood by realizing what constitutes moral reasoning.

The last of the traditional approaches is the "imperative" approach, the defense of the doctrine that moral judgments are fundamentally commands. The imperative theory, holding as it does that moral judgments are calls for agreement in feeling or attitude, does not allow for reasons; it finds no place for reason in ethics and consequently cannot account for the kind of dialogue that ensues when there are ethical disagreements. Like the objectivists and the subjectivists, the imperativist appears to be led into fallacy by the idea that if ethical judgments are to be true, they must be "about" some feature of the object or subject; hence, those who hold the imperative view argue that because there is no identifiable feature of object or subject with which moral terms are concerned, no moral judgment is true. The result, writes Toulmin, is a kind of pessimism.

The bright side of Toulmin's criticism of traditional views is that he recognizes an important emphasis in each of the three kinds of theories rejected: The objectivist theory emphasizes the need in moral argument for good reasons; the subjectivist emphasizes the importance of the feelings of approval and obligation; and the imperative approach calls attention to the rhetorical force of moral judgments.

Reasoning

In part 2, entitled "Logic and Life," Toulmin examines reasoning and its uses, experience and explanation, and reasoning and reality. He argues at the outset of his extensive discussion that the logic of utterances is inseparable from the point of the activity in which the utterances are used. He warns against supposing that there is but one kind of activity called "reasoning"; there are many ways of using language other than the descriptive use, and if close attention is paid to the variety of uses to which language is put (like a set of tools, to use philosopher Ludwig Wittgenstein's image, which Toulmin mentions), it becomes credible that the kind of reasoning involved in a purposive activity may involve for its expression a number of uses of language. This point is in line with Toulmin's insistence on looking afresh at ethical reasoning to discover what is happening there—a great deal more than simply describing objects and expressing feelings.

Toulmin offers an analysis of scientific reasoning to make the point that what serve as "good reasons" in science—namely, "those which are predictively reliable, coherent and convenient"—are bound up with the purposes of science. There is, thus, a relativity of reasons and of the value of reasons to the purpose of the activity in which the reasons play a part. For the same reason, as he argues in "Reasoning and Reality," it is nonsense to ask what is "really real"; scientific "reality" and artistic "reality" are not incompatible: Each relates to the distinctive purposive activity that generates talk about the real.

The question of whether ethics is a science is best approached, according to Toulmin, by noticing the difference in function between scientific and moral judgments. Scientific judgments are intended to alter expectations in experience; predictions are made that certain kinds of responses will follow from the activity of sensing various kinds of objects. Moral judgments, on the other hand, are intended to alter feelings and behavior. However, it has been a mistake to suppose that science involves the use of reason while ethics (or moral judgment) involves the use of rhetorical techniques and methods of rationalization. Both activities involve reason and the use of reasons; both may involve rhetoric and rationalization. What is important is to discover the difference between the two.

By examining the kinds of reasons given in support of moral claims, Toulmin concludes that two fundamental kinds of reasons (not necessarily distinct) count as "moral" reasons: those reasons that relate an act said to be a duty to the moral code of the community in which the reasons are advanced and those reasons that relate to the avoidance of the suffering, annoyance, or inconvenience of members of the community.

Accordingly, Toulmin argues that the idea of moral duty is intimately bound up with the practices adopted by a community to make living together possible and agreeable. Reasons relating to the moral code and reasons relating to human welfare come to the same thing: concern about harmonizing the interests and actions of the members of a community. Harmonizing interests requires procedures for settling conflicts of interest, and morality provides such procedures.

In the early stages of the development of a community's ethics, sets of principles are devised to regulate action. However, as it becomes evident through experience that some principles are not effective in harmonizing interests and that in particular situations, moral principles may conflict, the development enters a critical stage in which attention is paid to the "motives" of actions and the "results" of social practices. The consideration of consequences leads to modification of principles and hence to a more satisfactory moral code—that is, a moral code that is more successful in regulating conduct so as to prevent or minimize the suffering inflicted on people. Toulmin's emphasis is not on action intended to increase happiness, as with the utilitarians, but on action intended to settle conflicts of interest and reduce suffering.

Moral Reasoning

In his exposition of the "Logic of Moral Reasoning," Toulmin first explains that questions concerning whether a contemplated action is or is not right amount to questions about whether the action does or does not conform to a principle embedded in the community's moral code. Giving reasons in support of one's moral decisions, then, amounts to referring to a principle that governs action in such cases. The principle, of course, according to Toulmin, embodies accepted social practice.

Where there are conflicts of duties relative to principles, it may turn out that only by a comparison of estimated consequences can it be decided what would be the right thing to do. Rightness, however, is determined by the consideration of reasons, not by direct reference to consequences. The fundamental question is always whether a way of action is in accord with a principle established by conventional practice or is likely to harmonize interests or prevent suffering.

When the justice of a principle is called into question, it is relevant to consider the utility of the principle in harmonizing interests and preventing avoidable suffering, but it is not proper moral reasoning to decide whether an act in accordance with a principle is likely in a given case to have utility; there is already a reason for acting in a certain way, and it is a sufficient moral reason: namely, that the action is required by the principle.

It is possible that alternative courses of action might both satisfy the requirements of moral choice, either by both being in accord with the same principle (code) or having probable equally beneficial effects; in such a case, writes Toulmin, moral considerations no longer apply: If a choice is made, it is made on other grounds.

Toulmin argues that there is no need for a general answer to the question, "What makes a reason a good reason or an ethical argument a valid argument?" It is sufficient to consider what would constitute a good reason in a particular case. To be "reasonable" in the making of moral decisions is to decide on the basis of good reasons, that is, reasons that are based on principles derived from social practice. To be reasonable in the appraisal of existing practices is to consider the effects of such practices on those who make up the community. It would be a mistake in definition, Toulmin argues, to define the term "right" either by reference to principles or to utility; "right" is to be understood by reference to what is reasonable.

In arguing with a person whose self-love has "overpowered his sense of right," Toulmin declares, one finds oneself in a logical difficulty: If the sense of right has been overpowered, the appeal to reasons is futile. It does happen sometimes, however, that good reasons will weaken the hold of self-love and in that way restore the sense of right.

Toulmin discusses what he calls "equity in moral reasoning" and maintains that an ethical argument is an instance of moral reasoning only if it is worthy of acceptance by anyone; there must be a corresponding equity of moral principles—that is, the principles serve as general guides for anyone in the kinds of situations governed by the principles.

In part 4, "The Boundaries of Reason," Toulmin writes about philosophical ethics and then about reason and faith. Some ethical theories are "disguised comparisons," Toulmin argues; the debate between objectivists and subjectivists, although based on the mistake of thinking that the term "good" must refer either to an objective property or to a state of the speaker, nevertheless invites consideration of the degree to which the use of "good" is like (or unlike) property words and like or unlike words expressing feelings.

However, there is no need for ethical theories to be excursions into paradox, Toulmin contends. The study of moral reasoning yields explanatory accounts that are true and helpful; such accounts can correct whatever misconceptions may result from philosophical attempts to answer questions that themselves spring from mistaken assumptions.

Toulmin distinguishes between ethics and religion in this way: ethics provides *reasons* for choosing an action as "right"; religion uses concepts "spiritually"—to inspire people, enkindle their hearts, and give them the will to do the right thing.

Ian P. McGreal, updated by John K. Roth

Additional Reading

Bove, Paul A. "The Rationality of Disciplines: The Abstract Understanding of Stephen Toulmin." In *After Foucault: Humanistic Knowledge, Postmodern Challenges*. New Brunswick, N.J.: Rutgers University Press, 1988. This book discusses French literature from 1900 through the 1980's and includes material on Michel Foucault, the prose treatment of power, and human understanding in relation to the writings of Stephen Toulmin.

Dellapenna, Joseph W., and Kathleen M. Farrell. "Modes of Judicial Discourse: The Search for Argument Fields." In *Argumentation: Analysis and Practices*, edited by Frans H. van Eemeren et al. *Studies of Argumentation in Pragmatics and Discourse Analysis*. Dordrecht, Holland: Foris, 1987. This article uses the theories of Toulmin to examine legal argumentation and legal language.

Fromm, Harold. "Stephen Toulmin's Postmodernism. *Cosmopolis: The Hidden Agenda of Modernity*, by Stephen Toulmin." *The Hudson Review* 43, no. 4: 654-660. An in-depth discussion of Toulmin's book.

Fulkerson, Richard. "The Toulmin Model of Argument and the Teaching of Composition." In *Argument Revisited, Argument Redefined: Negotiating Meaning in the Composition Classroom*. Thousand Oaks, Calif.: Sage, 1996. The theories of argumentation of Toulmin are discussed in terms of language, stylistics, rhetoric, argumentation, and their relationship to the teaching of writing.

Kneupper, Charles W. "The Tyranny of Logic and the Freedom of Argumentation." *Pre/Text: A Journal of Rhetorical Theory* 5, no. 2 (1984): 113-121. This article discusses literary forms as well as the role of logic and the freedom of argumentation based on ideas of Toulmin.

Olson, Gary A. "Literary Theory, Philosophy of Science, and Persuasive Discourse: Thoughts from a Neo-Premodernist." *Journal of Advanced Composition* 13, no. 2 (1993): 238-309. This article includes an interview with Toulmin. Toulmin discusses the relationship of philosophy of science to literary theory and criticism.

Seibert, Thomas M. "The Arguments of a Judge." In *Argumentation: Analysis and Practices*, edited by Frans H. van Eemeren et al. *Studies of Argumentation in Pragmatics and Discourse Analysis*. Dordrecht, Holland: Foris, 1987. The article discusses judicial argumentation, language, and pragmatics using the theories of argumentation of Toulmin.

Skinner, Quentin. "*Cosmopolis* by Stephen Toulmin." *The New York Review of Books* 37, no. 6 (1990): 36. A full-length discussion of Toulmin's book.

Smith, P. Christopher. "Towards a Discursive Logic: Gadamer and Toulmin on Inquiry and Argument." In *The Specter of Relativism: Truth, Dialogue and Phronesis in Philosophical Hermeneutics*, edited by Lawrence K. Schmitt. *Northwestern University Studies in Phenomenology and Existential Philosophy*. Evanston, Ill.: Northwestern University Press, 1995. The article uses the theories of Hans-Georg Gadamer and Toulmin to examine the relationship of logic to hermeneutics.

Zappel, Kristiane. "Argumentation and Literary Text: Towards an Operational Model." In *Argumentation: Analysis and Practices*, edited by Frans H. van Eemeren et al. *Studies of Argumentation in Pragmatics and Discourse*. Dordrecht, Holland: Foris, 1987. The article applies the theories of argumentation advanced by Stephen Toulmin to general literature.

Paul C. L. Tang

Miguel de Unamuno y Jugo

Unamuno, an existentialist, described his struggle for faith and longing for immortality in his poetry, novels, drama, cultural criticism, and philosophy. He depicted a world in which people's desire for meaning and faith comes into conflict with science and rationality.

Principal philosophical works: *Paz en la guerra*, 1897 (*Peace in War*, 1983); *La esfinge*, wr. 1898, pr. 1909; *La venda*, wr. 1899, pb. 1913; *De la enseñanza superior en España*, 1899; *Nicodemo el fariseo*, 1899; *Tres ensayos*, 1900; *En torno al casticismo*, 1902; *Amor y pedagogía*, 1902; *De mi país*, 1903; *Vida de Don Quijote y Sancho, según Miguel de Cervantes Saavedra, explicada y comentada por Miguel de Unamuno*, 1905 (*The Life of Don Quixote and Sancho According to Miguel de Cervantes Saavedra Expounded with Comment by Miguel de Unamuno*, 1927); *Poesías*, 1907; *Recuerdos de niñez y de mocedad*, 1908; *Mi religión y otros ensayos breves*, 1910; *La difunta*, pr. 1910; *El pasado que vuelve*, wr. 1910, pr. 1923; *Fedra*, wr. 1910, pr. 1918 (*Phaedra*, 1959); *Rosario de sonetos líricos*, 1911; *Soliloquios y conversaciones*, 1911 (*Essays and Soliloquies*, 1925); *Contra esto y aquello*, 1912; *La princesa doña Lambra*, 1913; *Del sentimiento trágico de la vida en los hombres y en los pueblos*, 1913 (*The Tragic Sense of Life in Men and Peoples*, 1921); *Niebla*, 1914 (*Mist: A Tragicomic Novel*, 1928); *Abel Sánchez: Una historia de pasión*, 1917 (*Abel Sánchez*, 1947); *El Cristo de Velázquez*, 1920 (*The Christ of Velázquez*, 1951); *Tres novelas ejemplares y un prólogo*, 1920 (*Three Exemplary Novels and a Prologue*, 1930); *La tía Tula*, 1921 (*Tía Tula*, 1976); *Soledad*, wr. 1921, pr. 1953; *Raquel encadenada*, wr. 1921, pr. 1926; *Rimas de dentro*, 1923; *Teresa*, 1924; *L'Agonie du christianisme*, 1925 (*La agonía del Cristianismo*, 1931; *The Agony of Christianity*, 1928, 1960); *El otro*, wr. 1926, pr., pb. 1932 (*The Other*, 1947); *Cómo se hace una novela*, 1927 (*How to Make a Novel*, 1976); *Romancero del destierro*, 1928; *El hermano Juan: O, El mundo es teatro*, wr. 1927, pb. 1934; *Sombras de sueño*, 1930; *San Manuel Bueno, mártir*, 1931 (*Saint Manuel Bueno, Martyr*, 1956); *La ciudad de Henoc*, 1941; *Cuenca ibérica*, 1943; *Paisajes del alma*, 1944; *La enormidad de España*, 1945; *Visiones y commentarios*, 1949; *Poems*, 1952; *Cancionero*, 1953; *Teatro completo*, 1959, 1973; *Dos novelas cortas*, 1961; *The Last Poems of Miguel de Unamuno*, 1974.

Born: September 29, 1864; Bilbao, Spain
Died: December 31, 1936; Salamanca, Spain

Early Life

Miguel de Unamuno y Jugo was born September 29, 1864, in Bilbao, Spain, the first son and third of the six children of Félix de Unamuno and Salomé de Jugo. His father had gone to Mexico as a young man, accumulated some money, and then returned to marry his much younger niece, Salomé. He had also acquired several hundred books on philosophy, history, and the physical and social sciences, which helped form his son's mind. From an early age, death preoccupied Miguel. His father, two of Miguel's sisters, and a school friend died by 1873, producing fear in the young boy. Unamuno's struggle to accept his own mortality became one of the major themes of his religious, philosophical, and literary work.

Miguel completed a traditional Catholic secondary education at sixteen and then was enrolled in the Central University of Madrid, torn between his love for his childhood sweetheart, Concepción ("Concha") Lizárraga, and a mystical belief that God wanted him to become a priest. Fascinated with language since listening to his father talk with a man in French, Unamuno wrote his doctoral dissertation on the origins and prehistory of the Basque race. In Madrid, he applied reason to his religious faith and lost his faith. He struggled for the remainder of his life to overcome his doubt. After receiving his doctorate in 1884, he returned to Bilbao, competed for a university teaching position, taught private

Miguel de Unamuno y Jugo. *(Library of Congress)*

classes, and wrote for local periodicals. Impatient to wait until securing a permanent teaching position, he married Concha on January 31, 1891, and, under the influence of his wife and his mother, began religious observance again. In 1891, he also won a competition for the chair in Greek language and literature at the University of Salamanca.

Life's Work

In the provincial university town of twenty-three thousand, with the faded glory of its medieval university and magnificent, café-lined central plaza, Unamuno found the tranquillity to read voraciously and widely, ponder the human condition, write insatiably, and rear his family. Yet he

soon lost interest in teaching Greek: Given the desperate problems facing Spain, he decided that the nation really did not need more Hellenists. Although he conscientiously met his pedagogical responsibilities, Unamuno devoted the rest of his time to writing novels, poetry, and essays intended to illuminate the solution to Spain's problems and his own concerns about the human condition. He also associated himself with Spanish socialism, believing it offered the best hope of liberty through a religion of humanity, but refused to join the party. In fact, his interest in socialism was primarily religious and ethical; Unamuno in his heart was an anarchist.

Transcendental questions troubled Unamuno. In 1896, Raimundo Jenaro, the third of his nine children, was born, but shortly after birth the infant contracted meningitis, which produced fatal encephalitis, although the child lingered until 1902. His child's condition agonized Unamuno. Why was God punishing an innocent child? Was it because of Unamuno's own sins, perhaps for having abandoned his Catholic faith? He was desperate for consolation, spent days in meditation and prayer, yet remained anguished. God did not answer, and Unamuno was obsessed with suicide and beset with angina, insomnia, and depression. Not only was reason unable to bring him to a knowledge of God, but it told him that God did not exist, that death brought the finality of nothingness. Yet Unamuno's despair at the inevitability of death forced him to hope and led him to the paradoxical solution of creating God for himself through his own faith. When he began reading the works of Søren Kierkegaard in 1900, he discovered a kindred being, although Unamuno had already developed the fundamentals of his own thought.

Meanwhile, Unamuno poured forth articles for Spanish and Latin American periodicals, as well as novels, plays, and criticism to supplement his meager academic salary. In 1895, he published a series of essays, later reedited as *En torno al casticismo*, which urged a return to the bedrock of tradition, to the study of the Spanish people, as the first step in confronting the nation's decadence. *Peace in War*, sometimes called the first existentialist novel, reflected his experiences during the Carlist siege of Bilbao (1874-1876). Two plays, *La esfinge* and *La venda*, and an analysis of Spanish higher education, *De la enseñanza superior en España*, soon followed, as did *Nicodemo el fariseo*, which used Saint John's account of Nicodemus's meeting with Christ as a dramatic vehicle for stating the basic theme of all his remaining work: human beings' desire for God and their existential will to believe.

In 1900, Unamuno became rector of the university, despite opposition from conservatives who disliked the outsider from Bilbao for his socialist rhetoric and his unorthodox religious views. On taking office, he appointed himself to a new chair of the history of the Spanish language, declared that Spain was ready to be discovered, and urged that the students study popular culture. Dressed idiosyncratically in his "uniform," he appeared a cross between a Protestant minister and an owl; he wore a dark suit, with vest and white shirt buttoned to the top but no tie, and metal-rimmed eyeglasses. He had an aquiline nose and a closely cropped and pointed graying beard.

Unamuno energetically joined in the campaign of the Generation of 1898 to renew Spain following the loss of its last overseas colonies in 1898. Yet while others called for Spain to emulate the science, technology, and democracy of northern Europe and the United States, Unamuno rejected mass society and focused on the potential of the individual. He considered his essays, collected in *The Life of Don Quixote and Sancho According to Miguel de Cervantes Saavedra Expounded with Comment by Miguel de Unamuno*, to articulate a genuinely Spanish philosophy. Subjectively choosing parts of Cervantes's novel and ignoring relevant scholarship, Unamuno resurrected Quixote in his own image, a man who re-created the world around him through his own will to believe. Although some Spanish republicans looked to Unamuno to lead, or at least to participate in, a revolution against the decadent monarchy, he opposed all revolution except in the individual heart. He found José Ortega y Gasset and other

Spanish intellectuals too enamored of modern science and declared that Spain should let the northern Europeans invent and then apply their inventions.

Unamuno's religious thought received its fullest expression in *The Tragic Sense of Life in Men and Peoples*. Then, in 1914, the government unexpectedly and without explanation removed him as rector. Liberals and socialists supported him in the ensuing controversy. During World War I, he supported the Allied powers. His novel *Abel Sánchez* portrayed Cain as Abel's victim and questioned why God accepted the latter's smug offerings while rejecting those of his brother. In his powerful *The Christ of Velázquez*, art and spiritual longing seek in Christ the possibility of redemption from death, while Unamuno eschews all dogma and cult.

For publishing an article critical of the monarchy, a court in Valencia condemned Unamuno in 1920 to sixteen years of imprisonment. At the same time, he was presented in both Bilbao and Madrid as a candidate for the national parliament but refused to campaign and was not elected. With his sentence under appeal, the faculty at Salamanca elected him vice-rector in 1922. Then, to the dismay of his supporters, he agreed to meet with the king, leading to criticism that he was self-serving and only wanted the rectorship. While awaiting appeal of his sentence, he took care to avoid offending the monarchy but became convinced that Spain was headed for dictatorship. Time bore out his forebodings, and General Miguel Primo de Rivera seized power with the connivance of Alfonso XIII. In early 1924, Primo de Rivera exiled Unamuno to the Canary Islands, stripping him of his salary and positions at Salamanca despite national and international protests. At Fuerteventura, he planned with some French friends to escape, but Primo de Rivera granted him amnesty, although subjecting him to certain restrictions upon his return. Unamuno refused to return and went into voluntary exile in France to wait for the fall of the dictatorship.

Unamuno passed the years of exile first in Paris and then in Hendaye along the Basque border. They were years of despair and loneliness because he refused to let members of his family take turns living with him, wanting his exile to be a moral protest. While in Paris, he published *The*

Agony of Christianity, a difficult but intense and poetical restatement of his anguish caused by loving an unreachable God, from which torment the only respite was death. With Primo de Rivera's fall, Unamuno reentered Spain on February 9, 1930, and returned to Salamanca. Faculty, students, and workers demanded his reinstatement as rector. His greatest novel, *Saint Manuel Bueno, Martyr*, soon appeared. It tells the story of a priest who loses his faith but assumes the ethical obligation of protecting his parishioners from disbelief by setting an example of saintliness, teaching them to pray, and consoling himself by consoling them.

With the abdication of Alfonso XIII, Spain became a republic on April 14, 1931, and the municipal government of Salamanca named Unamuno an honorary magistrate for his role in the triumph of republicanism. The university cloister also appointed him rector, and some rumored that Unamuno wanted to be president of Spain. On April 27, the republic designated him president of the Council of Public Instruction, and Salamanca elected him as one of its representatives to the constituent assembly. Unamuno rarely participated in its deliberations except to stress unity, hoping to ward off regionalism. Increasingly disturbed by the factionalism and the anti- or irreligious stance of the leftists, he became openly critical of the republic, refused to be a candidate in the 1933 elections, and resigned from the Council of Public Instruction. Adding to his despondency were the deaths of his wife and eldest daughter in 1934. He retired from his university chair that September at age seventy, but the president of Spain decreed Unamuno rector of Salamanca for life and created a special chair in his name for him. The following year, the republic named him a citizen of honor, and in 1936, the University of Oxford gave him an honorary doctorate.

After the outbreak of the Spanish Civil War in July, 1936, the government removed Unamuno as rector because of his criticism of the republic. The Nationalists, however, soon captured Salamanca and rewarded Unamuno's support by reappointing him rector. Yet Unamuno had come to see the war as national insanity. In a ceremony on October 12, attended by faculty, some Nationalist military leaders, and townspeople, he coura-geously denounced the speech of a general who had exalted anti-intellectualism and death. Confined to his home for his protest, Unamuno died on December 31, 1936.

Influence

Paradoxical and prickly, egocentric and sincere, Unamuno inevitably generated controversy. In his fiction and poetry, he sacrificed art to philosophical concerns, especially his religious despair and struggle for faith. His philosophy was not systematic and careful, and his assertions were sometimes outlandish and exaggerated. Scholars and critics even disagree regarding Unamuno's religious views, some arguing that he was an atheist and others that his belief was sincere. Certainly, he constituted a thorny problem for Spanish Catholicism, which eventually banned several of his works.

Yet through the paradox, the rant, and the self-preoccupation, Unamuno's energy, determination, despair, and hope are unmistakable. The volume of his work was tremendous, and its breadth and weight placed him in the vanguard of Spanish intellectual life. With Kierkegaard and Friedrich Wilhelm Nietzsche, he laid out the existentialist dilemma, preparing the way for Martin Heidegger, Karl Jaspers, and Jean-Paul Sartre. He loved Spain deeply, despite its flaws, and became a sort of Quixote himself, tilting at transcendental windmills and giants that few had the courage or will to perceive.

Kendall W. Brown

The Tragic Sense of Life in Men and Peoples

Type of philosophy: Philosophy of religion, existentialism

First published: Del sentimiento trágico de la vida en los hombres y en los pueblos, 1913 (English translation, 1921)

Principal ideas advanced:

◇ Humanity's deepest urge is for immortality, particularly of the individual self.

◇ The tension between reason and irrationality, faith and doubt, is what makes life tragic.

◇ Pain creates awareness rather than pleasure; suffering makes existence real.

◇ Previous systems of philosophy offer only dissatisfying consolations.

◇ Meaning is salvation and perpetuation based on faith, hope, and charity.

Miguel de Unamuno y Jugo's first purpose in writing *The Tragic Sense of Life in Men and Peoples* was to establish a philosophical voice that was specifically Spanish. As he had in his previous works, he sought to fill a cultural void that unified and synthesized Spanish thought into an internationally recognized ideology. Reacting to the then dominating spirit of modernism, Unamuno hoped to integrate topical issues such as the loss of Spanish colonies, the fear of anarchism, and shifting definitions of Spanish identity into a larger, universal statement on the longing for immortality and the hunger for meaning beyond what was offered by the orthodox church and atheism. Echoing the literature of the period, Unamuno felt Spanish sensibilities would give a new direction in European philosophy, particularly his idea that impassioned personal experience is more important than abstract philosophical systems.

Wishing to free philosophy from old patterns of strict logic and rationality, Unamuno wrote this work in a uniquely subjective and personal style. He modestly referred to the collection as "these essays," realizing he was not creating a systematic philosophical approach to his subjects. Notable problems have resulted in critical complaints; for example, his approach to religion is often ambiguous and conflicting. He frequently zigzags from point to point, making personal digressions that keep the work from being a logically organized treatise. Still, *The Tragic Sense of Life in Men and Peoples* was Unamuno's most unified synthesis of his thinking, and the book does develop his themes in a largely coherent flow.

Recognizing the book's problems, Unamuno considered the 1921 English translation of the work an opportunity to clarify and revise the original text, written in 1912, and the English text is superior to the original version. Because much of the work refers to then topical and national issues and because he frequently refers to his other publications, new readers may find it help-ful to review Spanish culture at the beginning of the twentieth century to appreciate his points fully.

Humanity and Immortality

Throughout the series of twelve essays, Unamuno both defines his terms and recapitulates the ideas of past philosophic systems and religious doctrines to lead to the conclusions expressed in his final two essays. Unamuno begins with "Man of Flesh and Bone," emphasizing the theme that philosophy is closer to poetry than science but must be practical and helpful. Rooted in the subconscious, philosophy gives meaning and understanding to what logic explains if it discounts the abstract and is more passionate than reasoned. For Unamuno, analyzing rigidifies thought and kills identity.

In "The Hunger of Immortality," Unamuno reviews concepts of God put forward by Immanuel Kant, William James, Søren Kierkegaard, and Georg Wilhelm Friedrich Hegel. Unamuno states that rationality and perceptions of reality cannot prove an afterlife, but even with demonstrable facts, this reasoning would not support the truth of religion. Humanity is a concrete thing of unity and continuity, combining the memory of the individual and that of society. Identity of the self is dependent on existence within the context of society. To become something other than oneself is to cease to be.

Unamuno then addresses his primary concerns: the fear of dying altogether, the fear of resignation and despair, and the need to know what is true. Contradictions and tragedy create a tragic sense of life that makes humanity aware of health and disease. Consciousness is a disease, as is progress, illustrated by the biblical metaphor of Original Sin. We are dependent on knowledge to understand existence, and it is necessary to exist and emphasize personal survival.

However, Unamuno states, humankind desires more than mere survival and seeks dissatisfying paths for fame and immortality. A key source for philosophy is this hunger for an afterlife with a thirst for the eternal. However, philosophers are perverted and misled by intellectualism. By creating distinctions, they create confusion. In a practical and true philosophy, Unamuno asserts, nothing is more universal than individuality, and no human should sacrifice himself or herself. The process of sacrificing oneself for the next generation yields nothing for the individual and is false immortality. Rather, one should integrate society into oneself.

In "The Essence of Catholicism," Unamuno, like Saint Paul speaking to the Stoics, rejects reason to ponder resurrection. He determines that beauty and art are meaningless consolations, each only a shadow of what true immortality is. Further, human beings prefer to singularize themselves, hoping for fame in lieu of immortality. Philosophers, in Unamuno's opinion, are not interested in truth as much as they are interested in the systems they propose, gaining immortality by receiving credit for their creations, hoping to outshine their competitors. By attacking old masters, youth intends to capture a place in the pantheon of fame, seeking thereby to immortalize itself. These attempts lead to envy, which is more terrible than hunger, for it is spiritual hunger that matters.

Unamuno's next essay, "The Rationalist Disillusion," claims that the thirst for being greater than oneself has led to the creation of religion built on the fear of death. What distinguishes humanity is the need to guard the dead, and human beings can be seen as a series of phantoms going from nothingness to nothingness again. The mind seeks the dead because what is alive eludes understanding; science is the cemetery of dead ideas. There is no consolation in being submerged in the all, so we prefer to cling to the substance of our own selves. For Unamuno, existence in pain is better than oblivion in the Nirvana of Buddhism.

In a section dominated by Unamuno's characteristic loose ends, he states that philosophy is often abandoned for theology and worries about a new persecution of Christians in the climate of reason fostered by Baruch Spinoza. For Unamuno, the spirit engages in a lifelong battle to build the House of Life. Reason merely gives faith associations, as in war, the devouring of predators, which is how cultures learn to know the other.

Faith and God

Unamuno believed it is impossible to have a totally rational world without faith and vice versa.

As outlined in "Love, Suffering, Pity, and Personality," humanity needs love, sorrow, and pity, and we must be interconnected and must come to feel everything personally in order to arrive at universal compassion and universal pity. All consciousness is aware of death and suffering, and it is with pity that we find our common bond.

Unamuno further explores humanity's concepts of God by tracing deity in historical perspective, noting in "From God to God" that monotheism can be traced like monarchies. The monotheistic God evolved into a head god like the supreme godhead of paganism. Ultimately, God became known as the head of humanity, the God of people, and not of individuals.

Continuing this theme in "Religion, the Mythology of the Beyond and the Apocatastasis," Unamuno says that concepts of God changed when prophets gave divinity philosophy, which gave God ethics and rationality. However, saying God created everything only begs the question, answering nothing. Unamuno insists that we must move beyond monotheism, as unity is unstable. By defining God, theologians project the ideal into the real, but God is superfluous when we seek the reason for creation. If God is to interact with human lives, Unamuno theorizes, God must be arbitrary rather than rational because he cannot be contemplative. For Unamuno, who elsewhere defines God as universal, transcendent consciousness, God cannot be limited to ethics, dogmas, or personifications.

The heart of *The Tragic Sense of Life in Men and Peoples* appears in the essay "At the Bottom of the Abyss," in which Unamuno states that because reason cannot explain God, love of God must come first. The primary quest of philosophy is the hunger for God, the wish for God, realizing God does not exist but rather superexists. The keys to finding God are faith, hope, and charity, emphasizing trust in faith. Humanity must love God before knowing God. Embracing hope is noble and tragic, and charity, or doing good, is the important action humans must make to link with the community.

Again returning to biblical themes in "The Practical Problem," Unamuno states that divinity arises from suffering as in Jesus Christ, the ultimate symbol of suffering. Anguish is what leads us to God, breaking down the barrier of suffering that divides matter from consciousness. Evil is the inertia of the spirit, and each must take up his or her own cross of work and contribute to society.

Unamuno concludes by returning to his focus on Spanish culture, pointing to Miguel de Cervantes' fictional character Don Quixote as the archetypal symbol of the Spanish soul. Quixote's quest is parallel to Unamuno's quest for God, and his suffering is the heroism of comic irrationality. Unamuno restates his idea that spirituality must be sought in solitude, the hero able to withstand the ridicule of others. Quixote, about whom Unamuno wrote extensively in other works, moves beyond reason into superreason. However, his servant, Sancho Panza, is even more heroic, as his faith contains doubts, but he does not fail his course. Here, Unamuno successfully returns to his opening thesis on humanity as flesh and blood with a tragic sense of life, and Don Quixote is for Unamuno both the Spanish icon of soul searching and the universal Everyman, appropriately seeking what is impossible.

Voice of Spain

In the decades after the publication of *The Tragic Sense of Life in Men and Peoples*, Unamuno became internationally famous as the primary spokesperson for the soul of the Spanish people, although most critical response did not appear in print until the end of World War I. Although Unamuno's perspective clearly embraced Christian thought and was influenced by Saint Paul and the writings of Saint Augustine, his occasional comments on the rituals and trappings of the Catholic Church resulted in the book's being placed on the Church's Index as heretical, alongside other writings by Unamuno that failed to support Catholic dogma.

Although not considered an original thinker, Unamuno became known as an incarnation of his time and place, and general interest in his work was first viewed in the light of his political stance during his exile to France in the 1920's. In his home country, Unamuno's reputation was built on his work as a whole, and he was noted as a professor, philologist, political thinker, playwright, novelist, poet, as well as essayist, but *The Tragic Sense of Life in Men and Peoples* earned for him an international reputation as a leading

figure of the European twentieth century. Although he did not establish a new school of philosophical thought, some saw him as a precursor to religious existentialism, and he is noted as a singular voice in the tradition of writers examining the relationship of the self and organized society. His voice resonates themes that parallel changes in European social and political systems in the first half of the twentieth century, and his freshness and passion have earned for him notice as a reformer and major influence on Spanish culture.

After World War II, Unamuno's work continued to inspire scholarly interest, notably in his commentary on Don Quixote. On the occasions of the seventieth and hundredth anniversaries of his birth, conferences were held in the United States to assess his impact.

Wesley Britton

Additional Reading

Ellis, Robert R. *The Tragic Pursuit of Being: Unamuno and Sartre*. Tuscaloosa: University of Alabama Press, 1988. A short comparison of the existentialism of Miguel de Unamuno y Jugo and Jean-Paul Sartre.

Ferrater Mora, José. *Unamuno: A Philosophy of Tragedy*. Translated by Philip Silver. Berkeley: University of California Press, 1962. This book is an excellent, brief survey of Unamuno's philosophy. The author tries to understand Unamuno as the philosopher understood himself.

Ilie, Paul. *Unamuno: An Existentialist View of Self and Society*. Madison: University of Wisconsin Press, 1967. This work considers Unamuno's contributions to existentialism in relation to Søren Kierkegaard, Friedrich Nietzsche, Martin Heidegger, Karl Jaspers, and Jean-Paul Sartre.

Marías, Julían. *Miguel de Unamuno*. Translated by Frances M. López-Morillas. Cambridge, Mass.: Harvard University Press, 1942. This older but still insightful work analyzes Unamuno's contribution to philosophy, with occasional biographical references.

Nozick, Martin. *Miguel De Unamuno*. New York: Twayne, 1971. Together with a short biography, this work is an analysis of Unamuno's thought and an evaluation of his literary art. Contains a good bibliography.

Rudd, Margaret Thomas. *The Lone Heretic: A Biography of Miguel de Unamuno y Jugo*. Austin: University of Texas Press, 1963. At 349 pages, this is the most thorough biography in English but problematic in some of its details and interpretations. The work contains a good bibliography.

Wyers, Francis. *Miguel De Unamuno: The Contrary Self*. London: Tamesis Books Limited, 1976. This work attempts to make sense of the sometimes violent contradictions in Unamuno's thought and places him as a precursor to existentialism.

Kendall W. Brown, updated by Patrick S. Roberts

Giambattista Vico

Vico founded the philosophical study of history and elaborated the theoretical basis for socio-logical study.

Principal philosophical works: *De nostri temporis studiorum ratione*, 1709 (*On the Study Methods of Our Time*, 1965); *De antiquissima Italorum sapientia*, 1710 (*On the Most Ancient Wisdom of the Italians*, 1988); *De constantia jurisprudentis liber alter*, 1721; *Vita di Giambattista Vico scritta da sé medesimo*, wr. 1725-1728, 1731, pb. 1818 (*The Autobiography of Giambattista Vico*, 1944); *Principi di scienza nuova d'intorno alla natura delle nazioni per la quale si ritruovano i principi di altro sistema del diritto naturale delle genti*, 1725, rev. ed. 1730 (revised and enlarged as *Principi di scienza nuova d'intorno alla comune natura delle nazioni*, 1744; commonly known as *Scienza nuova*; *The New Science*, 1948); letter to Gherardo degli Angioli dated December 26, 1725, 1783; *Discoverta del vero Dante*, wr. c. 1728, pb. 1818 (*Discovery of the True Dante*, 1961).

Born: June 23, 1668; Naples
Died: January 23, 1744; Naples

Early Life

Giambattista Vico was one of eight children born to a Neapolitan bookshop owner and his scarcely literate wife. Vico was an energetic and prodigious child, already enrolled in school at the age of seven, when a fall from the top of a ladder fractured his skull. The fracture gave rise to a large tumor, and his doctor predicted that the boy would either die of it or grow up an idiot. Although Vico's convalescence was prolonged, neither part of the doctor's prediction came true. Vico came to credit the injury, however, with engendering his lifelong melancholic temperament, the sort of temperament, Vico said, that belongs to all people of ingenuity and depth.

Vico's early formal education was classical, which at the time meant indoctrination into medieval Christian Aristotelianism, but he also spent a great part of his youth in solitary study, which was doubtless encouraged by living upstairs from the family bookshop. At seventeen, Vico went, at his father's urging, to the University of Naples to study law. He read philosophy in his spare time and wrote ornate, metaphysical poetry for relaxation. He quickly grew impatient with the incessant note taking and memorization

of legal cases and quit his university lectures, saying that there was no true learning to be obtained from them. He resumed his devotion to private study of the works of great writers and supported himself by tutoring the nephews of the Bishop of Ischia in Vatolla. He continued to develop his ideas largely by himself for the ensuing nine years and developed passing enthusiasm for the philosophy of Epicurus, Plato, Cornelius Tacitus, Pierre Gassendi, Roger Bacon, René Descartes, and Baruch Spinoza, among others. In 1695, Vico returned to his native city and was appointed four years later to the professorship of rhetoric at the university. This was actually a minor post with a modest stipend; Vico kept the post until shortly before his death.

Life's Work

Vico's ideas gained rudimentary expression in two of the first tracts he published. In a 1709 oration, *On the Study Methods of Our Time*, Vico denied the applicability of the Cartesian geometrical method of analysis to the human studies of practical wisdom, ethics, politics, and law. What he wanted to put in its place emerged in a 1710 publication entitled *On the Most Ancient Wisdom of the Italians*. Vico focused on etymology as a source of clues to the truth about human development. Linguistic analysis utilized a sort of *inge-*

nium, the power of connecting separate and diverse elements, that Vico thought was necessary for human self-understanding and practical wisdom. This early work of Vico was met with a mixed reception; his critics complained of its obscurity. Nevertheless, Vico submitted it with an application for the chair of civil law at Naples when the post fell vacant in 1723. His rejection was a bitter disappointment and proved to be only the beginning of the neglect he had to endure throughout his career.

The first edition of Vico's magnum opus, *The New Science*, was published in 1725. Vico had hoped that this work would do for the study of humanity and culture what Isaac Newton's *Philosophiae naturalis principia mathematica* (1687; *The Mathematical Principles of Natural Philosophy*, 1729; best known as the *Principia*, 1848) had done for

mathematical physics. Dissatisfied with its reception, he recast it twice; subsequent editions were published in 1730 and (posthumously) in 1744.

The structure of the third edition of *The New Science* was quite unusual. It contained an elaborate allegorical drawing for a frontispiece, followed by a detailed explanation of the icon. A chronological table followed, which placed in parallel columns the major events in the histories of seven peoples. Next came a catalog of 114 axioms that summarized the assumptions and conclusions of the work. The three remaining sections developed a narrative of human history, the elaboration of Vico's theory that human history manifested three ages: the age of gods, the age of heroes, and the age of humans.

According to Vico, history was the gradual process of humanization. In prehistory, bestial giants roamed the endless forests of the earth. Their mental powers were dormant in their enormous bodies so that all thought was sensation. They lived strictly in the present, copulating at inclination and increasing in size by inhaling the vapors of their excrement. The first formation of thunder and lightning elicited a new emotion of fear in the giants; they trembled at the sky and named it Jove. Jove was the first thought. Thus began the age of gods. It is an age whose story was told by Herodotus, when people thought that everything either was a god or was made by gods. Religion brought forth primitive morality, which begot the "might makes right" age of heroes, as characterized by Homer. As human powers of reason were developed to control unruly passions, the age of humans was born.

Vico saw these ages as continuing in a never-ending cycle, or *ricorso*, that manifested an ineluctable, providential pattern that he called the "ideal eternal history" of humanity. Every culture, he believed, passed through these identical stages; each age had a characteristic

Giambattista Vico. *(Corbis/Bettmann)*

mode of expression, set of customs, kind of law, and type of religion.

Vico believed his discoveries about the evolution of human civilization to be scientific. The method of inquiry that yielded these results attended precisely to the aforementioned characteristic institutions of each group of people. One of Vico's deepest insights was that human beings may know themselves in a way such that they can never know what is external to them (that is, nature). Whatever is of humanity's own making speaks truth about humans; this includes cultural institutions, language, and even history itself. Vico expressed this principle by saying that the true (*verum*) and the made (*factum*) are convertible. Thus, a systematic, historical investigation of all the results of human will and contrivance would produce a true understanding of humanity. Vico believed that this was the only way for people to reach self-understanding.

According to Vico, language study plays a special role in human self-understanding. Vico's original and extraordinarily interesting views on linguistic interpretation were of a piece with his principle of *verum ipsum factum* ("the true is the made"). He believed that the terms people use, including abstract terms, could be traced to linguistic contrivances of the earliest humans. Etymology thus could illuminate earlier environmental conditions, psychological states, and commonplace activities of human ancestry. That was a result of the fact that language and thought were coextensive for Vico; language was a direct reflection of the development of thought, rather than a tool that was deliberately and artificially constructed.

Vico theorized that poetic figures, such as metaphor, in the language of his contemporaries had more directly expressed the experience of humans in earlier ages. Earlier people thought strictly in pictorial images, analogies, and personifications, and these formed the currency of their communication, which involved only gesturing and picture drawing. Vico designated such figures "imaginative universals," and they had a property that third-age ratiocinating people can scarcely recapture: that of invoking a universal image by means of a particular. The abstractions employed in the age of humans are the opposite of the imaginative universal. Abstrac-

tions hold only what many particulars have in common but which the particular alone can no longer express (with the exception, perhaps, of particular images in poetic contexts). Similarly, what third-age people call the extravagant fiction of mythology in fact expresses the most fundamental postulates and cognitive associations of the first humans. Vico referred to his own saga in *The New Science* as a myth in just this sense.

Although Vico occupied most of his mature years writing reincarnations of *The New Science* in the hope of satisfying his critics, he also penned in his fifty-seventh year an intellectual autobiography. This was a pioneering work of its genre and a fascinating philosophical document in its own right.

Vico gained a very limited fame in his time. He received the honorific recognition of royal historiographer from the sovereign Charles of Bourbon only after his memory was failing and he had been overcome by physical infirmity. After his death, a bizarre quarrel over who should have the honor of carrying his coffin to the grave erupted between the Royal University professors and the confraternity of Vico's parish. The intransigent confraternity took their leave, and as a result, the coffin remained at the family home for quite some time. Vico's son finally had to enlist the services of the cathedral to conduct the body to the sepulcher.

Influence

Vico's work was largely ignored by his contemporaries, most of whom were enthusiastic Cartesians. He was not without outspoken detractors, however, who ridiculed him as obscure, speculative, and slightly mad. Twentieth century thinkers, who have the benefit of hindsight, have said that Vico was simply too far ahead of his time to have had any immediate influence. Yet the relative neglect of Vico's work continued in posterity. A small group of later thinkers have remarked on the importance of Vico, including Karl Marx, Samuel Taylor Coleridge, William Butler Yeats, and Matthew Arnold, but their work did not reflect any direct and significant influence from Vician thought. A very few thinkers have based their thought on Vico's insights: Jules Michelet, Benedetto Croce, and to a certain extent, R. G. Collingwood and Ernst Cassirer.

Even though Vico must be credited with being the father of the social sciences and the philosophy of history, his work has yet to join the vanguard of seminal philosophical texts.

Most twentieth century thinkers have come to know Vico through James Joyce. Joyce referred readers who had difficulty with his works to Vico's *The New Science*. Joyce claimed that his imagination grew when he read Vico in a way that it did not from reading Sigmund Freud or Carl Gustav Jung. Joycean texts are replete with references to Vico, and they palpably appropriate Vico's cyclical theory of history as well as his theories of language and myth. Consequently, Vico's thought enjoyed something of an epiphany in the late twentieth century that helped legitimate his status as a great contributor to Western thought.

Patricia Cook

The New Science

Type of philosophy: Ethics, epistemology, philosophy of history

First published: Principi di scienza nuova d'intorno alla natura delle nazioni per la quale si ritruovano i principi di altro sistema del diritto naturale delle genti, 1725, rev. ed. 1730 (revised and enlarged as *Principi di scienza nuova d'intorno alla comune natura delle nazioni*, 1744; commonly known as *Scienza nuova; The New Science*, 1948)

Principal ideas advanced:

◇ The only way to know human beings is in terms of their creations: language, history, law, and religion.

◇ The new science consists of reasoning (philosophy) and investigation (philology, considered as the empirical study of language, history, and literature).

◇ After the Deluge, the world was dominated by giants; the giants lived like wild animals until storms turned their eyes toward heaven and led them to invent gods; this is the origin of religion.

◇ Because of their fear of the gods, people became ashamed of themselves; in acting accordingly, they created morality.

◇ The practice of burying the dead, undertaken for sanitary reasons, led to the belief in the immortality of the soul.

◇ All cultures must pass through three stages: the age of gods, the age of heroes, and the age of humans; corresponding to these stages are three kinds of customs, three kinds of laws, commonwealths, and religions.

Like many an eighteenth century scholar, Giambattista Vico was in agreement with literary figure Alexander Pope's slogan, "The proper study of mankind is man." However, whereas the typical representative of the Enlightenment thought that the way to study humanity was to apply the principles of Newtonian mechanics—for example, David Hartley's *Observations on Man* (1749); Julien Offroy de La Mettrie's *L'Homme-machine* (1747; *Man a Machine*, 1750; also known as *L'Homme Machine: A Study in the Origins of an Idea*, 1960)—Vico maintained that the only way to know humanity is in terms of humanity's creations—language, history, law, religion—in short, through the study of civilization.

Vico professed to be carrying on the work of the French philosopher René Descartes, and he took sharp issue with both the Cartesians and the Newtonians for supposing that nature is properly understandable by humans. Is it not true, he asked, that we can know only what we make? Then only God can understand nature, because it is his creation. Humans, on the other hand, can understand civilization because they have made it. This was Vico's Archimedean point, a truth beyond all question: "that the world of civil society has certainly been made by men, and that its principles are therefore to be found within the modification of our own human mind."

Vico professed, at the same time, to be an adherent of the method of Sir Francis Bacon; he claimed that he was merely carrying over into the study of civil affairs the method Bacon had applied to the study of nature. What he seems to have borrowed from Bacon, however, is not the inductive principle that most people associate with the English thinker, but the practice of turning to sensible evidence to verify one's theories. Vico explained that his science consisted of two parts, reasoning and investigation. The former, which he called "philosophy," had to do with the development of theories on the basis of axioms, definitions, and postulates. The latter, which he called "philology," was the empirical study of language, history, and literature. He maintained that because these latter studies are founded on memory and imagination and are mixed with emotion, they do not give us the truth; but when they are consulted by an intelligent investigator, who has a theory to test, they are of paramount importance and make possible a science of humanity.

The Role of the New Science

Vico's central thesis was that modern civilized humanity came into existence through a process that is intelligible in terms of certain tendencies inherent in the human constitution. He conceived that initially people roamed the forest like wild beasts, giving no evidence of reason or compassion or any of the traits that have come to distinguish them. Only gradually did people modify their passions and discipline their powers, learning reverence and devising the institutions and inventions with which they have subjugated the earth. Vico did not regard the process as accidental in any sense: It was all part of God's design. However, the elements that divine providence made use of were, in his opinion, simple and understandable, and finding them was the aim of the "new science." He emphasized the role of providence in history, in order to guard against the belief in fate and chance of the Stoics and Epicureans. In his view, however, providence was a rational principle immanent in the world, rather than a mysterious will transcendent over it.

The New Science opens with a long list of axioms and corollaries, which should be studied carefully before one reads the rest of the book. They purport to give the fundamental traits of human nature that provide the dynamism for cultural evolution, together with the traits that determine the habits of poets and chroniclers, whose creations must serve the scientist as sources. For example:

Because of the indefinite nature of the human mind, wherever it is lost in ignorance, man makes himself the measure of all things.

It is another property of the human mind that whenever men can form no idea of distant and unknown things, they judge them by what is familiar and at hand.

When men are ignorant of the natural causes producing things, they attribute their own nature to them.

When, on the basis of such axioms, Vico turned to study the myths and legends of the past and with their help to reconstruct the prehistory of the race, the results were hardly in agreement with the assumptions of the eighteenth century drawing room. It was the fashion to think of primitive humans as tender, rational creatures, who spontaneously worshiped the god of nature and knew none of the prejudices or vices of artificial civilizations. Moreover, people took it for granted that Homer was a cultivated philosopher and gentleman, well suited to be a tutor of their youth—except they could not understand why he attributed such scandalous behavior to his heroes and his gods. In Vico's opinion, however, Homer was sublime as a poet by virtue of the fact that he was no philosopher, but a poet with a childlike mind, the product of a childlike age. We must read Homer with this in view and make allowances when we use his material in any attempt to understand his times. Similarly, his gods and heroes must not be judged by our moral standards. They echo the memories of an age when reason and morality had scarcely begun to tame the savage spirit or soften the features of the gods people feared.

The Development of Civilization

Ransacking the myths of pagan peoples and fitting what he found into the biblical tradition, Vico constructed the following account. First, there seemed among all peoples to be a recollection of the Deluge; second, all traditions mentioned a time when the world was dominated by giants. Vico argued that God took the children of Shem to be the people of the Promise and conducted their development along supernatural lines that science was not designed to explain. However, the descendants of Ham and Japheth were permitted to wander abroad, unattended by divine grace, and to develop the civilization that was Vico's concern. They became a gigantic folk, said Vico, from the fact that after their mothers had weaned them, they left them to draw their nourishment from the earth. They became fierce and wild, cohabitating like beasts and fighting for their food. So it continued until climatic changes, which followed the drying out of the earth, brought thunderstorms into being. The lightning and roar of thunder astonished these savages, causing them to lift their eyes to heaven; and the fear that was in their hearts caused them to invent the first gods. Thus, according to Vico, religion came into being—the first step toward civilization.

The fear of the gods made humans take a look at themselves and made them ashamed of some of the things they did, particularly concerning matters of sex. When people stopped cohabitating like animals and instead entered caves as couples, they initiated a series of consequences that they could never have anticipated. In a word, they created morality, the second great principle of civilization, and by bringing their passions one by one under control, they liberated their higher capacities, notably reason.

The third principle of civilization recognized by Vico is witnessed by the universal practice among early people of burying their dead. Occasioned at first by the offensiveness of decaying corpses, it came to be the basis of belief in the immortality of the soul.

In opposition to the orthodox views of his day, Vico held that civilization originated independently in many different lands—a principle that had importance for the study of etymology, to which he gave so much attention. Because each language had a separate origin, it was useless to try to find common roots. On the other hand, different languages could be expected to show parallel developments. For example, because law originally came from God, the Greeks, who called God *Dios*, called divine things *diaïon* and law *dikaion*. Correspondingly, the Romans called God *Jove* and law *jus*, which is a contraction of *jous*.

It was a general principle with Vico that because of the unity of human nature, all cultures must pass through identical stages, namely, the age of gods, the age of heroes, and the age of humans. He found the existence of these stages attested not merely in mythology and epic poetry but also in the history of religion, in compilations of laws, and, above all, in etymologies. Following

these three ages, there are three kinds of natures characteristic of humans, three kinds of customs, three kinds of laws, commonwealths, religions, and so forth. Thus, in the first age human nature was fierce and cruel, in the second noble and proud, in the third benign and reasonable. Again, customs of the first age were tinged with religion, those of the second with punctilio (for example, Achilles), those of the third with civic responsibility.

Vico's Science

It was Vico's ambition to develop his science along seven different branches. First, he proposed to make it a "rational civil theology of divine providence." He was not alone, in the eighteenth century, in marveling at the "divine legislative mind" that fashions private vices into public virtues:

> Out of ferocity, avarice and ambition, the three vices that run through the human race, it creates the military, merchant, and governing classes and thus the strength, riches and wisdom of commonwealths. Out of these three great vices, which could certainly destroy all mankind on the face of the earth, it makes civil happiness.

Second, his science was to be a "philosophy of authority." In place of the usual speculation about social origins, contracts, the beginnings of property, and so forth, it offered a framework within which to trace the development of sovereignty and right—from the time when authority first sprang from the will of the gods, through the age when it was lodged with princes whose might obligated those who came to them for asylum, to the time when free people concluded by means of reason that authority resides in laws of nature.

Third, it was to be a "history of human ideas." Poetry, for Vico, was the wisdom of the heroic age, when people thought in images and confused fancies with memories. It was, however, the beginning of "the knowledge of good and evil," and all the ideas that speculative science was later to bring to refinement were present there in the rough.

The remaining four branches of the new science led to a speculative reconstruction of world history, including such matters as the span of time required for each period, the courses the nations run, the common elements of law and custom among the peoples, and, finally, the principles of universal history.

The Evolution of Civil Societies

Because Vico came to his investigations through the study of jurisprudence, he developed the implications of the new science more completely in that direction and in the field of political thought than in most others. He maintained that civil societies evolve through three stages. All begin as aristocracies, which come into being because of the tendency of the weak to seek asylum at the altars of the strong. The peace and prosperity that result from this arrangement gradually strengthen the productive classes, who demand guarantees from their superiors. In time, a republic of free people, governed by law, replaces the aristocracy. However, wealth and leisure breed effeminacy and greed. Citizens grow careless, and lawlessness prevails. Deliverance comes when a strong prince establishes order and takes authority into his hands. In Vico's words,

> Since in the free commonwealths all look out for their own private interests, into the service of which they press their public arms at the risk of ruin to their nations, to preserve the latter from destruction a single man must arise, as Augustus did at Rome, and take all public concerns into his own hands, leaving his subjects free to look after their private affairs. . . . Thus are the peoples saved when they would otherwise rush to their own destruction.

Vico regarded aristocracies and republics as unstable and maintained that states normally "come to rest under monarchies."

In the century of Frederick the Great, it was nothing unusual for an enlightened thinker to argue in favor of an absolute monarchy. Voltaire did also. However, the development described so far was, in Vico's view, only half a cycle. A nation might flourish for some time under a prince, as did Imperial Rome; but the fate of Rome serves notice that the irresponsibility of civilized people in an "age of reason" may pass all bounds and bring about the destruction of everything that

had been built up through the centuries. This was, in Vico's opinion, the eternal law of history. He saw civilization as a fragile achievement that divine providence frames out of violence, greed, and pride; but when the zenith has been passed, it is destroyed by these same forces, not by alien influences and external barbarians. A new "barbarism of reflection" turns civilized people into worse than beasts. Reason disintegrates into skepticism: "Learned fools fall to calumniating the truth." Civic loyalties forgotten, the restraints of morality are turned into jests. People throng together in cities and jostle each other at public festivals, but they live in deep solitude of spirit: Under soft words and polite embraces, they plot against one another's lives. Their factions grow into civil wars that decimate the land and let their cities return to forests. Those who survive are reduced again to "the barbarism of sense," until they learn once more the things necessary for life:

> Thus providence brings back among them the piety, faith, and truth which are the natural foundation of justice as well as the graces and beauties of the eternal order of God.

Vico gained only a limited fame in his own time. The curious manner in which many twentieth century points of view are anticipated in his work has, however, brought him belated recognition. Pragmatists can see their doctrine of knowledge in his contention that we know only what our minds contrive. Humanists find much wisdom in his account of civilization. Persons concerned with history as a science admire the way in which he combined hypothesis and investigation, and those whose interest is in plotting the cycles of cultures find fruitful suggestions in his work. James Joyce did much to popularize his name among students of literature. Inevitably, his account of the early giants creating their gods and fleeing in shame to caves has caught the attention of some existentialists.

Jean Faurot

Additional Reading

Adams, H. P. *The Life and Writings of Giambattista Vico.* London: Allen & Unwin, 1935. This biography is one of the few that attempt to integrate Vico's life and his thought. It is amusing and elegant, and includes translations of some of Vico's poems. Indexed.

Berlin, Isaiah. *Vico and Herder*. New York: Viking, 1976. A revised and expanded version of Berlin's influential assessment of Vico's philosophical ideas. Part 1 treats his "General Theory," part 2 "Vico's Theory of Knowledge and Its Sources." Berlin's introduction conveniently outlines several of Vico's key theses.

Burke, Peter. *Vico*. New York: Oxford University Press, 1985. A concise treatment of Vico's intellectual development, his main work, and his influence. Indexed, with a helpful list for further reading.

Caponigri, A. Robert. *Time and Idea: The Theory of History in Giambattista Vico*. London: Routledge & Kegan Paul, 1953. An excellent exposition of the main Vician themes of ideal eternal history, or *ricorso*, and the natural law. Densely packed and well indexed.

Croce, Benedetto. *The Philosophy of Giambattista Vico*. Translated by R. G. Collingwood. London: Howard Latimer, 1913. This now-classic commentary on the totality of Vico's thought may be too complex to serve introductory students, but it is a solid and reliable secondary source for issues not covered in more general literature. Well indexed.

Goetsch, James R. *Vico's Axioms: The Geometry of the Human World*. New Haven, Conn.: Yale University Press, 1995. A discourse on Vico's philosophy.

Lilla, Mark. *G. B. Vico: The Making of an Anti-Modern*. Cambridge: Harvard University Press, 1993. A detailed and comprehensive introduction to Vico that emphasizes many of his neglected early writings, which provide the basis for reinterpretation of *The New Science* as an antimodern work.

Mazzotta, Giuseppe. *The New Map of the World: The Poetic Philosophy of Giambattista Vico*. Princeton, N.J.: Princeton University Press, 1999. A good treatment of Vico's thoughts. Includes a bibliography and index.

Pompa, Leon. *Vico: A Study of "The New Science."* New York: Cambridge University Press, 1975. A very close analysis of Vico's text is offered here; this work is laced with quotations and helpful interpretations of passages in their context. Indexed, with a short bibliography.

Tagliacozzo, Giorgio, ed. *Vico and Contemporary Thought*. Atlantic Highlands, N.J.: Humanities Press, 1979. This collection of essays is an excellent example of many such works now available that mark a resurgence of interest in Vico's thought. These essays focus on the relevance of Vician insights to urgent twentieth century practical and philosophical concerns. Well indexed; contributors come from a wide range of disciplines.

Verene, Donald Phillip. *The New Art of Autobiography: An Essay on the Life of Giambattista Vico Written by Himself*. Oxford: Clarendon Press, 1991. The first full-length commentary on and interpretation of Vico's autobiography. Provides a biography of Vico and addresses his autobiography as both a literary and philosophical work.

_____, ed. *Vico and Joyce*. Albany: State University of New York Press, 1987. Essays discuss Vician themes not only in James Joyce's *Finnegans Wake* but also in *Ulysses* and *A Portrait of the Artist as a Young Man*. Accessible to beginning students of Joyce's literature and Vico's thought. Well indexed; contributors come from many disciplines.

Patricia Cook, updated by William Nelles

Swami Vivekananda

Teaching a nondualistic interpretation of Vedantic philosophy and emphasizing the universal reality underlying all religions, Vivekananda was the first Indian philosopher to gain a wide audience for Hinduism in the West.

Principal philosophical works: *Eight Lectures*, 1896 (commonly known as *Karma Yoga*); *Vedanta Philosophy: The Real and Apparent Man*, 1896; *My Master*, 1901; *The Science and Philosophy of Religion: A Comparative Study of Sankhya, Vedanta, and Other Systems of Thought*, 1908; *Inspired Talks*, 1908.

Born: January 12, 1863; Calcutta, India
Died: July 4, 1902; Calcutta, India

Early Life

Swami Vivekananda, whose birth name was Narendranath Datta, was raised in a liberal family atmosphere. His father, who was attorney-at-law in the high court of Calcutta, was a well-read man, with a deep appreciation of Islamic culture. It was through his father that Vivekananda developed his interest in other cultures. From his mother, who read to him from the Ramayana and Mahabharata, he gained a feeling for Hindu culture.

According to his own account, Vivekananda showed an interest in meditation from the age of seven or eight. He also showed some aptitude for classical Indian music, later coauthoring a manuscript about the tabla, a percussion instrument.

Vivekananda's disciples later claimed, with some encouragement from their master, that Vivekananda was considered a prodigy at high school and college, with a particular aptitude for philosophy. The truth appears to be more mundane. He was not an outstanding student and did not excel in examinations. Although he did study for a year at the Presidency College, the leading educational institution in India at the time, he had to transfer to the General Assembly's Institution, from which he graduated with a B.A. in 1884.

Life's Work

Vivekananda first met the revered holy man Ramakrishna, who was to dramatically influence his life, in 1881. When Vivekananda faced a crisis in 1884, he renewed his contact with Ramakrishna at the saint's ashram in Dakshineshwar. In that year, Vivekananda's father died, leaving no provision for his family. Facing poverty, Vivekananda attempted to find employment, but other than a one-month spell as a high school teacher, he was unsuccessful. Ramakrishna seems to have stepped into the void, becoming a father figure to Vivekananda, whom he regarded as his favorite disciple. In 1885, when Ramakrishna was taken ill, Vivekananda realized that the seer's mantle would pass to him, and it is from this date that his career as a monk began. Shortly before Ramakrishna died in 1886, the saint (according to the hagiographic accounts) passed all his spiritual powers to his disciple, who had supposedly earned them by his superhuman efforts and austerities.

Now the acknowledged inheritor of Ramakrishna's legacy, Vivekananda moved the master's devotees into a house in Baranagore, where they were to remain for six years. Embracing poverty, they survived by begging for a living, which was considered an acceptable practice for monks in India.

Vivekananda began to travel throughout India, a wandering monk observing everywhere he went the paradox of India's poverty and its heri-

Swami Vivekananda. *(Library of Congress)*

journey to Almora, he gained a vision of the oneness of the universe.

In January, 1891, Vivekananda traveled to Delhi and proceeded to Alwar, where he was recognized as a teacher and gave discourses on the Vedas and Upanishads and also the Bible. In south India, he visited Khetri in Rajasthan, where he met rulers and top officials. At Porbander, where he spent eleven months assisting a pandit in a translation of the Vedas, he first conceived the idea of traveling to the West. A year later, he completed his six years of pilgrimage, extending from the Himalayas in the north to Kanyakumair, the southernmost tip of India. It was at about this time that he assumed the name Vivekananda.

In 1893, his plan to visit the United States came to fruition. With his expenses paid by his followers, Vivekananda set off for the West, intending to convey Ramakrishna's message of a universal religion, the idea that all religions point to the same truth. He was to do this by proclaiming Advaita Vedanta, based on the Vedas and the Upanishads, which he believed contained the essence of all religion. Advaita, or nondualism, refers to the belief that in spite of the appearance of multiplicity in the world, the ultimate reality is unity, not diversity. Vivekananda also wished to raise money on his trip to help alleviate poverty in India.

When Vivekananda attended the World's Parliament of Religions held in Chicago in September, 1893, he proved to be a charismatic figure. With his handsome face, colorful attire—an orange robe and saffron turban—impressive bearing, and eloquent speech, he made a startling impression on everyone who met or heard him. His first words at the Parliament, "Sisters and Brothers of America," were met with thunderous applause. He went on to say that he was proud to belong to a religion, Hinduism, that has "taught the world both tolerance and universal acceptance. We believe not only in universal toleration, but we accept all religions as true."

Two days later, in his paper on Hinduism, Vivekananda explained the basic tenets of his religion, including the concepts of karma and reincarnation, the relationship between spirit and

tage of spiritual richness. He realized that India was in sore need of spiritual renewal. During these trips, Vivekananda studied a variety of subjects, including the Upanishads, Sanskrit, Jain and Muslim culture, and Christian theology. He also had mystical experiences. Reportedly, on a

matter, and unity and diversity. He concluded by pointing to the common center of all religion, which he believed was that at the heart of all faiths, the same truth reigns. He looked forward to the emergence of a universal religion,

> whose sun will shine upon the followers of Krishna and of Christ, on saints and sinners alike; which will not be Brahmanistic or Buddhistic, Christian or Mohammedan, but the sum total of all these, and still have infinite space for development.

Vivekananda also spoke about the problems facing India, sharply chiding Christian missionaries for thinking only of saving souls and not of feeding starving bodies. This was a criticism that Vivekananda would make frequently during his American stay, but he drew a distinction between a dogmatic, intolerant Christianity and the true teachings of Jesus, which he lauded.

By general agreement, Vivekananda was the finest spokesperson for Hinduism that the West had heard. He became a celebrity almost overnight, and legends seemed to grow up around him. Having suddenly become a national figure, Vivekananda was invited to give a lecture tour, and he visited the large cities on the East Coast and in the Midwest. So busy did his schedule become that at one point he was giving between twelve and fourteen lectures per week. He was sometimes shocked by the ignorance of Hinduism shown by his audiences, and not all his lectures were successful. In Detroit, in February, 1894, he angered many with his harsh comments about Christian missionaries. As he traveled the country, Vivekananda continued to study and to observe. He was impressed with Western science and technology but felt that materialism had adversely affected the West's spirituality.

Later in 1894, he decided to establish residence in New York, where the following year he gave free lectures and classes—the first time Vedanta had been taught in New York. Vivekananda also trained people in meditation. In the summer of 1895, he spent seven weeks at Thousand Island Park, an island in the St. Lawrence River, where he gave discourses on the Bhagavad Gita and the Upanishads to his growing band of disciples.

In August, 1895, Vivekananda sailed for London. He remained in London for a month, where

he met Margaret Noble, who was later to become one of his most prominent disciples, taking the name Sister Nivedita. Vivekananda returned to New York in December and concentrated on the teaching of karma yoga. He gave another series of public lectures in Madison Square Garden in early 1896 and an address to the graduating class of the philosophy department at Harvard University in March. As a result of this address, he was offered a chair of Eastern Philosophy at Harvard, which he declined. Before leaving the United States, Vivekananda founded the Vedanta Society of New York for the propagation of his work. In April, he sailed for London, where he gave more public lectures before leaving for India, via Naples, in December.

Arriving in India in January, 1897, he was given a hero's welcome. When he reached the railway station at Madras, he was received with wild enthusiasm by the populace. Crowds lined the streets as he made his way to the house where he was to stay. A similar reception greeted him when he left Madras for Calcutta in February. Wherever he spoke, he emphasized what he called practical Vedanta, which meant active concern for the material as well as the spiritual welfare of others. This year marked the beginning of the last period of Vivekananda's work, which centered on his plans for the spiritual revival of India and the establishment of the Ramakrishna Mission near Calcutta. Its purpose was to propagate the teachings of Ramakrishna, including the goal of fostering the knowledge that all religions are forms of the one eternal religion.

In 1899, Vivekananda interrupted his work in India to make another visit to the West. Now in poor health, he stayed in London, New York, Los Angeles, and San Francisco, giving lectures and training disciples. In the summer of 1900, he attended the Congress of the History of Religions in Paris. He returned to India in December, after which his health further deteriorated, and he died of heart disease and asthma in 1902.

Influence

As an expositor of Advaita Vedanta, the truth of which Vivekananda believed could be established by logical reasoning, Vivekananda laid out the philosophical basis for his dream of a universal religion. He envisioned a faith that would uphold differences in religious expression while honoring the underlying unity that gave rise to them. This idea, which Vivekananda developed from his master, Ramakrishna, has proved to be a powerful force in twentieth century Indian philosophical thought. It has found expression in figures such as the poet Rabindranath Tagore and the philosopher Sarvepalli Radhakrishnan. Radhakrishnan in particular was saturated in Vivekananda's thought as early as his school days, and this was not uncommon in Indian schools at the time. According to Radhakrishnan, collections of letters of Vivekananda were eagerly passed around by students in classrooms.

Like Vivekananda, Radhakrishnan would later come to the West; two generations after Vivekananda, he would be the leading interpreter of Vedanta to the West. Preaching the same idea of the common basis of all religion, Radhakrishnan often referred in his lectures to examples from Vivekananda's life and held him up as a symbol of India's spiritual heritage and goals.

In terms of his influence on the West, Vivekananda can be referred to as the founder of the American Vedanta movement. In spite of his celebrity, he did not win large numbers of overt converts, but he did sow the seeds for a more widespread understanding of Eastern philosophical thought and the common elements it shares with Western traditions. The work of Radhakrishnan is a testament to this goal, and Vivekananda's influence also lies indirectly behind the vogue for Vedantic teachings that accompanied the countercultural movement that swept the West during the 1960's. This was embodied in another Hindu monk, Maharishi Mahesh Yogi, who, like Vivekananda, also proclaimed a meeting point between East and West on the basis of direct experience of the unity of creation in the midst of diversity.

In India, Vivekananda is remembered as an Indian patriot who reawakened India's pride in its spiritual heritage. He is also honored for giving Vedanta a more practical orientation, as a philosophy concerned not only with personal liberation but also with the wide-ranging improvement of social conditions. His work is continued today by the Ramakrishna Mission in India and the Vivekananda Foundation in New York.

Bryan Aubrey

Karma Yoga

Type of philosophy: Indian philosophy, metaphysics, philosophy of religion
First published: Eight Lectures, 1896 (commonly known as *Karma Yoga*)
Principal ideas advanced:
◇ Karma yoga is a system of ethics that leads to the soul's freedom, the goal of all human nature, through work, or action.
◇ Action must be performed from a state of unselfishness, or nonattachment.
◇ Belief in God, or in a doctrine or metaphysical system, is not necessary for the path of karma yoga.

Swami Vivekananda began working on *Karma Yoga* when he returned to New York from London in December, 1895. It was not his habit to do much actual writing himself; a stenographer was employed to record his lectures. It is thanks to the efforts of the stenographer, J. J. Goodwin, an Englishman who became Vivekananda's disciple, that Vivekananda's teachings, including his exposition of karma yoga, have survived. *Karma Yoga* is one of four volumes by Vivekananda describing the different paths to enlightenment in Vedanta. The other volumes are on raja yoga (the principal system of yoga as taught by the ancient seer, Patanjali), jnana yoga (the way of knowledge), and bhakti yoga (the way of devotion).

Karma Yoga is divided into eight chapters. Vivekananda's style is simple, straightforward, and logical. In almost every chapter, he includes a story or anecdote from the Indian tradition to illustrate his main point. In keeping with his universalist outlook, Vivekananda also alludes to the Buddha and to Christian teachings. Sometimes he throws in an analogy drawn from science, especially physics, to make his point.

Karma and Karma Yoga
Vivekananda defines karma yoga as a system of ethics and religion intended to attain freedom (*moksha*) through unselfishness and good works. He does not exalt karma yoga as superior to other yogas, which include jnana and bhakti yoga. All yogas have the same goal, and each can lead to freedom independently of the others. He

also points out that karma yoga does not have to be practiced within a particular tradition. It makes no difference whether a person is a Hindu, a Christian, Jew, or Gentile.

In the first chapter, Vivekananda defines the word "karma." Derived from the Sanskrit word *kri*, to do, it simply means action, or work. The word is used in an all-inclusive sense; action includes the imprints of everything a person has done, thought, or felt. Everyone is performing karma all the time, and every thought and action leaves a mark on the doer. One's character is composed entirely of what one's karma, or one's actions, have been and are. Because actions are determined from within, according to thought and will, people are responsible for what they are and have the power to make themselves what they wish. It is therefore necessary to know that the highest form of action is motivated not by selfish goals such as money, fame, or power, but by unselfishness. If one works without selfish motive, one gains the highest reward and becomes a moral giant. The ideal is to act without being attached to the fruits of the action and to remain utterly calm and still even in the midst of activity. Here Vivekananda alludes to the Bhagavad Gita, one of the most important of Vedantic texts. Indeed, the whole of *Karma Yoga* might be described as a commentary on that central idea of nonattachment as expounded by Lord Krishna in the Bhagavad Gita.

In chapter 2, Vivekananda points to the relative nature of duty and morality; they differ in varying circumstances and various cultures. There are disparate callings in life, each with its own duties. The householder and the recluse each has a place; one is not better than the other. Nor is one stage in life better than another; the roles of student, householder, retiree, or *sanyasin* (one who has given up the world altogether) are equally valid in their due place.

Spiritual Help

Chapter 3 is devoted to a discussion of how a person may best be helped. According to Vivekananda, the highest aid that one can give is to help a person spiritually, because that is the only thing that will free the individual from want. Those who give spiritual knowledge are the great benefactors of humankind. After this in importance is intellectual knowledge. The least valuable help is physical, because if all one does if feed a hungry person, he or she will soon become hungry again.

The nature of spiritual help rests on the understanding of the central question of karma yoga: If everything is work (karma), how does one become free of the effects, both good and bad, that all action will produce? How does one step out of the turning wheel of karma, in which desire produces action, which in turn produces more desire in an eternal restless cycle? For the answer, Vivekananda returns to the Bhagavad Gita. The key passage, although Vivekananda does not refer to it directly, is chapter 2, verse 45, when Krishna counsels the warrior Arjuna to go beyond the "three gunas." The gunas, sattva, tamas, and rajas, are the three constituents of nature, present in everything. By taking his mind beyond them, Arjuna will be beyond the dualities of nature. He will realize the essential nature of his own being and the steadfastness of the universal self and no longer have attachment to the world. Krishna advises further (chapter 2, verse 48) that action must be performed from that realized state of being, in which case it will automatically result in nonattachment. As Vivekananda explains it, the message of the Bhagavad Gita is to perform the action, but not let the action or the thought behind it create a deep impression on the mind. To do anything less than this is to identify oneself with nature, which means that action results only in more slavery, not freedom. On a practical note, Vivekananda states that nonattachment can be cultivated by acting without the expectation of any reward. One must offer everything as a free gift; attachment comes when one expects something in return.

Duty

The tolerant universalism for which Vivekananda was noted is evident in chapter 4, which discusses the philosophy of duty. He first points out that the term is virtually impossible to define, because the same actions might be right in one context and wrong in another. However, the most universal guide is that one's duty is not to injure any living being and to do what will exalt and ennoble according to the tradition in which one has been born. It is important not to judge the customs of other cultures.

The purpose of performing duty is the same as in any other aspect of yoga, the object being to allow the higher self to shine through one's actions. Vivekananda then returns to his main theme: Duty only runs smoothly when it is motivated by love, and the only way to truly express love is to be nonattached.

In chapter 5, Vivekananda broaches one of the paradoxes often encountered in mystical thought. The paradox is that although working to help the world should be our highest motive and calling, the world does not need our help. The universe is just as it should be, and nothing we can do can alter that fact. Vivekananda likens the world to a dog with a curly tail; for all time, people have been trying to straighten it, but it always curls up again. Remembering this analogy is the antidote to fanaticism, which is incompatible with love.

Nonattachment

Chapter 6 returns to the central theme of nonattachment. Because action cannot be destroyed until it has produced its fruit and because all actions produce a mixture of good and bad effects, perfection can never emerge from work (karma). The consequence of this is that only the act of self-abnegation can produce happiness. Self-abnegation is *nivritti*, the "revolving away" from the self, and karma yoga is a means to that end and as such is the basis of all morality. Self-abnegation is another way of expressing the goal defined in the Bhagavad Gita as nonattachment in the performance of action, the art of being in the world but not of it. One must give up one's sense of ownership, because all that one thinks one owns does in fact belong to God. By nonattachment, one is able to deny the power of anything to act on one.

As if he is examining spokes of a wheel that all emanate from the same hub, Vivekananda explores nonattachment from a different angle in chapter 7. He points out that the will is free only when it is outside the sphere of time, space, and causation. Everything within that sphere is bound by the laws of cause and effect, which is another aspect of karma. In order to attain freedom, one must go beyond the limitations of this universe. This means transcending mind, thought, senses, and imagination, for real religion begins where the universe ends. There are two ways to accomplish this, the so-called *negative way*, through reasoning (jnana yoga), and the *positive way*, through karma yoga, the yoga of action. This is a gradual process, through which the mind learns by experience the nature of things until it lets them all go.

However, this does not mean one must give up all one's possessions. It is the state of one's mind that is the key. One could renounce the world and live in a desert but remain attached to the world of the senses. The converse is also true: a rich person could still live in a state of nonattachment.

Vivekananda adds that one way of cultivating nonattachment, if one is religious, is to give all the fruits of one's actions to the Lord, because this amounts to a perpetual sacrifice of the small self. However, it is possible to be successful on the path of karma yoga even if one does not believe in God or in any metaphysical or philosophical system.

Vivekananda rounds off his discussion of karma yoga, in chapter 8, with comments about freedom, morality, and metaphysics. He describes freedom as the goal of everything in the universe, from an atom to a person; it is why the saint prays and the robber robs. However, freedom can be gained only through unselfishness, which is the ground of all morality. When one has given up the self and is conscious only of others, one has gained an infinite expansion that is the goal of all philosophical and religious systems. This does not mean that such a person will be able to improve the world, however, because the sum total of good in the world always remains constant. It cannot be increased or decreased; the opposites of happiness and pain must always exist; they are only different expressions of the rising of the same wave. Everything in creation is a struggle between opposites. However, if one can stand inside the turning wheel of the world and learn the secret of karma yoga, one can attain the freedom that all seek.

Action and Nonattachment

Vivekananda's exposition of karma yoga was intended as much for his Western listeners as for students of philosophy and religion in his native India. Rather than expound abstruse or esoteric theories, he pursued a few overarching ideas, such as nonattachment in the performance of work, a concept with which many Westerners were unfamiliar up to that point. As a result, *Karma Yoga* has had an unquantifiable but lasting impact on Western attempts to understand the Vedantic philosophy.

In his homeland, Vivekananda's practice of extolling the virtues of work in the context of karma yoga earned him some rebuke from orthodox adherents of Advaita Vedanta, who put a greater emphasis on renunciation of worldly activity. Vivekananda's response was to claim that they were misunderstanding the nature of Vedanta, which did not advocate the abdication of social responsibility. The key, as always, lay in the concept of action performed in a mental state of nonattachment.

Bryan Aubrey

Additional Reading

Athalaye, D. A. *Swami Vivekananda: A Study*. New Delhi, India: Ashish Publishing House, 1979. A laudatory study of Vivekananda's life and work that sometimes sacrifices objectivity for unbridled enthusiasm about its subject. Contains useful analyses, mainly in paraphrase, of Vivekananda's major works on the four yogas.

His Eastern and Western Disciples. *The Life of Swami Vivekananda*. 2 vols. 5th ed. Calcutta: Advaita Ashrama, 1979-1981. First published in 1912, this biography, which runs more than thirteen hundred pages, contains the most comprehensive collection of materials on Vivekananda's life. It is unashamedly hagiographic in tone, its purpose being to inspire seekers on the spiritual path described by Vivekananda. Includes a bibliography, glossary, and many illustrations.

Kapoor, Satish K. *Cultural Contact and Fusion: Swami Vivekananda in the West (1893-96)*. Jalandhar, India: ABS Publications, 1987. The most detailed book on Vivekananda's journey to the West. Examines the nature of his mission, his interaction with Christians, and the extent of his impact.

Nivedita, Sister. *The Master as I Saw Him*. 12th ed. Calcutta: Udbodhan Office, 1977. Nivedita was formerly Margaret Noble, an Anglo-Irish woman who met Vivekananda in 1895, became his devotee, and later moved to Calcutta as his disciple.

Rao, V. K. R. V. *Swami Vivekananda: The Prophet of Vedantic Socialism*. New Delhi: Ministry of Information and Broadcasting, 1979. Concisely covers the life and teachings of Vivekananda. The biographical section is almost entirely based on the official biography by Vivekananda's disciples and never escapes its hagiographic excesses. The assessment of Vivekananda's ideas and his legacy in modern India is more original; Rao asserts that what Vivekananda called "practical Vedanta" closely resembles modern socialism.

Sil, Narasingha P. *Swami Vivekananda: A Reassessment*. Selinsgrove, Pa.: Susquehanna University Press, 1997. This is a corrective to hagiographic accounts of Vivekananda by his disciples. Sil tries to discover the real man behind the myth. Vivekananda is seen as a tragic figure, ambitious and impulsive, approaching his spiritual mission as if it were a Napoleonic conquest and ending up frustrated and isolated in his final years. This is a scholarly, well-researched book marred by the author's hostility to Vivekananda and his willingness to consistently place the swami's words and actions in the worst possible light.

Williams, George M. "Swami Vivekananda: Archetypal Hero or Doubting Saint?" In *Religion in Modern India*, edited by Robert D. Baird. New Delhi, India: Manohar, 1981. Williams is one of the few scholars who have tried to penetrate beyond the Vivekananda legend and to see in him a more human figure. Williams's Vivekananda survives spiritual crisis and angst to become an effective religious leader.

Bryan Aubrey

Voltaire

Voltaire encompasses in his work the extremes of rationalism during the Enlightenment. Until he was middle-aged, he was an Optimist, but in his sixties he rejected this philosophy in disgust and brilliantly argued the limitations of reason. He wrote prolifically in all literary forms during his lifetime, making critical commentary on prevailing social conditions and conventions.

Principal philosophical works: *Lettres philosophiques*, 1734 (originally published in English as *Letters Concerning the English Nation*, 1733; also known as *Philosophical Letters*, 1961); *Discours de métaphysique*, 1736; *Éléments de la philosophie de Newton*, 1738 (*The Elements of Sir Isaac Newton's Philosophy*, 1738); *Discours en vers sur l'homme*, 1738-1752 (*Discourses in Verse on Man*, 1764); *Zadig: Ou, La Destinée, Histoire orientale*, 1748 (originally published as *Memnon: Histoire orientale*, 1747; *Zadig: Or, The Book of Fate*, 1749); *Poème sur le désastre de Lisbonne*, 1756 (*Poem on the Lisbon Earthquake*, 1764); *Candide: Ou, L'Optimisme*, 1759 (*Candide: Or, All for the Best*, 1759; also known as *Candide: Or, The Optimist*, 1762; also as *Candide: Or, Optimism*, 1947); *Traité sur la tolérance*, 1763 (*A Treatise on Religious Toleration*, 1764); *Dictionnaire philosophique portatif*, 1764, 1769 (enlarged as *La Raison par alphabet*, also known as *Dictionnaire philosophique*; *A Philosophical Dictionary for the Pocket*, 1765; also known as *Philosophical Dictionary*, 1945, enlarged 1962).

Born: November 21, 1694; Paris, France
Died: May 30, 1778; Paris, France

Early Life

Voltaire was born François-Marie Arouet on November 21, 1694, in Paris. His father had migrated to the capital from Poitou and prospered there, holding a minor post in the treasury. Voltaire was educated at the Jesuit Collège Louis-le-Grand, and many years later the Jesuits were to be the objects of savage satire in his masterpiece *Candide*. Voltaire was trained in the law, which he abandoned. As a young man, during the first quarter of the century, Voltaire already exhibited two traits that have come to be associated with the Enlightenment: wit and skepticism. Louis XIV ruled France until 1715, and the insouciant Voltaire (not yet known by that name) and his circle of friends delighted in poking fun at the pretentious backwardness of the Sun King's court.

In 1716, when Voltaire was twenty-two, his political satires prompted the first of his several exiles, in this instance to Sully-sur-Loire. He was, however, unrepentant; in 1717, more satirical verses on the aristocracy caused his imprisonment by *lettre de cachet* (without trial). During his eleven months in the Bastille, Voltaire, like so many imprisoned writers before him, practiced his craft. He wrote *Œdipe* (1718; *Oedipus*, 1761), a tragedy that was a great success upon the stage following his release. A year later, when *Oedipus* appeared in print, the author took the name Voltaire, an approximate anagram of Arouet. Such was his fame, however, that the pseudonym afforded him little chance of anonymity. He came eventually to be known as François-Marie Arouet de Voltaire.

Life's Work

By the age of thirty, Voltaire was well established as a man of letters. For the next fifty years, he produced an enormous and varied body of work: tragic plays, satires in prose and verse, histories, philosophical tales, essays, pamphlets, encyclopedia entries, and letters by the thousands. Also by the age of thirty, he was a wealthy man. He speculated in the Compagnie des Indes with great success, and his fortune grew over the years. Voltaire's personal wealth afforded him an independence of which few writers of the period could boast.

Still, his penchant for religious and political controversy had him in trouble again by 1726. The chevalier de Rohan caused him to be beaten and incarcerated in the Bastille for a second time. He was subsequently exiled to England, where he spent most of the period from 1726 to 1729. There, he learned the English language, read widely in the literature, and became the companion of Alexander Pope and other Queen Anne wits. *La Henriade* (1728; *Henriade*, 1732), his epic of Henry IV, was published during this period, and his sojourn in Britain would eventually produce *Philosophical Letters*. Voltaire's great achievement during the years immediately following his return to France was his *Histoire de Charles XII* (1731; *The History of Charles XII*, 1732). This account of the Swedish monarch is often characterized as the first modern history.

Philosophical Letters implicitly attacked French institutions through its approbation of English institutions. For example, Voltaire wittily suggests therein that, despite the manifest benefits of inoculation against smallpox, the French reject the practice because the English have adopted it first. Again, Voltaire angered powerful enemies. His book was burned, he barely escaped imprisonment, and he was forced to flee Paris for a third time. He settled at Cirey in Lorraine, first as the guest and eventually as the companion of the brilliant Madame du Châtelet. There, for the next fifteen years, he continued to write in all genres, but, having become acquainted with the works of John Locke and David Hume, he turned increasingly to philosophical and scientific subjects. As revealed in his *Discourses in Verse on Man*, Voltaire embraced the philosophy of Optimism during these years, believing that reason alone could lead humanity out of the dark-

ness and into the millennium. Gradually, his reputation was rehabilitated within court circles. He had been given permission to return to Paris in 1735, he was named official historiographer of France in 1743, and he was elected to the French Academy in 1746. In 1748, he published his first philosophical tale, *Zadig*.

Madame du Châtelet died in 1749. The next year, believing that Louis XV had offered him insufficient patronage, Voltaire joined the court of Frederick the Great of Prussia at Potsdam. For three years, Voltaire lived in great comfort and luxury, completing during this period *Le Siècle de Louis XIV* (1751; *The Age of Louis XIV*, 1752). He and the Prussian king, however, were not well suited temperamentally. They quarreled, and the inevitable breach occurred in 1753. Shortly thereafter, Voltaire purchased Les Délices (the delights), a château in Switzerland, near Geneva.

Voltaire. *(Library of Congress)*

He stayed in the good graces of the Swiss for exactly as long as he had managed in Prussia, three years. There, his encyclopedia entry for Geneva was perceived as having a contemptuous tone. The national pride of his hosts was wounded, and he left the country.

He bought a great estate, Ferney, on French soil but just across the Swiss frontier. Ferney was the perfect retreat for a controversialist with Voltaire's volatile history; if the French authorities decided to act against him again, he could simply slip across the border. For the last twenty years of his life, Voltaire used the Ferney estate as the base from which he tirelessly launched his literary attacks upon superstition, error, and ignorance. He employed a variety of pseudonyms but made no effort to disguise his inimitable style and manner. This transparent device gave the authorities, by then indulgent and weary of attempting to muzzle him, an excuse not to prosecute.

The decade of the 1750's wrought a change in the middle-aged Voltaire's attitude far greater than any change he had undergone previously. He was deeply affected by the Lisbon earthquake of November 1, 1755. In this horrendous tragedy, perhaps as many as fifty thousand people died, many while worshiping in packed churches on All Saints' Day. Voltaire began to reexamine his concept of a rational universe that functioned according to fixed laws that humanity could apprehend and to which people could adapt themselves. He was now repulsed by the Optimists' theory that (to overstate it only slightly) this is the best of all possible worlds and therefore that any natural occurrence must be ultimately for the best. His first bitter attack on Leibnizian Optimism was *Poem on the Lisbon Earthquake*. His rebuttal of this smug philosophy culminated in his masterpiece of dark comedy, *Candide*.

Voltaire claimed to have written this wildly improbable picaresque novel in three days during 1758. It was published in 1759 and was immensely popular; it averaged two new editions per year for the next twenty years. Pangloss, tutor to the incredibly callow hero, is a caricature of the optimistic philosophers Gottfried Wilhelm Leibniz and Christian von Wolff, although Voltaire's temperamental archenemy, the social philosopher Jean-Jacques Rousseau, fancied himself the model for Pangloss. *Candide*'s satire is by no means limited to Optimism, and the novel reveals the best and worst of its author's character traits. Voltaire lashes out at his lifelong enemies: superstition, bigotry, extremism, hypocrisy, and (despite the fact that it accounted for most of his personal wealth) colonialism. Also readily apparent are his anti-Semitism, his anti-Catholicism, and his sexism.

The major work of Voltaire's later years was the *Philosophical Dictionary*. He also involved himself deeply in the day-to-day operations of Ferney, and he maintained his voluminous correspondence with virtually all the eminent persons of Europe. For the first time in almost three decades, Voltaire returned to Paris in 1778. He was afforded a tumultuous hero's welcome, but he was eighty-three and ill; the celebration was too much for him in his fragile state of health. He died on May 30, within weeks of his triumphal return to the city of his birth.

Despite the Catholic Church's opposition to Voltaire's burial in sanctified ground, he was secretly—and inappropriately, some have suggested—interred at a convent outside the city. A decade later came the French Revolution, and Voltaire's enemies had ostensibly become the French people's as well. He was exhumed and made a second grand entrance into Paris. He was reburied in the Panthéon next to his old rival Rousseau, an irony he might have enjoyed.

Influence

Voltaire's work is extremely varied, sometimes self-contradictory. His sentiments are often more personal than universal. He had had bad experiences with Jesuit priests, Protestant enthusiasts, and Jewish businesspeople; hence, Jesuits, Calvinists, and Jews are mercilessly lampooned in *Candide*. He apparently had good experiences with Anabaptists, and the generous and selfless Anabaptist Jacques, in his brief appearance, is one of the few admirable characters in the novel. Voltaire had been cured of Optimism by the horror of the Lisbon earthquake, the savagery of the Seven Years' War, and the reversals in his personal life. Yet he did not completely give way to pessimism. His philosophy in his later years seems to have been a qualified meliorism, as characterized by his famous injunction that every person should tend his or her own garden.

The famous and spurious quotation "I disagree with everything you say, but I shall fight to the death for your right to say it" will be forever associated with Voltaire's memory. Although he probably never uttered these precise words, they are an admirable summation of the way he lived his intellectual life. The surviving pictures of Voltaire, most in old age, represent him as thin, sharp-featured, and sardonic. He is the very embodiment of one aspect of the neoclassical period: skeptical, irreverent, and valuing personal freedom above all other things.

Patrick Adcock

Philosophical Dictionary

Type of philosophy: Ethics, philosophy of religion
First published: Dictionnaire philosophique portatif,
   1764 (*A Philosophical Dictionary for the Pocket,*
   1765; also known as *Philosophical Dictionary,*
   1945)
Principal ideas advanced:
◊ Superstition and fanaticism, as evidenced in the Christian religion, are evil forces that must be eliminated.
◊ The Judeo-Christian concept of a jealous, judgmental God is a false one.
◊ There is a deity, but that deity is an impersonal being, one who created the world and then put it under the control of natural law.
◊ Evil is a fact of human existence; there is no particular Providence to intervene in the affairs of an individual or a group.
◊ However, a general Providence has endowed human beings with reason and with an impulse toward benevolence.
◊ Human beings are expected to put their benevolence into practice by acting to eliminate the evils that result from the actions of individuals or of institutions.

The philosophes were a group of eighteenth century thinkers, writers, and scientists who were convinced that reason, not prejudice and superstition, is the best guide for individuals and for society. All of them, including Voltaire, had long been working on the huge *Encyclopédie: Ou, Dic-*tionnaire raisonné des sciences, des arts et des métiers (1751-1772; 17 volumes of text, 11 volumes of plates; partial translation *Selected Essays from the Encyclopedy,* 1772; complete translation *Encyclopedia,* 1965), the completion of which is considered one of the great intellectual achievements of the Enlightenment. However, on September 28, 1752, Frederick the Great of Prussia is said to have suggested to Voltaire that he compile a much shorter book in dictionary form, which would advance the same ideas but would be more accessible. Voltaire promptly got to work, submitting a number of articles to the king during the next several months, but after leaving Frederick's court, he put the book aside and did not resume work on it until 1762.

In 1764, the book finally appeared. Published anonymously in Geneva under the title *Dictionnaire philosophique portatif,* it consisted of seventy-three articles. Voltaire was wise not to claim authorship; the book was burned in Geneva, at The Hague, and in Paris, besides being proscribed by the Holy Office in Rome. However, its popularity can be judged by the fact that it was reprinted three times under the same title, with numerous revisions and additions, until in 1769 it appeared as a two-volume edition entitled *La Raison par alphabet* (reason by alphabet), which contained 120 articles, including the long imaginary dialogue "A, B, C." The 1769 edition, reprinted as *Dictionnaire philosophique,* is considered the final and complete version of the work. Peter Gay's translation (*Philosophical Dictionary,* 1962) was the first complete, authentic edition available in English.

Form and Content
Other than the fact that it is organized alphabetically, Voltaire's *Philosophical Dictionary* bears little resemblance to a reference work. The form is idiosyncratic, the tone is informal, there are deliberate inaccuracies, and while claiming to be directed against intolerance, it reflects the author's own prejudices.

One reason the *Philosophical Dictionary* can still fascinate readers is that Voltaire took such pains to vary the forms of his entries. Sometimes, as in "Abraham" and "Joseph," he retells a story from the Bible, inserting his own comments. At other times, he relates an anecdote or a fable, like the make-believe myth about the Syrians in search of a toilet in "All Is Good." "Atheism" is a fairly conventional essay, tracing the history of an idea, though it is considerably livelier than most other essays of the sort. By contrast, the entry called "Civil and Ecclesiastical Laws," which purports to reproduce some notes found "among the papers of a lawyer," is simply a series of short commands, each beginning with the word "Let." A number of the segments are more like plays than essays in an encyclopedia or a dictionary. There are imagined dialogues between the author and the reader, as in "Virtue," and others between two fictional characters, like the Indian and the Japanese in "Japanese Catechism." Sometimes several people take part in a discussion, as in "A, B, C," which is made up of seventeen conversations on as many topics.

Personal Observations

Though his store of information is impressive, Voltaire does not pretend to distance himself from his work, as a scholar would. He makes no attempt to avoid personal references. Thus, he begins "Judea" by informing us that he has never been to that particular place and thanking God for it. Often he chats with the reader, as in the entry on "Soul," in which he asks, "What, then, do you call your soul?" and presses his listener to "admit" that it is nothing more than "a power of feeling, of thinking." At other times, he uses tone to preclude disagreement, as when he says at the beginning of the entry "Martyr," "We are hoaxed with martyrs until we're ready to burst out laughing." It would be difficult to start an argument after that. Another example of Voltaire's highly personal approach to his subject is his habit of digressing at will. For instance, in "All Is Good," just when he is well launched into an attack on the philosopher Gottfried Wilhelm Leibniz and his philosophy of Optimism, he decides to explain why he does not like to use quotations.

There are defects in the *Philosophical Dictionary*. Sometimes Voltaire is deliberately inaccurate. For example, as Peter Gay points out, he presents the Shechemites as victims, omitting any reference to the fact, clearly stated in Genesis, that they had incurred the wrath of the Hebrews by raping Dinah. Gay also notes that Voltaire alters the story of Ananias in order to make the Christians appear greedy.

Intolerance and Religion

Moreover, for all his emphasis on tolerance, Voltaire clearly dislikes not just the Jewish faith but the Jews themselves. In "Jephthah or Human Blood Sacrifices," for instance, Voltaire points out the bloody results of the Jewish law and suggests that one judge a people not by their view of themselves but by their records. He applies that standard to such great Old Testament figures as Abraham, David, and Moses, all of whom he finds less than admirable. In "History of Jewish Kings and Chronicles," he attacks the idea that it was God who wrote the history of the Jewish people, then comments sarcastically that if God were indeed their historian, the Jews would be a superior people, and we should "prostrate ourselves" before any Jewish "peddler" who happens along. Voltaire's comments about the Jews, past or present, are always waspish, whether his subject is an eighteenth century peddler or the complaining Hebrews he describes in "Moses" as "unjust children of Jewish vagabonds." There can be no doubt about the anti-Semitism of someone who writes, in "Cannibals," that the Jews might as well have been cannibals, for that habit was all they needed to make them "the most abominable [people] on earth."

However, unlike many of the Christians of his time, Voltaire did not loathe the Jews because they had rejected Christ or were responsible for his death, as the ignorant liked to think, but because they had provided the basis of Christianity. Voltaire had to annihilate the Old Testament before he could demolish the New Testament and accomplish his stated goal, to wipe out "infamy." Voltaire was understandably careful in defining his opponent. "Infamy," he indicated, was made up of superstition, or any belief beyond the "worship of a supreme Being," as he defines it in his article, and fanaticism, which he compares to insanity. Significantly, there is no entry under "Christ" in the *Philosophical Dictionary*, and "Christianity," which is subtitled "Historical Research into Christianity," claims merely to look at evidence for Christian dogma and in the process to present a history of the Christian church. Voltaire had to be careful; as he points out in the

"Inquisition" article, it was not difficult to be burned at the stake. However, it is generally agreed that what Voltaire really meant by infamy was not just superstition or fanaticism but Christianity itself. Throughout the *Philosophical Dictionary*, Voltaire makes it evident that he thinks Christianity is a fraud, based on superstition and perpetuated by fanatics and fools, and that the results of the religion's influence are oppression, persecution, intolerance, corruption, hypocrisy, the denial of liberty, and general misery.

Voltaire displays his contempt for the God of the Jews in such articles as "Genesis" and "Jephthah or Human Blood Sacrifices." In fact, whenever he talks about characters and events from the Old Testament, Voltaire takes pains to picture the God revealed in its pages as jealous, bloodthirsty, unjust, and totally irrational. No sensible person, Voltaire suggests in "Ezekiel," can imagine worshiping a deity who commands a prophet to eat bread smeared with cow dung. The God Christians worship is no better. Though he is called a God of love, he condemns to eternal damnation most of the human race, those who have never heard of him, those who doubt some Church dogma, and those who in some way defy the Church, whom he permits to rule the Christian world. What Voltaire thinks of the institution that purports to do God's will is evident in his essay "On Popery," as well as in his article entitled "Inquisition," in which he defines his subject as an "admirable and wholly Christian invention to make the pope and the monks more powerful and turn a whole kingdom into hypocrites."

A Noninterventionist God

The God Voltaire worships is identified in "Creed" as a creator and a beneficent deity who does not discriminate among his children but has provided for all alike. He does not intervene in their affairs, for he has given them reason and "moral principles" so that they can govern their own conduct. Voltaire admits that he himself has no answer for the problem of evil. That issue alone would prevent him from believing either in a Christian Providence or in the Optimists' deity, whose actions are always for the best. At least, if God does not intervene in this world, one cannot accuse him of being unjust.

The best Voltaire can do is to admit that some evils cannot be prevented—the Lisbon earthquake, for example, or what in "War" he lists as two "gifts" of "Providence," famine and plague. However, the third great source of human misery, war, is under human control, and therefore it can be eradicated.

In "Philosopher," Voltaire outlines what God expects of individuals and of rulers alike. They are to devote themselves to virtue, thus setting an example for those who look up to them. They can work to prevent crime and to promote harmony, thus making their own lives and the lives of all who come into contact with them as happy as possible, given the limitations set by the Deity when he created the world.

The Dictionary's Impact

Though most readers think of Voltaire as the author of the philosophical tale *Candide*, the *Philosophical Dictionary* is his most comprehensive work and an invaluable revelation of his mature thought. Given its scope and its technical brilliance, it may indeed be his masterpiece.

Just as his *Philosophical Dictionary* embodies his view of the world and its institutions, so Voltaire himself embodies the spirit of his age. For this very reason, it is difficult to assess his influence. He was simply one of a number of philosophes who produced the *Encyclopedia*, for example. Similarly, though he risked his life to save those persecuted by state and church, he was not alone in such efforts. His works helped prepare the way for the American Revolution and the French Revolution, but he himself was not a republican but a monarchist, and he would never have approved of turning over the government to an ignorant mob. His ideal ruler would have been a benevolent philosopher-king.

However, even though one cannot identify an event that occurred or a literary work that was written solely as the result of Voltaire's writings or specifically because of his *Philosophical Dictionary*, he did make a difference. His crusade against "infamy" certainly influenced those who wrote the U.S. Constitution to make sure that church and state remain separate, while his campaign against tyranny, whatever its source, continues to inspire those who believe that the rights of individuals are always more important than the welfare of a powerful majority or the advancement of a powerful institution.

Rosemary M. Canfield Reisman

Additional Reading

Aldington, Richard. *Voltaire*. London: Routledge & Kegan Paul, 1925. Although old, this work remains one of the standard biographical-critical works. Part 1 (chapters 1-10) serves as a general biography of Voltaire. Part 2 (chapters 11-19) examines Voltaire as poet, dramatist, literary critic, historian, biographer, philosopher, pamphleteer, and correspondent. The volume also contains a chronological listing of Voltaire's works by genre, followed by a list of the English translations up to the time of publication and a select biography.

Ayer, A. J. *Voltaire*. London: Weidenfeld and Nicolson, 1986. This volume, by noted philosopher Ayer, takes a closer look at the philosophy and life of Voltaire.

Durant, Will, and Ariel Durant. *The Age of Voltaire*. New York: Simon & Schuster, 1983. Part of the noted series by husband and wife historians Will and Ariel Durant. Covering Voltaire as well as his historic contemporaries, this volume focuses on the philosophies who planted the seeds for the French Revolution. The Durants show how Voltaire's thinking influenced the rise of the Enlightenment.

Gay, Peter. *Voltaire's Politics: The Poet as Realist*. 1959. 2d ed. Princeton, N.J.: Princeton University Press, 1988. A work of intellectual history that attempts to trace the psychological, social, and intellectual origins of Voltaire's ideas. The author portrays Voltaire's politics as realistic and humanely relativistic; he argues that Voltaire's humane sympathies failed him only in the case of his anti-Semitism.

Gray, John. *Voltaire*. New York: Routledge, 1999. An excellent biographical introduction to the thoughts of the philosopher, clearly presented and requiring no special background. Bibliography.

Mason, Haydn. *Candide: Optimism Demolished*. New York: Twayne, 1992. This work presents a study of Voltaire's most famous work, *Candide*.

_____. *Voltaire: A Biography*. Baltimore, Md.: The Johns Hopkins University Press, 1981. Organized according to seven periods in Voltaire's life. Mason states that he has not attempted a comprehensive treatment of the life of Voltaire, which would easily require ten volumes. Instead, he has attempted to capture the essence of the man as revealed under the pressure of circumstances. Contains a helpful chronology and a select bibliography.

Richter, Petyton E., and Ilona Ricardo. *Voltaire*. Boston: Twayne, 1980. A general portrait of the philosopher and his beliefs. Solid introduction for newcomers to Voltaire.

Torrey, Norman L. *The Spirit of Voltaire*. New York: Columbia University Press, 1938. Argues for and seeks to document Voltaire's moral integrity while granting that a certain duplicity was a necessary condition of his life and work. Concludes with a long chapter on Voltaire's religion, probing whether he was a deist, a mystic, or a humanist.

Patrick Adcock, updated by Lisa A. Wroble

Max Weber

A German social scientist and theorist widely acclaimed as the "father of sociology," Weber is best known for his thesis of the Protestant ethic, which links the psychological effects of Calvinism with the development of modern capitalism.

Principal philosophical works: *Gesammelte Aufsätze zur Religionssoziologie*, 1920-1921 (volume 1 contains *Die protestantische Ethik und der Geist des Kapitalismus*, first pb. 1904-1905 [*The Protestant Ethic and the Spirit of Capitalism*, 1930]; *Die protestantischen Sekten und der Geist des Kapitalismus* [*The Protestant Sects and the Spirit of Capitalism*, 1946]; *Die Wirtschaftsethik der Weltreligionen*, first pb. 1915 [*The Social Psychology of the World Religions*, 1946, and *The Religion of China: Confucianism and Taoism*, 1951]; volume 2 contains *Hinduismus und Buddhismus*, 1921 [*The Religion of India: The Sociology of Hinduism and Buddhism*, 1958]; volume 3 contains *Das antike Judentum*, 1921 [*Ancient Judaism*, 1952]); *Die rationalen und soziologischen Grundlagen der Musik*, 1921 (*The Rational and Social Foundations of Music*, 1958); *Die Stadt*, 1922 (*The City*, 1958); *Wirtschaft und Gesellschaft*, 1922 (translations include *The Theory of Social and Economic Organization*, 1947; *Max Weber on Law in Economy and Society*, 1954; *The Sociology of Religion*, 1963; and *Economy and Society: An Outline of Interpretive Sociology*, 1968); *Wirtschaftsgeschichte*, 1923 (*General Economic History*, 1927); *From Max Weber: Essays in Sociology*, 1946; *Max Weber on the Methodology of the Social Sciences*, 1949; *Sociological Writings*, 1994.

Born: April 21, 1864; Erfurt, Prussia (now in Germany)
Died: June 14, 1920; Munich, Germany

Early Life

Max Weber was the first child of Max and Helen Fallenstein Weber. His father was a prominent lawyer and aspiring politician whose family had attained considerable wealth in the German linen industry. An ardent monarchist and Bismarckian within the German Reichstag, the elder Weber was to his son the epitome of a patriarchal, amoral creature of pleasure who knew real politics and the art of compromise. His mother, on the other hand, was a highly educated, moralistic woman, intensely preoccupied with religious and social concerns, particularly with charity work for the poor. The hedonistic father and humanitarian mother shared little in common, and Weber grew to maturity in a household charged with open tension and hostility.

Weber received an excellent early education in select German private schools. In addition, because of the political prominence of his father, a considerable circle of famous personalities—such as Wilhem Dilthey, Heinrich von Treitschke, Levin Goldschmidt, and Theodor Mommsen—frequented the Weber household. Meeting and engaging in political discussion with such men of prestige not only stimulated young Weber's intellectual curiosity but also provided him with contacts who would help promote his career in later life.

Weber began his university studies in 1882 at Heidelberg—his mother's home during her youth—taking courses in law, history, and theology. At his father's suggestion (and against his mother's wishes), he also joined the student fraternity, an activity that consumed much of his time in drinking bouts and duels. In 1883, Weber moved to Strasbourg to fulfill his one-year military obligation in the National Service. There, Weber visited and developed a close attachment to his aunt and uncle: Ida Baumgarten, a devout woman much like his mother, and Hermann Baumgarten, a professor of history who, unlike his father, was highly critical of the Bismarckian empire.

Hoping to extricate young Weber from the influence of the Baumgartens, the elder Weber encouraged his son to resume his studies back home at the University of Berlin. Weber returned to Berlin, and, except for one semester in school at Göttingen and several months away on military exercises, Weber spent the next eight years at home. In 1889, Weber was graduated magna cum laude and then began preparing for his *Habilitation* (a higher doctorate required to teach in German universities), which he received in 1891. While pursuing his advanced studies, Weber worked intermittently as a lawyer's assistant and a university assistant—two unremunerative apprenticeships. Hence at age twenty-nine, Weber was still residing in his parents' home, financially dependent on their income and con-

tinually subject to their conflicting claims on his loyalty.

In 1893, Weber married his second cousin, Marianne Schnitger, an intelligent woman who later achieved some prominence in the German feminist movement. The marriage lasted until Weber's death but was never consummated. Although their marriage was without affection, Weber and his wife were intellectually compatible. Following Weber's death, Marianne published a seven-hundred-page biography of her late husband that contained not a negative word regarding their union.

Life's Work

A workaholic with strong academic credentials and political contacts, Weber rose rapidly in the teaching profession. After a brief appointment in Berlin, Weber in 1894 became a full professor in economics at the University of Freiburg. Two years later, he was called to the University of Heidelberg to succeed the preeminent professor of political economy, Karl Knies. As a professor, Weber advocated what he called "freedom from value-judgment" in lecturing. This doctrine demanded that teachers present to their students the established empirical facts without expressing their evaluations as to whether the facts were satisfactory or unsatisfactory. Weber also was an avid researcher and writer. During these years, however, his research interests focused on rather mundane economic issues of immediate application.

Weber's academic career, however, was cut short in 1898 when he suffered a severe mental and physical breakdown that virtually incapacitated him for four years and prevented him from returning to the classroom until 1918. The symptoms of the illness included insomnia, inner tension, exhaustion, bouts of anxiety, and continual restlessness. Biographers have speculated that familial problems triggered this neu-

Max Weber. *(Library of Congress)*

rosis. In 1897, Weber had a violent dispute with his father over the authoritarian way his father treated his mother. Following the argument, his father stormed away from Weber's Heidelberg home, promising never to return. Shortly thereafter, the elder Weber died of a gastric hemorrhage. His mother quickly recovered from her grief, but Weber harbored intense feelings of guilt. Throughout his life, Weber had been intellectually torn between the moralistic idealism of his mother and the practical realism of his father. Outwardly, he resembled his father; inwardly, he aspired for the moral certitudes of his mother. Perhaps the tragic circumstances of his father's death locked the two sides of his personality in a paralyzing symbiosis.

Whatever the cause, Weber's neurotic breakdown had a dramatic impact upon his future thought and career. The prolonged agony of his personal crisis led him to develop insights into the relationship between religious ethics and social and economic processes that would distinguish his subsequent scholarship. His illness also freed him from the burden of the classroom. After a lengthy leave of absence, in 1903 Weber resigned from his university position and accepted the editorship of *Archiv für Sozialwissenschaft und Sozialpolitik* (social science and social political archives). This position provided Weber with a place to publish his own materials without passing an outside review. It also provided him with the leisure to write at his own pace. Except for a brief tenure as a German military hospital administrator during World War I, from the time of his partial recovery in 1903 until his return to academe in 1918, Weber was not obligated to any duties other than the editorial work he took on himself. All of Weber's most important works were written during these years between the worst part of his illness and his death. As tragic as his personal crisis was, without it he would not have achieved the greatness for which he is remembered.

Weber published his most famous piece, *The Protestant Ethic and the Spirit of Capitalism*, in the journal he edited during the years 1904 and 1905. In this work, Weber noted the correlation in German communities between the expansion of capitalism and Protestant ideology. He attributed this relationship to accidental psychological conse-

quences of the Puritan doctrine of predestination. This doctrine, Weber postulated, produced an extreme condition of anxiety among Calvinist believers, which served to motivate them to discipline their lives in every respect. Calvinists worked hard, avoided idleness and waste, and, as a consequence, accumulated considerable wealth. Ironically, however, as capitalism grew and Calvinists became rich, Puritanism began to fade. The Protestant ethic, in the end, transformed the world but in so doing eventually undermined itself.

After completing his study of Protestant ethics, Weber focused attention upon other world religions: Judaism, Confucianism, Daoism, Hinduism, and Buddhism. In all of his works on the sociology of religion, Weber emphasized the "universal historical relationship of religion and society." His studies attempted to show how different religious worldviews have affected the development of their cultures. In contrast to Karl Marx, who viewed religion as simply a reflection of the material basis of society, Weber argued that religious beliefs have significant impact on economic actions and, in the case of Protestantism, were themselves the basis for the emergence of modern capitalism.

In 1909, Weber agreed to edit a new edition of an academic encyclopedia intended to cover every area of economics. In addition to arranging other contributors for the project, Weber planned to write for the volume a section on the relationship between economy and society. Although he never finished this work, Weber's involvement in the project provided him with the occasion to work out a comprehensive sociology. At the time of his death, he had written nearly fifteen hundred pages of text, but the work still was incomplete. The disordered and fragmentary manuscript was edited and published posthumously as *Economy and Society: An Outline of Interpretive Sociology*. This book contains many of Weber's thoughts on politics, law, bureaucracy, and social stratification.

Perhaps Weber's greatest impact on his contemporaries came near the end of World War I, when he crusaded against Germany's annexationist war goals and policy of submarine warfare. His journalistic attacks at this time frequently placed him in conflict with the military censors. After Germany's defeat, Weber assisted in the drafting of the new constitution and in the founding of the German Democratic Party.

Weber briefly returned to the classroom, accepting in 1918 a professorship at the University of Vienna and the following year at the University of Munich. In early summer of 1920, Weber became ill with influenza, which soon turned into pneumonia. He died at his home in Munich on June 14, 1920.

Influence

In a strictly scientific sense, Weber did not develop a new sociological theory. His works instead consisted of a cloud of axioms, hypotheses, suggestions, and a few theorems—the details of which generally have been discredited by specialists in their respective fields. Weber also did not discover any new problematic area that had not been discovered by others before him. Sociologists previous to and independent of him, for example, had delved into matters relating to the origins and effects of modern capitalism. Moreover, largely because little of his work was published in book form while he was alive, Weber did not stand in the center of sociological discourse during his own life. Much to his dismay, few of his peers welcomed his "freedom from value-judgment" doctrine, which was Weber's major methodological contribution to social science disciplines.

Yet, today Weber is almost the canonized saint of sociology who is widely acclaimed as the most influential and, perhaps, the most profound of twentieth century social scientists. His greatness does not lie in cerebral consistency, for much of his work is ambiguous and inconclusive, if not contradictory. Instead, Weber's fame is a result of his multisided, far-reaching intellect. Weber was a genius whose work crossed all the boundaries of sociology, law, economics, history, and religion. His multidimensional works influenced thinkers as diverse as C. Wright Mills, H. Richard Niebuhr, György Lukács, and Carl Schmitt. Weber's works remain "classic" because they call scholars away from the narrow perspectives of their individual disciplines to ask the grand questions about the meaning of human culture for which there are no easy answers.

Terry D. Bilhartz

The Protestant Ethic and the Spirit of Capitalism

Type of philosophy: Ethics, philosophy of history, social philosophy

First published: Die protestantische Ethik und der Geist des Kapitalismus, 1904-1905, rev. ed. 1920 (*The Protestant Ethic and the Spirit of Capitalism*, 1930)

Principal ideas advanced:

◇ Human history can be understood only by way of multicausal analysis, including analysis of human values and beliefs.

◇ Modern capitalism is the historical product of economic, political, and social developments combined with an *ethos* that requires people to subordinate personal and traditional interests to the duties of their vocations and the needs of their business enterprises.

◇ The source of this ethic of duty in one's calling is the Protestantism of the seventeenth and eighteenth centuries, especially Puritanism, whose adherents sought relief from salvation anxiety by viewing success in their callings coupled with methodical personal asceticism as proof of their favorable status before God.

◇ These Protestants unintentionally helped set in motion the modern economic system, which gradually cast aside religion but continues to require methodical work in a calling.

Max Weber, one of the founders of modern sociology, and certainly one of the most brilliant and influential social thinkers of the twentieth century, was essentially unknown in the United States until the 1930 publication of Talcott Parsons's translation of *The Protestant Ethic and the Spirit of Capitalism*. Having first published the work in 1904-1905, Weber produced a revised edition shortly before his death in 1920. The book was Weber's entry into a number of contemporary debates, and this multidimensional quality contributes to its status as a classic. For example, with his book, Weber took a stand in an important methodological debate of his day known to historians of the social sciences as the *Methodenstreit*, or the struggle over method. In this debate between those who believed the social sciences should follow a method more in line with the natural sciences and those who argued for a method based on the historical approach to human phenomena, Weber demonstrated the possibilities of the latter with his groundbreaking historical analysis of the rise of modern capitalism.

On another front, Weber argued that religion had been a decisive determinant in Western economic development, thus disputing Marxist analyses that reduced ideological expression to primarily economic determinants. Perhaps most important, Weber entered into the debate concerning the nature of modernity itself. In his presentation of the "spirit" of the modern capitalist system, Weber attempted to present a clear and sober analysis of the origins, prospects, and cultural and personal costs of modern economic life.

The Protestant Ethic and the Spirit of Capitalism was only a small part of Weber's published and unpublished work. In order to place the book in the context of Weber's wider outlook, Parsons took an essay that Weber published in 1920 as an introduction to a separate set of sociological studies of religion and society and placed it at the beginning of his translation under the title "Author's Introduction." In that essay, Weber argued that only by way of the comparative study of cultures can the Western world historically comprehend itself and its own unique development, because what counts as "rational" is relative to the values and goals that structure a person's or group's action. Action that is rational from the perspective of consistent devotion to one value or goal may be completely irrational in the light of other values or goals. What is of special interest to Weber is how a sense of obligation to live consistently with a given set of values can emerge in the first place, how changes in what people consider to be rational can occur, and how contradictory goals and values intersect in people's lives, such that unintended consequences take developments in surprising directions.

Protestants and Modern Capitalism
It was commonly accepted among historians of Weber's day that territories with Protestant roots seemed to have outpaced Catholic territories in capitalist development. Moreover, in religiously mixed territories, Protestants seemed to outnumber Catholics in both the business classes and the stratum of skilled and technically trained work-

ers. After considering and discarding several possible explanations for these phenomena—for example, that Protestants enjoy less ecclesiastical control than Catholics and are thus freer to innovate and to pursue their economic interests, or that Catholics are more otherworldly and less materialistic than Protestants, who tend to be more progressive and life-affirming—Weber presents his own thesis.

Weber's position is not that modern capitalism was invented by the Protestants he discusses, nor that modern capitalism is the only sort of capitalism there is. Rather, Weber's view is that modern capitalism is the unique product of a complex web of material, technological, and ideological conditions. This leads him to oppose as too simplistic any Marxist causal overemphasis on the material substructure of human life. For Weber, as essential as material, political, and technological conditions are for the explanation of any social development, no explanation is complete that fails to take into account the meaning that people ascribe to their actions. People are motivated by the values they hold, and their actions play a causal role in historical change. It is this feature that Weber highlights in his book. He wants to understand what it is about Protestantism that seems to motivate people to act in ways that are congruent with the rationality required by modern capitalism.

A Calling
Referring to the writings of the eighteenth century American Benjamin Franklin, Weber argues that what is most distinctive about modern capitalism is not that it is characterized by greedier, more adventuresome capitalists than in previous eras, but rather that modern economic life is pervaded by the notion that it is one's paramount duty to work proficiently in one's "calling." When Franklin admonished his readers that "Time is money," he was expressing not merely a shrewd business maxim but an ethical stance toward life. This stance emphasized subordination of one's own interests to the interests of one's calling or one's business, diligence and discipline in economic matters, and abhorrence of idleness in both oneself and one's money. Modern capitalism emerged in part because sufficient numbers of people renounced the traditional estimation of

work as a mere means to maintain an accustomed way of life and instead adopted this ascetic ethic in their everyday working lives. They, like Franklin, came to think of careful reinvestment and relentlessly methodical labor in one's vocation as a testimony to one's moral and social worth. These people were bearers of the modern capitalist spirit. However, who were they, and where did they acquire this notion of calling?

Weber's argument is that Protestantism produced not capitalism, but rather this notion of a calling. During the Protestant Reformation, Martin Luther, with his doctrine of salvation by faith alone, undercut the medieval system of religious callings represented by various monastic orders and elevated service to others in secular callings as the primary arena for the practice of Christian love. However, it would be subsequent Protestant denominations in the seventeenth and eighteenth centuries that would become the bearers of the new economic outlook, especially Calvinism, Pietism, Methodism, and the various Anabaptist and Spiritualist sects. Weber singles out these denominations because of their emphasis on what he calls "innerworldly asceticism." Whereas medieval asceticism was primarily otherworldly—practiced within monastery walls—these Protestant groups required that their members give evidence of their faith by leading disciplined and diligent lives of service in the world by way of their secular vocations.

Weber thinks that of these groups, seventeenth century Calvinism produced the most intense incentive toward innerworldly asceticism. This was because the Calvinist emphasis on the doctrine of predestination, which holds that God has already determined from eternity who will be saved and who will be damned, cut off the traditional means of relief from salvation anxiety. No action, no experience, no magical intervention, no priestly mediation can alter one's eternal fate, forever sealed by God's primordial and inscrutable will. Calvinist Puritans were left with no avenues for the *achievement* of salvation. Nevertheless, there was one avenue left for *assurance* of their predetermined status: self-observation of one's relentless activity, proficiency, and diligence in one's calling. Inefficiency and wastefulness of one's time and one's assets were a sure sign that one was not one of the elect. Holding beliefs that

were functionally equivalent to predestination, the other three Protestant groups also managed to inculcate in the faithful—although to a somewhat lesser extent than Puritanism—the same notion that diligence in one's calling provided proof of one's favorable status before God.

The Work Ethic

Weber notes that even though medieval otherworldly asceticism demanded poverty of its individual devotees, nevertheless the monasteries were subject to ongoing waves of reform because their ascetic organization of time and work paradoxically generated greater productivity, greater wealth, and, inevitably, greater materialistic temptations. A similar consequence results from innerworldly asceticism. Wealth is generated by ceaseless and disciplined work, but, unlike the monk, the Protestant laborer does not renounce property with a vow of poverty. Property presents the Puritan not with an encumbrance on the road to salvation, but rather with a task to be performed in the world for God's glory. Certainly laborers must not become attached to their property and its fruits, but this is because they are to be stewards of God's bounty. The idolatrous use of wealth in luxurious and leisurely activity is a constant temptation, but the Puritan resists such attachments, reinvesting and thus multiplying this borrowed bounty.

To those steeped in the traditional medieval economic *ethos*, such activity appears to be the unnatural pursuit of wealth as an end in itself and thus represents the height of irrationality, if not the epitome of greed and avarice. To those laboring under the new *ethos*, however, it is assurance of their salvation that is at stake. Either way, one thing is clear: The traditional mode of production cannot compete with the new economic spirit. Traditionally operated enterprises, once confronted on a grand enough scale with this new breed of employer, along with sufficient numbers of exploitable but religiously dutiful employees, must conform or go under.

Weber now asks what all of this has to do with Ben Franklin, who, after all, was not a Puritan. His answer is that the union of Protestant innerworldly asceticism with the relevant material, political, and technological conditions helped transform the way people did business, and the resulting economic system gradually took on a life of its own. In the present, Weber points out, modern capitalism resists and tends to break down religious, traditional, and other forms of interference or restraint. Hence, men and women subordinate themselves to the tasks and sacrifices of their callings not because they are Protestants worried about their salvation, but because the system requires it, binding them to its rules like an "iron cage." Modern capitalism no longer requires people to be Protestants in belief, but it does require them to practice the Protestant "work ethic"—the discipline, efficiency, and busy-ness of innerworldly asceticism. Failure to do so means economic disadvantage or bankruptcy. The Puritans and related religious groups, of course, did not intend to play a role in the construction of the modern capitalist system, and they would surely be appalled by the materialistic values of modern economic life. However, nevertheless, unintentionally, in pursuit of otherworldly goals, the consequences of their practice far outlived the viability of their beliefs.

Weber's Legacy

Since its publication, nearly every aspect of Weber's thesis has been the subject of rigorous and relentless debate. Did Weber properly interpret Ben Franklin? Did he correctly interpret the various religious authors he used for his sources? Was his interpretation of the Protestant idea of calling accurate? Did he miss evidence that showed that modern capitalism may have developed much earlier than the so-called capitalist spirit appeared? If it did, does this negate his thesis? Is it true that Protestant territories were more advanced economically than Catholic ones, or was Weber taken in by the residual anti-Catholicism of Germany's earlier Kulturkampf? Did Weber ignore or misconstrue other sources of the capitalist spirit? Were the monasteries of medieval Western Christendom in fact seedbeds for economic asceticism? Is Weber's emphasis on the study of motives and meaning sufficient, appropriate, or relevant for his topic? Did Weber correctly identify the unique characteristics of modern economic life?

On all these issues, Weber has his detractors and defenders. In this respect, perhaps one of the greatest achievements of *The Protestant Ethic and the Spirit of Capitalism* has been the expansive debates it unleashed about the historical emergence of modernity. However, the book's continuing appeal cannot be explained only by the suggestiveness of its historical thesis. Many readers of the work find in its pages searing and haunting psychological, cultural, and philosophical insights into life in the modern economic system. They may well catch a glimpse of themselves in Weber's anxious and lonely Puritans or ponder Weber's sober appraisal of the human future. For many, there is something uncannily familiar in Weber's portrait of the Puritan's search for ultimate assurance through ceaseless rational efficiency and relentless productivity in a disenchanted and rationally inscrutable world.

Bradley Starr

Additional Reading

Albrow, Martin. *Max Weber's Construction of Social Theory*. New York: St. Martin's Press, 1990. Excellent extended introduction to most of the elements of Max Weber's social theory, including his personal, historical, and intellectual background. Carefully organizes and clarifies the many complicated thematic strands of Weber's work.

Bendix, Reinhard. *Max Weber: An Intellectual Portrait*. Garden City, N.Y.: Doubleday, 1960. An older, but useful extended overview of Weber's sociological works.

Brubaker, Rogers. *The Limits of Rationality: An Essay on the Social and Moral Thought of Max Weber*. London: George Allen & Unwin, 1984. Careful and persuasive presentation of Weber's profoundly influential concept of "rationalization" in its various forms. Presents Weber as an ethicist and analyst of modernity and its crises.

Collins, Randall. *Max Weber: A Skeleton Key*. Beverly Hills, Calif.: Sage, 1986. Superb brief introduction to Weber's life and thought as well as to some of the critical issues in Weber scholarship. Excellent starting point for further study.

Diggins, John Patrick. *Max Weber: Politics and the Spirit of Tragedy*. New York: Basic Books, 1996. A passionately and clearly written account of Weber's life as well as of his ethical and political perspective. Uses Weber's lifelong interest in the United States as a vehicle to explore his relevance to late twentieth century American thought and history.

Lehmann, Hartmut, and Guenther Roth, eds. *Weber's Protestant Ethic: Origins, Evidence, Contexts*. Cambridge, England: Cambridge University Press, 1995. Excellent collection of scholarly essays covering a wide range of late twentieth century assessments of Weber's famous Protestant ethic thesis.

Morrison, Ken. *Marx, Durkheim, Weber: Formations of Modern Social Thought*. London: Sage, 1995. Provides an accessible and careful survey of Weber's key works in sociology and methodology. Includes a helpful glossary of Weberian terminology.

Ritzer, George. *The McDonaldization of Society*. Rev. ed. Thousand Oaks, Calif.: Pine Forge Press, 1996. A stimulating, troubling, and highly readable application of the Weberian concept of rationalization in an analysis of the "iron cages" of late twentieth century life.

Weber, Marianne. *Max Weber: A Biography*. Translated by Harry Zohn. New York: Wiley, 1975. A haunting and profound account of Weber's life and times, amounting to an insightful intellectual portrait of Weber and post-World War I Germany by an intimate and intellectually astute participant.

Terry D. Bilhartz, updated by Bradley Starr

Cornel West

West, an advocate of the interpretation of philosophical pragmatism that he terms "prophetic pragmatism," holds that an amalgamation of Christianity and Marxism can overcome white racism and offer hope to the black community.

Principal philosophical works: *Prophesy Deliverance! An Afro-American Revolutionary Christianity*, 1982; *Prophetic Fragments*, 1988; *The American Evasion of Philosophy: A Genealogy of Pragmatism*, 1989; *The Ethical Dimensions of Marxist Thought*, 1991; *Prophetic Thought in Postmodern Times*, 1993; *Prophetic Reflections: Notes on Race and Power in America*, 1993; *Race Matters*, 1993; *Keeping Faith: Philosophy and Race in America*, 1993.

Born: June 2, 1953; Tulsa, Oklahoma

Early Life

Cornel Ronald West was born to a civilian U.S. Air Force administrator, Clifton Louis West, Jr., and his wife, Irene Bias West, an elementary schoolteacher and principal. The couple's older son, Clifton Louis III, remembers his brother as a gregarious youth who liked to go to two or three parties on a weekend, but only after he had read two or three books. The Wests had two daughters as well.

West was born in Tulsa, Oklahoma, but spent most of his formative years in Sacramento, California. A troubled youth, he received a six-month suspension from elementary school for striking a pregnant teacher who demanded that he say the Pledge of Allegiance, which he declined to do in protest against racial segregation in the United States. This crisis was resolved after some weeks when West was permitted to enroll in a local accelerated school.

By the age of eight, West was reading adult books voraciously. He particularly enjoyed a biography of Theodore Roosevelt, who became one of his childhood heroes. Roosevelt, like West, suffered from asthma as a child and spent sleepless nights propped up on pillows. Roosevelt overcame his infirmity and went to Harvard, which is precisely what the young West vowed he would do.

During his years in secondary school, West was exposed to the activist racial philosophy of the Black Panthers, whose headquarters were near the Baptist church he attended regularly. During this period, through the Black Panthers, he was introduced to the writings of Karl Marx, which influenced his thinking profoundly, particularly when he considered Marxist economics in the light of people in his Baptist congregation who were only a few generations removed from slavery and who, despite working hard, lived a marginal existence.

After finishing secondary school at the age of seventeen, West entered Harvard University, where he majored in Near Eastern languages and literature. He received the bachelor of arts degree magna cum laude in 1973, completing his studies in three years despite having to work two jobs during much of his Harvard career and despite a consuming social life of partygoing, music, and dancing. Jazz would remain a central factor in West's life and thought, and West came to identify music as an important restorative of his soul.

West continued his education at Princeton University, which granted him a master's degree in 1975 and a Ph.D. in 1980. Midway through his doctoral studies, West returned to Harvard as a Du Bois fellow. With encouragement from philosopher Richard Rorty, he worked during that year on a novel that has not been published.

Cornel West. *(Courtesy of West)*

Life's Work

In 1977, West became assistant professor of philosophy at New York City's Union Theological Seminary, a position he held until 1983, when he was granted tenure and promoted to associate professor. He joined the Divinity School of Yale University as an associate professor in the same year and remained there until 1987. West taught in France at the University of Paris during the spring of 1987. In 1988, he rejoined the faculty of Union Theological Seminary for another year of teaching before being appointed professor of religion and director of Afro-American Studies at

Princeton University in 1989. There, working with such luminaries as novelist Toni Morrison and biographer Arnold Rampersad, West turned his administrative talents to creating what was considered, by the mid-1990's, the United States' best program in African American studies. In 1997, West joined the Afro-American Studies Program at Harvard University.

A committed Christian labeling himself a progressive black Baptist, West also became a Marxist. He would explore race relations throughout his professional life and became convinced that a combination of Christianity and Marxism offers the most effective means of combating racism and male dominance in contemporary American society.

The academic community has been considerably more resistant to West's social views than have those outside the academy. A number of scholars have expressed concern about West's seeming conviction that certain religious texts are absolute, a posture they fear limits the objectivity and depth of his analyses. His approach, essentially deductive and frequently authoritarian, runs counter to the inductive approach that most current academic humanists adopt in their philosophical explorations. This concern arises, at least in part, from the fact that contemporary scholars seek to maintain an intellectual detachment and neutrality that someone professing an avowed Christian bias is unlikely to possess.

West's *Prophesy Deliverance! An Afro-American Revolutionary Christianity* encapsulates many of the social theories that the author presents in his later writing and lectures. The essence of West's argument is that the combination of Christianity and Marxism can power the United States' socioeconomic engine strongly enough to bring about significant changes in society.

This earliest of West's full-length philosophical studies was commended for its clear, crisp writing style as well as for marking "an entirely new stage of development in the movement of black liberation theology," as a reviewer for the academic book-review journal *Choice* wrote. West drew on such sources as the writings of W. E. B. Du Bois and Toni Morrison, intertwining them with Marxism, African American Christianity, and the philosophy of René Descartes in his attempt to create a critical framework for African American thought. Before West, African American thought often had been treated as though it was a monolith rather than the complex entity that any body of human thought necessarily is.

In considering black rage, which underlies such misfortunes as the race riots following the assassination of Martin Luther King, Jr., in 1968 and those following the beating of Rodney King in 1992, West identifies institutions through which black rage can be channeled. West may himself have expressed black rage when he struck his elementary school teacher in Sacramento, but his rage was soon channeled in such ways as to become a positive motivating force in his life. Reflecting on the question of black rage, West concludes that churches, including black mosques and synagogues, offer constructive means of channeling rage, as do black athletic apprenticeship networks. He considers religious institutions and black music two highly important outlets for channeling black rage into actions that benefit black society and society as a whole.

West is characterized by his ability to integrate sources from a variety of disciplines within a single work. For example, in *Prophetic Fragments*, an essay containing a socialist hypothesis on racism is followed immediately by one that presents black rap as the last form of transcendence available to young black ghetto dwellers.

Because West frequently moves quickly from one philosophical or social posture to another, his work has been described by one critic, Adolph Reed, as a thousand miles wide and about two inches deep, a criticism echoed in one way or another by many academicians. West counters such criticism by saying that it is not his style to wrestle for years with one idea. Rather, he claims that he wants to be a provocative intellectual who writes about many unsettling issues.

West's reputation as an intellectual gadfly seems secure. He forces people to think in original ways about pressing social issues and suggests, indeed at times creates, new contexts for their thinking. An example of this is found in his analysis of President George Bush's nomination of Clarence Thomas to the Supreme Court, a position for which many members of the legal profession considered Thomas unqualified. West points out that Bush placed the black community in the embarrassing position of being unwilling to protest this nomination despite the reservations many black people had regarding it. West, calling Bush's strategy cynical, argues that this nomination disoriented most black leaders, who could not utter publicly that a black Supreme Court nominee was unqualified. West contends that this reveals how captive black leaders are to white racist stereotypes about black intellectual talent. In time, of course, the National Association for the Advancement of Colored People did oppose the nomination, but its procrastination in expressing its disapproval buttresses West's insightful claim.

West's most ambitious and important book is *The American Evasion of Philosophy*, a study of American pragmatism offering keen insights into John Dewey's philosophy and discussing Ralph Waldo Emerson, C. S. Peirce, William James, and others. Much of his Marxist philosophy is amplified in *The Ethical Dimensions of Marxist Thought*, in which he quite effectively distances Marx's philosophy from the totalitarian manifestations of that philosophy in Communist nations throughout the world.

Prophetic Thought in Postmodern Times and *Prophetic Reflections: Notes on Race and Power in America* are both collections of West's speeches and interviews. In the same year that those two volumes appeared, West published *Race Matters*, a collection of previously published essays specifically aimed at a general audience. The book succeeded in focusing considerable public attention on West, who became a frequent participant on nationally televised talk shows and in other public arenas, achieving the role of a public intellectual concerned centrally with matters of race.

Influence

West's fresh social insights, delivered to large, general audiences much as Martin Luther King, Jr., did in the 1960's, proved him capable of forcing such audiences to revise their thinking about racial matters in ways that may one day change the entire social landscape of the United States, although many of West's social and economic theories may seem outrageously utopian and impractical.

West cannot be categorized facilely as liberal or conservative. He shares with neoconservatives a vision of the importance of the family in society. He departs from the neoconservatives, however, in eschewing the typical patriarchal family structure of many black homes because of its subordination of women and its characteristic homophobia.

West is crucially concerned with what he calls the maldistribution of wealth in the United States. He considers the impoverished to be despairing and the wealthy (into whose ranks, ironically, he has been catapulted) to suffer from paranoia. He contends that people cannot talk about race without talking about poverty and that they cannot talk about poverty without talking about the ways in which wealth and power are distributed. This stand makes West extremely critical of liberal capitalism but also distances him from conservatives, who generally support decreases in the sort of government regulation that the implementation of West's economic policies would necessarily entail.

West faults black liberals for considering race the fundamental, or even exclusive, factor in accounting for the current inferior position of African Americans in society. He also faults black conservatives who blame black inequality on behavioral characteristics and contend that if African Americans work hard enough and well enough, they will succeed in improving their status. West sees the truth lying somewhere in between these views. He points out that many black people do work hard but can barely satisfy their basic needs because they are confined to a particular level within the workforce. This situation exists partly because of their race, which, in the past, denied them educational opportunities equal to those available to nonblacks, particularly at the crucial levels where basic skills usually are acquired. That problem has been alleviated in part by relaxation of real estate restrictions, both overt and covert, that prevented African Americans from living in desirable neighborhoods with superior schools. The effects of this step toward racial equality, however, will take a generation or more to become evident.

R. Baird Shuman

The American Evasion of Philosophy

A Genealogy of Pragmatism

Type of philosophy: Ethics, pragmatism
First published: 1989
Principal ideas advanced:
◇ The roots of American pragmatism lie in Ralph Waldo Emerson's evasion of exclusionary philosophical concepts.
◇ The pragmatism of C. S. Peirce and William James was important but elitist.
◇ John Dewey articulated a more populist pragmatism than Peirce or James.
◇ Richard Rorty brought about a rebirth of American pragmatism but shrank from political activism.
◇ Combining Christian principles and Marxism offers the greatest hope to the oppressed masses in America.

Cornel West's *The American Evasion of Philosophy* appeared at a crucial point in his academic career. He had left his associate professorship at Yale University's Divinity School and had spent part of 1987 in France at the University of Paris. Back at New York City's Union Theological Seminary, where he had taught from 1977 until 1983, he was the leading candidate for the directorship of the Afro-American Studies Program at Princeton University, a position to which he was appointed in 1989, shortly after the appearance of this book, which is generally regarded as his most significant to date.

West's previous publications included two edited volumes, *Theology in the Americas: Detroit II Conference Papers* (1982) and *Post-Analytic Philosophy* (1985), as well as *Prophesy Deliverance! An Afro-American Revolutionary Christianity* (1982) and *Prophetic Fragments* (1988), a collection of essays. His most popular book, *Race Matters* (1993), directed toward general audiences, had not yet appeared.

An Agenda for Black Liberation
West's early work helped establish the philosophical agenda for black liberation following the Civil Rights movement of the 1960's and early 1970's. In his introduction to *The American*

Evasion of Philosophy, West expresses concern about the transformation of highly intelligent liberal intellectuals into tendentious neoconservatives with ethnic identity-based allegiances and neonationalist sentiments.

Later *Breaking Bread: Insurgent Black Intellectual Life* (1991), West's collaboration with educator bell hooks, strikes out at both liberals and conservatives who, in the authors' eyes, expect African Americans to make all the cultural and moral adjustments necessary for improved race relations without taking into consideration the incredible, long-term psychic pain that impoverished urban blacks had suffered as a result of racism. West and hooks considered the emerging black middle class decadent and deficient.

Combating Racism and Inequality

West's major social and philosophical effort has been to steer American society away from a tradition of racism and to find ways of offering social equality to members of minorities, notably African Americans but also homosexuals and members of other racial and ethnic minority groups. The avowed interest that has consumed him is racial equality, which he studies using his considerable intellect and broad grasp of the United States' socioeconomic and philosophical underpinnings. His overall conclusion is that American society, particularly black American society, can be changed for the better through a faith in God and an acceptance of Christianity combined with the economic and social philosophy of Karl Marx. A self-styled populist, West is concerned about the maldistribution of wealth in American society, a problem that the adoption of Marxist principles could, in his eyes, overcome.

The American Evasion of Philosophy is not for the philosophical neophyte. It deals with complex and difficult concepts. It would be impossible to present the interaction of its complex ideas in simpler terms without significantly distorting those ideas and interactions, thereby misleading readers. In its 279 pages, *The American Evasion of Philosophy* deals in some depth with thirteen philosophers. West attempts to demonstrate how Ralph Waldo Emerson's emphasis on innovation, refined and reshaped by such later philosophers as John Dewey, C. S. Peirce, William James, and others, when combined with pure Marxism and

the commitment of black churches to racial justice, will lead to an establishment of democratic radicalism that offers hope not only to oppressed black people in American society but to members of all minorities suffering discrimination.

Toward the end of *The American Evasion of Philosophy*, West places his vision of prophetic pragmatism within the Christian tradition, contending that "the Christian epic, stripped of static dogmas and decrepit doctrines, remains a rich source of existential empowerment and political engagement when viewed through modern lenses." West explains that his version of prophetic pragmatism is a part of the Christian tradition because existentially the understanding of self and of one's identity that this tradition informs during times of personal crisis is necessary to one's mental balance.

Oppression and Religion

On a political level, West observes that oppressed people throughout the world are deeply religious. He asserts that religious people have an increased understanding of oppressed people. Religion provided a focal point for slaves in the United States and offered them the only venue in which they could gather collectively.

West wants prophetic pragmatism to be more than a basis for academic conversation. He calls for it to become action-oriented, cautioning, however, that there should be no prophetic pragmatist movement:

> The translation of philosophic outlook into social motion is not that simple. In fact, it is possible to be a prophetic pragmatist and belong to different political movements, e.g., feminist, Chicano, black, socialist, left-liberal ones.

In *The American Evasion of Philosophy*, West attempts to revive what he identifies as a grand yet flawed tradition, drawing the best from populism, liberalism, and the Gospel, then applying it to the society of the oppressed. He is both brilliant and daunting in choosing to support his own overall solutions to the problem of racism by presenting the tenets of such a diverse group of philosophers as Emerson, Dewey, Peirce, and James, juxtaposed to writers such as Sidney Hook, C. Wright Mills, W. E. B. Du Bois, Reinhold

Niebuhr, Lionel Trilling, W. V. O. Quine, Richard Rorty, Roberto Unger, and Michel Foucault.

Early Pragmatism

Although Emerson is not generally considered a pragmatist, West situates him in the prehistory of the pragmatic movement because Emerson's primary concern was with empowering the human personality. Still, Emerson was restrained in regard to political involvement, making him less a liberal than a libertarian. West demonstrates how fundamentally Emerson's thought informed much of the thinking of the early pragmatists, who were essentially elitist East Coast intellectuals.

West is not blind to the class-bound social attitudes of the early pragmatists he considers in this book, but he views them historically, as products of a time when most American culture was the product of an East Coast social and intellectual establishment that was conservative, racist, isolationist, and elitist. West presents the writers he considers here honestly, making no attempt to obscure what might currently be regarded as their significant flaws; he considers their shortcomings within a forthright historical perspective.

West credits Peirce with mapping out the new terrain of American pragmatism while crediting James, through his forceful rhetoric, with bringing to the movement an appreciation of moral heroism and personal growth. It is Dewey, however, who receives West's strongest commendation for bringing a much-needed activism to the pragmatist movement. He writes, "if Emerson was the American [Giovanni Battista] Vico, James and Peirce our John Stuart Mill and Immanuel Kant, then Dewey is the American [Georg Wilhelm Friedrich] Hegel *and* Marx."

Modern Pragmatism

West also takes to task his Princeton mentor and friend Richard Rorty, who essentially brought about a renewed modern interest in pragmatism, particularly in the pragmatism of Dewey. Identifying Rorty's *Philosophy and the Mirror of Nature* (1979) as the most important book in American metaphilosophy since Dewey's *The Quest for Certainty* (1929), West proceeds to fault Rorty for retreating from communal to egocentric con-

cerns, accusing him of holding back when it comes to offering criticism of his culture. Calling Rorty's project pregnant with possibilities, he contends that the author refuses to give birth to the offspring his book conceives, charging him with retreating into the philosophical arena when cogent sociopolitical issues arise.

It is ironic that West criticizes Rorty in this way; West often does exactly that which he accuses Rorty of doing. Academic philosophy is usually nonactivist, which is perhaps a limitation of philosophical writing about populist issues. *The American Evasion of Philosophy*, with all its intimations about how the socioeconomic situations of oppressed people can be overcome through West's proposed blending of Christianity and Marxism, is less a call to action than a call to contemplation about the issues West raises.

Certainly, *The American Evasion of Philosophy* is concerned with the oppression of minorities and means of overcoming that oppression, but the book itself is written for academicians rather than for the audience upon whose problems it focuses. This observation is not intended to demean West's efforts, sincere and well informed as they obviously are. It is made instead to point out the futility of trying to deal with a subject as complicated as the development of American pragmatism and its potential for improving the lot of the oppressed in the sort of simplified terms that would make the book and its arguments accessible to those about whom it is written.

The very title of the book may confuse some readers. "Evasion" may seem on the surface to be a negative word choice, one calculated to denigrate American thought. West, however, chose this key word with a full appreciation of another application of it that might be appreciated by academics. The word refers to Emerson's refusal to bow to the philosophical quest for certainty, to the search for foundations. It stands as an affirmation of Emerson's populist outlook.

The evasion of philosophy, as West uses the term, marks the beginning of a new mode of criticizing American culture that would strip the profession of philosophy of the pretense and inherent elitism it is perceived as holding. In essence, then, the word "evasion," understood in this context, has populist overtones that are not immediately evident.

When *The American Evasion of Philosophy* appeared, it received considerable attention in the academic press and was in part responsible for West's being appointed to a full professorship and the directorship of the Afro-American Studies Program at Princeton University. West became a significant public intellectual, reaching broad audiences through media appearances and lectures throughout the world. The public that has received West so warmly is probably not the audience for a book as dense and specialized as *The American Evasion of Philosophy*. Instead, the general audience would be more likely to turn to West's *Race Matters*, a slim collection of some of his most important essays and lectures, which is aimed at a nonacademic audience. The two books, however, offer similar solutions for overcoming the racial strife that concerns West and colors his thinking. In both works, West expresses his conviction is that the most reasonable hope for the black masses in America is offered by the acceptance of Christian principles combined with the socioeconomic theories of Karl Marx.

R. Baird Shuman

Additional Reading

Allen, Norm R., Jr. "The Crisis of the Black Religious Intellectual." *Free Inquiry* 14 (Summer, 1994): 9-10. Allen discusses Stephen L. Carter and West, two significant black intellectuals whose orientation is religious. Both believe that for society to survive and progress, faith in God is crucial. They assess modern culture and past history from religious perspectives. Allen contends that their doing so limits their intellectual depth. He especially faults them for their insistence that their religious texts are absolute, sacred texts that should be accepted unconditionally.

Anderson, Jervis. "The Public Intellectual." *The New Yorker* 69 (January 17, 1994): 39-46. Anderson acknowledges West's appeal to young people. He cautions that despite his popular acceptance, West is viewed by many of his professional colleagues as superficial in his writing and thinking and so broad in the generalizations he makes as to compromise many of his philosophical conclusions.

Appiah, K. Anthony. "A Prophetic Pragmatism." *The Nation* 250 (April 9, 1990): 496-498. In this extensive review of *The American Evasion of Philosophy*, Appiah relates Rorty's attempts to come to an improved understanding of American philosophy to Hegel's attempts at the beginning of the eighteenth century to understand the past of philosophy in protonationalistic terms. He shows how West, whom he suggests may be the preeminent African American intellectual of his generation, strongly influenced by Rorty's thinking, combines cultural theory and the black community, showing the progressive potential of the black church. Appiah notes that West, like Rorty, considers Dewey the preeminent pragmatist in Western society.

Berube, Michael. "Public Academy." *The New Yorker* 70 (January 9, 1995): 73-80. In this article, Berube pays special attention to West, bell hooks, Michael Eric Dyson, and Derrick Bell. He comments on the fact that current African American intellectuals, unlike those of the past, have gained recognition as important critics of current culture; they have done so by participating in talk shows and in gatherings at various centers for black popular culture. He portrays the subjects of his articles as intellectuals who are neither stifled by scholarly tradition nor characterized by remoteness from the public.

Nichols, John. "Cornel West." *The Progressive* 61 (January, 1997: 26-29. In his extended interview with West, Nichols broaches questions about radical democracy, about whose future West is pessimistic. West calls on political progressives to respect the religious concerns of African Americans. He is not optimistic about the substantive help they might receive from the Democratic Party, despite black support of that party in the 1996 elections.

White, Jack E. "Philosopher with a Mission." *Time* 141 (June 7, 1993): 60-62. White pays special attention to West's *Race Matters*, identifying West as an intellectual and a rising civil rights leader. In *Race Matters*, West considers the status of race relations in the United States as the twentieth century draws to a close. West calls for an end to racism, sexism, and homophobia.

R. Baird Shuman

Alfred North Whitehead

Striving for a more comprehensive and unified system of human knowledge, Whitehead made major contributions to mathematical logic and produced a wholly original and modern metaphysics.

Principal philosophical works: *A Treatise on Universal Algebra: With Applications*, 1898; *On Mathematical Concepts of the Material World*, 1906; *Principia Mathematica*, 1910-1913 (with Bertrand Russell, 3 volumes); *An Introduction to Mathematics*, 1911; *The Organization of Thought*, 1917; *An Enquiry Concerning the Principles of Natural Knowledge*, 1919, rev. ed. 1925; *The Concept of Nature*, 1920; *The Principle of Relativity*, 1922; *Science and the Modern World*, 1925; *Religion in the Making*, 1926; *Symbolism, Its Meaning and Effect*, 1926; *The Aims of Education and Other Essays*, 1929; *The Function of Reason*, 1929; *Process and Reality: An Essay in Cosmology*, 1929; *Adventures of Ideas*, 1933; *Modes of Thought*, 1938; *Essays in Science and Philosophy*, 1947.

Born: February 15, 1861; Ramsgate, Isle of Thanet, Kent, England

Died: December 30, 1947; Cambridge, Massachusetts

Early Life

Alfred North Whitehead was born on February 15, 1861, in the town of Ramsgate on the Isle of Thanet, County of Kent, England. He was the last of four children born to Alfred Whitehead, a schoolmaster and clergyman, and Maria Sarah Buckmaster. Whitehead's father was a typical Victorian country vicar who tirelessly tended to the needs of the people of the island and was well loved by them. His grandfather, Thomas Whitehead, was more remarkable intellectually. The son of a prosperous farmer, he had single-handedly created a successful boys' school at Ramsgate, unusual for its time because of its emphasis on mathematics and science.

Ramsgate was a small, close-knit community in which history was a physical presence in the form of many ancient ruins, including Norman and medieval churches and Richborough Castle, built by the Romans when they occupied Britain. The surrounding waters were notoriously treacherous, and Whitehead remembered as a child hearing at night the booming of cannon and seeing rockets rise in the night sky, signaling a ship in distress. He believed that over the generations, this environment instilled in the people an obstinacy and a tendency toward lonely thought.

Because he was small for his age and appeared frail, young Whitehead was not allowed to attend school or participate in children's games. Instead, his father tutored him in Latin, Greek, and mathematics. Whitehead learned his lessons quickly and had free time for periods of solitary thought and rambles through the wild coastal countryside with its mysterious ruins.

In 1875, Whitehead left home and entered Sherborne in Dorsetshire, a well-regarded public school (more like an American private school or preparatory school than an American public school) from which both of his brothers had been graduated. He had grown to love mathematics, and he excelled at it enough to be excused from some of the standard courses in classical languages and literature in order to study it more deeply. Ignoring his frailty, he took up Rugby, developing his athletic skills with seriousness and tenacity. As captain of the team, he compensated for his size with intelligence and leadership and became one of the best forwards in the history of the school. Later in life, he said that being tackled in a Rugby game was an excellent paradigm for the "Real" as he meant the term philosophically.

Before his last year at Sherborne, he chose to take the grueling six-day scholarship examination for Trinity College, Cambridge, an examination that would determine not only entry and the needed financial assistance but, more important, eligibility for a fellowship and, therefore, his hopes for a career in mathematics. Whitehead took the examination a year earlier than necessary and passed.

Whitehead entered Trinity College in the autumn of 1880 as a participant in a special honors program that allowed him to study in his area of specialty, mathematics, exclusively for the full three years of undergraduate work. In the Cambridge of that time, however, perhaps more than today, important education also took place outside the classroom in lively, spontaneous discussions with other students, an experience that Whitehead described as being like "a daily Platonic Dialogue," and which sometimes ran late into the night and into the early morning, ranging over politics, history, philosophy, science, and the arts. For a time, Whitehead became intensely interested in Immanuel Kant's *Kritik der reinen Vernunft* (1781; *The Critique of Pure Reason*, 1838), in which one of Kant's primary aims was to explain how arithmetic and geometry, which appear to be self-consistent deductive systems without need of empirical verification, can yet give knowledge that can be reliably applied in the real world. This question was a central theme in much of Whitehead's own work, though he became disenchanted with Kant's explanations.

Although his mathematics teachers were all of the highest caliber, one in particular, William Davidson Niven, significantly influenced Whitehead's development by introducing him to the physics of James Clerk Maxwell, whose theories about electromagnetism called into question the all-encompassing explanatory power of the then-reigning Newtonian physics, opening the way to modern physics.

Life's Work

Whitehead's high scores on final examinations and his dissertation on Maxwell's *Treatise on Electricity and Magnetism* (1873) won for him a six-year fellowship, allowing him free room and board at Cambridge and unlimited freedom for mathematical research.

Unlike most research fellows, however, Whitehead did not become immediately productive. By character, he was not a piecemeal problem solver who worked in ever narrower and more refined areas of a subject, but rather an explorer seeking a wider and more unified perspective. He discovered and was impressed with the works of Hermann Günther Grassmann, an all-but-forgotten German mathematician who had developed a new kind of algebra. Grassmann's *Die lineale Ausdehnungslehre, ein neuer Zweig der Mathematik*

Alfred North Whitehead. *(Hulton Getty/Liaison Agency)*

(1844), along with George Boole's *The Mathematical Analysis of Logic* (1847) and William Hamilton's *The Elements of Quaternions* (1866), seemed to Whitehead to portend a whole new field of algebras of logic not limited to number and quantity and with exciting unexplored applications. Whitehead envisioned a work in which all these ideas would be brought together in a general theory that would include giving a spatial interpretation to logic, which would provide a more powerful general theory of geometry.

On a visit to his parents in Broadstairs in June of 1890, at a time when his great work did not seem to be going anywhere and he was contemplating conversion to Roman Catholicism, Whitehead was introduced to Evelyn Wade and fell in love. She was twenty-three years old, with black eyes and auburn hair and a vibrant personality. Though English, she spoke French as her native language, having been reared in a convent at Angers. Whitehead wasted no time and proposed to her—romantically, in a cave under the garden in his father's vicarage. They were married in December of 1891. Their marriage was to produce three children. The youngest would be tragically killed in aerial combat in 1918 during World War I. Evelyn loved and cared for Alfred and always made a place where he could work without interruption wherever they lived, but she had no interest in science or mathematics. Yet she perfectly complemented his analytic temperament with a deep interest in people and a wonderful aesthetic sense. Her example, according to Whitehead, taught him that "beauty, moral and aesthetic, is the aim of existence: and that kindness, and love, and artistic satisfaction are among its modes of attainment"—logic and science being important because they are useful in providing the conditions for periods of great art and literature. Whitehead's later worldview incorporated these ideas.

Marriage was good for Whitehead. He soon began work in earnest on his project, the first volume of which was published in 1898 as *A Treatise on Universal Algebra*. The second volume was never written, partly because of another momentous event that occurred in the same year as Whitehead's marriage: In 1890, Bertrand Russell entered Cambridge.

Whitehead, who happened to be reading examinations at the time, recognized Russell's po-

tential and, even though Russell's scores were disappointingly low, saw to it—some say by burning the scores—that Russell received a scholarship. Their future collaboration on *Principia Mathematica* was to be one of the most fruitful in the history of mathematics.

By 1903, Russell and Whitehead were colleagues. Russell had won a fellowship to Trinity College with a dissertation on the foundations of geometry. The two men found their individual interests and aims increasingly converging. With their wives, they attended the First International Congress of Philosophy in Paris in 1900 and met the great mathematician Giuseppe Peano, who had devised a symbolic notation that he was applying to the clarification of the foundations of mathematics. Russell, in his own work, had extended some of Peano's ideas and in 1903 published *The Principles of Mathematics*, in which he attempted to demonstrate that all mathematics, including geometry, could be deductively derived from a few concepts of logic. At the same time, Whitehead was working along similar lines in his projected second volume to his *A Treatise on Universal Algebra*. Their friendship and their intellectual excitement with what seemed to be a revolution in mathematics led inevitably toward collaboration, and they spent more and more time together.

At one point, the Russells even moved in with the Whiteheads. This arrangement, however, ultimately proved unsatisfactory. Russell fell secretly and unrequitedly in love with Evelyn Whitehead—he was by then very unhappy with his own wife—and the Russells, without anything coming into the open, moved out amiably. The collaboration was unaffected by this turn of events: The life of the mind was the greater passion for both men, and their work was proceeding well.

In 1903, they decided, rather than publish two separate additions to their own works, that they would concentrate on one joint work. This would become the monumental *Principia Mathematica*. They originally believed that it would take only about a year to complete. It took approximately nine. The manuscript ran to more than four thousand pages and required a fourwheeler to transport it to Cambridge Press. Whitehead, almost fifty, was now stooped from leaning over his desk for long periods. During the work on *Principia Mathematica*, Whitehead found time to write a short work that he considered to be his most original, "On Mathematical Concepts of the Material World." Published in 1906, it is concerned with "the possible relations to space of the ultimate entities which (in ordinary language) constitute the 'stuff' of space." Anticipating Albert Einstein's general theory of relativity, he criticized the classical concept of an absolute space occupied by pointlike atoms, defending instead a relativistic view that space is not independent of the things in it but is rather dependent for its structure on objects within it. Further, he proposed that the fundamental constituents of matter are not pointlike particles but are more complex entities such as lines of force, with particles being the result of the interactions of these lines. Neither this work nor *Principia Mathematica* met with great success when first published, being considered too philosophical by specialists.

In 1910, Whitehead rather mysteriously left his assured position at Trinity College and moved to London, where he had no position. Whitehead may simply have found himself in a rut; the reasons, however, are probably more complex. For one thing, he had become politically active in his last few years at Cambridge, speaking out for women's rights and adopting a liberal position that outraged the university elite with their bias toward the rich and titled. He and his wife were once pelted with oranges and rotten eggs while sitting behind a Labour Party speaker. A clue to his leaving Cambridge may also be found elsewhere. Years before, in 1887, as a member of the prestigious Cambridge Apostles discussion group, Whitehead had responded to the topic question, which asked which was more important in life, "Study or Marketplace?" with the terse comment, "Study with windows." Whitehead probably had begun to sense that he could not commit himself to the ivory-tower life of a don without trying to make some connection between his work and the wider world.

Indeed, his subsequent actions bear out this inference. Soon after settling in London, he wrote a popular exposition of mathematics for the nonspecialist, *An Introduction to Mathematics*, which was published in 1911. From 1911 to 1914, he taught at University College, London, and from

1914 to 1924, he held a professorship at the Imperial College of Science and Technology in Kensington, all the while serving on various committees and councils setting the policies for London education. The aim of these institutions was to bring education to the masses, rationally adapting it to their needs and circumstances. Whitehead believed that the old elitist structure of the university must give way to new forms and that no less than the salvation of civilization was at stake. He compared this enterprise of mass education to the activities of the monasteries of the Middle Ages. His ideas on this subject appeared later in his books *The Aims of Education and Other Essays* and *Essays in Science and Philosophy*. In 1923, another major shift occurred in Whitehead's life. While still at the Imperial College of Science and Technology, Whitehead received an invitation to come to Harvard University to join the philosophy department. This invitation was no doubt based on his reputation as a philosopher of science. Whitehead was then sixty-two years old, an age when most people are thinking of retirement. Whitehead, however, had never taught philosophy and liked the idea, and his wife wholeheartedly supported the move. It turned out to be the beginning of a massive creative surge in a new direction, reaching far beyond the specialized boundaries of the philosophy of science.

Beginning with *Science and the Modern World*, based on the Lowell lectures he gave in 1925 and published that year, Whitehead called into question the view that values have nothing to do with the basic constituents of nature, which, according to the prevailing view, which he called "scientific materialism," consisted really only of matter in motion. In 1929, continuing this trend toward an all-inclusive worldview, there followed *Process and Reality*, which is considered to be one of the greatest works of metaphysics of all time, as well as one of the most forbidding. It propounds what Whitehead called "the philosophy of organism," in a novel terminology. *Adventures of Ideas*, published in 1933, was his last major work and probably his most accessible book on philosophy, with extensive explorations of sociology, cosmology, philosophy, and civilization as revealed from the perspective of his new metaphysical views.

Whitehead's reception in the United States was warm, and it provided him with an audience for the products of his far-ranging and independent intellect that he perhaps could not have had in his native England. He is remembered fondly by students and faculty as rosy-cheeked and cherubic, giving freely of his time, meeting with students often on Sunday evenings, and lecturing widely at Eastern and Midwestern universities. His last work, a small, lucid, and accessible work titled *Modes of Thought*, was based on lectures he had given at Wellesley College and the University of Chicago. Whitehead died at Cambridge, Massachusetts, on December 30, 1947.

Influence

For more than fifty years, Whitehead applied his unique intellectual gifts successively to mathematics, education, and speculative philosophy and cosmology, always striving for an understanding of the nature of reality that could be applied to the betterment of humanity. Where he saw value in the ideas of others, he unselfishly helped those ideas to reach fruition. As a teacher, he brought out the best in his students, always with kindness and respect for their distinctive gifts. His later metaphysics is unique in the field for its scientific sophistication, yet it is free of the dogmatic rejection of the preeminence of human value in the world often found in the natural sciences.

Scott Bouvier

Process and Reality

An Essay in Cosmology

Type of philosophy: Metaphysics
First published: 1929
Principal ideas advanced:

◇ Only a philosophy of organism can describe a universe in which process, creativity, and interdependence are disclosed in immediate experience.

◇ Philosophy involves generalization from the concrete particulars to universals; it aims at a description of the dynamic process that is reality.

◇ A philosophical system should be logically consistent and coherent, and it should be grounded in immediate experience.

◇ The categories of this philosophy of organism are the category of the ultimate (creativity), the categories of existence (actual entities, prehensions, nexūs, subjective forms, eternal objects, propositions, multiplicities, and contrasts), the categories of explanation (twenty-seven in number), and the categories of obligation (nine in number).

◇ Everything but God is an actual entity occasioned by something; but God, although an actual entity, is not an actual occasion.

◇ Every event in the creative, interdependent process is qualified by past, present, and future.

◇ Process in reality is a creative advance in which feelings are integrated, actual occasions grow together toward a final phase of satisfaction, and God is conditioned by, and reciprocally affects, events in the temporal world.

The central aim in Alfred North Whitehead's chief work, *Process and Reality: An Essay in Cosmology*, is to replace the traditional philosophy of substance with a philosophy of organism. The author's thesis is that only a philosophy of organism can provide clarification of a universe in which process, dynamic actualization, interdependence, and creativity are disclosed as the primary data of immediate experience.

Although Whitehead expresses some far-reaching reservations regarding traditional modes of thought, he formulates his philosophy of organism through a dialogue with the great logicians, scientists, metaphysicians, and theologians of the past. He finds the thought of Greek philosopher Plato more decisive than that of German philosopher Immanuel Kant; he considers Henri Bergson more suggestive than Georg Wilhelm Friedrich Hegel; he contends that John Locke was closer to a philosophy of organism than René Descartes; and he is ready to choose Gottfried Wilhelm Leibniz over Aristotle. Western philosophy is defined by the author as a series of footnotes to Plato. Some of these footnotes he wishes to salvage and reformulate; others he is quite happy to see deleted. Of all the philosophical giants in the Western tradition, Kant is the least cordially received. The author makes it clear that his philosophy of organism constitutes a recurrence to pre-Kantian modes of thought. According to Whitehead, the "Copernican revolution" of Kant was not as revolutionary as many of his followers maintained it to be. Whitehead's philosophy is a speculative philosophy formulated into a coherent and logical system of general concepts that are intended to provide the categorial interpretation for any and all elements of human experience.

Descriptive Generalization

In examining the methodological foundations of Whitehead's system, we find first a procedure of descriptive generalization and second an epistemology that expresses both a rational and an empirical side. Philosophical method involves generalization, in which there is a movement from the concrete particular to the universal. This generalization is based on description rather than deduction. Whitehead considers it to be a mistake that deduction, the primary method of mathematics, has intermittently become the touchstone for philosophical inquiry. Deduction is for the author an auxiliary mode of verification that should never be given primacy in philosophical methodology. Applied in Whitehead's philosophy of organism, this method of descriptive generalization takes the form of a description of *dynamic process* rather than of static structure. Morphological description is replaced by description of dynamic life processes.

Whitehead's epistemology contains both rational and empirical elements. The rational criterion is coherence and logical consistency; the empirical criterion is applicability and adequacy. A philosophical system must be coherent and logical. No entity can be conceived in abstraction from all other entities, nor can an entity be understood as long as its relation to other entities is not specified according to logical rules. However, knowledge also demands an empirical justification. Categories must be applicable and adequate. They are applicable when they describe all related experience as exhibiting the same texture. They are adequate when they include all possible experience in their conceptual vision. Whitehead was deeply concerned to maintain an experiential basis for his philosophy: "The elucidation of

immediate experience is the sole justification for any thought." Philosophy should aim at generalization, but it should not overreach its mark and lose itself in abstractions that are not grounded in experience. One of the chief errors in philosophy, contends the author, is the "fallacy of misplaced concreteness." This fallacy results when an abstraction becomes an exemplification of the system and replaces the concrete entity of which it is an abstraction. The success of philosophy, continues the author, is commensurate with the degree to which it avoids this fallacy.

The Four Categories

Through the implementation of his method of descriptive generalization, Whitehead derives a categorial scheme that sets forth the governing concepts of his philosophy of organism. His categories are classified according to a fourfold schematic division: (1) the category of the ultimate; (2) categories of existence; (3) categories of explanation; and (4) categorial obligations.

The *category of the ultimate* is creativity. Creativity is the universal of universals, the ultimate metaphysical principle that underlies all things without exception. Every fact of the universe is in some way or another an exemplification of creativity. Even God is subordinate to the category of the ultimate. As the ultimate metaphysical principle, creativity is also the principle of *novelty*. It provides the reason for the emergence of the new. In its application to the novel situation, of which it is the origination, creativity expresses itself as the "creative advance."

The *categories of existence* are eight in number: (1) actual entities; (2) prehensions; (3) nexūs (plural of nexus); (4) subjective forms; (5) eternal objects; (6) propositions; (7) multiplicities; and (8) contrasts. *Actual entities*, which replace the traditional concept of particular substances, are the final facts of the universe; they are the real things of which the world is made up. *Prehensions* are the concrete facts of relatedness, exhibiting a "vector character," involving emotion, purpose, valuation, and causation. A *nexus* is a particular fact of togetherness of actual entities. *Subjective form* is the determining or defining quality of private matters of fact. *Eternal objects* are the pure potentials by reason of which facts are defined in their subjective forms. *Propositions* render meaningful the distinction between truth and false-hood; as abstract potentialities, they are sugges-tions about the concrete particularity of actual entities. *Multiplicities* indicate the disjunctions of diverse entities. *Contrasts* indicate the mode of synthesis that occurs in a prehension or a con-crete fact of relatedness. Along with these eight categories of existence, Whitehead delineates twenty-seven categories of explanation and nine categorial obligations.

Actual entities, which constitute Whitehead's first category of existence, are the building blocks of his organismic universe. Here the philosophy of organism inverts Baruch Spinoza. For Spinoza actual entities, as particulars, are inferior modes; only the Infinite Substance is ultimately real. In the philosophy of organism, actual entities are the ultimate facts. These actual entities are in a proc-ess of "perpetual perishing," but as they perish, they are somehow taken up in the creative ad-vance, pass into other actual entities through the operation of prehension, and achieve objective immortality. This interpretation of a universe of flux in which actual entities come to be and pass away must be understood, according to White-head, as simply an expansion of a sentence in Plato's Timaeos (last period dialogue, 360-347 B.C.E.; *Timaeus*, 1793), "However, that which is con-ceived by opinion with the help of sensation and without reason is always in the process of becom-ing and perishing and never really is." The uni-verse, as it is immediately disclosed, is a universe of becoming, flux, and perishing. The category of actual entities has universal applicability. It ap-plies to nonliving matter as well as to all in-stances of life. It applies to the being of humanity as well as to the being of God.

Actual Entities and Occasions

A significant implication of this doctrine is that God, for Whitehead, is not outside the system. He is within the reach and range of the catego-ries. However, God is differentiated from all other actual entities in that he is not occasioned by anything. Thus, all actual entities other than God are also occasions. God is an actual entity but not an actual occasion. Every actual occasion exhibits a dipolar structure consisting of a physi-cal pole and a mental pole. By reason of its physi-cal pole, the actual occasion prehends other ac-

tual occasions; by reason of its mental pole, a prehension of eternal objects is made possible. In this description of the bipolar structure of actual occasions, the author formulates an alternative to the Cartesian dualism of mind and body. God also exhibits a dipolar structure. He possesses two natures—a primordial nature and a conse-quent nature. His primordial nature, which con-sists of an envisagement of all the eternal objects and an appetition for their actualization, corre-sponds to the mental pole of actual occasions. His consequent nature, which is the consequence of the reaction of the world upon God, corresponds to the physical pole of actual occasions.

Actual occasions are grouped into societies or nexūs through the operation of prehension. A prehension, according to the eleventh category of explanation, consists of three factors: (1) the sub-ject that is prehending; (2) the datum that is pre-hended; and (3) the subjective form that desig-nates the manner in which the subject prehends its datum. A nexus, according to the fourteenth category of explanation, "is a set of actual entities in the unity of the relatedness constituted by their prehensions of each other." By reason of their physical poles, actual occasions can pre-hend each other and form societies or nexūs. There results an organismic coinherence in which every event in the universe is a factor in every other event. All things ultimately inhere in each other. There are no isolated events. For White-head the universe is an interdependent universe in which all parts are interrelated. The analogy of the organism replaces the analogy of the ma-chine. Not only, however, do actual occasions prehend each other by reason of their physical poles; they also prehend eternal objects by reason of their mental poles.

Eternal objects are permanent and immutable principles of determination, clearly reminiscent of the eternal forms or ideas in the philosophy of Plato. An eternal object is a pure potential that, in itself, remains neutral to any particular fact of ingression in the temporal order. There are no new eternal objects. They are fixed in the timeless primordial vision of God. However, each eternal object is a potentiality in the history of actual occasions. An actual occasion prehends an eter-nal object and thus the object becomes realized in time and space. Ingression refers to the particular mode in which the potentiality of an eternal object is realized in a particular entity, contributing to the structure and definition of that actual entity. Eternal objects contribute the necessary structure that keeps the organismic process from dissolving into an indeterminate and discontinuous succession. Process does not contradict structure in Whitehead's analysis. Process and structure are interdependent concepts.

Actual occasions, and the societies that they form, are in a process of growing together until they reach a final phase which is called "satisfaction." This process of growing together, in which new prehensions constantly take place, is designated by the author as "concrescence." "In a process of concrescence, there is a succession of phases in which new prehensions arise by integration of prehensions in antecedent phases. . . . The process continues until all prehensions are components in the one determinate integral satisfaction." Each actual occasion as it is objectified in the process of concrescence exhibits a claim upon the future. The future is in some sense constitutive of the being of every actual occasion. Whitehead expresses this when he describes an actual occasion as a "subject-superject." Every occasion is at once the subject experiencing and the superject of this experience; it is the present experiential datum, but it is also the future result or the aim of its present experience. This aim or future project is called the "subjective aim," which controls the becoming of the actual occasion and lures it to its final satisfaction.

All becoming thus occurs within a spatiotemporal continuum, in which all entities experience the bite of time. Each event in the universe is qualified by the past, present, and future. Although actual occasions perish, they enter into the internal constitution of other actual occasions, in which they become objectified. Every present fact of the universe is thus constituted by all antecedent phases. So also is every present fact constituted by its potentialities for future realization by its subjective aim. An actual entity is that which it can become. "That *how* an actual entity *becomes* constitutes *what* that actual entity *is;* so that the two descriptions of an actual entity are not independent. Its 'being' is constituted by its 'becoming.' This is the 'principle of process.'"

Flux and Permanence

That all things flow is the one ultimate generalization around which Whitehead develops his whole system. This doctrine of a fluent, becoming universe, remarks the author, was already suggested in the unsystematized insights of Hebrew literature (particularly the Psalms), as well as in the early beginnings of Greek philosophy (particularly Heraclitus). Coupled with this doctrine of flux, however, is a competing notion: the permanence of all things. These two notions, contends the author, constitute the complete problem of metaphysics.

Whitehead does not intend to reject the doctrine of permanence, but rather seeks to adapt it to his ultimate generalization that all things flow. This adaptation is expressed in two implicatory principles of his system: his doctrine of self-constituting identity and his doctrine of cosmic order. In his nine categorial obligations, the author formulates the category of objective identity, which asserts the essential self-identity of every actual entity as an individual constituent in the universe. Each actual entity is a cell with an atomic unity. In the process of concrescence, actual entities grow together but they do not sacrifice their atomic unity. They retain their self-identity and thus give expression to a life of their own. Viewing the organismic process from the side of the cellular and atomic units that comprise it, we need to acknowledge a self-constituting individuality that indicates a permanence within the flow of all things. As there is objective self-identity in Whitehead's philosophy of organism, so also is there preestablished harmony or universal cosmic order. The latter aspect of the universe is indicated in the author's seventh category of obligation, the category of subjective harmony. The process of concrescence exhibits a preestablished harmony in which all prehensions are viewed as being contributive to a stable cosmic order, informed by the eternal objects and directed by the subjective aim. Thus does the doctrine of permanence receive another expression in Whitehead's system.

Whitehead's elaboration of the notion of preestablished harmony has some interesting implications for his position on the nature of evil. Although he does not formulate an explicit theodicy, he veers in the direction of a Leibnizian resolution to the problem. Novelty is not to be identified with creativity. The emergence of novelty in the organismic process may inhibit and delay the creative advance and thus provide the condition for the rise of evil. Evil constitutes a real fact in Whitehead's universe. Spinoza's attempt to explain away evil as an illusion arising from our finite, modal point of view is thus rejected. When the creative advance attains its final phase or its satisfaction, the universe is the better off for the fact of evil. The satisfaction or the final phase is richer in content by reason of the particular cosmic disharmonies. All inhibiting novelties are somehow contributive to a greater good. In the creative advance of the world, particular evil facts are finally transcended.

The Primacy of Feeling

Whitehead's philosophy of organism occupies a unique position in the history of philosophy in that it makes the sentient quality of experience decisive. His theory of prehension and his doctrine of the creative advance are governed by a notion of the pervasiveness of feeling. In the final analysis, prehension involves an objectification of feelings, and the creative advance is a process in which these feelings are integrated in an exemplification of harmony. "In the place of the Hegelian hierarchy of categories of thought, the philosophy of organism finds a hierarchy of categories of feeling." This accent on the sentient quality of experience by Whitehead has both epistemological and metaphysical implications. It entails, first of all, a rejection of the subject-object dichotomy as the foundation for knowledge. Most traditional varieties of philosophy, claims the author, give priority to the intellect and the understanding. In such a view, the knowing subject is the primary datum and the philosophical task becomes a demonstration of the validity of propositions about the objects encountered by the subject. It was particularly in the Cartesian tradition that this subject-object form of statement became normative.

In Whitehead's philosophy of organism the subject is an emergent datum, rather than the foundational datum. The complex of feelings constitutes the primitive datum. The primitive element is sympathy, or feeling in another and feeling conformally with another. Intellect and consciousness arise only in the higher phases of concrescence. The universe is initially disclosed as a system of "vector feelings." This primacy of feeling is made explicit in Whitehead's doctrine of "presentational immediacy." In its immediate presentment, the world is *received* as a complex of feelings. Primitive experience must thus properly be understood in terms of *sense-reception* rather than *sense-perception*. In sense-reception, the interconnections of feelings are simultaneously disclosed. There is thus an internal bond between presentational immediacy and causal efficacy. Both David Hume and Immanuel Kant, in giving priority to the conscious subject, were unable to grasp this point. The sense-perception of the subject was for them the primary fact, and any apprehension of causation was somehow to be elicited from this primary fact

In the philosophy of organism, which gives primacy to sentient experience, causal relations are disclosed on the level of feelings. They are directly felt on a pretheoretical or precognitive level of experience. The types of feeling are indefinite and depend upon the complexity of the data that the feeling integrates. There are, however, three primary types of feeling that are constitutive of all more complex patterns: (1) physical feelings, (2) conceptual feelings, and (3) transmuted feelings. *Physical feelings* arise from the physical pole of the actual entity and have for their initial datum another actual entity. *Conceptual feelings* arise from the mental pole and have for their datum an eternal object. *Transmuted feelings* are akin to physical feelings in that they proceed from the physical pole, but their objective datum is a nexus of actual entities rather than a single entity. The creative advance integrates these various types of feeling in its progression toward satisfaction. This integration proceeds in such a manner that the earlier phases of feelings become components of later and more complex feelings. Thus, in each phase there is an emergence of novelty. This goes on until the final phase is reached, which is the complex satisfaction in which all earlier phases of feelings are taken up as formative constituents of a final and coordinated whole.

A Metaphysics of Theism

The categories of Whitehead's philosophy of organism receive their final exemplification in his metaphysics of theism. The doctrine of God completes Whitehead's system. In formulating his metaphysics of theism, he has no intention of submitting rationally demonstrative proofs for the existence of God; rather, he intends to provide a theoretic system that clarifies the immediate facts of religious experience. The touchstone of religious experience is love. The author finds the most decisive expression of this religious attitude in the Galilean origin of Christianity. The theism suggested in this Galilean origin must be contrasted, on one hand, with the theism of Aristotle, in which God is the unmoved mover who exhibits no concern for his creation and, on the other hand, with the theism of medieval theology, which, according to the author, gave to God the attributes that belonged exclusively to Caesar. Whitehead's intention is thus to formulate a theistic view that arises from a religious experience in which love is the governing datum.

In Whitehead's philosophy, this God of love is not to be treated as an exception to the categories and the metaphysical principles that they enunciate. God is the chief exemplification of the metaphysical system. In this role of chief exemplar, his nature can be viewed from two perspectives: as *primordial* and as *consequent*. As primordial, God is unlimited or infinite potentiality. He is a unity and plenum of conceptual feelings, in abstraction from any physical feelings, and hence lacks the fullness of actuality. God as primordial is deficient in actuality. As a unity of conceptual feelings and operations, he is a free creative act. He is in no way deflected by the particular occasions that constitute the actual world. The actual world presupposes the primordial nature, but the primordial nature does not presuppose the actual world. All that the primordial nature presupposes is the general and abstract character of creativity, of which it is the chief exemplification. As unlimited potentiality, the primordial nature includes the eternal objects and accounts for the order in their relevance to the process of creation. So also God in his primordial nature is the *lure* for feeling or the "object of desire." He provides the condition for each subjective aim and draws the process to its final satisfaction.

Coupled with God's primordial nature is his *consequent* nature. His consequent nature is derivative. It expresses the reaction of the world

upon God. The consequent nature is thus, in part, subject to the process of actualization in the actual world. Because of his consequent nature, God can share in the fullness of physical feelings of the actual world as these physical feelings become objectified in God. God shares with every actual occasion and every nexus its actual world. God is conditioned by the world. His nature is consequent upon the creative advance of actual occasions in the process of concrescence. The primordial nature is free, complete, eternal, actually deficient, and unconscious. The consequent nature is determined, incomplete, everlasting, fully actual, and conscious.

Because of his consequent nature, God establishes a providential relation to the world. His providential love is expressed through a tender care that nothing be lost. He saves everything in the world and preserves it in his own life. God's providence also manifests itself in the workings of divine wisdom. Through his infinite wisdom, he puts to use even that which in the temporal world would be considered mere wreckage. The consequent nature thus makes possible a continuing point of contact and a reciprocal relation between God and the world. The events in the temporal world are transformed through God's love and wisdom, and his love and wisdom then pass back into the world. God thus receives his final definition as the great companion—the fellow sufferer who understands.

Calvin O. Schrag

Additional Reading

Berthrong, John H. *Concerning Creativity: A Comparison of Chu Hsi, Whitehead, and Neville*. Albany: State University of New York Press, 1998. Berthrong employs the philosophies of Neville and Chu Hsi to offer a useful criticism of Whitehead's notions on God, world, and their relatedness.

Jones, Judith A. *Intensity: An Essay in Whiteheadian Ontology*. Nashville: Vanderbilt University Press, 1998. Jones offers an exacting analysis of Whitehead's metaphysical system. Aimed at graduate-level readers who are familiar with Whitehead's work.

Kraus, Elizabeth M. *The Metaphysics of Experience: A Companion to Whitehead's Process and Reality*. 2d ed. New York: Fordham University Press,

1998. An excellent guide to Whitehead's *Process and Reality*.

Kuntz, Paul Grimely. *Alfred North Whitehead*. Boston: Twayne, 1984. A clearly written and brief volume that provides an introduction to Alfred North Whitehead's thought.

Lowe, Victor. *Alfred North Whitehead: The Man and His Work*. Vol. 1, 1861-1910. Vol. 2, 1910-1947. Baltimore, Md.: The Johns Hopkins University Press, 1985. The fullest available account of Whitehead's life is found in these volumes. The first covers his life through his tenure at Cambridge. The second and more recent volume chronicles his life in London and at Harvard until his death. Lowe was a student of Whitehead and is an eminent authority on his work.

_____. *Understanding Whitehead*. Baltimore, Md.: The Johns Hopkins University Press, 1962. A collection of papers on Whitehead's thought in a volume aimed at the reader with little or no prior acquaintance with Whitehead's philosophy. Lowe tries to show what Whitehead's philosophy is about and why it is unique.

Rapp, Friedrich, and Reiner Wiehl. *Whitehead's Metaphysics of Creativity*. Albany: State University of New York Press, 1990. This book takes a critical look at Whitehead's metaphysics. The authors see Whitehead's speculative philosophy as going far beyond anything considered in contemporary analytic philosophy.

Ross, Stephen David. *Perspective in Whitehead's Metaphysics*. Albany: State University of New York Press, 1983. By elevating the role of perspective in Whitehead's thought, Ross attempts to eliminate many of the difficulties in Whitehead's philosophical system.

Russell, Bertrand. *The Autobiography of Bertrand Russell: 1872-1914*. Boston: Little Brown, 1951. Valuable for its account of the writing of *Principia Mathematica*, even though it is related from Russell's somewhat biased point of view.

Schilpp, Paul Arthur, ed. *The Philosophy of Alfred North Whitehead*. 1941. 2d ed. New York: Tudor, 1951. A collection of critical essays on Whitehead that includes Whitehead's autobiographical sketch and Lowe's insightful essay "The Development of Whitehead's Philosophy." Contains a complete bibliography of Whitehead's works.

Scott Bouvier, updated by Patrick S. Roberts

Elie Wiesel

Wiesel, a Jewish survivor of the Holocaust, published numerous works of philosophy, drama, and fiction based on his experiences. By writing and speaking out on behalf of the world's victims, he became a significant voice of conscience.

Principal philosophical works: *Un di Velt hot geshvign*, 1956, 1958 (as *La Nuit*, 1958; *Night*, 1960); *L'Aube*, 1960 (*Dawn*, 1961); *Le Jour*, 1961 (*The Accident*, 1962); *La Ville de la chance*, 1962 (*The Town Beyond the Wall*, 1964); *Les Portes de la forêt*, 1964 (*The Gates of the Forest*, 1966); *Les Juifs du silence*, 1966 (*The Jews of Silence*, 1966); *Le Chant des Morts*, 1966 (*Legends of Our Time*, 1968); *Le Mendiant de Jérusalem*, 1968 (*A Beggar in Jerusalem*, 1970); *Entre-deux soleils*, 1970 (*One Generation After*, 1970); *Célébration hassidique*, 1972 (*Souls on Fire*, 1972); *Ani Maamin: Un Chant perdu et retrouvé*, 1973 (*Ani Maamin: A Song Lost and Found Again*, 1973); *Le Serment de Kolvillàg*, 1973 (*The Oath*, 1973); *Célébration biblique*, 1975 (*Messengers of God: Biblical Portraits and Legends*, 1976); *Un Juif aujourd'hui*, 1977 (*A Jew Today*, 1978); *Four Hasidic Masters and Their Struggle Against Melancholy*, 1978; *Images from the Bible*, 1980; *Testament d'un poète juif assassiné*, 1980 (*The Testament*, 1981); *Five Biblical Portraits*, 1981; *Paroles d'étranger*, 1982; *Somewhere a Master*, 1982; *Le Cinquième Fils*, 1983 (*The Fifth Son*, 1985); *Le Crépuscule, au loin*, 1987 (*Twilight*, 1988); *Discours d'Oslo*, 1987; *The Six Days of Destruction: Meditations Towards Hope*, 1988 (with Albert H. Friedlander); *Silences et mémoire d'hommes: Essais, histoires, dialogues*, 1989; *L'Oublié*, 1989 (*The Forgotten*, 1992); *Evil and Exile*, 1990; *From the Kingdom of Memory: Reminiscences*, 1990; *A Journey of Faith*, 1990 (with John Cardinal O'Connor); *Sages and Dreamers: Biblical, Talmudic, and Hasidic Portraits and Legends*, 1991; *Tous les fleuves vont à la mer*, 1994 (*All Rivers Run to the Sea*, 1995).

Born: September 30, 1928; Sighet, Transylvania (now Romania)

Early Life

The journey that took Elie Wiesel through the Holocaust, the systematic destruction of nearly six million Jews by Nazi Germany during World War II, began in the town of Sighet, now part of Romania, where he was born on September 30, 1928. Raised in a religious home, Wiesel was the third child and only son born to his parents, Shlomo and Sarah Feig Wiesel. Sighet was in the northern area of a region known as Transylvania. Once a part of the Austrian Empire, it was ceded to Romania after World War I and then came under Hungarian control during World War II. During Wiesel's boyhood, Sighet's residents included some ten thousand Jews, about 40 percent of the population, and most of them were religiously Orthodox.

Sighet's Jews were subjected to Hungary's anti-Jewish policies, which included socioeconomic discrimination and deprivation of basic civil rights. Wiesel's father, a shopkeeper in Sighet, was jailed for a time because he helped rescue Polish Jews who had found their way to Hungary. Nevertheless, the young Wiesel's worlds of study, faith, and Jewish tradition remained relatively undisturbed until the Germans occupied the territory of their faltering Hungarian allies in March, 1944. Within a few weeks, the Jews of Sighet were ghettoized and then deported to Auschwitz in four transports between May 16 and May 22. Wiesel survived the shattering experience of that German death camp. His older sisters, Hilda and Bea, also escaped death during the Holocaust, but Wiesel's mother, father, and little sister, Tsiporah, did not.

Selected for slave labor, Wiesel and his father endured Auschwitz's brutal regime until January,

Elie Wiesel. *(Library of Congress)*

phy at the Sorbonne from 1948 to 1951. Albert Camus, Søren Kierkegaard, and Franz Kafka were among the writers who influenced him most. Wiesel spent time in India, too, hoping to write a dissertation on asceticism in the Jewish, Christian, and Hindu traditions. He wrote at length on the subject but was unable to complete all of his university work because he had to support himself. Finding work as a journalist, Wiesel wrote for Israeli, French, and American newspapers. His reporting assignments took him to Israel and then to New York in 1956 to cover the United Nations. That same year, he was struck by a taxicab in Times Square. When a long convalescence prevented him from making a required return to France to renew expired papers, Wiesel, a "stateless person" at the time, was persuaded to apply for U.S. citizenship. He was naturalized in 1963.

During the first decade after the war, writing of more than a scholarly or journalistic kind had been on Wiesel's mind. However, he had vowed to be silent about his Holocaust experiences for ten years, and thus it was only in 1956 that he published his first book. Written in Yiddish, *Un di Velt hot geshvign* (and the world remained silent) was a lengthy account of his life in Auschwitz. Two years later, he shortened this work considerably, translated the book into French, and published it as *La Nuit*. An English translation, *Night*, was published in 1960. Wiesel had found his voice and his themes. Both a wrenching account of the presence of evil and a terrifying indictment of God's injustice, *Night*, Wiesel's brief early memoir, remains his best-known book.

Life's Work

More than thirty of Wiesel's books have been published since *Night* appeared. None of the others focuses so explicitly on the Holocaust, but that event shadows everything he writes. All of his subsequent works are built around *Night*'s

1945. As Soviet troops approached the camp, the two were evacuated to Germany. Severely weakened by the death march to Buchenwald, Wiesel's father perished there, but the son was liberated by American troops on April 11, 1945. Eventually he was reunited with his older sisters. The horrors Wiesel witnessed during the Holocaust, the despair he felt, the protest he directed at God were all to be incorporated in his literary and philosophical writings.

After Wiesel's liberation from Buchenwald, he was assisted by French relief agencies and took up residence in Paris. With French as his adopted language, he plunged into literature and philoso-

testimony. Wiesel followed *Night* with two short novels presenting the anguish of those who survived the Holocaust: *Dawn* and *The Accident*. That every act is ambiguous and implies a loss of innocence and that "God commit[s] the most unforgivable crime: to kill without a reason" are central to the protagonists' conduct and outlook.

Gradually Wiesel's fiction became longer and more complex. His characters, moreover, come to realize that friendship can help them live in the post-Holocaust world. This is especially true in *The Town Beyond the Wall*, where, despite society's indifference to persecution and cruelty, loving and being a friend allow a kind of equilibrium. Questions about God, evil, and suffering, although they cannot be satisfactorily answered, must nevertheless be asked, because from the beginning, such a dialogue has been established between God and God's creation. By reconnecting with his religious community, Wiesel seems to suggest in *The Gates of the Forest*, the survivor may rediscover joy in spite of despair.

By 1965, Wiesel's literary accomplishments were winning book awards such as the French Prix Rivarol and the National Jewish Book Council Literary Award. His credits were enhanced further by *The Jews of Silence* and *Legends of Our Time*. Originally a series of newspaper articles, *The Jews of Silence* describes the first of Wiesel's many visits to the Soviet Union on behalf of persecuted Jews. *Legends of Our Time* brings together short pieces by Wiesel—many of them autobiographical—on a wide range of pre-and post-Holocaust themes, including "A Plea for the Dead," which contains some of Wiesel's most frequently quoted words: "At Auschwitz, not only man died, but also the idea of man. . . . It was its own heart the world incinerated at Auschwitz."

The prizewinning novel *A Beggar in Jerusalem* marked a turning point for Wiesel. The novel celebrates the Israeli victory in the Six-Day War and reaffirms that life must be loved. Wiesel dedicated *A Beggar in Jerusalem* to his future wife. In 1969, he married Marion Erster Rose, who was to become his principal translator—his writings are usually done originally in French—and with whom he would have a son, Shlomo Elisha, named for Wiesel's father.

Wiesel was appointed distinguished professor in the Department of Jewish Studies at City College of the City University of New York, a position he held from 1972 to 1976, when he became Andrew Mellon Professor in the Humanities at Boston University. In 1972, he also published one of his best-loved books, *Souls on Fire: Portraits and Legends of Hasidic Masters*. In this book and several others, Wiesel uses his post-Holocaust perspective to retell the stories of teachers who led a pre-Holocaust tradition of Jewish spirituality known as Hasidism. Especially strong in eastern Europe, Hasidism influenced Wiesel's town and family. Many followers of this tradition perished in the Holocaust. Wiesel strives to keep the memory of them and their Hasidic tradition alive. Emphasizing how Jewish spirituality finds ways to celebrate life in spite of persecutions, pogroms, and the Holocaust itself, Wiesel writes about biblical figures—Joseph, Job, Joshua, and Jeremiah, to name only a few—in ways that stress humanity's responsibility to be just and compassionate.

That message is also Azriel's, the main character in Wiesel's 1973 novel *The Oath*. This novel tells of Kolvillàg, a community that disappeared except for one surviving witness. A long record of testimony against violence had done little to restrain men and women—and even God—from further vengeance. Besieged by a pogrom in Kolvillàg, Azriel and other Jews were inspired by Moshe to try a different life-saving strategy: "By ceasing to refer to the events of the present, we would forestall ordeals in the future." Only Azriel survives. He bears the chronicles of Kolvillàg—one created with his eyes, the other in a book entrusted to him for safekeeping by his father, the community's historian. Torn between speech and silence but true to his promise, Azriel bears the oath of Kolvillàg as well. Years later, Azriel meets a young man who is about to kill himself in a desperate attempt to give his life significance by refusing to live it. Azriel decides to intervene, to find a way to make the waste of suicide impossible by breaking his oath and relating his own experience. Eventually his young friend recovers and testifies that "by allowing me to enter his life, [Azriel] gave meaning to mine."

Variations on Wiesel's theme of loving and choosing life appear in *A Jew Today*. Explaining what it means to be Jewish, Wiesel affirms that the Jew's task is not to make the world Jewish but to make it more fully human. In this book, Wiesel creates a series of distinctive dialogues. The dialogue in Wiesel's novels is often remarkable, but in *A Jew Today* and in other works, such as *One Generation After* and *From the Kingdom of Memory: Reminiscences*, he crafts a dialogue form that becomes a genre distinctively his own. The words and lines of these dialogues are spare and lean. Although the settings are unidentified and the characters unnamed, these simple and yet complex conversations communicate in powerfully moving ways the particularity of Wiesel's experience, memory, and concern.

Wiesel's dialogue is also particularly powerful in his play *Le Procès de Shamgorod tel qu'il se déroula de 25 février 1649* (1979; *The Trial of God: As It Was Held on February 25, 1649, in Shamgorod*, 1979). Wiesel is not a systematic theologian, but he takes religious questions with the utmost seriousness. In *Night*, he spoke of the flames that destroyed his faith forever, and yet that is not inconsistent with his continuing dialogue with God. If Auschwitz made it no longer possible to trust God simply, it made wrestling with God all the more important. Wiesel remains at odds with God because the only way he can be for God after Auschwitz is by also being against God. To accept God without protest would do too much to vindicate God and legitimize evil. Nowhere does Wiesel argue for those points more effectively than in *The Trial of God*.

Wiesel took on new responsibilities when President Jimmy Carter appointed him to chair the United States Holocaust Memorial Council, which is charged to honor the dead, remember the past, and educate the living. Wiesel served in this position from 1980 to 1986. Under his leadership, plans developed for the United States Holocaust Memorial Museum in Washington, D.C., which has received millions of visitors since its doors opened in April, 1993.

Wiesel's humanitarianism was uniquely recognized in ceremonies held in Oslo, Norway, in December, 1986, when he received the Nobel Peace Prize. He used his Nobel Prize to establish The Elie Wiesel Foundation for Humanity, which supports educational efforts to reduce hatred and the destructive conflict it produces. Such concerns continue to be dominant in novels such as *Twilight* and *The Forgotten* as well as in essays and reflections like those found in *Sages and Dreamers:*

Biblical, Talmudic, and Hasidic Portraits and Legends, the latter based on lectures that Wiesel has given for many years in New York.

No individual has done more than Wiesel to encourage thoughtful reflection about the Holocaust. His writings are declarations against injustice and indifference. Buttressing his words with deeds, Wiesel has spent much of his life protesting on behalf of oppressed people and interceding with world leaders to help those in need. Wiesel claims that he intended to be a witness but not necessarily a philosopher. In fact, he is both. Grounded in his Holocaust experiences, the philosophy to which he bears witness emphasizes questioning and remembering. It urges humankind to transform injustice into justice and compassion.

John K. Roth with Pierre L. Horn

All Rivers Run to the Sea

Type of philosophy: Ethics, Jewish philosophy, philosophy of religion
First published: Tous les fleuves vont à la mer, 1994 (English translation, 1995)
Principal ideas advanced:

◊ In a Holocaust-shattered time, the moral imperative is to do all that one can to mend the world.

◊ Unless indifference and despair are resisted, hatred and death will win victories they do not deserve.

◊ If we stop remembering, we stop being.

◊ Memory should be cultivated and intensified so that bitterness can be avoided, hatred resisted, truth defended, and justice served.

Autobiographies pour out names and faces, and memoirs contain details about encounters large and small. While conforming to those conventions, *All Rivers Run to the Sea* is unconventional because it shows how Elie Wiesel's moral and spiritual outlook emerged from the twentieth century's greatest darkness, the Holocaust. Three fundamental facts inform Wiesel's story: He is a Jew, a writer, and a survivor of the Holocaust, which was the systematic, state-sponsored persecution and murder of nearly six million Jews by Nazi Germany and its collaborators. Wiesel's reflections on these facts emphasize the importance of resisting hate, despair, and indifference.

A Rabbi's Prediction

One day when he was eight years old, Wiesel accompanied his mother, Sarah, when she went to see her rabbi. After speaking to her in the boy's presence, Rabbi Israel spent time with him alone. What was he learning about Judaism, the old man wanted to know. After the young Wiesel responded, Rabbi Israel spoke to his mother again—this time privately.

When Sarah Wiesel emerged from that encounter, she was sobbing. Try as he might, Elie Wiesel never persuaded her to say why. Twenty-five years later, and almost by chance, he learned the reason for his mother's tears. Anshel Feig, a relative in whom Wiesel's mother had confided on that day, told him that Elie's mother had heard the old rabbi say, "Sarah, know that your son will become a *gadol b'Israel*, a great man in Israel, but neither you nor I will live to see the day. That's why I'm telling you now."

Wiesel tells this story early in his memoirs. It reveals much about him and sets the autobiography's tone. For Wiesel, stories are important because they raise questions. Wiesel's questions, in turn, lead not so much to answers as to other stories. Typically, autobiographies settle issues; memoirs put matters to rest. Wiesel's plan is different. His storytelling invites readers to share his questions, but the questions his stories provoke lead to more stories and further questions that encourage protest against indifference and despair. Wiesel's life makes him wonder—sometimes in anger, frequently in awe, often in sadness, but always in ways that intensify memory so that bitterness can be avoided, hatred resisted, truth defended, and justice served. The stories within Wiesel's story can affect his readers in the same way. If few resolutions follow, greater moral sensitivity can be aroused.

Rabbi Israel was right about Elie Wiesel. The shy, religious, Jewish boy grew up to become an acclaimed author, a charismatic speaker, and a dedicated humanitarian. In 1986, he received the Nobel Peace Prize, one of the world's highest honors. In his particularity as a Jew—which in-cludes dedicated compassion for Jews who suffered under Soviet rule and passionate loyalty to Israel—as well as in his universality as a human being, Wiesel qualifies as "a great man."

Rabbi Israel was also right about Sarah Wiesel. Neither she, nor Rabbi Israel, nor Wiesel's father, Shlomo, lived to see his major accomplishments. Wiesel insists that none of his success is worth the violence unleashed, the losses incurred, the innocence demolished in a lifetime measured not simply by past, present, and future, but through time broken before, during, and after Auschwitz. He would be the first to say that it would have been better if his cherished little sister, Tsiporah, had lived and all of his many books had gone unwritten, for in that case the Holocaust might not have happened. Wiesel's honors weigh heavily upon him. They are inseparable from a question that will not go away: How can I justify my survival when my family and my world were destroyed?

A Holocaust Survivor

Wiesel did not expect to survive the Holocaust. He wonders how and why he did. At the same time, his Jewish tradition and his own experience underscore that events never happen purely by accident. And yet—Wiesel's two favorite words—especially where the Holocaust is concerned, the fact that events are linked by more than chance does not mean that everything can be explained or understood, at least not completely. Only by testifying about what happened in the Holocaust, only by bearing witness as truthfully and persistently as possible about what was lost, does Wiesel find that his survival makes sense. However, the sense that it makes can never be enough to remove the scarring question marks that the Holocaust has burned forever into Wiesel's experience, humanity's history, and God's creation.

Wiesel's memoirs are not triumphal vindications. They are drenched in sadness and melancholy. However, sadness and melancholy, and the despair to which they might yield, are not their last words. Out of those ingredients, Wiesel forges something much more affirmative. Optimism, faith, hope—those words are too facile to contain his outlook. Defiance, resistance, protest—those terms come closer, but even they have to be supplemented by an emphasis on friendship, dialogue, reaching out to others, helping people in need, working to make people free, and striving to mend the world.

This book's greatest contribution is ethical and spiritual. It shows how Wiesel found ways to transform his suffering into sharing, his pain into caring. These transformations do not mean that Wiesel forgives any more than he forgets. The Holocaust was too immense, too devastating, to be redeemed by forgiveness that God or anyone else can give. However, because the world has been shattered so severely, Wiesel believes that the moral imperative is to do all that one can to repair it. Otherwise, hatred and death win victories they do not deserve.

A Vanished Past

In 1964, Wiesel revisited his hometown. This return to Sighet, that place in Eastern Europe where his mother and Rabbi Israel had their fateful conversation, was anything but easy. After his liberation from Buchenwald in April, 1945, instead of returning to his hometown, Wiesel had gone to France, where he eventually became a reporter for an Israeli newspaper. Years later, his journalistic work took him to New York, where he became an American citizen.

Sighet was far away. The distance, however, did not involve mileage alone. Once a part of Romania, then annexed by Hungary, and once more under Romanian control, Sighet stood behind the Iron Curtain in the 1960's. Cold War politics made the journey difficult and dangerous. Nevertheless, Wiesel was determined to go back to Sighet, "the town beyond the wall," as one of his best novels calls it.

Memory drew him there, even though Wiesel already knew what his visit would confirm: Sighet no longer existed—at least not as it was when he was born there in 1928, or as he had known the place until he left it at the age of fifteen in 1944. More than time had passed. People had come and gone, but that fact only began to tell Sighet's story. Those things happen everywhere, but the way they happened in Sighet, the particularity and enormity of what happened there and in thousands of places like it, made Sighet's disappearance so devastating that the world itself could never again be what it was before.

Sighet vanished in the Holocaust's night and fog. Only traces remained of what once had been. Sighet's streets looked familiar to Wiesel in 1964, although one called the Street of Jews contained apartments that seemed as modest as they were empty at the time. His boyhood eyes, Wiesel realized, must have been unaware of the poverty that many of Sighet's Jews experienced.

The movie house still existed. The family house stood still. It had not been sold but taken; strangers occupied it. Wiesel found the Jewish cemetery. He lit candles at his grandfather's grave. Elsewhere, Sighet was filled with living people, but Wiesel's hometown was gone. As the Germans liked to say twenty years before, Sighet had become *judenrein* (cleansed of Jews). Along with hundreds of thousands of Hungarian Jews, the largest remaining community of European Jews that had not yet been decimated by the Nazis, the Jews of Sighet were deported to Auschwitz in the spring of 1944.

Wiesel and his two older sisters, Hilda and Bea, survived the Holocaust, but most of Sighet's Jews, including his father, mother, and little sister did not. Few of the survivors went back to Sighet after the Nazis surrendered in May, 1945. Poignantly, Wiesel reflects on all that was lost as he describes his visit to one of the few synagogues that was still open two decades later. Stacked inside were hundreds of books—Wiesel calls them "holy books"—that had been taken from abandoned Jewish homes and stored there. Wiesel began to look through them. Tucked inside one, he writes, were "some yellowed, withered sheets of paper in a book of Bible commentaries." Wiesel recognized the handwriting they contained. It was his. Summing up his sadness, his memoirs observe that the finding of those pages is "a commentary on the commentaries I had written at the age of thirteen or fourteen."

Remembering the Past

This story, the existence of yellow, withered sheets of paper, a boy's reflections on the Bible—all are part of a world that disappeared. Wiesel seeks to make it live again through memory, testimony, and writing. The episodes he records make questions explode: Why did the Allies refuse to bomb the railways to Auschwitz? Why did Wiesel's family not accept the help of their housekeeper, Maria? One of the very few Christians in Sighet who offered assistance to Sighet's Jews, she might have hidden the family successfully. Why was the world so indifferent to Jewish suffering? Why was God?

Wiesel's narrative does not follow a strictly chronological form. His story does not fit the usual style of beginning-middle-end. The memories of his life circle around each other too much for that. From time to time, Wiesel breaks this commentary on himself even further by reflecting on his dreams. In one of them, the Wiesel family has gathered for a holiday celebration. Elie is asked to sing, but he cannot remember the traditional songs. He is asked for a story, but the stories have been forgotten, too. "Grandfather," Wiesel calls out in his dream, "help me, help me find my memory!" Astonished, Wiesel's grandfather looks back at him. "You're not a child anymore," he says. "You're almost as old as I am."

Wiesel has lived for a long time. He has experienced and remembered more than most people, but he worries profoundly about forgetting. If we stop remembering, he warns, we stop being. Wiesel is older now than most of his extended family who perished in the Holocaust. He lives with the dead as well as with the living. Taking his memoirs' title from the biblical book of Ecclesiastes, which speaks of how generations come and go and of how the eye is not satisfied with seeing, nor the ear filled with hearing, Wiesel sounds a characteristically mystical note as he considers how all rivers run to the sea.

Beginning in obscurity, streams of experience and memory rush forth. As they grow and merge, life's currents become a flood that eventually pours into the ocean's awesome depth. Like Wiesel's memoirs, the sea does not yield all of its secrets. Instead its storms rage, its waves crash, its tides ebb and flow, and there are moments of beauty, calm, and silence. Through it all, the sea endures, which is not an answer but an invitation to more stories and to their questions about how and why.

Although Wiesel does not see himself primarily as a philosopher, theologian, or political theorist, he uses the storyteller's methods to express an influential ethical perspective. Storytellers can deal with ultimate questions, but they do not always answer them directly. That style attracts

Wiesel, because his Holocaust experience makes him suspicious of answers that put questions to rest. Such answers tend to oversimplify. They even falsify by settling what deserves to remain unsettled and unsettling. *All Rivers Run to the Sea* emphasizes these outlooks. It also underscores that Wiesel does not despair even though his Holocaust experiences give him many reasons to do so. Hatred, indifference, history itself, may do their worst, but Wiesel protests against that outcome. By remembering the particularity of what happened to his people under Nazi domination, and by acting on the imperatives that such memory enjoins, he believes there is a chance to mend the world. Wiesel's survival and the extensive body of writing that flows from it, including *All Rivers Run to the Sea*, embody that philosophy.

John K. Roth

Additional Reading

Berenbaum, Michael. *Elie Wiesel: God, the Holocaust, and the Children of Israel*. West Orange, N.J.: Behrman House, 1994. This reprint of *The Vision of the Void*, Berenbaum's thoughtful 1979 study of Elie Wiesel, emphasizes Wiesel's insights about Jewish tradition.

Berger, Alan L. *Crisis and Covenant: The Holocaust in American Jewish Fiction*. Albany: State University of New York Press, 1985. Contains important reflections on Wiesel's encounters with and impact on American Jewish life.

Brown, Robert McAfee. *Elie Wiesel: Messenger to All Humanity*. Rev. ed. Notre Dame, Ind.: University of Notre Dame Press, 1989. A leading Christian theologian provides an important overview and interpretation of Wiesel's multifaceted writing.

Cargas, Harry James. *Conversations with Elie Wiesel*. South Bend, Ind.: Justice Books, 1992. An updated and expanded edition of Cargas's 1976 interviews with Wiesel, this important book features Wiesel speaking not only about the Holocaust but also about his audience, craft, and mission as a witness and writer.

Ezrahi, Sidra DeKoven. *By Words Alone: The Holocaust in Literature*. Chicago: University of Chicago Press, 1980. Ezrahi insightfully discusses Wiesel's writings in the context of a wide range of Holocaust literature.

Horowitz, Sara. *Voicing the Void: Muteness and Memory in Holocaust Fiction*. Albany: State University of New York Press, 1997. Contains a helpful discussion of Wiesel's emphasis on the importance of memory.

Langer, Lawrence L. *The Holocaust and the Literary Imagination*. New Haven, Conn.: Yale University Press, 1975. A leading Holocaust scholar interprets Wiesel's work in ways that are insightful and accessible.

Patterson, David. *The Shriek of Silence: A Phenomenology of the Holocaust Novel*. Lexington: University Press of Kentucky, 1992. Patterson's book explores the distinctive ways in which Wiesel wrestles with the theme of silence as a feature of the Holocaust and its aftermath.

Rittner, Carol, ed. *Elie Wiesel: Between Memory and Hope*. New York: New York University Press, 1990. Philosophers, theologians, and literary critics respond to the ethical, religious, and philosophical themes explored in Wiesel's diverse writings.

Rosen, Alan, ed. *Celebrating Elie Wiesel: Stories, Essays, Reflections*. Notre Dame, Ind.: University of Notre Dame Press, 1998. Distinguished scholars reflect on the ethical and religious dimensions of Wiesel's essays and novels.

Rosenfeld, Alvin H., and Irving Greenberg, eds. *Confronting the Holocaust: The Impact of Elie Wiesel*. Bloomington: Indiana University Press, 1978. Including "Why I Write," a significant essay by Wiesel, this volume contains a balanced collection of worthwhile essays written by scholars from varied disciplines.

Roth, John K. *A Consuming Fire: Encounters with Elie Wiesel and the Holocaust*. Atlanta, Ga.: John Knox Press, 1979. This book explores key philosophical and religious themes in Wiesel's authorship, drawing out their implications for post-Holocaust Christianity.

Roth, John K., and Frederick Sontag. *The Questions of Philosophy*. Belmont, Calif.: Wadsworth, 1988. Wiesel's perspectives on the relationships among God, evil, and human responsibility are discussed in a chapter entitled "How Should I Deal with Evil and Death?"

John K. Roth

John Wisdom

Wisdom was a British analytic philosopher associated with Ludwig Wittgenstein. His writings, in vivid conversational style, deal especially with the nature of philosophy and with the philosophy of mind.

Principal philosophical works: *Interpretation and Analysis in Relation to Bentham's Theory of Definition*, 1931; *Logical Constructions*, 1931-1933 (serial), 1969 (book); *Problems of Mind and Matter*, 1934; *Other Minds*, 1952, 1965; *Philosophy and Psycho-Analysis*, 1953; *The Metamorphosis of Metaphysics*, 1961; *Paradox and Discovery*, 1965; *Proof and Explanation: The Virginia Lectures*, 1991.

Born: September 12, 1904; London, England
Died: December 9, 1993; Cambridge, England

Early Life

Arthur John Terence Dibben Wisdom attended private schools in England and then entered Cambridge University, where he studied moral science, as philosophy was called there. George Edward Moore and Charlie Dunbar Broad were the two professors of philosophy at Cambridge then; Ludwig Wittgenstein and Bertrand Russell, though no longer there, were influential through their writings. After earning his bachelor's degree in 1924, Wisdom did nonacademic work and then became lecturer at the University of St. Andrews in Scotland. To this period belong his early books *Interpretation and Analysis in Relation to Bentham's Theory of Definition*, *Problems of Mind and Matter*, and *Logical Constructions* (which first appeared in a journal before its publication in 1969 in book form). These writings show the influence of Moore and Russell; Wisdom agrees with them that logical analysis is the proper method in philosophy but tries to go beyond them in discussing what sort of translation from one form of words to another can express a logical analysis, and how such analyses can be illuminating.

Life's Work

In 1934, Wisdom returned to Cambridge as lecturer in philosophy. He took an M.A. from the university and became a fellow of Trinity College. Wittgenstein had returned to Cambridge in 1929, and Wisdom attended his classes and fell in with the new form of philosophical thinking Wittgenstein was developing. Outsiders heard rumors about Wittgenstein's revolutionary new ideas, but he published nothing in this period. Wisdom did publish, and consequently Wisdom's writings came to be a main source through which the wider world could gain glimpses of Wittgenstein's later thought. The journal articles that Wisdom wrote from the mid-1930's through the 1940's are collected in his books *Other Minds* and *Philosophy and Psycho-Analysis*, the most widely read of his works.

Wisdom was appointed professor at Cambridge early in the 1950's and continued teaching there until his retirement late in the 1960's. His book *Paradox and Discovery* contains articles written during the 1950's and 1960's. After retiring from Cambridge, he went to the United States and taught for several more years, mostly at the University of Oregon. He subsequently returned to live in Cambridge.

Wisdom was tall and genial, had a brilliant smile, and loved a good time. He had a passion for riding, and for a time he maintained a horse of his own. His wife, Pamela Strang, was a painter. His teaching was untraditional in style and content. He rarely spent time expounding any philosophical text. Generally, his classes consisted of spontaneous thinking efforts in which teacher and students joined in dialogue. His way of teaching is reflected in his mature writing style, which is informal and resembles dialogue.

Readers accustomed to didactic exposition sometimes become impatient with this style. They ask why Wisdom does not flatly state his own position instead of wasting time expressing conflicting viewpoints. The answer is that for Wisdom, as for Wittgenstein, philosophy is not a body of doctrine that can be flatly stated. For them, philosophy has to do with perplexities into which people fall through misunderstanding how their language works. Wittgenstein compared the person caught in philosophical perplexity to a fly in a flytrap: The victim, having the fixed idea that the way out must lie in a certain direction, struggles fruitlessly and with increasing desperation, despite the fact that in another direction the way has lain open all the time. If the victim can be brought to a new understanding of the structure of the situation, the trouble will disappear. With philosophical perplexities, though, merely telling the victim where the way out lies does little good, because the victim will not assimilate this news. A conceptual readjustment is needed that can be brought about only gradually and with difficulty, as a new perspective is built up to replace the fixed idea that generated the trouble.

Wisdom gave much of his attention to two philosophical perplexities, both of which had been of concern to Wittgenstein as well. These two issues are the nature of philosophy (where the paradox is that it looks as though philosophy is not a branch of knowledge, so how can it be of any value?) and the meaning of statements about mental phenomena (where the paradox is that it looks as though a person cannot really tell whether others are conscious, because all a person has to go on is others' bodily behavior).

In his striking paper "Philosophical Perplexity" (1936), Wisdom considers whether philosophical statements (for example, "One can't know what is in the mind of another") have meaning merely as expressions of verbal conventions, as the logical positivists were maintaining. Wisdom speaks both in favor of and in opposition to this purely verbal interpretation. This appears strange: Must not there be a definite answer one way or the other? Wisdom does not

think so. He insists that whatever one says about such a matter may be misleading. If one says that philosophical statements are purely verbal, the comparison is to paradigm examples of verbal statements that they only partly resemble; if one says that they are not verbal, they are contrasted with these examples, from which they only partly differ.

Wisdom urges that each thing a person says gets its point from the range of comparisons and contrasts that it proposes, and that any proposed comparison or contrast has the potential to mislead, because any two cases always are both different and similar. This does not mean that nothing useful can be said, but to speak illuminatingly, one must take care to bring out what is good about the better parallels and what is misleading about the poorer parallels. One can best advance by employing a rich variety of comparisons and contrasts, so that one gradually comes to see the type of case in question in its manifold relations of similarity and difference to many other kinds of cases.

Although Wisdom's writings strongly show the influence of Wittgenstein, Wisdom departed in one important way from Wittgenstein's view of philosophy. Wittgenstein made it appear as though philosophical perplexities are generated only through bad thinking by philosophers, and that the proper task of good philosophy is to dissolve those misunderstandings, after which there will be no further need for philosophy. Wisdom dissented, holding that philosophical paradoxes arise out of everyday thinking as well. He also held that they can have the power to illuminate, as well as to confuse, so they are to be welcomed, not simply eliminated. By first appreciating the force of a philosophical paradox and then by learning how to resolve it, one can gain a surer command of the conceptual terrain.

Wittgenstein was accustomed to having disciples who embraced his teachings unquestioningly, so he can hardly have been pleased at Wisdom's dissent. Wittgenstein seems to have been even more displeased later, when Wisdom, in his 1946 paper "Philosophy and Psycho-Analysis" (which became part of a book by the same title in 1953), compared the process of resolving philosophical perplexities to the process of Freudian psychoanalysis; in both, Wisdom says, insight is gained through reflecting on a range of phenomena so as to see new patterns in them. Wittgenstein probably regarded this comparison as belittling his work, though Wisdom had not intended it that way.

Wisdom's views about the philosophy of mind are more in line with Wittgenstein's. He, like Wittgenstein, tried to bring out how unsatisfactory is the idea of the soul as a little person within, watching an inner screen, as it were, on which are projected images that the person describes to himself or herself in a private language, while trying to infer from them conclusions about what exists in an outer world. This picture encourages absolute skepticism about one's ability to know the mind of another, and it fails to recognize that language must be in principle public, with public criteria for the correct application of its terms.

This may seem to point toward a behavioristic view according to which speaking of what is going on in the mind of another is just a shorthand way of speaking about that person's bodily behavior. Thus, "He's angry" would simply mean "He's flushed, shouting loudly, waving his fists, and that sort of thing." Wisdom rejected behaviorism of that sort, however, because it glosses over the crucial point that the chief way of settling whether a person is angry is by asking that person.

Wisdom held that an asymmetry between first-person and third-person mental ascriptions is built into language. This asymmetry is difficult to describe and is the main source of philosophical perplexity about the mental. The first-person locution "I'm angry," when uttered sincerely by someone who understands the language, carries a special weight toward settling whether that person is angry. It can outweigh extensive observations made by others of the person's bodily behavior. This does not have to mean that the subject inspects the private, inner contents of his or her mind to detect whether anger is present; rather, the person has been trained to use language, and under the rules of language his or her own word carries special weight because it is the word of a competent language user (of course, anyone who speaks could be lying, but that does not affect the point here). Through such an argument, Wisdom tried to avoid both the unduly mentalistic picture and the crudely behavioristic account of the meaning of statements about the mental.

In his widely read article "Gods" (published in *Philosophy and Psycho-Analysis*), Wisdom turns to the philosophy of religion. He does not take a stand in favor of religion; his aim is the modest one of refuting the criticism that religious statements are meaningless because observations cannot verify or falsify them. Wisdom notices that in earlier times religious statements sometimes were understood as implying specific observational predictions, and so were empirically testable. Wisdom grants, however, that most modern persons do not understand religious statements in this way. Thus, nowadays, when the prayers of religious believers are not answered, they do not regard this apparent lack of a literal answer as disconfirming their belief. Does this show that their religious statements have no factual meaning?

Wisdom urges that even after the stage in an inquiry is reached at which one no longer needs to collect further observational data, a question of fact can still remain unsettled. For example, two visitors may encounter a garden; they see no gardener but disagree about whether the garden is tended. One sees a pattern of disorder and judges that there is no gardener; the other sees suggestions of order and care and judges that there is a gardener, perhaps an invisible one. Their disagreement may reach a point where further collection of observations does not help, yet the disagreement continues. Wisdom says it can still be a disagreement about a matter of fact, because they may be disagreeing about what pattern is there in the phenomena: Is it a pattern of orderly care or not? This need not be merely a question about how they feel; it can be a question to be answered by thoughtful reflection on what is there, and one contender may be able to show the other something about the pattern that the latter had not previously seen.

Wisdom concludes that religious disagreements can be like this. They can be factual disagreements, even though they do not call for the collection of further observational data, and there can be reasonable discussion back and forth between the parties, as each undertakes to show the other patterns that the other had overlooked.

There can be a fact of the matter in such a case. Thus, the logical positivists, who dismissed religious statements as meaningless, were proceeding too hastily.

Influence

Wisdom originally came to prominence as a presenter of Wittgensteinian ideas to the public, and he did this in a vivid manner. Later, he was eclipsed in this role, as Wittgenstein began to speak for himself through the posthumous publication of large quantities of his own writings.

Wisdom should not, however, be regarded merely as a disciple of Wittgenstein, for he was an independent and creative thinker on his own. The enduring interest of his writings comes from their lively charm, their genial tolerance for conflicting viewpoints, and, above all, the insights they offer into central philosophical issues of enduring concern.

Stephen F. Barker

Philosophy and Psycho-Analysis

Type of philosophy: Epistemology, philosophy of language, philosophy of mind
First published: 1953
Principal ideas advanced:

◇ Philosophical questions are verbal in the sense that they turn on unconventional uses of language, but they are not merely verbal because, in virtue of their oddity, in the process of justifying their use, one's attention is called to matters obscured by conventional language.

◇ Metaphysical paradoxes and platitudes function as penetrating suggestions as to how language might be used to reveal what is hidden by the actual use of language.

◇ In philosophical analysis, penumbral facts (matters to which certain conventional sentences call attention) are compared to nonpenumbral facts (matters to which the penumbral are presumably reducible) to determine whether the switch from one kind of statement to another is advisable and illuminating.

◇ The goal of philosophy is the clarification of the structure of facts.

◇ Philosophers do not uncover new facts, but they show old facts in a new way.

The title of this book is somewhat misleading: Only two of the fifteen essays are concerned with psychoanalysis. Rather, Wisdom shows that there are certain similarities between the approach of the metaphysician and the approach of the psychoanalyst; he also shows that there are similarities between the approach of the metaphysician and that of the lawyer, or the mathematician, the logician, the scientist, the art critic, or even the novelist. Wisdom's design, therefore, is really to clarify the term "metaphysics." He suggests in one place that his task is one of "meta-metaphysics," that is, one of determining the status of metaphysical problems and metaphysical judgments. The essays are united in their common concern with this problem. They extend in time of publication from 1932 to 1953 and are arranged, roughly, in chronological order. Several are critical book reviews. Only one, the last, appears in print for the first time.

Philosophy and Linguistic Analysis
The importance of the book lies in the fact that it clarifies Wisdom's position in relation to the current attempts to define philosophy as some form of linguistic analysis. Although Wisdom was strongly influenced by Ludwig Wittgenstein, he did not believe, as Wittgenstein and many of the logical positivists did, that metaphysics is nonsense of some sort that becomes evident when its statements are properly analyzed; nor did he believe that metaphysical statements are merely linguistic and that all difficulties can be eliminated by substituting clear words for vague ones and precise grammatical constructions for ambiguous ones; nor did he follow the Oxford School in stressing either the "ordinary language" of the person in the street or his or her beliefs on certain philosophical matters as the final court of appeal for settling all philosophical disputes. He examines these views, as well as others that associate philosophical problems with their mode of expression, and endeavors to state his own view in contrast to them.

Philosophers pose questions such as "Can we really know what is going on in someone else's mind?," "Can we really know the causes of our sensations?," and "What is a chair?" The reader's task is to determine what philosophers seek when they ask such questions, and what they mean when they reply, "We can never really know what is going on in someone else's mind," "A chair is nothing but our sensations," or "A chair is something over and above our sensations."

In a sense, Wisdom says, philosophy gives rise to verbal disputes. To state that one cannot know what is going on in someone else's mind is to utter something that is obviously untrue unless one adopts an unusual meaning for the word "know." It might be said that one who makes a statement of this kind is uttering nonsense. Suppose that a philosopher asks whether two plus three can ever equal six? Again, the question becomes nonsense unless one adopts unconventional meanings for some of the words it contains. The fact that both statements are nonsensical does not mean that they are nonsensical in the same way. To determine how they differ in their portrayal of nonsense, one would need to make a study that would be at least partially verbal. Thus, philosophical clarification is achieved through an examination of language. Similarly, if a philosopher says that a chair is something over and above human sensations, he or she is not proposing a new definition of "chair" or a new use for chairs, but instead is suggesting the need for a clarification of the meaning of a word. Philosophical questions and answers, therefore, seem to be verbal.

Although the philosopher's statements are formulated in words, the intention is not to raise verbal issues; the philosopher is not taking over the role of the translator. A translator substitutes a sentence S for a sentence S_, for the purpose of telling the meaning of S_. Philosophers do not wish merely to substitute one statement of a fact for another; they wish to transmit insight—insight into the structure of the fact that is asserted by S_. They equate S with S_ because they believe that S better indicates the structure of a certain fact than does S_. This is not a verbal matter.

The nature of philosophical statements can be further clarified by distinguishing their *content* from their *point*. Suppose a philosophical statement contains the word "monarchy." Anyone who knows that "monarchy" means the same as

"set of persons ruled by the same king," and who also knows the meaning of *either* of these expressions, will find that the philosophical statement becomes clarified if one is substituted for the other. This involves merely clarification in *content* and is the concern of the decoder rather than that of the philosopher. The philosopher achieves clarification (the *point* of the utterance) only if the hearer already uses and understands the meaning of *both* "monarchy" and "set of persons ruled by the same king." Philosophical statements thus appear to be very curious: They provide information only if the hearer already knows what is being told to him or her. Philosophy is trying to show the "structure" of a monarchy by bringing together the sphere in which "monarchy" is used and the sphere in which "set of persons ruled by the same king" is used. These are different categories, and the philosophical problem is that of showing by means of the structure of the statement how they are related. Wisdom suggests a certain mnemonic device: "It's not the stuff, it's the style that stupefies." It is not *what* philosophers talk about that makes them unique, but the *form* in which they expresses themselves. Wisdom apologizes for a suspicion of smartness when he says, "Philosophers should be continually trying to say what cannot be said."

The Meaning of Analysis

What is really involved in this disclosure of "structure" can be understood only by an examination of what Wisdom means by *analysis* as the method of all philosophy. Because his use of this word is somewhat technical, the way may be prepared by an examination of the conception of the world that, according to Wisdom, is held by all metaphysicians. They believe, in his words, "that the actual world is made up solely of positive, specific, determinate, concrete, contingent, individual, sensory facts." They also believe, however, in an apparent "penumbra of fictional, negative, general, indeterminate, abstract, necessary, super-individual, physical facts." This penumbra is apparent only because observers have not penetrated deeply enough. Philosophers believe that there are not two ways of knowing—one for the nonpenumbral facts and another for the penumbral—yet they also believe that because the nonpenumbral and the penumbral are not identical, there *must* be two ways of knowing. This produces philosophical perplexity. In the following examples, what is given first may be designated as the penumbral fact, and what is given second as the nonpenumbral fact.

The height of the average man is simply the sum of the heights of the individual men divided by their number.

A chair is simply a collection of sense-data.

A person's mind is nothing more than his behavior.

The state is something over and above the individuals who make it up.

The statement "Not three people are interested in mathematical logic" may be expressed in this form: "If x is interested in mathematical logic, and y also is interested, and z also is interested, then x is identical with y, or y is identical with z, or x is identical with z."

"All men are mortal" can be reduced to "John is mortal, and George is mortal, and James is mortal, and so on."

"Time" means (G. E. Moore) that lunch is over, supper is to come, Smith's anger is past, and so on.

Analytic propositions are merely verbal propositions.

In these examples, average men, physical objects, minds, states, numerical statements, general statements, time, and analytic propositions are all penumbral. Actual men, sense-data, behavior, individual citizens, the identity of x's and y's, John and George being mortal, supper following lunch, and verbal propositions are nonpenumbral. Call the former "X facts" and the latter "Y facts." Then the question becomes simply this: Are X facts ultimate, or are they reducible to Y facts? If they are reducible, are they completely reducible? That is, are X facts equivalent to Y facts? If they are not completely reducible, are X facts something over and above Y facts?

Wisdom believes that it is misleading to formulate the problem in terms of facts, because that would suggest that the issue can be decided simply by examining the world, either the logical world or the natural world. This is not the case. The question should therefore be expressed in terms of propositions or sentences: Do X sentences stand for the same proposition as any combination of Y sentences? Are X sentences used in the same way as some combination of Y sentences? For a given X sentence, is there a Y sentence that serves the same purpose?

This approach suggests examining the sentences to see under what circumstances one would be inclined to answer the question with a "Yes" and under what circumstances with a "No." There is no right or wrong answer to these questions; however, dispute can be resolved by explaining what induces each disputant to claim what he or she does. Thus, statements that are metaphysical paradoxes and statements that are metaphysical platitudes are revealed to be not simply false statements and true statements, but penetrating suggestions as to how language *might be used* to reveal what is completely hidden by its *actual use*. "Thus it appears how it is that, to give metaphysicians what they want, we have to do little more than remove the spectacles through which they look at their own work. Then they see how those hidden identities and diversities which lead to the 'insoluble' reduction questions about forms, categories and predicates, have already been revealed, though in a hidden way."

Material and Philosophical Analysis

With such issues clarified, one is ready to turn to an examination of what Wisdom means by *analysis*. A distinction must first be made between *material* analysis and *philosophical* analysis. To give a material analysis is simply to give a definition, such as "*Wealth* is defined as *what is useful, transferable, and limited in supply.*" A definition of *wealth* as *riches* would not be materially analytic, for it does nothing to render explicit the connotation of the word defined. A philosophical analysis is given by a rule for translating sentences about any abstraction ("the state") into sentences about what it is an abstraction from ("the individual citizens"). A second distinction must be made between *formal* analysis and *philosophical* analysis. A formal analysis is the replacement of a sentence by another that more clearly indicates the form of the fact asserted: "Two horses passed him" means "A horse passed him and then another." This would not be a material analysis because *two* is not an adjective, and it is not a philosophical analysis because it merely exhibits more clearly the structure of something whose structure was not clear. The distinction between the three types of analysis can be illustrated by the statement "Two men are good." A *formal* analysis would be "A man is good and another man is good"; a *philosophical* analysis would be "A *mannish* pattern of states contains a high proportion of good ones and another *mannish* pattern does so also"; and a *material* analysis would be "A *mannish* pattern of states contains a high proportion of states likely to cause approval and another does so also."

Analysis (philosophical analysis) cannot be understood without explaining *ostentation*. Philosophers have always employed ostentation, though because of their preoccupation with philosophy they have had little time to talk about ostentation. Ostentation is a kind of substitution: It is used on a sentence S_ when one substitutes for S_ another sentence S that more clearly reveals the ultimate structure of the fact they assert. Take the sentence "England invaded France." This has a dyadic structure exhibited by "EIF," where "E" is a term, "I" is a relation, and "F" is another term. The sentence "EIF" does not, however, exhibit the *ultimate* structure of its fact. To show this, one would have to formulate sentences about Tom, Dick, and Harry, and about Henri, François, and Jean, and about the former being sent threateningly into land owned by the latter, and so on. One can say that "EIF" *directly* locates a fact of which England is an element, but it *indirectly* locates a fact of which Tom, Dick, and the rest are elements. The analysis of the sentence "EIF" into sentences about Englishmen and Frenchmen is a philosophical analysis because the predicates that are applicable to England are definable in terms of the predicates that are applicable to Englishmen. They are, of course, different *kinds* of predicates because they are exhibited in different *kinds* of structure. The sentences about Englishmen and Frenchmen become an ostentation of the sentence about England and France; S is an ostentation of S_. When this is the case, the facts displayed, though not two, are not identical.

The distinction between the penumbral and the nonpenumbral facts thus has been recognized, and the question as to whether the former can be "reduced" to the latter (whether the former are "logical constructions out of" the latter) can be discussed intelligently, pro and con. What is introduced by ostentation is not merely a clearer understanding of the structure of a fact but an increased clearness in the apprehension of the ultimate structure of the fact. One should not say that S is merely a translation of S_ but that S displays directly what S_ displays indirectly, or that S_ displays a fact that is secondary to the fact that S displays. The sentence about Tom, Dick, and the others displays directly what the sentence about England and France displays indirectly, or the fact displayed by the sentence about England and France is secondary to the fact displayed by the sentence about Tom, Dick, and the others. Wisdom concludes the discussion of this topic by stating that the philosopher makes a prayer: "Please give me clearer apprehension of the Arrangement of the Elements of the Fact finally located by the sentence 'aRb.'" (In this statement, Wisdom uses capital letters to indicate that what the philosopher is seeking is the ultimate arrangement of the ultimate elements of the ultimate fact, not merely the structure that is obviously exhibited by "aRb.")

The Penumbral and Nonpenumbral
The question of whether the penumbral can be reduced to the nonpenumbral has divided philosophers into two schools. On one hand are the naturalists, empiricists, and positivists. They accept the Verification Principle. On the other hand are the realists and the transcendentalists, who accept the Idiosyncrasy Platitude. The former maintain such statements as "A cherry is nothing but sensations and possibilities of more," "A mind is nothing but a pattern of behavior," and "There are no such things as numbers, only numerals." The latter argue that every statement has its own sort of meaning, and "everything is what it is and not another thing." Examples can be found in "Ethical propositions involve value predicates and are ultimate," "Mathematical propositions are necessary synthetic propositions—an ultimate sort of proposition," and "Statements about nations are not to be reduced

to statements about individuals; they are about a certain sort of concrete universal."

Wisdom's contention with regard to both of these principles is that a person should examine what he or she means when saying that either of them is true. To say this is to suppose that the principles in question can be confirmed or disconfirmed. This is not the case: Neither principle is a scientific theory. The issue should, therefore, be formulated in terms of the question whether one should accept the Verification Principle or the Idiosyncrasy Platitude. Now, however, what has the issue become? Can one say that the Verification Principle is a metaphysical theory? Yes, says Wisdom, in a certain sense. It is not so much a metaphysical theory as a recipe for framing metaphysical theories; it is a mnemonic device that tells those who accept it how to proceed in settling certain metaphysical issues. It draws their attention to "the deplorably old-fashioned clothes in which it presents itself," because it appears in the disguise either of a scientific discovery that removes a popular illusion or of a logical proposition from which deductions can be made. Furthermore, the principle serves to draw the attention of those who reject it to the fact that underneath its disguise it has obvious merits. The principle, therefore, has the characteristics of all metaphysical statements in that it covers up what it really intends to say. The same is true of the Idiosyncrasy Platitude. Whether either of these is called "metaphysical" is of no great importance; the point is that in examining the reasons for or against accepting one of these principles, one is led into the activity that is designed to eliminate metaphysical perplexities and to arrive at that clarification of structure which is the goal of philosophy.

Philosophy in Relation to Psychoanalysis

Finally, Wisdom attempts to show in what sense philosophical difficulties are like psychopathic difficulties. Wittgenstein said that he held no opinions in philosophy but tried to remove "a feeling of puzzlement, to cure a sort of mental cramp" associated with philosophical problems. Wisdom gives an example in which an individual wrestles with the problem of whether he can or cannot know what other creatures are thinking about. He points out that such an individual, first skeptical about the minds of other people, is led

inevitably into skepticism about his senses, and finally into a skepticism about everything. This is obviously an absurd position, however, and he develops a stress that is quite analogous to that of the businessperson who is trying to meet financial obligations and becomes neurotic as a result. In what respects are these stresses alike, and in what respect is the cure that the philosopher might administer to the puzzled thinker like the cure that the psychoanalyst might administer to the neurotic businessperson?

Philosophy has never been a purely psychogenic disorder, and it is not ordinarily considered to be a therapy. When philosophers proceed by trying to show "not new things but old things anew," however, they are adopting procedures much like those of the psychoanalyst. Philosophical discussion aims to bring out latent opposing forces, and not to teach what is behind closed doors or whether 235 times 6 equals 1,410. Philosophy often shows that behind the latent linguistic sources of confusion there are much more deeply hidden nonlinguistic forces, and that a purely linguistic treatment of philosophy therefore cannot be adequate. Philosophy also shows that the nonlinguistic sources are the same as those that trouble people elsewhere in their lives and therefore that the philosophical riddles are the true "riddles of the Sphinx."

Philosophy is concerned with what is paradoxical and unconventional. Such matters are not settled by experiment and observation. Many philosophers have said that questions that cannot be settled by experiment and observation are questions merely of words. In saying this, they are speaking wildly; however, so are those "scientists, philosophers, or poets who say one cannot stir a flower without troubling of a star. What they say is mad but there's method in it."

A. Cornelius Benjamin

Additional Reading

Bamborough, Renford, ed. *Wisdom: Twelve Essays.* Oxford, England: Blackwell, 1974. Contains twelve appreciative essays about Wisdom's philosophy by his friends and former students, along with a bibliography of Wisdom's writings. The essays by D.A.T. Gasking, Judith Thomson, and Keith Gunderson are especially helpful.

Broad, C. D. "The Local Historical Background of Contemporary Cambridge Philosophy." In *British Philosophy in the Midcentury*, edited by C. A. Mace. London: Allen & Unwin, 1957. This article contains Broad's reminiscences about the philosophical scene at Cambridge over much of the time when Wisdom was there. Broad makes scant mention of Wisdom, probably because they had little in common philosophically.

Gasking, D. A. T. "The Philosophy of John Wisdom, I and II." *Australasian Journal of Philosophy* (1954). A sympathetic account of Wisdom's way of doing philosophy.

Hacker, P. M. S. *Wittgenstein's Place in Twentieth-Century Analytic Philosophy*. Oxford, England: Blackwell, 1996. A careful and readable account of Wittgenstein's philosophy during his earlier and later periods. The book does not directly speak of Wisdom but sheds light indirectly on him.

Passmore, John. *A Hundred Years of Philosophy*. London: Gerald Duckworth, 1957. A broad survey of philosophy in the English-speaking world from the middle of the nineteenth to the middle of the twentieth century. See pages 367-368 and 434-438 for mention of Wisdom and his role in philosophical developments.

Urmson, J. O. *Philosophical Analysis*. Oxford, England: Clarendon Press, 1956. A short and incisive critical account of leading movements in analytic philosophy. Pages 76-85 and 169-182 pertain to Wisdom's earlier and later periods of work. Urmson recognizes Wisdom as an independent thinker and not merely an expositor of Wittgenstein.

Wittgenstein, Ludwig. *The Blue and Brown Books*. New York: Harper & Row, 1958. This volume is based on notes taken by students who attended Wittgenstein's lectures during the 1930's. The material was circulated privately in typescript for many years and was published only after Wittgenstein's death. It provides a view of what may have been the content of the lectures by Wittgenstein that Wisdom attended.

_____. *Philosophical Investigations*. New York: Macmillan, 1953. Published soon after Wittgenstein's death, this is the most polished and impressive of his writings. It contains the authoritative formulation of his later views concerning the philosophy of mind and the nature of philosophy, matters that were of central concern to Wisdom.

Stephen F. Barker

Ludwig Wittgenstein

Wittgenstein, who criticized many aspects of traditional philosophy, developed an account of the logical structure of language in his early period, then largely abandoned this view for one involving language-games. In his later years, he came to view philosophy as a therapeutic practice.

Principal philosophical works: "Logisch-philosophische Abhandlung," 1921 (best known by the bilingual German and English edition title of *Tractatus Logico-Philosophicus*, 1922, 1961); *Philosophische Untersuchungen/Philosophical Investigations*, 1953 (bilingual German and English edition); *Remarks on the Foundations of Mathematics*, 1956 (bilingual German and English edition); *The Blue and Brown Books*, 1958; *Philosophische Bemerkungen*, 1964 (*Philosophical Remarks*, 1975); *Lectures and Conversations on Aesthetics, Psychology, and Religious Belief*, 1966; *Zettel*, 1967 (bilingual German and English edition); *Philosophische Grammatik*, 1969 (*Philosophical Grammar*, 1974); *Über Gewißheit/On Certainty*, 1969 (bilingual German and English edition); *Vermischte Bemerkungen*, 1977 (*Culture and Value*, 1980); *Remarks on the Philosophy of Psychology*, 1980; *Last Writings on the Philosophy of Psychology*, 1982-1992 (2 volumes, bilingual German and English edition).

Born: April 26, 1889; Vienna, Austro-Hungarian Empire
Died: April 29, 1951; Cambridge, England

Early Life

Ludwig Josef Johann Wittgenstein was born into a prominent and highly cultured family in turn-of-the-twentieth-century Vienna. His father, Karl Wittgenstein, was a leading Austrian industrialist and had in fact made a fortune in the iron and steel industry. Originally educated at home, at the age of fourteen Wittgenstein entered school at Linz in Upper Austria and later attended the Technische Hochschule in Berlin-Charlottenburg. Wittgenstein developed a strong interest in physics, technology, and engineering.

In 1908, he went to England, where he experimented with kites at the Kite Flying Upper Atmosphere Station and became a student at the University of Manchester. His early studies explored airplane engine design, mathematics, and the philosophical and logical foundations of mathematics. He went to Jena, Germany, to visit Gottlob Frege (the father of modern logic), where he was advised to study with Bertrand Russell at the University of Cambridge. Russell had published *The Principles of Mathematics* in 1903, and, together with Alfred North Whitehead, had published in 1910 the first volume of their *Principia Mathematica* (1910-1913), a monumental and definitive work in modern logic. In 1912, Wittgenstein was accepted at the University of Cambridge and took up his formal studies there under Russell.

Although Russell and Wittgenstein later drifted apart, at this early period they had a closeness and a mutual seriousness that show themselves in many stories that date from this time. According to Russell, at the end of Wittgenstein's first term at Cambridge, he came to Russell and asked, "Do you think I am a complete idiot?" The idea was that Wittgenstein was thinking about becoming a pilot (if he was an idiot) and a philosopher (if he was not). Russell advised him to write a paper during the term break. Wittgenstein did, and when Russell saw it, he immediately said that Wittgenstein should not become a pilot. On another occasion, Wittgenstein came to Russell's rooms late one night and paced up and down, in a distraught mood, for hours. Russell asked him whether he was thinking about logic or his sins, and Wittgenstein answered "Both!" Russell was convinced that, although Wittgenstein was eccentric, he was a genius.

In 1913, Wittgenstein's father died and left him a huge fortune. This Wittgenstein gave away, some of it in the form of anonymous benefactions to Austrian poets and writers. Wittgenstein assumed a rather austere lifestyle, which he maintained for the rest of his life. He ate simply, dressed simply, had no family, and lived in very humble rooms.

Life's Work

Wittgenstein's early masterpiece, and the only philosophical book that he published during his lifetime, is best known by the title *Tractatus Logico-Philosophicus*. It was published as "Logisch-philosophische Abhandlung" in German in 1921 and appeared in an English-German bilingual edition in 1922 under the better-known title. Wittgenstein stated in the preface that the gist of the book lies in the following statement: "What can be said at all can be said clearly, and what we cannot talk about we must pass over in silence." The book is quite terse and follows a special numbering system in which each section (sometimes only a single sentence) receives a number based on its relative importance to the whole. The main statements are given the numbers 1 through 7. Number 1 says "The world is all that is the case"—that is, the world is the totality of facts or situations. One of the essential features of Wittgenstein's early philosophy, as expressed in the *Tractatus Logico-Philosophicus*, is that the most basic statements (or elementary propositions) of language achieve meaning by picturing facts. More complicated factual statements are built up from these. Thus, when all the true propositions have been stated, everything that can be said has been said; the rest is silence. As Wittgenstein claimed in the *Tractatus Logico-Philosophicus*, there are some things that are inexpressible—he spoke here of things that are mystical—and to try to express these in language will only result in nonsense.

Wittgenstein claimed that *Tractatus Logico-Philosophicus* solved the problems of philosophy. He therefore left philosophy and pursued vari-

ous other professions. He became a village schoolteacher in the Austrian mountains, a gardener in a monastery, and a worker in sculpture and architecture. In 1929, however, Wittgenstein returned to Cambridge and to philosophy. His *Tractatus Logico-Philosophicus*, already acknowledged as a classic work, was accepted as his doctoral dissertation, and he became first a research fellow and later a professor. Until his death in 1951, Wittgenstein wrote many volumes of philosophy (almost always in German) but did not publish any of these (or have them translated into English). He taught philosophy at Cambridge, but instead of lecturing he used a method of discussion and thinking aloud. Most of his influence—and it was considerable—occurred through the students who attended his discussions and those who took dictation from him (in English). Wittgenstein, however, found the atmosphere of Cambridge life to be sterile. He would sometimes leave to spend weeks and months in out-of-the-way places in Norway and Ireland and would write philosophy there.

The new philosophy that Wittgenstein developed in the 1930's and 1940's retained its focus on language but gave up the monolithic idea that language always functions in merely one way, that is, via the picturing relation. He came to emphasize the great variety of uses of language and the fact that language is intertwined with the rest of human life. His later work, best seen in his posthumously published *Philosophical Investigations*, provides some explicit criticism of the views earlier taken in the *Tractatus Logico-Philosophicus*. Wittgenstein went on to develop his thoughts in new and positive directions.

Wittgenstein's view of the nature of philosophical problems changed. He now came to see problems as tied to individuals. Thus he said, for example, that the philosopher's treatment of a problem is like the treatment of an illness. Just as in medicine there is always a patient (and never an illness alone) who is to be cured, in philosophy there is a person who is the bearer of philosophical questions or confusions. The doctor does not treat diseases in the abstract, and the philosopher does not treat problems in the abstract.

The later philosophy of Wittgenstein has been characterized as a therapeutic approach. A philosophical problem is seen as a sort of difficulty. A person who has such a problem is lost, in a sense, and Wittgenstein's aim is to show this person how to get out of the difficulty. One image he used was that of knots. Although philosophy should be simple, he said, in order to untie the knots of our thinking it must be at least as complicated as those knots.

Wittgenstein believed that language itself was exceedingly tricky and often extremely misleading. At one point he said that philosophy is a battle against the bewitchment of intelligence by means of language. In emphasizing the variety of ways in which language is used, Wittgenstein opposed the idea that any one form of language or thought—the scientific, for example—is in some sense basic or foundational. If anything is foundational, according to Wittgenstein, it is one's practice or way of life.

Wittgenstein believed that some of the areas where people are most likely to be misled occur in thinking and talking about mathematical abstractions, psychological concepts, and language itself. Although he did not confine his thought and writing to these areas, he did concentrate his attention on what he regarded as the temptations that are likely to appeal to thinkers in these areas and on the means of overcoming these temptations.

Influence

Wittgenstein's influence spread rapidly from Cambridge to other areas of the English-speaking world and to Scandinavia, largely through his students and by word of mouth. Since his death in 1951, more and more of his philosophical writings have been published, and the scope of his influence has grown, although it remains significantly stronger in English-speaking countries and in Scandinavia and weaker on the European continent, Latin America, and elsewhere.

It is not an exaggeration to say that Wittgenstein was a leader in a philosophical revolution focusing particular attention on language and on the ways in which people can be confused or misled, especially by ordinary language. "Ordinary language" philosophy takes its inspiration from Wittgenstein. In this area, the emphasis is on the ordinary meanings of customary terms, clarity of expression, and down-to-earth common

sense rather than special philosophical or technical terminology, impressive-sounding but vague language, and high-flown metaphysical notions.

Wittgenstein's own views and practice in philosophy changed over time, and many scholars distinguish sharply between the earlier and the later periods or approaches. One of his constant concerns, however, was with clarity of thought and expression. He considered these to be of the first importance and maintained throughout his career that nonsense is always to be rejected and sometimes fought against.

Stephen Satris

Tractatus Logico-Philosophicus

Type of philosophy: Epistemology, logic, metaphysics

First published: "Logisch-philosophische Abhandlung," 1921 (serial); *Tractatus Logico-Philosophicus*, 1922 (book, bilingual German and English edition)

Principal ideas advanced:

◇ The world is made up of atomic facts; atomic facts are facts that are incapable of being analyzed into more elemental facts.

◇ Propositions are logical pictures of (possible) facts; what is common to a proposition and the fact it pictures is logical structure.

◇ A proposition does not express the form of a possible fact; it shows it.

◇ To give the general form of proposition is to give the essence of all description and of the world; any proposition whatsoever can be formed by drawing from the class of elementary propositions and using various logical operations.

◇ Philosophy is a process of clarification; the propositions of natural science are meaningful, but the attempt to say something meaningful in ethics, aesthetics, or metaphysics is bound to fail, for any such attempt involves the impossible task of talking about the world from the outside.

This is an unusual book, both in content and in style. In content it is about logic, though Ludwig

Wittgenstein, in discussing this subject, manages to say much about the theory of signs, epistemology, metaphysics, and philosophy in general. Furthermore, Wittgenstein indicates that there are many things that we cannot say about logic, not because we do not know them or because we cannot find words by which to express them, but because they are literally *inexpressible* by means of *any* language. Consequently, we must remain silent about them.

The sentences (or sometimes groups of sentences) in this work are all numbered in accordance with a plan. For example, a certain sentence has the number 3; this follows sentences 1 and 2 in the order of the natural numbers. However, between 2 and 3 are sentences numbered, for example, 2.0122 and 2.151. Sentence 2.0122 is a statement referring to statement 2. Statement 2.151 follows statement 2.1 and is a comment on it; statement 2.1, in turn, is another comment on 2, and follows it. All statements are in this way arranged in a unique, linear order based on the decimal notation, and the reader is able to determine by the number attached to each sentence what *general* topic is being considered, what *special* aspect of this general subject is involved, and so on, sometimes to a fourth level of specialization.

Furthermore, because of the unusual meanings associated with many of the terms employed by the author, the editor chose to publish, on facing pages, the original German text and its parallel English translation. This design permits those who are familiar with German to improve their understanding of the text by comparing the English version with its German original, thereby in many cases detecting fine shades of meaning. In a book where such common words as "fact," "object," "meaning," and "truth" occur in great abundance and are employed with somewhat unusual connotations, the parallel translation is of great help. The book also contains a valuable introduction, written by Wittgenstein's mentor Bertrand Russell, that both summarizes the text and criticizes it on some important points.

Atomic Facts

For convenience of discussion, one can combine Wittgenstein's discussion of proposition 1 and the remarks on it with proposition 2 and all of the remarks contained in propositions numbered 2.0. Proposition 1 states that the world is everything that is the case; proposition 2 asserts that what is the case, or the fact, is the existence of atomic facts. The world, then, is made up of atomic facts and is constituted by them. Atomic facts are facts that are incapable of analysis into more elemental facts. This does not mean that atomic facts cannot be analyzed, but only that they cannot be analyzed into other atomic facts. An atomic fact is itself a combination of objects (entities, things), each of whose essence lies in its being a constituent of an atomic fact. However, the objects that are elements of atomic facts cannot themselves be analyzed because they form the substance of the world. If we take advantage of the illustration of an atomic fact that Russell gives in his introduction (Wittgenstein does not give illustrations of atomic facts), we may say that it is what is asserted by the proposition "Socrates is wise." This contains two objects, *Socrates* and *wise*, each of which, in its own unique way, unites with the other to form the atomic fact. Traditional philosophy would call these objects "substances" and "qualities."

Wittgenstein states that however different from the real world an imaginary world might be, it must have something, its form, in common with the real world. Because the form is given by the objects, we may presume Wittgenstein to be saying that any imaginable world would have to contain substances and qualities, however these might differ from those in the real world. The world is the totality of atomic facts; it also determines the nonexistence of atomic facts, for the nonexistence of an atomic fact is a kind of fact. Reality, therefore, is the totality of atomic facts plus the fact that these are *all* the atomic facts.

Propositions

Beginning with proposition 2.1, continuing more or less explicitly through proposition 4, and extending implicitly through the rest of the book, Wittgenstein examines what is meant by saying that a proposition is a picture of a fact. He describes this picturing relation variously as "modeling," "standing for," "representing," "corresponding with," "depicting," and "projecting." Note, however, that a proposition is itself a fact.

By this is not meant the propositional sign that expresses the fact, though Wittgenstein admits that propositions can be expressed perceptibly through the senses, but rather the *sense* of the proposition. The point is, of course, that the proposition is a *logical* picture of the fact, not a *visual* one or an *audible* one. He says that it represents the fact in "logical space"—a metaphor that he uses repeatedly throughout the book. Its representative character lies in its form or structure, which means a coordination of the elements in the picture with the objects in the fact, and an identity of logical form exhibited by both the picture and the fact.

Thus the proposition "Socrates is wise" pictures the fact of Socrates' wisdom because "Socrates" represents Socrates, and "wise" represents wisdom, and the form exhibited by "Socrates" and "wise" in the propositional relation is the same as that exhibited by Socrates and wisdom in the fact. That this is a logical form rather than a spatial form is to be seen in the fact that while the sentence "Socrates is wise" has a spatial order of its elements, neither the *meaning* of the sentence nor the *fact* asserted by the sentence is spatial; what is common to the meaning and the fact is a logical structure.

More precisely, the proposition does not strictly represent the fact but rather the *possibility* of the fact, the possibility of the existence and nonexistence of atomic facts. A proposition whose expression mentions a complex is not nonsense if this complex fails to exist but simply false. A proposition represents what it represents independently of its truth or falsity, through its form of representation, through its *sense*. Furthermore, by virtue of the identity of form that runs through various facts, the picture represents every reality whose form it has; thus "Socrates is wise" also pictures the fact that Plato is human.

"The logical picture of the facts is the thought" (proposition 3). To say that an atomic fact is thinkable means that we can imagine it, and if it is thinkable, it must also be logical, for anything that is "unlogical" could not be expressed at all. Language cannot express anything that "contradicts logic" any more than a spatial figure can represent anything that contradicts the laws of space or can represent the spatial coordinates of a point that does not exist.

The sign through which thoughts are expressed is the propositional sign. Both the proposition and the propositional sign are facts. In the propositional sign, the elements (the words) are combined in a definite way so that the objects of the thoughts correspond to the elements of the propositional sign. The simple signs used in propositional signs are called "names." Objects can only be named and spoken about; they cannot be asserted. Names cannot be further analyzed; they are primitive signs. They have meanings only in the context of propositions.

A propositional expression presupposes the forms of all propositions that it expresses, and thus it may be said to characterize a form and a content; the form is constant, and everything else is variable. If every constituent part of a proposition is changed into a variable, the logical form (the logical prototype) remains. Thus, to use an example that Russell gives elsewhere, if we change the proposition "Socrates drank hemlock" into the proposition "Coleridge ate opium," the form of the proposition, "*ARB*," remains. This may be called a "propositional variable."

A Logical Language

In the language of everyday life, the same word often signifies in two different ways, and different words signify in the same way. For example, the verb "to be" appears sometimes as the sign of equality, sometimes as the expression of existence, sometimes as an intransitive verb, and sometimes as a sign of identity. Words of this kind are the cause of some of the most fundamental confusions in thought, especially in philosophical thought. The only way to avoid these difficulties is to invent a special symbolism—a symbolism that obeys the rules of *logical* grammar (logical syntax). Such rules follow of themselves if we know how every sign signifies. Russell and the mathematician Gottlob Frege have invented such logical symbolisms, but even these do not exclude the possibility of error.

The great advantage of a logical language is that it calls our attention to formal properties of objects and facts. This is not because propositions express the form of facts, but because they "show it" and do not state it. No proposition is capable of representing its form of representation, for this would require something that is impossible—the picture would have to place itself outside its form of representation. "The proposition *shows* how things stand, *if* it is true." The existence of a structure in a possible state of affairs is not *expressed by* the proposition that presents the state of affairs; it is *shown in* the proposition by means of its structure. The identity of form that is exhibited by the proposition and by the fact accounts for the representation of the fact by the proposition, but this does not give the proposition a *formal property* of representing the fact. It would be as meaningless to ascribe a formal property to a proposition as to deny it of the proposition. It would be equally meaningless to assert that one form has a certain property and another form has a different property, for this assumes that there is sense in asserting that either form has either property. We do not ascribe properties to forms nor do we ascribe forms to propositions or states of affairs.

In this respect, formal concepts differ from proper concepts. The proper concept "man" can be expressed by a propositional function, for example, "x is a man"; but the formal concept "object" cannot be expressed by "x is an object." In this expression x is a sign of the pseudoconcept *object*, and to say that a rose is an object (thing, entity) is to utter nonsense. The same holds true of such words as "complex," "fact," "function," and "number," which should be represented in symbolism by variables, not by proper concepts. Recognizing these as variables shows the absurdity of making such statements as "There are objects" (supposedly patterned after "There are books") or "There is only one 1" (which according to Wittgenstein is as absurd as it would be to say "2 plus 2 is at 3 o'clock equal to 4"). To summarize, then, the great advantage of a precise logical symbolism is that it prevents us from talking nonsense. The correct use of the symbols, as was said above, follows immediately if we know how every sign signifies.

A further consequence of the notion that "object" is a pseudoconcept is the impossibility of finding some "property" that all "objects" possess. We have already seen that atomic facts are complex and contain objects as elements of a certain structure. These objects are unanalyzable. Consequently, to name a certain atomic fact is to presuppose the truth of a certain atomic proposi-

tion, namely, the proposition asserting the relatedness of the constituents of the complex; and this, in turn, presupposes the naming of the constituents (object) themselves. However, according to Wittgenstein, because the concept "object" is a pseudoconcept, there is no way that we can describe the totality of things that can be named. This means that we cannot say anything about the totality of what there is in the world. There is no property, such as self-identity, which all objects possess. To say that if all objects were exactly alike they would be identical, and there could be only one object in the world, is to assert not a logical truth, but an accidental characteristic of the world. Consequently, we cannot use self-identity as a property by which we can "locate" an object. Instead, we signify objects by means of letters, and different objects by different letters.

Types of Propositions

The simplest proposition, the elementary proposition, asserts the existence of an atomic fact. Such a proposition is a concatenation of names and is incapable of analysis into further propositions. One of Wittgenstein's important theses is that all propositions are truth-functions of elementary propositions and can be built up from them. (An elementary proposition is a truth-function of itself.) Truth-functions are obtained in the following way: Suppose all elementary propositions were given. Each of these could be either true or false. Therefore a proposition containing three elementary propositions p, q, r could have a truth-function T, T, F or T, F, T, and there would be eight such possible truth-functions. If there were four elementary propositions, there would be sixteen truth-functions. Starting with any group of elementary propositions, the truth-functions formed from them may be arranged in a series.

Of the propositions, two kinds are particularly important. One of them, a "tautology," is a type of proposition that is true for all the truth-possibilities of the elementary propositions. The other, a "contradiction," is a proposition that is false for all the truth-possibilities of the elementary propositions. The truth of a tautology is *certain*; the truth of a contradiction is *impossible*; the truth of all other propositions is *possible*. Here we have the serial arrangement of propositions that forms the basis for a theory of probability. An example of a tautology is "It is either raining or it is not raining"; this is always true regardless of whether the *p* and the *not-p* that it contains are true or false. A tautology, therefore, "says nothing" about the world, for it is true of all possible states of affairs. An example of a contradiction is "It is both raining and it is not raining"; this is false regardless of whether the *p* and the *not-p* that it contains are true or false. A contradiction therefore also "says nothing" about the world, for it is false for all possible states of affairs. Tautologies and contradictions are without sense. "Contradiction is the external limit of the propositions, tautology their substanceless center."

Logical operations are those that produce propositions from other propositions. For example, "denial" (not), "logical addition" (either/or), "logical multiplication" (and) are all logical operations. Thus, operations do not assert anything; the *result* of an operation, a proposition, does assert something; and what it asserts depends on the elementary propositions on which it is based. We can thus express the general form of all propositions; this is a propositional variable whose values would be all possible propositions. Wittgenstein states this form in abstract symbols; it means, according to Russell in the introduction, "whatever can be obtained by taking any selection of atomic propositions, negating them all, then taking any selection of the set of propositions now obtained, together with any of the originals—and so on indefinitely."

Logic

Language cannot express anything that contradicts logic. Wittgenstein now resumes discussion of this topic and points out that we cannot say what we cannot think. We cannot say that there is *this* in the world but there is not *that*, for such a statement would imply that logic can exclude certain possibilities from the world; but in such a case, logic would have to "get outside the limits of the world"; that is, it would have to consider these limits from both within and without the world. However, logic cannot go beyond itself: "Logic fills the world: the limits of the world are also its limits." This principle also has applications for solipsism. Solipsism is correct but can-

not be asserted; it can only be "shown." The subject who knows is the limit of the world; he or she does not belong to it. The best example of this theory is the field of vision: There is nothing *in the field of sight* that permits us to conclude that it is seen by an eye.

Reality, for Wittgenstein, proves to be very loose-knit. No atomic fact contradicts any atomic fact, and no atomic fact can be inferred from an atomic fact. There is no causal nexus in nature, and belief that there is such a thing is superstition. Induction is a process of assuming the simplest law that can be made to describe the regularities of nature. However, there is no necessity in this process. The only necessity is a *logical* necessity, and the only impossibility is a *logical* impossibility; and these presumably do not exist in the world.

The *sense* of the world lies outside the world. If there were *value*, it would have to "lie outside all happenings and being-so. For all happenings and being-so is accidental." As a consequence, ethics and aesthetics cannot be expressed, and are transcendental.

The Role of Philosophy

What, then, is philosophy? It seems to have two tasks. One is to show that every proposition is a picture of a fact. This cannot be *said*, for no proposition can say anything about itself. That a proposition has, for example, the subject-predicate form cannot be said in a proposition, and that a proposition has the form "*p* or *q*" cannot be said in a proposition. Nor can it be said how a proposition pictures reality. A sentence has no *apparent* pictorial character. However, neither does a musical score or a phonograph record; nor does a pattern of sound waves obviously picture the sound themselves. Yet all of these stand to that which they represent in a relation that can be seen in the similarity of structure holding between them and the facts. There is a "law of projection" that enables us to translate the picture into the fact, though this *law* cannot be stated. Because the law cannot be stated, we should not try to do so. Wittgenstein therefore concludes with proposition 7, "Whereof one cannot speak, thereof one must be silent."

However, there *is* another task for philosophy. Philosophy is not a theory, like one of the natural sciences, ending in a series of conclusions that can be called "philosophical propositions." It is an activity, a process of clarification, in which we try to delimit thoughts that are obscure and confused. If philosophy finds that the *answers* to its questions cannot be expressed, it should realize that its *questions* have not been properly expressed, for "if a question can be put at all, then it *can* also be answered." To doubt where there are no questions is absurd. To insist that the problems of life have not been touched by the sciences and yet to be unable to formulate these problems that remain in a language that is clear enough to permit an answer is really to say that there is no problem left. This is precisely what Wittgenstein says. "The solution of the problem of life is seen in the vanishing of this problem." The right method of philosophy is to turn all of the things that can be said over to the scientists, who will *say* them, and then when anyone asks a metaphysical question, to point out that the question is meaningless. Philosophy will then "see the world rightly."

A. Cornelius Benjamin

Philosophical Investigations

Type of philosophy: Epistemology, philosophy of language
First published: Philosophische Untersuchungen/ Philosophical Investigations, 1953 (bilingual German and English edition)
Principal ideas advanced:
◇ Language is best conceived as an activity involving the uses of words as tools.
◇ Words are used in a multiplicity of ways and are to be understood by engaging in the language "games" in which they are employed; words are not labels for things.
◇ For a large number of cases in which the word "meaning" is used, the meaning of a word is its use in the language.
◇ Discourse about sensations is understandable because there is a grammar of the word "sensations," and of such words as "pain" and "remember," which can be grasped by anyone acquainted with the relevant language-games;

no reference to what one has in mind or feels privately makes sense unless it makes sense in this way.
◇ Expecting, intending, remembering—these are ways of life made possible by the use of language; and language is itself a way of life.

Philosophical Investigations, published posthumously, contains in part 1 a body of work completed by Ludwig Wittgenstein by 1945. This material includes a preface in which he comments on the book, characterizing it as an "album" of "sketches of landscapes," in virtue of its being a collection of philosophical remarks that Wittgenstein used to attack the problems with which he concerned himself. Parts 2 and 3, written between 1947 and 1949, were added by the editors, G. E. M. Anscombe (who translated the work from the German) and R. Rhees. The German and English versions appear side by side.

Discussion of the work's contents preceded its publication because of the appearance of the "Blue Book" and the "Brown Book," collections of typescripts and notes based on Wittgenstein's lectures at Cambridge. In part, Wittgenstein became interested in publishing *Philosophical Investigations* during his lifetime because of a reluctance to rest his reputation on secondhand reports of his philosophical remarks.

An aura of mystery, therefore, surrounded *Philosophical Investigations* when it finally appeared—and something of the aura yet remains as arguments on the interpretation of the sense and direction of Wittgenstein's remarks tend to condition the understanding of the book. Nevertheless, there is little argument about the central theme; in spite of Wittgenstein's erratic and peripatetic method, the purpose of his remarks manages to become clear.

Understanding Language
The point of the book appears to be that language is best conceived as an activity involving the uses of words as tools. There is a multiplicity of uses to which words can be put. To understand the meaning of an utterance is to understand the use to which it is put. Consequently, it is misleading and confusing to think of language as being made up of words that stand for objects. Understanding the uses of words is like understanding

the rules of games, and just as confusion results when a player in a game makes up new rules, misapplies the rules, or conceives of the game in some static fashion, it causes confusion and perplexity when a user of language creates new rules, violates old ones, or misconceives language. To be clear about language, one must look to its uses.

However, if all that Wittgenstein meant to do was to say this, he could have done the job with a great deal less effort and at considerably less length. *Philosophical Investigations* is not so much a report of the results of Wittgenstein's philosophical investigations as it is an investigation *in progress*—and what it deals with and exhibits are philosophical investigations. In other words, Wittgenstein's remarks are used to show that certain philosophical problems arise because language is misconceived, and because of the author's adroit uses of language, we are led to conceive of language as instrumental. In a sense, then, the book *is* what it is *about*; its process, as a proof, is its evidence.

Investigations into Philosophy

What is it to investigate *philosophically*? Wittgenstein's answer is that it is *not* to seek theses or theories and it is *not* to find static meanings (objects) for which words are permanent labels; it is, rather, to understand by attending to the uses of language relevant to the problem at hand in order to discover how philosophical problems arise "when language *goes on holiday*"—that is, when a user of languages takes off in new, unpredictable directions as a result of failing to abide by the rules of a particular "language-game." One might support Wittgenstein at this point by saying that what poets do intentionally, in order to be poets, philosophers do in ignorance—and hence are philosophers.

In the preface, Wittgenstein declares that he had hoped to bring the remarks of the book into some coherent whole, but such an attempt, he came to realize, could never succeed. He suggests that philosophical investigation involves coming at a problem from a number of different directions.

Though it is true that escape from a static conception of language is made possible by a series of relevant demonstrations of the uses of language, there is no reason why the points of the book could not have been arranged serially for clarity, even if, to do so, eccentric uses of language would have been necessary. A number of problems could then have been dealt with in the Wittgenstein fashion, a fashion that has illuminated the eccentric uses of language. In fact, that is what *almost* happens in *Philosophical Investigations*: Now and then the reader catches Wittgenstein presenting a thesis, and it is clear that the problems he considers—suggested by his own odd uses of language in the expression of his theses—are intended to illustrate and support his points. Yet Wittgenstein had a streak of philosophical coyness (sometimes disguising itself as a kind of insight) which led him, presumably for theoretical reasons but more likely for effect, sometimes to withhold the moral of the tale, the destination of his philosophical wanderings.

Language as a Game and as a Tool

Wittgenstein uses two principal metaphors to make his meaning clear: the metaphor of language as a game and the metaphor of language as a tool—or, to be more accurate, the metaphors of languages as games or as tools. After describing a primitive language that could be described as involving a process of calling for objects by the use of words, Wittgenstein writes: "We can . . . think of the whole process of using words . . . as one of those games by means of which children learn their native language. I will call these games 'language-games' and will sometimes speak of a primitive language as a language-game. . . . I shall also call the whole, consisting of language and the actions into which it is woven, the 'language-game.'" (7) (In part 1, which comprises the largest section of the work, the remarks are numbered. For convenience in referring to the work—because there are no chapters, section headings, or other devices for locating oneself—these numbers are used here.) In 11, Wittgenstein writes: "Think of the tools in a toolbox: there is a hammer, pliers, a saw, a screwdriver, a rule, a glue-pot, glue, nails and screws.—The functions of words are as diverse as the function of these objects."

However, what is the point of using the expression language-game? Wittgenstein answers: "Here the term 'language-*game*' is meant to bring into prominence the fact that the *speaking* of language is part of an activity, or of a form of life." (23) He then presents a list of some of the functions of language—for example, giving orders, describing, reporting events, making up stories, translating—and comments: "It is interesting to compare the multiplicity of the tools in language and of the ways they are used, the multiplicity of kinds of word and sentence, with what logicians have said about the structure of language. (Including the author of the *Tractatus Logico-Philosophicus*.)" (23) He refers to his own earlier work, "Logisch-philosophische Abhandlung" (1921; published in the bilingual German and English edition as *Tractatus Logico-Philosophicus*, 1922), in which he defended a logical atomism—a philosophy that would elucidate problems by devising an ideal language in which for each simple object or property there would be a fixed, unambiguous symbol—ironically, the very conception of language that *Philosophical Investigations* examines and rejects.

The simile that using an utterance is like making a move in a game suggests the problem, "What is a game?" If language involves simply the use of names as labels, then there is a definite answer to that question. However, if the word "game" is used in various ways, it may very well be that there is no "object," no essential nature, to which the word "game" calls attention. Indeed, this conclusion is what Wittgenstein argues. In response to the supposition that there must be something common to the proceedings called "games," he urges everyone to *"look and see* whether there is anything common to all," and he ends a survey of games by remarking: "And the result of this examination is: we see a complicated network of similarities overlapping and criss-crossing: sometimes overall similarities, sometimes similarities of detail." (66) He introduces the expression "family resemblances" to characterize the similarities.

The point is that just as games form a "family," so do the various uses of an expression. To look for common meanings, then, is as fruitless as to look for the essential nature of games. The only way of making sense out of a problem having to do with the essence of language (or the meaning of a word) is by examining language as it is actually used in a multiplicity of ways.

Meaning

The theme of *Philosophical Investigations* is introduced shortly before the philosophical investigation into the essence of games: "For a *large* class of cases—though not for all—in which we employ the word 'meaning' it can be defined thus: the meaning of a word is its use in the language."

To understand this critical sentence is to understand *Philosophical Investigations*. At first the claim that, as the word "meaning" is often used, the meaning of a word is its use in the language might appear to be a variant of the familiar pragmatic claim that verbal disputes are resolved by decisions as to the practical use of language. Philosopher William James considered the question "Does the man go round the squirrel?" in an imagined situation in which, as the man walks round a tree, the squirrel moves about the tree trunk, keeping the tree between himself and the man. Some persons would be inclined to say that the man *does* go round the squirrel because the man's path enclosed the squirrel's path; but others would say that the man does *not* go round the squirrel because the squirrel keeps the same part of its body turned toward the man. James would settle the issue by deciding how to use the word "round." He did not *answer* the question, but he settled the problem; he settled it by resolving the issue as a problem. In an analogous fashion, it might seem, Wittgenstein proposed resolving problems, not by answering them, but by showing that they involve confusions concerning the use of language.

However, to interpret "the meaning is the use" in this manner is to fail to understand the function of the sentence in Wittgenstein's remarks. Wittgenstein is not suggesting that meanings be determined by reference to use or that meanings be explicated by reference to human attitudes in the use of language. What he suggests is what he says (but he says it oddly): The meaning of a word is its use in the language. For anyone who takes the word "meaning" as if the meaning of a term were an object, a class of objects, or a property of a class of objects—in other words, something to which a word, as a label, refers—it is nonsense to say "the meaning of a word is its use." If the word "human" means rational animal, for example, what would be the sense of saying, "The meaning of the word 'human,' namely, rational animal, is its use in the language"? However, if we take the word "meaning" as it is used in discourse about the *meaning* of conduct, the *meaning* of an act, the *meaning* of a form of life—then it makes sense to talk about the meaning of a word as being the use of the word in the language. It makes sense if by the "use" of something we mean what we would mean—more or less—in talking about the "purpose" of something. To understand a word, then, is much like understanding an act that makes no sense until one notices what the act does and, consequently, realizes what the act is *for*, what the purpose of it is, what *meaning* it has.

Words as Tools, not Names

There is no more difficult demand on philosophers accustomed to the sign-referent way of analyzing language than this demand that they stop thinking of words as names for objects and start thinking of words as tools that can be used in various ways and can be understood as bringing about certain changes in behavior or in ways of looking at things. Figurative description of language as a game is meant to stress "the fact that the *speaking* of language is part of an activity, or of a form of life": One does something with the use of a word that is much like what one does in making a move in a game; and just as it would be senseless to ask what the move *stands for* or *represents* (as if somehow it were a symbol for the victory toward which the player moves), so it is senseless to ask what the word, as used, *stands for* or *represents*. To be sure, conventional answers can be given to questions of the latter sort, but conventional answers are not illuminating; one comes to understand what language is and what language means in noticing (seeing) what is done with it (just as one can come to understand a machine by watching its operation).

This interpretation of Wittgenstein's remark that "the meaning of a word is its use in the language" gains strength with the realization that a considerable number of the remarks are directed against the idea that the meaning of a word is whatever the speaker has in mind or feels privately. Here again the problem "What is the essential nature of games?" is illuminating. By a survey of the various activities to which attention is called by various uses of the word "game," one

comes to understand the word "game" and games; and the problem dissolves because one is satisfied with the survey of the family of games, and there is nothing more about which to wonder. Similarly, to understand the meaning of the word "pain" is to have acquired the technique of using the word; there is nothing hidden or private about which to wonder.

However, this conclusion—that discourse about sensations is meaningful because the word "sensation" has a use in our language and that the word "sensation" cannot be part of a private language significant only to the speaker—is intolerable to philosophers who like to say that "Sensations are private," "Another person can't have my pains," or "I can only *believe* that someone else is in pain, but I *know* it if I am." (These are Wittgenstein's examples—which he discusses in a series of related remarks.) Wittgenstein realized that much of what he had to say is intolerable to some philosophers, but he writes that philosophers have the habit of throwing language out of gear; and sometimes the philosophical use of language is so extreme, so abnormal, that what is called for is *treatment* by one who understands that philosophical problems arise and philosophical theories are advanced when philosophers develop the disease of taking expressions that fit into the language in one way and then using the expressions in some other, problem-provoking, paradox-generating way. Hence, "The [enlightened] philosopher's treatment of a question is like the treatment of an illness." (255)

Thus, if someone comes forth with the philosophical "discovery" that "sensations are private," what he needs is treatment: A philosopher who talks about private sensations has made the error of confusing a discovery about the "grammar" (the systematic use) of the *word* "sensation" with a nonlinguistic fact. "The truth is: it makes sense to say about other people that they doubt whether I am in pain; but not to say it about myself." (246) However, it does not follow from the grammatical point—that it would be senseless to *say* that I doubt whether I am in pain—that therefore I *know* that I am in pain: The expression "I know I am in pain" has no use in our language—except, perhaps, to add emphasis to the expression "I am in pain." To confuse the use of the word "know" in such an expression as "I know he is in pain" (for he is writhing, clenching his teeth, and the like) with its use in the expression "I know I am in pain" is to breed perplexity that only an investigation into the multiplicity of uses of the word "know" can resolve.

Memory and Sensations

In his discussions of understanding, memory, and sensations, Wittgenstein characteristically sketches the range of uses of the terms "sensations," "understand," and "remember." He resists the tendency to settle on one use, one way of looking at things, one definition as somehow settling anything—for even if one considers what one takes to be a "single" use of a term, it soon develops that there are borderline cases, areas in which one use imperceptibly merges into another, so that any decision as to the use of language by way of definition settles nothing (the complex network remains) and may lead to further paradox. Philosophical difficulties in this area (as well as in others) arise when one kind of grammar is mistaken for another, when an expression appropriate in one context is used in another: "Perhaps the word 'describe' tricks us here. I say 'I describe my state of mind' and 'I describe my room.' You need to call to mind the differences between the language-games." (290)

Expecting, intending, remembering—these are ways of life made possible by the use of language; and language is itself a way of life. What we find when we try to find the criteria of these states are the uses of various expressions—or by noticing the uses of various expressions, we come to learn what kind of behavior prompts our use of these terms. No reference to *inner* thoughts, sensations, intentions, or memories is necessary.

For Wittgenstein, "*Essence* is expressed by grammar." (371) To understand the nature of something is to acquire the technique of using the language that prompted the question and the investigation concerning it. There are, however, no simple answers; in a sense, there are no answers at all. One gets acquainted with the multiplicity of uses and one surveys the scene accordingly: There is nothing left to wonder about.

Wittgenstein does not deny the existence of feelings—pains, memories, and expectations. In response to the charge that "you again and again reach the conclusion that the sensation itself is a

nothing," he responds, "Not at all. It is not a *something*, but not a *nothing* either! The conclusion was only that a nothing would serve just as well as a something about which nothing can be said. We have only rejected the grammar that tries to force itself on us here." (304) Again, in response to the query "Are you not really a behaviorist in disguise? Aren't you at bottom really saying that everything except human behavior is a fiction?" he replies, "If I do speak of a fiction, then it is of a *grammatical* fiction." (307)

The effort throughout is to argue against the tendency philosophers sometimes have to study "inner processes" in order to acquire knowledge about sensations, memory, and so forth; the proper procedure, according to Wittgenstein, is to attend to the use of the relevant terms. If we do observe the uses of such terms as "sensation," "pain," "think," "remember," and so forth, we come to see that the technique of using these terms in no way depends on introspecting private processes. An analogous mistake is made when it is assumed that to mean something is to think something. We can say that we meant a person to do one thing, and he did another—and we can say this even though we did not think of the possibility in question: "'When I teach someone the formation of the series . . . I surely mean him to write . . . at the hundreth place.'—Quite right; you mean it. And evidently without necessarily even thinking of it. This shows you how different the grammar of the verb 'to mean' is from that of 'to think.' And nothing is more wrong-headed than calling meaning a mental activity!" (693)

In part 2 of the *Investigations* the theme of the latter section of part 1 is made perfectly clear: meaning, intending, understanding, feeling, and seeing (whether it is visual apprehension or the understanding of something; and these are related) are techniques, forms of life, modes of action about which we could be clear were we not confused by misleading parallelisms of grammar. To understand, to see clearly, is to master techniques to which our attention is called when language is used; and the use of language is itself a technique.

Philosophical Investigations is Wittgenstein's mature discourse on method. It corrects the basic error of the *Tractatus Logico-Philosophicus*—the error of supposing that there are atomic facts involving unanalyzable simples, an error that arose from the mistaken conception of language as a naming of objects. This book not only makes the correction by conceiving of language as a tool and of the use of language as a form of life involving techniques, but it also exhibits the multifarious character of philosophical investigations by showing them as crisscrossing sight-seeing excursions made possible by tracing out families of similarities to which the multiplicity of language uses calls attention.

If there is a weakness in this revolutionary work, it is the weakness of glossing over the multiplicity of *limited* philosophical concerns. Not all philosophers can be satisfied with the restless philosophical excursions that so delighted Wittgenstein and at which he was so adept; many philosophers are more content to stay at home with their limiting and precising definitions, their fanciful speculations, their penchants for single uses of single terms. Nevertheless, Wittgenstein's work can serve as a foundation for argument against philosophic dogmatism; it makes possible an *enlightened* staying at home. From it philosophers can learn that there is more between heaven and earth than can be seen by the use of their vocabulary; and there is then some hope that, though they spend their days looking at the world from their single windows, they will not confuse the complexity of the world with the simplicity of some grammatical fiction.

Ian P. McGreal

On Certainty

Type of philosophy: Epistemology, philosophy of language

First published: Über Gewißheit/On Certainty, 1969 (bilingual German and English edition)

Principal ideas advanced:

◇ There are no items of commonsense knowledge, borne out by immediate sense experience, that can be known without possibility of doubt; thus philosopher G. E. Moore's "Here is one hand, and here is another," is not an example of absolute certainty.

◇ Psychological certainty is irrelevant to the truth of what we claim to know; however, epistemic certainty is objectively incontrovertible belief.

◇ Knowledge cannot be established as objectively certain in a way that would satisfy all imaginable grounds for doubt; however, knowledge with certainty or absolute certainty is not impossible.

◇ When a philosophically problematic word is used in everyday language-games in which it serves a pragmatically justified function, it presents no philosophical problems.

◇ The proper philosophical method is to place propositions in the appropriate ordinary language-games.

Ludwig Wittgenstein wrote a series of interconnected remarks on the concept of certainty from April, 1950, until April 27, 1951, two days before his death. Although he did not live to edit this work, which was published in 1969, his observations constitute a remarkably coherent discussion of what is arguably the central problem of epistemology: the question of whether, in what sense, and by what methods it may be possible to attain absolute certainty in knowledge.

The quest for certainty is a legacy of French philosopher René Descartes's seventeenth century rationalist philosophy. Philosophers have long sought to answer arguments brought by skepticism that knowledge, let alone certain or absolutely certain knowledge, is impossible. The problem of arriving at certain knowledge is carried forward by philosopher G. E. Moore's essays, including "A Defence of Common Sense" (1923), "Proof of an External World" (1939), and "Certainty" (1943). In these essays, Moore tries to argue that there are items of commonsense knowledge, ultimately justified by immediate sense experience, that can be known without possibility of doubt and that can thereby constitute the foundations for all other knowledge. Wittgenstein regards Moore's treatment of certainty as among his most important contributions to philosophy, yet he seems to appreciate the essays more as a statement of ordinary ways of thinking about the nature of certainty than for the philosophical conclusions Moore attempts to derive. Without defending skepticism, Wittgenstein mounts a devastating critique of Moore's attempt to gain certain knowledge for commonsense beliefs.

In a numbered series of reflections, Wittgenstein explores the implications and limitations of the concept of certainty. The problems of epistemology are a mainstay for most philosophers but an unusual topic for Wittgenstein. In his early masterwork, "Logisch-philosophische Abhandlung" (1921; best known by the bilingual German and English edition title of *Tractatus Logico-Philosophicus*, 1922, 1961), Wittgenstein explicitly separates the theory of knowledge from philosophy properly understood. There he writes: "Psychology is no nearer related to philosophy, than is any other natural science./ The theory of knowledge is the philosophy of psychology." (4.1121) Indeed, Wittgenstein does not address the traditional questions of epistemology outside *On Certainty*.

Psychological and Absolute Certainty

The book begins with Wittgenstein's admission that if we can grant Moore that we can know in holding up a hand before us that here is one hand, then everything else in Moore's argument for a commonsense theory of knowledge follows. This single example, amplified by a few digressions into related knowledge claims, provides the primary focus for Wittgenstein's criticism. Wittgenstein distinguishes between psychological certainty, as expressed in Moore's confident assertion of the existence of his hand, and epistemic certainty as objectively incorrigible or incontrovertible belief. Wittgenstein maintains that psychological certainty is irrelevant to the truth of what we claim to know. We participate in systems of beliefs, in which different kinds of propositions play different kinds of roles. To declare one's certainty in the truth of a particular selection of beliefs in such a system is to identify those judgments as being among a privileged set that are held fixed in our epistemic activity as not subject to revision. Wittgenstein explains: "Even if the most trustworthy of men assures me that he *knows* things are thus and so, this by itself cannot satisfy me that he does know. Only that he believes he knows. That is why Moore's assurance that he knows . . . does not interest us. The propositions, however, which Moore retails as ex-

amples of such known truths are indeed interesting. Not because anyone knows their truth, or believes he knows them, but because they all have a *similar* role in the system of our empirical judgments." (137)

Where a subjectively unshakable conviction in particular beliefs fails to guarantee their truth, Wittgenstein proposes that the attempt to establish certainty in the traditional philosophical sense requires objective criteria of absolute indubitability. Wittgenstein ultimately rejects the possibility of establishing knowledge as objectively certain in a way that would satisfy all imaginable grounds for doubt. However, he does not for this reason conclude that knowledge is impossible or even that knowledge with certainty or absolute certainty is impossible. Instead, he distinguishes between philosophical and extraphilosophical uses of the vocabulary of epistemic certainty. Moore, in holding up his hand and declaring "Here is one hand," is trying to make a philosophical point, thereby implicitly using the vocabulary of certainty in a philosophical way, by arguing that we can build a solid epistemic superstructure that will withstand the strongest possible skepticisms on a foundation of simple beliefs that no sane person could deny. However, what Wittgenstein discovers in Moore's use of commonsense language about belief is a distinctively nonphilosophical and therefore philosophically unproblematic way of calling attention to the special role that certain propositions play in our daily lives. Wittgenstein casts about for ordinary language contexts in which it would be sensible for someone to make such a pronouncement as Moore's "Here is one hand" outside of a philosophy lecture. He identifies several possibilities in communicating mundane facts, such as explaining the meaning of the word "hand," or giving notice to a visually impaired person that he or she is about to be touched. Yet none of these scenarios constitutes a situation in which objective certainty obtains with the absolute incorrigibility or incontrovertibility in the strong sense to which Moore in keeping with much of traditional epistemology aspires.

The Context of Language-Games

It is an essential element of Wittgenstein's later philosophical methodology to study difficult concepts by imagining language-games in which key terms and phrases can occur in everyday linguistic practice, where they are justified by fulfilling a definite purpose in the way people live, or in terms of what Wittgenstein refers to as a form of life. The results of examining the possible uses of epistemic vocabulary in language-games enable Wittgenstein to determine the salient features of the vocabulary's philosophical grammar. The principles of the philosophical grammar of the language of certainty establish that when a philosophically problematic vocabulary is contexted in the everyday language-games in which it serves a pragmatically justified function, it occasions no philosophical problems. It is only when we remove such terms and phrases from their legitimate application outside of philosophy in ordinary linguistic practice and try to understand them in isolation that philosophical puzzles and paradoxes arise. The only proper philosophical methodology is Wittgenstein's view is therefore one in which we try to arrive at a perspicuous representation of the appropriate ordinary language-games in which language use is naturally contexted. The activity of clarifying the pragmatically justified language-game provides a kind of therapy from the conceptual confusions that Wittgenstein attributes to philosophy as it is otherwise practiced, for example, as in Moore's arguments.

There are many different language-games in which certainty is attributed to beliefs. The most familiar of these are contexts in which we claim to know something that we cannot imagine to be false. Wittgenstein elaborates the grounds for this sense of psychological certainty in situations in which we cannot imagine doubting a proposition, or in which we cannot consistently doubt a given proposition without equally doubting the meanings of the terms in which the doubt is expressed, or in which we judge that the fact that we doubt could never be as certain for us as the beliefs we may try to doubt. According to Wittgenstein, in language-games in which we express knowledge or certainty, the claim that a belief is certain signals the role of a proposition as a stable foundation for other beliefs in a larger system of beliefs. However, it does not certify the proposition's truth in any higher philosophical sense that would remove it from all possibility of

doubt from the standpoint of a different imaginable belief system.

Belief Systems

Wittgenstein describes the entire system of beliefs that a person may accept as being made up of different kinds of propositions in various categories and with varying purposes. He articulates a polarity principle as part of the philosophical grammar of epistemic terminology, whereby it makes no sense to speak of a belief as capable of doubt except by contrast with other beliefs that are certain: "If you tried to doubt everything you would not get as far as doubting anything. The game of doubting itself presupposes certainty." (115) Within a belief system, some propositions may gain or lose credibility relative to other propositions about which are we are not prepared to entertain doubts. Beliefs that we are not prepared to doubt in a complex system of beliefs are those we designate in ordinary language-games as certain, as one of the main nonphilosophical uses of the word. This is the source of the mistaken philosophical idea that Moore among others in the history of philosophy tried to develop that we might also be able to attribute absolute certainty to special propositions in an even higher philosophical sense that would make them immune from any imaginable skepticism.

Wittgenstein captures the relation between the fixed and fluid propositions in an entire system of beliefs in one of his characteristically vivid metaphors, when he writes in 343: "If I want the door to turn, the hinges must stay put." The unquestioned, and in that sense objectively certain, propositions in a belief system are the hinges in Wittgenstein's analogy, and the propositions about which we may be prepared to consider doubts are the swinging door. However, if we work hard enough at it, we can always loosen and even remove the hinges.

Wittgenstein remarks on the origin of this privileging of certain beliefs in belief systems as inculcated from childhood and unconsciously adopted in many cases by individuals as part of their social acculturation. The justification for ordinary language-game attributions of certainty in Wittgenstein's pragmatic theory of meaning as applied here to the theory of knowledge is that as a result of our upbringing or involvement in a particular form of life, we simply act in such ways as to reflect the role of certain propositions as the fixed and stable part of a partly inherited belief system relative to which the truth of other propositions can intelligibly be questioned, doubted, or denied. The crucial point that Wittgenstein emphasizes is that even objective certainty does not go beyond this distinction between beliefs that are held fast in a system of beliefs so that others can be doubted, and in particular that there is no skeptic-proof philosophical sense of certainty in which absolutely certain knowledge can be attained or against which a higher standard knowledge can be measured.

An Answer to Skeptics

On Certainty attracted a wide philosophical audience. It was received as a sequel to Wittgenstein's *Philosophische Untersuchungen/Philosophical Investigations* (1953, bilingual German and English edition) and *Remarks on the Foundations of Mathematics* (1956, bilingual German and English edition), and as an unconventional contribution to epistemology in its own right. Wittgenstein's remarks on knowledge are extraordinarily rich in their variety of valuable observations about the nature and conditions of belief, certainty, and doubt.

Avrum Stroll, in his *Moore and Wittgenstein on Certainty* (1994), says of the "small but growing coterie of scholars" who have written book-length studies of Wittgenstein's text (to say nothing of the scores of articles in anthologies and essays in professional philosophical journals) that "they have . . . come to realize that there is more to *On Certainty* than merely a commentary on Moore." He adds: "They now realize that it contains a novel approach to the problem of certitude and to the sceptical challenges that any defender of certitude must face." Wittgenstein's treatment of the philosophical grammar of epistemic vocabulary in ordinary language-games in which knowledge and certainty are legitimately attributed to beliefs, by contrast with problematic uses of the same terminology by philosophers, continues to inspire Wittgenstein scholars to consider, interpret, and apply his penetrating investigations of the concept of certainty.

Dale Jacquette

Additional Reading

Fann, K. T., ed. *Ludwig Wittgenstein: The Man and His Philosophy*. New York: Dell, 1967. A collection of articles by friends, students, and scholars of Ludwig Wittgenstein. Included are articles on Wittgenstein as a person, a teacher, and a philosopher, and treatments of various aspects of Wittgenstein's philosophical work.

Hacker, P. M. S. *Wittgenstein*. New York: Routledge, 1999. An excellent biographical introduction to the thoughts of the philosopher, clearly presented and requiring no special background. Bibliography.

_____. *Wittgenstein's Place in Twentieth-Century Analytic Philosophy*. Oxford: Blackwell, 1996. A monumental work by a leading authority of Wittgenstein. This book thoroughly treats philosophical history before, during, and after the time of Wittgenstein.

Hallett, Garth L. *Essentialism: A Wittgensteinian Critique*. Albany: State University of New York Press, 1991. Strictly speaking, this book is an application of Wittgenstein's later thought rather than an introduction to it, but Hallett is so faithful to Wittgenstein's philosophy that the book is in fact a good guide to a correct understanding of it.

Janik, Allan, and Stephen Toulmin. *Wittgenstein's Vienna*. New York: Simon & Schuster, 1973. An illustrated survey showing the many connections between Wittgenstein's philosophical development and twentieth century movements in architecture, literature, music, psychoanalysis, and other fields, in the setting of late nineteenth century Viennese culture.

McGinn, Marie. *Wittgenstein and the "Philosophical Investigations."* New York: Routledge, 1997. A very useful and well-written introductory guide to Wittgenstein's *Philosophical Investigations*.

Malcolm, Norman. *Ludwig Wittgenstein: A Memoir*. 2d ed. New York: Oxford University Press, 1984. This book, written by Wittgenstein's most prominent American philosophical student, is a gem. Malcolm allows the reader to see the force of Wittgenstein's personality as well as his particular way of practicing philosophy. The second edition includes numerous letters that Wittgenstein wrote to Malcolm.

Monk, Ray. *Ludwig Wittgenstein: The Duty of Genius*. New York: Free Press, 1990. This is the definitive biography of Wittgenstein. It is thorough and detailed, examining Wittgenstein's private life as well as his philosophy.

Pitcher, George, ed. *Wittgenstein: The "Philosophical Investigations."* Garden City, N.Y.: Doubleday, 1966. Although many of the articles in this collection are rather technical, the book's first article is a general account of the historical context of Wittgenstein's philosophy. This is followed by several articles that are book reviews of his *Philosophical Investigations*.

Sluga, Hans, and David G. Stern, eds. *The Cambridge Companion to Wittgenstein*. Cambridge, England: Cambridge University Press, 1996. Some of the articles in this collection are rather narrowly focused, but the first two contain general introductions to Wittgenstein's life, his work, and his critical approach to philosophy.

Stroll, Avrum. *Moore and Wittgenstein on Certainty*. New York: Oxford University Press, 1994. This volume looks at the relationship between these two philosophers, particularly Wittgenstein's critical stance on G. E. Moore's views on certainty based on common sense.

Stephen Satris

Mary Wollstonecraft

In challenging British institutions to extend the political liberties of the American and French Revolutions to women, Wollstonecraft developed a comprehensive feminist program.

Principal philosophical works: *Thoughts on the Education of Daughters, with Reflections on Female Conduct in the More Important Duties of Life*, 1787; *Original Stories from Real Life: With Conversations Calculated to Regulate the Affections and Form the Mind to Truth and Goodness*, 1788; *The Female Reader: Or, Miscellaneous Pieces in Prose and Verse, Selected from the Best Writers, and Disposed Under Proper Heads: For the Improvement of Young Women*, 1789; *A Vindication of the Rights of Man, in a Letter to the Right Honourable Edmund Burke*, 1790; *A Vindication of the Rights of Woman, with Structures on Political and Moral Subjects*, 1792; *An Historical and Moral View of the Origin and Progress of the French Revolution*, 1794; *Letters Written During a Short Residence in Sweden, Norway, and Denmark*, 1796; *The Wrongs of Woman: Or, Maria*, 1798.

Born: April 27, 1759; London, England
Died: September 10, 1797; London, England

Early Life

Mary Wollstonecraft was born April 27, 1759, in London. She was the second of seven children born to Edward Wollstonecraft and his wife, Elizabeth, née Dickson. During the 1760's, her father sold his prosperous weaving business to become a spendthrift, hard-drinking gentleman farmer. As a result, Mary spent much of her childhood in fear of paternal fits and brutalities, often directed at her mother. A witness early in life to the precarious, helpless status of women, she lost her own chance at financial independence when the elder Wollstonecraft dissipated his daughters' legacies. Parental preference for the firstborn son, Edward, who was already favored by primogeniture, caused Mary later to attack the practice and contributed to her lasting resentment toward that brother. Though her formal education was limited to several years at the Yorkshire county day school, supplemented by shared lessons from the father of a friend, she engaged in continuous informal study casually directed by well-read acquaintances.

What turned out to be a lifelong headstrong bent facilitated Wollstonecraft's first attempt at economic independence. At the age of nineteen, she accepted, in defiance of her parents, the position of live-in companion to the wealthy, widowed Mrs. Dawson in Bath, where she remained until called home in 1781 to nurse her ailing mother. After the latter's death the following year, Wollstonecraft once more took charge of her future by giving up the secure but onerous job of companion in order to spend the next eighteen months in the congenial, albeit impoverished, home of her friend Fanny Blood.

Wollstonecraft's strong-willed character asserted itself again in 1784, when she brazenly removed her sister Eliza from an abusive husband and put her, together with another sister and Blood, to work in a hastily established school for girls, which she superintended until late 1785. At that time the consumptive Blood, now married and living in Lisbon, required constant care. Wollstonecraft courageously undertook the journey to Lisbon alone, attended her already dying friend, and returned to London several weeks after the funeral to find her school failing and bankrupt. To acquit herself of accumulated debts, she persisted in securing a publisher for a hurriedly composed tract, *Thoughts on the Education of Daughters*, thereby establishing contacts for her future writing career. She met most of the many subsequent crises in her life with equal resilience and resolution, often by challenging established mores.

In 1786, however, Wollstonecraft's literary prospects were as yet insufficient to vouchsafe a livelihood, and she reluctantly set out for Ireland as governess to the daughters of Lord and Lady Kingsborough. Her tenure in that fashionable environment lasted a mere ten months because of her refusal to acquiesce in the intrigues and whims of the lavish, aristocratic household. Instead, she invested her time completing the manuscript of her first novel. Determined never again to serve in a subservient capacity, she returned to London in search of an independent career, an audacious notion for a respectable, twenty-eight-year-old unmarried female.

Mary Wollstonecraft. *(Library of Congress)*

Life's Work

In searching for a publisher, Wollstonecraft had the good fortune to associate with Joseph Johnson, a member of the Radical Dissenters, Protestant skeptics who were dedicated to reason and receptive to extending authorship to women. Johnson engaged Wollstonecraft as reviewer for his new periodical, *The Analytical Review*, and brought her together with like-minded Dissenters. He also published her collection of pedagogical vignettes, *Original Stories from Real Life*, and her first novel, *Mary: A Fiction* (1788). The latter is a rather artless, stylistically inept tale chronicling Wollstonecraft's friendship with Blood but already demonstrative of her feminist spirit as she attempts to introduce a new kind of thinking heroine into the established genre of the sentimental novel. The author's belief that women should aspire to control their own lives is firmly incorporated into the plot.

Wollstonecraft's first controversial work came into being when her Dissenter friend Richard Price voiced his ardent support of the French Revolution. His implied criticism of the British ruling class so enraged the conservative Edmund Burke that he wrote *Reflections on the Revolution in France* (1790) in defense of the British status quo and against extension of political liberties. Wollstonecraft immediately entered the fray on the side of Price with *A Vindication of the Rights of Man*, which, though poorly reasoned and organized, was the first of many noted rebuttals to Burke, preceding Thomas Paine's *Rights of Man* (1791-1792), with which it is often associated. The popularity of her anonymously published essay encouraged Johnson to bring out a second, signed edition, and Wollstonecraft at once became famous and infamous, for she assailed the British parliament and the hereditary nobility in harsh, occasionally vituperative, language.

Society's amazement at seeing an unattached female engaged in rancorous political commentary motivated Wollstonecraft to address the gender inequality issue in *A Vindication of the Rights of Woman*. In analyzing how societal institutions and famous authors, particularly French social philosopher Jean-Jacques Rousseau, characterize women as beings of lesser value, she argued that these portraits are but expressions of how men wish to perceive women and called on members of her sex to reevaluate and assert themselves. At the same time, she expressed doubt that the middle-class woman, whom she especially wished to rescue from an inferior position, would be determined enough to rise above the strictures of social convention. Though her prose and frequently disorganized digressions barely match eighteenth century literary standards, the case for women's rights, including education and financial self-sufficiency, comes across clearly. By extension, the essay challenged all vested interests of society and evoked a storm of controversy. It represents the peak of Wollstonecraft's writing career in terms of public exposure.

Wollstonecraft's private life was much less satisfactory. While publicly encouraging women to become economically and emotionally independent, she herself sought stable personal bonds with men. Contemporaries describe her as a plain, purposeful woman of sober countenance and somewhat dowdy appearance, which some of the portraits used in the title pages of her books tried to soften and prettify. She was attractive to the opposite sex as a skilled and mettlesome conversationalist, but her tendency to be possessive and ever assertive strained intimate relationships. Her first ill-fated encounter was with the Swiss painter Henry Fuseli, to whom she became so deeply attached that, in her usual presumptuous fashion, she asked Fuseli's wife to take her into the household as his spiritual partner. Mrs. Fuseli's outraged refusal hastened Wollstonecraft's planned journey to France in 1792. Arriving in Paris at the height of the Jacobin terror, she moderated her former optimistic opinion about the efficacy of sudden social change, though in her formal account of that visit, *An Historical and Moral View of the Origin and Progress of the French Revolution*, she gamely holds to the liberal ideas set forth in previous publications.

Privately, Wollstonecraft was passionately involved with the American businessman Gilbert Imlay during her Paris stay. They had a child, Fanny (born 1794), and he registered her as his wife to afford her American protection during the

political upheavals. They were, however, never married. Imlay treated the affair lightly, while she demanded serious commitment. When he left her for another woman, she twice attempted suicide in 1795. After the first attempt, an alarmed Imlay sent her to Scandinavia as his business representative in the hope that new impressions would excite her authorial curiosity and restore her equilibrium. The resulting *Letters Written During a Short Residence in Sweden, Norway, and Denmark*, based on a personal journal Wollstonecraft wrote for Imlay, represents her best work from an artistic standpoint. Acknowledgment of her own vulnerability, recognition of the value of feelings, absence of polemics, and a genuine interest in the unfamiliar surroundings all very much enhance her writing.

Determined to satisfy her longing for enduring companionship, Wollstonecraft, upon returning to London, cultivated an intimate relationship with William Godwin, an old friend and political ally. Finding herself pregnant once more without benefit of matrimony, she married Godwin in 1797, even though both partners had earlier written impassionate denunciations of formal marriage. From all accounts, their life together was a satisfactory one, cut short by Wollstonecraft's death in childbirth on September 10, 1797. Her infant daughter Mary survived to become the spouse of the poet Percy Bysshe Shelley and an author in her own right.

In her last, incomplete work—the posthumously published *The Wrongs of Woman: Or, Maria*—Wollstonecraft returns to the genre of the sentimental novel in order to present her arguments for gender equality in a form women would widely read. Despite its fictional frame, the story chronicles a variety of abuses heaped on females by bourgeois institutions. Imaginary case histories, full of autobiographical events, cover a wide range of social classes, with special focus on a heroine who disregards convention and is subjected to moral censure. Another section details the injustices suffered by a working-class woman. Moreover, Wollstonecraft ventures into a frank, almost modern discussion of female sexuality. In its indictment of the status quo, the tale leaves the impression of a revolutionary manifesto. It was a fitting conclusion to the life of a feminist far ahead of her times.

Influence

Both the writings and the personal behavior of Mary Wollstonecraft reflect the belief in unalienable human rights that was given wide currency by the American and French Revolutions. Wollstonecraft dared extend this notion to members of her own sex at a time when neither established social values nor (with a few exceptions) radical libertarians considered such an extension. As a result, her arguments on behalf of women did not bring about any basic social changes or even engender a significant following. Not until John Stuart Mill's *The Subjection of Women* (1869) were many of the concerns raised by Wollstonecraft once again brought before a wide audience. That her feminist arguments appeared in print at all was primarily a result of her publisher Johnson's antiestablishment stance. Wollstonecraft's writings challenged the very fabric of aristocratic rule and as such were welcome matter for the Radical Dissenters.

A proper appreciation of Wollstonecraft's keen political and ethical insights is hampered by her cumbersome phrasing and a general inattention to aesthetic quality, perhaps the result of a meager formal education. In part, her roundabout reasoning also reflects confusion when frontally assaulting such a hallowed institution as marriage. She, too, had internalized to some degree prevailing cultural mores regarding the status of women. After returning from France with a daughter, she was careful to conceal her unwed state and lived as Mrs. Imlay. Her caution in this regard was well taken. When Godwin's memoirs later revealed the extent of her unconventional lifestyle, public opinion turned viciously against her and drowned her professional achievements in ridicule and abuse.

Only beginning in the twentieth century was proper recognition extended to Wollstonecraft. Her comprehensive approach, delineating the political and economic subjugation of women, their psychological and personal dependence, the contradictions embedded in conventional sexual morality, and the patriarchal nature of established institutions, corresponds to modern feminist aspirations. Hers was an early female voice giving reasoned articulation to woman suffrage, to reconsideration of the marriage contract and parental roles, to the desirability of blending motherhood with a professional career, and to female sexuality. She not only articulated many concerns still controversial in the late twentieth century but also advanced boldly enough ahead of her epoch to practice them.

Margot K. Frank

A Vindication of the Rights of Woman

With Structures on Political and Moral Subjects

Type of philosophy: Ethics, feminist philosophy, political philosophy
First published: 1792
Principal ideas advanced:
◇ Though women are inferior to men in physical strength, they have been rendered more inferior by the attitudes of society toward girls and women.
◇ Women are indeed guilty of many of the vices men attribute to them, but these vices arise not from their inimical natures but from their lack of education and understanding.
◇ Until women are recognized as rational beings and trained and educated from childhood, they will never be fit wives or mothers.
◇ As long as men who are advancing the cause of political revolution continue to oppress women, their plans for new governments based on rationality can never came to pass.

Mary Wollstonecraft began her political writing career in 1790 by publishing *A Vindication of the Rights of Man*, the first rebuttal of Edmund Burke's *Reflections on the Revolution in France* (1790). In this work, she refuted the conservative claims of Burke and his idealization of the English tradition, and she championed the French cause of revolution. *A Vindication of the Rights of Woman* can be seen as the logical sequel to *A Vindication of the Rights of Man*, and it takes up many of the same themes. Wollstonecraft dedicated the book to the French statesman Talleyrand, and throughout she points out the superiority of French society over English society. She also repeatedly stresses that a society built on respect for rationality and equality rather than inherited positions of superiority must deal with the issue of women and their place as rational beings in that society.

This book was written at a time of great political upheaval throughout the world, and Wollstonecraft hoped, like many, that France was following the United States to lead the world into a new era of enlightened social thought and practice. Though those dreams were not fulfilled, the work still stands as the most significant early feminist statement of the interrelatedness of gender, social class, and economics.

Women as Human Creatures

In Wollstonecraft's introduction to the work, she states the main themes she will treat, pointing out that women do have a great many faults she wishes to address but that, unlike other writers, she intends to consider women as human creatures, not as some separate species who have nothing in common with men. She also states that she will pay more attention to the middle class, as she sees the members of that class as most likely to benefit from the changes she proposes. Poor women are often courageous and strong but, because of monetary constraints, lack the opportunity to advance beyond sheer backbreaking toil. Rich women she sees as already so corrupted by luxury as to be beyond all hope of redemption.

In the dedication, she implores Talleyrand to contemplate her pleas for national education of women, on two basic grounds: first, that if women are not educated to be fit companions for the new class of rational men who she hopes will gain power, they will impede the progress of knowledge and the virtue it engenders; second, that if women are to be excluded from the rights of society with no evidence that they are not as rational as men, the injustice and tyranny of this exclusion will prove that the revolution and all its talk of equality and freedom are a lie.

Power and Corruption

In chapter 1, Wollstonecraft states that the only real basis for happiness among human beings is to be found in reason, virtue, and knowledge, and that knowledge and virtue can come only from the proper exercise of reason. She gives a brief overview of European history to point out that hereditary power has been the chief cause of misery and vice and that the new mode should stress rationality over any assumed prerogatives. Wollstonecraft points out that power always corrupts weak men, and therefore not only hereditary monarchies but also any professions subordinating by rank are injurious to morality, especially a standing army. Later she will develop the analogy of women and the army at greater length.

Debunking Women's Inferiority

Wollstonecraft uses her second chapter to point out the various arguments advanced over the ages to prove that women are substantially different from, and inferior to, men. She agrees that women are indeed guilty of many vices that men attribute to them, but she calls these vices the "natural effect of ignorance." She reprimands men for striving to keep women in a state of perpetual childhood and then scolding them for not acting more adult. The proper form of education cannot be achieved until society is differently constituted, she states, and this proper form would be an education that strengthens the body instead of making a virtue of weakness, and fits the mind for independence.

Finally, she evaluates the current attitudes of other writers, especially Jean-Jacques Rousseau (whom many account as a misogynist), toward women, and contends that they are blinded by their own desires and preconceptions. Though Rousseau and others stress the importance of reason and equality in political affairs, they assert that a woman should be only the toy of a man and bend all her efforts to please him. This is bound to end in disaster for all, declares Wollstonecraft, since a woman so constituted is not fit to be a wife, a mother, or a citizen. She ends the chapter by concluding that the argument that "it has ever been so" rebounds on the men who are opposing hereditary monarchies, institutions that have also existed unopposed for many years.

In chapter 3, Wollstonecraft responds particularly to Rousseau and his idealized character Sophia, the prototype of the helpless, weak, conniving female. She refutes his notion that girls are naturally drawn to dolls and to sewing, and points out that the habit of custom is more to blame for girls' actions than are their own desires. Further, women are not likely to endeavor to improve their minds when they are more likely to achieve social place and economic ease by feigning ignorance and weakness. Wollstonecraft stresses that if we can subject an entire sex to the arbitrary caprices of their husbands and fathers, where will this unjust subjection end? Though women and men may have different duties, they are both human and must be regulated by the same principles of order, reason, and independence.

A History of Discrimination

Chapter 4 analyzes some of the causes that lead to women's inferior state in society. First, Wollstonecraft points out that women have always been treated as either slaves or despots, and neither situation is conducive to reason. Second, pleasure is exalted as the business of women's lives, and while society continues to hold this view, women will continue to be weak. Third, women are praised and rewarded (usually by acquiring a husband) for being beautiful and useless. With nothing solid to occupy their minds, they occupy themselves with mindless coquetteries and exchange their liberty, health, and virtue for the sake of a man who provides them with physical sustenance but little else.

Wollstonecraft laments the fact that men spend their youth in preparing for and advancing in a profession, but women spend their time exciting their emotions, for this is the chief faculty for which they are awarded. This same focus on the emotions will unfit women for motherhood, as it disposes them to tantrums and to indulging their children and spoiling them. Further, for women who do not have husbands to meet their daily financial needs, their complete lack of training will lead them to become burdens on their relatives or even prostitutes, who further degrade society and the family bond.

Rebuttal of Rousseau

In chapter 5, Wollstonecraft responds specifically to several writers who have contributed to the problems women face in society, in her view. The first is Rousseau, already treated at some length. She greatly admired Rousseau's political writing

and his revolutionary spirit, but she finds his notions about women ludicrous and downright dangerous. She quotes Rousseau at length and dismantles most of his conclusions as arising not from observation or logic but from his own preconceptions and base desires. To his suggestion that girls are naturally flirtatious, she replies that they could not be otherwise, having been rewarded for such behavior from birth. His protestations of women's natural state of dependence and desire to be obedient she sees as the natural result of years of servitude forced on them; how could they be otherwise? Wollstonecraft also points out the flaw in Rousseau's reasoning. He states that beauty is valued only for a little while, yet friendship lasts and forms a deeper bond than romantic love between husbands and wives, as do children. If, then, beauty and artificial graces inevitably pall, why does he make the acquiring of them a woman's chief duty? Why does he discourage the very education and exercise of reason that would fit a woman to be a good friend and a worthy mother?

Wollstonecraft also dismisses the sermons of Dr. James Fordyce, a popular work of the time, as poorly written and argued nonsense. She points out that another popular text, by Dr. John Gregory, is not as ridiculous or as poorly written but argues from wrong principles. Wollstonecraft also lists several women with whose works she disagrees and cites the letters of Hester Chapone and Catherine Macaulay as worthy of praise.

Social Conditions of Women

In chapters 6 through 11, Wollstonecraft enumerates many problems common to women, as well as the societal conditions that she sees as giving rise to these conditions and helping to perpetuate them. She treats sexual morality at some length, and she contrasts true morality with the appearance of morality that women are urged to maintain by their training. She also stresses the deleterious effects of concentrating all thoughts of female morality on chastity alone, instead of on the whole person as a citizen and a human being. She underscores the fact that until women and men are praised and elevated in society only for discharging their duties with honor, society can never advance. She points out the failure to attend to duty of English politicians, soldiers, and society women alike. However, while they continue to be rewarded for improper behavior, one can hardly expect them to do otherwise. Wollstonecraft also finds this reciprocity in the parent-child bond and finds that women who are unfit for motherhood tend to raise children who do not respect them or take care of them when they are in need.

In chapter 12, Wollstonecraft points out the many failures of the educational system, particularly boarding schools, which she finds to encourage sloth, vice, and viciousness. She advances a system of day schools so that students may live at home. Further, these schools are to be nationally supported, so that teachers need not rely on parents for their salaries, which leads to bad educational practices. She also proposes co-education as a way of preparing boys and girls to live in society with each other. Each student should be allowed to rise on his or her own merit, and nothing else. Wollstonecraft also proposes that the class system be removed from the schools, and common respect for all humanity— and for animals—be part of the curriculum.

Argument for Women's Rights

In the final chapter, Wollstonecraft recaps her earlier arguments and advances the notion that only by repairing the defects created by the wrongful treatment of women can society truly be advanced to a state of moral rightness based on reason. With women prone to so much folly by their lack of understanding, their advancement to rationality would bring a host of benefits to both women and men, and to any nation. She concludes by stating that most of women's follies proceed from the tyranny of men, and if women are given their rights they will also acquire all the virtues needed to exercise them.

A Woman of Our Time

The impact of *A Vindication of the Rights of Woman* was initially limited, as Wollstonecraft's ideas were so radical for their time that many considered them nonsensical. Further, her personal life subjected her to much scorn in society and made espousing her views even more unpopular. However, with the rise of feminism in the twentieth century, Wollstonecraft was elevated to a great degree. She was often cited by early suffragists as

having provided the best argument for women's full participation in democracy.

It was only in the 1970's that she reached her full peak of influence. *A Vindication of the Rights of Woman* is now regarded as the first major text of feminist philosophy, and Wollstonecraft herself has been accorded an esteem she could not have dreamed of during her lifetime. The work was the first to maintain the interrelation of class, gender, and economics, an ideological position now taken as a given by most feminists. Ironically, many of the problems she cites still exist in modern society, and several of the solutions she proposed are still being sought by modern women. However, no matter what the future status of women in the world, this text will continue to be seen as the first comprehensive treatise on the state of woman in Western culture.

Vicki A. Sanders

Additional Reading

Conger, Syndy McMillen. *Mary Wollstonecraft and the Language of Sensibility*. Rutherford, N.J.: Fairleigh Dickinson University Press, 1994. A scholarly, well-documented assessment of Wollstonecraft's change in attitudes toward the language of emotions and feeling, from uncritical acceptance to critical rejection to a mature reacceptance and adaptation of it to new contexts, including feminism and political revolution. A corrective to standard twentieth century interpretations of Wollstonecraft that focus on the emphasis on reason during her middle years. Contains few details about her personal life and relationships.

Falco, Maria J., ed. *Feminist Interpretations of Mary Wollstonecraft*. University Park: Pennsylvania State University Press, 1996. A collection of twelve essays on a variety of political issues. Contains two essays that compare the thought of Rousseau and Wollstonecraft—one a fictional dialogue composed of passages from their works to illustrate how these two champions of human rights disagreed on women's rights. Includes essays dealing with liberalism, slavery, the evolution of women's rights since the time of Wollstonecraft, and the changing reactions to Wollstonecraft since her death.

Ferguson, Moira, and Janet M. Todd. *Mary Wollstonecraft*. Boston: Twayne, 1984. A volume in the Twayne authors series providing concise, scholarly, and well-documented accounts of both Wollstonecraft's life and her literary career. Includes an assessment of her ideas, style, and influence. Stresses her professional achievements more than her personal experience.

Flexner, Eleanor. *Mary Wollstonecraft: A Biography*. New York: Coward-McCann, 1972. Concentrates on Wollstonecraft's early life, associating her childhood disappointments and hardships with later behavior patterns, especially her relationships with and attitudes toward both parents. Emphasizes Edward Wollstonecraft's financial situation and its effect on his daughter. Well documented.

Kramnik, Miriam Brody. Introduction to *A Vindication of the Rights of Woman*. New York: Penguin Books, 1975. This lengthy introduction to Wollstonecraft's most famous work surveys her life and literary contributions. It discusses her within the framework of the history of feminism and compares her approach with the piecemeal efforts of nineteenth century feminists. Rather uncritical of Wollstonecraft's literary shortcomings.

Lorch, Jennifer. *Mary Wollstonecraft: The Making of a Radical Feminist*. New York: Berg, 1990. A concise account of Wollstonecraft's life, focusing on her relationships and her development as a feminist thinker. Stresses her personal experiences more than her professional achievements. Included is an analysis of her relevance to twentieth century feminism. Good documentation.

Poovey, Mary. *The Proper Lady and the Woman Writer: Ideology as Style in the Writings of Mary Wollstonecraft, Mary Shelley, and Jane Austen*. Chicago: University of Chicago Press, 1984. Describes Wollstonecraft from the vantage point of eighteenth century British bourgeois ideology, juxtaposing her to the prevailing cultural model of the middle-class married female. Shows how Wollstonecraft both rebelled against this unfulfilling state and became enmeshed in it. Sharp critiques of Wollstonecraft's reasoning and her style. Also analyzes English novelist Jane Austen and Wollstonecraft's daughter Mary Shelley within the context of their times.

Margot K. Frank,
updated by Kristen L. Zacharias

Xunzi

Through his development and modification of Confucian teachings, Xunzi built a synthesized and more realistic foundation for Confucian ideology that was influential throughout China during the Han Dynasty (207 B.C.E.-220 C.E.).

Principal philosophical works: *Xunzi*, latter half of third century B.C.E. (partial translation, *The Works of Hsüntze*, 1928; complete translation, *Xunzi*, 1988-1994, 3 volumes)

Born: c. 313 B.C.E.; Zhao, China
Died: After 238 B.C.E.; Lanling, China

Early Life

Although Xunzi is a great figure in Chinese philosophy, the basic facts of his life are controversial. According to most Chinese scholars, he was born in the northern state of Zhao around 313 B.C.E., and the period of his activities as a philosopher and politician covers sixty years, from 298 to 238 B.C.E. The most reliable sources about his life are his own writings, published posthumously, and Sima Qian's *Shi-ji* (first century B.C.E.; *Records of the Grand Historian of China*, 1960; rev. ed. 1993). Yet almost no information about his early life, his education, or even his family background can be found in these early sources, which provide an account of his life beginning at the age of fifty, when he first visited the state of Qi and joined a distinguished group of scholars from various philosophical schools at the Jixia Academy. This lack of information about his early life prompts some modern scholars to doubt the accuracy of Sima Qian's account and suggest that Xunzi first visited the Jixia Academy at the age of fifteen, not fifty. These scholars contend that either Xunzi's age was erroneously recorded in the first place or the text was corrupted.

Life's Work

Whether Xunzi first appeared on the stage of history at fifty or fifteen does not change much of his historical role, for he did not really affect his contemporaries or his immediate environment during his lifetime. Like his predecessors in the Confucian school, Confucius and Mencius specifically, Xunzi traveled from state to state, trying to persuade the rulers of Qi, Chu, Zhao, and even the Legalist Qin to adopt his brand of Confucian statecraft. The dating of his various visits to these states is again an area of endless academic debate.

There are, however, two reliable historical dates in Xunzi's public career. In 255 B.C.E., he was invited by Lord Chunshen of Chu to serve as the magistrate of Lanling. He was soon forced to resign the post when Lord Chunshen gave credence to some slanderous rumors about the potential danger of the benevolent Confucian policy. Xunzi then left for his native Zhao. He stayed as an honored guest in the Zhao court until Lord Chunshen apologized for his suspicion and invited him to resume the magistrateship. Xunzi remained in the position until 238 B.C.E., the year Lord Chunshen was assassinated. Xunzi was immediately dismissed from office, and he died in Lanling, probably soon after the coup.

The most immediate impact of Xunzi on the political situation of the ancient Chinese world came, ironically, from his two best students, Han Feizi and Li Si. Both men deviated from Xunzi's teachings of Confucian benevolence and turned his emphasis on pragmatic sociopolitical programming into realpolitik. Han Feizi became a synthesizer of Legalist thought, and Li Si became a prime minister who helped Emperor Zheng (also known as Shi Huangdi, or "first emperor") set up a totalitarian state after China was unified.

Xunzi's greatest contribution to Chinese civilization lies in the field of philosophy, or, more generally, in the intellectual formation of Chinese sociopolitical behavior. His writings were perhaps compiled by himself in his later years but were definitely supplemented with a few chapters from his disciples. The standard edition of Xunzi's works is the end product of a Han scholar, Liu Xiang, who collated and edited the available sources into thirty-two chapters. Because Xunzi lived through a period of fierce political strife, constant warfare, and tremendous social change on the eve of China's unification (also the golden age of Chinese philosophy known as the period of the Hundred Schools), his approach to the social and ethical issues of Confucian philosophy was markedly more realistic than those of Confucius and Mencius. In his defense of Confucian doctrine, he not only refuted the arguments and programs of other schools but also criticized the idealistic strain of thinking within his own camp, particularly in Mencius's philosophy. With an admirable command of scholarship and a powerful mind for critical analysis, Xunzi demonstrated the Confucian way of thinking in a most systematic and pragmatic manner.

In opposition to Mencius's contention that human nature is innately good and people need only go back to their original psychological urges to achieve goodness and righteousness, Xunzi states that human nature is evil and that only through education can people distinguish themselves from animals. Despondent as it appears, Xunzi's conception of human nature is quite complex and far removed from pessimism. For him, human nature, though evil, does not determine human destiny, for people have a capacity for reasoning and learning and for attaining a higher and more civilized order. That humanity has created civilization and sloughed off barbarism is clear testimony to the possibility of a brighter future for humankind, as long as the civilizing order is maintained and continued. The whole process of education and socialization thus becomes the focus of Xunzi's ethical concern.

It seems that when Xunzi addresses the question of human nature, he has no preconceived illusions and deals squarely with human psychology as such. The evil of which he speaks is simply a composite body of animal drives and has no likeness to the Judeo-Christian concept of Original Sin. With such a no-nonsense and down-to-earth approach, he is interested in human nature less as an ontological issue than as an epistemological one. His particular emphasis on "artificial endeavor" for humanity also attests this interest, which some scholars describe as a "moral epistemology."

Xunzi's interest in education and socialization centers on the Confucian concept of *li*, which has been translated in different contexts as propriety, decorum, rite, and etiquette. It is Xunzi's belief that proper social behavior is the foundation for morality in people and that institutionalized rites regulate human relations for a better society. Thus, education is not only a way of acquiring external knowledge for its own sake but also a process of internalizing all the knowledge for the molding of a good and moral person. On the other hand, society is not merely a background against which one develops his intellectual faculty or moral character: Society is the main source of personality development. Through interaction between the individual self and the social norm, a functioning structure takes shape and reveals a pattern of *li* that serves as the very basis of social order.

How did *li* first come into existence? Confucius did not talk about its origin, and this question did not interest Mencius. For Xunzi, however, this question was of primary importance. In his treatise on *li*, Xunzi offers the following explanation:

> Man is born with desires. If his desires are not satisfied for him, he cannot but seek some means to satisfy them himself. If there are no limits and measures of regulation in his seeking, then he will inevitably fall to wrangling with other men. From wrangling comes disorder and from disorder comes exhaustion. The ancient kings hated such disorder, and therefore they institutionalized *li* and righteousness in order to define the relationship between men, to train men's desires and to provide for their satisfaction.

This explanation supports his argument that human nature is evil and also shows Xunzi's concern for law and order.

For Confucius and Mencius, *li* is the internalized moral code that impels people to exhibit proper social behavior; it has nothing to do with the penal code, or law, imposed by government from outside to regulate social order. Xunzi's practical concern for institutionalized law and order greatly transformed this Confucian concept of *li*. Confucius and Mencius could not bear to see a society's peace and order being enforced by law, and Xunzi would acquiesce on this practical matter. Xunzi, however, was by no means a Legalist entrusting the programming of social order entirely to the institution of law; he always placed the benevolence of the ruling class, the moral behavior maintained by a gentlemanly social elite, and the education of the people ahead of the enforcement of law, a necessary evil.

Xunzi's concept of nature also complements his realistic approach to social and ethical issues. He believed that nature exists independent of human will. Heavenly matters have nothing to do with social and ethical issues, and therefore, human beings are solely responsible for their behavior. This attitude underlies logically his idea that human nature is evil and that good is the product of humanity's artificial endeavor. It also implies the unlimited potential of "evil-natured" humankind to do good and better the human world, because there is no supernatural force to hinder such a human endeavor. In this sense, Xunzi should be taken seriously as an ardent optimist with regard to human progress.

Influence

During his lifetime, Xunzi did not have any major effect on historical events. War, suffering, and political intrigue continued in his country. It was during this time of chaos and disintegration that Xunzi developed his systematic reinterpretation of the Confucian tradition. If the unification of China and the institutionalization of the Legalist program toward the end of the third century B.C.E. can only be partly credited to his students Han Feizi and Li Si, at least Xunzi can claim a lion's share in the formation of the Confucian system during the Han Dynasty, after the Legalist Qin Dynasty (221-207 B.C.E.) collapsed. This Han Confucian system, with its strong emphasis on the blending of practical sociopolitical institutions

with moral concerns, has served as the foundation of Chinese social and political norms for two millennia.

Pei-kai Cheng

Xunzi

Type of philosophy: Chinese philosophy, metaphysics, political philosophy
First transcribed: Xunzi, latter half of third century B.C.E. (partial translation, *The Works of Hsüntze*, 1928; complete translation, *Xunzi*, 1988-1994, 3 volumes)
Principal ideas advanced:
◇ Humanity is by nature evil; people are born with desires that tend to result in wantonness and strife.
◇ By education, training, and following the rules of conduct discovered by the sages, a human being can become virtuous.
◇ Learning begins with the recitation of the classics and ends with the ritual texts; one first becomes learned, then superior; one ends by becoming a sage.
◇ To rectify oneself, one needs to examine oneself, and one needs a teacher.
◇ The true king is benevolent and righteous; as a superior person, he forms a triad with Heaven and Earth; he attains order by following the rules of propriety.
◇ Rites are needed to provide guidance to people, who are born with desires that must be limited and ordered.
◇ Names should be used (and, where necessary, rectified) to identify the nature of things and to emphasize similarities and differences.

Although biographical information about Xunzi is scanty, some not entirely reliable reports of his life are available. One account of his life appears in Sima Qian's *Shi-ji* (first century B.C.E.; *Records of the Grand Historian of China*, 1960; rev. ed. 1993). The historian writes that Xunzi was a native of Zhao, an ancient feudal state in the south of Zhili and Shanxi; that he was born about 313 B.C.E. and died about 238 B.C.E.; and that the period of his principal activity was from about 298 B.C.E. until his death. The first note about him concerns his journey to Qi when he was fifty years old; apparently he went as a scholar-teacher, and he was so eminent as a scholar that he was three times honored by being appointed "to offer the wine at the Great Sacrifice"—that is to be the leader of the scholars and hence alone privileged to offer wine to Heaven. Reputedly, he was slandered, went to the state of Chu, and became magistrate of Lanling. His disciple, Li Si, became prime minister of Qin. Finally, after an extensive period of teaching and writing, during which Xunzi developed his Confucian views, he died and was buried in Lanling.

Xunzi is notable in his own right as one who recognized that people are not inherently good but rather are inclined to satisfy their own desires at the expense of others and in violation of laws and principles unless they can be shown that such a course is self-defeating. In emphasizing the potential for evil in people—and hence, in a sense, humanity's being born bad—Xunzi took exception to the philosophy of Mencius, who had argued that human beings are inherently and basically good, deriving their goodness from nature itself. Accordingly, Xunzi is perhaps more famous for his opposition to Mencius than he is for his positive views.

Xunzi is important in the history of Chinese philosophy not only because of his startling and unattractive proposition that humanity is naturally evil but also because his views influenced a disciple, Han Feizi, whose work became a masterpiece of Chinese philosophy. The disciple's *Han Feizi* is based on the principle that human beings are by nature inclined to the satisfaction of their selfish desires and that their primary objective is material profit.

The Importance of Learning

Xunzi begins with the proposition that for the superior person (the morally or spiritually exemplary person, whom Confucious called *junzi*) learning is an unending process. Just as a strip of wood may be given a new shape by bending it, and just as a sword can be sharpened, so a person can be made wise and his or her conduct become righteous through learning.

Learning is effective as the way to wisdom and virtue only to the degree to which it consists in

learning the *dao*, or Way, and learning the Way requires studying the classics (the works of the sages) and the ritual texts. One first becomes learned, then superior, then a sage. For Xunzi, learning is useless unless it manifests itself in action. If learning goes in the ear and comes out the mouth, he writes, it travels only four inches; what is needed is that it transform even a seven-foot body, and to do so learning must spread throughout the body and show itself in action.

One learns by associating with learned persons; books alone are not enough. When one has found the Way through learning, one's whole life is enhanced; even the senses will be more stimulated by what is right than by what ordinarily stimulates and delights them. Learned people have constancy of virtue, writes Xunzi; such people order themselves and can then respond to others; they are then complete people.

Xunzi's views were reflected in the writings of Han Feizi, but although Han Feizi argued that everyone is born with the love of profit and Xunzi emphasized the self-seeking desires of untutored people, he wrote in the *Xunzi*: "The gentleman is careless in the pursuit of profit but swift in avoiding harm. Timidly he shuns disgrace but he practices the principles of the Way with courage." Xunzi was able to argue in this way because he believed that despite people's original evil nature (a state of uncontrolled desire), they were subject to transformation through learning and were able to train themselves by reference to the sages and the Way and thus improve themselves and become superior persons.

For every vice, wrote Xunzi, there is a virtue that can be acquired through self-improvement; if one is hasty, develop restraint; if one is withdrawn, develop sincerity; if one is too forceful, acquire harmony. In short, order the temperament by following ritual and by learning from one's teacher.

Rules of Governance

Xunzi had advice for kings. A king must develop the habit of choosing well; he can then control others and survive. The ruler needs understanding and must be a superior person, transformed by learning, self-instruction, teaching, ritual, and practice. Rulers must be fair-minded, able to judge by finding the balance in the harmonious way. Equality is based upon inequality, the philosopher argued, in that relevant differences must be recognized and taken into account in acting; after all, even Heaven and Earth exemplify the principle of higher and lower and the possibility of unity and harmony.

As to the practical principles of governance, Xunzi argued that one must be alert to recognize merit: One must promote worthy people and punish the inferior. Unless the king loves the people, Xunzi writes, he will not survive; the people are the water that supports the ruler, who is the boat; just as they support him, so can they capsize him. However, if the common people can be made to feel safe and cared for, the ruler will be able to order the affairs of government and to survive.

A wise and prudent ruler acquires force in order not to have to use it; good will is more powerful than military might. The strongest ruler is the benevolent one; he is a king whose authority is strengthened by his righteousness. According to Xunzi, the king's regulations are the principles of benevolence, righteousness, and authority. The king's judgments become the king's laws; they are the judgments that lead no virtuous person to be unhonored, no person of ability to be unemployed, no guilty person to be unpunished.

Like inanimate things, writes Xunzi, people have energy; like the grass and the trees, people have life; like the birds and the beasts, people have intelligence—but of all that exists, only people have a sense of duty. Consequently, the human being is the noblest being on earth.

Society is necessary if there is to be order among people, and order is necessary if life is to be spent in something more constructive than struggling and fighting. However, where order is needed, the arrangement must be hierarchical; by obedience to the ritual principles, each thing will find its place and each person will be treated in a fair way.

What is true in time of peace is true in time of war, Xunzi claims; the proper way to conduct military affairs is to win the support of the people, to be benevolent, to order the state through honoring the rites and practicing righteousness, to reward those of merit, to punish the inferior and those who violate the principles, and to insist on obedience. Consequently, the superior person takes up arms only to put an end to violence; he or she wins respect and transforms the people.

The Way of Heaven

"Heaven's ways are constant," Xunzi writes at the beginning of one of the most important sections in *Xunzi* (chapter 17). Heaven (or nature) is affected by neither the good nor the bad; it does not serve the Sage King or fall before the tyrant. If the people respond to Heaven with peace and order, however, they will enjoy good fortune; otherwise, they will suffer for their disorder.

The sage does not compete with Heaven; he follows the Way, and so he enjoys good fortune. Order and disorder are not due to nature, Xunzi writes; order comes from following the Way, and disorder comes from neglecting it. However, following the Way is not a matter of simply admiring Heaven and singing praises. What is required, according to Xunzi, is that one respond to Heaven and make use of it, that one foster and regulate nature, that one transform things and utilize them, and that one encourage the full development of things.

Xunzi's conception of Heaven is naturalistic; he has nothing to say about the supernatural, and he sees no ethical principle in nature itself. The wise person utilizes what nature gives; following the Way is in part controlling it for one's benefit. Hence he asks, "Is it better to wait for things to increase of themselves, or to apply your talents and transform them?"

Human Nature, Rites, and Music

In chapter 19 of *Xunzi*, the philosopher's view of humanity's original nature is alluded to in the course of an explanation of the origin of rites. Humans are born with desires, writes Xunzi; accordingly, if the desires are not satisfied, they seek by their own actions to secure what they want; if they are interfered with, they contend with others and disorder reigns. The ancient kings established rules of proper conduct to put a limit to people's desires and to order human relationships.

According to Xunzi, the rites or rules of conduct have three bases: Heaven and earth, the basis of life; the ancestors, the basis of the family; and the rulers and teachers, the basis of order.

The rites not only make order possible and limit desires; but they also satisfy the emotions and encourage their proper expression (as in the rituals of burial and mourning). The sage understands the rites, and the superior person regards them as the way of humanity; the common people, who are comforted by them, assume them to pertain to spirits.

In opposition to Mozi, who regarded music as unimportant, Xunzi argues that music is joy expressed in an orderly and harmonious way. Accordingly, music serves to order the emotions, just as the rules of conduct order the desires. The transforming process that an individual needs to become a superior person is encouraged and disciplined by music in that music expresses the emotions and at the same time orders them. According to Xunzi, music "has the power to make good the hearts of the people, to influence men deeply, and to reform their ways and customs with facility." Music is the harmony of the emotions; *li* (rules of conduct) is the harmony of conduct according to reason.

The Mind

For people to understand the Way, Xunzi writes, they must have minds that are "empty, unified, and still." The mind is ready to understand when it is able to receive something new (when it is empty in that it is open), when it is the center of the understanding of differences (when it is unified), and when it is able to concentrate and is not diverted (when it is still). A mind that is in these ways empty, unified, and quiescent is able to perceive the Way.

The mind is "the ruler of the body and the master of its . . . intelligence," writes Xunzi: It determines what is to be accepted and what is to be rejected; it commands but is not subject to commands. If the mind acts freely and receptively, if it is not distracted but balanced and unified, it is capable of understanding human nature and subsequently the principles of all things. Such a mind does not suffer from the kind of blindness that afflicts those whose distracted and divided minds allow for no possibility of understanding.

The Rectification of Names

In chapter 22 of *Xunzi*, the author offers what would now be called a philosophy of language,

an epistemology (theory of knowledge), and the fundamentals of logic. He appears to have recognized the necessity of language to thought—that thinking is the process of verbalizing experience by using "names," that correcting errors in thought is what might be called the rectification of names.

As scholar Wing-tsit Chan points out, the rectification of names was a common subject for the Chinese philosophers, although for Xunzi's predecessors the interest was primarily social or moral. For Xunzi, however, the rectification of names became "some sort of systematic logical theory."

Confucius had urged that reality be made to correspond to the use of names; not only should the person called "emperor" *be* emperor—that is, act as an emperor should—but also, in all thinking and acting, the kind of order should prevail that the words require. The Western emphasis has been on fitting words to things—using the right words in description—but the Confucian emphasis was on fitting things to words: bringing conduct into line with titles. The theory of the rectification of names, then, bears some resemblance to the Platonic idea that the state, for example, should be harmonized by reference to the idea of the republic as a place of justice.

Xunzi's theory reverses the traditional Confucian emphasis in the consideration of the rectification of names. Instead of beginning with the names and urging that conduct be such as to realize the characters signified by names, his emphasis was on the course of knowledge, on the process of knowing—from the reception of sense impressions through the interpretation of them by the use of mind. "The mind gives meaning to impressions," Xunzi asserts; the faculty of knowing requires that the mind classify and that names be used to mark similarities and differences. "If a man simply allows his senses to record data but does not attempt to understand what they have recorded, or if he reaches an over-all understanding of the phenomenon but cannot put it into words, then everyone will call him an ignorant man," writes Xunzi, for whom knowing requires giving meaning to impressions, giving meaning requires classification and identification, and identification involves relating the use of names to the character of things.

Xunzi distinguished levels of generality, thereby laying the foundations for logical thinking. He also emphasized the accidental origin of names and their coming to have a place in language because of the habitual use of terms. (The disciplined uses of key terms were sometimes encouraged by directives from the king, Xunzi points out.) "Good" names are those that work well in discourse, clearly designating or classifying what they are used to describe.

Fallacies

Xunzi distinguished three groups of fallacies and proposed methods of logical analysis by which the fallacies could be eliminated and the paradoxes resolved. The first group of fallacies (illustrated by "To kill robbers is not to kill men") he describes as resulting from the practice of *using names to confuse names*. The second group (illustrated by "Mountains and abysses are on the same level") result from *using actualities to confuse the names*, Xunzi maintains. The third group (illustrated by "An ox and a horse are not a horse") result from *using names to confuse actualities*.

The cure for the first fallacious practice is to understand why names are used and what sorts of names they are. The remedy for the second error consists in discovering how similarities and differences are discovered and then seeing what names fit the actuality. The third fallacy can be prevented by following the agreements shown in the practice of using names; if one follows the agreements and rejects using names in odd ways, the fallacies will be avoided. (Xunzi's criticism applies to the paradoxes propounded by the followers of the logicians Hui Shi and Gongsun Long; his approach in criticism is thoroughly pragmatic and involves a naturalistic theory of name origins.)

Although language when properly used and understood is very important in teaching and learning, there are limits to its powers of persuasion, even as used by the most skillful of rhetoricians, Xunzi writes. Accordingly, because the ordinary people cannot be expected to understand the reasons behind injunctions that prescribe conduct in accordance with the Way, the enlightened ruler uses political power, including the threat of punishment, to persuade his subjects to obey the laws and commands.

Because people are originally evil in that they have desires that control the will, the remedy, according to Xunzi, is to eliminate the original ignorance of the Way through teaching, discipline, the use of right language, and prime examples of virtue. When all else fails, force must be used to maintain social order. (The theory that force is justified when no other practical expedient is available was subsequently acted on by Qin Shihuang and Li Si, Xunzi's disciple, in the burning of the books in 213 B.C.E., an effort to eliminate books of poetry, philosophy, and history in public circulation—many of them Confucian—in order that teachers representing the official position be more effective in indoctrinating the people.)

As a philosopher, Xunzi exhibited great analytic skill, the ability to distinguish similarities and differences and to relate the findings of empirical and philosophical inquiry in logically effective ways. His theory of humanity's evil nature and his naturalistic approach did not keep him from joining other Confucian scholars in calling for education, self-discipline, and the achievement of order by reference to the Way made clear by the sages.

Ian P. McGreal

Additional Reading

Cua, A. S. *Ethical Argumentation: A Study in Hsün-tzu's Moral Epistemology*. Honolulu: University of Hawaii Press, 1985. A philosophical look into Xunzi's ethical theory by a philosopher trained in the Western tradition. Includes a bibliography, notes, and an index.

De Bary, William Theodore, ed. *Sources of Chinese Tradition*. Vol. 1. New York: Columbia University Press, 1960. Includes a short selection from *Xunzi* and a brief article on Xunzi's rationalism and realism. Useful introduction.

Dubs, Homer H. *Hsün-tzu: The Moulder of Ancient Confucianism*. London: A. Probsthain, 1927. A classic work on Xunzi's life and philosophy. Provides a systematic approach based on traditional Chinese scholarship. Includes notes and an index.

Ivanhoe, Philip J. *Confucian Moral Self-Cultivation*. New York: Peter Lang, 1993. This work provides a very good introduction to important Confucian philosophers such as Confucius, Mencius, and Xunzi.

_____. *Chinese Language, Thought, and Culture: Nivison and His Critics.* La Salle, Ill.: Open Court, 1996. A collection of articles in honor of Nivison. Includes the articles "A Villain in the *Xunzi*" by Donald J. Munro and "Xunzi on Moral Motivation" by David B. Wong. Also includes a biography and an introduction.

Koller, John M., and Patricia Joyce Koller. *Asian Philosophies.* 3d ed. Upper Saddle River, N.J.: Prentice Hall, 1998. A general introduction to Asian philosophy. Contains a brief section on Xunzi's philosophy within a chapter on the main concepts in Confucianism. Good for beginners.

Machle, Edward J. *Nature and Heaven in the Xunzi: A Study of the Tian Lun.* SUNY Series in Chinese Philosophy and Culture. New York: State University of New York Press, 1993. This book contains a new translation of "The Discussion of Heaven," by Xunzi. Machle provides a very good philosophical discussion of the work.

Munro, Donald. J. *The Concept of Man in Early China.* Stanford: Stanford University Press, 1969. A valuable comparison between early Chinese and Western philosophies. This work focuses on Confucianism and Taoism and offers useful sections on Xunzi. Includes a bibliography, notes, a glossary, and an index.

Nivison, David S. *The Ways of Confucianism: Investigations in Chinese Philosophy.* Edited by Bryan Van Norden. La Salle, Ill.: Open Court, 1996. A collection of papers by Nivison on Chinese philosophy. Contains work on Xunzi's views on human nature, weakness of will, and moral motivation.

Schwartz, Benjamin I. *The World of Thought in Ancient China.* Cambridge, Mass.: Harvard University Press, 1985. A scholarly study that compares the major issues in Chinese philosophy with Western philosophical concepts. Includes a very helpful chapter on Xunzi. Provides a bibliography, notes, and an index.

Pei-kai Cheng, updated by Tammy Nyden-Bullock

Zeno of Elea

Although Zeno cannot be said to have succeeded in defending Parmenides' doctrine of the One, his paradoxes are still remembered, and his method of argument influenced all later philosophy.

Principal philosophical works: c. 465 B.C.E. (*Zeno of Elea: A Text*, 1936; commonly known as *The Paradoxes of Zeno*)

Born: c. 490 B.C.E.; Elea (now Velia, Italy)
Died: c. 440 B.C.E.; Elea (now Velia, Italy)

Early Life

Little is known of Zeno's life. In the early fifth century, when he was young, Greek philosophy was still in its cruder, experimental form, sometimes mythological, even borrowing from Asian lore, sometimes resembling primitive science by trying to explain the physical world and basing its conclusions on observation if not on experiment. One tendency was to try to explain all material phenomena as variations on one particular element. Thus, Thales of Miletus taught that all material things were derived from water; Anaximenes of Miletus taught that all things were derived from air; and Heraclitus of Ephesus, though his philosophy was by no means as simple as those of his predecessors, thought that all things were derived from fire. Empedocles, on the other hand, rejected the idea of any single element as the source of all and saw the material world as the result of the mixture and separation of four elements: earth, air, fire, and water.

Zeno's master, Parmenides, rejected this notion of multiplicity in favor of a fundamental unity. His arguments, which were placed in a mythological setting and expressed in hexameter verse, have survived only in fragments; they are exceedingly involved and hard to follow but perhaps can best be summarized as saying that multiplicity is illogical, self-contradictory, or merely unthinkable. This leaves the One, which is not water or air or fire but simply is "being"—"individual,

changeless, featureless, motionless, rock-solid being." Multiplicity, however, if contrary to logic, is nevertheless a fact of experience, and Parmenides apparently undertook to give a systematic account of it. A modern thinker might say that the world of reason and the world of experience were mutually exclusive and could never be reconciled.

Life's Work

Despite the paucity of biographical information about Zeno, Plato's dialogue *Parmenidēs* (middle period, 388-368 B.C.E.; *Parmenides*, 1793) reports the conversation of Socrates—then a young man—and the visiting Parmenides and Zeno. In that account, Zeno is described as "nearly forty years of age, tall and fair to look upon; in the days of his youth he was reported to have been beloved by Parmenides." In the dialogue, having finished reading aloud from his works, written in his youth, Zeno frankly explains their origin and his motive:

The truth is, that these writings of mine were meant to protect the arguments of Parmenides against those who make fun of him and seek to show the many ridiculous and contradictory results which they suppose to follow from the affirmation of the One. My answer is addressed to partisans of the many, whose attack I return with interest by retorting upon them that their hypothesis of the being of many, if carried out, appears to be still more ridiculous than the hypothesis of the being of One.

After Zeno confesses that his arguments were motivated not by "the ambition of an older man, but the pugnacity of a young one," Socrates endeavors to sum up Zeno's arguments:

> Do you maintain that if being is many, it must be both like and unlike, and that this is impossible, for neither can the like be unlike, nor the unlike like. . . . And if the unlike cannot be like, or the like unlike, then according to you, being could not be many, for this would involve an impossibility. In all that you say, have you any other purpose except to disprove the being of the many? And is not each division of your treatise intended to furnish a separate proof of this, there being as many proofs of the not-being of the many, as you have composed arguments?

In the dialogue, Zeno acknowledges that Socrates has correctly understood him. Zeno's defense of Parmenides thus consists not of evidence supporting Parmenides' position or even of positive arguments; rather, Zeno demonstrates that the opposite position is self-contradictory.

These proofs of the being of the One by proving the not-being of the many might not seem relevant in a scientific age, but some have survived and are known to those who are not otherwise learned in pre-Socratic philosophy. The most famous of Zeno's arguments, called the "Achilles," is summed up by Aristotle: "In a race, the quickest runner can never overtake the slowest, since the pursuer must first reach the point where the pursued started, so that the slower must always hold a lead." Almost as famous is the paradox of the arrow, which can never reach its target. According to Zeno's argument, at each point of its flight, the arrow must be at that point and at rest at that point. Thus, all motion, and therefore all change, is illusory.

Zeno's famed pugnacity was not limited to philosophy. After a plot in which he was involved against the tyrant Nearchus of Elea was discovered, the philosopher died under torture, and his death became the subject of various anecdotes. Some claim that he revealed the names of the tyrant's own friends as conspirators. Another story states that Zeno bit off his tongue and spit it out at the tyrant; in another, he bit off the tyrant's ear or nose.

Influence

Plato recognized in *Sophistēs* (middle period, 388-368 B.C.E.; *Sophist*, 1804) that there is something futile about such arguments as those of Zeno and that those who make them may simply be showing off:

Zeno of Elea. *(Archive Photos)*

Thus we provide a rich feast for tyros, whether young or old; for there is nothing easier than to argue that the one cannot be many, or the many one: and great is their delight in denying that a man is good; for man, they insist, is man and good is good. I dare say that you have met with persons who take an interest in such matters—they are often elderly men, whose meager sense is thrown into amazement by these discoveries of theirs, which they believe to be the height of wisdom.

Zeno can be defended in a number of ways. One could argue that his motives were good—that he wanted only to defend Parmenides. In doing so, he simply showed that trait of loyalty that brought about his death. More seriously, one could argue that his position in the history of philosophy excuses his failures, and one could praise him for raising issues and developing methods of argument that Aristotle took seriously. In Zeno's arguments, a recurring theme in philosophy can be seen: the conflict of reason and common sense. Periodically in philosophy, thinkers prove by logic things that ordinary people cannot accept. The empiricists—John Locke, George Berkeley, and David Hume—did this by stripping away the qualities of objects until the real world had to be defended as an illusion. In later years, the poststructuralists denounced the logocentric view of the world and wrote *sous rature*—the world may be described rationally, but that analysis must be voided because any logocentric analysis of the world by definition must be faulty. Periodically, it seems, logic and common sense must be at odds.

Nevertheless, in the twentieth century, Zeno found one eminent and eloquent defender, Bertrand Russell. Zeno, he said, for two thousand years had been pronounced an ingenious juggler and his arguments considered sophisms, when "these sophisms were reinstated, and made the foundations of a mathematical renaissance, by a German professor," Karl Weierstrass. Russell concluded, "The only point where Zeno probably erred was in inferring (if he did infer) that, because there is no change, therefore the world must be in the same state at one time as at another." Thus, at the dawn of philosophy, when philoso-

phers sometimes wrote in hexameters and were executed for their politics, Zeno expressed certain philosophical problems in a form that still amuses ordinary people and that still occasions profound debate among professional philosophers.

John C. Sherwood

The Paradoxes of Zeno

Type of philosophy: Logics, metaphysics
First transcribed: c. 465 B.C.E. (*Zeno of Elea: A Text*, 1936; commonly known as *The Paradoxes of Zeno*)
Principal ideas advanced:
◇ Reality cannot be a plurality, a many; reality must be one.
◇ Motion is impossible.
◇ Space cannot consist of points; time cannot consist of instants.
◇ The paradoxes of plurality: If the many have being and magnitude, they must be both large and small; if the many have no magnitude, they cannot be.
◇ If the units of the many be indivisible, they are nothing; if things are a many and divisible, they are both finite and infinite in number.
◇ The paradox of dichotomy: One cannot traverse an infinite number of points in a finite amount of time.
◇ The paradox of Achilles and the tortoise: A swifter runner cannot overtake a slower runner.
◇ The paradox of the arrow: An arrow in flight cannot move.
◇ The paradox of the stadium: If passage is relative to points, one set of moving things moving at the same velocity as another set can pass twice as many points as the other in the same amount of time: Double the time is equal to half the time.

Zeno of Elea is one of the most amazing figures in the history of philosophy. No fragments remain of what he wrote, and yet two and a half millennia after his time, professional philosophers and mathematicians continue to argue, as they have ever since he first propounded his paradoxes, about the point and validity of his arguments. Numerous historians and commentators, as well as philosophers, have written of Zeno's thought, and a review of Zeno's paradoxes may reasonably consist of constructions that represent what the consensus appears to be concerning the lines of argument that Zeno devised.

Speaking of Zeno, philosopher Bertrand Russell wrote that "by some care in interpretation it seems possible to reconstruct the so-called 'sophisms' which have been 'refuted' by every tyro from that day to this." Both Aristotle and Plato have something to say about Zeno. Simplicius, the scholarly historian of philosophy and commentator on Aristotle, tells us something of Zeno's arguments; but he was writing in the sixth century C.E., and although he may have had some reliable information about Zeno's views, no one knows for sure. In any case, what he writes is fascinating and promising, and he is often quoted as a source of Zeno's arguments. Diogenes Laërtius gives some information. Although these scattered passages do not bear evidence of authenticity, the arguments that emerge have a certain genius and integrity about them, leading scholars to be reasonably confident that if they do not thereby know Zeno, at least they know the shadow on the wall.

Before turning to the paradoxes themselves, however, we can hope to gain better understanding and appreciation of them by considering the probable point of their delivery. Zeno of Elea was a defender of Parmenides, also of Elea, who in his *Peri physeōs* (fifth century B.C.E., only fragments exist; *The Fragments of Parmenides*, 1869; commonly known as *On Nature*), developed a thoroughgoing monistic theory of reality to the effect that reality is a homogeneous sphere, eternal and indestructible; neither motion nor change is possible. Although sense experiences lead us to suppose that we observe a world of change and motion, such experiences are misleading. It is reasonable to suppose, then, that Zeno, as a disciple of Parmenides, used his paradoxical arguments to defend monism and to deny the pluralism of the Pythagoreans and other schools of his day.

The paradoxes as stated below are not in Zeno's words, of course; and it is entirely possible that the arguments do not correspond even in sense to Zeno's arguments, but the fragments of secondhand reports suggest arguments along the lines given below.

The Paradoxes of Plurality and of Space

Presuming (for the sake of argument) that there is a plurality of things, if the many are of no magnitude, then if one thing were added to another, there would be no change in size of the thing receiving the addition. Hence, what would be added would be nothing. If a thing of no magnitude were subtracted from another thing, the other would not at all be diminished; hence, what would be subtracted would be nothing. Hence, if there is a plurality, then each thing is of some magnitude.

However, if each thing in a plurality is of some magnitude, it is divisible into parts *ad infinitum*. Because there would be no end to its parts, such a thing would be infinitely large. Hence, because if there is a plurality, everything that exists is either of some magnitude or not, and if things of no magnitude are nothing, and if things of some magnitude are infinite in size, then, if there is a plurality, things are either so small as to be nonexistent or so large as to be infinitely large. Hence, it is false that there is a plurality of things.

Second, if there is a plurality, the number of things would have to be definite, but if the number is definite, then it could not be infinite because the infinite has no limit and is not definite. On the other hand, if there is a plurality, by the division of parts, one would arrive at an infinite number of things. Hence, if things are many, they are both finite and infinite in number, which is impossible. Hence, it is false that there is a plurality of things.

According to the paradox of space, if there is space, then everything that exists is in something—namely, space. However, then space would be in space, *ad infinitum*. Therefore, there is no space.

The Paradoxes of Motion

There are five paradoxes of motion, the dichotomy paradox, the paradox of Achilles and the tortoise, the arrow paradox, the stadium paradox, and the millet seed paradox.

According to the paradox of dichotomy (the

race course), before going the whole of any distance, a runner would first have to go half that distance. However, before going the half, the runner would have to cover the first half of that half (a quarter of the original distance). However, before going the first quarter of the course, the runner would have to go the first eighth. The number of requirements is infinite and cannot be satisfied in a finite amount of time. Therefore, the runner cannot even get started.

In the paradox of Achilles and the tortoise, in a race between Achilles, the swifter runner, and a tortoise that has taken the lead, Achilles cannot overtake the tortoise. Considering the situation at any instant in the race while the tortoise is in the lead, by the time Achilles reaches the point where the tortoise was at that instant, the tortoise (who keeps moving) will be some distance ahead. By the time Achilles reaches *that* point, the tortoise will have moved some distance ahead. Hence, because no matter how many points Achilles reaches at which the tortoise was, the tortoise will be some distance ahead. Achilles will never overtake the tortoise.

According to the arrow paradox, if an arrow is in flight, at any given instant, it is somewhere, occupying a space equal to its dimensions. However, anything occupying a space is at rest, and anything at rest is not in motion. Hence, an arrow in flight (a moving arrow) could not move. The arrow cannot move where it is; neither can it move where it is not.)

In the stadium paradox, in the middle of a stadium, there is a line of three stationary chariots (line *B*). A line of three moving chariots, *A*, approaching from one end of *B*, reaches a point at which the chariots are side by side with those of *B*; another line of three chariots, *C*, approaches at the same time from the other end of *B* and reaches a similar side by side position relative to *B*. (The lines of moving chariots accomplish this task at the same velocity.) Note that in the time it takes Chariot *A-1* to move from opposite *B-1* to opposite *B-3*, it passes only *one* chariot in *B*, namely *B-2*, but it passes *two* chariots in *C*, namely, *C-1* and *C-2*. Hence, in passing *B*, line of chariots *A* travels at half the speed with which it passes line *C*. If time is relative to motion, then half the time is equal to the whole. (See the accompanying table, "The Stadium Paradox.")

The Stadium Paradox

The Passing Chariots

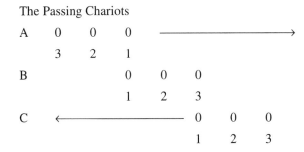

The Three Lines of Chariots in Line

A				0	0	0	→
				3	2	1	
B				0	0	0	
				1	2	3	
C	←		0	0	0		
			1	2	3		

If T represents the amount of time it takes a chariot in *A* to pass a chariot, then *T* (the amount of time taken to pass *B-2*) is equal to 2*T* (the amount of time taken to pass *C-1* and *C-2*).

The paradox of the millet seed looks at a single millet seed, which makes no noise when it falls. It would be impossible, then, for a number of seeds falling together (say, a bushelful) to make a noise (because the sum of any number of silences could hardly be a sound).

These are the principal paradoxes traditionally attributed to Zeno. Whatever the inaccuracies of the various accounts, the genius of Zeno comes through. Accordingly, philosophical critics—including geniuses who would not bother with trivial arguments—have given a great deal of thought over the centuries to Zeno's arguments: Some have supported Zeno, calling his arguments valid (at least as interpreted in their manner); others have found his arguments to be fallacious. Among those who support him are those who do so semantically, logically, or metaphysically; and among those who find him at fault are those who do so semantically, logically, or metaphysically. The literature of commentary has acquired much of the fascination and inspired something of the genius of Zeno's paradoxes as we know them.

Ian P. McGreal,
updated by John K. Roth

Additional Reading

Boardman, John, Jasper Griffin, and Oswyn Murray, eds. *The Oxford History of the Classical World*. Oxford: Oxford University Press, 1986. Martin West's article on "Early Greek Philosophy" is useful in placing Zeno in his historical and cultural context.

Copleston, Frederick. *A History of Philosophy: Greece and Rome*. Garden City, N.Y.: Doubleday, 1962. Copleston provides an instructive introduction in a brief chapter on Zeno and his famous paradoxes about time and motion.

Curd, Patricia, ed. *A Presocratics Reader: Selected Fragments and Testimonia*. Translations by Richard D. McKirahan, Jr. Indianapolis, Ind.: Hackett, 1996. Contains important texts and commentary that are important for understanding Zeno.

Faris, J. A. *The Paradoxes of Zeno*. Brookfield, Vt.: Avebury, 1996. A helpful study of the main logical paradoxes advanced by Zeno.

Grünbaum, Adolf. *Modern Science and Zeno's Paradoxes*. Middletown, Conn.: Wesleyan University Press, 1967. Grünbaum brings the resources of contemporary mathematics and physics to bear on paradoxes having to do with motion and time.

Hussey, Edward. *The Pre-Socratics*. Indianapolis, Ind.: Hackett, 1995. Includes a sympathetic analysis of Zeno, which focuses on concepts such as time, change, diversity, separation, and completeness.

McGreal, Ian Philip. *Analyzing Philosophical Arguments*. Corte Madera, Calif.: Chandler, 1967. McGreal offers a detailed analysis of Zeno's argument about Achilles and the tortoise, which concentrates on time and motion.

McKirahan, Richard D., Jr. *Philosophy Before Socrates: An Introduction with Texts and Commentary*. Indianapolis, Ind.: Hackett, 1994. An excellent study of pre-Socratic philosophy that includes a discussion of Zeno.

Salmon, Wesley C., ed. *Zeno's Paradoxes*. Indianapolis, Ind.: Bobbs-Merrill, 1970. This useful and intellectually entertaining anthology contains important articles by leading philosophers who deal with Zeno's paradoxes. Includes an excellent bibliography.

Schrempp, Gregory Allen. *Magical Arrows: The Maori, the Greeks, and the Folklore of the Universe*. Madison: University of Wisconsin Press, 1992. A comparative analysis that includes discussion of Zeno's reflections on time and motion.

John C. Sherwood, updated by John K. Roth

Zhuangzi

Zhuangzi was the greatest thinker of the Chinese Daoist school of philosophy. He went much beyond its founder, Laozi, in constructing an apolitical, transcendental philosophy designed to promote an individual's spiritual freedom.

Principal philosophical works: *Zhuangzi*, c. 300 B.C.E. (*The Divine Classic of Nan-hua*, 1881; also known as *The Complete Works of Chuang Tzu*, 1968; commonly known as *Zhuangzi*, 1991)

Born: c. 365 B.C.E.; Meng, Kingdom of Song, China
Died: c. 290 B.C.E.; Nanhua Hill, Caozhou, Kingdom of Chi, China

Early Life

Zhuangzi was born sometime around 365 B.C.E. According to historian Sima Qian, in *Shi-ji* (first century B.C.E.; *Records of the Grand Historian of China*, 1960; rev. ed. 1993). the philosopher was a native of the town of Meng in the Kingdom of Song. His personal name was Zhou. Beyond this, little is known regarding Zhuangzi's life and career. He was born into a time known as the Warring States period (475-221 B.C.E.), during which China had become divided into many small, fiercely competitive states as a result of the collapse of the Zhou Dynasty (1122-221 B.C.E.). Thus, Zhuangzi was a contemporary of the famous Confucian philosopher Mencius.

For a brief time, Zhuangzi served as a government official in Qiyuan, not far from his birthplace. He soon tired of public life, however, and resolved to pursue philosophical meditation and writing. Thereupon, he retired to the state of Qi, where he took up residence on Nanhua Hill, in the prefecture of Caozhou. There he spent the remainder of his life.

Zhuangzi's disillusionment with law and politics is apparent in an anecdote recorded in chapter 17 of the *Zhuangzi*:

Once, when Chuang Tzu [Zhuangzi] was fishing in the P'u [Pu] River, the king of Ch'u [Chu] sent two officials to go and announce to him: "I would like to trouble you with the administration of my realm."

Chuang Tzu held on to the fishing pole and, without turning his head, said, "I have heard that there is a sacred tortoise in Ch'u that has been dead for three thousand years. The king keeps it wrapped in cloth and boxed, and stores it in the ancestral temple. Now would this tortoise rather be dead and have its bones left behind and honored? Or would it rather be alive and dragging its tail in the mud?"

"It would rather be alive and dragging its tail in the mud," said the two officials.

Chuang Tzu said, "Go away! I'll drag my tail in the mud!"

A portrait of this stubbornly independent thinker has been preserved in Taipei's National Palace Museum. It shows a rather short, slightly built man with sparse hair and penetrating eyes. He stands with his hands clasped over his chest, a pose that conveys dignity and serenity.

Life's Work

The Daoism of Zhuangzi's time derived from the *I Ching* (*Yi Jing*, eighth to third century B.C.E.; English translation, 1876; also known as *Book of Change*, 1986), the ancient manual of divination based on the concept that the world and the laws of change are an ordered, interdependent unit, and from the *Dao De Jing* (late third century B.C.E.; *The Speculations on Metaphysics, Polity, and Morality, of "the Old Philosopher, Lau-Tsze,"* 1868), which described the workings of the *dao* (the Way), the primordial generative principle that is the mother of all things.

Dao was interpreted as "the Way of Heaven," or natural law, and the Daoists explained natural phenomena and the social order in reference to this principle. Proper human behavior consisted of not interfering with the *dao* but living in harmony with it. Therefore, the Daoists taught the doctrine of *wuwei* (not doing), or, more explicitly, *weiwuwei* (doing by not doing). This standard did not imply absolute quietism but rather acting intuitively, spontaneously, and effortlessly in imitation of the *dao*, which manages to accomplish everything naturally. Although some Daoists retired entirely from the world and lived as hermits, Daoism was not designed for the hermit but for the Sage King, who, though not withdrawing from the world, seeks to avoid interfering with it.

For the Daoists, then, the best government was the least government. Indeed, they reasoned, if all people acted in harmony with the *dao*, government as an institution would be unnecessary. Government by law and even the notions of good and evil were regarded by the Daoists as deviations from the *dao* and unwarranted interference with it. Such an attitude gave Daoists considerable independence in regard to politics and worldly affairs generally.

It is evident that Zhuangzi's decision to withdraw from political entanglements was amply supported by Daoist teachings. His interpretations of this and other doctrines have been passed down in the *Zhuangzi*, an imaginative compilation of anecdote and dialogue. In the words of a modern scholar, in the *Zhuangzi*, "animals speak, natural forces are personified, and dialogues which begin in soberness unexpectedly veer into humor, fantasy, and absurdity."

The *Dao De Jing* sets forth the universal *dao* as a political and social ideal, but the *Zhuangzi* is mostly concerned with individuals and their intellectual and spiritual freedom. Unlike the *Dao De Jing*, which is addressed to rulers, the *Zhuangzi* addresses anyone, ruler or private person, who wishes to become a member of the spiritual elite. To achieve this goal, the seeker must begin by achieving an awareness of the existence and workings of the universal *dao* and of his or her own relation to the scheme of things.

The *dao* is nameless; the name assigned to it is merely a convenient label. Though it is preexistent, formless, and imperceptible, it latently contains all forms, entities, and forces; it permeates all things. All being issues from it and returns to it. The life and death of human beings take part in this transformation from nonbeing into being and back again to nonbeing.

After accepting this metaphysical scheme, the seeker faces the second step on the ladder of knowledge: the realization of the importance of making full and free use of his or her natural ability. Whatever ability one possesses stems from one's *de*, the power within one that comes directly from the *dao*. The individual forms of things come from their *de*, which confers on them their natural properties and abilities. Things differ both in their nature and in their natural abilities. One kind of bird can fly a thousand miles; another kind has difficulty flying from one tree to another. It is no use for a person to discuss the ocean with a frog that has lived its whole life in a well.

It is important for the seeker to distinguish between what is heavenly—that is, of nature—and what is entirely human. What is heavenly is internal; what is human is external. The human is all that is artificial: the artifacts of humankind; institutions of government, education, and religion; and cultural codes of etiquette, law, and morals. All these artificialities involve restrictions on humanity's independence and freedom. To the extent that one can exercise one's natural abilities independently of or in spite of the restrictions imposed, one ought to do so. In so doing, one will achieve a measure of happiness, although it will be a relative, not an absolute, happiness. Interference with nature should be avoided, according to Zhuangzi's teachings. Government that seeks to rule people by strict laws and strong institutions is pictured as putting a halter around a horse's neck or a cord through an ox's nose. The use of violence by governments is like trying to lengthen the short legs of a duck or to shorten the long legs of a crane.

Relative happiness, then, can be attained by making good use of one's natural ability; yet, other factors such as avoiding injury and disease and overcoming fear of death are also necessary to happiness. If the seeker gains a proper understanding of the nature of things, he or she can greatly mitigate his anxiety regarding death as well as the grief felt when a loved one dies. Chapter 18 of the *Zhuangzi*, "Perfect Happiness," records an anecdote that illustrates this notion. Zhuangzi's wife had died, and Huizi had gone to pay his condolences to the philosopher. Upon entering his house, Huizi was amazed to find the master "sitting with his legs sprawled, pounding on a tub and singing." Scandalized, Huizi hastened to remind Zhuangzi that he had lived with his wife a long time, that she had borne and reared his children, and that she had grown old with him. Huizi reproached his friend: "It should be enough simply not to weep at her death. But pounding on a tub and singing—this is going too far, isn't it?" Zhuangzi replied:

You're wrong. When she first died, do you think I didn't grieve like anyone else? But I looked back to her beginning and the time before she was born. Not only the time before she was born, but the time before she had a body. Not only the time before she had a body, but the time before she had a spirit. In the midst of the jumble of wonder and mystery a change took place and she had a spirit. Another change and she had a body. Another change and she was born. Now there's been another change and she's dead. It's just like the progression of the four seasons, spring, summer, fall, winter.

Now she's going to lie down peacefully in a vast room. If I were to follow after her bawling and sobbing, it would show that I don't understand anything about fate. So I stopped.

Thus, death is simply a phase in the turning of the wheel of fortune that is the *dao*. The turning of the wheel voids the identity and disintegrates the material body of the dead person. From the standpoint of the *dao*, however, no state of being is more desirable than another. As a natural event in the cycle of human life, death is neither to be feared nor to be sorrowed over.

How does the seeker reach the third and last rung of the upward way? To answer this question, Zhuangzi proposed an epistemology, a theory of knowledge. Knowledge, he said, is of two kinds: lower and higher. The lower involves sense perception, reason, and language; it depends on relativity, finitude, and memory. Higher knowledge involves suprasensible perception, intuition, and silence; it depends on the unity of opposites, infinitude, and forgetfulness. Lower knowledge lacks understanding. Higher knowledge is filled with understanding, a condition in which everything is illuminated by "the light of Heaven."

To achieve higher knowledge, people must forget the knowledge that they have acquired. They must transcend all relativity, finitude, and apparent contradictions implied in conventional opposites such as right and wrong, great and small, life and death. They can transcend such distinctions when they realize that the *dao* makes them all one. Once they have attained this realization, they have no use for categories. Where "ordinary men discriminate and parade their discriminations before others," the enlightened person "embraces things." Thus, forgetfulness and "no-knowledge" constitute the highest wisdom.

The lower level of knowledge permits the use of speech. Good language is dispassionate and calm; bad language is "shrill and quarrelsome." At the higher level of knowledge, however, language is inadequate: "The Great Way is not named; Great Discriminations are not spoken. . . . If discriminations are put into words, they do not suffice." The holy person does not speak; silence reigns supreme. The holy person, content because he or she has forgotten the self and the world, may be said to have entered Heaven and achieved absolute happiness.

Influence

If the real Zhuangzi is a barely perceptible shadow cast by the dim light of history, he is brightly visible in the pages of the *Zhuangzi*. Here he emerges as a living, breathing, dynamic human being, radiant of mind, wide-ranging in imagination, full of wit and humor. The *Zhuangzi* is a monumental book and a great classic of Chinese literature. Its style is brilliant, full of clever rhetorical devices, satire, fantasy, metaphor, jokes, dreams, and parody. Although it is a work of philosophy, it may also be termed "protofictional." It not only uses historical characters, such as Confucius, fictionally, but also creates fictional characters as foils for its protagonist. In this way, the *Zhuangzi* contributed to the development of later Chinese fictional genres such as *xiaoshuo* and *zhiguai*.

Philosophically, Zhuangzi went beyond the *Dao De Jing* in offering a clear alternative to the philosophies of his age. He emphasized the personal ideal of the emancipation of individuals for their own sake in place of the social ideal of the harmonious society ruled by the Sage King. Although the *Zhuangzi* never gained the popularity and influence of the *Dao De Jing*, it continued to command the interest and admiration of Chinese rulers and philosophers. The neo-Daoist philosophers Xiang Xiu and Guo Xiang both wrote commentaries on the *Zhuangzi*, seeking to reconcile the social ideal of Confucius with the private ideal of Zhuangzi. Despite their criticism of Zhuangzi, they performed the important service of transmitting his work and preserving it for posterity.

In the West, the *Zhuangzi* has made a decided impression on numerous prominent thinkers, beginning perhaps with the great German philosopher Georg Wilhelm Friedrich Hegel, who in 1816 lectured at the University of Heidelberg on Daoism and Confucianism, based on the *I Ching* and the *Zhuangzi*. His concept of the absolute as a process rather than a source and his description of the dialectical process (thesis and antithesis merging into a synthesis) are reminiscent of Zhuangzi's concept of the *dao* and the underlying unity of opposites. Later thinkers such as Pierre Teilhard de Chardin, Carl Gustav Jung, Jacques Maritain, Jacques Lacan, and Thomas Merton all show evidence in their writing of an intimate acquaintance with Daoism and the thought of Zhuangzi.

Richard P. Benton

Zhuangzi

Type of philosophy: Chinese philosophy, ethics, metaphysics
First transcribed: Zhuangzi, c. 300 B.C.E. (*The Divine Classic of Nan-hua*, 1881; also known as *The Complete Works of Chuang Tzu*, 1968; commonly known as *Zhuangzi*, 1991)

Principal ideas advanced:

◊ *Dao* is the universal Way of things, the all-pervading principle of all that exists; the virtue or power of every individual is a manifestation of *dao*.

◊ Distinctions between people or things, between right and wrong, are seen to be false once the universal presence of *dao* is recognized.

◊ The only way to salvation (tranquillity) is to identify oneself with the orderly process of all being, the *dao*.

◊ Death is nothing to fear, for people live as long as their essence, the *dao*, lives; and the *dao* is eternal.

◊ The True Person retains the unspoiled simplicity of a child; rather than concern the self with political action, the individual allows the *dao* to take its course; the True Person abstains from intellectual analysis and the study of abstract ideas.

The name of Zhuangzi (Zhuang Zhou)—together with that of Laozi, to whom legend attributes the *Dao De Jing* (late third century B.C.E.; *The Speculations on Metaphysics, Polity, and Morality, of "the Old Philosopher, Lau-Tsze,"* 1868)—has become synonymous with classical Daoism. Zhuangzi was probably one of the many eccentric recluses who challenged the intellectual authority of Confucius during the Warring States period (475-221 B.C.E.). Disgusted with the prevailing chaos and weary of the self-styled sages' moral preachings, these recluses saw the only salvation in "letting things be what they are." Legends about Zhuangzi tell of his refusal to serve in the capacity of prime minister, his mystic wanderings, and his cryptic speeches. The anecdotes involving him and the statements attributed to him are extremely imaginative in character; and his words often soar to dazzling metaphysical heights. Like the *Dao De Jing*, the thirty-three chapters of the *Zhuangzi* contain much poetry in which appear many images identifiable with the poetic tradition founded in ancient China along the Yangzi (Chang Jiang) River valley or in relatively southern parts of China.

The Dao

Like the *Dao De Jing*, this work expounds a theory based on the mystic universal principle called *dao*. *Dao* is the beginning of all being; hence, it could be understood as nonbeing. Having no begetter, *dao* is best expressed by what is spontaneous. From these ideas, the workings of *dao* can be seen as actually nonactivity, or doing nothing that is not done by itself. In short, *dao* is the all-pervading principle that exists before the existence of the universe, and it is to be found in everything, no matter how trivial or base. The manifestation of this first principle in each individual thing is called *de* (virtue, power). *Dao* and *de*, thus, are actually of one essence, the former being the universal essence, and the latter the share of the former deposited in every individual being.

Zhuangzi constructed his view of the universe on this mystic concept of *dao*. He does so very rarely by direct logical exposition, using instead a multitude of anecdotes, imaginary dialogues, and metaphorical parables. The universe comes into existence in accordance with *dao*, and the myriad beings in the universe each partake of *dao*. In their essence, the loftiest sage and the humblest of people are the same, their distinctions being artificial, impermanent, and never absolute. The Himalayas and the threshold of a peasant's hut are actually of the same height; the greatest of birds, the roc, really has no reason for laughing at the tiniest wren when they compare their ranges of flight. Because each follows its own Way as *dao* makes it, each is as important as the other. This is Zhuangzi's theory of relativity with which he defies the existing social institutions, all of which make distinctions. These distinctions, in Zhuangzi's view, are all false, and he viewed the concern of the Confucians and the School of Names with the distinction between names and reality as totally irrelevant and useless.

Even the notions of right and wrong do not exist for Zhuangzi. Right is right only because of the existence of wrong; nothing is absolutely right. Furthermore, everything is simultaneously itself (when it looks at itself) and something else (when looked upon by something else); consequently, there cannot be an absolute "this" or "that." Everything is "this" and "that" at the same time.

When someone challenged Zhuangzi to explain how he could make such an assertion and claim it to be right when his assertion was a denial of the notion of right, Zhuangzi dismissed the question by saying that he was not concerned with settling such an argument. He did not believe that there was any argument to be settled. He was merely proposing a third course of action or a third view transcending the ordinary right-wrong dualism.

The Way

Why is there no need to settle any argument? To begin with, everything follows *dao*. Because *dao* is always right, by virtue of the fact that it always "is so," everything is always right also. If there is conflict, then the conflict itself is also right. Zhuangzi believed that conflict arises when people depart from *dao* and try to act contrary to the natural Way. He asserts, without trying to prove his assertion, that everything in the universe is inclined toward order; therefore, he denies the validity of the accepted legends about how the ancient Sage Kings "worked" to bring about peace and order. Zhuangzi preferred to see the abolition of all the human-made social and political institutions because he believed that only then could the Way (*dao*) prevail. *Dao* will always ultimately prevail; whatever humankind can do will not make any lasting difference.

The Way is constant, and its constancy is revealed in the ceaseless change that cannot be obstructed in the universe. Every being is involved in this process of change, from one species to another, one appearance to another, or one form of its existence to another form of existence. Hence, nothing is improving or degenerating, but everything is involved in this universal cyclical motion. Humankind is no exception. The only way to obtain salvation (tranquillity) is for people to understand this process and to identify themselves with *dao*. In doing so, people are able to attain the axis of the wheel from which they could view the perpetual disturbance in the universe with transcendental calm. They would, then, achieve tranquillity in chaos. In this very respect, Zhuangzi's system comes close to Buddhism.

Recalling that Zhuangzi compares a person to a clod, one may say that Zhuangzi's is not a very edifying view of humanity, but it is consistent with his fundamental concept of *dao*. According to him, humanity is part of *dao*'s making. Humanity has a share of *dao* just as a clod of dirt does. If one preserves this share of *dao*, one will not be lost. The way to cling to *dao* is by retaining one's original unspoiled simplicity—the state of mind of a child.

Zhuangzi arrives at this conclusion along several lines of argument: First, the commonly accepted cultivation of the mind drives people to acquire a knowledge of artificial distinctions without real meaning. Such knowledge is not true knowledge; the only true knowledge lies in the comprehension of *dao*. Second, the artificial knowledge that people acquire serves no other purpose than to create confusion and strife. People are led by their false sense of righteousness to combat what they erroneously consider wrong. They are encouraged by their illusion about greatness to strive for what may be actually small. Third, there is nothing that is absolutely complete except *dao* itself. Humanity's artificial effort to construct anything or create anything is necessarily incomplete. People cannot attain perfect construction of anything through their own efforts. Hence, whatever they undertake to complete, they leave something undone. What is more, the moment they make a move, they injure something, and also themselves. Hence, Zhuangzi insists on the importance of an uncarved block, and he praises the perfection of music from a lute that has no strings.

Life and Death
Consistent with his theory of relativity and cyclical change, Zhuangzi shows indifference toward death and suggests that there may be great joy after death. He decries the common practice of mourning because, as he puts it, the mourner assumes knowledge of the unknown and pretends his dislike of it. The famous story in chapter 18 about the death of Zhuangzi's wife is a graphic illustration of this attitude. Zhuangzi refuses to weep; instead, he sits with his legs crossed and beats on an inverted pot to accompany his singing. Through this unconventional behavior, Zhuangzi expresses his idea about immortality.

Strictly speaking, the question of immortality does not exist in Zhuangzi's system. If life and death are but phases in an irresistible cycle of change, then there is no difference between the living and the dead, or between the mortal and the immortal. Mortality becomes a problem and a source of sorrow only because people cannot free themselves from the artificially constructed straitjacket of their view of life and existence. In the physical sense, people must die and there is no escape. However, if people can understand the Way and embrace *dao*, then they live as long as *dao* lives; hence, they are immortal. Zhuangzi defies death by saying that if (after death) his left arm became a rooster, he would simply use it to mark the time of night. People may die indeed, but their essence, as part of the universal essence, lives on forever. This is the metaphysical view of immortality in the *Zhuangzi*.

There is also a mystic explanation of immortality offered by Zhuangzi. A person who has succeeded in preserving his or her original simplicity and in maintaining his or her share of *dao* is called in Zhuangzi's terms, a True Person. In order to achieve this stage, a person has to rid himself or herself of intellectual knowledge by "fasting his mind" and "contemplating on emptiness." If the person succeeds in forgetting that there are "things" in the world, he or she will have discarded manmade distinctions in the universe and will have come close to a union with *dao*. What the person senses will be merely an emptiness and a vastness; his or her appearance will resemble that of the stupid. Then the individual will have attained the "mysterious power in nature."

So far this seems to be only an exaggerated metaphorical statement of Zhuangzi's vision of perfect self-discipline and cultivation, but the mysticism surrounding him thickens when he goes on to describe the True Person's capacities. The best of these True People, so says Zhuangzi, are ethereal. They sense no heat in fire and no chill in ice. They can "mount on clouds, ride on the sun and moon, and wander at ease beyond the seas." Consequently, neither life nor death can affect them. There are many parallel stories told of this kind of spirit-travel in other ancient Chinese writings. They seem to be part of the common primitive Daoist-shamanistic traditions shared by the Chinese, particularly those in the central Yangzi (Chang Jiang) River valley, where Zhuangzi is said to have lived. In this book,

Zhuangzi attempts to give a metaphysical explanation to these legends. He stresses the importance of "preserving oneself" by following the natural bends of things; consequently, one achieves immortality because one does not wear oneself out. This theory is illustrated in his story about the perfect butcher whose carving knife remains perpetually sharp because it always goes between the bones and tissues and never meets any resistance.

Emptying the Mind
Although the physical liberation of a True Person, if taken literally, amounts to a mystic vision that can hardly be rationally explained, the liberation of a person's mind in the Daoist fashion is not difficult to comprehend. Zhuangzi has no use for intellectual knowledge. To him "things are what they are," and they do what nature dictates them to do. Humanity should live as part of nature together with all other things in nature and desist from the futile pursuit of seeing, reading, and analyzing the universe in abstraction. The moment people cease to confuse themselves with the useless puzzles that other people have created, their minds will be liberated. Then and only then will they be ready to comprehend *dao*.

By emptying the mind of intellectual prejudices, people can see the similarity of all things. Hence, the individual and the myriad things will be one, and people will feel that the universe is within them. Whatever they do or do not do will cause no concern or anxiety. They will thus be free to move in the universe. At this stage, these people's happiness is true and supreme, because there is nothing about them that is not in accord with nature.

The kind of extreme happiness that Zhuangzi speaks of is also a result of emotional liberation. Having been intellectually liberated, one no longer sees any cause for alarm, worry, or sorrow. Following a course completely in accord with nature, one depends on nothing and seeks nothing. One is totally free. It is this total freedom projected into time and space that Zhuangzi describes in his stories about the True Person. Zhuangzi's ideal freedom is threefold: an intellectual liberation from humanity's prejudices and manmade restrictions, an emotional liberation through a thorough understanding of the Way of

all lives, and finally a total liberation when one feels no restriction because one accepts every natural course of events.

Zhuangzi and Other Philosophers
Although this work does not deal with the various aspects of what has become known as magical Daoism, Zhuangzi's theory of the True Person and his notion of *qi* (gaseous matter, spirit) provide it with ample inspiration. Zhuangzi's vague formula to achieve the state of being a True Person mentions the physical discipline of sitting in meditation and the mental discipline of discarding abstract ideas. He also urges people to "listen" with their *qi* or to react to the outside world with their spirit, while sparing their ordinary senses. These suggestions can be related to some primitive practice of breathing exercise to aid mental concentration and ward off distracting influence. It has been said that this aspect of Daoism is a bridge between Zhuangzi's mysticism and that of Mencius. We must not overlook, however, the fundamental difference between these two philosophers. Both believed in a mystical perfection of humanity through the cultivation of *qi*, but while Mencius saw the road to salvation through doing socially good deeds, Zhuangzi absolutely denied the validity of altruism.

A comparison of Zhuangzi with Laozi will show their parallelism at almost every point. As we have noted, Laozi and Zhuangzi are recognized as cofounders of the Daoist school of thought, and there is rarely any mention of one without the other. There is nevertheless one important difference between them. In advocating nonactivity, Laozi stresses the difference between two extremes and warns of the disaster that inevitably follows extremity. In urging the same thing, Zhuangzi denies any real difference between extremes. Again, Laozi advises the ruler to govern by noninterference because he believes in the inevitable reversal from one extreme to the other; hence, complete lack of rule will automatically bring rule. Zhuangzi, on the other hand, believes in noninterference as an ideal for governing because of an alleged propensity toward order in everything.

Insofar as Zhuangzi repeatedly criticized his contemporary moralists as useless do-gooders, his anti-intellectual attitude was clearly a reaction against the overbearing Confucians and the many other voices that at the time vied with one another in offering political cure-alls and social panaceas. Most of these moralists sought to bring order to society by urging altruism and redefinition of terms; Zhuangzi was diametrically opposed to such activities. However, in opposing his contemporary thinkers, Zhuangzi was not unconcerned with the signs of his time; he also offered a political recipe of his own that he believed could solve all the prevalent problems. It should be noted that the *Zhuangzi* remains an extremely important source for the study of many other less well-known schools of thought in ancient China. In several cases, Zhuangzi's comments on some of his contemporaries provide the only information available on their philosophies.

The Power of Metaphor

In many ways, this work has exerted even greater influence on the Chinese mind than has the *Dao De Jing*. It has been able to do so because of the numerous imaginary and metaphorical anecdotes it contains. The metaphysical poetry of the *Dao De Jing* is fascinating, but often it is too cryptic to be grasped. The metaphors in the *Zhuangzi*, however, have found their way into the common pool of metaphors in Chinese literature and even in the daily language where, although their original Daoist color has been diluted through use, they have had a subtle influence on the configuration of the Chinese mind. On a higher level, such notions as the purity of the human heart (mind) and the calmness of emotions have become the core of quietism that has found eloquent expression in the undying poems of Tao Qian and Wang Wei. The principles of quietude, simplicity, detachment, and leisureliness that have made these poets immortal also laid the foundation for the development of Chan (Zen) Buddhism in China and for the theory and practice of the Chinese landscape painting—the most important Chinese contribution to art.

In daily life, this school of thought acts as an ever-present balancing influence on the Chinese mind, providing a measure of practical wisdom. Zhuangzi's allegorical tales on the themes of relativity and cyclical change appear in many later

works in infinite variations. For instance, the story about the death of Zhuangzi's wife appears in a famous seventeenth century collection of traditional short stories; it again appears in an opera still being staged in modern times. One of these stories is often quoted by someone trying to comfort a friend over the loss of a dear one. Another story is used, in the form of a proverb, to advise people never to take worldly affairs too seriously. A third anecdote enables people to live through the most trying of crises when they recall and believe in Zhuangzi's saying that "This, too, is Nature's way."

Kai-yu Hsu

Additional Reading

Allinson, Robert E. *Chuang Tzu for Spiritual Transformation: An Analysis of the Inner Chapters*. Albany: State University of New York Press, 1989. Allinson discusses the writing style of the *Zhuangzi* and how it relates to the text's philosophical commitment to spiritual transformation.

Ames, Roger T., ed. *Wandering at Ease in the Zhuangzi*. SUNY Series in Chinese Philosophy and Culture. Albany: State University of New York Press, 1998. This book offers eleven essays dealing with topics from the role of humor in the *Zhuangzi* to comparative studies with the writings of Confucius.

Creel, H. G., ed. *What Is Taoism? And Other Studies in Chinese Cultural History*. 1970. Reprint. Chicago: University of Chicago Press, 1982. A collection of essays worth the reader's attention including Creel's important essay "The Great Cold: A Taoist Conception of the Universe."

De Bary, William Theodore, ed. *Sources of Chinese Tradition*. Vol. 1. New York: Columbia University Press, 1960. Includes a short selection from the *Zhuangzi* and a very brief article on Zhuangzi's skepticism and mysticism. Good introduction.

Ivanhoe, Philip J., and Paul Kjellberg, eds. *Essays on Skepticism, Relativism, and Ethics in the Zhuangzi*. Albany: State University of New York Press, 1996. This excellent collection consists of six essays that take various approaches to the question: "How did Zhuangzi remain so cheerful given his apparent dismal philosophy?" Several essays discuss Zhuangzi's philosophy of language. Others compare him to philosophers such as Plato and Jacques Derrida.

Koller, John M., and Patricia Joyce Koller. *Asian Philosophies.* 3d ed. Upper Saddle River, N.J.: Prentice Hall, 1998. A general introduction to Asian philosophy. Contains a brief section on Zhuangzi's philosophy within a chapter on the main concepts in Taoism. Good for beginners.

Mair, Victor, ed. *Experimental Essays on Chuang-tzu.* Honolulu: University of Hawaii Press, 1983. A collection including articles by Chad Hansen, A. C. Graham, and Lee Yearley.

Van Norden, Bryan W. "Competing Interpretations of the Inner Chapters." *Philosophy East and West* 46, no. 2 (April, 1996), 247-268. Provides a running commentary on the opening of the *Zhuangzi.*

Wu, Kuang-ming. *Butterfly as Companion.* Albany: State University of New York Press, 1990. This work is great for beginning students. It contains the Chinese text, a literal translation, and several essays on the *Zhuangzi.*

_____. *Chuang-tzu: World Philosopher at Play.* New York: Crossroad, 1982. This book takes a revolutionary approach to Zhuangzi and raises several interesting questions. It considers the relevance of Zhuangzi's philosophy to contemporary times.

Richard P. Benton,
updated by Tammy Nyden-Bullock

Chronological List of Philosophers

This chronology of world philosophers offers an interesting perspective on the progress of thought from ancient to modern times. Although the arrangement is chronological on the basis of birth years and not according to historical movements or schools of thought, the proximity of contemporaries provides students of the history of philosophy with some insights into potential influences and contemporaneous developments. Philosophers covered in these volumes appear in **boldface;** also listed and boldfaced are the five texts covered in these volumes, whose authorship is uncertain, by probable date of transcription.

—*J.K.R.*

900-600 B.C.E.

Homer (early ninth century B.C.E.-late ninth century B.C.E.)
I Ching (transcribed eighth to third century B.C.E.)
Thales of Miletus (c. 624 B.C.E.-c. 548 B.C.E.)
Anaximander (c. 610 B.C.E.-c. 547 B.C.E.)
Dao De Jing (transcribed sixth to third century B.C.E.)
Pythagoras (c. 580 B.C.E.-c. 500 B.C.E.)
Confucius (551 B.C.E.-479 B.C.E.)
Heraclitus of Ephesus (c. 540 B.C.E.-c. 480 B.C.E.)
Parmenides (c. 515 B.C.E.-after 436 B.C.E.)
Anaxagoras (c. 500 B.C.E.-c. 428 B.C.E.)

599-300 B.C.E.

Leucippus (fifth century B.C.E.)
Mozi (fifth century B.C.E.)
The Doctrine of the Mean (transcribed fifth to fourth century B.C.E.)
Zeno of Elea (c. 490 B.C.E.-c. 440 B.C.E.)
Empedocles (c. 490 B.C.E.-c. 430 B.C.E.)
Democritus (c. 460 B.C.E.-c. 370 B.C.E.)
Hippocrates (c. 460 B.C.E.-c. 370 B.C.E.)
Plato (c. 427 B.C.E.-347 B.C.E.)
Aristotle (384 B.C.E.-322 B.C.E.)
Mencius (c. 372 B.C.E.-c. 289 B.C.E.)
Hui Shi (c. 370 B.C.E.-c. 310 B.C.E.)
Zhuangzi (c. 365 B.C.E.-c. 290 B.C.E.)
Pyrrhon of Elis (c. 360 B.C.E.-c. 272 B.C.E.)
Epicurus (341 B.C.E.-270 B.C.E.)
Euclid (335 B.C.E.-270 B.C.E.)
Gongsun Long (c. 320 B.C.E.-c. 250 B.C.E.)
Xunzi (c. 313 B.C.E.-after 238 B.C.E.)

299 B.C.E.-299 C.E.

Han Feizi (280 B.C.E.-233 B.C.E.)
Chrysippus (c. 279 B.C.E.-206 B.C.E.)
Bhagavad Gita (transcribed c. 200 B.C.E.-200 C.E.)
Dong Zhongshu (c. 170 B.C.E.-c. 104 B.C.E.)
Cicero (106 B.C.E.-43 B.C.E.)
Lucretius (c. 98 B.C.E.-October 15, 55 B.C.E.)
Philo Judaeus (c. 20 B.C.E.-c. 45 C.E.)
Lucius Annaeus Seneca (c. 4 B.C.E.-c. 65 C.E.)
Wang Chong (27 C.E.-c. 100 C.E.)
Epictetus (c. 55-c. 135)
The Great Learning (transcribed c. end of first century B.C.E.)
Marcus Aurelius (April 26, 121-March 17, 180)
Galen (129-c. 199)
Sextus Empiricus (c. 140-160 -c. 220-230)
Nāgārjuna (c. 150-c. 200)
Quintus Septimius Florens Tertullian (c. 160-c. 220)
Origen (c. 185-c. 254)
Plotinus (205-270)
Wang Bi (c. 226-c. 249)

300-1199

Guo Xiang (died 312)
Diogenes Laërtius (c. 300-c. 350)
Saint Augustine (November 13, 354-August 28, 430)
Hypatia (370-415)
Boethius (c. 480-524)
Pseudo-Dionysius (fl. c. 500 C.E.)
Xuan Zang (c. 602-664)
Huineng (638-713)

Han Yu (768-824)
Kūkai (774-835)
Samkara (788-820)
Kindi, Abu Yusuf Ya'qub ibn Ishaq al-
(c. 800-866)
Johannes Scotus Erigena (c. 810-c. 877)
Israeli, Isaac ben Solomon (c. 855-955)
al-Razi (c. 864-c. 925)
Muhammad ibn Tarkhan al-Farabi (870-950)
Saadia Gaon (882-942)
Avicenna (August or September, 980-1037)
Shao Yong (1011-1077)
Rāmānuja (c. 1017-1137)
Solomon ben Yehuda Ibn Gabirol (c. 1020-
c. 1058)
Zhang Zai (1020-1077)
Cheng Hao (1032-1089)
Cheng Yi (1033-1107)
Saint Anselm (c. 1033-April 21, 1109)
al-Ghazzālī (1058-1111)
Peter Abelard (1079-April 21, 1142)
Abu Bakr Ibn Bājja (c. 1090-1138)
Joseph ben Jacob Ibn-Zaddik (died 1149)
Hildegard von Bingen (1098-September 17,
1179)
Abū Bakr Ibn Tufayl (died 1185)
John of Salisbury (1115-1180)
Averroës (1126-1198)
Zhu Xi (1130-1200)
Moses Maimonides (March 30, 1135-
December 13, 1204)
Shihab Suhrawardi (1155-1191)
Puril Pojo Chinul (1158-1210)
Robert Grosseteste (c. 1160-1253)
Moses Nahmanides (1194-1270)
Madhva (1197-1276)

1200-1499
Dōgen (1200-1253)
Saint Albertus Magnus (c. 1200-1280)
Jalāl al-Dīn Rūmī (September 30,
1207-December 17, 1273)
Saint Bonaventure (1217 or 1221-July 15, 1274)
Roger Bacon (c. 1220-c. 1292)
Saint Thomas Aquinas (1224 or 1225-March 7,
1274)
Meister Eckhart (c.1260-1327 or 1328)
Dante Alighieri (1265-1321)

John Duns Scotus (c. March, 1266-November 8,
1308)
William of Ockham (c. 1285-1347 or 1349)
Gersonides (1288-1344)
Ibn Khaldun (1332-1406)
Nicholas of Cusa (1401-August 11, 1464)
Isaac ben Judah Abravanel (1437-1509)
Judah Abravanel (c. 1460/65-1500/25)
Giovanni Pico della Mirandola (1463-1494)
Desiderius Erasmus (October 28, 1466?-July 12,
1536)
Cajetan (Tommaso de Vio, 1468-1534)
Niccolò Machiavelli (May 3, 1469-June 21, 1527)
Wang Yangming (1472-1529)
Sir Thomas More (February 7, 1478-July 6, 1535)
Martin Luther (1483-1546)

1500-1599
John Calvin (1509-1564)
Saint Teresa of Ávila (1515-1582)
Michel Eyquem de Montaigne (February 28,
1533-September 13, 1592)
Isaac Luria (1534-1572)
Luis de Molina (1535-1600)
Saint John of the Cross (June 24, 1542-
December 14, 1591)
Tycho Brahe (1546-1601)
Giordano Bruno (1548-February 17, 1600)
Francisco Suárez (1548-1617)
Francisco Sanches (1551-1623)
Richard Hooker (1553-1600)
Jacobus Arminius (1560-1609)
Francis Bacon (January 22, 1561-April 9, 1626)
Galileo Galilei (1564-1642)
Johannes Kepler (1571-1630)
Mulla Sadra (1571-1640)
Jakob Böhme (1575-1624)
Hugo Grotius (1583-1645)
Hayashi Razan (1583-1657)
Thomas Hobbes (April 5, 1588-December 4,
1679)
Pierre Gassendi (1592-1655)
René Descartes (March 31, 1596-February 11,
1650)

1600-1699
Antoine Arnauld (1612-1694)
Henry More (1614-1687)
Kumazawa Banzan (1619-1691)

World Philosophers and Their Works

Wang Fuzhi (1619-1692)
Blaise Pascal (June 19, 1623-August 19, 1662)
Itō Jinsai (1627-1705)
Anne Conway (c. 1630-1679)
Samuel von Pufendorf (1632-1694)
John Locke (August 29, 1632-October 28, 1704)
Baruch Spinoza (November 24, 1632-
February 21, 1677)
Nicolas Malebranche (August 6, 1638-
October 13, 1715)
Isaac Newton (December 25, 1642-March 20,
1727)
Gottfried Wilhelm Leibniz (July 1, 1646-
November 14, 1716)
Pierre Bayle (November 18, 1647-December 28,
1706)
Giambattista Vico (June 23, 1668-January 23,
1744)
Bernard Mandeville (c. 1670-1733)
Third Earl of Shaftesbury (February 26, 1671-
February 15, 1713)
Samuel Clarke (1675-1729)
George Berkeley (March 12, 1685-January 14,
1753)
Emanuel Swedenborg (1688-1772)
Charles-Louis de Secondat Montesquieu
(1689-1755)
Joseph Butler (May 18, 1692-June 16, 1752)
Francis Hutcheson (1694-1747)
Voltaire (November 21, 1694-May 30, 1778)

1700-1799
Jonathan Edwards (October 5, 1703-March 22,
1758)
Benjamin Franklin (1706-1790)
Samuel Johnson (1709-1784)
Julien Offroy de La Mettrie (December 25,
1709-November 11, 1751)
Thomas Reid (April 26, 1710-October 7, 1796)
David Hume (May 7, 1711-August 25, 1776)
Jean-Jacques Rousseau (June 28, 1712-July 2,
1778)
Denis Diderot (October 5, 1713-July 31, 1784)
Étienne Bonnot de Condillac (1714-1780)
Claude-Adrien Helvétius (1715-1771)
Dai Zhen (1723-1777)
Adam Ferguson (1723-1816)
Adam Smith (June 5, 1723-July 17, 1790)
Immanuel Kant (April 22, 1724-February 12, 1804)

Gotthold Ephraim Lessing (1729-1781)
Moses Mendelssohn (1729-1786)
Edmund Burke (1729-1797)
Joseph Priestley (1733-1804)
Thomas Paine (1737-1809)
Marquis de Condorcet (1743-1794)
William Paley (1743-1805)
Thomas Jefferson (1743-1826)
Johann Gottfried Herder (1744-1803)
John Jay (December 12, 1745-May 17, 1829
Jeremy Bentham (February 15, 1748-June 6,
1832)
Pierre-Simon Laplace (1749-1827)
Johann Wolfgang von Goethe (1749-1832)
James Madison (March 16, 1751-June 28, 1736)
Salomon Maimon (c. 1752-1800)
Dugald Stewart (1753-1828)
Comte Joseph de Maistre (1754-1821)
Alexander Hamilton (January 11, 1755-July 12,
1804)
William Blake (1757-1827)
Friedrich Schiller (1759-1805)
Mary Wollstonecraft (April 27, 1759-
September 10, 1797)
Claude-Henri Saint-Simon (1760-1825)
Yagyong Chong (1762-1836)
Johann Gottlieb Fichte (May 19, 1762-
January 27, 1814)
Pierre François Maine de Biran (1766-1824)
Thomas Robert Malthus (February 13, 1766-
December 23, 1834)
Friedrich Schleiermacher (1768-1834)
Georg Wilhelm Friedrich Hegel (August 27,
1770-November 14, 1831)
David Ricardo (1772-1823)
Friedrich von Schlegel (1772-1829)
Samuel Taylor Coleridge (1772-1834)
Friedrich Wilhelm Joseph Schelling (1775-1854)
Arthur Schopenhauer (February 22, 1788-
September 21, 1860)
Sarah Grimké (1792-1873) and Angelina Grimké
(1805-1879)
Auguste Comte (January 19, 1798-September 5,
1857)

1800-1849
John Henry Newman (February 21, 1801-
August 11, 1890)
Harriet Martineau (1802-1876)

Ralph Waldo Emerson (May 25, 1803-April 27, 1882)

Ludwig Feuerbach (July 28, 1804-September 13, 1872)

John Stuart Mill (May 20, 1806-May 7, 1873)

Harriet Taylor Mill (1807-1858)

Pierre-Joseph Proudhon (1809-1865)

Charles Darwin (February 12, 1809-April 19, 1882)

Margaret Fuller (1810-1850)

Søren Kierkegaard (May 5, 1813-November 11, 1855)

Mikhail Bakunin (1814-1876)

George Boole (1815-1864)

Charles Renouvier (1815-1903)

Henry David Thoreau (1817-1862)

Rudolf Hermann Lotze (1817-1881)

Karl Marx (May 5, 1818-March 14, 1883)

George Eliot (Mary Ann Evans, 1819-1880)

Friedrich Engels (1820-1895)

Herbert Spencer (April 27, 1820-December 8, 1903)

Fyodor Dostoevski (1821-1881)

Thomas Henry Huxley (1825-1895)

Leo Tolstoy (September 9, 1828-November 20, 1910)

Nishi Amane (1829-1897)

Chauncey Wright (1830-1875)

James Clerk Maxwell (1831-1879)

Helena Petrovna Blavatsky (1831-1891)

Konstantin Leontyev (1831-1891)

Lewis Carroll (Charles Lutwidge Dodgson, 1832-1898)

Wilhelm Dilthey (November 19, 1833-September 30, 1911)

Thomas Hill Green (1836-1882)

Sri Ramakrishna (1836-1886)

Franz Clemens Brentano (1838-1917)

Charles Sanders Peirce (September 10, 1839-April 19, 1914)

Oliver Wendell, Jr. Holmes (1841-1935)

Hermann Cohen (1842-1918)

William James (January 11, 1842-August 26, 1910)

Friedrich Nietzsche (October 15, 1844-August 25, 1900)

Georg Cantor (1845-1918)

F. H. Bradley (January 30, 1846-September 18, 1924)

Borden Parker Bowne (1847-1910)

Bernard Bosanquet (1848-1923)

Vilfredo Pareto (1848-1923)

Gottlob Frege (November 8, 1848-July 26, 1925)

1850-1874

Alexius Meinong (1853-1931)

Ferdinand Tönnies (1855-1936)

Josiah Royce (November 20, 1855-September 14, 1916)

Lucien Lévy-Bruhl (1857-1939)

Ferdinand de Saussure (November 26, 1857-February 22, 1913)

Georg Simmel (1858-1918)

Max Planck (1858-1947)

Émile Durkheim (April 15, 1858-November 15, 1917)

Samuel Alexander (1859-1938)

Edmund Husserl (April 8, 1859-April 27, 1938)

Henri Bergson (October 18, 1859-January 4, 1941)

John Dewey (October 20, 1859-June 1, 1952)

Jane Addams (1860-1935)

Pierre Duhem (1861-1916)

Alfred North Whitehead (February 15, 1861-December 30, 1947)

Rabindranath Tagore (May 7, 1861-August 7, 1941)

Raimundo de Farias Brito (1862-1917)

David Hilbert (1862-1943)

Swami Vivekananda (January 12, 1863-July 4, 1902)

George Herbert Mead (February 27, 1863-April 26, 1931)

George Santayana (December 16, 1863-September 26, 1952)

Ferdinand Canning Scott Schiller (1864-1937)

Max Weber (April 21, 1864-June 14, 1920)

Miguel de Unamuno y Jugo (September 29, 1864-December 31, 1936)

Lev Shestov (1866-1938)

Benedetto Croce (February 25, 1866-November 20, 1952)

Frederick James Eugene Woodbridge (1867-1940)

Zhang Binglin (Chuang Ping-lin, 1868-1936)

W. E. B. Du Bois (February 23, 1868-August 27, 1963)

Rudolf Otto (1869-1937)

Emma Goldman (1869-1940)

Mohandas K. Gandhi (October 2, 1869-January 30, 1948)

Vladimir Ilich Lenin (1870-1924)

Kitarō Nishida (June 17, 1870-June 7, 1945)

D. T. Suzuki (October 18, 1870-July 12, 1966)

Rosa Luxemburg (1871-1919)

Harold Arthur Prichard (1871-1947)

Marcel Mauss (May 10, 1872-February 10, 1950)

Bertrand Russell (May 18, 1872-February 2, 1970)

Sri Aurobindo Ghose (August 15, 1872-December 5, 1950)

G. E. Moore (November 4, 1873-October 24, 1958)

Max Scheler (1874-1928)

Ernst Cassirer (1874-1945)

Nikolai Berdyaev (1874-1948)

1875-1899

Rainer Maria Rilke (1875-1926)

Giovanni Gentile (1875-1944)

Carl Jung (July 26, 1875-June 6, 1961)

Ralph Barton Perry (1876-1957)

José Ingenieros (1877-1925)

Muhammad Iqbal (1877-1938)

Hatano Seiichi (1877-1950)

William D. Ross (1877-1971)

Ananda Kentish Coomaraswamy (August 22, 1877-September 9, 1947)

Martin Buber (February 8, 1878-June 13, 1965)

Albert Einstein (1879-1955)

Oswald Spengler (1880-1936)

Pierre Teilhard de Chardin (1881-1955)

Hans Kelsen (1881-1973)

Mordecai Menahem Kaplan (1881-1983)

Moritz Schlick (1882-1936)

Virginia Woolf (1882-1941)

Nicolai Hartmann (1882-1950)

Ernst Mach (1883-1916)

Franz Kafka (1883-1924)

John Maynard Keynes (1883-1946)

Karl Jaspers (February 23, 1883-February 26, 1969)

C. I. Lewis (April 12, 1883-February 3, 1964)

José Ortega y Gasset (May 9, 1883-October 18, 1955)

Henry Nelson Wieman (1884-1975)

Étienne Gilson (1884-1978)

Gaston Bachelard (June 27, 1884-October 16, 1962)

Lizzie Susan Stebbing (1885-1943)

Niels Bohr (1885-1962)

Tanabe Hajime (1885-1962)

Xiong Shi-li (1885-1968)

Georg Lukács (1885-1971)

Ernst Bloch (1885-1977)

Karl Barth (1886-1968)

Paul Tillich (August 20, 1886-October 22, 1965)

Franz Rosenzweig (December 25, 1886-December 10, 1929)

Erwin Schrödinger (1887-1961)

C. D. Broad (1887-1971)

T. S. Eliot (1888-1965)

Sarvepalli Radhakrishnan (September 5, 1888-April 17, 1975)

Watsuji Tetsurō (1889-1960)

F. A. von Hayek (1889-1992)

R. G. Collingwood (February 22, 1889-January 9, 1943)

Ludwig Wittgenstein (April 26, 1889-April 29, 1951)

Martin Heidegger (September 26, 1889-May 26, 1976)

Gabriel Marcel (December 7, 1889-October 8, 1973)

Edith Stein (1891-1942)

Hans Reichenbach (1891-1953)

Francisco Romero (1891-1962)

Hu Shi (1891-1962)

Michael Polanyi (1891-1976)

Antonio Gramsci (January 23, 1891-April 27, 1937)

Rudolf Carnap (May 18, 1891-September 14, 1970)

Walter Benjamin (1892-1940)

Brand Blanshard (1892-1987)

Reinhold Niebuhr (June 21, 1892- June 1, 1971)

Karl Mannheim (1893-1947)

Roman Ingarden (1893-1970)

I. A. Richards (1893-1979)

Mao Zedong (December 26, 1893-September 9, 1976)

H. Richard Niebuhr (1894-1962)

Max Horkheimer (1895-1973)

Fung Yu-lan (1895-1990)

Jiddu Krishnamurti (May 12, 1895-February 17, 1986)

Lin Yutang (October 10, 1895-March 26, 1976)
Mikhail Bakhtin (November 16, 1895-March 7, 1975)
Jean Piaget (1896-1980)
Charles Hartshorne (born June 5, 1897)
Georges Bataille (September 10, 1897-July 8, 1962)
C. S. Lewis (1898-1963)
Oets Kolk Bouwsma (1898-1978)
Herbert Marcuse (1898-1979)
Alfred Schutz (April 13, 1899-May 20, 1959)
H. H. Price (May 17, 1899-November 26, 1984)
Leo Strauss (September 20, 1899-October 18, 1973)

1900-1924
Erich Fromm (1900-1980)
Hans-Georg Gadamer (born February 11, 1900)
Keiji Nishitani (February 27, 1900-November 24, 1990)
Gilbert Ryle (August 19, 1900-October 6, 1976)
Paul Weiss (born 1901)
Werner Heisenberg (1901-1976)
Charles Morris (1901-1979)
Ernest Nagel (1901-1985)
Jacques Lacan (April 13, 1901-September 9, 1981)
Michael Oakeshott (December 11, 1901-December 19, 1990)
Alexander Kojève (1902-1968)
Talcott Parsons (1902-1979)
Alfred Tarski (1902-1983)
Fernand Braudel (1902-1985)
Herbert Feigl (1902-1988)
Karl Raimund Popper (July 28, 1902-September 17, 1994)
Joseph Dov Soloveitchik (1903-1993)
Alonzo Church (1903-1995)
Hans Jonas (born May 10, 1903)
Theodor Adorno (September 11, 1903-August 6, 1969)
Bernard Lonergan (1904-1984)
Karl Rahner (1904-1984)
B. F. Skinner (1904-1990)
John Wisdom (September 12, 1904-December 9, 1993)
Patrick Devlin (1905-1992)
Carl G. Hempel (born 1905)
Ayn Rand (February 2, 1905-March 6, 1982)

Viktor Emil Frankl (March 26, 1905-September 2, 1997)
Jean-Paul Sartre (June 21, 1905-April 15, 1980)
Kurt Gödel (1906-1978)
Léopold Sédar Senghor (born 1906)
Emmanuel Lévinas (January 12, 1906-December 25, 1995)
Dietrich Bonhoeffer (February 4, 1906-April 9, 1945)
Nelson Goodman (born August 7, 1906)
Hannah Arendt (October 14, 1906-December 4, 1975)
Mircea Eliade (1907-1986)
Germaine Brée (born 1907)
Abraham Joshua Heschel (January 11, 1907-December 23, 1972)
H. L. A. Hart (July 18, 1907-December 19, 1992)
Maurice Blanchot (born September 22, 1907)
C. L. Stevenson (1908-1979)
William K. Frankena (1908-1994)
Claude Lévi-Strauss (born 1908)
Simone de Beauvoir (January 9, 1908-April 14, 1986)
Maurice Merleau-Ponty (March 14, 1908-May 4, 1961)
W. V. O. Quine (born June 25, 1908)
Simone Weil (1909-1943)
Isaiah Berlin (June 6, 1909-November 5, 1997)
Richard B. Brandt (born 1910)
Marjorie Grene (born 1910)
A. J. Ayer (October 29, 1910-June 27, 1989)
Norman Malcolm (1911-1990)
J. L. Austin (March 26, 1911-February 8, 1960)
Jean Améry (1912-1978)
Arne Naess (born January 27, 1912)
Wilfrid S. Sellars (May 20, 1912- July 2, 1989)
Alan Gewirth (born November 28, 1912)
Charlotte Delbo (1913-1985)
Paul Ricœur (born 1913)
Takeuchi Yoshinori (born 1913)
Aimé Césaire (born June 25, 1913)
Albert Camus (November 7, 1913-January 4, 1960)
Arthur Prior (1914-1969)
Stuart N. Hampshire (born 1914)
John Passmore (born 1914)
Masao Abe (born February 9, 1915)
Roland Barthes (November 12, 1915-March 26, 1980

Roderick M. Chisholm (born 1916)
Emil L. Fackenheim (born June 22, 1916)
Donald Davidson (born March 6, 1917)
Louis Althusser (October 16, 1918-October 22, 1990)
Primo Levi (1919-1987)
Leon Festinger (1919-1989)
R. M. Hare (born 1919)
G. E. M. Anscombe (born 1919)
Iris Murdoch (July 15, 1919-February 8, 1999)
Mary Midgley (born September 13, 1919)
Peter Strawson (born November 23, 1919)
Philippa Foot (born 1920)
William P. Alston (born 1921)
Kenneth Arrow (born 1921)
Betty Friedan (born 1921)
Ruth Barcan Marcus (born 1921)
John E. Smith (born 1921)
John Rawls (born February 21, 1921)
Paulo Freire (September 19, 1921-May 2, 1997)
Imre Lakatos (1922-1974)
Philip Hallie (1922-1994)
John Hick (born 1922)
Stephen Toulmin (born March 25, 1922)
Thomas S. Kuhn (July 18, 1922-June 17, 1996)
Anthony Flew (born 1923)
Mary Mothersill (born 1923)
Israel Scheffler (born 1923)
Paul Feyerabend (1924-1994)
Arthur Danto (born 1924)
Mary Hesse (born 1924)
Frederick Sontag (born 1924)
Mary Warnock (born 1924)
Richard L. Rubenstein (born January 8, 1924)
Jean-François Lyotard (August 10, 1924-April 21, 1998)

1925-1954
Malcolm X (Malcolm Little, 1925-1965)
Zygmunt Bauman (born 1925)
John B. Cobb, Jr. (born 1925)
Gilles Deleuze (January 18, 1925-November 4, 1995)
Michael Dummett (born June 27, 1925)
Frantz Fanon (July 20, 1925-December 6, 1961)
David M. Armstrong (born 1926)
Hilary Putnam (born July 31, 1926)
Stanley Cavell (born September 1, 1926)
Michel Foucault (October 15, 1926-June 25, 1984)

Lawrence Kohlberg (1927-1987)
Leszek Kolakowski (born 1927)
Noam Chomsky (born 1928)
Mary Daly (born 1928)
Hans Kung (born 1928)
Nicholas Rescher (born July 15, 1928)
Elie Wiesel (born September 30, 1928)
Jean Baudrillard (born 1929)
Robert Coles (born 1929)
Hubert Dreyfus (born 1929)
Virginia Held (born 1929)
Nel Noddings (born 1929)
Adrienne Rich (born 1929)
Dorothee Soelle (born 1929)
Judith Jarvis Thomson (born 1929)
Bernard Williams (born 1929)
Alasdair MacIntyre (born January 12, 1929)
Martin Luther King, Jr. (January 15, 1929-April 4, 1968)
Jürgen Habermas (born June 18, 1929)
Annette C. Baier (born October 11, 1929)
Luce Irigaray (born 1930)
Jacques Derrida (born July 15, 1930)
Pierre Bourdieu (born August 1, 1930)
Keith Donnellan (born 1931)
Charles Taylor (born 1931)
Richard Rorty (born October 4, 1931)
John S. Mbiti (born November 30, 1931)
Ronald Dworkin (born December 11, 1931)
Richard J. Bernstein (born 1932)
Fred Dretske (born 1932)
Umberto Eco (born 1932)
John R. Searle (born July 31, 1932)
Alvin Plantinga (born November 15, 1932)
David Kaplan (born 1933)
Berel Lang (born 1933)
Ruth Millikan (born 1933)
Audre Lorde (1934-1992)
Sarah Kofman (1934-1994)
Sissela Bok (born 1934)
Don Cupitt (born 1934)
Jaegwon Kim (born 1934)
D. Z. Phillips (born 1934)
Richard Swinburne (born 1934)
Tenzin Gyatso (Fourteenth Dalai Lama, born 1935)
Sandra Harding (born 1935)
Sara Ruddick (born 1935)
Barry Stroud (born 1935)

Michael Walzer (born 1935)
Jerry A. Fodor (born April 22, 1935)
Carol Gilligan (born 1936)
Keith Lehrer (born 1936)
Robert M. Adams (born 1937)
Hélène Cixous (born 1937)
Thomas Nagel (born July 4, 1937)
Gilbert Harman (born 1938)
Brian Skyrms (born 1938)
Robert Nozick (born November 16, 1938)
Robert Neville (born 1939)
Tzvetan Todorov (born March 1, 1939)
Jon Elster (born 1940)
Jean-Luc Nancy (born 1940)
Carole Pateman (born 1940)
Ernest Sosa (born 1940)
Saul Kripke (born November 13, 1940)
Jean Bethke Elshtain (born 1941)
David K. Lewis (born 1941)
V. Y. Mudimbe (born 1941)
Onora O'Neal (born 1941)
Julia Kristeva (born June 24, 1941)

Ned Block (born 1942)
Paul M. Churchland (born 1942)
Paulin J. Hountondji (born 1942
Derek Parfit (born 1942)
Daniel C. Dennett (born March 28, 1942)
Alison M. Jagger (born September 23, 1942)
Marilyn M. Adams (born 1943)
Patricia Smith Churchland (born July 16, 1943)
Angela Davis (born 1944)
William G. Lycan (born 1945)
Tyler Burge (born 1946)
Andrea Dworkin (born 1946)
Catharine A. MacKinnon (born 1946)
Gillian Rose (1947-1998)
Susan Bordo (born 1947)
Martha Craven Nussbaum (born May 6, 1947)
Penelope Maddy (born 1950)
bell hooks (Gloria Watkins, born 1952)
Tsenay Serequeberhan (born May 18, 1952)
Susan Griffin (born 1953)
Kwame Anthony Appiah (born May 8, 1954)
Judith Butler (born 1956)

More World Philosophers

The following 341 philosophers, in addition to those covered in these volumes, are among those most likely to be encountered by those beginning a study of world philosophy. They are listed in alphabetical order, followed by their years of birth and death and the areas of philosophical inquiry for which they are known.

—J.K.R.

Abravanel, Isaac ben Judah (1437-1509): Jewish philosophy, metaphysics, political philosophy

Abravanel, Judah (c. 1460/65-1500/25): Jewish philosophy, metaphysics, philosophy of love

Adams, Marilyn M. (born 1943): Metaphysics, philosophy of religion, philosophical theology

Adams, Robert M. (born 1937): Metaphysics, philosophy of religion, philosophical theology

Addams, Jane (1860-1935): Ethics, social philosophy

Albertus Magnus, Saint (c. 1200-1280): Ethics, logic, metaphysics, philosophical theology

Alexander, Samuel (1859-1938): Metaphysics

Alston, William P. (born 1921): Epistemology, philosophy of religion

Améry, Jean (1912-1978): Ethics, Jewish philosophy, philosophy of history

Anscombe, G. E. M. (born 1919): Ethics, epistemology, philosophy of language

Arminius, Jacobus (1560-1609): Metaphysics, philosophical theology

Armstrong, David M. (born 1926): Epistemology, philosophy of mind

Arnauld, Antoine (1612-1694): Epistemology, metaphysics

Arrow, Kenneth (born 1921): Arrow's paradox, decision theory, epistemology, logic

Bacon, Roger (c. 1220-c. 1292): Epistemology, philosophy of science

Bakunin, Mikhail (1814-1876): Anarchism, ethics, political philosophy

Barth, Karl (1886-1968): Epistemology, philosophy of religion, philosophical theology

Baudrillard, Jean (born 1929): Epistemology, ethics, social philosophy

Bauman, Zygmunt (1925): Ethics, social philosophy

Benjamin, Walter (1892-1940): Aesthetics, ethics, Jewish philosophy, social philosophy

Berdyaev, Nikolai (1874-1948): Philosophy of religion, metaphysics

Bernstein, Richard J. (born 1932): Epistemology, pragmatism, social philosophy

Blake, William (1757-1827): Aesthetics, metaphysics, philosophy of religion

Blanshard, Brand (1892-1987): Epistemology, idealist metaphysics, value theory

Blavatsky, Helena Petrovna (1831-1891): Metaphysics, philosophical theology, theosophy

Bloch, Ernst (1885-1977): Ethics, philosophy of religion, social philosophy

Block, Ned (born 1942): Epistemology, philosophy of mind

Böhme, Jakob (1575-1624): Metaphysics, philosophical theology

Bohr, Niels (1885-1962): Epistemology, philosophy of science, quantum mechanics

Bok, Sissela (born 1934): Ethics, social philosophy

Boole, George (1815-1864): Boolean algebra, epistemology, logic, philosophy of mathematics

Bordo, Susan (born 1947): Ethics, feminist philosophy, social philosophy

Bosanquet, Bernard (1848-1923): Logic, idealist metaphysics, social philosophy

Bouwsma, Oets Kolk (1898-1978): Epistemology, philosophy of language

Bowne, Borden Parker (1847-1910): Metaphysics, personalism, philosophy of religion

Brahe, Tycho (1546-1601): Epistemology, philosophy of science, scientific method

Brandt, Richard B. (born 1910): Epistemology, ethics

Braudel, Fernand (1902-1985): Ethics, philosophy of history

Brée, Germaine (born 1907): Ethics, existentialism

Brentano, Franz Clemens (1838-1917): Ethics, philosophical psychology, philosophy of mind

Broad, C. D. (1887-1971): Epistemology, philosophy of science

Burge, Tyler (born 1946): Epistemology, philosophy of mind

Burke, Edmund (1729-1797): Ethics, political philosophy, social philosophy

Butler, Judith (born 1956): Ethics, feminist philosophy, social philosophy

Cajetan (Tommaso de Vio, 1468-1534): Logic, metaphysics, philosophical theology

Calvin, John (1509-1564): Ethics, philosophical theology

Cantor, Georg (1845-1918): Epistemology, logic, philosophy of mathematics, set theory

Carneades (c. 213 B.C.E.-c. 128 B.C.E.): Epistemology, ethics, skepticism, philosophical theology

Carroll, Lewis (Charles Lutwidge Dodgson, 1832-1898): Author of *Alice in Wonderland*, epistemology, logic, philosophy of mathematics

Cassirer, Ernst (1874-1945): Aesthetics, epistemology, social philosophy

Cheng Hao (1032-1089): Chinese philosophy, Confucian ethics and social philosophy

Cheng Yi (1033-1107): Chinese philosophy, Confucian ethics and social philosophy

Chinul, Puril Pojo (1158-1210): Buddhist metaphysics, Chinese philosophy, philosophy of religion

Chisholm, Roderick M. (born 1916): Epistemology, philosophy of mind, skepticism

Chomsky, Noam (born 1928): Epistemology, philosophy of language

Chong, Yagyong (1762-1836): Confucian ethics, Korean philosophy, political philosophy

Chrysippus (c. 279 B.C.E.-206 B.C.E.): Epistemology, ethics, Stoicism

Church, Alonzo (1903-1995): Epistemology, logic, philosophy of language, philosophy of mathematics

Cicero (106 B.C.E.-43 B.C.E.): Ethics, logic, rhetoric, social philosophy

Cixous, Hélène (born 1937): Feminist philosophy, metaphysics, philosophy of language, social philosophy

Clarke, Samuel (1675-1729): Ethics, philosophical theology

Cobb, John B., Jr. (1925): Ethics, metaphysics, philosophical theology, philosophy of religion

Cohen, Hermann (1842-1918): Epistemology, Jewish philosophy, philosophy of religion

Coleridge, Samuel Taylor (1772-1834): Aesthetics, ethics, literary theory, philosophy of religion

Coles, Robert (born 1929): Ethics, philosophy of education, social philosophy

Condillac, Étienne Bonnot de (1714-1780): Epistemology, logic, theories about sense perception

Condorcet, Marquis de (1743-1794): Epistemology, philosophy of mathematics, social philosophy, theories about progress

Conway, Anne (c. 1630-1679): Metaphysics, philosophical theology

Cupitt, Don (born 1934): Metaphysics, philosophy of religion, philosophical theology

Dai Zhen (1723-1777): Chinese philosophy, Confucian ethics, history of philosophy

Daly, Mary (born 1928): Ethics, feminist philosophy, philosophy of religion, philosophical theology

Dante Alighieri (1265-1321): Author of the *Divine Comedy*, aesthetics, ethics, philosophy of religion

Danto, Arthur (born 1924): Aesthetics, epistemology, ethics

Davis, Angela (born 1944): Ethics, feminist philosophy, social philosophy

Delbo, Charlotte (1913-1985): Epistemology, ethics, philosophy of history

Devlin, Patrick (1905-1992): Ethics, philosophy of law

Diogenes Laërtius (c. 300-c. 350): History of philosophy, metaphysics

Dōgen (1200-1253): Epistemology, Japanese philosophy, Zen Buddhism

Dong Zhongshu (c. 170 B.C.E.-c. 104 B.C.E.): Chinese philosophy, Confucian ethics and social philosophy

Donnellan, Keith (born 1931): Epistemology, philosophy of language

Dostoevski, Fyodor (1821-1881): Aesthetics, ethics, philosophy of literature, philosophy of religion

Dretske, Fred (born 1932): Epistemology, philosophy of mind

Dreyfus, Hubert (born 1929): Epistemology, philosophy of mind

Duhem, Pierre (1861-1916): Epistemology, philosophy of science

Dworkin, Andrea (born 1946): Ethics, feminist philosophy, social philosophy

Eco, Umberto (born 1932): Ethics, philosophy of history, social philosophy

Einstein, Albert (1879-1955): Epistemology, metaphysics, relativity and quantum theory

Eliade, Mircea (1907-1986): Epistemology, philosophy of religion

Eliot, George (Mary Ann Evans, 1819-1880): Aesthetics, ethics, novelist, philosophy of religion

Eliot, T. S. (1888-1965): Aesthetics, literary criticism, metaphysics, philosophy of religion, social philosophy

Elshtain, Jean Bethke (born 1941): Ethics, political philosophy, social philosophy

Elster, Jon (born 1940): Epistemology, philosophy of mind, social philosophy

Engels, Friedrich (1820-1895): Communist theory, ethics, philosophy of economics, political philosophy, social philosophy

Euclid (335 B.C.E.-270 B.C.E.): Logic, philosophy of mathematics

Farabi, Muhammad ibn Tarkhan al- (870-950): Epistemology, Islamic philosophy, metaphysics, political philosophy

Farias Brito, Raimundo de (1862-1917): Latin American philosophy, metaphysics, philoophical psychology, philosophy of religion

Feigl, Herbert (1902-1988): Epistemology, logical positivism, philosophy of mind, philosophy of science

Ferguson, Adam (1723-1816): Ethics, philosophy of history, social philosophy

Festinger, Leon (1919-1989): Cognitive dissonance, epistemology, ethics, social philosophy

Feyerabend, Paul (1924-1994): Epistemology, philosophy of science

Flew, Anthony (born 1923): Epistemology, philosophy of language, philosophy of religion

Foot, Philippa (born 1920): Epistemology, ethics, logic, philosophy of language

Frankena, William K. (1908-1994): Ethics, philosophy of language

Franklin, Benjamin (1706-1790): Ethics, social philosophy

Friedan, Betty (born 1921): Ethics, feminist philosophy, social philosophy

Fromm, Erich (1900-1980): Ethics, philosophical psychology, social philosophy

Fuller, Margaret (1810-1850): Ethics, feminist philosophy, political philosophy

Fung Yu-lan (1895-1990): Chinese philosophy, ethics, metaphysics, philosophy of history

Galen (129-c. 199): Ethics, philosophy of education, philosophy of science

Galileo Galilei (1564-1642): Epistemology, philosophy of science, scientific method

Gassendi, Pierre (1592-1655): Epistemology, philosophy of science, skepticism

Gentile, Giovanni (1875-1944): Idealist metaphysics, philosophy of education, social philosophy

Gersonides (1288-1344): Jewish philosophy, metaphysics, philosophical theology

Ghazzālī, al- (1058-1111): Islamic philosophy, metaphysics, mysticism, philosophical theology

Gilligan, Carol (born 1936): Ethics, feminist philosophy, philosophy of education, social philosophy

Gilson, Étienne (1884-1978): History of philosophy, metaphysics, philosophy of religion

Gödel, Kurt (1906-1978): Epistemology, Gödel's theorem, logic, philosophy of mathematics

Goethe, Johann Wolfgang von (1749-1832): Aesthetics, metaphysics, natural philosophy, philosophy of religion

Goldman, Emma (1869-1940): Ethics, political philosophy, social philosophy

Green, Thomas Hill (1836-1882): Ethics, idealist metaphysics, social philosophy

Grene, Marjorie (born 1910): Ethics, existentialism

Griffin, Susan (born 1953): Ethics, feminist philosophy, social philosophy

Grimké, Sarah (1792-1873): and **Angelina Grimké** (1805-1879): Ethics, feminist philosophy, social philosophy

Grosseteste, Robert (c. 1160-1253): Metaphysics, philosophy of science, scientific method

Grotius, Hugo (1583-1645): Ethics, international law, philosophy of law, social philosophy

Guo Xiang (died 312): Chinese philosophy, Daoist ethics and metaphysics

Gyatso, Tenzin (Fourteenth Dalai Lama, born 1935): Buddhist ethics and metaphysics, Tibetan philosophy

Ha-Levi, Judah (c. 1075-1141): Jewish philosophy, metaphysics, philosophical theology, philosophy of religion

Hallie, Philip (1922-1994): Ethics, social philosophy

Hampshire, Stuart N. (born 1914): Epistemology, philosophy of mind

Han Yu (768-824): Chinese philosophy, Confucian epistemology and metaphysics

Harding, Sandra (born 1935): Ethics, feminist philosophy, social philosophy

Hare, R. M. (born 1919): Ethics, political philosophy

Harman, Gilbert (born 1938): Ethics, epistemology

Hartmann, Nicolai (1882-1950): Ethics, metaphysics

Hatano Seiichi (1877-1950): Japanese philosophy, metaphysics, philosophy of religion

Hayashi Razan (1583-1657): Confucian ethics, Japanese philosophy

Hayek, F. A. von (1889-1992): Epistemology, philosophy of economics, social philosophy

Heisenberg, Werner (1901-1976): Epistemology, philosophy of science, quantum mechanics

Held, Virginia (born 1929): Ethics, feminist philosophy, social philosophy

Helvétius, Claude-Adrien (1715-1771): Epistemology, philosophical psychology, social philosophy

Hempel, Carl G. (born 1905): Epistemology, logical positivism, philosophy of science

Herder, Johann Gottfried (1744-1803): Aesthetics, ethics, philosophy of history, social philosophy

Hesse, Mary (born 1924): Epistemology, philosophy of science

Hick, John (born 1922): Epistemology, metaphysics, philosophy of religion

Hilbert, David (1862-1943): Epistemology, logic, philosophy of mathematics

Holmes, Oliver Wendell, Jr. (1841-1935): Epistemology, philosophy of law, pragmatism

Homer (early ninth century B.C.E.-late ninth century B.C.E.): Ethics, metaphysics, philosophy of religion, traditional author of the *Iliad* and the *Odyssey*

Hooker, Richard (1553-1600): Ethics, natural law theory, political philosophy

hooks, bell (Gloria Watkins, born 1952): Ethics, feminist philosophy, social philosophy

Horkheimer, Max (1895-1973): Critical theory, epistemology, ethics

Hu Shi (1891-1962): Chinese philosophy, epistemology, pragmatism

Hui Shi (c. 370 B.C.E.-c. 310 B.C.E.): Chinese philosophy, epistemology, logic

Hutcheson, Francis (1694-1747): Ethics, philosophy of religion

Huxley, Thomas Henry (1825-1895): Agnosticism, epistemology, philosophy of biology, philosophy of science

Hypatia (370-415): Metaphysics

Ibn Bājja, Abu Bakr (c. 1090-1138): Ethics, Islamic philosophy, metaphysics

Ibn Gabirol, Solomon ben Yehuda (c. 1020-c. 1058): Ethics, Jewish philosophy, metaphysics

Ibn Khaldun (1332-1406): Ethics, Islamic philosophy, philosophy of history, social philosophy

Ibn Tufayl, Abū Bakr (died 1185): Islamic philosophy, metaphysics, philosophy of religion

Ibn-Zaddik, Joseph ben Jacob (died 1149): Jewish philosophy, metaphysics, philosophical theology

Ingarden, Roman (1893-1970): Aesthetics, epistemology, phenomenology

Ingenieros, José (1877-1925): Ethics, Latin American philosophy, metaphysics

Iqbal, Muhammad (1877-1938): Aesthetics, Islamic philosophy, metaphysics

Israeli, Isaac ben Solomon (c. 855-955): Jewish philosophy, metaphysics, philosophical theology

Itō Jinsai (1627-1705): Japanese philosophy, Confucian ethics, metaphysics

Jefferson, Thomas (1743-1826): Ethics, political philosophy, social philosophy

John of Salisbury (1115-1180): Epistemology, logic, social philosophy

Johnson, Samuel (1709-1784): Ethics, philosophy of religion

Kafka, Franz (1883-1924): Ethics, existentialism, social philosophy

Kaplan, David (born 1933): Epistemology, logic

Kaplan, Mordecai Menahem (1881-1983): Ethics, founder of Reconstruction in Judaism, Jewish philosophy, philosophy of religion

Kelsen, Hans (1881-1973): Epistemology, legal positivism, philosophy of law, social philosophy

Kepler, Johannes (1571-1630): Founder of modern astronomy, metaphysics, philosophy of science, scientific method

Keynes, John Maynard (1883-1946): Epistemology, philosophy of economics, philosophy of probability, social philosophy

Kim, Jaegwon (born 1934): Epistemology, philosophy of mind

Kindi, Abu Yusuf Ya'qub ibn Ishaq al- (c. 800-866): Ethics, Islamic philosophy, metaphysics

Kofman, Sarah (1934-1994): Ethics, feminist philosophy, philosophical psychology

Kohlberg, Lawrence (1927-1987): Ethics, philosophy of education, social philosophy

Kojève, Alexander (1902-1968): Metaphysics, philosophy of history, social philosophy

Kolakowski, Leszek (born 1927): Epistemology, metaphysics, philosophy of religion

Kūkai (774-835): Buddhist metaphysics and ethics, Japanese philosophy

Kumazawa Banzan (1619-1691): Confucian ethics and social philosophy, Japanese philosophy

Kung, Hans (born 1928): Metaphysics, philosophy of religion, philosophical theology

Lakatos, Imre (1922-1974): Epistemology, logic, philosophy of mathematics

Lang, Berel (born 1933): Aesthetics, ethics, philosophy of history

Laplace, Pierre-Simon (1749-1827): Astronomer, epistemology, mathematician, philosophy of science

Lehrer, Keith (born 1936): Epistemology, freedom and determinism, philosophy of mind

Lenin, Vladimir Ilich (1870-1924): Communist theory, metaphysics, political philosophy, social philosophy

Leontyev, Konstantin (1831-1891): Aesthetics, metaphysics, philosophy of history

Lessing, Gotthold Ephraim (1729-1781): Aesthetics, philosophy of history, metaphysics

Leucippus (fifth century B.C.E.): Epistemology, metaphysics

Levi, Primo (1919-1987): Ethics, Jewish philosophy, philosophy of history

Lévi-Strauss, Claude (born 1908): Ethics, social philosophy, structuralism

Lévy-Bruhl, Lucien (1857-1939): Ethics, social philosophy

Lewis, C. S. (1898-1963): Aesthetics, metaphysics, philosophy of literature, philosophy of religion

Lewis, David K. (born 1941): Epistemology, logic, philosophy of mind, possible worlds

Lonergan, Bernard (1904-1984): Epistemology, metaphysics, philosophical theology

Lorde, Audre (1934-1992): Ethics, feminist philosophy, social philosophy

Lotze, Rudolf Hermann (1817-1881): Idealist metaphysics, philosophy of religion

Lukács, Georg (1885-1971): Aesthetics, metaphysics, political philosophy

Luria, Isaac (1534-1572): Jewish philosophy, metaphysics, mysticism

Luther, Martin (1483-1546): Ethics, philosophical theology, social philosophy

Luxemburg, Rosa (1871-1919): Ethics, Marxist philosophy, philosophy of economics

Lycan, William G. (born 1945): Epistemology, philosophy of mind

Mach, Ernst (1883-1916): Epistemology, philosophy of science

MacKinnon, Catharine A. (born 1946): Ethics, feminist philosophy, political philosophy

Maddy, Penelope (born 1950): Epistemology, logic, philosophy of mathematics

Madhva (1197-1276): Indian philosophy, metaphysics, Hindu theology

Maimon, Salomon (c. 1752-1800): Epistemology, Jewish philosophy

Maine de Biran, Pierre François (1766-1824): Epistemology, philosophical psychology

Maistre, Comte Joseph de (1754-1821): Philosophy of religion, political philosophy

Malcolm, Norman (1911-1990): Epistemology, philosophy of language

Malcolm X (Malcolm Little, 1925-1965): Ethics, Islamic philosophy, philosophy of religion, social philosophy

Mandeville, Bernard (c. 1670-1733): Ethics, social philosophy

Mannheim, Karl (1893-1947): Ethics, social philosophy, theories about ideology

Marcus, Ruth Barcan (born 1921): Epistemology, logic

Marcuse, Herbert (1898-1979): Ethics, political philosophy

Martineau, Harriet (1802-1876): Ethics, social philosophy

Maxwell, James Clerk (1831-1879): Epistemology, philosophy of science

Meinong, Alexius (1853-1931): Metaphysics, philosophical psychology

Mendelssohn, Moses (1729-1786): Aesthetics, Jewish philosophy, metaphysics, philosophy of religion

Mill, Harriet Taylor (1807-1858): Ethics, feminist philosophy

Millikan, Ruth (born 1933): Epistemology, philosophy of language, philosophy of mind

Molina, Luis de (1535-1600): Freedom and determinism, metaphysics, philosophical theology

Montesquieu, Charles-Louis de Secondat (1689-1755): Ethics, philosophy of law, social philosophy

More, Henry (1614-1687): Metaphysics, philosophy of religion

Morris, Charles (1901-1979): Epistemology, logic, theory of signs

Mothersill, Mary (born 1923): Aesthetics, ethics, philosophy of language

Mudimbe, V. Y. (born 1941): African philosophy, epistemology, social philosophy

Mulla Sadra (1571-1640): Islamic philosophy, metaphysics

Nāgārjuna (c. 150-c. 200): Buddhist metaphysics, Indian philosophy

Nagel, Ernest (1901-1985): Epistemology, philosophy of science

Nahmanides, Moses (1194-1270): Jewish philosophy, metaphysics

Nancy, Jean-Luc (born 1940): Metaphysics

Neville, Robert (born 1939): Metaphysics, philosophy of religion

Niebuhr, H. Richard (1894-1962): Ethics, philosophical theology, social philosophy

Nishi Amane (1829-1897): Ethics, history of philosophy, Japanese philosophy, logic

Noddings, Nel (born 1929): Ethics, feminist philosophy, philosophy of education

O'Neal, Onora (born 1941): Ethics, political philosophy

Otto, Rudolf (1869-1937): Metaphysics, philosophy of religion

Paine, Thomas (1737-1809): Ethics, political philosophy

Paley, William (1743-1805): Ethics, philosophical theology

Pareto, Vilfredo (1848-1923): Ethics, Pareto efficiency, social philosophy

Parfit, Derek (born 1942): Ethics, philosophy of language, philosophy of mind

Parsons, Talcott (1902-1979): Ethics, social philosophy

Passmore, John (born 1914): Ethics, history of philosophy, philosophy of education

Pateman, Carole (born 1940): Ethics, feminist philosophy, political philosophy

Perry, Ralph Barton (1876-1957): Ethics, pragmatism, social philosophy

Phillips, D. Z. (born 1934): Ethics, philosophy of language, philosophy of religion

Philo Judaeus (c. 20 B.C.E.-c. 45 C.E.): Jewish philosophy, philosophical theology

Piaget, Jean (1896-1980): Epistemology, philosophy of education

Pico della Mirandola, Giovanni (1463-1494): Ethics, humanism, social philosophy

Planck, Max (1858-1947): Epistemology, philosophy of science

Polanyi, Michael (1891-1976): Epistemology, metaphysics

Prichard, Harold Arthur (1871-1947): Ethics, epistemology

Priestley, Joseph (1733-1804): Metaphysics, philosophy of science

Prior, Arthur (1914-1969): Epistemology, logic

Proudhon, Pierre-Joseph (1809-1865): Ethics, social philosophy

Pseudo-Dionysius (fl. c. 500 C.E.): Metaphysics, philosophical theology

Pufendorf, Samuel von (1632-1694): Ethics, international law, philosophy of law

Pyrrhon of Elis (c. 360 B.C.E.-c. 272 B.C.E.): Epistemology, skepticism

Rahner, Karl (1904-1984): Metaphysics, philosophy of religion

Ramakrishna, Sri (1836-1886): Hindu metaphysics, Indian philosophy

Rāmānuja (c. 1017-1137): Hindu metaphysics, Indian philosophy

Razi, al- (c. 864-c. 925): Ethics, Islamic philosophy, metaphysics

Reichenbach, Hans (1891-1953): Epistemology, philosophy of science, probability theory

Renouvier, Charles (1815-1903): Epistemology, ethics

Ricardo, David (1772-1823): Ethics, philosophy of economics

Rich, Adrienne (born 1929): Aesthetics, ethics, feminist philosophy, social philosophy

Richards, I. A. (1893-1979): Aesthetics, epistemology, literary theory

Ricœur, Paul (born 1913): Epistemology, hermeneutics, philosophy of religion

Rilke, Rainer Maria (1875-1926): Aesthetics, ethics

Romero, Francisco (1891-1962): Latin American philosophy, metaphysics

Rose, Gillian (1947-1998): Ethics, Jewish philosophy, political philosophy

Ross, William D. (1877-1971): Ethics

Ruddick, Sara (born 1935): Ethics, feminist philosophy, political philosophy

Saadia Gaon (882-942): Epistemology, Jewish philosophy, philosophical theology

Saint-Simon, Claude-Henri (1760-1825): Ethics, philosophy of history, social philosophy

Sanches, Francisco (1551-1623): Epistemology, skepticism

Scheffler, Israel (born 1923): Epistemology, philosophy of education, philosophy of science

Scheler, Max (1874-1928): Epistemology, phenomenology, social philosophy

Schelling, Friedrich Wilhelm Joseph (1775-1854): Aesthetics, metaphysics

Schiller, Ferdinand Canning Scott (1864-1937): Epistemology, pragmatism

Schiller, Friedrich (1759-1805): Aesthetics, epistemology

Schlegel, Friedrich von (1772-1829): Ethics, philosophy of history

Schleiermacher, Friedrich (1768-1834): Epistemology, philosophical theology, philosophy of religion

Schlick, Moritz (1882-1936): Epistemology, ethics, philosophy of language

Schrödinger, Erwin (1887-1961): Epistemology, philosophy of science

Seneca, Lucius Annaeus (c. 4 B.C.E.-c. 65 C.E.): Ethics, Stoicism

Senghor, Léopold Sédar (born 1906): African philosophy, ethics, political philosophy

Shao Yong (1011-1077): Chinese philosophy, Confucian metaphysics, philosophy of history

Shestov, Lev (1866-1938): Epistemology, philosophy of religion

Simmel, Georg (1858-1918): Ethics, phenomenology, social philosophy

Skinner, B. F. (1904-1990): Behaviorism, ethics, philosophical psychology, philosophy of science

Skyrms, Brian (born 1938): Decision theory, epistemology, philosophy of mind

Smith, John E. (born 1921): Metaphysics, philosophy of religion, pragmatism

Soelle, Dorothee (born 1929): Ethics, philosophical theology, philosophy of religion

Soloveitchik, Joseph Dov (1903-1993): Epistemology, Jewish philosophy, philosophy of religion

Sontag, Frederick (born 1924): Existentialism, metaphysics, philosophy of religion

Sosa, Ernest (born 1940): Epistemology, metaphysics, philosophy of mind

Spengler, Oswald (1880-1936): Ethics, philosophy of history

Stebbing, Lizzie Susan (1885-1943): Epistemology, logic, philosophy of science

Stein, Edith (1891-1942): Epistemology, phenomenology, philosophy of religion

Stevenson, C. L. (1908-1979): Emotivism, epistemology, ethics

Stewart, Dugald (1753-1828): Epistemology, philosophy of language, philosophy of religion

Stroud, Barry (born 1935): epistemology, philosophy of language

Suárez, Francisco (1548-1617): Metaphysics, philosophical theology, philosophy of law

Suhrawardi, Shihab (1155-1191): Epistemology, Islamic philosophy, metaphysics

Swedenborg, Emanuel (1688-1772): Metaphysics, philosophical theology, theosophy

Swinburne, Richard (born 1934): Epistemology, philosophy of religion, philosophy of science

Takeuchi Yoshinori (born 1913): Buddhist ethics and metaphysics, Japanese philosophy

Tanabe Hajime (1885-1962): Epistemology, Japanese philosophy, logic, philosophy of science

Tarski, Alfred (1902-1983): Epistemology, logic, philosophy of mathematics

Taylor, Charles (born 1931): Ethics, political philosophy

Teilhard de Chardin, Pierre (1881-1955): Cosmic evolution, metaphysics, philosophical theology

Teresa of Ávila, Saint (1515-1582): Metaphysics, mysticism, philosophical theology

Tertullian, Quintus Septimius Florens (c. 160-c. 220): Metaphysics, philosophical theology

Thales of Miletus (c. 624 B.C.E.-c. 548 B.C.E.): Metaphysics, philosophy of science

Thomson, Judith Jarvis (born 1929): Ethics, feminist philosophy, social philosophy

Thoreau, Henry David (1817-1862): Ethics, Transcendentalism, social philosophy

Tönnies, Ferdinand (1855-1936): Ethics, social philosophy

Walzer, Michael (born 1935): Ethics, political philosophy, social philosophy

Wang Chong (27-c. 100): Chinese philosophy, Daoist metaphysics, ethics

Wang Fuzhi (1619-1692): Chinese philosophy, materialist metaphysics

Wang Bi (c. 226-c. 249): Chinese philosophy, Daoist metaphysics

Wang Yangming (1472-1529): Chinese philosophy, Confucian epistemology and ethics

Warnock, Mary (born 1924): Ethics, existentialism

Watsuji Tetsurō (1889-1960): Ethics, Japanese philosophy

Weil, Simone (1909-1943): Ethics, philosophy of religion, philosophical theology

Weiss, Paul (born 1901): Metaphysics

Wieman, Henry Nelson (1884-1975): Ethics, metaphysics, philosophical theology

Williams, Bernard (born 1929): Ethics, metaphysics, philosophy of mind

Woodbridge, Frederick James Eugene (1867-1940): Epistemology, metaphysics

Woolf, Virginia (1882-1941): Aesthetics, ethics, feminist philosophy, social philosophy

Wright, Chauncey (1830-1875): Metaphysics, pragmatism, philosophy of science

Xiong Shi-li (1885-1968): Chinese philosophy, Confucian ethics and metaphysics

Xuan Zang (c. 602-664): Chinese philosophy, Buddhist metaphysics

Zhang Binglin (Chuang Ping-lin, 1868-1936): Chinese philosophy, Confucian epistemology, history of philosophy

Zhang Zai (1020-1077): Chinese philosophy, Confucian ethics and metaphysics

Zhu Xi (1130-1200): Chinese philosophy, Confucian ethics, metaphysics, social philosophy

Glossary

a posteriori: Term for the type of proposition that can be verified only "after the fact." A proposition whose truth or falsity is contingent and dependent on experience.

a posteriori statement: A factual statement. An empirical statement, one to be confirmed or disproved by reference to evidence acquired through experience. Opposite of an a priori statement.

a priori: That which precedes and conditions experience, such as a form of intuition (as in the philosophy of Immanuel Kant). Or, whatever is true independently of experience. Opposite of a posteriori.

a priori statement: A universally and necessarily true statement, a statement that is true independently of any factual state of affairs. Opposite of an a posteriori statement.

absolute: Unconditioned, free of all qualifications, totally independent, perfect, nonrelative, eternal, and all-inclusive. God, as entirely unconditioned.

absolute idealism: The doctrine that reality is entirely spiritual or mental and that every aspect of reality has its being and its character only as an aspect of the whole.

abstraction: The process of forming an idea of a characteristic common to, or possibly common to, a number of objects. Also, the idea that is formed.

absurd: The pointless, hopeless, irrational, meaningless character that human life sometimes assumes. A quality or condition that presents philosophy with the problem of justifying the value of human existence.

accident: A characteristic that is not one of the defining characteristics of the object to which it belongs.

aesthetic attitude: The contemplation of an object for the sake of the experience of contemplating it.

aesthetics: The philosophy of art, beauty, and criticism.

agent: In ethics, the person who acts.

agnostic: One who believes that the existence of God, gods, or a spiritual world is unknown or unknowable.

ahimsa: Noninjury and nonviolence toward any living thing, a view stressed in Buddhism and Jainism.

Allah: The one God of Islam.

allegory: A type of story used for teaching, in which the relations between the people, things, and events in the story stand symbolically for an altogether separate, often abstract, state of affairs.

altruism: The idea human beings can and, according to some theories, should set self-interest aside and act in the interests of others. In psychological altruism, the idea that people "naturally" act in the interests of others.

ambiguity: An expression, situation, or condition whose possible meanings make it unclear.

amoral: Neither moral nor immoral.

analogy, argument from: An argument intended to show that two things are similar in certain important ways and thus are probably alike in other respects as well.

analytic statement: A statement that is true because of the meanings of its terms. A statement whose contradictory is an inconsistency. A statement that must be true and cannot be false. Opposite of synthetic statement.

analytical: Referring to the method of inquiry that divides things or ideas into their simplest parts and studies the relations that hold among those parts.

anātman: No self; no soul. Buddhist denial of an ultimate, substantial soul.

animism: The belief that nature is full of spirits.

antecedent: That which is before. In logic, the conditional (if) clause in a conditional (if . . . then) statement.

anthropomorphism: The attribution of human characteristics to God or to inanimate objects.

antinomy: A contradiction between two conclusions drawn from equally credible premises.

anxiety: Apprehension, fearful anticipation. In existentialism, a human condition stemming from the uncertainty of the future and the unavoidability of decision making and responsibility that freedom places upon us.

apology: A defense by the use of intellectual argument.

appearance and reality: A traditional distinction in epistemology and metaphysics that contrasts things as they seem to be and things as they actually are.

archetype: An original essence, an ideal pattern of which individual things are copies, a universal.

argument: Unlike the ordinary connotation of a dispute between two or more persons, a sustained inquiry composed of systematic reasoning from one claim to another and aimed at an exposition and analysis of the subject matter.

argumentum ad feminen or ad hominem: An argument that directs critical attack against an opponent instead of against his or her argument.

asceticism: Renunciation of the comforts of society. A way of life emphasizing austerity and self-discipline.

atheism: The philosophical position that denies the existence of God or gods.

ātman: In Hinduism, the individual self, soul, essence, or nature of a person.

attribute: A property or characteristic necessary to a thing of a certain sort, an essential property. Or, any property or characteristic.

avidya: Indian term for ignorance, in particular ignorance about the universe and the self.

axiom: A statement that is self-evidently true. Neither requiring or even capable of proof, such statements are often regarded as the first principles from which proofs begin.

bad faith: In existentialism, a term for the various ways in which people attempt to evade responsibility for their lives by denying the reality of their own freedom.

begging the question: The fallacy of assuming the conclusion of an argument by using the conclusion as a premise.

behaviorism: A method in psychology that limits empirical investigation of the mind to the study of human behavior.

being: An existing thing. Also, what all existing things possess in common and what is referred to by the various senses and tenses of the verb "to be."

belief: An attitude of confidence about the truth of a proposition, whether this confidence is justified or not. A disposition to confirm some particular opinion as knowledge of the truth.

Brahman: The universal reality or world soul. The supreme, all-pervasive essence and ground of the universe.

Buddha-nature: The doctrine that all sentient beings have within them something of the Buddha. Through meditation and other ascetic practices, this nature can shine forth.

Buddhism: The philosophy or religion based on the teachings of Gautama Siddhartha. The Four Noble Truths teach that life is suffering, that desire is the cause of suffering, that suffering can be eliminated, and that the way to rid oneself of suffering is by following the eightfold path to nirvana. The eightfold path involves right understanding, right resolve, right speech, right conduct, right living, right effort, right intuition, and right concentration.

Calvinism: The theology based on the teachings of John Calvin. The doctrines include belief in humankind's sinful condition, predestination, irresistibility of grace, and the absolute sovereignty of God.

capitalism: An economic system based on open competition, free markets, private ownership of the means of production and distribution, and accumulation and reinvestment of profits.

Cartesianism: The philosophy of René Descartes. Descartes used a method of systematic doubt by which he arrived at the idea that served as the foundation of his philosophy: *Cogito, ergo sum*, "I think, therefore I exist."

categorical imperative: In the philosophy of Immanuel Kant, the unconditional moral law for all rational beings, the purely formal principle of moral action: "Act only according to a maxim by which you can at the same time will that it shall become a universal law."

category: A fundamental concept. One of the primary ideas to which all other ideas can be reduced.

catharsis: In Aristotle, the purgation or elimination of the emotions of pity and fear by the dramatic resolution in tragedy.

cause: An entity, process, or principle that is taken to determine or explain how or why things happen. In Aristotelian philosophy, four kinds of cause are distinguished: material cause, that out of which something is made; formal cause, the plan or idea by reference to which something is made; final cause, the purpose for which something is made; and efficient cause, the act or event which produces the result.

certainty: The state of mind that is confident in its belief and free of doubt to such an extent that no reasons for doubt could be raised.

chance: The element of uncertainty and unpredictability in human experience and perhaps in existence itself.

choice: An act of self-determination, a free and conscious decision between real alternatives.

citizen: A person possessing the rights and duties that belong to him or her as a member of a nation or sovereign state.

civil disobedience: A nonviolent method for protesting against the power of the state.

class: A collection that results if a number of entities possess a common property. An empty class is a potential collection, a class that has no members.

cogito, ergo sum: See Cartesianism.

cognition: Any kind of knowledge process. Or, the product of the knowledge process.

coherence theory of truth: The theory that truth is a property not of individual statements or propositions but of the totality of ideas or of the absolutely inclusive idea.

communism: A theory advocating a classless society in which private ownership of the means of production is abolished and in which labor is organized for the common advantage of all the members of a society.

concept: Any idea. Or, any universal that can be the object of thought.

conceptualism: The theory that universals neither exist independently nor are mere names but exist as concepts in the mind.

conditional statement: Any statement of the form "If . . . then."

connotation: The properties common to whatever is designated by a particular term. The defining properties of a term. Or, the ideas and images associated with the use of a particular term.

consequent: That which is after. In logic, the closing clause of a conditional statement.

consistency: The logical relation that holds between propositions that are not contradictory. Or, the relation between entities that may be parts of a whole.

content of consciousness: Whatever is directly apprehended in experience, as distinguished from awareness, the act of experiencing content. The datum of experience.

contingency: A state of affairs that need not occur or may or may not occur.

contradiction: The logical relation that holds between two statements or propositions that cannot both be true and cannot both be false in that the truth of either involves the falsity of the other.

correspondence theory of truth: The theory that a statement or proposition is true if it corresponds to a matter of fact. To correspond to a fact, a statement must somehow designate the fact.

cosmogony: A theory concerning the creation of the universe.

cosmological argument: An argument that claims to prove the existence of God by maintaining that there must have been a first cause that initiated the causal sequence of contingent things.

cosmology: The philosophic study of basic causes and processes in the universe. An inquiry into the structure of the universe.

covenant: A binding agreement. A contract or bond between God and God's people that specifies mutual rights and duties.

critical realism: The theory that most existing things do not depend for their existence on being perceived or conceived in mind. The theory that knowledge of independently existing things is possible even when the ideas by which things are known differ in existence and in character from the things known.

Dao: The Way. The natural, proper, and true path of events. In Confucian philosophy, the way of life found in Confucius's teachings. In Daoism, ultimate reality and also the natural and proper path of life human beings should follow.

datum: The given element. Or, whatever is presented as the content of consciousness.

deduction: Reasoning that involves passing from one or more propositions to other propositions logically implied by the former.

definition: The process of explaining the meaning of a term. Or the expression used to explain the meaning of a term.

deism: The belief that God created the world but thereafter has no involvement in it.

democracy: The form of government in which authority resides in the people, who act through direct vote or elected representatives.

denotation: The class of entities to which a term refers. Whatever a term designates.

deontological ethics: Any theory about right and the wrong that relates moral value not to the consequences of human action but to the formal nature of the act. An ethics that regards an act as right if it conforms to moral principle.

determinism: The theory that every event depends on one or more other events that are its causes and that the character of any event is entirely a function of its causes.

dharma: In Indian philosophy, the cosmic law, virtue, the right.

Dharma: In Buddhism, the eternal truth about reality.

dialectic: The use of questions and answers as a method of philosophical inquiry, weighing the strengths and weaknesses of differing or opposing viewpoints with the aim of reaching a new, more complete, and more balanced understanding.

ding an sich: The thing-in-itself, whatever exists independently of human knowledge.

doubt: The state of mind that is highly aware of the potential for error, deception, misconception, and misperception in the sphere of ordinary judgments.

dualism: Any metaphysical theory that takes two ultimate and irreducible principles to be necessary to explain experience, the world, or being.

duty: An action that must be performed, either because a person has freely undertaken an ob-ligation to do the action, or because a person accepts the authority of a rule or law requiring that action.

egocentric predicament: The peculiar situation in which any knower exists when he or she attempts to discover something whose existence does not depend on its being known.

egoism, ethical: The theory that one ought to act so as to secure the greatest possible good for oneself.

egoism, psychological: The theory that human beings are so constituted that they must act to secure whatever they regard as best for themselves.

élan vital: The life force, the basic creative principle of all living things. Or, the evolutionary principle as operative in nature.

emanation: The creative process in which all being is derived in a nontemporal fashion from a single source of being.

emotive meaning: The capacity of an utterance to express or to communicate feeling.

empathy: The assumption of the attitude, motion, or state of mind of another as if one were the other.

empirical statement: A statement that can be verified or shown to be false by reference to facts revealed by experience.

empiricism: The theory that all knowledge, except for certain logical truths and principles of mathematics, comes from experience.

end: A thing or state of affairs considered as a practical objective or as a desirable outcome. The purpose for which an action or series of actions is performed.

enlightenment: Freedom from ignorance. Discerning the ultimate truth about reality. The highest goal of many Daoist, Buddhist, and Hindu philosophies. Typically enlightenment involves the elimination of selfishness and an emphasis on tranquility, insight, and action that serves others.

Enlightenment: An important philosophical trend in seventeenth and eighteenth century Europe. It stressed confidence in human reason and individual liberty.

Epicureanism: The theory that happiness is the greatest good and that happiness is to be achieved by living a life of moderation in which the contemplative pleasures are preferred to the sensuous pleasures.

epiphenomenalism: The theory that mental events reflect bodily changes but have no causal influence on the body.

epistemological dualism: The theory that the content of consciousness and the object known are distinct in existence even though they may be alike in essence.

epistemological monism: The theory that the content of consciousness and the aspect of the object known are one in existence as well as in essence.

epistemology: The theory of knowledge. The attempt to clarify ideas about knowledge and the methods for securing knowledge.

eschatology: The theological study of such final matters as death, immortality, divine judgment, and the end of the world.

essence: The distinctive nature of a thing.

eternity: The infinite temporal duration that includes all time. Or, a state that transcends time.

ethical hedonism: The theory that acts are right insofar as they contribute to happiness or pleasure and wrong insofar as they contribute to unhappiness or suffering.

ethical relativism: The theory that the rightness and wrongness of acts are relative to, or functions of, the attitudes of persons or cultures judging the acts.

ethics: The part of philosophy that deals with questions about the nature and source of right and wrong, good and evil, and what should and should not be done.

eudaemonism: The theory that acts are right insofar as they contribute to human well-being or happiness. The emphasis in eudaemonism is not upon pleasure, as in hedonistic ethics, but upon the way of life most suited to human nature.

evidence: Reasons, usually experiential ones, for belief.

evil: Imperfection, disharmony, cruelty, corruption, destruction, wrong-doing.

evolution: A gradual process in which something changes into a different and typically more complex or better form.

excluded middle, principle of: The principle that a proposition is either true or it is false.

existence: Actuality or factuality. The state or fact of being.

existentialism: A philosophy that emphasizes the radical extent of human freedom and attempts to deal with its consequences for people's day-to-day existence. Existentialism sometimes distinguishes between existence and essence and claims that in human life existence precedes essence.

experiment: A situation designed to test a hypothesis.

faith: In theology, belief and trust in God.

fallacy: An unsound argument or an error in reasoning.

fallibilism: The philosophical view that certainty is a practical impossibility and that human judgments must be tested and evaluated because they are prone to error.

fatalism: The belief that all or some events are determined by some supernatural being or power. Or, the vague belief that somehow certain events are decided upon as historical facts prior to their occurrence.

final cause: The end or purpose for which something was done.

finite: Limited, having bounds. Existing or enduring for a limited time only, impermanent.

first mover: The being or power that initiated creation or change in the universe, the first cause.

first principle: The first cause of all contingent beings. Or, a necessary truth which serves as the foundation of a system of ideas.

form: The structure of a thing. What identifies a particular thing or a kind of thing.

forms: Plato's term for his conception of universals, the eternal, transcendent ideas in which particular entities participate and which must be grasped if we are to have knowledge of the truth.

free will: The capacity to make decisions that are uncoerced or not simply determined by antecedent causes.

freedom: Conceived positively, the ability to originate action independently from other causal factors. Conceived negatively, the absence of obstacles to one's course of action.

generalization: An inductive conclusion drawn from the observation of particulars.

genocide: The intended destruction of a national, ethnic, racial, or religious group.

gestalt: Shape, form. The whole considered as more than the sum of its parts.

God: The deity of the Judeo-Christian tradition, to whom is attributed the creation and sustaining of the universe.

good: The ideal state of perfection, satisfaction, harmony, or justice, which ethics aims to bring about within human life.

hedonism: The view that in human experience, pleasure is the ultimate good.

heresy: A controversial or unorthodox opinion or doctrine, especially beliefs at odds with established religious teachings.

history: The chronological development of human societies.

hope: An attitude of desire toward some outcome, coupled with the expectation that this outcome will actually follow even in the absence of evidence to support that view.

humanism: The belief that no better authority, either religious or supernatural, exists for the grounding of human knowledge and the solution of human problems than human experience and intelligence themselves.

hypothesis: An explanation that accounts for a set of facts and that can be tested by further inquiry. A view that is taken to be true for the purpose of argument or inquiry.

hypothetical imperative: Any conditional obligation of the form "If you want . . . , then you must do . . . " Often contrasted with the term "categorical imperative."

idea: In Platonic philosophy, an eternal essence, a universal archetype of things. In Berkeleian philosophy, any sense object directly known in experience.

ideal: A concept or principle that embodies a vision of some kind of perfection or excellence and serves to direct human conduct and awareness towards goals of higher than ordinary significance.

idealism: Any theory that holds reality to be mental, spiritual, or mind-dependent. Such theories usually affirm that reality is perfectly rational in its structure.

identity, principle of: The logical principle that

anything is itself, that any symbol is equivalent in meaning to itself.

identity of indiscernibles: The principle that no two things can be absolutely identical.

ideology: A body of ideas and values that reflect the needs and aspirations of an individual, group, class, or culture.

immanent: Being within, part of, indwelling. The opposite of transcendent.

immaterialism: The view that nonmaterial beings exist. Its strong version holds that only nonmaterial beings exist.

imperative: A prescriptive proposition, ethical principle, law, or rule that specifies what it is a person's duty to do in a given situation.

implication: The logical relation that holds between one proposition and another whenever it could not be the case that the one is true and the other false.

incoherent: Lacking logical or meaningful order.

indeterminism: The theory, often applied to acts of will, that at least some events are not caused by antecedent conditions and may not be predictable.

individualism: The political view that the fundamental unit of society is the individual, and that certain rights belong to each individual.

induction: A type of inference that begins with particulars and moves from lesser to greater generality. A typical form of induction moves from the observation that A, B, and C all have the property x to the conclusion that all members of the class y, of which A, B, and C are members, have the property x.

inference: The process of reasoning—deductive or inductive—that moves from premises to a conclusion. Inference is a kind of activity. Implication is a logical relationship.

infinite: Having no boundaries or limits, immeasurably great, unlimited.

infinite regress: A sequence of causes or explanations that never reaches a stopping point.

innate ideas: Beliefs or knowledge with which a person is born.

interactionism: The theory that body and mind causally affect each other.

interpretation: A way of viewing or understanding that emphasizes an observer's situation or a thinker's perspective.

intrinsic property: A nonrelational property. Or,

the intuitable character of an experience.

intuition: The faculty of knowing by mental inspection and without recourse to reason. Direct and immediate knowing or awareness that is neither deductive nor inductive. Or, the product of intuitive recognition.

invalid: Not valid. A property of arguments when they fail to follow agreed-upon rules of inference.

irrational: Contrary to reason, violating the rules of reason, illogical.

judgment: The movement of thought by which we assert or deny that something is the case.

justice: The principle of moral rightness. Equity; conformity to moral rightness in action or attitude.

justification: The procedure by which a knowledge claim is rationally defended.

Kabbalah: Meaning "received tradition," the term refers to the tradition of Jewish mysticism, which is based on esoteric meanings of Hebrew scripture.

karma: In Hindu and Buddhist philosophy, action, the moral law of cause and effect; the total effect of a person's actions and conduct during successive phases of his or her existence, regarded as determining one's destiny.

knowledge: Accurate and true information and understanding about something. The sum or range of what has been accurately and truly perceived, discovered, or learned.

knowledge, theory of. *See* epistemology.

koan: In Zen Buddhism, a riddle, phrase, or word that cannot be understood by reason or intellect; it is used as an exercise to show and break the limitations of reason and thought.

lamas: Religious leaders in Tibetan Buddhism.

language games: A term, popularized by Ludwig Wittgenstein, that refers to the variety of activities that can be performed using language.

law: A customary practice or norm that is taken to be universally binding on all members of a community or social order.

li: In Chinese philosophy, ritual, propriety, rules of conduct. Or, the rational principle, reason as law, the key to achieving universal harmony. A key element in Confucius's thought.

linguistic analysis: A philosophical approach holding that philosophical issues can be clarified and even eliminated by paying close attention to the uses of language in ordinary, day-to-day life.

logic: The part of philosophy that studies and clarifies the structure of arguments, especially the rules for valid inference and inductive generalization.

logical principles: The principles on which the analysis of the structure of arguments depends. Namely, the principles of identity, contradiction, and excluded middle.

materialism: The doctrine that everything is composed of matter. The belief that matter alone is real and that everything that exists can be understood as a form of matter. In ethics, the doctrine that material well-being and self-interest should always govern individual actions.

matter: That which is in itself undifferentiated and formless and which, as the subject of change and development, receives form and thus becomes something particular.

maya: In Hindu philosophy, the power of creation and illusion.

means: A thing considered for its usefulness or expediency. Something that might be helpful in the process of attaining an end or a desired outcome.

metalanguage: A language devised to describe another language.

metaphysics: The part of philosophy concerned with the study of the ultimate nature of reality and that which is most basic and fundamental in reality. Metaphysics includes analysis of general concepts such as existence, reality, freedom, mind, and God. It may also involve speculative inquiry about philosophical matters that lie beyond the range of empirical investigations.

mind-body problem: The issue of how the mental/conscious and physical/material aspects of reality are related. A fundamental topic in metaphysics and epistemology.

miracle: An event that defies the usual laws of nature and is taken as evidence for the existence of God or other divinities.

moksha: In Hinduism, release or liberation from the cycle of existence.

monism: The metaphysical view that all reality is basically of one substance.

monotheism: The belief in one god.

moral philosophy: The study of right and wrong, ethical values and principles.

morality: Standards for right and wrong conduct. A set of ethical principles and practices regarded as universally valid or as basic to a particular culture or society.

motive: A reason for acting. A basic interest or need that action aims to fulfill.

mysticism: The belief that knowledge, especially of the divine or ultimately real, can be gained through subjective or supernatural insight, intuition, or revelation. The discipline that leads to such awareness.

myth: A traditional story, usually of unknown origin but claiming a basis in history, that is used to explain, illustrate, or justify some belief or practice.

naïve realism: The conventional opinion that the world is directly known and that it has whatever character we perceive it to have.

natural law: A law or body of laws derived from nature and regarded as binding upon human actions apart from or in conjunction with laws established by human authority.

natural theology: Theology, or philosophy concerning God, based on ordinary experience and not dependent on revelation.

naturalism: The theory that reality is understandable in terms of scientifically verifiable concepts and without reference to the supernatural.

naturalistic ethics: Any philosophical theory concerning right and wrong, good and the bad, claiming that value terms and moral judgments are empirically definable and verifiable.

naturalistic fallacy: The fallacy defined by G. E. Moore as the error of identifying some property common to good things with goodness itself, which, in Moore's view, is a nonnatural quality that cannot be defined by anything else.

nature: The material world. The forces and process that control what happens in the material world. Also, the essential characteristics and qualities of a person or thing.

necessary truth: A truth that cannot be otherwise, not even in one's imagination.

Neoplatonism: A philosophic movement stated in the beginning of the third century, it combines Platonic and Aristotelian ideas with certain conceptions from Eastern philosophy and maintains that reality is an absolute oneness, that matter is the negation of being, and that the One creates orders of being by a nontemporal process of emanation.

Nirvana: The state of enlightenment attained by Buddha. A state of perfect bliss and peacefulness, gained through meditation, which extinguishes individual attachments and releases one from the cycle of existence.

nominalism: The theory that only particulars are real and that abstract concepts, general terms, or universals have no objective reference but serve only as names for observable likenesses among the things we experience.

nonnaturalistic ethics: Any ethics that regards value as unique and unanalyzable and views intuition as the only way of knowing the truth of moral claims.

nonviolent resistance: The technique of social protest designed to express opposition to the status quo while avoiding the waste of life that results from violence.

normative: Evaluative, judgmental. A type of statement that attributes moral or aesthetic qualities such as superiority or inferiority, rightness or impropriety, to a thing, action, or state of affairs.

noumenon: In the philosophy of Immanuel Kant, a thing-in-itself, the unknowable reality behind phenomena.

objective truth: Truth independent of personal opinions and demonstrable to anyone who inquires properly.

occasionalism: The theory that God causes mental phenomena to accompany physical events.

Ockham's razor: A scientific and philosophical principle, introduced by William of Ockham, which holds that the explanation involving the fewest assumptions is to be preferred.

omnipotence: Often attributed to God, the absolute ability to control events.

omniscience: Often attributed to God, the characteristic of knowing everything.

One: In philosophy, the One is the universe considered as the divine unity of all being.

ontological argument: In the philosophy of Saint Anselm, the argument that since God is the being than which no greater can be conceived, God must exist, for it is better to exist than not to exist, and it is better to exist necessarily than to exist contingently.

ontology: The exploration of being as such. The study of what existence itself is, considered apart from any question as to the nature of any particular existent. The attempt to discover the fundamental categories of all being.

optimism: An outlook that anticipates the best outcome in any given situation and believes that good triumphs over evil.

ordinary language: A central concept in linguistic analysis and the philosophy of language. An idea that emphasizes the variety of ways in which language is actually used.

panpsychism: The doctrine that everything has a mind or soul.

pantheism: The doctrine that everything is an aspect of God.

paradox: A seemingly contradictory statement that may nonetheless by true. A self-contradictory conclusion based on seemingly good argumentation.

parallelism: In connection with the mind-body problem, the theory that mental and physical events occur concomitantly but are not causally related.

particular: An individual thing. A member of a class, a thing of a kind, as distinguished from the class, the kind, the universal.

Pascal's wager: The argument advanced by Blaise Pascal for the rationality of belief in God: Namely, that although a wrong belief in the existence of God could do no harm, a wrong disbelief could result in losing the opportunity to live a life rich in religious significance.

percept: A given element in perceptual experience, a sensation or sense-datum.

personalism: The philosophy that regards personality as the highest good and God as the divine personality.

pessimism: An outlook that stresses the inevitability of misfortune.

phenomenology: Primarily originating with Edmund Husserl, a philosophy emphasizing the description, content, and structure of all that can appear within human experience.

phenomenon: An appearance, as distinguished from a thing-in-itself.

philosophy: Literally, the love of—and, consequently, search for—wisdom. The intellectual attempt to resolve problems having to do with the nature of matters of common experience and concern. Thus, the attempt to make basic ideas clear and to justify descriptions of reality. The major fields of philosophy are metaphysics, epistemology, and ethics.

Platonic realism: The theory that universals, or general characteristics, have a reality of their own and subsist eternally, apart from the things that embody them.

pluralism: Any theory that emphasizes the variety of realities in existence and that may regard the universe as composed of or dependent on more than one ultimate reality.

polytheism: Any theory claiming that there is more than one God.

postmodernism: Any of a number of trends or movements in the arts, literature, philosophy, or theology in reaction to or rejection of principles and practices whose roots are found especially in seventeenth and eighteenth century Western thought.

potentiality: An unrealized or latent capacity or power. Opposite of actuality.

power: The ability to influence and control the course of events and the behavior of others.

pragmatism: The philosophical movement founded by the Americans Charles Sanders Peirce, William James, and John Dewey and based on the assumption that the pursuit of truth is a practical ongoing and an unfinalizable process, limited by the finite capacities of human reason and guided and determined by the concrete practical interests of human beings.

pratītya samutpāda: The Buddhist teaching of interdependent origination, which holds that all elements of reality arise in conjunction with each other.

predestination: The doctrine that all events are determined by the action of God's will. Or, the doctrine that God has foreordained the eternal life or damnation of some persons.

preestablished harmony: In the philosophy of Gottfried Wilhelm von Leibniz, the theory that individual souls (monads) know reality contemporaneously with other monads, even though monads have no access to external events, because of God's causing the experiences of all monads to be harmonious with one another.

premise: A proposition on which, at least in part, the conclusion of an argument is based.

primary qualities: In the philosophy of John Locke, characteristics regarded as inseparable from physical objects and as belonging to them quite apart from any relation to other objects or to knowing minds: solidity, extension, figure, motion or rest, and number.

principle of noncontradiction: The principle in logic that a proposition and its contradiction cannot both be true simultaneously.

principle of sufficient reason: A principle stating that a series of contingent events (events that need not have occurred) must be accounted for by reference to some reason or cause other than that supplied by any of the contingent events in the series.

problem of evil: The issue that emerges from trying to reconcile the presence of suffering and evil in the world with the claim that God is omnipotent, omniscient, and just.

progress: The concept of the betterment of the human condition through the process of history.

proof: Reasoning that shows how a conclusion is validly drawn from evidence and established rules of inference.

property: Any characteristic. More specifically, any characteristic that is essential, defining, or relational.

proposition: A declarative sentence. Or a potential belief or claim to knowledge about the world, expressed in words and capable of being tested against both the observable facts and some standard of meaningfulness.

providence: The care, guardianship, and control of the world and, in particular, human history exercized by a deity.

quality: A particular and observable attribute of an object that, in combination with other qualities, composes our conception of the object.

Qur'an: The sacred scripture of Islam, believed to contain the revelations made by Allah to Mohammed.

radical empiricism: The theory, named by William James, which claims that all things and the relations between things are matters of direct experience. Hence, the theory that all terms are meaningful by reference to experience.

rational: Logical, consistent with or based on reason.

rationalism: The theory that knowledge of reality is possible through the use of reason without reference to matters of sense experience.

rationality: The capacity to think and act in accord with plans and goals. More specifically, the ability to think and act logically, clearly, and soundly.

realism: In metaphysics, the doctrine that physical objects exist independently of being thought or perceived. Also, the doctrine that universals exist (subsist) apart from things.

reality: The totality of all that is actual. Or a person, event, or thing that is actual.

reason: The capacity for rational thought, inference, or discrimination.

reasons: Evidence or arguments that explain or justify a belief, theory, decision, or action.

redemption: Often regarded as coming from the grace of God, the transformation of evil into good.

reductio ad absurdum: The method of proving a proposition by showing that its contradictory involves an inconsistency or of disproving a proposition by showing that the proposition involves an inconsistency.

refute: To prove to be false, invalid, or erroneous.

relation: A term referring to the various ways in which things can be connected to one another.

relational characteristic: A characteristic understandable only by relating the object possessing the characteristic to some person as knowing subject. A characteristic understandable only in terms of the experiences a person would have were he or she to be affected by the object possessing the characteristic.

relations, principle of the internality of: The principle that all relations are interdependent, that the nature of any one thing affects the nature of everything else in the universe.

relativism: The theory that truth and values are neither absolute nor independent of human experience but are dependent upon individual, historical, or cultural perspectives.

religion: The beliefs, practices, and institutions that express human experience and idea of that which is taken to be holy, divine, sacred, or ultimate in power and value.

ren: Compassion, virtue, benevolence, love. A key virtue in Confucian philosophy.

responsibility: The state, quality, or fact of being legally or ethically accountable for one's choices, decisions, and actions.

revelation: Knowledge gained from a divine source.

right: Morally proper or just. Also, a justified claim to be free to act in a certain way, to pursue certain ends, or to expect certain behavior of others.

rule: A prescriptive guideline specifying what can or is to be done by a person under certain conditions.

samadhi: Intense mental concentration without awareness of thoughts or sensations. The culminating state in Hinduism or Buddhism in which saving insight is obtained.

samsāra: The cycle of birth, death, and rebirth from which one can escape only by achieving Nirvana.

satori: In Zen Buddhism, the moment of enlightenment, the sudden recognition of the unity of being.

scientific method: Refers to procedures used to advance human knowledge by collecting data through observation and experiment and by formulating, testing, and confirming hypotheses by appealing to such data.

secondary qualities: In the philosophy of John Locke, those characteristics of physical objects that do not belong to the physical objects themselves except as powers to cause sensations. The secondary qualities are the colors, sounds, tastes, and smells of things.

self: The object of the idea of personal identity. An individual's consciousness of his or her own being or identity, a personal individual.

self-contradictory: An idea or statement, or a set of ideas or statements, containing contradictory elements.

self-evident: Requiring no proof or explanation.

self-interest: Regard for one's personal advantage or interest.

semiotics: The study of signs and symbols. Semiotics includes pragmatics, the study of the uses of signs; semantics, the study of the meanings of signs; and syntactics, the study of the forms of linguistic expressions.

sense-datum: The given content of a sense experience, a sense image. Or, the given content of any experience.

skepticism: The critically developed philosophical position of one who doubts that knowledge is not possible. Or, the view that all knowledge is merely probable, never certain.

social contract: A theory of the justification of the right of a state to govern, based on the assumption that citizens permit such authority by their explicit or tacit consent, and that such authority implies a reciprocal obligation of the state to recognize certain rights for its citizens.

solipsism: The belief that only oneself exists.

sophism: Fallacious and deceptive reasoning. Or, a fallacious and deceptive argument.

sophist: In fifth century B.C.E., a Greek teacher of rhetoric, the art of politics, and basic scientific knowledge. Or, one who, at the expense of moral integrity, emphasizes success in argument or politics.

soul: The animating part of a human being, sometimes regarded as immaterial and immortal.

state of nature: A hypothetical condition of human beings prior to their being brought under the administration of a sovereign state.

Stoicism: An ethical doctrine endorsing a life of virtue, action in accordance with the rational way of the universe, and endurance in the face of unavoidable difficulties.

subjective idealism: The doctrine that knowledge of the world is limited to the world as a complex system of sensations. The view that matter is a complex of sensations. The claim by George Berkeley that *esse es percipi*, to be is to be perceived.

subjective truth: A belief that an individual, but perhaps no one else, takes to be true. A belief that is held passionately but may not be true or false objectively.

subjectivism: A view maintaining that the personal or cultural concepts we bring to experience determine to a larger extent our sense of reality.

subsistence: The mode of existence, involving neither temporal nor spatial location, which is peculiar to universals, ideas, archetypes, and other abstract entities.

substance: The unchanging unity underlying the qualities of things in the world. That which has properties. The enduring system of properties considered as a system in abstraction from the properties.

summum bonum: The highest good, that which is intrinsically better than any other good and which is thus qualified to serve as the end of human conduct.

syllogism: The type of deductive inference forming the core of Aristotelian logic, composed of a major premise stating a categorical fact ("All men are mortal") and a minor premise stating a particular matter of fact ("Socrates is a man"), and concluding with the inference derived from combining the two premises ("Socrates is mortal").

symbol: An object that is taken to stand for or suggest something other than itself, especially an object used to represent an abstract quality.

synthetic statement: A statement whose truth value cannot be determined by logical analysis but requires comparison to the empirical phenomenon it is supposed to describe. A statement in which the subject does not imply the predicate.

tabula rasa: In John Locke's philosophy, the term, meaning "blank tablet," used to describe the mind at birth as being without innate ideas.

tautology: An analytically true statement, a statement that can be shown to be true by logical analysis.

teleological argument: An argument devised to prove God's existence by maintaining that evidence of design or purpose in nature suggests the existence of a cosmic designer.

teleology: Any theory of ends or purposes. Or, the study of events as signs of purpose.

temporal: As opposed to eternal, that which changes and is not permanent.

theism: The view of reality maintaining that a transcendent power grounds all finite being. Belief in the existence of a god or gods, espe-

cially belief in a personal God as creator and ruler of the world.

theodicy: A theory about the relationship between God and human life that seeks to reconcile the existence of evil in the world with the doctrine of God's goodness.

theology: Often closely related to philosophy, intellectual inquiry about God and problems concerned with God. Natural theology limits itself to empirical evidence. Revealed theology depends on revelation.

theory: A system of ideas devised to analyze, predict, or otherwise explain and account for realities within the world or even reality itself.

transcendent: Separate and distinct from the natural world. Opposite of immanent.

transcendental philosophy: Philosophy that studies either the a priori form of experience or experience as formed a priori. Or, philosophy that regards the spiritual as the essence of reality or as a mode of being transcending the empirical and the physical.

transubstantiation: The changing of one substance into another, or the substitution of one substance for another without a change of properties.

truth: Agreement between concepts and reality, between the world as represented through language and the world as it actually is.

tychism: In the philosophy of Charles Sanders Peirce, the doctrine that chance events occur. The doctrine that some events are uncaused.

uniformity of nature: The complete regularity of events in nature.

universal: A concept or idea that applies to many particular things. Forms, essences, absolute generalities. Concepts denoting those properties characteristic of, or forming the common essence of, particular entities of various kinds.

universalizability: The ability to be applied to all persons at all times without exception. A concept often linked to ideas about duty, obligation, and responsibility in ethical theories.

universe: In philosophy, this term often refers to everything that exists.

unmoved mover: The first cause, or mover, not itself moved. God, as the prime mover.

Upanishads: A key series of ancient texts in Hindu philosophy and theology.

utilitarianism: The ethical position, advanced by Jeremy Bentham and elaborated by John Stuart Mill, which takes the object of moral judgment to be the consequences of actions, the contents of the good to be pleasure or satisfaction, and the aim of moral agency to be the production of the greatest good for the greatest number of persons.

utopia: A fictional, ideal state, society, or means of organizing social life that pursues the aims of universal harmony and satisfaction.

validity: The property an argument possesses when it correctly follows accepted rules of inference. The property of an argument in which the premises imply the conclusion.

value: A principle, standard, or quality considered worthwhile or desirable. The property of being desirable or necessary for human existence. The relative importance of a thing in relation to human needs and desires.

value, immediate: The value that something has as a result of being a direct cause of pleasure or satisfaction. Thus, aesthetic value is one kind of immediate value.

value, instrumental: The value that something has because it is a means to something intrinsically good.

value, intrinsic: The value of something that is worthwhile on its own account and not merely as a means.

vedanta: The Indian philosophy based on the Upanishads, the philosophic writings which made up the last of the Vedas.

Vedas: The most ancient of Hinduism's sacred writings.

verification: Corroboration, confirmation. The correlation of sentences with empirical evidence that lends credibility to their claim to represent truth. Showing some statement to be true by appealing to empirical evidence in its favor, or to formal rules of reasoning that guarantee the validity of its derivation from other statements that can themselves be checked against empirical evidence.

via negativa: A method that attempts to understand the nature of God or absolute reality by discerning what it is not.

virtue: Moral excellence, a particularly good and beneficial quality of character.

volition: The cause of purposeful human activity. The ability to will or intend some state of affairs. The capacity of a human being to initiate events causally connected with his or her own body and according to the individual's own purposes.

voluntarism: The theory that the will is universe's basic reality, controlling power, or explanatory principle.

will: The power of consciousness by which one deliberately chooses or decides upon a course of action.

will to power: The view of Friedrich Nietzsche that human life is driven by a desire to control and master the world.

wisdom: Knowledge and understanding that show us how to live rightly and well.

world: The universe, the system of totality of whatever exists. The subject matter of experience, the totality of things that can possibly engage the attention and interest of human beings.

world ground: That power, or basic reality, which sustains and directs the universe.

world soul: The spirit or creative principle that makes life possible and endows contingent things with reality and order.

worldview: A way of looking at the world. A comprehensive view of the world, usually reflecting a particular perspective.

worship: Veneration, ritual celebration, or idolization of some ideal or deity.

wu-wei: Nonaction. In Daoism, the proper way of desireless action, which constitutes the core of the Daoist ethic.

yi: Duty, obligation, right relationship. A key virtue in Confucian philosophy.

yin and yang: In Chinese philosophy, two fundamental energy principles. Yin is feminine, passive, dark, and negative, while yang is masculine, active, bright, and positive. Everything that exists is presumed to exhibit the interplay of yin and yang.

yoga: In Hinduism, any systematic discipline of meditation aimed at the realization of religious truth.

zazen: Sitting in meditation; a part of Zen Buddhist training.

World Philosophers
and
Their Works

CATEGORIZED LIST OF WORKS

Subject Headings Used in List

Aesthetics, III
African Philosophy, III
Buddhism, III
Chinese Philosophy, III
Epistemology, IV
Ethics, V
Existentialism, VII
Feminist Philosophy, VII
Indian Philosophy, VII
Islamic Philosophy, VII
Japanese Philosophy, VII
Jewish Philosophy, VII
Logic, VII
Metaphysics, VII

Phenomenology, IX
Philosophical Psychology, IX
Philosophical Theology, IX
Philosophy of Education, IX
Philosophy of History, X
Philosophy of Language, X
Philosophy of Law, X
Philosophy of Mathematics, X
Philosophy of Mind, X
Philosophy of Religion, X
Philosophy of Science, XI
Political Philosophy, XI
Pragmatism, XI
Social Philosophy, XI

Overviews of the titles listed under these twenty-seven categories appear in the body of this work, immediately following essays on the philosopher's life or essays on the authorship of the work.

Aesthetics
Aesthetic as Science of Expression and General
    Linguistic (Benedetto Croce)
Art as Experience (John Dewey)
Characteristics of Men, Manners, Opinions,
    Times (Third Earl of Shaftesbury)
The Critique of Judgment (Immanuel Kant)
The Dialogic Imagination (Mikhail Bakhtin)
In My Father's House (Kwame Anthony
    Appiah)
Inner Experience (Georges Bataille)
Mythologies (Roland Barthes)
Philosophy in a New Key (Suzanne K. Langer)
Poetics (Aristotle)
The Postmodern Condition (Jean-François
    Lyotard)
The Psychoanalysis of Fire (Gaston Bachelard)
The Sense of Beauty (George Santayana)
The Sufi Path of Love (Jalāl al-Dīn Rūmī)
Ways of Worldmaking (Nelson Goodman)
What Is Art? (Leo Tolstoy)
The Writing of the Disaster (Maurice Blanchot)

African Philosophy
African Philosophy (Paulin J. Hountondji)
African Religions and Philosophy (John S. Mbiti)
The Hermeneutics of African Philosophy
    (Tsenay Serequeberhan)
In My Father's House (Kwame Anthony Appiah)

Buddhism. *See also* **Philosophy of Religion**
An Inquiry into the Good (Kitarō Nishida)
The Platform Sutra of the Sixth Patriarch
    (Huineng)
Religion and Nothingness (Keiji Nishitani)
Zen and Western Thought (Masao Abe)
Zen Buddhism (D. T. Suzuki)

Chinese Philosophy
Analects (Confucius)
The Doctrine of the Mean
Gongsun Longzi
The Great Learning
Han Feizi
I Ching

The Importance of Living (Lin Yutang)
Menzi (Mencius)
Mozi
The Platform Sutra of the Sixth Patriarch
  (Huineng)
Xunzi
Zhuangzi

Epistemology
Aesthetic as Science of Expression and General
  Linguistic (Benedetto Croce)
"Apology for Raimond Sebond" (Michel
  Eyquem de Montaigne)
The Book of Deliverance (Avicenna)
Brainstorms (Daniel Dennett)
Collected Papers of Charles Sanders Peirce
  (Charles Sanders Peirce)
The Concept of Law (H. L. A. Hart)
The Construction of Social Reality (John R.
  Searle)
Course in General Linguistics (Ferdinand de
  Saussure)
The Critique of Pure Reason (Immanuel Kant)
Difference and Repetition (Gilles Deleuze)
Discourse on Method (René Descartes)
An Essay Concerning Human Understanding
  (John Locke)
An Essay on Metaphysics (R. G. Collingwood)
Essays on Actions and Events (Donald
  Davidson)
Essays on the Intellectual Powers of Man *and*
  Essays on the Active Powers of Man (Thomas
  Reid)
First Principles (Herbert Spencer)
The Foundations of Arithmetic (Gottlob Frege)
The Foundations of Indian Culture (Sri
  Aurobindo Ghose)
Glosses on Porphyry (Peter Abelard)
Gongsun Longzi
Gorgias (Plato)
The Hermeneutics of African Philosophy
  (Tsenay Serequeberhan)
An Historical and Critical Dictionary (Pierre
  Bayle)
How to Do Things with Words (J. L. Austin)
The Idea of a University Defined and Illustrated
  (John Henry Newman)
Ideas (Edmund Husserl)
Individuals (Peter Strawson)

An Inquiry into Meaning and Truth (Bertrand
  Russell)
An Introduction to Metaphysics (Henri Bergson)
The Journey of the Mind to God (Saint
  Bonaventure)
The Language of the Self (Jacques Lacan)
Language, Truth, and Logic (A. J. Ayer)
The Logic of Scientific Discovery (Karl Raimund
  Popper)
Meaning in History (Wilhelm Dilthey)
Meditations on First Philosophy (René Descartes)
Memories, Dreams, Reflections (Carl Jung)
Meno (Plato)
Mind and the World-Order (C. I. Lewis)
Monologion *and* Proslogion (Saint Anselm)
Must We Mean What We Say (Stanley Cavell)
Mythologies (Roland Barthes)
Naming and Necessity (Saul Kripke)
Negative Dialectics (Theodor Adorno)
The New Science (Giambattista Vico)
Novum Organum (Francis Bacon)
Objectivity (Nicholas Rescher)
Of Gramatology (Jacques Derrida)
On Certainty (Ludwig Wittgenstein)
The Origin of Species by Means of Natural
  Selection (Charles Darwin)
Our Knowledge of the External World (Bertrand
  Russell)
Outline of a Theory of Practice (Pierre Bourdieu)
Outlines of Pyrrhonism (Sextus Empiricus)
Perception (H. H. Price)
Phenomenology of Perception (Maurice
  Merleau-Ponty)
The Phenomenology of Spirit (Georg Wilhelm
  Friedrich Hegel)
The Phenomenology of the Social World (Alfred
  Schutz)
Philosophical Investigations (Ludwig
  Wittgenstein)
Philosophy and Logical Syntax (Rudolf Carnap)
Philosophy and Psycho-Analysis (John Wisdom)
Philosophy and the Mirror of Nature (Richard
  Rorty)
Philosophy in a New Key (Suzanne K. Langer)
The Positive Philosophy of Auguste Comte
  (Auguste Comte)
The Postmodern Condition (Jean-François
  Lyotard)
Pragmatism (William James)

The Principles of Psychology (William James)
Protagoras (Plato)
The Psychoanalysis of Fire (Gaston Bachelard)
The Quest for Certainty (John Dewey)
Realism with a Human Face (Hilary Putnam)
RePresentations (Jerry A. Fodor)
Science, Perception, and Reality (Wilfrid Sellars)
Selected Essays (Gottlob Frege)
Sophist (Plato)
The Structure of Scientific Revolutions (Thomas S. Kuhn)
Theaetetus (Plato)
Thoughts on the Interpretation of Nature (Denis Diderot)
Three Dialogues Between Hylas and Philonous (George Berkeley)
Tractatus Logico-Philosophicus (Ludwig Wittgenstein)
A Treatise Concerning the Principles of Human Knowledge (George Berkeley)
A Treatise of Human Nature (David Hume)
Truth and Method (Hans-Georg Gadamer)
The View from Nowhere (Thomas Nagel)
The Vocation of Man (Johann Gottlieb Fichte)
Warrant and Proper Function (Alvin Plantinga)
Ways of Worldmaking (Nelson Goodman)
William of Ockham: Selections (William of Ockham)
Word and Object (W. V. O. Quine)

Ethics
Aesthetic as Science of Expression and General Linguistic (Benedetto Croce)
African Philosophy (Paulin J. Hountondji)
African Religions and Philosophy (John S. Mbiti)
After Auschwitz (Richard L. Rubenstein)
After Virtue (Alasdair MacIntyre)
All Rivers Run to the Sea (Elie Wiesel)
The American Evasion of Philosophy (Cornel West)
Analects (Confucius)
Anarchy, State, and Utopia (Robert Nozick)
Apology (Plato)
Art as Experience (John Dewey)
An Autobiography (Mohandas K. Gandhi)
Being and Nothingness (Jean-Paul Sartre)
Beyond Good and Evil (Friedrich Nietzsche)
Bhagavad Gita

Characteristics of Men, Manners, Opinions, Times (Third Earl of Shaftesbury)
Civilization and Its Discontents (Sigmund Freud)
The Concept of Law (H. L. A. Hart)
The Consolation of Philosophy (Boethius)
The Crest Jewel of Wisdom (Samkara)
The Critique of Judgment (Immanuel Kant)
The Critique of Practical Reason (Immanuel Kant)
Crito (Plato)
Dao De Jing
Dark Night of the Soul (Saint John of the Cross)
The Dialogic Imagination (Mikhail Bakhtin)
Discourse on Colonialism (Aimé Césaire)
Discourses *and* Encheridion (Epictetus)
The Doctrine of the Mean
Ecology, Community, and Lifestyle (Arne Naess)
Either/Or (Søren Kierkegaard)
An Enquiry Concerning the Principles of Morals (David Hume)
An Essay on the Principle of Population (Thomas Robert Malthus)
Essays (Ralph Waldo Emerson)
Essays on the Intellectual Powers of Man *and* Essays on the Active Powers of Man (Thomas Reid)
Ethics (Baruch Spinoza)
An Ethics of Sexual Difference (Luce Irigaray)
Euthyphro (Plato)
An Examination of the Place of Reason in Ethics (Stephen Toulmin)
Facing the Extreme (Tzvetan Todorov)
The Federalist (Alexander Hamilton, James Madison, and John Jay)
Feminist Politics and Human Nature (Alison M. Jaggar)
Fifteen Sermons Preached at the Rolls Chapel (Joseph Butler)
Foundations of the Metaphysics of Morals (Immanuel Kant)
Four Essays on Liberty (Isaiah Berlin)
The Fragility of Goodness (Martha Craven Nussbaum)
The Future Lasts Forever (Louis Althusser)
The Gift (Marcel Mauss)
God's Presence in History (Emil L. Fackenheim)
Gorgias (Plato)
The Great Learning
Han Feizi

The Wretched of the Earth (Frantz Fanon)
The Writing of the Disaster (Maurice Blanchot)
Zen Buddhism (D. T. Suzuki)
Zhuangzi

Existentialism
Being and Nothingness (Jean-Paul Sartre)
Being and Time (Martin Heidegger)
Concluding Unscientific Postscript (Søren
　Kierkegaard)
The Courage to Be (Paul Tillich)
Either/Or (Søren Kierkegaard)
Man's Search for Meaning (Viktor Emil Frankl)
The Mystery of Being (Gabriel Marcel)
Phenomenology of Perception (Maurice
　Merleau-Ponty)
Philosophical Fragments (Søren Kierkegaard)
Reason and Existenz (Karl Jaspers)
The Rebel (Albert Camus)
The Second Sex (Simone de Beauvoir)
The Tragic Sense of Life in Men and Peoples
　(Miguel de Unamuno y Jugo)
What Is Philosophy? (José Ortega y Gasset)

Feminist Philosophy
An Ethics of Sexual Difference (Luce Irigaray)
Feminist Politics and Human Nature (Alison M.
　Jaggar)
The Second Sex (Simone de Beauvoir)
A Vindication of the Rights of Woman (Mary
　Wollstonecraft)

Indian Philosophy
An Autobiography (Mohandas K. Gandhi)
The Crest Jewel of Wisdom (Samkara)
The Foundations of Indian Culture (Sri
　Aurobindo Ghose)
An Idealist View of Life (Sarvepalli
　Radhakrishnan)
Karma Yoga (Swami Vivekananda)
The Religion of Man (Rabindranath Tagore)
Think on These Things (Jiddu Krishnamurti)
Time and Eternity (Ananda Kentish
　Coomaraswamy)

Islamic Philosophy
The Book of Deliverance (Avicenna)
The Incoherence of the Incoherence (Averroës)
The Sufi Path of Love (Jalāl al-Dīn Rūmī)

Japanese Philosophy. *See also* Buddhism
An Inquiry into the Good (Kitarō Nishida)
Religion and Nothingness (Keiji Nishitani)
Zen and Western Thought (Masao Abe)
Zen Buddhism (D. T. Suzuki)

Jewish Philosophy. *See also* Philosophy of
　Religion
After Auschwitz (Richard L. Rubenstein)
All Rivers Run to the Sea (Elie Wiesel)
God's Presence in History (Emil L. Fackenheim)
The Guide of the Perplexed (Moses Maimonides)
I and Thou (Martin Buber)
Man Is Not Alone (Abraham Joshua Heschel)
The Star of Redemption (Franz Rosenzweig)

Logic
Collected Papers of Charles Sanders Peirce
　(Charles Sanders Peirce)
The Foundations of Arithmetic (Gottlob Frege)
Gongsun Longzi
The Logical Basis of Metaphysics (Michael
　Dummett)
Naming and Necessity (Saul Kripke)
Organon (Aristotle)
The Paradoxes of Zeno (Zeno of Elea)
Philosophy and Logical Syntax (Rudolf Carnap)
Science of Logic (Georg Wilhelm Friedrich Hegel)
Selected Essays (Gottlob Frege)
Tractatus Logico-Philosophicus (Ludwig
　Wittgenstein)
William of Ockham: Selections (William of
　Ockham)
Word and Object (W. V. O. Quine)

Metaphysics
Anaximander: Fragment (Anaximander)
Appearance and Reality (F. H. Bradley)
Being and Nothingness (Jean-Paul Sartre)
Being and Time (Martin Heidegger)
Bhagavad Gita
The Book of Deliverance (Avicenna)
Brainstorms (Daniel Dennett)
The City of God (Saint Augustine)
The Concept of Mind (Gilbert Ryle)
Concerning the Cause, Principle, and One
　(Giordano Bruno)
Concluding Unscientific Postscript (Søren
　Kierkegaard)

Science, Perception, and Reality (Wilfrid Sellars)
Secrets of God (Hildegard von Bingen)
Sophist (Plato)
The Star of Redemption (Franz Rosenzweig)
Statesman (Plato)
Summa Contra Gentiles (Saint Thomas Aquinas)
Summa Theologica (Saint Thomas Aquinas)
Symposium (Plato)
Theodicy (Gottfried Wilhelm Leibniz)
Think on These Things (Jiddu Krishnamurti)
Three Dialogues Between Hylas and Philonous (George Berkeley)
Thus Spake Zarathustra (Friedrich Nietzsche)
Timaeus (Plato)
Time and Eternity (Ananda Kentish Coomaraswamy)
Totality and Infinity (Emmanuel Lévinas)
Tractatus Logico-Philosophicus (Ludwig Wittgenstein)
A Treatise Concerning the Principles of Human Knowledge (George Berkeley)
A Treatise on God as First Principle (John Duns Scotus)
Truth and Method (Hans-Georg Gadamer)
The View from Nowhere (Thomas Nagel)
The Vocation of Man (Johann Gottlieb Fichte)
The Way of Truth and The Way of Opinion (Parmenides)
Ways of Worldmaking (Nelson Goodman)
What Is Philosophy? (José Ortega y Gasset)
The World and the Individual (Josiah Royce)
The World as Will and Idea (Arthur Schopenhauer)
Xunzi
Zen and Western Thought (Masao Abe)
Zhuangzi

Phenomenology
Ideas (Edmund Husserl)
Phenomenology of Perception (Maurice Merleau-Ponty)
The Phenomenology of the Social World (Alfred Schutz)

Philosophical Psychology
Civilization and Its Discontents (Sigmund Freud)
The Language of the Self (Jacques Lacan)
Man's Search for Meaning (Viktor Emil Frankl)
Memories, Dreams, Reflections (Carl Jung)

Mind, Self, and Society (George Herbert Mead)
On the Soul (Aristotle)
The Principles of Psychology (William James)
The Psychoanalysis of Fire (Gaston Bachelard)

Philosophical Theology. See also Philosophy of Religion
The City of God (Saint Augustine)
Concerning the Cause, Principle, and One (Giordano Bruno)
Confessions (Saint Augustine)
Dark Night of the Soul (Saint John of the Cross)
The Divine Relativity (Charles Hartshorne)
The Enneads (Plotinus)
Freedom of the Will (Jonathan Edwards)
Glosses on Porphyry (Peter Abelard)
The Guide of the Perplexed (Moses Maimonides)
I and Thou (Martin Buber)
The Incoherence of the Incoherence (Averroës)
The Journey of the Mind to God (Saint Bonaventure)
Letters and Papers from Prison (Dietrich Bonhoeffer)
Monologion and Proslogion (Saint Anselm)
The Nature and Destiny of Man (Reinhold Niebuhr)
Of Learned Ignorance (Nicholas of Cusa)
On Detachment (Meister Eckhart)
On First Principles (Origen)
On the Division of Nature (Johannes Scotus Erigena)
On the Freedom of the Will (Desiderius Erasmus)
Pensées (Blaise Pascal)
Secrets of God (Hildegard von Bingen)
The Sufi Path of Love (Jalāl al-Dīn Rūmī)
Summa Contra Gentiles (Saint Thomas Aquinas)
Summa Theologica (Saint Thomas Aquinas)
Theodicy (Gottfried Wilhelm Leibniz)
A Treatise on God as First Principle (John Duns Scotus)
William of Ockham: Selections (William of Ockham)

Philosophy of Education
The Idea of a University Defined and Illustrated (John Henry Newman)
Pedagogy of the Oppressed (Paulo Freire)

Philosophy of History

The City of God (Saint Augustine)
An Essay on Metaphysics (R. G. Collingwood)
Facing the Extreme (Tzvetan Todorov)
The Future Lasts Forever (Louis Althusser)
Lectures on the Philosophy of History (Georg Wilhelm Friedrich Hegel)
The Life of Reason (George Santayana)
Meaning in History (Wilhelm Dilthey)
The New Science (Giambattista Vico)
The Phenomenology of Spirit (Georg Wilhelm Friedrich Hegel)
The Protestant Ethic and the Spirit of Capitalism (Max Weber)
Selected Works (Karl Marx)

Philosophy of Language

The Concept of Mind (Gilbert Ryle)
Course in General Linguistics (Ferdinand de Saussure)
How to Do Things with Words (J. L. Austin)
The Language of the Self (Jacques Lacan)
Language, Truth, and Logic (A. J. Ayer)
The Logical Basis of Metaphysics (Michael Dummett)
Must We Mean What We Say (Stanley Cavell)
Naming and Necessity (Saul Kripke)
On Certainty (Ludwig Wittgenstein)
Philosophical Investigations (Ludwig Wittgenstein)
Philosophy and Logical Syntax (Rudolf Carnap)
Philosophy and Psycho-Analysis (John Wisdom)
Science, Perception, and Reality (Wilfrid Sellars)
Selected Essays (Gottlob Frege)
Word and Object (W. V. O. Quine)

Philosophy of Law

The Concept of Law (H. L. A. Hart)
Han Feizi
Taking Rights Seriously (Ronald Dworkin)

Philosophy of Mathematics

The Foundations of Arithmetic (Gottlob Frege)
Principia (Isaac Newton)
Pythagoras: Philosophy (Pythagoras)

Philosophy of Mind

Brainstorms (Daniel Dennett)
The Concept of Mind (Gilbert Ryle)

The Construction of Social Reality (John R. Searle)
The Engine of Reason, the Seat of the Soul (Paul M. Churchland)
Essays on Actions and Events (Donald Davidson)
Neurophilosophy (Patricia Churchland)
Philosophy and Psycho-Analysis (John Wisdom)
RePresentations (Jerry A. Fodor)

Philosophy of Religion. *See also* Philosophical Theology

African Religions and Philosophy (John S. Mbiti)
After Auschwitz (Richard L. Rubenstein)
All Rivers Run to the Sea (Elie Wiesel)
"Apology for Raimond Sebond" (Michel Eyquem de Montaigne)
Beyond Good and Evil (Friedrich Nietzsche)
Bhagavad Gita
Concluding Unscientific Postscript (Søren Kierkegaard)
The Consolation of Philosophy (Boethius)
The Courage to Be (Paul Tillich)
Dialogues Concerning Natural Religion (David Hume)
Dialogues on Metaphysics and on Religion (Nicolas Malebranche)
The Divine Relativity (Charles Hartshorne)
Euthyphro (Plato)
God's Presence in History (Emil L. Fackenheim)
An Historical and Critical Dictionary (Pierre Bayle)
The Idea of a University Defined and Illustrated (John Henry Newman)
The Importance of Living (Lin Yutang)
Inner Experience (Georges Bataille)
Karma Yoga (Swami Vivekananda)
Man Is Not Alone (Abraham Joshua Heschel)
Pensées (Blaise Pascal)
Philosophical Dictionary (Voltaire)
Philosophical Fragments (Søren Kierkegaard)
Principles of the Philosophy of Future (Ludwig Feuerbach)
Religion and Nothingness (Keiji Nishitani)
The Religion of Man (Rabindranath Tagore)
The Star of Redemption (Franz Rosenzweig)
The Tragic Sense of Life in Men and Peoples (Miguel de Unamuno y Jugo)
The Two Sources of Morality and Religion (Henri Bergson)

Warrant and Proper Function (Alvin Plantinga)
The Will to Believe and Other Essays in Popular
     Psychology (William James)
Zen and Western Thought (Masao Abe)

Philosophy of Science
The Engine of Reason, the Seat of the Soul (Paul
     M. Churchland)
First Principles (Herbert Spencer)
The Logic of Scientific Discovery (Karl Raimund
     Popper)
Neurophilosophy (Patricia Churchland)
Novum Organum (Francis Bacon)
The Origin of Species by Means of Natural
     Selection (Charles Darwin)
Physics (Aristotle)
Principia (Isaac Newton)
RePresentations (Jerry A. Fodor)
The Structure of Scientific Revolutions (Thomas
     S. Kuhn)
Thoughts on the Interpretation of Nature (Denis
     Diderot)

Political Philosophy
Analects (Confucius)
Anarchy, State, and Utopia (Robert Nozick)
Dao De Jing
Discourse on Colonialism (Aimé Césaire)
The Federalist (Alexander Hamilton, James
     Madison, and John Jay)
Feminist Politics and Human Nature (Alison M.
     Jaggar)
Four Essays on Liberty (Isaiah Berlin)
The Future Lasts Forever (Louis Althusser)
The Great Learning
Han Feizi
The Hermeneutics of African Philosophy
     (Tsenay Serequeberhan)
Laws (Plato)
Leviathan (Thomas Hobbes)
Mozi
Natural Right and History (Leo Strauss)
Of Civil Government (John Locke)
On Contradiction (Mao Zedong)
On Liberty (John Stuart Mill)
The Origins of Totalitarianism (Hannah Arendt)
Politics (Aristotle)
The Prince (Niccolò Machiavelli)
Prison Notebooks (Antonio Gramsci)

The Rebel (Albert Camus)
Republic (Plato)
Statesman (Plato)
Taking Rights Seriously (Ronald Dworkin)
A Theory of Justice (John Rawls)
A Treatise on the Social Contract (Jean-Jacques
     Rousseau)
Utopia (Thomas More)
A Vindication of the Rights of Woman (Mary
     Wollstonecraft)
Xunzi

Pragmatism
The American Evasion of Philosophy (Cornel
     West)
Collected Papers of Charles Sanders Peirce
     (Charles Sanders Peirce)
Human Nature and Conduct (John Dewey)
Mind and the World-Order (C. I. Lewis)
Pragmatism (William James)
The Quest for Certainty (John Dewey)
Realism with a Human Face (Hilary Putnam)
The Will to Believe and Other Essays in Popular
     Psychology (William James)

Social Philosophy
African Philosophy (Paulin J. Hountondji)
An Autobiography (Mohandas K. Gandhi)
Civilization and Its Discontents (Sigmund Freud)
The Construction of Social Reality (John R.
     Searle)
The Dialogic Imagination (Mikhail Bakhtin)
Ecology, Community, and Lifestyle (Arne Naess)
An Essay on the Principle of Population
     (Thomas Robert Malthus)
Facing the Extreme (Tzvetan Todorov)
First Principles (Herbert Spencer)
The Gift (Marcel Mauss)
Mengzi (Mencius)
Mind, Self, and Society (George Herbert Mead)
On Human Conduct (Michael Oakeshott)
Outline of a Theory of Practice (Pierre Bourdieu)
Pedagogy of the Oppressed (Paulo Freire)
The Phenomenology of the Social World (Alfred
     Schutz)
The Positive Philosophy of Auguste Comte
     (Auguste Comte)
The Postmodern Condition (Jean-François
     Lyotard)

Title Index

Index